T0310386

TURFGRASS

BIBLIOGRAPHY

TURFGRASS BIBLIOGRAPHY

FROM

1672 to 1972

Compiled and Edited by

James B. Beard,

Harriet J. Beard,

and

David P. Martin

MICHIGAN STATE UNIVERSITY PRESS

1977

Michigan State University Press
Library of Congress Catalog Card Number: 75–21100
ISBN: 0–87013–195–8
MANUFACTURED IN THE UNITED STATES OF AMERICA

Preface

This Turfgrass Bibliography was compiled over a ten-year period by the senior editor while assembling supporting literature to write the textbook, *Turfgrass: Science and Culture,* published by Prentice-Hall, Inc. After completion of the textbook, it seemed appropriate that this collection of literature be made available to the general public since less than ten percent of the over 16,000 references were actually cited in the textbook. Because the Turfgrass Bibliography has only a limited sales potential, publication was assumed by the Michigan State University Press, a non-profit organization, with financial assistance given by the O.J. Noer Research Foundation, Inc., the United States Golf Association Green Section Research and Education Fund, Inc., the Michigan Golf Association, and the Michigan Seniors Golf Association. Publication of this Turfgrass Bibliography would not have been possible without the encouragement and financial backing of these five organizations. Acknowledgement is given to Lyle Blair, Charles G. Wilson, Alexander M. Radko, and James Standish, Directors of these organizations.

This is the first time that an extensive bibliography of turfgrass literature has been published. The Turfgrass Bibliography contains over 16,000 references listed alphabetically by author. These references are then cross indexed on a subject basis containing more than 40,000 entries. The Bibliography contains a compilation of scientific, semi-technical, and popular writings covering all phases of turfgrass science, culture, and management. A significant portion of this turfgrass literature appears in obscure state and regional turfgrass publications that are not included in such standard reference sources as Biological Abstracts, Herbage Abstracts, Agricultural Index, Horticultural Abstracts, Bioresearch Index, and Crop Science Abstracts. The Bibliography should be a valuable reference source for scholars of turfgrass culture; private and commercial turfgrass researchers; teachers and adult extension workers; serious students of turfgrass culture and management; and practicing professional turfmen involved in the preparation of articles and talks concerning turfgrass culture and management.

While the Turfgrass Bibliography probably is not all encompassing, every attempt has been made to seek out the available publications in the turfgrass field. The focal point for this effort has been the O. J. Noer Memorial

Turfgrass Library at Michigan State University. The concept was first developed in 1966 when the O. J. Noer Research Foundation donated Dr. Noer's lifetime collection of turfgrass literature to the Michigan State University Library. Dr. Richard Chapin, Director of the Michigan State University Library and Dr. Madalin Cabalin, Assistant Director, subsequently played vital leadership roles in processing, cataloguing, and placing the collection in the Michigan State University Library. Additional sizeable private collections of turfgrass literature were donated by Thomas Mascaro and Dr. James R. Watson. Since these initial contributions Charles Wilson and James Latham of the O. J. Noer Research Foundation have been active in contacting people concerning donations to the library. Many valuable books and publications have been donated as a result of their efforts. These contributions are too numerous to acknowledge individually. More recently an O. J. Noer Regional Turfgrass Library has been established at Texas A&M University. Finally, the assistance of many Michigan State University students in the final processing of the author and subject cards is gratefully acknowledged. Special recognition should be given to John Bartelt, Larry Carleton, and Ron Yoder.

JAMES B. BEARD
Texas A&M University

AUTHOR INDEX

1. Aaamodt, O. S. War among plants. Turf Culture. 2(4):240–244. 1942.

2. Aaron, F. Flood problems down the drain. Golfdom. 42(2):50–52. 1968.

3. Abbott, E. V. and R. L. Tippett. Additional hosts of sugarcane mosaic virus. Plant Disease Reporter. 48(6):443–445. 1964.

4. Abburquerque, H. E. Leaf area index, light penetration, and carbohydrate reserves during growth of Kentucky 31 tall fescue (*Festuca arundinacea* Schreb.). M.S. Thesis, Virginia Polytechnic Institute. 1967.

5. Aberg, E., R. H. Porter, and W. A. Robbins. Further experiments with the Iowa air blast seed separator for the analysis of small-seeded grasses. Iowa Agricultural Experiment Station Research Bulletin 340. 1945.

6. Abernethy, R. R. Design and economy comparisons of turf systems. Proceedings Midwest Regional Turf Conference. pp. 86–88. 1966.

7. ______. Economic conditions of modern irrigation designs. Proceedings Texas Turfgrass Conference. 21:13–16. 1966.

8. ______. What kind of system does my course need. International Turfgrass Conference Proceedings. 39:54–55. 1968.

9. Abid El-Rahman, A. A. and M. O. El-Monayeri. Growth and water requirements of some range plants under controlled conditions. Plant and Soil. 29(1):119–131. 1968.

10. Ablon, L. Responsibility of the sprinkler irrigation contractor. Proceedings Annual Turfgrass Sprinkler Irrigation Conference. 5:47–48. 1967.

11. Abramson, S. C. Weeds and their control. Proceedings Florida Turf-Grass Management Conference. 10:162–170. 1962.

12. Abruna, F., Pearson, R. W., and Elkins, C. B. Quantitative evaluation of soil reaction and base status changes resulting from field application of residually acid-forming nitrogen fertilizers. Soil Science Society of America Proceedings. 22(6):539–542. 1958.

13. Adams, B., B. Lester, C. Mendenhall, and B. Elmer. Maintaining bermuda grass fairways. Central Plains Turfgrass Conference Proceedings. p. 4. 1961.

14. Adams, E. B. Wyoming lawn handbook. Wyoming Agricultural Experiment Station Bulletin 495. 24 p. 1969.

15. Adams, F., and R. W. Pearson. Neutralizing soil acidity under bermudagrass sod. Soil Science Society of America Proceedings. 33(5):737–742. 1969.

16. Adams, J. A. Master planning your insect control program. New York State Turf Association Bulletin 13. 49–52 pp. 1950.

17. ______. Turf pests of southeastern New York. Proceedings Southeastern New York Turf School. pp. 37–46. 1950.

18. Adams, J. E. Influence of mulches on runoff, erosion, and soil moisture depletion. Soil Science Society of America Proceedings 30(1):110–114. 1966.

19. Adams, M. W. Cross- and self-incompatibility in relation to seed setting in *Bromus inermis.* Botanical Gazette. 115(2):-95–105. 1953.

20. Adams, P. B. and F. L. Howard. An evaluation of turfgrass disease control chemicals in 1961. Park Maintenance. 15(1):14–19. 1962.

21. ______. Residual control of gray *(Typhula)* snow mold of bentgrass. Golf Course Reporter. 31:20–22. 1963.

22. ______. Methyl arsine oxide. Golf Course Reporter. 32:32–34. 1964.

23. ______. Advance in turfgrass pathology. Rhode Island Agriculture. 10:5. 1964.

24. ______. Rhode Island's 1964 fungicide trials. Park Maintenance. 18(2):18–22. 1965.

25. Adams, P. R. How much does it cost to—mow and fertilize golf greens? Exposition Conference—California. 3 pp. 1966.

26. Adams, R. E. Weed control in lawns Gardeners Chronicle. 159(15):343–345. 1966.

27. Adams, W. A., V. I. Stewart, and D. J. Thornton. The assessment of sands suitable for sportsfields. Journal Sports Turf Research Institute. 47:77–85. 1971.

28. Adams, W. E. and M. Twersky. Effect of soil fertility on winter killing of Coastal bermudagrass. Agronomy Journal. 52(6):325–326. 1959.

29. Adams, W. E., A. W. White, and R. N. Dawson. Influence of lime sources and rates on 'Coastal' bermudagrass production, soil profile reaction, exchangeable Ca and Mg. Agronomy Journal. 59(2):147–149. 1967.

30. ______. Coastal bermudagrass forage production and chemical composition as influenced by potassium source, rate, and frequency of application. Agronomy Journal. 59(3):247–250. 1967.

31. Adamson, R. M. Weeds in turf. Research Report National Weed Committee, Western Section (Canada). pp. 114–118. 1961.

32. ______. Chemical control of *Veronica filiformis* in a lawn. Research Report National Weed Committee, Western Section (Canada). p. 206. 1968.

33. ______. Sensitivity of seedlings of twelve bluegrass varieties to ioxynil. Research Report National Weed Committee, Western Section (Canada). p. 208. 1968.

34. ______. Weed control in new turfgrass plantings. Northwest Turfgrass Conference Proceedings. 25:49–54. 1971.

35. Adamson, R. M. and R. H. Turley. The relative effect of herbicides upon white Dutch clover. Research Report National Weed Committee, Western Section. 9:105–108. 1962.

36. ______. Chemical control of English daisy *(Bellis perennis).* Research Report National Weed Committee, Western Section. 9:-106–107. 1962.

37. ______. Chemical control of *Veronica filiformis.* Research Report National Weed Committee, Western Section. 9:-107–108. 1962.

38. ______. Reaction of fescue varieties to herbicide applications. Research Report National Weed Committee, Western Section. 9:113. 1962.

39. ______. The relative effect of herbicides upon lawn grasses and *Holcus lanatus.* Research Report National Weed Committee, Western Section. 9:114–115. 1962.

40. Adegbola, A. A. and C. M. McKell. Effect of nitrogen fertilization on the carbohydrate content of coastal bermudagrass *(Cynodon dactylon* (L.), Pers.). Agronomy Journal. 58(1):60–64. 1966.

41. ______. Regrowth potential of coastal bermudagrass as related to previous nitrogen fertilization. Agronomy Journal. 58(2):145–146. 1966.

42. Adojaan, A. Types of lawn in Estonia. 1st Czechoslovak Symposium on Sports Turf Proceedings. pp. 189–196. 1969.

43. Affeldt, E. F. Equipment for eighteen holes. The National Greenkeeper. 1(11):21–22. 1927.

44. Agar, D. M. Seeds and germination The Groundsman. 17(1):15–19. 1963.

45. Agbakoba, S. C. O. and J. R. Goodin. Effect of paraquat on the nitrogen content and regrowth of coastal bermudagrass *(Cynodon dactylon* (L.) Pers.). Agronomy Journal. 59(6):605–607. 1967.

46. Ahlgren, G. H. The effect of adding vitamin B_1 (Thiamin) to several grass species. Journal American Society of Agronomy. 33:-572–576. 1941.

47. ______. Influence of Thiamin additions on germination and growth of certain grasses and of white clover. New Jersey Agricultural Experiment Station Bulletin 692. 1942.

49. ______. Now's the time to re-make the lawn. New Jersey Agriculture. 26:7. 1944.

50. ______. 21 problems to trouble the greenkeeper. Golfdom. 20(4):31–32, 75. 1946.

51. ______. Factors that influence clover population. Rutgers University Short Course in Turf Management. 18:66–68. 1950.

52. ______. Some Eastern ideas on turf production and management. State College of Washington Annual Turf Conference. 4:-10–14. 1951.

53. ______. Research. Golfdom. 27(10):-45–46. 1953.

54. ______. Your lawn. Grounds for Living. Rutgers University Press. 91–111 pp. 1956.

55. Ahlgren, G. H. and H. R. Cox. Destroying lawn weeds with 2,4–D. New Jersey Agricultural Experiment Station Bulletin 725. 1946.

56. Ahlgren, G. H. and R. E. Engel. Spring care of established lawns. New Jersey Agricultural Experiment Station Circular 524:1–4. 1949.

57. ______. Summer care of the lawn. New Jersey Agriculture Experiment Station Circular. 525:1–4. 1951.

58. Ahlgren, H. L. Effect of fertilization, cutting treatments, and irrigation on yield of forage and chemical composition of the rhizomes of Kentucky bluegrass *(Poa pratensis* L). Journal of American Society of Agronomy. 30(8):683–691. 1938.

59. Ahlgren, H. L. and O. S. Aamodt. Harmful root interactions as a possible explanation for effects noted between various species of grasses and legumes. Journal of American Society of Agronomy. 31(11):982–985. 1939.

60. Ahlgren, H. L., D. C. Smith, and E. L. Nielsen. Behavior of various selections of Kentucky bluegrass, *Poa pratensis* L. when grown as spaced plants and in mass seedings. Journal of American Society of Agronomy. 37(4):268–281. 1945.

61. Altman, J. Turf disease research in Colorado—1967–68. Rocky Mountain Regional Turfgrass Conference Proceedings. 12–16 pp. 1968.

62. Ahmed, M. K. Cytogenetic studies of Kentucky bluegrass *(Poa pratensis)*. Rutgers University Short Course in Turf Management Proceedings. pp. 55–56. 1971.

63. Ahrens, J. F. Residual effects of preemergence crabgrass killers on crabgrass and turf. New England Agricultural Chemical Conference and Herbicide Workshop. 1:31. 1964.

64. ______. Effects of preemergence herbicides on new turf seedings. New England Agricultural Chemical Conference and Herbicide Workshop. 1:36. 1964.

65. ______. New herbicides for preemergence control of crabgrass in turf. Proceedings Northeastern Weed Control Conference. 19:473–477. 1965.

66. ______. Persistence and counteraction of bensulide in turf. Proceedings Northeastern Weed Control Conference. 23:405. 1969.

67. Ahrens, J. F. and R. J. Lukens. Studies on the chemical control of *Poa annua* in C1–C19 putting green turf. Proceedings Northeastern Weed Control Conference. 20:-547–551. 1966.

68. Ahrens, J. F. and A. R. Olson. Comparisons of preemergence herbicides for the control of crabgrass. Proceedings Northeastern Weed Control Conference 15:276–279. 1961.

69. ______. Comparison of preemergence herbicides for the control of crabgrass. Weed Abstracts. 12(3):137. 1963.

70. Ahrens, J. F., R. J. Lukens, and A. R. Olson. Control of crabgrass and other weeds in turf. Connecticut Agricultural Experiment Station Bulletin. 649:1–18. 1962.

71. ______. Preemergence control of crabgrass in turf with fall and spring treatments. Proceedings Northeastern Weed Control Conference. 16:511–518. 1962.

72. ______. Single and repeated applications of preemergence crabgrass killers on turf. Proceedings Northeastern Weed Control Conference. 17:483–484. 1963.

73. Ahring, R. The influence of glume constituents on seed germination in two Old World bluestems. Ph.D. Thesis. University of Nebraska. 1972.

74. Ahring, R. M. and R. M. Irving. A laboratory method of determining cold hardiness in bermudagrass, *Cynodon dactylon* (L.) Pers. Crop Science. 9(5):615–618. 1969.

75. Aikman, J. M. The effect of aspect of slope on climatic factors. Iowa State College Journal Science. 15:161–167. 1940.

76. Aikman, J. W. The use of native midwestern grasses for highway purposes. Ohio Short Course on Roadside Development. 19:-71–79. 1960.

77. Aimi, J. The club manager and the golf course superintendent: their relationship to each other. Proceedings Mid-Atlantic Association of Golf Course Superintendents Conference. pp. 28–30. 1964.

78. Ainslie, G. G. The bluegrass webworm. United States Department of Agriculture Technical Bulletin 173. 1930.

79. Aitken, J. A. Instructions on the application of bituminous membranes cover for soil stabilization by grass seeding. Proceedings, School of Soils, Fertilization and Turf Maintenance, Green Section, Royal Canadian Golf Association. pp. 36–41. 1955.

80. Aiton, E. W. Our public relations. Proceedings Mid-Atlantic Association of Golf Course Superintendents Conference. pp. 27–28. 1964.

81. Akamine, E. K. Germination of Hawaiian range grass seeds. Hawaii Station Technical Bulletin. p. 2. 1944.

82. Akerberg, E. Seed production of the "*Poa*" species. Herbage Reviews. 6:228–233. 1938.

83. ______. Apomictic and sexual seed formation in *Poa pratensis.* Hereditas. 25:-359–370. 1939.

84. ______. Cytogenetic studies in *Poa pratensis* and its hybrid with *Poa alpina.* Hereditas. 28:1–126. 1942.

85. Akulova, E. A. Light transmission through a forest canopy in relation to incident radiation and tree-crown density. Fiziologiia Rastenii. 11(5):818–823. 1964.

86. Al-Aish, M. and W. V. Brown. Grass germination responses to isopropyl-phenyl carbamate and classification. American Journal of Botany. 45:16–23. 1958.

87. Alban, E. K. Vegetation control in the Ohio highway research project. 23rd Short Course on Roadside Development. Ohio State University. pp. 89–96. 1964.

88. Alberda, T. The effects of cutting, light intensity and night temperature on growth and soluble carbohydrate content of *Lolium perenne* L. Plant and Soil. 8(3):199–230. 1957.

89. ______. The problems of relating greenhouse and controlled environmental work to sward conditions. Journal of the British Grassland Society. 20(1):41–48. 1965.

90. ______. The influence of temperature, light intensity and nitrate concentration on drymatter production and chemical composition of *Lolium perenne* L. Netherlands Journal of Agricultural Science. 13(4):335–360. 1965.

91. ______. The influence of reserve substance on dry matter production after defoliation. Proceedings 10th International Grassland Congress. pp. 140–147. 1966.

92. Albert, W. B. Studies on the growth of alfalfa and some perennial grasses. Journal of the American Society of Agronomy. 19:-624–654. 1927.

93. ______. Control of little barley in coastal bermudagrass with atrazine and paraquat. Weeds. 13:375–376. 1965.

94. Albrecht, H. R. Strain differences in tolerance to 2,4–D in creeping bentgrasses. Journal of the American Society of Agronomy. 39:163–165. 1947.

95. ______. Adapted grasses. Pennsylvania State College Turf Conference. 18:48–51. 1949.

96. Albrecht, W. A. The living soil. The Golf Course Reporter. 23(4):14–17, 20–21. 1955.

97. Aldag, R. W. and J. L. Young. Aspects of D-leucine and D-lysine metabolism in maize and ryegrass seedlings. Oregon Agricultural Experiment Station. Technical Paper No. 2729. pp. 187–201. 1970.

98. Alder, E. F. and R. B. Bevington. Diphenatrile, dipropalin, and trifluralin as preemergent turf herbicides. Proceedings Northeastern Weed Control Conference. pp. 505–510. 1962.

99. Alderfer, R. B. Soil conditions affecting drainage and compaction. Proceedings Pennsylvania State College Turfgrass Conference. 18:21–30. 1949.

100. ______. The influence of soil compaction on the intake and runoff of water.

Proceedings Pennsylvania State College Turfgrass Conference. 19:52–58. 1950.

101. ______. Soil compaction—some basic causes and effects. Proceedings Pennsylvania State College Turfgrass Conference. 20:80–86. 1951.

102. ______. Compaction of turf soils—some causes and effects. USGA Journal and Turf Management. 4(2):25–28. 1951.

103. ______. Penn State soil technician—discusses turf compaction. Midwest Turf News and Research. 6(2):3–5. 1952.

104. ______. Compaction and moisture problems in turf. Proceedings Midwest Regional Turf Conference. pp. 51–54. 1952.

105. ______. Soil relationships in turf production. Proceedings Pennsylvania State College Annual Turfgrass Conference. 21:-20–31. 1952.

106. ______. Soil conditioners. 1953 Annual Conference Mid-Atlantic Association of Golf Course Superintendents. pp. 5–7. 1953.

107. ______. Physical condition of the soil affects fertilizer utilization. Better Crops with Plant Food. p. 24. 1954.

108. ______. Effects of soil compaction on bluegrass turf. Proceedings Pennsylvania State College Turfgrass Conference. 23:31–32. 1954.

109. ______. Soil compaction. Rutgers University Short Course in Turf Management. pp. 1–3. 1955.

110. ______. Building the lawn. Handbook on Lawns. Brooklyn Botanic Garden. pp. 134–144. 1956.

111. ______. Soil relationships in turf production. Proceedings Pennsylvania State College Turfgrass Conference. 25:101–104. 1956.

112. ______. Productive soils must breathe. Parks and Recreation. 40(7):15–16. 1957.

113. ______. It's the holes that count. Parks and Recreation. 40(8):7–9. 1957.

114. ______. The living soil. Rutgers University Short Course in Turf Management. 3 pp. 1957.

115. ______. Infiltration, retention and movement of water in soils. Parks and Recreation. 41(1):15. 1958.

116. ______. Obtaining the best from the soil. Rutgers University Short Course in Turf Management. pp. 1–2. 1960.

117. ______. Soil compaction—a major turf problem. Turf Clippings. 1(5):A–16 to A–18. 1960.

118. ______. Water movement and retention in soils. Rutgers University Short Course in Turf Management. pp. 41–42. 1963.

119. ______. Water movement and retention in soils. Rutgers University Short Course in Turf Management. pp. 41–42. 1964.

120. ______. Behavior of water in the soil. Rutgers University Short Course in Turf Management. pp. 1–3. 1969.

121. ______. Behavior of water in the soil. Rutgers University. College of Agriculture and Environmental Science. Lawn and Utility Turf Section. pp. 7–9. 1969.

122. Alderfer, R. B. and F. G. Merkle. The comparative effects of surface application vs. incorporation of various mulching materials on structure, permeability, runoff, and other soil properties. Soil Science Society of America Proceedings. 8:79–86. 1943.

123. Aldous, A. E. Effect of different clipping treatments on the yield and vigor of prairie grass vegetation. Journal of the American Society of Agronomy. 19:624–654. 1927.

124. Aldrich, D. G. Relationship of the university to the turfgrass industry. Proceedings Southern California Turfgrass Institute. pp. 22–25. 1960.

125. ______. Relationship of the university to the turfgrass industry. California Turfgrass Culture. 11(4):25–27. 1961.

126. Aldrich, D. T. A. Testing ryegrass varieties for British agriculture. Proceedings First International Turfgrass Research Conference. pp. 45–50. 1969.

127. Aldrich, J. M. European frit fly in North America. Journal of Agriculture Research. 18(9):451–474. 1920.

128. Aldrich, S. M. Maintaining greens on sandy soil. The National Greenkeeper 1(12):25. 1927.

129. Aldrich, S. R. What's in the fertilizer bag. Illinois Turfgrass Conference. pp. 2–11. 1960.

130. ———. Urea-formaldehyde nitrogenous fertilizers. Illinois Turfgrass Conference. pp. 6–9. 1961.

131. Alexander, C. W. and D. E. McCloud. CO² uptake (net photosynthesis) as influenced by light intensity of isolated bermudagrass leaves contrasted to that of swards under various clipping regimes. Crop Science. 2:132–135. 1962.

132. Alexander, J. P. and J. Q. Lynd. Response of four strains of Bermudagrass to different rates of nitrogen fertilizer. Oklahoma Agricultural Experiment Station. Processed Series P-485. 16 pp. 1964.

133. Alexander, M. Persistence and biological reaction of pesticides in soils. Soil Science Society of America Proceedings. 29(1):-1–7. 1965.

134. Alexander, M. M. and R. E. Bowling. Preliminary investigation—composition of roadside litter in Georgia. Georgia Highway Department Research Assistance Project No. 1–68. pp. 1–25. 1970.

135. Alexander, P. M. Preventive maintenance vs. curative practices. Southeastern Turfgrass Conference. 22:11–16. 1968.

136. ———. Maleic hydrazide and overseeding of Tifgreen bermudagrass putting greens. Clemson University Agricultural Research. 11(2):6. 1964.

137. ———. Nematode and fairy ring control on Tifgreen bermuda. Golf Course Reporter. 32(5):12–14. 1964.

138. ———. Comparison of grasses for overseeding. Turf-Grass Times. 3(8):12, 14. 1968.

139. ———. Successful control in practice greens and fairways. 40th International Turfgrass Conference and Show Proceedings. pp. 70–73. 1969.

140. ———. Anthracnose—serious disease problem. USGA Green Section Record. 7(5):8–9. 1969.

141. ———. *Poa annua* and its control. Twenty-First Annual RCGA National Turfgrass Conference. pp. 1–3. 1970.

142. ———. The golf course superintendent's continuing education and the G.C.S.A.A. 23rd Annual RCGA National Turfgrass Conference. pp. 1–4. 1972.

143. Alexander, P. M. and W. Gilbert. Winter damage to bermuda greens. Golf Course Reporter. 31(9):50–53. 1963.

144. Alexander, P. M. and J. G. Wright. Aided by maleic hydrazide. Golf Course Reporter. 32(9):36–40. 1964.

145. Alexander, T. M. W. Peat—Its origin and types. The Groundsman. 17(7):18–20. 1964.

146. Alizai, H. U. and L. C. Hulbert. Effects of soil texture on evaporative loss and available water in semi-arid climates. Soil Science. 110(5):328–332. 1970.

147. Aljibury, F. K. Adapting automatic irrigation into existing systems. Proceedings of Turf, Tree Landscape, and Nursery Conference. pp. 17–1 to 17–2. 1966.

148. ———. Turf and soil water—air relationship. California Turfgrass Culture. 17(3):19. 1967.

149. ———. Turf, water management. Proceedings Annual Turfgrass Sprinkler Irrigation Conference. 5:35–36. 1967.

150. Aljibury, F. K. and D. D. Evans. Water permeability of saturated soils as related to air permeability at different moisture tensions. Soil Science Society of America Proceedings. 29:366–369. 1965.

151. Allan, C. "Dead" land restored to life by golf turf program. Golfdom. 24(3):-50–51. 1950.

152. Allard, H. A. and M. W. Evans. Growth and flowering of some tame and wild grasses in response to different photoperiods. Journal of Agricultural Research. 62(4):193–228. 1941.

153. Allard, H. A. and W. W. Garner. Further observations of the response of various species of plants to length of day. United States Department of Agriculture Technical Bulletin 727. 64 pp. 1940.

154. Allen, A. *Poa annua*—friend or foe. Turf Clippings. 1(5):6–7. 1960.

155. Allen, C. The value of the proper use of lime. Turf Clippings. 1(5):11–12. 1960.

156. Allen, K. Mulch as an aid to erosion control. 21st Short Course on Roadside Development. Ohio State University. pp. 96–97. 1962.

157. Allen, S. E., and C. M. Hunt. Controlled-release fertilizers for turfgrasses. Agronomy Abstracts. p. 99. 1965.

158. Allen, S. E., D. A. Mays, and G. L. Terman. Low cost slow-release fertilizer developed. Crops and Soils. 21(3):13–15. 1968.

159. Allen, T. C., and A. H. Freiberg. Symmetrical dichlorotetrafluoroacetone, a synthetic organic rust chemotherapeutant. Phytopathology. 54:580–583. 1964.

160. Allan, W. C. White grub in Ontario. Guelph Turfgrass Conference Proceedings. pp. 12–15. 1959.

161. Allen, W. W. Summary of disease incidence in the Southwest in 1960. Oklahoma Turfgrass Conference Proceedings. pp. 56–58. 1960.

162. ______. Turfgrass survey. Proceedings Texas Turfgrass Conference. 15:46–49. 1960.

163. ______. Factors limiting turf quality. U.S.G.A. Journal and Turf Management. 14(3):30–31. 1961.

164. ______. Outline of presentation on effects of traffic on soil. Proceedings Southeastern Turfgrass Conference. 17:15–17. 1963.

165. ______. St. Augustinegrass management. Proceedings Annual Texas Turfgrass Conference. 19:62–64. 1964.

166. ______. Control of diseases. Proceedings Annual Texas Turfgrass Conference. 21:27–28. 1966.

167. Allen, W. W., R. A. Kilpatrick, and E. C. Bashaw. A technique for screening St. Augustine grass for tolerance to *Rhizoctonia solani.* The Plant Disease Reporter. 50(8):-622–623. 1966.

168. Allen, W. W., J. A. Long and E. C. Holt. Control of brown patch in St. Augustinegrass. Texas Agricultural Progress. 5(6):-10. 1959.

169. Allinson, D. W. Influence of photoperiod and thermoperiod on the IVDMD and cell wall components of tall fescue. Crop Science. 11(3):456–458. 1971.

170. Allison, F. E. The fate of nitrogen applied to soils. Advances in Agronomy. 18:-219–258. 1966.

171. Allison, F. E. and M. S. Anderson. The use of sawdust for mulches and soil improvement. USDA Circular No. 891. 19 pp. 1951.

172. Allison, F. E. and R. M. Murphy. Comparative rates of decomposition in soil of wood and bark particles of several species of pines. Soil Science Society of America Proceedings. 27(3):309–312. 1963.

173. Allison, L. E. Salinity in relation to irrigation. Advances in Agronomy. 16:139–180. 1964.

174. Allison, J. L., H. S. Sherwin, I. Forbes, and R. E. Wagner. *Rhizoctonia solani,* a destructive pathogen of Alta fescue, smooth brome grass, and birdsfoot trefoil. Phytopathology. 39(1):1. 1949.

175. Allott, D. J. Turf research at Levington. Parks, Golf Courses & Sports Grounds. 22(9):548, 555. 1957.

176. ______. Weed control in a parks department. Park Administration. 23(4):173–176. 1958.

177. ______. Soil structure in relation to plant nutrition. The Groundsman. 15(1):8–10, 20. 1961.

178. ______. Turf nutrition and nutrient availability. The Groundsman. 15(3):10–16. 1961.

179. ______. The root of turf management. The Groundsman. 16(1):6–8. 1962.

180. ______. Recent advances in worm control. The Groundsman. 16(9):4–6, 18. 1963.

181. Atsatt, P. R., and L. C. Bliss. Some effects of emulsified hexa-octadecanol on germination, establishment, and growth of Kentucky bluegrass. Agronomy Journal. 55(6):-533–537. 1963.

182. Altman, J. Nitrogen in relation to turf diseases. Rocky Mountain Regional Turfgrass Conference Proceedings. Colorado State University. 10:25–38. 1963.

183. ______. Nitrogen in relation to turf diseases. Golf Course Reporter. 33(5):16–30. 1965.

184. ______. Diseases of bluegrass with particular reference to Colorado. Technical Bulletin. Agricultural Experiment Station. Colorado State University. 93:1–11. 1966.

185. ______. Diseases of bluegrass with particular reference to Colorado. Rocky Mountain Regional Turfgrass Conference. pp. 47–54. 1966.

186. ______. Turf disease research in Colorado. Scotts Turfgrass Research Seminar. pp. 6–10. 1968.

187. ______. Environmental factors influencing turfgrass diseases. Proceedings Scotts Turfgrass Research Conference. 2:1–12. 1971.

188. ______. Effects of the environment on turf diseases in the Rocky Mountain region. 18th Annual Rocky Mountain Regional Turfgrass Conference Proceedings. pp. 69–82. 1972.

189. ______. Environmental factors influencing turfgrass diseases. Turf Bulletin. 9(3):6–9. 1972.

190. Altom, J. D. Persistence of picloram, dicamba, and four phenoxy herbicides in soil and grass. M. S. Thesis. Oklahoma State University. 1972.

191. Alves, G. Golf course maintenance. The National Greenkeeper. 3(2):27–30. 1929.

192. ______. Rehabilitating old golf courses. The National Greenkeeper. 7(4):-5–7, 26. 1933.

193. Amadeo, R. C. Kikuyu grass can be disastrous to southern courses. The Golf Superintendent. 34(4):26–28, 54. 1966.

194. Ames, R. W. Insects and disease problems in turf. Parks and Recreation. 46(8):281. 1963.

195. Ames, R. B. and C. R. Skogley. Pre- and post-emergence crabgrass control in lawn turf. Proceedings Northeastern Weed Control Conference. 16:528–535. 1962.

196. Ames, R. W. Problems in insect and disease control. Southern California Turfgrass Institute Proceedings. pp. 17–21. 1960.

198. Anapu, A. Value of a St. Augustine grass grading program. Proceedings Annual University of Florida Turf-Grass Management Conference. 8:64. 1960.

199. Anderson, A. E. Turf management at Brae Burn. U.S.G.A. Green Section Record. 2(5):3–5. 1965.

200. Anderson, A. L. Turfgrass diseases and their control. Michigan Forestry and Park Conference Proceedings. 43:24–25. 1969.

201. Andersen, A. L. and D. M. Huber. The plate-profile technique for isolating soil fungi and studying their activity in the vicinity of roots. Phytopathology. 55(5): 592–594. 1965.

202. Andersen, A. M. Development of the female gametophyte and caryopsis of *Poa pratensis* and *Poa compressa.* Journal of Agricultural Research. 34(11): 1001–1018. 1927.

203. ______. The effect of removing the glumes on the germination of seeds of *Poa compressa.* American Journal of Botany. 19(10):835–836. 1932.

204. ______. Comparison of methods used in germinating seed of *Poa compressa.* Proceedings International Seed Testing Association. 10:307–315. 1938.

205. ______. Some factors influencing the germination of seed of *Poa compressa* L. Proceedings Association of Official Seed Analysts. 37:134–143. 1947.

206. ______. The effect of certain fungi and gibberellin on the germination of Merion Kentucky bluegrass seed. Proceedings Association Official Seed Analysts. 47:145–153. 1957.

207. Anderson, B. R. Breeding and selection of turfgrasses. Turf Clippings. 1(7): 8-A to 13-A. 1962.

208. Anderson, B. R., and S. R. McLane. Control of annual bluegrass and crabgrass in turf with fluorophenoxyacetic acids. Weeds. 6(1):52–58. 1958.

209. Anderson, C. Winter kill a problem. The Greenkeepers' Reporter. 7(3):13. 1939.

210. ______. Dollar spot. The Greenkeeper's Reporter. 12(3):16–17. 1944.

212. Anderson, C. J., C. Walter, and W. C. Mitchell. Effect of maleic hydrazide as a growth retardent on maintained lawns. North Central Weed Control Conference p. 151. 1953.

213. Anderson, C. R. Inhibitors for economic maintenance. 22nd Short Course on Roadside Development. pp. 74–76. 1962.

214. Anderson, C. R. and R. C. Moffett. Chemical mowing by the Maryland State Roads Commission. Proceedings Northeastern Weed Control Conference. 17:393–396. 1963.

215. Anderson, D. O. Growth retardant chemicals. 29th Short Course on Roadside Development. pp. 93–97. 1970.

216. ______. Maintenance with growth retardant chemicals. Park Maintenance. 25(8):15–16. 1972.

217. Anderson, E. How to select a power sprayer. Grounds Maintenance. 2(12):57–59, 106–108. 1967.

218. Anderson, J. Don't forget fall topdressing. The National Greenkeeper. 3(9):-25–26. 1929.

219. ______. Soils. The National Greenkeeper 6(12):5. 18. 1932.

220. ______. Ten major phases of greenkeeping. The Greenkeeper's Reporter. 4(3):3–7, 12–14. 1936.

221. ______. Modern equipment and costs. The Greenkeepers' Reporter. 5(8):12–14. 1937.

222. ______. Lawn maintenance. The Greenkeepers' Reporter. 6(3):17–18, 32–33. 1938.

223. ______. The Greenkeeper and cost of golf. The Greenkeepers' Reporter. 6(4):20, 22. 1938.

224. ______. Turf problems in New Jersey. The Greenkeepers' Reporter. 6(5):17–19. 1938.

225. ______. To topdress or not. Greenkeeper's Reporter. 9(4):19–20. 1941.

226. Anderson, J. L. The origin of soils. Rocky Mountain Regional Turfgrass Conference Proceedings. Colorado State University. 6:7–10. 1959.

227. Anderson, J. U. Estimation of soil pH by indicators. New Mexico Agricultural Experiment Station. Research Report 48. 9 pp. 1961.

228. Anderson, K. L. Establishing turf to control erosion on slopes. Central Plains Annual Turf Conference. Kansas State College. 2:31–37. 1951.

229. ______. Time of burning as it affects soil moisture in an ordinary upland bluestem prairie in the Flint Hills. Journal of Range Management. 18(6):311–316. 1965.

230. Anderson, K. L., E. F. Smith, and C. E. Owensby. Burning bluestem range. Journal of Range Management. 23:84–92. 1970.

231. Anderson, L. E. Weed identification lab. Central Plains Annual Turf Conference. Kansas State University. 11:1. 1961.

232. Anderson, L. G. and W. R. Kneebone. Differential responses of *Cynodon dactylon* (L.) Pers. selections to three herbicides. Crop Science. 9(5):599–601. 1969.

233. Anderson, M. C. Studies of the woodland light climate. II. Seasonal variation in the light climate. The Journal of Ecology. 52(3):643–663. 1964.

234. Anderson, M. S. Sewage sludge for soil improvement. USDA Circular No. 972. 27 pp. 1955.

235. ______. Sawdust and other natural organics for establishing turf and soil improvement. USDA. ARS 41–18. 8 pp. 1957.

236. ______. History and development of soil testing. Journal of Agricultural and Food Chemistry. 8(2):84–87. 1960.

237. Anderson, M. S., S. F. Blake, and A. L. Mehring. Peat and muck in agriculture. USDA Circular No. 888. 31 pp. 1951.

238. Anderson, O. E., L. S. Jones, and F. C. Boswell. Soil temperature and source of nitrogen in relation to nitrification in sodded and cultivated soils. Agronomy Journal. 62(2):206–211. 1970.

239. Anderson, S. R., K. L. Bader, R. Guarasci, A. E. Hoffman, and R. W. Miller. Turf renovation and management of the Ohio State University football stadium. Mimeographed Sheet, Progress Report, Ohio State University. September, 1964.

240. Anderson, S. R., K. L. Bader, R. Guarasci, A. E. Hoffman, and R. W. Miller. Turf renovation and management of the Ohio State University football stadium. Turf Bulletin. Massachusetts Turf and Lawn Grass Council. 4(3):19–20. 1967.

241. Anderson, W. A., and P. R. Henderlong. Feasibility of identifying Kentucky bluegrass varieties via the disc electrophoresis technique. Agronomy Abstracts. p. 48. 1971.

242. Anderson, W. B. Trace elements. Proceedings Annual Texas Turfgrass Conference. 19:37–38. 1964.

243. Andresen, M. H. Observations on Australian Greenkeeping practices. New Zealand Institute for Turf Culture Newsletter. 65:21, 23–25. 1970.

244. Andrews, O. N. and R. Dickens. Turf-recommended practices—Alabama. 22nd Annual Southern Weed Conference Research Report. p. 84. 1969.

245. Andrews, O. N., L. E. Foote, and J. A. Jackobs. Turf establishment on Illinois roadsides as influenced by seeding mixtures and time of seeding. Agronomy Abstracts. p. 98–99. 1964.

246. Andrews, O. N., and J. A. Jackobs. Establishing turf on Illinois roadsides. Illinois Research. 7(3):6–7. 1965.

247. ———. Establishing turf on Illinois roadsides. Turf Bulletin. Massachusetts Turf and Lawn Grass Council. 4(2):14–15. 1966.

248. Andrews, O. N. and C. L. Murdoch. Evaluating grass and legume species for roadside turf. Agronomy Abstracts. p. 48. 1965.

249. Angstrom, A. The albedo of various surfaces of ground. Geografiska Annaler. 7:-323–342. 1925.

250. Anonymous. Have a weed-free lawn all year long with Weedone brand lawn and garden weed killers. Amchem Products, Inc. 23pp.

251. ———. Weed control for large turf areas. Amchem Products, Inc. Ambler, Pennsylvania. 11 pp.

252. ———. Put "K"uality in your lawn. American Potash Institute Publication. Washington, D.C.

253. ———. New ideas in roadside turf. American Seed Trade Association Publication. 11 pp.

254. ———. Fertilizing program for bentgrass greens. Bob Dunning-Jones Incorporated Publication. 7 pp.

255. ———. Grass sowing under bitumen emulsion. British Bitumen Emulsions, Ltd. Slough, England. 71 pp. 1950.

256. ———. Turf and its management for football, cricket, and hockey fields. Illinois Sporting Review. 13 pp.

257. ———. Modern equipment for putting green upkeep. Jacobsen Manufacturing Company. Wisconsin. 24 pp.

258. ———. The ring nematode, *Criconemoides ornatus,* on peach and centipede grass. Journal of Nematology. 2(3):204–208. 1970.

259. ———. Quality bentgrass proves compatible with bluegrass in the 4-year turf tests. Lawn/Garden/Outdoor Living. 2 pp.

260. ———. Lawn beauty with Merion sod. Merion Bluegrass Association Publication, New York. 4 pp.

261. ———. Milarsenite for weed control on golf course turf. Bulletin No. 4. Turf Service Bureau, Milwaukee Sewerage Commission. pp. 1–15.

262. ———. Milorganite: a fertilizer that produces better turf. Milwaukee Sewerage Commission Publication. 12 pp.

263. ———. Owner's manual for lawn care. Nursery Sod Growers Association (Ontario). 6 pp.

264. ———. Planning and building the golf course. National Golf Foundation, Inc. 28 pp.

265. ———. Sod growing in Nebraska. Yard and Garden Tips. University of Nebraska. 5 pp.

266. ———. Hybrid bermuda lawns. North Haven Gardens. Dallas, Texas. 3 pp.

267. ———. How to make a lawn. Peter Henderson and Company. New York. 8 pp.

268. ———. Weed information from Scotts Research. O. M. Scott and Son Publication. 25 pp.

269. ______. Quick tips about Milorganite lawn and garden fertilizer. Sewerage Commission: Fertilizer Division Publication. 18 pp.

270. ______. Turf tips. Milwaukee Sewerage Commission Publication. No. 6–67. 2 pp.

271. ______. The identification of grasses by the leaf method. Sutton and Sons. Reading, England. 7 pp. 1950.

272. ______. Turf disease handbook Mallinckrodt Chemical Works Publication. St. Louis, Mo. 1957.

273. ______. Lawn weed control. Department of Horticulture, University of Wisconsin. 3 pp.

274. ______. U-3 bermudagrass. USGA Green Section Mimeo.

275. ______. Lawngrass mixtures for Virginia. USDA and Immigration of Virginia Bulletin. No. 203. pp. 6–9.

276. ______. Improving athletic field turfgrass. West Point Products Corporation Publication. 24 pp.

277. ______. Turf, field and farm weekly. Turf, Field and Farm Weekly. New York. Vol. 6. 1868.

278. ______. Connecticut grasses. Connecticut Agricultural Experiment Station. 12th Annual Report. Part II. pp. 95–104. 1888.

279. ______. Grasses. Florida Agricultural Experiment Station Bulletin. pp. 5–15. 1888.

280. ______. Grasses, clovers, and forage crops and grasses of New York. New York (Geneva) Agricultural Experiment Station Bulletin 14. pp. 75–103. 1888.

281. ______. Beautify the lawn to reflect your personality. Luther Burbank Society. Santa Rosa, California. 28 pp. 1915.

282. ______. Making and maintaining a lawn. Bureau of Plant Industry. Seed Distribution. Government Printing Office. 6 pp. 1916.

283. ______. The maintenance of lawns, applicable to golf courses. C. H. Potter and Company, Inc. Washington, D.C. 28 pp. 1916.

284. ______. Making a new lawn. Virginia Agriculture Department Bulletin. 126:-139–141. 1918.

285. ______. Norfolk lawns and how to grow them. Vogue Printing Company. Norfolk, Virginia. 27 pp. 1918.

286. ______. Movement, price, and quality of timothy, redtop, Kentucky bluegrass, orchard grass, meadow fescue, and white clover seed. United States Seed Reporter. 3(3):7. 1919.

287. ______. Making and maintaining a lawn. USDA Circular 49. pp. 1–6. 1919.

288. ______. The seeding and care of golf courses. O. M. Scott and Sons Co. Publication. Marysville, Ohio. 55 pp. 1923.

289. ______. Low fertilizing value of peat. USGA Green Section Bulletin. 3(1):16. 1923.

290. ______. Winter seedings. USGA Green Section Bulletin. 3(1):21. 1923.

291. ______. Spring treatment for new vegetative greens. USGA Green Section Bulletin. 3(1):21. 1923.

292. ______. Growing bermuda grass on sandy soil. USGA Green Section Bulletin. 3(1):21. 1923.

293. ______. Providing bent stolons for vegetative planting. USGA Green Section Bulletin. 3(1):22. 1923.

294. ______. Burning over turf for controlling crabgrass. USGA Green Section Bulletin. 3(1):22. 1923.

295. ______. Eradication of dandelions and plantain from putting greens. USGA Green Section Bulletin. 3(1):23. 1923.

296. ______. Vegetative propagation of bent grasses. USGA Green Section Bulletin. 3(5):152. 1923.

297. ______. Bent greens in Kansas. USGA Green Section Bulletin. 3(5):153. 1923.

298. ______. Reseeding bent greens; use of redtop in reseeding. USGA Green Section Bulletin. 3(5):153. 1923.

299. ______. Should putting greens be kept closely cut at all times? USGA Green Section Bulletin. 3(11):291–293. 1923.

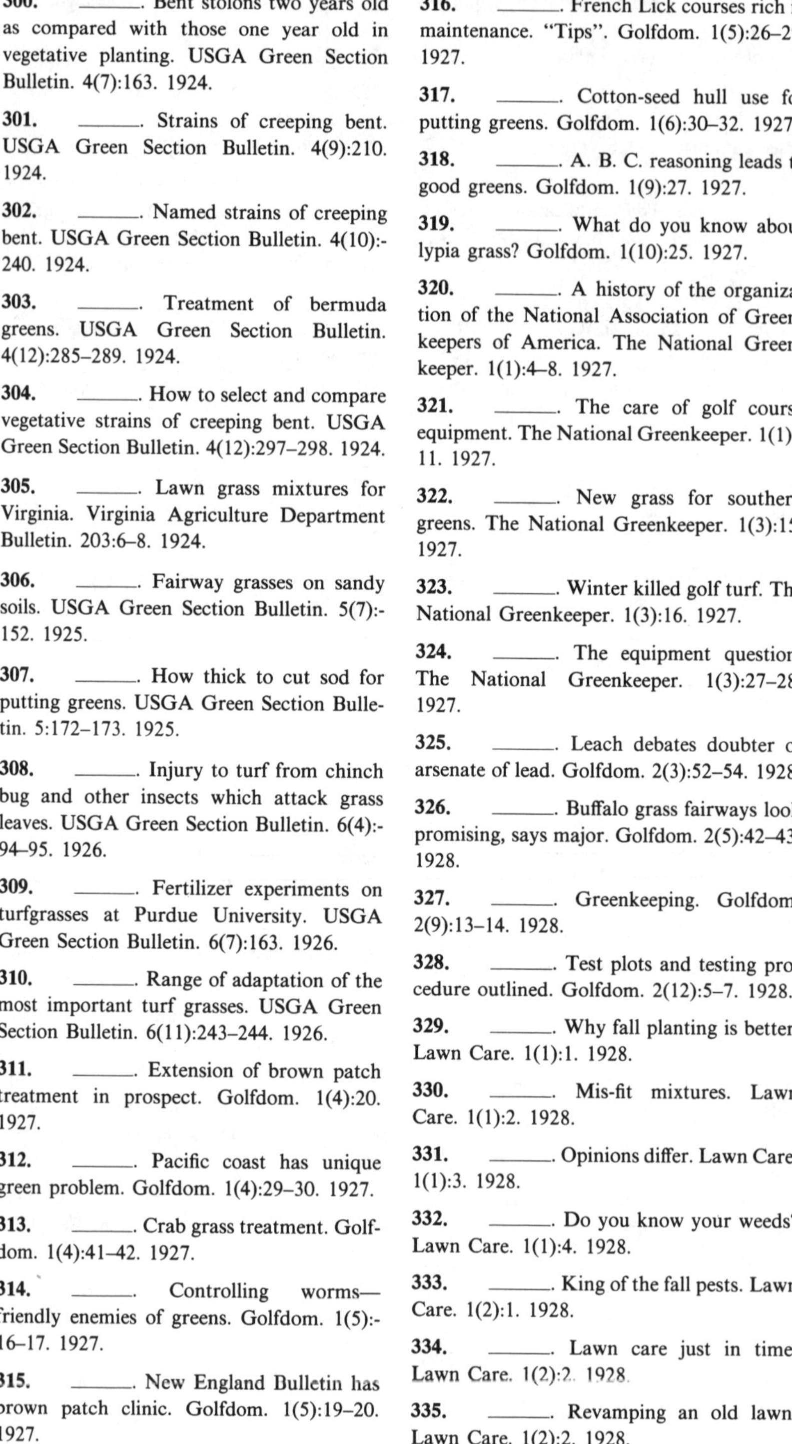

300. ———. Bent stolons two years old as compared with those one year old in vegetative planting. USGA Green Section Bulletin. 4(7):163. 1924.

301. ———. Strains of creeping bent. USGA Green Section Bulletin. 4(9):210. 1924.

302. ———. Named strains of creeping bent. USGA Green Section Bulletin. 4(10):-240. 1924.

303. ———. Treatment of bermuda greens. USGA Green Section Bulletin. 4(12):285–289. 1924.

304. ———. How to select and compare vegetative strains of creeping bent. USGA Green Section Bulletin. 4(12):297–298. 1924.

305. ———. Lawn grass mixtures for Virginia. Virginia Agriculture Department Bulletin. 203:6–8. 1924.

306. ———. Fairway grasses on sandy soils. USGA Green Section Bulletin. 5(7):-152. 1925.

307. ———. How thick to cut sod for putting greens. USGA Green Section Bulletin. 5:172–173. 1925.

308. ———. Injury to turf from chinch bug and other insects which attack grass leaves. USGA Green Section Bulletin. 6(4):-94–95. 1926.

309. ———. Fertilizer experiments on turfgrasses at Purdue University. USGA Green Section Bulletin. 6(7):163. 1926.

310. ———. Range of adaptation of the most important turf grasses. USGA Green Section Bulletin. 6(11):243–244. 1926.

311. ———. Extension of brown patch treatment in prospect. Golfdom. 1(4):20. 1927.

312. ———. Pacific coast has unique green problem. Golfdom. 1(4):29–30. 1927.

313. ———. Crab grass treatment. Golfdom. 1(4):41–42. 1927.

314. ———. Controlling worms—friendly enemies of greens. Golfdom. 1(5):-16–17. 1927.

315. ———. New England Bulletin has brown patch clinic. Golfdom. 1(5):19–20. 1927.

316. ———. French Lick courses rich in maintenance. "Tips". Golfdom. 1(5):26–29. 1927.

317. ———. Cotton-seed hull use for putting greens. Golfdom. 1(6):30–32. 1927.

318. ———. A. B. C. reasoning leads to good greens. Golfdom. 1(9):27. 1927.

319. ———. What do you know about lypia grass? Golfdom. 1(10):25. 1927.

320. ———. A history of the organization of the National Association of Greenkeepers of America. The National Greenkeeper. 1(1):4–8. 1927.

321. ———. The care of golf course equipment. The National Greenkeeper. 1(1):-11. 1927.

322. ———. New grass for southern greens. The National Greenkeeper. 1(3):15. 1927.

323. ———. Winter killed golf turf. The National Greenkeeper. 1(3):16. 1927.

324. ———. The equipment question. The National Greenkeeper. 1(3):27–28. 1927.

325. ———. Leach debates doubter of arsenate of lead. Golfdom. 2(3):52–54. 1928.

326. ———. Buffalo grass fairways look promising, says major. Golfdom. 2(5):42–43. 1928.

327. ———. Greenkeeping. Golfdom. 2(9):13–14. 1928.

328. ———. Test plots and testing procedure outlined. Golfdom. 2(12):5–7. 1928.

329. ———. Why fall planting is better. Lawn Care. 1(1):1. 1928.

330. ———. Mis-fit mixtures. Lawn Care. 1(1):2. 1928.

331. ———. Opinions differ. Lawn Care. 1(1):3. 1928.

332. ———. Do you know your weeds? Lawn Care. 1(1):4. 1928.

333. ———. King of the fall pests. Lawn Care. 1(2):1. 1928.

334. ———. Lawn care just in time. Lawn Care. 1(2):2. 1928.

335. ———. Revamping an old lawn. Lawn Care. 1(2):2. 1928.

336. ______. Fall fertilizing. Lawn Care. 1(2):3. 1928.

337. ______. Late mowing. Lawn Care. 1(2):3. 1928.

338. ______. Should lawns be covered in winter? Lawn Care. 1(2):4. 1928.

339. ______. Leaves for protection. Lawn Care. 1(2):4. 1928.

340. ______. Plantain killer. Lawn Care. 1(2):4. 1928.

341. ______. Newly planted bent greens. The National Greenkeeper. 2(6):23–25. 1928.

342. ______. Roseman silent co-operator. Roseman Tractor Mower Company. 30 pp. 1928.

343. ______. Hastening recovery of grass on divots by fertilization and marking spots so treated. USGA Green Section Bulletin. 8(3):63. 1928.

344. ______. The fairway fertilization problem. USGA Green Section Bulletin. 8(6):110–112. 1928.

345. ______. Water systems and watering. USGA Green Section Bulletin. 8(7):130–132. 1928.

346. ______. Parasitic control of the Japanese beetle. USGA Green Section Bulletin. 8(11):231. 1928.

347. ______. Authority tells of Astoria bent. Golfdom. 3(8):53–54. 1929.

348. ______. Get busy killing chickweed, says Adalink. Golfdom. 3(9):42. 1929.

349. ______. Bermuda grass care. Golfdom. 3(12):22. 1929.

350. ______. Fairway renovation. Greenkeepers Club of New England Newsletter. 1(4):2. 1929.

351. ______. The commercial bent grasses. Greenkeepers Club of New England Newsletter. 1(7):2–3. 1929.

352. ______. Pittsburgh demonstration plots. Greenkeepers Club of New England Newsletter. 1(8):3–6. 1929.

353. ______. The spring lawn menu. Lawn Care 2(1):1. 1929.

354. ______. Dandelion delirium. Lawn Care. 2(1):2. 1929.

355. ______. Winter drouth and its effects on grass. Lawn Care. 2(1):2. 1929.

356. ______. The simple art of mowing. Lawn Care. 2(1):3. 1929.

357. ______. Does it pay to lime your lawn? Lawn Care. 2(1):4. 1929.

358. ______. Good plant food—not lime needed. Lawn Care. 2(1):4. 1929.

359. ______. Moss—where it grows and what to do about it. Lawn Care. 2(2):2. 1929.

360. ______. Spraying with iron sulfate. Lawn Care. 2(2):2. 1929.

361. ______. Recommended leaf mold for shady lawns. Lawn Care. 2(2):2. 1929.

362. ______. Weeding is a waste of money. Lawn Care. 2(2):2. 1929.

363. ______. Turf vs. grass. Lawn Care. 2(2):3. 1929.

364. ______. Nurse crop unnecessary. Lawn Care. 2(2):4. 1929.

365. ______. Chickweed from sheep manure. Lawn Care. 2(2):4. 1929.

366. ______. Grub proofing your lawn. Lawn Care. 2(3):1. 1929.

367. ______. Now is the time to fight crab grass. Lawn Care. 2(3):1–2. 1929.

368. ______. Summer fertilization. Lawn Care. 2(3):2. 1929.

369. ______. Chickweed: varieities and cures. Lawn Care. 2(4):1–2. 1929.

370. ______. Advantages of fall seeding. Lawn Care. 2(4):3. 1929.

371. ______. Turf Builder does wonders. Lawn Care. 2(4):3–4. 1929.

372. ______. Death to dandelions. Lawn Care. 2(4):4. 1929.

373. ______. When shall I sow seed? Lawn Care. 2(5):2. 1929.

374. ______. Late mowing of lawns. Lawn Care. 2(5):2–3. 1929.

375. ______. Creeping bent as a lawn grass. Park and Cemetery. 39(10):305–307. 1929.

376. ______. Everything for the garden. Peter Henderson and Co. New York. p. 208. 1929.

377. ______. The maintenance and renovation of turf on golf courses. Sports Turf for Golf Courses and Athletic Fields. Peter Henderson and Co. pp. 21–23. 1929.

378. ______. Drainage, and its relation to sports turf. Sports Turf for Golf Courses and Athletic Fields. Peter Henderson and Company. p. 25. 1929.

379. ______. Weeds and their eradication. Sports Turf for Golf Courses and Athletic Fields. Peter Henderson and Co. p. 26. 1929.

380. ______. Controlling turf diseases. Sports Turf for Golf Courses and Athletic Fields. Peter Henderson and Co. p. 27. 1929.

381. ______. Ridding sports turf of insects and other pests. Sports Turf for Golf Courses and Athletic Fields. Peter Henderson and Co. p. 28. 1929.

382. ______. Top dressing materials: how to make a compost pile. Sport Turf for Golf Courses and Athletic Fields. Peter Henderson and Co. pp. 29. 1929.

383. ______. Caring for trees on the golf course. USGA Green Section Bulletin. 9(1):-19. 1929.

384. ______. Research work planned in Great Britain. USGA Green Section Bulletin. 9(6):106–108. 1929.

385. ______. Green section summer meetings. USGA Green Section Bulletin. 9(9):158–163. 1929.

386. ______. The use of peat, muck, and humus on golf courses. USGA Green Section Bulletin. 9(11):191–192. 1929.

387. ______. Rutgers prof. discusses weed control problem. Golfdom. 4(5):106–107. 1930.

388. ______. Puts spotlight on grass disease findings. Golfdom. 4(6):91–93. 1930.

389. ______. Audubon makes quick time with new fairways. Golfdom. 4(8):74, 76. 1930.

390. ______. Characteristic adaptations of the more important turf grasses. Golfdom. 4(9):27. 1930.

391. ______. Meeting with New England agronomists. Greenkeepers Club of New England Newsletter. 2(12):2–3. 1930.

392. ______. Lawn making methods revised. Horticulture. 8:402. 1930.

393. ______. A common lawn pest and how to kill it. Lawn Care. 3(1):1–2. 1930.

394. ______. Spring seeding, rolling, and fertilizing. Lawn Care. 3(1):3–4. 1930.

395. ______. Friend and foe is this weed. Lawn Care. 3(2):1–2. 1930.

396. ______. Dandelion eradication. Lawn Care. 3(2):3–4. 1930.

397. ______. Exterminating earthworms. Lawn Care. 3(3):1–2. 1930.

398. ______. Summer maintenance. Lawn Care. 3(3):3. 1930.

399. ______. Summer feeding. Lawn Care. 3(3):4. 1930.

400. ______. A persistent weed. Lawn Care. 3(4):1–2. 1930.

401. ______. Using iron sulfate. Lawn Care. 3(4):2. 1930.

402. ______. More about crab grass. Lawn Care. 3(4):2–3. 1930.

403. ______. 10–6–4 is best. Lawn Care. 3(4):3. 1930.

404. ______. Ants: how to rid your lawn of them. Lawn Care. 3(5):1–2. 1930.

405. ______. Fall seeding best hundred years ago. Lawn Care. 3(5):3. 1930.

406. ______. Top dressing for lawns. Park and Cemetery. 39(12):374. 1930.

407. ______. Drainage and soils. Parks and Recreation. 13(4):184–185. 1930.

408. ______. Seeds and grasses. Parks and Recreation. 13(4):186–187. 1930.

409. ______. Lawns (adapted to the northern part of the United States). U.S. Bur. of Plant Industry. Office of Forage Crops and Diseases. Washington, D.C. 1930.

410. ______. Identifying strains of creeping bent. USGA Green Section Bulletin. 10(3):51–54. 1930.

411. ______. The bluegrass webworm. USGA Green Section Bulletin. 10(6):115–116. 1930.

412. ______. Japanese beetle spread. USGA Green Section Bulletin. 10(6):116. 1930.

413. ______. Searching in the orient for new turf grasses. USGA Green Section Bulletin. 10(10):178–183. 1930.

414. ______. Asiatic beetles as turf pests. USGA Green Section Bulletin. 10(10):185–190. 1930.

415. ______. Sources of golf course grass seed. USGA Green Section Bulletin. 10(12):-218–224. 1930.

416. ______. Many weed seeds retain vitality for years. USGA Green Section Bulletin. 10(12):228. 1930.

417. ______. Synthetic nitrogen notes fertilizer developments. Golfdom. 5(1):56. 1931.

418. ______. Brown-patch, worms, scald, and *Pythium* fight greensmen. Golfdom. 5(9):19–20. 1931.

419. ______. What is wrong with the grass. Golf Turf of High Quality. Stump & Water Co. pp. 10–11. 1931.

420. ______. Individual grass varieties. Golf Turf of High Quality. Stumpp & Walter Co. pp. 17–19. 1931.

421. ______. How to identify the grasses in your turf. Golf Turf of High Quality. Stumpp & Walter Co. pp. 20–22. 1931.

422. ______. Hints on planting stolons of creeping bent. Golf Turf of High Quality. Stumpp & Walter Co. p. 23. 1931.

423. ______. Hints on sowing grass seeds. Golf Turf of High Quality. Stumpp & Walter Co. p. 23. 1931.

424. ______. When to sow grass seeds. Golf Turf of High Quality. Stumpp & Walter Co. p. 24. 1931.

425. ______. Weeds in newly sown turf. Golf Turf of High Quality. Stumpp & Walter Co. p. 25. 1931.

426. ______. How to eradicate weeds. Golf Turf of High Quality. Stumpp & Walter Co. pp. 26–28. 1931.

427. ______. Winter-kill. Golf Turf of High Quality. Stumpp & Walter Co. p. 29. 1931.

428. ______. Turfing and turf nurseries. Golf Turf of High Quality. Stumpp & Walter Co. p. 30. 1931.

429. ______. Turf in the southern states and tropics. Golf Turf of High Quality. Stumpp & Walter Co. p. 31. 1931.

430. ______. Worms in putting greens. Golf Turf of High Quality. Stumpp & Walter Co. p. 38. 1931.

431. ______. It may be brown-patch! Golf Turf of High Quality. Stumpp & Walter Co. p. 39. 1931.

432. ______. Remedies for sundry turf pest. Golf Turf of High Quality. Stumpp & Walter Co. p. 41. 1931.

433. ______. Barbak 211, insures perfect greens, eliminating the dreaded brown patch. Greenkeepers Club of New England Newsletter. 3(2):8. 1931.

434. ______. Seed production results at the Rhode Island Experiment Station. Greenkeepers Club of New England Newsletter. 3(4):8. 1931.

435. ______. Brown-patch control. Greenkeepers Club of New England Newsletter. 3(5):6. 1931.

436. ______. Brown-patch notes. Greenkeepers Club of New England Newsletter. 3(7):4–6. 1931.

437. ______. Suggestions for a reference library on turf management. Greenkeepers Club of New England Newsletter. 3(7):8. 1931.

438. ______. Brown-patch notes. Greenkeepers Club of New England Newsletter. 3(8):2–6. 1931.

439. ______. An experiment in composition of nutrient solution and growth of grass. Greenkeepers Club of New England Newsletter. 3(10):8. 1931.

440. ______. Brown-patch discussion. Greenkeepers Club of New England Newsletter. 3(12):4–6. 1931.

441. ______. December meeting. Greenkeepers Club of New England Newsletter. 3(12):6–8. 1931.

442. ______. Seaside turf experiments. Journal of the Board of Greenkeeping Research. 2(5):106–111. 1931.

443. ______. Speedwell. A world-wide lawn pest can be controlled. Lawn Care. 4(1):1–2. 1931.

444. ______. When winter goes. Lawn Care. 4(1):3. 1931.

445. ______. Creeping buttercup. Lawn Care. 4(2):1–2. 1931.

446. ______. Dandelions and plantain dispelled. Lawn Care. 4(2):2. 1931.

447. ______. Fighting weeds at the source. Lawn Care. 4(2):3. 1931.

448. ______. Grass growing in dense shade. Lawn Care. 4(2):3–4. 1931.

449. ______. Moles, potent destroyers of good turf. Lawn Care. 4(3):1–3. 1931.

450. ______. Sodium chlorate is not common salt. Lawn Care. 4(3):3. 1931.

451. ______. Knot grass. Lawn Care. 4(5):1–2. 1931.

452. ______. More bad news for moles. Lawn Care. 4(5):2–3. 1931.

453. ______. Introduction to the chemistry of fertilizers. USGA Green Section Bulletin. 11(3):54–57. 1931.

454. ______. Dictionary of fertilizers and fertilizer terms. USGA Green Section Bulletin. 11(4):75–102. 1931.

455. ______. The use of fertilizers on putting greens. USGA Green Section Bulletin. 11(5):106–109, 113. 1931.

456. ______. Moisture requirements of grass, with figures on rainfall for 1925–1930 inclusive. USGA Green Section Bulletin. 11(8):154–162. 1931.

457. ______. Some problems of southern golf courses. USGA Green Section Bulletin. 11(9):176–181. 1931.

458. ______. Simple upkeep on MacGregor course gives championship condition. Golfdom. 6(10):8–9. 1932.

459. ______. Key to identify grasses in turf. Greenkeepers Club of New England Newsletter. 4(1):9–10. 1932.

460. ______. Golf show and convention. Greenkeepers Club of New England Newsletter. 4(2):2–10. 1932.

461. ______. Rhode Island field day. Greenkeepers Club of New England Newsletter. 4(6):5–6. 1932.

462. ______. Sheep sorrel. Lawn Care. 5(1):1–2. 1932.

463. ______. Seed early. Lawn Care. 5(1):3. 1932.

464. ______. Quack-grass. Lawn Care. 5(2):1–3. 1932.

465. ______. Spotted spurge. Lawn Care. 5(3):1. 1932.

466. ______. Watch for web worms. Lawn Care. 5(3):3–4. 1932.

467. ______. Yellow trefoil. Lawn Care. 5(4):1–2. 1932.

468. ______. Vital facts on mowing. Lawn Care. 5(4):2. 1932.

469. ______. Goose grass. Lawn Care. 5(5):1–2. 1932.

470. ______. Brown spots. Lawn Care. 5(5):2–3. 1932.

471. ______. Date of seeding. Lawn Care. 5(5):3. 1932.

472. ______. Building a golf course. Parks and Recreation. 15(6):347–355. 1932.

473. ______. Hints on building a golf course. Parks and Recreation. 15(7):447–450. 1932.

474. ______. Lawn making and maintenance. O. M. Scott & Sons Co. 59 pp. 1932.

475. ______. The delicate question of watering turf. USGA Green Section Bulletin. 12(2):22–25. 1932.

476. ______. When is a bentgrass a creeping bent? USGA Green Section Bulletin. 12(2):37–38. 1932.

477. ______. Merits of Velvet bent are presented. Golfdom. 7(1):34–35. 1933.

478. ______. Mixed German bent seed is often a costly gyp. Golfdom. 7(5):57–58. 1933.

479. ______. Some facts regarding velvet bent grass. Greenkeepers Club of New England Newsletter. 5(1):6. 1933.

480. ______. Turf field day at the New Jersey Agricultural Experiment Station. Greenkeepers Club of New England Newsletter. 5(7):4–5. 1933.

481. ______. Meeting at experimental plots. Greenkeepers Club of New England Newsletter. 5(10):2–3. 1933.

482. ______. Summary, root development of perennial grasses and its relation to soil conditions. Greenkeepers Club of New England Newsletter. 5(11):2–3. 1933.

483. ______. Report on results of research work carried out in connection with soil acidity and the use of sulphate of ammonia as a fertilizer for putting greens and fairways. Journal of the Board of Greenkeeping Research. 3(9):65–78. 1933.

484. ______. Nimblewill. Lawn Care. 6(1):1–2. 1933.

485. ______. Compost for lawn topdressing. Lawn Care. 6(1):2–3. 1933.

486. ______. Knawel. Lawn Care. 6(2):-1–2. 1933.

487. ______. The terrace problem. Lawn Care. 6(3):1–4. 1933.

488. ______. Shepherd's purse. Lawn Care. 6(4):1–2. 1933.

489. ______. Chinch bugs attack turf. Lawn Care. 6(5):1–2. 1933.

490. ______. A classification of peats. USGA Green Section Bulletin. 13(4):111–118. 1933.

491. ______. Cocoos bent as compared with Washington bent. USGA Green Section Bulletin. 13(4):119. 1933.

492. ______. Fertilizer recommendations for New York. Cornell Extension Bulletin. 281:33–38. 1934.

493. ______. Nebraska seed big producer of Kentucky blue seed. Golfdom. 8(3):71. 1934.

494. ______. Government and dealers tell why seed prices are rising. Golfdom. 8(9):31–35. 1934.

495. ______. How to identify the grasses in your turf. Golf Turf. Stumpp and Walter Company, New York. pp. 8–10. 1934.

496. ______. Description of fertilizer materials. Greenkeepers Club of New England Newsletter. 6(5):8–10. 1934.

497. ______. A grass destroying fungus new to America. Greenkeepers Club of New England Newsletter. 6(5):12–14. 1934.

498. ______. Purchasing grass seed for your golf course. Greenkeepers Club of New England Newsletter. 6(11):3. 1934.

499. ______. Snow-mold. Greenkeepers Club of New England Newsletter. 6(11):4. 1934.

500. ______. Care of velvet bent turf. Greenkeepers Club of New England Newsletter. 6(11):4–6. 1934.

501. ______. Grass seed notes. Greenkeepers Club of New England Newsletter. 6(12):4–5. 1934.

502. ______. Sedge. Lawn Care. 7(1):-1–2. 1934.

503. ______. Temperature vitally affects plant growth. Lawn Care. 7(1):3. 1934.

504. ______. The problems of shaded lawns. Lawn Care. 7(2):1–3. 1934.

505. ______. The problems of shaded lawns. Lawn Care. 7(3):1–2. 1934.

506. ______. The problems of shaded lawns. Lawn Care. 7(4):1–2. 1934.

507. ______. Purslane. Lawn Care. 7(5):-1–2. 1934.

509. ______. How to take care of a lawn. Stumpp & Walter Co. New York. p. 40. 1934.

510. ______. Lawns in the vicinity of Washington, D.C. U.S. Bureau of Plant Industry Division of Forage Crops and Diseases. 4 pp. 1934.

511. ______. Lime. Golfdom. 9(2):24–26. 1935.

512. ______. Jersey field day reveals helpful data. Golfdom. 9(9):21–22. 1935.

513. ______. Production and marketing of redtop. Greenkeepers Club of New England Newsletter. 7(1):8–10. 1935.

514. ______. North woods bent. Greenkeepers Club of New England Newsletter. 7(9):5. 1935.

515. ______. Fertilizing. Greenkeepers Club of New England Newsletter. 7(9):8–10. 1935.

516. ______. You can't grow grass on the sidewalk! Greenkeepers Club of New England Newsletter. 7(10):8–10. 1935.

517. ______. Liming. Greenkeepers Club of New England Newsletter. 7(9):10. 1935.

518. ______. Top-dressing. Greenkeepers Club of New England Newsletter. 7(9):10. 1935.

519. ______. Plant count excites research interest. The Greenkeepers' Reporter. 3(1):-9–10. 1935.

520. ______. Peppergrass. Lawn Care. 8(1):1–2. 1935.

521. ______. Spring maintenance hints. Lawn Care. 8(1):3–4. 1935.

522. ______. Good lawns in the shade. Lawn Care. 8(2):1–8. 1935.

523. ______. Control of crabgrass. Lawn Care. 8(3):1–8. 1935.

524. ______. Summer injury to turf. Lawn Care. 8(4):1–3. 1935.

525. ______. Turf experiments. F. H. Woodruff and Sons. Milford, Connecticut. 43 pp. 1936.

526. ______. Can't make bent slant uphill, Monteith tells Diegel. Golfdom. 10(4):64. 1936.

527. ______. Rhode Island bent. Greenkeepers Club of New England Newsletter. 8(2):10. 1936.

528. ______. Feeding turf early is best. Greenkeepers Club of New England Newsletter. 8(6):4–5. 1936.

529. ______. Crabgrass. Greenkeepers Club of New England Newsletter. 8(6):5–6. 1936.

530. ______. Concerning weeds in general. Greenkeepers Club of New England Newsletter. 8(7):3–4. 1936.

531. ______. Applying corrosive suplimate and calomel to turf. Greenkeepers Club of New England Newsletter. 8(9):3–4. 1936.

532. ______. Good lawns and their construction and maintenance. Greenkeepers Club of New England Newsletter. 8(9):5–6. 1936.

533. ______. Fall seeding. Greenkeepers Club of New England Newsletter. 8(10):8–10. 1936.

534. ______. White clover in lawns. Lawn Care. 9(1):1–2. 1936.

535. ______. "*Poa annua*"—grass or weed? Lawn Care. 9(2):1–3. 1936.

536. ______. Henbit. Lawn Care. 9(3):-1–2. 1936.

537. ______. Why seed lawns in the fall? Lawn Care. 9(4):1–2. 1936.

538. ______. Foxtail. Lawn Care. 9(5):-1–2. 1936.

539. ______. Snowmold disease. Turf Culture. 1(1):2–3. 1936.

540. ______. Weed control tests. Turf Culture. 1(1):3. 1936.

541. ______. Seasonal reminders. Turf Culture. 1(1):3–5. 1936.

542. ______. The control of ants in turf. Turf Culture. 1(2):1–4. 1936.

543. ______. Unusual weather conditions in 1936. Turf Culture. 1(2):4–5. 1936.

544. ______. Bermuda grass seed. Turf Culture. 1(2):6. 1936.

545. ______. Cutworms and army worms. Turf Culture. 1(2):6–8. 1936.

546. ______. Controlling clover. Turf Culture. 1(2):8–9. 1936.

547. ______. Seasonal reminders. Turf Culture. 1(2):9–11. 1936.

548. ______. A 15-year miracle. Turf Culture. 1(3):1. 1936.

549. ______. The library of grass. Turf Culture. 1(3):2–12. 1936.

550. ______. Applying corrosive sublimate and calomel to turf. Turf Culture. 1(4):-1–2. 1936.

551. ______. Controlling webworms. Turf Culture. 1(4):2. 1936.

552. ______. Copper fungicides. Turf Culture. 1(4):2. 1936.

553. ______. Winter sports for the golf club. Turf Culture. 1(6):2. 1936.

554. ______. A moderate crop of Kentucky bluegrass seed is reported. Turf Culture. 1(4):3. 1936.

555. ______. Seasonal reminders. Turf Culture. 1(4):3–4. 1936.

556. ______. The use of soil analyses. Turf Culture. 1(5):1. 1936.

557. ______. Collecting and shipping soil samples. Turf Culture. 1(5):1–2. 1936.

558. ______. Winter injury to turf. Turf Culture. 1(6):1–2. 1936.

559. ______. Greenkeepers' convention. Turf Culture. 1(6):2. 1936.

560. ______. Purchase grass seed on a basis of quality. Turf Culture. 1(5):2–3. 1936.

561. ______. Vacuum machine for harvesting buffalo grass seed. Turf Culture. 1(5):3. 1936.

562. ______. Seasonal reminders. Turf Culture. 1(5):3–4. 1936.

563. ______. Winter injury to turf. Turf Culture. 1(6):1–2. 1936.

564. ______. Turf injury from excess moisture. Greenkeeper's Reporter. 5(9):20–22, 24–25. 1937.

565. ______. Texas finds bent is OK. Golfdom. 11(4):21–22. 1937.

566. ______. Turf in the southern states and tropics. Golf Turf. Stumpp and Walter Company, New York. p. 10. 1937.

567. ______. Control of chinch bugs on lawns. Greenkeepers Club of New England Newsletter. 9(3):11. 1937.

568. ______. Bowling greens. Greenkeepers Club of New England Newsletter. 9(7):10–12. 1937.

569. ______. Notes on the use of a level. The Greenkeepers' Reporter. 5(6):7–9. 1937.

570. ______. Copper fungicides. Greenkeepers' Reporter. 5(6):15. 1937.

571. ______. Fourth annual report on greenkeeping research. The Greens Research Committee of the New Zealand Golf Association. Palmerston North, New Zealand. 30 pp. 1937.

572. ______. Honeycombed soil. Lawn Care. 10(1):1. 1937.

573. ______. Control of grubs. Lawn Care. 10(2):5–8. 1937.

574. ______. Orchard grass. Lawn Care. 10(3):9–10. 1937.

575. ______. About soils. Lawn Care. 10(4):13–16. 1937.

576. ______. Turf injury from excess moisture. Lawn Care. 10(5):17–20. 1937.

577. ______. The maintenance and renovation of turf on golf courses. Sports Turf. Peter Henderson and Company, New York. pp. 3–4. 1937.

578. ______. Preparation of the soil for sports turf on a golf course or athletic field. Sports Turf. Peter Henderson and Company, New York. p. 6. 1937.

579. ______. Drainage, and its relation to sports turf. Sports Turf. Peter Henderson and Company, New York. p. 7. 1937.

580. ______. Irrigation for perfect turf on the golf course and athletic field. Sports Turf. Peter Henderson and Company, New York. p. 13. 1937.

581. ______. Weed and their eradication. Sports Turf. Peter Henderson and Company, New York. p.21. 1937.

582. ______. Ridding sports turf of insects and other pests. Sports Turf. Peter Henderson and Company, New York. p.22. 1937.

583. ______. Top dressing materials. Sports Turf. Peter Henderson and Company, New York. p.27. 1937.

584. ______. Controlling turf diseases. Sports Turf. Peter Henderson and Company, New York. p.29. 1937.

585. ______. You can have a good lawn. Chicago Park District, Modern Recreation Series. 28 pp. 1938.

586. ______. DuPont C. C. to open second 18 this spring. Golfdom. 12(1):35–36. 1938.

587. ______. Spike discs grow increasingly popular as maintenance aid. Golfdom. 12(5):27. 1938.

588. ______. Greenkeepers spring bulletin. Greenkeepers Club of New England Newsletter. 10(4):10–12. 1938.

589. ______. Questions and answers about lawn seed and lawn care. Greenkeepers Club of New England Newsletter. 10(8):8–12. 1938.

590. ______. Snow mold. Greenkeepers Club of New England Newsletter. 10(12):-4–5. 1938.

591. ______. Metropolitan bent disease. The Greenkeepers' Reporter. 6(5):34. 1938.

592. ______. The carotene-xanthophyll ratio in fresh and dried grass. Journal of the Society of Chemical Industry. 57:457–460. 1938.

593. ______. Liming acid soils. Lawn Care. 48:1–3. 1938.

594. ______. The dandelion. Lawn Care. 49:1–4. 1938.

595. ______. Chinch bugs. Lawn Care. 50:1–3. 1938.

596. ______. Protecting seedings with burlap. Lawn Care. 51:1–3. 1938.

597. ______. Wild garlic. Lawn Care. 52:1–2. 1938.

598. ______. Grading lawn seed mixtures. The Modern Cemetarian. 48(7):128–129. 1938.

599. ______. Controlling turf troubles. Sports Turf. Peter Henderson and Company, New York. p. 29. 1938.

600. ______. The effect of watering on brownpatch. Turf Culture. p. 3. 1938.

601. ______. Spread of the Japanese beetle. Turf Culture. pp. 3–4. 1938.

602. ______. Chinch bugs. Turf Culture. pp. 4–5. 1938.

603. ______. The use of arsenate of lead. Turf Culture. p. 6. 1938.

604. ______. Seasonal reminders—excess stolons, dollarspot, excess watering, brownpatch, etc. Turf Culture. pp. 7–8. 1938.

605. ______. Rules and recommendations for testing seeds. USDA Circular 480:-1–24. 1938.

606. ______. Soil adaptations of the more important turf grasses. Golfdom. 13(2):28. 1939.

607. ______. Jap beetles doomed. Golfdom. 13(7):7–9. 1939.

608. ______. Brown patch. Golf Turf. Stumpp and Walter Company, New York. p. 25. 1939.

609. ______. The harmful effects of winter play on putting greens. The Greenkeepers' Reporter. 7(1):13, 54. 1939.

610. ______. The nematode parasite of the Japanese beetle. The Greenkeepers' Reporter. 7(4):7, 40. 1939.

611. ______. Japanese beetle. The Greenkeepers' Reporter. 7(5):7–8. 1939.

612. ______. Japanese beetle. Greenkeeper's Reporter. 7(5):8–9. 1939.

613. ______. Turf field day in N. J. The Greenkeepers' Reporter. 7(6):18. 1939.

614. ______. Chickweed. Lawn Care. 53:1–4. 1939.

615. ______. Sow early. Lawn Care. 53:4. 1939.

616. ______. The science of mowing. Lawn Care. 54:1–3. 1939.

617. ______. New threat to dandelions. Lawn Care. 55:1–2. 1939.

618. ______. Take a tip from nature. Seed your lawn this fall. Lawn Care. 56:1–4. 1939.

619. ______. Poison ivy. Lawn Care. 57:-1–3. 1939.

620. ______. Helpful hints for better maintenance. The Modern Cemetery. 49(1):-12. 1939.

621. ______. Grasses for parks. Parks and Recreation. 23(1):7–8. 1939.

622. ______. Seed annual 1939. Stumpp & Walter Co. New York. 118 pp. 1939.

623. ______. What others write on turf-research. Turf Culture. 1(1):80–89. 1939.

624. ______. What others write on turf-research. Turf Culture. 1(2):144–149. 1939.

625. ______. GSA covers fairway problems. Golfdom. 14(3):61–64. 1940.

626. ______. Greensman hear Arlington report. Golfdom. 14(10):23–24. 1940.

627. ______. Snowmold injury to turf. Greenkeepers Club of New England Newsletter. 12(11):2–3. 1940.

628. ______. To topdress or not. Greenkeepers' Reporter. 8:9–10, 32. 1940.

629. ______. The spring lawn program. Lawn Care. 58:1–4. 1940.

630. ______. Watering lawns. Lawn Care. 60:1–4. 1940.

631. ______. Excessive rains are damaging to turf. Lawn Care. 61:3. 1940.

632. ______. Plant hormones and vitamins. Lawn Care. 62:1–4. 1940.

633. ______How winter affects grass. Lawn Care. 63:1–3. 1940.

634. ______. Why lawns go bad. Lawn Care. 63:3. 1940.

635. ______. Day length affects bluegrass. Ohio Agricultural Experiment Station Bulletin 617:13–14. 1940.

636. ______. Tear gas kills weed seed. Ohio Agricultural Experiment Station Bulletin. 617:14–15. 1940.

637. ______. Pasture and fine turf. Pennsylvania Agricultural Experiment Station Bulletin. 399:48–51. 1940.

638. ______. Avoid excessive watering. Timely Turf Topics. p. 1. May, 1940.

639. ______. Brown patch control. Timely Turf Topics. p. 1. June, 1940.

640. ______. Cutworms and army worms. Timely Turf Topics. p. 1. September, 1940.

641. ______. Dollarspot control. Timely Turf Topics. p. 1. May, 1940.

642. ______. Drainage improvements. Timely Turf Topics. p. 1. December, 1940.

643. ______. Dye for grass. Timely Turf Topics. p. 1. June, 1940.

644. ______. Extreme brownpatch injury. Timely Turf Topics. p. 1. September, 1940.

645. ______. Japanese beetle control. Timely Turf Topics. p. 1. July, 1940.

646. ______. *Pythium* disease. Timely Turf Topics. p. 1. August, 1940.

647. ______. Snowmold injury to turf. Timely Turf Topics. p. 1. October, 1940.

648. ______. Spiking turf. Timely Turf Topics. p. 1. July, 1940.

649. ______. Summer fungicide rates. Timely Turf Topics. p. 1. July, 1940.

650. ______. Webworms. Timely Turf Topics. p. 1. June, 1940.

651. ______. White grubs. Timely Turf Topics. p. 1. May, 1940.

652. ______. Ants in turf. Timely Turf Topics. p. 2. August, 1940.

653. ______. Earthworms. Timely Turf Topics. p. 2. July, 1940.

654. ______. Height of cut. Timely Turf Topics. p. 2. July, 1940.

655. ______. Improve drainage now. Timely Turf Topics. p. 2. October, 1940.

656. ______. Insect pests. Timely Turf Topics. p. 2. July, 1940.

657. ______. Japanese beetles. Timely Turf Topics. p. 3. June, 1940.

658. ______. Leafspot on bluegrass. Timely Turf Topics. p. 2. May, 1940.

659. ______. Mercury fungicides. Timely Turf Topics. p. 2–3. May, 1940.

660. ______. Rainfall affects turf maintenance. Timely Turf Topics. p. 2. May, 1940.

661. ______. Weed control with arsenicals. Timely Turf Topics. p. 2. September, 1940.

662. ______. Chinch bugs. Timely Turf Topics. p. 3. July, 1940.

663. ______. Fairy rings. Timely Turf Topics. p. 3. October, 1940.

664. ______. Fall fertilizing. Timely Turf Topics. p. 3. August, 1940.

665. ______. Green scum on turf. Timely Turf Topics. p. 3. August, 1940

666. ______. Mercury vs. copper fungicides. Timely Turf Topics. p. 3. July, 1940.

667. ______. Southern June bug. Timely Turf Topics. p. 3. August, 1940.

668. ______. Skating, skiing do not harm turf. Golfdom. 15(1):11. 1941.

669. ______. Proper feeding—first step to lawn beauty. Lawn Care. 64:1–4. 1941.

670. ______. Moneywort. Lawn Care. 65:1–2. 1941.

671. ______. Fall seeding controls weeds. Lawn Care. 66:1–2. 1941.

672. ______. Mallow. Lawn Care. 67:-1–2. 1941.

673. ______. Spiking benefits turf. Lawn Care. 67:2–3. 1941.

674. ______. Underground lawn irrigation at green lawn. The Modern Cemetery. 51(5):74. 1941.

675. ______. Pasture and fine turf. Pennsylvania Agricultural Experiment Station Bulletin. 414:37–39. 1941.

676. ______. Brownpatch in the South. Timely Turf Topics. p. 1. February 1941.

677. ______. Drainage. Timely Turf Topics. p. 1. February, 1941.

678. ______. Mole crickets. Timely Turf Topics. p. 1. May, 1941.

679. ______. *Poa annua* a serious pest. Timely Turf Topics. p. 1. July, 1941.

680. ______. Snowmold injury. Timely Turf Topics. p. 1. May, 1941.

681. ______. Spring rolling. Timely Turf Topics. p. 1. February, 1941.

682. ______. Dry weather alters disease control. Timely Turf Topics. p. 1. July, 1941.

683. ______. Good air circulation necessary for healthy turf. Timely Turf Topics. p. 2. November, 1941.

684. ______. Mole cricket control. Timely Turf Topics. p. 2. November, 1941.

685. ______. Moss—an indication of starved turf. Timely Turf Topics. p. 2. February, 1941.

686. ______. Prevent crabgrass invasion. Timely Turf Topics. p. 2. May, 1941.

687. ______. Prevention of sun-scald. Timely Turf Topics. p. 2. July, 1941.

688. ______. Spring fertilizing. Timely Turf Topics. p. 2. February, 1941.

689. ______. Webworms on greens in dry weather. Timely Turf Topics. p. 2. July, 1941.

690. ______. Cutworms and army worms. Timely Turf Topics. p. 3. May, 1941.

691. ______. Snowmold disease. Timely Turf Topics. p. 3. February, 1941.

692. ______. Spring seeding. Timely Turf Topics. p. 3. February, 1941.

693. ______. Winter-kill of turf. Timely Turf Topics. p. 3. February, 1941.

694. ______. Snowmold treatment. Timely Turf Topics. p. 4. November, 1941.

695. ______. Zoysia. Timely Turf Topics. p. 4. November, 1941.

696. ______. Turf manual. United States Golf Association Greens Section. 141 pp. 1941.

697. ______. Mineral out; organic in. Golfdom. 16(9):13–16. 1942.

698. ______. Tree feeding—an aid to lawns. Lawn Care. 69:1–4. 1942.

699. ______. Crabgrass: the increasing menace. Lawn Care. 70:1–4. 1942.

700. ______. Chemical warfare on crabgrass. Lawn Care. 71:1–3. 1942.

701. ______. Fall is the time. Lawn Care. 71:3. 1942.

702. ______. Devil's paint brush. Lawn Care. 72:1–2. 1942.

703. ______. Sodium fluoride on crabgrass. Lawn Care. 72:2. 1942.

704. ______. Leaves should be removed. Lawn Care. 72:3. 1942.

705. ______. Domestic grass seed may replace imports. Pennsylvania Agricultural Experiment Station Bulletin. 429:24. 1942.

706. ______. Centipede grass. Timely Turf Topics. p. 1. November, 1942.

707. ______. Organic fertilizer for turf. Timely Turf Topics. p. 2. November, 1942.

708. ______. Tetramethyl thiuramdisulfide. Timely Turf Topics. p. 2. June, 1942.

709. ______. Turf specialists working on airfields. Timely Turf Topics. p. 2. August, 1942.

710. ______. Conserve fungicides. Timely Turf Topics. p. 3. March, 1942.

711. ______. *Dichondra repens*—weed or grass substitute? Timely Turf Topics. p. 3. August, 1942.

712. ______. Other possible mercury substitutes. Timely Turf Topics. p. 3. June, 1942.

713. ______. Can watering be reduced. Timely Turf Topics. p. 4. March, 1942.

714. ______. Fairways to sheep pastures. Timely Turf Topics. p. 4. August, 1942.

715. ______. Milky white disease of Japanese beetle grubs. Timely Turf Topics. p. 4. November, 1942.

716. ______. Mowing height. Timely Turf Topics. p. 4. March, 1942.

717. ______. Nitrogen fertilizers. Timely Turf Topics. p. 5. June, 1942.

718. ______. Tetramethyl thiuramdisulfide acclaimed as good mercury substi-

tute. Timely Turf Topics. p. 5. November, 1942.

719. ______. Earth mounds of southern green June beetles troublesome on turf. Timely Turf Topics. p. 6. November, 1942.

720. ______. What others write on turf-research. Turf Culture. 2(4):253–258. 1942.

721. ______. Green section tells of turf material status. Golfdom. 17(1):31. 1943.

722. ______. Green section hit by war. Golfdom. 17(2):20–21, 24. 1943.

723. ______. For weeds: ammonium sulfamate. Golfdom. 17(7):13–14. 1943.

724. ______. Turf experiments at Rhode Island. Greenkeeper's Reporter. 2(3):20–21. 1943.

725. ______. Lawn pennywort. Lawn Care. 75:1–2. 1943.

726. ______. Winter damage to lawns. Lawn Care. 77:1–3. 1943.

727. ______. Grass selection promises control of turf disease. Pennsylvania Agricultural Experiment Station Bulletin. 446:25. 1943.

728. ______. The use of turf on airports. Principles of highway construction as applied to airports, flight strips, and other landing areas for aircraft. Public Roads Administration Federal Works Agency. pp. 315, 344. 1943.

729. ______. Dollarspot and brownpatch control on ryegrass greens in Georgia. Timely Turf Topics. p. 1. December, 1943.

730. ______. Remove mat of excess stolons by vigorous raking. Timely Turf Topics. p. 1. September, 1943.

731. ______. Spiking may improve localized spots of dying bent. Timely Turf Topics. p. 1. September, 1943.

732. ______. Victory gardens and the golf course. Timely Turf Topics. p. 1. March, 1943.

733. ______. Charcoal treatments on greens. Timely Turf Topics. p. 2. December, 1943.

734. ______. Mole crickets troublesome in turf in the south. Timely Turf Topics. p. 2. June, 1943.

735. ______. Maintenance practices influence snowmold. Timely Turf Topics. p. 3. September, 1943.

736. ______. Proper topdressing may help avoid layering. Timely Turf Topics. p. 3. September, 1943.

737. ______. Minimum maintenance of golf holes and courses closed to play. Timely Turf Topics. pp. 4–6. March, 1943.

738. ______. Forking and charcoal treatment in putting green maintenance. Timely Turf Topics. p. 5. June, 1943.

739. ______. Iowa authority gives course care tips. Golfdom. 18(2):11. 1944.

740. ______. Rhode Island plans course maintenance battle. Golfdom. 18(7):30, 32, 34. 1944.

741. ______. Maintenance of turf and erosion control measures in the fourth service command. The Greenkeeper's Reporter. 12(4):4–8, 28–29. 1944.

742. ______. Four year summary of ratings of bents on experimental greens. The Greenkeeper's Reporter. 12(5):10–12. 1944.

743. ______. Dry weather affects lawns. Lawn Care. 79:1–3. 1944.

744. ______. Scientist urges high cutting. Lawn Care. 79:3–4. 1944.

745. ______. Chinch bugs as lawn pests. Lawn Care. 80:1–3. 1944.

746. ______. Early fall lawn program. Lawn Care. 81:1–3. 1944.

747. ______. Problems of watering. Lawn Care. 81:3. 1944.

748. ______. Buckhorn and plantain—lawn saboteurs. Lawn Care. 82:1–3. 1944.

749. ______. Zoysia grasses. Lawn Care. 82:4. 1944.

750. ______. Distributing arsenate of lead on hillsides. Timely Turf Topics. p. 1. August, 1944.

751. ______. Growth—regulating substances give promising results as turf herbicides. Timely Turf Topics. p. 1–2. November, 1944.

752. ______. Scarification advisable before hot weather. Timely Turf Topics. p. 1. June, 1944.

753. ______. Spores of milky white disease available commercially in Japanese beetle control. Timely Turf Topics. p. 1. June, 1944.

754. ______. Establishment and care of a stolon nursery. Timely Turf Topics. p. 2. August, 1944.

755. ______. Lawn pennywort control. Timely Turf Topics. p. 2. November, 1944.

756. ______. Possible fire hazard of ammonium nitrate used as a fertilizer. Timely Turf Topics. p. 2. July, 1944.

757. ______. Four-year summary of ratings of creeping bents on experimental greens. Timely Turf Topics. p. 2–5. June, 1944.

758. ______. Carbowax—a carrier for organic pesticides. Timely Turf Topics. p. 3. November, 1944.

759. ______. Narrow-leaf plantain and dandelion control. Timely Turf Topics. p. 3. November, 1944.

760. ______. Serious chinch bug injury imminent in dry seasons. Timely Turf Topics. p. 3. July, 1944.

761. ______. Clover control in turf. Timely Turf Topics. pp. 4–5. November, 1944.

762. ______. Early dollarspot attacks. Timely Turf Topics. p. 5. June, 1944.

763. ______. Preparation of carbowax—growth regulator herbicide solution. Timely Turf Topics. p. 5. November, 1944.

764. ______. Grau to direct Greens Section's new program. Golfdom. 19(8):25, 28. 1945.

765. ______. Green Section reports on tough-wearing grasses. Golfdom. 19(9):61, 63. 1945.

766. ______. Clover control in turf. The Greenkeeper's Reporter. 13(1):12. 1945.

767. ______. Wake up your lawn! Lawn Care. No. 83. pp. 1–2. 1945.

768. ______. Control of ants. Lawn Care. No. 84. pp. 1–3. 1945.

769. ______. Spring '46 lawn program. Lawn Care. No. 87. pp. 1–2. 1945.

770. ______. Hints on Jap beetle control. The Modern Cemetery. 55(8):231. 1945.

772. ______. 2, 4–D what is it? Timely Turf Topics. p. 1. July, 1945.

773. ______. Scarification advisable before hot weather. Timely Turf Topics. p. 1. June, 1944.

774. ______. Response of turfweeds to 2, 4–D. Timely Turf Topics. p. 2–3. July, 1945.

775. ______. Response of grasses to 2, 4–D. Timely Turf Topics. p. 2–3. August, 1945.

776. ______. Comparison of 2, 4–D formulations. Timely Turf Topics. p. 3. August, 1945.

777. ______. When to use 2, 4–D. Timely Turf Topics. p. 3. July, 1945.

778. ______. Effect of climatic factors on herbicidal properties of 2, 4–D. Timely Turf Topics. p. 4. July, 1945.

779. ______. Repeated applications of 2, 4–D may be advisable. Timely Turf Topics. p. 4. August, 1945.

780. ______. Seasonal variations in weed sensitivity to 2, 4–D. Timely Turf Topics. p. 4. July, 1945.

781. ______. Dust vs. spray applications of 2, 4–D. Timely Turf Topics. pp. 5–6. July, 1945.

782. ______. Zoysia for wear-resistant turf. Timely Turf Topics. pp. 5–6. August, 1945.

783. ______. Report of the preliminary studies for the examination of the structural benefits of turf on airfields. War Department. Corps of Engineers, Ohio River Division Laboratory. 1945.

784. ______. Beautiful lawns with less work. Firestone Tire and Rubber Company. pp. 1–22. 1946.

785. ______. Hot weather: creeping red fescue. Golfdom. 20(3):26. 1946.

786. ______. New Jersey reports results of 2½ years DDT use. Golfdom. 20(5):40, 44. 1946.

787. ______. Southwest turf program is set up by Grau-Noer trip. Golfdom. 20(9):-48–50, 52. 1946.

788. ______. Good lawns made easier. Lawn Care. No. 89. pp. 1–4. 1946.

789. ______. Agronomists report on foundation research; test bents on fairway. Midwest Turf News and Research. 1 p. October, 1946.

790. ______. Turf problems aired in Midwest Turf: four issues each year. Midwest Turf-News and Research. p. 1. Oct. 1946.

791. ______. DDT gets ants on greens for Detroit greenkeepers. Midwest Turf-News and Research. p. 2. October, 1946.

792. ______. Try these tips for a top course. Midwest Turf News and Research. 3 pp. October, 1946.

793. ______. Proper sand for construction and topdressing. Timely Turf Topics. p. 1–2. October-November, 1946.

794. ______. Present seed market as affecting seeding rates. Timely Turf Topics. p. 2–3. October-November, 1946.

795. ______. 2–4–D-fertilizer mixtures. Timely Turf Topics. p. 3. May-June, 1946.

796. ______. Sabadilla. Timely Turf Topics. p. 3. January, 1946.

797. ______. Roots in airfield and roadside sod. Timely Turf Topics. p. 4. January, 1946.

798. ______. Highlights—Penn State "speaker statements." Timely Turf Topics. p. 5–7. March-April, 1946.

799. ______. Highlights—Maryland "speaker statements." Timely Turf Topics. p. 8–9. March-April, 1946.

800. ______. Highlights—Iowa "speaker statements." Timely Turf Topics. p. 9–10. March-April, 1946.

801. ______. Highlights—Midwest "speaker statements." Timely Turf Topics. p. 12–13. March-April, 1946.

802. ______. Report of traffic test, turf base shoulder investigation at Maxwell Field, Ala. War Department. Corps of Engineers. 1946.

803. ______. Report of traffic tests on turf base investigational areas at Mac Dill Field, Florida. War Department. Corps of Engineers. 1946.

804. ______. Firestone lawn and garden booklet; helpful information on lawns, flowers, shrubs. Firestone Tire and Rubber Company. 22 pp. 1947.

805. ______. Exmoor introduces bent grass into watered fairways. Golfdom. 21(4):-41. 1947.

806. ______. Research, education programs stressed at turf meetings. Golfdom. 21(10):91–92. 1947.

807. ______. Effect of isopropyl-phenyl carbamate on quackgrass stolons. The Greenkeeper's Reporter. 15(4):9–10. 1947.

809. ______. Centipedegrass for lawns. Mimeo Paper No. 48. University of Georgia. 1947.

810. ______. Your lawn and plantings. Housing Commission. Detroit. 7 pp. 1947.

811. ______. Cooperative trials with methoxone 1946. Journal of the Board Greenkeeping Research. 7:38–40. 1947.

812. ______. Solving the shade problem. Lawn Care. No. 93. pp. 1–4. 1947.

813. ______. Weed-feed simultaneously. Lawn Care. No. 94. pp. 1–3. 1947.

814. ______. M.R.T.F. March conference spotlights turf problems. Midwest Turf News and Research. 1(1):1. 1947.

815. ______. Agronomist reports '46 test results of sixty-six bentgrasses at Purdue. Midwest Turf News and Research. 1(1):3–4. 1947.

816. ______. The role of lime in turf management. Turf Service Bureau, Milwaukee Sewerage Commission. 1:1–23. 1947.

817. ______. Control turf diseases by use of fungicides advises Noer in talk. Midwest Turf News and Research. 1(2):4. 1947.

818. ______. Grau discusses drainage provisions for greens at conference meeting. Midwest Turf News and Research. 1(2):1, 4. 1947.

819. ______. 1947 was bad for turf on bent greens. Midwest Turf News and Research. 1(4):2, 4. 1947.

820. ______. How to build, repair and maintain lawns. Northrup, King & Co. Berkeley, California. 12 pp. 1947.

821. ______. Availability of nitrogen from various carriers. Pennsylvania State University Mimeo. 1947.

822. ______. Lawn, its making and maintenance. Purdue Agricultural Extension Bulletin. 254:1–16. 1947. (rev.)

823. ______. Make-up and use of fertilizers for putting greens, grass tennis courts, and bowling greens in Rhode Island. Rhode Island University Mimeo. 1947.

824. ______. Turf maintenance tip No. 1. Rhode Island Agricultural Experiment Station. 1947.

825. ______. Turf for sport. No. 1. Sutton and Sons. Reading, England. 1947.

826. ______. Improving poor soil conditions on putting greens. Timely Turf Topics. p. 1. February, 1947.

827. ______. Spring care of bentgrass putting greens. Timely Turf Topics. p. 1. March, 1947.

828. ______. Lovegrasses for roughs in the southwest. Timely Turf Topics. p. 1. April, 1947.

829. ______. What is the value of lime? Timely Turf Topics. p. 2. April, 1947.

830. ______. Standards of maintenance suggested for best playing conditions. Timely Turf Topics. p. 1. May, 1947.

831. ______. Soil aeration improves utilization of fertilizers. Timely Turf Topics. p. 1. June, 1947.

832. ______. Summer care of bentgrass putting greens. Timely Turf Topics. p. 1. July, 1947.

833. ______. Topdressing survey. Timely Turf Topics. pp. 2–4. July, 1947.

834. ______. Mowing survey report. Timely Turf Topics. pp. 2–3. October, 1947.

835. ______. Effect of nitrogen and irrigation on clover populations in bluegrass sod. Timely Turf Topics. p. 1. November, 1947.

836. ______. Lead arsenate for the control of crabgrass. Timely Turf Topics. p. 2. November, 1947.

837. ______. Value of nurse grasses in seed mixtures. Timely Turf Topics. p. 2. November, 1947.

838. ______. Summary of ureaform experiments. USDA mimeo. 1947.

839. ______. Planting: Turf. U.S. Engineer Dept. (It's Engineering Manual For War Department Construction). U.S. Gov't. Printing Office. 23 pp. 1947.

840. ______. How soil reaction affects the supply of plant foods. Virginia Polytechnic Institute and USDA Cooperating Extension Bulletin. 136:1–18. 1947.

841. ______. Turf base shoulder investigation, Maxwell Field, Montgomery, Alabama. War Department. Corps of Engineers. Mobile, Alabama. May, 1947.

842. ______. Centipede grass seed production. University of Georgia Mimeo. 1948.

843. ______. The influence of various nitrogen sources upon the yields of dry clippings of centipedegrass grown on a Tifton sandy loam. University of Georgia Mimeo. 1948.

844. ______. DDT for controlling larvae of the Japanese beetle. Golf Course Reporter. 16(1):34. 1948 .

845. ______. Ten hints for good lawns. Golf Course Reporter. 16(3):12. 1948.

846. ______. Soil conditions show need for aeration programs. Golfdom. 22(5):54, 56. 1948.

847. ______. Advances in turf management reported at GSA convention. Golfdom. 22(3):46–50, 96–109. 1948.

848. ______. Cooperative trials with 2, 4–D, 1947. Journal Board of Greenkeeping Research. 7(24):133–141. 1948.

849. ______. Origin of lawn seed. Lawn Care. 98:1–3. 1948.

850. ______. Where weeds come from. Lawn Care. 101:1–3. 1948.

851. ______. Fall is lawn fix-up time. Lawn Care. 102:1–2. 1948.

852. ______. Annual foundation conference features aids for turfmen. Midwest Turf News and Research. 2(2):1, 3, 4. 1948.

853. ______. Annual conference features control of many turf problems. Midwest Turf News and Research. 2(3):1–2. 1948.

854. ______Results of 1947 Purdue bent tests given. Midwest Turf News and Research. 2(3):3. 1948.

855. ______. New weed eradication method. The Modern Cemetery. 57(11):125. 1948.

856. ______. Watering the lawn. The Modern Cemetery. 58(4):39–40. 1948.

857. ______. New insecticide for soil and turf. The Modern Cemetery. 58(8):87–88. 1948.

858. ______. Scientists make progress in crabgrass control methods. New Jersey Agriculture. 30:3. 1948.

859. ______. Weed chemicals—guidance in use and effect. Park Maintenance. 1(3):-15–16. 1948.

860. ______. Turf tips for top shape golf courses. Park Maintenance. 1(4):5–7. 1948.

861. ______. Cutting fescue seed early reduces shattering losses. Pennsylvania Agricultural Experiment Station Bulletin. 502:17. 1948.

862. ______. Centipede, a city lawn grass. Southern Seedsman. 1948.

863. ______. 2, 4–D investigations. USGA Journal and Turf Management. 1(3):-14. 1948.

864. ______. Summer turf troubles. USGA Journal and Turf Management. 1(4):-16–18. 1948.

865. ______. Control of weeds in special-purpose turf with 2, 4–D. USGA Journal and Turf Management. 1(5):16. 1948.

866. ______. Turf field day at Beltsville. USGA Journal and Turf Management. 1(6):-15–17. 1948.

867. ______. Kentucky bluegrass bent tests. USGA Journal and Turf Management. 1(6):17. 1948.

868. ______. Report on management practices responsible for turf improvement at the Country Club of the Everglades. Florida University Mimeo. 1949.

869. ______. Lawns and grass plots. Garden Guide. A. T. DeLaMarc Co., Inc. New York. pp. 33–41. 1949.

870. ______. Comparative Performance of a number of bermudagrass selections. University of Georgia Mimeo. 1949.

871. ______. Hints on brownpatch control. Golf Course Reporter. 17(4):37. 1949.

872. ______. Summary of information of turf diseases. Golf Course Reporter. 17(5):-26–27. 1949.

873. ______. National turf field day. Golf Course Reporter. 17(6):31–33. 1949.

874. ______. Washington State holds second annual turf conference. Golfdom. 23(3):31–33, 106. 1949.

875. ______. Shot-making turf tests on north-south mixture. Golfdom. 23(3):48. 1949.

876. ______. Greenkeepers bring courses through tough summer. Golfdom. 23(10):52–53. 1949.

877. ______. Safeguarding against damage by winter wind and moisture. Golfdom. 23(10):81. 1949.

878. ______. Winter lawns in the South. Lawn Care. 107:2. 1949.

879. ______. Winter protection of no value to lawns. Lawn Care. 107:2–3. 1949.

880. ______. Maryland lawn culture. Maryland Agricultural Extension Bulletin. 129:1–10. 1949.

881. ______. Highlights listed for '49 turf meet. Midwest Turf News and Research. 3(1):3. 1949.

882. ______. Turf conferees hear lecture during sectional meetings. Midwest Turf News and Research. 3(2):1. 1949.

883. ______. Turf conferees hear lecture during sectional meetings. Midwest Turf News and Research. 3(2):1–3. 1949.

884. ______. Claims U-3 bermuda a hot weather grass. Midwest Turf News and Research. 3(3):1–2. 1949.

885. ______. Control of weeds in special purpose turf with 2, 4–D. Progress Report No. 1. New York Agricultural Experiment Station. 1949.

886. ______. Hints on brownpatch control. USGA Journal and Turf Management. 2(4):31. 1949.

887. ______. Observations on turf maintenance in 1949. USGA Journal and Turf Management. 2(6):25–29. 1949.

888. ______. Second annual national turf field day. USGA Journal and Turf Management. 2(6):29–31. 1949.

889. ______. Brief report on the status of B-27 bluegrass. USGA Journal and Turf Management. 2(6):32. 1949.

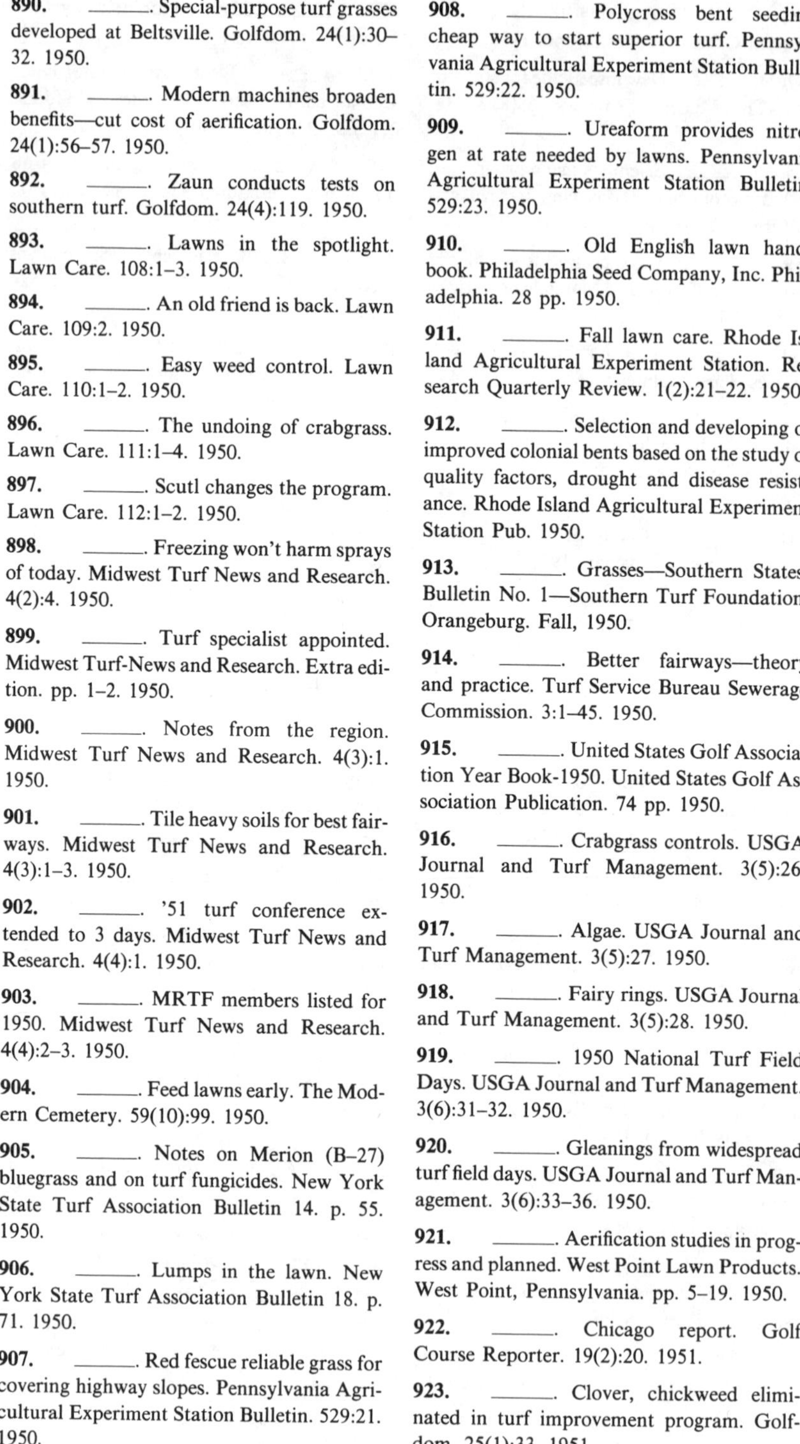

890. ———. Special-purpose turf grasses developed at Beltsville. Golfdom. 24(1):30–32. 1950.

891. ———. Modern machines broaden benefits—cut cost of aerification. Golfdom. 24(1):56–57. 1950.

892. ———. Zaun conducts tests on southern turf. Golfdom. 24(4):119. 1950.

893. ———. Lawns in the spotlight. Lawn Care. 108:1–3. 1950.

894. ———. An old friend is back. Lawn Care. 109:2. 1950.

895. ———. Easy weed control. Lawn Care. 110:1–2. 1950.

896. ———. The undoing of crabgrass. Lawn Care. 111:1–4. 1950.

897. ———. Scutl changes the program. Lawn Care. 112:1–2. 1950.

898. ———. Freezing won't harm sprays of today. Midwest Turf News and Research. 4(2):4. 1950.

899. ———. Turf specialist appointed. Midwest Turf-News and Research. Extra edition. pp. 1–2. 1950.

900. ———. Notes from the region. Midwest Turf News and Research. 4(3):1. 1950.

901. ———. Tile heavy soils for best fairways. Midwest Turf News and Research. 4(3):1–3. 1950.

902. ———. '51 turf conference extended to 3 days. Midwest Turf News and Research. 4(4):1. 1950.

903. ———. MRTF members listed for 1950. Midwest Turf News and Research. 4(4):2–3. 1950.

904. ———. Feed lawns early. The Modern Cemetery. 59(10):99. 1950.

905. ———. Notes on Merion (B–27) bluegrass and on turf fungicides. New York State Turf Association Bulletin 14. p. 55. 1950.

906. ———. Lumps in the lawn. New York State Turf Association Bulletin 18. p. 71. 1950.

907. ———. Red fescue reliable grass for covering highway slopes. Pennsylvania Agricultural Experiment Station Bulletin. 529:21. 1950.

908. ———. Polycross bent seeding cheap way to start superior turf. Pennsylvania Agricultural Experiment Station Bulletin. 529:22. 1950.

909. ———. Ureaform provides nitrogen at rate needed by lawns. Pennsylvania Agricultural Experiment Station Bulletin. 529:23. 1950.

910. ———. Old English lawn handbook. Philadelphia Seed Company, Inc. Philadelphia. 28 pp. 1950.

911. ———. Fall lawn care. Rhode Island Agricultural Experiment Station. Research Quarterly Review. 1(2):21–22. 1950.

912. ———. Selection and developing of improved colonial bents based on the study of quality factors, drought and disease resistance. Rhode Island Agricultural Experiment Station Pub. 1950.

913. ———. Grasses—Southern States. Bulletin No. 1—Southern Turf Foundation. Orangeburg. Fall, 1950.

914. ———. Better fairways—theory and practice. Turf Service Bureau Sewerage Commission. 3:1–45. 1950.

915. ———. United States Golf Association Year Book-1950. United States Golf Association Publication. 74 pp. 1950.

916. ———. Crabgrass controls. USGA Journal and Turf Management. 3(5):26. 1950.

917. ———. Algae. USGA Journal and Turf Management. 3(5):27. 1950.

918. ———. Fairy rings. USGA Journal and Turf Management. 3(5):28. 1950.

919. ———. 1950 National Turf Field Days. USGA Journal and Turf Management. 3(6):31–32. 1950.

920. ———. Gleanings from widespread turf field days. USGA Journal and Turf Management. 3(6):33–36. 1950.

921. ———. Aerification studies in progress and planned. West Point Lawn Products. West Point, Pennsylvania. pp. 5–19. 1950.

922. ———. Chicago report. Golf Course Reporter. 19(2):20. 1951.

923. ———. Clover, chickweed eliminated in turf improvement program. Golfdom. 25(1):33. 1951.

924. ______. Study shows effect of height of cut on roll of golf ball. Golfdom. 25(3):-28–29. 1951.

925. ______. Root systems get air-treated. Golfdom. 25(5):44–45. 1951.

926. ______. Electrical soil warming as an anti-frost measure for sports turf. Journal Sports Turf Research Institute. 8(27):25–44. 1951.

927. ______. Growing grass on slopes. Lawn Care. 118:1–3. 1951.

928. ______. Winter lawn injury. Lawn Care. 118:4. 1951.

929. ______. Notes on annual Purdue Turf Conference. Midwest Turf News and Research. 5(1):1–5. 1951.

930. ______. Who attends the turf Conference? Midwest Turf News and Research. 5(1):6. 1951.

931. ______. What about bermuda? Midwest Turf News and Research. 5(3):1. 1951.

932. ______. Plan C.C.S.A. fall tourney with M.R.T.F. field day. Midwest Turf News and Research. 5(3):6. 1951.

933. ______. New chemicals control clover. Midwest Turf News and Research. 5(3):6. 1951.

934. ______. Buy fertilizer now. Midwest Turf-News and Research. 5(4):5. 1951.

935. ______. List articles written on turf disease control. Midwest Turf News and Research. 5(4):5. 1951.

936. ______. Vetch with grass is best cover for highway slopes. Pennsylvania Agricultural Experiment Station Bulletin. 540:28. 1951.

937. ______. Grass and fine turf. Pennsylvania Agricultural Experiment Station Bulletin. 540:29–30. 1951.

938. ______. Be proud of your lawn. Popular Mechanics. 95:166–171. 1951.

939. ______. How to make a lawn. Rhode Island Agricultural Experiment Station. Research Quarterly Review. 2(1):8–10. 1951.

940. ______. U–3 bermuda grass. Southern California Turf Culture. 1(1):3. 1951.

941. ______. Crabgrass meets its match. Southern Seedsman. 14(6):24, 48. 1951.

942. ______. Leveling tests on soil surfaces under turf cover. U.S. Air Force Base, Chanute Air Force Base, Rantoul, Illinois, in cooperation with West Point Products. West Point, Pennsylvania. 20 pp. 1951.

943. ______. Soil survey manual. USDA Handbook. 18:1–503. 1951.

944. ______. Turf research review, 1951. The U.S. Golf Association Green Section, Plant Industry Station, Beltsville, Maryland.

945. ______. Improved turf grasses. USGA Journal and Turf Management. 3(7):-33–34. 1951.

946. ______. They aerify for better turf in Philadelphia. USGA Journal and Turf Management. 4(1):25–27. 1951.

947. ______. Fertilizer—seed mixtures. USGA Journal and Turf Management. 4(1):-29. 1951.

948. ______. Better bluegrass with Zoysia? USGA Journal and Turf Management. 4(3):25–26. 1951.

949. ______. Turf management hints for August. USGA Journal and Turf Management. 4(4):25–28. 1951.

950. ______. Turf management hints for September. USGA Journal and Turf Management. 4(5):27–28. 1951.

951. ______. Aerification and efficient turf maintenance. USGA Journal and Turf Management. 4(5):29–30. 1951.

952. ______. Report of 1951 National Turf Field Days. USGA Journal and Turf Management. 4(6):25–27. 1951.

953. ______. Plant diseases—two diseases of turf. Agriculture Gazette. NSW. 63:-200–203. 1952.

954. ______. USDA manual for testing agricultural and vegetable seed. Agriculture Handbook. 30:218. 1952.

955. ______. The rotary mower in California. California Turfgrass Culture. 2(2):2. 1952.

956. ______. From the USGA Green Section. Golf Course Reporter. 20(2):36–38. 1952.

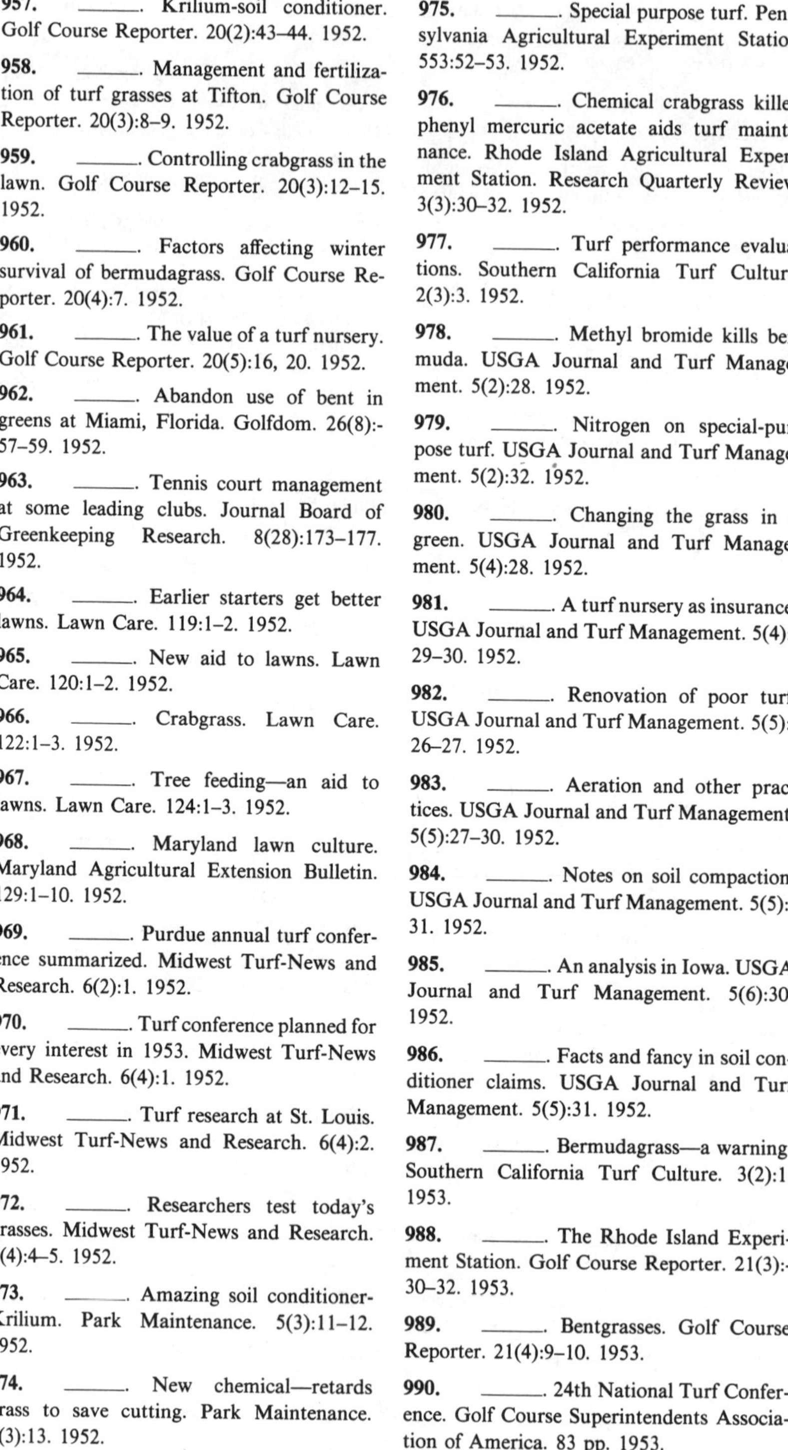

957. ______. Krilium-soil conditioner. Golf Course Reporter. 20(2):43–44. 1952.

958. ______. Management and fertilization of turf grasses at Tifton. Golf Course Reporter. 20(3):8–9. 1952.

959. ______. Controlling crabgrass in the lawn. Golf Course Reporter. 20(3):12–15. 1952.

960. ______. Factors affecting winter survival of bermudagrass. Golf Course Reporter. 20(4):7. 1952.

961. ______. The value of a turf nursery. Golf Course Reporter. 20(5):16, 20. 1952.

962. ______. Abandon use of bent in greens at Miami, Florida. Golfdom. 26(8):-57–59. 1952.

963. ______. Tennis court management at some leading clubs. Journal Board of Greenkeeping Research. 8(28):173–177. 1952.

964. ______. Earlier starters get better lawns. Lawn Care. 119:1–2. 1952.

965. ______. New aid to lawns. Lawn Care. 120:1–2. 1952.

966. ______. Crabgrass. Lawn Care. 122:1–3. 1952.

967. ______. Tree feeding—an aid to lawns. Lawn Care. 124:1–3. 1952.

968. ______. Maryland lawn culture. Maryland Agricultural Extension Bulletin. 129:1–10. 1952.

969. ______. Purdue annual turf conference summarized. Midwest Turf-News and Research. 6(2):1. 1952.

970. ______. Turf conference planned for every interest in 1953. Midwest Turf-News and Research. 6(4):1. 1952.

971. ______. Turf research at St. Louis. Midwest Turf-News and Research. 6(4):2. 1952.

972. ______. Researchers test today's grasses. Midwest Turf-News and Research. 6(4):4–5. 1952.

973. ______. Amazing soil conditioner-Krilium. Park Maintenance. 5(3):11–12. 1952.

974. ______. New chemical—retards grass to save cutting. Park Maintenance. 5(3):13. 1952.

975. ______. Special purpose turf. Pennsylvania Agricultural Experiment Station. 553:52–53. 1952.

976. ______. Chemical crabgrass killer; phenyl mercuric acetate aids turf maintenance. Rhode Island Agricultural Experiment Station. Research Quarterly Review. 3(3):30–32. 1952.

977. ______. Turf performance evaluations. Southern California Turf Culture. 2(3):3. 1952.

978. ______. Methyl bromide kills bermuda. USGA Journal and Turf Management. 5(2):28. 1952.

979. ______. Nitrogen on special-purpose turf. USGA Journal and Turf Management. 5(2):32. 1952.

980. ______. Changing the grass in a green. USGA Journal and Turf Management. 5(4):28. 1952.

981. ______. A turf nursery as insurance. USGA Journal and Turf Management. 5(4):-29–30. 1952.

982. ______. Renovation of poor turf. USGA Journal and Turf Management. 5(5):-26–27. 1952.

983. ______. Aeration and other practices. USGA Journal and Turf Management. 5(5):27–30. 1952.

984. ______. Notes on soil compaction. USGA Journal and Turf Management. 5(5):-31. 1952.

985. ______. An analysis in Iowa. USGA Journal and Turf Management. 5(6):30. 1952.

986. ______. Facts and fancy in soil conditioner claims. USGA Journal and Turf Management. 5(5):31. 1952.

987. ______. Bermudagrass—a warning. Southern California Turf Culture. 3(2):1. 1953.

988. ______. The Rhode Island Experiment Station. Golf Course Reporter. 21(3):-30–32. 1953.

989. ______. Bentgrasses. Golf Course Reporter. 21(4):9–10. 1953.

990. ______. 24th National Turf Conference. Golf Course Superintendents Association of America. 83 pp. 1953.

991. ______. Mild winter—mixed blessing to lawn. Lawn Care. 127:1–2. 1953.

992. ______. Questions—1. Grasses and their adaptation, 2. Fertilizers, soils and amendments, 3. Renovating, aerifying and irrigating, 4. Weeds and weedy grasses, 5. Disease and insects, and 6. labor incentives. Proceedings of Midwest Regional Turfgrass Conference. pp. 57–78. 1953.

993. ______. Report of 1953 field day. Midwest Turf News and Research. 1:1–2. 1953.

994. ______. Rutgers research aimed at improving turf management. New Jersey Agriculture. 35(5):15–16. 1953.

995. ______. Roadside vegetative cover research project. New York State Department of Public Worker. 43 pp. 1953.

996. ______. Seeding formula for Milwaukee's new Braves Park. Park Maintenance. 6(5):10. 1953.

997. ______. Fungicides—when and how to apply them. Park Maintenance. 6(6):20–21. 1953.

998. ______. Phenyl mercurials effective on crabgrass. Park Maintenance. 6(9):16–17. 1953.

999. ______. Asphalt mulch will bring new grass through. Park Maintenance. 6(10):15–17. 1953.

1000. ______. Phenyl mercuric acetate aids turf maintenance. Parks and Recreation. 36(10):20–21. 1953.

1001. ______. The seeding and care of lawns in Saskatchewan. Plant Industry Branch, Department of Agriculture. Saskatchewan. 11 pp. 1953.

1002. ______. *Helminthosporium* and *Curvularia* turfgrass blights controlled. Rhode Island Agricultural Experiment Station. Research Quarterly Review. 3(4):42–43. 1953.

1003. ______. New chemical slows lawn grass growth. Rhode Island Agricultural Experiment Station. Research Quarterly Review. 4(3):27, 33. 1953.

1004. ______. Notes on turf management in autumn and early winter. Sports Turf Bulletin. 22:1–4. 1953.

1005. ______. Artificial production of *Fusarium* patch disease. Sports Turf Bulletin. 23:1–2. 1953.

1006. ______. Golf in frosty weather. Sports Turf Bulletin. 23:2. 1953.

1007. ______. Turf for winter sports. Sports Turf Bulletin. 23:2. 1953.

1008. ______. Hints for lawn owners (and others!). Sports Turf Bulletin. 23:3. 1953.

1009. ______. Plant disease. USDA Yearbook. Washington, D. C. 940 pp. 1953.

1010. ______. 2,4-D at usual rates harmless to soils. USGA Journal and Turf Management. 6(3):32. 1953.

1011. ______. 25th National Turf Conference and Show. Golf Course Superintendents Association of America. 68 pp. 1954.

1012. ______. Texas Turf Association summary of test plot showings. Golfdom. 28(3):102. 1954.

1013. ______. Course superintendents advised on turf problems in "cool" zone. Golfdom. 28(3):109–111. 1954.

1014. ______. Weeds of the North Central states. University of Illinois Agricultural Experiment Station Circular 718:1–239. 1954.

1015. ______. Notes on the use of foliar nutrients. Journal Sports Turf Research Institute. 8:429–431. 1954.

1016. ______. Fall field days. Midwest Turf-News and Research. 3:1–2. 1954.

1017. ______. Rutgers research helps prevent diseases of golf greens. New Jersey Agriculture. 36(3):10–14. 1954.

1018. ______. Roadside vegetation cover research project. New York State Department of Public Works. 65 pp. 1954.

1019. ______. Soils and irrigation. North California Turf Conference. pp. 41–61. 1954.

1020. ______. Autumn and the leatherjacket. Parks, Golf Courses and Sports Grounds. 20(1):19–20. 1954.

1021. ______. Winter turf maintenance. Parks, Golf Courses and Sports Grounds. 20(3):165–166. 1954.

1022. ______. Growth control possible with MH-40 agent. Park Maintenance. 7(7):-16. 1954.

1023. ______. How to take care of your lawn. Popular Mechanics Magazine. Chicago. 32 pp. 1954.

1024. ______. The chigger. Purdue University Agricultural Extension Service. Department of Entomology. Mimeo E-34:1–2. 1954.

1025. ______. Johnson grass control. Purdue University Agricultural Extension Service. Extension Leaflet. 369:1–16. 1954.

1026. ______. Question and answer clinic—irrigation and its application. Proceedings Southern California Turfgrass Conference. pp. 32–34. 1954.

1027. ______. Question and answer clinic—grasses and weeds. Proceedings of the Southern California Turfgrass Conference. pp. 35–40. 1954.

1028. ______. Question and answer clinic—diseases and insects. Proceedings Southern California Turfgrass Conference. pp. 41–46. 1954.

1029. ______. Question and answer clinic—soils and nutrition. Proceedings Southern California Turfgrass Conference. pp. 46–51. 1954.

1030. ______. The bowling green. Southern California Turfgrass Culture. 4(3):1. 1954.

1031. ______. Association football, rugby, and hockey pitches. Sports Turf Bulletin. 24:1–2. 1954.

1032. ______. Bowling greens. Sports Turf Bulletin. 24:2. 1954.

1033. ______. Cricket squares. Sports Turf Bulletin. 24:3. 1954.

1034. ______. Tennis courts. Sports Turf Bulletin. 24:3. 1954.

1035. ______. Golf courses. Sports Turf Bulletin. 24:3–4. 1954.

1036. ______. Further work in the pathology laboratory. Sports Turf Bulletin. 24:4. 1954.

1037. ______. Turf diseases. Sports Turf Bulletin. 25:1. 1954.

1038. ______. Seeding down new sports fields and lawns. Sports Turf Bulletin. 25:1–2. 1954.

1039. ______. Weed control. Sports Turf Bulletin. 25:3. 1954.

1040. ______. Watering. Sports Turf Bulletin. 25:4. 1954.

1041. ______. Silver jubilee conference: 1st July, 1954. Sports Turf Bulletin. 26:1–2. 1954.

1042. ______. Turf management reminders. Sports Turf Bulletin. 26:2–3. 1954.

1043. ______. Care is needed in constructional work. Sports Turf Bulletin. 26:3. 1954.

1044. ______. Turf diseases in autumn. Sports Turf Bulletin. 26:3. 1954.

1045. ______. Grass growth stunting. Sports Turf Bulletin. 27:1. 1954.

1046. ______. Aspects of the winter management programme. Sports Turf Bulletin. 27:1–2. 1954.

1047. ______. Drainage troubles. Sports Turf Bulletin. 27:2. 1954.

1048. ______. Dollar spot disease. Sports Turf Bulletin. 27:3. 1954.

1049. ______. Frost protection of football grounds. Sports Turf Bulletin. 27:3. 1954.

1050. ______. Water in relation to plant growth. Proceedings Annual Texas Turfgrass Conference. 9:50–58. 1954.

1051. ______. Diagnosis and improvement of saline and alkali soils. USDA Handbook. 60. 1954.

1052. ______. New grasses from Pennsylvania. USGA Journal and Turf Management. 7(4):31. 1954.

1053. ______. Fertilizing bermudagrass. USGA Green Section. Southwestern Turfletter. 3:1. 1954.

1054. ______. Ants on the golf course. USGA Green Section. Southwestern Turfletter. 3:3. 1954.

1055. ______. More about water. USGA Green Section. Southwestern Turfletter. 4:-1–2. 1954.

1056. ______. Permeability—can gypsum help you? USGA Green Section. Southwestern Turfletter. 4:1–2. 1954.

1057. ______. Lawns. Western Garden Book. Lane Publishing Co. California. pp. 103–114. 1954.

1058. ______. Growing grass under eucalyptus. California Turfgrass Culture. 5(1):4. 1955.

1059. ______. New-experimental putting green. Florida Turf Association Bulletin. 2(2):1. 1955.

1060. ______. Turf renovation with new soil fumigant. Golf Course Reporter. 23(7):-34–35. 1955.

1061. ______. 26th National Turfgrass Conference and Show. Golf Course Superintendents Association of America. 60 pp. 1955.

1062. ______. Lawns in Kansas. Kansas Agricultural Experiment Station Circular 327:1–30. 1955.

1063. ______. How to install and care for your lawn. Lane Publishing Company. Menlo Park, California. 64 pp. 1955.

1064. ______. Grass and trees can live together. Lawn Care. Northern States Edition. 142:1–2. 1955.

1065. ______. Foundation membership reaches 254 in 1954! Midwest Turf News and Research. No. 6. 1955.

1066. ______. Lawns for Albuquerque and northern New Mexico. New Mexico Agricultural Extension Circular. 258:1–8. 1955.

1067. ______. Lawns as you like them. New Mexico Agricultural Extension News. 35:8. 1955.

1068. ______. Roadside vegetative cover research project. New York State Department of Public Works. 51 pp. 1955.

1069. ______. A non-selective weed killer. Parks, Golf Courses and Sports Grounds. 20(7):428. 1955.

1070. ______. Turf maintenance in the spring. Parks, Golf Courses and Sports Grounds. 20(7):454–457. 1955.

1071. ______. Telvar W-new general weed killer. Parks, Golf Courses and Sports Grounds. 20(10):660. 1955.

1072. ______. Improving a poor putting green by lifting and relaying. Parks, Golf Courses & Sports Grounds. 21(2):106–109. 1955.

1073. ______. Sitting around the table with the turf researchers. Park Maintenance. 8(1):13–14. 1955.

1074. ______. Chemical kill of crabgrass object of Kentucky tests. Park Maintenance. 8(3):34–35. 1955.

1075. ______. Fertilizer that works all season. Park Maintenance. 8(7):10. 1955.

1076. ______. Merion bluegrass rust is not fatal if right treatment is applied. Park Maintenance. 8(8):19. 1955.

1077. ______. One-shot fungus killer. Park Maintenance. 8(9):23. 1955.

1078. ______. Milwaukee tests turf. Park Maintenance. 8(10):48. 1955.

1079. ______. Control of cutworms. Purdue University Agricultural Extension Service. Entomology Department Mimeo E–48. pp. 1–2. 1955.

1080. ______. Maleic hydrazide of limited use on turf. Rhode Island Agriculture. 1(4):7, 9. 1955.

1081. ______. Broad-spectrum turf fungicide effective against many turf fungi. Rhode Island Agriculture. 1(4):10. 1955.

1082. ______. Weeds in sports areas; their prevention and control. Department of Agriculture, Division of Plant Industry, New South Wales. 14 pp. 1955.

1083. ______. The importance of timeliness. Sports Turf Bulletin. 28:2–3. 1955.

1084. ______. New school playing fields. Sports Turf Bulletin. 28:3–5. 1955.

1085. ______. The grass seed position for 1955. Sports Turf Bulletin. 28:5. 1955.

1086. ______. The experiment ground in winter. Sports Turf Bulletin. 28:5–6. 1955.

1087. ______. Bag trolleys on the golf course. Sports Turf Bulletin. 28:7. 1955.

1088. ______. Be prepared! Some suggestions for spring work. Sports Turf Bulletin. 28:8–9. 1955.

1089. ______. Seed renovation trials. Sports Turf Bulletin. 29:2–3. 1955.

1090. ______. Following up on winter pitch renovations. Sports Turf Bulletin. 29:-3–4. 1955.

1091. ______. Annual meadow grass—bane or blessing? Sports Turf Bulletin. 29:4. 1955.

1092. ______. Some points about mosses. Sports Turf Bulletin. 29:4–6. 1955.

1093. ______. Weedkilling. Sports Turf Bulletin. 29:6. 1955.

1094. ______. Dollar spot disease. Sports Turf Bulletin. 29:7. 1955.

1095. ______. Re-making the ring on the Yorkshire Agricultural Society's show ground. Sports Turf Bulletin. 30:3–5. 1955.

1096. ______. Some points about playing fields construction. Sports Turf Bulletin. 30:-5–6. 1955.

1097. ______. Autumn work. Sports Turf Bulletin. 30:7–9. 1955.

1098. ______. Selective weedkillers. Sports Turf Bulletin. 30:10. 1955.

1099. ______. Improving a poor putting green by lifting and re-laying. Sports Turf Bulletin. 31.5–7. 1955.

1100. ______. Some notes on autumn and winter maintenance programmes. Sports Turf Bulletin. 31:7–10. 1955.

1101. ______. Turf diseases. Sports Turf Bulletin. 31:10–11. 1955.

1102. ______. Establishment and care of Meyer zoysia lawns. Field Crops Research Branch. U.S. Agricultural Research Service. 2 pp. 1955.

1103. ______. Control of winter annuals. USGA Green Section. Southwestern Turfletter. 1:1–2. 1955.

1104. ______. Removal of thatch. USGA Green Section. Southwestern Turfletter. 1:2. 1955.

1105. ______. Merion bluegrass seed production. U.S.G.A. Journal and Turf Management. 8(1):27–32. 1955.

1106. ______. West Point-modern turfgrass tools. West Point Products Corporation. 100 pp. 1955.

1107. ______. Committee on terminology. Agronomy Journal. 48:608. 1956.

1108. ______. The Mott hammer knife mower. California Turfgrass Culture. 6(1):7. 1956.

1109. ______. Malazide, plant growth regulator. Fisons Chemicals Ltd., London. 1956.

1111. ______. In New Jersey turf is big business. Golf Course Reporter. 24(8):11. 1956.

1112. ______. 27th National Turfgrass Conference and Show. Golf Course Superintendents Association of America. 68 pp. 1956.

1113. ______. Experts exchange ideas for maintenance progress. Golfdom. 30(2):62–66. 1956.

1114. ______. Tell use and effect of Dowfume MC-2 in turf renovation. Golfdom. 30(3):88–92. 1956.

1115. ______. Dollar spot—fungicide trial, 1956. Journal Sports Turf Research Institute. 9:353–354. 1956.

1116. ______. Lawn care, building and maintaining, 2nd Ed. O. M. Scott & Sons. Marysville, Ohio. 109 pp. 1956.

1117. ______. Grants for research increase. Midwest Turf-News and Research. 9:-1–2. 1956.

1118. ______. Field days—September 17, repeated September 18. Midwest Turf-News and Research. 12:1–2. 1956.

1119. ______. New insecticide promises turf insect relief to park managers and their staffs. Parks & Recreation. 39(6):18–19. 1956.

1120. ______. Turf is big business. New Jersey Agriculture. 38(1):8–11. 1956.

1121. ______. Latest data on brown patch. Park Maintenance. 9(7):16–18. 1956.

1122. ______. Future killer of crabgrass being tested. Park Maintenance. 9(10):31. 1956.

1123. ______. Try this warm climate zoysia. Park Maintenance. 9(11):5. 1956.

1124. ______. A report on *Fusarium* patch disease. Parks, Golf Courses and Sports Grounds. 21(11):710–713. 1956.

1125. ______. New nitrogenous fertilizer. Parks, Golf Courses and Sports Grounds. 22(3):169. 1956.

1126. ______. Fatty acids, new nematocide for agriculture. Rhode Island Agriculture. 2(3):4, 10. 1956.

1127. ______. For best lawns; kind, mixtures of grasses important. Rhode Island Agriculture. 2:6–7. 1956.

1128. ______. Compost. Sports Turf Bulletin. 32:5–6. 1956.

1129. ______. Frost holes. Sports Turf Bulletin. 32:6–7. 1956.

1130. ______. Seasonal notes for lawn owners. Sports Turf Bulletin. 32:7. 1956.

1131. ______. Leather jackets. Sports Turf Bulletin. 32:9–10. 1956.

1132. ______. Some suggestions for spring work on the bowling green. Sports Turf Bulletin. 32:10–11. 1956.

1133. ______. Renovation of football pitches. Sports Turf Bulletin. 32:11. 1956.

1134. ______. Control of *Fusarium* patch disease in France. Sports Turf Bulletin. 33:5. 1956.

1135. ______. Keeping the frost out of football grounds—salt, straw and soil warming. Sports Turf Bulletin. 33:6–7. 1956.

1136. ______. How to make the most of an advisory visit. Sports Turf Bulletin. 33:-7–8. 1956.

1137. ______. Mowing. Sports Turf Bulletin. 33:8–9. 1956.

1138. ______. Summer work on football and rugby pitches. Sports Turf Bulletin. 33:-9–10. 1956.

1139. ______. Management of cricket squares during the playing season. Sports Turf Bulletin. 33:10. 1956.

1140. ______. Fever flies. Sports Turf Bulletin. 33:10–11. 1956.

1141. ______. Turf diseases. Sports Turf Bulletin. 34:3–9. 1956.

1142. ______. Drought. Sports Turf Bulletin. 34:9–11. 1956.

1143. ______. Grass aphides. Sports Turf Bulletin. 34:11. 1956.

1144. ______. Making use of expert advice. Sports Turf Bulletin. 35:5–6. 1956.

1145. ______. Samples or specimens for evaluation. Sports Turf Bulletin. 35:6–8. 1956.

1146. ______. Earthworms. Sports Turf Bulletin. 35:8–9. 1956.

1147. ______. Green earthworms. Sports Turf Bulletin. 35:9–10. 1956.

1148. ______. Moss. Sports Turf Bulletin. 35:10–11. 1956.

1149. ______. Grasses to withstand drouth. Texas Agricultural Experiment Station, Texas Agricultural Progress. 2(1):12–13. 1956.

1150. ______. Turf research at Massachussetts. Turf Clippings. 1(1):21. 1956.

1151. ______. Bermudagrass encroachment in bent greens. USGA Green Section. Southwestern Turfletter. 5:1. 1956.

1152. ______. Grubs. USGA Green Section. Southwestern Turfletter. 5:2. 1956.

1153. ______. Bermudagrass names. USGA Green Section. Southwestern Turfletters. 6:1. 1956.

1154. ______. Mowing and the thatch problem. USGA Journal and Turf Management. 9(4):31–32. 1956.

1155. ______. Your lawn. Better Crops with Plant Food. 41(5):20. 1957.

1156. ______. New liquid applicators for turfgrass. California Turfgrass Culture. 7(3):-17. 1957.

1157. ______. Vermiculite for building and maintaining turf. Golf Course Reporter. 25(6):10–11. 1957.

1158. ______. 28th National Turfgrass Conference and Show. Golf Course Superintendents Association of America. 72 pp. 1957.

1159. ______. Why feed a lawn? Lawn Care. Northern Edition. 148:2–3. 1957.

1160. ______. Nature's tip. . . . seed in the fall! Lawn Care. Northern Edition. 152:1. 1957.

1161. ______. Turf disease handbook. Mallinckrodt Chemical Works. 27 pp. 1957.

1162. ______. Field days—September 16, repeated September 17. Midwest Turf-News and Research. 17:1–2. 1957.

1163. ______. Slow nitrogen release from uramite fertilizer brings improved turf. Park Maintenance. 10(4):14–16. 1957.

1164. ______. Fall is time to kill crab-grass. Park Maintenance. 10(7):30. 1957.

1165. ______. Zoysia evaluation. Park Maintenance. 10(9):22–23. 1957.

1166. ______. DuPont manual is aid to effective use of fertilizer on turf. Park Maintenance. 10(10):46–51. 1957.

1167. ______. Michigan State on crab-grass and rust control. Park Maintenance. 10(10):64. 1957.

1168. ______. Herbicides. Park Maintenance. 10(10):71–72. 1957.

1169. ______. A new general purpose weed killer based on simazin. Parks, Golf Courses & Sports Grounds. 22(6):355–356. 1957.

1170. ______. St. Ives creeping red fescue (Fr. 10). Parks, Golf Courses and Sports Grounds. 22(7):422. 1957.

1171. ______. A new grass. Parks, Golf Courses & Sports Grounds. 22(11):697. 1957.

1172. ______. Controlling fairy rings in turf. Parks, Golf Courses & Sports Grounds. 23(2):92–94. 1957.

1173. ______. Lawn and garden book. Popular Mechanics Press. Chicago. 192 pp. 1957.

1174. ______. Grass seeding method tested. Rhode Island Agriculture. 3(3). 3. 1957.

1175. ______. Sponginess in turf. Rhode Island Agriculture. 4(1):5. 1957.

1176. ______. Methods of aeration. Sports Turf Bulletin. 36:5–7. 1957.

1177. ______. Some reminders for early spring work. Sports Turf Bulletin. 36:7–12. 1957.

1178. ______. Rotary scarification. Sports Turf Bulletin. 37:5. 1957.

1179. ______. Some points to be watched in the construction of new playing fields. Sports Turf Bulletin. 37:5–8. 1957.

1180. ______. A pearlwort bowling green. Sports Turf Bulletin. 37:9–10. 1957.

1181. ______. Keep the pin moving. Sports Turf Bulletin. 37:10. 1957.

1182. ______. Gypsum. Sports Turf Bulletin. 37:11. 1957.

1183. ______. Weedkilling with selective weed killers. Sports Turf Bulletin. 38:5. 1957.

1184. ______. Slowing down new turf areas. Sports Turf Bulletin. 38:6. 1957.

1185. ______. Summer work on winter pitches. Sports Turf Bulletin. 38. 7. 1957.

1186. ______. Mowing. Sports Turf Bulletin. 38:8. 1957.

1187. ______. Hockey. Sports Turf Bulletin. 38:8–9. 1957.

1188. ______. Turf diseases on the private lawn. Sports Turf Bulletin. 38:9–10. 1957.

1189. ______. Watering. Sports Turf Bulletin. 38:11. 1957.

1190. ______. Golf in frosty weather. Sports Turf Bulletin. 39:6–7. 1957.

1191. ______. Turf for winter games. Sports Turf Bulletin. 39:7–9. 1957.

1192. ______. Fairy rings. Sports Turf Bulletin. 39:9–12. 1957.

1193. ______. Crabgrass control. Sports Turf Bulletin. 39:12. 1957.

1194. ______. Production of chewing's fescue seed and browntop seed in New Zealand. Journal of the Sports Turf Research Institute. 9:318–321. 1957.

1195. ______. *Corticium* disease fungicide trial, 1957. Journal Sports Turf Research Institute. 9(33):367–368. 1957.

1196. ______. Problems and discussions. Texas Turfgrass Conference Proceedings. 12:19–20. 1957.

1197. ______. Your disease control program. USGA Mid-Continent Turfletter. 1:1. 1957.

1198. ______. The collar of the green. USGA Mid-Continent Turfletter. 1:2. 1957.

1199. ______. Preventive control of diseases. USGA Mid-Continent Turfletter. 2:1. 1957.

1200. ______. Crabgrass. USGA Mid-Continent Turfletter. 2:2. 1957.

1201. ______. How serious are nematodes. USGA Mid-Continent Turfletter. 2:2. 1957.

1202. ______. Liquid fertilizers. USGA Mid-Continent Turfletter. 2:2. 1957.

1203. ______. Irrigation. USGA Mid-Continent Turfletter. 2:3. 1957.

1204. ______. Grubs in turf. USGA Mid-Continent Turfletter. 3:1. 1957.

1205. ______. More about Mondo grass. USGA Mid-Continent Turfletter. 3:2. 1957.

1206. ______. Where are your tree feeder roots? USGA Mid-Continent Turfletter. 3:2. 1957.

1207. ______. Disease damage on fairways. USGA Mid-Continent Turfletter. 3:3. 1957.

1208. ______. Protect against fungi now. USGA Mid-Continent Turfletter. 4:1. 1957.

1209. ______. "Green plasma" with "instant green". USGA Mid-Continent Turfletter. 4:2. 1957.

1210. ______. Soil tests. USGA Mid-Continent Turfletter. 4:2. 1957.

1211. ______. Seed supplies. USGA Mid-Continent Turfletter. 4:3. 1957.

1212. ______. Turfgrass meetings. USGA Mid-Continent Turfletter. 5:1. 1957.

1213. ______. Plastic pipe for irrigation. USGA Mid-Continent Turfletter. 5:2. 1957.

1214. ______. Berkshires grass. USGA Mid-Continent Turfletter. 5:3. 1957.

1215. ______. United States Golf Association Year Book 1957. United States Golf Association Publication. 101 pp. 1957.

1216. ______. Gibberellic acid effects on bluegrass dormancy. What's New in Crops and Soils. p. 21. 1957.

1217. ______. Sod and turf nursery producers pest control panel. Proceedings of University of Florida Turf Management Conference. 6:58–61. 1958.

1218. ______. Penncross bent. Golf Course Reporter. 26(1):12. 1958.

1219. ______. Golf course drainage. Golf Course Reporter. 26(1):28–30. 1958.

1220. ______. *Nimisila*—a new bentgrass. Golf Course Reporter. 26(3):26–28. 1958.

1221. ______. *Veronica filiformis*—and its control. Golf Course Reporter. 26(3):32–33. 1958.

1222. ______. DSMA control dallisgrass. Golf Course Reporter. 26(5):30. 1958.

1223. ______. Plan now for turf renovation. Golf Course Reporter. 26(6):10–13. 1958.

1224. ______. Soil fumigation. Golf Course Reporter. 26(6):16, 18. 1958.

1225. ______. New staple in golf course construction—vermiculite. Golfdom. 32(5):-103. 1958.

1226. ______. L. A. Dodgers use quick turf method. Landscaping. 4(2):4, 21. 1958.

1227. ______. Use of a soil fumigant for weed control purposes. Landscaping. 4(3):9. 1958.

1228. ______. To give your lawn new life—seed now. Lawn Care. North Central Edition. 3–585:1–2. 1958.

1229. ______. Lawn weed control. Michigan State University Cooperative Extension Service. 9 pp. 1958.

1230. ______. The '58 conference stresses research accomplishments. Midwest Turf-News and Research. 18:1. 1958.

1231. ______. New machine used to control environment in turf studies. New Jersey Agriculture. 40(1):10–11. 1958.

1232. ______. The nematode: how to kill it. Park Maintenance. 11(1):7–10. 1958.

1233. ______. Soil tests help solve turf problems. Park Maintenance. 11(2):66–68. 1958.

1234. ______. Grau, Daniel, Riddle tell of economical types of turf for slopes. Park Maintenance. 11(3):56–58. 1958.

1235. ______. *Veronica* victim of weed chemicals, Cornell research. Park Maintenance. 11(6):12. 1958.

1236. ______. No soggy turf for champion Milwaukee Braves. Park Maintenance. 11(6):20–21. 1958.

1237. ______. Powdered urea-form fertilizers overcome previous disadvantages. Park Maintenance. 11(6):41–42. 1958.

1238. ______. A new approach to sports turf. Parks, Golf Courses and Sports Grounds. 23(6):366–368. 1958.

1239. ______. Weeds or grasses? Parks, Golf Courses and Sports Grounds. 23(10):-623–624. 1958.

1240. ______. Gibberellins and gibberellic acid. Parks, Golf Courses, and Sports Grounds. 24(3):181–182. 1958.

1241. ______. Ureaform—new turfgrass fertilizer. Rhode Island Agriculture. 4(3):3. 1958.

1242. ______. Report of the committee on transactions in seeds. Sports Turf Bulletin. 40:4–8. 1958.

1243. ______. Keeping the frost out of football grounds. Sports Turf Bulletin. 40:-8–9. 1958.

1244. ______. Mainly for Scotland. Sports Turf Bulletin. 40:9–10. 1958.

1245. ______. Fertilizers. Sports Turf Bulletin. 40:10–11. 1958.

1246. ______. Drainage troubles. Sports Turf Bulletin. 40:12. 1958.

1247. ______. The importance of timeliness. Sports Turf Bulletin. 41:5–7. 1958.

1248. ______. Control of dollar spot disease by cadmium chloride/Urea fungicide. Sports Turf Bulletin. 41:7. 1958.

1249. ______. Mowing. Sports Turf Bulletin. 41:8–9. 1958.

1250. ______. Leather jackets. Sports Turf Bulletin. 41:9. 1958.

1251. ______. Lichens. Sports Turf Bulletin. 41:10. 1958.

1252. ______. Thoughts on fertilizers. Sports Turf Bulletin. 41:10–11. 1958.

1253. ______. A new fungicide formulation. Sports Turf Bulletin. 42:5–6. 1958.

1254. ______. Summer weed control. Sports Turf Bulletin. 42:7. 1958.

1255. ______. Summer management on winter playing areas. Sports Turf Bulletin. 42:8–9. 1958.

1256. ______. Seasonal notes for the lawn owner. Sports Turf Bulletin. 42:9–10. 1958.

1257. ______. Weed greens. Sports Turf Bulletin. 42:10. 1958.

1258. ______. Notes after a visit to Holland. Sports Turf Bulletin. 42:11. 1958.

1259. ______. Snails but no phosphate. Sports Turf Bulletin. 42:11. 1958.

1260. ______. *Fusarium* patch. Sports Turf Bulletin. 43:4–7. 1958.

1261. ______. *Ophiobolus* patch disease. Sports Turf Bulletin. 43:7. 1958.

1262. ______. Pitch reconstruction. Sports Turf Bulletin. 43:8–9. 1958.

1263. ______. Soil warming. Sports Turf Bulletin. 43:9–11. 1958.

1264. ______. Take care of your sprayer. Sports Turf Bulletin. 43:11. 1958.

1265. ______. Salt problems in irrigated soils. USDA Information Bulletin 190. 1958.

1266. ______. Golf course maintenance costs. USGA Journal and Turf Management. 10(7):30. 1958.

1267. ______. Question and Answer session. USGA Journal and Turf Management. 11(1):31–32. 1958.

1268. ______. Question and answer session. USGA Journal and Turf Management. 11(2):32. 1958.

1269. ______. The cost of golf. USGA Mid-Continent Turfletter. 1:1. 1958.

1270. ______. A new tool for weed control? USGA Mid-Continent Turfletter. 1:1. 1958.

1271. ______. Gibberellic acid on zoysia grasses. USGA Mid-Continent Turfletter. 1:2. 1958.

1272. ______. The rainmakers. USGA Mid-Continent Turfletter. 1:2. 1958.

1273. ______. Nutrition and turfgrass diseases. USGA Mid-Continent Turfletter. 1:3. 1958.

1274. ______. Reminders. USGA Mid-Continent Turfletter. 2:1–3. 1958.

1275. ______. Winterkill of bermudagrass. USGA Mid-Continent Turfletter. 3:1. 1958.

1276. ______. Poison information centers. USGA Mid-Continent Turfletter. 3:2. 1958.

1277. ______. Watering putting greens. USGA Mid-Continent Turfletter. 4:1. 1958.

1278. ______. Homegrown sheep fescue seed. USGA Mid Continent Turfletter. 4:2. 1958.

1279. ______. Mechanical trap raking. USGA Mid Continent Turfletter. 4:2. 1958.

1280. ______. Thoughts on renovation procedures. USGA Mid-Continent Turfletter. 5:1. 1958.

1281. ______. Putting greens. USGA Mid-Continent Turfletter. 5:1–2. 1958.

1282. ______. Fairway renovation. USGA Mid-Continent Turfletter. 5:2. 1958.

1283. ______. Snow molds. USGA Mid-Continent Turfletter. 6:1–2. 1958.

1284. ______. Hormone insecticides? USGA Mid-Continent Turfletter. 6:3. 1958.

1285. ______. Fall renovation of greens and fairways. West Point Products Corporation. 62 pp. 1958.

1286. ______. Some questions about irrigation. California Turfgrass Culture. 9(3):18. 1959.

1287. ______. Recovery of diseased turf grown on sand and heavy clay soil. California Turfgrass Culture. 9(3):24. 1959.

1288. ______. Better bent greens: fertilization and management. Turf Service Bureau, Milwaukee Sewerage Commission. 2:-1–33. 1959.

1289. ______. MSU turf meet touches Dutch elm, mower care, greens. Golf Course Reporter. 27(2):30–33. 1959.

1290. ______. Musser testimonial tops outstanding Penn State meeting. Golf Course Reporter. 27(2):48–51. 1959.

1291. ______. Salute to Stockbridge. Golf Course Reporter. 27(7):10–13. 1959.

1292. ______. Seeded blankets introduced. Landscaping. 5(5):2–3. 1959.

1293. ______. Some questions about irrigation. Landscaping. 5(6):4. 1959.

1294. ______. Golf course drives for top efficiency with irrigation automation. Landscaping. 5(8):14. 1959.

1295. ______. Old wives' tales about watering. Lawn Care. North Central Edition. 3–593:6. 1959.

1296. ______. How do they keep golf greens so green? Lawn Care. North Central Edition. 3–594:1–2. 1959.

1297. ______. Is your lawn infested with crabgrass? Lawn Care. North Central Edition. 3–594:4–5. 1959.

1298. ______. 1958 grants, membership. Midwest Turf-News and Research. 22:1–2. January, 1959.

1299. ______. Lawn care and maintenance. Oregon State Cooperative Extension Service. 1959.

1300. ______. Lawn pests and problems. Oregon State College Extension Circular. 658:1–10. 1959.

1301. ______. Starting a new lawn. Oregon State College Extension Circular. 656:-1–10. 1959.

1302. ______. Midwest Regional Turf Field Day. Park Maintenance. 12(1):24. 1959.

1303. ______. Plot against spread of Johnson grass. Park Maintenance. 12(5):24. 1959.

1304. ______. Turf annual-fertilizers. Park Maintenance. 12(7):22–23. 1959.

1305. ______. Turf annual-Irrigation notes. Park Maintenance. 12(7):28. 1959.

1306. ______. Soil fumigant passes control tests on turf. Park Maintenance. 12(12):8. 1959.

1307. ______. Urea-form fertilizer. Parks, Golf Courses and Sports Grounds. 24(4):249–250. 1959.

1308. ______. Propagation of the turf fungi. Parks, Golf Courses and Sports Grounds. 24(5):304. 1959.

1309. ______. Fisons introduce a total weedkiller. Parks, Golf Courses and Sports Grounds. 24(6):394. 1959.

1310. ______. "Greenlay"—lawn seed in rolls. Parks, Golf Courses & Sports Grounds. 24(7):474. 1959.

1311. ______. A turf nursery from seed. Parks, Golf Courses and Sports Grounds. 24(9):608. 1959.

1312. ______. Dowpon—a specialized weedkiller. Parks, Golf Courses, and Sports Grounds. 25(1):44. 1959.

1313. ______. Basic steps to a good lawn. You Can Grow a Good Lawn; The American Potash Institute. pp. 16–17. 1959.

1314. ______. Maintenance of interstate highway roadsides as affected by work operations. "Roadside Development" Highway Research Board, National Academy of Science, National Research Council. 697:27–29. 1959.

1315. ______. Quiz the experts—questions on turf research. Proceedings Southeastern Turfgrass Conference. 13:54–74. 1959.

1316. ______. Uses for zoysiagrasses in the Southwest. Southern California Turfgrass Culture. 9(4):29. 1959.

1317. ______. Propagation of turf fungi. Sports Turf Bulletin. 44:6–7. 1959.

1318. ______. Winter tees. Sports Turf Bulletin. 44:7. 1959.

1319. ______. Winter care of the mower. Sports Turf Bulletin. 44:7–8. 1959.

1320. ______. Early spring maintenance. Sports Turf Bulletin. 44:8–9. 1959.

1321. ______. Witch-craft. Sports Turf Bulletin. 44:9–10. 1959.

1322. ______. Notes after a visit to Germany. Sports Turf Bulletin. 44:11. 1959.

1323. ______. For the lawn owner. Sports Turf Bulletin. 45:3–4. 1959.

1324. ______. Bag trolleys on the golf course. Sports Turf Bulletin. 45:5. 1959.

1325. ______. Renovation of winter pitches. Sports Turf Bulletin. 45:6–7. 1959.

1326. ______. The mower in summer. Sports Turf Bulletin. 45:7. 1959.

1327. ______. A turf nursery from seed. Sports Turf Bulletin. 45:8–10. 1959.

1328. ______. Muddy fairways. Sports Turf Bulletin. 45:10. 1959.

1329. ______. *Agrostis tenuis.* Sports Turf Bulletin. 45:11. 1959.

1330. ______. Cable-laying for soil warming. Sports Turf Bulletin. 46:5–6. 1959.

1331. ______. Looking ahead: notes on golf green management in autumn and early winter. Sports Turf Bulletin. 46:8–9. 1959.

1332. ______. Chewings' fescue. Sports Turf Bulletin. 46:10. 1959.

1333. ______. Chewings' fescue and browntop from the U.S.A. Sports Turf Bulletin. 46:11. 1959.

1334. ______. Creeping red fescue. Sports Turf Bulletin. 47:5. 1959.

1335. ______. Sheep's fescue. Sports Turf Bulletin. 47:5–6. 1959.

1336. ______. The control of sea-side chickweed. Sports Turf Bulletin. 47:6–7. 1959.

1337. ______. Guarding golf greens against frost damage. Sports Turf Bulletin. 47:7–8. 1959.

1338. ______. Notes on bowling green management in autumn and early winter. Sports Turf Bulletin. 47:8–9. 1959.

1339. ______. Playing field construction. Sports Turf Bulletin. 47:11–12. 1959.

1340. ______. Mixing of herbicides with insecticides, pesticides, or other herbicides. Stockbridge School Turf Clippings. Conference Proceedings. pp. 18–19. 1959.

1341. ______. Desiccation. USGA Mid-Continent Turfletter. 1:1–2. 1959.

1342. ______. Fertilization of bentgrass greens. USGA Mid-Continent Turfletter. 1:2. 1959.

1343. ______. Knotweed *Polygonum aviculare* L. USGA Mid-Continent Turfletter. 1:3. 1959.

1344. ______. Crabgrass is coming. USGA Mid-Continent Turfletter. 2:1–2. 1959.

1345. ______. Disease on bermudagrass. USGA Mid-Continent Turfletter. 2:3. 1959.

1346. ______. Some thoughts on traffic damage. USGA Mid-Continent Turfletter. 3:1–2. 1959.

1347. ______. Observations by Al Radko. USGA Mid-Continent Turfletter. 3:3. 1959.

1348. ______. How to deal with winterkill. USGA Mid-Continent Turfletter. 4:1. 1959.

1349. ______. Early season injury overcome. USGA Mid-Continent Turfletter. 4:2. 1959.

1350. ______. Nematocide helps in Minnesota. USGA Mid-Continent Turfletter. 4:2. 1959.

1351. ______. Spray rig innovation. USGA Mid-Continent Turfletter. 4:2. 1959.

1352. ______. Adversity shows up weaknesses. USGA Mid-Continent Turfletter. 4:3. 1959.

1353. ______. Nematode literature. USGA Mid-Continent Turfletter. 5:1. 1959.

1354. ______. Orchard Lake Country Club builds a putting green. USGA Mid-Continent Turfletter. 5:1. 1959.

1355. ______. Switch to fertilizer for surer footing. USGA Mid-Continent Turfletter. 5:1. 1959.

1356. ______. Kentucky bluegrass seed production down. USGA Mid-Continent Turfletter. 5:2. 1959.

1357. ______. Seaside bent seeding helps to restore greens. USGA Mid-Continent Turfletter. 6:1. 1959.

1358. ______. Treatment of winterkill. USGA Mid-Continent Turfletter. 6:1. 1959.

1359. ______. Fairways respond to careful management. USGA Mid-Continent Turfletter. 6:2. 1959.

1360. ______. Mammalian toxicity and persistence of pesticides. USGA Mid-Continent Turfletter. 6:3. 1959.

1361. ______. United States Golf Association Year Book—1959. United States Golf Association Publication. 110 pp. 1959.

1362. ______. A handbook of agronomy. Virginia Polytechnic Institute Bulletin. 97:-167. 1959.

1363. ______. How thick should sod be cut. Warren's Turf Nursery Publication. pp. 1–21. 1959.

1364. ______. Response of Meyer zoysia to lime and fertilizer treatments. California Turfgrass Culture. 10(3):22. 1960.

1365. ______. Houston convention; research men have their day. Golfdom. 34(3):-40–46. 1960.

1366. ______. Nematodes won't attend PGA tourney. Golfdom. 34(7):28, 80–81. 1960.

1367. ______. Report of overseeding trials at East Lake, Sea Island, Ga. Golfdom. 34(10):38. 1960.

1368. ______. A selected bibliography. Highway Research Board. 26:11–17. 1960.

1369. ______. Conventional turfing method finds new market in the West. Landscaping. 5(10):6, 31, 35. 1960.

1370. ______. Mystery grass now being made available. Landscaping. 5(11):4. 1960.

1371. ______. New net product proves material aid to landscaping. Landscaping. 5(12):4, 6, 17. 1960.

1372. ______. How high should you cut? Lawn Care. North Central Edition. 3–602:6. 1960.

1373. ______. Can you water too often? Lawn Care. North Central Edition. 3–602:7. 1960.

1374. ______. Better fairways: theory and practice. Turf Service Bureau, Milwaukee Sewerage Commission. 3:1–45. 1950.

1375. ______. State's 200,000 acres of turf worth $340,000,000. New Jersey Agriculture. 42(4):4–5. 1960.

1376. ______. Weed control. New Zealand Institute for Turf Culture Newsletter. 6:1–3. 1960.

1377. ______. Pre-emergents may be more effective with overhead irrigation methods. Park Maintenance. 13(1):14. 1960.

1378. ______. Use of polythene on golf greens. Parks, Golf Courses and Sports Grounds. 25(7):500. 1960.

1379. ______. New lawn mix from Woodwards. Parks, Golf Courses and Sports Grounds. 25(7):509. 1960.

1380. ______. Weed control in flower and ornamental crops. Parks, Golf Courses and Sports Grounds. 25(10):750–754. 1960.

1381. ______. Weedazol T-L for couch control. Parks, Golf Courses and Sports Grounds. 25(10):760. 1960.

1382. ______. Ureaform nitrogen suggested for full season turf growth. Pennsylvania Agricultural Experiment Station. Science for the Farmer. 8:15. 1960.

1383. ______. Which lawn grass is best? South Carolina Agricultural Research. 7:2. 1960.

1384. ______. Weed control recommendations for 1960 fairway turf. California Turfgrass Culture. 10(1):8. 1960.

1385. ______. Newport Kentucky bluegrass. California Turfgrass Culture. 10(2):16. 1960.

1386. ______. Golf courses—some hints. Sports Turf Bulletin. 48:5. 1960.

1387. ______. Smooth stalked meadow grass. Sports Turf Bulletin. 48:7. 1960.

1388. ______. Rough stalked meadow grass. Sports Turf Bulletin. 48:8. 1960.

1389. ______. Gall midges. Sports Turf Bulletin. 48:9. 1960.

1390. ______. *Poa annua.* Sports Turf Bulletin. 49:6–8. 1960.

1391. ______. Turf damage from foot traffic. Sports Turf Bulletin. 49:8–9. 1960.

1392. ______. The renovation of winter pitches. Sports Turf Bulletin. 49:9–10. 1960.

1393. ______. The meadow-grasses. Sports Turf Bulletin. 50:7–8. 1960.

1394. ______. Summer and autumn management on the golf course. Sports Turf Bulletin. 50:9–10. 1960.

1395. ______. Lawn hints. Sports Turf Bulletin. 50:10–11. 1960.

1396. ______. Perennial ryegrass. Sports Turf Bulletin. 51:6–7. 1960.

1397. ______. Alien lawn weeds. Sports Turf Bulletin. 51: 7–8. 1960.

1398. ______. Notes on winter maintenance of sports turf. Sports Turf Bulletin. 51:9–11. 1960.

1399. ______. Our answers to your questions—lime reduces nematodes. Sunshine State Agricultural Research Report. 5(2):18–19. 1960.

1400. ______. Soil classification: a comprehensive system. 7th approximation. USDA. US Government Printing Office. Washington, D.C. 265 pp. 1960.

1401. ______. Specifications for a method of putting green construction. USGA Journal and Turf Management. 13(5):24–28. 1960.

1402. ______. Visits to green section visiting service subscribers. USGA Mid-Continent Turfletter. 1:1. 1960.

1403. ______. Spring is just around the corner. USGA Mid-Continent Turfletter. 1:-2–3. 1960.

1404. ______. Winter kill problems with bermudagrass. USGA Mid-Continent Turfletter. 3:1. 1960.

1405. ______. Deep-drilling for greens. USGA Mid-Continent Turfletter. 3:2. 1960.

1406. ______. Gnats damage greens in Phoenix. USGA Mid-Continent Turfletter. 3:2. 1960.

1407. ______. Specification for construction of greens. USGA Mid-Continent Turfletter. 4:1. 1960.

1408. ______. The value of a nursery. USGA Mid-Continent Turfletter. 4:1. 1960.

1409. ______. Ball washer mounts. USGA Mid-Continent Turfletter. 4:2. 1960.

1410. ______. Eight miles of strip-sodding at Westwood. USGA Mid-Continent Turfletter. 4:2. 1960.

1411. ______. Records. USGA Mid-Continent Turfletter. 4:2. 1960.

1412. ______. Superintendent's ingenuity saves large tree. USGA Mid-Continent Turfletter. 4:3. 1960.

1413. ______. Recent turfgrass conferences. USGA Mid-Continent Turfletter. 5:1. 1960.

1414. ______. Seed supplies. USGA Mid-Continent Turfletter. 5:2. 1960.

1415. ______. Consider the services of the green section. USGA Mid-Continent Turfletter. 5:3. 1960.

1416. ______. USGA Open championship annual. Peerless Printing Co., Denver. 224 pp. 1960.

1417. ______. United States Golf Association year book. USGA Publication. 113 pp. 1960.

1418. ______. Your lawn in hours. Warren's Turf Nursery. 29 pp. 1960.

1419. ______. Herbicide screening trials on field crops and turf. Arkansas Agricultural Experiment Station. Mimeograph Series 105:1–15. 1961.

1420. ______. Seedling vigor and rate of emergence in two sources of Newport Kentucky bluegrass. Crop Science. 1:305–306. 1961.

1421. ______. Another look at golf cars. Golf Course Reporter. 29(8):12–20. 1961.

1422. ______. Researchers discuss chemicals, cautions. Golfdom.. 35(3):44–48. 1961.

1423. ______. 15 Speakers appear on this program. Golfdom. 35(3):108–120. 1961.

1424. ______. Inspection of commercial fertilizers. Indiana Agricultural Experiment Station. Purdue University. Inspection Report 31. 1961.

1425. ______. Kentucky research results in brief—insects attacking grasses. Kentucky Farm and Home Science. 7(1):7. 1961.

1426. ______. The underground story of grass. Lawn Care. North Central Edition. 3–613. 1961.

1427. ______. The Midwest Regional Turf Foundation for research, education, and training. Midwest Turf-News and Research. 1(revised):1–2. 1961.

1428. ______. 1960 grants, membership. Midwest Turf-News and Research. 24:1–3. 1961.

1429. ______. Experiment station diversifies program. Nevada Ranch and Home Review. 2(3):4–5. 1961.

1430. ______. Turf culture. New Zealand Institute for Turf Culture. Palmerston North, New Zealand. 179 pp. 1961.

1431. ______. What rolling should be done. New Zealand Institute for Turf Culture Newsletter. 15:10. 1961.

1432. ______. Lawn and ornamental days. Ohio Agricultural Experiment Station, Wooster, Ohio. 21 pp. 1961.

1433. ______. Turf grass recommendations. Pacific Northwest Turf Conference Proceedings. 15:93–94. 1961.

1434. ______. Turf annual—fertilization. Park Maintenance. 14(7):21–23. 1961.

1435. ______. Renovation is topic at turf conference. Park Maintenance. 14(9):6. 1961.

1436. ______. Cut costs as Ontario department does by mechanized seeding and sodding. Park Maintenance. 14(10):10,14. 1961.

1437. ______. Working with weedkillers. Sports Turf Bulletin. 54:5–7. 1961.

1438. ______. Ten rules when spraying with selective weedkillers. Sports Turf Bulletin. 54:7. 1961.

1439. ______. Timothy. Sports Turf Bulletin. 54:9–10. 1961.

1440. ______. *Ophiobolus* patch disease in the U.S.A. Sports Turf Bulletin. 54:12. 1961.

1441. ______. Progress report: Preemerge chemicals of the control of crabgrass. Stockbridge School Turf Clippings Conference Proceedings. 1(6):A–70—A–71. 1961.

1442. ______. Seeds. USDA. Yearbook of Agriculture. US Government Printing Office, Washington D.C. 591 pp. 1961.

1443. ______. Quarter for water. USGA Journal and Turf Management. 13(7):24–30. 1961.

1444. ______. Be ready—spring is just around the corner. USGA Mid-Continent Turfletter. 1:1. 1961.

1445. ______. Consider the rate. USGA Mid-Continent Turfletter. 1:2. 1961.

1446. ______. Fungicides for *Fusarium* patch. USGA Mid-Continent Turfletter. 1:2. 1961.

1447. ______. Green section educational meeting. USGA Mid-Continent Turfletter. 1:2. 1961.

1448. ______. The green section visiting service. USGA Mid-Continent Turfletter. 1:3. 1961.

1449. ______. Soil test results reflect fertilization practices. USGA Mid-Continent Turfletter. 2:1. 1961.

1450. ______. Timeliness. USGA Mid-Continent Turfletter. 2:1. 1961.

1451. ______. Drift of pesticides. USGA Mid-Continent Turfletter. 2:3. 1961.

1452. ______. National golf week. USGA Mid-Continent Turfletter. 2:3. 1961.

1453. ______. Kentucky bluegrass seed crop forecast. USGA Mid Continent Turfletter. 4:1. 1961.

1454. ______. California research. USGA Mid Continent Turfletter. 4:2. 1961.

1455. ______. Traffic barriers. USGA Mid-Continent Turfletter. 4:3. 1961.

1456. ______. Your winter reading. USGA Mid-Continent Turfletter. 5:1. 1961.

1458. ______. Turf conferences. USGA Mid-Continent Turfletter. 5:2. 1961.

1459. ______. Agronomists view St. Louis turf research. USGA Mid-Continent Turfletter. 6:1. 1961.

1460. ______. Mowing trials in New Zealand. USGA Mid-Continent Turfletter. 6:1. 1961.

1461. ______. Now where did I put those pruning tools? USGA Mid-Continent Turfletter. 6:2. 1961.

1462. ______. Nomenclature of some plants associated with turfgrass management. Agronomy Journal. 54:275–276. 1962.

1463. ______. Summary of terms. Crop Science. 2(1):85–87. 1962.

1464. ______. Annual Membership Directory of the Golf Course Superintendents Association of America-1962. Golf Course Superintendents Association of America. Jacksonville Beach, Fla. 123 pp. 1962.

1465. ______. Al suggests hideout for troubled turfmen. Golfdom. 36(3):56–60. 1962.

1466. ______. Crabgrass annoys superintendents but 3 out of 4 tolerate it. Golfdom. 36(8):19–20,72,74. 1962.

1467. ______. Consultants suggest three-stage program for club expansion. Golfdom. 36(9):21–22. 1962.

1469. ______. Notes on experimental bentgrasses. Iagreen. 1(1):8–9. 1962.

1470. ______. Turfgrass nutrition—disease control studies. Iagreen. 1(1):12–24. 1962.

1471. ______. Turfgrass ecological studies. Iagreen. 1(1):25–26. 1962.

1472. ______. Warm season grass evaluation trial. Iagreen. 1(1):27–28. 1962.

1473. ______. Bluegrass evaluation trial. Iagreen. 1(1):29–30. 1962.

1474. ______. Pre-emergence crabgrass control trials. Iagreen. 1(1):32–33. 1962.

1475. ______. *Ophiobolus* patch disease. Journal of Sports Turf Research Institute. 10(38):467–468. 1962.

1476. ______. Lawn grasses. Kansas State University Agricultural Experiment Station. Progress Report 80:43–44. 1962.

1477. ______. Kentucky research results in brief—weed control in turf. Kentucky Farm and Home Science. 8(1):7. 1962.

1478. ______. Difficulties sometimes encountered in growing grass in the shade. Lawn Care. North Central Edition. 3–622:5. 1962.

1479. ______. Experiments on seeding and mulching for roadside erosion control. Minnesota Department of Highways Investigation No. 614. 38 pp. 1962.

1480. ______. 1962 New Jersey fertilizer and lime recommendations for average soil conditions. New Jersey Agricultural Experiment Station. Extension Bulletin 365:1–20. 1962.

1481. ______. New York Times Garden Book. A. A. Knopf. New York. 198–200 pp. 1962.

1482. ______. Summer sports. New Zealand Institute for Turf Culture Newsletter. 17:3–4. 1962.

1483. ______. Earthworms and their influence on playing turf. New Zealand Institute for Turf Culture Newsletter. 18:4–6. 1962.

1484. ______. Influence of acidity on sports turf texture. New Zealand Institute for Turf Culture Newsletter. 18:18–20. 1962.

1485. ______. Soil acidification. New Zealand Institute for Turf Culture Newsletter. 21:10–11. 1962.

1486. ______. Quality of irrigation water. Oregon State University Cooperative Extension Service. Extension Bulletin 808:1–8. 1962.

1487. ______. Turf annual—diseases. Park Maintenance. 15(7):17–40. 1962.

1488. ______. Turf annual—fertilization. Park Maintenance. 15(7):24–28. 1962.

1489. ______. Turf annual—grasses. Park Maintenance. 15(7):28–32. 1962.

1490. ______. Turf annual—insecticides. Park Maintenance. 15(7):32–33. 1962.

1491. ______. Turf annual—irrigation. Park Maintenance. 15(7):33–34. 1962.

1492. ______. Turf annual—management aids. Park Maintenance. 15(7):34–37. 1962.

1493. ______. Turf annual—weeds. Park Maintenance. 15(7):37–40. 1962.

1494. ______. Lawn bowling—an analysis of public operations. Parks and Recreation. 45(2):86–87. 1962.

1495. ______. Breeding superior varieties of Kentucky bluegrass, red fescue, and creeping bentgrass. Seventy-fourth Annual Report of the Pennsylvania Agricultural Experiment Station. Bulletin 681:7. 1962.

1497. ______. Evaluation of existing and new types and varieties of Kentucky bluegrass, fescue, and bentgrasses for special purpose turf. Seventy-fourth Annual Report of the Pennsylvania Agricultural Experiment Station. Bulletin 681:7. 1962.

1498. ______. Compost. Sports Turf Bulletin. 56:5–6. 1962.

1500. ______. The fulfilment of a dream. Sports Turf Bulletin. 57:8–10. 1962.

1501. ______. The need for water. Sports Turf Bulletin. 58:8–9. 1962.

1502. ______. Surface renovation. Sports Turf Bulletin. 59:4–5. 1962.

1503. ______. The maintenance of a rugby football ground. Turf for Sport. 4(2):-3–7. 1962.

1504. ______. Monthly hints on turf for sport. Turf for Sport. 4(2):8–9. 1962.

1505. ______. Respiratory devices for protection against certain pesticides. USDA. ARS–33–76. 13 pp. 1962.

1506. ______. Soil survey manual. USDA Handbook (Supplement). 18:173–188. 1962.

1507. ______. *Poa annua* as a winter fairway. USGA Mid-Continent Turfletter. 2:1. 1962.

1508. ______. Buffer strips between bent and bermuda. USGA Mid-Continent Turfletter. 2:2. 1962.

1509. ______. Fluffy turf on aprons. USGA Mid-Continent Turfletter. 2:2. 1962.

1510. ______. Dallas golf courses keep records. USGA Mid-Continent Turfletter. 3:2. 1962.

1511. ______. After effects of winter. USGA Mid-Continent Turfletter. 3:3. 1962.

1512. ______. New bermudagrass pests. USGA Mid-Continent Turfletter. 3:3. 1962.

1513. ______. School for golf course workers. USGA Mid-Continent Turfletter. 4:1. 1962.

1514. ______. Bermudagrass winterkill—causes and cures. USGA Mid-Continent Turfletter. 4:2. 1962.

1515. ______. Kentucky bluegrass. USGA Mid-Continent Turfletter. 4:3. 1962.

1516. ______. Some thoughts on organic matter. USGA Mid-Continent Turfletter. 5:1. 1962.

1517. ______. Seed forecast. USGA Mid-Continent Turfletter. 5:2. 1962.

1518. ______. Protection against snow mold. USGA Mid-Continent Turfletter. 5:3. 1962.

1519. ______. Causes of cold injury in turfgrass. USGA Mid-Continent Turfletter. 6:1. 1962.

1520. ______. Water movement in soils. USGA Mid-Continent Turfletter. 6:2. 1962.

1521. ______. Chinch bugs moving to midwest; here's way to identify them. Weeds and Turf. p. 6. September, 1962.

1522. ______. How to use new pre-emergent herbicides in turf. Weeds and Turf. pp. 8–10. September, 1962.

1523. ______. How to control turf diseases. Weeds and Turf. pp. 1, 3–6, 11. November, 1962.

1524. ______. Identifying grasses in Wisconsin turf. Wisconsin Extension Service. Special Circular. 69:1–12. 1962.

1526. ______. Irrigation symposium. Golf Course Reporter. 31(6):14–36. 1963.

1527. ______. Changes coming in fertilizer labels and calculations. Golf Course Reporter. 31(8):48–52. 1963.

1528. ______. Midwest turfmen describe 1961–62 winterkill damage. Golfdom. 37(1):-79. 1963.

1529. ______. Uclans tell of studies in turf technology. Golfdom. 37(3):96–102. 1963.

1530. ______. Warren's business is turf production but pastime is research. Golfdom. 37(6):28–30, 97–98. 1963.

1531. Astrup, M. H. Mulching practices and materials. Highway Research Record No. 23:50–59. 1963.

1532. Anonymous. Procedure for introducing a variety. Illinois Turfgrass Conference Proceedings. 4:18. 1963.

1533. ______. Continuing home audit: lawn maintenance. Marketing Research Department, Los Angeles Times. 1963.

1534. ______. Notes from sod growers discussion. Proceedings Midwest Regional Turf Conference. p. 53. 1963.

1535. ______. 1962 grants and memberships. Midwest Turf-News and Research. No. 26. 1963.

1536. ______. Minimum maintenance: lawns. Minimum Maintainance Landscaping. Jacobsen Mfg. Co. pp. 28–29. 1963.

1537. ______. New bowling greens from old. New Zealand Institute for Turf Culture Newsletter. 23:2–7. 1963.

1538. ______. Golf green renovation. New Zealand Institute for Turf Culture Newsletter. 23:7–8. 1963.

1539. ______. Manurial treatments of greens. New Zealand Institute for Turf Culture Newsletter. 23:8–9. 1963.

1540. ______. Influence of colour on temperatures under rubber bowls mats. New Zealand Institute for Turf Culture Newsletter. 23:11–12. 1963.

1541. ______. Carolina lawns. North Carolina Agricultural Extension Service Circular 292. 12 pp. 1953.

1542. ______. Experimental data on soil-wetting agents and practical use and principle of wilt control by biochemical action on stomata openings. Oklahoma Turfgrass Conference Proceedings. pp. 5–8. 1963.

1543. ______. Suggestions for removing ice from golf course greens. Park Maintenance. 16(2):49. 1963.

1544. ______. Nematode-capturing fungus found by USDA. Park Maintenance. 16(5):8. 1963.

1545. ______. Diseases. Park Maintenance. 16(7):14–18. 1963.

1546. ______. Fertilization. Park Maintenance. 16(7):18–21. 1963.

1547. ______. Grasses. Park Maintenance. 16(7):21–23. 1963.

1548. ______. Insecticides. Park Maintenance. 16(7):23–24. 1963.

1549. ______. Irrigation. Park Maintenance. 16(7):25–26. 1963.

1550. ______. Management aids. Park Maintenance. 16(7):26. 1963.

1551. ______. Weeds. Park Maintenance. 16(7):26–28. 1963.

1552. ______. The protection of sports pitches in winter. Parks, Golf Courses and Sports Grounds. 28(4):244–245. 1963.

1553. ______. Rotavators to remove ice. Parks, Golf Courses and Sports Grounds. 28(8):588. 1963.

1554. ______. Grass seeds suitable for sports turf. Parks, Golf Courses and Sports Grounds. 28(9):656–660. 1963.

1555. ______. Inorganic nitrogenous fertilizers. Sports Turf Bulletin. 60:7–9. 1963.

1556. ______. Organic nitrogenous fertilizers. Sports Turf Bulletin. 61:7–10. 1963.

1557. ______. Matted turf. Sports Turf Bulletin. 62:5. 1963.

1558. ______. Phosphatic fertilizers—bone products. Sports Turf Bulletin. 62:6–7. 1963.

1559. ______. Greenkeeping on common land. Sports Turf Bulletin. 62:8–9. 1963.

1560. ______. Ten rules when spraying with selective weedkillers. Sports Turf Bulletin. 62:11. 1963.

1561. ______. Drainage—new playing fields—part I. Sports Turf Bulletin. 63:5–6. 1963.

1562. ______. Controlling lawn weeds with herbicides. USDA. Home and Garden Bulletin. 79:1–16. 1962.

1563. ______. Green section educational meetings. USGA Mid-Continent Turfletter. 1:1. 1963.

1564. ______. How drainage affects temperature. USGA Mid-Continent Turfletter. 1:1. 1963.

1565. ______. Act now to prevent winterkill on bermudagrass. USGA Mid-Continent Turfletter. 1:2. 1963.

1566. ______. Plan now for months ahead. USGA Mid-Continent Turfletter. 1:2. 1963.

1567. ______. Soil testing service offered by Green Section. USGA Green Section Record. 1(4):11–12. 1963.

1568. ______. New fertilizer labels coming. USGA Green Section Record. 1(4):12–13. 1963.

1569. ______. How to identify and control insect pests in turf. Weeds and Turf. pp. 10, 12, 14, 16. February, 1963.

1570. ______. How to identify and control insect pests in turf—part 2. Weeds and Turf. pp. 14–15, 26. March, 1963.

1571. ______. How to identify and control chinch bugs. Weeds and Turf. pp. 16, 18–20, 22, 25. May, 1963.

1572. ______. 535 at '63 Wooster field day updated on lawns, ornamentals. Weeds and Turf. p. 12. November, 1963.

1573. ______. Vacuum cooling of sod aids shipping problem. American Nurseryman. 120(6):52–54. 1964.

1574. ______. Penncross bent. Anthos. 4(1):39–40. 1965.

1575. ______. Chemical weed-control program for hard-to-mow areas saves money and improves housekeeping. Better Roads. 34:15–16. 1964.

1576. ______. New fertilizer labels coming. California Turfgrass Culture. 14(1):6. 1964.

1578. ______. Maintenance calendar. Club Operations. 2(3):G–16. 1964.

1579. ______. Weed research. Colorado Farm and Home Research, Colorado State University Experiment Station. 15(3):5–8. 1964.

1580. ______. Several new herbicides tested. Colorado Farm and Home Research, Colorado State University Experiment Station. 15(1):5. 1964.

1581. ______. Lawn and garden insect control manual. Geigy Chemical Corporation. Geigy Agricultural Chemicals. Ardsley, N.Y. 39 pp. 1964.

1582. ______. Winter damage repair should be made in April. Golfdom. 38(4):-30–32. 1964.

1583. ______. Element deficiency diseases. The Groundsman. 17(9):6–8. 1964.

1584. ______. Observations on the construction of a new green. The Groundsman. 18(1):20–23. 1964.

1585. ______. What causes the dew to fall? Lawn Care. North Central Edition. 641:11. 1964.

1586. ______. Is soil testing worthwhile? Lawn Care. North Central Edition. 642:6. 1964.

1587. ______. The role of soil. Lawn Care. North Central Edition. 642:6. 1964.

1588. ______. A report on the Better Homes & Gardens ideas study. Research Division, Meridith Publishing Company. 17 pp. 1964.

1589. ______. 1963 annual report of memberships and grants. Midwest Turf-News and Research. No. 27. 1964.

1590. ______. Two great experiment stations report on turfgrass fungicides for 1963. Park Maintenance. 17(4):36–39. 1964.

1591. ______. Automatic irrigation on golf courses. Parks, Golf Courses and Sports Grounds. 29(5):316–318. 1964.

1592. ______. Renovating a multi-purpose sports stadium. Parks, Golf Courses and Sports Grounds. 29(5):339–342. 1964.

1593. ______. Chemical verge control. Park, Golf Courses and Sports Grounds. 30(2):128–132. 1964.

1594. ______. The effects of cloudiness on evaporation. Rhodesian Meteorological Service, Agricultural Meteorology Notes. 11:2. 1964.

1595. ______. Fabric mesh cuts erosion problems. Rural and Urban Roads. 2(5):49. 1964.

1596. ______. A scheme for golf greenkeeper apprenticeship. Sports Turf Bulletin. 64:3–6. 1964.

1597. ______. Winter injury. Sports Turf Bulletin. 64:6–7. 1964.

1598. ______. Notes on the maintenance of hard porous surfaces for sport. Sports Turf Bulletin. 65:4–6. 1964.

1599. ______. Buying grass seeds. Sports Turf Bulletin. 65:6–9. 1964.

1600. ______. Problems of excess fibre formation. Sports Turf Bulletin. 66:9–11. 1964.

1601. ______. Drainage-new playing fields. Part II. Sports Turf Bulletin. 67:5–9. 1964.

1602. ______. Earthworms. Sports Turf Bulletin. 67:11–12. 1964.

1603. ______. Lawns and ground covers. Sunset Book No. 350. Menlo Park, California. 112 pp. 1964.

1604. ______. Turfgrass maintenance cost in Texas. Texas Agricultural Experiment Station. Bulletin B-1027. 20 pp. 1964.

1605. ______. Sub-Surface irrigation for turf areas. Turf Bulletin. Massachusetts Turf and Lawn Grass Council. 2(5):8. 1964.

1606. ______. Is it rye or ryegrass? Turf Bulletin. Massachusetts Turf and Lawn Grass Council. 2(5):6. 1964.

1607. ______. Danger—poison!! The relative toxicity of agricultural chemicals. Turf Bulletin. Massachusetts Turf and Lawn Grass Council. 2(5):15–16. 1964.

1608. ______. Nematodes—biology, host range, and life cycle. Turf Bulletin. 2(6):9–12. 1964.

1609. ______. Kingston bent. Turf Bulletin. Massachusetts Turf and Lawn Grass Council. 2(8):7. 1964.

1610. ______. A grass killer? Turf Bulletin. Massachusetts Turf and Lawn Grass Council. 2(8):9. 1964.

1611. ______. Virus may hit turf grasses. Turf Bulletin. Massachusetts Turf and Lawn Grass Council. 2(8):12. 1964.

1612. ______. Chemistry and our lawns. Turf Bulletin. Massachusetts Turf and Lawn Grass Council. 2(9):13–14. 1964.

1613. ______. Damage to turf from the army worm. USGA Green Section Bulletin. 4(7):166–169. 1964.

1614. ______. Golf course vacuum cleaner. USGA Green Section Record. 1(5):3. 1964.

1615. ______. Care of sprayers. USGA Green Section Record. 1(5):12. 1964.

1617. ______. Chemistry and our lawns. Velsicol Bulletin ADS #14. Velsicol Chemical Corp. 1964.

1618. ______. Rules for testing seeds. Proceedings of Association of Official Seed Analyst. 54:2. 1965.

1619. ______. Planning areas and facilities for health, physical education and recreation. The Athletic Institute and American Association for Health, Physical Education and Recreation, Washington, D. C. pp. 1–272. 1965.

1620. ______. Herbicides for weed control. Auburn University Annual Turfgrass Short Course. pp. 18–19. 1965.

1621. ______. Cutting roadside maintenance costs. Better Roads. 35(8):25. 1965.

1622. ______. Around the course. Club Operations. 3(1):G–1, G–29. 1965.

1623. ______. Care and feeding of bermuda planting. Club Operations. 3(1):G–11. 1965.

1624. ______. Superintendents use ingenuity, science to solve tough problems. Club Operations. 3(1):G–13-G–14. 1965.

1625. ______. Make your tees a turf show window. Club Operations. 3(2):G–8–G–9. 1965.

1626. ______. How one course licked its insect problem. Club Operations. 3(2):G–18–G–19. 1965.

1627. ______. The science of building good greens. Club Operations. 3(3):16–19, 25. 1965.

1628. ______. Systemized procedures in sure quality maintenance efficiency. Club Operations. 3(3):32–33. 1965.

1629. ______. Spray early for crabgrass. Colorado Farm and Home Research & Colorado State University. 15(5):7. 1965.

1630. ______. All about lawns and roses. Elanco Products Co. Indianapolis. 22 pp. 1965.

1631. ______. Bibliography on roadside development. Highway Research Board. pp. 10–14. 1965.

1632. ______. Irrigation installation, minimum standards. Proceedings Midwest Regional Turf Conference. pp. 36–37. 1965.

1633. ______. How does Zoysia look for midwestern lawns? Midwest Turf News and Research. No. 10. (4th Revision). 1965.

1634. ______. 1964 Annual report of memberships and grants. Midwest Turf-News and Research. No. 30. 1965.

1635. ______. Maintenance of bentgrass for private putting greens and lawns. Midwest Turf News and Research. No. 32. 1965.

1636. ______. Plant and weed identification. Mississippi State University Cooperative Extension Service. Publication 476. 1965.

1637. ______. Sports ground construction—specifications for playing facilities. The National Playing Fields Association and the Sports Turf Research Institute. 1965.

1639. ______. Turfgrass review—diseases, fertilization, grasses, insecticides, irrigation, management, and weeds. Park Maintenance. 18(7):17–44. 1965.

1640. ______. Grass takes time. Parks, Golf Courses and Sports Grounds. 30(7):510. 1965.

1641. ______. Susceptibility of bluegrass to root knot nematodes. Plant Disease Reporter. 49:89–90. 1965.

1642. ______. Timing the construction of new sports grounds, etc. Sports Turf Bulletin. 68:11–12. 1965.

1643. ______. Why not use your watering system? Sports Turf Bulletin. 69:8–10. 1965.

1644. ______. What's in a fertilizer, other than plant foods? Sports Turf Bulletin. 69:10–12. 1965.

1645. ______. Weedkilling? "Take good care"!! Sports Turf Bulletin. 70:10–12. 1965.

1646. ______. Moss. Sports Turf Bulletin. 71:4–6. 1965.

1647. ______. *Fusarium* and its control. Sports Turf Bulletin. 71:6–8. 1965.

1648. ______. Cyst nematode attacks St. Augustinegrass. Sunshine State Agricultural Research Report. 10(3):12. 1965.

1649. ______. Found: the light switch for plant growth. Turf Bulletin. Massachusetts Turf & Lawn Grass Council. 2(11):7. 1965.

1650. ______. Selecting fertilizers. Turf Bulletin. Massachusetts Turf & Lawn Grass Council. 2(11):18–22. 1965.

1651. ______. Establishing and keeping athletic field grasses. Turf Bulletin. Massachusetts Turf & Lawn Grass Council. 2(11):-20–22. 1965.

1652. ______. Maintenance of bentgrass for private putting greens and lawns. Turf Bulletin. Massachusetts Turf & Lawn Grass Council. 2(12):7–8. 1965.

1653. ______. Velsicol herbicide—Banvel D 4–S. Turf Bulletin. Massachusetts Turf & Lawn Grass Council. 2(12):8. 1965.

1654. ______. Aerification and spiking. Turf Bulletin. Massachusetts Turf & Lawn Grass Council. 2(12):12, 19, 22. 1965.

1655. ______. 2, 4–D may increase nitrates in plants. Turf Bulletin. Massachusetts Turf & Lawn Grass Council. 2(12):24. 1965.

1656. ______. Durar hard fescue for erosion control. Turf Bulletin. Massachusetts Turf & Lawn Grass Council. 2(12):24. 1965.

1658. ______. "Mr. Golfer" helps. Turf Bulletin. Massachusetts Turf and Lawn Grass Council. 2(13):24. 1965.

1659. ______. Controlling lawn weeds with herbicides. USDA. Bulletin 79:1–16. 1965.

1660. ______. Adequate drainage key to holding courses during 1964 heat and humidity. USGA Green Section Record. 2(5):10–12. 1965.

1661. ______. How to ready soil for the next crop. Weeds, Trees, and Turf. 4(9):20–22. 1965.

1662. ______. WIT survey shows sod industry headed for vast expansion, increased sales. Weeds, Trees, and Turf. 4(8):22–25. 1965.

1663. ______. Economics of large scale turf-irrigation. Sec. 1. Turf maintenance costs, components and trends. Western Landscaping News. 5. 1965.

1664. ______. Economics of large scale turf irrigation—Part IX. The Cemeterian. 4:-9–10, 39–40. 1966.

1665. ______. Preventing winter turf damage. The Cemeterian. 12:11–12, 45–46. 1966.

1666. ______. Glossary of turf terms. Golf Course Operations. 4(1):15. 1966.

1667. ______. Turf nursery program at Cherry Hills. Golf Course Operations. 4(1):-23–24. 1966.

1668. ______. Adapting turfgrass to shade. Golf Course Operations. 4(1):25, 34–35. 1966.

1669. ______. The cost of large scale turf maintenance. Economics Research Associates, Thompson Mfg. Co., Los Angeles. p. 27. 1966.

1670. ______. Playing fields and hard surface areas. Department of Education and Science Building Bulletin. 28. 1966.

1671. ______. All fairways fertilized in two hours! Golf Course Operations. 4(2):8–9. 1966.

1672. ______. Course cost system. The Golf Superintendent. 34(1):52–53. 1966.

1673. ______. Correspondence course in turf recommended by GCSAA. The Golf Superintendent. 34(4):20–22, 56. 1966.

1674. ______. Poisons—symptoms and antidotes. The Golf Superintendent. 34(6):-30–32, 40. 1966.

1675. ______. 40th Anniversary of GCSAA. The Golf Superintendent. 34(9):-16–18. 1966.

1676. ______. Guide for fertilizing shade and ornamental trees. The Golf Superintendent. 34(10):28–30. 1966.

1677. ______. Controlling bentgrass diseases. Grounds Maintenance. 1(4):26–28. 1966.

1678. ______. Engine troubleshooting guide. Grounds Maintenance. 1(8):13–14. 1966.

1679. ______. Post-installation highway work. Grounds Maintenance. 1(10):14–17. 1966.

1680. ______. Colorants assure green turf. Grounds Maintenance. 1(11):10. 1966.

1681. ______. Users evaluate small mowers. Grounds Maintenance. 1(12):4–7. 1966.

1682. ______. Hockey pitch maintenance for keen, firm and true surfaces. The Groundsman. 20(3):14–22. 1966.

1683. ______. What is a turf disease? The Groundsman. 20(3):26–28. 1966.

1684. ______. The art and science of roadside development. Highway Research Board Special Report 88. Washington, D. C. 81 pp. 1966.

1685. ______. Turfgrass growth characteristics. Iagreen. Iowa State University. pp. 9–13. 1966.

1686. ______. Turfgrass growth responses. Iagreen. Iowa State University. pp. 14–15. 1966.

1687. ______. Evaluation of turfgrass management practices. Iagreen. Iowa State University. pp. 15–17. 1966.

1688. ______. Turfgrass fertilization. Iagreen. Iowa State University. pp. 17–18. 1966.

1689. ______. Turfgrass weed control. Iagreen. Iowa State University. pp. 18–21. 1966.

1690. ______. Turfgrass disease control. Iagreen. Iowa State University. pp. 21–23. 1966.

1691. ______. International rules for seed testing. International Seed Testing Association Proceedings. 31:1. 1966.

1692. ______. New gimmicks for stadium grasses. Landscape Design and Construction. 12(3):12, 20. 1966.

1693. ______. Lawns without soil. Landscape Design and Construction. 12(3):13, 21. 1966.

1695. ______. A report on first annual golf turf symposium on winter injury. Milwaukee Milorganite. Winter Injury Bulletin 5:1–26. 1966.

1696. ______. Turf, turfgrasses, and their cultivation objectives. Mitt. d. Gesellschaft f. Rasenforschung 1, H. 4, 7–12. 1966.

1697. ______. Your lawn. Ohio Cooperative Extension Service Bulletin 271. 1966.

1698. ______. Pomona's automatic sprinkling cuts park costs. Park Maintenance. 19(7):8–10. 1966.

1699. ______. Two golf courses highlight $10 million Pipestem State Park. Park Maintenance. 19(7):12–16. 1966.

1700. ______. Turf annual—Forward, disease, fertilizer, grasses, insects and pests, irrigation, management, and weeds. Park Maintenance. 19(7):17–40. 1966.

1701. ______. Turf maintenance costs. Parks and Recreation. 1(3):239–241, 289. 1966.

1702. ______. Turfgrass survey. Pennsylvania Crop Reporting Service. Pennsylvania Department of Agriculture. Harrisburg. 36 pp. 1966.

1703. ______. Seeding deep cuttings. Roads and Road Construction (London). 44(524):240. 1966.

1704. ______. 1966 Ryan report on sod and turf grasses. Ryan Rumors. 12(4):1–10. 1966.

1706. ______. Chemicals for weed control on non-grass areas. Sports Turf Bulletin. 65:9–11. 1964.

1707. ______. Hints on playing field construction. Sports Turf Bulletin. 73:8–12. 1966.

1708. ______. What is a turf disease? Sports Turf Bulletin. 74:10–12. 1966.

1709. ______. The bowling green in autumn. Sports Turf Bulletin. 75:6–7. 1966.

1710. ______. Drainage and soil permeability. Sports Turf Bulletin. 75:7–9. 1966.

1711. ______. Maintenance of turf equipment. Sports Turf Bulletin. 75:9–12. 1966.

1712. ______. Minimum installation specifications for turf sprinkler irrigation systems. Sprinkler Irrigation Association. Number A–66:1–8. 1966.

1713. ______. Proposal for a more adequate turfgrass research program in Texas. The Texas Turfgrass Association. 8 pp. 1966.

1714. ______. Lawn seed division members updated on turfgrass evaluation and management. Turf Bulletin. Massachusetts Turf & Lawn Grass Council. 3(1):11. 1966.

1715. ______. Chemicals to kill waterweeds. Turf Bulletin. Massachusetts Turf & Lawn Grass Council. 3(2):13–15, 18. 1966.

1716. ______. 250 Maryland farms cultivate sod for sale. Turf Bulletin. Massachusetts Turf & Lawn Grass Council. 3(2):21. 1966.

1717. ______. Guidelines for a herbicide program. Turf Bulletin. Massachusetts Turf & Lawn Grass Council. 3(2):22–23. 1966.

1718. ______. Hints on playing field construction in Great Britain. Turf Bulletin. Massachusetts Turf & Lawn Grass Council. 3(3):9–10. 1966.

1719. ______. Turf maintenance costs. Turf Bulletin. Massachusetts Turf and Lawn Grass Council. 4(2):11–13. 1966.

1720. ______. Gain in golf cars or loss in course upkeep? Turf-Grass Times. 1(3):1, 7, 15. 1966.

1721. ______. Trends in golf course numbers, cost, design and maintenance. Turf-Grass Times. 1(5):3–8. 1966.

1722. ______. How they grow sod in Colorado. Turf-Grass Times. 1(5):14. 1966.

1723. ______. Grass under glass? Turf-Grass Times. 2(1):1–5. 1966.

1724. ______. Heating cold turf. Turf-Grass Times. 2(2):1–3. 1966.

1725. ______. Latest irrigation installation techniques. Turf-Grass Times. 2(2):4–5, 15. 1966.

1726. ______. Canadian golf superintendents form national. Turf-Grass Times. 2(2):-16. 1966.

1727. ______. Lawn weed control with herbicides. USDA Home and Garden Bulletin. No. 123. 24 pp. 1967.

1728. ______. Spot and strip sodding techniques. USGA Green Section Record. 3(5):3. 1966.

1729. ______. The case for temporary greens. USGA Green Section Record. 3(5):-11–13. 1966.

1730. ______. The green section on golf carts. USGA Green Section Record. 4(2):-7–13. 1966.

1731. ______. Wisconsin turfmen hear how hardiness, potash content affect wintering grasses. Weeds, Trees and Turf. 5(6):-34–35. 1966.

1732. ______. Bluegrass perils, all-in-one harvester shown at Rutgers sod and research field days. June 20–22. Weeds, Trees and Turf. 5(8):24–29. 1966.

1733. ______. OSU says DMA, AMA for crabgrass control. Weeds, Trees and Turf. 5(8):36. 1966.

1734. ______. Maryland turf expert advises overseeding now. Weeds, Trees and Turf. 5(8):38. 1966.

1735. ______. "No-mow" is hit of Texas A&M Turfgrass Day. Weeds, Trees and Turf. 5(8):42–43. 1966.

1736. ______. Law aids sod certification. Weeds, Trees and Turf. 5(9):6. 1966.

1737. ______. Weibullsholsm Vaxtforadlingsanstalt intensifierar sin grasforadling. Weibulls Aktuellt om Gras. 1. 1966.

1738. ______. Vanderhoof east seeding. British Columbia Department of Highways, Victoria. pp. 1–7. 1967.

1739. ______. Fertilizer material solubility. California Turfgrass Culture. 17(1):6–8. 1967.

1740. ______. Observations on the mowing problem. The Cemeterian. 31(7):11, 12, 45. 1967.

1741. ______. Lawn and Garden Book. Chevron Chemical Company, Ortho Division. 1967.

1742. ______. The economics of large scale turf irrigation. Economics Research Associates, Thompson Mfg. Co., Los Angeles. 27 pp. 1967.

1743. ______. Golf course operations: how does yours compare? Florida Turfgrass Association Bulletin. 14(1):6–8. 1967.

1744. ______. Grass thrives under plexiglass sheets. Florist and Nursery Exchange. 147:16. 1967.

1745. ______. Superintendents' long green. Golfdom. 41(5):36–37. 1967.

1746. ______. Snowmobiles—friend or foe? The Golf Superintendent. 35(2):10, 49. 1967.

1747. ______. Asphalt subsoil water barrier. The Golf Superintendent. 35(2):40, 56. 1967.

1748. ______. A comparison of hydraulic vs. electrical valves. Golf Superintendent. 35(3):71. 1967.

1749. ______. History and purpose of the GCSAA scholarship and research fund. The Golf Superintendent. 35(5):36–42. 1967.

1750. ______. Golf course chemical warfare takes to the air. The Golf Superintendent. 35(7):8–9. 1967.

1751. ______. A tribute to John Morley. The Golf Superintendent. 35(8):20, 21, 42. 1967.

1752. ______. Winter injury in Canada. The Greenmaster. 3(6):4, 6–8. 1967.

1753. ______. Heavy rains plague greenmasters. The Greenmaster. 3(9):9–10. 1967.

1754. ______. Weeds and weed control. The Greenmaster. 3(12):4, 6–9. 1967.

1755. ______. Chelated iron keeps plants from starving. Grounds Maintenance. 2(1):-39. 1967.

1756. ______. Air pollution damage to plants. Grounds Maintenance. 2(4):7–9, 58–61. 1967.

1757. ______. Super-sized mowers. Grounds Maintenance. 2(4):34–36. 1967.

1758. ______. Toxicity of insecticides. Grounds Maintenance. 2(4):38. 1967.

1759. ______. Wettable powder controls crabgrass. Grounds Maintenance. 2(4):48–49. 1967.

1760. ______. How to control chickweed. Grounds Maintenance. 2(6):13–14. 1967.

1761. ______. How to control dandelions. Grounds Maintenance. 2(7):24, 26. 1967.

1762. ______. Toxicity of insecticides. Grounds Maintenance. 2(7):34. 1967.

1763. ______. How to control bindweed. Grounds Maintenance. 2(9):13–14. 1967.

1764. ______. How to control chinch bugs. Grounds Maintenance. 2(10):23–24. 1967.

1765. ______. Applying turf colorants. Grounds Maintenance. 2(10):28–29. 1967.

1766. ______. How to control white grubs and Japanese beetle larvae. Grounds Maintenance. 2(11):28–29. 1967.

1767. ______. Applying turf colorants. Grounds Maintenance. 2(12):63. 1967.

1768. ______. Hydraulic mulching . . . a growing business. Landscape Design and Construction. 12(12):18–19, 34–35. 1967.

1769. ______. This racetrack turf is for go! Landscape Design and Construction. 13(2):12–13, 33. 1967.

1770. ______. Keep it cool, man (sod, that is). Landscape Design and Construction. 13(3):23. 1967.

1771. ______. Lawn weed control. Michigan State University Cooperative Extension Service. Extension Folder F-261. 1967.

1772. ______. The role of lime in turf management. Milwaukee Milorganite Bulletin. Turf Service Bureau. Sewerage Commission. 1:1–23. 1967.

1773. ______. The home lawn. Minnesota Agricultural Extension Service Folder 165. 1967.

1774. ______. Golf Operators Handbook. National Golf Foundation, Inc. Chicago, Illinois. 104 pp. 1967.

1775. ______. Seasonal notes. New Zealand Institute for Turf Culture Newsletter. 48:14–17. 1967.

1776. ______. Turf annual-diseases. Park Maintenance. 20(7):20–24. 1967.

1777. ______. Turf annual—fertilizers. Park Maintenance. 20(7):24–28. 1967.

1778. ______. Turf annual—grasses. Park Maintenance. 20(7):28–32. 1967.

1779. ______. Turf annual—insects and pests. Park Maintenance. 20(7):32–33. 1967.

1780. ______. Turf annual—irrigation. Park Maintenance. 20(7):33–36. 1967.

1781. ______. Turf annual—management. Park Maintenance. 20(7):36–39. 1967.

1782. ______. Turf annual—weed control. Park Maintenance. 20(7):39–43. 1967.

1783. ______. Trends in turfgrass irrigation. Park Maintenance. 20(7):47. 1967.

1784. ______. Fore! National Golf Foundation cites course maintenance trends throughout U.S.A. Park Maintenance. 20(8):12–13. 1967.

1785. ______. A look at campus maintenance on SIU's 850 acres of grounds. Park Maintenance. 20(10):18–20. 1967.

1786. ______. Autumn football in December with electric soil warming. Park Maintenance. 20(10):74–75. 1967.

1787. ______. For instant ground cover, let us spray: wood fiber mulch, hydro-seeding do job. Park Maintenance. 20(11):16–17. 1967.

1788. ______. New "pop-up" irrigation system for St. Andrews. Parks Golf Courses & Sports Grounds. 32(11):957–958. 1967.

1789. ______. Turf grass varieties. Sports Turf Bulletin. 76:7–8. 1967.

1790. ______. Preparing for spring. Sports Turf Bulletin. 76:8–10. 1967.

1791. ______. Management of golf fairways. Sports Turf Bulletin. 76:10–12. 1967.

1792. ______. Maintenance of racecources. Sports Turf Bulletin. 77:4–7. 1967.

1793. ______. Earthworms and their control. Sports Turf Bulletin. 77:7–9. 1967.

1794. ______. All hands on deck. Sports Turf Bulletin. 77:9–12. 1967.

1795. ______. Croquet lawns. Sports Turf Bulletin. 78:4–6. 1967.

1796. ______. Maintenance of polo grounds. Sports Turf Bulletin. 78:6–8. 1967.

1797. ______. Newer herbicides. Sports Turf Bulletin. 78:9–11. 1967.

1798. ______. The importance of timing in the construction of new sports turf areas. Sports Turf Bulletin. 78:11–12. 1967.

1799. ______. End of summer renovation on the sports ground. Sports Turf Bulletin. 79:4–6. 1967.

1800. ______. Sports turf in Wales. Sports Turf Bulletin. 79:7–9. 1967.

1801. ______. A longer football season. Swedish Football Association Publication. pp. 1–6. 1967.

1802. ______. How to repair a ball mark. Turf Bulletin. Massachusetts Turf & Lawn Grass Council. 4(3):10–11. 1967.

1803. ______. Sulphur-containing fertilizers—what they are—how they are used. Turf Bulletin. 4(6):5–6. 1967.

1804. ______. Factors affecting the volatilization of ammonia formed from urea in soil. Turfgrass News. p. 3. 1967.

1805. ______. Soil testing important after a drought year. Turf-Grass Times. 2(3):1, 15. 1967.

1806. ______. Certified sod production doubles in Florida. Turf-Grass Times. 2(3):5, 8. 1967.

1807. ______. Promote dormant seeding. Turf-Grass Times. 2(3):14. 1967.

1808. ______. European chafer beetle continues to spread. Turf-Grass Times. 2(4):-1,3. 1967.

1809. ______. Spring dead spot is still a mystery. Turf-Grass Times. 2(4):6–11, 18–24. 1967.

1810. ______. Mites are resisting miticides. Turf-Grass Times. 2(5):13. 1967.

1811. ______. Flood tolerant grasses. Turf-Grass Times. 2(5):20. 1967.

1812. ______. Lighting adds 1000 golf hours. Turf-Grass Times. 2(5):20. 1967.

1813. ______. Spring deadspot tour is made. Turf-Grass Times. 2(6):8, 20. 1967.

1814. ______. Guidelines for assistants and apprentices. Turf-Grass Times. 3(2):5. 1967.

1815. ______. Colorado research rates Windsor. Turf Talks. Scotts. Marysville, Ohio. p. 1. November, 1967.

1816. ______. Turf seed history. Turf Talks. Scotts. Marysville, Ohio. pp. 1–2. January, 1967.

1817. ______. Progress in controlling stripe smut. Turf Talks. Scotts. Marysville, Ohio. p. 2. August, 1967.

1818. ______. News from Scotts research. Turf Talks. Scotts. Marysville, Ohio. p. 3. January, 1967.

1819. ______. Bluegrass variety studies. Turf Talks. Scotts. Marysville, Ohio. p. 4. August, 1967.

1820. ______. Eugene's novel approach. USGA Green Section Record. 4(6):8–12. 1967.

1821. ______. Herbicide handbook. Weed Society of America. W. F. Humphrey Press Inc., Geneva, New York. 293 pp. 1967.

1822. ______. Turfgrass management training. Part I. Weeds, Trees, and Turf. 6(2):8–11. 1967.

1823. ______. Richlawn's "Turfmaster" eases sod harvesting. Weeds, Trees and Turf. 6(2):26–28. 1967.

1824. ______. Sodmen move to form national group. Weeds, Trees and Turf. 6(3):-26–30. 1967.

1825. ______. Turfgrass management training—part II. Weeds, Trees, and Turf. 6(4):24–26. 1967.

1826. ______. Highway maintenance—multiphased management task faced by our 50 states. Weeds, Trees and Turf. 6(5):8–11. 1967.

1827. ______. Adequate turf stands under shade are possible with careful culture. Weeds Trees and Turf. 6(5):26–27. 1967.

1828. ______. Turfgrass management training. Part III. Weeds, Trees, and Turf. 6(6):6–7. 1967.

1829. ______. Turfgrass management training. Part IV. Weeds, Trees, and Turf. 6(7):12–13. 1967.

1830. ______. American Sod Association stages first field day. Weeds Trees and Turf. 6(8):26–29. 1967.

1831. ______. Sodman leases land and adapts local grass. Weeds, Trees and Turf. 6(9):8–11. 1967.

1832. ______. Chemicals help Kansas battle weeds. Better Roads. 38(9):23. 1968.

1833. ______. Herbicides—a boon to highways. Carolina Highways. 22(9):14–15. 1968.

1834. ______. Now is the time for lawn rebuilding chores. The Cemeterian. 32(8):7, 8, 45. 1968.

1835. ______. Proturf broad spectrum insecticide. Cemeterian. 32:9–10. 1968.

1836. ______. How much nitrogen for your course? Golf Businessman's Almanac. 1:44. 1968.

1837. ______. Don't forget that lime. Golf Businessman's Almanac. 1:46. 1968.

1838. ______. Don't overwater. Golf Businessman's Almanac. 1:49. 1968.

1839. ______. Topdressing tips. Golf Businessman's Almanac. 1:52. 1968.

1840. ______. Truce on crabgrass? Golf Businessman's Almanac. 1:60. 1968.

1841. ______. Analyze your turf and save money. Golfdom. 42(8):56. 1968.

1842. ______. Pest control in Canada. The Greenmaster. 4(6):3–5. 1968.

1843. ______. *Pythium* blight strikes U.S.A. The Greenmaster. 4(10):12. 1968.

1844. ______. Speaking of irrigation—spacings spell success. Grounds Maintenance. 3(1):16–17. 1968.

1845. ______. How to control earthworms. Grounds Maintenance. 3(1):18–20. 1968.

1846. ______. *Fusarium* blight. Grounds Maintenance. 3(3):29. 1968.

1847. ______. How to control sowbugs and pillbugs. Grounds Maintenance. 3(4):23–24. 1968.

1848. ______. Athletic fields: turf renovation. Grounds Maintenance. 3(4):66–68. 1968.

1849. ______. How to control sod webworm. Grounds Maintenance. 3(8):23–24. 1968.

1850. ______. Better lawns. Home and Garden Bulletin No. 51. Supt. of Documents, U.S. Govt. Printing Office, Washington, D.C. 1968b.

1851. ______. Lawn weed control with herbicides. Home and Garden Bulletin No. 123. Supt. of Documents, U.S. Govt. Printing Office, Washington, D.C. 1968a.

1852. ______. Keeping a lawn. University of Illinois. College of Agriculture. Cooperative Extension Service Circular 982. 15 pp. 1968.

1853. ______. The establishment of crownvetch as influenced by several grasses used as a companion crop. Illinois Cooperative Highway Research Program. Project 1HR–67. pp. 15–16. 1968.

1854. ______. Experiment 007—the establishment of legumes and grass species in pots of soil from highway slopes near Urbana and Lawrenceville, Ill. Illinois Cooperative Highway Research Program Project 1HR–67. pp. 16–19. 1968.

1855. ______. Experiment 008—The effect of various temperatures upon germination of seeds of a large number of legume and grass species. Illinois Cooperative Highway Research Program Project 1HR–67. pp. 19–24. 1968.

1856. ______. Experiment 012—The effect of seed size, planting depth, and soil type upon the establishment of crown vetch, *Coronilia varia.* Illinois Cooperative Highway Research Program Project 1HR–67. p. 25. 1968.

1857. ______. Experiment 014.—Transplant of 4 species or varieites to replace zoysia experiment 004 on Interstate 74 at Urbana. Illinois Cooperative Highway Research Program Project 1HR–67. pp. 27–30. 1968.

1858. ______. Experiment 015: A comparison of temporary and permanent seeding mixtures when seeded every two weeks through the grading season. Illinois Cooperative Highway Research Program Project IHR–67. p. 31. 1968.

1859. ______. Experiment 016: A study of the causes of the failure of plants to become established on certain Illinois subsoils. Illinois Cooperative Highway Research Program Project IHR–67. pp. 33–34. 1968.

1860. ______. Experiment 019: Grass species for southern Illinois trial Union County, Interstate 57. Illinois Cooperative Highway Research Program Project IHR–67. p. 35. 1968.

1861. ______. Experiment 020: A bermuda grass clone and zoysia variety trial Union County, Interstate 57. Illinois Cooperative Highway Research Program Project IHR–67. p. 36. 1968.

1862. ______. Experiment 021: bluegrass variety trial. Illinois Cooperative Highway Research Program. Project IHR–67. pp. 37–39. 1968.

1863. ______. Establishment of vegetation (Phase 1). Mississippi State University, Mississippi Highway Department and Bureau of Public Roads, Final Report. 1968.

1864. ______. Annual report on golf statistics. National Golf Foundation. Chicago, Ill. 1968.

1865. ______. Power coring demonstration. New Zealand Institute for Turf Culture. 57:3–9. 1968.

1866. ______. Seasonal notes: winter playing fields. New Zealand Institute for Turf Culture. 57:16–21. 1968.

1867. ______. Varieties of grasses. N.I.A.B. Farmers leaflet No. 16. 1968.

1870. ______. Most golf greens recovered from winter injury. Ohio Turfgrass Foundation Newsletter. No. 12. p. 2. 1968.

1871. ______. Turfgrass production and management research progress report, 1967. Oklahoma Agricultural Experiment Station. Processed Series P–580. 24 pp. 1968.

1872. ______. Turf tests point to control of *Veronica.* Park Maintenance. 21(5):24. 1968.

1873. ______. Motorway verge maintenance. Parks, Golf Courses and Sports Grounds. 33(7):565–566, 569. 1968.

1874. ______. Pay-as-you go financing for golf courses. Parks and Recreation. 3(5):-24, 66. 1968.

1875. ______. A rug of grass for easy maintenance. Parks and Recreation. 3(5):25, 67. 1968.

1876. ______. Lighted golf course allows night play. Parks and Recreation. 3(5):25, 66–67. 1968.

1877. ______. Specifications, roadside development. Pennsylvania Highway Department. Section 800.0–804.3. 1968.

1878. ______. Rhode Island annual turfgrass field days. Agricultural Experiment Station, University of Rhode Island. 37:1–40. 1968.

1879. ______. Soil amendment study—putting green. Scotts Turfgrass Research Seminar. p. 21. 1968.

1880. ______. Hydraulic seeding or hydro seeding. Sports Turf Bulletin. 80:5–7. 1968.

1881. ______. Controlled plot trials. Sports Turf Bulletin. 80:8–9. 1968.

1882. ______. Cricket pitches. Sports Turf Bulletin. 80:9–12. 1968.

1883. ______. Sports turf in Ireland. Sports Turf Bulletin. 81:5–6. 1968.

1884. ______. Diseases of established turf. Sports Turf Bulletin. 81:7–9. 1968.

1885. ______. Seasonal tips April-June. Sports Turf Bulletin. 81:9–11. 1968.

1886. ______. Grass seed supplies. Sports Turf Bulletin. 81:12. 1968.

1887. ______. Topdressing. Sports Turf Bulletin. 83:5–7. 1968.

1888. ______. Seasonal tips (October-December). Sports Turf Bulletin. 83:10–12. 1968.

1889. ______. Small tractor service manual. (Second Edition). Technical Publications Division Intertec Publishing Corporation. pp. 1–216. 1968.

1890. ______. Sulphur—containing fertilizers. Turf Bulletin. Massachusetts Turf and Lawn Grass Council. 4(6):5–6. 1967.

1891. ______. Ruby creeping red fescue promising new turf grass. Turf Bulletin. Massachusetts Turf and Lawn Grass Council. 4(8):23. 1968.

1892. ______. Temporary soil sterilants. Turf Bulletin. Massachusetts Turf and Lawn Grass Council. 5(1):10–11. 1968.

1898. ______. Definitions and standards for sprinkler irrigation equipment. Annual

Turfgrass Sprinkler Irrigation Conference Proceedings. 6:29–36. 1968.

1899. ______. Hot water bath controls nematodes in sod. Turf-grass Times. 3(5):18. 1968.

1900. ______. Sterilizing a stadium. Turf-Grass Times. 3(6):2–3. 1968.

1901. ______. Protection against lightning on golf courses. Turf-Grass Times. 3(7):-14–15. 1968.

1902. ______. San Diego stadium solid sodded. Turf-Grass Times. 3(8):3. 1968.

1903. ______. Turf diseases in Colorado. Turf-Grass Times. 3(8):7. 1968.

1904. ______. The miracle of *Poa pratensis.* Turf Talks. p. 1. November, 1968.

1905. ______. Rhizome initiation and development of Windsor, Merion, and Delta Kentucky bluegrass. Turf Talks. p. 1. March, 1968.

1906. ______. Turf on sand. Turf Talks. p. 1. May, 1968.

1907. ______. Golf course greens recovering from winter injury? Turf Talks. p. 2. May, 1968.

1908. ______. Seed protection from stripe smut. Turf Talks. p. 2. September, 1968.

1909. ______. Successful spring seedings! Turf Talks. p. 2. March, 1968.

1910. ______. Vigorous rhizoming and rooting in 4 types of soil. Turf Talks. p. 3. January, 1968.

1911. ______. Key to the native perennial grasses—midwest region east of the Great Plains. USDA. Soil Conservation Service. Superintendent of Documents. Washington, D. C. 116 pp. 1968.

1912. ______. Standard specifications for construction of airports. U.S. Department of Commerce. Civil Aeronautics Administration, Washington, D.C. 1968.

1915. ______. System of management underway at Summit Hall to protect sod root zone and eliminate reseeding. Weeds, Trees and Turf. 7(1):25–26. 1968.

1916. ______. Washington State finds dacthal effective in postemergence trial. Weeds, Trees and Turf. 7(3):34–36. 1968.

1917. ______. Calabasas course exemplifies design and installation technology. Weeds, Trees, and Turf. 7(4):8, 10, 12. 1968.

1918. ______. Irrigation roundup. Weeds, Trees, and Turf. 7(4):13, 14, 16. 1968.

1919. ______. Modern irrigation system on 850 acres aids quality sod production at Emerald Valley. Weeds, Trees and Turf. 7(4):32–35. 1968.

1920. ______. Helicopter is versatile tool. Weeds, Trees, and Turf. 7(5):16. 1968.

1921. ______. Needed chemical deicers damage highway vegetation. Weeds, Trees, and Turf. 7(5):28. 1968.

1922. ______. Field to lawn sod handling equipment is basis for new Minni Turf Corporation. Weeds, Trees and Turf. 7(5):30–31. 1968.

1923. ______. Manage fertilizer for more heat tolerant bent. Weeds, Trees and Turf. 7(5):35–38. 1968.

1924. ______. Golf course designed for senior citizens. Weeds, Trees, and Turf. 7(6):-10–13 & 34. 1968.

1925. ______. Turf quality begins at farm level. Weeds, Trees, and Turf. 7(9):10–13, 38. 1968.

1926. ______. Grass identification is key to proper care. Weeds, Trees, and Turf. 7(9):-26. 1968.

1927. ______. Golf green construction. Weeds, Trees, and Turf. 7(10):10. 1968.

1928. ______. High flotation tires solve problems at New Jersey blue grass lawn farms. Weeds, Trees, and Turf. 7(10):30. 1968.

1929. ______. Sod growers invited to attend ASPA annual. Weeds, Trees and Turf. 7(12):50–52. 1968.

1930. ______. The Weibullshom plant breeding institute intensifies its grass breeding. Weibulls Grass Topics. 4 pp. 1968.

1932. ______. Can your turf (lawn) take it this year? Better Crops with Plant Food. 53(1):16–18. 1969.

1933. ______. Chemical spray helps reduce weed-control costs. Better Roads. 39(9):32–34. 1969.

1934. ______. Herbicide controls roadside vegetation in California. Better Roads. 40(2):24–26. 1970.

1935. Bures, I. F. Establishment and maintenance of sporting places under grass cover. First Czechoslovak Symposium on Sportturfs Proceedings. 284 pp. 1969.

1936. Anonymous. From the American Potash Institute. The Golf Superintendent. 37(1):88. 1969.

1937. ______. Snowmobiles: should they be permitted on golf courses? The Greenmaster. 5(3):3–5. 1969.

1938. ______. The Canadian Open 1969. The Greenmaster. 5(8):4, 6–7. 1969.

1939. ______. Sizing up the turf industry. Grounds Maintenance. 5(9):10, 12–13. 1970.

1940. ______. 2, 4–D, the workhorse for weeds. Grounds Maintenance. 4(1):15–16. 1969.

1941. ______. Hydraulic mulching. Grounds Maintenance. 4(5):9–10. 1969.

1942. ______. Fogger and sprayer attachments for mowers and small tractors. Grounds Maintenance. 4(5):17, 20. 1969.

1943. ______. The functional spectrum of plants . . . precipitation and humidity control. Grounds Maintenance. 4(5):47. 1969.

1944. ______. Creating sports turf on clay soil. The Groundsman. 22(12):21. 1969.

1945. ______. Soils and plants nutrition. The Groundsman. 23(2):30–31. 1969.

1946. ______. Small engines service manual. Ninth edition. Technical Publications Div. Intertec Publishing Corp. 1–328 pp. 1969.

1947. ______. The seven links in turfgrass management. Kellogg Supply, Inc. Bulletin. 3(4):1–5. 1969.

1948. ______. What we should know about micronutrients. Kellogg Supply, Inc. Bulletin. 3(4):6–8. 1969.

1949. ______. Don't guess plant food needs—soil test to be sure. Lakeshore News. 1(3):5. 1969.

1950. ______. Cougar Kentucky bluegrass. Lakeshore News. 1(3):9. 1969.

1951. ______. These new lawn edgings are a mark of distinction. Landscape Industry. 14(1):40–41. 1969.

1952. ______. Special fall advice on bluegrass. Lawn Care. Michigan Edition. p. 5. 1969.

1953. ______. Hot, dry weather may bring undesirable lawn visitors. Lawn Care. Michigan Edition. pp. 6–7. 1969.

1954. ______. Does some of your grass fade away in the heat of summer? Lawn Care. Michigan Edition. pp. 8–9. 1969.

1955. ______. If your builder gives you a choice of lawns. Lawn Care. Michigan Edition. p. 9. 1969.

1956. ______. Safe power lawn mower throws debris forward. Machine Design. October, 1969.

1958. ______. Sod industry research 1968–1969. Michigan Agricultural Experiment Station Research Report 104. pp. 1–7. 1969.

1959. ______. Lawn weed control. Farm Science Series. Cooperative Extension Service Extension Bulletin E–653. 4 pp. 1969.

1960. ______. High use turf areas exposed to compaction, Purdue. Midwest Regional Turf Conference Proceedings. p. 20. 1969.

1961. ______. System 9—the Purr-Wick system. Midwest Regional Turf Foundation Turf Conference Proceedings. pp. 21–22. 1969.

1962. ______. Fertilization program for the bluegrasses. Northwest Turfgrass Topics. 11(1):11. 1969.

1963. ______. Sportveldenonderzoek: Deel 2. N.S.F.-K.N.V.B.-K.N.H.M. 80 pp. 1969.

1964. ______. Sportveldenonderzoek: Deel 1. N.S.F.-K.N.V.B.-K.N.H.M. Publication. 87 pp. 1969.

1965. ______. How about fine turf for roadside beauty. Park Maintenance. 22(2):-19. 1969.

1966. ______. Guide analyzes costs of golf course development. Park Maintenance. 22(4):44. 1969.

1967. ______. 1969 turf research and irrigation annual. Park Maintenance. 22(7):-17–36. 1969.

1968. ______. Guideline specifications soil preparation and sodding. Cooperative Extension Service, University of Maryland and Virginia Polytechnic Institute. 12 pp. 1969.

1969. ______. Lawn care programs. Cooperative Extension Service, Purdue University. AY–173. 2 pp. 1969.

1970. ______. Rhode Island annual turfgrass field days. Agricultural Experiment Station, University of Rhode Island. 38:1–40. 1969.

1971. ______. Choice of mowing machine for fine turf. Sports Turf Bulletin. 84:-5–7. 1969.

1972. ______. Golf tees. Sports Turf Bulletin. 84:7–10. 1969.

1973. ______. Seasonal tips (January-March). Sports Turf Bulletin. 84:10–12. 1969.

1974. ______. The value of good varieties. Sports Turf Bulletin. 85:4–8. 1969.

1975. ______. Maintenance of hard porous surfaces. Sports Turf Bulletin. 85:10–12. 1969.

1976. ______. Weed control for the groundsman and greenkeeper. Sports Turf Bulletin. 86:5–6. 1969.

1977. ______. The main diseases of turf. Sports Turf Bulletin. 86:7–9. 1969.

1978. ______. Tips on grass tennis courts. Sports Turf Bulletin. 86:10–12. 1969.

1979. ______. Understanding the basic fertilizer spreader: spreading relationships. Turf Bulletin, Massachusetts Turf and Lawn Grass Council. 5(3):9–12, 17. 1969.

1980. ______. TVA shows sulphur coated urea. Turf Bulletin, Massachusetts Turf and Lawn Grass Council. 5(3):13–16, 26. 1969.

1981. ______. Over 11 million golfers. Turf-Grass Times. 4(3):23. 1969.

1982. ______. Crownvetch for highway turf. Turf-Grass Times. 4(6):1, 7. 1969.

1983. ______. Classification of turf equipment. Turfgrass Times. 4(6):8, 10. 1969.

1984. ______. Metamorphosis of seed quality. Turf Talks. pp. 1–2. March, 1969.

1985. ______. Rutgers University scientist is the first to substantiate control for stripe smut disease. Turf Talks. pp. 1–2. July, 1969.

1986. ______. Sod webworms in turf. Turf Talks. pp. 3–4. July, 1969.

1987. ______. How to buy lawn seed. USDA Consumer and Marketing Service. 169:4. 1969.

1988. ______. Ready market for Long Island grower. Weeds, Trees and Turf. 8(2):-36–37. 1969.

1989. ______. Automatic irrigation system. Weeds, Trees, and Turf. 8(3):6. 1969.

1990. ______. Sod industry survey. Weeds, Trees and Turf. 8(3):36–40. 1969.

1991. ______. Sod winterkill extensive. Weeds, Trees, and Turf. 8(6):31–33. 1969.

1992. ______. Golf course maintenance headed toward total turfgrass perfection. Weeds, Trees, and Turf. 8(7):14–15. 1969.

1993. ______. Sand-based greens, grid field renovation. Weeds, Trees and Turf. 8(7):20–23. 1969.

1994. ______. How to cut sod-delivery costs in half. Weeds, Trees, and Turf. 8(12):-50–52. 1969.

1995. ______. Non-selective weed control for the golf course. The Bonnie Greensward. pp. 2–4. 1970.

1996. ______. California turfgrass culture index. California Turfgrass Culture. 20(1):4–8. 1970.

1997. ______. Using powered vehicles. Golf Superintendent. 38(2):48–49. 1970.

1998. ______. New variety highlight chewings fescue. The Greenmaster. 6(4):30. 1970.

1999. ______. Sizing up the turf industry. Grounds Maintenance. 5(9):10. 1970.

2000. ______. Experiment harmonizes real—synthetic turf. Grounds Maintenance. 5(2):60–61. 1970.

2001. ______. Planning approach areas. Grounds Maintenance. 5(3):22–23. 1970.

2002. ______. How to build a pitching mound. Grounds Maintenance. 5(3):24. 1970.

2003. ______. A 'mixture' of top-dressing techniques. Grounds Maintenance. 5(3):-33, 35. 1970.

2004. ______. Maintenance facts study. Grounds Maintenance. 5(3):76–78. 1970.

2005. ______. Turf aeration. Part I. The Groundsman. 23(6):19, 21. 1970.

2006. ______. Physiological and color aspects of turfgrasses with fall and winter nitrogen. Kellogg Supply, Inc. 4(6):1–5. 1970.

2007. ______. Effects of nitrogen of winter root growth of bent grass. Kellogg Supply, Inc. 4(6):6–7. 1970.

2008. ______. Effects of N, P, and K tissue levels and late fall fertilization on the cold hardiness of Tifgreen bermudagrass. Kellogg Supply, Inc. 4(6):8–10. 1970.

2009. ______. '*Poa Annua*'—three effective ways to control this tough turf pest. Lakeshore News. 2(3):9. 1970.

2010. ______. Dacthal—constant improvement on a well proven herbicide. Lakeshore News. 2(4):7. 1970.

2011. ______. Daconil 2787 gets new clearance on turf, ornamentals. Lakeshore News. 2(7):12–14. 1970.

2012. ______. '*Poa Annua*'—three effective ways to control this tough turf pest. Lakeshore News. 2(7):15. 1970.

2013. ______. Good greens are no accident. Lakeshore News. 2(8):7, 9. 1970.

2014. ______. Improving athletic field turfgrass. Lakeshore News. 2(10):1, 4, 10. 1970.

2015. ______. Dacthal applied post-emerge on turf, controls creeping speedwell in tests. Lakeshore News. 2(10):2. 1970.

2016. ______. Grubworms cause dead brown grass. Lakeshore News. 2(11):1970.

2017. ______. Notes to the bluegrass buff. Lawn Care. Lower Michigan Edition. p. 9. February/March, 1970.

2018. ______. The successful seeder's motto: "Have patience—and keep the soil moist". Lawn Care. Lower Michigan Edition. p. 4. April/May, 1970.

2019. ______. Mowing—how high and how often? Lawn Care. Lower Michigan Edition. p. 6. April/May, 1970.

2020. ______. To help you choose lawn seed wisely. Lawn Care. Lower Michigan Edition. pp. 4–5. Fall, 1970.

2021. ______. The miracle of grass. Lawn Care. Lower Michigan Edition. pp. 8–9. Fall, 1970.

2023. ______. *Poa compressa.* New Zealand Institute for Turf Culture Newsletter. 66:29–30. 1970.

2024. ______. Research progress report. Ohio Turfgrass Foundation Newsletter. No. 18. pp. 4–6. 1970.

2025. ______. New soil heating system. Parks, Golf Courses and Sports Grounds. 5(10):878–883. 1970.

2026. ______. Sevin with one blow kills lawn devastating trio. Park Maintenance. 9(6):34–36. 1970.

2027. ______. Turf research and irrigation annual. Park Maintenance. 23(7):11–26. 1970.

2028. ______. Penncross creeping bentgrass—a triumph of breeding. The Penncross Story. The Rudy-Patrick Company. pp. 1–3. 1970.

2029. ______. Seeding and managing penncross. The Penncross Story. The Rudy-Patrick Company. pp. 4–6. 1970.

2030. ______. Penncross breeding and other bentgrass varieties. The Penncross Story. The Rudy-Patrick Company. p. 7. 1970.

2031. ______. The birth of a bluegrass. Seed World. 106(8):20. 1970.

2032. ______. Commercial turf production. Sports Turf Bulletin. 90:6–10. 1970.

2033. ______. Moss and its control. Sports Turf Bulletin. 91:4–7. 1970.

2034. ______. Earthworm control. Sports Turf Bulletin. 91:7–8. 1970.

2035. ______. Does your turf need lime? Sports Turf Bulletin. 91:10–12. 1970.

2036. ______. Turfgrass and the environment. Turf Talks. Scotts. Marysville, Ohio. p. 1. May, 1970.

2037. ______. Trouble shooting spring brown spots. Turf Talks. Scotts. Marysville, Ohio. p. 2. May, 1970.

2038. ______. Activities of Scotts Research Stations and personnel. Turf Talks. Scotts. Marysville, Ohio. pp. 3–4. May, 1970.

2039. ______. Guide for the chemical control of turfgrass diseases and turfgrass weeds. Virginia Polytechnic Institute. Extension Division C. Control Series 76. 10 pp. 1970.

2040. ______. The truth about weeds in lawns. Weeds Today. 1(2):15–17. 1970.

2041. ______. Second national sod industry survey. Weeds, Trees, and Turf. 9(11):-17–20. 1970.

2042. ______. Perlite is carrier in new bulk-blend fertilizer process. Weeds, Trees, and Turf. 9(1):20–21. 1970.

2043. ______. Sand/bark greens and tees. Weeds, Trees and Turf. 9(2):24–25. 1970.

2044. ______. Minimum installation specifications for turf sprinkler irrigation systems. Weeds, Trees and Turf. 9(3):14–16. 1970.

2045. ______. Guideline specifications—soil preparation and sodding. Weeds, Trees, and Turf. 9(4):30–31. 1970.

2046. ______. How Cal-Turf moves sod. Weeds, Trees, and Turf. 9(8):30–31. 1970.

2047. ______. Managing a lawn. University of Alaska Cooperative Extension Service Publication 35. 1971.

2048. ______. Grass problem solved by accident. The Bull Sheet. 25(11):6. 1972.

2049. ______. A summary of hybrid bermuda mowing trials. Florida Turf. 4(2):4–5. 1971.

2050. ______. The migs maintenance system. The Greenmaster. 7(8):22–23. 1971.

2051. ______. Scientists back golfers on green. The Greenmaster. 7(10):22–23. 1971.

2052. ______. Turf disease digest. Grounds Maintenance. 6(6):32. 1971.

2053. ______. Turf pest digest. Grounds Maintenance. 6(7):32. 1971.

2054. ______. Soil structure. The Groundsman. 24(6):26–27. 1971.

2055. ______. Soil organisms, drainage and mat. The Groundsman. 24(7):18–19. 1971.

2056. ______. Study of erosion in roadside drainage channels in North Carolina. Highway Research Abstracts. 41(2):12. 1971.

2057. ______. The establishment of vegetation on nontopsoiled highway slopes in Washington. Highway Research Abstracts. 41(3):6. 1971.

2058. ______. Erosion control on highway rights-of-way in Arkansas. Highway Research Abstracts. 41(6):3. 1971.

2059. ______. Get the drop on erosion control. Highway Research Abstracts. 41(6):4. 1971.

2060. ______. A technical glossary of horticultural and landscape terminology. Horticultural Research Institute, Inc., Washington, D. C. 109 pp. 1971.

2061. ______. 1972 suggested insecticide guide: Insect control by the homeowner. Illinois Circular 900. University of Illinois. 6 pp. 1971.

2062. ______. Growing a vigorous, strong root system on cool season turfgrasses. Kellogg Supply, Inc. 7(2):1–2. 1971.

2063. ______. The relationship of several amended soils and compaction rates on vegetative growth, root development and cold resistance of 'Tifgreen' bermudagrass. Kellogg Supply, Inc. 7(2):3–5. 1971.

2064. ______. Nitrogen effects on root development. Kellogg Supply, Inc. 7(2):6–8. 1971.

2065. ______. pH acidall. Kellogg Supply, Inc. 7(2):9. 1971.

2066. ______. Post emergent control of crabgrass or goosegrass. Kellogg Supply, Inc. 7(2):9–10. 1971.

2067. ______. Controlling annual bluegrass *(Poa annua)*. Kellogg Supply, Inc. 7(2):10. 1971.

2068. ______. Wetting agents may help in more ways than one. Kellogg Supply, Inc. 7(2):11. 1971.

2069. ______. Review of some papers from the 1971 American Society of Agronomy meeting. Kellogg Supply, Inc. 7(4):1–3. 1971.

2070. ______. Start *Poa annua* control programs in January. Kellogg Supply, Inc. 7(4):6–7. 1971.

2071. ______. Goosegrass can be controlled! Kellogg Supply, Inc. 7(4):7. 1971.

2072. ______. Pre-emergent crabgrass control. Kellogg Supply, Inc. 7(4):7. 1971.

2073. ______. Cold weather fertilization. Kellogg Supply, Inc. 7(4):8. 1971.

2074. ______. Winter broadleaf weed control. Kellogg Supply, Inc. 7(4):8. 1971.

2075. ______. Apply long-lasting fertilizers with nitrohumus or topdressing mixes. Kellogg Supply, Inc. 7(4):9. 1971.

2076. ______. Clear plastic tarps with holes can speed winter germination and/or growth. Kellogg Supply, Inc. 7(4):9. 1971.

2077. ______. Bluegrasses can be mowed lower during colder weather. Kellogg Supply, Inc. 7(4):9–10. 1971.

2078. ______. Winter dormancy and desiccation. The Keynoter. Pennsylvania Turfgrass Council. 4:1. 1971.

2080. ______. Agronomy tips. Lakeshore News. 3(12):6. 1971.

2081. ______. The big "cover-up" of large tracts. Landscape Industry. 16(2): 14–16, 53, 1971.

2082. ______. Innovation: sod laid mechanically. Landscape Industry. 16(2): 26, 55. 1971.

2083. ______. Bringing along a new lawn. Lawn Care. Lower Michigan Edition. pp.4–5. Summer, 1971.

2084. ______. Late spring or early summer seedings can be successful—if moisture needs are met. Lawn Care. Lower Michigan Edition. p. 7. Summer, 1971.

2085. ______. What to consider as spring moves into summer. Lawn Care. Lower Michigan Edition. pp. 8–9. Summer, 1971.

2086. ______. Some problems of older lawns. Lawn Care. Lower Michigan Edition. pp.10–11. Summer, 1971.

2087. ______. Why fertilize in fall? There are many reasons—some of them underground. Lawn Care. Lower Michigan Edition. pp.4–5. Fall, 1971.

2088. ______. Phosphorus—friend or foe? Lawn Care. Lower Michigan Edition. p.6. Fall, 1971.

2089. ______. Golf facilities in the United States. National Golf Foundation Information Sheet STI. 8pp. 1971.

2092. ______. The adaptation of selected cool season grasses and crownvetch to eastern Nebraska roadsides. State of Nebraska Department of Roads Research Program. pp. 7–17. 1971.

2093. ______. The adaptation of selected cool season grasses and crownvetch to western Nebraska roadsides. State of Nebraska Department of Roads Research Program. pp. 18–23. 1971.

2094. ______. Evaluation of nitrogen fertilizers for maintenance of common Kentucky bluegrass sod growing under roadside conditions. State of Nebraska Department of Roads Research Program. pp. 105–118. 1971.

2098. ______. Turf yellowing. Ohio Turfgrass Foundation Newsletter. No. 22. p. 7. 1971.

2099. ______. Colored growth often due to slime molds. Ohio Turfgrass Foundation Newsletter. No. 24. p. 4. 1971.

2100. ______. Turf research and irrigation annual. Park Maintenance. 24(7):16–25. 1971.

2101. ______. New grass strain. Parks, Golf Courses and Sports Grounds. 36(10):-985–986. 1971.

2102. ______. Grass concrete. Parks, Golf Courses and Sports Grounds. 37(3):270. 1971.

2103. ______. New method of turf production. Parks, Golf Courses & Sports Grounds. 37(3):276. 1971.

2104. ______. What to look for in 1971. A Patch of Green. p. 7. February, 1971.

2105. ______. Major contributions to turfgrass culture by the MSU turfgrass research group. A Patch of Green. pp. 8, 10. February, 1971.

2106. ______. Snow and ice removal. A Patch of Green. p. 4. March, 1971.

2107. ______. A winter disease of Kentucky bluegrass. A Patch of Green. p. 13. May, 1971.

2108. ______. Micropore release fertilizer packets. A Patch of Green. pp. 10–12. June, 1971.

2109. ______. Question of chemical pollution closing in. A Patch of Green. pp. 7–8, 14, 17. July, 1971.

2110. ______. Let some grass grow under your feet. A Patch of Green. pp. 5–6. September, 1971.

2111. ______. Controlling moss in lawns. A Patch of Green. p. 13. November, 1971.

2112. ______. Cutworm problems on turfs in Michigan. A Patch of Green. p. 14. November, 1971.

2113. ______. Rhode Island annual turfgrass field days. Agricultural Experiment Station, University of Rhode Island. 40:1–57. 1971.

2114. ______. Special discussion session on turfgrass disease problems. Proceedings of Scotts Turfgrass Research Conference. 2:69–84. 1971.

2115. ______. Nerf Nerf Turf Farm accounting system. The Sod Grower. 1(1):8–13. 1971.

2116. ______. Fertilizer recommendations for sod production in Michigan. The Sod Grower. 1(1):17. 1971.

2117. ______. Advantages and disadvantages of palletizing. The Sod Grower. 1(2):6. 1971.

2118. ______. The 2, 4, 5–T story. The Sod Grower. 1(2):8–9. 1971.

2119. ______. Why thirty cents—tradition or habit. The Sod Grower. 1(2):11. 1971.

2120. ______. Looking back at 1971. The Sod Grower. 1(4):5–7, 17. 1971.

2121. ______. The worst sod pest. The Sod Grower. 1(4):9. 1971.

2122. ______. Profit or no. The Sod Grower. 1(4):10. 1971.

2123. ______. S.G.A.M. Board to propose steps toward more orderly sod market. The Sod Grower. 1(4):11–13. 1971.

2124. ______. Rugby pitch management. Sports Turf Bulletin. 92:5–7. 1971.

2125. ______. Damage to fine turf from winter traffic. Sports Turf Bulletin. 92:7–9. 1971.

2126. ______. Drainage—winter pitches. Sports Turf Bulletin. 92:9–12. 1971.

2127. ______. The importance of correct fertilizer treatment. Sports Turf Bulletin. 93:-4–5. 1971.

2128. ______. To roll or not to roll. Sports Turf Bulletin. 93:6–8. 1971.

2129. ______. News on grass varieties. Sports Turf Bulletin. 93:8–12. 1971.

2130. ______. Difficulties with excess fibre—the value of scarification. Sports Turf Bulletin. 94:4–7. 1971.

2131. ______. *Corticium* or red thread disease. Sports Turf Bulletin. 94:7–9. 1971.

2132. ______. Weed control in turf. Sports Turf Bulletin. 94:9–12. 1971.

2133. ______. Management of cricket outfields. Sports Turf Bulletin. 95:5–8. 1971.

2134. ______. Sports turf aeration. Sports Turf Bulletin. 95:8–10. 1971.

2135. ______. *Fusarium* patch disease. Sports Turf Bulletin. 95:10–12. 1971.

2136. ______. Fertility research plots demonstrate method of weed control. Turf Talks. Scotts. Marysville, Ohio. p. 1. September, 1971.

2137. ______. Activities of Scotts Research Stations and personnel. Turf Talks. Scotts. Marysville, Ohio. p. 2. September, 1971.

2138. ______. Fall program for crabgrass. Turf Talks. Scotts. Marysville, Ohio. p. 2. September, 1971.

2139. ______. Watering tips for fall seedings. Turf Talks. Scotts. Marysville, Ohio. p. 2. September, 1971.

2140. ______. Demand increases for Virginia sod. Virginia Department of Agriculture and Commerce. Bulletin. p. 7. March, 1971.

2141. ______. Guideline specifications for sodding. American Sod Producers Association Publication. 1972.

2142. ______. Bluegrass won't thicken? Blame day length? Crops and Soils. 24(8):21. 1972.

2143. ______. Turf blankets might protect turf from winter damage. Crop and Soils Magazine. 25(1):24. 1972.

2144. ______. Extend your season and profit. Golfdom. 46(6):37, 40. 1972.

2145. ______. Spring 1972. The Greenmaster. 8(6):15, 18–32. 1972.

2146. ______. Iron in plants, soils, fertilizers. Grounds Maintenance. 7(6):20, 23. 1972.

2147. ______. Watering small, specialized areas. Grounds Maintenance. 7:32–33. 1972.

2148. ______. Winter protection for greens. Grounds Maintenance. 7(12):90–91. 1972.

2149. ______. Gypsum counteracts salt in roadside soil tests. Highway Research Abstracts. 42(2):6. 1972.

2150. ______. Guide for the custom application of pesticides. Departments of Horticulture, Agriculture, Entomology, and Plant Pathology. University of Illinois. 12 pp. 1972.

2151. ______. Topdressing. Iowa Golf Course Superintendents Reporter. 5(4):1. 1972.

2152. ______. Aerification. Iowa Golf Course Superintendents Association Reporter. 5(7):1. 1972.

2153. ______. Seeding a new lawn in late summer or early fall. Iowa State University Cooperative Extension Service Pamphlet 331. 1972.

2154. ______. Guideline specifications for sodding. Turf Grass Times. 8(2):9–10. 1972.

2155. ______. Soil microbes and organic amendments. Kellogg Supply, Incorporated. 8(2):1–7. 1972.

2156. ______. The use of iron in turfgrass management. Kellogg Supply, Inc. 8(2):8–11. 1972.

2157. ______. Diseases and insects. Kellogg Supply, Inc. 8(2):12. 1972.

2158. ______. Bermuda grass from bentgrass. Kellogg Supply, Inc. 8(2):13. 1972.

2159. ______. Aerate before laying sod. Kellogg Supply, Inc. 8(2):14. 1972.

2160. ______. Controlling nutgrass and morning glory in ground cover and shrub beds. Kellogg Supply, Inc. 8(2):14. 1972.

2161. ______. Deep aerification by trenching. Kellogg Supply, Inc. 8(2):14. 1972.

2162. ______. Turfgrass diseases: The relationship of potassium. Kellogg Supply, Inc. 8(3):6–7. 1972.

2163. ______. Controlling annual bluegrass in golf and bowling greens. Kellogg Supply, Inc. 8(3):8. 1972.

2164. ______. Cultural control of crabgrass, annual bluegrass, and other weedy grasses and broadleaf weeds in turfgrasses. Kellogg Supply, Inc. 8(3):10. 1972.

2165. ______. Thatch and methods for its control. Kellogg Supply, Inc. 8(4):2. 1972.

2166. ______. The miracle of spring. Lawn Care. Lower Michigan Edition. pp. 2–3. Spring, 1972.

2167. ______. Early spring—the only time you can prevent crabgrass in this year's lawn. Lawn Care. Lower Michigan Edition. pp. 4–5. Spring, 1972.

2168. ______. Late spring supplement. Lawn Care. Lower Michigan Edition. pp. 18–19. Spring, 1972.

2169. ______. Causes of winter injury on turfgrasses. Turf-Grass Times. 8(2):16. 1972.

2170. ______. Sod industry research. Michigan State University Agricultural Experiment Station. pp. 58–61. 1972.

2171. ______. Why topdress. Mid-Atlantic Newsletter. 23(10):3. 1972.

2172. ______. Seventh report on greenkeeping research. New Zealand Institute for Turf Culture. Palmerston North, New Zealand. 80 pp.

2173. ______. Bentgrass varieties vary in tolerance. Ohio Turfgrass Foundation Newsletter. No. 28. p. 2. 1972.

2174. ______. Turf disease notes. Ohio Turfgrass Foundation Newsletter. No. 30. pp. 5–6. 1972.

2175. ______. The importance of proper training. A Patch of Green. Michigan and Border Cities GCSA Publication. pp. 8–9. 1972.

2176. ______. May meeting. A Patch of Green. pp. 6, 11. 1972.

2177. ______. Beard chooses Pennlawn for shaded areas. Park Maintenance. 25(3):-29. 1972.

2178. ______. Broadleaved weeds. Park Maintenance. 25(7):19–20. 1972.

2179. ______. Rhode Island annual turfgrass field days. Agricultural Experiment Station, University of Rhode Island. 41:1–43. 1972.

2180. ______. The ABC's of lawn sprinkler systems. A. C. "Chet" Sarsfield, Pub., Lafayette, California. 145 pp. 1972.

2181. ______. Centipedegrass better when cut lower. Turf-Grass Times 8(2):16. 1972.

2182. ______. Management of golf fairways. Sports Turf Bulletin. 96:8–11. 1972.

2183. ______. Unfrozen winter pitches. Sports Turf Bulletin. 96:11–12. 1972.

2184. ______. Current work on grass varieties and mixtures. Sports Turf Bulletin. 97:4–7. 1972.

2185. ______. Some observations on turf culture in the U.S.A. Sports Turf Bulletin. 97:7–10. 1972.

2186. ______. Hockey pitches. Sports Turf Bulletin. 97:10–12. 1972.

2187. ______. Crested dogstail. Sports Turf Bulletin. 98:4–5. 1972.

2188. ______. Soil cultivation in playing field construction. Sports Turf Bulletin. 98:-6–8. 1972.

2189. ______. Sand slits to improve drainage. Sports Turf Bulletin. 98:8–9. 1972.

2190. ______. Grass tennis courts. Sports Turf Bulletin. 99:4–7. 1972.

2191. ______. Mole drainage. Sports Turf Bulletin. 99:7–9. 1972.

2192. ______. Checking the germination of seed. Sports Turf Bulletin. 99:9–10. 1972.

2193. ______. Vegetative propagation. Sports Turf Bulletin. 99:11–12. 1972.

2194. ______. Old English Lawn Handbook. The Stanford Seed Co. 35 pp. 1972.

2195. ______. New standard seed specifications. Turf-Grass Times. 8(1):17. 1972.

2196. ______. Rutgers University scientist documents outstanding control for leaf spot disease on Kentucky bluegrass. Turf Talks. Scotts. Marysville, Ohio. pp. 1–2. April, 1972.

2197. ______. Quotes from here and there. Turf Talks. Scotts. Marysville, Ohio. p. 2. April, 1972.

2198. ______. Activities of Scotts Research Stations and personnel. Turf Talks. Scotts. Marysville, Ohio. pp. 2–3. April, 1972.

2199. ______. Fertilizer, time and patience . . . a remedy for striped lawn. Turf Talks. Scotts. Marysville, Ohio. p. 3. April, 1972.

2200. ______. Grass varieties in the United States. USDA Agricultural Handbook. No. 170. 124 pp. 1972.

2201. ______. New foam frost protection. Turf-Grass Times. 8(2):16. 1972.

2202. ______. Sod now leading crop in Maryland. Turf-Grass Times. 8(2):16. 1972.

2203. ______. Atrazine in lawns. Weeds Today. 3(4):17. 1972.

2204. ______. The search for shade tolerant turf. Weeds, Trees, and Turf. 11(2):19, 36, 42. 1972.

2205. ______. Turf pest control and the environment. Weeds, Trees and Turf. 11(2):-28, 62. 1972.

2206. ______. Turf from a Yorkshire Lagoon. Turf-Grass Times. 8(2):21. 1972.

2207. ______. You can't gamble with turf. Weeds, Trees and Turf. 11(7):18, 34–35. 1972.

2208. ______. Birth of a bluegrass. Weeds, Trees and Turf. 11(8):46–47. 1972.

2209. ______. Slow release nitrogen. Weeds, Trees and Turf. 11(9):22, 32–33. 1972.

2210. ______. Grooming the monster. Weeds, Trees and Turf. 11(10):12, 20–21. 1972.

2211. ______. A ryegrass that cuts clean. Weeds, Trees and Turf. 11(11):12–13. 1972.

2212. ______. Sod for a mobile home estate. Weeds, Trees and Turf. 11(12):16–17. 1972.

2213. ______. Fall is the time to plant a lawn. Seed World. 85(7):29. 1959.

2214. ______. Planting the fall lawn. Seed World. 85(8):26. 1959.

2215. ______. Tips on lawn and garden care. Seed World. 86(12):23. 1960.

2216. ______. Matting protects grass plantings. Seed World. 87(5):29–30. 1960.

2217. ______. Spring fever will save your lawn. Seed World. 88(11):59. 1961.

2218. ______. Prevent lawn "indigestion" with balanced diet. Seed World. 88(12):27. 1961.

2219. ______. Lawnmakers feud over spring vs. fall fertilization. Seed World. 89(2):19–20. 1961.

2220. ______. Fall is the time to plant a lawn. Seed World. 89(7):28. 1961.

2221. ______. Snow mold. Seed World. 90(7):3. 1962.

2222. ______. "Fading out" disease on lawn grasses. Seed World. 93(6):21. 1963.

2223. ______. Lawns need fall fertilizing. Seed World. 93(7):21. 1963.

2224. ______. Lawn seed labeling. Seed World. 93(10):21. 1963.

2225. ______. Natural turf and glare-free lighting possible in stadiums with domes. Seed World. 100(7):24. 1967.

2226. ______. Fall is lawn care time. Seed World. 103(4):18. 1968.

2227. ______. Versatile lawngrasses. Seed World. 103(5):20. 1968.

2228. ______. Have both lawn and shade. Seed World. 103(6):20. 1968.

2229. ______. Crabgrass in your lawn. Seed World. 105(7):20. 1969.

2230. Ansaldo, R. Soil, sawdust and turfgrass. Turf Clippings. University of Massachussets. 1(5):15. 1960.

2231. Ansari, A. Q. and W. E. Loomis. Leaf temperatures. American Journal of Botany. 46(10):713–717. 1959.

2232. Anslow, R. C. Seed formation in perennial ryegrass. Journal of the British Grassland Society. 18:90–96. 1963.

2233. Anslow, R. C. and H. L. Back. Grass growth in mid-summer and light interception and growth rate of a perennial ryegrass sward. Journal of the British Grassland Society. 22(2):108–111. 1967.

2234. Anslow, R. C. and J. O. Green. The seasonal growth of pasture grasses. Journal of Agricultural Science. 68(1):109–122. 1967.

2235. Antipov, V. G. Gas resistance of lawn grasses. Botanicheskii Zhurnal. 44:990–992. 1959.

2236. Antognini, J., R. A. Gray, J. D. Wright, and B. H. Lake. Weed control in grass and dichondra turfs with betasan. Agronomy Abstracts. p. 104. 1964.

2237. Aono, S. Microclimate of the green, part 1. K. G. U. Green Section Turf Research Bulletin. 4:41–48. 1963.

2239. Appleby, A. P. The action of applied herbicides. Proceedings of the 20th Annual Northwest Turfgrass Conference. pp. 17–21. 1966.

2240. ______. Herbicide selectivity. Weeds Today. 1(3):20–22. 1970.

2241. Apt, W. J. and R. Goss. Nematode problems in turf areas. Pacific Northwest Turf Conference Proceedings. pp. 25–29. 1959.

2242. Apt, W. J., H. M. Austenson, and W. D. Courtney. Use of herbicides to break the life cycle of the bentgrass nematode *Anguina agrostis* (Steinbuck 1799) Filipjev 1936. The Plant Disease Reporter. 44(7):524–526. 1960.

2243. Arber, A. Monocotyledons: A morphological study. Cambridge Botany Handbooks. Cambridge, England. 258 pp. 1925.

2244. ______. The *Graminae.* Cambridge at the University Press. 480 pp. 1934.

2245. Archbold, H. K. Fructosans in the monocotyledons. A review. The New Phytologists. 39:185–219. 1940

2246. Archibald, J. A., R. A. Cline and H. J. Reissman. Soil moisture and temperature relationships as influenced by surface mulching. Report of the Ontario Horticultural Experiment Station Production Laboratory. pp. 23–28. 1966.

2247. Archibald, J. G. The chemical composition of grass plots fertilized and grazed intensively. Journal of Agricultural Research. 41:491–501. 1930.

2248. ______. Influence of weather on the sugar content of forage crops. Journal of Dairy Science. 44(3):511–514. 1961.

2249. Archibald, J. G. and E. Bennett. Yield and chemical composition of certain species of grass. Journal of Agricultural Research. 50:711–715. 1935.

2250. Archibald, J. G., and P. R. Nelson. The chemical composition of grass plots fertilized and grazed intensively. Journal of the American Society of Agronomy. 21(6):686–700. 1929.

2251. Archibald, J. G., P. R. Nelson, and E. Bennett. A three year study of the chemical composition of grass from plots fertilized and grazed intensively. Journal of Agricultural Research. 45:627–640. 1932.

2252. Arditti, J., R. Ernst, and P. L. Healey. Biological effects of surfactants. Plant Physiology Abstracts. 47:31. 1971.

2253. Arikado, H. Studies on the development of the ventilating system in relation to the tolerance against excess moisture injury in various crops. 13. Difference between Italian ryegrass and oats in the tolerance against excess-moisture injury. Proceedings Crop Science Society of Japan. 32(4):353–357. 1964.

2254. Armacost, R. B. Agrosto—logic. Turf Clippings—Stockbridge School Conference Proceedings. 1(10):51–57. 1965.

2255. Armiger, W. H. Effects of urea-form fertilizer on turf. Golf Course Reporter. 16:32–34. 1948.

2256. Armiger, W. H., K. G. Clark, F. O. Lundstrom, and A. E. Blair. Urea-form: Greenhouse studies with perennial ryegrass. Agronomy Journal. 43(3)123–127. 1951.

2257. Armiger, W. H., I. Forbes, R. E. Wagner, and F. O. Lundstrom. Urea-form—a nitrogenous fertilizer of controlled availability: Experiments with turf grasses. Journal of the American Society of Agronomy. 40(4):342–356. 1948.

2258. Armstrong, J. M. A cytolotgical study of the genus *Poa.* Canadian Journal of Research. 15:281–287. 1937.

2259. Arnold, C. Y. Understanding soils. Illinois Turfgrass Conference Proceedings. pp. 1–2. 1961.

2260. Arnold, E. H. Insect pests of greens. New Zealand Institute for Turf Culture Newsletter. 7:1–3. 1960.

2261. ______. Turf diseases. New Zealand Institute for Turf Culture Newsletter. 22:13–14. 1962.

2262. ______. Turf diseases. New Zealand Institute for Turf Culture Newsletter. 23:19. 1963.

2263. ______. Choice of soils for top-dressing. New Zealand Institute for Turf Culture Newsletter. 24:15–16. 1963.

2264. ______. Turf diseases. New Zealand Institute for Turf Culture Newsletter. 27:14–15. 1963.

2265. ______. Turf diseases. New Zealand Institute for Turf Culture Newsletter. 28:5–6. 1963.

2266. ______. Turf diseases. New Zealand Institute for Turf Culture Newsletter. 30:14–15. 1964.

2267. Arnold, K. Hydro-mulching adapts to landscaping. Landscape Industry. 15(1):16–17. 1970.

2268. ______. Grass seed sprayed on Kentucky Golf Estates. Weeds, Trees, and Turf. 9:22. 1970.

2269. Arnold, W. J. Snail and lawn pest control with zectran pesticide Down to Earth. 18(3):20–24. 1962.

2270. Arnott, R. A. The effect of seed weight and depth of sowing on the emergence and early seedling growth of perennial ryegrass. Journal of British Grasslands Society. 24(2):104–110. 1969.

2271. Arrowood, J. L. A fertilizing program for good greens maintenance. Golfdom. 23(6):75. 1949.

2272. Arsjad, S. and J. Giddens. Effect of added plant tissue on decomposition of soil organic matter under different wetting and drying cycles. Soil Science Society of America Proceedings. 30:457–460. 1966.

2273. Arthur, A. P. A skipper *Thymelicus lineola (Ochs.) (Lepidoptera: Hesperiidae)* and its parasites in Ontario. Canadian Entomologist. 94:1082–1089. 1962.

2274. Arthur, J. H. New Zealand chewing's fescue and browntop. Journal of Greenkeeping Research. 7(25):236–243. 1949.

2275. Ashby, W. C. and H. Hellmers. Flowering and growth responses to photoperiod and temperature for six southern California grasses. Botanical Gazette. 120(3):151–157. 1959.

2277. Ashley, R. A. and E. M. Rahn. Persistence of atrazine at two locations as affected by soil incorporation and certain additives. Proceedings of the Northeastern Weed Control Conference. pp. 557–562. 1967.

2278. Ashworth, L. J., and J. V. Amin. A mechanism for mercury tolerance in fungi. Phytopathology. 54(12):1459–1463. 1964.

2279. Ashworth, L. J., B. C. Langley, and W. H. Thames, Jr. Long-term inhibition of *Rhizoctonia solani* by a nematicide, 1,2-dibromo-3-chloropropane. Phytopathology. 54:187–191. 1964.

2280. Asplund, A. E. Greenkeeping in the north of Minnesota. Greenkeepers' Reporter. 6:22, 32. 1938.

2281. ———. Watering bent greens. Golf Course Reporter. 21:14. 1953.

2282. Atsatt, P. R. and L. C. Bliss. Some effects of emulsified hexa-octadecanol on germination, establishment, and growth of Kentucky bluegrass. Agronomy Journal. 55(6):-533–537. 1963.

2283. Aston, A. R., and C. H. M. van Bavel. Soil surface water depletion and leaf temperature. Agronomy Journal. 64(3):368–373. 1972.

2284. Aston, J. L. and A. D. Bradshaw. Natural variation in *Agrostis stolonifera* L. (creeping bent) and the value of this grass in turf. Journal of the Sports Turf Research Institute. 11(39):7–18. 1963.

2285. Astrup, M. H. Maintenance of interstate highway roadsides as affected by highway design. "Roadside Development", Highway Research Board, National Academy of Sciences—National Research Council, Publication 697:31–33. 1959.

2286. Atkins, J. G. Forage crop *Rhizoctonia* cross inoculation tests (Abstr.). Phytopathology. 42:282. 1952.

2287. Atkins, M. D., and J. J. Coyle. Grass waterways in soil conservation. USDA Leaflet No. 477. Soil Conservation Service. 8 pp. 1960.

2288. Atkins, W. R. G. The measurement of daylight in relation to plant growth. Empire Forestry Journal. 11:42–52. 1932.

2289. Atkins, W. R. G. and H. H. Poole. Photo-electric measurements of illumination in relation to plant distribution. Part 4. Changes in the colour composition of daylight in the open and in shaded situations. Royal Dublin Society. Scientific Proceedings. 20:13–48. 1931.

2290. Atkinson, R. E. How to grow *Dichondra*. Lasca Leaves. 14(3):65–66. 1964.

2291. Atwell, S. D., G. L. Bieber, and C. Y. Ward. Effects of mulches on microenvironment temperatures and moisture. Proceedings, Southern Agricultural Workers. 65:47–48. 1968.

2292. Aubertin, G. M. and G. W. Gorsline. Effect of fatty alcohol on evaporation and transpiration. Agronomy Journal. 56(1):-50–52. 1964.

2293. Aubertin, G. M., and L. T. Kardos. Root growth through porous media under controlled conditions. II. Effect of aeration levels and rigidity. Soil Science Society of America. 29(4):363–365. 1965.

2294. Aubertin, G. M., R. W. Rickman, and J. Letey. Differential salt-oxygen levels influence plant growth. Agronomy Journal. 60(4):345–349. 1968.

2295. Auda, H., R. E. Blaser and R. H. Brown. Tillering and carbohydrate contents of orchardgrass as influenced by environmental factors. Crop Science. 6:139–143. 1966.

2296. Audus, L. J. Plant Growth Substances. Leonard Hill, Ltd., London. 553 pp. 1963.

2297. ______. ed. The Physiology and Biochemistry of Herbicides. Academic Press, Inc., New York. 555. pp. 1964.

2298. Augustine, M. T. Vegetative slope and channel stabilization. Agronomy Abstracts. p. 122. 1965.

2299. Augustine, M. T. and W. C. Sharp. Effect of several fertilizer treatments on the production of American beachgrass culms. Agronomy Journal. 61(1):43–45. 1969.

2300. Augustine, M. T., R. B. Thornton, J. M. Sanborn, and A. T. Leiser. Response of American beachgrass to fertilizers. Journal of Soil and Water Conservation. 19:112–115. 1964.

2301. Ault, E. B. Comparison of water sources. USGA Journal and Turf Management. 13(1):29–30. 1960.

2302. Aunapu, A. The grass grading committee's recommendations concerning grading of St. Augustinegrass. Proceedings, Annual University of Florida Turf-Grass Management Conference. 9:127–128. 1961.

2303. Austenson, H. M. Progress report on turf work at Western Washington Experiment Station. Pacific Northwest Turf Conference Proceedings. pp. 47–50. 1955.

2304. ______. Turfgrass adaptation studies in western Washington. Northwest Turf Conference Proceedings. 11:15–16. 1957.

2306. Austin, J. Our drainage problem. The Greenkeepers' Reporter. 5(10):6. 1937.

2307. Austin, N. Greens levelling procedure. New Zealand Institute for Turf Culture Newsletter. 7:2. 1960.

2308. Avnimelech, Y. Nitrate transformation in peat. Soil Science. 111(2):113–118. 1971.

2309. Axtell, J. D. and L. D. Doneen. The use of gypsum in irrigation water. Better Crops with Plant Food Magazine. 33(9):16–18. 1949.

2310. Ayer, M. T. The effect of two preemergence herbicides on the rooting and establishment of "Tifgreen" and 'Tifway' bermudagrass. Proceedings, Florida Turfgrass Management Conference. 18:106–108. 1970.

2311. Ayer, M. T. and G. C. Horn. Developments in overseeding. Florida Turfgrass Management Conference Proceedings. 19:125–126. 1971.

2312. Ayer, M. T., G. C. Horn, and G. S. Smith. Phytotoxicity of preemergence herbicides to *Poa annua*, 5 overseeded cool season grasses and 'Tifgreen' bermudagrass. Agronomy Abstracts. p. 45. 1971.

2313. Ayers, A. D. Seed germination as affected by soil moisture and salinity. Agronomy Journal. 44(2):82–84. 1952.

2314. Ayers, A. D. and H. E. Hayward. A method for measuring the effects of soil salinity on seed germination with observations on several crop plants. Soil Science Society of America Proceedings. 13:224–226. 1948.

2315. Aylor, D. Noise reduction by vegetation and ground. Highway Research Abstracts. 42(5):1. 1972.

2316. Aylsworth, J. Q. Pinpoint your sod harvesting costs. Weeds, Trees & Turf. 7(2):-8–9, 41. 1968.

2317. Ahlgren, G. H. and R. E. Engel. Planting and caring for the lawn. New Jersey Bulletin 724. 1949.

2318. Ahlgren, G. H. "Your lawn" ground for living. Rutgers University Press. New Jersey. 1949.

2319. Albrecht, H. R. Strain Differences in tolerance to 2,4-D in creeping bentgrasses. American Society of Agronomy Journal. 39(2):163–165. 1947.

2320. Allen, G. P. The effect of July applications of dalapon on the growth and botanical composition of an *Agrostis/Lolium* pasture. Weed Research. 8:309–320. 1968.

2321. Baartaja, O. Survival of *Fusarium, Pythium,* and *Rhizoctonia* in very dry soil. Bi-monthly Report. Department of Forestry. Canada. 20(6):3. 1964.

2322. Babbage, J. Arsenate of lead. The National Greenkeeper. 2(5):36. 1928.

2323. Babcock, C. I. Ammonium nitrate behavior in fires. National Fire Protection Association Quarterly. 1:15. 1960.

2324. Baber, A. A. Review of herbicides for turf weed control. Stockbridge School Conference Proceedings. Turf Clippings. A:53–54. 1968.

2325. Bachelor, P. L. School playing field maintenance. Journal of the Sports Turf Research Institute. 9(31):98–104. 1955.

2326. Bachelder, S. Rutgers turf fungicide trials. Golf Course Reporter. 31:11–20. 1961.

2327. Bachelder, S. and R. E. Engel. 1958 New Jersey fungicide trials. Golf Course Reporter. 29:22–29. 1959.

2328. ______. 1959 turf fungicide trials. Golf Course Reporter. 28:50–56. 1960.

2329. ______. 1961 turf fungicide trials. Park Maintenance. 15:38–43. 1962.

2330. ______. 1962 turf fungicide trials. Park Maintenance. 16(4):38–44. 1963.

2331. ______. 1963 turf fungicide trials. Rutgers University Three-day Turf Course Proceedings. pp. 62–71. 1963.

2332. ______. 1963 turf fungicide trials. Rutgers University Short Course in Turf Management. 32:1–8. 1964.

2333. Bachelder, S., R. E. Engel and H. D. Snyder. 1956 turf fungicide trials. Rutgers University Turfgrass Short Course. 1957.

2334. Badenhuizen, N. P., and E. N. Lawson. Lethal synthesis in *Cynodon dactylon* growing in southern Africa. American Journal of Botany. 49(2):158–167. 1962.

2335. Bader, K. L., R. R. Davis, and O. L. Musgrave. Turf for heavy use areas. Ohio Cooperative Extension Service. Columbus, Ohio. Leaflet 115. 1964.

2336. Badgley, J. E. Panel discussion—drainage problems. Rutgers University Annual Short Course in Turf Management. 19:-55–59. 1952–1953.

2337. Baier, W. and G. W. Robertson. Estimating supplemental irrigation water requirements from climatological data. Canadian Agricultural Engineering. 9(1):46–50. 1967.

2338. Bailey, B. Budget preparation. Proceedings University of Florida Turf-Grass Management Conference. 10:110–115. 1962.

2339. Bailey, L. F. Some water relations of three western grasses. I. The transpiration ratio. II. Drought resistance. III. Root developments. American Journal of Botany. 27:-122–135. 1940.

2340. Bailey, R. E. Evaluation of grass species and mulches for erosion control on Oklahoma highways. M. S. Thesis, Oklahoma State University. 1966.

2341. Bailey, R. H. Behind the scene in turf-grass seed production. Turf-Grass Times. 2(1):3, 18–20. 1966.

2342. ______. Ultraviolet light helps decode ryegrass species. Weeds, Trees and Turf. 11(5):14. 1972.

2343. Bailey, T. B. Effect of three selected growth regulators on Penncross bentgrass (*Agrostis palustris* Hud.). M. S. Thesis, University of Minnesota. 73 pp. 1969.

2344. Bain, C. Dealing death to earth worms. The National Greenkeeper. 1(4):29–30. 1927.

2345. ______. Greenkeeping during World War 1. Greenkeepers' Reporter. 11(2):9. 1943.

2346. Bain, D. C. *Sclerotinia* blight of bahia and Coastal bermuda grasses. Plant Disease Reporter. 46:55–56. 1962.

2347. ______. *Puccinia zoysiae* in Mississippi. The Plant Disease Reporter. 50(10):-770. 1966.

2348. Bain, D. C., B. N. Patel, and M. V. Patel. Blast of ryegrass in Mississippi. The Plant Disease Reporter. 56(3):210. 1972.

2350. Bains, S. S., and M. Fireman. Effects of exchangeable sodium percentage on the growth and absorption of essential nutrients and sodium by five crop plants. Agronomy Journal. 56:432–435. 1964.

2351. Bair, R. A. Minor elements stimulate grasses in Florida. Timely Turf Topics. USGA Green Section. p. 3. May, 1947.

2352. ______. Minor elements in turf production. Golf Course Reporter. 16:28–31. 1948.

2353. ______. Turf research work being carried on under actual playing conditions on an experimental golf course. Florida Greenkeeping Superintendents Association and the

Southeastern Turf Conference. Turf Management Conference. pp. 12–19. 1949.

2354. ______. Grasses for lawns, recreational areas, parks, airports, and roadsides. Annual Report. Florida State Project 533. 1948–1949.

2355. ______. Turf progress at the Everglades experiment station. Florida Greenkeeping Superintendents Association Turf Management Conference. pp. 5–21. 1950.

2356. ______. Fertility problems—minor elements, the importance of micro-nutrient balance in growing healthy grass. University of Florida Turf-Grass Management Conference. 3:112–117. 1955.

2357. Baird, W. J. Crab grass control. Golf Course Reporter. 16(2):8. 1948.

2358. Baker, A. S. One dealer's problem. Proceedings of Midwest Regional Turf Conference. pp. 35–38. 1952.

2359. Baker, A. V., D. N. Maynard, B. Mioduchowska, and A. Buch. Ammonium and salt inhibition of some physiological processes associated with seed germination. Physiologia Plantarum. 23(5):898–907. 1970.

2360. Baker, B. S. Growth of four perennial grasses as influenced by environmental conditions. M. S. Thesis, West Virginia University. 1966.

2361. ______. Growth and some metabolic responses of four perennial grasses as influenced by temperature. Ph.D. Thesis, West Virginia University. 82 pp. 1969.

2362. Baker, B. S. and G. A. Jung. Effect of environmental conditions on the growth of four perennial grasses. I. Response to controlled temperature. Agronomy Journal. 60(2):155–158. 1968.

2363. ______. Effect of environmental conditions on the growth of four perennial grasses. II. Response to fertility, water, and temperature. Agronomy Journal. 60(2):158–162. 1968.

2364. Baker, C. W. Something about turf . . . F. H. Woodruff & Sons, Grass Seed Division. Milford, Connecticut. 47 pp. 1936.

2365. ______. Seed in her time . . . for zoysia! Southern Seedsman. 13(8):16, 44. 1950.

2366. ______. Plant grass seed mixes. Proceedings of University of Florida Turf-Grass Management Conference. 8:100–105. 1960.

2368. ______. Grasses from the commercial angle. The Greenkeepers' Reporter. 6(3):20, 22. 1938.

2369. ______. Big news in grasses! Southern Seedsman. 12(3):16, 65. 1949.

2370. ______. The grass seed outlook. New York State Turf Association. Bulletin 16. pp. 61–62. 1950.

2371. ______. Grasses for turf purposes. Proceedings of Southeastern New York Turf School. pp. 8–14. 1950.

2372. ______. Report on southern grasses. Golfdom. 25(2):62–63. 1951.

2373. ______. The potential and demand for seeding grasses and grass seed mixtures in Florida. Proceedings of University of Florida Turfgrass Management Conference. 5:99–102. 1957.

2374. ______. Retailing lawnseed mixtures. Proceedings of University of Florida Turfgrass Management Conference. 7:64–68. 1959.

2375. ______. The 1961 lawn grass seed story and the prospects for 1962. Proceedings of University of Florida Turfgrass Management Conference. 9:144–150. 1961.

2376. ______. The advantages and disadvantages of Bahiagrass for large lawn areas. Proceedings of University of Florida Turfgrass Management Conference. 10:101–106. 1962.

2377. ______. A comparison of seeded grasses. Proceedings of University of Florida Turfgrass Management Conference. 11:92–97. 1963.

2378. ______. Seeded lawns. Proceedings of Florida Turfgrass Management Conference. 14:93–95. 1966.

2379. ______. Seeding lawns. Proceedings Florida Turfgrass Management Conference. 14:126–128. 1966.

2380. ______. Soil preparation for and planting of Bahiagrass for turf. Proceedings of Florida Turfgrass Management Conference. 17:67–74. 1969.

2381. Baker, H. K. 1957 studies on the root development of herbage plants. Journal of British Grassland Society. 12:197–207. 1957.

2382. Baker, H. K. and G. L. David. Winter damage to grass. Agriculture. 70(8):-380. 1963.

2383. Baker, J. Lawns: the head of the garden. Plants Are Like People. Nash Publishing. California. pp. 17–88. 1971.

2384. Baker, K. F. Treatment of soil by aerated steam. Proceedings of Turf, Tree Landscape, and Nursery Conference. pp. 18–1 to 18–3. 1966.

2385. Baker, K. F., N. T. Flentje, C. M. Olsen, and H. M. Stretton. Effect of antagonists on growth and survival of *Rhizoctonia solani* in soil. Phytopathology. 57(6):591–597. 1967.

2386. Baker, O. S. Fertilization practices. University of Florida Turfgrass Management Conference Proceedings. 3:72–75. 1955.

2387. Bakke, A. L. Looking ahead to chemical control of common weeds on golf courses. Journal Paper No. J-1198. Iowa Agricultural Experiment Station. 8 pp. 1943.

2388. ______. Chemical control of common weeds on golf courses. Golfdom. 19(2):-42–46. 1945.

2389. Baldwin, H. I. A comparison of the available moisture in sod and open soil by the soil-point method. Torrey Botanical Club Bulletin. 55:251–255. 1928.

2390. Baldwin, R. L. and S. T. Cockerham. Lawn planting and care in Ventura County. University of California College of Agriculture Extension Service Publication. pp. 1–24.

2391. Ball, J. K. Lawns and their care. Arkansas Agricultural Extension Service Leaflet 309. 1961.

2392. ______. Lawns and their care. University of Arkansas Agricultural Extension Service. Leaflet 309. 1964.

2393. ______. Lawns and their care. Arkansas Agricultural Extension Service. Leaflet 309. 1971.

2394. ______. Turf—recommended practices—Arkansas. 19th Annual Southern Weed Conference. Research Report. pp. 109–110. 1966.

2395. Ballard, W. R. It pays extra dividends—invest in a good lawn. Maryland Agricultural Extension Service. Circular 81:3. 1930.

2396. Ballentine, W. O. Semi-automatic irrigation systems. Golf Course Reporter. 30(6):38, 40. 1962.

2397. Baltensperger, A. A. Initiating a bermuda grass breeding program at the University of Arizona. Arizona Turf Conference Proceedings. pp. 20–21. 1959.

2398. ______. Evaluation of bermuda grass varieties and strains. Arizona Agricultural Experiment Station. Turfgrass Report 203. pp. 3–14. 1961.

2399. ______. Prolonged winter greenness of bermudagrass by use of plastic covers and electric soil heating. Arizona Agricultural Experiment Station. Turfgrass Report 203. pp. 40–44. 1961.

2400. ______. Bermudagrass seed mixture study. Arizona Agricultural Experiment Station. Turfgrass Research Report 203. pp. 48–49. 1961.

2401. ______. Reduced dormancy of bermudagrass by soil heating. Agronomy Abstracts. 54:100. 1962.

2402. ______. Evaluation of bermudagrass varieties and strains. Arizona Agricultural Experiment Station. Turfgrass Research Report. 212:17. 1962.

2403. ______. Reduce dormancy of bermudagrass by soil heating. Arizona Agricultural Experiment Station. Turfgrass Research Report. 212:18–22. 1962.

2404. Bandel, V. A. Phosphorus in soils and plants. Turf Bulletin. 4(4):19. 1967.

2405. ______. How to buy lime and fertilizer. Grounds Maintenance. 4(2):32, 34, 36, 38, 39. 1969.

2406. Bando, P. Irrigation and athletics. Midwest Regional Turf Conference Proceedings. pp. 56–57. 1970.

2407. Banerjee, A. C. and R. Randell. Sod webworm infestation in relation to turf grass management. Illinois Turfgrass Conference Proceedings. pp. 8–11. 1966.

2408. Bangs, D. Reports from the field. Turf Talks. Scotts. Marysville, Ohio. p. 4. 1967.

2409. Bangs, W. J. Crown vetch—pros and cons as an erosion control plant. Ohio Short Course on Roadside Development. 30:-93–95. 1971.

2410. Banin, A. and P. F. Low. Simultaneous transport of water and salt through clays: 2. steady-state distribution of pressure and applicability of irreversible thermodynamics. Soil Science. 112(2):69–88. 1971.

2411. Bannerman, L. E., R. E. Engel and R. J. Aldrich. Effectiveness of potassium cyanate dusts for crabgrass control. Proceedings Northeastern Weed Control Conference. pp. 267–269. 1952.

2412. Bannerman, L. W. A study of the effect of surface active agents on the efficiency of certain herbicides. Masters Thesis. Rutgers University. New Brunswick, New Jersey. 1953.

2413. Barauskas, A. A. You can do something about the "Whether." USGA Green Section Record. 9(2):35–41. 1971.

2414. Barber, S. A. Basic principles with phosphorus. Proceedings of the Midwest Regional Turf Conference. pp. 47–49. 1963.

2415. ______. Liming materials and practices. In R. W. Pearson and F. Adams (ed.). Soil Acidity and Liming. Agronomy. 12:125–160. 1967.

2416. Barbour, M. Early growth in annual and perennial ryegrass. Agronomy Journal. 59(2):204–205. 1967.

2417. Bardsley, H. C. Handling customer problems. Proceedings of Florida Turfgrass Management Conference. 12:123–125. 1964.

2418. Barker, G. J. and E. Truog. Improvement of stiff-mud clays through pH control. Journal of the American Ceramic Society. 21(9):326–329. 1938.

2419. Barkley, D. G. Comparison of various mulches for turf establishment. Virginia Turfgrass Conference. pp. 4–5. 1963.

2420. Barkley, D. G., R. E. Blaser, and R. E. Schmidt. Effect of mulches on microclimate and turf establishment. Agronomy Journal. 57:189–192. 1965.

2421. Barley, K. P., and E. L. Greacen. Mechanical resistance as a soil factor influencing the growth of roots and underground shoots. Advances in Agronomy. 19:-1–43. 1967.

2422. Barling, D. M. Biological studies in *Poa angustifolia.* Watsonia. 4(4):147–168. 1959.

2423. Barlow, J. N. and H. C. Lock. A review of disease control in turf. Control of Weeds, Pests and Diseases of Cultivated Turf Proceedings. 1:20–24. 1967.

2424. Barnard, C. Floral histogenesis in the monocotyledons. I. The *Gramineae.* Australian Journal of Botany. 5:1–20. 1957.

2425. ______. Grasses and grasslands. Macmillan and Co. Ltd. London. 269 pp. 1964.

2426. Barnard, G. K. Drainer's dilemma —cutting costs in clay. Parks, Golf Courses and Sports Grounds. 32(10):855–859. 1967.

2427. Barnes, E. G. Maintenance of lawns on industrial properties. Rutgers University Three-day Turf Course Proceedings. pp. 11–17. 1963.

2428. ______. Maintenance of lawns on industrial properties. Rutgers University Short Course in Turf Management. 32:11–17. 1964.

2429. Barnes, H. F. Gall midges and grass seed production. Journal of the Board of Greenkeeping Research. 6:118–120. 1940.

2430. ______. Gall midges living at the base of grasses. Journal of the Sports Turf Research Institute. 9(34):430–436. 1958.

2431. Barnes, O. K., R. L. Lang, and A. A. Beetle. Dryland grass seeding in Wyoming. Wyoming Agricultural Experiment Station Bulletin. 299:1–22. 1950.

2432. Barnett, A. P., E. G. Diseker, and E. C. Richardson. Evaluation of mulching methods for erosion control on newly prepared and seeded highway backslopes. Agronomy Journal. 59(1):83–85. 1967.

2433. Barnett, F. L. Effects of gibberellic acid on dwarfs on lowland switchgrass, *Panicum virgatum* L. Crop Science. 12(3):331–334. 1972.

2434. Barnett, N. M. and A. W. Naylor. Amino acid and protein metabolism in bermudagrass during water stress. Plant Physiology. 41(7):1222–1230. 1966.

2435. Barrer, P. R. Control of pests in turf (summary). New Zealand Institute for Turf Culture Newsletter. 5:5. 1960.

2436. Barnett. H. L. and H. C. Hanson. Control of leafy spurge and review of literature on chemical weed control. North Dakota Agricultural Experiment Station. Bulletin 277. 1934.

2437. Barrett, J. R., and W. H. Daniel. Electrically warmed soils for sports turfs—second progress report. Midwest Turf News and Research. No. 33. 1965.

2438. ______. Turf heating with electric cable. Agricultural Engineering. 47(10):526. 1966.

2439. ______. Turf heating with electric cables. Turf Clippings. University of Massachussetts. 2(1):A–1 to A–8. 1966.

2440. Barrett, J. R. and R. Freeborg. Turf Heating in action. Midwest Regional Turf Foundation Turf Conference Proceedings. pp. 97–101. 1969.

2441. Barrett, R. Why golf courses? The Greenmaster. 7(7):5–8. 1971.

2442. Barron, L. Lawns and how to make them. Doubleday, Page & Company. New York. 174 pp. 1906.

2443. ______. Lawn making. Doubleday, Doran and Company, Inc. New York. 176 pp. 1923.

2444. ______. Lawn making. Doubleday, Doran & Company, Inc. 176 pp. 1928.

2445. Barron, L. and F. F. Rockwell. Lawns and grading. The Complete Book of Garden Magic. Tudor Publishing Co. pp. 28–39. 1948.

2446. Barrons, K. C. Correct spraying methods cut cost of 2, 4–D results. Golfdom. 21(5):76, 78, 80. 1947.

2447. ______. Grass control, new chemical, TCA, is promising. Park Maintenance. 2(6):20–22. 1949.

2448. ______. Practices that will reduce damage with 2, 4–D spray. Park Maintenance. 3(3):15. 1950.

2449. Barrow, N. J. Influence of solution concentration of calcium on the adsorption of phosphate, sulfate, and molybdate by soils. Soil Science. 113(3):175–180. 1972.

2450. Barrows, E. M. Good turf for landscape use. Landscape Architecture. 18(3):-204–211. 1928.

2451. ______. Studying types of putting green turf. The Greenkeeper's Reporter. 3:-1–7. 1935.

2452. ______. Patent grasses. National Association of Greenkeepers of America Conference Proceedings. 10:89–100. 1936.

2453. Barrows, E. M. and L. J. Feser. The plant count and what it may mean. Greenkeepers Reporter. 2(8–9):4–8. 1934.

2454. Bartels, L. F. A comparison of gypsum blocks and evaporimeters for irrigation control. Australian Journal of Experimental Agriculture and Animal Husbandry. 5(19):453–457. 1965.

2455. Bartle, W. H. March with caution. Parks, Golf Courses, and Sports Grounds. 23(6):350, 356. 1958.

2456. ______. New machinery. Journal of the Sports Turf Research Institute. 11(39):29–44. 1963.

2457. ______. New machinery. Journal of the Sports Turf Research Institute. No. 40:81–94. 1964.

2458. ______. Aeration and top-dressing. Gardeners Chronicle. 158(8):204. 1965.

2459. ______. New machinery. Journal of the Sports Turf Research Institute. No. 41:59–75. 1965.

2460. ______. Records which will make the charts. Parks, Golf Courses, and Sports Grounds. 30(6):421–422. 1965.

2461. ______. New machinery. Journal of the Sports Turf Research Institute. 40:-61–80. 1967.

2462. ______. New machinery. The Journal of the Sports Turf Research Institute. 45:75–89. 1969.

2463. Bartlett, N. Can you work with *Poa annua?* The Golf Superintendent. 35(2):-30–37, 53. 1967.

2464. Bartlett, N. F. and J. Troll. Can you work with *Poa annua?* Turf Bulletin. 4(3):5–9. 1967.

2465. Barton, C. G. My experience with bent greens. The National Greenkeeper. 1(1):14–15. 1927.

2466. Barton, J. H. Perennial warm season grass test, lower Rio Grande valley of Texas. Texas Agricultural Experiment Station Progress Report. 1698:1–3. 1954.

2467. Barton, W. L. Part I—membership relations. Proceedings, University of Florida Turf Conference. 2:55–57. 1954.

2468. Bartonek, F. A. Pre-emergent crabgrass controls. Grounds Maintenance. 2(2):37–40. 1967.

2469. ______. Pre-emergent crabgrass controls. Grounds Maintenance. 2(12):65–68. 1967.

2470. Bar-Yosef, B., U. Kafkafi, and N. Lahav. Relationships among adsorbed phosphate, silica, and hydroxyl II during drying and rewetting of kaolinite suspension. Soil Science Society of America Proceedings. 33(5):672–676. 1969.

2471. Baskin, C. Watering greens. Golf Course Reporter. 25(5):28–29. 1957.

2472. Baskovic, P. Grass playgrounds in Yugoslavia and the possibilities of their improvement. 1st Czechoslovak Symposium on Sportsturf Proceedings. pp. 57–68. 1969.

2473. Bass, L. N. Effect of light intensity and other factors on germination of seeds of Kentucky bluegrass (*Poa pratensis* L.) Proceedings of the Association of Official Seed Analysts. 41:83–86. 1951.

2474. ______. Relationships of temperature, time and moisture content to the viability of seeds of Kentucky bluegrass. Iowa Academy of Science. 60:86–88. 1953.

2475. ______. Effect of various concentrations of gibberellic acid on the germination of Kentucky bluegrass and Merion Kentucky bluegrass seed. Mimeograph Leaflet. Iowa State College. Ames, Iowa. 1958.

2476. Bateman, L. Part I—what the player expects. Proceedings University of Florida Turf Management Conference. 4:45–47. 1956.

2477. Bateman, P. L. A. Worm control —a new material. The Groundsman. 21(12):-18–27. 1968.

2478. Bates, T. E. and A. D. Scott. Control of potassium release and reversion associated with changes in soil moisture. Soil Science Society of America Proceedings. 33(4):566–568. 1969.

2479. Baughman, R. W. Effect of clipping on the development of roots and tops of various grass seedlings. M. S. Thesis. 39 pp. 1939.

2480. Baum, W. A. On the vertical distribution of mean temperature within the microclimatic layer. Bulletin of the American Meteorological Society. 29:424–426. 1948.

2481. ______. On the relation between mean temperature and height in the layer of air near the ground. Ecology. 30:104–107. 1949.

2482. Bauman, M. Weed problems on golf courses. State College of Washington Annual Turf Conference. 4:29–30. 1951.

2483. ______. Draining turfgrass areas. Proceedings of the 16th Annual Pacific Northwest Turf Conference, pp. 19–20. 1962.

2484. ______. Architectural plans and their transfer to the ground. Proceedings of the 20th Annual Northwest Turfgrass Conference. pp. 83–85. 1966.

2485. Baumgardner, T. M. Fairway management in the South. Golf Course Reporter. 16(2):5–7. 1948.

2486. ______. Southern fairway management methods outlined. Golfdom. 22(4):37, 92, 95. 1948.

2487. ______. Landscaping of golf courses. Turf Management Conference—Florida Greenkeeping Superintendents Association. pp. 21–23. 1950.

2488. ______. Part I—north Florida and south Georgia. Proceedings of the Second Annual University of Florida Turf Conference. 2:33–36. 1954.

2489. ______. Progress and problems of golf operations in resort areas. Proceedings University of Florida Turf Management Conference. 4:54–56. 1956.

2490. ______. Tifgreen. Proceedings University of Florida Turf Management Conference. 6:28–30. 1958.

2491. ———. Maintenance of ryegrass-bermudagrass greens. Southeastern Turfgrass Conference. 13:19–23. 1959.

2492. ———. Overseeding at Sea Island Golf Club. Proceedings of University of Florida Turf-Grass Management Conference. 9:86. 1961.

2493. ———. Overseeding bermudagrass greens. Proceedings Fifteenth Southeastern Turfgrass Conference. pp. 28–32. 1961.

2494. ———. Overseeding winter greens at Sea Island. Golf Course Reporter. 30(9):-48, 50, 1962.

2495. ———. Winter grass overseeding —on greens at Sea Side Island Golf Club. 33rd International Turf-Grass Conference Proceedings. p. 9. 1962.

2496. ———. Overseeding bermudagrass greens. Proceedings Sixteenth Southeastern Turfgrass Conference. pp. 28–30. 1962.

2497. ———. Landscaping fairways. Proceedings University of Florida Turf-Grass Management Conference. 10:92–94. 1962.

2498. ———. Overseeding panel: mixtures. Proceedings University of Florida Turfgrass Management Conference. 14:79–80. 1966.

2499. ———. Living with the problem-greens. 40th International Turfgrass Conference and Show Proceedings. p. 66–67. 1969.

2500. Baumgardner, T. M., C. Danner, P. Grandison, E. Maples, and J. M. Latham. Building and planting putting greens—a summary. Southeastern Turfgrass Conference. 11:9–12. 1957.

2501. Baumgardt, J. P. Ground covers you should consider. Ground Maintenance. 2(2):30–32. 1967.

2502. ———. Systemics—a new line of defense. Grounds Maintenance 2(3):44–63. 1967.

2503. ———. How to make a soil test. Ground Maintenance. 2(11):32–34. 1967.

2504. ———. Keep fringe areas from draining your budget. Grounds Maintenance. 4(6):9–10, 13. 1969.

2505. ———. Renovating bluegrass lawns. Grounds Maintenance. 4(8):39–40. 1969.

2506. Baumiller, S. W. New trends in planting design. Seventeenth Short Course on Roadside Development. Ohio State University and Ohio Department of Highways. Columbus, Ohio. pp. 8–10. 1958.

2507. Bayless, B. Fertilizer injection—how it works. Turfgrass Sprinkler Irrigation Conference. p. 17–18. 1971.

2508. Bayliss, J. S. Observations on *Marasmius oreades* and *Clitocybe gigantea* as parasitic fungi causing "fairy rings". Journal of Economic Biology. 6(4):111–132. 1911.

2509. Baynton, H. W. Temperature structure in and above a tropical forest. Quarterly Journal of the Royal Meteorological Society. 91:225–232. 1965.

2510. Beach, G. A. Irrigation of lawns. Colorado State University Experiment Station. General Series 685. pp. 1–11.

2511. ———. Lawns. Colorado Agricultural Experiment Station. Extension Bulletin 303A. pp. 1–8. 1929.

2512. ———. Lawns; planting and maintenance in Colorado. Colorado Agricultural Experiment Station Bulletin. 420:1–12. 1936.

2513. ———. Planting and maintaining Colorado lawns. Colorado Agricultural Experiment Station Bulletin. 442:1–16. 1938.

2514. ———. Colorado lawns; planting and maintenance. Colorado Agricultural Experiment Station Extension Bulletin 392A. pp. 1–21. 1947.

2515. ———. Your irrigation problems are different. Rocky Mountain Regional Turf Conference Proceedings. pp. 15–19. 1954.

2516. ———. Turfgrass irrigation. Rocky Mountain Regional Turfgrass Conference Proceedings. pp. 11–14. 1956.

2517. ———. Management practices in the care of lawns. Rocky Mountain Regional Turfgrass Conference Proceedings. pp. 42–45. 1963.

2518. ———. Which is the best turfgrass? Rocky Mountain Regional Turfgrass Conference Proceedings. pp. 30–32. 1964.

2519. Beach, G. A. and C. M. Drage. Colorado lawns, planting and maintenance. Colorado Agricultural Experiment Station. Extension Bulletin 392A. pp. 1–24. 1953.

2520. Beach, W. S. Seed treatments for control of damping-off fungi. Penn State College Twentieth Annual Turfgrass Conference Proceedings. pp. 32–36. 1951.

2521. ______. Seed treatment of turfgrass. Penn State College Twenty-Second Annual Turfgrass Conference Proceedings. pp. 51–54. 1953.

2522. ______. Seed treatment of turfgrass. Pennsylvania State College Turf Conference. 23:51–54. 1954.

2523. Beal, W. J. Some selections of grasses promising for field and lawn. Proceedings of the Thirteenth Annual Meeting of the Society for the Promotion of Agricultural Science. 6(6):393–397. 1892.

2524. ______. How to know our common grasses of pasture and lawn previous to flowering. Agricultural Science Proceedings. 9:137–138. 1892.

2525. ______. Mixtures of grasses for lawns. Proceedings of the Fourteenth Annual Meeting of the Society for the Promotion of Agricultural Science. 14:28–33. 1893.

2526. ______. Grasses of North America. Henry Holt and Co., New York. Volume 1. 457 pp. 1896.

2527. ______. Lawn-grass mixtures as purchased in the markets compared with a few of the best. Agricultural Science Proceedings. 12:59–63. 1898.

2528. Beale, R. The practical greenkeeper. Carters Tested Seeds. Boston. 101 pp.

2529. ______. Lawns for sports. Simpkin, Marshall, Hamilton, Kent and Co. Ltd. 276 pp. 1924.

2530. ______. The Book of The Lawn. Cassell and Company, Ltd. London. 151 pp. 1931.

2531. ______. British turf expert compares maintenance conditions. Golfdom. 7(6):42–43. 1933.

2532. Bean, A. G. M. Water distribution by irrigation sprinklers. Journal of Agricultural Engineering Research. 10(4):314–321. 1965.

2533. Bean, E. W. The influence of light intensity upon the growth of an S.37 cocksfoot *(Dactylis glomerata)* sward. Annals of Botany. N. S. 28(111):427–443. 1964.

2534. Bean, G. A. The pathogenicity of *Helminthosporium* spp. and *Curvularia* spp. on bluegrass in the Washington, D. C. area. The Plant Disease Reporter. 48(12):978–979. 1964.

2535. ______. The use of dimethyl sulfoxide (DMSO) with certain fungicides for controlling *Helminthosporium* diseases of Kentucky bluegrass. The Plant Disease Reporter. 49(10):810–811. 1965.

2536. ______. *Pythium* and *Fusarium* blight. Mid-Atlantic Superintendents Conference Proceedings. pp. 28–29. 1969.

2537. ______. *Fusarium* blight of turfgrasses. The Golf Superintendent. 34(10):32–34. 1966.

2538. ______. Observations and studies on *Fusarium* blight disease of turfgrass. Phytopathology. 56:583. 1966.

2539. ______. Observations on *Fusarium* blight of turfgrasses. The Plant Disease Reporter. 50(12):942–945. 1966.

2540. ______. *Fusarium* blight—disease of turf grasses. Turf Clippings. University of Massachussetts. 2(1):A–35 to A–38. 1966.

2541. ______. Observations on *Fusarium* blight of turfgrass. Turf Bulletin. 4(4):15, 18. 1967.

2542. ______. The role of moisture and crop debris in the development of *Fusarium* blight of Kentucky bluegrass. Phytopathology. 59(4):479–481. 1969.

2543. ______. Adequate water can reduce *Fusarium* severity. Park Maintenance. 23(7):13. 1970.

2544. Bean, G. A. and A. J. Powell. *Pythium* blight. Professional Turf News. Borden Greens and Fairways. 1(3):1. 1970.

2545. Bean, G. A., and R. D. Wilcoxson. *Helminthosporium* leaf spot of bluegrass. Pathogenicity of three species of *Helminthosporium* on roots of bluegrass. Phytopathology. 54(9):1065–1070. 1964.

2546. ______. Pathogenicity of three species of *Helminthosporium* on roots of blue-

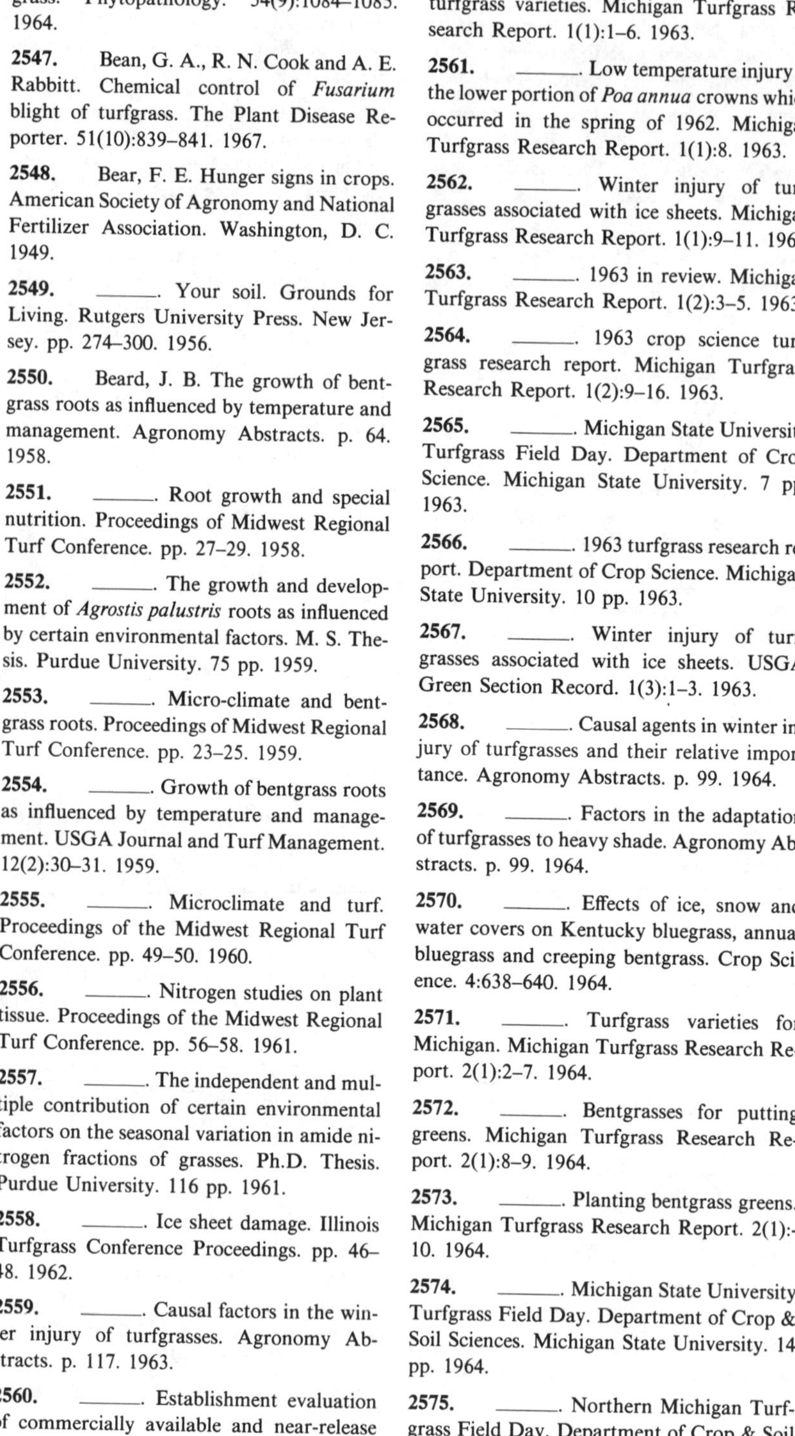

grass. Phytopathology. 54(9):1084–1085. 1964.

2547. Bean, G. A., R. N. Cook and A. E. Rabbitt. Chemical control of *Fusarium* blight of turfgrass. The Plant Disease Reporter. 51(10):839–841. 1967.

2548. Bear, F. E. Hunger signs in crops. American Society of Agronomy and National Fertilizer Association. Washington, D. C. 1949.

2549. ———. Your soil. Grounds for Living. Rutgers University Press. New Jersey. pp. 274–300. 1956.

2550. Beard, J. B. The growth of bentgrass roots as influenced by temperature and management. Agronomy Abstracts. p. 64. 1958.

2551. ———. Root growth and special nutrition. Proceedings of Midwest Regional Turf Conference. pp. 27–29. 1958.

2552. ———. The growth and development of *Agrostis palustris* roots as influenced by certain environmental factors. M. S. Thesis. Purdue University. 75 pp. 1959.

2553. ———. Micro-climate and bentgrass roots. Proceedings of Midwest Regional Turf Conference. pp. 23–25. 1959.

2554. ———. Growth of bentgrass roots as influenced by temperature and management. USGA Journal and Turf Management. 12(2):30–31. 1959.

2555. ———. Microclimate and turf. Proceedings of the Midwest Regional Turf Conference. pp. 49–50. 1960.

2556. ———. Nitrogen studies on plant tissue. Proceedings of the Midwest Regional Turf Conference. pp. 56–58. 1961.

2557. ———. The independent and multiple contribution of certain environmental factors on the seasonal variation in amide nitrogen fractions of grasses. Ph.D. Thesis. Purdue University. 116 pp. 1961.

2558. ———. Ice sheet damage. Illinois Turfgrass Conference Proceedings. pp. 46–48. 1962.

2559. ———. Causal factors in the winter injury of turfgrasses. Agronomy Abstracts. p. 117. 1963.

2560. ———. Establishment evaluation of commercially available and near-release turfgrass varieties. Michigan Turfgrass Research Report. 1(1):1–6. 1963.

2561. ———. Low temperature injury to the lower portion of *Poa annua* crowns which occurred in the spring of 1962. Michigan Turfgrass Research Report. 1(1):8. 1963.

2562. ———. Winter injury of turfgrasses associated with ice sheets. Michigan Turfgrass Research Report. 1(1):9–11. 1963.

2563. ———. 1963 in review. Michigan Turfgrass Research Report. 1(2):3–5. 1963.

2564. ———. 1963 crop science turfgrass research report. Michigan Turfgrass Research Report. 1(2):9–16. 1963.

2565. ———. Michigan State University Turfgrass Field Day. Department of Crop Science. Michigan State University. 7 pp. 1963.

2566. ———. 1963 turfgrass research report. Department of Crop Science. Michigan State University. 10 pp. 1963.

2567. ———. Winter injury of turfgrasses associated with ice sheets. USGA Green Section Record. 1(3):1–3. 1963.

2568. ———. Causal agents in winter injury of turfgrasses and their relative importance. Agronomy Abstracts. p. 99. 1964.

2569. ———. Factors in the adaptation of turfgrasses to heavy shade. Agronomy Abstracts. p. 99. 1964.

2570. ———. Effects of ice, snow and water covers on Kentucky bluegrass, annual bluegrass and creeping bentgrass. Crop Science. 4:638–640. 1964.

2571. ———. Turfgrass varieties for Michigan. Michigan Turfgrass Research Report. 2(1):2–7. 1964.

2572. ———. Bentgrasses for putting greens. Michigan Turfgrass Research Report. 2(1):8–9. 1964.

2573. ———. Planting bentgrass greens. Michigan Turfgrass Research Report. 2(1):-10. 1964.

2574. ———. Michigan State University Turfgrass Field Day. Department of Crop & Soil Sciences. Michigan State University. 14 pp. 1964.

2575. ———. Northern Michigan Turfgrass Field Day. Department of Crop & Soil

Sciences. Michigan State University. 5 pp. 1964.

2576. ______. 1964 turfgrass research report. Department of Crop Science. Michigan State University. 3 pp. 1964.

2577. ______. Turf stress-cool and cold conditions. Proceeding of Midwest Regional Turf Conference. pp. 22–27. 1964.

2578. ______. The problem of winter injury. Stockbridge School Turf Clippings Conference Proceedings. 1(9):A–13–A–20. 1964.

2579. ______. A comparison of mulches for turf establishment on light soils. Agronomy Abstracts. p. 48. 1965.

2580. ______. Factors in the adaptation of turfgrasses to shade. Agronomy Journal. 57:457–459. 1965.

2581. ______. Bentgrass varietal tolerance to ice cover injury. Agronomy Journal. 57:513. 1965.

2582. ______. Effects of ice covers in the field on two perennial grasses. Crop Science. 5:139–140. 1965.

2583. ______. Michigan State University Turfgrass Field Day. Department of Crop & Soil Sciences. Michigan State University. 18 pp. 1965.

2584. ______. Northern Michigan Turfgrass Field Day. Department of Crop & Soil Sciences. Michigan State University. 12 pp. 1965.

2585. ______. Bentgrass variety evaluations. Michigan Turfgrass Research Report. 3(1):2. 1965.

2586. ______. Winter damage of turfgrasses. Proceedings of the 19th Annual Northwest Turfgrass Conference. pp. 38–51. 1965.

2587. ______. Selecting turfgrass maintenance level—part I. The Cemeterian. pp. 9, 10, 39, 40. May, 1966.

2588. ______. Selecting turfgrass maintenance level—part II. The Cemeterian. pp. 9–10, 47–48. June, 1966.

2589. ______. Selected turfgrass variety evaluations—part III. The Cemeterian. pp. 7–8, 45–46. July, 1966.

2590. ______. Selecting turfgrass maintenance level—part V. The Cemeterian. pp. 13, 14, 51. November, 1966.

2591. ______. Winter injury. The Golf Superintendent. 34(1):24, 26–27, 30. 1966.

2592. ______. Northern Michigan Turfgrass Field Day. Department of Crop and Soil Sciences. Michigan State University. 9 pp. 1966.

2593. ______. A comparison of mulches for erosion control and grass establishment on light soil. Quarterly Bulletin. Michigan State University. 48(3):369–376. 1966.

2594. ______. Direct low temperature injury of nineteen turfgrasses. Quarterly Bulletin. Michigan State University. 48(3):377–383. 1966.

2595. ______. Fungicide and fertilizer applications as they affect "*Typhula*" snow mold control on turf. Quarterly Bulletin. Michigan State University. 49(2):221–228. 1966.

2596. ______. Selecting the level of turfgrass maintenance. Michigan Turfgrass Research Report. 3(1):2–4. 1966.

2597. ______. Management of bentgrass putting greens. Michigan Turfgrass Research Report. 3(1):5–6. 1966.

2598. ______. Selected turfgrass variety evaluations. Michigan Turfgrass Research Reports. 3(1):7–9. 1966.

2599. ______. Turf annual—1966. Park Maintenance. 19(7):17–18. 1966.

2600. ______. Why lawns don't grow well in the shade. Seed World. 98(8):21. 1966.

2601. ______. Shade grasses and maintenance. California Turfgrass Culture. 17(4):-29–32. 1967.

2602. ______. Shade grasses and maintenance. 38th Int. Turfgrass Conference & Show. pp. 31–36. 1967.

2603. ______. Michigan State University Turfgrass Field Day. Department of Crop Science. Michigan State University. 20 pp. 1967.

2604. ______. Plant-water relationships. First Ohio Turfgrass Conference Proceedings. pp. 4–9. 1967.

2605. ______. Winter injury and prevention. Turf Bulletin. 4(4):8–11, 20–21. 1967.

2606. ______. Turfgrass research review. Golfdom. 42(1):18, 23. 1968.

2607. ______. Turfgrass research review. Golfdom. 42(2):18, 76–86. 1968.

2608. ______. Turfgrass research review. Golfdom. 42(3):28, 30, 74. 1968.

2609. ______. Turfgrass research review. Golfdom. 42(4):23, 56. 1968.

2610. ______. Turfgrass research review. Golfdom. 42(5):23–24. 1968.

2611. ______. Turfgrass research review. Golfdom. 42(6):17–18. 1968.

2612. ______. Turfgrass research review. Golfdom. 42(7):27–28, 30. 1968.

2613. ______. Turfgrass research review. Golfdom. 42(8):29–30. 1968.

2614. ______. Turfgrass research review. Golfdom. 42(9):21–22. 1968.

2615. ______. Turfgrass research review. Golfdom. 42(10):23, 65, 81. 1968.

2616. ______. Northern Michigan Turfgrass Field Day. Department of Crop & Soil Sciences. Michigan State University. 10 pp. 1968.

2617. ______. 1968 turfgrass research summary. Department of Crop Science. Michigan State University. 27 pp. 1968.

2618. ______. Turfgrass varieties. Michigan Turfgrass Research Report. 3(1):2–8. 1968.

2619. ______. Turf annual—1968. Park Maintenance. 21(7):16. 1968.

2620. ______. Winter injury of turfgrasses, causes and preventions. RCGA National Turfgrass Conference. 19:1–7. 1968.

2621. ______. Effect of temperature stress on *Poa annua.* USGA Green Section Record. 6(2):10–12. 1968.

2622. ______. Low temperature and *Poa annua.* USGA Green Section Record. 6(4):-10–11. 1968.

2623. ______. Covers for the protection of turfgrasses against winter desiccation and direct low temperature injury. Agronomy Abstracts. p. 52. 1969.

2624. ______. Effect of temperature stress on *Poa annua.* California Turfgrass Culture. 19(1):1–2. 1969.

2625. ______. Winter fertilization: a new concept. Golfdom. 43(2):67. 1969.

2626. ______. The plant, its habits and the way we propagate it. 40th International Turfgrass Conference and Show. p. 47. 1969.

2627. ______. Lawn care for parks. Michigan Forestry and Park Conference Proceedings. 43:20–22. 1969.

2628. ______. Steps in turfgrass establishment. Michigan Forestry and Park Conference Proceedings. 43:27–30. 1969.

2629. ______. Sod and turf—Michigan's $350 million carpet. Michigan Science and Action Series. 2. 23 pp. 1969.

2630. ______. Michigan State University Sod Producers Field Day. Department of Crop & Soil Sciences. Michigan State University. 18 pp. 1969.

2631. ______. Michigan State University Turfgrass Field Day. Department of Crop & Soil Sciences. Michigan State University. 26 pp. 1969.

2632. ______, ed. Michigan Upper Peninsular Turfgrass Field Day. Department of Crop & Soil Sciences. Michigan State University. 12 pp. 1969.

2633. ______. 1969 turfgrass research summary. Department of Crop Science. Michigan State University. 25 pp. 1970.

2634. ______. Effects of environmental stress. Michigan State University Agricultural Experiment Station Research Report 104. p. 5. 1969.

2636. ______. Low temperatures and *Poa annua.* New York Turfgrass Association Bulletin 83. pp. 323–324. 1969.

2639. ______. Winter injury of turfgrasses. Proceedings of the First International Turfgrass Research Conference. pp. 226–234. 1969.

2640. ______. Turfgrass shade adaptation. Proceedings of the First International Turfgrass Research Conference. pp. 273–282. 1969.

2641. ______. University education. Proceedings of the First International Turfgrass Research Conference. pp. 422–425. 1969.

2642. ______. Sod production and utilization. Annual RCGA National Turfgrass Conference Summary. 20:1–6. 1969.

2643. ______. Environmental stresses of turfgrasses, causes and prevention. Annual RCGA National Turfgrass Conference Summary. 20:7–10. 1969.

2645. ______. The delicate art of turfgrass cultivation. Golfdom. 44(5):44–46, 84. 1970.

2646. ______. Turfgrass research review. Golfdom. 44(9):24, 26, 28. 1970.

2647. ______. Controlling bluegrass during bermudagrass overseeding. Golfdom. 44(10):29–41. 1970.

2648. ______. Turf research is international. 41st International Turfgrass Conference and Show. pp. 10–13, 1970.

2649. ______. Sod industry research 1969–1970. Michigan State University Agricultural Experiment Station Report 120. 12 pp. 1970.

2650. ______, ed. Northern Michigan Turfgrass Field Day. Department of Crop & Soil Sciences. Michigan State University. 18 pp. 1970.

2651. ______. Protecting turfs against winter injury. Michigan Turfgrass Research Report. pp. 7–10. Winter, 1970.

2652. ______. Plant-water relations and root growth. Twenty-first Annual RCGA National Turfgrass Conference. 21:4–7. 1970.

2653. ______. The plant characteristics, dissemination, environmental adaptation, and cultural requirements of *Poa annua* L. Turf-Gazon. 2:33–35. 1970.

2654. ______. An ecological study of annual bluegrass. USGA Green Section Record. 8(2):13–18. 1970.

2655. ______. Turfgrass research review. Golfdom. 45(1):30, 39, 42–43. 1971.

2666. ______. Turfgrass research review. Golfdom. 45(5):32, 35, 38. 1971.

2667. ______. Turfgrass research review. Golfdom. 45(6):16–20. 1971.

2668. ______. Turfgrass research review. Golfdom. 45(7):18. 1971.

2669. ______. Turfgrass research review. Golfdom. 45(8):21–30. 1971.

2670. ______. Turfgrass research review. Golfdom. 45(9):19–23. 1971.

2671. Beard, J. B., D. P. Martin, J. E. Kaufmann, and J. A. Fischer. Improved establishment and maintenance of roadside vegetation in Michigan. Michigan State University-Agricultural Experiment Station Research Report 144. pp. 1–66. 1971.

2672. Beard, J. B., ed. Michigan State University Sod Producer's Field Day. Department of Crop & Soil Sciences. Michigan State University. 34 pp. 1971.

2673. ______, ed. Michigan State University Turfgrass Field Day. Department of Crop & Soil Sciences. Michigan State University. 38 pp. 1971.

2674. ______. Seed germination and environmental conditions effecting germination. Ohio Turfgrass Conference Proceedings. pp. 15–20. 1971.

2675. ______. Winter covers. Park Maintenance. 24(7):22–23. 1971.

2676. ______. Turfgrass research review. Golfdom. 46(1):14. 1972.

2677. ______. Turfgrass research review. Golfdom. 46(2):26, 29–31. 1972.

2678. ______. Turfgrass research review. Golfdom. 46(3):16, 101–102. 1972.

2679. ______. Superintendents: Are you making wasteful purchases? Golfdom. 46(3):-43–44, 49. 1972.

2680. ______. Turfgrass research review. Golfdom. 46(4):14, 17. 1972.

2681. ______. Turfgrass research review. Golfdom. 46(5):17, 20, 1972.

2682. ______. Turfgrass research review. Golfdom. 46(6):24, 26–27. 1972.

2683. ______. Turfgrass research review. Golfdom. 46(7):18, 20, 22, 1972.

2684. ______, Ed. Northern Michigan Turfgrass Field Day. Department of Crop & Soil Sciences. Michigan State University. 22 pp. 1972.

2685. ______. Principles of turfgrass renovation and reestablishment. 42nd Annual Michigan Turfgrass Conference Proceedings. 1:86–88. 1972.

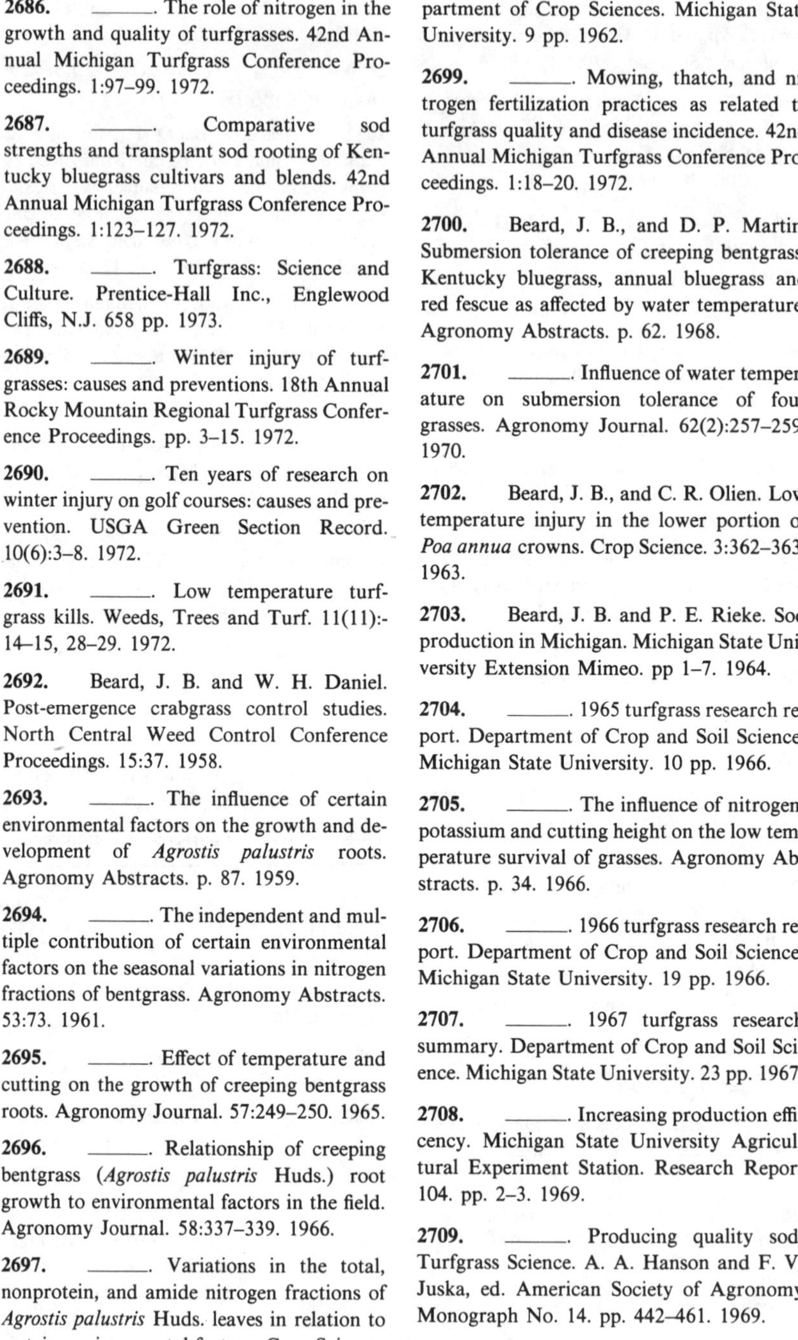

2686. ______. The role of nitrogen in the growth and quality of turfgrasses. 42nd Annual Michigan Turfgrass Conference Proceedings. 1:97–99. 1972.

2687. ______. Comparative sod strengths and transplant sod rooting of Kentucky bluegrass cultivars and blends. 42nd Annual Michigan Turfgrass Conference Proceedings. 1:123–127. 1972.

2688. ______. Turfgrass: Science and Culture. Prentice-Hall Inc., Englewood Cliffs, N.J. 658 pp. 1973.

2689. ______. Winter injury of turfgrasses: causes and preventions. 18th Annual Rocky Mountain Regional Turfgrass Conference Proceedings. pp. 3–15. 1972.

2690. ______. Ten years of research on winter injury on golf courses: causes and prevention. USGA Green Section Record. 10(6):3–8. 1972.

2691. ______. Low temperature turfgrass kills. Weeds, Trees and Turf. 11(11):-14–15, 28–29. 1972.

2692. Beard, J. B. and W. H. Daniel. Post-emergence crabgrass control studies. North Central Weed Control Conference Proceedings. 15:37. 1958.

2693. ______. The influence of certain environmental factors on the growth and development of *Agrostis palustris* roots. Agronomy Abstracts. p. 87. 1959.

2694. ______. The independent and multiple contribution of certain environmental factors on the seasonal variations in nitrogen fractions of bentgrass. Agronomy Abstracts. 53:73. 1961.

2695. ______. Effect of temperature and cutting on the growth of creeping bentgrass roots. Agronomy Journal. 57:249–250. 1965.

2696. ______. Relationship of creeping bentgrass (*Agrostis palustris* Huds.) root growth to environmental factors in the field. Agronomy Journal. 58:337–339. 1966.

2697. ______. Variations in the total, nonprotein, and amide nitrogen fractions of *Agrostis palustris* Huds. leaves in relation to certain environmental factors. Crop Science. 7(2):111–115. 1967.

2698. Beard, J. B. and W. J. Eaton. Report of 1962 Michigan Turfgrass Trials. Department of Crop Sciences. Michigan State University. 9 pp. 1962.

2699. ______. Mowing, thatch, and nitrogen fertilization practices as related to turfgrass quality and disease incidence. 42nd Annual Michigan Turfgrass Conference Proceedings. 1:18–20. 1972.

2700. Beard, J. B., and D. P. Martin. Submersion tolerance of creeping bentgrass, Kentucky bluegrass, annual bluegrass and red fescue as affected by water temperature. Agronomy Abstracts. p. 62. 1968.

2701. ______. Influence of water temperature on submersion tolerance of four grasses. Agronomy Journal. 62(2):257–259. 1970.

2702. Beard, J. B., and C. R. Olien. Low temperature injury in the lower portion of *Poa annua* crowns. Crop Science. 3:362–363. 1963.

2703. Beard, J. B. and P. E. Rieke. Sod production in Michigan. Michigan State University Extension Mimeo. pp 1–7. 1964.

2704. ______. 1965 turfgrass research report. Department of Crop and Soil Science. Michigan State University. 10 pp. 1966.

2705. ______. The influence of nitrogen, potassium and cutting height on the low temperature survival of grasses. Agronomy Abstracts. p. 34. 1966.

2706. ______. 1966 turfgrass research report. Department of Crop and Soil Science. Michigan State University. 19 pp. 1966.

2707. ______. 1967 turfgrass research summary. Department of Crop and Soil Science. Michigan State University. 23 pp. 1967.

2708. ______. Increasing production efficency. Michigan State University Agricultural Experiment Station. Research Report 104. pp. 2–3. 1969.

2709. ______. Producing quality sod. Turfgrass Science. A. A. Hanson and F. V. Juska, ed. American Society of Agronomy Monograph No. 14. pp. 442–461. 1969.

2710. Beard, J. B., J. W. King, and P. E. Rieke. Sod laying techniques. Michigan State University Agricultural Experiment Station Research Report 104. p. 4. 1969.

2711. Beard, J. B., P. E. Rieke, and J. W. King. Sod production of Kentucky bluegrass. Proceedings of the First International Turfgrass Research Conference. pp. 509–513. 1969.

2712. Beard, J. B., K. T. Payne, P. E. Rieke, and D. P. Martin. Lawn establishment. Michigan Cooperative Extension Service Bulletin E–673. Farm Science Series. 8 pp. 1970.

2713. Beard, J. B., P. E. Rieke, D. P. Martin, and R. C. Shearman. Michigan lawn care. Michigan Cooperative Extension Service Bulletin E-646. Farm Science Series. 8 pp. 1972.

2714. Beard, J. B., P. E. Rieke, D. P. Martin, and A. J. Turgeon. Lawn care. Michigan Cooperative Extension Service Bulletin E-646. Farm Science Series. 8 pp. 1970.

2715. Beard, J. B., M. B. Tesar, J. W. Thomas, C. J. Flegal, B. A. Good, M. G. Yang, and W. G. Hoag. Sod clipping utilization. Michigan State University Agricultural Experiment Station. Research Report 104. p. 5. 1969.

2716. Beardsley, I. A. Maintenance of mowing equipment. New Zealand Institute for Turf Culture Newsletter. 48:10. 1967.

2717. Beasley, J. L. Massachusetts progress report on research with maleic hydrazide. Proceedings of the Northeastern Weed Control Conference. 15:452–456. 1961.

2718. ______. Massachusetts progress report on research with maleic hydrazide. Stockbridge School Turf Clippings Conference Proceedings. pp. A-57-A-62. 1961.

2719. ______. Realistic restoration of nature in highway roadside design and maintenance: progressive or passive. Twenty-second Short Course on Roadside Development. pp. 71–73. 1963.

2720. ______. Chemicals for highway roadside only, to assist in realistic restoration of nature. Turf Bulletin. Massachusetts Turf and Lawn Grass Council. 2(7):10–12. 1964.

2721. ______. What highway supervisors want from the contract applicators. Weeds Trees and Turf. 4(4):12–14, 26. 1965.

2722. Beasley, R. P. Sub-surface irrigation systems for lawns and turf. Proceedings of the 7th Annual Missouri Lawn and Turf Conference. pp. 23–25. 1966.

2723. Beaton, J. D. New concepts in turfgrass fertilizers. Proceedings of the Northwest Turfgrass Conference. 21:38–59. 1967.

2724. Beaton, J. D., W. A. Hubbard, and R. C. Speer. Comparison of ammonium salt of oxidized nitrogen enriched coal, glycoluril, hexamine, oxamine, resin coated urea, thiourea, and urea formaldehyde with ammonium nitrate and urea for seven harvests of orchardgrass in the growth chamber. Agronomy Abstracts. p. 101. 1965.

2725. ______. Coated urea, thiourea, urea-formaldehyde, hexamine, oxamide, glycoluril, and oxidized nitrogen-enriched coal as slowly available sources of nitrogen for orchardgrass. Agronomy Journal. 59(2):-127–133. 1967.

2726. Beatty, R. H. Control of weeds in turf. Annual Conference Mid-Atlantic Association of Greenkeepers. pp. 45–47. 1950.

2727. Beatty, R. H., and B. H. Davis. Factors in controlling crabgrass with potassium cyanate. USGA Journal and Turf Management. 3(7):31–33. 1951.

2728. Beatty, R. H., J. E. Gallagher, and C. Jack. A comparison of several chemicals for chickweed control. Agronomy Abstracts. p. 64. 1958.

2729. Beatty, R. H., R. J. Otten, and J. E. Gallagher. Summary of 1959 cooperative pre-emergence crabgrass control trials with 2, 3, 6-trichlorophenylacetic acid. Agronomy Abstracts. 51:88. 1959.

2730. ______. Pre-emergence crabgrass trials for 1960. Agronomy Abstracts. p. 69. 1960.

2731. Beaty, E. R. Sprouting of coastal bermudagrass stolons. Agronomy Journal. 58(5):555–556. 1966.

2732. Beaty, E. R., R. A. McCreery, and J. D. Powell. Response of 'Pensacola' bahiagrass to nitrogen fertilization. Agronomy Journal. 52(8):453–455. 1960.

2733. Beaty, E. R., R. L. Stanley and J. Powell. Effect of height of cut on yield of Pensacola bahiagrass. Agronomy Journal. 60(4):356–358. 1968.

2734. Beavers, J., A. L. Cox, M. D. Swanner, H. T. Barr, and C. L. Mondart.

Erosion control study. Louisiana State University, Louisiana Department of Highways and Bureau of Public Roads. pp. 1–44.

2735. Beavington, R. B. Upland grass production in north-east Scotland in relation to soil and site conditions. Journal of the British Grassland Society. 24(1):31–40. 1969.

2736. Beck, E. W. The control of bermuda and Rhodes grass scales. Southeastern Turfgrass Conference. 9:34–39. 1955.

2737. Beck, M. Why we developed the big roll system. Weeds, Trees and Turf. 10(10):26–28. 1971.

2738. Beck, W. F. Brown patch studied by doctor. Golfdom. 3(12):32, 35. 1929.

2739. Beckett, H. Covering bermuda greens for winter protection. USGA Green Section Bulletin. 9(10):175–178. 1929.

2740. Beckley, M. S., and T. Byrne. Budgeting your fertilizer needs for turfgrass. California Turfgrass Culture. 12(2):10–11. 1962.

2741. Beddows, A. R. Seed setting and flowering of various grasses. Welch Plant Breeding Station Bulletin. 12:5–99. 1931.

2742. Bedker, E. J., and L. C. Stilwell. Golf course design and construction. Agronomy Abstracts. p. 162. 1972.

2743. Beecher, A. S. Design of the home grounds. University of Maryland Cooperative Extension Service. 191:26 pp. 1962.

2744. Beer, C. Kansas—in the transition zone. Turf Clippings. University of Massachussetts. 1(8):10. 1963.

2745. Beers, Z. H. Fertilizers an important factor in establishing and maintaining roadside turf. Ohio Short Course on Roadside Development. 21:94–95. 1962.

2747. Beeson, K. C., L. Gray, and M. B. Adams. The absorption of mineral elements by forage plants: 1. The phosphorus, cobalt, manganese, and copper content of some common grasses. Journal of the American Society of Agronomy. 39:356–362. 1947.

2748. Beetle, A. A. Distribution of the native grasses of California. Hilgardia. 17(9):-309–357. 1947.

2749. Beetle, A. A. and M. May. Grasses of Wyoming. Wyoming Agricultural Experiment Station Research Journal. 39:151. 1971.

2750. Beever, S. L., and J. P. Cooper. Influence of temperature on growth and metabolism of ryegrass seedlings. I. Seedling growth and yield components. II. Variation in metabolites. Crop Science. 4:139–146. 1964.

2751. Begg, E. M. and H. C. Purdy. Large scale weed control with arsenic acid. Turf Culture. 1(1):44–52. 1939.

2752. Begg, J. E. and M. J. Wright. Growth and development of leaves from intercalary meristems in *Phalaris arundinacea* L. Nature. 194:1097–1098. 1962.

2753. Beistel, P. Developing new parks and recreation areas. Proceedings of the Annual Northwest Turfgrass Conference. 21:-25–28. 1967.

2754. Belcher, W. C. Managing the mowing operation. Agronomy Abstracts. p. 163. 1972.

2755. Bell, A. A. Fungi associated with root and crown rots of *Zoysia japonica.* The Plant Disease Reporter. 51(1):11–14. 1967.

2756. Bell, A. A. and L. R. Krusberg. Occurrence and control of a nematode of the genus *Hypsoperine* on zoysia and bermuda grasses in Maryland. The Plant Disease Reporter. 48(9):721–722. 1964.

2757. Bell, A. A. and R. R. Muse. The usefulness of tetrachloroisophthalonitrile and tetrachloronitroanisole for control of *Helminthosporium* and rust diseases of Kentucky bluegrass. The Plant Disease Reporter. 49(4):323–326. 1965.

2758. Bell, D. M. Fairway renovation forum. Penn State College Nineteenth Annual Turfgrass Conference Proceedings. pp. 35–37. 1950.

2759. Bell, R. S. Turf management in Rhode Island. Rhode Island Agricultural Experiment Station. Miscellaneous Publication. 26:1–12. 1945.

2760. Bell, R. S., and J. A. DeFrance. Influence of fertilizers on the accumulation of roots from closely clipped bent grasses and on the quality of turf. Soil Science. 58:17–24. 1944.

2761. Bell, R. S. and J. C. F. Tedrow. The control of wind erosion by the establishment of turf under airport conditions. Rhode Island Agricultural Experiment Station Bulletin 295. 22 pp. 1945.

2762. Bell, R. S., W. H. Lachman, E. M. Rahn, and R. D. Sweet. Life history studies as related to weed control in the Northeast: 1—nutgrass. Rhode Island Agricultural Experiment Station Bulletin. 364:1–33. 1962.

2763. Bellew, W. I. Planning turf facilities for university programs. Proceedings of the University of Florida Turf Grass Management Conference. 7:81–83. 1959.

2764. Bellingham, F. J. Hydraulic seeding on motorway, verges and other marginal areas as practiced in England. Ohio Short Course on Roadside Development. 23:44–48. 1964.

2765. ______. A new method of seeding. The Groundsman. 18(9):24–26. 1965.

2766. Bembower, W. Lawns for Hawaii. Hawaii Agricultural Extension Service Circular. 255:1–8. 1948.

2767. ______. Lawns for Hawaii. Hawaii Agricultural Extension Service Circular. 255:1–12. 1951.

2768. Bement, R. E., D. F. Harvey, A. C. Everson, and C. O. Hyoton. Use of asphalt—emulsion mulches to hasten grass-seeding establishment. Journal of Range Management. 14:102–109. 1961.

2769. Bendixon, L. E. and C. S. Oxender. Growth regulators for perennial weed control. Ohio Report on Research and Development. 54(4):60–61. 1969.

2770. Benedict, H. M. Growth of some range grasses in reduced light intensities at Cheyenne, Wyoming. Botanical Gazette. 102(3):582–589. 1941.

2771. ______. Effect of day length and temperature on the flowering and growth of four species of grasses. Journal of Agricultural Research. 61:661–761. 1940.

2772. Benedict, H. M. and G. D. Brown. The growth and carbohydrate responses of *Agropyron smithii* and *Bouteloua gracilis* to changes in nitrogen supply. Plant Physiology. 19:481–494. 1944.

2773. Bengeyfield, W. H. Make hay in early autumn. USGA Journal and Turf Management. 8(4):32. 1955.

2774. ______. What's going on in turf research. Northwest Turf Conference Proceedings. 11:1–4. 1957.

2775. ______. Wetting agents and their place in turf management. 12th Annual Pacific Northwest Turf Conference. 12:9–12. 1958.

2776. ______. Fertilization—its part in management. Proceedings of the Southern California Turfgrass Institute. pp. 13–16. 1960.

2777. ______. What to look for in fertilizers in 1961. Proceedings Northern California Turfgrass Institute. pp. 12–15. 1961.

2778. ______. Turf management in Hawaii and Japan. 15th Annual Northwest Turf Conference Proceedings. 15:21–24. 1961.

2779. ______. Organic matter, there's nothing quite like it. 16th Annual Northwest Turf Conference Proceedings. 15–17. 1962.

2780. ______. How to meet winter course maintenance problems. Club Operations. 1(1):34. 1963.

2781. ______. Professional self improvement. Proceedings of the Texas Turfgrass Conference. 18:8–13. 1963.

2782. ______. The traffic problem. USGA Green Section Record. 1(1):1–2. 1963.

2783. ______. Instant scoreboard. USGA Green Section Record. 1(3):4–5. 1963.

2784. ______. Trends in golf architecture. Proceedings of the 18th Annual Northwest Turfgrass Conference. 18:33–35. 1964.

2785. ______. Course maintenance centers on the putting green. USGA Green Section Record. 1(6):2–3. 1964.

2786. ______. Pesticide laws and the golf course. USGA Green Section Record. 2(2):-1–3. 1964.

2787. ______. Are you a good boss? Proceedings of the 19th Annual Northwest Turfgrass Conference. 19:64–67. 1965.

2788. ______. Can grass survive the traffic? USGA Green Section Record. 3(3):-1–6. 1965.

2789. ______. West coast panel tells how to analyze turf costs. The Golf Superintendent. 34(4):13–18. 1966.

2790. ______. The USGA Green Section—past, present, and future. Proceedings of the 20th Annual Northwest Turfgrass Conference. pp. 52–57. 1966.

2791. ______. Analyzing my turf costs. University of California Turf, Landscape Tree, and Nursery Conference Proceedings. pp. 6–1 to 6–5. 1966.

2792. ______. Nationwide cart survey. USGA Green Section Record. 4(2):1–6. 1966.

2793. ______. We are going to be challenged. Proceedings of the Annual Northwest Turfgrass Conference. 21:21–25. 1967.

2794. ______. Reviving a controversy—bentgrass overseeding. USGA Green Section Record. 5(2):10–11. 1967.

2795. ______. The USGA Green Section specifications. How have they done? California Turfgrass Culture. 18(1):1–3. 1968.

2796. ______. We are being challenged! The Golf Superintendent. 36(2):29, 64–65. 1968.

2797. ______. So you want to build a golf course. Proceedings 22nd Annual Northwest Turfgrass Conference pp. 31–34. 1968.

2798. ______. Turf establishment—stolonizing. Turf Bulletin. 4(8):18. 1968.

2799. ______. Topdressing putting greens: old fashioned or not? Turf Bulletin. 4(8):25–26. 1968.

2800. ______. Turf establishment—stolonizing. USGA Green Section Record. 5(6):16–17. 1968.

2801. ______. The turfgrass situation on the West Coast of the U.S.A. Proceedings of the First International Turfgrass Research Conference. p. 32. 1969.

2802. ______. Turfgrass soils and their modification: USGA green mixes. Proceedings of the First International Turfgrass Research Conference. pp. 149–150. 1969.

2803. ______. The USGA Green Section advisory service. Proceedings of the First International Turfgrass Research Conference. p. 426. 1969.

2804. ______. Cultural systems on golf courses. Proceedings of the First International Turfgrass Research Conference. pp. 506–508. 1969.

2805. ______. Topdress greens and see the difference. USGA Green Section Record. 7(1):1–4. 1969.

2806. ______. Research and you. USGA Green Section Record. 8(5):1. 1970.

2807. ______. Honestly, can one budget be compared with another? USGA Green Section Record. 9(2). 11. 1971.

2808. ______. Books on golf course turf management. USGA Green Section Record. 9(4):11. 1971.

2809. Bengeyfield, W. H., H. Clarke, C. Regele and J. Lee. Irrigation systems—operation. USGA Green Section Record. 4(3):-1–2. 1966.

2810. Bengeyfield, W. H., J. Sirianni, H. Hardin, and J. Zoller. The good and not so good of triplex putting green mowers. USGA Green Section Record. 10(2):25–29. 1972.

2811. Bengtson, J. W. and F. F. Davis. Experiments with fertilizers on bent turf. Turf Culture. 1(3):192–213. 1939.

2812. Bennett, A. W. The fertilization of grasses. Gardener's Chronicle and Agricultural Gazette. No. 11. pp. 362, 400, 401. 1873.

2813. Bennett, D. G. Summer maintenance of bermuda greens. Golf Course Reporter. 21(4):5–8. 1953.

2814. Bennett, F. T. *Fusarium* species on British cereals. Annals of Applied Biology. 20:272–290. 1933.

2815. ______. *Fusarium* patch disease of bowling and golf greens. Journal of the Board of Greenkeeping Research. 3:79–86. 1933.

2816. ______. *Corticium* disease of turf. Journal of the Board of Greenkeeping Research. 4:32–39. 1935.

2817. ______. Dollarspot disease of turf and its causal organism, *Sclerotinia homeocarpa,* n. sp. Annals of Applied Biology. 24:-236–257. 1937.

2818. Bennett, H. H. Relation of grass cover to erosion control. Journal of the American Society of Agronomy. 27(3):173–179. 1935.

2819. Bennett, H. W. Uredospore storage in breeding for crown rust resistant annual ryegrass. Crop Science. 8(5):627–628. 1968.

2820. Bennett, H. W., O. R., Hammons, and W. R. Weissinger. Identification of certain Mississippi grasses by vegetable morphology. Mississippi State College of Agricultural Experiment Station Technical Bulletin. 31:1–108. 1952.

2821. Bennett, I. Monthly maps of mean daily insolation for the United States. Solar Energy. 9:145–158. 1965.

2822. Bennett, J. W. The worming of fairways. Journal of the Board of Greenkeeping Research. 3:29–31. 1933.

2823. Bennett, O. L. and B. D. Doss. Effect of soil moisture level on root distribution of cool season forage species. Agronomy Journal. 52:204–207. 1960.

2824. Bennett, O. L., E. L. Mathias, and P. R. Henderlong. Effects of north- and south-facing slopes on yield of Kentucky bluegrass (*Poa pratensis* L.) with variable rate and time of nitrogen application. Agronomy Journal. 64(5):630–635. 1972.

2825. Bennett, O. L., B. D. Doss, D. A. Ashley, V. J. Kilmer and E. C. Richardson. Effects of soil moisture regime on yield, nutrient content, and evapotranspiration for three annual forage species. Agronomy Journal. 56(2):195–198. 1964.

2826. Bennett, R. H. Introductory remarks: Roadside development and research. 19th Short Course on Roadside Development. Ohio State Univ. pp. 33–34. 1960.

2827. Bennett, W. J. Fertilizer problems. Turf clippings. University of Massachussetts. 1(8):A-70 to A-71. 1963.

2828. Benoit, G. R., and J. Bornstein. Freezing and thawing effects on drainage. Soil Science Society of America Proceedings. 34(4):551–557. 1970.

2829. Benson, D. O. Mowing grass with a reel-type machine. California Turfgrass Culture. 13(2):11–14. 1963.

2830. Benson, N. and R. M. Barnette. Leaching studies with various sources of nitrogen. Journal of the American Society of Agronomy. 31:44–54. 1939.

2831. Beresford, W. Sprinkler types for golf courses. USGA Journal and Turf Management. 13(2):28–29. 1960.

2832. Berg, H. W. Fertilizing a golf course through an irrigation system. Stockbridge School Turf Clippings Conference Proceedings. 1(9):A-6-A-11. 1964.

2833. Berger, K. C. Micronutrient deficiencies in the United States. Agricultural and Food Chemistry. 10(3):178–181. 1962.

2834. Berggren, F. Wartime methods studied at Purdue turf meet. Golfdom. 25(5):-58, 60–61. 1951.

2835. ______. Research Results Reviewed at Purdue conference. Golfdom. 26(4):72, 74. 1952.

2836. ______. MRTF turf researchers freeze-tests zoysia. Midwest Turf-News and Research. 6(3):3. 1952.

2837. Berggren, F. and E. G. Sharvelle. Sharvelle describes fungicide progress. Midwest Turf-News and Research. 5(3):2. 1951.

2838. Berggren, G. H. Observations of weed control in crownvetch. The Pennsylvania State University Second Crownvetch Symposium, Agronomy Mimeo. 6:15–21. 1968.

2839. Berghorn, A. Turf diseases. Greenkeepers Club of New England Newsletter. 9(8):10–12. 1937.

2840. Berkenkamp, B. Extracellular ribonuclease production by fungi. Proceedings, Scotts Turfgrass Research Conference. 21:95–99. 1971.

2841. Bernard, J. L. Jack Bernard explains his method of overseeding. Golfdom. 35:72. 1961.

2842. Bernard, J. B. Rhodesgrass scale, new Florida headache. Golfdom. 36(7):54. 1962.

2843. Bernard, J. D. Lawns. Rinehart's Garden Library. New York. 94 pp. 1954.

2844. Bernstein, L. Salt tolerance of grasses and forage legumes. Agriculture Information Bulletin 194. 7 pp. 1958.

2845. ______. Salt tolerance of plants. Agriculture Information Bulletin 283. 23 pp. 1964.

2846. Bernstein, L., and H. E. Hayward.

Physiology of salt tolerance. Annual Review of Plant Phsyiology. 9:25–46. 1958.

2847. Berry, C. D. Testing bluegrass seedlings. Proceedings of the Midwest Regional Turf Conference. pp. 14–15. 1963.

2848. ______. Research in bluegrass. Proceedings of the Midwest Regional Turf Conference. pp. 50–51. 1964.

2849. ______. Progress in bluegrass research. Proceedings of the Midwest Regional Turf Conference. pp. 60–61. 1965.

2850. Berry, R. F. and C. S. Hoveland. Summer defoliation and autumn-winter production of *Phalaris* species and tall fescue varieties. Agronomy Journal. 61(4):493–497. 1969.

2851. Berry, C. D. and R. T. Gudauskas. Susceptibility of tall fescue. *Festuca arundinacea* Schreb., to crown rust. Crop Science. 12(1):101–102. 1972.

2852. Berry, C. D., D. V. Glover and W. H. Daniel. Phenotypic and genotypic variation and covariation of some quantitative turf characters of *Poa pratensis* L. Crop Science. 9(4):470–473. 1969.

2853. Bertoni, J. "Weather" or not—you care! A Patch of Green. Michigan and Border Cities USGA Publication. pp. 11–14. November, 1972.

2854. Bertramson, B. R. Let's put the grasses to work. Proceedings of the 6th Annual Pacific Northwest Turf Conference. 6:-40–45. 1952.

2855. Besemer, S. T. A comparison of resin-fertilizer with non-coated soluble fertilizers on bentgrass putting green turf. California Turfgrass Culture. 13(1):3–5. 1963.

2856. ______. Mechanical gopher control on golf courses. California Turfgrass Culture. 14(2):16. 1964.

2857. Besemer, S. T. and D. H. Close. Drainage of turf-grass areas. Turf-Grass Times. 2(2):10–13. 1966.

2858. Besley, H. E. and C. H. Reed. Urban wastes management. Journal of Environmental Quality. 1(1):78–81. 1972.

2859. Bessey, E. A. A nematode disease of grasses. Science N.S. 21 (532):391–392. 1905.

2860. Beutel, J., and F. Roewekamp. Turfgrass survey of Los Angeles County. Bulletin Southern California Golf Association. 12 pp. 1954.

2861. Beveridge, R. Technical maintenance of sports grounds. New Zealand Institute for Turf Culture Newsletter. 67:3–11. 1970.

2862. Bevilacqua, D. W. Susceptibility of Merion bluegrass to stripe smut. Turf clippings. University of Massachussetts. 1(5):18. 1960.

2863. Bews, J. W. The world's grasses. Longmans, Green and Co., London, England. 408 pp. 1929.

2864. Bhimaya, C. P., R. N. Kaul, and B. N. Gearguli. Sand dune rehabilitation in western Rajasthan. Science and Culture. 27:-224–229. 1961.

2865. Bibbey, R. O. Weed control of fairways. Proceedings of the School of Soils, Fertilization and Turf Maintenance. Green Section, Royal Canadian Golf Association. pp. 28–31. 1951.

2866. Bibby, F. F., and D. M. Tuttle. Notes on phytophagous and predatory mites of Arizona. Journal of Economic Entomology. 52(2):186–190. 1959.

2867. Bickowsky, E. R., and V. B. Youngner. Chemicals for lawn renovation. California Turfgrass Culture. 6(1):3. 1956.

2869. Bidwell, W. Reducing thatch brings back healthy turf. Golfdom. 26(3):78, 80, 82. 1952.

2870. ______. Top researchers report at turf conference. Park Maintenance. 6(3):12–15, 25. 1953.

2871. ______. Don't say it—write it. 38th International Turfgrass Conference and Show. pp. 1–2. 1967.

2872. ______. Eight million chances. The Penncross Story. The Rudy-Patrick Company. pp. 8–19. 1970.

2873. Bieber, G. L. Crownvetch establishment as affected by phytotoxicity of companion species. PhD. Thesis, Auburn University. 79pp. 1967.

2874. ______. Mulches for turf areas. 28th Short Course on Roadside Development, (Ohio). 28:108–109. 1969.

2875. Bieber, G. L., and K. L. Anderson. Soil moisture in bluestem grassland following burning. Journal of Soil and Water Conservation. 16(4):186–187. 1961.

2876. Bieber, G. L. and C. S. Hoveland. Phytotoxicity of plant materials on seed germination of crownvetch, *Coronilla varia* L. Agronomy Journal. 60(2):185–188. 1968.

2877. Bieberly, F. G., E. A. Cleavinger, and L. E. Willoughby. Warm season grasses in Kansas. Kansas State College Extension Service Circular No. 258. 16 pp. 1957.

2878. Bieberly, F. G., E. A. Cleavinger, H. D. Wilkins, J. V. Baird, and G. W. Wright. Cool season grasses in Kansas. Kansas Agricultural Extension Circular No. 257. 12 pp. 1962.

2879. Billet, R. W. Weed control studies. Proceedings of the University of Florida Turf Grass Management Conference. 7:44–50. 1959.

2880. Bing, A. Chemicals in preparation for new turf seedings. New England Agricultural Chemical Conference and Herbicide Workshop. 1:32–33. 1964.

2881. Bingaman, D. Subsurface irrigation. Midwest Regional Turf Foundation Turf Conference Proceedings. pp. 47–50. 1967.

2882. ______. Sands for rootzones. Midwest Regional Turf Conference Proceedings. pp. 68–70. 1968.

2883. Bingaman, D. E. Relationships between pore space and water behavior of compacted sands and three constituent sand particle dimensions. MS Thesis, Purdue University. 1973.

2884. Bingaman, D. E., and H. Kohnke. Sand as a growth medium for athletic turf. Agronomy Abstracts. p. 56. 1968.

2885. ______. Sand as a growth medium for athletic turf. Midwest Regional Turf Conference Proceedings. pp. 18–22. 1969.

2886. ______. Evaluating sands for athletic turf. Agronomy Journal. 62(4):464–467. 1970.

2887. Bingham, F. C. Watering program for bermuda greens. Golf Course Reporter. 25(6):32. 1957.

2888. Bingham, F. T., J. P. Martin, and J. A. Chastain. Effects of phosphorus fertilization of California soils on minor element nutrition of citrus. Soil Science. 86(1):24–31. 1958.

2889. Bingham, S. W. Hawkweed control with turf herbicides. Proceedings of the Northeastern Weed Control Conference. pp. 486–490. 1965.

2890. ______. Wild garlic control in bermudagrass turf. Proceedings of the Northeastern Weed Control Conference. pp. 508–510. 1965.

2891. ______. Turf-recommended practices—Virginia. 19th Annual Southern Weed Conference Research Report. pp. 115–117. 1966.

2892. ______. Goosegrass control in fairway bermudagrass turf. Virginia Turfgrass Conference Proceedings. 8:19–20. 1967.

2893. ______. Effect of repeated treatments for broadleaf weed control on bluegrass root and shoot development. Virginia Turfgrass Conference Proceedings. 8:21–22. 1967.

2894. ______. Annual bluegrass control in bermudagrass greens. Virginia Turfgrass Conference Proceedings. 8:23–24. 1967.

2895. ______. Annual treatments for crabgrass control on Seaside bentgrass. Virginia Turfgrass Conference Proceedings. 8:-25–26. 1967.

2896. ______. Kentucky 31 fescue control in bluegrass. Virginia Turfgrass Conference Proceedings. 8:27. 1967.

2897. ______. Evaluation of new formulations of herbicides for turf. Virginia Turfgrass Conference Proceedings. 8:28. 1967.

2898. ______. Inactivation of bensulide for planting turfgrasses. Virginia Turfgrass Conference Proceedings. 8:30–31. 1967.

2899. ______. Influence of herbicides on root development of bermudagrass. Weeds. 15(4):363–365. 1967.

2900. ______. Goosegrass control in fairway bermudagrass turf. Results of 1967 Research Program for Control of Weeds and Diseases of Turfgrasses and Ornamentals. Information Note 101-A. Department Plant

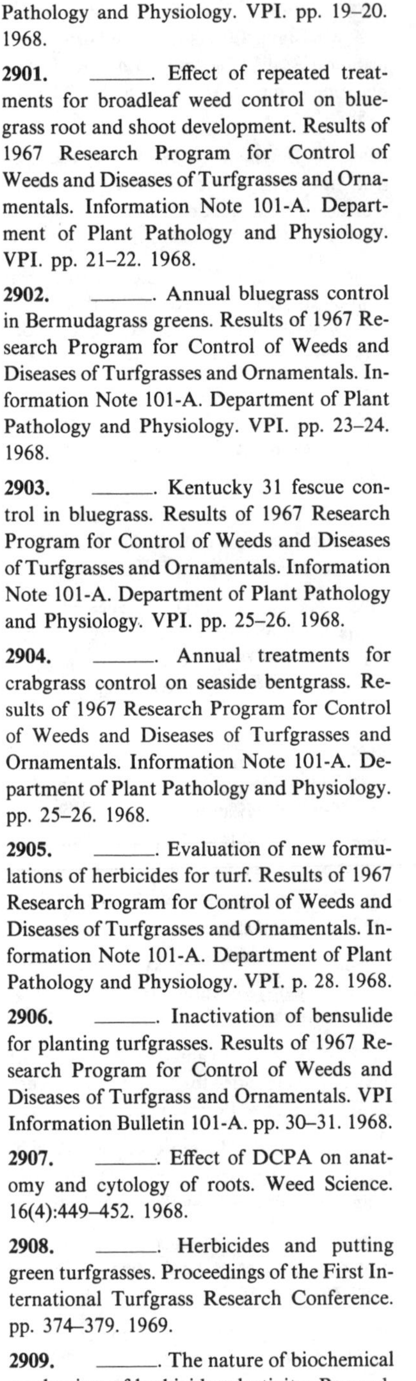

Pathology and Physiology. VPI. pp. 19–20. 1968.

2901. ______. Effect of repeated treatments for broadleaf weed control on bluegrass root and shoot development. Results of 1967 Research Program for Control of Weeds and Diseases of Turfgrasses and Ornamentals. Information Note 101-A. Department of Plant Pathology and Physiology. VPI. pp. 21–22. 1968.

2902. ______. Annual bluegrass control in Bermudagrass greens. Results of 1967 Research Program for Control of Weeds and Diseases of Turfgrasses and Ornamentals. Information Note 101-A. Department of Plant Pathology and Physiology. VPI. pp. 23–24. 1968.

2903. ______. Kentucky 31 fescue control in bluegrass. Results of 1967 Research Program for Control of Weeds and Diseases of Turfgrasses and Ornamentals. Information Note 101-A. Department of Plant Pathology and Physiology. VPI. pp. 25–26. 1968.

2904. ______. Annual treatments for crabgrass control on seaside bentgrass. Results of 1967 Research Program for Control of Weeds and Diseases of Turfgrasses and Ornamentals. Information Note 101-A. Department of Plant Pathology and Physiology. pp. 25–26. 1968.

2905. ______. Evaluation of new formulations of herbicides for turf. Results of 1967 Research Program for Control of Weeds and Diseases of Turfgrasses and Ornamentals. Information Note 101-A. Department of Plant Pathology and Physiology. VPI. p. 28. 1968.

2906. ______. Inactivation of bensulide for planting turfgrasses. Results of 1967 Research Program for Control of Weeds and Diseases of Turfgrass and Ornamentals. VPI Information Bulletin 101-A. pp. 30–31. 1968.

2907. ______. Effect of DCPA on anatomy and cytology of roots. Weed Science. 16(4):449–452. 1968.

2908. ______. Herbicides and putting green turfgrasses. Proceedings of the First International Turfgrass Research Conference. pp. 374–379. 1969.

2909. ______. The nature of biochemical mechanism of herbicide selectivity. Proceedings of Scotts Turfgrass Research Conference. 3:27–47. 1972.

2910. Bingham, S. W. and J. S. Coartney. Control broadleaf weeds in turfgrass. Weeds Today. 1(2):18. 1970.

2911. Bingham, S. W. and C. L. Foy. Use the right chemical tool for weed control in lawns. Weeds, Trees and Turf. 6(4):12–15, 23, 46. 1967.

2912. Bingham, S. W. and R. E. Schmidt. Crabgrass control in turf. 17th Annual Southern Weed Conference Proceedings. pp. 113–122. 1964.

2913. ______. Crabgrass control in turf. Vesicol Bulletin ADS#11, Vesicol Chemical Corporation. 1964.

2914. ______. Broadleaved weed control in turf. Agronomy Journal. 57(3):258–260. 1965.

2915. ______. Broadleaf weed control in turf. 18th Annual Southern Weed Conference Proceedings. pp. 130–134. 1965.

2916. ______. Residue of bensulide in turfgrass soil following annual treatments for crabgrass control. Agronomy Journal. 59(4):-327–329. 1967.

2917. ______. Perennial grass control in bluegrass turf. Weed Science. p. 78. 1969.

2918. Bingham, S. W., R. E. Schmidt, and C. Curry. Annual bluegrass control in bermudagrass putting green turf. Agronomy Abstracts. p. 62. 1968.

2919. ______. Annual bluegrass control in overseeded bermudagrass putting green turf. Agronomy Journal. 61(6):908–911. 1969.

2920. Binnie, A. Fall fertilization. The National Greenkeeper. 5(9):11–12. 1931.

2921. Biocourt, A. W. Lawn maintenance. Massachusetts Agricultural Extension Special Circular. 137:1–2. 1946.

2922. Birchfield, W. and W. J. Martin. Survival of root knot and reniform nematodes studied. Louisiana Agriculture. 13(4):-14–15. 1970.

2923. Birth, G. S. and G. R. McVey. Measuring the color of growing turf with a reflectance spectrophotometer. Agronomy Journal. 60(6):640–643. 1968.

2924. Biswell, H. H. and J. E. Weaver. Effect of frequent clipping on the development of roots and tops of grasses in prairie sod. Ecology. 14:368–390. 1933.

2925. Biswell, H. H., A. M. Schultz, D. W. Hedrick and J. I. Mallory. Frost heaving of grass and brush seedlings on burned chamise brushlands in California. Journal of Range Management. 6:172–180. 1953.

2926. Bittle, G. H. Turf management problems on highways. Proceedings of the 18th Annual Oklahoma-Texas Turf Conference. 18:96–100. 1963.

2927. Bjorklund, B. Snow mould in lawns. Weibulls Grastips. pp. 22–23. 1971.

2928. Black, A. L. Nitrogen and phosphorus fertilization for production of crested wheatgrass and native grass in Northeastern Montana. Agronomy Journal. 60(2):213–216. 1968.

2929. Black, A. P. Lawn and turf irrigation systems: the water source. University of Florida Turfgrass Conference Proceedings. 4:74–78. 1956.

2930. ______. Water in Florida. Proceedings of the Annual University of Florida Turfgrass Management Conference. 13:19–27. 1965.

2931. Black, C. C. and E. G. Rodgers. Response of Pensacola bahiagrass to herbicides. Weeds. 8:71–77. 1960.

2932. Black, G. A. Grasses of the genus *Axonopus.* Advancing Frontiers of Plant Sciences. Vol. 5. 186 pp. 1963.

2933. Black, S. Plenty of misery: but we worked our way out o.k. Golfdom. 3(4):23–24. 1929.

2934. Blackledge, J. L. Part IV—topdressing. Proceedings of the Second Annual University of Florida Turf Conference. 2:-52–54. 1954.

2935. ______. Mower classification and usage. Proceedings University of Florida Turf Management Conference. 6:7–9. 1958.

2936. ______. Fundamentals in turf grass production. University of Florida Turfgrass Management Conference Proceedings. 7:6–7. 1959.

2937. ______. Public parks. Proceedings of the 8th Annual University of Florida Turf-Grass Management Conference. 8:108–109. 1960.

2938. ______. Specialized equipment. Proceedings of the 13th Annual Florida Turfgrass Management Conference. 13:124–26. 1965.

2939. ______. Watering and mowing. Proceedings of the 17th Annual University of Florida Turfgrass Management Conference. 17:51–54. 1969.

2940. Blacklow, W. M., and W. S. McGuire. Influence of gibberellic acid on the winter growth of varieties of tall fescue (*Festuca arundinacea* Schreb.). Crop Science. 11(1):19–22. 1971.

2941. Blackman, G. E. An ecological study of closely cut turf treated with ammonium and ferrous sulphates. Annals of Applied Biology. 19:204–220. 1932.

2942. ______. A comparison between the effects of ammonium sulfate and other forms of nitrogen on the botanical composition of closely cut turf. Annals of Applied Biology. 19(4):443–461. 1932.

2943. ______. The ecological and physiological action of ammonium salts on the clover content of turf. Annals of Botany. 48:-975–1001. 1934.

2944. ______. The influence of temperature and available nitrogen supply on the growth of pasture in the spring. The Journal of Agricultural Science. 26(4):620–647. 1936.

2945. Blackman, G. E. and W. G. Templeman. The interaction of light intensity and nitrogen supply in the growth and metabolism of grasses and clover *(Trifolium repens).* II. The influence of light intensity and nitrogen supply on the leaf production of frequently defoliated plants. Annals of Botany. 2:765–791. 1938.

2946. ______. The interaction of light intensity and nitrogen supply in the growth and metabolism of grasses and clover *(Trifolium repens).* IV. The relation of light intensity and nitrogen supply to the protein metabolism of the leaves of grasses. Annals of Botany N.S. 4(15):533–587. 1940.

2947. Blackwell, P. L. Maintenance of turf shoulders. Highway Research Board, Committee on Roadside Development. 1947.

2948. Blaine, W. M. New golf course

management practices. Illinois Turfgrass Conference Proceedings. pp. 43–45. 1969.

2949. Blair, A. M. Herbicides for control of grass weeds when establishing ryegrass. British Weed Control Conference Proceedings. 10(2):495–499. 1970.

2950. Blair, I. Control of diseases in turf. New Zealand Institute for Turf Culture Newsletter. 5:5–6. 1960.

2951. Blair, R. Turf progress at the Everglades Experiment Station. Florida Greenkeeping Superintendents Association Turf Management Conference. pp. 5–21. 1950.

2952. Blake, A. K. Viability and germination of seeds and early life history of prairie plants. Ecological Monographs. 5(4):407–460. 1935.

2953. Blake, G. R. Soil compaction and soil structure. Rutgers University 19th Annual Short Course in Turf Management. pp. 14–17. 1951.

2954. ______. Fundamentals of irrigation. Rutgers University 20th Annual Short Course in Turf Management. pp. 68–70. 1952–53.

2955. Blake, R. C. Renovation program at Whitinsville Golf Club. Turf Clippings. University of Massachussetts. 1(1):18–19. 1956.

2956. ______. Turf professions and education. Turf Bulletin. Massachusetts Turf and Lawn Grass Council. 3(1):3. 1966.

2957. ______. Personal observations on winter kill. The Golf Superintendent. 35(1):-17. 1967.

2958. ______. Be a better leader. 38th International Turfgrass Conference & Show. pp. 75–78. 1967.

2959. ______. What does a superintendent expect from the club. USGA Green Section Record. 9(2):19–21. 1971.

2960. Blanchard, J. L. Burial trends affecting cemetery turf management. Proceedings University of Florida Turf-Grass Management Conference. 10:119–121. 1962.

2961. Blandy, R. V. The control of mosses in lawns and sports turf. Parks, Golf Courses and Sports Grounds. 20(2):93–97. 1954.

2962. ______. Further developments in moss control. Parks, Golf Courses & Sports Grounds. 22:160–165. 1956.

2963. Blaney, H. F. and W. D. Criddle. Determining water requirements in irrigated areas from climatological and irrigation data. U.S. Soil Conservation Service Technical Bulletin 96:1–44. 1950.

2964. Blaser, R. E. Establishment and maintaining turf and soil cover along newly constructed highways. Proceedings of the 1967 West Virginia Turfgrass Conference. West Virginia Agricultural Experiment Station Miscellaneous Publication. 5:11–16. 1968.

2965. ______. Fertilizer practices and species adaptation for steep road cuts in Virginia. Agronomy Abstracts. p. 64. 1958.

2966. ______. Green roadbanks take plenty of plant food. Better Crops. 42(10):5. 1958.

2967. ______. Methods of maintaining and reseeding deteriorated highway slopes. Ohio Short Course on Roadside Development. 21:87–93. 1962.

2968. ______. Soil mulches for grasses. Roadside Development, Highway Research Board. Publication 1030. pp. 15–20. 1962.

2969. ______. Principles of making turf mixtures for roadside seedings. Highway Research Record 23, Highway Research Board, Washington, D.C. 23:79–84. 1963.

2970. ______. Principles of making turf mixtures for roadside seedings. Virginia Polytechnic Institute. Virginia Agricultural Experiment Station. Reprint Number 54. September, 1964.

2971. ______. Establishing and maintaining turf and soil cover along newly constructed highways. West Virginia Turfgrass Conference Proceedings. pp. 11–16. 1967.

2972. ______. Liming and fertilizing turfgrasses. West Virginia Turfgrass Conference Proceedings. pp. 21–26. 1967.

2973. ______. Soil and air temperatures and fertilizing turf. Ohio Turfgrass Conference Proceedings. pp. 45–49. 1969.

2974. Blaser, R. E. and W. E. Stokes. Effect of fertilizer on growth and composition of carpet and other grasses. Florida Agricultural Experiment Station Bulletin. 390. 31 pp. 1943.

2975. Blaser, R. E., and D. G. Barkley. The effect of various mulches on microclimate and turf establishment. Agronomy Abstracts. p. 117. 1963.

2976. Blaser, R. E., and R. E. Schmidt. In the mid-Atlantic. Golf Course Reporter. 27(7):32–33. 1959.

2977. ______. Effect of nitrogen on organic food reserves and some physiological responses of bentgrass and bermudagrass grown under various temperatures. Agronomy Abstracts. p. 99. 1964.

2978. ______. The ecology of nitrogen activity in turf soils. Golf Course Reporter. 32:12. 1964.

2979. Blaser, R. E. and C. Y. Ward. Seeding highway slopes as influenced by lime, fertilizers and adaptation of species. Report of Committee on Roadside Development. Highway Research Board. pp. 21–39. 1958.

2980. Blaser, R. E., and J. M. Woodruff. The need for specifying two- or three-step seeding and fertilization practices for establishing sod on highways. Highway Research Record No. 246. Roadside Development. pp. 44–49. 1968.

2981. Blaser, R. E., R. H. Brown, and H. T. Bryant. The relationship between carbohydrate accumulation and growth of grasses under different microclimates. Proceedings, 10th International Grassland Congress. pp. 147–150. 1966.

2982. Blaser, R. E., R. E. Schmidt and F. B. Stewart. Rate and seasons of applying nitrogen on turf quality and physiology. Agronomy Abstracts. p. 50. 1967.

2983. Blaser, R. E., W. H. Skrdla, and T. H. Taylor. Ecological and physiological factors in compounding seed mixtures. Advances in Agronomy. 4:179–216. 1952.

2984. Blaser, R. E., D. G. Barkley, W. H. McKee, and E. W. Carson. Mulching, seed mixtures and fertilization for grassing highway sloping cuts. Agronomy Abstracts. p. 101. 1962.

2985. Blaser, R. E., G. W. Thomas, C. R. Brooks, G. J. Shoop, and J. B. Martin. Turf establishment and maintenance along highway cuts. Virginia Council of Highway Investigation and Research. Reprint 36. 19 pp. 1962.

2986. Blatt, J., W. Hylen, and R. Page. Panel on lakes and ponds. Golf Superintendent. 38(1):34–40. 1970.

2987. Blazek, O. The application of herbicides to playground and park swards. 1st Czechoslovak Symposium on Sportsturf Proceedings. pp. 223–229. 1969.

2988. Bleak, A. T. and W. Keller. Effects of seed age and preplanting seed treatment on seedling response in crested wheatgrass. Crop Science. 9(3):296–302. 1969.

2989. ______. Field emergence and growth of crested wheatgrass from pretreated vs nontreated seeds. Crop Science. 10(1):85–87. 1970.

2990. Bledsoe, R. W. Some fundamental aspects of plant physiology as related to the growth of turf grasses. University of Florida Turfgrass Conference Proceedings. pp. 5–7. 1953.

2991. Bliss, L. C. Microenvironment and grass adaptation. Illinois Turfgrass Conference Proceedings. pp. 4–6. 1962.

2992. Bloch, A. Keeping turf healthy through preparation without irrigation. Proceedings of Midwest Regional Turf Conference. pp. 22–23. 1956.

2993. Blomquist, H. L. The grasses of North Carolina. Duke University Press. Durham. 276 pp. 1948.

2994. Bloodgood, J. A. Quality of seed and germination. Proceedings 1970 3-Day Turf Courses. Rutgers University. pp. 27–28. 1970.

2995. ______. A look at turfgrass seeds. Proceedings 1972 3-Day Turf Courses, Rutgers University. pp. 45–47. 1972.

2996. Bloodworth, M. E. Sand, clay, organic in green mixture. Golfdom. 34:116–118. 1960.

2997. Bloom, J. R. and H. B. Couch. Influence of pH, nutrition and soil moisture on the development of large brown patch. Phytopathology. 48:260. 1958.

2998. ______. Influence of environment on diseases of turf-grasses. Effect of nutrition,

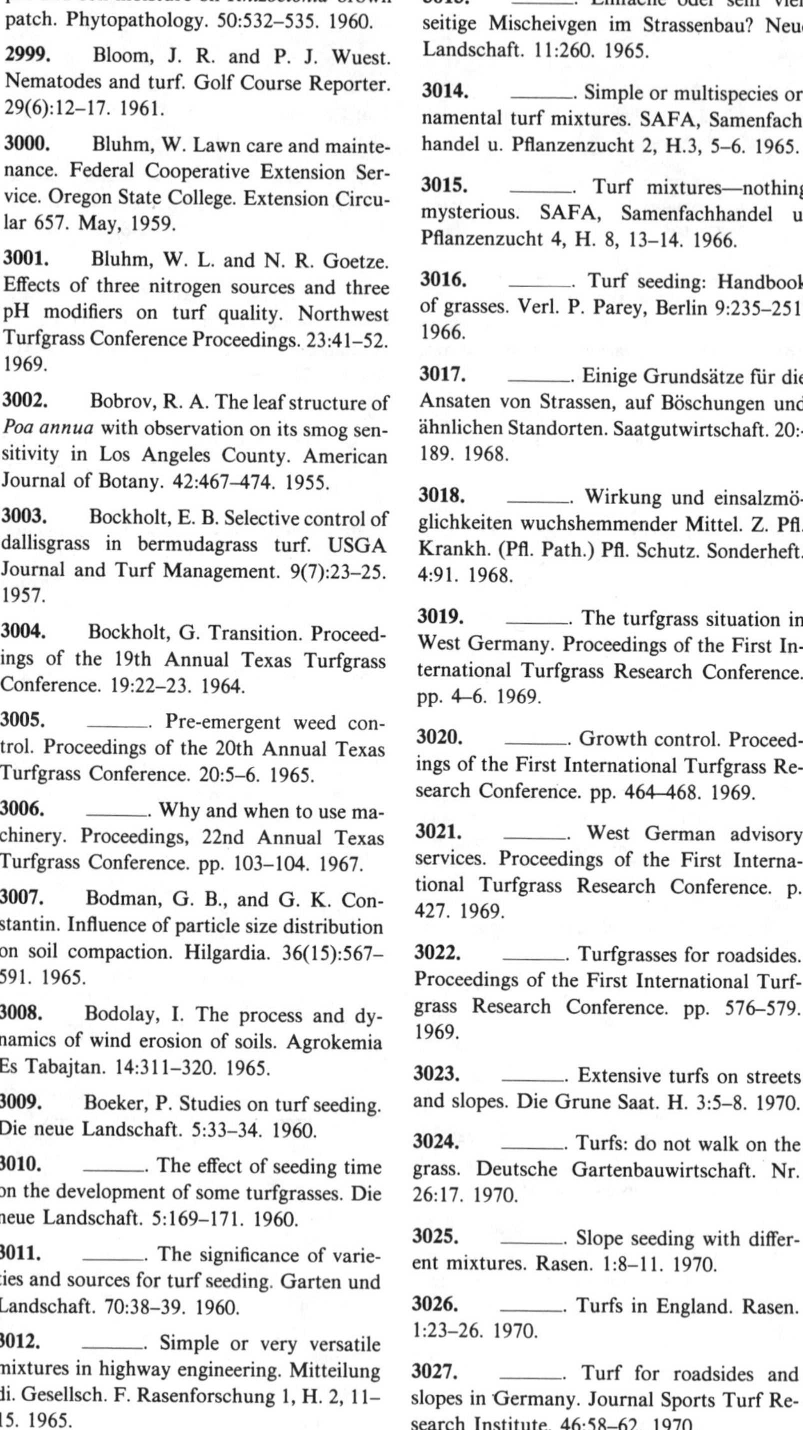

pH and soil moisture on *Rhizoctonia* brown patch. Phytopathology. 50:532–535. 1960.

2999. Bloom, J. R. and P. J. Wuest. Nematodes and turf. Golf Course Reporter. 29(6):12–17. 1961.

3000. Bluhm, W. Lawn care and maintenance. Federal Cooperative Extension Service. Oregon State College. Extension Circular 657. May, 1959.

3001. Bluhm, W. L. and N. R. Goetze. Effects of three nitrogen sources and three pH modifiers on turf quality. Northwest Turfgrass Conference Proceedings. 23:41–52. 1969.

3002. Bobrov, R. A. The leaf structure of *Poa annua* with observation on its smog sensitivity in Los Angeles County. American Journal of Botany. 42:467–474. 1955.

3003. Bockholt, E. B. Selective control of dallisgrass in bermudagrass turf. USGA Journal and Turf Management. 9(7):23–25. 1957.

3004. Bockholt, G. Transition. Proceedings of the 19th Annual Texas Turfgrass Conference. 19:22–23. 1964.

3005. ______. Pre-emergent weed control. Proceedings of the 20th Annual Texas Turfgrass Conference. 20:5–6. 1965.

3006. ______. Why and when to use machinery. Proceedings, 22nd Annual Texas Turfgrass Conference. pp. 103–104. 1967.

3007. Bodman, G. B., and G. K. Constantin. Influence of particle size distribution on soil compaction. Hilgardia. 36(15):567–591. 1965.

3008. Bodolay, I. The process and dynamics of wind erosion of soils. Agrokemia Es Tabajtan. 14:311–320. 1965.

3009. Boeker, P. Studies on turf seeding. Die neue Landschaft. 5:33–34. 1960.

3010. ______. The effect of seeding time on the development of some turfgrasses. Die neue Landschaft. 5:169–171. 1960.

3011. ______. The significance of varieties and sources for turf seeding. Garten und Landschaft. 70:38–39. 1960.

3012. ______. Simple or very versatile mixtures in highway engineering. Mitteilung di. Gesellsch. F. Rasenforschung 1, H. 2, 11–15. 1965.

3013. ______. Einfache oder sehr vielseitige Mischeivgen im Strassenbau? Neue Landschaft. 11:260. 1965.

3014. ______. Simple or multispecies ornamental turf mixtures. SAFA, Samenfachhandel u. Pflanzenzucht 2, H.3, 5–6. 1965.

3015. ______. Turf mixtures—nothing mysterious. SAFA, Samenfachhandel u. Pflanzenzucht 4, H. 8, 13–14. 1966.

3016. ______. Turf seeding: Handbook of grasses. Verl. P. Parey, Berlin 9:235–251. 1966.

3017. ______. Einige Grundsätze für die Ansaten von Strassen, auf Böschungen und ähnlichen Standorten. Saatgutwirtschaft. 20:-189. 1968.

3018. ______. Wirkung und einsalzmöglichkeiten wuchshemmender Mittel. Z. Pfl. Krankh. (Pfl. Path.) Pfl. Schutz. Sonderheft. 4:91. 1968.

3019. ______. The turfgrass situation in West Germany. Proceedings of the First International Turfgrass Research Conference. pp. 4–6. 1969.

3020. ______. Growth control. Proceedings of the First International Turfgrass Research Conference. pp. 464–468. 1969.

3021. ______. West German advisory services. Proceedings of the First International Turfgrass Research Conference. p. 427. 1969.

3022. ______. Turfgrasses for roadsides. Proceedings of the First International Turfgrass Research Conference. pp. 576–579. 1969.

3023. ______. Extensive turfs on streets and slopes. Die Grune Saat. H. 3:5–8. 1970.

3024. ______. Turfs: do not walk on the grass. Deutsche Gartenbauwirtschaft. Nr. 26:17. 1970.

3025. ______. Slope seeding with different mixtures. Rasen. 1:8–11. 1970.

3026. ______. Turfs in England. Rasen. 1:23–26. 1970.

3027. ______. Turf for roadsides and slopes in Germany. Journal Sports Turf Research Institute. 46:58–62. 1970.

3028. ______. Rohrschwingle (fescus) is no turfgrass! Deutsche Gartenbauwirtschaft. Nr. 4:79. 1971.

3029. ______. Erfahrungen an die praxis (Results on usage). Deutsche Gartenbauwirtschaft. Nr. 7:152–153. 1971.

3030. ______. Passable turfroads in horticulture and gardening. Rasen. 2:1–5. 1971.

3031. ______. Fescue as forage or turfgrass. Wurtt. Wochenbl. f. Landwirtschaft Nr. 8:433. 1971.

3032. Boeker, P., W. Richter, and G. Sauer. Beobachtungen auf Versuchen mit urichshemmenden Mitteln entlang der Autobahnen und Bundesstrassen. Z. Pfl. Krankh. (Pfl. Path.) Pfl. Schutz. Sonderheft. III p. 341. 1965.

3033. ______. Observations or studies with growth retarding agents along motorhighways and state maintained streets. Sonderheft III, Zeitschr. F. Pflanzenkrankheiten U. Pflanzenschutz. pp. 341–345. 1965.

3034. Boelter, D. H. Physical properties of peats as related to degree of decomposition. Soil Science Society of America Proceedings. 33(4):606–609. 1969.

3035. Bogart, J. E. Factors influencing competition of annual bluegrass (*Poa annua* L.) within established turfgrass communities and seedling stands. M.S. Thesis, Michigan State University. 75 pp. 1972.

3036. ______. Turf management in urban areas. The Voice of M. A. N. 17(4):4. 1972.

3037. Bogart, J. E., and J. B. Beard. Competitive factors influencing the encroachment of *Poa annua* in turfs. 42nd Annual Michigan Turfgrass Conference Proceedings. 1:21–23. 1972.

3038. Bogdan, A. V. Cultivated varieties of tropical and sub-tropical herbage plants in Kenya. East African Agricultural and Forestry Journal. 30:330–338. 1965.

3039. ______. Turfgrasses in Kenya. Proceedings of the First International Turfgrass Research Conference. pp. 51–56. 1969.

3040. Bogdan, K. Die *Agrostis canina*—Wiesen in Nordbosnien. Advancing Frontiers of Plant Sciences. 2:1–7. 1963.

3041. Boggs, A. Has hunch on eradication of brown-patch. Golfdom. 6(7):60–61. 1932.

3042. Bohart, R. M. Sod webworms and other lawn pests in California. Hilgardia. 17(8):267–308. 1947.

3044. Bohling, H. Planting large lawn areas. Proceedings of Midwest Regional Turf Conference. pp. 11–13. 1952.

3045. Bohne, P. W. and B. S. Morgan. The present status of MH-30 as a management tool for highway turf. Agronomy Abstracts. p. 101. 1962.

3046. Bollen, W. B., and D. W. Glennie. Sawdust, bark and other wood wastes for soil conditioning and mulching. Forest Products Journal. 11:38–46. 1961.

3047. Bolton, J. L. and R. E. McKenzie The effect of early spring flooding on certain forage crops. Scientific Agriculture. 26(3):-99–105. 1946.

3048. Bommer, D. "Samen"—vernzlisation perennierender gräserarten. Zeitschrift für Pflanzensüchtung. 46:105–111. 1961.

3049. Bond, B. The football pitch. The Groundsman. 22(3):26–27. 1968.

3050. Bond, J. J. and W. O. Willis. Soil water evaporation: first stage drying as influenced by surface residue and evaporation potential. Soil Science Society of America Proceedings. 34(6):924–927. 1970.

3051. Bond, R. R. How to plant creeping bent stolons and produce putting greens. Old Orchard Turf Nurseries. Wisconsin.

3052. ______. How to plant stolons and develop putting surface. Golf Course Reporter. 16(2):42–43, 48. 1948.

3053. ______. How to establish new stolon bent greens quickly. Golfdom. 22(5):49, 52. 1948.

3054. ______. How to obtain quick establishment of stolon bents. Proceedings of Midwest Regional Turf Conference. pp. 28–31. 1948.

3055. ______. Stolon planting, requires skilled preparation. Park Maintenance, 2:8–10. 1949.

3056. ______. How to plant creeping bent stolons and produce putting greens. Southern California Turf Culture 3(4):3–4. 1953.

3057. ______. Experience hasn't justified mixed green hopes. Golfdom. 29(6):38, 40–41. 1955.

3058. ______. Veteran turf nurseryman reviews C-19 and C-1. Golfdom. 29(9):41, 44. 1955.

3059. Boocock, D. F. Laying a lawn with turf. Gardeners Chronicle. 156(23):572, 586. 1964.

3060. Booher, L. J. Liquid fertilization of turfgrass. California Turfgrass Culture. 12(3):17–18. 1962.

3061. Booker, D. R. Sources of weather information available for golf course use. Proceedings of the Mid-Atlantic Association of Golf Course Superintendents Conference. pp. 3–4. 1963.

3062. Boosalis, M. G. A soil infestation method for studying spores of *Helminthosporium sativum.* Phytopathology. 50(11): 860–865. 1960.

3063. Booterbaugh, T. Sound northern practice is successful basis in South. Golfdom. 26(3): 82, 84. 1952.

3064. Bor, N. L. The grasses of Burma, Ceylon, India and Pakistan. Permagon Press, New York. 767 pp. 1960.

3065. Border, E. G. Fairway mowing and fertilization. Exposition Conference. Southern California. 2 pp. 1966.

3066. ______. Know your costs. The Golf Superintendent. 35(3):67. 1967.

3067. ______. Costs for fairway mowing, fertilization. Park Maintenance. 21(2):32. 1968.

3068. Borders, H. I. Effect of some fungicide mixtures on sod webworms in south Florida turfgrasses. Florida Entomologist. 48(2):133. 1965.

3069. ______. Control of plant diseases in Florida lawns and gardens. Soap and Chemical Specialties Journal. 40(4):105–109.

3070. ______. Diseases of warm-season grasses. Annual Research Report of the Institute of Food and Agricultural Sciences. University of Florida. p. 206. 1970.

3071. Bordewick, B. E. Chemicals control St. Augustine grass in bermudagrass turf in Texas tests. Weeds Trees and Turf. 6(10):-23–25. 1967.

3072. Borrill, M. Inflorescence initiation and leaf size in some *Gramineae.* Annals of Botany. N. S. 23:217–27. 1959.

3073. ______. The developmental anatomy of leaves in *Lolium lemulentum.* Annals of Botany. N. S. 25:1–11. 1961.

3074. Bosemark, N. O. The influence of nitrogen on root development. Physiologia Plantarum. 7:497–502. 1954.

3075. Bosshart, R. P. Effects of soil moisture, mulch, slope-facing, and surface temperature on grass seedlings. M. S. Thesis, Virginia Polytechnic Institute. 69 pp. 1967.

3076. Bosshart, R. P., and W. H. McKee. Grass seedling response to moisture and soil surface temperature stresses as affected by wood cellulose mulch. Agronomy Abstracts. 58:25. 1966.

3077. Boster, D. O. Pennsylvania turfgrass survey. Pennsylvania Department of Agriculture. Publication CRS-42. 36 pp. 1966.

3078. Boswell, V. R. What seeds are and do. USGA Journal and Turf Management. 14(5):30–32. 1961.

3079. Boughman, R. W. Effect of clipping on the development of roots and tops of various grass seedlings. M.S. Thesis, Iowa State College. 1939.

3080. Bouyoucos, G. J. An investigation of soil temperature and some of the most important factors influencing it. Michigan State University Agricultural Experiment Station. Technical Bulletin 17. 1913.

3081. ______. Soil temperature. Michigan Agricultural Experiment Station Technical Bulletin. 26:688–816. 1916.

3082. Boswell, V. R. What seeds are and do. Sports Turf Bulletin. 56:7–10. 1962.

3083. Bouyoucos, G. J. Determining soil colloids by the hydrometer. First International Congress of Soil Science Proceedings. pp. 17–19. 1927.

3084. ______. Hydrometer method improved for making particle size analyses of soils. Agronomy Journal. 54:464–465. 1962.

3085. Bouyoucos, G. F. and M. M. McCool. The correct explanation for the heaving of soils, plants and pavements. Journal of the American Society of Agronomy. 20:480–491. 1928.

3086. Bove, F. Cost of maintaining greens and tees. University of California Turf, Landscape Tree, and Nursery Conference Proceedings. p. 6. 1966.

3087. ______. Cost analysis—southwest. International Turfgrass Conference and Show. 39:59–60. 1968.

3088. Boving, P. A. Irrigation. Illinois Turfgrass Conference Proceedings. pp. 19–21. 1962.

3089. Bowen, P., and R. L. Morris. Broad leaf weed control in turf: mixtures of dicamba with 2,4-D and MCPA. Proceedings of 1st International Turfgrass Research Conference, Harrogate, England. pp. 380–392. 1969.

3090. Bowen, T. R. Eras and fads in maintenance. Greenkeepers Reporter. 8(3):-24–27. 1940.

3091. Bower, C. A. Diagnosing soil salinity. USDA. Agricultural Information Bulletin. 279:1–12. 1963.

3092. Bower, C. A., G. Ogata, and J. M. Tucker. Growth of sudan and tall fescue grasses as influenced by irrigation water salinity and leaching fraction. Agronomy Journal. 62(6):793–794. 1970.

3093. Bower, C. D. Vertical turbine pumps . . . analysis and correction of basic problems. Sprinkler Irrigation Association Annual Technological Conference Proceedings. pp. 85–87. 1965.

3094. Bowers, A. H. A happy New Year —for plant food supplies. Midwest Turf News and Research. 4(1):4–5. 1950.

3095. Bowers, L. M. A lawn program that works. Proceedings of the 1966 Midwest Regional Turf Conference. pp. 60–62. 1966.

3097. Bowers, W. H. Fully automatic irrigation equipment. Proceedings of Annual Florida Turfgrass Management Conference. 13:47–49. 1965.

3098. ______. Automatic irrigation. From skepticism to enthusiasm in a decade. Golfdom. 43(9):50–53. 1969.

3099. Bowler, D. G. Some important considerations in the improvement of wet soils. New Zealand Institute for Turf Culture. 81:153–156. 1972.

3100. Bowman, R. E. and T. R. Flanagan. Density-frequency distribution of weeds on golf greens. Proceedings of the Northeastern Weed Control Conference. pp. 490–497. 1967.

3101. Bowmer, W. J. and W. G. McCully. Can herbicides be effectively impregnated into asphalt. Weeds, Trees and Turf. 5(5):22, 23. 1966.

3102. ______. Establishment of bermudagrass seeded with annual ryegrass. Texas Agricultural Experiment Station. Progress Report PR-2556. pp. 1–18. 1968.

3103. Bowyer, T. H., and M. C. Shurtleff. Fungicide evaluation on bentgrass putting green turf. University of Illinois Turfgrass Field Day. pp. 22–25. 1972.

3104. Boyce, J. H. The care of lawns. Division of Forage Crops. Central Experimental Farm, Ottawa, Canada. 13 pp.

3105. ______. The construction of new lawns. Division of Forage Crops. Central Experimental Farms, Ottawa, Canada. 10 pp.

3106. ______. The establishment and maintenance of turf on putting and bowling greens. Division of Forage Crops. Central Experimental Farm. Ottawa, Canada 21 pp.

3107. ______. Development of lawn and turf. The Modern Cemetery. 55(10):258–260. 1945.

3108. ______. Development of lawn and turf. The Modern Cemetery. 56(2):19. 1946.

3109. ______. Development of lawn and turf. The Modern Cemetery. 56(4):41–42. 1946.

3110. ______. The construction and care of lawns. Canada Department of Agriculture, Ottawa. 22 pp. 1950.

3111. ______. Winter injury and snow mold problems in Canada. Proceedings, School of Soils, Fertilisation, and Turf Maintenance. Green Section, Royal Canadian Golf Association. pp. 16–23. 1952.

3112. ______. Turf research at Central Experimental Farm, Ottawa. Guelph Turfgrass Conference Proceedings. pp. 38–40. 1959.

3113. ______. Turfgrass research in Canada. The Greenmaster. 8(12):3–13. 1972.

3114. Boyd, B. Burning bermuda greens. Proceedings, Third Annual Tennessee Turfgrass Conference. pp. 30–31. 1969.

3115. Boyd, E. Success with zoysia. Midwest Regional Turf Conference Proceedings. pp. 60–61. 1970.

3116. Boyd, F. T., V. N. Schroder, and V. G. Perry. Interaction of nematodes and soil temperature on growth of three tropical grasses. Agronomy Journal. 64(4):497–500. 1972.

3117. Boyd, L. and A. G. Law. 1971 wear trials on bluegrass varieties, Pullman. Northwest Turfgrass Conference Proceedings 25:76–78. 1971.

3118. Boyd, P. Weed control. New Zealand Institute for Turf Culture. Newsletter 42:3. 1966.

3119. Boyd, T. Club superintendent lists requirements for fairway changes. Midwest Regional Turf Foundation. 2(4):1–2. 1948.

3121. ______. Records on a course. Proceedings of Midwest Regional Turf Conference. pp. 19–22. 1951.

3122. ______. Seeks suggestions to boost members. Midwest Turf-News and Research. 6(2):6. 1952.

3123. ______. Report on experimental green. Proceedings of Midwest Regional Turfgrass Conference. pp. 21–22. 1955.

3124. ______. Lord, am I confused. Golf Course Reporter. 25(6):30–31. 1957.

3125. ______. Labor management and daily planning. USGA Journal and Turf Management. 11(2):26–28. 1958.

3126. ______. Turf service for club members. Proceedings of Midwest Regional Turf Conference. pp. 29–33. 1959.

3127. Boyde, E. Success with zoysia. The Golf Superintendent. 38:46–47. 1970.

3128. Boyle, A. M. Lawn diseases in Arizona. Arizona Agricultural Experiment Station Technical Bulletin. 136:1–16. 1959.

3129. ______. Bermudagrass and disease susceptibility. Agricultural Experiment Station Turfgrass Report 203. University of Arizona. pp. 23–24. 1961.

3130. Boyle, A. M., and A. D. Davison Control of summer blight in common bermuda. Report on Turfgrass Research, Arizona Agricultural Experiment Station. Report 240. pp. 13–14. 1966.

3131. Boyns, B. M. Concentrated fertilisers—ammonium phosphate. Journal of the Board of Greenkeeping Research. 4:280–288. 1936.

3132. ______. Concentrated fertilisers—urea. Journal of the Board of Greenkeeping Research. 5:34–37. 1937.

3133. Boysen, W. R. Automatic irrigation in the west. The Golf Course Reporter. 33(6):35–40. 1965.

3134. ______. The past, present and future of the golf course superintendent. Proceedings of the Annual Northwest Turfgrass Conference. 21:6–13. 1967.

3135. Brach, G. A. Management practices in the care of lawns. Rocky Mountain Regional Turfgrass Conference Proceedings. Colorado A & M. pp. 42–45. 1963.

3136. Bracken, J. W. Post-emergence weed control. Proceedings of the 20th Annual Texas Turfgrass Conference. 20:7–8. 1965.

3137. Brackett, C. E. Availability, quality, and present utilization of fly ash. Fly Ash Utilization Proceedings. Bureau of Mines I.C. 8348. pp. 16–36. 1967.

3138. Bradbury, J. Our problem. The Groundsman. 15(8):18–20. 1962.

3139. ______. Cricket squares in spring. The Groundsman. 18(7):24–29. 1965.

3140. ______. Autumn work on the cricket square. The Groundsman. 22(12):18–20. 1969.

3141. ______. William Webb Ellis—are you mad? The Groundsman. 24(5):10–12. 1971.

3142. Braden, P. Factors affecting choice of pipe for sprinkler systems. Southern California Turfgrass Institute Mimeo. p. 4. 1957.

3143. Bradfield, R. Enter the soil conditions. New York State Turf Association Bulletin 38. pp. 147–148. 1952.

3144. Bradley, C. K. Working with weather. Golfdom. 10(1):9–10. 1936.

3145. ______. Evens turf wear. Golfdom. 11(5):37–38. 1937.

3146. ______. Air fields from the grounds viewpoint. The Greenkeeper's Reporter. 13:10–13. 1945.

3147. Bradley, J. K. and W. K. Thompson. Determination of 2, 4-dichlorophenoxyacetic acid and 2, 4, 5-trichlorophenoxyacetic acid in lawn fertilisers. Journal of the Science of Food and Agriculture. 15(10):673–677. 1964.

3148. Bradley, K. The harmful effects of winter play on putting greens. Greenkeepers' Reporter. 7(1):13, 54. 1939.

3150. Bradshaw, A. D. Populations of *Agrostis-tenuis* resistant to lead and zinc poisoning. Nature. 169:1098. 1952.

3151. ______. Natural hybridization of *Agrostis tenuis Sibth* and *A. stolonifera* L. New Phytologists. 57:66–84. 1958.

3152. ______. Studies of variation in bent grass species. I. Hybridization between *Agrostis tenuis* and *A. stolonifera.* Journal Sports Turf Research Institute. 9:422–429. 1958.

3153. ______. Population differentiation in *Agrostis tenuis* Sibth. I. Morphological differentiation. New Phytologist. 58:208–227. 1959.

3154. ______. Studies of variation in bent grass species, II. Variation within *Agrostis tenuis.* Journal Sports Turf Research Institute. 10:6–12. 1959.

3155. ______. Experimental investigations into the mineral nutrition of several grass species. III. Phosphate level. Journal of Ecology. 48:631–637. 1960.

3156. ______. Population differentiation in *Agrostis tenuis* Sibth. III. Populations in varied environments. New Phytologists. 59:-92–103. 1960.

3157. ______. The mineral nutrition of grass species. Annual of Applied Biology. 50:354. 1962.

3158. ______. Turf grass species and soil fertility. Journal Sports Turf Research Institute. 10:372–384. 1962.

3159. Bradshaw, A. D., and R. W. Snaydon. Population differences within plant species in response to soil factors. Nature. 183:-129–130. 1959.

3160. Bradshaw, J. Better lawns. Bolens Division, FMC Corp. 47 pp. 1965.

3161. Brady, E. P. Maintenance under pressure. Golf Course Reporter. 29:(1)96–104. 1961.

3162. Brady, G. T. Summit Hall Turf Farm situated amidst megalopolis of 30 million. Weeds, Trees and Turf. 5(6):27–30. 1966.

3163. ______. Sod production is not for sissies. Turf-Grass Times. 3(4):1,18. 1968.

3164. Brandon, A. L. Establishment of turf and erosion control. The Greenskeepers' Reporter. 13:7, 8, 20, 21. 1945.

3165. Brandt, G. H. Potential impact of sodium and calcium chloride de-icing mixtures on roadside soils and plants. Highway Research Abstracts. 42(12):46. 1972.

3166. Brandt, J. Problems in golf course management. Illinois Turfgrass Conference. pp. 44–46. 1960.

3167. ______. Preparation for motorized carts. Proceedings of Midwest Regional Turf Conference. pp. 28–29. 1955.

3168. ______. Arsenicals and their uses. Proceedings of the Midwest Regional Turf Conference. pp. 59–61. 1959.

3169. ______. Second year crabgrass control. Proceedings of the Midwest Regional Turf Conference. pp. 19–21. 1960.

3170. ______. Unwatered fairways. Proceedings of Midwest Regional Turf Conference. pp. 24–26. 1965.

3171. ______. Ten years of decisions. Midwest Regional Turf Conference Proceedings. pp. 57–60. 1969.

3173. ______. Expanding responsibility and authority. Midwest Regional Turf Conference Proceedings. pp. 15–18. 1972.

3174. Brandt, S. A. The effects of spray droplet size on the efficacy of 2, 4-D sprays. M. S. Thesis. University of Saskatchewan. 1972.

3175. Brank, V. C. J. R. Mackay, S. Freyman, D. G. Pearce. Needle ice and seedling establishment in southwestern British Columbia. Canadian Journal of Plant Science. 47:135–139. 1967.

3176. Brann, W. R. Soil and water conservation in an urban city. Proceedings, Fourth Annual Tennessee Turfgrass Conference. p. 52–53. 1970.

3177. Brannen, F. A. The trend in seed mixes. Proceedings of University of Florida Turf-Grass Management Conference. 8:94–96. 1960.

3178. Branson, F. A. Two new factors of affecting resistance of grasses to grazing. Journal of Range Management. 6(3):165–171. 1953.

3179. Branson, F. A., R. F. Miller, and I. S. McQueen. Plant communities and soil moisture relationships near Denver, Colorado. Ecology. 46(3):311–319. 1965.

3180. Branson, R. L. Soil amendments—what can they really do? Southern California Turfgrass Institute Proceedings. pp. 16–17. 1959.

3181. ______. Soil amendments—what can they really do? Northern California Turfgrass Institute Proceedings. pp. 16–17. 1960.

3182. ______. Salinity in relation turfgrass. California Turfgrass Culture. 11(4):-27–28. 1961.

3183. ______. Soil amendments—what can they really do? California Turfgrass Culture. 11(1):7–8. 1961.

3184. ______. Better answers with soil and plant analyses. University of California Nursery, Landscape Tree, and Turf Conference Proceedings. pp. 13–1 to 13–3. 1965.

3185. ______. Better answers with soil and plant analyses. California Turfgrass Culture. 16(1):1–2. 1966.

3186. ______. Water quality for turfgrass irrigation. Proceedings 6th Annual Turfgrass Sprinkler Irrigation Conference. 6:18–21. 1968.

3187. Brant, F. H. Mulching practices and materials. Roadside Development. 928:-24–36. 1961.

3188. Brant, F. H. and M. H. Ferguson. Safety and beauty for highways. Yearbook Separate 2036. pp. 315–318. 1948.

3189. Brant, R. E. Hard seed in crownvetch. Second Crownvetch Symposium—The Pennsylvania State University. 6:57–59. 1968.

3190. Brant, R. E., G. W. McKee, and R. W. Cleveland. Effect of chemical and physical treatment on hard seed of Penngift crownvetch. Crop Science. 11(1):1–6. 1971.

3191. Brantley, C. O. The Japanese beetle bows out. Golfdom. 19(3):18. 1945.

3192. ______. Japanese beetle grub control. The Greenkeeper's Reporter. 13:19. 1945.

3193. Brathwaite, C. W. D. *Colocasia esculenta,* a new host of *Meloidogyne incognita* in Trinidad. The Plant Disease Reporter. 56(7):618. 1972.

3194. Brauen, S. E. Seed coat histology, germination, dormancy, and seedling drouth tolerance of Lehman lovegrass, *Eragrostis lehmanniana* Nees. PhD. Thesis. University of Arizona. 148 pp. 1967.

3195. Bray, J. R. The chlorophyll content of some native and managed plant communities in Central Minnesota. American Journal of Botany. 48:313–333. 1960.

3196. Bray, R. H. Nitrates tests for soils and plant tissues. Soil Science. 60:219–221. 1945.

3197. Brazeau, W. C. Changing to turf management. Midwest Regional Turf Conference Proceedings. pp. 13–15. 1972.

3198. Breakwell, E. Popular description of grasses: The rye or *Lolium* grasses. Agricultural Gazette. N.S. Wales. 29:274–281. 1918.

3199. Brecheen, K. G. Transmission of short wave radiation through forest canopy. Research Note. U.S. Weather Bureau Coop. Snow Investigation. p. 115. 1951.

3200. Bredakis, E. J. Interaction between height of cut and various nutrient levels on the development of turfgrass roots and tops. M.S. Thesis. University of Massachusetts. 91 pp. 1959.

3201. ______. Uptake of potassium. Turf

Clippings. University of Massachusetts. 1(8):A-59 to A-61. 1963.

3202. ______. Stabilization of fly ash by means of vegetation and its possible use as a soil amendment. Final Report. Department of Plant and Soil Science. University of Massachusetts. pp. 1–18. 1966.

3203. Bredakis, E. J. and H. Page. Can flyash support plant life? Turf Bulletin. Massachusetts Turf & Lawn Grass Council. 3(3):-3–4. 1966.

3204. Bredakis, E. J. and E. C. Roberts. The response of turfgrass roots to clipping and fertilization practices. Agronomy Abstracts. p. 88. 1959.

3205. Bredakis, E. J. and J. E. Steckel. Breakdown of organic nitrogen fertilizers used in turf production. Agronomy Abstracts. p. 69. 1960.

3206. ______. Leachable nitrogen from soils incubated with turfgrass fertilizers. Agronomy Journal. 55(2):145–146. 1963.

3207. Bredakis, E. J. and J. M. Zak. Timing of seeding throughout the growing season. Ohio Short Course on Roadside Development. 24:65–69. 1965.

3208. ______. Timing of seeding. Turf Bulletin. Massachusetts Turf & Lawn Grass Council. 3(1):18–20. 1966.

3209. ______. Turf along Massachusetts highways. Turf Bulletin. Massachusetts Turf & Lawn Grass Council. 3(2):3–4. 1966.

3210. Bredakis, E. J., W. G. Colby, and H. Page. Stabilization of fly ash by means of vegetation. Agronomy Abstracts. p. 34. 1966.

3211. Bredakis, E. J., W. G. Colby, and M. E. Weeks. The utilization of potassium from different sources by four turfgrass species. Agronomy Abstracts. p. 104. 1964.

3212. Breece, J. B. Winter green turf. Divot News. 9(7):2. 1970.

3213. Breece, J. R., W. B. Davis, and V. B. Youngner. Overseeding bermudagrass fairways. California Turfgrass Culture. 20(3):17–19. 1970.

3214. Breed, C. H. J. Crownvetch as an aid to strip mine reclamation. Mining Congress Journal. 47(4):70–71. 1961.

3215. Breland, H. L. The collection and handling of soil samples. Proceedings 3rd Annual University of Florida Turf-Grass Management Conference. 3:104–107. 1955.

3216. Brennan, E. Air pollution damage to vegetation in New Jersey with a consideration of turfgrasses. Rutgers University Short Course in Turf Management Proceedings. pp. 1–4. 1971.

3217. Brennan, E. and P. M. Halisky. Response of turfgrass cultivators to ozone and sulfur dioxide in the atmosphere. Rutgers University Journal Series. Paper No. 3953. May, 1970.

3218. Brennan, F. J. Water systems for golf courses. Proceedings of the Mid-Atlantic Association of Golf Course Superintendents. pp. 22–27. 1954.

3219. Brescia, B. R. Public golf operation and artificial grass. 40th International Turfgrass Conference and Show. pp. 11–13. 1969.

3220. Bresler, E. and W. D. Kemper. Soil water evaporation as affected by wetting methods and crust formation. Soil Science Society of America Proceedings. 34(1):3–8. 1970.

3221. Bresler, E., W. D. Kemper, and R. J. Hanks. Infiltration, redistribution, and subsequent evaporation of water from soil as affected by wetting rate and hysteresis. Soil Science Society of America Proceedings. 33(6):832–839. 1969.

3222. Brett, C. H. What every turf man should know about turf insects. Proceedings of the Annual Oklahoma-Texas Turf Conference. 5:69–75. 1950.

3223. Bretzlaff, C. Fungicide herbicide use on fairways. Proceedings of Midwest Regional Turf Conference. pp. 45–46. 1959.

3224. Brewster, J. L. and P. B. Tinker. Nutrient cation flows in soil around plant roots. Soil Science Society of America. 34(3):-421–426. 1970.

3225. Brewster, R. H. An economic study of the Florida cut sod industry. M.S.A. Thesis. University of Florida, Gainesville. 33 pp. 1965.

3226. Brien, R. M. Diseases of turf and their control. New Zealand Institute for Turf Culture Newsletter. 30:10–11. 1964.

3227. Briggs, G. R. Lawns. Gardening in the South. A.T. De La Mare Co., Inc. New York. pp. 31–44. 1931.

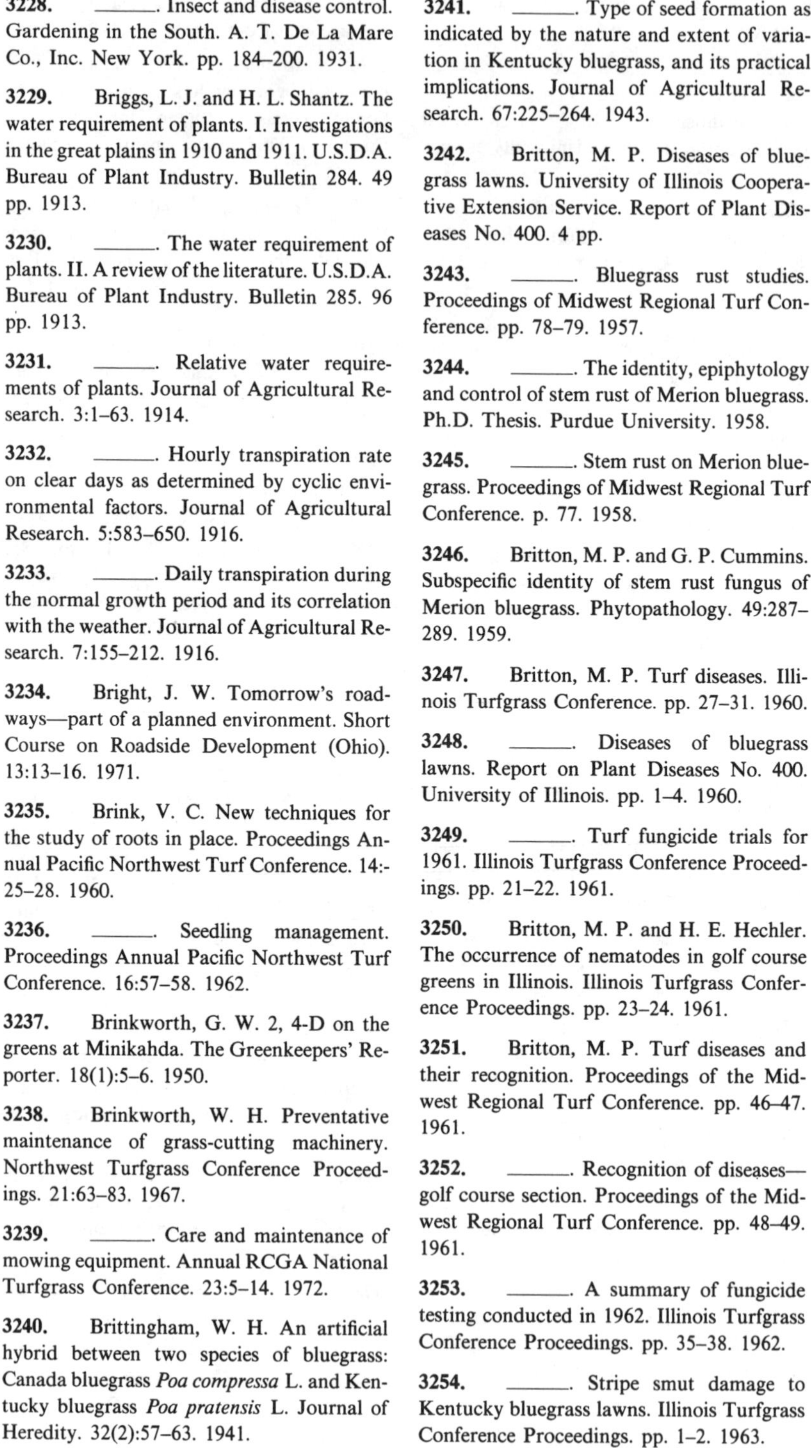

3228. ______. Insect and disease control. Gardening in the South. A. T. De La Mare Co., Inc. New York. pp. 184–200. 1931.

3229. Briggs, L. J. and H. L. Shantz. The water requirement of plants. I. Investigations in the great plains in 1910 and 1911. U.S.D.A. Bureau of Plant Industry. Bulletin 284. 49 pp. 1913.

3230. ______. The water requirement of plants. II. A review of the literature. U.S.D.A. Bureau of Plant Industry. Bulletin 285. 96 pp. 1913.

3231. ______. Relative water requirements of plants. Journal of Agricultural Research. 3:1–63. 1914.

3232. ______. Hourly transpiration rate on clear days as determined by cyclic environmental factors. Journal of Agricultural Research. 5:583–650. 1916.

3233. ______. Daily transpiration during the normal growth period and its correlation with the weather. Journal of Agricultural Research. 7:155–212. 1916.

3234. Bright, J. W. Tomorrow's roadways—part of a planned environment. Short Course on Roadside Development (Ohio). 13:13–16. 1971.

3235. Brink, V. C. New techniques for the study of roots in place. Proceedings Annual Pacific Northwest Turf Conference. 14:-25–28. 1960.

3236. ______. Seedling management. Proceedings Annual Pacific Northwest Turf Conference. 16:57–58. 1962.

3237. Brinkworth, G. W. 2, 4-D on the greens at Minikahda. The Greenkeepers' Reporter. 18(1):5–6. 1950.

3238. Brinkworth, W. H. Preventative maintenance of grass-cutting machinery. Northwest Turfgrass Conference Proceedings. 21:63–83. 1967.

3239. ______. Care and maintenance of mowing equipment. Annual RCGA National Turfgrass Conference. 23:5–14. 1972.

3240. Brittingham, W. H. An artificial hybrid between two species of bluegrass: Canada bluegrass *Poa compressa* L. and Kentucky bluegrass *Poa pratensis* L. Journal of Heredity. 32(2):57–63. 1941.

3241. ______. Type of seed formation as indicated by the nature and extent of variation in Kentucky bluegrass, and its practical implications. Journal of Agricultural Research. 67:225–264. 1943.

3242. Britton, M. P. Diseases of bluegrass lawns. University of Illinois Cooperative Extension Service. Report of Plant Diseases No. 400. 4 pp.

3243. ______. Bluegrass rust studies. Proceedings of Midwest Regional Turf Conference. pp. 78–79. 1957.

3244. ______. The identity, epiphytology and control of stem rust of Merion bluegrass. Ph.D. Thesis. Purdue University. 1958.

3245. ______. Stem rust on Merion bluegrass. Proceedings of Midwest Regional Turf Conference. p. 77. 1958.

3246. Britton, M. P. and G. P. Cummins. Subspecific identity of stem rust fungus of Merion bluegrass. Phytopathology. 49:287–289. 1959.

3247. Britton, M. P. Turf diseases. Illinois Turfgrass Conference. pp. 27–31. 1960.

3248. ______. Diseases of bluegrass lawns. Report on Plant Diseases No. 400. University of Illinois. pp. 1–4. 1960.

3249. ______. Turf fungicide trials for 1961. Illinois Turfgrass Conference Proceedings. pp. 21–22. 1961.

3250. Britton, M. P. and H. E. Hechler. The occurrence of nematodes in golf course greens in Illinois. Illinois Turfgrass Conference Proceedings. pp. 23–24. 1961.

3251. Britton, M. P. Turf diseases and their recognition. Proceedings of the Midwest Regional Turf Conference. pp. 46–47. 1961.

3252. ______. Recognition of diseases—golf course section. Proceedings of the Midwest Regional Turf Conference. pp. 48–49. 1961.

3253. ______. A summary of fungicide testing conducted in 1962. Illinois Turfgrass Conference Proceedings. pp. 35–38. 1962.

3254. ______. Stripe smut damage to Kentucky bluegrass lawns. Illinois Turfgrass Conference Proceedings. pp. 1–2. 1963.

3255. ______. Some important turf diseases. Illinois Turfgrass Conference Proceedings. pp. 1–3. 1964.

3256. ______. Influence of management and microenvironment on turfgrass disease incidence. Agronomy Abstracts. p. 44. 1965.

3257. ______. The selection and use of fungicides for disease control on bentgrass. Sixth Illinois Turfgrass Conference Proceedings. pp. 1–4. 1965.

3258. ______. Factors influencing turfgrass disease development. 9th Illinois Turfgrass Conference Proceedings. pp. 1–6. 1968.

3259. Britton, M. P. and J. D. Butler. Resistance of seven Kentucky bluegrass varieties to stem rust. The Plant Disease Reporter. 49(8):708–710. 1965.

3260. ______. Control of bentgrass diseases. Illinois Research. 8(1):10–11. 1966.

3261. Britton, M. P. and G. B. Cummins. The reaction of species of *Poa* and other grasses to *Puccinia striiformis.* Plant Disease Reporter. 40(7):643–645. 1956.

3262. Britton, M. P. and D. P. Rogers. *Olpidium brassicae* and *Polymorpha graminis* in roots of creeping bent in golf putting greens. Mycologia. 55(6):758–763. 1963.

3263. Britton, M. P. and M. C. Shurtleff. Turfgrass disease control. Proceedings of the Midwest Regional Turf Conference. pp. 23–27. 1963.

3264. Britton, W. E. Three injurious insects recently introduced into Connecticut. Journal of Economic Entomology. 19(3):-540–545. 1926.

3265. Broach, R.V.D. and F. E. Terrio. An aid to establishing vegetation in waterways. Ohio Short Course on Roadside Development. 19:66–69. 1960.

3266. Broadbent, F. E. Variables affecting A values as a measure of soil nitrogen availability. Soil Science. 110(1):19–23. 1970.

3267. Broadbent, F. E. and T. E. Lewis. Salt formation as a basis of urea retention in soils. Soil Science Society of America Proceedings. 28:292–294. 1964.

3268. Broadbent, F. E. and T. Nakashima. Plant recovery of immobilized nitrogen in greenhouse experiments. Soil Science Society of America Proceedings. 29:55–60. 1965.

3269. ______. Nitrogen immobilization in flooded soils. Soil Science Society of America Proceedings. 34(2):218–221. 1970.

3270. Broadbent, F. E., G. N. Hill, and K. B. Tyler. Movement of urea in soils. California Agriculture. 12(12):9–10. 1958.

3271. Broadfoot, W. C. Experiments on the chemical control of snow-mould of turf in Alberta. Scientific Agriculture. 16:615–618. 1936.

3272. ______. Snow-mould of turf in Alberta. Journal of Board of Greenkeeping Research. 5:182–183. 1938.

3273. Broadfoot, W. C. and M. W. Cormack. A low-temperature *Basidiomycete* causing early spring killing of grasses and legumes in Alberta. Phytopathology. 31:-1058–1059. 1941.

3274. Broadhurst, N. A., M. L. Montgomery, and V. H. Freed. Metabolism of 2-methoxy-3,6-dichlorobenzoic acid (dicamba) by wheat and bluegrass plants. Journal of Agricultural and Food Chemistry. 14(6):585–588. 1966.

3275. Brock, J. R. Grass under plastic. Golf Course Reporter. 32(10):62–64. 1964.

3276. ______. Grass under plastic. Parks, Golf Courses and Sports Grounds. 30(7):512,514. 1965.

3277. Brock, T. D. Antibiotics field extended to combat plant fungi. Golfdom. 27(6):60, 62. 1953.

3278. Brockman, J. S. The growth rate of grass as influenced by fertilizer nitrogen and stage of defoliation. Proceedings of the International Grassland Congress. 10:234–240. 1966.

3279. Brockman, J. S., C. M. Rope, and M. T. Stevens. A mathematical relationship between nitrogen input and output in cut grass swards. Journal of the British Grassland Society. 26(1):75–77. 1971.

3280. Brockman, J. S., P. G. Shaw, and K. M. Wolton. Fertilizer N and the yield of cut grass swards in eastern England. Journal of the British Grassland Society. 26(1):17–24. 1971.

3281. Brodie, B. B. and G. W. Burton. Nematode population reduction and growth response of bermuda turf as influenced by organic pesticide applications. The Plant Disease Reporter. 51(7):562–566. 1967.

3282. Brogdon, J. E. Are you handling pesticides safely. Florida Turf Association Bulletin. 2(1):3–5. 1955.

3283. ———. Insect problems. Control. University of Florida Turfgrass Conference Proceedings. 3:130–132. 1955.

3284. ———. Are you handling pesticides safely? Golf Course Reporter. 23(7):-16–21. 1955.

3285. ———. Insect development and principles of control. University of Florida Turfgrass Conference Proceedings. 5:27–29. 1957.

3286. ———. Lawn pest control guide. Florida Agricultural Extension Circular. 181:1–8. 1958.

3287. ———. Insect problems and control. University of Florida Turfgrass Conference Proceedings. 7:51–52. 1959.

3288. ———. Current lawn pest control recommendations. Proceedings of University of Florida Turf-Grass Management Conference. 8:88–89. 1960.

3289. ———. Lawn insect control recommendations for 1961–62. Proceedings of University of Florida Turf-Grass Management Conference. 9:154–156. 1961.

3290. ———. Lawn insect control recommendations for 1962–63. Proceedings University of Florida Turf-Grass Management Conference. 10:134–136. 1962.

3291. ———. The rest of the pests. Proceedings of University of Florida Turf-Grass Management Conference. 11:28–33. 1963.

3292. ———. Panel: pest control on greens. Proceedings Annual University of Florida Turf-Grass Management Conference. 12:84–86. 1964.

3293. ———. Pest control. Proceedings Annual University of Florida Turf-Grass Management Conference. 12:93–96. 1964.

3294. ———. Diagnosing lawn problems; insects. Proceedings 13th Annual University of Florida Turf-Grass Management Conference. 13:98–99. 1965.

3295. ———. Pesticide regulations and the turf-grass industry. Proceedings University of Florida Turf-Grass Management Conference. 18:42–44. 1970.

3296. Brogden, J. E., and S. H. Kerr. Home gardeners lawn insect control guide. Florida Agricultural Experiment Station Circular 213A. 1964.

3297. Brook, V. Use soap to vanquish cricket moles. Golfdom. 7(6):20. 1933.

3298. Brooks, C. R. Nitrogen nutrition and fertilization. Proceedings of the Annual Texas Turfgrass Conference. 19:27–30. 1964.

3299. ———. Growth of roots and tops of bermudagrass as related to aeration and drainage in stratified golf-green soils. Ph.D. Thesis, Texas A & M. 123 pp. 1966.

3300. Brooks, C. R. and R. E. Blaser. Effect of fertilizer slurries used with hydroseeding on seed viability. Highway Research Record. 53:30–34. 1963.

3301. Brooks, C. R. and J. R. Runkles. Growth of bermudagrass (*Cynodon dactylon* L.) as related to aeration and drainage in stratified golf green soils. Agronomy Abstracts. p. 57. 1968.

3302. Brooks, C., R. E. Blaser, and W. W. Moschler. The effect of fertilizer solutions on seed germination. Agronomy Abstracts. p. 88. 1959.

3303. Brooks, D. Is irrigation water the cause of your turf problems? Golf Course Operations. 4(1):12–14. 1966.

3304. Brooks, L. E. and E. C. Holt. Cool-season grasses in the Wichita valley. Texas Agricultural Experiment Station Progress Report. 1716:1–4. 1954.

3305. ———. Warm season grass tests in the Wichita valley. Texas Agricultural Experiment Station Progress Report. 1792:1–3. 1955.

3306. Brooks, W. F. Sprinkling the fairway. USGA Green Section Bulletin. 3(11):-288–290. 1923.

3307. Brooks, W. P. Top-dressing permanent mowings. 23rd Annual Report Massachusetts Agricultural Experiment Station. pp. 10–17. 1911.

3308. Brougham, R. W. Effect of intensity of defoliation on regrowth of pasture. Australian Journal of Agricultural Research. 7:377–387. 1956.

3309. ______. Interception of light by the foliage of pure and mixed stands of pasture plants. Australian Journal of Agricultural Research. 9(1):39–52. 1958.

3310. ______. The effects of season and weather on the growth rate of a ryegrass and clover pasture. New Zealand Journal of Agricultural Research. 2(2):283–296. 1959.

3311. ______. The relationship between the critical leaf area, total chlorophyll content, and maximum growth-rate of some pasture and crop plants. Annals of Botany. N.S. 24(96):463–474. 1960.

3312. Brougham, R. W. and A. C. Glenday. Grass growth in mid-summer: a re-interpretation of published data. Journal of the British Grassland Society. 22(2):100–107. 1967.

3313. Brower, P. Care of machinery. Proceedings Annual Texas Turfgrass Conference. 22:69–71. 1967.

3314. Brown, A. Beauty, upkeep, status push turf irrigation. Weeds, Trees and Turf. 9(3):26. 1970.

3315. ______. Mowing specifications and specifications of mowing costs. Proceedings of Southern California Turfgrass Institute. pp. 80–90. 1971.

3316. Brown, B. A. The effect of fertilizer on the soil, the botanical and chemical composition of the herbage, and the seasonal and total production of grassland in Connecticut. Report of 4th International Grassland Congress. 4:313–317. 1937.

3317. ______. Grasses for lawns, parks and athletic fields. Connecticut Agricultural College Extension Folder. 22:1–8. 1948.

3318. Brown, B. A. and R. I. Munsell. An evaluation of Kentucky bluegrass. Journal of the American Society of Agronomy. 37(4):259–267. 1945.

3319. Brown, B. A., and W. L. Slate. Maintenance and improvement of permanent pastures. Connecticut (Storrs) Agricultural Experiment Station Bulletin. 155:153–250. 1929.

3320. Brown, B. A., R. I. Munsell, and A. V. King. Fertilization and renovation of grazed permanent pastures. University of Connecticut Experiment Station Bulletin. 350:1–27. 1960.

3321. Brown, B. A., R. I. Munsell, R. F. Holt, and A. V. King. Soil reactions at various depths as influenced by time since application and amounts of limestone. Soil Science Society America Proceedings. 20:518–522. 1956.

3322. Brown, C. S. What happens to the potassium we use? University of Maine Turf Conference Proceedings. pp. 55–57. 1968.

3323. Brown, D. Methods of surveying and measuring vegetation. Bulletin 42 Commonwealth Bureau of Pastures and Field Crops, Farnham Royal, Bucks, England. pp. 43–49. 1954.

3324. ______. Where are we with grasses? Proceedings of the Midwest Regional Turf Conference. pp. 34–36. 1960.

3325. ______. Surveying the pre-emergent chemicals and ideas. Proceedings Midwest Regional Turf Conference. pp. 20–22. 1968.

3326. Brown, D. M. Seeds—facts and fancy. Midwest Regional Turf Conference Proceedings. pp. 74–75. 1971.

3327. Brown, E. Germination of Kentucky bluegrass. USDA Office of Experiment Stations Bulletin. 115:105–110. 1902.

3328. ______. The seeds of the bluegrasses. I. The germination, growing, handling, and adulteration of bluegrass seeds. USDA Bureau of Plant Industry Bulletin. 84:14. 1905.

3329. Brown, E. M. Some effects of temperature on the growth and chemical composition of certain pasture grasses. Missouri Agricultural Experiment Station Research Bulletin. 299:3–76. 1939.

3330. ______. Seasonal variations in the growth and chemical composition of Kentucky bluegrass. Missouri Agricultural Experiment Station. Research Bulletin 360:1–53. 1943.

3331. Brown, E. O. and R. N. Porter. An improved method of testing seeds of Kentucky bluegrass. Proceedings Association of

Official Seed Analysts of America. 27:44–49. 1935.

3332. Brown, G. E., H. Cole, and R. R. Nelson. Pathogenicity of *Curvularia* sp. to turfgrass. The Plant Disease Reporter. 56(1):59–63. 1972.

3333. Broslaw, J. Which kind of pipe? Developments in plastic pipe. Golf Course Reporter. 32 (6):36–38. 1964.

3334. Brown, H. E. and J. R. Thompson Summer water use by aspen, spruce and grassland in western Colorado. Journal of Forestry. 63(10):756–760. 1965.

3335. Brown, H. T. and W. E. Wilson. On the thermal emissivity of a green leaf in still and moving air. Proceedings of the Royal Society of London. Series B. 76(507):122–137. 1905.

3336. Brown, J. L. Some physical properties of organic soil materials. M.S. Thesis. University of Minnesota. 1972.

3337. Brown, J. R. Fertilizers and their behavior in soils. Proceedings of the Annual Missouri Lawn and Turf Conference. 8:17–28. 1967.

3338. Brown, K. W., and R. L. Duble. Physical characteristics of golf greens built to USGA Green Section specifications. Agronomy Abstracts. p. 61. 1972.

3339. Brown, L. A. A study of phosphorus penetration and availability in soils Soil Science. 39:277–287. 1935.

3340. Brown, L. D. Role of potash in turf production. Turf Clippings. University of Massachusetts. 4(1):A-17 to A-27. 1969.

3341. ______. Producing sturdy turf with potash. Annual RCGA National Turfgrass Conference. 21:8. 1970.

3342. Brown, L. R. Budgeting for golf course operations. Annual RCGA National Turfgrass Conference. 23:15–17. 1972.

3343. Brown, M. A. Report on overseeding studies. Proceedings of University of Florida Turf-Grass Management Conference. 9:87–88. 1961.

3344. ______. Effects of high phosphorus and arsenic on growth of Tifgreen and Everglades bermudagrasses. Proceedings University of Florida Turf-Grass Management Conference. 10:74–76. 1962.

3345. ______. Turf fertilizers for the future. Southern Turfgrass Association Conference Proceedings. pp. 38–41. 1967.

3346. ______. Fertility requirements of bermudagrass. Proceedings Florida Turfgrass Management Conference. 18:52–57. 1970.

3347. Brown, M. J., R. E. Luebs, and P. F. Pratt. Effect of temperature and coating thickness on the release of urea from resin-coated granules. Agronomy Journal. 58(2):-175–178. 1966.

3348. Brown, P. Panel on fertilizers for turf areas. Northwest Turf Conference Proceedings. 11:31–32. 1957.

3349. Brown, P. D. and L. Fryer. Turf fertilizer. Proceedings Annual Pacific Northwest Turf Conference. 7:32–35. 1953.

3350. Brown, P. E. Fertilizing lawn and garden soils. Iowa Agricultural Experiment Station Circular. 24:1–15. 1916.

3351. Brown, P. H. Ohio's progress report on roadside research. Ohio Short Course on Roadside Development. 21:81–86. 1962.

3352. Brown, R. Unusual fertility problems and their causes. Illinois Turfgrass Conference Proceedings. pp. 22–26. 1970.

3353. Brown, R. A. Lead arsenate vs. calcium arsenate for pre-emergent crabgrass control. Golf Course Reporter. 26(3):36. 1958.

3354. ______. Arsenicals. Proceedings of the Midwest Regional Turf Conference. pp. 54–55. 1959.

3355. Brown, R. H. Control of broadleaf weeds in turf. Research Report of the National Weed Committee. Eastern Section. 6:-134. 1961.

3356. ______. Control of chickweed in turf. Research Report of the National Weed Committee. Eastern Section. 6:135. 1961.

3357. ______. Control of broadleaf weeds in turf. Research Report of the National Weed Committee. Eastern Section. 7:-97–99. 1962.

3358. ______. Control of chickweed in turf. Research Report of the National Weed Committee. Eastern Section. 7:99–100. 1962.

3359. ______. Crabgrass control in turf. Research Report of the National Weed Committee. Eastern Section. 7:100–102. 1962.

3360. ______. Postemergence crabgrass control in turf. Research Report of the National Weed Committee. Eastern Section. 8:-112–113. 1963.

3361. ______. Weed control with mixtures of 2, 4-D, MCPP, MCPA, and/or dicamba. Research Report of the National Weed Committee. Eastern Section. 8:114. 1963.

3362. ______. Weed control in turf. Research Report of the National Weed Committee. Eastern Section. 8:114–116. 1963.

3363. ______. Factors that influence grass growth. Southeastern Turfgrass Conference. 23:1–14. 1969.

3364. Brown, R. H., and R. E. Blaser. Relationships between reserve carbohydrate accumulation and growth rate in orchardgrass and tall fescue. Crop Science. 5:577–582. 1965.

3365. ______. Soil moisture and temperature effects on growth and soluble carbohydrates of orchardgrass *(Dactylis glomerata).* Crop Science. 10(3):213–216. 1970.

3366. Brown, R. H. and V. E. Gracen. Distribution of the post-illumination CO_2 burst among grasses. Crop Science. 12(1):-30–33. 1972.

3367. Brown, R. H., R. B. Cooper, and R. E. Blaser. Effects of leaf age on efficiency. Crop Science. 6:206–209. 1966.

3368. Brown, R. H. S. Large scale renovations Leicester City football pitch. Journal of the Greenkeeping Research Institute. 7:-244–250. 1949.

3369. Brown, R. H. W. Lawns and grasslands. Gardening Complete. Fabor and Fabor London. pp. 313–331. 1968.

3370. Brown, R. L. and A. L. Hafenrichter. Factors influencing the production and use of Beachgrass and Dunegrass clones for erosion control: I. Effect of date of planting. Journal of the American Society of Agronomy. 40(6):512–521. 1948.

3371. ______. Factors influencing the production and use of Beachgrass and dunegrass clones for erosion control. II. Influence of density of planting. Journal of the American Society of Agronomy. 40(7):603–609. 1948.

3372. ______. Factors influencing the production and use of beachgrass and dunegrass clones for erosion control. III. Influence of kinds and amounts of fertilizer and production. Journal of the American Society of Agronomy. 40(8):677–684. 1948.

3373. Brown, W. L. Chromosome complements of five species of *Poa* with an analysis of variation in *Poa pratensis.* American Journal of Botany. 26:717–723. 1939.

3374. ______. The cytogenetics of *Poa pratensis.* Annual Missouri Botanical Garden. 28:493–522. 1941.

3375. ______. The practical aspects of sexual and asexual reproduction in turf grasses. Turf Culture. 2(4):246–252. 1942.

3376. Brown, W. V. Leaf anatomy and grass systematics. Botanical Gazette. 119:-170–178. 1958.

3377. ______. The epiblast and coleoptile of the grass embryo. Bulletin of Torrey Botanical Club. 86:13–16. 1959.

3378. Brown, W. V. and W. H. P. Emery. Persistent nucleoli and grass systematics. American Journal of Botany. 44:585–590. 1957.

3379. Brown, W. V. and S. C. Johnson. The fine structure of the grass guard cells. American Journal of Botany. 49:110. 1962.

3380. Brown, W. V., C. Heinsch, and W. H. P. Emery. The organization of the grass shoot apex and systematics. American Journal of Botany. 44:590–595. 1957.

3381. Bruce, D. A. Flexibility of controls. 41st International Turfgrass Conference and Show. pp. 31–32. 1970.

3382. ______. Spring pump tips. A Patch of Green. Michigan and Border Cities CGSA Publication. pp. 4–5. April, 1971.

3383. ______. Irrigation drainage time. A Patch of Green. Michigan and Border Cities GCSA Publication. pp. 7–8. November, 1971.

3384. Bruneau, A. H. Morphological and cytological study of cultivars of red fescue. M.S. Thesis. University of Rhode Island. 39 pp. 1970.

3385. Brussell, G. E. and V. Perry. New developments in nematode control. Parts 3 and 4. Turf-Grass Times. 1(2):18–19. 1965.

3386. Bryan, O. C. Yellowing of centipede grass and its control. University of Florida Agricultural Experiment Station Press Bulletin. 450. 1933.

3387. Bryan, P. J. Is there a future for meadow grasses in sports fields? Parks, Golf Courses, and Sports Grounds. 38(1):44–48. 1972.

3388. Bryan, W. E. Hastening the germination of Bermuda grass seed by the sulfuric acid treatment. Journal of the American Society of Agronomy. 10:279–281. 1918.

3389. Bryant, C. New chemical herbicides for weeds and grasses. Greenkeeping Superintendents Association. National Turf Conference. 21:65–71. 1950.

3390. Bryant, H. T., R. E. Blaser, and J. R. Peterson. Effect of trampling by cattle on bluegrass yield and soil compaction of a meadowville loam. Agronomy Journal. 64(3):331–334. 1972.

3391. Bryant, J. P. Phosphorus behavior in plants and soils. Ohio Turfgrass Conference Proceedings. pp. 27–32. 1970.

3392. ______. The soil chemically. Midwest Regional Turf Conference Proceedings. pp. 53–55. 1971.

3393. Bryant, M. D. Lawn grasses for New Mexico. New Mexico Agricultural Extension Service. 1963.

3394. Bryant, T. A. Disappearance of atrazine, DCPA, diuron, linuson, norea, prometryne, triluralia from the soil. M. S. Thesis. University of Tennessee. 117 pp. 1967.

3395. Bryant, W. Your budget, fact or fiction. USGA Green Section Record. 9(2):-6–7. 1971.

3396. Bryson, H. R. Insect control on turf areas. Central Plains Turfgrass Conference Proceedings. pp. 74–80. 1950.

3397. Brzeski, M. W., C. W. Laughlin, J. M. Vargas, Jr., D. K. McCallu, and M. K. Hanna. Occurrence of cyst nematodes *(Heterodera spp.)* in Michigan. The Plant Disease Reporter. 55(5):399. 1971.

3398. Buch, M. L. Some roadside comments. Midwest Regional Turf Conference Proceedings. pp. 72–73. 1970.

3399. Buchanan, W. D. Lawn and turf pests in Utah. Weeds Trees and Turf. 11(8):-34. 1972.

3400. Buchanan, W. G. Research and innovation means economy. USGA Green Section Record. 9(6):6–8. 1971.

3401. ______. Bridges serve the golf course. USGA Green Section Record. 10(5):-11–13. 1972.

3402. Buchanan, W. G., and S. J. Zontek. 1971—A year of unique problems. Proceedings, 1972 3-Day Turf Courses, Rutgers University. pp. 54–55. 1972.

3403. Bucher, G. E. and A. P. Arthur. Disease in a field population of the introduced Essex skipper, *Thymelicus lineola (Ochs) (Lepidoptera: Hesperidae).* Canadian Entomologist. 93(11):1048–1049. 1961.

3404. Buck, R. A. Speedy golf. Midwest Regional Turf Conference Proceedings. pp. 13–14. 1970.

3405. Buckholtz, K. P. The sensitivity of quackgrass to various chlorinated benzoic acids. WSSA Abstract. pp. 33–34. 1958.

3406. Buckley, H. E. Semi-automatic irrigation equipment. University of Florida Turfgrass Management Conference Proceedings. 13:50–53. 1965.

3407. ______. Understanding irrigation terminology. Turf-Grass Times. 2(2):6. 1966.

3408. ______. Sprinkler distribution patterns. Turf-Grass Times. 2(3):10, 13. 1967.

3409. ______. Irrigation talk: engineering of system effects cost of growing turf. Turf-Grass Times. 2(5):9, 18. 1967.

3410. ______. Sprinkler spacing. Turf-Grass Times. 2(6):9, 14. 1967.

3411. ______. Irrigation talk. Turf-Grass Times. 3(1):6, 17. 1967.

3412. ______. Tips on buying an irrigation system. Turf-Grass Times. 3(2):9–12. 1967.

3413. ______. Watering practices. University of Florida Turfgrass Management Conference Proceedings. 17:30–35. 1969.

3414. ______. The high cost of transpiration. Turf-grass Times. 5(6):6, 22. 1970.

3415. Buckner, R. C. Cross-compatibility of annual and perennial ryegrass with tall fescue. Agronomy Journal. 52(7):409–410. 1960.

3416. ______. Use of polyethylene tubes for selfing tall fescue. Agronomy Journal. 52(7):410–411. 1960.

3417. Buckner, R. C. and P. B. Burrus. Tall fescue improvement. Kentucky Agricultural Experiment Station Annual Report. 73:18–19. 1960.

3418. ______. Bluegrass breeding. Kentucky Agricultural Experiment Station Annual Report. 73:19–20. 1960.

3419. ______. Tall fescue improvement. Kentucky Agricultural Experiment Station Annual Report. 74:24–25. 1961.

3420. ______. Kentucky bluegrass improvement. Kentucky Agricultural Experimental Station Annual Report. 74:25–26. 1961.

3421. ______. Kentucky bluegrass varieties. Kentucky Agricultural Experiment Station Annual Report. 75:16–17. 1962.

3422. ______. Yields of orchardgrass varieties. Kentucky Agricultural Experiment Station Annual Report. 75:17. 1962.

3423. ______. Tall fescue improvement. Kentucky Agricultural Experiment Station Annual Report. 75:17–18. 1962.

3424. ______. Tall fescue improvement. Kentucky Agricultural Experiment Station Annual Report. 76:27–28. 1963.

3425. ______. Kentucky bluegrass improvement. Kentucky Agricultural Experiment Station Annual Report. 76:28–29. 1963.

3426. ______. Tall fescue improvement. Kentucky Agricultural Experiment Station Annual Report. 77:28–29. 1964.

3427. ______. Kentucky bluegrass improvement. Kentucky Agricultural Experiment Station Annual Report. 77:33. 1964.

3428. ______. Tall fescue improvement. Kentucky Agricultural Experiment Station Annual Report. 78:26. 1965.

3429. ______. Kentucky bluegrass improvement. Kentucky Agricultural Experiment Station Annual Report. 78:26–27. 1965.

3430. ______. Tall fescue breeding. Kentucky Agricultural Experiment Station Annual Report. 79:27–28. 1966.

3431. ______. Kentucky bluegrass breeding. Kentucky Agricultural Experiment Station Annual Report. 79:28–29. 1966.

3432. ______. Breeding in cool season grasses for turf improvement. Kentucky Agricultural Experiment Station Annual Report. 81:31. 1968.

3433. Buckner, R. C., H. D. Hill and P. B. Burrus. Some characteristics of perennial and annual ryegrass X tall fescue hybrids and of the *Amphidiploid* progenies of annual ryegrass X tall fescue. Crop Science. 1:75–80. 1961.

3434. Buckner, R. C., G. T. Webster and P. B. Burrus. Breeding of pasture, hay, and turf grasses. Kentucky Agricultural Experiment Station Annual Report. 84:24–25. 1971.

3435. Buckner, R. C., P. B. Burrus, L. Bush and G. T. Webster. Breeding of pasture, hay and turf grasses. Kentucky Agricultural Experiment Station Annual Report. 83:21–22. 1970.

3436. Buckner, R. C., B. C. Pass, P. B. Burrus and J. R. Todd. Reaction of Kentucky bluegrass strains to feeding by the sod webworm. Crop Science. 9(6):744–746. 1969.

3437. Buckner, R. C., C. M. Rincker, P. B. Burrus, R. M. Cressman, and C. S. Garrison. Effects of two diverse environments on seed production characteristics of tall fescue hybrid derivatives. Crop Science. 12(3):264–268. 1972.

3438. Buckner, W. A. Golf course irrigation. The National Greenkeeper. 1(8):13–14, 38. 1927.

3439. Budd, E. G. Preliminary studies into the biology and cultural control of *Poa trivialis* in cereal and grass seed crops. 10th British Weed Control Conference Proceedings. 1:314–319. 1970.

3440. ______. The selective control of *Poa trivialis, Poa annua, Alopecurus myosuroides* and some broad leaved weeds in grass crops grown for seed. 10th British Weed Control Conference Proceedings. 2:500–505. 1970.

3441. ______. Seasonal germination patterns of *Poa trivialis* L. and subsequent plant behavior. Weed Research. 10(3):243–249. 1970.

3442. Budd, E. G. and J. P. Shildrick. Preliminary report of studies on *Poa trivialis* (rough-stalked meadow grass) in grass seed crop. 9th British Weed Control Conference Proceedings. 1:520–526. 1968.

3443. Budd, J. How southern greensmen meet their special course problems. Golfdom. 14(8):13–16, 31–34. 1940.

3444. Bugsch, J. A. Installation of high quality sod. Rutgers University. College of Agriculture and Environmental Science. Lawn and Utility Turf Section. p. 43. 1969.

3445. Bukey, F. S. and J. E. Weaver. Effects of frequent clipping on the underground food reserves of certain prairie grasses. Ecology. 20(2):246–252. 1939.

3446. Bull, F. L. Soil conservation. Proceedings of the Mid-Atlantic Association of Greenkeepers Conference. pp. 58–60. 1950.

3447. Bull, T. A. Photosynthetic efficiencies and photorespiration in calvin cycle and C_4-dicarboxylic acid plants. Crop Science. 9(6):726–731. 1969.

3448. Bunn, L. Management practices help control turf diseases. Turf Clippings, University of Massachusetts. 4(1):3–4. 1969.

3449. Burch, L. Nematodes in the turf. The Greenkeepers' Reporter. 24(5):5–7. 1956.

3450. Burdett, P. E. How is your potash today? The Greenkeepers' Reporter. 6(4):26, 42–43. 1938.

3451. ______. Report Lawn Sinox effective in weed control. Golfdom. 20(2):49–50. 1946.

3452. ______. New materials and the commercial dealer. Midwest Regional Turf Conference Proceedings. pp. 32–34. 1952.

3453. ______. Weed control for healthy turf. Midwest Regional Turf Conference Proceedings. pp. 25–28. 1956.

3454. Bures, I. F. A method for investigating and evaluating lawns on sports grounds. CSc. Leipzig. East Germany. 1966.

3455. ______. The course for caretakers of lawn-covered grounds. Praha. Czechoslovakia. 1967.

3456. ______. Method of analyzing and evaluating the lawn sports grounds. Praha. 1967.

3457. ______. The present state and problems relating to research of lawns in Czechoslovakia. Bruno. 1969.

3458. ______. The influence of mowing mechanisms on playground grass stands in the year of sowing. First Czechoslovak Symposium of Sportturf Proceedings. pp. 157–165. 1969.

3459. ______. Reaction of Czechoslovak grass varieties to varying height and frequency of mowing. First Czechoslovak Symposium of Sportturf Proceedings. pp. 209–216. 1969.

3460. ______. Establishment and maintenance of sporting places under grass cover. Praha. 1969.

3461. Burgess, A. C. Effect of over-acidity on sports turf. New Zealand Institute for Turf Culture Newsletter. 12:10–11. 1961.

3462. ______. Effect of fertilizers on grass establishment. New Zealand Institute for Turf Culture Newsletter. 13:11. 1961.

3463. ______. Height of mowing is important on greens. New Zealand Institute for Turf Culture Newsletter. 33:14–15. 1964.

3464. ______. Soils and their management in greenkeeping. New Zealand Institute for Turf Culture Newsletter. 37:3–4. 1965.

3465. Burgess, R. F. Ditch liners, their ability to prevent erosion. 28th Short Course on Roadside Development. Ohio Department of Highways. 28:109–112. 1969.

3466. Burgis, D. S. Nut grass control with 2, 4-D in Florida. University of Florida Agricultural Experiment Station Circular. S–38:1–5. 1951.

3467. Burke, F. C. Erosion control with helicopter, ingenuity and hydraulic mulching. Ohio Short Course on Roadside Development. 30:97–100. 1971.

3468. Burke, M. Vegetative vs. seeded greens. The National Greenkeeper. 1(3):19–20. 1927.

3469. ______. Some tips on new construction. The National Greenkeeper. 2(3):-10, 38. 1928.

3470. Burkhardt, F. A. Brown patch from compost. The National Greenkeeper. 2(12):15–16. 1928.

3471. Burkhardt, H. A. Water and how to use it. The National Greenkeeper. 3(7):28. 1929.

3472. Burkhart, L. Highlights of the Arizona Turf Conference. Arizona Turf Conference Proceedings. pp. 1–2. 1959.

3473. Burman, P. D. and T. L. Loudon. Evapotranspiration and irrigation efficiency studies. Wyoming Agricultural Experiment Station Research Journal. 10:16. 1967.

3475. Burnett, W. F. Sports grounds: Maintenance of grass cover. The West of Scotland Agricultural College Advisory Leaflet No. 20.

3476. Burnett, W. R. Krilium experiments. Annual Northwest Turf Conference Proceedings. 7:37–38. 1953.

3477. Burns, E. R. and R. Dickens. Turf: recommended practices—additions or changes. Southern Weed Science Society Research Report. 24:81. 1971.

3478. ______. Turf: preliminary evaluation of herbicides. Southern Weed Science Society Research Report. 24:86. 1971.

3479. ______. Turf: recommended practices. Southern Weed Science Society Research Report. 25:112. 1972.

3480. ______. Turf: preliminary evaluation of herbicides. Southern Weed Science Society Research Report. 25:117. 1972.

3481. Burns, F. C. Arsenicals for preemergence crabgrass control. Midwest Regional Turf Conference Proceedings. p. 57. 1959.

3482. Burns, J. C., H. D. Gross, W. W. Woodhouse, and L. A. Nelson Seasonal dry matter distribution and annual yields of a cool-season sward as altered by frequency and rate of nitrogen application. Agronomy Journal. 62(4):453–458. 1970.

3483. Burns, R. E. Response of three bermudagrass varieties and reduced light intensity. Agronomy Abstracts. p. 68. 1970.

3484. ______. Yield and quality of different vertical layers of a tall fescue sward. Agronomy Journal. 62(6):803–804. 1970.

3485. ______. Turfgrass research reports 1969–1970, Georgia. Southern Regional Turf Research Committee Report, Virginia Polytechnic Institute. 6 pp. 1970.

3486. ______. Environmental factors affecting root development of bermudagrass cuttings. Agronomy Abstracts. p. 45. 1971.

3487. ______. Methods of improving late season rooting of bermudagrass sod. Agronomy Abstracts. p. 61. 1972.

3488. ______. Environmental factors affecting root development and reserve carbohydrates of bermudagrass cuttings. Agronomy Journal. 64(1):44–45. 1972.

3489. Burr, R. J. Factors influencing the effectiveness of activated carbon used to protect newly seeded grasses from herbicides. M.S. Thesis, Oregon State University. 57 pp. 1970.

3490. Burr, S. British economic grasses. Edward Arnold, London. 1933.

3492. Burris, J. S. and E. W. Carson. Carbohydrate metabolism in orchardgrass *(Dactylis glomerata* L.) as affected by age. Crop Science. 11(2):171–174. 1971.

3493. Burris, J. S., R. H. Brown and R. E. Blaser. Evaluation of reserve carbohydrates in Midland bermudagrass (*Cynodon dactylon* L.). Crop Science. 7(1):22–24. 1967.

3494. Burson, B. L. and H. W. Bennett. Chromosome numbers, microsporogenesis, and mode of reproduction of seven *Paspalum* species. Crop Science. 11(2):292–294. 1971.

3497. Burt, E. O. New herbicides on the horizon. University of Florida Turfgrass Management Conference Proceedings. 2:22–24. 1954.

3498. ______. Weed problems: control. University of Florida Turfgrass Management Conference Proceedings. 3:150–151. 1955.

3499. ______. Special weed problems. University of Florida Turfgrass Management Conference Proceedings. 4:94–98. 1956.

Entries numbered 3567a to 3599a appear after 3598.

3500. ______. A. Factors causing weed problems. Proceedings University of Florida

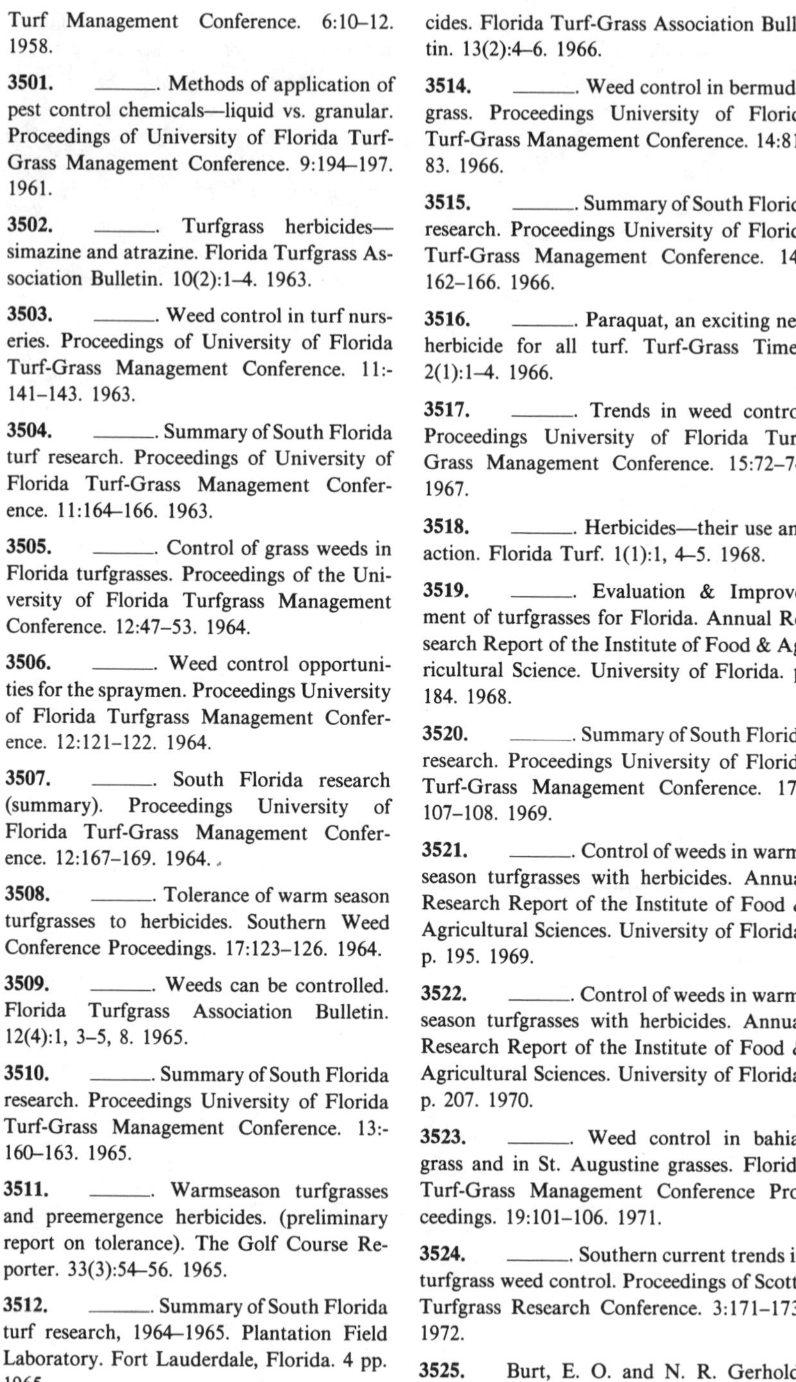

Turf Management Conference. 6:10–12. 1958.

3501. ______. Methods of application of pest control chemicals—liquid vs. granular. Proceedings of University of Florida Turf-Grass Management Conference. 9:194–197. 1961.

3502. ______. Turfgrass herbicides—simazine and atrazine. Florida Turfgrass Association Bulletin. 10(2):1–4. 1963.

3503. ______. Weed control in turf nurseries. Proceedings of University of Florida Turf-Grass Management Conference. 11:-141–143. 1963.

3504. ______. Summary of South Florida turf research. Proceedings of University of Florida Turf-Grass Management Conference. 11:164–166. 1963.

3505. ______. Control of grass weeds in Florida turfgrasses. Proceedings of the University of Florida Turfgrass Management Conference. 12:47–53. 1964.

3506. ______. Weed control opportunities for the spraymen. Proceedings University of Florida Turfgrass Management Conference. 12:121–122. 1964.

3507. ______. South Florida research (summary). Proceedings University of Florida Turf-Grass Management Conference. 12:167–169. 1964.

3508. ______. Tolerance of warm season turfgrasses to herbicides. Southern Weed Conference Proceedings. 17:123–126. 1964.

3509. ______. Weeds can be controlled. Florida Turfgrass Association Bulletin. 12(4):1, 3–5, 8. 1965.

3510. ______. Summary of South Florida research. Proceedings University of Florida Turf-Grass Management Conference. 13:-160–163. 1965.

3511. ______. Warmseason turfgrasses and preemergence herbicides. (preliminary report on tolerance). The Golf Course Reporter. 33(3):54–56. 1965.

3512. ______. Summary of South Florida turf research, 1964–1965. Plantation Field Laboratory. Fort Lauderdale, Florida. 4 pp. 1965.

3513. ______. Progress report on control of perennial grasses with non-selective herbicides. Florida Turf-Grass Association Bulletin. 13(2):4–6. 1966.

3514. ______. Weed control in bermudagrass. Proceedings University of Florida Turf-Grass Management Conference. 14:81–83. 1966.

3515. ______. Summary of South Florida research. Proceedings University of Florida Turf-Grass Management Conference. 14:-162–166. 1966.

3516. ______. Paraquat, an exciting new herbicide for all turf. Turf-Grass Times. 2(1):1–4. 1966.

3517. ______. Trends in weed control. Proceedings University of Florida Turf-Grass Management Conference. 15:72–74. 1967.

3518. ______. Herbicides—their use and action. Florida Turf. 1(1):1, 4–5. 1968.

3519. ______. Evaluation & Improvement of turfgrasses for Florida. Annual Research Report of the Institute of Food & Agricultural Science. University of Florida. p. 184. 1968.

3520. ______. Summary of South Florida research. Proceedings University of Florida Turf-Grass Management Conference. 17:-107–108. 1969.

3521. ______. Control of weeds in warm-season turfgrasses with herbicides. Annual Research Report of the Institute of Food & Agricultural Sciences. University of Florida. p. 195. 1969.

3522. ______. Control of weeds in warm-season turfgrasses with herbicides. Annual Research Report of the Institute of Food & Agricultural Sciences. University of Florida. p. 207. 1970.

3523. ______. Weed control in bahiagrass and in St. Augustine grasses. Florida Turf-Grass Management Conference Proceedings. 19:101–106. 1971.

3524. ______. Southern current trends in turfgrass weed control. Proceedings of Scotts Turfgrass Research Conference. 3:171–173. 1972.

3525. Burt, E. O. and N. R. Gerhold. "*Poa annua*" control in bermuda turf with kerb. Southern Weed Science Society Proceedings. 23:122–126. 1970.

3527. Burt, E. O. and J. A. Simmons. Germination and growth of turfgrass seedlings following pre-emergence herbicides. North Central Weed Control Conference Proceedings. 19:52. 1962.

3528. Burt, E. O., and G. H. Snyder. Nitrogen fertilization of bermudagrass turf though the irrigation system. Agronomy Abstracts. p. 61. 1972.

3529. Burt, E. O., R. W. White, and J. A. Simmons. Tolerance of some trees and shrubs in newly sprigged and established St. Augustinegrass to atrazine and simazine. Southern Weed Conference Proceedings. 15:119–120. 1962.

3531. Burton, G. Breeding better grasses. Proceedings of University of Florida Turf-Grass Management Conference. 8:5. 1960.

3532. Burton, G. W., and J. E. Elsner. Tifdwarf—a new bermudagrass for golf greens. Florida Turf-Grass Association Bulletin. 12(2):7–8. 1965.

3533. Burton, G. W. Scarification studies on southern grass seeds. Journal of the American Society of Agronomy. 31(3):179–187. 1939.

3534. ______. Observations on the flowering habits of four *Paspalum* species. American Journal of Botany. 29(10):843–848. 1942.

3535. ______. A comparison of the first year's root production of seven southern grasses established from seed. Journal of the American Society of Agronomy. 35(3):192–196. 1943.

3536. ______. Factors influencing seed setting in several Southern Grasses. Journal of the American Society of Agronomy. 35(6):465–474. 1943.

3537. ______. Seed production of several southern grasses as influenced by burning and fertilization. Journal of the American Society of Agronomy 36(6):523–529. 1944.

3538. ______. Breeding bermudagrass for the Southeastern United States. Journal of the American Society of Agronomy. 39(7):-551–569. 1947.

3539. ______. Southern turf grasses. Golfdom. 21(4):48. 1947.

3540. ______. 2, 4-D aids the establishment of southern turf grasses. Timely Turf Topics. p. 3. August, 1947.

3541. Burton, G. W. and D. G. Sturkie. Greenswards in the warmer regions. U.S. Agriculture Yearbook. pp. 311–314. 1948.

3542. Burton, G. W. Artificial fog facilitates *Paspalum* emasculation. Journal of American Society of Agronomy. 40(3):281–282. 1948.

3543. ______. The method of reproduction in common bahia grass. Journal of the American Society of Agronomy. 40(5):443–452. 1948.

3544. ______. A method for producing chance crosses and polycrosses of Pensacola bahia grass, *Paspalum notatum.* Journal of the American Society of Agronomy. 40(5):-470–472. 1948.

3545. ______. Centipede lawns from seed. Southern Seedsman. 12(1):15, 28. 1949.

3546. ______. Carpet for farm lawns. Southern Seedsman. 12(2):15, 50. 1949.

3547. ______. Bermuda: turf toughie! Southern Seedsman. 12(3):17, 56–57. 1949.

3548. ______. St. Augustine is shady lawn grass. Southern Seedsman. 12(4):15, 34. 1949.

3549. Burton, G. W. and B. P. Robinson. Breeding bermudagrass turf. Georgia Mimeo. 1950.

3550. Burton, G. W. What makes grass grow. Southern Turf Foundation Bulletin. 1950.

3551. ______. Breeding grasses for better turf. Proceedings of the 5th Annual Texas Turf Conference 5:37–44. 1950.

3552. ______. Nitrogen is essential in centipedegrass production. Victory Farm Forum. 1950.

3553. ______. The adaptability and breeding of suitable grasses for the southeastern states. Advances in Agronomy. 3:197–241. 1951.

3554. Burton, G. W., and E. H. DeVane. Effect of rate and method of applying different sources of nitrogen upon yield and chemical composition of bermudagrass, *Cynodon* *dactylon.* Abstracts of American Society of Agronomy Annual Meeting. p. 23. 1951.

3555. Burton, G. W. Intra- and interspecific hybrids in bermudagrass. Journal of Heredity. 42:152–156. 1951.

3556. ______. SSA grant spurs turf improvement program. Southern Seedsman. 14(12):38, 60. 1951.

3557. Burton, G. W., and B. P. Robinson. The story behind Tifton 57 bermuda. Southern Turf Foundation Bulletin. 1951.

3558. Burton, G. W. Quantitative inheritance in grasses. Genetics and Breeding. A:7. 1952.

3559. Burton, G. W., and B. P. Robinson. Tifton 57 bermudagrass for lawns, athletic fields and parks. Mimeo Paper No. 68. 1952.

3560. ______. Tifton 57 bermuda grass for lawns, athletic fields, and parks. Georgia Coastal Plain Experiment Station. Mimeo Paper No. 78. 1952.

3561. Burton, G. W. Quantitative inheritance in grasses. Proceedings Sixth International Grassland Congress. 1:277–283. 1952.

3562. Burton, G. W., R. L. Carter and E. H. DeVane. Grass root penetration and activity as measured with radiophosphorus. Annual Phosphorus Work Conference at Auburn, Alabama. 1952.

3563. Burton, G. W., E. H. DeVane, and R. L. Carter. Differential penetration and activity of roots of several southern grasses as measured by yields, drought symptoms, and P32 uptake. Agronomy Abstracts. p. 106. 1953.

3564. Burton, G. W. and E. H. DeVane. Estimating heritability in tall fescue *(Festuca arundinacea)* from replicated clonal material. Agronomy Journal. 45(10):478–481. 1953.

3565. Burton, G. W. Ten easy steps to a good lawn. Atlanta Journal. 1953.

3566. ______. Let's take a look at southern lawn grasses. Flower Grower. Georgia. 1953.

3567. Burton, G. W., E. H. DeVane, and R. L. Carter. Sawdust as a source of organic matter for top-dressing. Golf Course Reporter. 21(5):5–10. 1953.

3568. Burton, G. W. Better turfgrasses can be produced by breeding. USGA Journal and Turf Management. 8(4):28–29. 1955.

3569. Burton, G. W., E. H. DeVane, and R. L. Carter. Sawdust as a source of organic matter for topdressing. Southern Turf Foundation Bulletin No. 4. 1953.

3570. Burton, G. W., and E. H. DeVane. Fertilizing bermudagrass. Victory Farm Forum. 1953.

3571. Burton, G. W., E. H. DeVane and R. L. Carter Root penetration, distribution and activity in southern grasses measured by yields, drought symptoms and P^{32} uptake. Agronomy Journal. 46(5):229–233. 1954.

3572. Burton, G. W. Coastal bermudagrass. Georgia Agricultural Experiment Station Bulletin. N.S. 2:1–31. 1954.

3573. ______. "Hocus-pocus" in grass breeding. Proceedings of Midwest Regional Turf Conference. pp. 11–14. 1954.

3574. ______. Better bermudas for the south. Southern Seedsman. 17(6):47–48, 63. 1954.

3575. ______. Factors limiting growth of turf grasses. USGA Journal and Turf Management. 8(5):29–32. 1955.

3577. ______. Drought resistance and rooting habits of several southern grasses. Southeastern Turfgrass Conference. 9:1–8. 1955.

3578. ______. Lawn grasses for the south. Handbook on Lawns. Brooklyn Botanic Garden. pp. 156–167. 1956.

3579. ______. Lawn grasses for the South. Plants and Gardens. 12(2):156–167. 1956.

3580. ______. Breeding bermuda grass for turf. Southeastern Turfgrass Conference. 10:1–2. 1956.

3581. Burton, G. W., G. M. Prine, and J. E. Jackson. Studies of drouth tolerance and water use of several southern grasses. Agronomy Journal. 49(9):498–503. 1957.

3582. Burton, G. W., J. E. Jackson, and F. E. Knox. The influence of light reduction upon the production, persistence and chemical composition of coastal bermudagrass,

Cynodon dactylon. Agronomy Journal. 51(9):537–542. 1959.

3583. Burton, G. W. Tifway bermudagrass. USGA Journal and Turf Management. 13(3):28–30. 1960.

3584. Burton, G. W., and I. Forbes. The genetics and manipulation of obligate apomixis in common bahiagrass *(Paspalum notatum).* Proceedings 8th International Grassland Congress. pp. 66–71. 1960.

3585. Burton, G. W. Bermuda grass for fairways. Central Plains Turfgrass Conference. pp. 3–4. 1961.

3586. ______. Breeding bermuda for turf. Central Plains Turfgrass Conference. p. 4. 1961.

3587. Burton, G. W. and J. E. Jackson. A method for measuring sod reserves. Agronomy Journal. 54(1):53–55. 1962.

3588. Burton, G. W. Conventional breeding of dallisgrass, *Paspalum dilatatum* Poir. Crop Science. 2(6):491–494. 1962.

3589. Burton, G. W., and J. E. Jackson. Radiation breeding of apomictic prostrate dallisgrass. *Paspalum dilatatum* var. *pauciciliatum.* Crop Science. 2(6):495–497. 1962.

3590. Burton, G. W. and E. E. Deal. Shade studies on Southern grasses. Golf Course Reporter. 30:26–27. 1962.

3591. ______. Shade problems in the South and the new grasses. International Turf-grass Conference Proceedings. 33:12–13. 1962.

3592. Burton, G. W. The shade problem and what you can do about it. Southeastern Turfgrass Conference. 16:31–33. 1962.

3593. Burton, G., J. E. Jackson, and R. H. Hart. Effects of cutting frequency on nitrogen, yield, in vitro digestibility, and protein, fibre, and carotene content of 'Coastal' bermudagrass. Agronomy Journal. 55(5):-500–502. 1963.

3594. Burton, G. W. Effects of traffic on turf. Southeastern Turfgrass Conference. 17:-18–20. 1963.

3595. Burton, G. W. and J. E. Jackson. Effect of shading lower leaves on the yield, height, and sod reserves of coastal bermudagrass. Crop Science. 4(3):259–262. 1964.

3596. Burton, G. W., H. Inglis, E. Jensen and T. M. Baumgardner. Cultural control of weeds. Southeastern Turfgrass Conference. 18:22–27. 1964.

3597. Burton, G. W. Grasses around the world. Proceedings 18th Southeastern Turfgrass Conference. pp. 39–40. 1964.

3598. ______. Tifgreen bermudagrass for golf greens. USGA Green Section Record. 2(1):11–13. 1964.

3567a. Cabler, J. F. Possibilities for chemical growth retardants in turf management. Proceedings of University of Florida Turf-Grass Management Conference. 10:77–86. 1962.

3568a. ______. A comparison of vegetative grasses. Proceedings of University of Florida Turf-Grass Management Conference. 11:89–91. 1963.

3569a. ______. Growth retardants. Proceedings of University of Florida Turf-Grass Management Conference. 11:171–173. 1963.

3570a. ______. Chemical growth substances as substitutes for high light intensities on 'Tifgreen' bermudagrass. Proceedings of the Florida State Horticultural Society. 76:-470–474. 1963.

3571a. ______. Soil testing is necessary for a successful turf management program. Florida Turfgrass Association Bulletin. 11(1):3. 1964.

3572a. ______. Soluble salts and turf grasses. Florida Turfgrass Association Bulletin. 11(2):5–6. 1964.

3573a. ______. Foliar feeding of plant nutrients. Florida Turfgrass Association Bulletin. 11(2):7–8. 1964.

3574a. ______. Weed identification. Proceedings University of Florida Turf Grass Management Conference. 12:32–37. 1964.

3575a. ______. Measuring and calculating the size of turf areas. Proceedings University of Florida Turf-Grass Management Conference. 12:67–69. 1964.

3576a. Cabler, J. F., and G. C. Horn. Chemical growth retardants for turf-grasses. Golf Course Reporter. 31(1):35–44. 1963.

3577a. Cachan, P. Vertical and seasonal microclimatic variations in the evergreen forest of the lower Ivory Coast. Ecological significance of the vertical microclimatic variations in the evergreen forest. Ann. Fac. Sci., Univ. Dakar. 8:5–155. 1963.

3578a. Cahill, W. R. Preparing, presenting, and selling a reasonable budget. Proceedings 15th Annual University of Florida Turf-Grass Management Conference. 15:43–46. 1967.

3579a. Caid, J. A. Types and uses of plastic pipes. Proceedings, Texas Turfgrass Conference. 22:43–46. 1967.

3580a. Cain, R. B. The microbiology of the soil: 5, The effect of soil treatment. Gardeners Chronicle. 150(19):354. 1961.

3582a. Cairncross, A. C. The systems approach as applied to golf courses. Annual RCGA National Turfgrass Conference. 23:-18–27. 1972.

3583a. Cairns, E. J. Nematodes affecting turfgrass and methods of control. Auburn University Annual Turfgrass Short Course. pp. 28–35. 1960.

3584a. Cake, E. W. Some aspects of sod production and marketing. Proceedings University of Florida Turf Management Conference. 6:44–49. 1958.

3585a. Cale, E. B. Development of turf on stabilized soils. Report of Committee on Roadside Development. Highway Research Board. 83–109. 1948.

3586a. ______. Grass establishment on stabilized airport soils. Turf Management Conference—Florida Greenkeeping Superintendents Association. pp. 24–26. 1950.

3587a. ______. Physical properties of the soil. University of Florida Turfgrass Conference Proceedings. 5:8–14. 1957.

3588a. Caley, G. H. Aeration of turf is important in conditioning program. Golfdom. 6(8):52, 54. 1932.

3589a. Calhoun, C. R. and E. C. Roberts "Artificial" soil mixtures for putting greens. Agronomy Abstracts. p. 52. 1969.

3590a. Calhoun, C. R., J. T. Pesek, and E. C. Roberts. The effect of ureaformaldehyde nitrogen in the presence of varying phosphorus and potassium levels on the yield and nutrient content of a Kentucky bluegrass turf. Agronomy Abstracts. p. 69. 1960.

3591a. ______. Effect of phosphorus, potassium and ureaformaldehyde nitrogen on predictions of quality in bluegrass turf. Agronomy Abstracts. p. 105. 1964.

3592a. Call, L. E. Turf and lawn grass experiments. Kansas Agricultural Experiment Station. Director's Report 1924–1926. pp. 47–48. 1926.

3593a. ______. Lawns. Kansas State University Agricultural Experiment Station Bulletin 468. pp. 48–49. 1964.

3594a. Callahan, L. M. Secondary effects of pesticides. Ohio Turfgrass Conference Proceedings. pp. 82–86. 1971.

3595a. ______. The effects of three phenoxyalkylcarboxylic acid compounds on the physiology and survival of turfgrasses. Ph.D. Thesis, Rutgers University. 129 pp. 1969.

3596a. ______. Turf-evaluation of new herbicides—Tennessee. Southern Weed Conference Research Report. 19:120–123. 1966.

3597a. ______. Disease control in fine turfgrasses. Proceedings, Turf and Landscape Clinic, Tennessee Turfgrass Association. pp. 4–7. 1966.

3598a. ______. Weed control and plant tolerances. Proceedings, Turf and Landscape Clinic, Tennessee Turfgrass Association. pp. 13–15. 1966.

3599a. ______. Select herbicides carefully—turfgrass tolerances do differ. Weeds, Trees and Turf. 5(11):6–7, 17. 1966.

Entries numbered 3600a to 3699a appear after 3699.

3600. Burton, G. W., J. C. Morcock, C. Walls, and R. L. Carter. Mechanics of fertilizing golf courses through irrigation equipment. Southeastern Turfgrass Conference. 19:37–41. 1965.

3601. Burton, G. W. and J. E. Elsner. Tifdwarf—a new bermudagrass for golf greens. USGA Green Section Record. 2(5):-8–9. 1965.

3602. Burton, G. W. Tifway (Tifton 419) bermudagrass (Reg. #7). Crop Science. 6(1):93–94. 1966.

3603. ______. Tifdwarf bermudagrass (Reg. #8). Crop Science. 6(1):94. 1966.

3604. Burton, G. W. and C. Lance. Golf car versus grass. The Golf Superintendent. 34(1):66–70. 1966.

3605. Burton, G. W. and R. H. Hart. Use of self-incompatibility to produce commercial seed-propagated F_1 bermudagrass hybrids. Crop Science 7(5):524–527. 1967.

3606. Burton, G. W., W. S. Wilkinson and R. L. Carter. Effect of nitrogen, phosphorus, and potassium levels and clipping frequency on the forage yield and protein, carotene, and xanthophyll content of Coastal bermudagrass. Agronomy Journal. 61(1):60–63. 1969.

3607. Burton, G. W. Developing new varieties for southern golf courses. 40th International Turfgrass Conference and Show Proceedings. pp. 28–31. 1969.

3608. ———. Grasses for the golf course. Southeastern Turfgrass Conference. 23:15–18. 1969.

3609. Burton, G. W., I. Forbes, and J. Jackson. Effect of ploidy on fertility and heterosis in Pensacola bahiagrass. Crop Science. 10(1):63–66. 1970.

3610. Burton, G. W. Turf research reports 1969–1970, Georgia. Southern Regional Turf Research Committee Report, Virginia Polytechnic Institute. 5 pp. 1970.

3611. Burton, G. W. and J. B. Powell. Better bermudagrass to meet golf's demands. USGA Green Section Record. 9(6):9–11. 1971.

3612. Burton, M. and R. E. Hutchins. Insect damage of lawns checked. Mississippi Farm Research. 21(11):1, 7. 1958.

3613. Busch, C. D. A comparison of sprinkler and subsurface irrigation of bermudagrass. Turfgrass Research. Arizona Agricultural Experiment Station. Report 219:-3–7. 1963.

3615. Buscher, F. K. The importance of soil testing. Ohio Agricultural Research and Development Center. Research Summary 48:27–28. 1970.

3616. Bush-Brown, J. Soils and soil improvement. America's Garden Book. Charles Scribner's Sons. New York. pp. 154–172. 1965.

3617. ———. Plant diseases and insect pests. America's Garden Book. Charles Scribner's Sons, New York. pp. 610–676. 1965.

3618. Bush, L., R. Buckner, P. Burrus. Physiological studies of fescue and ryegrass genotypes. Kentucky Agricultural Experiment Station Annual Report. 83:22–23. 1970.

3619. Bushey, D. J. Lawns. A Guide to Home Landscaping. McGraw-Hill. New York. Chapter 5. pp. 60–81. 1956.

3620. Bussart, J. E. Development, labeling and distribution of turfgrass pesticide chemicals. Proceedings of the Texas Turfgrass Conference. 15:40–45. 1960.

3621. ———. Development, labeling, distribution of turfgrass pesticide chemicals. USGA Green Section Record. 2(2):4–9. 1964.

3622. Butler, B. The reclamation of colliery wastes to playing fields, public open spaces and agriculture without the use of soil. The Groundsman. 16(9):24–34. 1963.

3623. Butler, G. D. Turf insect problems. Proceedings of the Annual Arizona Turf Conference. pp. 32–35. 1953.

3624. ———. Scale insects on turfgrass. Proceedings of the Arizona Turfgrass Conference. pp. 7–9. 1954.

3625. ———. Variations in the response of bermudagrass strains to eriophyid mite infestation. Turfgrass Research. Arizona Agricultural Experiment Station. Report 203:15–19. 1961.

3627. ———. Some observations of populations of insects and mites on turfgrass experimental plots. Turfgrass Research. Arizona Agricultural Experiment Station. Report 203:32–34. 1961.

3628. ———. The introduction of insects during 1961 for biological control of turf pests. Turfgrass Research. Arizona Agriculture Experiment Station. Report 203:35–36. 1961.

3629. Butler, G. D., and D. M. Tuttle. New mite is damaging to bermudagrass. Progress Agriculture Arizona. 13(1):11. 1961.

3630. Butler, G. D. and A. A. Baltensperger. Eriophyid mite, *Aceria neocynodonis* Keifer, control on bermudagrass. Agronomy Abstracts. p. 101. 1962.

3631. Butler, G. D. The distribution and control of the bermudagrass eriophyid mite. Turfgrass Research. Arizona Agricultural Experiment Station. Report 212:1–9. 1962.

3632. ______. Variations in response of bermudagrass strains to bermudagrass eriophyid mite infestations. Turfgrass Research. Arizona Agricultural Experiment Station. Report 212:10–11. 1962.

3633. ______. Control of eriophyid mite on bermudagrass. Turfgrass Research. Arizona Agricultural Experiment Station. Report 203:25–31. 1961.

3634. ______. Biological control of puncturevine. Turfgrass Research. Arizona Agricultural Experiment Station. Report 212:30. 1962.

3635. Butler, G. W., P. C. Barclay, and A. C. Glenday. Genetic and environmental differences in the mineral composition of ryegrass herbage. Plant Soil. 16:214–228. 1962.

3637. Butler, G. D. The biology of the bermudagrass eriophyid mite. Turfgrass Research. Arizona Agricultural Experiment Station. Report 219:8–13. 1963.

3638. Butler, G. D., J. L. Stroehlein and L. Moore. The control of the bermudagrass eriophyid mite. Turfgrass Research. Arizona Agricultural Experiment Station. Report 219:14–25. 1963.

3639. Butler, G. D. Laboratory studies on the systemic activity of diazinon. Turfgrass Research. Arizona Agricultural Experiment Station. Report 219:29–33. 1963.

3640. Butler, G. D. and A. A. Baltensperger. The bermudagrass eriophyid mite. California Turfgrass Culture. 13(2):9–11. 1963.

3641. Butler, J. D. and F. W. Slife. Lawn weeds: identification and control. Illinois Agricultural Extension Circular. 873:1–27. 1963.

3642. Butler, G. D., and W. R. Kneebone. Variations in response of bermudagrass varieties to bermudagrass mite infestations with and without chemical control. Turfgrass Research. Arizona Agricultural Experiment Station. Report 230:7–10. 1965.

3643. Butler, G. D., and T. Scanlon. Evaluation of materials for the control of the bermudagrass mite. Turfgrass Research. Arizona Agricultural Experiment Station. Report 230:11–16. 1965.

3644. Butler, G. D. Progress report on the biological control of puncture-vine with weevils. Turfgrass Research. Arizona Agricultural Experiment Station. Report 230:17–20. 1965.

3645. Butler, G. D., and P. D. Johnson. Life cycle studies on a Rhodesgrass scale parasite. Turfgrass Research. Arizona Agricultural Experiment Station. Report 230:21–23. 1965.

3646. Butler, J. D. Seeding rates and some factors in the spring establishment of turf. Illinois Turfgrass Conference Proceedings. pp. 13–14. 1961.

3648. ______. Some effects of different levels of shade on several grasses and weeds. Illinois Turfgrass Conference Proceedings. pp. 22–25. 1962.

3649. ______. Some characteristics of the more commonly grown creeping bentgrasses. Illinois Turfgrass Conference Proceedings. pp. 23–25. 1963.

3650. Butler, J. D. and M. P. Britton. Fungicides and turf disease control—1964. Illinois Turfgrass Conference Proceedings. pp. 26–30. 1964.

3651. Butler, J. D. Thatch—as a problem in turf management. Illinois Turfgrass Conference Proceedings. pp. 1–3. 1965.

3652. ______. Turf weeds—why we have them. Wisconsin Turfgrass Conference. pp. 1–4. 1965.

3653. Campbell, R. W. Spray compatibility. Central Plains Turfgrass Conference. pp. 1–2. 1961.

3654. Butler, J. D., and J. M. Ackley. Highway right-of-way maintenance spraying. University of Illinois Agricultural Engineering Series, Illinois Cooperative Highway Research Program No. 63. 11 pp. 1966.

3655. Butler, J. D. and H. J. Hopen. Weed control in turf. Illinois Turfgrass Conference Proceedings. pp. 28–30. 1966.

3656. Butler, J. D. Kentucky bluegrass today. Illinois Turfgrass Conference Proceedings. pp. 36–38. 1966.

3657. ______. Important weeds of turf areas in the North Central states. Weed Abstracts. p. 74. 1966.

3658. Butler, J. D. and H. J. Hopen. Perennial grass weeds are serious turf problem. The Golf Superintendent. 35(9):32–35. 1967.

3659. Butler, J. D. Review of bluegrasses. The Golf Superintendent. 35(9):35. 1967.

3660. ______. Equipment and techniques for roadside spraying. University of Illinois Project IHR-58. Agricultural Engineering Series No. 67. 36 pp. 1967.

3661. Butler, J. D. and W. M. Blaine. Starting a lawn. Illinois Agricultural Extension Service. Circular 963. 15 pp. 1967.

3662. Butler, J. D. and H. J. Hopen. Weed control in turf—1967. Illinois Turfgrass Conference Proceedings. pp. 4–7. 1967.

3663. Butler, J. D. A look at the creeping bentgrasses. Illinois Turfgrass Conference Proceedings. pp. 10–12. 1967.

3664. Butler, J. D. and H. J. Hopen. A review of turf weed control—1968. Illinois Turfgrass Conference Proceedings. pp. 7–10. 1968.

3665. Butler, J. Turfgrass research at the University of Illinois. Scotts Turfgrass Research Seminar. pp. 28–29. 1968.

3666. ______. Care in starting a lawn pays big dividends. Illinois Turfgrass Conference Proceedings. pp. 19–22. 1969.

3668. ______. Recent advances and problems in turf weed control. Illinois Turfgrass Conference Proceedings. pp. 11–13. 1970.

3669. Butler, J. D., T. D. Hughes, G. D. Sanks, and P. R. Craig. Salt causes problems along Illinois Highways. Illinois Research. Illinois Agricultural Experiment Station. 13(4):1971.

3670. Butler, J. D. Turf problems and ecology. Missouri Lawn and Turf Conference Proceedings. 12:8–11. 1971.

3671. ______. Disease problems in lawns and general turf. Missouri Lawn and Turf Conference Proceedings. 12:48–51. 1971.

3672. ______. Choosing Kentucky bluegrasses for turf areas. Rocky Mountain Regional Turfgrass Conference Proceedings. 18:35–43. 1972.

3673. ______. Choosing Kentucky bluegrass for turf areas. Western Landscaping News. 12(10):30–32, 34, 36. 1972.

3674. Butler, W. E. P. Coring of golf greens. New Zealand Institute for Turf Culture Newsletter. 24:9–10. 1963.

3675. ______. Golf course management. New Zealand Institute for Turf Culture. Newsletter. 36:11–13. 1965.

3676. ______. Greens construction. New Zealand Institute for Turf Culture Newsletter. 48:3–4. 1967.

3677. Butterfield, H. M. and H. W. Shepherd. Lawn making and maintenance. California Extension Service Publication. pp. 1–11.

3678. Butterfield, H. M. Past research in California turf grasses. Northern California Turf Conference Report. pp. 1–3. 1950.

3679. Butterfield, H. M., W. Schoonover, and H. W. Shepherd. Lawn planting and care. California Agricultural Extension Service. Circular 181:1–38. 1951.

3680. Butterfield, H. M. Lawn-grass substitutes in California. University of California (Berkeley) Mimeo. 7 pp. 1963.

3681. Butters, E. A. Analysis of grass seed mixtures. Rutgers University Turfgrass Short Course. 2 pp. 1957.

3682. Butterworth, B. Injection equipment for turf. Parks, Golf Courses, and Sports Grounds. 37(8):794, 796. 1972.

3683. Butterworth, C. Trends in merchandising in garden supply stores. Proceedings of the University of Florida Turfgrass Management Conference. 12:99–103. 1964.

3684. Button, E. F. Ferti-seeding. Crops & Soils. 10(7):17–18. 1958.

3685. ______. Effect of gibberellic acids on laboratory germination of creeping red fescue. Agronomy Journal. 51(1):60–61. 1959.

3686. ______. Hydraulic ferti-seeding. Park Maintenance. 12(3):74–78. 1959.

3687. ______. Applied conservation on Connecticut highways. Journal of Soil and Water Conservation. 15(6):278–279. 1960.

3688. ______. Observations on highway turf establishment and maintenance. Turf Clippings. University of Massachusetts. 1(6):A-62–70. 1961.

3689. Button, E. F. and K. Potharst. Comparison of mulch material for turf establishment. Journal of Soil and Water Conservation. 17(4):166–169. 1962.

3690. Button, E. F. The modern "complete highway"—its challenge to the agronomic profession. Agronomy Abstracts. p. 99. 1964.

3691. Button, E. F. and C. F. Moyes. Effect of a seaweed extract upon emergence and survival of seedlings of creeping red fescue. Agronomy Journal. 56(4):444–445. 1964.

3692. Button, E. F. Establishing slope vegetation. Public Works Magazine. 1964.

3693. ______. Hydroplanting highway turf. Turf-Grass Times. 1(4):1, 17. 1966.

3694. Buxton, D. R. and W. F. Wedin. Establishment of perennial forages: 1. Subsequent yields. Agronomy Journal. 62(1):93–97. 1970.

3695. ______. Establishment of perennial forages: II. Subsequent root development. Agronomy Journal. 62(1):97–100. 1970.

3696. Byers, R. A. Biology and control of a spittlebug, *Prosapia bicincta* (Say) on Coastal bermudagrass. Georgia Agricultural Experiment Station Technical Bulletin N.S. 42:1–26. 1965.

3698. Byrne, T. and P. Lert. The drainage problem in sodded turf. Turfgrass Times. 5(5):10. 1970.

3699. Byrne, T. G., and O. R. Lunt. Controlled availability fertilizers. IV. Urea formaldehyde. California Agriculture. 16(3):10–11. 1962.

3600a. ______. Turf research at the University of Tennessee. Southern Turfgrass Association Conference Proceedings. 33–34. 1967.

3601a. ______. Turf-recommended practices—Tennessee. Southern Weed Conference Research Report. 20:93–94. 1967.

3602a. ______. Turfgrass research at the University of Tennessee. Scotts Turfgrass Research Seminar. pp. 60–66. 1968.

3603a. ______. Combating today's diseases. Southern Turfgrass Association Conference Proceedings. pp. 35–37. 1968.

3604a. ______. Turf research at the University of Tennessee. Southern Turfgrass Association Conference Proceedings. pp. 40–41. 1968.

3605a. ______. Fungicide trials at the University of Tennessee. Proceedings Tennessee Turfgrass Conference. pp. 32–33. 1968.

3606a. ______. Highlights of synthetic turf. Proceedings, Tennessee Turfgrass Conference. 3:19–20. 1969.

3607a. ______. Turfgrass research reports 1969–1970, University of Tennessee. Southern Regional Turf Research Committee Report. Virginia Polytechnic Institute. pp. 32–40 1970.

3608a. ______. Weed control in lawns. Proceedings Tennessee Turfgrass Conference. 4:27–31. 1970.

3609a. ______. Are diseases really to blame. Weeds Today. 1(2):19–21. 1970.

3610a. ______. Phytotoxicity of herbicides in a Penncross bent green. Agronomy Abstracts. p. 52. 1971.

3611a. ______. *Poa annua* in the transition zone. Missouri Lawn and Turf Conference Proceedings. 12:32–34. 1971.

3612a. ______. Sod webworm research in Tennessee. Missouri Lawn and Turf Conference Proceedings. 12:36–42. 1971.

3613a. ______. Turf—recommended practices—Tennessee. Southern Weed Science Society Research Report. 24:85. 1971.

3614a. ______. Are diseases really to blame? Tennessee Turfgrass Conference. 5:-25–27. 1971.

3615a. ______. Phytotoxicity of herbicides in a Tifgreen bermudagrass green and to cool season grass overseedings. Agronomy Abstracts. p. 61. 1972.

3616a. ______. The real culprit behind turf diseases. The Golf Superintendent. 40(5):12–16. 1972.

3617a. ______. Turf-recommended practices—Tennessee. Southern Weed Science Society Research Report. 25:116. 1972.

3618a. Callahan, L. M. and R. E. Engel. The control of chickweed and clover by phenoxypropionics and dicamba compounds in bentgrass. Proceedings Northeastern Weed Control Conference. 18:535–539. 1964.

3619a. ______. The effects of phenoxy herbicides on the physiology and survival of turfgrass. USGA Green Section Record. 3(1):1–6. 1965.

3620a. ______. Tissue abnormalities induced in roots of colonial bentgrass by phenoxyalkylcarboxylic acid herbicides. Weeds. 13:336–338. 1965.

3621a. Callahan, L. M. and D. M. Gossett. Turf-recommended practices—Tennessee. Southern Weed Conference Research Report 19:114–115. 1966.

3622a. Callahan, L. M., R. E. Engel, and R. D. Illnicki. Environmental influence on bentgrass treated with silvex. Turf Bulletin. 5(1):12–15. 1968.

3623a. ______. Environmental influence on bentgrass treated with silvex. Weed Science. 16(2):193–196. 1968.

3625a. Callahan, L., R. Ilnicki, and R. Engel. Phenoxy compounds and turf injury. USGA Green Section Record. 2(2):12–13. 1964.

3626a. Caltrider, P. G. and D. Gottlieb. Respiratory activity and enzymes for glucose catabolism in fungus spores. Phytopathology. 53(9):1021–1030. 1963.

3627a. Camenga, B. C. Sprinkler irrigation design manual. Moist 'O matic, Riverside, California. p. 92. 1965.

3628a. Cameron, R. S. Turf-grass weevil on annual bluegrass—a problem or panacea. Turf-grass Times. 5(7):10–11, 18. 1970.

3629a. Cameron, M. C. How the assistant superintendent should work with the superintendent. Proceedings of the 37th Annual Turfgrass Conference and Show. pp. 6–8. 1966.

3631a. Cameron, R. S. Getting the bugs out. Golfdom. 44(6):48–50. 1970.

3632a. ______. Control of a species of Hyperodes. New York Turfgrass Association Bulletin. 86:333–334. 1970.

3633a. ______. Biology and control of a species of Hyperodes. Rutgers University Short Course in Turf Management pp. 33–34. 1970.

3634a. ______. Biology and control of a species of *Hyperodes*. USGA Green Section Record. 8(3):7–9. 1970.

3635a. Cameron, R. S. and N. Johnson. Biology and control of turfgrass weevil. Cornell University. Extension Bulletin 1226. pp. 1–8 1971.

3636a. Cameron, R. S., H. J. Kastl, and J. F. Cornman. *Hyperodes* weevil damages annual bluegrass. New York Turfgrass Association Bulletin. 79: 307–308. 1968.

3637a. Cameron, S. Long Island "turfgrass weevil" prefers *Poa annua* to other grasses. Park Maintenance. 23(7):21. 1970.

3638a. Campbell, C. B. Establishing color on a golf course. Proceedings of the Texas Turfgrass Conference. 20:66–67. 1965.

3639a. ______. Program planning and handling. Proceedings Annual Texas Turfgrass Conference. 21:67–69. 1966.

3640a. Campbell, J. K. The value of compost. The Golf Superintendent. 34(9):53. 1966.

3641a. ______. Club members ask: how can I turn my fine lawn into my own, private putting green. The Golf Superintendent. 35(3):56–58. 1967.

3642a. ______. Automatic greens irrigation. The Golf Superintendent. 35(7):43–44. 1967.

3643a. ______. Maintenance program at the royal and ancient golf club. Annual RCGA National Turfgrass Conference. 20:-11–17. 1969.

3644a. ______. Golf course maintenance at St. Andrews, Scotland. Turf Clippings. 4(1):A-68 to A-75. 1969.

3645a. ______. Problems of maintenance. Golf Superintendent. 38(2):28–29. 1970.

3646a. ______. The royal and ancient—St. Andrews 41st International Turfgrass Conference and Show Proceedings. pp. 52–57. 1970.

3647a. ______. The value of compost. Lakeshore News. 3(9):11, 13. 1971.

3648a. ______. Our soil fertility program at St. Andrews. Annual RCGA National Turfgrass Conference. 23:28–29. 1972.

3649a. Campbell, J. O. Mid-summer methods in Nebraska. Golfdom. 1(6):10–11. 1927.

3650a. ______. Greenkeeping yesterday and today. Golfdom. 6(2):46–47. 1932.

3651a. Campbell, R. B., and L. A. Richards. Some moisture and salinity relationships in peat soils. Agronomy Journal. 42:-582–585. 1950.

3652a. Campbell, R. L. Biological studies of *Ionopus rubriceps* (Macquart): *Diptera: Stratiomyidae*. Ph.D. Thesis, University of California, Berkeley. 1968.

3653a. Butler, J. D. and F. W. Slife. Postemergence herbicides on spring—seeded Kentucky bluegrass. Weeds. 13:370–371. 1965.

3654a. Campbell, R. W., and R. A. Keen. Report and tour of turfgrass research. Central Plains Turfgrass Conference. pp. 1–2. 1961.

3655a. Campbell, R. W. and T. B. Shackelford. Responses from herbicidal applications to a bermudagrass athletic field. North Central Weed Control Conference Proceedings. 19:51–52. 1962.

3656a. Campbell, R. W. and R. K. Singh. Notes on nimblewill control. North Central Weed Control Conference Proceedings. 19:-51. 1962.

3657a. ______. Henbit and chickweed studies. North Central Weed Control Conference Proceedings. 19:52–53. 1962.

3658a. Campbell, W. Everglades No. 1. Proceedings University of Florida Turf Management Conference. 6:25–27. 1958.

3659a. Campbell, W. C. A golfer's view of greens. USGA Green Section Record. 5(6):2–5. 1968.

3660a. Campbell, W. F. Turf management in Utah. Utah State University Agricultural Experiment Station. Utah Science. 32(4):130–134. 1971.

3661a. Canavan, D. Construction by contract and the role of the superintendent. Turf Clippings. University of Massachusetts. 3(3):A39–41. 1968.

3662a. Cane, D. S. Lawns. Garden Design of To-Day. Charles Scribner's Sons. New York. pp. 90–92. 1936.

3663a. Canode, C. L. Grass seed production as influenced by cultivation, gapping, and postharvest residue management. Agronomy Journal. 64(2):148–151. 1972.

3664a. ______. Germination of grass seed as influenced by storage condition. Crop Science. 12(1):79–81. 1972.

3665a. Canode, C. L. and W. C. Robocker. Annual weed control in seedling grasses. Weeds. 14(4):306–309. 1966.

3666a. ______. Chemical control of red sorrel in Kentucky bluegrass seed fields. Weeds. 15(4):351–353. 1967.

3667a. ______. Selective weed control in seedling cool-season grasses. Weed Science. 18(2):288–291. 1970.

3668a. Canode, C. L., A. G. Law and J. D. Maguire. Post-harvest drying rate and germination of Kentucky bluegrass seed. Crop Science. 10(3):316–317. 1970.

3669a. Canode, C. L., M. A. Maun, and I. D. Teare. Initiation of inflorescences in cool-season perennial grasses. Crop Science. 12(1):19–22. 1972.

3670a. Candoe, C. L., W. C. Robocker, and T. J. Muzik. Annual grass weed control in grass seed production. Washington State Weed Conference Proceedings. pp. 38–39. 1961.

3671a. ______. Grass seed production as influenced by chemical control of downy brome. Weeds. 10:216–219. 1962.

3672a. Cannaday, J. E. Brown spot. The National Greenkeeper. 2(12):7–9. 1928.

3673a. ______. Fungus diseases and why. The National Greenkeeper. 3(6):10–17, 34. 1929.

3674a. Capizzi, O. Winter injury on home lawn. Turf Clippings. University of Massachusetts. 1(5):A-12. 1960.

3675a. Caplan, I. Some chinch bugs aren't. Weeds, Trees, and Turf. 7(8):31–32. 1968.

3676a. Capps, H. J. Maintenance of commercial or industrial turf equipment. Proceedings University of Florida Turf-Grass Management Conference. 10:87–91. 1962.

3677a. Caranahan, H. L. and H. D. Hill. *Lolium perenne* L. X tetraploid *Festuca elatior* L. triploid hybrids and colchicine treatments for inducing autoallohexaploids. Agronomy Journal. 47(6):258–262. 1955.

3678a. Card, F. W., M. A. Blake, and H. L. Barnes. Lawn experiment. Rhode Island Agricultural Experiment Station. 19th Annual Report. Part 2. pp. 162–166. 1906.

3679a. Carder, A. C. Field trials with dalapon on quackgrass. Weeds. 15:201–203. 1967.

3680a. Carey, T. Mowing by the book. Golfdom 41(4):52–54. 1967.

3681a. ______. Are your grounds too green? Golfdom 41(10):46–50, 88–91. 1967.

3682a. Carleton, R. M. You can kill growing crabgrass but not the dormant seed. Park Maintenance. 8(4):26–27. 1955.

3683a. ______. New way to kill weeds in your lawn and garden. Arco Publishing Co. Inc. New York, N.Y. 112 pp. 1957.

3684a. ______. Your lawn and how to make it and keep it. D. Van Nostrand Company, Inc. New Jersey. 165 pp. 1959.

3685a. ______. The grasses that make up our lawns. Seed World. 90(1):4. 1962.

3686a. ______. Snow mold: A problem in home lawns. Seed World. 90(3):25. 1962.

3687a. ______. Pre-emergence crabgrass control. Seed World. 90(5):27–28. 1962.

3688a. ______. Fertilizers for home lawns. Seed World. 90(7):27–28. 1962.

3689a. ______. How to mow a lawn. Seed World. 90(9):22–23. 1962.

3690a. ______. Broadleaved weed control in lawns. Seed World. 90(11):22–23. 1962.

3691a. ______. Is it crab grass . . . or isn't it? Seed World. 91(2):30. 1962.

3692a. ______. Fall feeding recommended for lawns. Seed World. 91(4):21. 1962.

3693a. ______. Now is the time to control snow mould on lawns. Seed World. 91(6):20–21. 1962.

3694a. ______. Turfgrass and chemicals. Seed World. 91(8):26. 1962.

3695a. ______. Winter lawn care—a neglected activity. Seed World. 91(10):26. 1962.

3696a. ______. Ratings of cool season grasses. Seed World. 91(12):20–21. 1962.

3697a. ______. Chickweed *Poa annua* and knotweed. Seed World. 92(4):19. 1963.

3698a. ______. Common chickweed—a spring puzzler. Seed World. 92(6):26. 1963.

3699a. ______. Growing lawns on problem soils. Seed World. 92(8):22. 1963.

Entries numbered 3700a to 3705a appear after 3799.

3700. ______. Urea formaldehyde. California Turfgrass Culture. 12(3):19–20. 1962.

3701. Byrne, T. G., W. B. Davis, L. J. Booker, and L. F. Werenfels. A further evaluation of the vertical mulching method of improving old greens. California Turfgrass Culture. 15(2):9–11. 1965.

3702. ______. Vertical mulching for improvement of old golf greens. Turf Bulletin. 2(13):18–20. 1965.

3703. Byrne, T. G. A low-application sprinkler system for bowling greens. Proceedings of Turf, Landscape Tree, and Nursery Conference. pp. 3–1 to 3–3. 1966.

3704. ______. A low-application sprinkler system for bowling greens. Western Landscape News. 7(3):28. 1967.

3705. Byrne, T. G. and A. H. McCain. Systemic control of bluegrass rust. California Turfgrass Culture. 18(4):28. 1968.

3706. Carr, A. J. H. Virus diseases of grasses. Span. 11:2. 1968.

3707. Carrier, L. The identification of grasses by their vegetative characters. USDA Bulletin 461. 30 pp. 1917.

3708. ______. The Bordeaux treatment for brown patch. USGA Green Section Bulletin. 3(6):163–164. 1923.

3709. ______. Winterkilling of turf. USGA Green Section Bulletin. 3(10):254–255. 1923.

3710. ______. Florida greenkeeping. The National Greenkeeper. 1(10):19–20. 1927.

3711. ______. The history of *Poa bulbosa.* The National Greenkeeper. 1(9):9–10. 1927.

3712. ______. Vegetative planting. The National Greenkeeper. 1(8):26, 38. 1927.

3713. ______. Golf grasses III. The bent family. The National Greenkeeper. 2(4):17–19. 1928.

3714. ______. Golf grasses. The National Greenkeeper. 2(1):7, 34. 1928.

3715. ______. Turf research at Davis. North California Turf Conference. pp. 75–77. 1951.

3716. Carrier, L. and K. S. Bort. The history of Kentucky bluegrass and white clover in the United States. Journal of American Society of Agronomy. 8(4):256–266. 1916.

3717. Carrier, L. and R. A. Oakley. The management of bluegrass pastures. Virginia Agricultural Experiment Station Bulletin. 204. 1914.

3718. Carriere, R. History of golf and its evolution in Quebec. Annual RCGA National Turfgrass Conference. 20:18–22. 1969.

3719. Carroll, J. C. Atmospheric drought test of some pasture and turf grasses. Journal of American Society of Agronomy. 35(1):77–79. 1943.

3720. ______. Effects of drought, temperature, and nitrogen on turfgrasses. Plant Physiology. 18:19–36. 1943.

3721. Carrol, J. C., and F. A. Welton. Effect of heavy and late applications of nitrogenous fertilizer on the cold resistance of Kentucky bluegrass. Plant Physiology. 14(2):297–307. 1939.

3722. Carrow, R. N. Soil factors influencing arsenic soil tests and growth of selected turfgrasses. Ph.D. Thesis, Michigan State University. 223 pp. 1972.

3723. ______. Factors affecting the adaptation and competitiveness of *Poa annua* L. Turf Bulletin. 9(3):3–4. 1972.

3724. Carrow, R. N. and P. E. Rieke. The effects of phosphorus and tricalcium arsenate on the germination and growth of four cool season grasses. Agronomy Abstracts. p. 68. 1970.

3725. ______. Effects of tricalcium arsenate, phosphorus, and soil pH on the arsenic soil test results and growth of turfgrasses. Agronomy Abstracts. p. 45. 1971.

3726. ______. Arsenic toxicity on *Poa annua* L. as influenced by soil type and soil reactions. Agronomy Abstracts. p. 61. 1972.

3727. ______. Phosphorus and potassium nutrition in turfgrass culture. 42nd Annual Michigan Turfgrass Conference Proceedings. 1:100–105. 1972.

3728. ______. Soil factors affecting arsenic toxicity on *Poa annua.* 42nd Annual Michigan Turfgrass Conference Proceedings. 1:24–29. 1972.

3729. Carson, E. W. and R. E. Blaser. The effect of nitrogen fertilization and grass association on the establishment of "*Lespedeza cuneata.*" Agronomy Abstracts. 54:-101. 1962.

3730. ______. Establishing *Sericea* on highway slopes. Roadside Development, Highway Research Board. pp. 22–43. 1962.

3731. Carson, G. P. The repair and maintenance of turf equipment. Proceedings of Midwest Regional Turf Conference. pp. 22–26. 1949.

3732. Carson, R. L. Lawn equipment rentals. Proceedings University Florida Turf-Grass Management Conference. 7:69. 1959.

3733. Carter, A. S. Ideas about seed quality. Proceedings of the Midwest Regional Turf Conference. pp. 59–60. 1962.

3734. ______. Seed mixtures—a review. Proceedings Midwest Regional Turf Conference. pp. 53–54. 1965.

3735. ______. Ideas about seed quality. Turf Bulletin. Massachusetts Turf and Lawn Grass Council. 7(1):15–17, 19, 20. 1970.

3736. Carter, D. L., and C. D. Fanning. Mulches help remove salts. Crops and Soils. 16(8):26. 1964.

3737. Carter, D. L., and H. B. Peterson. Sodic tolerance of tall wheatgrass. Agronomy Journal. 54(5):382–384. 1962.

3738. Carter, J. C. Recognizing and combating diseases. Proceedings of Midwest Regional Turf Conference. pp. 49–55. 1951.

3739. Carter, J. C., and A. G. Law. The effect of clipping upon the vegetative development of some perennial grasses. Journal of the American Society of Agronomy. 40(12):-1084–1091. 1948.

3740. Carter, R. L. Soil problems on the golf course. Proceedings Southeastern Turfgrass Conference. pp. 46–50. 1965.

3741. Carver, R. B., M. C. Rush, and G. D. Lindberg. An epiphytotic of ryegrass blast in Louisiana. The Plant Disease Reporter. 56(2):157–159. 1972.

3742. Casey, E. J. Water distribution systems. USGA Journal and Turf Management. 13(1):27–28. 1960.

3743. ______. Bunker renovation. USGA Green Section Record. 4(6):22. 1967.

3744. Casey, N. M. The effects of air pollution on urban air temperature. M.S. Thesis, University of Missouri. 1971.

3745. Casida, J. E. Toxicology of insecticides commonly used in turf maintenance. Proceedings of Scotts Turfgrass Research Conference. 1:1–14. 1969.

3746. Caskey, G. B. Rochelle's watering system laid out with eye to future expansion. Golfdom. 5(2):55–58. 1931.

3747. ______. Caskey gives further details of Rochelle's watering system. Golfdom. 5(3):118, 120–121. 1931.

3748. ______. Speed, uniformity and thrift in treating your greens. Golfdom. 7(7):-15–17. 1933.

3749. ______. Postwar maintenance picture. Golfdom. 20(3):40, 42, 61. 1946.

3750. ______. Some aspects of post-war golf course maintenance. Parks & Recreation. 29(3):133–135, 173–176. 1946.

3751. Cassel, D. K., D. R. Nielsen and J. W. Biggar. Soil-water movement in response to imposed temperature gradients. Soil Science Society of America Proceedings. 33(4):-493–500. 1969.

3752. Cassidy, D. How we control vegetation at the California division of highways. Weeds, Trees and Turf. 5(3):15–16. 1966.

3753. Cassidy, P. I. Should putting greens be cut by hand or power? Greenkeepers Club of New England Newsletter. 8(4):-10–14. 1936.

3755. Castronovo, V. Managing grass to reduce care. Illinois Turfgrass Conference Proceedings. pp. 50–52. 1969.

3756. Cepikova, A. Root systems of perennial herbage plants and when they die out. Proceedings of the Lenin Academy of Agricultural Science. 9(10):28–29. 1942.

3757. Cerns, W. G. Effect of dextrorotary isomer of 4-chloro-2-methyl phenoxy propionic acid (Compitox) on chickweed. North Central Weed Control Conference Proceedings. 17:103–104. 1960.

3758. Chada, H. L., and E. A. Wood. Biology and control of the rhodesgrass scale. USDA Technical Bulletin 1221. 21 pp. 1960.

3759. Chadwick, D. L., and G. W. Todd. Effect of wind on plant respiration in the dark. Plant Physiology Abstracts. 47:31. 1971.

3760. Chadwick, L. C. The importance of plant ecology for roadside plantings. 21st Short Course on Roadside Development, (Ohio). pp. 57–59. 1962.

3761. Chamberlain, H. E. Development of an herbicide for the selective removal of bentgrass from bluegrass turf. Rocky Mountain Regional Turfgrass Conference Proceedings. pp. 33–35. 1964.

3762. ______. Comparative toxicities and mode of action of pre-emergence crabgrass herbicides to bluegrass *(Poa pratensis)* seedlings. Dissertation Abstracts. 26(2):646. 1965.

3763. Chamberlain, H. E. and J. L. Fults. The effect of preemergence crabgrass herbicides on bluegrass seedlings of different ages. Research Progress Report of Western Weed Control Conference. pp. 30–31. 1962.

3764. ______. An evaluation of several techniques for the greenhouse evaluation of preemergence crabgrass herbicides. Research Progress Report, Western Weed Control Conference. pp. 31–32. 1962.

3765. Chamberlain, H. E., J. L. Fults, and J. W. May. Carryover effect of bandane for the control of crabgrass. Research Progress Report, Western Weed Control Conference. p. 28. 1963.

3766. ______. A technique for the greenhouse evaluation of preemergence herbicides.

Research Progress Report, Western Weed Control Conference. pp. 28–29. 1963.

3767. ______. The use of Banvel D on miscellaneous turf weeds. Research Progress Report, Western Weed Control Conference. p. 29. 1963.

3768. Chamberlain, H. E., J. L. Fults, and M. A. Ross. The effects of five preemergence herbicides on Kentucky bluegrass seeded at intervals after herbicide treatment. Research Progress Report, Western Weed Control Conference. pp. 28–29. 1962.

3769. Chamberlin, R. E. Inhibitors for roadside maintenance. 22nd Short Course on Roadside Development, (Ohio). p. 77. 1963.

3770. Champness, S. S. Effect of microclimate on the establishment of timothy grass. Nature. 165:325. 1950.

3771. Chamrad, A. D. and T. W. Box. Drought associated mortality of range grasses in south Texas. Ecology. 46(6):780–785. 1965.

3772. Chan, A. P. Turfgrass research. R.C.G.A. Sports Turfgrass Conference. 16:-1–3. 1965.

3773. Chan, F. J. Direct seeding—an alternative for establishing woody plants in the landscape. Proceedings of the 1972 Turf and Landscape Horticulture Institute. pp. 60–62. 1972.

3774. Chan, G., and J. Folkner. Highway seeding tests. Arizona Turf Conference Proceedings. 6:7–8. 1959.

3775. Chanderlin, C. C. Grass seeds in a nutshell. The National Greenkeeper. 1(8):8. 1927.

3776. ______. Grass seeds in a nutshell. The National Greenkeeper. 1(9):29–30, 36. 1927.

3777. Chapman, A. G. Experimenting in Kentucky. USGA Green Section Bulletin. 7(12):228–231. 1927.

3778. Chapman, C. J. What fertilizers for lawns and gardens. Wisconsin Agricultural Extension Bulletin 92. 4 pp. 1929.

3779. Chapman, R. A. Trends of populations of certain ectoparasitic plant nematodes in turf. Kentucky Agricultural Experiment Station Annual Report. 73:17. 1960.

3780. Bingham, S. W. Weed control—up to date–1963. Virginia Turfgrass Conference Proceedings. 8:31–34. 1963.

3781. Chappell, W. E., and R. E. Schmidt. Pre-and postemergence crabgrass and *Poa annua* control studies in turf. Proceedings of the 14th Southern Weed Control Conference. 9–97. 1961.

3782. ______. Phytotoxic effects of certain preemergence crabgrass control treatments on seedling turf grasses. Proceedings of the Northeastern Weed Control Conference. 16:474–478. 1962.

3783. Charles, A. H. Production of early grass. Journal of Agricultural Society, University College, Wales. 36:57–63. 1955.

3784. ______. Effects of method of establishment on tall fescue and Italian ryegrass mixtures in the following year. Journal of the British Grassland Society. 22(4):245–251. 1967.

3785. ______. Control of weed grasses by the selective effects of fertilizer application and management. 9th British Weed Control Conference Proceedings. 3:1223–1230. 1968.

3786. Charriere, J. Disease and pest control by sprinkler irrigation or by spraying. Revue Horticole Suisse. 38:272–274. 1965.

3787. Chase, A. The first book of grasses. Smithsonian Institute, Washington, D. C. 127 pp. 1959.

3788. Chaster, G. D. Stabilized turf—an answer to traffic? The Golf Course Reporter. 33(4):52–56. 1965.

3789. Chatterjee, B. N. Analysis of ecotypic differences in tall fescue *(Festuca arundinacea* Schreb). Annals of Applied Biology. 49:560–562. 1961.

3790. Chen, T. M., R. H. Brown, and C. C. Black. Photosynthetic activity of chloroplasts isolated from bermudagrass (*Cynodon dactylon* L.). as species with a high photosynthetic capacity. Plant Physiology. 44(5):649–654. 1969.

3791. ______. Photosynthetic $^{14}CO_2$ fixation products and activities of enzymes related to photosynthesis in bermudagrass and other plants. Plant Physiology. 47(2):-199–203. 1971.

3792. Chenoweth, A. K. Consider organic matter in soil for healthy turf. Golfdom. 2(4):28–32. 1928.

3793. Chepil, W. S., N. P. Woodruff, F. H. Siddoway, D. W. Fryrear and D. V. Armbrust. Vegetative and nonvegetative materials to control wind and water erosion. Soil Science Society of America Proceedings. 27(1):-86–89. 1963.

3794. Chepil, W. S., N. P. Woodruff, F. H. Siddoway, and L. Lyles. Anchoring vegetative mulches. Agricultural Engineering. 41(11):754–755, 759. 1960.

3795. Cherewick, W. J. Studies on the biology of *Erysiphe graminis* D. C. Canadian Journal of Research. 22:52–86. 1944.

3796. Cherry, C. E. The maintenance & management of sea-washed turf bowling greens. Journal of Board Greenkeeping Research. 7(23):70–79. 1947.

3797. Chesebro, J. W. and D. J. Porteous. Evaluation of dursban 2E emulsifiable insecticide for phytotoxicity to bentgrass turf. Down to Earth. 28(3):1–2. 1972.

3798. Cheesman, J. H. How to meet winter course maintenance problems: Southwest. Club Operations. 1(1):34–35. 1963.

3799. Cheesman, J. H. Effects of nitrogen and moisture stress on disease incidence in Merion bluegrass. Iagreen. Iowa Turfgrass Conference Proceedings. pp. 11–12. 1963.

3700a. ______. Do demonstration lawn plots pay? Seed World. 92(11):32. 1963.

3701a. ______. Grasses for shade. Seed World. 93(2):15. 1963.

3703a. Carnahan, R. Care, operation and overhauling of 2-cycle engines. Proceedings University of Florida Turf Management Conference. 4:27–31. 1956.

3704a. Carpenter, P. L. Using post-emergence turf herbicides near woody ornamentals. Grounds Maintenance. 5(7):14–17. 1970.

3705a. Carper, J. Thatch—its causes and removal. Proceedings Pacific Northwest Turf Conference. 15:79–80. 1961.

3801. Cheesman, J. Early morning golfer. The Golf Superintendent. 35(9):19, 23. 1967.

3802. Cheesman, J. Organizing and preparing your budget. Turfgrass Times. 5(2):-6–7. 1969.

3803. Cheesman, J. H. and E. C. Roberts. Effect of nitrogen level and moisture stress on *Helminthosporium* infection in Merion bluegrass. Agronomy Abstracts. 105. 1964.

3804. Cheesman, J. H., and E. C. Roberts. Effects of nitrogen and moisture stress on disease incidence in Merion bluegrass. Iagreen. Iowa Turfgrass Conference Proceedings. 30:11–12. 1964.

3805. Cheesman, J. H., E. C. Roberts, and L. H. Tiffany. Effects of nitrogen level and osmotic pressure of the nutrient solution on incidence of *Puccinia graminis* and *Helminthosporium sativum* infection in Merion kentucky bluegrass. Agronomy Journal. 57(6):599–602. 1965.

3806. Chessman, R. A. Lawns for town and country. Oklahoma Agricultural Experiment Station. Forage Crops Leaflet. 10:1–4. 1952.

3807. Chessmore, R. A. Lawns for town and country. Oklahoma Agricultural Experiment Station Publication. 1954.

3808. Chevalier, L. Comportement du *Cynodon dactylon* vis-vis d'um parasite *Ustilago cynodontis* (Pass.) P. Henn. Naturalia Monspel, Ser. Bot. 12:3–12. 1960.

3809. Chibe, Y. Shade tolerance on the growth of turfgrasses. K.G.U. Green Section Turf Research Bulletin. 16:77–91. 1969.

3810. Chilcote, D. O. Burning fields boosts grass seed yields. Crops and Soils. 21(8):18. 1969.

3811. Childers, N. F. An ideal tropical lawn grass. Agriculture in the Americas. 6:-145–147. 1946.

3812. Childers, N. F. and D. G. White. Manila Grass for lawns. Federal Experiment Station. Mayaguez, Puerto Rico. Circular No. 26. 16 pp. 1947.

3813. Childers, P. E. Maintenance of greens in Southern Arizona. Golf Course Reporter. 17(2):36. 1949.

3814. Childs, E. C. Concepts of soil water phenomena. Soil Science. 113(4):246–253. 1972.

3815. Chiles, R. E., W. W. Huffine, and J. Q. Lynd. Effect of planting depth and type of root storage on germination of four varieties of Bermudagrass. Oklahoma Agricultural Experiment Station. Processed Series P-487. 30 pp. 1964.

3816. Chiles, R. E., W. W. Huffine and J. Q. Lynd. Differential response of *Cynodon* varieties to type of sprig storage and planting depth. Agronomy Journal. 58(2):231–234. 1966.

3818. Chin, W., and W. Kroontje. Urea hydrolysis and subsequent loss of ammonia. Soil Science Society of America Proceedings. 27(3):316–318. 1963.

3819. Chinery, W. D. Lime—for or against. The National Greenkeeper. 3(4):18–19. 1929.

3820. Chinn, S. H. F. and R. J. Ledingham. A laboratory method for testing the fungicidal effects of chemicals on fungal spores in soil. Phytopathology. 52(10):1041–1044. 1962.

3821. Chippindale, H. G. The operation of interspecific competition in causing delayed growth of grasses. Annals of Applied Biology. 19(2):221–242. 1932.

3822. Chippindale, H. G. Environment and germination in grass seeds. Journal of the British Grassland Society. 4(1):57–61. 1949.

3823. Chippindall, L. K. A. The grasses and pastures of South Africa. Part 1. A guide to the identification of grasses in South Africa. Central News Agency, Cape Town, South Africa. 1955.

3824. Chisholm, A. R. A Canadian examines Pennsylvania State research plots. R.C.G.A. Sports Turfgrass Conference. 16:5. 1965.

3825. Chittenden, D. B., and E. C. Roberts. Relationship between sodium as a percent of total soluble salts in the nutrient solution and response of two roadside grasses grown in solution culture. Agronomy Abstracts. 52. 1969.

3826. Chlevin, B. Golf for industry, a planning guide. National Golf Foundation, Inc. (1957).

3827. Choate, R. G. Underground drainage of flatwood soils. Sunshine State Agricultural Research Report. 8(4):11. 1963.

3828. Cholava, R. The soils of the principal stadia in Czechoslovakia and their shortcomings. 1st Czechoslovak Symposium on Sportsturf Proceedings. pp. 37–44. 1969.

3829. Christiansen, E. E. Irrigation by sprinkling. University of California Agricultural Experiment Station Bulletin. 670:1–124. 1942.

3830. Christiansen, J. E. Lawn-sprinkler systems. California Agricultural Extension Circular. 134:1–18. 1947.

3831. Christiansen, P. A., and R. Q. Landers. Notes on prairie species in Iowa. I. Germination and establishment of several species. Proceedings of Iowa Academy of Science. 73:51–59. 1966.

3832. ______. Notes on prairie species in Iowa. II. Establishment by sod and seedling transplants. Proceedings of Iowa Academy of Science. 76:94–104. 1969.

3833. Christie, J. R. and V. G. Perry. A low-phytotoxic nematocide of the organic phosphate group. Plant Disease Reporter. 42(1):74–75. 1958.

3834. Christie, R. J., J. M. Good, and G. C. Nutter. Nematodes associated with injury to turf. Proceedings of the Soil Science Society of Florida. 14:167–169. 1954.

3835. Chubb, R. Proper irrigation by new method of flow control. Golf Course Reporter. 25:22–25. 28. 1957.

3836. Church, G. L. Meiotic phenomena in certain *Gramineae.* Botanical Gazette. 87:-608–629. 1929.

3837. ______. Cytological studies in the *Gramineae.* American Journal of Botany. 23:12–15. 1936.

3838. Chwala, A. and V. Anger. Surfactants. Endeavour. 30(110):97–99. 1971.

3839. Cissel, M. S. The Cissels employ a turf bird. Weeds, Trees and Turf. 8(7):26–27. 1969.

3840. Clapham, A. J. Growth responses of a mixed stand of perennial grasses treated with maleic hydrazide. M. S. Thesis, University of Rhode Island. pp. 1–81. 1967.

3841. Clapham, A. J., S. Kenyon and R. S. Bell. Chemical control of vegetation under highway guardrails in Rhode Island. Proceedings of the Northeastern Weed Control Conference. pp. 395–400. 1967.

3842. ______. Chemical control of vegetation under highway guardrails. Proceedings of Northeastern Weed Control Conference. 22:342–345. 1968.

3843. Clapham, A. J., R. C. Wakefield, and R. S. Bell. The effect of maleic hydrazide on the growth of turf grasses. University of Rhode Island Agricultural Experiment Station. Bulletin 399:1–22. 1969.

3844. Clapp, A. W. Suggestions for evaluating and choosing a lawn seed. Turf Bulletin. Massachusetts Turf and Lawn Grass Council. 2(12):20–22. 1965.

3845. Clapp, J. G., Jr., D. S. Chamblee, and H. D. Gross. Interrelationships between defoliation systems, morphological characteristics, and growth of 'Coastal' bermudagrass. Agronomy Abstracts. p. 34. 1965.

3846. Clapp, R. and G. P. Steinbauer. How to make and keep a good lawn. Maine Agricultural Extension Bulletin. 349. 15 pp. 1947.

3847. Clark, D. G. Influence of vitamin B_1 on the growth of *Agrostis tenuis* and *Brassica alba.* Plant Physiology. 17(1):137–140. 1942.

3848. Clark, H. Irrigation systems. Central Plains Turfgrass Conference. pp. 4–5. 1963.

3849. Clark, H. E. The requirements for grass growth. Rutgers University Short Course in Turf Management. pp. 1–5. 1960.

3850. ______. Grass nutrition. Rutgers University Annual Short Course in Turf Management. 19:59–62. 1952–1953.

3851. ______. The structure and growth of the plant. Rutgers University Turfgrass Short Course. pp. 7–9. 1966.

3852. ______. Drainage at Twickenham. Journal of the Sports Turf Research Institute. 46:14–16. 1970.

3853. Clark, H. M. Irrigation pipe materials. Golf Course Reporter. 30(6):26, 28, 30. 1962.

3854. Clark, J. N. The equipment needs in maintenance of parks and other large landscape areas. Proceedings University of Florida Turf-Grass Management Conference. 9:177–182. 1961.

3855. Clark, K. G., V. L. Gaddy, F. O. Lundstrom, and J. Y. Yee. Solubility relationships and nitrification characteristics of urea-form. Journal of Agricultural and Food Chemistry. 4(2):135–140. 1956.

3856. Clark, K. G., V. L. Gaddy, and K. D. Jacob. Availability of water-insoluble nitrogen in mixed fertilizers. Agronomy Journal. 43(2):57–61. 1951.

3857. Clark, W. H. Lawns and ground covers. Gardening the Small Place. Little, Brown, and Co. Boston. pp. 209–230. 1952.

3858. ______. On bent. The Golf Superintendent. 35(9):28. 1967.

3859. Clarke, E. S. *Cotula* and starweed greens. New Zealand Institute for Turf Culture. 42:11–12. 1966.

3860. Clarke, G. L. Elements of ecology. Wiley, New York. 1954.

3861. Clarke, S. Fairway verticutting. Proceedings University of Florida Turfgrass Management Conference. 12:88–89. 1964.

3863. ______. How I get the most from my triplex green mowers. USGA Green Section Record. 8(6):6–8. 1970.

3864. Clarke, S. E. and P. L. Frank. Tifdwarf evaluation. Proceedings University of Florida Turf Grass Management Conference. 14:69–72. 1966.

3865. Clarke, S. E., J. A. Campbell, and W. Shevkenek. The identification of certain native and naturalized grasses by their vegetative characteristics. Canada Department of Agriculture Publication 762. Technical Bulletin 50. 1944.

3866. ______. The identification of certain native and naturalized grasses by their vegetative characters. Canada Department of Agriculture Publication No. 762. Technical Bulletin No. 50. 129 pp. 1950.

3867. Clausen, J. New bluegrasses by combining and rearranging genomes of contrasting *Poa* species. Proceedings International Grassland Congress. 6:216–221. 1952.

3868. ______. How spray program protects turf against weeds. Club Operations. 3(2):G-16—G-17. 1965.

3869. Clausen, J., W. Hiesey, and M. A. Nobs. The *Poa* program. Carnegie Institute, Washington, Yearbook No. 53:151–156. 1943–1954.

3870. Clausen, J., D. D. Keck, and W. M. Hiesey. Experimental studies on the nature of species. I. Effect of varied environments on western North American plants. Carnegie Institute, Washington, Publication No. 520. Washington, D. C. 1940.

3871. ______. Experimental taxonomy. Carnegie Institute, Washington, Yearbook No. 43:69–81. 1944.

3872. ______. Experimental studies on the nature of species, III. Carnegie Institute, Washington, Publication 581. 129 pp. 1948.

3873. Cleary, J. L. Disease and wilt control in *Poa annua* and bent. Proceedings, Tennessee Turfgrass Conference. 3:15–18. 1969.

3874. Clemans, D. Maintaining a tight bluegrass turf. Proceeding of the Midwest Regional Turf Conference. pp. 37–38. 1964.

3875. ______. Developing bluegrass fairways—my program. Proceedings Midwest Regional Turf Conference. pp. 41–42. 1965.

3876. ______. Replacing weeds with turf —2nd report. Proceedings Midwest Regional Turf Conference. pp. 59–60. 1966.

3877. ______. Programed watering on 36 holes. Proceedings of the Annual Missouri Lawn and Turf Conference. 7:5–6. 1966.

3878. ______. Successful control in practice-greens. 40th International turfgrass conference and show proceedings. pp. 53–54. 1969.

3879. Clements, H. F., and H. G. Heggeness. Arsenic toxicity to plants. Hawaii Agricultural Experiment Station Annual Report. pp. 77–78. 1939.

3880. Clements, H. F. and J. Munson. Arsenic toxicity studies in soil and in culture solution. Pacific Science. 1(1):151–171. 1947.

3881. Dawson, R. B. Common weeds of turf. Journal of the Board of Greenkeeping Research. 3(11):197–199. 1934.

3882. Clements, R. H. and S. H. Kerr. Pest control. Florida Research Report. 37(10):26, 28, 30. 1969.

3883. Clements, S. Hydro-sprigging—New method of planting courses. Club Operations. 4(1):16–18, 30. 1966.

3884. Clerke, P. M. Engineering aspects for night lighting a golf course. Turf Clippings. 1(10):57–64. 1965.

3885. Clifford, E. O. and R. G. Howe. Reclaiming polyfilm tarp following soil fumigation of seedbeds. Down to Earth. 19(2):-11–12. 1963.

3886. Clinton, G. P. The *Ustilagineae,* or smuts of Connecticut. Connecticut State Geological and Natural History Survey Bulletin 5. 43 pp. 1905.

3887. Clissold, E. J. Jap beetle killer now sold under U.S. patent. Golfdom. 18(2):34, 38. 1944.

3888. Cooper, A. E. Establishing the new lawn. Pennsylvania Agricultural Extension Circular. 407:1–12. 1955.

3889. ______. The value of a consistent program of soil testing on Pennsylvania golf courses. Pennsylvania State College Turf Conference. 25:70–74. 1956.

3890. Cooper, C. S., M. G. Klages, and J. Schulz-Schaeffer. Performance of six grass species under different irrigation and nitrogen treatments. Agronomy Journal. 54(4):-283–288. 1962.

3891. Cooper, C. S. and M. Qualls. Morphology and chlorophyll content of shade and sun leaves of two legumes. Crop Science. 7(6):672–673. 1967.

3892. Cooper, G. Chemical weed control. Park Maintenance. 8(5):33–37. 1955.

3893. Cooper, J. Phosphorus. Lakeshore News. 2(3):11. 1970.

3894. Cooper, J. F. Rust resistant ryegrass released by University of Florida. Turfgrass Times. 2(1):5. 1966.

3895. Cooper, J. P. Resistance to inanition in grass seedlings. Nature. 161:894–895. 1948.

3896. ______. Day-length and head formation in the ryegrasses. Journal of the British Grassland Society. 5(2):105–112. 1950.

3897. ______. Studies on growth and development in *Lolium.* II. Pattern of bud de-

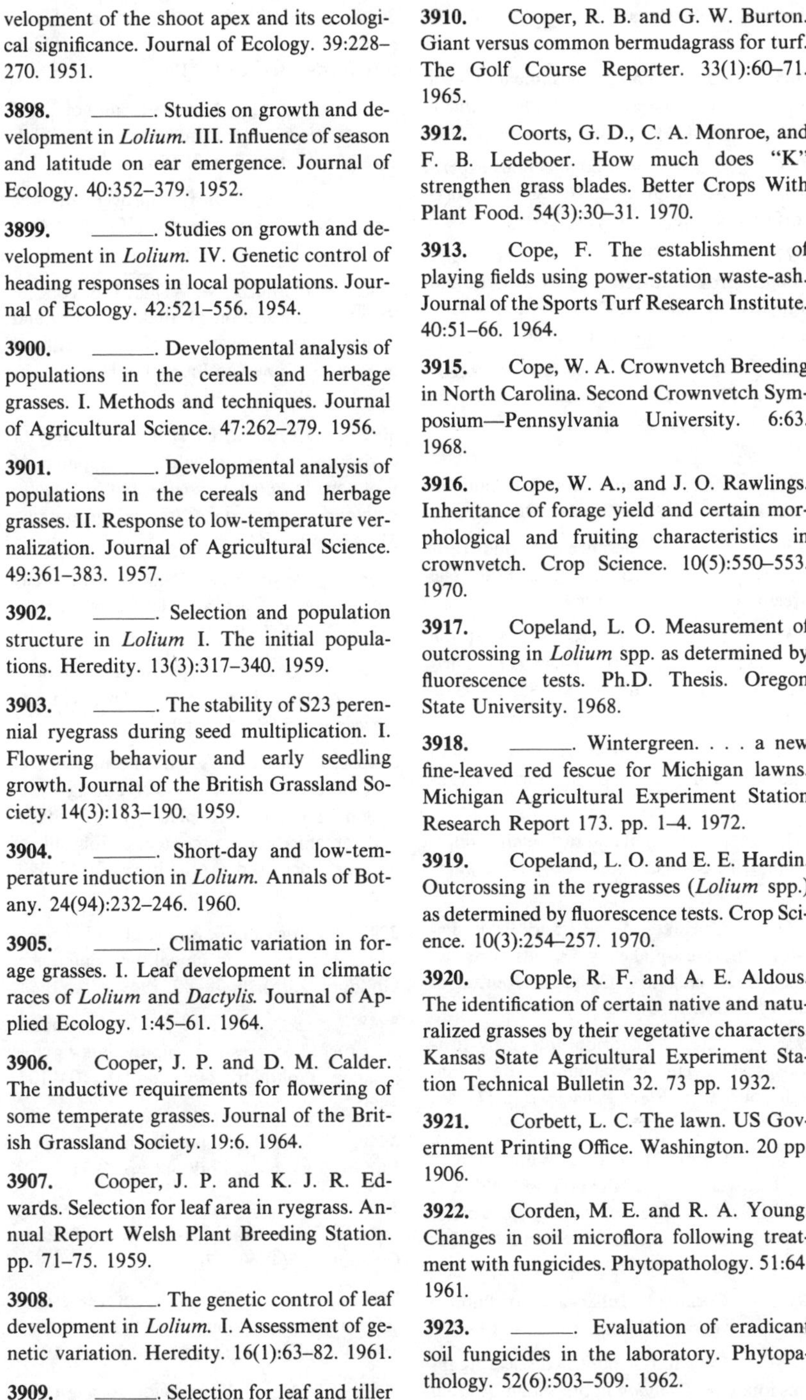

velopment of the shoot apex and its ecological significance. Journal of Ecology. 39:228–270. 1951.

3898. ______. Studies on growth and development in *Lolium.* III. Influence of season and latitude on ear emergence. Journal of Ecology. 40:352–379. 1952.

3899. ______. Studies on growth and development in *Lolium.* IV. Genetic control of heading responses in local populations. Journal of Ecology. 42:521–556. 1954.

3900. ______. Developmental analysis of populations in the cereals and herbage grasses. I. Methods and techniques. Journal of Agricultural Science. 47:262–279. 1956.

3901. ______. Developmental analysis of populations in the cereals and herbage grasses. II. Response to low-temperature vernalization. Journal of Agricultural Science. 49:361–383. 1957.

3902. ______. Selection and population structure in *Lolium* I. The initial populations. Heredity. 13(3):317–340. 1959.

3903. ______. The stability of S23 perennial ryegrass during seed multiplication. I. Flowering behaviour and early seedling growth. Journal of the British Grassland Society. 14(3):183–190. 1959.

3904. ______. Short-day and low-temperature induction in *Lolium.* Annals of Botany. 24(94):232–246. 1960.

3905. ______. Climatic variation in forage grasses. I. Leaf development in climatic races of *Lolium* and *Dactylis.* Journal of Applied Ecology. 1:45–61. 1964.

3906. Cooper, J. P. and D. M. Calder. The inductive requirements for flowering of some temperate grasses. Journal of the British Grassland Society. 19:6. 1964.

3907. Cooper, J. P. and K. J. R. Edwards. Selection for leaf area in ryegrass. Annual Report Welsh Plant Breeding Station. pp. 71–75. 1959.

3908. ______. The genetic control of leaf development in *Lolium.* I. Assessment of genetic variation. Heredity. 16(1):63–82. 1961.

3909. ______. Selection for leaf and tiller development. Annual Report Welsh Plant Breeding Station. p. 18. 1962.

3910. Cooper, R. B. and G. W. Burton. Giant versus common bermudagrass for turf. The Golf Course Reporter. 33(1):60–71. 1965.

3912. Coorts, G. D., C. A. Monroe, and F. B. Ledeboer. How much does "K" strengthen grass blades. Better Crops With Plant Food. 54(3):30–31. 1970.

3913. Cope, F. The establishment of playing fields using power-station waste-ash. Journal of the Sports Turf Research Institute. 40:51–66. 1964.

3915. Cope, W. A. Crownvetch Breeding in North Carolina. Second Crownvetch Symposium—Pennsylvania University. 6:63. 1968.

3916. Cope, W. A., and J. O. Rawlings. Inheritance of forage yield and certain morphological and fruiting characteristics in crownvetch. Crop Science. 10(5):550–553. 1970.

3917. Copeland, L. O. Measurement of outcrossing in *Lolium* spp. as determined by fluorescence tests. Ph.D. Thesis. Oregon State University. 1968.

3918. ______. Wintergreen. . . . a new fine-leaved red fescue for Michigan lawns. Michigan Agricultural Experiment Station Research Report 173. pp. 1–4. 1972.

3919. Copeland, L. O. and E. E. Hardin. Outcrossing in the ryegrasses (*Lolium* spp.) as determined by fluorescence tests. Crop Science. 10(3):254–257. 1970.

3920. Copple, R. F. and A. E. Aldous. The identification of certain native and naturalized grasses by their vegetative characters. Kansas State Agricultural Experiment Station Technical Bulletin 32. 73 pp. 1932.

3921. Corbett, L. C. The lawn. US Government Printing Office. Washington. 20 pp. 1906.

3922. Corden, M. E. and R. A. Young. Changes in soil microflora following treatment with fungicides. Phytopathology. 51:64. 1961.

3923. ______. Evaluation of eradicant soil fungicides in the laboratory. Phytopathology. 52(6):503–509. 1962.

3924. Cordukes, W. E. Compaction and wear of turf grasses. Greenhouse Garden

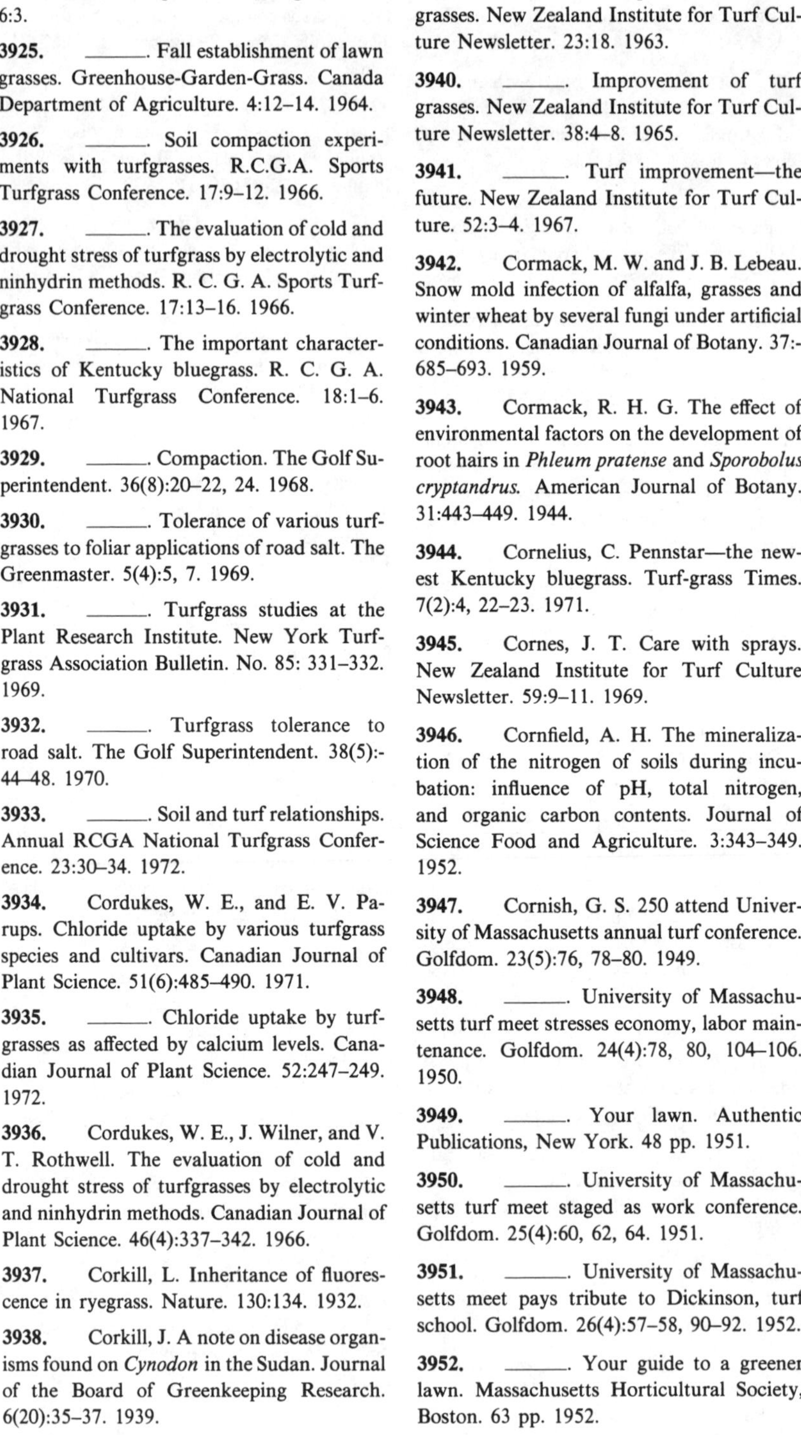

Grass. Canada Department of Agriculture. 6:3.

3925. ______. Fall establishment of lawn grasses. Greenhouse-Garden-Grass. Canada Department of Agriculture. 4:12–14. 1964.

3926. ______. Soil compaction experiments with turfgrasses. R.C.G.A. Sports Turfgrass Conference. 17:9–12. 1966.

3927. ______. The evaluation of cold and drought stress of turfgrass by electrolytic and ninhydrin methods. R. C. G. A. Sports Turfgrass Conference. 17:13–16. 1966.

3928. ______. The important characteristics of Kentucky bluegrass. R. C. G. A. National Turfgrass Conference. 18:1–6. 1967.

3929. ______. Compaction. The Golf Superintendent. 36(8):20–22, 24. 1968.

3930. ______. Tolerance of various turfgrasses to foliar applications of road salt. The Greenmaster. 5(4):5, 7. 1969.

3931. ______. Turfgrass studies at the Plant Research Institute. New York Turfgrass Association Bulletin. No. 85: 331–332. 1969.

3932. ______. Turfgrass tolerance to road salt. The Golf Superintendent. 38(5):-44–48. 1970.

3933. ______. Soil and turf relationships. Annual RCGA National Turfgrass Conference. 23:30–34. 1972.

3934. Cordukes, W. E., and E. V. Parups. Chloride uptake by various turfgrass species and cultivars. Canadian Journal of Plant Science. 51(6):485–490. 1971.

3935. ______. Chloride uptake by turfgrasses as affected by calcium levels. Canadian Journal of Plant Science. 52:247–249. 1972.

3936. Cordukes, W. E., J. Wilner, and V. T. Rothwell. The evaluation of cold and drought stress of turfgrasses by electrolytic and ninhydrin methods. Canadian Journal of Plant Science. 46(4):337–342. 1966.

3937. Corkill, L. Inheritance of fluorescence in ryegrass. Nature. 130:134. 1932.

3938. Corkill, J. A note on disease organisms found on *Cynodon* in the Sudan. Journal of the Board of Greenkeeping Research. 6(20):35–37. 1939.

3939. Corkill, L. Improvement of turf grasses. New Zealand Institute for Turf Culture Newsletter. 23:18. 1963.

3940. ______. Improvement of turf grasses. New Zealand Institute for Turf Culture Newsletter. 38:4–8. 1965.

3941. ______. Turf improvement—the future. New Zealand Institute for Turf Culture. 52:3–4. 1967.

3942. Cormack, M. W. and J. B. Lebeau. Snow mold infection of alfalfa, grasses and winter wheat by several fungi under artificial conditions. Canadian Journal of Botany. 37:-685–693. 1959.

3943. Cormack, R. H. G. The effect of environmental factors on the development of root hairs in *Phleum pratense* and *Sporobolus cryptandrus.* American Journal of Botany. 31:443–449. 1944.

3944. Cornelius, C. Pennstar—the newest Kentucky bluegrass. Turf-grass Times. 7(2):4, 22–23. 1971.

3945. Cornes, J. T. Care with sprays. New Zealand Institute for Turf Culture Newsletter. 59:9–11. 1969.

3946. Cornfield, A. H. The mineralization of the nitrogen of soils during incubation: influence of pH, total nitrogen, and organic carbon contents. Journal of Science Food and Agriculture. 3:343–349. 1952.

3947. Cornish, G. S. 250 attend University of Massachusetts annual turf conference. Golfdom. 23(5):76, 78–80. 1949.

3948. ______. University of Massachusetts turf meet stresses economy, labor maintenance. Golfdom. 24(4):78, 80, 104–106. 1950.

3949. ______. Your lawn. Authentic Publications, New York. 48 pp. 1951.

3950. ______. University of Massachusetts turf meet staged as work conference. Golfdom. 25(4):60, 62, 64. 1951.

3951. ______. University of Massachusetts meet pays tribute to Dickinson, turf school. Golfdom. 26(4):57–58, 90–92. 1952.

3952. ______. Your guide to a greener lawn. Massachusetts Horticultural Society, Boston. 63 pp. 1952.

3953. ______. Course construction. The Golf Course Reporter. 26(6):22–28. 1958.

3954. ______. Turf construction methods and equipment. New York State Turf Association Bulletin. 61:237–238. 1958.

3955. ______. What's new in fertilizers. Turf Clippings. 1(8):A-40, A-41. 1963.

3956. Cornish, G. and W. Robinson. Custom-made municipals. Golfdom. 40(8):-22–26. 1966.

3957. ______. Renovation and rebuilding. The Golf Superintendent. 34(8):20–24. 1966.

3958. ______. Course modernization. The Greenmaster. 2(9):2. 1966.

3959. ______. Renovation and rebuilding. Turf Bulletin. 3(2):9–10. 1966.

3960. ______. Good landscaping is an asset. Golfdom 41(4):36–40. 1967.

3961. ______. Design for maintenance. Golfdom. 41(6):36–39, 70. 1967.

3962. Cornish, G. S. Problems in renovation and rebuilding. University of Maine Turf Conference Proceedings. 6:32–35. 1968.

3963. ______. Contemporary design standards. Turf Clippings. University of Massachusetts. 3(3):A34–36. 1968.

3964. Cornish, G. S. and W. G. Robinson, Golf course design, an introduction. Cornish and Robinson. (1971).

3965. Cornman, J. F. Home lawn. Cornell Agricultural Extension Bulletin 469. 22 pp. 1941.

3966. ______. Home lawn. Cornell Agricultural Extension Bulletin 469. 22 pp. 1946(rev.).

3967. ______. Home lawn. Cornell Agricultural Extension Bulletin 469. 22 pp. 1949 (rev.).

3968. ______. Fall tips on lawns and fairways. New York State Turf Association. Bulletin 5:17. 1949.

3969. ______. Fertilizers for turf areas. New York State Turf Association. Bulletin 8:29–30. 1949.

3970. ______. Spring work on lawns New York State Turf Association. Bulletin 11:41–42. 1950.

3971. ______. Maleic hydrazide. New York State Turf Association. Bulletin 15:58. 1950.

3972. ______. Crabgrass killers as I see them. New York State Turf Association. Bulletin 15:59. 1950.

3973. ______. What to do about high seed prices. New York State Turf Association. Bulletin 16:62–63. 1950.

3974. ______. Cornell turf research in 1950. New York State Turf Association. Bulletin 17:65–66. 1950.

3975. ______. About liquid fertilizers. New York State Turf Association Bulletin. 20:78. 1950.

3976. ______. Grass seed mixtures. Proceedings of Southeastern New York Turf School. pp. 24–28. 1950.

3977. ______. Fertilizers for turf. Proceedings of Southern New York Turf School. pp. 5–7. 1950.

3978. ______. Mat formation on putting greens. New York State Turf Association Bulletin. 29:112–114. 1951.

3979. ______. Eliminating mat on putting greens. New York State Turf Association Bulletin. 30:117–118. 1951.

3980. ______. Merion bluegrass—an appraisal. New York State Turf Association Bulletin. 32:123–125. 1951.

3981. ______. Mat formation on putting greens. Golf Course Reporter. 20(4):8–14. 1952.

3982. ______. Endothal, 2,4,5–T tests show effective clover control. Golfdom. 27(5):86–87. 1953.

3983. ______. Cornell lawn seed recommendations—their basis. New York State Turf Association Bulletin. 45:171–173. 1953.

3984. ______. Fertilizers for turf. New York State Turf Association Bulletin. 46:-175–176. 1953.

3985. ______. Cornell conference answers many turf problems. Golfdom. 29(5):-76,78. 1955.

3986. ______. Home lawns. Cornell Agricultural Extension Bulletin 922. 32 pp. 1954.

3987. ______. Zoysias as lawn grasses in New York. New York State Turf Association Bulletin. 57:222. 1957.

3988. ______. Home lawns. Cornell Agricultural Extension Bulletin 922. 32 pp. 1958.

3989. ______. In the Northeast. Golf Course Reporter. 27(7):28–31. 1959.

3990. ______. Chemical control of crabgrass 1959 Cornell recommendations. New York State Turf Association Bulletin. 63:246. 1959.

3991. ______. Watering recommendations unchanged. New York State Turfgrass Association Bulletin. 65:251–252. 1959.

3992. ______. Fall lawn care. Merion Bluegrass Association. 27(7). 1959.

3993. Cornman, J. F. and R. G. Mower. Pre-emergence and post-emergence crabgrass control. Proceedings Northeastern Weed Control Conference. 14:271–277. 1960.

3994. Cornman, J. F. Home lawns. Cornell Agricultural Extension Bulletin 922. 32 pp. 1961 (rev.).

3995. ______. Practical turfgrass fertilization. International Turf-Grass Conference Proceedings. 32:11. 1961.

3996. Cornman, J. F. and J. A. Weidhass. 1962 Cornell recommendations for turfgrass. New York State College of Agriculture at Cornell University. Cooperative Extension Service. April, 1962.

3997. Cornman, J. F. Algae in turf. USGA Green Section Mid-Continent Turfletter. No. 5. p. 3. 1961.

3998. ______. Practical turfgrass fertilization. Golf Course Reporter. 29(4):35–40. 1961.

3999. ______. *Veronica filiformis* and its control. New York State Turf Association Bulletin. 68:263–264. 1961.

4000. ______. Practical turfgrass fertilization. New York State Turf Association Bulletin. 67:257–258. 1961.

4001. Clissold, E. J. Control of Japanese beetle grub. The Greenkeepers' Reporter. 12(1):5,31. 1944.

4002. Cloud, B. Designing more effective sprinkler systems. Proceedings Turfgrass Sprinkler Irrigation Conference. 4:1–5. 1966.

4003. ______. Specifications: their importance and make-up. Proceedings Turfgrass Sprinkler Irrigation Conference. 5:28–34. 1967.

4004. Clough, J. How to select a sprinkler irrigation system. Grounds Maintenance. 1(4):10–14. 1966.

4005. Clough, J. and S. Scanlon. Synthetic turf is here to stay. Grounds Maintenance. 4(6):14–20. 1969.

4006. Clouston, D. The identification of grasses by leaf anatomy. Thesis for D.Sc. University Library, Edinburgh. 1935.

4007. ______. The establishment and care of fine turf for lawns and sports grounds. D. Wylie & Son. Aberdeen. 121 pp. 1937.

4008. ______. Identification of grasses in non-flowering condition. Journal of the Sports Turf Research Institute. 10(36):146–155. 1960.

4009. ______. Identification of grasses in non-flowering condition. Journal of the Sports Turf Research Institute. 10(37):254–263. 1961.

4010. Coartney, J. S., and A. H. Kates. What type 2, 4-D to use? Weeds, Trees and Turf. 8(7):16–18. 1969.

4011. Coats, G. E. and C. Y. Ward. Response of bermudagrass cultivars to preemergence herbicides. Southern Weed Science Society Proceedings. 25:193. 1972.

4012. Cobb, G. Architectural design of golf courses for practical maintenance and the superintendent's role in establishment. Proceedings of University of Florida Turf-Grass Management Conference. 8:29–32. 1960.

4013. Cockerham, K. L. The control of lawn insects. Southern Seedsman. 21(2):20–21,48,50–51. 1958.

4014. Cockerham, S. T. Evaluation of Kentucky bluegrasses in California. Cal-Turf, Inc., Camarillo, Cal. 1972.

4015. ______. Growth retardants. Park Maintenance. 25(7):17. 1972.

4016. ______. *Poa annua.* Park Maintenance. 25(7):19. 1972.

4017. Cockerham, S. T., and D. Barlow. Evaluation of turfgrass growth retardant chemicals. California Turfgrass Culture. 21(3):23. 1971.

4018. Cockerham, S. T. and J. W. Whitworth. Germination and control of annual bluegrass. The Golf Superintendent. 35(5):-10–17, 45–46. 1967.

4019. Cockerham, S. T., R. W. Chase, and T. Grether. Development of a commercial by-product from turfgrass clippings. Agronomy Abstracts. p. 62. 1972.

4020. Codd, L. E. W. Seed setting and strain building in grass. With special reference to "Makari-kari" grass. Farming in South Africa. 14:277–279. 1939.

4021. Coelho, R. C. Seed dormancy in western wheatgrass. M.S. Thesis, Mississippi State University. 1971.

4022. Coffin, C. Memorial parks. Proceedings University of Florida Turf-Grass Management Conference. 8:112–115. 1960.

4024. Coffman, B. S., and P. H. Brown. A study of roadside maintenance and its effect on highway design and construction. Engineering Experiment Station Report. Ohio State University. 189(2):95 pp. 1963.

4025. Coffman, B. S. and W. F. Edwards. A study of roadside maintenance and its effect on highway design and construction. Ohio Short Course on Roadside Development. 22:65–70. 1962.

4026. Coffman, B. S., and J. S. Sawhney. Fertilization and erosion on a new highway. Highway Research Record. 93:2–23. 1965.

4027. Coffman, B. S., P. H. Brown, and G. B. Tobey. A study of roadside maintenance and its effect on highway design and construction. Engineering Experiment Station Report. Ohio State University. Report 189–1. 127 pp. 1962.

4028. Cohen, Y. and N. H. Tadmor. Effects of temperature on the elongation of seedling roots of some grasses and legumes. Crop Science. 9(2):189–192. 1969.

4029. Coith, A. T. Maintaining turf facilities in municipal parks. University of Florida Turfgrass Conference Proceedings. 7:88–89. 1959.

4031. Colbaugh, P. The influence of management practices on turfgrass diseases. II. Proceedings of the 1972 Turf and Landscape Horticulture Institute. p. 52. 1972.

4032. Colburn, B. Maintenance fertilization of bermuda grass. Proceedings University of Florida Turf-Grass Management Conference. 17:49–50. 1969.

4033. Colburn, W. E. Fertilization of T-419 (Tifway) bermudagrass on high sandy soils. Proceedings University of Florida Turf-Grass Management Conference. 10:95–97. 1962.

4034. ______. What about topdressing. Proceedings of University of Florida Turf-Grass Management Conference. 11:56–57. 1963.

4035. ______. Fairway verticutting. Proceedings University of Florida Turf-Grass Management Conference. 12:90. 1964.

4036. ______. Comparison of lawn sprinklers. Proceedings University of Florida Turf-Grass Management Conference. 13:75–76. 1965.

4037. Colby, W. G. Conserving soil for a good lawn. Turf clippings. University of Massachusetts. 1(5):A–27 to A–28. 1960.

4038. Colby, W. G. and E. J. Bredakis. The feeding power of four turf species for exchangeable and non-exchangeable potassium. Agronomy Abstracts. p. 35. 1966.

4039. Colby, W. G., and L. J. Zanoni. Levels of soluble reserve carbohydrates in some cool season grasses. Agronomy Abstracts. p. 57. 1968.

4040. Cole, B. Employee motivation. Central Plains Turfgrass Conference. pp. 3–4. 1961.

4041. Cole, F. D. Establishment of roadside vegetation along Arizona highways. Arizona University and Highway Department. HPR–1(3), 4B. 1967.

4042. Cole, H. Fungicide resistance and pathogenic specialization among isolates of the *Sclerotinia* dollar spot causal organism *Sclerotinia homoeocarpa.* Rutgers University. College of Agriculture and Environmental Science. Lawn and Utility Turf Section. pp. 65–66. 1969.

4043. ______. Fungicide resistance and pathogenic specialization among isolates of the "*Sclerotinia*" dollar spot causal organism

"*Sclerotinia homoeocarpa.*" Rutgers University Short Course in Turf Management. 37:-1-2. 1969.

4044. ______. Pesticides, a pollution paradox. Ohio Turfgrass Conference Proceedings. pp. 6–10. 1970.

4045. ______. A grass roots view of pesticides. The Keynoter. Pennsylvania Turfgrass Council. pp. 2–3. 1971.

4046. Cole, H., and P. M. Anderson. Carbon dioxide-powered plot sprayer for turfgrass disease control fungicide application. Plant Disease Reporter. 52(9):678–682. 1968.

4047. Cole, H. and O. D. Burke. Control turf and lawn diseases. Pennsylvania Agricultural Extension Circular. 492:1–8. 1959.

4048. Cole, H. and H. Couch. Control turfgrass diseases. Pennsylvania Agricultural Extension Circular. 510:1–32.

4049. Cole, H., S. W. Braverman, and J. Duich. *Fusaria* and other fungi from seeds and seedlings of Merion and other turf-type bluegrasses. Phytopathology. 58(10):1415–1419. 1968.

4050. Cole, H., L. B. Massie and J. Duich. Bentgrass varietal susceptibility to *Sclerotinia* dollar spot and control with 1-(butylcarbamoyl)-2-benzimidazole carbamic acid, methyl ester, a new systemic fungicide. The Plant Disease Reporter. 52(5):410–414. 1968.

4051. ______. Control of stripe smut in Merion Kentucky bluegrass turf with Benomyl. The Plant Disease Reporter. 54(2):146–150. 1970.

4052. Cole, H., A. T. Perkins and J. Duich. *Sclerotinia* dollarspot on bentgrass-varietal susceptibility to infection and influence of variety on fungicide effectiveness. The Plant Disease Reporter. 51(1):40–42. 1967.

4053. Cole, H., J. M. Duich, L. B. Massie and W. D. Barber. Influence of fungus isolate and grass variety on *Sclerotinia* dollarspot development. Crop Science. 9(5):567–570. 1969.

4054. Cole, H., J. Duich, B. Taylor and G. Brown. Fungicide programs for the control of *Helminthosporium* leafspot and crown rot on Kentucky bluegrass. The Plant Disease Reporter. 53(6):462–466. 1969.

4055. Cole, S. W. The action of the sulphates of ammonia and iron on grasses and weeds. Journal of the Board of Greenkeeping Research. 1(2):79–88. 1930.

4056. Coleman, V. R. Insect control on golf greens. Southeastern Turfgrass Conference. 21:46–47. 1967.

4057. Coleman, C. Y., and E. L. McWhirter. Turfgrass research report 1970, Mississippi. Southern Regional Turf Research Committee Report, Virginia Polytechnic Institute. pp. 15–18. 1970.

4058. Coles, W. H. Modern methods of lawn irrigation by automatic sprinkling. Park and Cemetery. 41(10):294–295. 1931.

4059. Collins, C. Herbicides new and old —using them effectively. Proceedings Missouri Lawn and Turf Conference. 8:10–13. 1967.

4060. Collins, J. B., E. P. Whiteside, and C. E. Cress. Seasonal variability of pH and lime requirements in several southern Michigan soils when measured in different ways. Soil Science Society of America Proceedings. 34(1):56–61. 1970.

4061. Collins, W. Herbicides and herbicide equipment. Proceedings of University of Florida Turf Grass Management Conference. 12:171–177. 1964.

4062. Colt, H. S., and C. H. Alison. Some essays on golf course architecture. Charles Schribner's Sons, London. 1920.

4063. ______. Some essays on golf-course architecture. Country Life—George Newnes Ltd. London, England. 69 pp. 1920.

4064. Coltharp, J. L. Herbicide evaluation for the selective control of annual bluegrass in bermudagrass turf. M.S. Thesis, Oklahoma State University. 24 pp. 1970.

4065. Coltharp, J. L., and W. W. Huffine. Herbicide evaluation for the selective control of annual bluegrass in bermudagrass turf. Agronomy Abstracts. p. 52. 1969.

4066. Comar, C. L. and C. G. Barr. Evaluation of foliage injury and water loss in connection with use of wax and oil emulsions. Plant Physiology. 19(1):90–104. 1944.

4067. Combe, G. A. Lifting, renovating and relaying a putting green. New Zealand Institute for Turf Culture. Newsletter 41:11–12. 1966.

4068. Combellack, J. H., and N. J. Gelbertson. Weed control in turf with hydroxybenzonitriles. Proceedings, Victorian Weeds Conference. 1968.

4070. Compton, C. C. Chlordane in fertilizer for soil-insects control. USGA Journal and Turf Management. 2(4):32. 1949.

4071. Condo, J. K. What turf grass certification means to the state plant board. Proceedings University of Florida Turf Management Conference. 5:33–35. 1957.

4072. ______. A report on the turf grass certification program. Proceedings University of Florida Turf Management Conference. 6:41–43. 1958.

4073. ______. Floratine St. Augustinegrass release. Florida Turfgrass Management Conference Proceedings. 7:37–39. 1959.

4074. ______. Present status of the certification program. Proceedings University of Florida Turf-Grass Management Conference. 8:61–63. 1960.

4075. ______. The Florida turf-grass certification program—Now and the future. Proceedings University of Florida Turf-Grass Management Conference. 9:115–117. 1961.

4076. ______. Present status of the turfgrass certification program. Proceedings University of Florida Turf-Grass Management Conference. 10:191–194. 1962.

4077. ______. The progress of certification. Proceedings University of Florida Turf-Grass Management Conference. 11:136–137. 1963.

4078. Conger, G. H. Bermuda in Oklahoma. The National Greenkeeper. 2(1):6, 27. 1928.

4079. Conlin, C. B. Stabilization of a sand blow area. Turf Bulletin. Massachusetts Turf and Lawn Grass Council. 2(9):3–4. 1964.

4080. Conn, P. W. H. Cultivation and maintenance of grass areas. Parks, Golf Courses & Sports Grounds. 22(10):627, 636–639. 1957.

4081. Connell, C. H. and M. T. Garrett. Disinfection effectiveness of heat drying of sludge. Journal Water Pollution Control Federation. pp. 1262–1268. 1963.

4082. Connell, R. P. Eradication of tall fescue. New Zealand Journal of Agriculture. 40:93–99. 1930.

4084. Conner, C. N. Road surfaces for club grounds. The Greenkeepers' Reporter. 5(5):3–8, 15. 1937.

4085. Conner, H. E. Variation in leaf anatomy in *Festuca novaezelandiae* (Hack.) Cockayne and *F. matthewsii* (Hack.) Cheeseman. New Zealand Journal of Science. 3(3):-468–509. 1960.

4086. Conner, S. D. New and old lawns. Purdue Agricultural Extension Leaflet. 149:4. 1929.

4087. Conner, S. D. and M. L. Fisher. How to make and maintain a lawn. Purdue Agricultural Extension Leaflet. 41:1–6. 1922.

4088. ______. How to make and maintain a lawn. Purdue Agricultural Extension Leaflet. 41:1–6. (2d. rev. ed.) 1926.

4089. ______. How to make and maintain a lawn. Purdue Agricultural Extension Leaflet. 41:1–6. (3rd rev. ed.) 1928.

4090. ______. How to make and maintain a lawn. Purdue Agricultural Extension Leaflet. 41:1–6. (4th rev.) 1931.

4091. ______. How to make and maintain a lawn. Purdue Agricultural Extension Leaflet. 41:1–6. (5th rev. ed.) 1937.

4092. Conover, C. A. Some useful conversion factors and short-cuts in calculation. Florida Turf. 2(3):4–8. 1969.

4093. Conover, H. S. Seeding and care of lawns, pastures and borrow pits. Public Grounds Maintenance Handbook. Tennessee Valley Authority. pp. 9–69. 1953.

4094. ______. Weeds. Public Grounds Maintenance Handbook. Tennessee Valley Authority. pp. 209–270. 1953.

4095. ______. Soil erosion. Public Grounds Maintenance Handbook. Tennessee Valley Authority. pp. 271–312. 1953.

4096. ______. Grounds maintenance handbook. F. W. Dodge Corporation, New York. 501 pp. 1958.

4097. ______. Grounds maintenance handbook. McGraw-Hill Book Company, Inc., New York. Tennessee Valley Authority. 501 pp. 1953.

4098. Conover, T. Sulphate as a fertilizer. The National Greenkeeper. 6(9):13–14. 1932.

4099. Conquest, A. H. Cost of mowing and fertilizing memorial parks. Exposition Conference. Southern California. 3 pp. 1966.

4100. Conrad, B. A. *Poa annua* greens in Denver. Greenkeepers' Reporter. 11(3):15. 1943.

4101. Conrad, J. P. and C. N. Adams. Retention by soils of the nitrogen of urea and some related phenomena. Journal of the American Society of Agronomy. 32(1):48–54. 1940.

4102. Conrad, W. E. Restoration of native growth along the interstate highway by hydraulic seedings. Ohio Short Course on Roadside Development. 22:58–64. 1963.

4103. Congers, E. S., L. P. Wilding, and E. O. McLean. Influence of chemical weathering on basal spacings of clay minerals. Soil Science Society of America Proceedings. 33(4):518–523. 1969.

4104. Cook, C. W. A study of the roots of *Bromus inermis* in relation to drought resistance. Ecology. 24:169–182. 1943.

4105. Cook, W. C., I. B. Jensen, G. B. Colthorp and E. M. Larson. Seeding methods for Utah roadsides. Utah Agricultural Experiment Station, Utah Resources Series 52. pp. 3–22. 1970.

4106. Cook, D. I. and D. F. VanHaverbeke. Trees and shrubs for noise abatement. University of Nebraska College of Agriculture the Agricultural Experiment Station Research Bulletin 246. pp. 1–77. 1971.

4107. Cook, G. D., J. R. Dixon and A. C. Leopold. Transpiration: its effects on plant's leaf temperature. Science. 144:546–47. 1964.

4108. Cook, J. Wellesley College's melting pot of machinery, grounds. Grounds Maintenance. 3(4):56–58. 1968.

4109. Cook, J. B. Controlling gophers with poison and traps. California Turfgrass Culture. 12(2):16. 1962.

4110. Cook, R. L. and M. M. McCool. Rate of intake, accumulation, and transformation of nitrate nitrogen by small grains and Kentucky bluegrass. Journal of the American Society of Agronomy. 22(9):757–764. 1930.

4111. Cook, R. N. The effect of nitrogen carriers on growth and disease of bentgrass turf cut at ¼ inch. Rutgers University Short Course in Turf Management. 27:1–2. 1959.

4112. Cook, R. N. and R. E. Engel. The effect of nitrogen carriers on the incidence of disease on bentgrass turf. Agronomy Abstracts. 51:88. 1959.

4113. ______. Nitrogen fertilizer studies. Rutgers University Short Course in Turf Management. 28:1–2. 1960.

4114. Cook, R. N., R. E. Engel, and S. Bachelder. A study of the effect of nitrogen carriers on turfgrass disease. The Plant Disease Reporter. 48(4):254–255. 1964.

4115. Cook, W. H. and A. C. Halferdahl. Chemical weed killers. A Review, National Research Council of Canada Bulletin 18. 1937.

4116. Cook, W. L. A light on golf. Parks and Recreation. 46(9):312–313. 1963.

4117. Cook, W. L. and R. Hollard. Public golf courses. American Institute of Park Executives, Inc. 1964.

4118. Cooke, I. J. Soil conditions and turf establishment. The Groundsman. 15(8):-14–16. 1962.

4119. ______. Looking after the roots. The Groundsman. 15(9):18–20. 1962.

4120. ______. Damage to plant roots caused by urea and anhydrous ammonia. Nature. 194(4835):1262–1263. 1962.

4121. Coombe, D. E. The spectral composition of shade light in woodlands. Journal of Ecology. 45:823–830. 1957.

4122. Cooney, J. C., and E. Pickard. Comparative tick control field tests—land between the lakes. Down to Earth. 28(1):9–11. 1972.

4123. Cordukes, W. E., and A. J. MacLean. Tolerance of some turfgrasses to different concentrations of salt in soils. C.D.A. Plant Research Institute Contribution No. 931 and Soil Research Institute Contribution No. 436. 1972.

4124. Cooper, A. E. Turf on athletic fields. Greenkeepers' Reporter. 17(6):26–28. 1949.

4125. ______. Turf on athletic fields New York State Turf Association. Bulletin 9. pp. 33–34, 42–43. 1949.

4126. ______. Turf extension program in Pennsylvania. Proceedings of Midwest Regional Turf Conference. pp. 66–69. 1950.

4127. ______. Establishing the new lawn. Pennsylvania Agricultural Extension Circular. 407:1–9. 1952.

4128. ______. Lawn management. Pennsylvania State College Agricultural Extension Service Circular 412. pp. 1–14. 1953.

4129. ______. Soil testing and golf course fertilization. Pennsylvania State College Twenty-Second Annual Turfgrass Conference Proceedings. pp. 22–25. 1953.

4130. ______. Turf on athletic fields. New York State Turf Association Bulletin 39 & 40. p. 158. 1953.

4131. ______. Soil testing and golf course fertilization. Pennsylvania State College Turf Conference. 23:22–25. 1954.

4132. Cornman, J. F. 1961 chemical control of crabgrass. New York State Turf Association Bulletin. 66:254, 256. 1961.

4133. ______. You can have a beautiful lawn, if you get rid of these weeds. Cornell Agricultural Extension Bulletin 1079. 4 pp. 1962.

4134. ______. 1962 Pre-emergence crabgrass control. New York State Turf Association Bulletin. 70:270–271. 1962.

4135. ______. Weeds in golf course turf and their control. Turf Clippings 1(9):A1–A3. 1964.

4136. ______. Weeds in golf course turf and their control. Turf Bulletin. Massachusetts Turf and Lawn Grass Council. 2(7):6, 14. 1964.

4137. ______. Home lawns. Cornell Agricultural Extension Bulletin 922. 32 pp. 1965.

4138. ______. Annual bluegrass—a turfgrass enigma. Cornell Plantations. 21(4):66–68. 1966.

4139. ______. Preemergence crabgrass control in old and new turf in 1965. Proceedings of the Northeastern Weed Control Conference. p. 510–513. 1966.

4140. ______. Residual effects of R-4461 on perennial turfgrasses. North East Weed Control Conference Proceedings. 20:552–553. 1966.

4141. ______. Preemergence crabgrass control results in 1966. Proceedings of the Northeastern Weed Control Conference. p. 483. 1967.

4142. ______. 1967 Cornell recommendations for turfgrass. New York Agricultural Extension Service Publication. 1967.

4143. ______. The influence of maintenance practices on thatch formation by Merion Kentucky bluegrass turf. Agronomy Abstracts. p. 53. 1969.

4144. ______. Turfgrass management in the north-eastern United States. Proceedings of the First International Turfgrass Research Conference. pp. 17–18. 1969.

4145. ______. Thatch, cultivation and top-dressing of high-cut turf. Proceedings of the First International Turfgrass Research Conference. pp. 502–503. 1969.

4146. ______. Turf research in New York State. Rutgers University. College of Agriculture and Environmental Science. Lawn and Utility Turf Section. pp. 74–76. 1969.

4147. ______. Turf research in New York state. Rutgers University Short Course in Turf Management. 37:1–3. 1969.

4148. ______. The nature of turf herbicides—dicamba. Rutgers University Short Course in Turf Management Proceedings. 21 pp. 1971.

4149. ______. Some thoughts on control of turf weeds—chickweeds, clover, and wild onion. Rutgers University Short Course in Turf Management Proceedings. p. 22. 1971.

4150. Cornman, J. F. and J. A. Jagschitz. Endothal for clover control—1952 trials. New York State Turf Association Bulletin 39 & 40. pp. 151–156. 1953.

4151. ______. 2, 4, 5, —T for clover control in October. New York State Turf Association Bulletin 39 & 40. p. 157. 1953.

4152. Cornman, J. F., and R. C. O'Knefski. Commercial turfgrass sod production. New York Turfgrass Association Bulletin. 78:301–303. 1967.

4153. Cornman, J. F., F. M. Madden, and N. J. Smith. Tolerance of established lawn grasses, putting greens, and turfgrass seeds to preemergence crabgrass control chemicals. Proceedings Northeastern Weed Control Conference. 18:519–522. 1964.

4154. Corns, W. G. Chemical weed control. Second Western Turf Conference at University of Alberta, Edmonton. pp. 27–30. 1953.

4155. ______. Effects of foliage treatment with gibberellin on forage yield of alfalfa, Kentucky bluegrass and winter wheat. Canada Journal of Plant Science. 38:314–319. 1958.

4156. Corns, W. G. and R. Schraa. Effects of trifluralin and Banvel D as preemergent treatments on greenhouse seedlings of chickweed, white Dutch clover, creeping red fescue, Kentucky bluegrass, and several herbaceous ornamentals. Research Report National Weed Committee, Western Section. 9:197. 1962.

4157. Corns, W. G., W. H. Vanden Born, and R. J. Schraa. Selective chemical control of couchgrass and bromegrass in Kentucky bluegrass sod. Canadian Journal of Plant Science. 44(3):296–297. 1964.

4158. Cory, E. N. Directions for the control of insect pests on golf courses. Greenkeepers Club of New England Newsletter. 11(6):2–3. 1939.

4159. ______. Economy in insect control. Proceedings of National Turf Field Days. pp. 56–57. 1950.

4160. Cott, A. E. Turfgrass fertility. Yard and Garden Series. Iowa State University Cooperative Extension Service. 1965.

4161. ______. Turfgrasses and ground covers for parks and recreation areas. Weeds, Trees and Turf. 5(9):12–14. 1966.

4162. ______. Turfgrasses and ground cover for parks and recreation areas. Turf Bulletin. 4(1):12–14. 1966.

4163. ______. Sodding a new lawn with bluegrass sod. Iowa Cooperative Extension Service, Folder No. 491. 1970.

4164. Cott, A. E., and E. C. Roberts. Lawns for better living. Iowa State University. Pamphlet 312. 1964.

4165. Cotton, H. E. Drainage. The National Greenkeeper. 4(9):5–7. 1930.

4166. Couch, H. B. Control of rust on Merion Kentucky bluegrass. Pennsylvania State College Turf Conference. 25:13–14. 1956.

4167. ______. Melting-out of Kentucky bluegrass—Its cause and control. Golf Course Reporter. 25(7):5–7. 1957.

4168. ______. The control of bluegrass and fescue diseases. New York State Turf Association Bulletin 58. pp. 223–225. 1957.

4169. ______. Nitrogen application in brown patch control. Golfdom. 31:64. 1958.

4170. ______. Fundamentals of turfgrass disease control. Proceedings of the Midwest Regional Turf Conference. pp. 43–45. 1961.

4171. ______. Latest developments in turfgrass disease research. Seed World. 89 (12):4,6. 1961.

4172. ______. Effect of nutrition on turf diseases. Turf Clippings. University of Massachusetts. 1(6):A-31–32. 1961.

4173. ______. Diseases of turfgrasses. Reinhold Publishing Corporation, New York. 289 pp. 1962.

4174. ______. Diagnosis and control of turf-grass diseases. Golf Course Reporter. 30(5):9–14. 1962.

4175. ______. Diagnosis and control of turf-grass diseases. International Turf-Grass Conference Proceedings. 33:2–3. 1962.

4176. ______. *Fusarium* blight of turfgrass. New York Turfgrass Association Bulletin. 77:297–298. 1964.

4177. ______. *Fusarium* blight, new and destructive disease of turfgrasses. Pennsylvania Agricultural Experiment Station. Science for the Farmer. 11:12–13. 1964.

4178. Couch, H. B. and E. R. Bedford. Influence of nutrition and soil moisture on the development of *Fusarium* blight of turfgrasses. Phytopathology. 54:890 1964.

4179. Couch, H. B. Effects of nutrition and pH on turfgrass disease incidence. Agronomy Abstracts. p. 44. 1965.

4180. ______. A guide for chemical control of turfgrass diseases. Club Operations. 3(1):G–32. 1965.

4181. ______. Turfgrass diseases. Golf Course Reporter. 33(3):78. 1965.

4182. ______. Relationship between soil moisture, nutrition and severity of turfgrass diseases. Journal of the Sports Turf Research Institute. No. 42: pp. 54–64. 1966.

4183. ______. Developing a turfgrass disease control program. First Ohio Turfgrass Conference Proceedings. pp. 73–76. 1967.

4184. ______. Developing a turfgrass disease control program. West Virginia Turfgrass Conference Proceedings. pp. 17–20. 1967.

4185. ______. Fairy rings. Plant Disease Control Notes. Control Series 57. 3 pp. 1969.

4186. ______. Red leaf spot of bentgrasses. Plant Disease Control Notes. Control Series 58. 1 p. 1969.

4187. ______. Stripe smut. Plant Disease Control Notes. Control Series 59. 1 p. 1969.

4188. ______. Melting-out of Kentucky bluegrass. Plant Disease Control Notes. Control Series 60. 1 p. 1969.

4189. ______. Slime molds. Plant Disease Control Notes. Control Series 61. 1 p. 1969.

4190. ______. *Helminthosporium* blight (netblotch) of fescues. VPI. Plant Disease Control Notes. Control Series 74. 1 p. 1969.

4191. ______. *Fusarium* blight of turfgrasses. Rutgers University. College of Agriculture and Environmental Science. Lawn and Utility Turf Section. pp. 83–84. 1969.

4192. ______. *Fusarium* blight of turfgrasses. Rutgers University Short Course in Turf Management. 37:1–2. 1969.

4193. ______. Trends in turfgrass disease control. Illinois Turfgrass Conference Proceedings. 34–36 pp. 1970.

4194. ______. *Sclerotinia* dollar spot. Park Maintenance. 24(7):18. 1971.

4195. ______. Turfgrass disease control in the twentieth century. Golf Superintendent. 39(10):23–26. 1971.

4196. ______. The development of coordinated turfgrass disease control programs. R.C.G.A. National Turfgrass Conference. 22:4–6. 1971.

4197. Couch, H. B. and E. R. Bedford. *Fusarium* blight of turfgrasses. Phytopathology. 56:781–786. 1966.

4198. Couch, H. B. and J. R. Bloom. Influence of soil moisture, pH, and nutrition on the alteration of disease proneness in plants. Transactions New York Academy of Science. 20 (Ser. II):432. 1958.

4199. ______. Turfgrass disease control. New York State Turf Association Bulletin 64. pp. 248–250. 1959.

4201. ______. Influence of environment on diseases of turfgrasses. II. Effect of nutrition, pH, and soil moisture on *Sclerotinia* dollar spot. Phytopathology. 50(10):761–763. 1960.

4202. Couch, H. B., and R. R. Muse. Results of 1967 turfgrass fungicide trials. Virginia Turfgrass Conference Proceedings. 8:-123–125. 1967.

4203. ______. Results of 1967 turfgrass fungicide trials. Results of 1967 Research Program for Control of Weeds and Diseases of Turfgrasses and Ornamentals. Information Note 101-A. Department of Plant Pathology and Physiology. VPI. pp. 123–125. 1968.

4204. Couch, H. B. and A. S. Williams. Guide for the chemical control of turfgrass diseases and turfgrass weeds. VPI Department of Plant Pathology and Physiology No. 1034. 1967.

4205. Couch, H. B. and H. Cole. Chemical control of melting—out of Kentucky bluegrass. USDA Plant Disease Reporter. 41(3):205–208. 1957.

4206. Couch, H. B. and L. D. Moore. Broad spectrum fungicides tested for control of melting-out of Kentucky bluegrass and *Sclerotinia* dollar spot of seaside bentgrass. The Plant Disease Reporter. 44(7):506–509. 1960.

4207. Couch, R. W., R. I. D. Murphy, D. E. Davis, and H. H. Funderburk. The control of catsear, dallisgrass, carpetgrass, and other lawn weeds in bermudagrass turf. Southern Weed Conference Proceedings. 17:107–111. 1964.

4208. Couch, H. B., W. W. Osborne, J. S. Coartney, and S. W. Bingham. Guide for the chemical control of turfgrass diseases and turfgrass weeds. Virginia Polytechnic Institute Extension Division, Control Series 76. 9 pp. 1969.

4209. Couch, H. B., E. R. Bedford, L. D. Moore, J. C. Rogowicz, and R. R. Muse. Results of '61–62 turfgrass fungicide trials. Golf Course Reporter. 31(5):24–34. 1963.

4211. Coughran, S. J. Mow, mow, mow your slope, gently down the green. Highway Research Abstracts. 42(10):3. 1972.

4212. Coull, D. T. How water helps better turf campaign. Golfdom. 4(2):72. 1930.

4213. Coulthard, T. L. and J. R. Stein. Water quality survey. American Society of Agricultural Engineers. 13(4):430–432. 1970.

4214. Counsell, J. Preparing the golf course for a new season. Greenkeepers Club of New England Newsletter. 9(5):4–5. 1937.

4215. Counterman, C. C. Maintaining large turf areas. Proceedings of Midwest Regional Turf Conference. pp. 12–14. 1968.

4216. Coupland, R. T. Weed control. Proceedings School of Soils, Fertilisation & Turf Maintenance, Green Section, Royal Canadian Golf Association. pp. 65–67. 1954.

4217. Coursen, B. W. and W. R. Jenkins. Host-parasite relationships of the pin nematode *Paratylenchus projectus,* on tobacco and tall fescue (Abs.). Phytopathology. 48:460. 1958.

4218. Court, M. N., R. C. Stephen and J. S. Waid. Nitrite toxicity arising from the use of urea as a fertilizer. Nature. 194(4835):-1263–1265. 1962.

4219. ______. Toxicity as a cause of the inefficiency of urea as a fertilizer. I. Review. Journal of Soil Science. 15(1):42–48. 1964.

4220. ______. Toxicity as a cause of the inefficiency of urea as a fertilizer. II. Experimental. Journal of Soil Science. 15(1):49–65. 1964.

4221. Courtillot, M. Effectiveness of parathion against ryegrass rust. (in French). Academie d'Agriculture de France. Bulletin des Sciences. 51:223–228. 1965.

4222. Courtney, W. D. and H. B. Howell. Investigations on bentgrass neatmode *Anguina agrostis* (Steinbuck 1799) Filipjev 1936. U.S.D.A. Plant Disease Reporter. 36(3):74–83. 1952.

4223. Courtney, W. D., D. V. Peabody, Jr., and H. M. Austenson. Effect of herbicides on nematodes in bentgrass. The Plant Disease Reporter. 46(4):256–257. 1962.

4224. Coverston, D. Y. A return to the campus. Turf-Grass Times. 1(2):4, 9. 1965.

4225. Cowan, I. R. Mass and heat transfer in laminar boundary layers with particular reference to assimilation and transpiration in leaves. Agricultural Meteorology. 10(4/5):311–329. 1972.

4226. Cowan, J. R. Tall fescue. Advances in Agronomy. 8:283–320. 1956.

4227. Cowling, D. W. and L. H. P. Jones. A deficiency in soil sulfur supplies for perennial ryegrass in England. Soil Science. 110(5):346–354. 1970.

4228. Cox, H. R. Better lawns. New Jersey Agricultural Extension Bulletin. 54:1–8. 1926.

4229. ______. Better lawns. New Jersey Agricultural Extension Bulletin. 76:1–8. 1930.

4230. ______. Better lawn grass seed for New Jersey. New Jersey Agriculture. 12:3. 1930.

4231. Cox, J. R. Topdressing. Greenkeepers' Reporter. 9(1):40. 1941.

4232. Cox, L. D. and R. E. Owens. Maintenance costs of public golf courses. Bulletin of the New York State College of Forestry. 15(1):38. 1942.

4233. Crabb, R. Introducing a new bluegrass into the North American market. Proceedings of the Midwest Regional Turf Conference. pp. 63–65. 1962.

4234. Crafts, A. S., and R. S. Rosenfels. Toxicity studies with arsenic in eighty California soils. Hilgardia. 12(3):177–200. 1939.

4235. Craig, P. Large area turf weed control. Illinois Turfgrass Conference Proceedings. pp. 57–59. 1969.

4236. ______. How, why, and when of mowing and irrigation. USGA Green Section Record. 5(6):23–25. 1968.

4237. Craig, R. B. Air-conditioned fairways. Proceedings of the Midwest Regional Turf Conference. pp. 33–34. 1966.

4238. ______. Expanding responsibility and authority. Midwest Regional Turf Conference Proceedings. pp. 20–21. 1972.

4239. Craig, W. R. Turf on school grounds. Southeastern New York Turf School. pp. 33–37. 1950.

4240. Craig, W. S. New insect problems in turf. Proceedings of the Annual Missouri Lawn and Turf Conference. 7:20. 1966.

4241. Crain, A. W. Fertilizer program for athletic fields. Oklahoma-Texas Turf Conference Proceedings. pp. 32–34. 1949.

4242. ______. How climate influences the management of turf grasses. Proceedings of the 6th Annual Texas Turf Conference. pp. 9–13. 1951.

4243. ______. Grasses (other than bermuda) for use on parks, schools, cemeteries, lawns, etc. (other than golf courses). Proceedings of the Nineteenth Annual Texas Turfgrass Conference. 19:60–61. 1964.

4244. ______. Surfactants and their use with herbicides. Proceedings of the Twentieth Annual Texas Turfgrass Conference. 20:20–23. 1965.

4245. ______. Essentials of proper St. Augustine lawn management. Alpha Termite and Pest Control Lawn Division. Houston, Texas. 1966.

4246. ______. Water conservation in turf irrigation. Proceedings Texas Turfgrass Conference. 22:33–38. 1967.

4247. Crain, A. W., and R. C. Potts. What every turf man should know about grasses. Oklahoma-Texas Turf Conference Proceedings. pp. 33–39. 1950.

4248. Cramer, R. and J. A. Wilson. Scientific sewage disposal at Milwaukee. Industrial and Engineering Chemistry. 20(1):-15. 1928.

4249. Crampton, B. Recognizing weedy grasses. Proceedings Northern California Turfgrass Institute. pp. 21–22. 1961.

4250. ______. Three roadside grasses as records for Sacramento, El Dorado and Placer counties, California. Madrono. 19(6):-224. 1968.

4251. Crane, F. A. How plants use nitrogen, phosphorus, and potassium. Golf Course Reporter. 23(3):33–36. 1955.

4252. Cranstoun, W. M. Sod certification procedures. Rutgers University Short Course in Turf Management. 32:19–20. 1964.

4253. Crawford, C. S., and R. F. Harwood. Bionomics and control of insects affecting Washington grass seed fields. Washington Agricultural Experiment Station Technical Bulletin 44. pp. 1–25. 1964.

4255. Creed, A. W. How do you do? The Greenkeepers' Reporter. 7(3):25,43. 1939.

4256. Criddle, W. D. Methods of computing consumptive use of water. Proceedings ASCE, Irrigation and Drainage Division Journal Paper 1507. 1958.

4257. Criddle, W. D., S. Davis, C. H. Parr, and D. G. Schockley. Methods for evaluating irrigation systems. USDA Handbook. 82:1–17. 1965.

4258. Crider, F. J. Root-growth stoppage resulting from defoliation of grass. U.S.D.A. Technical Bulletin. 1102:1–23. 1955.

4259. Crissinger, H. L. Control of diseases and natural enemies. The Greenmaster. 4(7):12–13. 1968.

4260. ______. Food and the N.P.K. mentality. The Greenmaster. 4(10):6,8–9. 1968.

4261. Croal, D. T. Proper nitrate of soda use in greenkeeping. Golfdom. 2(5):60–61. 1928.

4262. Crocker, R. L. and P. M. Martin. Competition between perennial ryegrass and meadow fescue under field-plot conditions. Journal of the British Grassland Society. 19:-27–29. 1964.

4263. Crofts, A. S. New developments in weed control. Greenkeeping Superintendents Association National Turf Conference. 20:-86–91. 1949.

4264. Croley, C. E. Grass problems created by ornamental plants. Oklahoma Turfgrass Conference Proceeding. pp. 11–15. 1960.

4265. ______. Potassium—that mysterious macronutrient. USGA Journal and Turf Management. 14(7):27–30. 1962.

4266. Crolius, P. C. Mechanized erosion control. Park Maintenance. 12(2):10–11. 1959.

4267. Crombie, E. A. Dandelion and plantain eradication. The National Greenkeeper. 5(1):14. 1931.

4268. Cromroy, H. L., and F. A. Johnson. A new look at the bermudagrass stunt mite in Florida. Florida Turfgrass Association. 6(2):6–7. 1972.

4269. Cronin, T. *Poa annua* will be controlled. The Bull Sheet. 24(10):2. 1971.

4270. ______. *Poa annua* programs. *Poa annua* will be controlled! A Patch of Green. Michigan and Border Cities GCSA Publication. pp. 8–9. June, 1971.

4271. Crookston, R. K. Physiological characteristics and leaf anatomy of C_4 and C_3 species. Ph.D. Thesis, University of Minnesota. 1972.

4272. Crosier, W. and B. Cullinan. Some observations in the germination of grass seeds. Proceedings of the Association of Official Seed Analysts. 33:69–74. 1941.

4273. Crossley, G. K. and A. D. Bradshaw. Differences in response to mineral nutrients of populations of ryegrass, *Lolium perenne* L., and orchardgrass, *Dactylis glomerata* L. Crop Science. 8(3):383–387. 1968.

4274. Crowder, L. V. Making a lawn in Georgia. Georgia Agricultural Experiment Station Press Bulletin. 613:1–2. 1949.

4275. ______. A survey of meiotic chromosome behavior in tall fescue grass. American Journal of Botany. 40:348–354. 1953.

4276. ______. Interspecific and intergeneric hybrids of *Festuca* and *Lolium.* Journal of Heredity. 44:195–203. 1953.

4277. ______. A simple method for distinguishing tall and meadow fescue. Agronomy Journal. 45(8):453–454. 1953.

4278. Crowder, L. V., O. E. Sell, and E. M. Parker. The effect of clipping, nitrogen application, and weather on the productivity of fall-sown oats, ryegrass, and crimson clover. Agronomy Journal 47(2):51–54. 1955.

4279. Crowl, R. N. Banvel and bandane for turf weeds. Weeds, Trees, and Turf. 4(9):-24. 1965.

4280. Crowley, D. Keeping greens in winter play. Golfdom. 3(10):16. 1929.

4281. Crum, R. W. and F. Burggraf. Highway research abstracts. Highway Research Board, National Research Council. 17(11). 1947.

4282. Crummett, D. O. Plant tissue testing. First Annual Fall Field Day on Turf Culture. (UCLA) pp. 13–19. 1949.

4283. Cruzado, H. J., and T. J. Mysik. Effect of maleic hydrazide on some tropical lawn grasses. Weeds. 6:329–330. 1958.

4284. Cubbon, M. H. Clover in acid soils. Greenkeepers Club of New England Newsletter. 3(10):2. 1931.

4285. ______. Factors affecting accumulation of nitrates in soil. Golfdom. 6(2):47–49. 1932.

4286. ______. Nitrogen—what is it? The National Greenkeeper. 6(3):8,10–11. 1932.

4287. ______. Soil nutrients and soil acidity. The National Greenkeeper. 6(12):-6–9,18. 1932.

4288. ______. The makeup of the soil. The National Greenkeeper. 7(1):7–10. 1933.

4289. ______. Effects of organic matter in soil. The National Greenkeeper. 7(2):8–11. 1933.

4290. Cullinan, B. Germinating seeds of Southern grasses. Proceedings of the Association of Official Seed Analysts. 33:74–76. 1941.

4291. Cummins, G. B. Aids through the microscope. Proceedings of the Midwest Regional Turf Conference. pp. 19–20. 1963.

4292. Cunningham, G. H. Control of fairy rings. Greens Research Committee, New Zealand Golf Association, 2nd Annual Report. pp. 44–46. 1934.

4293. Cunningham, G. T. Experience with creeping bent in Virginia. USGA Green Section. Bulletin. 8:179–181. 1928.

4294. Cunningham, H. S. Study of the histologic changes induced in leaves by certain leaf-spotting fungi. Phytopathology. 18(9):717–751. 1928.

4295. Cunningham, S. A. Lawns, golf courses, polo fields, and how to treat them. The Coe-Mortimer Company. New York. 31 pp. 1914.

4296. Cunningham, T. Proper watering of greens is elusive subject. Golf Course Reporter. 21(6):14–15. 1953.

4297. Currie, W. B. Lawn making and maintenance. Park and Cemetery. 39(9):270–272. 1929.

4298. Currier, F. W. Getting the greens you want. Golfdom. 1(6):11–12. 1927.

4300. Curry, C. Aerification, topdressing, and vertical mowing greens. University of Maine Turf Conference Proceedings. 7:26. 1969.

4301. Curry, R. J., L. E. Foote, O. N. Andrews, and J. A. Jackobs. Lime and fertilizer requirements as related to turf establishment along the roadside. Highway Research Record. 53:26–29. 1963.

4302. Curtis, D. V., H. H. Iruka, E. W. Muller, E. Secor and D. Ward. Herbicide work on New York state highways. Proceedings of the Northeastern Weed Control Conference. 9:463–470. 1955.

4303. Curtis, L. C. Deleterious effects of guttated fluids on foliage. American Journal of Botany. 30:778–781. 1943.

4304. ______. The Influence of guttation fluid on pesticides. Phytopathology. 34:196–205. 1944.

4305. ______. The exudation of glutamine from lawn grass. Plant Phsyiology. 19(1):1–5. 1944.

4306. Curtis, R. W. and J. A. DeFrance. Lawns: construction and maintenance. Cornell Agricultural Extension Bulletin 296. 52 pp. 1934.

4307. Custead, J. R. Night lighting. Grounds Maintenance. 2(2):42–44. 1967.

4308. Cuthbert, L. A. Guide to growing lawns and hedges. Cassell, London. 32 pp. 1954.

4309. ______. Spring work on a sports centre. The Groundsman. 21(8):30–31. 1968.

4310. Cutright, N. J. and M. B. Harrison. Chemical control of *Fusarium* blight of Merion Kentucky bluegrass turf. The Plant Disease Reporter. 54(9):771–773. 1970.

4311. ______. Some environmental factors affecting *Fusarium* blight of Merion Kentucky bluegrass. The Plant Disease Reporter. 54(12):1018–1020. 1970.

4312. Czarnowski, M. and J. Slomka. Some remarks on the percolation of light through the forest canopy. Ecology. 40:312–315. 1959.

4313. Dahl, A. S. Snow-mold. U.S.G.A. Green Section Bulletin. 8(10):198–200. 1928.

4314. ______. Zonate eye-spot disease of turf grasses. U.S.G.A. Green Section Bulletin. 9(4):71–75. 1929.

4315. ______. Results of snow-mold work during winter of 1928–1929. U.S.G.A. Green Section Bulletin. 9(8):134–136. 1929.

4316. ______. Snow mold and its control. The National Greenkeeper. 5(1):10,12–13,30. 1931.

4317. ______. Effect of watering putting greens on occurrence of brown patch. U.S.-G.A. Green Section Bulletin. 13(3):62–66. 1933.

4318. ______. Effect of temperature and moisture on occurrence of brownpatch. U.S.-G.A. Green Section Bulletin. 13:53–61. 1933.

4319. ______. Relationship between fertilizing and drainage in the occurrence of brownpatch. U.S.G.A. Green Section Bulletin. 13(5):136–139. 1933.

4320. ______. Effect of temperature on brown patch of turf. Pytopathology 23(1):8. 1933.

4321. ______. Snowmold of turf grasses as caused by *Fusarium nivale*. Phytopathology. 24(3):197–214. 1934.

4322. Dahlsson, S. The frit fly—harmful to lawns. Weibulls Grästips. pp. 3–8. 1971.

4323. ______. Test your soil! On sampling for soil analysis. Weibulls Grästips. pp. 28–29. 1971.

4324. ______. New fertilizer declaration. Weibulls Grästips. p. 30. 1971.

4325. Dahm, P. A. New and old spray materials for insect control. Central Plains Turfgrass Conference. pp. 61–68. 1951.

4326. Dahnke, W. C., O. J. Attoe, L. E. Engelbert, and M. D. Groskopp. Controlling release of fertilizer constituents by means of coatings and capsules. Agronomy Journal. 55(3):242. 1963.

4327. Daigle, L. T. The use of the proper equipment for the job. Proceedings of the Annual University of Florida Turf-grass Management Conference. 13:92–94. 1965.

4328. ______. Establishing St. Augustine grass lawns. Proceedings 17th Annual University of Florida Turf-Grass Management Conference. 17:57–59. 1969.

4329. Dale, J. L. Infection of St. Augustine grass with virus causing maize dwarf mosaic. The Plant Disease Reporter. 50(6):441–442. 1966.

4330. ______. A blight disease of zoysia. The Plant Disease Reporter. 51(5):376. 1967.

4331. ______. A spotting and discoloration condition of dormant bermudagrass. The Plant Disease Reporter. 56(4):355–357. 1972.

4332. Dale, J. L. and C. Diaz. New disease of bermudagrass lawns and turf. Arkansas Farm Research. 12(6):6. 1963.

4333. Dale, J. L. and C. E. McCoy. The relationship of scale insect to death of bermudagrass in Arkansas. The Plant Disease Reporter. 48(3):228. 1964.

4334. Dale, J. L. and G. E. Templeton. Downy mildew of small grains and grasses in Arkansas. Plant Disease Reporter. 44(3):-206–207. 1960.

4335. Dale, J. L. and C. L. Murdoch. *Polymyxa* infection of bermuda grass. The Plant Disease Reporter. 53(2):130–131. 1969.

4336. Dale, M. Hybridization of Kentucky bluegrass with Canada bluegrass. Park Maintenance. 23(7):18. 1970.

4337. ______. Hybridization of Kentucky bluegrass with Canada bluegrass. Rutgers University Short Course in Turf Management. 38:5–7. 1970.

4338. ______. An evaluation of taxonomic characters and turf performance of interspecific hybrids between Kentucky bluegrass and Canada bluegrass. M.S. Thesis, Rutgers University. 1971.

4339. Dale, M. R., and M. K. Ahmed. Identification of Kentucky bluegrass varieties. Rutgers University Short Course in Turf Management Proceedings. pp. 12–15. 1971.

4340. Dale, M. R., M. K. Ahmed, and C. R. Funk. Interspecific hybridization of Kentucky bluegrass (*Poa pratensis* L.) and Canada bluegrass (*P. compressa* L.) for turf improvement. Agronomy Abstracts. p. 46. 1971.

4341. Damanakis, M., D. S. Drennan, J. D. Fryer, and K. Holly. The toxicity of paraquat to a range of species following uptake by the roots. Weed Research. 10(3):278–283. 1970.

4342. Damon, S. C. The Planting and care of lawns. Rhode Island Agricultural Extension Bulletin. 13:1–8. 1922.

4343. ______. Making and care of lawns. Rhode Island Agricultural Extension Bulletin. 48:1–13. 1927.

4344. Dana, M. N. Uninvited guests in your turf—how to handle weeds? 1962 Wisconsin Turfgrass Conference Proceedings. 2 pp. 1962.

4345. ______. Keys to turf weed control. 1962 Wisconsin Turfgrass Conference Proceedings. 5 pp. 1963.

4346. Dana, M. N. and R. Newman. New products for post-emergence weed control. North Central Weed Control Conference Proceedings. 20:51. 1964.

4347. Daniel, E. Turf, its importance and maintenance in a park service. New Mexico Turfgrass Conference Proceedings. 3:10–14. 1957.

4348. ______. Cemetery turf. Proceedings of the Fifteenth Annual Texas Turfgrass Conference. 15:28–30. 1960.

4349. Daniel, W. H. Bluegrass fairway? Yes! If! Midwest Turf Leaflet. No. 29. 4 pp. 1964.

4353. ______. A progress report. Midwest Turf-News and Research. 4(3):2,4. 1950.

4354. ______. Plan this winter for scarce labor. Midwest Turf-News and Research. 4(4):1–2. 1950.

4355. ______. Research. Proceedings of National Turf Field Days. pp. 37–38. 1950.

4356. ______. The effects of irrigation and mowing practices on the quality of fairway turf. USGA Journal and Turf Management. 3(5):30. 1950.

4357. ______. Turf management in shade tree areas. Arborist's News. 16(9): 1951.

4358. ______. How to measure soil moisture and conserve water, labor. Golfdom. 25(3):36–37,40. 1951.

4359. ______. 35 on program; confab stretched. Midwest Turf-News and Research. 5(1):1–7. 1951.

4360. ______. Study turf research at fall field day. Midwest Turf News and Research. 5(4):1–3. 1951.

4361. ______. Study of turf research at Fall Field Day. Midwest Regional Turf Foundation. pp. 1–3. October, 1951.

4362. ______. Review reading in former issues. Midwest Turf-News and Research. 5(4):6. 1951.

4363. ______. Notes from the region. Midwest Turf-News and Research. 6(3):4–5. 1951.

4364. ______. The control of clover in turf with 2, 4, 5-T. Agronomy Abstracts. p. 39. 1952.

4366. ______. Research on *Poa annua.* G.C.S.A. Conference. 1952.

4367. ______. The golf course superintendent and turf insurance. The Golf Course Reporter. 20(1):5–7. 1952.

4368. Daniel, W. H. and L. Munzenmaier. Research on *Poa annua.* Golf Course Reporter. 20(2):14–15. 1952.

4369. Daniel, W. H. You can control clover in fairways. Midwest Regional Turf Foundation. pp. 2–3. October, 1952.

4370. ______. Questions for research. Proceedings of Midwest Regional Turf Conference. pp. 38–40. 1952.

4371. ______. The turf management college course at Purdue University. Proceedings of Midwest Regional Turf Conference. pp. 49–51. 1952.

4372. ______. What is Krilium? Midwest Turf News and Research. 6(1):1–2. 1952.

4373. ______. What about compaction? Northern California Turf Conference. pp. 15–17. 1952.

4374. ______. The use of 2, 4, 5-T for clover control in turf. Proceedings of the Annual Southern California Turf Conference. pp. 38–40. 1952.

4375. ______. What makes perfect turf? Golf Course Reporter. 21(8):7–9. 1953.

4376. ______. National chemical crabgrass controls in 1952. Golf Course Reporter. 21(3):14–17. 1953.

4377. ______. 2,4,5—T for clover control in turf. Golf Course Reporter. 21(3):-27–28. 1953.

4378. ______. Report on national crabgrass control tests in 1952. Golfdom. 27(5):-64,66,68. 1953.

4379. ______. Modern lawn maintenance. Indiana Nurserymen. 14(29). 1953.

4380. ______. Soil conditioners and turf. Lake States Park Institute Proceedings. 1953.

4381. ______. Industry and today's turf. Proceedings of Midwest Regional Turf Conference. pp. 13–14. 1953.

4382. ______. 2, 4, 5–T for clover control in turf. New York State Turf Association Bulletins 39 and 40. pp. 156–157. 1953.

4383. ______. The use of 2,4,5–T for clover control in turf. Proceedings, Pacific Northwest Turf Conference. 7:10–12. 1953.

4384. ______. Characteristics and habits of the common turf grasses. Proceedings. School of Soils, Fertilization & Turf Maintenance Green Section, Royal Canadian Golf Assoc. pp. 41–43. 1953.

4385. ______. Living with and controlling *Poa annua.* Proceedings, School of Soils, Fertilization & Turf Maintenance Green Section, Royal Canadian Turf Assoc., pp. 47–50. 1952.

4386. ______. The use of 2,4,5–T for clover control in turf. Southern California Turf Culture. 3(3):1–3. 1953.

4387. ______. Chemical crabgrass controls in 1952. USGA Journal and Turf Management. 6(5):25–28. 1953.

4388. ______. An appraisal of Merion bluegrass for lawns in the midwest. Midwest

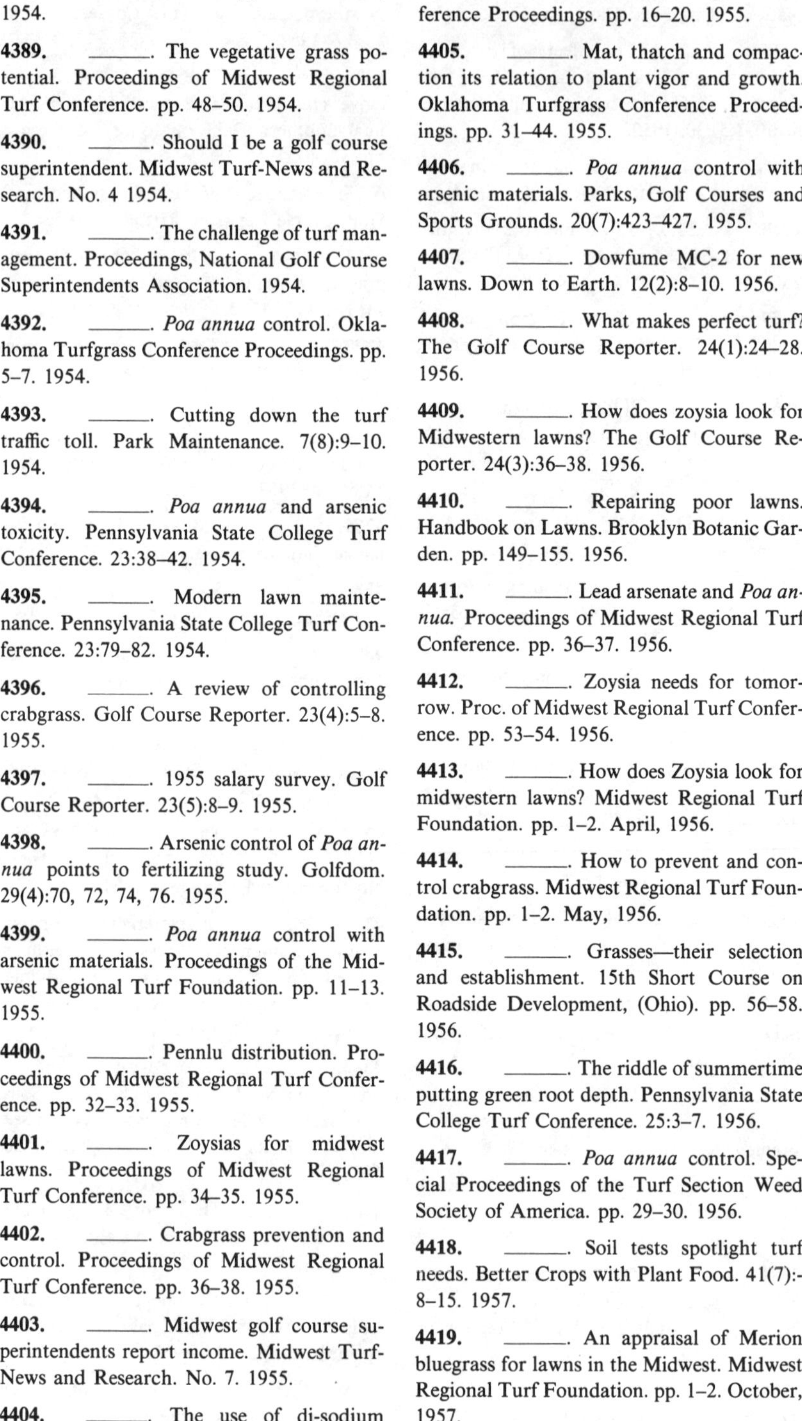

Regional Turf Foundation. pp. 1–2. October, 1954.

4389. ______. The vegetative grass potential. Proceedings of Midwest Regional Turf Conference. pp. 48–50. 1954.

4390. ______. Should I be a golf course superintendent. Midwest Turf-News and Research. No. 4 1954.

4391. ______. The challenge of turf management. Proceedings, National Golf Course Superintendents Association. 1954.

4392. ______. *Poa annua* control. Oklahoma Turfgrass Conference Proceedings. pp. 5–7. 1954.

4393. ______. Cutting down the turf traffic toll. Park Maintenance. 7(8):9–10. 1954.

4394. ______. *Poa annua* and arsenic toxicity. Pennsylvania State College Turf Conference. 23:38–42. 1954.

4395. ______. Modern lawn maintenance. Pennsylvania State College Turf Conference. 23:79–82. 1954.

4396. ______. A review of controlling crabgrass. Golf Course Reporter. 23(4):5–8. 1955.

4397. ______. 1955 salary survey. Golf Course Reporter. 23(5):8–9. 1955.

4398. ______. Arsenic control of *Poa annua* points to fertilizing study. Golfdom. 29(4):70, 72, 74, 76. 1955.

4399. ______. *Poa annua* control with arsenic materials. Proceedings of the Midwest Regional Turf Foundation. pp. 11–13. 1955.

4400. ______. Pennlu distribution. Proceedings of Midwest Regional Turf Conference. pp. 32–33. 1955.

4401. ______. Zoysias for midwest lawns. Proceedings of Midwest Regional Turf Conference. pp. 34–35. 1955.

4402. ______. Crabgrass prevention and control. Proceedings of Midwest Regional Turf Conference. pp. 36–38. 1955.

4403. ______. Midwest golf course superintendents report income. Midwest Turf-News and Research. No. 7. 1955.

4404. ______. The use of di-sodium methyl arsonate. Oklahoma Turfgrass Conference Proceedings. pp. 16–20. 1955.

4405. ______. Mat, thatch and compaction its relation to plant vigor and growth. Oklahoma Turfgrass Conference Proceedings. pp. 31–44. 1955.

4406. ______. *Poa annua* control with arsenic materials. Parks, Golf Courses and Sports Grounds. 20(7):423–427. 1955.

4407. ______. Dowfume MC-2 for new lawns. Down to Earth. 12(2):8–10. 1956.

4408. ______. What makes perfect turf? The Golf Course Reporter. 24(1):24–28. 1956.

4409. ______. How does zoysia look for Midwestern lawns? The Golf Course Reporter. 24(3):36–38. 1956.

4410. ______. Repairing poor lawns. Handbook on Lawns. Brooklyn Botanic Garden. pp. 149–155. 1956.

4411. ______. Lead arsenate and *Poa annua.* Proceedings of Midwest Regional Turf Conference. pp. 36–37. 1956.

4412. ______. Zoysia needs for tomorrow. Proc. of Midwest Regional Turf Conference. pp. 53–54. 1956.

4413. ______. How does Zoysia look for midwestern lawns? Midwest Regional Turf Foundation. pp. 1–2. April, 1956.

4414. ______. How to prevent and control crabgrass. Midwest Regional Turf Foundation. pp. 1–2. May, 1956.

4415. ______. Grasses—their selection and establishment. 15th Short Course on Roadside Development, (Ohio). pp. 56–58. 1956.

4416. ______. The riddle of summertime putting green root depth. Pennsylvania State College Turf Conference. 25:3–7. 1956.

4417. ______. *Poa annua* control. Special Proceedings of the Turf Section Weed Society of America. pp. 29–30. 1956.

4418. ______. Soil tests spotlight turf needs. Better Crops with Plant Food. 41(7):-8–15. 1957.

4419. ______. An appraisal of Merion bluegrass for lawns in the Midwest. Midwest Regional Turf Foundation. pp. 1–2. October, 1957.

4420. ______. Soil test summaries show turf needs. Midwest Regional Turf Foundation. pp. 1–2. July, 1957.

4421. ______. Killing crabgrass in 1958. Golf Course Reporter. 26(3):24. 1958.

4422. ______. Microclimatic report feature of Midwest field days. Golfdom. 32(10):-50. 1958.

4423. ______: How bluegrass grows. Proceedings of Midwest Regional Turf Conference. pp. 29–30. 1958.

4424. ______. Why soak grass seed? Proceedings of Midwest Regional Turf Conference. pp. 30–31. 1958.

4425. ______. Arsenic toxicity to weedy grasses. Proceedings of Midwest Regional Turf Conference. pp. 51–54. 1958.

4426. ______. Bermudagrass use in the Midwest. Midwest Regional Turf Foundation. pp. 1–2. August, 1958.

4427. ______. Preventing crabgrass in turf-areas. North Central Weed Control Conference Proceedings. 15:35–36. 1958.

4428. ______. Preventing crabgrass in turf areas. Proceedings North Central Weed Control Conference. 15:35–36. 1958.

4429. ______. Agricultural chemicals in efficient turf management. USGA Journal and Turf Management. 11(1):27–29. 1958.

4430. ______. Fertilizing for top quality lawns. You Can Grow a Good Lawn; The American Potash Institute. pp. 18–24. 1959.

4431. ______. Principles of roadside fertilization. Better Crops with Plant Food. 43(1):14. 1959.

4432. ______. In the Midwest. Golf Course Reporter. 27(7):36–37. 1959.

4433. ______. Mechanical renovation of grasses. Proceedings of the Midwest Regional Turf Conference. pp. 46–47. 1959.

4434. ______. Arsenic toxicity to weedy grasses. Proceedings of the Midwest Regional Turf Conference. pp. 61–63. 1959.

4435. ______. Preventing crabgrass in turf areas. Midwest Regional Turf Foundation. pp. 1–2. January, 1959.

4436. ______. Weedy grass control with arsenicals. Midwest Regional Turf Foundation. No. 22. 2 pp. 1959.

4437. ______. Cutting sod for rhizome values. Rural Roads. 9(1):38. 1959.

4438. ______. How thick should sod be cut? Warren's Turf Nursery. Palos Park, Illinois. pp. 9–10. 1959.

4439. ______. Solving the pesky *Poa annua* problem. Golf Course Reporter. 28:-24–28. 1960.

4440. ______. *Poa annua* problem. Golf Course Reporter. 28(1):68–69. 1960.

4441. ______. Managing good turf. Illinois Turfgrass Conference. pp. 13–16. 1960.

4442. ______. Solving the *Poa annua* problem. Proceedings of the Midwest Regional Turf Conference. pp. 23–27. 1960.

4443. ______. Newsletter. Midwest Turf-News and Research. pp. 1–3. May, 1960.

4444. ______. Principles in use of sod for erosion control. 19th Short Course on Roadside Development (Ohio). pp. 83–84. 1960.

4445. ______. Solving the *Poa annua* problem. Park Maintenance. 13:42–47. 1960.

4446. ______. Fertilizers and their contribution to roadsides. Roadside Development. Highway Research Board. Publication 774. pp. 11–13. 1960.

4447. ______. An evaluation of varieties, strains, and types of Kentucky bluegrasses. Proceedings of the Midwest Regional Turf Conference. pp. 30–35. 1961.

4448. ______. Aids in understanding nitrogen nutrition. Proceedings of the Midwest Regional Turf Conference. pp. 65–67. 1961.

4449. ______. Potentials with growth control with chemicals on cool season fairway grasses. Proceedings of the Midwest Regional Turf Conference. pp. 71–70. 1961.

4450. ______. An evaluation of varieties, strains and types of Kentucky bluegrass. Seed World. 88(7):4–9. 1961.

4451. ______. Sod production. Proceedings of the Midwest Regional Turf Conference. pp. 71–73. 1962.

4452. ______. Preventing crabgrass in 1962. Proceedings of the Midwest Regional Turf Conference. pp. 74–75. 1962.

4453. ______. Purdue stadium renovation. Proceedings Midwest Regional Turf Conference. pp. 86–87. 1962.

4454. ______. Preventing crabgrass in 1962. Proceedings Midwest Regional Turf Conference. pp. 74–75. 1962.

4455. ______. Ideas about building a golf course. Midwest Turf News and Research. No. 18. pp. 1–4. 1962.

4456. ______. Current trend in the control of *Poa annua.* Oklahoma Turfgrass Conference Proceedings. p. 9. 1962.

4457. ______. Green leaves make turf. 1962. Wisconsin Turfgrass Conference Proceedings. pp. 1–2. 1962.

4458. ______. Principles of sod production. 1962 Wisconsin Turfgrass Conference Proceedings. pp. 1–2. 1962.

4459. ______. Bluegrass fairways. Central Plains Turfgrass Conference. p. 1. 1963.

4460. ______. Bluegrass today and tomorrow. Central Plains Turfgrass Conference. p. 3. 1963.

4461. ______. Evansville creeping bentgrass—certification plans as of March, 1963. Proceedings of the Midwest Regional Turf Conference. p. 7. 1963.

4462. ______. Proposed release for Midwest zoysia—1963. Proceedings of the Midwest Regional Turf Conference. pp. 7–8. 1963.

4463. ______. Maintaining nutrient balance. Proceedings of the Midwest Regional Turf Conference. p. 52. 1963.

4464. ______. Principles in maintaining athletic turf. Oklahoma Turfgrass Conference Proceedings. pp. 21–23. 1963.

4465. ______. Turfgrass review. Park Maintenance. 16:13–28. 1963.

4466. ______. Prescription rootzones with calcined clays. Proceedings of the Eighteenth Annual Texas Turfgrass Conference. 18:17–18. 1963.

4467. ______. Principles in maintaining athletic turf. Proceedings of the Eighteenth Annual Texas Turfgrass Conference. 18:21–23. 1963.

4468. ______. Review and preview—Purdue Stadium. Proceedings of 1964 Midwest Regional Turf Conference. pp. 17–19. 1964.

4469. ______. *Poa annua* and arsenic toxicity. Proceedings of Midwest Regional Turf Conference. pp. 53–57. 1964.

4470. ______. Bluegrass fairway? Yes! If! Midwest Turf News and Research. No. 29. pp. 1–4. 1964.

4471. ______. Bluegrass fairways? Yes! . . . If! Golf Course Reporter. 33(8):41–46. 1965.

4472. ______. Midwest zoysia—second report. Proceedings of the 1965 Midwest Regional Turf Conference. pp. 65. 1965.

4473. ______. Purdue stadium progress report. Proceedings of the 1965 Midwest Regional Turf Conference. p. 66. 1965.

4474. ______. Turf research. Proceedings of the 1965 Midwest Regional Turf Conference. pp. 66–67. 1965.

4475. ______. Competition for space in turf. Northern Ohio Turfgrass News. 7(8):1. 1965.

4476. ______. Promoting turf growth wisely. Park Maintenance. 17(10):104–107. 1964.

4477. Daniel, W. H. and J. R. Barrett. On the research front—soil warming for turf areas. U.S.G.A. Green Section Record. 3(2):-12–13. 1965.

4478. Daniel, W. H. I'm tired of *Poa annua.* The Golf Superintendent. 34(8):16–18. 1966.

4479. Daniel, W. H., and J. R. Barrett. Soil warming and turf use. Proceedings Midwest Regional Turf Conference. pp. 79–82. 1966.

4480. Daniel, W. H. Crabgrass and goosegrass prevention—1966. Proceedings of the 1966 Midwest Regional Turfgrass Conference. p. 89. 1966.

4481. ______. Watch out! salt concentrates by freezing. Midwest Regional Turf Foundation Newsletter. p. 1–2. November, 1966.

4482. ______. Bluegrass fairway? Yes! If! Turf Bulletin. 3(1):20–22. 1966.

4483. ______. Bentgrass today. First Ohio Turfgrass Conference Proceedings. pp. 38–40. 1967.

4484. ______. Thatch control or making room for new growth. First Ohio Turfgrass Conference Proceedings. pp. 61–66. 1967.

4485. ______. Turf specialist wants you to grow better weeds. Park Maintenance. 20(10):22–24. 1967.

4486. ______. Nitrogen release from buried cloth containers. Agronomy Abstracts. 60:57. 1968.

4487. ______. Par for the grass. Bull Sheet. 21(9):10. 1968.

4488. ______. Summary of ten ways to construct high use turf areas exposed to compaction. Midwest Regional Turf Conference Proceedings. p. 71. 1968.

4489. ______. Sodco bluegrass. Midwest Regional Turf Conference Proceedings. p. 79. 1968.

4490. Daniel, W. H., and T. P. Riordan. Improvement of Kentucky bluegrass through breeding and selection. Purdue and Indiana State Highway Commission JHRP No. 24. 9 pp. 1968.

4491. Daniel, W. H. Soil test summaries show turf needs. Midwest Turf Leaflet. No. 16. 2 pp. 1968.

4492. ______. Summer watering practices. Turf-Grass Times. 3(7):1–2. 1968.

4493. ______. You and the new turfgrasses. West Virginia Turfgrass Conference Proceedings. pp. 1–2. 1968.

4494. ______. Controlling "*Poa annua*" —The failure grass. West Virginia Turfgrass Conference Proceedings. pp. 49–51. 1968.

4495. ______. Renewing worn out turf. Illinois Turfgrass Conference Proceedings. pp. 14–16. 1969.

4496. ______. Maintenance of football fields. Illinois Turfgrass Conference Proceedings. pp. 40–42. 1969.

4497. ______. Turfgrass in the Midwestern United States. Proceedings of the First International Turfgrass Research Conference. pp. 27–28. 1969.

4498. ______. The evaluation of a new turfgrass. Proceedings of the First International Turfgrass Research Conference. pp. 57–64. 1969.

4499. ______. Viewpoints on control methods and precautions—Midwest. Proceedings of the International Turfgrass Conference. 40:58–60. 1969.

4500. ______. Soil warming in North America. Proceedings of the First International Turfgrass Research Conference. pp. 235–240. 1969.

4501. ______. The "Purr-Wick" rootzone system for compacted turf areas. Proceedings of the First International Turfgrass Research Conference. pp. 323–325. 1969.

4502. ______. Annual grass weed control. Proceedings of the First International Turfgrass Research Conference. pp. 393–395. 1969.

4503. ______. Vertical drainage for compacted turf areas. The Journal of the Sports Turf Research Institute. 45:41–47. 1969.

4504. ______. Controlling *Poa annua* with arsenates. Mid-Atlantic Superintendents Conference Proceedings. pp. 36–40. 1969.

4505. ______. Calcinated aggregates. Midwest Regional Turf Conference Proceedings. pp. 13–14. 1969.

4506. ______. Sponge rubber. Midwest Regional Turf Conference Proceedings. p. 14. 1969.

4507. ______. Activated charcoal. Midwest Regional Turf Conference Proceedings. p. 15. 1969.

4508. ______. Summary of ten ways to construct high use turf areas exposed to compaction. Midwest Regional Turf Conference Proceedings. p. 20. 1969.

4509. ______. System 9—the Purr-Wick system. Midwest Regional Turf Conference Proceedings. pp. 21–22. 1969.

4510. ______. Sodco bluegrass. Midwest Regional Turf Conference Proceedings. p. 81. 1969.

4511. ______. Controlling *Poa annua.* Midwest Regional Turf Conference Proceedings. pp. 86–90. 1969.

4512. ______. *Poa annua.* Turf Bulletin. 5(3):23–25. 1969.

4513. ______. Control program *Poa annua.* Weeds, Trees and Turf. 8(4):12–16. 1969.

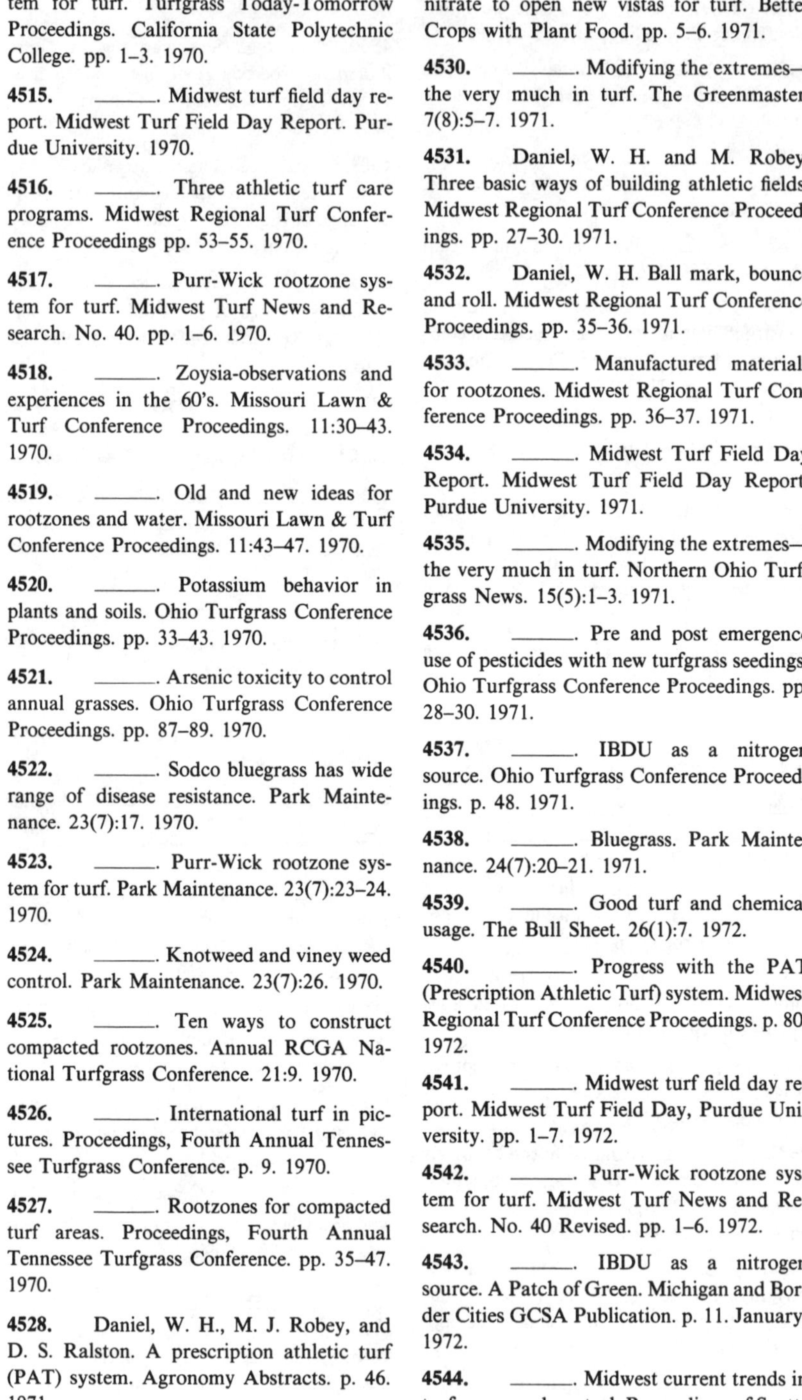

4514. ______. Purr-Wick-Rootzone system for turf. Turfgrass Today-Tomorrow Proceedings. California State Polytechnic College. pp. 1–3. 1970.

4515. ______. Midwest turf field day report. Midwest Turf Field Day Report. Purdue University. 1970.

4516. ______. Three athletic turf care programs. Midwest Regional Turf Conference Proceedings pp. 53–55. 1970.

4517. ______. Purr-Wick rootzone system for turf. Midwest Turf News and Research. No. 40. pp. 1–6. 1970.

4518. ______. Zoysia-observations and experiences in the 60's. Missouri Lawn & Turf Conference Proceedings. 11:30–43. 1970.

4519. ______. Old and new ideas for rootzones and water. Missouri Lawn & Turf Conference Proceedings. 11:43–47. 1970.

4520. ______. Potassium behavior in plants and soils. Ohio Turfgrass Conference Proceedings. pp. 33–43. 1970.

4521. ______. Arsenic toxicity to control annual grasses. Ohio Turfgrass Conference Proceedings. pp. 87–89. 1970.

4522. ______. Sodco bluegrass has wide range of disease resistance. Park Maintenance. 23(7):17. 1970.

4523. ______. Purr-Wick rootzone system for turf. Park Maintenance. 23(7):23–24. 1970.

4524. ______. Knotweed and viney weed control. Park Maintenance. 23(7):26. 1970.

4525. ______. Ten ways to construct compacted rootzones. Annual RCGA National Turfgrass Conference. 21:9. 1970.

4526. ______. International turf in pictures. Proceedings, Fourth Annual Tennessee Turfgrass Conference. p. 9. 1970.

4527. ______. Rootzones for compacted turf areas. Proceedings, Fourth Annual Tennessee Turfgrass Conference. pp. 35–47. 1970.

4528. Daniel, W. H., M. J. Robey, and D. S. Ralston. A prescription athletic turf (PAT) system. Agronomy Abstracts. p. 46. 1971.

4529. Daniel, W. H. Prilled potassium nitrate to open new vistas for turf. Better Crops with Plant Food. pp. 5–6. 1971.

4530. ______. Modifying the extremes—the very much in turf. The Greenmaster. 7(8):5–7. 1971.

4531. Daniel, W. H. and M. Robey. Three basic ways of building athletic fields. Midwest Regional Turf Conference Proceedings. pp. 27–30. 1971.

4532. Daniel, W. H. Ball mark, bounce and roll. Midwest Regional Turf Conference Proceedings. pp. 35–36. 1971.

4533. ______. Manufactured materials for rootzones. Midwest Regional Turf Conference Proceedings. pp. 36–37. 1971.

4534. ______. Midwest Turf Field Day Report. Midwest Turf Field Day Report. Purdue University. 1971.

4535. ______. Modifying the extremes—the very much in turf. Northern Ohio Turfgrass News. 15(5):1–3. 1971.

4536. ______. Pre and post emergence use of pesticides with new turfgrass seedings. Ohio Turfgrass Conference Proceedings. pp. 28–30. 1971.

4537. ______. IBDU as a nitrogen source. Ohio Turfgrass Conference Proceedings. p. 48. 1971.

4538. ______. Bluegrass. Park Maintenance. 24(7):20–21. 1971.

4539. ______. Good turf and chemical usage. The Bull Sheet. 26(1):7. 1972.

4540. ______. Progress with the PAT (Prescription Athletic Turf) system. Midwest Regional Turf Conference Proceedings. p. 80. 1972.

4541. ______. Midwest turf field day report. Midwest Turf Field Day, Purdue University. pp. 1–7. 1972.

4542. ______. Purr-Wick rootzone system for turf. Midwest Turf News and Research. No. 40 Revised. pp. 1–6. 1972.

4543. ______. IBDU as a nitrogen source. A Patch of Green. Michigan and Border Cities GCSA Publication. p. 11. January, 1972.

4544. ______. Midwest current trends in turfgrass weed control. Proceedings of Scotts

Turfgrass Research Conference. 3:155–160 1972.

4545. Daniel, W. H., J. R. Barrett, and L. H. Coombs. Electrically warmed soils for sport turfs—a progress report. Midwest Turf News and Research. No. 28. 6 pp. 1964.

4546. Daniel, W. H. and J. R. Barrett. Soil warming for turf areas. Agronomy Abstracts. 56:100. 1964.

4547. ______. Electricity warms soils for sport turf. Weeds, Trees, and Turf. 5:14–16. 1966.

4548. Daniel, W. H., and R. P. Freeborg. The PAT (Prescription Athletic Turf) System—initial installations. Agronomy Abstracts. 2:62. 1972.

4549. Daniel, W. H. and N. R. Goetze. Subjective versus objective measurements of turf qualities. Agronomy Abstracts. 49:76. 1957.

4550. ______. Heavy nitrogen fertilization of cool-season turfgrasses. Agronomy Abstracts. 52:69. 1960.

4551. Daniel, W. H. and R. Montgomery. Rootzone mixtures for turf. Agronomy Abstracts. 53:74. 1961.

4552. Daniel, W. H. and D. S. Ralston. Zero tension and subsurface irrigation for turf. Agronomy Abstracts. 60:57. 1968.

4553. Daniel, W. H., and T. P. Riordan. Kentucky bluegrass *(Poa pratensis)* improvement through breeding and selection. Agronomy Abstracts. 61:53. 1969.

4554. Daniel, W. H. and E. C. Roberts. Turfgrass management in the United States. Advances in Agronomy. 18:259–326. 1966.

4555. Daniel, W. H., J. R. Barrett, and L. H. Coombs. Electrically warmed soils for sport turfs—a progress report. Midwest Turf News and Research. No. 28. pp. 1–6. 1964.

4556. ______. Electrically warmed soils for sport turfs—a progress report. Proceeding of Midwest Regional Turf Conference. pp. 1–6. 1964.

4558. Daniel, W. H., R. B. Hull, O. C. Lee, and E. G. Sharvelle. The lawn its making and maintenance. Purdue University Agricultural Extension Service Bulletin 254 (4th revision). pp. 1–19. 1952.

4559. ______. The lawn: how to establish and maintain. Purdue Agricultural Extension Service Bulletin 254 (5th Revision) pp. 1–21. 1955.

4560. Daniel, W. H., H. W. Gilbert, O. C. Lee, E. G. Sharvelle, G. E. Lehkers, G. C. Oderkirk. Lawn, how to establish and maintain. Purdue Agricultural Extension Circular. 438:1–27. 1957.

4562. Daniels, M. A. The control of ants. The National Greenkeeper. 2(5):33–34. 1928.

4563. Danielson, L. L. Comparative performance of herbicide sprays, granules and glomules. Proceedings of the Northeastern Weed Control Conference. p. 71. 1967.

4564. Danielson, R. A. Your greensmower and its care. Southern Turfgrass Association Conference Proceedings. pp. 16–18. 1964.

4565. Danielson, R. E. Water, wetting agents, and soil physics. Rocky Mountain Regional Turfgrass Conference Proceedings. 9:17–22. 1962.

4566. ______. Factors affecting turfgrass irrigation. Rocky Mountain Regional Turfgrass Conference Proceedings. 18:16–23. 1972.

4567. Danner, C. Bermuda-rye greens conversion at Nashville. Golfdom. 22(2):68. 1948.

4568. ______. Converting to bent in Tennessee saves on maintenance. Golfdom. 25(3):44. 1951.

4569. ______. Bent can be grown in the South. Golfdom. 33(3):50–54. 1959.

4570. ______. Management of bent in the south. 30th National Turfgrass Conference and Show. pp. 10–11. 1959.

4571. ______. Establishment and management of bentgrass greens for the South. Southeastern Turfgrass Conference. 9:40–43. 1955.

4572. ______. Using bent as a permanent grass for greens. Proceedings Thirteenth Southeastern Turfgrass Conference. pp. 24–28. 1959.

4573. ______. Golf-green irrigation. Southeastern Turfgrass Conference. 21:33–37. 1967.

4574. ______. Bentgrass greens for the South. USGA Journal and Turf Management. 6(1):28–31. 1953.

4575. Daray, J. Special maintenance duties of the southern greenskeeper. Golfdom. 1(9):20–21. 1927.

4576. Darling, H. Record late snows have N.E. Superintendents puzzled. Golfdom. 30(5):48. 1956.

4577. Darlington, C. D. and E. K. Janaki Ammal. Chromosome atlas of cultivated plants. Allen and Unwin, London. 397 pp. 1945.

4578. Darrow, R. A. Effect of soil temperature, pH, and nitrogen nutrition on the development of *Poa pratensis.* Botanical Gazette. 101:109–127. 1939.

4579. Daubenmire, R. F. Temperature gradients near the soil surface with reference to techniques of measurement in forest ecology. Journal of Forestry. 41(8):601–603. 1943.

4580. Daubenmire, R. Ecology of fire in grasslands. Advances in Ecological Research. 5:209–266. 1968.

4581. Daul, A. S. The relation between rainfall and injuries to turf—Season 1933. The Greenkeepers' Reporter. 2(2):1–4. 1934.

4582. Davenport, D. C. Effects of phenylmercuric acetate on transpiration and growth of small plots of grass. Nature. 212(5064):801–802. 1966.

4583. ______. Effects of chemical antitranspirants on transpiration and growth of grass. Journal of Experimental Botany. 18(55):332–337. 1967.

4584. Davenport, D. C., M. A. Fisher, and R. M. Hagan. Some counteractive effects of antitranspirants. Plant Physiology. 49(5):-722–724. 1972.

4585. Davenport, D. C., R. M. Hagan, and P. E. Martin. Antitranspirants . . . uses and effects on plant life. California Turfgrass Culture. 19(4):25–27. 1969.

4586. Davidson, H. Organic matter and nursery soil management. Michigan State Nursery Notes. No. 5. 1970.

4587. Davidson, J. H. The use of odorized methyl bromide for turf improvement. Proceedings of Midwest Regional Turf Conference. pp. 30–33. 1956.

4588. Davidson, J. L. and F. L. Milthorpe. The effect of defoliation on the carbon balance in *Dactylis glomerata.* Annals of Botany. 30:185–197. 1966.

4589. ______. Leaf growth in *Dactylis glomerata* following defoliation. Annals of Botany. 30(118):173–184. 1966.

4590. Davidson, J. R. Cost development for sweeping, aerating, and renovating memorial park lawns. Exposition Conference. Southern California. 4 pp. 1966.

4591. Davidson, R. M. Nutritional and fungicidal tests for *Ophiobolus* control. Northwest Turfgrass Topics. 14(2):4–5. 1971.

4592. Davidson, R. M., Jr. and R. L. Goss. Effects on P, S, N, lime, chlordane, and fungicides on *Ophiobolus* patch disease of turf. The Plant Disease Reporter. 56(7):565–567. 1972.

4593. Davies, A. The growth of varieties of perennial ryegrass in the seeding year. Journal of the British Grassland Society. 15(1):12–20. 1960.

4594. Davies, A., and D. M. Calder. Patterns of spring growth in swards of different grass varieties. Journal of the British Grasslands Society. 24(2):215–225. 1969.

4595. Davies, I. The use of epidermal characteristics for the identification of grasses in the leafy stage. Journal of the British Grassland Society. 14(1):7–16. 1959.

4596. Davies, J. G. Seed rates and interspecific competion in seed mixtures. Australian and New Zealand Association for Advancement of Science Report. 22:316. 1936.

4597. Davies, W. Modern concepts of grassland improvement. Herbage Review. 5:-194–199. 1937.

4599. Davies, W. E. The breeding affinities of some British species of *Agrostis.* British Agricultural Bulletin. 5:313. 1953.

4600. Davis, A. G. and B. F. Martin. Observations on the effect of artificial flooding on certain herbage plants. Journal of the British Grassland Society. 4(1):63–64. 1949.

4601. Davis, A. M. Lawn grass evaluation. Arkansas Farm Research. 6(1):10. 1957.

4602. Davis, B. A. Lawns. The Southern Garden. J. B. Lippincott Co. New York. pp. 178–186. 1971.

4603. Davis, C. S. Control of pests of trees, shrubs and turf. Parks and Recreation. 47(3):112–113, 125–126. 1964.

4604. Davis, D. E. Effects of herbicides on plant physiological processes. Proceedings of Scotts Turfgrass Research Conference. 3:-49–74. 1972.

4605. Davis, D. L. Changes in soluble protein fraction during cold acclimation plus the effects of certain nutrients and stress conditions on winterkill of *Cynodon* spp. PhD. Thesis, North Carolina State University. 75 pp. 1967.

4606. Davis, D. L. and W. B. Gilbert. Changes in the soluble protein fractions during cold acclimation of bermudagrass. Agronomy Abstracts. 59:50–51. 1967.

4607. Davis, F. F. What's been observed in the tests of 2,4-D on weeds. Golfdom. 19(9):11–13, 15,17. 1945.

4608. ______. Growth regulator makes promising turf herbicide. Greenkeepers' Reporter. 12(6):12–15. 1944.

4609. Davis, F. F., and G. E. Harrington. Sod is ideal for playing fields. Grass, 1948 Yearbook of Agriculture. United States Department of Agriculture. pp. 295–302. 1948.

4610. Davis, G. Insect control panel (summary of remarks). Texas Turfgrass Conference Proceedings. 13:52–55. 1958.

4611. ______. Insect ecology. Proceedings of the Eighteenth Annual Texas Turf Conference. 18:26–30. 1963.

4612. ______. Insects and insecticides. Proceedings of the Nineteenth Annual Texas Turfgrass Conference. 19:48–50. 1964.

4613. ______. Insects, insecticides and new developments. Proceedings of the Twentieth Annual Texas Turfgrass Conference. 20:18–19. 1965.

4614. ______. Classification of insects that may attack turf and ornamentals. Texas Turfgrass Conference Proceedings. 23:23–25. 1968.

4615. Davis, J. J. Pests which disfigure turf. Midwest Turf News and Research. 1(3):4. 1947.

4616. ______. How to destroy ants in turf. Midwest Turf-News and Research. 1(4):3. 1947.

4617. Davis, J. R. Efficiency factors in sprinkler system design. Sprinkler Irrigation Association Open Technical Conference Proceedings. pp. 15–30. 1963.

4619. Davis, R. Nutritional studies of turf grasses. Proceedings of Midwest Regional Turf Conference. pp. 42–44. 1949.

4620. ______. Experiments in fertilizing. Midwest Turf News and Research. 3(1):1–3. 1949.

4622. Davis, R. R. The physical condition of putting green soils and other environmental factors affecting the quality of greens. Ph.D. Thesis, Purdue University. 1950.

4623. ______. Golf greens, good bad. Proceedings of Midwest Regional Turfgrass Conference. pp. 85–87. 1951.

4624. ______. Garden expert answers: crabgrass. Household. 52(8). 1952.

4625. ______. Physical condition of putting-green soils and other environmental factors affecting greens. USGA Journal and Turf Management. 5(1):25–27. 1952.

4626. ______. Lawn care—culture. Pesticide News. 7(2):1954.

4627. Davis, R. R. Experiences with fairway improvements. Proceedings of Midwest Regional Turf Conference. pp. 23–24. 1955.

4628. ______. Questions and answers on features of Meyer zoysiagrass. Ohio Farm Research. 41:44–45. 1956.

4629. ______. An evaluation of grasses for unirrigated fairways and lawns. Pennsylvania State College Turf Conference. 25:48–51. 1956.

4630. ______. The effect of other species and mowing heights on persistence of lawn grasses. Agronomy Abstracts. 50:64. 1958.

4631. ______. The effect of other species and mowing height on persistence of lawn grasses. Agronomy Journal. 50:671–673. 1958.

4632. ______. The weed content of Kentucky bluegrass as influenced by variety, mowing height and seedling stand. Agronomy Abstracts. 52:69. 1960.

4633. ______. The roots get hurt. Golfdom. 35(5):38–40, 109. 1961.

4634. ______. Turfgrass mixtures—influence of mowing height and nitrogen. Illinois Turfgrass Conference. pp. 42–45. 1961.

4635. ______. Clipping heights and rooting depths. International Turf-Grass Conference Proceedings. 32:9–10. 1961.

4636. ______. Turfgrass mixtures—influence of mowing height and nitrogen. Proceedings of the Midwest Regional Turf Conference. pp. 27–29. 1961.

4637. ______. Pre-emergence herbicides for crabgrass control in turf. North Central Weed Control Conference Proceedings. 18:-82. 1961.

4638. ______. Advancement in erosion control protection by seeding. 20th Short Course on Roadside Development, (Ohio). pp. 102–105. 1961.

4639. ______. Nitrogen fertilization of turfgrasses. Agronomy Abstracts. 54:102. 1962.

4640. ______. A look at the practical significance of turfgrass research results in Ohio. Iagreen. 1(2):18–21. 1962.

4641. ______. Caring for your lawn. Ohio Agricultural Extension Service. Bulletin 271. 1–17 pp. October, 1962.

4642. ______. Turfgrass research and developments in Ohio. Rutgers University. 1963 Three-day Turf Course Proceedings. pp. 29–35. 1963.

4643. ______. Effects of traffic on soils. USGA Green Section Record. 1(1):10. 1963.

4644. ______. Turfgrass mixtures and their response to mowing height and nitrogen fertilization. 1962 Wisconsin Turfgrass Conference Proceedings. p. 1. 1963.

4645. ______. Nitrogen fertilization of turfgrasses. 1962 Wisconsin Turfgrass Conference Proceedings. pp. 1–2. 1963.

4646. ______. Turfgrass research and developments in Ohio. Rutgers University Short Course in Turf Management. 32:29–35. 1964.

4647. ______. Forms of nitrogen for fertilizing Kentucky bluegrass in Ohio. Golf Course Reporter. 33(5):42–50. 1965.

4648. ______. Your lawn. Ohio State University Extension Bulletin 271. 31 pp. 1966.

4649. ______. Lawn grasses, mixtures, and blends. Lawn and Ornamentals Research—1966. Ohio Agricultural Research and Development Center. Research Summary 16. pp. 1–2. 1966.

4650. ______. Fairway nitrogen sources. Royal Canadian Golf Association Sports Turfgrass Conference. 17:55–68. 1966.

4651. ______. Grass mixtures for lawn and golf courses. Lawn and Ornamentals Research—1967. Ohio Agricultural Research and Development Center. Research Summary 24. pp. 1–8. 1967.

4652. ______. Blends and mixtures of turfgrass. First Ohio Turfgrass Conference Proceedings. pp. 41–47. 1967.

4653. ______. Population changes in Kentucky bluegrass—red fescue mixtures. Agronomy Abstracts. 59:51. 1967.

4654. ______. Grass mixtures for lawns and golf courses. West Virginia Turfgrass Conference Proceedings. pp. 34–40. 1967.

4655. ______. Grass mixtures for lawns. The Cemeterian. 32(6):11. 1968.

4656. ______. Grass mixtures for lawns and golf courses. West Virginia University Miscellaneous Publication. 5:34. 1968.

4657. ______. Cool-season turfgrass communities in the United States. Proceedings of the First International Turfgrass Research Conference. pp. 104–109. 1969.

4658. ______. Tissue analyses as indicators of turfgrass nutrition. Proceedings of the First International Turfgrass Research Conference. pp. 196–199. 1969.

4659. ______. Turfgrass field days as a technique for education. Proceedings of the First International Turfgrass Research Conference. pp. 428–429. 1969.

4660. ______. Nutrition and fertilizers. Turfgrass Science. ASA Monograph No. 14. 1970.

4661. Davis, R. R. and D. D. Bondarenko. New chemicals kill lawn weeds.

Ohio State University Agricultural Experiment Station. Ohio Farm and Home Research. 45(3):41,47. 1960.

4662. Davis, R. R., and J. B. Jones, Jr. Prospects for a plant analysis program for turfgrasses—problems and potential. Agronomy Abstracts. 60:58. 1968.

4663. Davis, R. R. and R. W. Miller. Bentgrass varieties for golf courses and lawns. Lawn and Ornamentals Research. Ohio Agricultural Research and Development Center. Research Summary 6. pp. 7–8. 1965.

4664. ______. Maintenance fertilization of Kentucky bluegrass. Lawn and Ornamentals Research. Ohio Agricultural Research and Development Center. Research Summary 6. pp. 13–15. 1965.

4665. Davis, R. R., and J. B. Polivka. Better lawns result from proper mowing, fertilizing and weed control. Ohio Farm and Home Research. 38(281):37–38. 1953.

4666. Davis, R. R., and H. A. Runnels. Merion bluegrass, new strains of fescue, and polycross bent. Ohio Farm and Home Research. 1954.

4667. ______. Some facts about Merion bluegrass. Ohio Farm and Home Research. 1954.

4668. ______. Merion bluegrass must be handled properly to produce good lawn. Ohio Farm and Home Research. 40(292):10–12. 1955.

4669. Davis, R. R. and E. W. Stroube. Chemicals for difficult broadleaf weeds. Ohio Lawn and Ornamental Days. p. 10. 1963.

4670. Davis, R. R. and C. J. Willard. Both cultural and chemical practices needed to prevent crabgrass in lawns. Ohio Farm and Home Research. 37(274):5–7. 1952.

4671. Davis, R. R., J. C. Caldwell, and G. R. Gist. Caring for your lawn. Ohio Agricultural Experiment Station Research Bulletin 271. 17 pp. 1960.

4672. Davis, R. R., R. W. Miller and M. H. Niehaus. Kentucky bluegrass for Ohio lawns. Ohio Report on Research and Development. 51(2):19,31. 1966.

4673. Davis, R. R., V. H. Ries, and C. J. Willard. Your lawn. Ohio Agricultural Extension Bulletin. 271:1–17. 1960.

4674. Davis, R. R., E. W. Stroube, and K. L. Bader. Crabgrass can be controlled with chemicals. Ohio State University Agricultural Experiment Station. Ohio Farm and Home Research. 47(2):19,31. 1962.

4675. Davis, R. R., E. W. Stroube, and R. W. Miller. Well tended lawns can be invaded by knotweed. Ohio Farm and Home Research. 49(2):28–29. 1964.

4676. Davis, R. R., K. L. Bader, J. L. Caldwell, R. P. Holdsworth, B. F. Janson, O. L. Musgrave, R. E. Partyka, and E. W. Stroube. Starting your lawn. Ohio Cooperative Extension Service Bulletin 271. pp. 1–31. 1964.

4677. Davis, S. Identification of turf diseases. Oklahoma Turfgrass Conference Proceedings. pp. 14–16. 1953.

4678. Davis, S. H. Lawn disease control. Agricultural Extension Service, Rutgers University. Leaflet No. 166.

4679. ______. A report on the 1949 national cooperative turf fungicide trials. Rutgers University Short Course in Turf Management. 18:51–57. 1950.

4680. ______. Turf fungicide trials—1950. Proceedings of the Mid-Atlantic Turf Conference. pp. 11–19. 1951.

4681. ______. Tests of turf fungicides in New Jersey. Pennsylvania State College Turfgrass Conference Proceedings. 20:21–30. 1951.

4682. ______. Turf fungicide trials—1950. Rutgers University Short Course in Turf Management. 19:108–116. 1951.

4683. ______. Diseases of turf grasses and the 1942 fungicide trials. Golfdom. 27(6):66,68,79–84. 1953.

4684. ______. 1953 turf fungicide trials. New Jersey Agricultural Experiment Station Mimeograph Report. 1953.

4685. ______. A review of turf diseases common in New Jersey. Rutgers University Short Course in Turf Management. pp. 15–19. 1952–1953.

4686. ______. Disease control on fine turf (bents). New Jersey Agricultural Experiment Station Bulletin. 816:108–109. 1966.

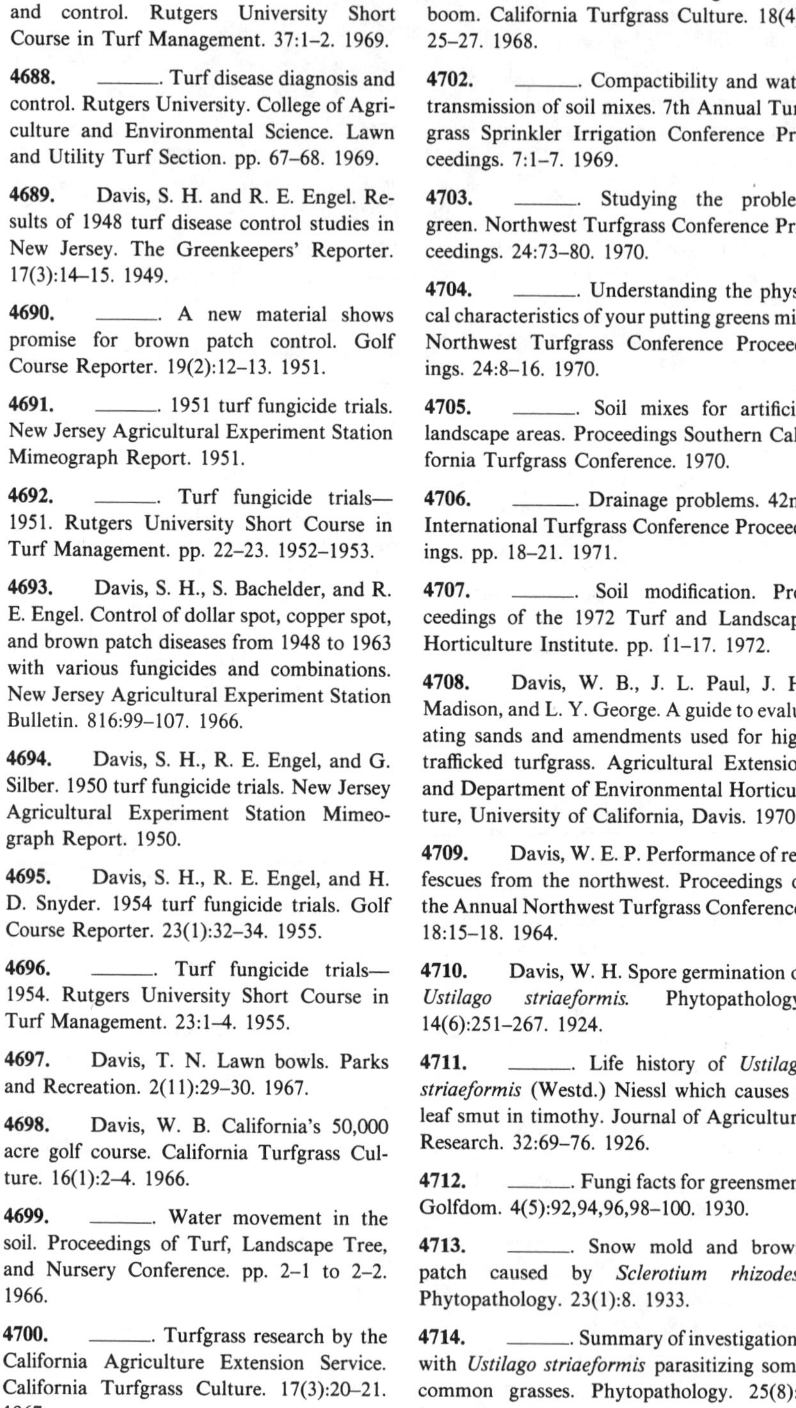

4687. ______. Turf disease: diagnosis and control. Rutgers University Short Course in Turf Management. 37:1–2. 1969.

4688. ______. Turf disease diagnosis and control. Rutgers University. College of Agriculture and Environmental Science. Lawn and Utility Turf Section. pp. 67–68. 1969.

4689. Davis, S. H. and R. E. Engel. Results of 1948 turf disease control studies in New Jersey. The Greenkeepers' Reporter. 17(3):14–15. 1949.

4690. ______. A new material shows promise for brown patch control. Golf Course Reporter. 19(2):12–13. 1951.

4691. ______. 1951 turf fungicide trials. New Jersey Agricultural Experiment Station Mimeograph Report. 1951.

4692. ______. Turf fungicide trials—1951. Rutgers University Short Course in Turf Management. pp. 22–23. 1952–1953.

4693. Davis, S. H., S. Bachelder, and R. E. Engel. Control of dollar spot, copper spot, and brown patch diseases from 1948 to 1963 with various fungicides and combinations. New Jersey Agricultural Experiment Station Bulletin. 816:99–107. 1966.

4694. Davis, S. H., R. E. Engel, and G. Silber. 1950 turf fungicide trials. New Jersey Agricultural Experiment Station Mimeograph Report. 1950.

4695. Davis, S. H., R. E. Engel, and H. D. Snyder. 1954 turf fungicide trials. Golf Course Reporter. 23(1):32–34. 1955.

4696. ______. Turf fungicide trials—1954. Rutgers University Short Course in Turf Management. 23:1–4. 1955.

4697. Davis, T. N. Lawn bowls. Parks and Recreation. 2(11):29–30. 1967.

4698. Davis, W. B. California's 50,000 acre golf course. California Turfgrass Culture. 16(1):2–4. 1966.

4699. ______. Water movement in the soil. Proceedings of Turf, Landscape Tree, and Nursery Conference. pp. 2–1 to 2–2. 1966.

4700. ______. Turfgrass research by the California Agriculture Extension Service. California Turfgrass Culture. 17(3):20–21. 1967.

4701. ______. California's golf course boom. California Turfgrass Culture. 18(4):-25–27. 1968.

4702. ______. Compactibility and water transmission of soil mixes. 7th Annual Turfgrass Sprinkler Irrigation Conference Proceedings. 7:1–7. 1969.

4703. ______. Studying the problem green. Northwest Turfgrass Conference Proceedings. 24:73–80. 1970.

4704. ______. Understanding the physical characteristics of your putting greens mix. Northwest Turfgrass Conference Proceedings. 24:8–16. 1970.

4705. ______. Soil mixes for artificial landscape areas. Proceedings Southern California Turfgrass Conference. 1970.

4706. ______. Drainage problems. 42nd International Turfgrass Conference Proceedings. pp. 18–21. 1971.

4707. ______. Soil modification. Proceedings of the 1972 Turf and Landscape Horticulture Institute. pp. 11–17. 1972.

4708. Davis, W. B., J. L. Paul, J. H. Madison, and L. Y. George. A guide to evaluating sands and amendments used for high trafficked turfgrass. Agricultural Extension and Department of Environmental Horticulture, University of California, Davis. 1970.

4709. Davis, W. E. P. Performance of red fescues from the northwest. Proceedings of the Annual Northwest Turfgrass Conference. 18:15–18. 1964.

4710. Davis, W. H. Spore germination of *Ustilago striaeformis.* Phytopathology. 14(6):251–267. 1924.

4711. ______. Life history of *Ustilago striaeformis* (Westd.) Niessl which causes a leaf smut in timothy. Journal of Agriculture Research. 32:69–76. 1926.

4712. ______. Fungi facts for greensmen. Golfdom. 4(5):92,94,96,98–100. 1930.

4713. ______. Snow mold and brown patch caused by *Sclerotium rhizodes.* Phytopathology. 23(1):8. 1933.

4714. ______. Summary of investigations with *Ustilago striaeformis* parasitizing some common grasses. Phytopathology. 25(8):-810–817. 1935.

4715. Davis, W. and M. T. Thomas. The behavior of grasses in the seeding year, when sown in pure plots: establishment, rate of growth, and palatability. Welsh Journal of Agriculture. 4:206–221. 1928.

4716. Davison, A. D., and C. J. Gould. Turfgrass diseases and their control. Northwest Turfgrass Conference Proceedings. 22:-52–56. 1968.

4718. Dawson, J. E. Organic soils. Advances in Agronomy. 8:377–401. 1956.

4719. Dawson, J. R. Steam-air mixtures for the heat treatment of soil. Parks, Golf Courses and Sports Grounds. 33(7):570–577. 1968.

4720. Dawson, R. B. Some greenkeeping problems and practices, the programme of the research station and the factors influencing growth of turf. Journal of Board of Greenkeeping Research. 1(1):12–23. 1929.

4721. ______. Bermuda grass in India: an interesting experience. Journal of Board of Greenkeeping Research. 1(1):26–27. 1929.

4722. ______. Worm killing: A summary of four methods. Journal of Board of Greenkeeping Research. 1(2):60–64. 1930.

4723. ______. Creeping grasses and turf formation from them. Journal of Board of Greenkeeping Research. 1(2):71–73. 1930.

4724. ______. Culture of grasses for sports purposes. Journal of Board of Greenkeeping Research. 1(2):74–78. 1930.

4725. ______. Weed eradication and old turf. Journal of the Board of Greenkeeping Research. 2(4):41–43. 1931.

4726. ______. The importance of clean seed for sowing putting greens. Journal of the Board of Greenkeeping Research. 2(5):125–139. 1931.

4727. ______. Leather jackets. Journal of the Board of Greenkeeping Research. 2(6):-183–195. 1932.

4728. ______. The mole draining of golf courses on heavy land. Journal of the Board of Greenkeeping Research. 2(7):249–255. 1932.

4729. ______. Common weeds of turf. Journal of the Board of Greenkeeping Research. 2(7):282–288. 1932.

4730. ______. Common weeds of turf. Journal of the Board of Greenkeeping Research. 3(8):44–48. 1933.

4731. ______. Common weeds of turf. Journal of the Board of Greenkeeping Research. 3(9):90–93. 1933.

4732. ______. A short account of the four and a half year's work at the St. Ives Research Station. Journal of the Board of Greenkeeping Research. 3(10):121–132. 1934.

4733. ______. Common weeds of turf. Journal of the Board of Greenkeeping Research. 3(10):161–163. 1934.

4734. ______. Forking as an aid to turf recovery after drought. Journal of the Board of Greenkeeping Research. 3(11):233–241. 1934.

4735. ______. Making lawns from seed. Landscape and Garden. 1(4):38–39. 1934.

4736. ______. Some common errors in lawn management and how to avoid them. Journal of the Board of Greenkeeping Research. 4(12):25–31. 1935.

4737. ______. Common weeds of turf. Journal of the Board of Greenkeeping Research. 4(12):73–76. 1935.

4738. ______. Common weeds of turf. Journal of the Board of Greenkeeping Research. 4(13):108–109. 1935.

4739. ______. The camomile lawn. Journal of the Board of Greenkeeping Research. 4(14):185–192. 1936.

4740. ______. Compost and fertilisers in relation to greenkeeping. Journal of the Board of Greenkeeping Research. 4(14):198–199. 1936.

4741. ______. Common weeds of turf. Journal of the Board of Greenkeeping Research. 4(14):200–202. 1936.

4742. ______. Common weeds of turf. Journal of the Board of Greenkeeping Research. 4(15):271–273. 1936.

4743. ______. Common weeds of turf. Journal of the Board of Greenkeeping Research. 5(16):38–40. 1937.

4744. ______. Practical lawn craft. Crosby Lockwood & Son, Ltd., London. 320 pp. 1939.

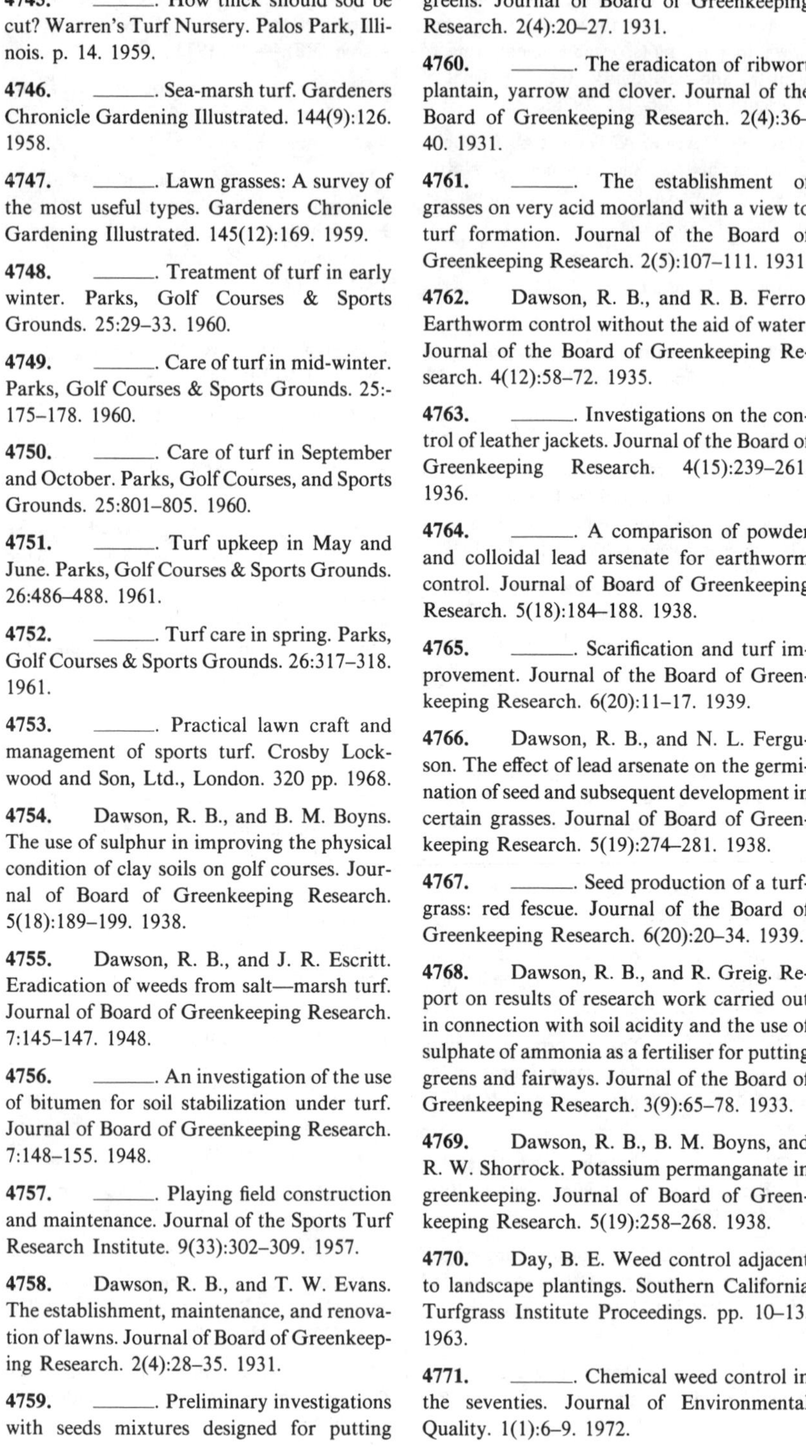

4745. ______. How thick should sod be cut? Warren's Turf Nursery. Palos Park, Illinois. p. 14. 1959.

4746. ______. Sea-marsh turf. Gardeners Chronicle Gardening Illustrated. 144(9):126. 1958.

4747. ______. Lawn grasses: A survey of the most useful types. Gardeners Chronicle Gardening Illustrated. 145(12):169. 1959.

4748. ______. Treatment of turf in early winter. Parks, Golf Courses & Sports Grounds. 25:29–33. 1960.

4749. ______. Care of turf in mid-winter. Parks, Golf Courses & Sports Grounds. 25:-175–178. 1960.

4750. ______. Care of turf in September and October. Parks, Golf Courses, and Sports Grounds. 25:801–805. 1960.

4751. ______. Turf upkeep in May and June. Parks, Golf Courses & Sports Grounds. 26:486–488. 1961.

4752. ______. Turf care in spring. Parks, Golf Courses & Sports Grounds. 26:317–318. 1961.

4753. ______. Practical lawn craft and management of sports turf. Crosby Lockwood and Son, Ltd., London. 320 pp. 1968.

4754. Dawson, R. B., and B. M. Boyns. The use of sulphur in improving the physical condition of clay soils on golf courses. Journal of Board of Greenkeeping Research. 5(18):189–199. 1938.

4755. Dawson, R. B., and J. R. Escritt. Eradication of weeds from salt—marsh turf. Journal of Board of Greenkeeping Research. 7:145–147. 1948.

4756. ______. An investigation of the use of bitumen for soil stabilization under turf. Journal of Board of Greenkeeping Research. 7:148–155. 1948.

4757. ______. Playing field construction and maintenance. Journal of the Sports Turf Research Institute. 9(33):302–309. 1957.

4758. Dawson, R. B., and T. W. Evans. The establishment, maintenance, and renovation of lawns. Journal of Board of Greenkeeping Research. 2(4):28–35. 1931.

4759. ______. Preliminary investigations with seeds mixtures designed for putting greens. Journal of Board of Greenkeeping Research. 2(4):20–27. 1931.

4760. ______. The eradicaton of ribwort plantain, yarrow and clover. Journal of the Board of Greenkeeping Research. 2(4):36–40. 1931.

4761. ______. The establishment of grasses on very acid moorland with a view to turf formation. Journal of the Board of Greenkeeping Research. 2(5):107–111. 1931.

4762. Dawson, R. B., and R. B. Ferro. Earthworm control without the aid of water. Journal of the Board of Greenkeeping Research. 4(12):58–72. 1935.

4763. ______. Investigations on the control of leather jackets. Journal of the Board of Greenkeeping Research. 4(15):239–261. 1936.

4764. ______. A comparison of powder and colloidal lead arsenate for earthworm control. Journal of Board of Greenkeeping Research. 5(18):184–188. 1938.

4765. ______. Scarification and turf improvement. Journal of the Board of Greenkeeping Research. 6(20):11–17. 1939.

4766. Dawson, R. B., and N. L. Ferguson. The effect of lead arsenate on the germination of seed and subsequent development in certain grasses. Journal of Board of Greenkeeping Research. 5(19):274–281. 1938.

4767. ______. Seed production of a turfgrass: red fescue. Journal of the Board of Greenkeeping Research. 6(20):20–34. 1939.

4768. Dawson, R. B., and R. Greig. Report on results of research work carried out in connection with soil acidity and the use of sulphate of ammonia as a fertiliser for putting greens and fairways. Journal of the Board of Greenkeeping Research. 3(9):65–78. 1933.

4769. Dawson, R. B., B. M. Boyns, and R. W. Shorrock. Potassium permanganate in greenkeeping. Journal of Board of Greenkeeping Research. 5(19):258–268. 1938.

4770. Day, B. E. Weed control adjacent to landscape plantings. Southern California Turfgrass Institute Proceedings. pp. 10–13. 1963.

4771. ______. Chemical weed control in the seventies. Journal of Environmental Quality. 1(1):6–9. 1972.

4772. Day, B. E., and L. S. Jordan. Spray retention by bermudagrass. Weeds. 9:351–355. 1961.

4773. Day, B. E. and R. C. Russell. The effect of drying on survival of nutgrass tubers. California Agricultural Experiment Station Bulletin 751. 4 pp. 1955.

4774. Day, F. Turfgrass problems in public areas. New Mexico Turfgrass Conference Proceedings. 1:6–8. 1955.

4775. Day, H. M. Sources of water supply. USGA Green Section Record. 4(1):1–8. 1966.

4776. Day, M. H. Buy quality grass seed for sod production. Weeds, Trees and Turf. 5(12):37–38. 1966.

4777. O'Donnell, J. L. and J. R. Love. Effects of time and height of cut on rooting activity of Merion Kentucky bluegrass as measured by radioactive phosphorus uptake. Agronomy Journal. 62(3):313–316. 1970.

4778. Deakin, O. A. Experimental stabilized turf shoulders for New Jersey parkways. Report on Committee on Roadside Development. Highway Research Board. pp. 56–62. 1948.

4779. Deal, A. S. The problem of insects. Parks and Recreation. 1(9):732–735. 1966.

4780. ______. The problem of insects. Turf Bulletin. 4(2):7–10. 1966.

4781. ______. Some tips on turfgrass pest control for 1971. Divot News. 10(2):2. 1971.

4782. ______. Two pests of St. Augustine grass. California Turfgrass Culture. 22(3):19. 1972.

4783. ______. Regulating growth of 'Merion' Kentucky bluegrass (*Poa Pratensis* L.) turf with cultural and management techniques. PhD. Thesis, Rutgers University. Dissertation Abstracts. 24(3):2643. 1963.

4784. Deal, E. E. Regulating growth of Merion Kentucky bluegrass *(Poa pratensis)* turf with cultural and management techniques. Dissertation Abstracts. 24:2643–4. 1964.

4785. ______. Turf on athletic fields and play areas. Maryland Agricultural Extension Service Fact Sheet 168. 1965.

4786. ______. Turf management. Turf Bulletin. 2(12):22. 1965.

4787. ______. Bermudagrass fertilization. The Golf Superintendent. 34(6):34. 1966.

4788. ______. Maryland turfgrass research report. Mid-Atlantic Superintendents Conference Proceedings. pp. 23–25. 1966.

4789. ______. Control of crabgrass, goosegrass and annual bluegrass with preemergence herbicides. Proceedings of the Northeastern Weed Control Conference. pp. 537–546. 1966.

4790. ______. Turf management. Turf Bulletin. 3(1):17. 1966.

4791. ______. Crabgrass control. Turf Bulletin. 3(2):8. 1966.

4792. ______. Watch for variability in crabgrass control chemicals. Turf-Grass Times. 1(5):1. 1966.

4793. ______. Sod industry—big business in Maryland. Weeds, Trees, and Turf. 5:19–20. 1966.

4794. ______. Tufcote bermudagrass establishment using preemergence herbicides. Agronomy Abstracts. 59:56. 1967.

4795. ______. Grass dyes coloring compounds. The Golf Superintendent. 35(1):71–72. 1967.

4796. ______. Crabgrass control chemicals. Golf Superintendent. 35(1):94–95. 1967.

4797. ______. Phosphorus fertilization. The Golf Superintendent. 35(7):39–41. 1967.

4798. ______. Soil preparations for sod production. Proceedings of the International Turfgrass Conference. 38:50–52. 1967.

4799. ______. Annual bluegrass Turf Bulletin. 4(4):22. 1967.

4800. ______. Grass dyes—coloring compounds. Turf-Grass Times. 3(2):1. 1967.

4801. ______. Bermudagrasses in the transitional zone. USGA Green Section Record. 6(4):12–13. 1968.

4802. ______. Atmospheric pollution and annual bluegrass. The Golf Superintendent. 37(1):37. 1969.

4803. ______. Recent developments in turf. Mid-Atlantic Superintendents Conference Proceedings. pp. 19–20. 1969.

4805. ______. Control broadleaf weeds. Golf Superintendent. 38(1):102. 1970.

4806. Deal, E. E., and R. E. Engel. Effects of four soil moisture regimes on growth of 'Merion' Kentucky bluegrass *(Poa pratensis* L.). Agronomy Abstracts. 54:102. 1962.

4807. ______. Iron, manganese, boron and zinc: effects on growth of Merion Kentucky bluegrass. Agronomy Journal. 57:553–555. 1965.

4809. Dearie, E. B. "Zero hour" for new turf. Golfdom. 2(8):29–32. 1928.

4810. ______. Florida reclaims sea and jungle for golf. Golfdom. 3(3):48–50. 1929.

4811. ______. Conditioning new course is case of local study. Golfdom. 5(2):72, 74. 1931.

4812. ______. Fairway-watering as a greenkeeper sees it. Golfdom. 6(12):10–11, 14. 1932.

4813. ______. Club's drastic treatment brings weedless fairway. Golfdom. 13(8):12. 1939.

4814. ______. Where does economy start? The National Greenkeeper. 2(3):7–8. 1928.

4815. ______. Selecting the right site. The National Greenkeeper. 2(6):5–6. 1928.

4816. ______. Where does economy start? The National Greenkeeper. 2(7):22. 1928.

4817. ______. Bringing the new course along. The National Greenkeeper. 2(9):14, 16. 1928.

4818. ______. Golf course construction from the greenkeeper's standpoint. Selecting the site. The National Greenkeeper. 4(4):5–7, 9–10, 12. 1930.

4819. ______. Golf course construction from the greenkeeper's standpoint. Chapter II. Designing the course. The National Greenkeeper. 4(5):20–26. 1930.

4820. ______. Golf course construction from the greenkeeper's standpoint. Chapter III. Moulding the course. The National Greenkeeper. 4(6):15–21. 1930.

4821. ______. Golf course construction from the greenkeeper's standpoint. Chapter IV. Drainage on the golf course. The National Greenkeeper. 4(7):11–16. 1930.

4822. ______. Golf course construction from the greenkeeper's standpoint. Chapter V. Irrigating the golf course. The National Greenkeeper. 4(8):20–25. 1930.

4823. ______. Golf course construction from the greenkeeper's standpoint. Chapter VI. Conditioning the golf course. The National Greenkeeper. 4(9):11–17. 1930.

4824. ______. Golf course construction from the greenkeeper's standpoint. Chapter VII. Landscaping the Golf Course. The National Greenkeeper. 4(10):19–22. 1930.

4825. ______. Golf course construction from the greenkeepers standpoint. Chapter VIII. Bringing the new course along. The National Greenkeeper, 4(12):9–10, 12. 1930.

4826. ______. Drainage. The National Greenkeeper. 5(7):5–6, 8. 1931.

4827. Dearie, G. Fairway renovation, how and why. Proceedings of the Midwest Regional Turf Conference. pp. 63–65. 1959.

4828. Deatrick, E. P. The spotting method of weed eradication. Lawn Care. 4(4):3–4. 1931.

4829. de Belle, G. Roadside erosion and resource implications in Prince Edward Island. Highway Research Abstracts. 42(11):6. 1972.

4830. DeBoer, G. An evaluation of soil tests for available iron. M.S. Thesis, University of California, Davis. 1972.

4831. Debona, A. C. and L. J. Audus. Studies on the effects of herbicides on soil nitrification. Weed Research. 10(3):250–263. 1970.

4832. Decker, A. M. and H. J. Retzer. Bluegrass pasture sod seeded with crownvetch. Second Crownvetch Symposium—Pennsylvania State University. 6:108–114. 1968.

4833. Decker, A. M., and T. S. Ronningen. Heaving in forage stands and in bare ground. Agronomy Journal. 49:412–415. 1957.

4834. Decker, G. C. Turf insect pests. The Greenkeepers' Reporter. 7(2):17–20, 46. 1939.

4835. ______. Identify—then get busy. Golfdom. 13(5):21–24. 1939.

4836. ______. How to control rodent and insect turf destroyers. Golfdom. 20(3):21–22, 65–66. 1946.

4837. De Cugnac, A. Research on the sugars of grasses. Annals des Sciences Naturelles Botanique. 13:1–129. 1931.

4838. Dedrick, A. R., N. P. Swanson, and A. E. Dudeck. Mulches for steeply constructed slopes to control erosion and to establish grass. Nebraska Quarterly. 12(4):9–10. 1966.

4839. DeFrance, J. A. What is new in weed control? Greenkeepers Club of New England Newsletter. 9(1):6–9. 1937.

4840. ______. The effect of different fertilizer ratios on colonial, creeping, and velvet bent grasses. Proceedings of the American Society for Horticultural Science. 36:773–780. 1938.

4841. ______. Turf making and lawn management in Rhode Island. Rhode Island Agricultural Experiment Station Miscellaneous Publication 6. 1940.

4842. ______. A comparison of grasses for athletic fields and the effect on the turf of peat incorporated with the soil. Proceedings of the American Society for Horticultural Science. 39:433–438. 1941.

4843. ______. Weed control on closely cut turf-Part I. Greenkeepers Club of New England Newsletter. 13(6):4–5. 1941.

4844. ______. Weed control on closely cut turf-Part II. Greenkeepers Club of New England Newsletter. 13(7):4–5. 1941.

4845. ______. A comparison of bent turf from self- and open-pollinated seed and from stolons. Turf Culture. 2:169–177. 1941.

4846. ______. Growing velvet bent grass seed in Rhode Island for commercial use. Rhode Island Agricultural Experiment Station, Rhode Island State College. Miscellaneous Publication No. 12. pp. 1–5. 1942.

4847. ______. Effect of certain chemicals on the germination of crabgrass seed when plants are treated during the period of seed formation. Proceedings of the American Society of Horticultural Science. 43:331–335. 1943.

4848. ______. The killing of weed seed in compost by the use of certain fertilizers and chemicals. Proceedings of the American Society for Horticultural Science. 43:336–342. 1943.

4849. ______. How to kill weed seeds in compost. Golfdom. 17(5):13–14. 1943.

4850. ______. How to kill weed seeds in compost. Golfdom:17(7):20–21, 24. 1943.

4851. ______. Controlling weeds in turf with 2, 4-D. Rhode Island Agricultural Experiment Station Miscellaneous Publication 30. 1946.

4852. ______. Rhode Island field day. Golfdom. 21(1):40–41,58. 1947.

4853. ______. Water-soluble mercurials for crabgrass control in turf. The Greenkeeper's Reporter. 15:30–31. 1947.

4854. ______. Weed free compost and seedbeds for turf. Rhode Island Agricultural Experiment Station Miscellaneous Publication 31. 15 pp. 1947.

4855. ______. Effect of certain chemicals on the killing of putting-green turf and their influence on various methods of reseeding. The Greenskeepers' Reporter. 16(2):36–38. 1948.

4856. ______. Special fertilizers. The Greenkeepers' Reporter. 16(3):42–43. 1948.

4857. ______. Methods and materials that develop weed free turf. Golfdom. 22(9):-30, 31, 56, 58. 1948.

4858. ______. Crabgrass control in turf. Northeastern Weed Control Conference Proceedings. 2:99–112. 1948.

4859. ______. Turf experiments result in better types of grasses. Park Maintenance. 1:5–7. 1948.

4861. ______. Weed-free compost and seedbeds for turf. Rhode Island Agricultural Experiment Station Miscellaneous Publication 31. 15 pp. 1948 (rev.).

4862. ______. Crabgrass control in turf with chemicals. Proceedings of the American Society for Horticultural Science. 53:546–554. 1949.

4863. ______. Crabgrass, its chemical control in turf. Park Maintenance. 2:6–7. 1949.

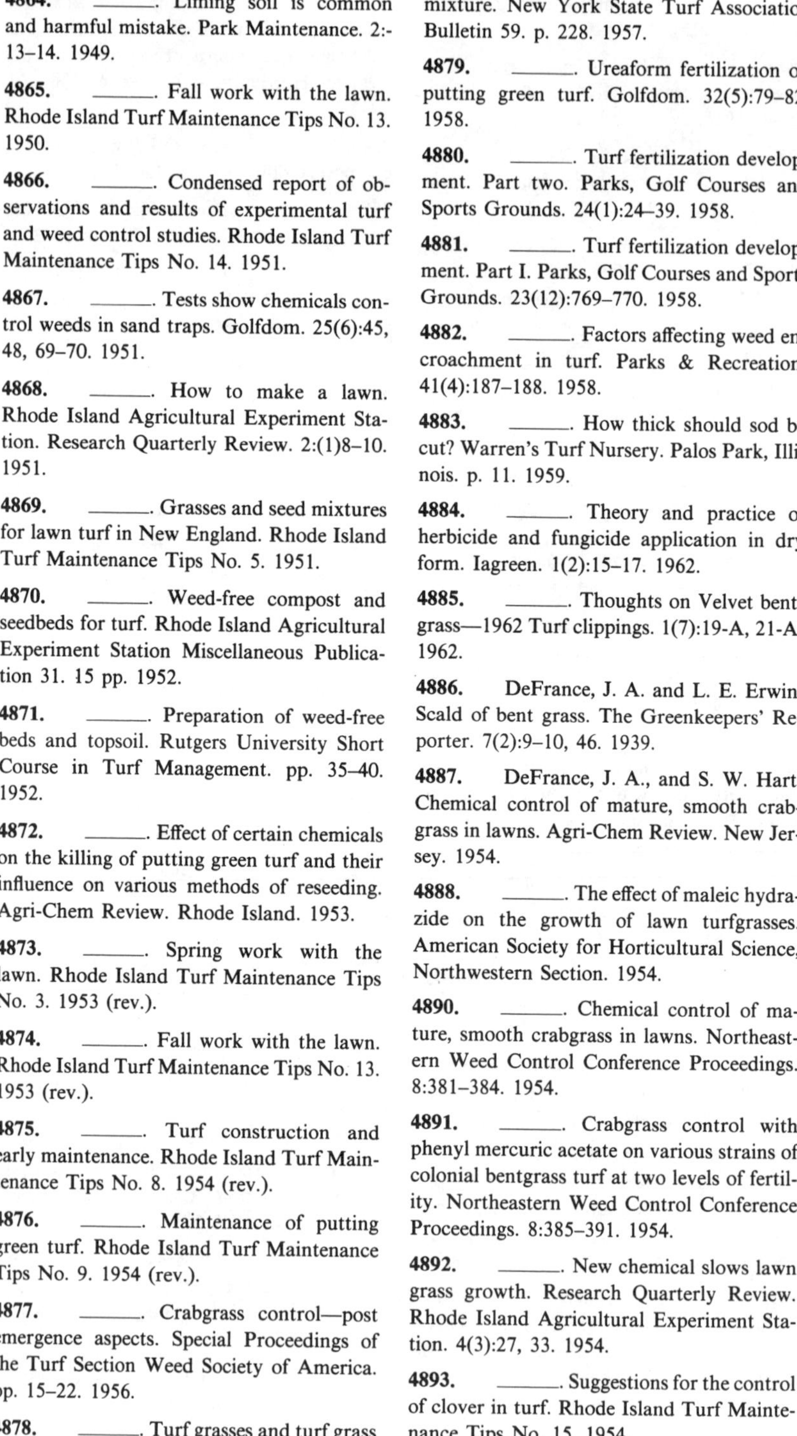

4864. ______. Liming soil is common and harmful mistake. Park Maintenance. 2:-13–14. 1949.

4865. ______. Fall work with the lawn. Rhode Island Turf Maintenance Tips No. 13. 1950.

4866. ______. Condensed report of observations and results of experimental turf and weed control studies. Rhode Island Turf Maintenance Tips No. 14. 1951.

4867. ______. Tests show chemicals control weeds in sand traps. Golfdom. 25(6):45, 48, 69–70. 1951.

4868. ______. How to make a lawn. Rhode Island Agricultural Experiment Station. Research Quarterly Review. 2:(1)8–10. 1951.

4869. ______. Grasses and seed mixtures for lawn turf in New England. Rhode Island Turf Maintenance Tips No. 5. 1951.

4870. ______. Weed-free compost and seedbeds for turf. Rhode Island Agricultural Experiment Station Miscellaneous Publication 31. 15 pp. 1952.

4871. ______. Preparation of weed-free beds and topsoil. Rutgers University Short Course in Turf Management. pp. 35–40. 1952.

4872. ______. Effect of certain chemicals on the killing of putting green turf and their influence on various methods of reseeding. Agri-Chem Review. Rhode Island. 1953.

4873. ______. Spring work with the lawn. Rhode Island Turf Maintenance Tips No. 3. 1953 (rev.).

4874. ______. Fall work with the lawn. Rhode Island Turf Maintenance Tips No. 13. 1953 (rev.).

4875. ______. Turf construction and early maintenance. Rhode Island Turf Maintenance Tips No. 8. 1954 (rev.).

4876. ______. Maintenance of putting green turf. Rhode Island Turf Maintenance Tips No. 9. 1954 (rev.).

4877. ______. Crabgrass control—post emergence aspects. Special Proceedings of the Turf Section Weed Society of America. pp. 15–22. 1956.

4878. ______. Turf grasses and turf grass mixture. New York State Turf Association Bulletin 59. p. 228. 1957.

4879. ______. Ureaform fertilization on putting green turf. Golfdom. 32(5):79–82. 1958.

4880. ______. Turf fertilization development. Part two. Parks, Golf Courses and Sports Grounds. 24(1):24–39. 1958.

4881. ______. Turf fertilization development. Part I. Parks, Golf Courses and Sports Grounds. 23(12):769–770. 1958.

4882. ______. Factors affecting weed encroachment in turf. Parks & Recreation. 41(4):187–188. 1958.

4883. ______. How thick should sod be cut? Warren's Turf Nursery. Palos Park, Illinois. p. 11. 1959.

4884. ______. Theory and practice of herbicide and fungicide application in dry form. Iagreen. 1(2):15–17. 1962.

4885. ______. Thoughts on Velvet bentgrass—1962 Turf clippings. 1(7):19-A, 21-A. 1962.

4886. DeFrance, J. A. and L. E. Erwin. Scald of bent grass. The Greenkeepers' Reporter. 7(2):9–10, 46. 1939.

4887. DeFrance, J. A., and S. W. Hart. Chemical control of mature, smooth crabgrass in lawns. Agri-Chem Review. New Jersey. 1954.

4888. ______. The effect of maleic hydrazide on the growth of lawn turfgrasses. American Society for Horticultural Science, Northwestern Section. 1954.

4890. ______. Chemical control of mature, smooth crabgrass in lawns. Northeastern Weed Control Conference Proceedings. 8:381–384. 1954.

4891. ______. Crabgrass control with phenyl mercuric acetate on various strains of colonial bentgrass turf at two levels of fertility. Northeastern Weed Control Conference Proceedings. 8:385–391. 1954.

4892. ______. New chemical slows lawn grass growth. Research Quarterly Review. Rhode Island Agricultural Experiment Station. 4(3):27, 33. 1954.

4893. ______. Suggestions for the control of clover in turf. Rhode Island Turf Maintenance Tips No. 15. 1954.

4894. ______. A comparison of turfgrass from strains of conlonial bent at two levels of Fertility. The Golf Course Reporter. 24(3):-18–24. 1956.

4895. DeFrance, J. A. and J. R. Kollett. Annual bluegrass *(Poa annua)* L. control with chemicals. Golf Course Reporter. 27(1):14–18. 1959.

4896. DeFrance, J. A. and T. E. Odland. A comparison of nitrogen carriers for bentgrass fertilization. Proceedings of the American Society for Horticultural Science. 37:-1084–1090. 1939.

4897. ______. Seed yields of velvet bent, *Agrostis canina* L. as influenced by the kind of fertilizer applied. Journal of the American Society of Agronomy. 34:205–210. 1942.

4898. DeFrance, J. A. and J. A. Simmons. Factors in producing good turf quickly. Golfdom. 24(5):40, 42, 44, 80, 82, 84. 1950.

4899. ______. Crabgrass control with PMAS on colonial bent putting-green turf and on seedling turf in lawns. Northeastern Weed Control Conference Proceedings. 4:-231–238. 1950.

4900. ______. Emergence and initial growth of turf grasses under field conditions. Rhode Island Turf Maintenance Tips No. 11. 1950.

4901. ______. Inhibiting weeds in seedbeds with chemicals. Proceedings of the American Society for Horticultural Science. 57:355–360. 1951.

4902. ______. Relative period of emergence and initial growth of turf grasses and their adaptability under field conditions. Proceedings of the American Society for Horticultural Science. 57:439–442. 1951.

4903. ______. Effect of chemical treatment of seedbeds for weed control and on subsequent plantings of grass at various intervals after treatment. Rhode Island Agricultural Experiment Station Contribution 775. 1951.

4904. ______. Inhibiting weeds in seedbeds with chemicals. Agri-Chem Review. Rhode Island. 1952.

4905. ______. Preliminary results of a study on velvet bentgrass putting-green turf under different levels of limestone and compost. Agronomy Abstracts. p. 40. 1952.

4906. ______. Comparison of various chemicals for crabgrass control in turf. Proceedings of the American Society for Horticultural Science. 59:479–482. 1952.

4907. ______. A comparison of chemicals for crabgrass control and a study of some factors related to the control of crabgrass with phenyl mercury compounds. Proceedings of the Northeast Weed Control Conference. pp. 67–75. 1952.

4908. DeFrance, J. A. and A. J. Wisniewski. Control of crabgrass and other common lawn weeds. Handbook on Lawns. Brooklyn Botanic Garden. pp. 102–109. 1956.

4909. DeFrance, J. A., C. H. Allen, Jr. and J. A. Simmons. Crabgrass control in turf with PMAS. New York State Turf Association Bulletin 14. pp. 53–55. 1950.

4910. ______. Crabgrass control in turf with PMAS. Rhode Island Turf Maintenance Tips No. 10. 1950.

4911. DeFrance, J. A., R. S. Bell, and T. E. Odland. Killing weed seeds in the grass seedbed by the use of fertilizers and chemicals. Journal of the American Society of Agronomy. 39:530–535. 1947.

4912. DeFrance, J. A., H. B. Musser, and R. E. Engel. Crabgrass control. Greenkeeping Superintendents Association National Turf Conference. 21:90–95. 1950.

4913. DeFrance, J. A., T. E. Odland, and R. S. Bell. Improvement of velvet bentgrass by selection. Agronomy Journal. 44:376–378. 1952.

4914. DeFrance, J. A., J. A. Simmons and C. H. Allen. Preparation, planting and developing a putting green with stolons. Rhode Island Turf Maintenance Tips No. 12. 1950.

4915. ______. Stolon method of planting and developing putting greens. Golfdom. 25(7):50–52, 54. 1951.

4916. deGruchy, J. H. B. Water fluctuations as a factor in the life of the higher plants of 3,300 acre lake in the Permian Red Beds of central Oklahoma. Ph.D. Thesis, Oklahoma State University. 117 pp. 1952.

4917. DeMonsabert, C. J. New Orleans —a look at the Sugar Bowl. Golf Course Reporter. 3(8):16. 1963.

4918. Dekle, G. W. What is an insect. Proceedings University of Florida Turf-Grass Management Conference. 11:5–7. 1963.

4919. Delaune, R. D. and W. H. Patrick. Urea conversion to ammonia in waterlogged soils. Soil Science Society of America Proceedings. 34(4):603–607. 1970.

4920. DeLoach, R. J. H. Fertilizers for golf courses. USGA Green Section Bulletin. 1(9):186–187. 1921.

4921. ______. Why minerals in fertilizers. Parks & Recreation. 14(7):349–352. 1931.

4922. ______. Why minerals in fertilizers. The National Greenkeeper. 5(6):15–21. 1931.

4923. ______. Why minerals in fertilizers. The National Greenkeeper. 5(7):12–17. 1931.

4924. ______. Arrays authorities in presenting virtues of mineral fertilizer. Golfdom. 5(3):74, 81–82, 84. 1931.

4925. Delouche, J. C. Germination of Kentucky bluegrass harvested at different stages of maturity. Proceedings of the Association of Official Seed Analysts. 48:81–84. 1958.

4926. DeMur, A. R. Effect of several environmental factors on the toxicity of the herbicide Siduron and mechanism of its action. Ph.D. Thesis, University of California. 1971.

4927. Dener-Madsen, G. Football pitches by the gravel bed method. Weibulls Grästips. pp. 24–27. 1971.

4928. Denmark, W. L. Weather forecasting. Illinois Turfgrass Conference Proceedings. pp. 29–31. 1962.

4929. Denmead, O. T. Evaporation sources and apparent diffusivities in a forest canopy. Journal of Applied Meteorology. 3:-383–389. 1964.

4930. Dennis, G. Insecticides are rated as to their poisonous effect. Park Maintenance. 15(10):80–81. 1962.

4931. Dennis, R. The fascinating story of herbicide action. Turf Bulletin. Massachusetts Turf & Lawn Grass Council. 2(9):9–10. 1964.

4932. DePencier, R. R. Automatic irrigation. U.S.G.A. Green Section Record. 4(3):10–12. 1966.

4934. DeRopp, R. S. Studies in physiology of leaf growth. II. Growth and structure of the first leaf of rye when cultivated in isolation or attached to the intact plant. Annals of Botany. 10:31–40. 1946.

4935. Derrick, S. *Poa annua* control with Dacthal. Midwest Regional Turf Conference Proceedings. pp. 37–38. 1970.

4936. Derwyn, R., B. Whalley and C. M. McKell and L. R. Green. Seedling vigor and the early nonphotosynthetic stage of seedling growth in grasses. Crop Science. 6(2):147–150. 1966.

4937. Desmond, G. A. Future of powered lawn and garden equipment industry. Turf-Grass Times. 3(1):1–3. 1967.

4938. Dest, W. Post emergence control of crab grass on putting green turf. Turf Clippings. University of Massachussetts. 1(2):15–16. 1956.

4939. ______. Grasses for tees and their management. Turf Clippings. 1(9):A31, A-32. 1964.

4940. De Tata, T. Sell your club on proper watering. Golf Course Reporter. 21(5):21–22. 1953.

4941. DeVane, E. H., M. Stelly, and G. W. Burton. Effect of fertilization and management of different types of bermuda and bahia grass sods on the nitrogen and organic matter content of Tifton sandy loam. Agronomy Journal. 44(4):176–179. 1952.

4942. Devine, J. R. and M. R. J. Holmes. Field experiments comparing ammonium nitrate and ammonium sulphate as top-dressings for winter wheat and grassland. Journal of Agricultural Science. 62:377–379. 1964.

4943. ______. Field experiments comparing winter and spring applications of ammonium sulphate, ammonium nitrate, calcium nitrate, and urea to grassland. Journal of Agricultural Science. 4:101–107. 1965.

4944. deVries, D. A. and J. W. Birch. The modification of climate near the ground by irrigation for pastures on the Riverine Plain. Australian Journal of Agricultural Research. 12(2):260–272. 1961.

4945. Dewald, C. L., L. W. Fancher, and B. H. Lake. Betasan, a promising new herbicide for use on turf. Proceedings Southern Weed Conference. 16:110–114. 1963.

4946. Dewees, T. General maintenance of sprinkler systems. Proceedings Turfgrass Sprinkler Irrigation Conference. 5:5–6. 1967.

4947. DeWerth, A. F. Care and maintenance of school and playground turf. Proceedings of the Annual Texas Turf Conference. 6:76–81. 1951.

4948. ______. Ground covers in lieu of grass. Proceedings of the Annual Texas Turfgrass Conference. 21:55–60. 1966.

4949. Dewey, D. R. Salt tolerance of twenty-five strains of *Agropyron.* Agronomy Journal. 52(11):631–635. 1960.

4950. ______. Polyembryony in *Agropyron.* Crop Science. 4(3):313–317. 1964.

4951. ______. Inheritance of a seedling marker in tetraploid crested wheatgrass. Crop Science. 8(4):495–498. 1968.

4952. ______. Improved selfing techniques for crested wheatgrass. Crop Science. 9(4):481–483. 1969.

4953. ______. Wide hybridization: a radical approach to grass breeding. Utah State University Agricultural Experiment Station. Utah Science. 31(1):3–6. 1970.

4954. Dewey, J. E. Herbicide toxicity. New York Turfgrass Association Bulletin. 83:322. 1969.

4955. ______. Practical toxicology in consumer use of turfgrass herbicides. Proceedings of Scotts Turfgrass Research Conference. 3:133–147. 1972.

4956. Dewey, W. G. and R. F. Nielson. Control snowmold by speeding snowmelt. Crops and Soils. 23(5):8–9. 1971.

4957. DeWitt, J. L., C. L. Canode, and J. K. Patterson. Effects of heating and storage on the viability of grass seed harvested with high moisture content. Agronomy Journal. 54(5):126–128. 1962.

4958. Denton, S. Wetting agents. Turf Bulletin. 4(7):3–15. 1968.

4959. Dexter, S. T. Response of quack grass to defoliation and fertilization. Plant Physiology. 11:843–851. 1936.

4960. ______. The drought resistance of quack grass under various degrees of fertilization with nitrogen. Journal of the American Society of Agronomy. 29:568–577. 1937.

4961. Deyo, M. E. When courses are flooded what's a little thing like *Pythium.* Golfdom 39(6):22–80. 1965.

4962. ______. The Credit Island Park disaster. Park Maintenance. 18(10):16–20. 1965.

4963. Dhonau, G. D. Experience with lawn grasses. Park and Cemetery. 39(9):275–276. 1929.

4964. Dickens, J. Moles and molehills. Gardener's Chronicle. 154(16):288. 1963.

4965. Dickens, R. Time of planting and mixtures of crown vetch in Alabama. Second-Crownvetch Symposium—Pennsylvania State University Agronomy Mimeo 6. 1968.

4966. ______. Turfgrass research reports 1969–70, Alabama. Southern Regional Turf Research Committee Report. Virginia Polytechnic Institute. pp. 2–4. 1970

4967. Dickens, R., G. A. Buchanan. Old weed in new home: that's cogongrass. Alabama Agricultural Experiment Station. 18(2):4. 1971.

4968. Dickens, R., and A. E. Hiltbold. Movement and persistence of methanearsonates in soil. Weeds. 15(4):299–304. 1967.

4969. Dickerson, O. J. Some observations on *Hypsoperine graminis* in Kansas. Plant Disease Reporter. 50:396–398. 1966.

4970. Dickerson, T. Small power tool edgers. Grounds Maintenance. 4(4):33. 1969.

4971. Dickinson, B. C. Study shows long range beneficial effects of repeated ethion treatment on turfgrass. Weeds, Trees, and Turf. 6(9):23–24. 1967.

4972. Dickinson, L. S. Lawn; the culture of turf in park, golfing and home areas. Gardener's Chronicle. 87:458. 1930.

4973. ______. Fall seeding factors that chart successful policy. Golfdom. 4(8):64–68. 1930.

4974. ______. Uneven pre-seeding fertilization is hidden cause of trouble. Golfdom. 5(7):66, 68, 81. 1931.

4975. ______. Lawns and lawn grasses and lawn management. Massachusetts Agricultural Experiment Station Bulletin 260. p. 359. 1930.

4976. ______. Seeds and grasses. The National Greenkeeper. 4(4):29–31. 1930.

4977. ______. A new phase in the control of large brown patch. The National Greenkeeper. 4(6):5–7. 1930.

4978. ______. Winterplay on permanent greens. The National Greenkeeper. 5(1):8. 1931.

4979. ______. The lawn. Orange Judd Publishing Company, Inc. New York. 128 pp. 1930.

4980. ______. The effect of air temperature on the pathogenicity of *Rhizoctonia solani* parasitizing grasses on putting green turf. Phytopathology. 20(8):597–608. 1930.

4981. ______. The lawn. Orange Judd Publishing Company, Inc. New York. 128 pp. 1931.

4982. ______. Lawn management. Massachusetts Agricultural Extension Leaflet 85. 14 pp. (Rev.) 1933.

4983. ______. The seed bed of a lawn. The National Greenkeeper. 7(5):8–9. 1933.

4984. ______. Park and cemetery turf. The National Greenkeeper. 7(6):9–10. 1933.

4985. ______. Fertilizing fine grasses. The National Greenkeeper. 7(7):9–12. 1933.

4986. ______. Weeds and other lawn pests. The National Greenkeeper. 7(8):11–12. 1933.

4987. ______. General turf maintenance. The National Greenkeeper. 7(9):9–10. 1933.

4988. ______. If there's seeding to do, do it in the fall. Golfdom. 8(9):13–14. 1934.

4989. ______. Winter injury to turf. Greenkeepers Club of New England Newsletter. 7(3):14. 1935.

4990. ______. Artificial watering of fine turf grasses. Greenkeepers Club of New England Newsletter. 8(8):3. 1936.

4991. ______. Availability and life of fertilizers. Golfdom. 11(2):59–60. 1937.

4992. ______. Artificial watering of turf grasses. Golfdom. 11(2):63–64. 1937.

4993. ______. Keep within turf's tolerance. Golfdom. 11(5):74, 76. 1937.

4994. ______. Massachusetts Agricultural Extension Leaflet 85. 14 pp. 1940.

4995. ______. Lawn management. Massachusetts Agricultural Extension Leaflet 85. 14 pp. (Rev.) 1948.

4996. ______. Practical training for turf maintenance. Golf Course Reporter. 18(4):-24–28. 1950.

4997. Dicks, O. W., and A. J. Turgeon. Evaluation of various growth retardants on Kentucky bluegrass and tall fescue turfs. University of Illinois Turfgrass Field Day. pp. 17–18. 1972.

4998. Dickerson, L. S. The forgotten fertilizer's opportunity. Greenkeeper's Reporter. 11(3):11–12. 1943.

4999. Dickson, E. G. Turbo-rain gives 24-hour unattended large-area irrigation. Weeds, Trees and Turf. 9(3):22–24. 1970.

5001. Dickson, W. K. Regional testing of Kentucky bluegrass varieties. Rutgers University Short Course in Turf Management Proceedings. pp. 16–20. 1971.

5002. Dickson, W. K., and M. K. Ahmed. Breeding "*Poa trivialis.*" Proceedings 1972 3-Day Turf Courses, Rutgers University. pp. 5–9. 1972.

5003. Dickson, W. K. and C. R. Funk. Shade tolerance of turfgrass species, varieties and mixtures. Rutgers University Short Course in Turf Management. 5 pp. 1969.

5004. ______. Shade tolerance of turfgrass species, varieties and mixtures. Rutgers University. College of Agriculture and Environmental Science. Lawn and Utility Turf Section. pp. 51–55. 1969.

5006. ______. Shade tolerance of turfgrass species, varieties and mixtures. The Golf Superintendent. 38(9):16–17. 1970.

5007. ______. Performance of Kentucky bluegrass and fine fescue varieties at Rutgers. Proceedings 1972 3-Day Turf Courses, Rutgers University. pp. 10–15. 1972.

5008. Di Edwardo, A. A. The nematode problem in the turf nursery. Proceedings of

University of Florida Turf-Grass Management Conference. 9:129–130. 1961.

5009. ______. Recognition and control of nematodes in turf. Proceedings of University of Florida Turf-Grass Management Conference. 9:190–193. 1961.

5010. ______. Nematode control. Proceedings, University of Florida Turf-Grass Management Conference. 9:225. 1961.

5011. ______. Distribution of nematodes on turf in Florida. Proceedings University of Florida Turf-Grass Management Conference. 10:23–27. 1962.

5012. ______. Nematode research. Proceedings University of Florida Turf-Grass Management Conference. 10:195–197. 1962.

5013. ______. Nematode research. Proceedings of University of Florida Turf-Grass Management Conference. 11:147–149. 1963.

5014. ______. Pathogenicity and host-parasite relationships of nematodes on turf in Florida. Florida Agricultural Experiment Station Annual Report. p. 109. 1963.

5015. DiEdwardo, A. A. and V. G. Perry. *Heterodera leuceilyma* n. sp. *(Nemata: Heteroderidae),* a severe pathogen of St. Augustinegrass in Florida. Florida Agricultural Experiment Station Bulletin 687. 35 pp. 1964.

5016. Dieter, L. C. Golf course maintenance and traffic problems. Proceedings of the Mid-Atlantic Association of Golf Course Superintendents Conference. pp. 21–22. 1964.

5017. ______. Living with *Poa annua.* Mid-Atlantic Superintendents Conference Proceedings. pp. 33–34. 1969.

5018. Dietrich, I. T. Grasses for wet sites. North Dakota State Cooperative Extension Service Circular A-478. 1969.

5019. Dietrich, J. A. Developing and maintenance of grassed areas. Parks & Recreation. 31(7):373–376. 1948.

5021. Diseker, E. G., and E. C. Richardson. Highway erosion research studies. Short Course on Roadside Development. 20:65–75. 1961.

5022. Ditmer, W. P. Observation of a seed analyst on crownvetch seed. Second Crownvetch Symposium—Pennsylvania State University 6:54–56. 1968.

5023. Dittmer, H. J. Lawn problems of the Southwest. University of New Mexico Publications in Biology Number 4. University of New Mexico Press, Albuquerque. 76 pp. 1950.

5025. Doan, J. Courses become disaster areas as *Pythium* strikes. Golfdom. 38(9):-28–29, 84–85. 1964.

5026. ______. Drainage renovation stressed. Golfdom. 39(8):32, 34, 62, 64, 66. 1965.

5027. ______. Water. The Golf Superintendent. 34(1):16–20 and 72. 1966.

5028. ______. Bringing back a beat-up course. Golfdom. 41(7):26–30. 1967.

5029. Dobie, F. Thoughts on automatic irrigation. The Golf Superintendent. 36(6):-28. 1968.

5030. ______. Urea formaldehyde for golf course use. Ohio Turfgrass Conference Proceedings. pp. 49–51. 1971.

5031. Dodd, A. V. Temperature distribution in the microclimatic layer. M.S. Thesis, Pennsylvania State University. 41 pp. 1950.

5032. Dodd, J. D. and H. H. Hopkins. Yield and carbohydrate content of blue grama grass as affected by clipping. Transactions of the Kansas Academy Science. 61:-280–287. 1958.

5033. Dodge, A. D. The mode of action of the bipyridylium herbicides, paraquat and diquat. Endeavour. 30(111):130–135. 1971.

5034. Dodman, R. L., K. R. Barker, and J. C. Walker. Modes of penetration by different isolates of *Rhizoctonia solani.* Phytopathology. 58(1):31–32. 1968.

5035. Doe, H. H. Water pricing. Turf-Grass Times. 1(5):10. 1966.

5036. Doerer, T. A. The club manager, the pro, and the golf course superintendent their relationship to each other. Proceedings of the Mid-Atlantic Association of Golf Course Superintendents Conference. pp. 14–15. 1964.

5037. ______. Professional and superintendent relations. The Golf Course Reporter. 33(1):44–50. 1965.

5038. ______. Manager versus straw-boss. USGA Green Section Record. 10(2):9. 1972.

5039. Doerschuk, V. C. Ask about winter-kill. Golfdom. 10(9):17–18, 32. 1936.

5040. Dolan, C. H. Which kind of pipe? —asbestos cement. Golf Course Reporter. 32(6):28–32. 1964.

5042. Dolling, H. and W. D. Shrader. Comparison of fiber glass and other mulch materials for erosion control on highway backslopes in Iowa. Ohio Short Course on Roadside Development. 23:83–88. 1964.

5043. Domogalla, B. P., C. Juday and W. H. Peterson. The forms of nitrogen found in certain lake waters. The Journal of Biological Chemistry. 63(2):269–285. 1925.

5044. Doogue, L. J. Making a lawn. McBride, Nast and Company, New York. 51 pp. 1912.

5045. Doolittle, R. and H. Tiedebohl. Lawns. Southwest Gardening. University of New Mexico Press. pp. 62–69. 1967.

5046. Dore, A. T. and R. C. Wakefield. Growth retardants. Park Maintenance. 25(7):16–17. 1972.

5047. Dore, A. T., R. C. Wakefield and J. A. Jagschitz. Effect of four growth retardants on Kentucky bluegrass and red fescue used for roadside turf. Northeastern Weed Science Society Proceedings. pp. 123–130. 1971.

5048. Dore, W. G. The glass in grass. The Greenmaster. 4(1):4–5. 1967.

5049. Dorman, F. W. Observations on golf turf in Scotland and Ireland. California Turfgrass Culture. 12(1):6–8. 1962.

5050. Dorman, F. W. and C. L. Hemstreet. Compacted golf greens respond to deep aeration, controlled irrigation. California Agriculture. 18(6):9–10. 1964.

5051. Dorman, F. W., C. L. Hemstreet, and T. M. Little. Controlling dry spots on golf greens. California Agriculture. 18(8):-2–3. 1964.

5052. Dosdall, L. Factors influencing the pathogenicity of *Helminthosporium sativum.* Minnesota Agricultural Experiment Station Technical Bulletin 17. 47 pp. 1923.

5053. Doss, B. D. and H. M. Taylor. Evapotranspiration and drainage from the root zone of irrigated coastal bermudagrass (*Cynodon dactylon* L. Pers.) on coastal plains soils. American Society of Agricultural Engineers Journal. 13(4):426–429. 1970.

5054. Doss, B. D., D. A. Ashley and O. L. Bennett. Effect of soil moisture regime on root distribution of warm season forage species. Agronomy Journal. 52(10):569–571. 1960.

5055. Doss, B. D., O. L. Bennett, and D. A. Ashley. Moisture use by forage species as related to pan evaporation and net radiation. Soil Science. 98(5):322–327. 1964.

5056. Doss, B. D., O. L. Bennett, D. A. Ashley and H. A. Weaver. Soil moisture regime effect on yield and evapotranspiration from warm season perennial forage species. Agronomy Journal. 54(5):239–242. 1962.

5057. Doty, E. W. How much it costs and where it goes. The National Greenkeeper. 3(5):22–23. 1929.

5059. Dowling, S. E. Irrigation systems. Proceedings Florida Turfgrass Management Conference. 7:16–19. 1957.

5060. ______. Temporary vs. permanent irrigation measures. Proceedings of University of Florida Turf-Grass Management Conference. 8:97–98. 1960.

5061. ______. Water supply sources and development. Golf Course Reporter. 30(6):-8–18. 1962.

5062. ______. Sod irrigation. Proceedings University of Florida Turf-Grass Management Conference. 10:171–174. 1962.

5063. ______. Manual irrigation equipment. Proceedings 13th Annual Florida Turfgrass Management Conference. 13:54–57. 1965.

5064. Downes, J. D. Conventional irrigation versus frequent light sprinkling. Michigan State University Horticultural Report No. 30. 7 pp. 1966.

5065. Downing, C., H. H. Williams, V. A. Gibeault, J. Van Dam, and A. H. Lange. Studies on the initial effect and residual characteristics of several selective preemergent herbicides in relation to overseeding and *Poa annua* control. California Turfgrass Culture. 20(4):25–28. 1970.

5066. Downs, W. G. and J. M. Duich. Pre- and postemergence effect of siduron on crabgrass. Proceedings of the Northeastern Weed Control Conference. pp. 519–526. 1966.

5067. Dowtin, J. M. Lighted golf courses: meeting the demand for divot space. Proceedings 13th Annual Florida Turfgrass Management Conference. 13:58–64. 1965.

5068. ______. Commercial lighting: brighten your plant and recreational area's future. Proceedings 13th Annual Florida Turfgrass Management Conference. 13:107–116. 1965.

5069. Drablos, C. J. W. and W. R. Oschwald. Factors affecting irrigation practices. Illinois Turfgrass Conference Proceedings. pp. 31–39. 1967.

5070. Drachman, P. E. Merion bluegrass experiences. Proceeding of the Midwest Regional Turf Conference. pp. 25–26. 1955.

5071. ______. Zoysia for lawns and nurseries. Proceedings of Midwest Regional Turfgrass Conference. pp. 27–28. 1955.

5072. Drage, C. M. What kind of turf cover do you want? Rocky Mountain Regional Turf Conference Proceedings. pp. 25–28. 1954.

5073. ______. Three square meals. Rocky Mountain Regional Turfgrass Conference Proceedings. pp. 15–18. 1955.

5074. ______. Turfgrass fertilizer demonstrations. Rocky Mountain Regional Turfgrass Conference Proceedings. pp. 15–18. 1956.

5075. ______. Soil preparation for sodding. Rocky Mountain Regional Turfgrass Conference. 12:19–22. 1966.

5076. ______. Seedbed preparation. Rocky Mountain Regional Turfgrass Conference. 12:41–44. 1966.

5077. ______. No shortcut for good lawn. Seed World. 99(3):22. 1966.

5078. Drage, C. M. and G. Beach. Lawn care. Colorado Agricultural Extension Circular. 198A:1–10. 1959.

5079. ______. Care of lawns. Colorado State University Extension Service Bulletin. 1960.

5080. ______. Planting bluegrass lawns. Colorado State University Agricultural Extension Service Circular 197-A. 9 pp. 1960.

5081. ______. Care of lawns. Colorado State University Agricultural Extension Service Bulletin 452-A. 12 pp. 1961.

5082. Drage, C. M., R. D. Heil, and W. G. Macksam. Iron chlorosis in yards and gardens. Colorado State University Pamphlet 118. 1968.

5084. Drechsler, C. Zonate eyespot of grasses caused by *Helminthosporium giganteum.* Journal of Agricultural Research. 37(8):473–492. 1928.

5085. ______. Occurrence of the zonate-eyespot fungus *Helminthosporium giganteum* on some additional grasses. Journal of Agricultural Research. 39(2):129–135. 1929.

5086. ______. Leaf spot and foot rot of bluegrass. USGA Green Section Bulletin. 9(7):120–123. 1929.

5087. ______. Leaf spot and foot rot of Kentucky bluegrass caused by *Helminthosporium vagans.* Journal of Agricultural Research. 40(5):447–456. 1930.

5089. ______. A leafspot of bentgrasses caused by *Helminthosporium erythiospilum* n. sp. Phytopathology. 25(3):344–361. 1935.

5090. Dreesen, J. Advancement in chemical control of vegetation. Ohio Short Course on Roadside Development. 20:117–119. 1961.

5093. Drum, T. E. Turf management problems of cemeteries. Oklahoma-Texas Turf Conference Proceedings. pp. 95–96. 1950.

5094. Drumm, T. Cemetery turf maintenance. Texas Turf Conference Proceedings. pp. 19–22. 1950.

5095. Dryness, C. T. Grass-legume mixtures for roadside soil stabilization. U. S. Forest Service Pacific Northwest Research Note PNW-71. 19 pp. 1961.

5096. Drysdale, A. C. Golf course landscaping. R.C.G.A. Sports Turfgrass Conference. 17:1–4. 1966.

5097. Drysadale, R. Canada seeks better grass for golfers. The Golf Course Reporter. 33(9):46–47. 1965.

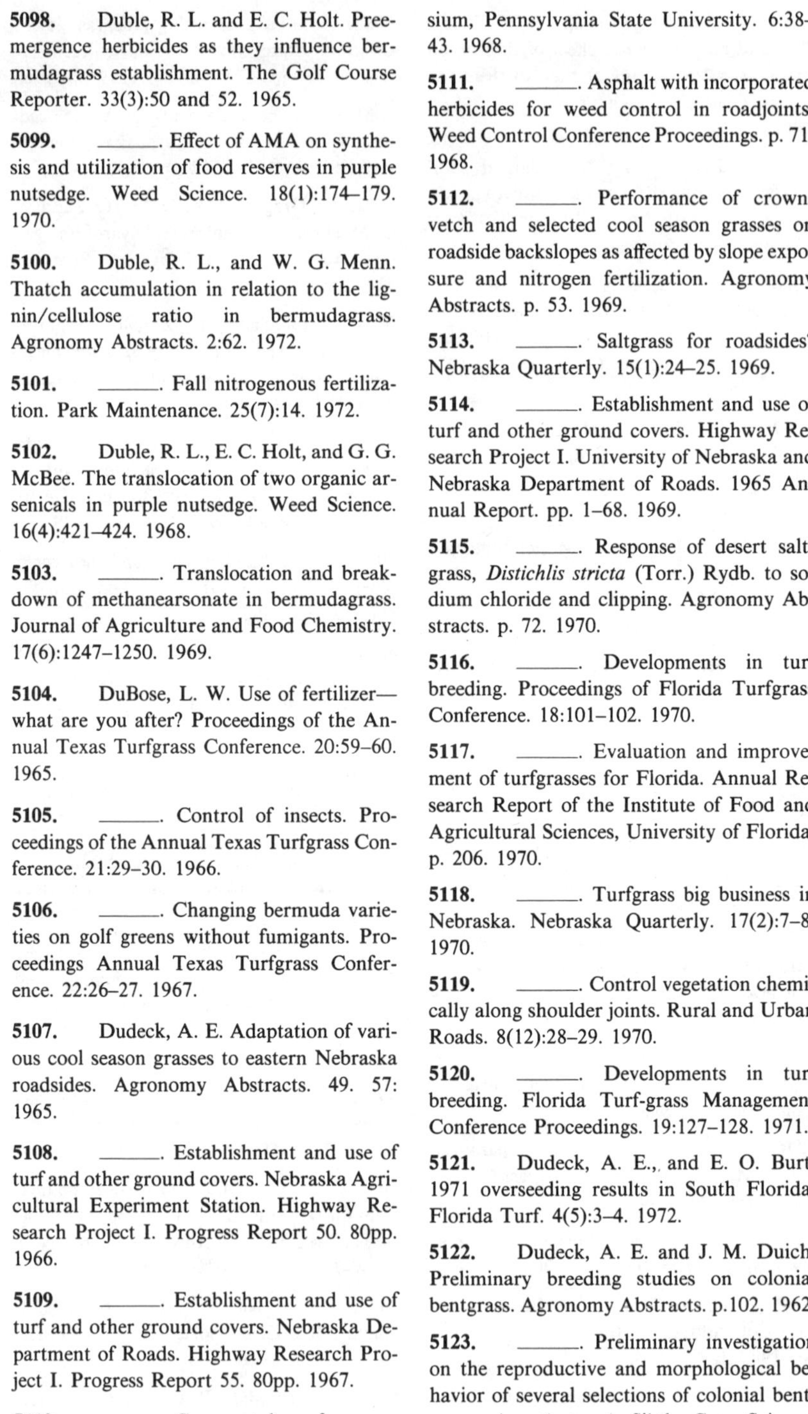

5098. Duble, R. L. and E. C. Holt. Preemergence herbicides as they influence bermudagrass establishment. The Golf Course Reporter. 33(3):50 and 52. 1965.

5099. ______. Effect of AMA on synthesis and utilization of food reserves in purple nutsedge. Weed Science. 18(1):174–179. 1970.

5100. Duble, R. L., and W. G. Menn. Thatch accumulation in relation to the lignin/cellulose ratio in bermudagrass. Agronomy Abstracts. 2:62. 1972.

5101. ______. Fall nitrogenous fertilization. Park Maintenance. 25(7):14. 1972.

5102. Duble, R. L., E. C. Holt, and G. G. McBee. The translocation of two organic arsenicals in purple nutsedge. Weed Science. 16(4):421–424. 1968.

5103. ______. Translocation and breakdown of methanearsonate in bermudagrass. Journal of Agriculture and Food Chemistry. 17(6):1247–1250. 1969.

5104. DuBose, L. W. Use of fertilizer—what are you after? Proceedings of the Annual Texas Turfgrass Conference. 20:59–60. 1965.

5105. ______. Control of insects. Proceedings of the Annual Texas Turfgrass Conference. 21:29–30. 1966.

5106. ______. Changing bermuda varieties on golf greens without fumigants. Proceedings Annual Texas Turfgrass Conference. 22:26–27. 1967.

5107. Dudeck, A. E. Adaptation of various cool season grasses to eastern Nebraska roadsides. Agronomy Abstracts. 49. 57: 1965.

5108. ______. Establishment and use of turf and other ground covers. Nebraska Agricultural Experiment Station. Highway Research Project I. Progress Report 50. 80pp. 1966.

5109. ______. Establishment and use of turf and other ground covers. Nebraska Department of Roads. Highway Research Project I. Progress Report 55. 80pp. 1967.

5110. ______. Crownvetch performance in Nebraska. Second Crownvetch Symposium, Pennsylvania State University. 6:38–43. 1968.

5111. ______. Asphalt with incorporated herbicides for weed control in roadjoints. Weed Control Conference Proceedings. p. 71. 1968.

5112. ______. Performance of crownvetch and selected cool season grasses on roadside backslopes as affected by slope exposure and nitrogen fertilization. Agronomy Abstracts. p. 53. 1969.

5113. ______. Saltgrass for roadsides? Nebraska Quarterly. 15(1):24–25. 1969.

5114. ______. Establishment and use of turf and other ground covers. Highway Research Project I. University of Nebraska and Nebraska Department of Roads. 1965 Annual Report. pp. 1–68. 1969.

5115. ______. Response of desert saltgrass, *Distichlis stricta* (Torr.) Rydb. to sodium chloride and clipping. Agronomy Abstracts. p. 72. 1970.

5116. ______. Developments in turf breeding. Proceedings of Florida Turfgrass Conference. 18:101–102. 1970.

5117. ______. Evaluation and improvement of turfgrasses for Florida. Annual Research Report of the Institute of Food and Agricultural Sciences, University of Florida. p. 206. 1970.

5118. ______. Turfgrass big business in Nebraska. Nebraska Quarterly. 17(2):7–8. 1970.

5119. ______. Control vegetation chemically along shoulder joints. Rural and Urban Roads. 8(12):28–29. 1970.

5120. ______. Developments in turf breeding. Florida Turf-grass Management Conference Proceedings. 19:127–128. 1971.

5121. Dudeck, A. E., and E. O. Burt. 1971 overseeding results in South Florida. Florida Turf. 4(5):3–4. 1972.

5122. Dudeck, A. E. and J. M. Duich. Preliminary breeding studies on colonial bentgrass. Agronomy Abstracts. p.102. 1962.

5123. ______. Preliminary investigation on the reproductive and morphological behavior of several selections of colonial bentgrass. *Agrostis tenuis* Sibth. Crop Science. 7(6):605–610. 1967.

5124. Dudeck, A. E., and J. O. Young. Establishment and use of turf and other ground covers. 1967 Annual Report. Progress Report 62 HPR-1(5). Highway Research Project 1. Nebraska Department of Roads. 25pp. 1968.

5125. ______. Establishment and use of turf and other ground covers. 1968 Annual Report. Nebraska Department Roads Progress Report 68 HPR-1(6). 30pp. 1969.

5126. ______. Establishment and use of turf and other ground covers. Highway Research Project I. University of Nebraska and Nebraska Department of Roads. 1968 Annual Report. pp. 1–30. 1969.

5127. ______. Performance of crownvetch and selected cool season grasses on roadside backslopes as affected by slope exposure and nitrogen fertilization. Agronomy Journal. 62(3):397–399. 1970.

5128. Dudeck, A. E., N. P. Swanson, and A. R. Dedrick. Protecting steep construction slopes against water erosion. II. Effect of selected mulches on seedling stand, soil temperature and soil moisture relations. Agronomy Abstracts. p. 38. 1966.

5129. ______. Mulches for grass establishment on fill slopes. Agronomy Abstracts. p. 51. 1967.

5130. ______. Mulches for grass establishment on steep construction slopes. Highway Research Board Roadside Development, Highway Research Record No. 206. p. 53. 1967.

5131. ______. Mulch performance on steep construction slopes. Rural and Urban Roads. pp. 59–62. 1967.

5132. ______. Mulches for erosion control and grass establishment on steep construction slopes. Nebraska Department of Roads. Nebraska Study No. 64–1. 1969.

5133. ______. Mulches for erosion control and grass establishment on steep construction slopes. Turfgrass Times. 6(1):4,12,-13. 1970.

5134. Dudeck, A. E., N. P. Swanson, L. N. Mielke, and A. R. Dedrick. Mulches for grass establishment on fill slopes. Agronomy Journal. 62(6):810–812. 1970.

5135. Dudley, D. I. Warm-season grasses for north-central Texas. Texas Agricultural Experiment Station Miscellaneous Publication. 52. 2pp. 1950.

5136. Dudley, J. W. Overseeding with bentgrass. Proceedings Thirteenth Southeastern Turfgrass Conference. pp. 29–30. 1959.

5137. ______. Overseeding with bentgrass. USGA Journal and Turf Management. 13(4):31. 1960.

5138. ______. (Moderator) Care and handling of golf carts. Proceedings 17th Southeastern Turfgrass Conference. pp. 23–31. 1963.

5139. ______. Experience with maleic hydrazide. USGA Green Section Record. 1(3):12. 1963.

5141. Dudley, J. W. Forty years with a drainage problem. USGA Green Section Record. 5(2):8–9. 1967.

5142. Dudley, J. and C. Danner. Overseeding bermudagrass greens with cool-season grasses. Proceedings 19th Southeastern Turfgrass Conference. pp.51–58. 1965.

5143. Dudley, R. G. Developing a community college campus. Midwest Regional Turf Conference Proceedings. pp. 71–72. 1972.

5144. Duell, R. W. Utilization of fertilizer by six pasture grasses. Agronomy Journal. 52(5):277–278. 1960.

5145. ______. Bermudagrass has multipleleaved nodes. Crop Science. 1(3):230–231. 1961.

5146. Duff, D. T. Tall fescue and tall fescue-Kentucky bluegrass turf as influenced by cutting height, nitrogen application and irrigation. M.S. thesis, Ohio State University. 1964.

5147. ______. Fall nitrogenous fertilization. Park Maintenance. 25(7):14. 1972.

5148. ______. *Poa annua.* Park Maintenance. 25(7):18. 1972.

5149. Duff, D. T. and J. B. Beard. Effects of air movement and syringing on the microclimate of bentgrass turf. Agronomy Journal. 58(5):495–497. 1966.

5150. ______. Some effects of supraoptimal temperatures upon creeping bentgrass

(*Agrostis palustris* Huds.). Agronomy Abstracts. p. 51. 1967.

5151. ______. Air movement and syringing—effects on the microenvironment of bentgrass turf. The Golf Superintendent. 36(3):20–21, 47. 1968.

5152. Duguid, G. Experience with glass mat on new seeding. Proceedings of the 1965 Midwest Regional Turf Conference. pp. 67–68. 1965.

5153. ______. Fairway irrigation. The Greenkeeper's Reporter. 2(4):5–6. 1934.

5154. ______. Part III—the role of the superintendent. Proceedings University of Florida Turf Management Conference. 4:50–51. 1956.

5155. Duich, J. M. and H. B. Musser. Commercial vs. selected types and strains of seeded bents for putting greens. Pennsylvania State College Turf Conference. 23:74–78. 1954.

5156. Duich, J. M. 1955 tests of new materials for crabgrass control in Pennsylvania. Pennsylvania State College Turf Conference. 25:23–35. 1956.

5157. ______. Rates of seeding and five year summary of establishment of crown vetch. Ohio Short Course on Roadside Development. 16:64–67. 1957.

5158. ______. Variation in Merion Kentucky bluegrass. Proceedings of Midwest Regional Turf Conference. pp. 33–34. 1958.

5159. ______. Seeding and establishing roadside turf. Proceedings of Midwest Regional Turf Conference. pp. 34–36. 1958.

5160. ______. Good lawn management. You Can Grow A Good Lawn. The American Potash Institute. pp.28–32. 1959.

5161. ______. Preemergence crabgrass results in Pennsylvania 1959. Proceedings of the Northeastern Weed Control Conference. pp. 268–270. 1960.

5162. ______. Grass varieties and seed mixtures. Golf Course Reporter. 29(3):18–27. 1961.

5163. ______. Grass varieties and seed mixtures. International Turf-Grass Conference Proceedings. 32:10. 1961.

5164. ______. Selecting progeny of Merion Kentucky bluegrass. Agronomy Abstracts. p. 102. 1962.

5165. ______. Penncross bentgrass. Turf Clippings. 1(7):13-A to 16-A. 1962.

5167. ______. Soil modification research. 38th International Turfgrass Conference. pp. 25–30. 1967.

5168. ______. Turfgrass is big business in Pennsylvania. Midwest Regional Turf Conference Proceedings. pp. 7–8. 1968.

5169. ______. Particle size and density—a review. Midwest Regional Turf Conference Proceedings. pp. 51–53. 1968.

5171. ______. Soil modification research. Proceedings 1968 Turf Conference. Midwest Regional Turf Foundation. pp. 61–63. 1968.

5172. ______. Breeding and evaluation of Kentucky bluegrass for turf. Eighty-first Annual Report of the Pennsylvania Agricultural Experiment Station Bulletin 752. p.5. 1968.

5173. ______. Understanding and using fertilizers. Golfdom. 43(2):32–33, 51. 1969.

5174. ______. Kentucky bluegrass varieties. Park Maintenance. 25(7):15. 1972.

5175. ______. Perennial ryegrass. Park Maintenance. 25(7):15. 1972.

5176. Duich, J. M. and H. Cole. Etiology, epidemiology and control of turfgrass diseases. Eighty-first Annual Report of the Pennsylvania Agricultural Experiment Station Bulletin 752. p .5. 1968.

5177. Duich, J. M. and B. R. Fleming. Weed control in special purpose turf. Seventy-fourth Annual Report of the Pennsylvania Agricultural Experiment Station Bulletin 681. p. 8. 1962.

5178. ______. The breeding, genetics, and evaluation of turfgrass. Seventy-seventh Annual Report of the Pennsylvania Agricultural Experiment Station Bulletin 718. p. 7. 1965.

5179. Duich, J. M. and E. L. Moberg. Penn State reports results of lawn fertilizer test. Park Maintenance. 23(7):14. 1970.

5180. Duich, J. M. and H. B. Musser. Response of creeping bentgrass turf under putting green management to urea-form and other nitrogenous fertilizers. Agronomy Abstracts. p. 64. 1958.

5181. ______. Response of creeping bentgrass turf under putting-green management to ureaform and other nitrogenous fertilizers. Agronomy Abstracts. p. 89. 1959.

5182. Duich, J. M. and H. B. Musser. The extent of aberrants produced by Merion Kentucky bluegrass as determined by first and second generation progeny tests. Agronomy Journal. 51(7):421–424. 1959.

5183. ______. Response of Kentucky bluegrass, creeping red fescue, and bentgrass to nitrogen fertilizers. Pennsylvania State University Agricultural Experiment Station. Progress Report 214:1–20. 1960.

5184. Duich, J. M. and A. T. Perkins. Effect of preemergence chemicals on *Poa annua* and bentgrass. Proceedings of the Northeastern Weed Control Conference. pp. 484–489. 1967.

5185. Duich, J. M. and D. V. Waddington. Evaluation of experimental and commercial preemergence crabgrass chemicals for turf. Northeastern Weed Science Society Proceedings. pp. 97–101. 1971.

5186. ______. Crabgrass. Park Maintenance. 24(7):25. 1971.

5187. Duich, J. M., W. G. Downs and B. R. Fleming. Pre- and postemergence effect of 1–(2–methylcyclohexyl)–3–phenylurea on crabgrass and five turfgrass species. Proceedings of the Northeastern Weed Control Conference. pp. 511–517. 1965.

5188. Duich, J. M., B. R. Fleming, and A. E. Dudeck. The effect of preemergence chemicals on crabgrass and bluegrass, fescue and bentgrass turf. Proceedings North East Weed Control Conference. 15:268–275. 1961.

5189. Duich, J. M., B. R. Fleming, and F. Lukezic. Disease control investigations on Kentucky bluegrass, red fescue, and bentgrasses. Seventy-fourth Annual Report of the Pennsylvania Agricultural Experiment Station Bulletin 681. p. 7. 1962.

5190. Duich, J. M., B. R. Fleming, and F. Sirianni. The use of several phenoxy compounds for weed control on bentgrass. Proceedings Northeastern Weed Control Conference. 18:530–534. 1964.

5191. Duich, J. M., A. T. Perkins and H. Cole. Registration of Pennfine perennial ryegrass (Reg. No. 26). Crop Science. 12(2):257. 1972.

5192. Duich, J. M., G. J. Shoop and B. R. Fleming. 1964 preemergence crabgrass control results in Pennsylvania. Proceedings of the Northeastern Weed Control Conference. pp. 478–485. 1965.

5193. ______. 1964 preemergence crabgrass control results. The Golf Course Reporter. 33(3):58–64. 1965.

5194. Duich, J. M., D. V. Waddington, and B. R. Fleming. Grass mixtures for special purpose turf. Seventy-fourth Annual Report of the Pennsylvania Agricultural Experiment Station. Bulletin 681. p. 7. 1962.

5195. ______. Maintenance practices of Fairway turf. Seventy-fourth Annual Report of the Pennsylvania Agricultural Experiment Station Bulletin 681. p.7. 1962.

5196. ______. Ureaform as a source of nitrogen for special purpose turf. Seventy-fourth Annual Report of the Pennsylvania Agricultural Experiment Station. Bulletin 681. p. 7. 1962.

5197. ______. Broadleaf weed control in turf. Proceedings of the Northeastern Weed Control Conference. pp. 490–495. 1966.

5198. Duich, J. M., D. V. Waddington, and E. L. Moberg. Slow release nitrogen sources. Park Maintenance. 24(7):19. 1971.

5199. Duich, J. M., D. V. Waddington, and T. A. Perkins. 1965 preemergence crabgrass control results in Pennsylvania. Proceedings of the Northeastern Weed Control Conference. pp.514–518. 1966.

5200. ______. 1966 crabgrass control results in Pennsylvania. Proceedings of the Northeastern Weed Control Conference. pp. 478–481. 1967.

5201. ______. 1966 broadleaf weed control results in Pennsylvania. Proceedings of the Northeastern weed control conference. pp. 503–507. 1967.

5202. ______. Turfgrass weed controls recommended. Pennsylvania State University Agricultural Experiment Station. Bulletin 747:42–43. 1966–67.

5203. ______. Turfgrass weed control. Eighty-first Annual Report of the Pennsylvania Agricultural Experiment Station Bulletin 752. p. 5. 1968.

5204. Duich, J. M., B. R. Fleming, A. E. Dudeck, and G. J. Shoop. The effect of certain preemergence chemicals on grass germination and seedling grasses. North East Weed Control Conference Proceedings. 16:-479–483. 1962.

5205. ______. 1963 crabgrass control results in Pennsylvania. Proceedings Northeastern Weed Control Conference. 18:507–510. 1964.

5206. Duich, J. M., B. R. Fleming, L. J. Kardos, and W. I. Thomas. Soil modification for turfgrass establishment and maintenance. Seventy-fourth Annual Report of the Pennsylvania Agricultural Experiment Station Bulletin 681. p. 8. 1962.

5207. Duich, J. M., B. R., Fleming, B. R., Dudeck, G. J. Shoop, and J. Boyd. 1961 preemergence crabgrass results. Proceedings Northeastern Weed Control Conference. 16:-495–497. 1962.

5208. Duke, R. Maintenance by contract. Proceedings of the Midwest Regional Turf Conference. pp. 67–68. 1966.

5209. Duke, R. B. Yard parks program in Indianapolis. Proceedings of Midwest Regional Turf Conference. pp. 19–21. 1952.

5210. Duke, R. M. Our turf and landscape program. Proceedings of the Midwest Regional Turf Conference. pp. 71–73. 1961.

5211. Duley, F. L. and L. L. Kelly. Effect of soil type, slope and surface conditions on intake of water. University of Nebraska Agricultural Experiment Station Research Bulletin 112. 16pp. 1939.

5212. Duling, J. Maintenance by contract. Proceedings of the Midwest Regional Turf Conference. pp. 68–69. 1966.

5213. Dumas, W. T. Factors affecting nozzle orifice wear. Highlights of Agricultural Research. 13(4):7. 1966.

5214. Dunavin, L. S. Bermudagrass. Sunshine State Agricultural Research Report. 8(1):36. 1963.

5215. Duncan, C. C. The effect of temperature and nitrate level on nitrogen metabolism in various grasses. M.S. Thesis, University of California, Riverside. 1972.

5216. Duncan, G. W. Construction of greens, tees and fairways. New Zealand Institute for Turf Culture Newsletter. 59:27–29. 1969.

5217. Dunlap, F. Superintendents' relations. Proceedings of Midwest Regional Turf Conference. pp. 28–33. 1951.

5218. ______. Renovate fairways to eliminate *Poa annua.* Golfdom. 26(6):66–67. 1952.

5219. ______. Fall renovation on the golf course. Golf Course Reporter. 31(7):44–47. 1963.

5220. Dunlap, J. Proper chemical application. Northern Ohio Turfgrass News. 11(2):1–3. 1968.

5221. ______. Proper chemical application. International Turfgrass Conference and Show. 39:33–36. 1968.

5222. ______. The role of the superintendent in development. 41st International Turfgrass Conference and Show. pp. 28–29. 1970.

5223. Dunn, A. C. Turf problems in cemetery operation. Golf Course Reporter. 17(1):5–7. 1949.

5224. Dunn, E. A. A completely automatic sprinkling system at the Seattle Golf Club. USGA Journal and Turf Management. 13(3):25–27. 1960.

5225. Dunn, J. H. M. U. turfgrass research—1970. Missouri Lawn & Turf Conference Proceedings. 11:19–26. 1970.

5226. ______. M.U.turfgrass research—1971. Missouri Lawn and Turf Conference Proceedings. 12:14–18. 1971.

5227. ______. Winter hardiness in warm-season turfgrasses. Missouri Lawn and Turf Conference Proceedings. 12:20–23. 1971.

5228. ______. Kentucky bluegrass in the transition zone. Park Maintenance. 25(7):14–15. 1972.

5229. ______. Yellow nutsedge control. Park Maintenance. 25(7):20. 1972.

5230. Dunn, J. H., and R. E. Engel. Bentgrass turf growth response to urea nitrogen impregnated on hydrocarbons and vermiculite carriers. New Jersey Agricultural Experiment Station. 816:22–40. 1966.

5231. ______. Rooting ability of Merion Kentucky bluegrass sod grown on mineral and muck soil. Agronomy Abstracts. p. 58. 1968.

5232. ______. Rooting ability of Merion Kentucky bluegrass sod grown on mineral and muck soil. Agronomy Journal. 62(4):-517–520. 1970.

5233. ______. Root response of Merion Kentucky bluegrass sods to various nitrogen applications near the time of transplanting. Agronomy Journal. 62(5):623–625. 1970.

5234. ______. Effect of defoliation and root-pruning on early root growth from Merion Kentucky bluegrass sods and seedlings. Agronomy Journal. 63(5):659–663. 1971.

5235. ______. Nitrogen and sod. Park Maintenance. 24(7):19. 1971.

5236. Dunn, J. H. and C. J. Nelson. Chemical changes occurring in rhizomes of three bermudagrass turf cultivars during fall and winter. Agronomy Abstracts. p. 46. 1971.

5237. Dunn, J. H., N. K. Das, and D. D. Hemphill. Chemical control of yellow nutsedge in a mixed common bermudagrass—common Kentucky bluegrass lawn turf. North Central Weed Control Conference Proceedings. 25:83–84. 1970.

5238. ______. Chemical control of yellow nutsedge in a mixed lawn turf of common Kentucky bluegrass and tall fescue. North Central Weed Control Conference Proceedings. 26:89. 1971.

5239. Dunn, R. Antedote to a drainer's dilemma!! Parks, Golf Courses, and Sports Grounds. 32(12):1077–1081. 1967.

5240. Dunn, S., G. K. Gruendling, and A. S. Thomas. Effect of light on the life cycles of crabgrass and barnyardgrass. Weed Science. 16(1):58–60. 1968.

5241. Dunning, B. Turf development procedure that's successful in S. W. Golfdom. 27(9):28–29, 32, 68–70. 1953.

5242. ______. Development of turf for specialized purposes. Oklahoma Turfgrass Conference Proceedings. 8:7–8. 1953.

5243. ______. Green construction. Golfdom. 30(9):25–26, 28, 45. 1956.

5244. ______. Soil mixing for greens. Oklahoma Turfgrass Conference Proceedings. 14:19–25. 1959.

5245. ______. The A B C's of green construction. Southern Turfgrass Association Conference Proceedings. pp. 1–8. 1960.

5246. ______. Full package deal for improved maintenance. Golfdom. 35(1):66, 68. 1961.

5247. Dunning, B., and R. Plummer. Bentgrass green construction. Oklahoma-Texas Turf Conference Proceedings. pp. 76–79. 1950.

5248. Dunning, R. C. Practical aspects of fertilizing lawns and fairways. Southwest Turf Conference Proceedings. pp. 11–19. 1948.

5249. ______. Fertilizing bent grass putting greens. Southwest Turf Conference Proceedings. pp. 91–95. 1948.

5250. ______. Bermuda grass greens. Southwest Turf Conference Proceedings. pp. 96–100. 1948.

5251. Dunning, R. Basic concepts of green construction. Golf Course Reporter. 30(4):16–34. 1962.

5252. Dupont, C. Helicopter spraying—tomorrow or today. International Turfgrass Conference & Show. 39:86–89. 1968.

5253. Durkin, J. J. Turf insect problems. New Mexico Turfgrass Conference Proceedings. 42–46 pp. 1955.

5254. ______. Control your lawn insects, if you can find them. New Mexico Agricultural Extension News. 39:7. 1959.

5255. Durrell, L. W. Common weeds of Colorado lawns. Colorado Agricultural Experiment Station Bulletin 310. 8pp. 1926.

5256. Dury, P. Cricket on a sandy soil. The Groundsman. 18(7):36–38. 1965.

5257. ______. Building a cricket square. The Groundsman. 23(10):15, 17. 1970.

5258. ______. Notes on fungi. The Groundsman. 23(10):16–17. 1970.

5259. ______. Notes on grasses. The Groundsman. 23(9):19. 1970.

5260. ______. Work study and cricket wicket preparation. The Groundsman. 24(7):44–45. 1971.

5261. Dustman, R. B. Soil practice for lawns. Ohio Agricultural Extension Timely Soil Topics. 46:4. 1922.

5262. Dutton, R. D. Looking ahead on drainage, sod and weeds pays. Golfdom. 5(6):80–81. 1931.

5263. Dwinell, V. Minnesota's athletic field maintenance program. Park Maintenance. 16(11):8–9. 1963.

5264. Dybing, C., J. L. Fults, and R. Block. A test of chlordane, chlorobromepropane and hexachlorocyclopentadiene (P-162) for pre-emergence control of crabgrass, *Digitaria sanguinalis* (L) and other annual grasses. Colorado State University Scientific Journal Series Article No. 445.

5265. Dybing, C. D., J. L. Fults, and R. M. Blouch. Chlordane, chlorobromopropene, and hexachlorocyclopentadiene for preemergence of crabgrass *(Digitaria sanguinalis* L.) and other annual grasses. Weeds. 3(4):377–386. 1954.

5266. Dye, P. Building new golf courses. Proceedings of the Midwest Regional Turf Conference. pp. 49–52. 1966.

5267. Dymond, J. R. Lawn grass mixtures. Agricultural Gazette of Canada. 4(5):-359. 1917.

5268. Eagle, J. Irrigation system design. Proceedings of the Annual Texas Turfgrass Conference. 21:5–6. 1966.

5269. Eakin, J. H. Frost seeding of crownvetch. Second Crownvetch Symposium —Pennsylvania State University. 6:48–49. 1968.

5270. Easley, E. E. Cost analysis—automatic versus manual. International Turfgrass Conference & Show. 39:62. 1968.

5271. Eastman, A. L. Prepare now against snow mold. Golfdom. 11(9):13–14. 1937.

5272. ______. Hollow fork technique. Golfdom. 12(4):27–30. 1938.

5273. Ebara, K. The breeding of turf grasses. KGU Green Section Turf Research Bulletin. 7:1–14. 1964.

5274. ______. The cultural managements on turfgrasses. K.G.U. Green Section Turf Research Bulletin. 13:1–22. 1967.

5275. Ebel, T. The effect of fertility and mulching on the establishment of four plant species, grown alone and in various combinations on highway cuts. Illinois Cooperative Highway Research Program IHR-67. pp. 2–10. 1961.

5276. ______. Experiment 003–the effect of straw mulch on the establishment of grasses and legumes when seeded in established and newley planted black locust. Illinois Cooperative Highway Research Program Project IHR-67. pp. 10–11. 1961.

5277. Edwards, C. R. Fluorescence and the Federal Seed Act. Weeds, Trees and Turf. 11(5):52, 58. 1972.

5278. Eck, H. V., R. F. Dudley, R. H. Ford, and C. W. Gantt, Jr. Sand dune stabilization along streams in the southern Great Plains. Journal of Soil and Water Conservation. 23(4):131–134. 1968.

5279. Eckert, E. C. Michigan's program in roadside development. Ohio Short Course on Roadside Development. 21:42–47. 1962.

5280. Eckert, W. Modernizing Maple Bluff. Midwest Regional Turf Conference Proceedings. pp. 9–10. 1970.

5281. Eckhoff, H. C. A look into the future of golf. Proceedings, 11th Annual University of Florida Turf-Grass Management Conference. 11:41–47. 1963.

5282. ______. Guide lines for planning a golf course. New York Turfgrass Association Bulletin. 76:293–295. 1964.

5283. ______. Fairway irrigation survey. The Golf Superintendent. 34(9):22. 1966.

5284. ______. What's happening in golf. R.C.G.A. Sports Turfgrass Conference. 17:-49–53. 1966.

5285. ______. Financing the renovation. USGA Green Section Record 4(6):24–25. 1967.

5286. ______. Trends in golf course development. International Turfgrass Conference and Show. 39:36–38. 1968.

5287. ______. Golf facility development and operation take new direction. Annual RCGA National Turfgrass Conference. 20:-23–26. 1969.

5288. Eckstein, C. N. Budgeting and accounting. USGA Journal and Turf Management. 11(2):28–30. 1958.

5289. ______. Putting green design. USGA Green Section Record. 1(6):4–5. 1964.

5290. Ede, A. L. Trenchless drainage. The Groundsman. 22(12):14–17. 1969.

5291. Ede, A. N. Soil heating system using warm air. Journal of the Sports Turf Research Institute. 46:76–91. 1970.

5292. Eden, F. M. Lawn irrigation systems. Rutgers University. College of Agriculture and Environmental Science. Lawn and Utility Turf Section. pp. 12–14. 1969.

5293. ______. Lawn irrigation systems. Rutgers University Short Course in Turf Management. 3pp. 1969.

5294. Eden, W. G. Insects of turfgrass and their control. Auburn University Annual Turfgrass Short Course. 21–27pp. 1960.

5295. ______. Turf insects and their control. Auburn University Turfgrass Short Course. pp. 12–17. 1961.

5296. ______. Undesirable pesticide residues. Proceedings 18th Annual Florida Turfgrass Management Conference. 18:32–41. 1970.

5297. Eden, W. G. and R. L. Self. Watch out for chinch bugs. Highlights of Agricultural Research. 7(2):16. 1960.

5298. ______. Controlling chinch bugs on St. Augustine grass lawns. Auburn University Agricultural Experiment Station Progress Report 79. 3pp. 1960.

5299. Edgecombe, S. W. Iowa greenkeeping notes. The Greenkeepers' Reporter. 7(4):22–23, 27–29. 1939.

5300. Edler, G. C. Bent seed production in Germany. USGA Green Section Bulletin. 10(11):205. 1930.

5301. Edmond, D. B. and S. T. Coles. Some long term effects of fertilizers on mown turf of brown top and chewing's fescue. New Zealand Journal of Agricultural Research. 1(5):665–674. 1956.

5302. Edmondson, J. B. A comparison of the herbicidal activity of 2, 4-D and dicamba. M. S. Thesis, University of Illinois. 36 pp. 1966.

5303. Edmonston, T. K. Why do we resort to topdressing practices? Proceedings of University of Florida Turf-Grass Management Conference. 11:58–59. 1963.

5304. Edmunds, S. E. Sub-irrigated greens at the St. Louis Country Club. USGA Green Section Bulletin. 1(5):85–87. 1921.

5305. Edwards, D. C. Three ecotypes of *Pennisetum clandestinum* Hochst. (Kikuyugrass). Empire Journal of Experimental Agriculture. 5(20):371–377. 1937.

5306. Edwards, G. E. and C. C. Black. Isolation of mesophyll cells and bundle sheath cells from *Digitaria sanguinalis* (L.) Scop. leaves and a scanning microscopy study of the internal leaf cell morphology. Plant Physiology. 47(1):149–156. 1971.

5307. Edwards, J. H., Regrowth, total available carbohydrates and total nitrogen of coastal bermudagrass roots *Cynodon dactylon* (L. Pers.) as affected by nitrogen and potassium fertilization and clipping interval. M.S. Thesis, University of Georgia. 87pp. 1970.

5308. Edwards, J. H., and H. D. Barnes. Changing greens from common bermudagrass to Tifgreen. USGA Journal and Turf Management. 11(5):25–32. 1958.

5309. Edwards, K. J. R. and J. P. Cooper. The genetic control of leaf development in *Lolium.* II. Response to selection. Heredity. 18(3):307–317. 1963.

5310. Edwards, R. D. Physical and chemical soil factors affecting the performance of bentgrass. M.S. Thesis, North Carolina State University. 1972.

5311. Eggens, J. L. Turf studies University of Guelph. The Greenmaster. 5(1):4–6. 1968.

5312. Eggens, J. L. Ground covers for Ontario golf courses. Annual RCGA National Turfgrass Conference. 19:8–9. 1968.

5313. ______. Turf research at University of Guelph. Scotts Turfgrass Research Seminar. pp. 73–77. 1968.

5314. ______. Cultivars: a review of various selections, strains and varieties licensed for sale in Canada. Annual RCGA National Turfgrass Conference. 20:27–29. 1969.

5315. ______. Turfgrass identifying characteristics, their uses and special features. Annual RCGA National Turfgrass Conference. 20:30–32. 1969.

5316. ______. Turfgrass variety trials 1968–1970. Ontario Agricultural College, University of Guelph. 8 pp. 1970.

5317. ______. The grass plant—anatomy, nutrition and growth. Annual RCGA National Turfgrass Conference. 21:10–13. 1970.

5318. ______. Problems encountered in turf management–1970. R.C.G.A. National Turf Conference. 22:7–10. 1971.

5319. ______. Foreman or superintendent. Annual RCGA National Turfgrass Conference. 23:35–38. 1972.

5320. Eggens, J. L. and N. McCollum. Turfgrass variety trials 1968–1971. Ontario Agricultural College, University of Guelph. 9 pp. 1971.

5321. Eggleton, W. G. E. The assimilation of inorganic nitrogenous salts, including sodium nitrite, by the grass plant. Biochemistry Journal. 29:1389–1397. 1935.

5323. Egley, G. H. and B. J. Rogers. Some effects of chlordane on germination and growth of turf grasses. Proceedings North Central Weed Control Conference. 15:35. 1958.

5324. Egner, H. Radioaktiva Gödselmedel. Meddelande No. 294 Pran Centralanstalten för försöksväsendet pä Jordbruksomradet. Kemiska Avbelningen No 36. Stockholm. 28 pp. 1925.

5325. Ehara, K. Summer etiolation on zoysia turf at Miyazaki golf course. KGU Green Section Turf Research Bulletin. 5:89–91. 1963.

5326. ______. Turfgrasses and turf establishment and management. Yokendo Co., Tokyo. 1968.

5327. ______. Characteristics and practice of bermuda grass. K.G.U. Green Section Turf Research Bulletin. 22(2):1–6. 1972.

5328. Ehara, K., and N. Maeno. Physiological and ecological studies on the regrowth of herbage plants. 5. Effect of light on the utilization of food reserves in regrowth of bahiagrass *(Paspalum notatum* Flugge and Italian ryegrass *(Lolium multiflorum* Lam.). Journal of Japanese Society of Grassland Science. 12(1). 1966.

5329. ______. Physiological and ecological studies on the regrowth of herbage plants. 6. Utilization ratio and regrowth in some grasses. Journal of Japanese Society of Grassland Science. 12(1). 1966.

5330. Ehara, K., and S. Tanaka. Effect of temperature on the growth, behavior, and chemical composition of the warm and cool season grasses. Proceedings of the Crop Science Society of Japan. 29:304–306. 1961.

5331. Ehara, K., H. Ikeda, and N. Maeno. Physiological and ecological studies on the regrowth of herbage plants. 7. Studies on regrowth behavior of oats *(Avena sativa L.)* after defoliation at the internode elongation stage. Journal of Japanese Society of Grassland Science. 13(3). 1967.

5332. Ehara, K., H. Nabeshima, and W. Agata. The study on the effects of perlite on the growth of green turfgrass. Journal of the Japanese Institute of Landscape Architects. 27(1): 1963.

5333. Ehara, K., T. Sasaki, and H. Ikeda. Physiological and ecological studies on the regrowth of herbage plants. I. Effects of food reserves and temperature on the regrowth of orchardgrass. Journal of Japanese Society of Grassland Science. 10(3). 1965.

5334. Ehara, K., Y. Yamada, and N. Maeno. Physiological and ecological studies on the regrowth of herbage plants. 4. The evidence of utilization of food reserves during the early stage of regrowth in bahiagrass. Journal of Japanese Society of Grassland Science. 12(1). 1966.

5335. Ehara, K., T. Miyoshi, and M. Mizuki, and H. Ikeda. Physiological and ecological studies on the regrowth of herbage plants. 3. Effect of macronutrients and time of top dressing of nitrogen on the regrowth of Bahiagrass *(Paspalum notatum* Flugge.). Journal of Japanese Society of Grassland Science. 11(3). 1965.

5336. Ehara, K., T. Sasaki, H. Ikeda, and Y. Nata. Physiological and ecological studies on the regrowth of herbage plants. 2. Effect of changes in food reserves, temperature, light and plant nutrients on the regrowth of orchardgrass and bahiagrass under dark conditions. Journal of Japanese Society of Grassland Science. 10(3). 1965.

5338. Ehrenreich, J. H., and J. M. Aikman. An ecological study of the effect of certain management practices on native prairie in Iowa. Ecology Monograph. 33(2):113–130. 1963.

5339. Eichmeier, A.H., R.Z. Wheaton, and E.H. Kidder. Local variation in precipitation induced by minor topographical differences. Michigan Agricultural Experiment Station Quarterly Bulletin. 47(4):533–541. 1965.

5340. Eichner, R. How much does it cost to renovate golf greens? Exposition Conference. Southern California. 2 pp. 1966.

5341. ______. Renovating greens? Park Maintenance. 20(5):14–15. 1967.

5343. Eisele, C. H. Rasen gras und Grünflächen. Parey, Berlin. 135 pp. 1962.

5344. ______Richtlinien zur Prüfung von Rasensaatgut. Mitteilungen der Gesellschaft für Rasenforschung. pp. 2:3, 72. 1967.

5345. ______. Seeds for sportsturf. First Czechoslovak Symposium on Sportturf Proceedings. pp. 129–135. 1969.

5346. ______. Seed testing of turfgrasses in West Germany. Proceedings of the First International Turfgrass Research Conference. pp. 132–136. 1969.

5347. Eisenmenger, W.S. The relative permanent toxicity of insecticides, fungicides and weedicides. Greenkeepers Club of New England Newsletter. 12(7):4–8. 1940.

5348. ______. Residual poisons. Greenkeeper's Reporter. 8(2):17–18, 38–39. 1940.

5349. Ekern, P. C. Evapotranspiration by Bermudagrass sod *(Cynodon dactylon* L. Pers.) in Hawaii. Agronomy Journal. 58(4):-387–390. 1966.

5350. Ekeson, A. Balan for weed control in lawns and golf courses. Lakeshore News. 2(4):2. 1970.

5351. Elder, W.C. Trichloroacetate (TCA) for Bermudagrass and Johnson grass control. USGA Journal and Turf Management. 2(3):31. 1949.

5352. ______. Fumigating with gas controls bermuda grass in greens. Golfdom. 24(4):37, 40–41. 1950.

5353. ______. Soil sterilization for weed control. Oklahoma-Texas Turf Conference Proceedings. pp. 79–83. 1950.

5354. ______. Turf grasses—their development and maintenance in Oklahoma. Oklahoma Agricultural Experiment Station. Bulletin B-425:1–32. 1954.

5355. Eldridge, J.D. An outline of weed control. Golfdom. 8(8):38–43. 1934.

5356. Elgabaly, M. M., W. M. Elghamry. Air permeability as related to particle size and bulk density in sand systems. Soil Science. 110(1):10–12. 1970.

5357. Eliovson, S. The lawn. The Complete Gardening Book. Howard Timmins. Cape Town, South Africa. pp. 115–128. 1970.

5358. Elkins, D. M. and T. L. Kitowski. Chemical mowing. Crops and soils. 24(8):-12–13. 1972.

5359. Elkins, D. M., J. K. Leasure and J. J. Faix. Herbicides for spring establishment of crownvetch (*Coronilla varia* L.). Crop Science. 10(1):95–97. 1970.

5360. Elkins, D. M., D. L. Suttner, and T. L. Kitowski. The use of growth retardants to control grass growth. Agronomy Abstracts. 2:164. 1972.

5361. Ellet, W. B., and L. Carrier. The effect of frequent clipping on total yield and composition of grasses. Journal of the American Society of Agronomy. 7:85–87. 1915.

5362. Elling, L. J. Burning studies on Kentucky bluegrass and timothy in northern Minnesota. Agronomy Abstracts. p. 49. 1969.

5363. Elliot, C. R. Registration of 'Boreal' red fescue (Reg. #6). Crop Science. 8:-398. 1968.

5364. ______. Floral induction and initiation in three perennial grasses. Ph.D. Thesis, University of Saskatchewan. 98 pp.

5365. Elliott, J. B. Preliminary studies on sand amelioration of soil under sports turf used in winter. Journal Sports Turf Research Institute. 47:66–76. 1971.

5366. ______. Sand amelioration of soil under sports turf. Parks, Golf Courses, and Sports Grounds. 37(10):998–1004. 1972.

5367. Elliot, J. G., and J. D. Fryer. Dalapon for control of grass weeds. Agriculture. 65(3):119–124. 1958.

5368. Elliot, N. R. Lawn. Kentucky Agricultural Extension Circular. 256:1–8. 1932.

5369. ______. Planting and care of the lawn. Kentucky Agricultural Extension Circular. 381:1–15. 1942.

5370. ______. Planting and care of the lawn. Kentucky Agricultural Extension Circular. 381:1–15. 1949.

5371. ______. Lawn. Kentucky Agricultural Extension Leaflet. 172:1–5. 1956.

5372. Elliot, S. Greenkeeping on a heathland course in Scotland. Journal of the Board of Greenkeeping Research. 4(12):43–49. 1935.

5373. Elliott, E. S. The effect of soil fertility on the development of Kentucky bluegrass diseases. Phytopathology. 52(11):1218. 1962.

5374. ______. Fertilizer—disease interrelationships in turf grasses. West Virginia Turfgrass Conference Proceedings. pp. 62–66. 1968.

5375. Ellis, L. W. Creeping bent plugs. USGA Green Section Bulletin. 2(12):328. 1922.

5376. Ellis, R. Automatic irrigating and fertilizing for Hollywood Park's new turf track. Grounds Maintenance. 2(5):38–40. 1967.

5377. Ellis, S. P. Present status and problems in turf development and management for parks. Proceedings of the Annual Texas Turf Conference. 15:31–35. 1960.

5378. Ellison, B. R. Fungi attacking turf grass and management problems complicated by them. Kelly-Western Seed Division. p.8. 1957.

5380. Elmore, C. L. Soil environment—pesticides. Proceedings of the 1972 Turf and Landscape Horticulture Institute. pp. 23–30. 1972.

5381. Elmore, C. L., L. Frey, K. Gowans, and J. Van Dam. A progress report. California Turfgrass Culture. 22(1):5–7. 1972.

5382. Elmore, C. L., K. Gowans, E. Johnson and W. B. McHenry. Preemergence and postemergence control of broadleaf weeds in your grass culture. California Turfgrass Culture. 21(4):27–29. 1971.

5383. Elmore, C. L., K. Mueller, K. Gowans, and B. Fischer. Progress report on crabgrass control in turf 1971. California Turfgrass Culture. 22(2):14–16. 1972.

5384. Elsaid, H. M., and J. B. Sinclair. Adapted tolerance to organic fungicides by an isolate of *Rhizoctonia solani.* Phytopathology. 52(8):731. 1962.

5385. Elstad, M. T. How to maintain turf machinery. Midwest Turf-News and Research. 6(1):5–6. 1951.

5386. ______. Elstad discusses machinery care. Midwest Turf-News and Research. 6(3):3. 1951.

5387. ______. It's not always the machine. Proceedings University of Florida Turf Management Conference. 4:25–26. 1956.

5388. ______. Why equipment manufacturers are concerned about small engine maintenance. International Turfgrass Conference and Show. 39:46–47. 1968.

5389. Elwood, P. H. Lawns: their making and maintenance. Massachusetts Agricultural Extension Service Leaflet 14. 4 pp.

5390. Ely, J., B. Johnson, and A. Overland. Contract maintenance of turfgrass and ornamentals. Northwest Turfgrass Conference Proceedings. 22:57–74. 1968.

5392. Emerson, W. W. Water conduction by severed grass roots. Journal of Agricultural Science. 45:241–245. 1954.

5393. Emmons, J. W. Establishing new lawns. University of Florida Turfgrass Conference Proceedings. 5:69–71. 1957.

5394. Emslie, L. The fertilizing of greens and fairways. The Greenkeeper's Reporter. 3(3):10–12. 1935.

5395. Endo, R. M. The relation of fertility to turf diseases. Proceedings of the Southern California Turfgrass Conference. pp. 23–26. 1959.

5396. ______. The relation of fertility to turf diseases. North California Turf Conference. pp. 23–26. 1960.

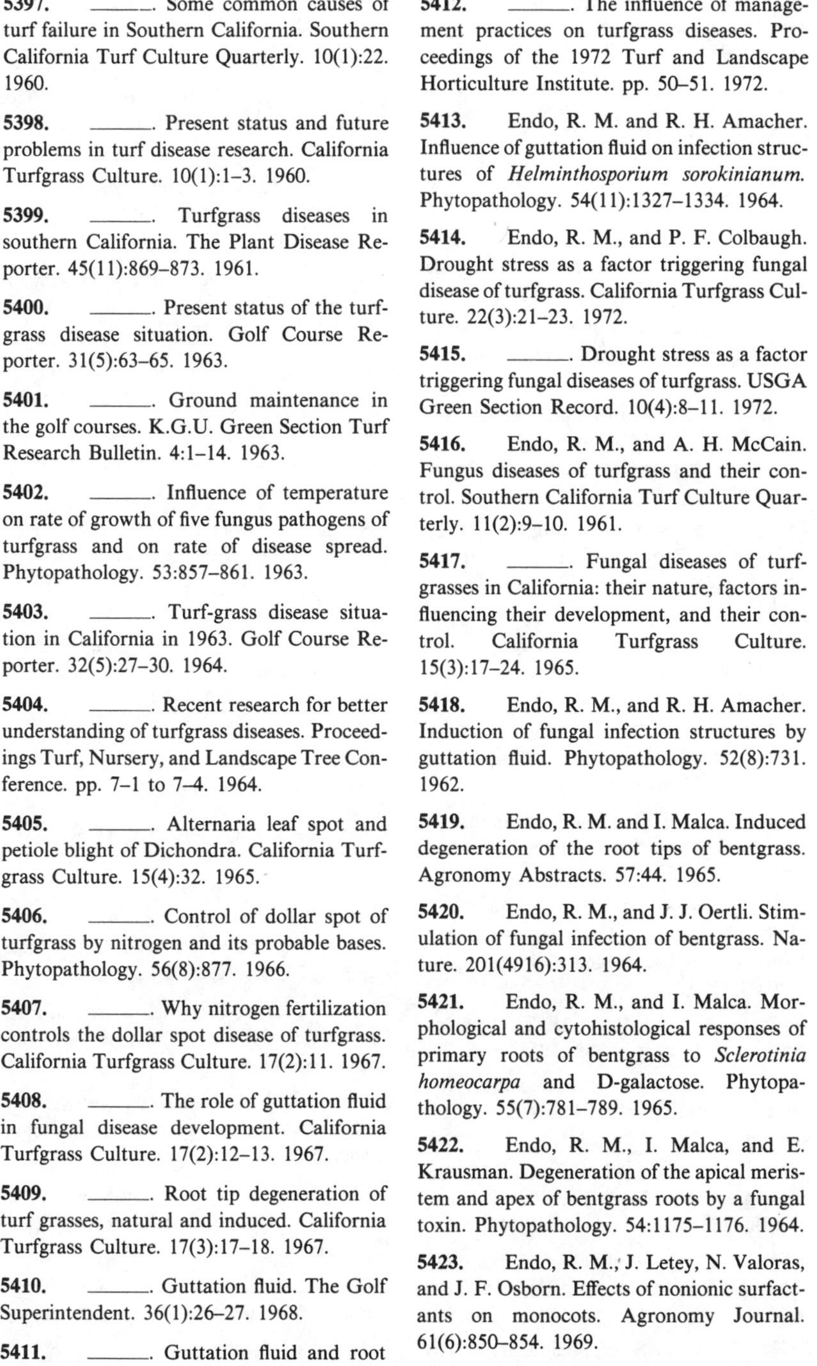

5397. ———. Some common causes of turf failure in Southern California. Southern California Turf Culture Quarterly. 10(1):22. 1960.

5398. ———. Present status and future problems in turf disease research. California Turfgrass Culture. 10(1):1–3. 1960.

5399. ———. Turfgrass diseases in southern California. The Plant Disease Reporter. 45(11):869–873. 1961.

5400. ———. Present status of the turfgrass disease situation. Golf Course Reporter. 31(5):63–65. 1963.

5401. ———. Ground maintenance in the golf courses. K.G.U. Green Section Turf Research Bulletin. 4:1–14. 1963.

5402. ———. Influence of temperature on rate of growth of five fungus pathogens of turfgrass and on rate of disease spread. Phytopathology. 53:857–861. 1963.

5403. ———. Turf-grass disease situation in California in 1963. Golf Course Reporter. 32(5):27–30. 1964.

5404. ———. Recent research for better understanding of turfgrass diseases. Proceedings Turf, Nursery, and Landscape Tree Conference. pp. 7–1 to 7–4. 1964.

5405. ———. Alternaria leaf spot and petiole blight of Dichondra. California Turfgrass Culture. 15(4):32. 1965.

5406. ———. Control of dollar spot of turfgrass by nitrogen and its probable bases. Phytopathology. 56(8):877. 1966.

5407. ———. Why nitrogen fertilization controls the dollar spot disease of turfgrass. California Turfgrass Culture. 17(2):11. 1967.

5408. ———. The role of guttation fluid in fungal disease development. California Turfgrass Culture. 17(2):12–13. 1967.

5409. ———. Root tip degeneration of turf grasses, natural and induced. California Turfgrass Culture. 17(3):17–18. 1967.

5410. ———. Guttation fluid. The Golf Superintendent. 36(1):26–27. 1968.

5411. ———. Guttation fluid and root tip degeneration in turfgrasses. Proceedings of Scotts Turfgrass Research Conference. 2:-85–94. 1971.

5412. ———. The influence of management practices on turfgrass diseases. Proceedings of the 1972 Turf and Landscape Horticulture Institute. pp. 50–51. 1972.

5413. Endo, R. M. and R. H. Amacher. Influence of guttation fluid on infection structures of *Helminthosporium sorokinianum.* Phytopathology. 54(11):1327–1334. 1964.

5414. Endo, R. M., and P. F. Colbaugh. Drought stress as a factor triggering fungal disease of turfgrass. California Turfgrass Culture. 22(3):21–23. 1972.

5415. ———. Drought stress as a factor triggering fungal diseases of turfgrass. USGA Green Section Record. 10(4):8–11. 1972.

5416. Endo, R. M., and A. H. McCain. Fungus diseases of turfgrass and their control. Southern California Turf Culture Quarterly. 11(2):9–10. 1961.

5417. ———. Fungal diseases of turfgrasses in California: their nature, factors influencing their development, and their control. California Turfgrass Culture. 15(3):17–24. 1965.

5418. Endo, R. M., and R. H. Amacher. Induction of fungal infection structures by guttation fluid. Phytopathology. 52(8):731. 1962.

5419. Endo, R. M. and I. Malca. Induced degeneration of the root tips of bentgrass. Agronomy Abstracts. 57:44. 1965.

5420. Endo, R. M., and J. J. Oertli. Stimulation of fungal infection of bentgrass. Nature. 201(4916):313. 1964.

5421. Endo, R. M., and I. Malca. Morphological and cytohistological responses of primary roots of bentgrass to *Sclerotinia homeocarpa* and D-galactose. Phytopathology. 55(7):781–789. 1965.

5422. Endo, R. M., I. Malca, and E. Krausman. Degeneration of the apical meristem and apex of bentgrass roots by a fungal toxin. Phytopathology. 54:1175–1176. 1964.

5423. Endo, R. M., J. Letey, N. Valoras, and J. F. Osborn. Effects of nonionic surfactants on monocots. Agronomy Journal. 61(6):850–854. 1969.

5424. Enfield, G. H. Agronomists help gridiron with fertilizer, new grass. Midwest Turf News and Research. 3(3):1, 3–4. 1949.

5425. ______. Field lives up to expectations. Midwest Turf-News and Research. 3(4):1. 1949.

5426. ______. Agronomist tells when to buy your fertilizer. Midwest Turf News and Research. 5(1):1–2. 1951.

5427. ______. Soil testing doubles in 10 years. Turf Bulletin. 4(7):9. 1968.

5430. Engel, R. E. Turf program at New Jersey. Golf Course Reporter. 18(3):24–25. 1950.

5431. ______. New Jerseys' turf program unites research, teaching. Golfdom. 24(6):68, 70. 1950.

5432. ______. Turf program at New Jersey. National Turf Conference of the Greenkeeping Superintendents Association. 21:18–21. 1950.

5433. ______. Trial plantings of U-3 bermuda grass. Farm Crops Department Report, Rutgers University. 1950.

5434. ______. Control of broad-leaved weeds two years after 2, 4-D treatment. Rutgers University Short Course in Turf Management. 18:5–7. 1950.

5435. ______. Trial plantings of U-3 bermudagrass. Rutgers University Short Course in Turf Management. 18:47–50. 1950.

5436. ______. Status of chemicals for crabgrass control in turf. Rutgers University Short Course in Turf Management. 18:69–72. 1950.

5437. ______. Methods for *Poa annua* control require cooperation. Golf Course Reporter 19(6):5–6. 1951.

5438. ______. Merion (B27) bluegrass. New Jersey Mimeo Leaflet. 1951.

5439. ______. Fertilizer studies in New Jersey. Proceedings of the Mid-Atlantic Turf Conference. pp. 31–36. 1951.

5440. ______. Trial plantings of U3 bermuda grass. New York State Turf Association Bulletin 29. pp. 111–112. 1951.

5441. ______. Studies of turfgrass cultivation. Ph.D. Thesis, Rutgers University. 100 pp. 1951.

5442. ______. Some preliminary results from turf cultivation. Rutgers University Short Course in Turf Management. pp. 17–22. 1951.

5443. ______. Improved and experimental grasses. Rutgers University Short Course in Turf Management. pp. 23–30. 1951.

5444. ______. Crabgrass control in 1950. Rutgers University Short Course in Turf Management. pp. 47–52. 1951.

5445. ______. Research big need on *Poa annua* chemical control. Golfdom. 26(3):64, 66. 1952.

5446. ______. Meeting golfer's demand for short-cut fairways. Golfdom. 26(6):42–43. 1952.

5447. ______. Controlling crabgrass in the lawn. New Jersey Agricultural Extension Leaflet. 92:1–7. 1952.

5448. ______. Thatch control. Golfdom. 27(10):46. 1953.

5449. ______. *Poa annua* and clover control. Proceedings of the Mid-Atlantic Association of Golf Course Superintendents. pp. 7–10. 1953.

5450. ______. Turf cultivation. Rutgers University Short Course in Turf Management. pp. 9–11. 1952–1953.

5451. ______. Observations on fertilizer treatments. Rutgers University Short Course in Turf Management. pp. 11–15. 1952–1953.

5452. ______. Thatch on turf and its control. The Golf Course Reporter. 22(5):12–14. 1954.

5453. ______. Performance of bentgrasses cut to one-quarter inch. Golf Course Reporter 22(2):20–22. 1954.

5454. ______. Crabgrass control in turf. Proceedings of Midwest Regional Turf Conference. pp. 43–44. 1954.

5455. ______. Controlling crabgrass in the lawn. New Jersey Agricultural Extension Leaflet. 120:1–7. 1954.

5456. ______. Management, weather and disease. The Golf Course Reporter. 23(4):-12–13. 1955.

5457. ______. Lawn care. New Jersey Agricultural Extension Bulletin. 286:1–10. 1955.

5458. ______. Resist disease, close cutting Merion bluegrass. New Jersey Agricultural Experiment Station. 37(2):10–11. 1955.

5459. ______. Grass identification. Rutgers University Short Course in Turf Management. 23:1–5. 1955.

5460. ______. Care of lawns in shade and on steep slopes. Handbook on Lawns. Brooklyn Botanic Garden. pp. 145–148. 1956.

5461. ______. Choose the right lawn seed mixture. New Jersey Agricultural Extension Leaflet. 155:1–4. 1956.

5462. ______. Crabgrass control with pre-emergence treatments. Special Proceedings of the Turf Section Weed Society of America. pp. 12–14. 1956.

5463. ______. Reason why chemical treatments fail. Rutgers University Short Course in Turf Management. 3 pp. 1957.

5464. ______. Four years of herbicidal treatment of *Poa annua* in bentgrass turf. Proceedings of the Northeastern Weed Control Conference. 12:140–141. 1958.

5465. ______. Management factors affecting turfgrass diseases. Parks and Recreation. 41(4):184–185. 1958.

5466. ______. Fertilizer applications, techniques. Golf Course Reporter. 27(7):24–26. 1959.

5467. ______. Turf developments. Proceedings of Midwest Regional Turf Conference. pp. 16–19. 1959.

5468. ______. 1957 research at Rutgers. New York State Turf Association Bulletin 64. p. 247. 1959.

5469. ______. Nitrogen and turfgrass production. Rutgers University Short Course in Turf Management. 27:1–3. 1959.

5470. ______. Good drainage for greens. USGA Journal and Turf Management. 12(1):27–29. 1959.

5471. ______. The turfgrass plots at Rutgers. Annual Mid-Atlantic Golf Course Superintendent's Conference Proceedings. pp. 41–48. 1960.

5472. ______. Seedbed preparation and seeding practices. Rutgers University Short Course in Turf Management. 28:1. 1960.

5473. ______. Grasses for golf turf. Rutgers University Short Course in Turf Management. 28:1–2. 1960.

5474. ______. Turfgrass culture and soil water relationships. USGA Journal and Turf Management. 13(2):26–28. 1960.

5475. ______. Competition of turfgrass species seeded in mixtures. Agronomy Abstracts. p. 74. 1961.

5476. ______. Water: friend or foe? Golf Course Reporter. 29(5):23–25. 1961.

5477. ______. Agronomic requirements of water distribution factors. Golf Course Reporter. 30(6):20–24. 1962.

5478. ______. What it takes to make a fabulous lawn. House Beautiful. 104(5):188–191. 1962.

5479. ______. Recent developments in turfgrass production. Illinois Turfgrass Conference Proceedings. pp. 44–48. 1963.

5480. ______. Research development and turfgrass production. Proceedings of the Mid-Atlantic Association of Golf Course Superintendents. p. 2. 1963.

5481. ______. Crabgrass control obtained on turf treated with several new and developmental preemergence herbicides. Proceedings Northeastern Weed Control Conference. 17:490–492. 1963.

5483. ______. Characteristics of the turf grasses. Rutgers University Annual Short Course in Turf Management. 19:62–65. 1952–1953.

5484. ______. Turf fertilization. Rutgers University Annual Short Course in Turf Management. 19:65–68. 1952–1953.

5485. ______. Establishing turf. Rutgers University Annual Short Course in Turf Management. 19:71–73. 1952–1953.

5486. ______. Management, weather, and disease. Proceedings of Midwest Regional Turf Conference. pp. 62–64. 1964.

5487. ______. Summer injury on turf from drought, heat, traffic, and chemicals. Rutgers University Short Course in Turf Management. 32:36. 1964.

5488. ______. Use of preemergence herbicides on turf. The Golf Course Reporter. 33(4):16–18. 1965.

5489. ______. Turfgrass watering related to soil-climate-management. The Golf Course Reporter. 33(6):44–46. 1965.

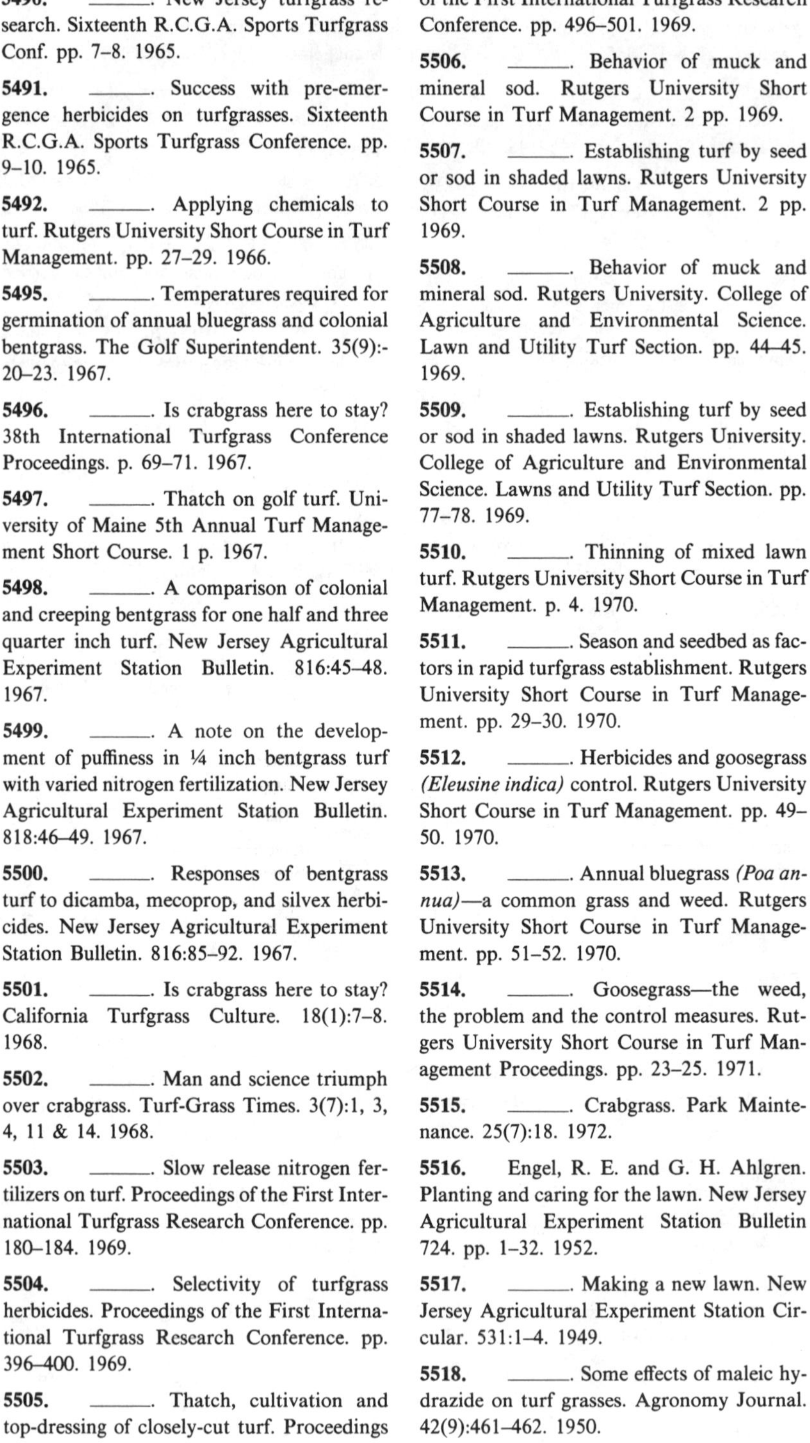

5490. ______. New Jersey turfgrass research. Sixteenth R.C.G.A. Sports Turfgrass Conf. pp. 7–8. 1965.

5491. ______. Success with pre-emergence herbicides on turfgrasses. Sixteenth R.C.G.A. Sports Turfgrass Conference. pp. 9–10. 1965.

5492. ______. Applying chemicals to turf. Rutgers University Short Course in Turf Management. pp. 27–29. 1966.

5495. ______. Temperatures required for germination of annual bluegrass and colonial bentgrass. The Golf Superintendent. 35(9):-20–23. 1967.

5496. ______. Is crabgrass here to stay? 38th International Turfgrass Conference Proceedings. p. 69–71. 1967.

5497. ______. Thatch on golf turf. University of Maine 5th Annual Turf Management Short Course. 1 p. 1967.

5498. ______. A comparison of colonial and creeping bentgrass for one half and three quarter inch turf. New Jersey Agricultural Experiment Station Bulletin. 816:45–48. 1967.

5499. ______. A note on the development of puffiness in ¼ inch bentgrass turf with varied nitrogen fertilization. New Jersey Agricultural Experiment Station Bulletin. 818:46–49. 1967.

5500. ______. Responses of bentgrass turf to dicamba, mecoprop, and silvex herbicides. New Jersey Agricultural Experiment Station Bulletin. 816:85–92. 1967.

5501. ______. Is crabgrass here to stay? California Turfgrass Culture. 18(1):7–8. 1968.

5502. ______. Man and science triumph over crabgrass. Turf-Grass Times. 3(7):1, 3, 4, 11 & 14. 1968.

5503. ______. Slow release nitrogen fertilizers on turf. Proceedings of the First International Turfgrass Research Conference. pp. 180–184. 1969.

5504. ______. Selectivity of turfgrass herbicides. Proceedings of the First International Turfgrass Research Conference. pp. 396–400. 1969.

5505. ______. Thatch, cultivation and top-dressing of closely-cut turf. Proceedings of the First International Turfgrass Research Conference. pp. 496–501. 1969.

5506. ______. Behavior of muck and mineral sod. Rutgers University Short Course in Turf Management. 2 pp. 1969.

5507. ______. Establishing turf by seed or sod in shaded lawns. Rutgers University Short Course in Turf Management. 2 pp. 1969.

5508. ______. Behavior of muck and mineral sod. Rutgers University. College of Agriculture and Environmental Science. Lawn and Utility Turf Section. pp. 44–45. 1969.

5509. ______. Establishing turf by seed or sod in shaded lawns. Rutgers University. College of Agriculture and Environmental Science. Lawns and Utility Turf Section. pp. 77–78. 1969.

5510. ______. Thinning of mixed lawn turf. Rutgers University Short Course in Turf Management. p. 4. 1970.

5511. ______. Season and seedbed as factors in rapid turfgrass establishment. Rutgers University Short Course in Turf Management. pp. 29–30. 1970.

5512. ______. Herbicides and goosegrass *(Eleusine indica)* control. Rutgers University Short Course in Turf Management. pp. 49–50. 1970.

5513. ______. Annual bluegrass *(Poa annua)*—a common grass and weed. Rutgers University Short Course in Turf Management. pp. 51–52. 1970.

5514. ______. Goosegrass—the weed, the problem and the control measures. Rutgers University Short Course in Turf Management Proceedings. pp. 23–25. 1971.

5515. ______. Crabgrass. Park Maintenance. 25(7):18. 1972.

5516. Engel, R. E. and G. H. Ahlgren. Planting and caring for the lawn. New Jersey Agricultural Experiment Station Bulletin 724. pp. 1–32. 1952.

5517. ______. Making a new lawn. New Jersey Agricultural Experiment Station Circular. 531:1–4. 1949.

5518. ______. Some effects of maleic hydrazide on turf grasses. Agronomy Journal. 42(9):461–462. 1950.

5519. ______. Better lawn seed mixtures. New Jersey Agricultural Extension Leaflet. 114:1–7. 1953.

5520. ______. Making a new lawn. New Jersey Agricultural Experiment Station Circular 553. 4 pp. 1953.

5521. ______. Turf management on athletic fields. New Jersey Agricultural Extension Leaflet. 119:1–8. 1954.

5522. ______. Making a new lawn. New Jersey Agricultural Experiment Station Circular 556. 4 pp. 1954.

5523. ______. Engel, R. E. and R. B. Alderfer. The effect of cultivation, topdressing lime, nitrogen and wetting agent on thatch development in ¼ inch bentgrass turf over a ten-year period. New Jersey Agricultural Experiment Station Bulletin. 818:32–45. 1967.

5524. Engel, R. E. and R. J. Aldrich. Three new compounds for controlling weeds in turf. Proceedings, Northeast Weed Control Conference. No. 5. p. 151–153. 1951.

5526. ______. Effectiveness of chemical combinations for crabgrass control. Proceedings of the Northeastern Weed Control Conference. pp. 265–266. 1952.

5527. ______. Control of annual bluegrass *(Poa annua)* in fairway type turf. Proceedings Northeastern Weed Control Conference. 9:353–355. 1955.

5528. ______. Preliminary results of chemical control of goosegrass *(Eleusine indica)* in greens-type turf. Rutgers University Short Course in Turf Management. 23:1–2. 1955.

5529. ______. Control of annual bluegrass *(Poa annua)* in fairway-type turf. Rutgers University Short Course in Turf Management. 23:1–3. 1955.

5530. ______. Reduction of annual bluegrass, *Poa annua,* in bentgrass turf by the use of chemicals. Golf Course Reporter. 28(4):-15–18. 1960.

5531. ______. Reduction of annual bluegrass, *Poa annua,* in bentgrass turf by the use of chemicals. Weeds. 8(1):26–28. 1960.

5532. Engel, R. E. and L. M. Callahan. Kentucky bluegrass response to pre-emergence herbicide residues in a turfgrass soil. Agronomy Abstracts. p. 105. 1964.

5533. ______. Merion Kentucky bluegrass response to soil residue of preemergence herbicides. Weeds. 15(2):128–130. 1967.

5534. Engel, R. E., and J. H. Dunn. 1965 pre-emergence treatments for goosegrass control. New Jersey Agricultural Experiment Station Bulletin. 816:93–98. 1966.

5535. ______. Promising preemergence herbicides tested for crabgrass control in 1965. Proceedings of the Northeastern Weed Control Conference. pp. 506–509. 1966.

5536. ______. Promising pre-emergence herbicides tested for crabgrass control in 1965. Rutgers University Short Course in Turf Management. pp. 18–21. 1966.

5537. ______. Preemergence herbicides for control of goosegrass in cool-season turfgrasses for a series of tests over seven seasons. New Jersey Agricultural Experiment Station Bulletin. 818:93–112. 1967.

5538. Engel, R. E., and E. E. Evaul. The history of turf at the New Jersey Experimental Station. Golf Course Reporter. 16(1):22–23, 38–41. 1948.

5539. Engel, R. E. and C. R. Funk. Performance of red fescue types. New Jersey Agricultural Experiment Station Bulletin. 816:-68–71. 1966.

5540. Engel, R. E. and H. W. Indyk. Better lawn seed mixtures. New Jersey Agricultural Experiment Station. Extension Bulletin. 357. 8 pp.

5541. ______. Making a new lawn. New Jersey Agricultural Extension Leaflet. 308:-1–4. 1961.

5542. Engel, R. E. and R. D. Ilnicki. Injury to established turfgrasses from preemergence herbicides. Proceedings of the Northeastern Weed Control Conference. 17:493. 1963.

5543. ______. Performance of experimental herbicides applied preemergence for crabgrass control in turf. Proceedings of the Northeastern Weed Control Conference. pp. 470–472. 1965.

5544. ______. Performance of experimental herbicides applied preemergence for

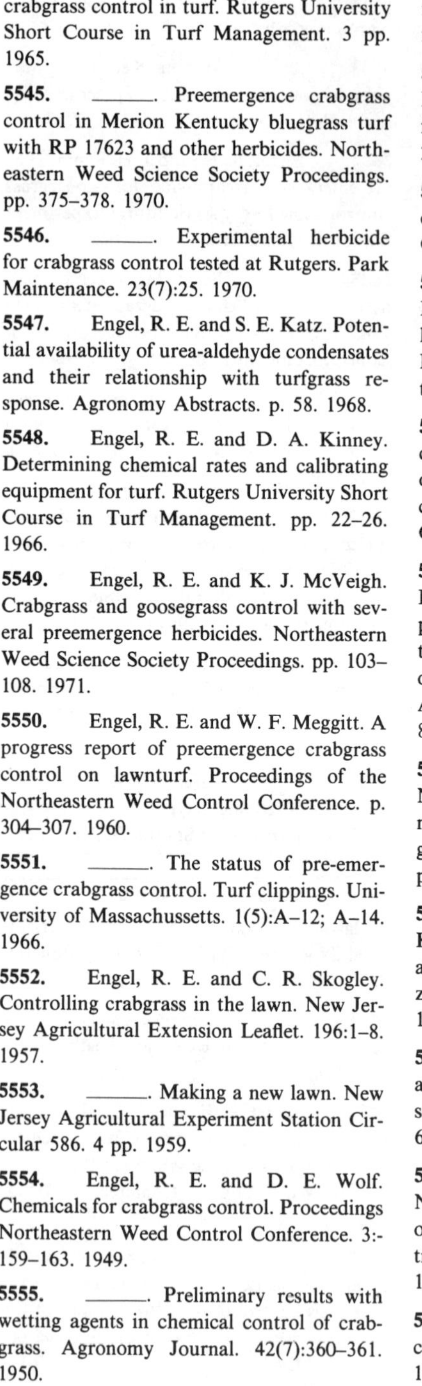

crabgrass control in turf. Rutgers University Short Course in Turf Management. 3 pp. 1965.

5545. ______. Preemergence crabgrass control in Merion Kentucky bluegrass turf with RP 17623 and other herbicides. Northeastern Weed Science Society Proceedings. pp. 375–378. 1970.

5546. ______. Experimental herbicide for crabgrass control tested at Rutgers. Park Maintenance. 23(7):25. 1970.

5547. Engel, R. E. and S. E. Katz. Potential availability of urea-aldehyde condensates and their relationship with turfgrass response. Agronomy Abstracts. p. 58. 1968.

5548. Engel, R. E. and D. A. Kinney. Determining chemical rates and calibrating equipment for turf. Rutgers University Short Course in Turf Management. pp. 22–26. 1966.

5549. Engel, R. E. and K. J. McVeigh. Crabgrass and goosegrass control with several preemergence herbicides. Northeastern Weed Science Society Proceedings. pp. 103–108. 1971.

5550. Engel, R. E. and W. F. Meggitt. A progress report of preemergence crabgrass control on lawnturf. Proceedings of the Northeastern Weed Control Conference. p. 304–307. 1960.

5551. ______. The status of pre-emergence crabgrass control. Turf clippings. University of Massachussetts. 1(5):A–12; A–14. 1966.

5552. Engel, R. E. and C. R. Skogley. Controlling crabgrass in the lawn. New Jersey Agricultural Extension Leaflet. 196:1–8. 1957.

5553. ______. Making a new lawn. New Jersey Agricultural Experiment Station Circular 586. 4 pp. 1959.

5554. Engel, R. E. and D. E. Wolf. Chemicals for crabgrass control. Proceedings Northeastern Weed Control Conference. 3:-159–163. 1949.

5555. ______. Preliminary results with wetting agents in chemical control of crabgrass. Agronomy Journal. 42(7):360–361. 1950.

5556. ______. Results of testing chemicals for crabgrass control in 1949. Proceedings of the Northeastern Weed Control Conference. pp. 239–243. 1950.

5557. Engel, R. E., R. J. Aldrich, and G. H. Ahlgren. A comparison of five chemicals for crabgrass control in turf. Weeds. 2(1):-27–32. 1953.

5558. ______. A comparison of five chemicals for crabgrass control in turf. Agri-Chem Review, New Jersey. 1954.

5559. Engel, R. E., R. N. Cook and R. D. Ilnicki. Crabgrass control obtained in established turf with preemergence herbicides. Proceedings of the Northeastern Weed Control Conference. 16:543–544. 1962.

5560. ______. The effect of three spring dates of preemergence herbicide application on crabgrass control in established turf. Proceedings of the Northeastern Weed Control Conference. 16:545. 1962.

5561. Engel, R. E., J. H. Dunn, and R. D. Ilnicki. Preemergence crabgrass herbicide performance as influenced by dry vs. spray treatments and variation of application date of spring treatments on lawn turf. New Jersey Agricultural Experiment Station Bulletin. 818:112–121. 1967.

5562. Engel, R. E., J. H. Dunn, and A. Neuberger. Effect of varied defoliation on a mixed stand of Kentucky bluegrass, bentgrass, and red fescue. Agronomy Abstracts. p. 53. 1969.

5563. Engel, R. E., C. R. Funk, and D. Kinney. The effect of varied rates of atrazine and simazine on the establishment of several zoysia strains. Agronomy Abstracts. p. 38. 1966.

5564. ______. Effect of varied rates of atrazine and simazine on the establishment of several zoysia strains. Agronomy Journal. 60(3):261–262. 1968.

5565. Engel, R. E., R. D. Ilnicki, and R. N. Cook. Pre-emergence crabgrass control on turfgrasses. North East Weed Control Conference Proceedings. 15:280–283. 1961.

5566. ______. Preemergence crabgrass control on turfgrass. Weed Abstracts. 12(3):-139. 1963.

5567. Engel, R. E., R. D. Ilnicki and J. H. Dunn. Preemergence crabgrass herbicides performance as influenced by dry vs. spray treatment and variation of application date of mid-spring treatments of lawn turf. Proceedings of the Northeastern Weed Control Conference. p. 482. 1967.

5568. Engel, R. E., K. J. McVeigh, and R. W. Duell. Growth regulation. Park Maintenance. 24(7):22. 1971.

5569. Engel, R. E., W. F. Meggitt and J. R. Fulwider. Influence of winter and spring applications of preemergence herbicides on control of crabgrass. Proceedings of the Northeastern Weed Control Conference. pp. 147–148. 1959.

5570. ______. Influence of winter and spring applications of pre-emergence herbicides on control of crabgrass. Rutgers University Short Course in Turf Management. 27:1–2. 1959.

5571. Engel, R. E., A. Morrison, and R. D. Ilnicki. Pre-emergence chemical effects in annual bluegrass. Golf Superintendent. 36(2):20–21, 39. 1968.

5572. Engel, R. E., E. R. Steiniger, and G. H. Ahlgren. The zoysias as turf grasses in New Jersey. The Golf Course Reporter. 20(3):25–26. 1952.

5573. ______. Zoysias as turf grasses in New Jersey. New York State Turf Association Bulletin 37. pp. 143–144. 1952.

5574. Engel, R. E., K. J. McVeigh, R. M. Schmit and R. W. Duell. The effect of growth regulators on turfgrass species. Northeastern Weed Science Society Proceeding. p. 131–140. 1971.

5575. Engelbert, V. Reproduction in some *Poa* species. Canadian Journal of Research. 18 (Sect. C) (10):518–521. 1940.

5576. Engholm, D. The business of servicing lawns. Rocky Mountain Regional Turfgrass Conference Proceedings. pp. 45–47. 1961.

5577. Engibous, J. C., W. J. Friedmann, and M. B. Gillis. Yield and quality of pangolagrass and bahiagrass as affected by rate and frequency of fertilization. Soil Science Society of America Proceedings. 22:423–425. 1958.

5578. England, J. M., T. H. Taylor, W. C. Templeton. Effects of paraquat, cacodylic acid and dalapon on Kentucky bluegrass sod and on the establishment of legumes planted immediately after herbicidal application. Kentucky Agricultural Experiment Station Annual Report. 76:30. 1963.

5579. English, J. P. Modernizing for demands of the game. USGA Green Section Record. 4(6):2–3. 1967.

5580. English, K. R. Effects of nitrogen fertilization on the sod development of Kentucky bluegrass on Houghton muck as measured by several nitrogen responses. M. S. Thesis, Michigan State University. 1971.

5581. English, K. R., and P. E. Rieke. The effects of nitrogen treatments on soil nitrogen tests and Merion Kentucky bluegrass grown for sod on Houghton muck. Agronomy Abstracts. 2:62. 1972.

5582. English, L. L. Sod webworms. Illinois Turfgrass Conference Proceedings. pp. 32–34. 1962.

5583. Enlow, C. R. Winter grass experiments at Gainesville, Florida. USGA Green Section Bulletin. 8(11):224–226. 1928.

5584. ______. Turf studies at the Florida Experimental Station. USGA Green Section Bulletin. 8(12):246–247. 1928.

5585. ______. Fertilizing program for Florida's special needs. Golfdom. 3(10):13–14. 1929.

5586. Enlow, C. R. and W. E. Stokes. Lawns in Florida. Florida Agricultural Experiment Station Bulletin 209. 20 pp. 1929.

5587. Ennis, W. B. and F. L. Timmons. Safe use of herbicides on right-of-way and other noncrop areas. Ohio Short Course on Roadside Development. 19:92–97. 1960.

5588. Eno, C. F. The transformation of various sources of nitrogen in the soil. Proceedings of University of Florida Turf-Grass Management Conference. 9:17–24. 1961.

5589. ______. For good turf know your soils. Proceedings 14th Annual University of Florida Turfgrass Management Conference. 14:20–23. 1966.

5590. Entriken, H. L. Bermuda grass experiences at Enid, Oklahoma. USGA Green Section. Bulletin. 5:245. 1925.

5591. Entrup, E. L. Turfgrass breeding in West Germany. Proceedings of the First

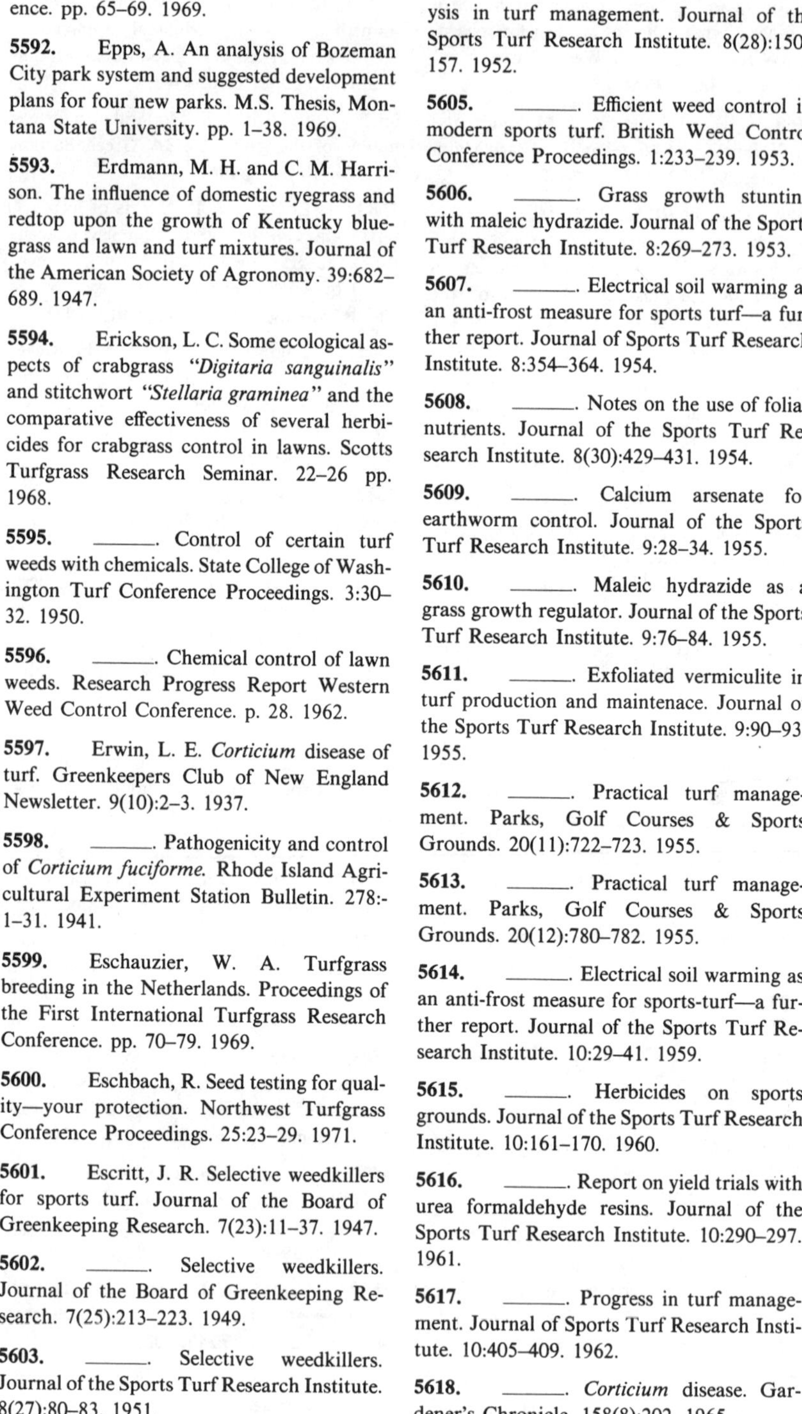

International Turfgrass Research Conference. pp. 65–69. 1969.

5592. Epps, A. An analysis of Bozeman City park system and suggested development plans for four new parks. M.S. Thesis, Montana State University. pp. 1–38. 1969.

5593. Erdmann, M. H. and C. M. Harrison. The influence of domestic ryegrass and redtop upon the growth of Kentucky bluegrass and lawn and turf mixtures. Journal of the American Society of Agronomy. 39:682–689. 1947.

5594. Erickson, L. C. Some ecological aspects of crabgrass "*Digitaria sanguinalis*" and stitchwort "*Stellaria graminea*" and the comparative effectiveness of several herbicides for crabgrass control in lawns. Scotts Turfgrass Research Seminar. 22–26 pp. 1968.

5595. ———. Control of certain turf weeds with chemicals. State College of Washington Turf Conference Proceedings. 3:30–32. 1950.

5596. ———. Chemical control of lawn weeds. Research Progress Report Western Weed Control Conference. p. 28. 1962.

5597. Erwin, L. E. *Corticium* disease of turf. Greenkeepers Club of New England Newsletter. 9(10):2–3. 1937.

5598. ———. Pathogenicity and control of *Corticium fuciforme.* Rhode Island Agricultural Experiment Station Bulletin. 278:-1–31. 1941.

5599. Eschauzier, W. A. Turfgrass breeding in the Netherlands. Proceedings of the First International Turfgrass Research Conference. pp. 70–79. 1969.

5600. Eschbach, R. Seed testing for quality—your protection. Northwest Turfgrass Conference Proceedings. 25:23–29. 1971.

5601. Escritt, J. R. Selective weedkillers for sports turf. Journal of the Board of Greenkeeping Research. 7(23):11–37. 1947.

5602. ———. Selective weedkillers. Journal of the Board of Greenkeeping Research. 7(25):213–223. 1949.

5603. ———. Selective weedkillers. Journal of the Sports Turf Research Institute. 8(27):80–83. 1951.

5604. ———. Soil fertility and soil analysis in turf management. Journal of the Sports Turf Research Institute. 8(28):150–157. 1952.

5605. ———. Efficient weed control in modern sports turf. British Weed Control Conference Proceedings. 1:233–239. 1953.

5606. ———. Grass growth stunting with maleic hydrazide. Journal of the Sports Turf Research Institute. 8:269–273. 1953.

5607. ———. Electrical soil warming as an anti-frost measure for sports turf—a further report. Journal of Sports Turf Research Institute. 8:354–364. 1954.

5608. ———. Notes on the use of foliar nutrients. Journal of the Sports Turf Research Institute. 8(30):429–431. 1954.

5609. ———. Calcium arsenate for earthworm control. Journal of the Sports Turf Research Institute. 9:28–34. 1955.

5610. ———. Maleic hydrazide as a grass growth regulator. Journal of the Sports Turf Research Institute. 9:76–84. 1955.

5611. ———. Exfoliated vermiculite in turf production and maintenace. Journal of the Sports Turf Research Institute. 9:90–93. 1955.

5612. ———. Practical turf management. Parks, Golf Courses & Sports Grounds. 20(11):722–723. 1955.

5613. ———. Practical turf management. Parks, Golf Courses & Sports Grounds. 20(12):780–782. 1955.

5614. ———. Electrical soil warming as an anti-frost measure for sports-turf—a further report. Journal of the Sports Turf Research Institute. 10:29–41. 1959.

5615. ———. Herbicides on sports grounds. Journal of the Sports Turf Research Institute. 10:161–170. 1960.

5616. ———. Report on yield trials with urea formaldehyde resins. Journal of the Sports Turf Research Institute. 10:290–297. 1961.

5617. ———. Progress in turf management. Journal of Sports Turf Research Institute. 10:405–409. 1962.

5618. ———. *Corticium* disease. Gardener's Chronicle. 158(8):202. 1965.

5619. ______. *Fusarium* patch. Gardener's Chronicle. 158(8):202–203. 1965.

5620. ______. Grasses for sports turf. The Groundsman. 19(1):14–18. 1965.

5621. ______. Personal problems of the groundsman. The Groundsman. 19(8):4–10. 1966.

5622. ______. The relationship between management practices and the control of weeds, pests and diseases. Proceedings of the First Symposium on the Control of Weeds, Pests and Diseases of Cultivated Turf. pp. 2–7. 1967.

5623. ______. The relationship between management practices and the control of weeds, pests and diseases. Parks, Golf Courses and Sports Grounds. 33(7):584–585. 1968.

5624. ______. Construction and maintenance of golf courses in Europe. Northwest Turfgrass Conference Proceedings. 22:6–20. 1968.

5625. ______. Lawn and sports turf in Europe. Northwest Turfgrass Conference Proceedings. 22:74–90. 1968.

5626. ______. Management practice and the control of weeds, pests and diseases. The Groundsman. 21(6): 18–22. 1968.

5627. ______. Turfgrass conditions in Britain. Proceedings of the First International Turfgrass Research Conference. p. 14–16. 1969.

5628. ______. Soil warming in the United Kingdom. Proceedings of the First International Turfgrass Research Conference. pp. 241–242. 1969.

5629. ______. Turfgrass education in the British Isles. Proceedings of the First International Turfgrass Research Conference. pp. 430–431. 1969.

5630. ______. Sports ground construction. Proceedings of the First International Turfgrass Research Conference. pp. 554–558. 1969.

5631. Escritt, J. R. and J. H. Arthur. Earthworm control. Journal of the Board of Greenkeeping Research. 7(24):162–172. 1948.

5632. Escritt, J. R. and D. C. Legg. Investigations on annual meadow-grass control. Journal of the Sports Turf Research Institute. No.44. pp. 5–18. 1968.

5633. ______. Gradual release nitrogen fertilizers for use on fine turf. Journal of the Sports Turf Research Institute. No.44. pp. 66–77. 1968.

5634. ______. Fertilizer trials at Bingley. Proceedings of the First International Turfgrass Research Conference. pp. 185–190. 1969.

5635. Escritt, J. R. and H. J. Lidgate. An investigation of the suitability of a urea formaldehyde fertilizer product for use on turf. Journal of the Sports Turf Research Institute. 10(38):385–393. 1962.

5636. ______. Report on fertilizer trials. Journal of the Sports Turf Research Institute. No. 40:7–42. 1964.

5637. ______. Further report on the suitability of a urea formaldehyde fertilizer product for use on turf. Journal of the Sports Turf Research Institute. No. 41:5–24. 1965.

5638. Escritt, J. R. and A. R. Woolhouse. Fungal diseases of turf in Britain. Proceedings of the First International Turfgrass Research Conference. pp. 346–350. 1969.

5639. Eshbaugh, F. P. The building and maintenance of lawns. Oklahoma Panhandle Agricultural Experiment Station. Bulletin 14:3–6. 1930.

5640. Espenschied, R. F. Selecting ground maintenance equipment. Illinois Turfgrass Conference Proceedings. pp. 26–29. 1969.

5641. Esser, R. P. Turf nematode survey. Proceedings University of Florida Turf-Grass Management Conference. 10:38–42. 1962.

5642. ______. Vernacular name for *Hypsoperine graminis.* Nematology Newsletter. 10(3):17. 1964.

5643. Esser, R. P. and E. B. Sledge. New rootknot nematodes associated with sodgrass in Flordia. Proceedings University of Florida Turf-Grass Management Conference. 10:30–37. 1962.

5644. Esson, M. J. Turf pests and their control. New Zealand Institute for Turf Culture Newsletter. 76:181–185. 1971.

5645. Ethridge, L. The suppliers role in the irrigation industry and the importance of manufacturer's specifications. Proceedings Turfgrass Sprinkler Irrigation Conference. 3pp. 1966.

5646. Etter, A. G. How Kentucky bluegrass grows. Annals of the Missouri Botanical Garden. 38(3):293–375. 1951.

5647. Evans, A. C. Earthworms Journal of the Board of Greenkeeping Research. 7(23):49–54. 1947.

5648. ______. The importance of earthworms. Grass Productivity. Philosophical Library, New York. pp. 45–46. 1948.

5649. Evans, A. C. and W. J. McL. Guild. Studies on the relationships between earthworms and soil fertility. I. Biological studies in the field. Annals of Applied Biology. 34(3):307–330. 1947.

5650. Evans, D. W., and C. L. Canode. Influence of nitrogen fertilization, gapping, and burning on seed production of Newport Kentucky bluegrass. Agronomy Journal. 63(4):575–580. 1971.

5651. Evans, E. M., L. E. Ensminger, B. D. Doss, and O. L. Bennett. Nitrogen and moisture requirements of coastal bermuda and Pensacola bahia. Auburn University Agricultural Experiment Station Bulletin 337. 19 pp. 1961.

5652. Evans, E. M., R. D. Rouse and R. T. Gudauskas. Low soil potassium sets up coastal for a leaf spot disease. Highlights of Agricultural Research. 11(2):14. 1964.

5653. Evans, G. Chromosome complements in grasses. Nature. 118:841. 1926.

5654. Evans, G. C. Ecological studies on the rain forest of Southern Nigeria. II. The atmospheric environmental conditions. Journal of Ecology 27:436–482. 1939.

5655. ______. An area survey method of investigating the distribution of light intensity in woodlands, with particular reference to sunflecks. Journal of Ecology. 44:391–428. 1956.

5656. Evans, G. and R. A. Calder. Manuring pedigree grasses for seed production. Welsh Journal of Agriculture. 7:195–208. 1931.

5657. Evans, G. C. and D. E. Coombe. Hemispherical and woodland canopy photography and the light climate. Journal of Ecology 47:103. 1959.

5658. Evans, G. C., T. C. Whitmore, and Y. K. Wong. The distribution of light reaching the ground vegetation in a tropical rain forest. Journal of Ecology. 48:193–204. 1960.

5660. Evans, L. M. Putting greens on heavy clay soil. USGA Green Section Bulletin. 8(9):183–184. 1928.

5661. ______. Prince Edward Island bent. The National Greenkeeper. 3(1):27. 1929.

5662. ______. Beetles at Cedarbrook. The National Greenkeeper. 3(8):14–15. 1929.

5663. Evans, L. T. Inflorescence initiation in *Lolium temulentum* L. Australian Journal of Biological Sciences. 13(4):429–440. 1960.

5664. ______. The influence of temperature on flowering in species of *Lolium* and in *Poa pratnosis.* Journal of Agricultural Science. 54:410–416. 1960.

5665. ______. The influence of environmental conditions on inflorescence development in some long-day grasses. New Phytologist. 59:163–174. 1960b.

5666. Evans, M. W. The life history of timothy. USDA Bulletin 1450. 56 pp. 1927.

5667. ______. Relation of latitude to certain phases of the growth of timothy. American Journal of Botany. 26:212–218. 1939.

5668. ______. The grasses: their growth and development. Ohio Agricultural Experiment Station. Agronomy Mimeograph. No. 105. 1946.

5669. ______. Kentucky bluegrass. Ohio Agricultural Experiment Station Research Bulletin. 681:1–39. 1949.

5670. Erb, L. Iron sulphate. The National Greenkeeper. 7(6):5–8. 1933.

5671. Evans, M. W. and J. E. Ely. Usefulness of Kentucky bluegrass and Canada bluegrass in turfs as affected by their habits and growth. USGA Green Section Bulletin. 13(5):140–143. 1933.

5672. ______. The rhizomes of certain species of grasses. Journal of the American Society of Agronomy. 27:791–797. 1935.

5673. Evans, M. W. and F. O. Grover. Developmental morphology of the growing point of the shoot and the inflorescence in grasses. Journal of Agricultural Research. 61(7):481–520. 1940.

5674. Evans, M. W., and J. M. Watkins. The growth of Kentucky bluegrass and of Canada bluegrass in late spring and in autumn as affected by the length of day. Journal of the American Society of Agronomy. 31:-767–774. 1939.

5675. Evans, P. S. A comparison of some aspects of the anatomy and morphology of Italian ryegrass (*Lolium multiforum* Lam.) and perennial ryegrass (*L. perenne* L.). New Zealand Journal of Botany. 2(2):120–130. 1964.

5676. Evans, S. The herbicidal control of broad-leaved and grass weeds in established grassland. Journal of British Grassland Society. 19(2):205–211. 1964.

5677. Evans, S. A. Dalapon for the control of "couch" *(Agropyron repens, Agrostis gigantea* and *Agrostis stolonifera).* British Weed Control Conference Proceedings. 1:287–300. 1960.

5678. Evans, T. W. Some principles of manuring for turf. Journal of the Board of Greenkeeping Research. 2(4):44–50. 1931.

5679. ______. The root development of New Zealand browntop, chewing's fescue, and fine-leaved sheep's fescue under putting green conditions. Journal of the Board of Greenkeeping Research. 2(5):119–124. 1931.

5680. ______. Renovationg golf greens. Journal of the Board of Greenkeeping Research. 2(6):181–182. 1932.

5681. ______. The cutting and fertility factors in relation to putting green management. Journal of the Board of Greenkeeping Research. 2(6):196–209. 1932.

5682. ______. Composts and fertilisers in relation to greenkeeping. Journal of the Board of Greenkeeping Research. 2(7):268–272. 1932.

5683. ______. Composts and fertilisers in relation to greenkeeping. Journal of the Board of Greenkeeping Research. 3(8):34–38. 1933.

5684. ______. Composts and fertilisers in relation to greenkeeping. Journal of the Board of Greenkeeping Research. 3(10):169–172. 1934.

5685. ______. Composts and fertilizers in relation to greenkeeping. Journal of the Board of Greenkkeeping Research. 3(11):-220–223. 1934.

5686. ______. Composts and fertilizers in relation to greenkeeping. Journal of the Board of Greenkeeping Research. 4(13):104–107. 1935.

5687. Evans, W. F. Herbicides for turf. Midwest Regional Turf Conference Proceedings. 91–93 pp. 1969.

5688. Evans, W. F. and R. J. Otten. Sindone herbicides for preemergence crabgrass control in turf. 20th Annual Southern Weed Conference Proceedings. pp. 64–68. 1967.

5689. Evans, W. F. and J. F. Koerwer. Brominal for seedling turfgrass. North Central Weed Control Conference Proceedings. 24:58. 1969.

5690. Evans, W. H. Weed destruction by means of chemicals. USDA Experiment Station Work. 1:19. 1902.

5691. Evaul, E. E. Management of bentgrass lawns. New Jersey Agriculture. 10:7. 1928.

5692. ______. Bentgrasses—when and how to use them. New Jersey Agriculture. 10:10. 1928.

5693. ______. About that lawn in winter. New Jersey Agriculture. 10:13. 1928.

5694. ______. A brief on renovating poor turf. Golfdom. 3(6):28. 1929.

5695. Evelyn, J. Kalendarium hortense. J. Martyn and J. Allestry, London. Second edition, 247 pp. 1670.

5696. ______. Directions for the gardener at Sayo-court, but which may be of use for other gardens. Edited by Geoffrey Keynes (London) Nonesuch Press, 109 pp. 1932.

5697. Everett, T. H. Lawns and landscaping handbook. Arco Publishing Co., Inc. New York. 144 pp. 1956.

5698. ______. Lawns and landscaping handbook. Fawcett. Greenwich, Conn. 144 pp. 1956.

5699. Evers, R. A. Prairie and prairie plants. Illinois Turfgrass Conference Proceedings. pp. 3–9. 1963.

5700. Everson, A. C. Effects of frequent clipping at different stubble heights on western wheatgrass (*Agropyron smithii* Rybd.). Agronomy Journal. 58(1):33–35. 1966.

5701. Evison, J. R. B. The good lawn. Gardeners Chronicle. 141(9):244. 1957.

5702. ———. The lawn from seed. Gardeners Chronicle. 141(10):271. 1957.

5703. ———. The lawn from turves. Gardeners Chronicle. 141(11):294. 1957.

5704. ———. Grasses for lawns. Gardeners Chronicle. 142(13):241. 1957.

5705. ———. Fertilisers for the lawn. Gardeners Chronicle. 142(14):261. 1957.

5706. ———. Turf weeds and their eradication: 1. Gardeners Chronicle. 143(1):15. 1958.

5707. ———. Turf weeds and their eradication: 2. Gardeners Chronicle. 143(4):61. 1958.

5708. ———. Common diseases of turf. Gardeners Chronicle. 143(9):143. 1958.

5709. ———. Common pests of turf. Gardeners Chronicle Gardening Illustrated. 143(12):195. 1958.

5710. Evvard, J. M. Simple vs. complex minerals on bluegrass. Iowa Agricultural Experiment Station Leaflet. 3:1–4. 1925.

5711. Eyles, T. W. Wormkilling on the downs. Journal of the Board of Greenkeeping Research. 1(2):69. 1930.

5712. Fahey, T. Winchester bent. Greenkeepers Club of New England Newsletter. 1(1):3. 1929.

5713. Fairbrothers, D. E. The naturalization of *Eragrostis curvula* (weeping lovegrass) in New Jersey. Bulletin of Torrey Botanical Club. 87:216–218. 1960.

5715. Fairchild, M. L. Control of soil insects in lawns and turf. Proceedings Missouri Lawn and Turf Conference. pp. 24–26. 1962.

5716. Faix, J. J. Crownvetch establishment on a simulated roadcut using two seeding methods and two nursegrasses and establishment for forage yield as influenced by lime and fertilizer placement on an acid soil. M.S. Thesis, Southern Illinois University. 34 pp. 1969.

5717. Faix, J. J., D. M. Elkins and H. J. Jones. Crownvetch seedling growth on an acid soil as influenced by soil preparation and lime placement. Agronomy Journal. 62(4):485–487. 1970.

5718. Fallows, R. S. Herbicides—their types and uses. The Groundsman. 20(8):34. 1967.

5719. ———. Herbicides—their types and uses. The Groundsman. 20(11):16–17. 1967.

5720. Farber, E., and R. R. Hind. Process for converting sawdust into fertilizer. Forest Products Journal. 60(10):340–343. 1959.

5721. ———. Sawdust into fertilizer. Golf Course Reporter. 29(1):107–114. 1961.

5722. Farley, G. A. Golf course commonsense. Farley Libraries, Cleveland Heights, Ohio. p. 1. 1931.

5723. ———. Some hints on maintaining traps and rough. Golfdom. 5(2):101–102, 104, 106. 1931.

5724. Farmer, R. E. Budgeting the golf course. The National Greenkeeper. 7(5):5–7. 1933.

5725. Farmer, R. P. Creation of maintenance problems. Proceedings Fifth Annual Tennessee Turfgrass Conference. pp. 17–18. 1971.

5726. Farnham, M. E. Fall in the fertilizer program. The National Greenkeeper. 5(9):12–13. 1931.

5727. ———. Maintenance of improved turf. The Pennsylvania State College Eighteenth Annual Turf Conference. pp. 60–71. 1949.

5728. ———. Aerification of greens and fairways. Greenkeeping Superintendents Association National Turf Conference. 21:117–120. 1950.

5729. ———. Athletic fields. Proceedings of Midwest Regional Turf Conference. pp. 40–44. 1951.

5730. ———. Athletic field turf management. Proceedings of Midwest Regional Turf Conference. pp. 59–63. 1951.

5731. ______. Crabgrass control cultural practices. Pennsylvania State College Turfgrass Conference Proceedings. 20:91–99. 1951.

5732. Farnham, M. E. and C. K. Hallowell. Weed control experiments. The Greenkeepers' Reporter. 14(1):5–6. 1946.

5733. ______. Additional weed control test with 2,4–D. The Greenkeepers' Reporter. 15(1):28–29. 1947.

5734. ______. Fairway renovation with weed control practices. Timely Turf Topics. USGA Green Section. August. p. 2. 1947.

5735. Farnham, R. S. Nitrogen fertilization of turf grasses. Minnesota Farm and Home Science. 22(1):11–12. 1964.

5736. Farrar, L. L. Symptoms, soil analysis and treatment for nematode control. Auburn University Short Course. pp. 29–34. 1967.

5738. Fassett, N. C. Grasses of Wisconsin. University of Wisconsin Press, Madison. 178 pp. 1951.

5739. Fatum, C. H. Golf course maintenance cost survey. USGA Green Section Record. 1(3):6–7. 1963.

5740. ______. The control of diseases, insects, and weeds in golf course fairways. Rutgers University Short Course in Turf Management Proceedings. pp. 63–66. 1971.

5741. Faubion, J. L. and E. C. Holt. Purple nutsedge control in bermudagrass with organic arsenicals. Agronomy Abstracts. p. 105. 1964.

5742. Faubion, J. L., J. Letey, F. A. Klingerman, and W. C. Morgan. Sand—organic mixes for putting green construction. Agronomy Abstracts. p. 68. 1970.

5743. Faulkner, R. P. The science of turf cultivation. Technical Press, London. 64 pp. 1950.

5744. Faust, J. L. The New York Times Book of Lawn Care. Alfred A. Knopf, Inc., New York. 85 pp. 1957.

5745. ______. The New York Times Book of Lawn Care. Alfred A. Knopf, Inc., New York. 85 pp. 1964.

5746. Fazio, S. Lawns for Arizona. Arizona Agricultural Extension Circular. 135:-1–21. 1948.

5747. ______. 1953 Turf plot report, Tucson. Proceedings of the Arizona Turf Conference. pp. 28–30. 1953.

5748. ______. Merion bluegrass—both good and bad. Progressive Agriculture in Arizona. 1954.

5749. Fazio, S. and H. F. Tate. Lawns for Arizona. Arizona Agricultural Extension Circular. 135:1–23. 1951 (rev.)

5750. Featherly, H. I. Grasses of Oklahoma. Oklahoma Agricultural Experiment Station Technical Bulletin. 3. 1–131. 1938.

5751. Feddersen, R. L. Herbicide drift damage and its control. Ohio 29th Short Course on Roadside Development. pp. 98–101. 1970.

5753. Fedorov, A. K. On the response of perennial grasses to vernalization. Soviet Plant Physiology. 15(3):394–399. 1968.

5754. Feed, F. J. Lawns and playing fields. Faber and Faber, London. 212 pp. 1950.

5755. Feinot, R. Softening hard soil areas. Proceedings of the Midwest Regional Turf Conference. pp. 27–28. 1969.

5756. Fejer, S. O. Effects of gibberellic acid, indoleacetic acid, coumarin and perloline on perennial ryegrass (*Lolium perenne* L.) New Zealand Journal of Agricultural Research. 3(4):734–743. 1960.

5757. Feldmesser, J. and A. M. Golden. Control of nematodes damaging home lawn grasses in two counties in Maryland. The Plant Disease Reporter. 56(6):476–480. 1972.

5758. Fendall, R. K. and C. L. Canode. Dormancy-related growth inhibitors in seeds of orchardgrass *(Dactylis glomerata L.)* Crop Science. 11(5):727–730. 1971.

5759. Fenn, M. G. Control of *Fusarium* patch disease in France. Parks, Golf Courses & Sports Grounds, 21(8):497–498. 1956.

5760. ______. Turf upkeep in central France. Journal of the Sports Turf Research Institute. 10(37):319–325. 1961.

5761. Fenne, S. B. Controlling lawn and turfgrass diseases. Virginia Agricultural Extension Circular. 802:1–10. 1959.

5762. Fennell, G. R. Control of *Cotula*. New Zealand Institute for Turf Culture Newsletter. 5:4. 1960.

5763. Fenemore, P. G. Control of soil insects in turf. New Zealand Institute for Turf Culture. Newsletter No. 27. pp. 11–12. 1963.

5764. Fennemore, P. G. Recent developments in pest control. New Zealand Institute for Turf Culture Newsletter. 53:9–10. 1968.

5765. Fenster, C. R. and L. R. Robison. Calibrating a sprayer. The Golf Superintendent. 35(7):26. 1967.

5766. Fenstermacher, J. M. and N. Jackson. New fungicides. Park Maintenance. 24(7):18. 1971.

5767. Fenwick, H. S. Soil fumigation: How and why it works. University of Idaho Agricultural Extension Service. Bulletin 528. 1971.

5768. Fergus, E. N. Kentucky 31 fescue—culture and use. Kentucky Agricultural Experiment Station Circular 497:1–16. 1952.

5769. Ferguson, A. Color in plant life. The Greenkeepers' Reporter. 5(6):11–13, 26. 1937.

5770. Ferguson, A. C. Bent grasses. Turf Research Project, University of Manitoba. pp. 2–10. 1958–62.

5771. ______. Bentgrass variety and strain trials. Turf Research Project, University of Manitoba. pp. 10–11. 1958–62.

5772. ______. Soil mix experiment. Turf Research Project, University of Manitoba. p. 11. 1958–62.

5773. ______. Fungicide treatments for control of snow mold. Turf Research Project, University of Manitoba. p. 12. 1958–62.

5774. ______. Polyethylene as winter cover on golf greens. Turf Research Project, University of Manitoba. pp. 12–14. 1958–62.

5775. ______. Lawn and fairway grasses. Turf Research Project, University of Manitoba. pp. 14–15. 1958–62.

5776. ______. Variety and strain trial of lawn and fairway grasses. Turf Research Project, University of Manitoba. pp. 15–16. 1958–62.

5777. ______. Clover control in lawns and fairways. Turf Research Project, University of Manitoba. p. 17. 1958–62.

5778. ______. Winter injury north of the 49th. The Golf Superintendent. 34(8):38–39. 1966.

5779. ______. Some observations on winter injury in turfgrass experiments at the University of Manitoba. 18th Annual R. C. G. A. National Turfgrass Conference. pp. 7–12. 1967.

5780. ______. Winter injury—some possible preventatives. Annual RCGA National Turfgrass Conference. 21:14–15. 1970.

5781. ______. Highlights of our turfgrass research program. R.C.G.A. National Turf Conference. 22:11–13. 1971.

5782. ______. Turfgrass seeds (species, mixtures, and blends for specific purposes). Annual RCGA National Turfgrass Conference. 23:39–40. 1972.

5783. Ferguson, J. W. Soil management. Short Course on Roadside Development (Ohio). 14:93–100. 1955.

5785. Ferguson, M. H. Bentgrass for lawns. USDA-USGA Publication. 2 pp. 1950.

5786. ______. What's new in turf. Proceedings of Midwest Regional Turf Conference. pp. 3–6. 1948.

5787. ______. Crabgrass control in parks and lawns. Proceedings of Midwest Regional Turf Conference. pp. 61–62. 1948.

5788. ______. Soil factors affecting the absorption and utilization of soil nutrients by grass. Proceedings of the Mid-Atlantic Association of Greenkeepers Conference. pp. 16–22. 1950.

5789. ______. Compaction, drainage and aeration. U.S.G.A. Journal and Turf Management. 3(2):32–33. 1950.

5790. ______. Soil water and soil air: Their relationship to turf production. USGA Journal and Turf Management. 3(3):35–36. 1950.

5791. ______. Review of the research of 1950. Proceedings of the Mid-Atlantic Association of Greenkeepers Conference. pp. 36–42. 1951.

5792. ______. Weed control by use of chemicals with special emphasis on crabgrass control. Proceedings of the 5th Annual Texas Turf Conference. pp. 93–101. 1951.

5793. ______. Bermudagrass. Park Maintenance. 6(10):13, 54. 1953.

5794. ______. The green section research program. USGA Journal and Turf Management. 6(4):25–26. 1953.

5795. ______. Scale attacks bermudagrass putting greens. U.S.G.A. Journal and Turf Management. 6(5):29–30. 1953.

5796. ______. Be sure your new seeding produces turf. USGA Journal and Turf Management. 6(5):30–32. 1953.

5797. ______. Watering in winter. U.S.-G.A. Journal and Turf Management. 6(6):-25–26. 1953.

5798. ______. Summary of the Texas turfgrass conference. Proceedings of the Annual Texas Turfgrass Conference. 9:79–84. 1954.

5799. ______. National golf fund supports turf research. USGA Journal and Turf Management. 7(1):31–32. 1954.

5800. ______. The turfgrass research program at Texas A & M. U.S.G.A. Journal and Turf Management. 7(4):27–29. 1954.

5801. ______. Now is the time. USGA Journal and Turf Management. 7(5):27–29. 1954.

5802. ______. Turfgrass for Oklahoma. Oklahoma Turfgrass Conference Proceedings. pp. 5–10. 1955.

5803. ______. Everett Queen: his golf course and his methods. USGA Journal and Turf Management. 8(4):24–27. 1955.

5804. ______. Mister chairman. USGA Journal and Turf Management. 8(5):25–28. 1955.

5805. ______. When you build a putting green make sure the soil mixture is a good one. USGA Journal and Turf Management. 8(6):26–29. 1955.

5806. ______. Fertilization of turfgrasses. U.S.G.A. Journal and Turf Management. 8(4):30–32. 1955.

5807. ______. What research has done to improve golf turf. Golfdom. 30(4):51–53. 1956.

5808. ______. Turfgrass research at Texas A. & M. The Greenkeepers' Reporter. 24(1):18–22. 1956.

5809. ______. Trends in golf course maintenance. USGA Journal and Turf Management. 9(3):25–30. 1956.

5810. ______. Soil modification. Golf Course Reporter. 25(8):5–7. 1957.

5811. ______. Soil modification: practices with putting green soils. Proceedings of Midwest Regional Turf Conference. pp. 19–22. 1957.

5812. ______. Golf course problems of the southwest. Rutgers University Turfgrass Short Course. 2 pp. 1957.

5813. ______. Structural characteristics of the grass plant as related to adaptation. Proceedings of the Texas Turfgrass Conference. 12:39–42. 1957.

5814. ______. Beautification by means of trees and shrubs. USGA Journal and Turf Management. 10(4):25–29. 1957.

5815. ______. The role of water in plant growth. Parks and Recreation. 41(1):16. 1958.

5816. ______. Effects of golf shoe soles on putting green turf. USGA Journal and Turf Management. 11(6):25–28. 1958.

5817. ______. Turf will be good for the open championship at Southern Hills. USGA Open Championship Annual. Allied Printers and Publishers. Tulsa. 87, 195, 215. 1958.

5818. ______. Manfestations of traffic effects on turf and the measurement of these effects. Agronomy Abstracts. p. 89. 1959.

5819. ______. Western turf advancement. Arizona Turf Conference Proceedings. pp. 28–30. 1959.

5820. ______. Turf research in action. Golf Course Reporter. 27(1):33–56. 1959.

5821. ______. How many sprigs should you plant? Golf Course Reporter. 27(1):64. 1959.

5822. ______. Turf establishment and management. Oklahoma Turfgrass Conference Proceedings. pp. 28–29. 1959.

5823. ______. Structural characteristics of the grass plant as related to adaptation. Proceedings of the Midwest Regional Turf Conference. pp. 78–79. 1959.

5824. ______. Shoe sole tests to be broadened. USGA Journal and Turf Management. 11(7):29–30. 1959.

5825. ______. Soils. USGA Journal and Turf Management. 12(1):29–30. 1959.

5826. ______. *Poa annua* control. USGA Journal and Turf Management. 12(5):25–28. 1959.

5827. ______. Turf damage from foot traffic. USGA Journal and Turf Management. 12(5):29–32. 1959.

5828. ______. The role of water in plant growth. USGA Journal and Turf Management. 12(6):30–32. 1959.

5829. ______. Effect of weather on diseases. Oklahoma Turfgrass Conference Proceedings. pp. 54–56. 1960.

5830. ______. Turfgrass soil mixtures. Rocky Mountain Regional Turfgrass Conference Proceedings. 7:15–21. 1960.

5831. ______. Summary of Texas turfgrass conference. Proceedings of the Texas Turfgrass Conference. 15:77–80. 1960.

5832. ______. The role of water in plant growth. USGA Journal and Turf Management. 13(2):30. 1960.

5833. ______. Golf course design and construction. Central Plains Turfgrass Conference. pp. 2–3. 1961.

5834. ______. Specific care of dormant turf—Southern Grasses. International Turfgrass Conference Proceedings. 32:18. 1961.

5835. ______. Turf research in America. Rocky Mountain Regional Turfgrass Conference Proceedings. 8:38–43. 1961.

5836. ______. Soils. Proceedings Fifteenth Southeastern Turfgrass Conference. pp. 1–4. 1961.

5837. ______. The need for planning for traffic control. Proceedings of the Annual Texas Turf Conference. 16:16–18. 1961.

5838. ______. Why keep records? USGA Journal and Turf Management. 14(6):27–32. 1961.

5839. ______. Role of proper management practices in weed control. Oklahoma Turfgrass Conference Proceedings. pp. 10–13. 1962.

5840. ______. How much did you put on? USGA Journal and Turf Management. 15(4):29–32. 1962.

5841. ______. Plants and light. USGA Journal and Turf Management. 15(6):26–29. 1962.

5843. ______. The need for planning for traffic control. Proceedings 17th Southeastern Turfgrass Conference. pp. 3–5. 1963.

5844. ______. Importance of turfgrass in Texas. Proceedings of the 18th Annual Texas Turfgrass Conference. 18:31–36. 1963.

5845. ______. Effects of traffic on turf. USGA Green Section Record. 1(1):3–5. 1963.

5846. ______. Role of proper management practices in weed control. USGA Journal and Turf Management. 15(7):26–28. 1963.

5847. ______. Fertilizers—basic information. USGA Journal and Turf Management. 15(7):28–30. 1963.

5848. ______. Soils for putting greens. Virginia Turfgrass Conference. pp. 35–36. 1963.

5849. ______. Physiological mechanisms of winter injury to plants. Agronomy Abstracts. p. 100. 1964.

5850. ______. The role of non-nitrogen fertilizer elements. Golf Course Reporter. 32(4):24–30. 1964.

5851. ______. Preparing and caring for temporary greens. Southern Turfgrass Association Conference Proceedings. pp. 7–8. 1964.

5852. ______. Mat and thatch cause, effect and remedy. USGA Green Section Record. 1(5):10–12. 1964.

5853. ______. Pesticides—boon or bane? USGA Green Section Record. 2(2):10–11. 1964.

5854. ______. Bentgrass for the South—varieties. USGA Green Section Record. 2(3):6–8. 1964.

5855. ______. Bentgrass for the South—management. USGA Green Section Record. 2(3):9–11. 1964.

5856. ______. Fertilizer—how much? USGA Green Section Record. 2(4):6–12. 1964.

5857. ———. Mat, thatch, aerification. Southern Turfgrass Association Conference Proceedings. pp. 22–23. 1965.

5858. ———. Maintaining bermuda greens in the fall and winter. Southern Turfgrass Association Conference Proceedings. pp. 24–25. 1965.

5859. ———. The golf course at Bellerive. USGA Green Section Record. 3(2):8–10. 1965.

5860. ———. The troubles we've seen. USGA Green Section Record. 3(3):10–13. 1965.

5861. ———. After five years: the green section specification for a putting green. USGA Green Section Record. 3(4):1–7. 1965.

5862. ———. Chester Mendenhall and the trees of Mission Hills. USGA Green Section Record. 3(4):10–12. 1965.

5863. ———. Trends in golf course management. USGA Journal and Turf Management. 18(3). 1965.

5864. ———. Study winterkill, then fight it! Golfdom. 40(1):39–40, 42. 1966.

5865. ———. The proper slant on pesticides. Golfdom. 40(7);38–40, 62–66. 1966.

5866. ———. Anatomy of turf plants. Proceedings of the Midwest Regional Turf Conference. pp. 21–23. 1966.

5867. ———. Evapotranspiration—turf and weather. Proceedings of the 1966 Midwest Regional Turf Conference. pp. 26–27. 1966.

5868. ———. Building new golf courses. Proceedings of the Annual Texas Turfgrass Conference. 21:38–41. 1966.

5869. ———. Phosphorus. Turf Clippings. University of Massachussetts. 2(1):A–14 to A–16. 1966.

5870. Ferguson, M. H., G. Daniel, A. Miller, and J. B. Moncrief. Water systems—engineering and installation. USGA Green Section Record. 4(3):3–6. 1966.

5871. Ferguson, M. H. Design and use of irrigation systems. Golfdom. 41(8):22–24, 48–50. 1967.

5872. ———. Experiments and experience with soil mixes—a review and evaluation. University of Missouri Lawn and Turf Conference. pp. 29–32. 1967.

5873. ———. Soil amendments. Proceedings of the Annual Texas Turfgrass Conference. 22:57–58. 1967.

5874. ———. Zoysia use and management. Turf-Grass Times. 2(6):20. 1967.

5875. ———. Why renovate or revise? USGA Green Section Record. 4(6):2. 1967.

5876. ———. Principles governing putting green construction. Agronomy Abstracts. p. 58. 1968.

5877. ———. Fertilizer—how much? Golfdom. 42(7):34–35, 38, 59. 1968.

5878. ———. Experiments and experience with soil mixes: a review and evaluation. Proceedings of the Midwest Regional Turf Conference. pp. 59–61. 1968.

5879. ———. Experiments and experience with soil mixes—a review and evaluation. Southern Turfgrass Association Conference Proceedings. pp. 44–46. 1968.

5880. ———. Fertilizing golf greens and fairways. Turf Bulletin. Massachusetts Turf and Lawn Grass Council. 4(8):16–17. 1968.

5881. ———. Evolution of a putting green. Turf Bulletin. Massachusetts Turf and Lawn Grass Council. 4(8):32–33. 1968.

5882. ———. Building golf holes for good turf management. United States Golf Association, New York, N.Y. 55 pp. 1968.

5883. ———. Putting green design—please golfers, ease maintenance. USGA Green Section Record. 5(6):6–7. 1968.

5884. ———. Evolution of a putting green. USGA Green Section Record. 6(1):-1–4. 1968.

5885. ———. Experiments and experience with soil mixes. Parks, Golf Courses and Sports Grounds. 34(7):604–628. 1969.

5887. Ferguson, M. H. and I. Forbes. Bentgrass for lawns. USDA Mimeo Leaflet.

5888. Ferguson, M. H. and F. V. Grau. The history and development of controls for major disease of bentgrass on putting greens. USGA Journal and Turf Management. 2(1):-25–30. 1949.

5889. ______. What about liquid fertilizers? USGA Journal and Turf Management. 3(6):29–30. 1950.

5890. ______. U-3 bermudagrass. USGA Journal and Turf Management. 4(1):-31. 1951.

5891. Ferguson, M. H. and H. E. Hampton. Permeability—the key to verdant turf. Proceedings of the Texas Turfgrass Conference. 20:54–58. 1965.

5892. Ferguson, M. H. and C. G. Wilson. Crabgrass control. USGA Journal and Turf Management. 3(7):27–31. 1951.

5893. Ferguson, M. H., J. B. Beard, and J. G. Lebeau. On the research front. USGA Green Section Record. 2(4):13. 1964.

5894. Ferguson, M. H., Howard, L., and Bloodworth, M. E. Laboratory methods for evaluation of putting green soil mixtures. USGA Journal and Turf Management. 13(5):30–32. 1960.

5895. Ferguson, M. H., J. L. Holmes, S. Moore, and A. Virtuoso. Construction of putting greens. USGA Green Section Record. 1(6):7–8. 1964.

5896. Ferguson, N. L. Annual meadow-grass (*Poa annua* L.). Greenkeeping Section of New Zealand Golf Institute. pp. 9–12. 1936.

5897. ______. A greenkeepers guide to the grasses—the meadow grasses. Journal of the Board of Greenkeeping Research. 4(15):-274. 1936.

5898. ______. A greenkeeper's guide to the grasses. Journal of the Board of Greenkeeping Research. 5(16):41–46. 1937.

5899. Ferguson, W. S. and R. A. Terry. The effect of nitrogenous fertilizers on the non-protein nitrogenous fraction of grassland herbage. Journal of Agricultural Science. 48(2):149–152. 1956.

5900. Ferme, J. J. The course thru the green. Greenkeepers Club of New England Newsletter. 2(7):2–3. 1930.

5901. Ferro, R. B. An improved instrument for turf sampling. Journal of the Board of Greenkeeping Research. 4(13):119–120. 1935.

5902. ______. Some factors affecting earthworm activity in turf. Journal of Board Greenkeeping Research. 5(17):86–98. 1937.

5903. Fertig, S. N. Broadleaf weed problems of the Northeast Weed Control Conference. Proceedings of Northeastern Weed Control Conference. 22:19–26. 1968.

5904. Fertig, S. N. and M. R. Vega. The inhibiting effect of maleic hydrazide (MH–40) on lawn grasses. Central Experiment Station Contribution No. 1868. University of Phillipines Mimeo. 11 pp.

5905. Feser, Leo J. Good turf. Park Maintenance. 6(4):14–16. 1953.

5906. Feser, R. Phosphates—their use and effect in turf management. Golf Course Reporter. 25(3):18–20. 1957.

5907. Feston, P. M. Scouts, visitors, and supplies equal turf restoration. Park Maintenance. 11(10):70–72. 1958.

5908. Feucht, J. R. Trends in landscape management that affect the turfsman. Annual Rocky Mountain Regional Turfgrass Conference Proceedings. 18:56–60. 1972.

5909. Fides, B. A look at liquid fertilizers on the golf course. University of Maine Turf Conference Proceedings. 6:36–38. 1968.

5910. Fieger, P. Curasol to fight erosion. 29th Ohio Short Course on Roadside Development. pp. 87–92. 1972.

5912. Fifield, E. Discusses lawn bowling —plan, construction, care. Midwest Turf News and Research. 6(3):1–2. 1952.

5913. Fields, J. Bermuda grass. Oklahoma Agricultural Experiment Station Bulletin. 55:1–11. 1902.

5914. ______. Bermuda for lawns. Oklahoma Agricultural Experiment Station Bulletin. 70. pp. 3–4. 1906.

5915. Fields, M. L., R. Der, and D. D. Hemphill. Influence of DCPA on selected soil microorganisms. Weeds. 15(3):195–197. 1967.

5916. Fifield, W. M. The experiment stations' interest in turf. Turf Management Conference—Florida Greenkeeping Superintendents Association, pp. 27–32. 1950.

5917. Filer, T. H. Nitrogen management studies for bermuda putting green turf. Proceedings of the Texas Turfgrass Conference. 12:32–35. 1957.

5918. ______. Snowmold control and other disease studies in eastern Washington. Proceedings 14th Annual Northwest Turf Conference. 14:7–9. 1960.

5919. ______. Parasitic aspects of a fairy ring fungus. *Marasmius oreades.* Phytopathology. 55:1132–1134. 1965.

5920. ______. Damage to turfgrasses caused by cyanogenic compounds produced by *Marasmius oreades,* a fairy ring fungus. The Plant Disease Reporter. 49(7):571–574. 1965.

5921. ______. Effect of grass and cereal seedlings of hydrogen cyanide produced by mycelium and and sporophores of *Marasmius oreades.* Plant Disease Reporter. 50:-264–266. 1966.

5922. ______. Red thread found on bermuda grass. The Plant Disease Reporter. 50(7):525–526. 1966.

5923. Filer, T. H. and A. G. Law. Snowmold investigations in eastern Washington. Proceedings 15th Annual Northwest Turf Conference. 15:7–8. 1961.

5924. Filmer, R. S. Controlling hairy chinch bug, increasing peril to turf. Golfdom. 20(2):40, 61. 1946.

5925. Filmer, R. S. and C. L. Smith. Activated Sabadilla, a new control of chinch bugs in turf. Golfdom. 19(8):9. 1945.

5926. Finger, J. S. The new golf course and the superintendent. Turf Bulletin. 3(3):-5–7, 10. 1966.

5927. ______. Breaking in the new golf course. Turf-Grass Times. 2(6):12–14. 1967.

5928. ______. The business end of building or rebuilding a golf course. Joseph S. Finger. 48 pp. 1972.

5930. Fink, R. J. Phytotoxicity of herbicide residues in soils. Agronomy Journal. 64(6):804–805. 1972.

5931. Finn, B. J., S. J. Bourget, K. F. Nielsen and B. K. Dow. Effects of different soil moisture tensions on grass and legume species. Canadian Journal Soil Science. 41(1):16–23. 1961.

5932. Finn, C. O. New techniques in turf establishment. Short Course on Roadside Development (Ohio). 14:115–120. 1955.

5933. ______. Fast turf establishment—through the use of mulch and hydraulic seeding. Proceedings of Midwest Regional Turf Conference. pp. 41–44. 1957.

5934. ______. Mulches in turf establishment. Proceedings of the Midwest Regional Turf Conference. pp. 69–70. 1965.

5935. ______. Hydroseeding turf areas over the world. Proceedings of the Midwest Regional Turf Conference. pp. 70–72. 1965.

5936. Finn, G. Snowmobiles on the golf course, the con's. Turf-Grass Times. 8(1):22. 1972.

5937. Fiori, B. J., H. Tashiro, and K. Personius. The bluegrass billbug. New York Turfgrass Association Bulletin. 81:314–315. 1968.

5938. Firsching, J. G. Maintaining turf in parks and playgrounds. Central Plains Turfgrass Conference. pp. 55–58. 1951.

5939. ______. Shade turf. Central Plains Turfgrass Conference. p. 3. 1961.

5940. Fischer, G. W. Fundamental studies of the stripe smut of grasses *(Ustilago striaeformis)* in the Pacific Northwest. Phytopathology. 30(2):93–118. 1940.

5941. ______. A local, winter-time epidemic of blister smut. *Entyloma crastophilum* on Kentucky bluegrass at Pullman, Washington. Plant Disease Reporter. 35(2):88. 1951.

5942. Fischer, J. A. Evaluation of high temperature effects on annual bluegrass (*Poa annua* L.). M. S. Thesis, Michigan State. 42 pp. 1967.

5943. ______. Sand trap maintenance. Proceedings of the Midwest Regional Turf Conference. pp. 69–70. 1972.

5944. Fischer, R. Economic trends and their influence on the construction and sod industries. 42nd Annual Michigan Turfgrass Conference Proceedings. 1:117–118. 1972.

5945. Fish, V. C. Are you getting your money's worth. Proceedings of Texas Turfgrass Conference. 15:72–76. 1960.

5946. ______. Mowing economics: important steps to follow to save time, money. Turf-Grass Times. 1(5):16–17. 1966.

5947. Fisher, B. S. The leaf anatomy and vegetative characters of certain South African grasses: the Chloridae. Ph.D. Thesis, University of South Africa. 1940.

5948. Fisher, G. G. Aberystwyth "S" strains of grasses. Journal of the Sports Turf Research Institute. 8(27):50–55. 1951.

5950. Fisher, J. E. The growth of rhizomes in Kentucky bluegrass. Forage Notes. 7(1):11–12. 1961.

5951. ______. Evidence of circumnutational growth movements of rhizomes of *Poa pratensis* L. that aid in soil penetration. Canada Journal of Botany. 42:293–299. 1964.

5952. ______. Morphologically distinct states in the growth and development of rhizomes of *Poa pratensis* L. and their correlation with specific geotropic responses. Canadian Journal of Botany. 43:1163–1175. 1965.

5953. ______. The growth of rhizomes in Kentucky bluegrass. 1. Initiation and early growth. Greenhouse-Garden-Grass. Canada Department of Agriculture. 5:3:1–7. 1965.

5954. ______. The growth of rhizomes in Kentucky bluegrass. 2. Form and structure during the main stages of growth. Greenhouse-Garden-Grass Canada Department of Agriculture. 5:4:1–6. 1965.

5955. Fisher, R. F. The mysterious fairy ring. Illinois Research. 14(1):8–9. 1972.

5956. Fiske, J. G. Substitute home mixtures for just grass seed and rejoice in a velvety lawn. New Jersey Agriculture. 4:4. 1922.

5957. ______. Our common lawn weeds. New Jersey Agriculture. 8:10–11. 1926.

5958. Fitts, J. W. Preparation is key to successful turf. Park Maintenance. 9(6):20. 1956.

5959. Fitts, O. B. Early morning watering as an aid to brown patch control. U.S.-G.A. Green Section Bulletin. 4:159. 1924.

5960. ______. A preliminary study of root growth of five grasses under turf conditions. USGA Green Section Bulletin. 5:58–62. 1925.

5961. ______. June experiments at Arlington Experimental Turf Garden with chlorophenol mercury compounds. (Semesan and Uspulun). USGA Green Section Bulletin. 5:-147–148. 1925.

5962. ______. How to prevent or overcome grainy and fluffy conditions of turf in vegetative greens. USGA Green Section Bulletin. 5:195–196. 1925.

5963. ______. Water as an essential in growing and maintaining good turf. USGA Green Section Bulletin. 5:206–207. 1925.

5964. ______. Converting established turf to creeping bent by broadcasting stolons and topdressing USGA Green Section Bulletin. 5:223–224. 1925.

5965. ______. The vital importance of topdressing in the maintenance of satisfactory creeping bent greens. USGA Green Section Bulletin. 5:242–245. 1925.

5966. ______. Top-dressing of putting greens. American Fertilizer. 64:54. 1926.

5967. ______. Seepage water, a menace to good turf maintenance. USGA Green Section Bulletin. 7(3):46–48. 1927.

5968. ______. Your lawn. Nature. 12:-108–113. 1928.

5969. ______. What fertilizer study is doing to improve course standards. Golfdom. 5(4):25–27. 1931.

5970. ______. Records warn mild winters mean summer turf woes. Golfdom. 6(4):-21–23. 1932.

5971. Fizzell, J. A. A dozen weeds in your lawn. Illinois Agricultural Extension Circular. 847:1–11. 1962.

5972. Flack, H. Spring work in the county cricket ground. The Groundsman. 21(8):28–39. 1968.

5973. Flaherty, J. R. Irrigation practices on *Poa annua.* Turf Clippings. University of Massachusetts. 2(2):A-9–10. 1967.

5974. ______. Condition of fairways concurrent with the use of tri-calcium arsenate for annual bluegrass control. Proceedings 1970 3-Day Turf Courses, Rutgers University. pp. 40–41. 1970.

5975. Flaig, W. Organic compounds in soil. Soil Science. 111(1):19–33. 1971.

5976. Flannagan, T. R. and R. J. Bartlett. Soil compaction associated with alternating green and brown stripes on turf. Agronomy Journal. 53(6):404–405. 1961.

5977. Fleischman, G. Notes on bents. USDA, Washington D.C. 4 pp. 1946.

5978. Fleming, B. R. Mechanical practices today. Southern Turfgrass Association Conference Proceedings. pp. 47–48. 1968.

5979. ______. Turfgrass research at Tennessee Tech. Proceedings Third Annual Tennessee Turfgrass Conference. pp. 28–29. 1969.

5980. ______. Advantages of an automatic irrigation system. Proceedings Fifth Annual Tennessee Turfgrass Conference. pp. 36–38. 1971.

5981. Fleming, B. R., J. M. Duich, and G. J. Shoop. Soil modification for turfgrass. New York Turfgrass Association Bulletin. 72:278–279. 1963.

5982. ______. Clover and knotweed control. Proceedings of the Northeastern Weed control Conference. pp. 496–499. 1965.

5983. Fleming, W. E. How to kill the beetle. The National Greenkeeper. 6(6):5–6, 8. 1932.

5984. ______. Preventing injury from Japanese and Asiatic beetle larvae to turf in parks and other large areas. U.S. Department of Agriculture Circular 403:11 pp. 1936.

5985. ______. Chlordane controls Japanese beetle larvae in turf. Golfdom. 24(4):-52–54, 98–100. 1950.

5986. ______. Protection of turf from damage by Japanese beetle grubs. USDA Leaflet. 290:1–8. 1950.

5987. Fleming, W. E. and F. E. Baker The effectiveness of various arsenicals in destroying larvae of the Japanese beetle in sassafras sandy loam. Journal of Agricultural Research. 52(7):495–503. 1936.

5988. Fleming, W. E. and F. W. Metzger. Control of the Japanese beetle and its grub in home yards. U.S. Department of Agriculture Circular 401. 15 pp. 1936.

5989. Fleming, W. E. and M. R. Osburn. Control of larvae of the Japanese and the Asiatic beetles in lawns and golf courses. U.S. Department of Agriculture Circular 238:1–10. 1932.

5990. Fletcher, F. W. How to fumigate for turf weed control. Weeds and Turf. 2(2):-8–9, 27. 1963.

5991. Fletcher, H. L. V. The lawn. The Pleasure Garden. Hodder and Stoughton. England pp. 11–17. 1967.

5992. Flife, F. W. Herbicides to cut upkeep. Illinois Turfgrass Conference Proceedings. 10:62–63. 1969.

5995. Flood, V. Turning nature's forces upside down. The National Greenkeeper. 1(4):25, 26, 42. 1927.

5997. Florence, Paul. Windsor—the pony grass that went to town. Proceedings of the Midwest Regional Turf Conference. pp. 79–80. 1969.

5998. Floyd, V. Growing grass on coral rock. Golfdom. 40(4):26–29. 1966.

5999. ______. From bermuda grass to bent. Golfdom. 40(5):26–27, 30–31. 1966.

6000. ______. Smooth greens on the Gulf. Golfdom. 40(6):40–42. 1966.

6001. ______. Building greens to last. Golfdom. 40(7):26, 27, 30, 31. 1966.

6002. ______. "Super sheds" for course maintenance. Golfdom 41(1):38–40. 1967.

6003. ______. Tamers of the desert sand. Golfdom. 41(9):26–29. 1967.

6004. Flynn, J. Beating wash-out problems. Golf Course Reporter. 26(4):30–32. 1958.

6005. Flynn, J. F. How to grow and keep a better lawn. HART Publishing Company, Inc. New York City. 89 pp. 1951.

6007. Foard, D. E., and A. H. Haber. Use of growth characteristics in studies of morphologic relations. I. Similarities between epiblast and coleorhiza. American Journal of Botany. 49:520–523. 1962.

6008. Fogg, J. M. Weeds of lawn and garden. University of Pennsylvania Press, Philadelphia. 1945.

6009. Foley, D. The establishment of 29 species of grasses and legumes on a highway slope east of Urbana, Illinois on Interstate 74. Illinois Cooperative Highway Research Program Project IHR–67. 11–14. 1961.

6010. ______. Use of mulches for turf establishment. Illinois Turfgrass Conference Proceedings. 10:49–50. 1969.

6011. Foley, D. J. Building a lawn. Gardening for Beginners. Funk and Wagnalls, New York. pp. 207–214. 1972.

6012. Folkner, J. S. Overseeding trials. Arizona Agricultural Experiment Station Turfgrass Report 203. pp. 45–47. 1961.

6013. ______. Select the right grass. Proceedings of the Arizona Turfgrass Conference. pp. 5–7. 1954.

6014. ______. Maleic hydrazide, an aid in summer-winter turf transition. Golf Course Reporter. 24(6):5–7. 1956.

6015. ______. Tells use of maleic hydrazide in summer-winter turf transition. Golfdom. 30(8):24–25, 69. 1956.

6016. ______. Construction renovation and management of athletic fields. Arizona Agricultural Experiment Station. Report No. 158. 1957.

6017. ______. Construction, renovation and management of athletic fields. Arizona Agricultural Experiment Station Report No. 158. 1959.

6018. ______. The southern approach. Golf Course Reporter. 28(6):32–34, 45–48. 1960.

6019. ______. Overseeding trials—1961–62. Turfgrass Research, Report 212, University of Arizona. pp. 26–29. 1962.

6020. Fonder, J. F. Brutal season emphasizes care in grass selection. Golfdom. 5(10):-60–63. 1931.

6021. ______. Physical and chemical factors in proper topdressing. Golfdom. 6(4):84, 86. 1932.

6022. ______. Unbalanced feeding, not excess diet, fertilizing danger. Golfdom. 7(7):12–13. 1933.

6023. Fons, W. L. Influence of forest cover on wind velocity. Journal of Forestry. 38(6):481–486. 1940.

6024. Fontenot, D. L. Native materials can be used. USGA Green Section Record. 3(5):4–11. 1966.

6025. Foote, L. E. The effects of fertilizer rates on the amount of bare ground and roadside turf components. Agronomy Abstracts. p. 38. 1966.

6026. ______. Formulation of erosion prevention recommended for new construction. Minnesota Department of Highways Special Bulletin No. 1. 18 pp. 1967.

6027. ______. Fertilizer aids turf, reduces weeds and erosion. Turf-Grass Times. 3(1):1, 15. 1967.

6028. ______. Fertilizer placement with sodding. Agronomy Journal. 61(6):965–966. 1969.

6029. Foote, L. E. and B. F. Himmelman. Maleic hydrazide as a growth retardant. Minnesota Department of Highways Investigation No. 616. Final Report. 50 pp. 1965.

6030. ______. Vegetation control along fence lines with maleic hydrazide. Weeds. 15(1):38–41. 1967.

6031. ______. Fence line vegetation control. Weeds, Trees, and Turf. 6(9):17–19. 1967.

6032. Foote, L. E., and A. G. Johnson. Seedling vigor of five strains of crownvetch. Journal Soil and Water Conservation. 20:-220–221. 1965.

6033. Foote, L. E. and D. L. Kill. Turf establishment on highway right-of-way slopes. Short Course on Roadside Development (Ohio). 27:83–93. 1968.

6034. ______. Comparing mulches: the long and short of it. Weeds, Trees, and Turf. 8(3):12–18. 1969.

6035. ______. Turf species: growth patterns and adaptations. Better Roads. 40:24–28. 1970.

6036. Foote, L. E. and D. B. White. Communication of biological and engineering concepts in highway research. Agronomy Abstracts. p. 100. 1964.

6037. Foote, L. E., B. F. Himmelman, and D. L. Kill. Vegetation and erosion control for highway slopes and ditches. Minnesota Department of Highways Investigation No. 614. Interim Report. 39 pp. 1966.

6038. Foote, L. E., D. L. Kill, and A. H. Bolland. Erosion prevention and turf establishment manual. Minnesota Department of Highways. Office of Materials, Construction Division. 44 pp. 1970.

6039. Foote, L. E., J. A. Jackobs, C. N. Hittle, and D. Graffis. The effect of fertility and different plant species on establishment of turf on highway cuts. Agronomy Abstracts. p. 56. 1962.

6040. Foote, L. E., J. A. Jackobs, J. Shepherd, and E. Gould. Instrumentation and techniques for research in roadside development. Ohio Short Course on Roadside Development. 23:63–78. 1964.

6041. Forbes, E. B., A. C. Whittier, and R. C. Collison. The mineral nutrients in bluegrass. Ohio Agricultural Experiment Station. Bulletin 222. pp. 39–53. 1910.

6042. Forbes, I. The Zoysia grasses breeding program. Proceedings of National Turf Field Days. pp. 39–42. 1950.

6043. ______. Chromosome numbers and hybrids in zoysia. Agronomy Journal. 44(4):194–199. 1952.

6044. ______. Vegetative certification of turfgrasses—what it is, what it means. Proceedings University of Florida Turf-Grass Management Conference. 3:37–40. 1955.

6045. ______. Zoysia management. Proceedings Twelfth Southeastern Turfgrass Conference. pp. 16–19. 1958.

6046. Forbes, I., and G. W. Burton. Induction of tetraploidy and rapid field method of detecting induced tetraploidy in Pensacola bahiagrass. Crop Science. 1(5):383–384. 1961.

6047. Forbes, I. and M. H. Ferguson. Observations on the zoysia grasses. The Greenskeepers' Reporter. 15(2):7–9. 1947.

6048. ______. Effects of strain differences, seed treatment, and planting depth on seed germination of *Zoysia* Spp. Journal of the American Society of Agronomy. 40:725–732. 1948.

6049. Forbes, I., B. P. Robinson, and J. W. Latham. Emerald zoysia. Golf Course Reporter. 23(2):22. 1955.

6050. ______. Emerald zoysia—improved hybrid lawn grass for the South. U.S.G.A. Journal and Turf Management. 7(7):-23–26. 1955.

6051. Forbes, J. O. Problems of highway weed control. Proceedings of 1st Western Canada Roadside Development Conference. pp. 45–50. 1964.

6052. Ford, D. R. The influence of temperature and light intensity on the photosynthetic rate and chemical composition of *Festucae arundinacea* and *Dactylus glomerata* M.S. Thesis, Purdue University. pp. 9–11. 1967.

6053. Ford, R. Graininess in Seaside bent greens. Greenkeeper's Reporter. 11(5):24–25. 1943.

6054. Ford, R. E. Maize dwarf mosaic virus susceptibility of Iowa native perennial grasses. Phytopathology. 57(4):450–451. 1967.

6055. Forde, B. J. Effect of various environments on the anatomy and growth of perennial ryegrass and cocksfoot. 1. Leaf growth. New Zealand Journal Botany. 4(4):-455–468. 1966.

6056. ______. Effect of various environments on the anatomy and growth of perennial ryegrass and cocksfoot. 2. Apical and sub-apical growth. New Zealand Journal of Botany. 4(4):469–78. 1966.

6057. ______. Translocation in grasses. I. Bermudagrass. New Zealand Journal of Botany. 4(4):479–495. 1966.

6058. Fordham, H. C. Soil amendments related to turf. Turf Bulletin. Massachusetts Turf and lawn grass Council. 4(4):26, 28. 1967.

6059. ______. Lawn construction and insect problems. Turf Clippings. University of Massachussetts. 1(8):A–71 to A–72. 1963.

6060. Fortner, J. L. Bag vs. bulk fertilizer. Proceedings Florida Turfgrass Management Conference. 14:49–51. 1966.

6061. ______. Maintenance fertilization of Bahia. Proceedings University of Florida Turfgrass Management Conference. 17:75–81. 1969.

6063. Fortney, W. R. and A. P. Dye. Crabgrass control studies. Annual Report of West Virginia Agricultural Experiment Station. Parts 2–3:5–10. 1962.

6064. ______. Crabgrass control studies. West Virginia University Agricultural Experiment Station Bulletin 481, Parts 2 and 3. 5, 10. 1963.

6065. Foster, C. A. The influence of planting date on the seed bearing capacity of tillers of perennial ryegrass spaced plants grown for seed. Journal of the British Grasslands Society. 24(3):271–277. 1969.

6066. Foulis, J. Hot weather hints on course care. Golfdom. 1(6):13. 1927.

6067. Fountaine, D. Suggests simple foils of winter kill and brown-patch. Golfdom. 3(3):44. 1929.

6068. Foutch, H. W. Response of cool season perennial grasses to temperature. Ph.D Thesis, Auburn University. 1971.

6069. Fowells, H. A. The temperature profile in a forest. Journal of Forestry. 46(12):897–899. 1948.

6070. Fox, C. Roadside councils role in the federal highway beautification program. Short Course on Roadside Development (Ohio). 13:17–18. 1971.

6071. Fox, C. J. S. Long-term effects of insecticides on wireworms *(Agriotes* spp.) of grassland in Nova Scotia. Canadian Journal of Plant Science. 44(1):32–36. 1964.

6072. Fox, D. F. Plant growth regulators for use on roadsides. Short Course on Roadside Development (Ohio). 27:104–105. 1968.

6073. Fox, G. L., D. S. Metcalfe, and C. M. Sacamano. Turfgrass management training in Arizona—available and potential. Proceedings of Arizona Turfgrass Conference. pp. 9–10. 1972.

6074. Fox, H. Japanese beetles; seasonal trends in relative abundance of—in the soil during the annual life cycle. Journal of the New York Entomological Society. 45(1):-115–126. 1937.

6075. Fox, R. C. An oil-wax-surfactant system for retarding the evaporation of water. Nature. 205(4975):1004–1005. 1965.

6076. Fox, W. M. Getting the most out of your help. Turf-Grass Times. 2(3):6, 7, 12. 1967.

6077. Foy, C. L. and D. W. Jones. The influence of potassium and other mineral nutrients on the action of herbicides in turfgrasses. Agronomy Abstracts. p. 51. 1967.

6079. Foy, C. L., G. E. Coats, and T. O. Evrard. Further studies on grass growth inhibition. Virginia Turfgrass Conference Proceedings. 8:29. 1967.

6080. ______. Control of bermudagrass in pavement. Virginia Turfgrass Conference Proceedings. 8:32. 1967.

6081. ______. Further studies on grass growth inhibition. Results of 1967 Research Program for Control of Weeds and Diseases of Turfgrass and Ornamentals. Information Bul. 101–A. Dept. of Plant Pathology and Physiology. VPI. p. 29. 1968.

6082. ______. Control of bermudagrass in pavement. Results of 1967 Research Program for Control of Weeds and Diseases of Turfgrass and Ornamentals. Information Note 101-A. Department of Plant Pathology and Physiology. VPI. p. 32. 1968.

6083. ______. Soil sterilant studies along highway rights of way. Results of 1967 Research Program for Control of Weeds and Diseases of Turfgrasses and Ornamentals. Dept. of Plant Pathology and Physiology. VPI. Pp. 35–39. 1968.

6084. Foy, N. R. Chewings fescue; history, seed production, and seed-export problems. New Zealand Journal of Agriculture. 31:356–370. 1925.

6085. ______. History of chewings fescue. New Zealand Journal of Agriculture. 33:52. 1926.

6086. ______. Use of ultra-violet light in diagnosis of types of ryegrasses in New Zealand. New Zealand Journal of Agriculture. 43:389–400. 1931.

6087. ______. Deterioration problems in New Zealand chewings fescue. New Zealand Journal of Agriculture. 49:10–24. 1934.

6088. ______. Deterioration problems in New Zealand chewings fescue. Greenkeepers Club of New England Newsletter. 7(5):10. 1935.

6089. Frakes, R. V. Seedling vigor and rate of emergence in two sources of 'Newport' Kentucky bluegrass. Crop Science. 1(4):305–306. 1961.

6090. Frame, J. and I. V. Hunt. The effect of companion grasses and seed rate on the productivity of a tall-fescue sward. Journal of British Grassland Society. 19:330–335. 1964.

6091. Francis, C. K. and R. O. Baird. A study of bermuda grass. Oklahoma Agricultural Experiment Station Bulletin. 90:1–19. 1910.

6092. Francis, C. W., D. F. Grigal. A rapid and simple procedure using Sr^{85} for determining cation exchange capacities of soils and clays. Soil Science. 112(1):17–21. 1971.

6093. Francis, T. Facts about . . . planning a golf course. The Groundsman. 22(8):-36–37. 1969.

6094. ______. Grass seeds in turfculture. The Groundsman. 22(10):21. 1969.

6095. Franchi, B. Automatic irrigation systems. Proceedings of the Texas Turfgrass Conference. 18:19–20. 1963.

6096. Frank, A. B. Effects of some preemergence herbicides on the growth of Kentucky bluegrass (*Poa pratensis* L.) and a study of persistence of siduron (1-2—methylcyclohexal)—3—phenylurea in the soil. M. S. Thesis, Ohio State University. 42 pp. 1966.

6098. Frank, A. B., R. W. Miller, and S. R. Anderson. Effect of several preemergence herbicides on growth of Kentucky bluegrass *Poa pratensis* L. Agronomy Abstracts. p. 62. 1968.

6099. Frank, E. Questions relating to cultivation of lawn grasses. First Czechoslovak Symposium on Sportturf Proceedings. pp. 253–257. 1969.

6100. Frank, P. L. The pros and cons of topdressing greens. Proceedings GCSAA Annual Turfgrass Conference. 40:15–16. 1969.

6101. Franks, J. H. Turf management equipment. The Groundsman. 20(12):20–21. 1967.

6102. Frankowski, P. Success with arsenics on 50 acres. Proceedings of the Midwest Regional Turf Conference. pp. 24–26. 1970.

6103. Frans, R. E. Turf—evaluation of new herbicides—Arkansas. 19th Annual Southern Weed Conference Research Report. pp. 118–119. 1966.

6104. Frans, R. E., and T. M. Fullerton. Herbicides for weed control in Bermuda grass turf. Arkansas Agricultural Station. Report Series. 164:1–12. 1967.

6105. Frans, R. E. and E. L. Holifield. Herbicide field evaluation trials on field crops and turf. Arkansas Agricultural Experiment Station. 241. 1963.

6106. ______. Herbicide field evaluation trials on field crops and turf. Arkansas Agricultural Experiment Station. 241. 1964.

6107. Frans, R. E. and M. A. Sprague. Chemical control of Kentucky bluegrass. Agronomy Journal. 45(3):121–122. 1953.

6108. Frans, R. E., H. R. Smith, and T. M. Fullerton. Herbicide field evaluation trials on field crops and turf. Arkansas Agricultural Experiment Station. 281. 1965.

6110. Frazer, R. L. Landscape development and maintenance around a clubhouse. Proceedings of the Texas Turfgrass Conference. 20:35–36. 1965.

6111. Frazier, S. L. How grass seedlings make turf. Proceedings of the Midwest Regional Turf Conference. pp. 43–44. 1960.

6112. Frazier, S. L., and W. H. Daniel. Turfgrass seedling development under measured environment and management conditions. Agronomy Abstracts. p. 70. 1960.

6114. Frederiksen, S. The case for preventive turf disease control. Rocky Mountain Regional Turfgrass Conference Proceedings. 8:26–38. 1961.

6115. ______. Top tips on turf disease control. International Turfgrass Conference Proceedings. 33:4. 1962.

6116. ______. The case for preventive turf disease control. Proceedings Missouri Lawn and Turf Conference. pp. 11–18. 1962.

6117. ______. Disease identification. Central Plains Turfgrass Conference. p. 1. 1962.

6118. ______. The mystery and madness of spring dead spot. Proceedings of the Midwest Regional Turf Conference. pp. 28–31. 1963.

6119. ______. Practical turf disease identification. Proceedings Missouri Lawn and Turf Conference. pp. 1–9. 1963.

6120. ______. Spring dead spot a progress report. Golf Course Reporter. 32(8):38–44. 1964.

6121. ______. Principles of snow mold control. Second Annual Intermountain Turf

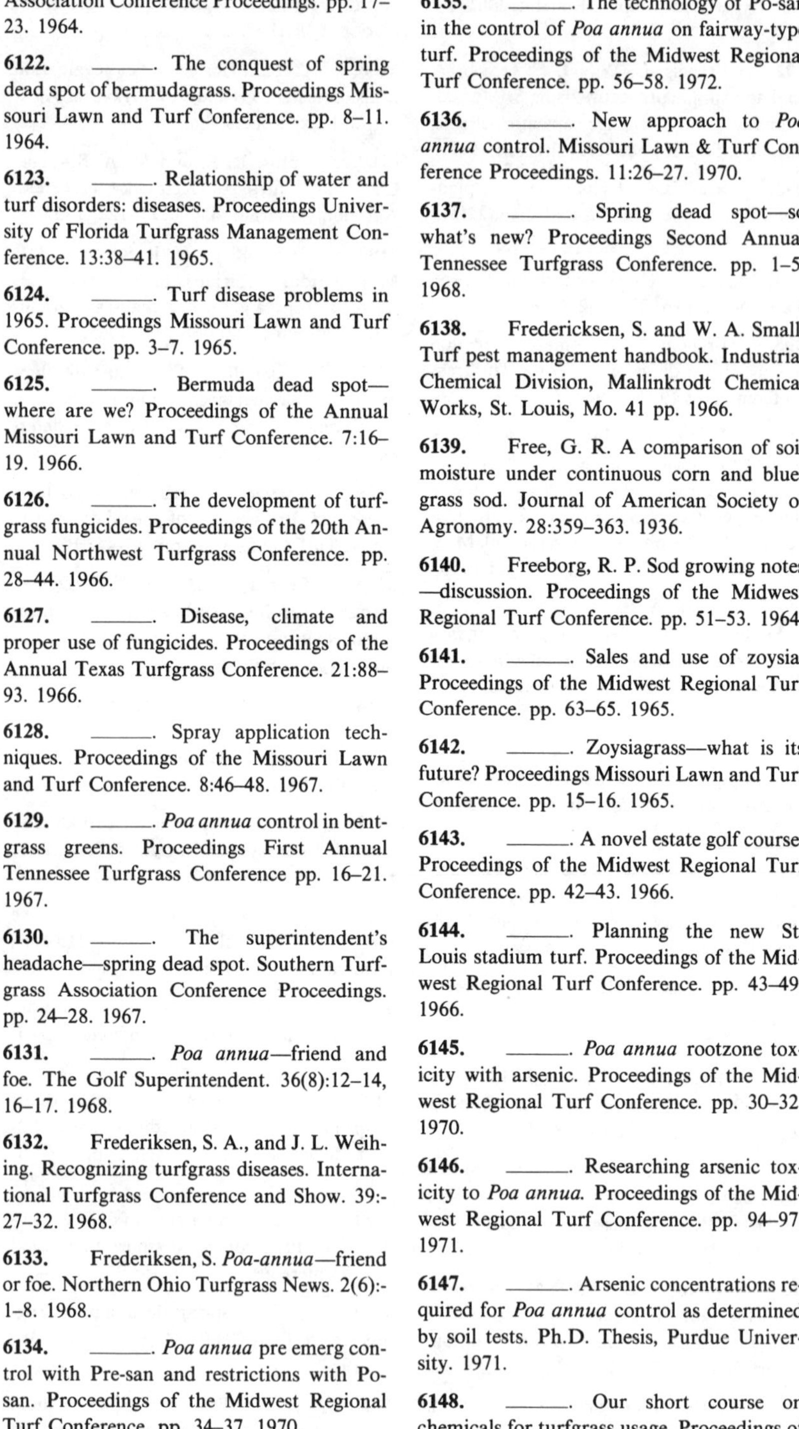

Association Conference Proceedings. pp. 17–23. 1964.

6122. ______. The conquest of spring dead spot of bermudagrass. Proceedings Missouri Lawn and Turf Conference. pp. 8–11. 1964.

6123. ______. Relationship of water and turf disorders: diseases. Proceedings University of Florida Turfgrass Management Conference. 13:38–41. 1965.

6124. ______. Turf disease problems in 1965. Proceedings Missouri Lawn and Turf Conference. pp. 3–7. 1965.

6125. ______. Bermuda dead spot—where are we? Proceedings of the Annual Missouri Lawn and Turf Conference. 7:16–19. 1966.

6126. ______. The development of turfgrass fungicides. Proceedings of the 20th Annual Northwest Turfgrass Conference. pp. 28–44. 1966.

6127. ______. Disease, climate and proper use of fungicides. Proceedings of the Annual Texas Turfgrass Conference. 21:88–93. 1966.

6128. ______. Spray application techniques. Proceedings of the Missouri Lawn and Turf Conference. 8:46–48. 1967.

6129. ______. *Poa annua* control in bentgrass greens. Proceedings First Annual Tennessee Turfgrass Conference pp. 16–21. 1967.

6130. ______. The superintendent's headache—spring dead spot. Southern Turfgrass Association Conference Proceedings. pp. 24–28. 1967.

6131. ______. *Poa annua*—friend and foe. The Golf Superintendent. 36(8):12–14, 16–17. 1968.

6132. Frederiksen, S. A., and J. L. Weihing. Recognizing turfgrass diseases. International Turfgrass Conference and Show. 39:-27–32. 1968.

6133. Frederiksen, S. *Poa-annua*—friend or foe. Northern Ohio Turfgrass News. 2(6):-1–8. 1968.

6134. ______. *Poa annua* pre emerg control with Pre-san and restrictions with Po-san. Proceedings of the Midwest Regional Turf Conference. pp. 34–37. 1970.

6135. ______. The technology of Po-san in the control of *Poa annua* on fairway-type turf. Proceedings of the Midwest Regional Turf Conference. pp. 56–58. 1972.

6136. ______. New approach to *Poa annua* control. Missouri Lawn & Turf Conference Proceedings. 11:26–27. 1970.

6137. ______. Spring dead spot—so what's new? Proceedings Second Annual Tennessee Turfgrass Conference. pp. 1–5. 1968.

6138. Fredericksen, S. and W. A. Small. Turf pest management handbook. Industrial Chemical Division, Mallinkrodt Chemical Works, St. Louis, Mo. 41 pp. 1966.

6139. Free, G. R. A comparison of soil moisture under continuous corn and bluegrass sod. Journal of American Society of Agronomy. 28:359–363. 1936.

6140. Freeborg, R. P. Sod growing notes —discussion. Proceedings of the Midwest Regional Turf Conference. pp. 51–53. 1964.

6141. ______. Sales and use of zoysia. Proceedings of the Midwest Regional Turf Conference. pp. 63–65. 1965.

6142. ______. Zoysiagrass—what is its future? Proceedings Missouri Lawn and Turf Conference. pp. 15–16. 1965.

6143. ______. A novel estate golf course. Proceedings of the Midwest Regional Turf Conference. pp. 42–43. 1966.

6144. ______. Planning the new St. Louis stadium turf. Proceedings of the Midwest Regional Turf Conference. pp. 43–49. 1966.

6145. ______. *Poa annua* rootzone toxicity with arsenic. Proceedings of the Midwest Regional Turf Conference. pp. 30–32. 1970.

6146. ______. Researching arsenic toxicity to *Poa annua.* Proceedings of the Midwest Regional Turf Conference. pp. 94–97. 1971.

6147. ______. Arsenic concentrations required for *Poa annua* control as determined by soil tests. Ph.D. Thesis, Purdue University. 1971.

6148. ______. Our short course on chemicals for turfgrass usage. Proceedings of the Midwest Regional Turf Conference. pp. 12–13. 1972.

6149. Freeborg, R. P. and W. H. Daniel. Improving the stadium field. Proceedings of the Midwest Regional Turf Conference. p. 43. 1967.

6150. ______. Atomic absorption to measure arsenic rates controlling *Poa annua* L. North Central Weed Control Conference Proceedings. 25:84–85. 1970.

6151. ______. A test to determine soil concentrations of arsenic toxic to *Poa annua.* Agronomy Abstracts. p. 46. 1971.

6152. ______. Arsenic rates for "*Poa annua*" restriction determined by soil analysis. North Central Weed Control Conference Proceedings. 26:90. 1971.

6153. ______. Arsenic retention in golf course soils. Agronomy Abstracts. 2:62. 1972.

6154. Freeborn, W. E. The sale of sod grasses in Georgia. Proceedings University of Florida Turfgrass Conference. 7:56–63. 1959.

6155. Freed, V. H. Control in lawn and turf areas. Proceedings 5th Annual Northwest Turf Conference. 5:31–33. 1951.

6156. ______. Weed control in lawn and turf areas. State College of Washington Annual Turf Conference. 4:31–33. 1951.

6157. Freeland, K. H. A new manpower source. USGA Green Section Record. 4(5):-6–8. 1967.

6158. Freeman, T. E. The turf disease situation. Proceedings University of Florida Turfgrass Conference. 4:91–93. 1956.

6159. ______. Progress on turf disease problems. Proceedings University of Florida Turf Management Conference. 5:88–90. 1957.

6160. ______. A new *Helminthosporium* disease of bermudagrass. Plant Disease Reporter. 41(5):389–391. 1957.

6161. ______. Diagnosis and control of common turf diseases. Proceedings University of Florida Turf Management Conference. 6:18–20. 1958.

6162. ______. Progress in disease problems. Proceedings University of Florida Turf Management Conference. 6:109–112. 1958.

6163. ______. Florida isolates of dollarspot fungus stand hot weather. Florida Agricultural Experiment Station Research Report. 4(3):3. 1959.

6164. ______. Bermudagrass diseases. Proceedings University of Florida Turfgrass Conference. 7:31–32. 1959.

6165. ______. Progress on disease problems. Proceedings University of Florida Turfgrass Conference. 7:98–100. 1959.

6166. ______. A leaf spot of St. Augustinegrass caused by *Corcospora fusimaculans.* Phytopathology. 49:160–161. 1959.

6167. ______. Control dollarspot by fertilization. Sunshine State Agricultural Research Report. 5(4):17. 1960.

6168. ______. Disease control. Proceedings of University of Florida Turf-Grass Management Conference. 8:119–121. 1960.

6169. ______. Effects of temperature on cottony blight of ryegrass. Phytopathology. 50:575. 1960.

6170. ______. Fungicides and the commercial sprayman. Proceedings of University of Florida Turf-Grass Management Conference. 9:198–200. 1961.

6171. ______. Disease control. Proceedings of University of Florida Turf-Grass Management Conference. 9:222–224. 1961.

6172. ______. Gray leafspot on St. Augustinegrass. Florida Agricultural Experiment Station Research Report. 7(2):8–9. 1962.

6173. ______. Dollarspot, disease of turfgrasses in Florida. Florida Turf-Grass Association Bulletin. 9(4):4–5. 1962.

6174. ______. Disease control recommendations. Proceedings University of Florida Turf-Grass Management Conference. 10:160–161. 1962.

6175. ______. Turf disease research. Proceedings University of Florida Turf-Grass Management Conference. 10:198–200. 1962.

6176. ______. Gray leafspot. Florida Turfgrass Association Bulletin. 10(1):6–7. 1963.

6177. ______. Turf grass disease research. Proceedings of University of Florida Turf-Grass Management Conference. 11:-152–154. 1963.

6178. ______. Age of ryegrass in relation to damage by *Pythium aphanidermatum.* The Plant Disease Reporter. 47(9):844. 1963.

6179. ______. Disease. Proceedings of the Florida Turfgrass Management Conference. 12:87. 1964.

6180. ______. Turf disease research. Proceedings University of Florida Turf-Grass Management Conference. 12:142–145. 1964.

6181. ______. Age of ryegrass in relation to damage by *Pythium aphanidermatum.* Florida Turfgrass Association Bulletin. 11(1):7. 1964.

6182. ______. *Helminthosporium* diseases of bermudagrass. Golf Course Reporter. 32(5):24–26. 1964.

6183. ______. Influence of nitrogen on severity of *Piricularia grisea* infection of St. Augustinegrass. Phytopathology. 54:1187–1189. 1964.

6184. ______. Turf-disease research, 1964–65. Proceedings University of Florida Turf Grass Management Conference. 13:-133–138. 1965.

6185. ______. Rust of *zoysia* spp. in Florida. The Plant Disease Reporter. 49(5):-382. 1965.

6186. ______. A rust disease of zoysiagrass new to Florida. Florida Turf-Grass Association Bulletin, 13(1):1. 1966.

6187. ______. Turf disease research: 1965–66. Proceedings University of Florida Turf Grass Management Conference. 14:-159–161. 1966.

6188. ______. Diseases of southern turf grasses. Florida Agricultural Experiment Station Bulletin. 773:1–31. 1967.

6189. ______. Control of gray leafspot disease of St. Augustinegrass. Florida Turf Association Bulletin. 4(4):6. 1957.

6190. ______. Evaluation of turf fungicides. Proceedings University of Florida Turf-Grass Management Conference. 15:-102–104. 1967.

6191. ______. Factors affecting occurrence of turf diseases. Florida Turf. 1(3):3–4. 1968.

6192. ______. Developments in disease control. Proceedings of the University of Florida Turfgrass Management Conference. 16:85–86. 1968.

6193. ______. New fungicides for *Pythium* control. Florida Turf-Grass. 7:4–5. 1968.

6194. Freeman, T. E. and H. G. Meyers. *Pythium* blight of turfgrasses. Florida Turf Grower. 3(1):6. 1968.

6195. Freeman, T. E. Diseases of southern turfgrasses. Florida Agricultural Experimental State Bulletin. 713A. 31 pp. 1969.

6196. ______. Diseases of turfgrasses. Annual Research Report of the Institute of Food & Agricultural Sciences, Univ. of Florida. p. 112. 1969.

6197. ______. Algae control with fungicides. Florida Turf. 2(1):1. 1969.

6198. ______. Developments in turfgrass disease control. Proceedings Florida Turfgrass Management Conference. 17:91–93. 1969.

6199. ______. Diseases of turfgrasses in warm-humid regions. Proceedings First International Turfgrass Research Conference. 340–345. 1969.

6200. ______. Influence of nitrogen sources on growth of *Sclerotinia homeocarpa.* Phytopathology. 59(2):114. 1969.

6201. ______. Diseases of warm season grasses. Annual Research Report of the Institute of Food & Agricultural Sciences, University of Florida. p. 117. 1970.

6202. ______. Developments in disease control. Proceedings Florida Turfgrass Management Conference. 18:94–95. 1970.

6203. ______. A seed disorder of bermuda grass caused by *Helminthosporium spiciferum.* The Plant Disease Reporter. 54(5):358–359. 1970.

6204. ______. Development in disease control. Florida Turf-Grass Management Conference Proceedings. 19:121–122. 1971.

6205. ______. Diseases of warm-season turfgrasses. Proceedings of Scotts Turfgrass Research Conference. 2:31–41. 1971.

6206. Freeman, J. F. and P. Frields. Herbicides on bluegrass sod for production of corn without tillage. Kentucky Agricultural Experiment Station Annual Report. 78:29. 1965.

6207. Freeman, T. E. and G. C. Horn. Reaction of turfgrasses to attack by *Pythium aphanidermatum* (Edson) Fitzpatrick. The Plant Disease Reporter. 47(5):425–427. 1963.

6208. ______. Reaction of turfgrasses to attack by *Pythium aphanidermatum* (Edson) Fitzpatrick. Florida Turfgrass Association Bulletin. 12(4):7–8. 1965.

6209. ______. Promising new fungicides for *Pythium* control. Florida Turf-Grass Association Bulletin. 13(4):7. 1966.

6210. ______. *Pythium* fungicides. Golf Superintendent. 35(2):58–60. 1967.

6211. ______. Effect of temperature on development of cottony blight of annual ryegrass. Sourcebook of Laboratory Exercises in Plant Pathology. pp. 387. 1967.

6212. Freeman, T. E., and H. H. Luke. Effect of light on sporulation of *Helminthosporium stenspilum.* Phytopathology. 57:811. 1967.

6213. ______. Influence of light on sporulation by *Helminthosporium stenospilum.* Phytopathology. 59(3):271–273.

6214. Freeman, T. E. and H. G. Meyers. Control of cottony blight disease *(Pythium)* on southern golf courses. Southern Golf Courses. 1(1):6, 8.

6215. ______. Control of *Pythium* blight. Golf Superintendent. 37(5):24–25, 44–45. 1969.

6216. Freeman, T. E., and R. T. Miller. Turf diseases. Proceedings University of Florida Turf-Grass Management Conference. 16:19–21. 1968.

6217. Freeman, T. E. and R. S. Mullin. Turfgrass disease control guide. Florida Agricultural Extension Circular. 221:1–7. 1962.

6218. ______. Turfgrass diseases and their control. Florida Agricultural Extension Circular 221B. 1966.

6219. ______. Turfgrass diseases and their control. Florida Agricultural Extension Circular. 221–C. 1968.

6220. Freeman, J. F. and C. H. Slack. Response of seedling Kentucky bluegrass to siduron. Kentucky Agricultural Experiment Station. Annual Report. 79:20. 1965.

6221. Freeman, J. F., R. E. Sigafus and T. W. Waldrep. Control of red sorrel and *Galium pedemontanum* in seed fields of Kentucky bluegrass. Kentucky Agricultural Experiment Station Annual Report. 76:24. 1963.

6222. Frelich, J. R. Emergence force of forage seedlings and emergence of grass seedlings through wax crusts. M.S. Thesis, University of Nevada. 1969.

6223. French, D. F. Environmental consideration—a common sense approach to planning. Short Course on Roadside Development (Ohio). 13:4–12. 1971.

6224. French, G. T. Spraying to eradicate dandelions from lawns. New York (Geneva) Agricultural Experiment Station. Bulletin No. 335. p. 35–43. 1911.

6226. Freyman, S. The nature of ice-sheet injury to forage plants. Ph.D. Thesis, University of British Columbia. pp. 1–100. 1967.

6227. ______. Effects of clipping on pinegrass. Canadian Journal of Plant Science. 50(6):736–739. 1970.

6228. Freyman, S. and V. C. Brink. Low temperature injury of turfgrass. Proceedings of the 19th Annual Northwest Turfgrass Conference. pp. 32–38. 1965.

6229. ______. Ice-sheet injury to turf. Proceedings of the 20th Annual Northwest Turfgrass Conference. pp. 64–68. 1966.

6230. Fribourg, H. A., R. H. Brown, G. M. Prine, and T. H. Taylor. Aspects of the microclimate at five locations in the southeastern United States. Southern Cooperative Series Bulletin 124. 72 pp. 1967.

6231. Friday, D. T. New fertilizers and techniques for application to the roadside. Short Course on Roadside Development (Ohio). 13:67–74. 1954.

6232. ______. Advancement in erosion control protection by fertilizer. Ohio Short Course on Roadside Development. 20:106–113. 1961.

6233. Friend, R. B. The Asiatic beetle in Connecticut; *Anomala orientalis* as a lawn pest. Connecticut Agricultural Experiment Station Bulletin. 304:858–664. 1929.

6234. Frierson, P. E. The medfly and similar problems in the movement of turf nursery stock. Proceedings University of Florida Turfgrass Conference. 4:69–73. 1956.

6235. ______. Turf certification at the retail level. Proceedings University of Florida Turf-Grass Management Conference. 9:141–143. 1961.

6236. ______. The place of turf certification, now and in the future. Proceedings University of Florida Turf-Grass Management Conference. 10:17–19. 1962.

6237. Frisch, D. M. and M. A. Charles. Deamination of 4-aminopyrimidine nucleosides by extracts of rye grass *(Lolium perenne).* Plant Physiology. 41(3):475–478. 1966.

6238. Frischknecht, N. C. Seedling emergence and survival of range grasses in central Utah. Agronomy Journal. 43(4):177–182. 1951.

6239. ______. Effects of presowing vernalization on survival and development of several grasses. Journal of Range Management. 12:280–286. 1959.

6242. Frost, K. R. Efficiency of sprinkler irrigation. Sprinkler Irrigation Association Open Technical Conference Proceedings. pp. 33–37. 1964.

6243. Fry, A. W. and E. J. Hunter. How to buy an irrigation system for a sod farm. Weeds, Trees and Turf. 5(9):20–21. 1966.

6244. Fryer, J. D., and R. J. Chancellor. Effect of dalapon on *Agropyron repens, Agrostis gigantea,* and *A. stolonitera.* British Weed Control Conference Proceedings. pp. 208–213. 1960.

6245. Fuchigami, T. Dallisgrass control. California Turfgrass Culture. 7(1):8. 1957.

6246. ______. Chemical calculations in turfgrass management. Southern California Turfgrass Culture. 7(3):22–24. 1957.

6247. ______. How to remove 2,4–D from spray equipment. Landscaping. 3(8):-16–17. 1957.

6248. ______. Vegetative propation of grasses. Southern California Turf Culture Quarterly. 8(3):19–20. 1958.

6249. ______. Application rates for selective herbicides. Landscaping. 3(8):16–17. 1958.

6250. Fuchigami, T. and V. T. Youngner. Kikuyugrass, *Pennisetum clandestinum* and its control. California Turfgrass Culture. 3(4):31. 1953.

6251. ______. Kikuyugrass, *Pennisetum clandestinum* and its control. Southern California Turf Culture Quarterly. 8(4):31–32. 1958.

6252. ______. Crabgrass control tests-1959. Southern California Turf Culture. 9(4):32. 1959.

6253. Fuchs, E. J. Artificial turf—care and usage. Proceedings of the Midwest Regional Turf Conference. pp. 77–79. 1972.

6254. Fuchs, W. W. A fundamental lesson on plant diseases. Proceedings of the Annual Missouri Lawn and Turf Conference. 7:11–12. 1966.

6255. Fudge, J. G. Some facts about fertilizers. Golf Course Reporter. 21(1):5–8. 1953.

6256. Fugina, C. E. How Arcadia builds sand greens that satisfy member demand. Golfdom. 5(7):42, 46, 48. 1931.

6257. Fujioka, G. Winter control and irrigation in golf course. KGU Green Section Turf Research Bulletin. 6:1–21. 1964.

6258. Fujioka, Y. Turf diseases in Hiroshima prefecture. KGU Green Section Turf Research Bulletin. 15:39–44. 1968.

6259. ______. Spore-types of *Curvularia* sp. KGU Green Section Turf Research Bulletin. 18:35–40. 1970.

6260. Fukuchi, F. K. Stadium turf problems solved by work, ingenuity. Park Maintenance. 9(9):6–8. 1956.

6261. Fuller, W. H. Alkali conditions affecting turf culture. Proceedings of the Arizona Turfgrass Conference. pp. 17–20. 1953.

6262. ______. Alkali conditions affecting turf culture. Golf Course Reporter. 23(3):-13–16. 1955.

6263. Fuller, W. H. and K. G. Clark. Microbiological studies on urea-formaldehyde preparations. Soil Science Society of America Proceedings. 12:198–202. 1947.

6264. Fuller, W. W., W. C. Elder, B. B. Tucker, and W. E. McMurphy. Tall fescue in

Oklahoma. Oklahoma Agricultural Experiment Station. Progress Report P-650. 1–22. 1971.

6265. Fullerton, T. M., A. M. Davis and R. E. Frans. The effect of selected preemergence herbicides and fertilizer levels on the establishment of several turfgrasses. 20th Annual Southern Weed Conference Proceedings. pp. 69–74. 1967.

6266. Fullerton, T. M., A. E. Spooner, C. L. Murdoch, and R. E. Frans. DCPA effects on establishment and winter hardiness of bermudagrass as influenced by date of planting. Agronomy Abstracts. p. 63. 1968.

6267. Fullmer, F. S. Metering dry fertilizers and soil amendments into irrigation systems. Better Crops with Plant Food. pp. 8–14. 1950.

6268. Fulton, J. Birds, big greens aid, deserve fullest club protection. Golfdom. 5(5):-86, 88–89. 1931.

6269. Fults, J. L. Somatic chromosome complements in *Bouteloua.* American Journal of Botany. 29:45–55. 1942.

6270. ______. Outsmarting weeds. Rocky Mountain Regional Turf Conference Proceedings. 1:3–10. 1954.

6271. ______. Colorado turfgrasses. Colorado Agricultural and Mechanical College Extension Service. Circular 2663. 28 pp. 1956.

6272. ______. Basic facts about grasses and a key for identification; Colorado turfgrasses. Colorado Agricultural Extension Circular. 201A:1–28. 1959.

6273. ______. Colorado turfgrasses; basic facts about grasses and a key for identification. Colorado State University Agricultural Extension Service Circular 201–A. 28 pp. 1961.

6274. ______. The crabgrass problem—a progress report. Rocky Mountain Regional Turfgrass Conference Proceedings. 8:48–50. 1961.

6275. ______. The crabgrass problem—a progress report. Research Progress Western Weed Control Conference. pp. 32–34. 1962.

6276. ______. The crabgrass problem-1966. Proceedings of GCSAA Annual Turfgrass Conference. 37:37–41. 1966.

6277. ______. Importance of weed, disease, and insect control in sod production. Rocky Mountain Regional Turfgrass Conference. 12:18. 1966.

6278. ______. Grasses for saline and alkali areas. Annual Rocky Mountain Regional Turfgrass Conference Proceedings. 18:44–55. 1972.

6279. Fults, J. L., J. May, and A. Moser. Synergism, antagonism, and compatibility between preemergence grass herbicides. Proceedings Western Weed Control Conference. pp. 15–16. 1963.

6280. Fulwider, J. Topdressing experiences with greens at Century. Turf Clippings. University of Massachussetts. 1(5):A–5 to A–6. 1960.

6281. ______. Golf course tee maintenance. Turf Clippings. University of Massachusetts. 1(9):A–32 to A–33. 1964.

6282. ______. Topdressing. USGA Green Section Record. 5(6):26–27. 1968.

6283. ______. Topdressing. Proceedings GCSAA Annual Turfgrass Conference. 40:-13–14. 1969.

6284. Fulwider, J. R. and R. E. Engel. Preemergence control of goosegrass in turf areas. Proceedings of the Northeastern Weed Control Conference. pp. 138–139. 1958.

6285. ______. The effect of temperature and light on germination of seed of goosegrass *(Eleusine indica).* Weeds. 7(3):359–361. 1959.

6286. ______. Seed characteristics and control of goosegrass, *Elusine indica.* USGA Journal and Turf Management. 12(7):24–27. 1960.

6287. Funk, C. R. New turfgrass varieties. Rutgers University Short Course in Turf Management. 32:57–58. 1964.

6288. ______. Red fescue for New Jersey lawns. Rutgers University Short Course in Turf Management. 1 p. 1965.

6289. ______. Ryegrass for New Jersey lawns. Rutgers University Short Course in Turf Management. 3 pp. 1965.

6290. ______. Kentucky bluegrass for New Jersey lawns. Rutgers University Short Course in Turf Management. 12 pp. 1965.

6291. ______. Expression of apomixis in Kentucky bluegrass *(Poa pratensis* L.) Turfgrass Research, New Jersey Agricultural Experiment Station. Bulletin 816. pp. 5–7. 1966.

6292. ______. Turfgrass breeding. Seed World. 98(10):16–18. 1966.

6293. ______. Turfgrass breeding in New Jersey. Turfgrass Research. New Jersey Agricultural Experiment Station. Bulletin 816. pp. 3–5. 1966.

6294. ______. Advances in breeding cool season turfgrasses. Proceedings GCSAA Annual Turfgrass Conference. 40:24–28. 1969.

6295. ______. New turfgrass varieties. Mid-Atlantic Superintendents Conference Proceedings. pp. 22–24. 1969.

6296. ______. Blending bluegrass varieties. Ohio Turfgrass Conference Proceedings. pp. 5–8. 1969.

6297. ______. Turfgrasses for the seventies. Turf-grass Times. 5(3):20, 34. 1970.

6298. ______. New bluegrasses and ryegrasses. USGA Green Section Record. 8(2):-22–24. 1970.

6299. ______. Turfgrass breeding at Rutgers. Green World. 1:6–7. 1971.

6300. ______. Fluorescence and ryegrass breeding. Weeds, Trees and Turf. 11(5):28. 1972.

6301. Feucht, J. R. Winter watering. The Golf Superintendent. 41(1):34. 1973.

6302. Funk, C. R. and M. K. Ahmed. New varieties of Kentucky bluegrass. Green World. 1(2):1–2. 1971.

6303. ______. How the turfgrass plant reproduces. Proceedings 1972 3-Day Turf Courses, Rutgers University. pp. 23–27. 1972.

6304. Funk, C. R., and R. E. Engel. Performance of Kentucky bluegrass varieties and various sources of common Kentucky bluegrass. Rutgers University Turfgrass Short Course. pp. 21–28. 1963.

6305. ______. Effect of cutting height and fertilizer on species composition and turf quality ratings of various turfgrass mixtures. Rutgers University Turfgrass Short Course. pp. 47–56. 1963.

6306. ______. Performance of Kentucky bluegrass varieties and various sources of common Kentucky bluegrass—1957 test. Rutgers University Short Course in Turf Management. 32:21–28. 1964.

6307. ______. Effect of cutting height and fertilizer on species composition and turf quality ratings of various turfgrass mixtures. Rutgers University Short Course in Turf Management. 32:47–56. 1964.

6308. ______. Influence of variety, fertility level and cutting height on weed invasion of Kentucky bluegrass. Proceedings of the Northeastern Weed Control Conference. pp. 480–485. 1966.

6309. ______. Influence of variety, fertility level and cutting height on weed invasion of Kentucky bluegrass. Rutgers University Turfgrass Short Course. 34:10–17. 1966.

6310. ______. Performance of Kentucky bluegrass, perennial ryegrass and tall fescue varieties. Turfgrass Research. New Jersey Agricultural Experiment Station. Bulletin 818. pp. 67–71. 1967.

6311. Funk, C. R. and S. J. Han. Recurrent intraspecific hybridization: a proposed method of breeding Kentucky bluegrass, *Poa pratensis.* Turfgrass Research. New Jersey Agricultural Experiment Station. Bulletin 818. pp. 3–14. 1967.

6312. Funk, C. R. and G. W. Pepin. New developments in Kentucky bluegrass. The Golf Superintendent. 39(6):22–26. 1971.

6313. Funk, C. R., W. K. Dickson, and M. K. Ahmed. Kentucky bluegrass blends for sod. Proceedings 1972 3-Day Turf Courses, Rutgers University. pp. 18–22. 1972.

6314. ______. Kentucky bluegrass blends for sod. Western Landscaping News. 12:6–14. 1972.

6315. Funk, C. R., R. E. Engel, and W. K. Dickson. Promising new turfgrass varieties for New Jersey. Rutgers University. College of Agriculture and Environmental Science. Lawn and Utility Turf Section. pp. 31–35. 1969.

6316. ______. Promising new turfgrass varieties for New Jersey. Rutgers University Short Course in Turf Management. 5 pp. 1969.

6317. Funk, C. R., R. E. Engel, and P. M. Halisky. Performance of Kentucky bluegrass varieties as influenced by fertility level and cutting height. Turfgrass Research. New Jersey Agricultural Experiment Station. Bulletin 816. pp. 7–21. 1966.

6318. ______. Performance of bentgrass varieties and selections. Turfgrass Research. New Jersey Agricultural Experiment Station. Bulletin 816. pp. 41–44. 1966.

6319. ______. Clonal evaluation of selections of Kentucky bluegrass, *Poa pratensis* L. Turfgrass Research. New Jersey Agricultural Experiment Station. Bulletin 818. pp. 55–67. 1967.

6320. ______. Summer survival of turfgrass species as influenced by variety, fertility level and disease incidence. Turfgrass Research. New Jersey Agricultural Experiment Station. Bulletin. pp. 71–77. 1967.

6321. ______. Ecological factors affecting turf performance and disease reaction of varietal blends of Kentucky bluegrass. Agronomy Abstracts. p. 63. 1968.

6322. ______. Regional adaptation of bluegrass blends. Park Maintenance. 23(7):-17–18. 1970.

6323. Funk, C. R. and R. E. Engel, and H. W. Indyk. Ryegrass in New Jersey. Turfgrass Research. New Jersey Agricultural Experiment Station. Bulletin 816. pp. 59–67. 1966.

6324. Funk, C. R., P. M. Halisky, and P. L. Babinsky. *Helminthosporium* leaf spot and crown rot of Kentucky bluegrass. USGA Green Section Record. 8(5):7–10. 1970.

6325. Funk, C. R., S. J. Han and W. J. Siebels. Effect of pollen parent on progeny performance and expression of apomixis in Kentucky bluegrass, *Poa pratensis* L. Turfgrass Research. New Jersey Agricultural Experiment Station. Bulletin 818. pp. 20–31. 1967.

6326. Funk, C. R., A. M. Radko, and R. J. Peterson. Bonnieblue—A new bluegrass. USGA Green Section Record. 10(5):5–6. 1972.

6327. Funk, C. R., W. K. Dickson, M. K. Ahmed, and K. J. McVeigh. Kentucky bluegrass varieties for use on New Jersey golf courses. Proceedings 1972 3-Day Turf Courses, Rutgers University. p. 28. 1972.

6328. Funk, C. R., R. E. Engel, P. M. Halisky, and W. K. Dickson. Evaluation of Kentucky bluegrass blends for turf performance, disease reaction and varietal composition. Rutgers University. College of Agriculture and Environmental Science. Lawn and Utility Turf Section. pp. 19–30. 1969.

6329. ______. Evaluation of Kentucky bluegrass blends for turf performance, disease reaction and varietal composition. Rutgers University Short Course in Turf Management. 2 pp. 1969.

6330. Funk, C. R., R. E. Engel, P. M. Halisky, R. W. Duell, and W. K. Dickson. Kentucky bluegrass varieties in New Jersey. Proceedings 1970 3-Day Short Courses, Rutgers University. pp. 8–26. 1970.

6331. Furrer, J. D. A summary of three years performance for commonly used preemergence lawn weed control herbicides under Nebraska conditions. North Central Weed Control Conference Proceedings. 24:-56–57. 1969.

6332. Furrer, J. D. and N. E. Shafer. Crabgrass control in lawns. Nebraska Agricultural Extension Circular. 159:1–4. 1950.

6333. Furtick, W. R. and F. E. Phipps. Sheep sorrel *(Rumex acetoselia)*. Research Progress Report Western Weed Control Conference. p. 8. 1962.

6336. Fushtey, S. G. Experiments on the chemical control of snow mold in turf. Canadian Plant Distribution Survey. 41(5):291–296. 1961.

6337. ______. Nematodes—are they a problem in turf? RCGA National Turfgrass Conference. 19:10–12. 1968.

6338. Gabriels, D. M. Physical properties of soils as affected by synthetic soil conditioners. M.S. Thesis, Iowa State University. 1971.

6339. Gaillard, G. E. and R. Laird. Winged Foot's new program produced fine turf. Golfdom. 29(4):56, 58. 1955.

6340. Galaktionov, I. I. Mnogoletnie gazony srednei Polosy rsfsr; ustroĭstvo iukhod ministerstva kommunal nogo khozīaīstra rsfsr. moskva. 38 pp. 1963.

6341. Gale, J. Studies on plant anti-transpirants. Plant Physiology. 14:777–786. 1961.

6342. Gallagher, F. That's not what I said. Turf Clippings. University of Massachusetts. 2(2):39–43. 1967.

6343. Gallagher, J. E. Herbicide tests. First Annual Fall Field Day on Turf Culture. U.C.L.A. pp. 28–31. 1949.

6344. ______. 2,4-D for the control of Dichondra in bentgrasses. Southern California Turf Culture. 1(3):1–2. 1951.

6345. ______. The turf plots during the past year. Southern California Turf Culture. 1(3):3. 1951.

6346. ______. Soil amendments and fertilizers. Southern California Conference on Turf Culture. pp. 11–21. 1950.

6347. ______. Fertilizers and herbicides. Southern California Conference on Turf Culture. pp. 3–5. 1951.

6348. ______. The outlook in chemical weed control on fine turf. Stockbridge School Turf Clipping, Conference Proceedings. pp. A-24–A-26. 1951.

6349. ______. Methyl bromide fumigation for turf weed control. Southern California Turf Culture. 2(1):1. 1952.

6351. ______. Patience needed to solve the compaction problem. Southern California Turf Culture. 2(4):4. 1952.

6352. ______. Methods of crabgrass control. Proceedings of the 23rd Annual Penn State Turfgrass Conference. pp. 12–21. 1954.

6353. ______. Select the right grass. Proceedings of the Southern California Turfgrass Conference. pp. 7–11. 1954.

6354. ______. Healthy turf through weed control. Proceedings of Midwest Regional Turf Conference. pp. 28–30. 1956.

6355. ______. Weed control for turf grasses. New Mexico Turfgrass Conference Proceedings. 1:9–13. 1956.

6356. ______. Weed control for turf grasses. Rocky Mountain Regional Turfgrass Conference Proceedings. 3:7–14. 1956.

6357. ______. Chemical weed control in turf. Golf Course Reporter. 25(5):5–10. 1957.

6358. ______. Chemicals for crabgrass control. Proceedings of Midwest Regional Turf Conference. pp. 48–52. 1957.

6359. ______. Control of common turf weeds. Proceedings University of Florida Turf Management Conference. 6:13–15. 1958.

6360. ______. Pre and post-emergent control of undesirables. Oklahoma Turfgrass Conference Proceedings. pp. 12–17. 1958.

6361. ______. Turfgrass weed control. Proceedings Twelfth Southeastern Turfgrass Conference. 12:11–15. 1958.

6362. ______. Turfgrass weed control. Arizona Turf Conference Proceedings. pp. 16–19. 1959.

6363. ______. Weed control—problems and control. Oklahoma Turfgrass Conference Proceedings. pp. 30–32. 1959.

6364. ______. Turfgrass weed control—current recommendations. Proceedings Northwest Turf Conference. 13:67–70. 1959.

6365. ______. Weed killer and how they act. Central Plains Turfgrass Conference. p. 2. 1961.

6366. ______. Weed control. Proceedings of University of Florida Turf-Grass Management Conference. 9:201–207. 1961.

6367. ______. Weed control. Proceedings Missouri Lawn and Turf Conference. pp. 23–28. 1961.

6368. ______. Pre-emergence crabgrass control. Golf Course Reporter. 30(3):10–12, 14, 16–17. 1962.

6369. ______. Pre-emergence control now approaches the ultimate. Golfdom. 36(4):64–66. 1962.

6370. ______. Review of pre-emergence crabgrass control. International Turfgrass Conference Proceedings. 33:8. 1962.

6371. ______. Weeds are turf problems everywhere. Turf-Grass Times. 2(6):3–5. 1967.

6372. ______. Golf-course chemicals—Yesterday, today, and tomorrow. Southeastern Turfgrass Conference Proceedings. 22:-17–22. 1968.

6373. Gallagher, J. E., and Beard, J. B. Recognizing weeds in turf. Proceedings of the Midwest Regional Turf Conference. pp. 29–31. 1960.

6374. Gallagher, J. E. and B. H. Emerson. Di sodium methyl arsonate vs. crabgrass. New York State Turf Association Bulletin 51. pp. 195–196. 1955.

6375. Gallagher, J. E., and C. C. Jack. Chickweed control test 1956–57. Proceedings 12th North Eastern Weed Control Conference. pp. 151–153. 1958.

6376. ______. Chickweed control tests 1956–1957. Proceedings of the Northeastern Weed Control Conference. pp. 151–153. 1958.

6377. Gallagher, J. E. and M. Z. Mahdi. Crabgrass trials of 1951. Southern California Turf Culture. 2(2):1–2. 1952.

6378. Gallagher, J. E. and R. J. Otten. New chemicals for preemergence crabgrass control. Proceedings of the Northeastern Weed Control Conference. pp. 149–154. 1959.

6379. ______. Preemergence crabgrass control trials, 1960. Proceedings Northeastern Weed Control Conference. 15:303–311. 1961.

6380. ______. Preemergence crabgrass control trials, 1961. Proceedings Northeastern Weed Control Conference. 16:498–501. 1962.

6381. Gallagher, J. E., R. J. Otten, and R. H. Beatty. Chemical control of *Poa annua* in bermudagrass turf. Agronomy Abstracts. p. 102. 1962.

6382. Gallagher, W. E. and F. J. Murphy. Turf preparation for the '64 Open. USGA Green Section Record. 2(1):8–9. 1964.

6383. Gallaway, B. M. Development of stablized surfaces for heavy traffic areas. Proceedings of the Texas Turfgrass Conference. 16:19–24. 1961.

6384. Galle, F. C. The control of weeds and use of soluble fertilizer. Southeastern Turfgrass Conference. 9:55–59. 1955.

6385. Galloway, H. M. and J. E. Yahner. Soils—their development and adaption to suburban uses. Proceedings of the Midwest Regional Turf Conference. pp. 50–51. 1968.

6386. Gamble, M. D. Inundation tolerance of bermudagrass. Agronomy Abstracts. p. 37. 1958.

6387. Gambrell, F. L. European chafer: a soil-inhabiting pest of grasses and nursery plantings. Farm Research. 20(4):2–3. 1954.

6388. ______. European chafer continues its fight with New York lawns. Farm Research, New York Agricultural Experiment Station. April-September:8–9. 1967.

6389. Gambrell, F. L., S. C. Mendall, and E. H. Smith. A destructive European insect new to the United States. Journal of Economic Entomology. 35(2):289. 1942.

6390. Gammon, H. Deeper roots give Bermuda new life. Golfdom. 39(8):24. 1965.

6391. Gandert, D. Rasen. Bedeutung, anlage, pflege. Deutscher Landwirtschaftsverlag. Berlin. 156 pp. 1960.

6392. Gandert, K. D., and H. Roth. The utilization of lawn areas on sports grounds. First Czechoslovak Symposium on Sportturf Proceedings. pp. 69–76. 1969.

6393. Gane, R. The effect of temperature, humidity and atmosphere on the viability of chewings fescue grass seed in storage. Journal of Agricultural Science. 38(1):90–92. 1948.

6394. Ganem, R. Modernizing—when, why, how. Golfdom. 41(3):24–26, 92–112. 1967.

6395. Garabedian, S. Maintaining a night lighted course. Turf Clippings. University of Massachusetts. 1(10):A65–A66. 1965.

6397. Gardiner, J. G. "Wetter" water solves turf compaction problem. Park Maintenance. 10(4):28–30. 1957.

6398. Gardner, A. L. and I. V. Hunt. Inter-varietal competition in perennial ryegrass swords. Journal of the British Grassland Society. 18:285–291. 1963.

6399. Gardner, C. The operation and maintenance of internal combustion engines commonly used in turf maintenance. Proceedings of Midwest Regional Turf Conference. pp. 14–32. 1950.

6400. Gardner, F. P. and W. E. Loomis. Floral induction and development in orchard grass. Plant Physiology. 28(2):201–217. 1953.

6402. Gardner, J. L. Studies in tillering. Ecology. 23:162–174. 1942.

6403. Gardner, W. H. Synthetic soil conditioners and their applications. Proceedings 6th Annual Northwest Turf Conference. 6:-13–19. 1952.

6404. ______. How water moves in the soil. Crops and Soils. pp. 7–9. 1962.

6405. ______. How water moves in the soil. Turf Bulletin. 7(1):3–8. 1970.

6406. Gardner, W. H. and J. C. Hatch. Water movement in soils. California Turfgrass Culture. 12(1):5. 1962.

6407. Gardner, W. R. Dynamic aspects of water availability to plants. Soil Science. 89:63–73. 1960.

6408. ______. Measurement of capillary conductivity and diffusivity with a tensiometer. 7th International Congress of Soil Science Transactions. 1:300–305. 1960.

6409. Garman, H. and E. C. Vaughn. The curing of bluegrass seeds as affecting their viability. Kentucky Agricultural Experiment Station Bulletin. 198:27–39. 1916.

6410. Garmen, W. L. A study of the physical properties of golf greens in Oklahoma. Oklahoma-Texas Turf Conference Proceedings. pp. 44–47. 1949.

6411. ______. Physical properties of soil as applied to turf management. Oklahoma-Texas Turf Conference Proceedings. pp. 89–94. 1950.

6412. ______. Permeability of various grades of sand and peat and mixtures of these with soil and vermiculite. USGA Journal and Turf Management. 5(1):27–28. 1952.

6413. Garmhausen, W. J. Establishing turf on Ohio's roadsides. Proceedings of Midwest Regional Turf Conference. pp. 55–60. 1948.

6414. ______. New thoughts on roadside turf. Landscape Architecture. 49(2):86–90. 1958.

6415. ______. Parkway and roadside development modern methods of maintenance. Park Maintenance. 20(9):16–18. 1967.

6416. Garmhausen, W. J. and W. H. Collins. Highway medians. Parks and Recreation. 3(9):47, 98, 99. 1968.

6417. Garnder, W. A. Effect of light on germination of light-sensitive seeds. Botanical Gazette. 71(4):249–288. 1921.

6418. Garner, E. S. Kikuyu grass. USGA Green Section Bulletin. 5:252–253. 1925.

6419. ______. The low-down on bent grass. The National Greenkeeper. 2(12):5–6, 20. 1928.

6420. ______. Stolons vs. seeds. The National Greenkeeper. 3(4):25–28. 1929.

6421. ______. Turf experiments at Rhode Island Experiment Station. USGA Green Section Bulletin. 8(12):254–255. 1929.

6422. Garner, E. S., and S. C. Damon. The persistence of certain lawn grasses as affected by fertilization and competition. Rhode Island Agricultural Experiment Station Bulletin 217. 22 pp. 1929.

6424. Garrett, J. C. Planting and care of lawns. Oklahoma Agricultural Extension Circular. 545:1–8.

6425. ______. Better lawns for Oklahoma. Oklahoma Agricultural Extension Circular. 703:1–23. 1960.

6426. Garrett, R. C. Buried aluminum irrigation pipe. Turf Clippings. University of Massachusetts. 1(10):A15–A21. 1965.

6427. Garrison, C. S. Seed production studies with crownvetch. Second Crownvetch Symposium. Pennsylvania State University. 6:50–52. 1968.

6428. Gartner, J. B. and J. D. Butler. A soil test survey of golf greens. Illinois Turfgrass Conference Proceedings. 9:24–34. 1968.

6429. Garton, J. E. Calculation of amount of fertilizer for lawns. Oklahoma Agricultural Experiment Station Miscellaneous Publication. 38:1–4. 1954.

6430. Garwood, E. A. Growth, water-use, and nutrient uptake from the subsoil by a grass sward. Experiments in Progress. The Grassland Research Institute. Annual Report for 1963–1964. 17:51–52. 1965.

6431. ______. Seasonal variation in appearance and growth of grass roots. Journal of the British Grassland Society. 22(2):121–130. 1967.

6432. ______. Some effects of soil water conditions and soil temperature on the roots of grasses. Journal of the British Grassland Society. 22(3):176–181. 1967.

6433. Garwood, E. A. and T. E. Williams. Soil water use and growth of a grass sward. Journal of Agricultural Science. 68(2):281–292. 1967.

6434. ______. Growth, water use, and nutrient uptake from the subsoil by grass swards. Journal of Agricultural Science. 69(1):125–130. 1967.

6435. Gary, J. E. The vegetative establishment of four major turfgrasses and the response of stolonized "Meyer" zoysiagrass (*Zoysia japonica* var. Meyer) to mowing height, nitrogen fertilization, and light intensity. M.S. Thesis, Mississippi State University, pp. 1–50. 1967.

6436. Gary, J. E., and C. Y. Ward. The influence of shading on the establishment of Meyer zoysiagrass. Proceedings of the Association of Southern Agricultural Workers. 64:70. 1967.

6437. Gaskin, T. A. Abnormalities of grass roots and their relationship to root knot nematodes. Plant Disease Reporter. 43(1):-25–26. 1959.

6438. ______. To introduce a turfgrass. Illinois Turfgrass Conference Proceedings. 4:16–18. 1963.

6439. ______. Effect of shading on turfgrass. Agronomy Abstracts. p. 101. 1964.

6440. ______. Effect of pre-emergence crabgrass herbicides on rhizome development in Kentucky bluegrass. Agronomy Journal. 56(3):340–342. 1964.

6441. ______. Methods of testing turfgrasses. Illinois Turfgrass Conference Proceedings. 5:64–74. 1964.

6442. ______. How bluegrass develops. Proceedings of the Midwest Regional Turf Conference. pp. 45–48. 1964.

6443. ______. Growing turfgrass in shade. Park Maintenance. 17(10):90–94. 1964.

6444. ______. Susceptibility of bluegrass to root-knot nematodes. The Plant Disease Reporter. 49(1):89–90. 1965.

6445. ______. Varietal reaction of creeping bentgrass to stripe smut. The Plant Disease Reporter. 49(3):268. 1965.

6446. ______. Varietal reaction of Kentucky bluegrass to *Septoria* leaf spot *(Septoria macropoda).* The Plant Disease Reporter. 49(9):802. 1965.

6447. ______. Varietal resistance to flag smut in Kentucky bluegrass. The Plant Disease Reporter. 49(12):1017. 1965.

6448. ______. Effect of pre-emergence crabgrass herbicides on rhizome development in Kentucky bluegrass. Turf Bulletin. Massachusetts Turf & Lawn Grass Council. 2(12):11–12. 1965.

6449. ______. Testing for drought and heat resistance in Kentucky bluegrass. Agronomy Journal. 58(4):461–462. 1966.

6450. ______. Evidence for physiologic races of stripe smut *(Ustilago striiformis)* attacking Kentucky bluegrass. The Plant Disease Reporter. 50(6):430–431. 1966.

6451. ______. Bluegrass. Park Maintenance. 24(7):20. 1971.

6452. Gaskin, T. A. and M. P. Britton. The effect of powdery mildew on the growth of Kentucky bluegrass. Plant Disease Reporter. 46(10):724–725. 1962.

6453. Gaskin, T. A. and J. A. Simmons. Chemical control of stripe smut on Kentucky bluegrass. Agronomy Abstracts. p. 38. 1966.

6454. Gasser, J. K. R., and A. Penny. The value of urea nitrate and urea phosphate as nitrogen fertilizers for grass and barley. Journal of Agricultural Science. 69(1):139–148. 1967.

6455. Gates, A. J. The health of turf (in a satisfactory and an inferior turf-grass area) a comparative study. B.S. Thesis, University of British Columbia. 1969.

6456. Gates, D. H. Revegetation of a high-altitude, barren slope in Northern Idaho. Journal of Range Management. 15(6):314–318. 1962.

6457. Gauch, H. G. What makes grass grow. Proceedings of the Mid-Atlantic Association of Greenskeepers Conference. pp. 49–53. 1951.

6458. Gault, J. Golf courses—scenic effect and hazards. The Greenkeepers' Reporter. 7(1):34, 36. 1939.

6459. ______. Wartime turf maintenance in England. The Greenkeeper's Reporter. 11(1):11–12. 1943.

6460. Geer, W. C. Moles. USGA Green Section Bulletin. 3(11):295. 1923.

6461. Geisler, F. A study of pollen grains of thirty-two species of grasses. Butler University Botanical Studies. 7:65–73. 1945.

6462. Gentry, C. E., L. Henson and R. A. Chapman. Relationship between certain fungal diseases and perloline content of tall fescue. Kentucky Agricultural Experiment Station Annual Report. 81:81. 1968.

6463. ______. Alkaloids in tall fescue. Kentucky Agricultural Experiment Station Annual Report. 81:81–82. 1968.

6464. Gentry, C. E., R. A. Chapman, L. Henson, and R. C. Buckner. Factors affecting the alkaloid content of tall fescue (*Festuca arundinacea* Schreb.) Agronomy Journal. 61(2):313–316. 1969.

6465. Gentry, W. E. Fertilizers—major elements. Proceedings of the Annual Texas Turfgrass Conference. 21:94–98. 1966.

6466. George, V. Creeping bent greens at the County Club of LaFayette. Ind. USGA Green Section Bulletin. 8(9):194–195. 1925.

6467. ______. Applying chemicals to greens. The National Greenkeeper. 2(10):10. 1928.

6468. ______. "When autumn comes." Golfdom. 3(8):17–18. 1929.

6469. ______. Animal vs. chemical fertilizers. The National Greenkeeper. 3(3):25–30. 1929.

6470. Gephart, D. D. Dallisgrass control. Western Landscaping News. 7(3):16. 1967.

6471. Gerber, R. Sharpening and adjusting mowers. The Greenkeepers' Reporter. 5(2):42. 1937.

6472. Gernert, W. B. Native grass behavior as affected by periodic clipping. Agronomy Journal. 28:447–456. 1936.

6473. Getzendaner, M. E. Answering critical questions about residues of agricultural chemicals. Down to Earth. 28(1):24–29. 1972.

6474. Geyer, R. My experiences in using newer grasses. Proceedings of the Midwest Regional Turf Conference. pp. 70–71. 1971.

6475. Geyer, W. A., C. E. Long, N. W. Miles, J. K. Greig, E. B. Nilson and L. D. Leuthold. Chemical weed control—herbicides for lawn and turf. Kansas State University Agricultural Experiment Station. Bulletin 533. pp. 15–17. 1970.

6476. Ghaster, G. D. Stabilized turf. Golfdom. 36(4):88–90. 1962.

6477. Gianfagna, A. J. and A. M. S. Pridham. Experiments with crabgrass seed. New York State Turf Association Bulletin 29. p. 114. 1951.

6478. ______. Some aspects of dormancy and germination of crabgrass seed, *Digitaria sanguinalis* Scop. Proceedings of the American Society for Horticultural Science. 58:-291–297. 1951.

6479. ______. Some aspects of dormancy and germination of crabgrass seed *Digitaria sanguinalis* Scop. Agri-Chem Review. 1954.

6480. Gibbens, F. W. Weed control in fine turf. New Zealand Institute for Turf Culture Newsletter. 69:9–13. 1970.

6481. ______. Modern sprays and spraying techniques. New Zealand Institute For Turf Culture Newsletter. 73:81–83. 1971.

6482. ______. Turfing v. seeding. New Zealand Institute for Turf Culture Newsletter. 74:108–109. 1971.

6483. ______. When weeds are taking over. New Zealand Institute for Turf Culture Newsletter. 77:27–33. 1972.

6484. ______. Establishment and management of turf. New Zealand Institute for Turf Culture Newsletter. 81:165–166. 1972.

6485. Gibeault, V. A. Annual meadow-grass—a major weed of fine turf? Journal of the Sports Turf Research Institute. 41:48–52. 1965.

6486. ______. The selective control of colonial bentgrass (*Agrostis tenuis* L.) with DMPA and trifluralin and the effect of DMPA on turfgrass root growth. M.S. Thesis, University of Rhode Island. 46 pp. 1965.

6487. ______. Investigations on the control of annual meadow-grass. Journal of Sports Turf Research Institute. 42:17–40 (1967). 1966.

6488. ______. A new irrigation system: who is responsible for what? Divot News. p. 5. 1970.

6489. ______. Management of newly planted areas. Southern California Turfgrass Council. California State Polytechnic College. pp. 1–4. 1970.

6490. ______. Perenniality in *Poa annua* L. Ph.D. Thesis, Oregon State University. 1971.

6491. ______. Specifications for turfgrass species. Proceedings of Southern California Turfgrass Institute. pp. 4–9. 1971.

6492. ______. Calculating irrigation needs. California Turfgrass Culture. 22(4):-28–30. 1972.

6493. ______. Guides for developing an irrigation program. Calculating irrigation needs. Turfgrass Sprinkler Irrigation Conference Proceedings. 10:35–41. 1972.

6494. Gibeault, V. A. and N. R. Goetze. Morphological characteristics of perennial plant types in the species *Poa annua* L. Agronomy Abstracts. p. 47. 1971.

6495. Gibeault, V. A. and C. R. Skogley. Effects of DMPA (Zytron) on colonial bentgrass, Kentucky bluegrass, and red fescue root growth. Crop Science. 7(4):327–329. 1967.

6496. Gibeault, V. A., and J. Van Dam. An evaluation of perennial ryegrass varieties for winter overseeding. California Turfgrass Culture. 22(2):11–13. 1972.

6497. Gibeault, V. A., J. Van Dam, and S. Spaulding. An evaluation of turfgrass mixes in the Antelope Valley. California Turfgrass Culture. 21(1):7–8. 1971.

6498. Gibeault, V. A., V. B. Youngner, and D. R. Donaldson. Tall fescue in California. California Turfgrass Culture. 22(4):25–26. 1972.

6499. Gibeault, V. A., V. B. Youngner, R. Baldwin, and J. Breece. Perennial ryegrass in California. California Turfgrass Culture. 22(2):9–11. 1972.

6500. Gibson, J. W. Weed control with repeated applications of Tordon herbicides. Turf Bulletin. Massachusetts Turf and Lawn Grass Council. 6(2):9–11. 1970.

6501. Gibson, N. H. The encyclopedia of golf. A. S. Barnes and Company, New York, N. Y. p. 15. 1958.

6502. Giddens, J., W. E. Adams, and R. N. Dawson. Nitrogen accumulation in fescuegrass sod. Agronomy Journal. 63(3):451–454. 1971.

6503. Giddens, J., H. E. Perkins, and L. C. Walker. Movement of nutrients in Coastal Bermudagrass. Agronomy Journal. 54(5):-379. 1962.

6504. Giddens, J., R. D. Hauck, W. E. Adams, and R. N. Dawson. Forms of nitrogen and nitrogen availability in fescuegrass sod. Agronomy Journal. 63(3):458–460. 1971.

6505. Gilbert, B. E. An analytical study of the putting greens of Rhode Island golf courses. Rhode Island Agricultural Experiment Station. Bulletin 212. 15 pp. 1928.

6506. Gilbert, B. E., and F. R. Pember. Tolerance of certain weeds and grasses to toxic aluminum. Soil Science. 39:425–429. 1935.

6508. Gilbert, J. H. Note on the occurrence of "fairy rings". Journal of the Linnean Society of Botany. 15(81):17–24. 1875.

6509. Gilbert, F. A., A. H. Bowers, and M. D. Sanders. Effect of nitrogen sources in complete fertilizers on bluegrass turf. Agronomy Journal. 50(6):320–323. 1958.

6510. Gilbert, W. B. Winter injury to tifgreen—history and present status. The Golf Course Reporter. 33(9):12–18. 1965.

6511. ______. Turfgrass research in the south-eastern United States. Proceedings of the First International Turfgrass Research Conference. pp. 19–26. 1969.

6512. ______. Turfgrass establishment on roadsides. Proceedings of the First International Turfgrass Research Conference. pp. 583–591. 1969.

6513. ______. Turfgrass research in the Southeast. Proceedings GCSAA Annual Turfgrass Conference. 40:31–37. 1969.

6514. Gilbert, W. B. and D. L. Davis. Relationship of potassium nutrition and temperature stresses on turfgrasses. Agronomy Abstracts. p. 52. 1967.

6515. ______. An investigation of critical problems of establishing and maintaining a satisfactory sod cover along North Carolina highways. Project ERD-110-S Final Report (1962–1966). North Carolina State University Highway Research Program. 100 pp. 1967.

6516. ______. Influence of fertility ratios on winter hardiness of bermudagrass. Agronomy Journal. 63(4):591–593. 1971.

6517. ______. Make bermudagrass winter-tough with right balanced fertility. Better Crops with Plant Food. 15(4):22–24. 1971.

6518. Gilbert, W. B. and E. E. Deal. Temporary ditch liners for erosin control and sod establishment. Agronomy Abstracts. p. 101. 1964.

6519. Gilbert, W. B. and R. D. Edwards. Physical and chemical soil factors affecting the growth of bentgrass. Agronomy Abstracts. p. 47. 1971.

6520. Giles, F. A. Grass substitutes. Illinois Turfgrass Conference Proceedings. 10:-22–25. 1969.

6521. Gill, D. The slicing machine. New Zealand Institute for Turf Culture Newsletter. 59:23. 1969.

6522. Gill, J. B. Conservation of water through use of sprinklers. Proceedings of the Annual Texas Turfgrass Conference. 9:43–49. 1954.

6523. Gill, W. J. An evaluation of overseeding procedures for southern lawns. M.S. Thesis, Mississippi State University. pp. 1–60. 1964.

6524. Gill, W. J., W. R. Thompson, and C. Y. Ward. Species and methods for overseeding bermudagrass greens. The Golf Superintendent. 35(9):10–17. 1967.

6525. Gillard, P. H. The object of the exercise. The Groundsman. 19(10):27. 1966.

6526. ______. The object of the exercise (part 2). The Groundsman. 19(11):4–8. 1966.

6527. ______. An introduction to golf course maintenance. The Groundsman. 19(11):17–22. 1966.

6528. ______. The object of the exercise (part 3). The Groundsman. 19(12):14–20. 1966.

6529. ______. Bowling green maintenance. The Groundsman. 20(1):4–12. 1966.

6530. ______. The object of the exercise (Part 4). The Groundsman. 20(1):24. 1966.

6531. ______. The object of the exercise (Part 5). The Groundsman. 20(2):8–10. 1966.

6532. ______. The object of the exercise (Part 6). The Groundsman. 20(3):12. 1966.

6533. ______. Theory v. practice. The Groundsman. 20(4):4–6. 1966.

6534. ______. Golf courses revisited. The Groundsman. 21(10):12–13. 1968.

6535. Gillespie, N. Turf grasses—panel discussion. North California Turf Conference. pp. 34–41. 1951.

6536. ______. Never too late to save a lawn; but the battle is a tough one. Southern Seedsman. 20(9):30–31. 1957.

6537. ______. A lawn where you live. 1001 Western Garden Questions Answered. D. Van Nostrand Co. New Jersey. pp. 22–40. 1966.

6538. Gillham, L. B. Effects of asphalt emulsions and vegetative mulches on the viability of bermudagrass sprigs. M. S. Thesis. Oklahoma State University. 42 pp. 1970.

6539. Gillham, L. B., and W. W. Huffine. Effects of asphalt emulsions and vegetative mulches on the viability of bermudagrass sprigs. Agronomy Abstracts. p. 53. 1969.

6540. Gillie, R. E. Progress with athletic fields. Proceedings of the Midwest Regional Turf Conference. pp. 72–74. 1972.

6541. Gilliland, H. B. Experiments on the vegetative propagation of *Cynodon* species. Better Turf Through Research, African Explosives and Chemical Industries Limited. pp. 86–90. 1948.

6542. Gilmour, J., F. R. Horne, E. L. Little, F. A. Staflen, and R. H. Richens. International code of nomenclature of cultivated plants—1969. International Bureau for Plant Taxonomy and Nomenclature. 32 pp. 1969.

6543. Giordano, P. M. and J. A. DeFrance. Chickweed control in lawn turf with chemicals. Proceedings of the Northeastern Weed Control Conference. pp. 300–303. 1960.

6544. Giordano, P. M. and C. R. Skogley. A study of the effects of various formulations of chlordane on new stands of turfgrass. Proceedings Northeastern Weed Control Conference. 15:254–257. 1961.

6545. ______. A study of the effects of various rates and formulations of chlordane on new stands of turfgrass. Weed Abstracts. 12(3):139. 1963.

6546. Gipson, C. E. Maintenance in Mexico. Golf Course Reporter. 31(4):92–94. 1963.

6547. Gipson, S. K. Installing and using intimate mixes. Proceedings of the Midwest Regional Turf Conference. pp. 44–47. 1971.

6548. Girth, H. G. The nematode parasite of the Japanese beetle. Greenkeeper's Reporter. 7(4):40. 1939.

6549. Gist, G. R., and R. M. Smith. Root development of several common forage grasses to depth of eighteen inches. Journal of the American Society of Agronomy. 40:1036. 1948.

6550. Glenday, A. C. Soil testing of playing areas. New Zealand Institute for Turf Culture Newsletter. 31:2–3. 1964.

6551. Glenn, J. 25% saving through maintenance analysis and controls in Los Angeles. Park Maintenance. 21(1):22–26. 1968.

6552. Glenn, W. A controlled, balanced program for feeding putting greens. Turf and Landscape Clinic Proceedings, Tennessee Turfgrass Association. pp. 8–12. 1966.

6553. Glissman, H. C. An experiment put me into zoysia business. Golfdom. 27(4):-105–107. 1953.

6554. ______. Z–52 Zoysia—makes good combination with bluegrass. Parks & Recreation. 37(4):6–7. 1954.

6555. Glissmann, H. W. Maintaining turf on athletic fields. Central Plains Turfgrass Conference. pp. 58–60. 1951.

6556. Glover, W. H. Flood waters at Shawnee C. C. Greenkeeper's Reporter. 5(2):12–13, 38–40. 1937.

6557. ______. Behavior of named bents under playing use. Golfdom. 24(3):68–70, 101–105. 1950.

6558. ______. Management and environment as they effect the control of disease on bentgrass greens. Proceedings of the Mid-Atlantic Association of Greenkeepers. Conference. pp. 22–24. 1950.

6559. ______. The behavior of named strains of bentgrasses under actual play. Greenkeeping Superintendents Association National Turf Conference. 21:72–77. 1950.

6560. ______. Labor management on my course. Proceedings of Midwest Regional Turfgrass Conference. pp. 22–27. 1951.

6561. ______. Construction of bent greens with special reference to soil management. Proceedings School of Soils, Fertilization & Turf Maintenance Green Section, Royal Canadian Golf Association. pp. 5–9. 1952.

6562. ______. Mid-Atlantic "operation zoysia" exhibit "A" in cooperation. Golfdom. 27(3):65, 68–70, 110–112. 1953.

6563. ______. Operation zoysia. Park Maintenance. 7(5):18–22. 1954.

6564. Glowa, T. Turf maintenance at West Point Military Academy. Greenkeeping Superintendents Association National Turf Conference. 21:104–110. 1950.

6565. Goatley, J. L. and R. W. Lewis. Composition of guttation fluid from rye, wheat and barley seedlings. Plant Physiology. 41:373–375. 1966.

6566. Godfrey, G. H. Experiments on the control of brown-patch with chlorophenol mercury. Boyce Thompson Institute for Plant Research. Professional Paper No. 1. 5 pp. 1925.

6567. ______. Experiments on the control of brown-patch with chlorophenol mercury. USGA Green Section Bulletin. 5:83–87. 1925.

6568. Godwin, H. F. Making and using a bent nursery. The National Greenkeeper. 2(5):15–19. 1928.

6569. ______. Bent fairway planting in Michigan. Golfdom. 2(4):32. 1928.

6570. ______. Turf nursery operating method that pay. Golfdom. 2(5):65–68. 1928.

6571. Goetz, A. J. Brown-patch and its control at St. Louis. USGA Green Section Bulletin. 9(10):179–183. 1929.

6572. Goetze, N. R. Athletic field management. Proceedings Northwest Turf Conference. 14:45–49. 1960.

6573. ______. Research on *Poa annua* control. Proceedings of Midwest Regional Turf Conference. pp. 37–38. 1956.

6574. ______. Nitrogen fertility research. Proceedings of Midwest Regional Turf Conference. pp. 79–84. 1957.

6575. ______. Nitrogen in plant metabolism. Proceedings of Midwest Regional Turf Conference. pp. 14–16. 1958.

6576. ______. *Poa annua* research continues. Proceedings of Midwest Regional Turf Conference. pp. 50–51. 1958.

6577. ______. "*Poa annua*" control in turf. North Central Weed Control Conference Proceedings. 15:36–37. 1958.

6578. ______. Gleanings from the Midwest Turf Association. Proceedings Northwest Turf Conference. 13:41–43. 1959.

6579. ______. Heavy nitrogen fertilization of cool season turfgrasses. Ph.D. Thesis, Purdue University. 76 pp. 1960.

6580. ______. Controlling weedy grasses. Proceedings Northern California Turfgrass Institute. pp. 23–26. 1961.

6581. ______. Varieties, characteristics, and adaptation. Proceedings 16th Annual Northwest Turf Conference. 16:53–56. 1962.

6582. ______. Maintenance fertilization. Proceedings 16th Annual Northwest Turf Conference. 16:75–78. 1962.

6583. ______. Turfgrass seeds: how to know and find quality. Golf Course Reporter. 31(3):36–42. 1963.

6584. ______. Management of golf turf in the Pacific Northwest. 34th International Turfgrass Conference Proceedings. p. 10. 1963.

6585. ______. Which grasses are best for turf. Northwest Turfgrass Conference Proceedings. 17:5–7. 1963.

6586. Goetze, N. R. How to recognize quality turfgrass seeds. Illinois Turfgrass Conference Proceedings. 5:84–88. 1964.

6587. ______. Limiting factors in selective annual bluegrass control. Proceedings of the 18th Annual Northwest Turfgrass Conference. pp. 13–15. 1964.

6588. ______. Maintenance of athletic grounds. Proceedings of the 19th Annual Northwest Turfgrass Conference. pp. 68–75. 1965.

6589. ______. Grasses for school turf. Turf Management Handbook. Washington State University. p. 9. 1965.

6590. ______. Principles of chemical weed control. Turf Management Handbook, Washington State University. pp. 10–11. 1965.

6591. ______. Maintenance programs for athletic fields. Turf Management Handbook, Washington State University. pp. 12–13. 1965.

6592. ______. Survey of Oregon golf facilities. Proceedings of the 20th Annual Northwest Turfgrass Conference. pp. 21–27. 1966.

6593. ______. Turfgrass (Oregon). Oregon State University Fertilizer Guide No. 47. 2 pp. 1970.

6594. Goetze, N. R. and W. H. Daniel. Turf quality as influenced by nitrogen fertilization. Agronomy Abstracts. p. 77. 1957.

6595. ______. Nitrogen fertilizer research for fairways. Golf Course Reporter. 25(1):5–8. 1957.

6596. Goetze, N. R. and R. C. Pickett. A comparison of methods of evaluating zoysia turf breeding material. Agronomy Abstracts. p. 65. 1958.

6597. Goit, K. E. Aeration and healthy turf. Park Maintenance. 6(10):22–24. 1953.

6598. Goit, W. and R. Shaffer. Grass. Golf Course Equipment Co., Chicago. 30 pp. 1932.

6599. Goldberg, C. W. An evaluation of two benzimidazole fungicides on several turfgrass diseases. M.S. Thesis, Pennsylvania State University. 75 pp. 1969.

6601. Goldberg, C. W., H. Cole, and J. Duich. Comparative effectiveness of thiabendazole and benomyl for control of *Helminthosporium* leafspot and crown rot, red thread, *Sclerotinia* dollar spot, and *Rhizoctonia* brown patch of turfgrass. The Plant Disease Reporter. 54(12):1080–1084. 1970.

6602. Golovach, A. G. Gazony, ikh ustro īstvo i soderzhanie. Akademiia Nauk USSR. 336 pp. 1955.

6603. Gomide, J. A., C. H. Noller, G. O. Mott, J. H. Conard, and D. L. Hill. Mineral composition of six tropical grasses as influenced by plant age and nitrogen fertilization. Agronomy Journal. 61(1):120–123. 1969.

6604. Gomm, F. B. Reseeding studies at a small high altitute park in Southwestern Montana. Montana Agricultural Experiment Station. Bulletin 568. 16 pp. 1962.

6605. Gooch, R. B. Athletics facilities—new developments. Journal of the Sports Turf Research Institute. 46:92–96. 1970.

6606. Good, J. M., J. R. Christie, and J. C. Nutter. Identification and distribution of plant parasitic nematodes in Florida and Georgia. Phytopathology. 43(1):13. 1956.

6607. Good, J. M., A. E. Steele and T. J. Ratcliffe. Occurrence of plant parasitic nematodes in Georgia turf nurseries. Plant Disease Reporter. 43(2):236–238. 1959.

6608. Goodey, B. Gall-forming nematodes of grasses in Britain. Journal of the Sports Turf Research Institute. 10(35):54–60. 1959.

6609. Goodey, T. Plant parasitic nematodes and the diseases they cause. E. P. Dutton and Company, New York. 306 pps. 1933.

6610. Goodin, J. R. Chemical control of flowering of *Pennisetum clandestinum,* kikuyugrass. Southern California Turf Culture Quarterly. 9(3):17. 1959.

6611. Gooding, D. G. Weed control by spraying. The Groundsman. 21(3):12–13. 1967.

6612. ______. Weed control by spraying. The Groundsman. 22(9):24–27. 1969.

6613. ______. The ground we tread. The Groundsman. 24(8):30–36. 1971.

6614. Gooding, H. J. Prevention of brown patch. The Greenkeeper's Reporter. 3(3):8–9. 1935.

6615. Goodman, A. M. Tile drainage. New York State Turf Association Bulletin 36. pp. 139–142. 1952.

6616. Goodwin, R. H., and W. Stepka. Growth and differentiation in the root tip of *Phleum pratense.* American Journal of Botany. 32:36–46. 1945.

6617. Gordan, J. H. Turf—basic principles of nutrition. Turf Bulletin. 5(5):18–19. 1969.

6618. Gordon, R. A golf course under seaside conditions. Journal of the Board of Greenkeeping Research. 3(10):164–168. 1934.

6619. Gordon, R. L. Opening remarks at panel discussion—representing suppliers. Proceedings of the Turfgrass Sprinkler Irrigation Conference. 5:45. 1967.

6620. ______. Developement of a complete system. Proceedings GCSAA Annual Turfgrass Conference. 41:25–27. 1970.

6621. ______. Proper specifications for irrigation systems. Proceedings, 24th Northwest Turfgrass Conference. 24:37–45. 1970.

6622. ______. A consultant's approach to sprinkler irrigation. Proceedings of Southern California Turfgrass Institute. pp. 99–101. 1971.

6623. Gordon, W. C. and C. Y. Ward. Six months progress report for establishment of vegetation. Mississippi State University Department of Agronomy and Horticulture. Report No. 2. 81 pp. 1964.

6624. Gordon, W. F. Design with respect to maintenance practices. USGA Journal and Turf Management. 12(2):27–29. 1959.

6625. Górska, A. Monograph of Polish playgrounds sown with Polish-type grass seed. First Czechoslovak Symposium on Sportturf Proceedings. pp. 197–208. 1969.

6626. Goss, R. L. Turf research progress at WSC. Northwest Turf Conference Proceedings. 11:5–8. 1957.

6627. ______. "Delayed action" fertilizers. Northwest Turf Conference Proceedings. 11:9–10. 1957.

6628. ______. Turf research in progress at Pullman and Puyallup, Washington. Proceedings, Northwest Turf Conference. 12:-3–7. 1958.

6629. ______. Research progress report. Proceedings Northwest Turf Conference. 13:7–13. 1959.

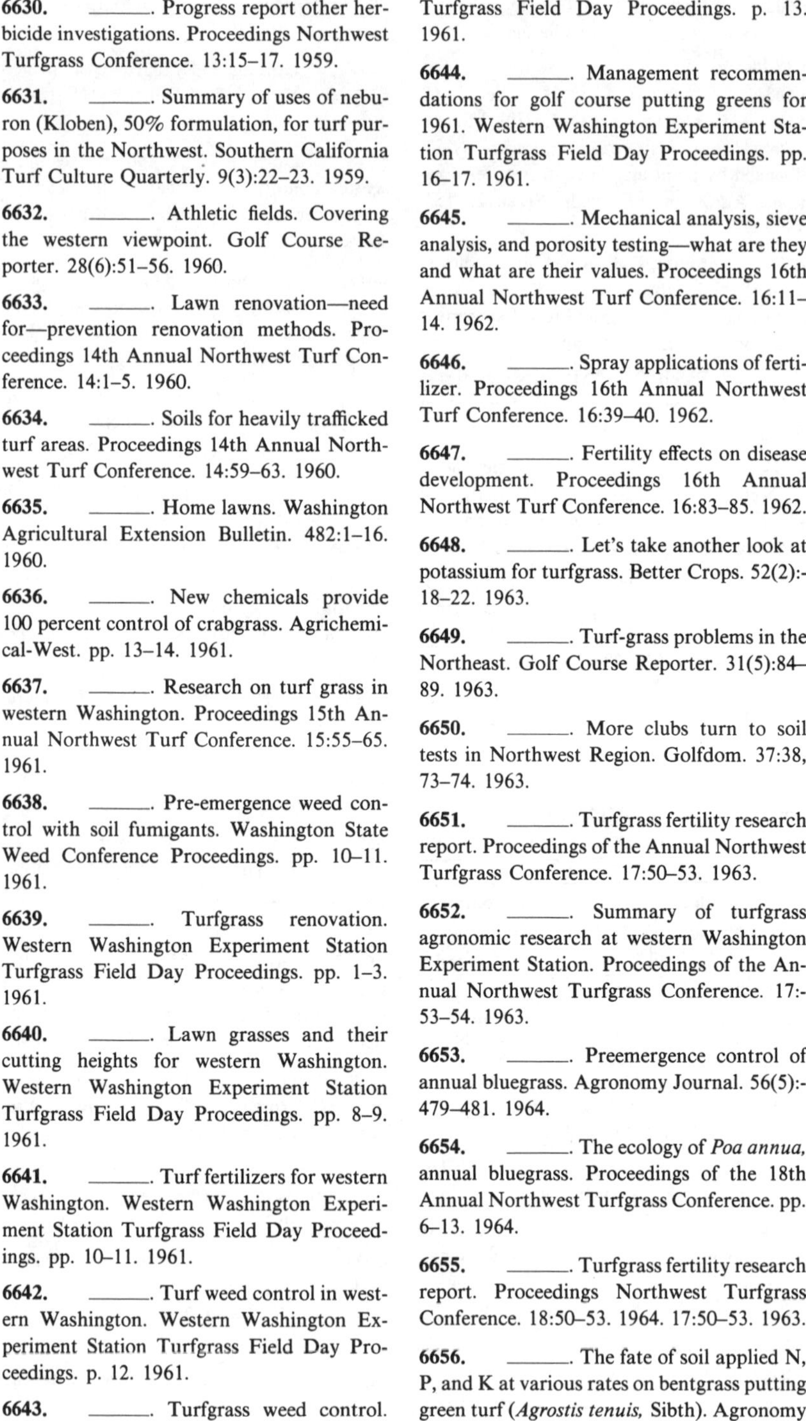

6630. ______. Progress report other herbicide investigations. Proceedings Northwest Turfgrass Conference. 13:15–17. 1959.

6631. ______. Summary of uses of neburon (Kloben), 50% formulation, for turf purposes in the Northwest. Southern California Turf Culture Quarterly. 9(3):22–23. 1959.

6632. ______. Athletic fields. Covering the western viewpoint. Golf Course Reporter. 28(6):51–56. 1960.

6633. ______. Lawn renovation—need for—prevention renovation methods. Proceedings 14th Annual Northwest Turf Conference. 14:1–5. 1960.

6634. ______. Soils for heavily trafficked turf areas. Proceedings 14th Annual Northwest Turf Conference. 14:59–63. 1960.

6635. ______. Home lawns. Washington Agricultural Extension Bulletin. 482:1–16. 1960.

6636. ______. New chemicals provide 100 percent control of crabgrass. Agrichemical-West. pp. 13–14. 1961.

6637. ______. Research on turf grass in western Washington. Proceedings 15th Annual Northwest Turf Conference. 15:55–65. 1961.

6638. ______. Pre-emergence weed control with soil fumigants. Washington State Weed Conference Proceedings. pp. 10–11. 1961.

6639. ______. Turfgrass renovation. Western Washington Experiment Station Turfgrass Field Day Proceedings. pp. 1–3. 1961.

6640. ______. Lawn grasses and their cutting heights for western Washington. Western Washington Experiment Station Turfgrass Field Day Proceedings. pp. 8–9. 1961.

6641. ______. Turf fertilizers for western Washington. Western Washington Experiment Station Turfgrass Field Day Proceedings. pp. 10–11. 1961.

6642. ______. Turf weed control in western Washington. Western Washington Experiment Station Turfgrass Field Day Proceedings. p. 12. 1961.

6643. ______. Turfgrass weed control. Western Washington Experiment Station Turfgrass Field Day Proceedings. p. 13. 1961.

6644. ______. Management recommendations for golf course putting greens for 1961. Western Washington Experiment Station Turfgrass Field Day Proceedings. pp. 16–17. 1961.

6645. ______. Mechanical analysis, sieve analysis, and porosity testing—what are they and what are their values. Proceedings 16th Annual Northwest Turf Conference. 16:11–14. 1962.

6646. ______. Spray applications of fertilizer. Proceedings 16th Annual Northwest Turf Conference. 16:39–40. 1962.

6647. ______. Fertility effects on disease development. Proceedings 16th Annual Northwest Turf Conference. 16:83–85. 1962.

6648. ______. Let's take another look at potassium for turfgrass. Better Crops. 52(2):-18–22. 1963.

6649. ______. Turf-grass problems in the Northeast. Golf Course Reporter. 31(5):84–89. 1963.

6650. ______. More clubs turn to soil tests in Northwest Region. Golfdom. 37:38, 73–74. 1963.

6651. ______. Turfgrass fertility research report. Proceedings of the Annual Northwest Turfgrass Conference. 17:50–53. 1963.

6652. ______. Summary of turfgrass agronomic research at western Washington Experiment Station. Proceedings of the Annual Northwest Turfgrass Conference. 17:-53–54. 1963.

6653. ______. Preemergence control of annual bluegrass. Agronomy Journal. 56(5):-479–481. 1964.

6654. ______. The ecology of *Poa annua,* annual bluegrass. Proceedings of the 18th Annual Northwest Turfgrass Conference. pp. 6–13. 1964.

6655. ______. Turfgrass fertility research report. Proceedings Northwest Turfgrass Conference. 18:50–53. 1964. 17:50–53. 1963.

6656. ______. The fate of soil applied N, P, and K at various rates on bentgrass putting green turf (*Agrostis tenuis,* Sibth). Agronomy Abstracts. 57:45. 1965.

6657. ______. Nitrogen-potassium team on turf grasses. Better Crops With Plant Food. 49(2):34. 1965.

6658. ______. Preemergence control of annual bluegrass (*Poa annua* L.). The Golf Course Reporter. 33(3):24–30. 1965.

6659. ______. Does your turf use everything you feed it? Proceedings of the 19th Annual Northwest Turfgrass Conference. pp. 15–21. 1965.

6660. ______. Agronomic research report for the northwest turfgrass conference. Proceedings of the 19th Annual Northwest Turfgrass Conference. pp. 22–24. 1965.

6661. ______. Some reasons for summer turfgrass losses. Northwest Turfgrass Topics. 7(2):3–7. 1965.

6662. ______. Fertilization of play and athletic areas. Turf Management Handbook, Washington State University. pp. 1–3. 1965.

6663. ______. Draining turfgrass areas. Turf Bulletin. Massachusetts Turf & Lawn Grass Council. 2(12):9–10. 1965.

6664. ______. Soils for play and athletic fields. Turf Management Handbook, Washington State University. pp. 5–6. 1965.

6665. ______. Reclaiming the approaches. The Golf Superintendent. 34(1):23. 1966.

6666. ______. Does your turf use everything you feed it? Proceedings of the Midwest Regional Turf Conference. pp. 4–8. 1966.

6667. ______. Turfgrass research in the Pacific Northwest. Proceedings of the Midwest Regional Turf Conference. pp. 9–12. 1966.

6668. ______. Some physical and chemical considerations in construction. Proceedings of the 20th Annual Northwest Turfgrass Conference. pp. 74–79. 1966.

6669. ______. Some physiological effects of soil salinity. Turf Bulletin. Massachusetts Turf and Lawn Grass Council. 3(3):11. 1966.

6670. ______. Some effects on soil pH and calcium levels from fertilizer applications to soil producing putting green turf. Journal of the Sports Turf Research Institute. 43:-23–27. 1967.

6671. ______. Specifications for turfgrass installations. Proceedings of the Annual of 21st Northwest Turfgrass Conference. 21:-102–107. 1967.

6672. ______. Plant food and your dollars. Northwest Turfgrass Topics. 9(1):7–8. 1967.

6673. ______. Recent developments with Banvel-D. Northwest Turfgrass Topics. 9(2):6–7. 1967.

6674. ______. The effects of urea on soil pH and calcium levels. Northwest Turfgrass Topics. 9(3):1, 4. 1967.

6675. ______. The value and use of turfgrass surveys in research and teaching programs. Agronomy Abstracts. p. 59. 1968.

6676. ______. The soil environment. Northwest Turfgrass Topics. 10(1):2, 6. 1968.

6677. ______. Turfgrass research in the Pacific Northwest. Proceedings Annual GCSAA Turfgrass Conference. 40:21–24. 1969.

6678. ______. Viewpoints on control methods and precautions—Northwest. Proceedings GCSAA Annual Turfgrass Conference. 40:61–62. 1969.

6679. ______. Some inter-relationships between nutrition and turfgrass diseases. Proceedings of the First International Turfgrass Research Conference. pp. 351–361. 1969.

6680. ______. The value of turf in the state of Washington—a turfgrass survey. Northwest Turfgrass Conference Proceedings. 23:13–20. 1969.

6681. ______. International Turfgrass Research Conference and European Turfgrass Tour. Northwest Turfgrass Conference Proceedings. 23:79–88. 1969.

6682. ______. Repairing winter damage to turfgrass areas. Northwest Turfgrass Topics. 11(1):1, 3. 1969.

6683. ______. New herbicides for *Poa annua* seedhead. Northwest Turfgrass Topics. 11(2):6–7. 1969.

6684. ______. Fall weed control. Northwest Turfgrass Topics. 11(2):9. 1969.

6685. ______. Pre- and post-emergence controls for *Poa annua*. Proceedings, 24th Annual Northwest Turfgrass Conference. 24:81–88. 1970.

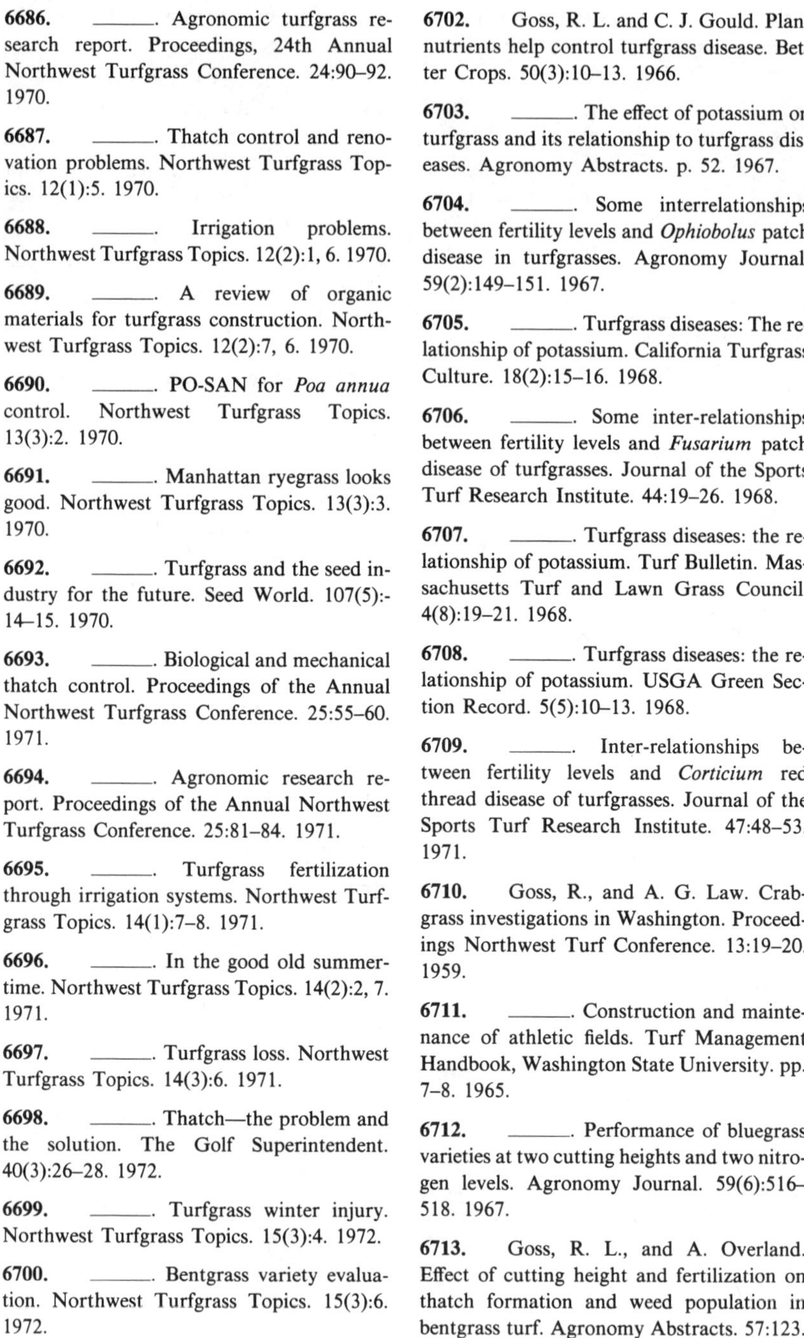

6686. ______. Agronomic turfgrass research report. Proceedings, 24th Annual Northwest Turfgrass Conference. 24:90–92. 1970.

6687. ______. Thatch control and renovation problems. Northwest Turfgrass Topics. 12(1):5. 1970.

6688. ______. Irrigation problems. Northwest Turfgrass Topics. 12(2):1, 6. 1970.

6689. ______. A review of organic materials for turfgrass construction. Northwest Turfgrass Topics. 12(2):7, 6. 1970.

6690. ______. PO-SAN for *Poa annua* control. Northwest Turfgrass Topics. 13(3):2. 1970.

6691. ______. Manhattan ryegrass looks good. Northwest Turfgrass Topics. 13(3):3. 1970.

6692. ______. Turfgrass and the seed industry for the future. Seed World. 107(5):-14–15. 1970.

6693. ______. Biological and mechanical thatch control. Proceedings of the Annual Northwest Turfgrass Conference. 25:55–60. 1971.

6694. ______. Agronomic research report. Proceedings of the Annual Northwest Turfgrass Conference. 25:81–84. 1971.

6695. ______. Turfgrass fertilization through irrigation systems. Northwest Turfgrass Topics. 14(1):7–8. 1971.

6696. ______. In the good old summertime. Northwest Turfgrass Topics. 14(2):2, 7. 1971.

6697. ______. Turfgrass loss. Northwest Turfgrass Topics. 14(3):6. 1971.

6698. ______. Thatch—the problem and the solution. The Golf Superintendent. 40(3):26–28. 1972.

6699. ______. Turfgrass winter injury. Northwest Turfgrass Topics. 15(3):4. 1972.

6700. ______. Bentgrass variety evaluation. Northwest Turfgrass Topics. 15(3):6. 1972.

6701. Goss, R., and H. Austenson. Testing and selecting for better turfgrasses. Proceedings Northwest Turf Conference. 12:33–34. 1958.

6702. Goss, R. L. and C. J. Gould. Plant nutrients help control turfgrass disease. Better Crops. 50(3):10–13. 1966.

6703. ______. The effect of potassium on turfgrass and its relationship to turfgrass diseases. Agronomy Abstracts. p. 52. 1967.

6704. ______. Some interrelationships between fertility levels and *Ophiobolus* patch disease in turfgrasses. Agronomy Journal. 59(2):149–151. 1967.

6705. ______. Turfgrass diseases: The relationship of potassium. California Turfgrass Culture. 18(2):15–16. 1968.

6706. ______. Some inter-relationships between fertility levels and *Fusarium* patch disease of turfgrasses. Journal of the Sports Turf Research Institute. 44:19–26. 1968.

6707. ______. Turfgrass diseases: the relationship of potassium. Turf Bulletin. Massachusetts Turf and Lawn Grass Council. 4(8):19–21. 1968.

6708. ______. Turfgrass diseases: the relationship of potassium. USGA Green Section Record. 5(5):10–13. 1968.

6709. ______. Inter-relationships between fertility levels and *Corticium* red thread disease of turfgrasses. Journal of the Sports Turf Research Institute. 47:48–53. 1971.

6710. Goss, R., and A. G. Law. Crabgrass investigations in Washington. Proceedings Northwest Turf Conference. 13:19–20. 1959.

6711. ______. Construction and maintenance of athletic fields. Turf Management Handbook, Washington State University. pp. 7–8. 1965.

6712. ______. Performance of bluegrass varieties at two cutting heights and two nitrogen levels. Agronomy Journal. 59(6):516–518. 1967.

6713. Goss, R. L., and A. Overland. Effect of cutting height and fertilization on thatch formation and weed population in bentgrass turf. Agronomy Abstracts. 57:123. 1965.

6714. Goss, R. L. and J. Roberts. A compaction machine for turfgrass areas. Agronomy Journal. 56(5):522. 1964.

6715. Goss, R. L. and F. Zook. New approach for *Poa annua* control. The Golf Superintendent. 39(1):46–48. 1971.

6716. Goss, R. L., R. M. Blanchard, and W. R. Melton. The establishment of vegetation on nontopsoiled highway slopes in Washington. Washington State Highway Commission, Washington State University Agricultural Research Center, and Federal Highway Administration. Research Project Y-1009. 29 pp. 1970.

6717. Goss, R. L., J. K. Patterson, and A. G. Law. The response of bluegrass varieties to two cutting heights and two nitrogen levels. Agronomy Abstracts. p. 89. 1959.

6718. Goss, R. L., E. C. Wilcox, and A. G. Law. Washington turfgrass survey—1967. Washington Cooperative Extension Service EM 3135. 46 pp. 1969.

6719. Goss, R. L., C. J. Gould, O. Maloy, A. G. Law, and K. J. Morrison. Recommendation for turfgrass management in Washington. Washington State University Extension Manual 2783. pp. 1–12. 1967.

6720. Goss, R. L., K. J. Morrison, A. G. Law, C. B. Harston, B. F. Roche, D. H. Brannon, M. R. Harris, and C. J. Gould. Home lawns. Washington State University Extension Bulletin 482. 16 pp. 1962.

6721. Goss, S. H. No grounds for weed growth. The Groundsman. 20(8):32–33. 1967.

6722. Gossens, A. P., and W. J. Stapleberg. A brief note on the macroscopic aspect of some western Transvaal grasses. South African Journal of Science. 30:212–219. 1933.

6723. Gossett, D. M. and L. M. Callahan. Turf—recommended practices—Tennessee. 22nd Annual Southern Weed Conference Research Report. pp. 89–90. 1969.

6724. ______. Turf—recommended practices—Tennessee. 22nd Annual Southern Weed Conference Research Report. pp. 91–92. 1969.

6725. Gotz, H. J. and F. A. Haskins. Evaluation of cross-fertilization in forage crops. Crop Science. 11(5):731–734. 1971.

6726. Gough, F. J. and M. E. McDaniel. Zoysia rust in Texas. The Plant Disease Reporter. 53(3):232. 1969.

6727. Gould, C. J. Turf diseases in western Washington. Golf Course Reporter. 25(1):18–20. 1957.

6728. ______. Turf disease research in western Washington. Northwest Turf Conference Proceedings. 11:11–14. 1957.

6729. ______. Turf diseases in western Washington in 1955 and 1956. Plant Disease Reporter. 41(4):344–347. 1957.

6730. ______. Turf disease research at the Western Washington Experiment Station. Proceedings Northwest Turf Conference. 12:29–31. 1958.

6731. ______. Turf disease research during 1959 in Western Washington. Proceedings Northwest Turf Conference. 13:31–36. 1959.

6732. ______. Turf disease studies in western Washington. Proceedings 14th Annual Northwest Turf Conference. 14:11–14. 1960.

6733. ______. Some pathological pitfalls in practice. Proceedings 15th Annual Northwest Turf Conference. 15:29–33. 1961.

6734. ______. Turf diseases in western Washington. Western Washington Experiment Station Turfgrass Field Day Proceedings. pp. 4–7. 1961.

6735. ______. Panel discussion on fundamentals of turfgrass disease and insect occurrence. Proceedings 16th Annual Northwest Turf Conference. 16:101–108. 1962.

6736. ______. Some practical aspects of disease control. Golf Course Reporter. 31(5):66–71. 1963.

6737. ______. Some practical aspects of turf disease control. 34th International Turfgrass Conference Proceedings. p. 10. 1963.

6738. ______. Developments in fungicides and disease control. University of Maine Turf Conference Proceedings. 1:8 pp. 1963.

6739. ______. How climate affects our turfgrass disease. Proceedings of the Annual Northwest Turfgrass Conference. 17:29–42. 1963.

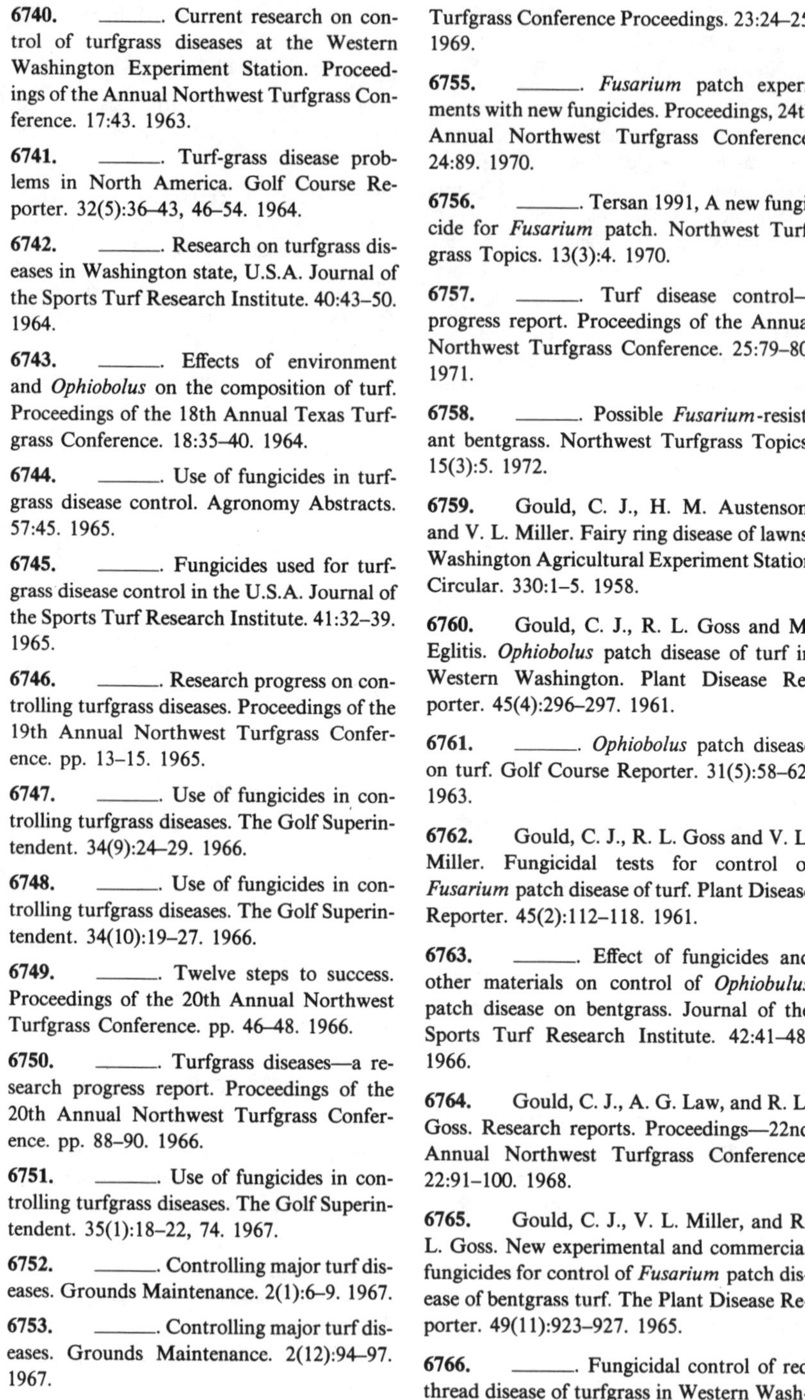

6740. ———. Current research on control of turfgrass diseases at the Western Washington Experiment Station. Proceedings of the Annual Northwest Turfgrass Conference. 17:43. 1963.

6741. ———. Turf-grass disease problems in North America. Golf Course Reporter. 32(5):36–43, 46–54. 1964.

6742. ———. Research on turfgrass diseases in Washington state, U.S.A. Journal of the Sports Turf Research Institute. 40:43–50. 1964.

6743. ———. Effects of environment and *Ophiobolus* on the composition of turf. Proceedings of the 18th Annual Texas Turfgrass Conference. 18:35–40. 1964.

6744. ———. Use of fungicides in turfgrass disease control. Agronomy Abstracts. 57:45. 1965.

6745. ———. Fungicides used for turfgrass disease control in the U.S.A. Journal of the Sports Turf Research Institute. 41:32–39. 1965.

6746. ———. Research progress on controlling turfgrass diseases. Proceedings of the 19th Annual Northwest Turfgrass Conference. pp. 13–15. 1965.

6747. ———. Use of fungicides in controlling turfgrass diseases. The Golf Superintendent. 34(9):24–29. 1966.

6748. ———. Use of fungicides in controlling turfgrass diseases. The Golf Superintendent. 34(10):19–27. 1966.

6749. ———. Twelve steps to success. Proceedings of the 20th Annual Northwest Turfgrass Conference. pp. 46–48. 1966.

6750. ———. Turfgrass diseases—a research progress report. Proceedings of the 20th Annual Northwest Turfgrass Conference. pp. 88–90. 1966.

6751. ———. Use of fungicides in controlling turfgrass diseases. The Golf Superintendent. 35(1):18–22, 74. 1967.

6752. ———. Controlling major turf diseases. Grounds Maintenance. 2(1):6–9. 1967.

6753. ———. Controlling major turf diseases. Grounds Maintenance. 2(12):94–97. 1967.

6754. ———. Promising new fungicides for control of *Fusarium* patch. Northwest Turfgrass Conference Proceedings. 23:24–25. 1969.

6755. ———. *Fusarium* patch experiments with new fungicides. Proceedings, 24th Annual Northwest Turfgrass Conference. 24:89. 1970.

6756. ———. Tersan 1991, A new fungicide for *Fusarium* patch. Northwest Turfgrass Topics. 13(3):4. 1970.

6757. ———. Turf disease control—progress report. Proceedings of the Annual Northwest Turfgrass Conference. 25:79–80. 1971.

6758. ———. Possible *Fusarium*-resistant bentgrass. Northwest Turfgrass Topics. 15(3):5. 1972.

6759. Gould, C. J., H. M. Austenson, and V. L. Miller. Fairy ring disease of lawns. Washington Agricultural Experiment Station Circular. 330:1–5. 1958.

6760. Gould, C. J., R. L. Goss and M. Eglitis. *Ophiobolus* patch disease of turf in Western Washington. Plant Disease Reporter. 45(4):296–297. 1961.

6761. ———. *Ophiobolus* patch disease on turf. Golf Course Reporter. 31(5):58–62. 1963.

6762. Gould, C. J., R. L. Goss and V. L. Miller. Fungicidal tests for control of *Fusarium* patch disease of turf. Plant Disease Reporter. 45(2):112–118. 1961.

6763. ———. Effect of fungicides and other materials on control of *Ophiobulus* patch disease on bentgrass. Journal of the Sports Turf Research Institute. 42:41–48. 1966.

6764. Gould, C. J., A. G. Law, and R. L. Goss. Research reports. Proceedings—22nd Annual Northwest Turfgrass Conference. 22:91–100. 1968.

6765. Gould, C. J., V. L. Miller, and R. L. Goss. New experimental and commercial fungicides for control of *Fusarium* patch disease of bentgrass turf. The Plant Disease Reporter. 49(11):923–927. 1965.

6766. ———. Fungicidal control of red thread disease of turfgrass in Western Washington. The Plant Disease Reporter. 51(3):-215–219. 1967.

6767. Gould, C. J., V. L. Miller, and D. Polley. Fair ring disease of lawns. Golf Course Reporter. 23(8):16–20. 1955.

6768. ______. Fairy ring disease of lawns. Proceedings 9th Annual Northwest Turf Conference. 9:22–26. 1955.

6769. Gould, C. J., N. A. Maclean, I. C. MacSwan, and T. Filer. Panel discussion of northwest turfgrass disease. Proceedings 15th Annual Northwest Turf Conference. 15:9–19. 1961.

6771. Gould, F. W. Grass systematics. McGraw Hill Co., New York. 382 pp. 1968.

6772. Gourlay, D. Course maintenance at the Royal and Ancient Golf Club. Seventeenth R.C.G.A. Sports Turfgrass Conference. pp. 17–19. 1966.

6773. ______. A visit to St. Andrews. The Greenmaster. 3(4):10–12. 1967.

6774. ______. A sensible fertilizer programme. The Greenmaster. 7(8):8, 10, 12–13. 1971.

6775. ______. A calendar for golf course maintenance. Annual RCGA National Turfgrass Conference. 23:41–46. 1972.

6776. Gowans, K. D. Phosphate needs for turfgrass establishment. Park Maintenance. 23(7):14, 16–17. 1970.

6777. ______. Turfgrass seeds by the pound. California Turfgrass Culture. 22(3):-23–24. 1972.

6778. ______. Turfgrass seeds by the pound. Turf Bulletin. 9(3):10–11. 1972.

6779. Gowden, L. V. Starve by mowing. Golfdom. 6(3):88. 1932.

6780. Graber, L. F. Injury from burning off old grass on established bluegrass pastures. Journal of American Society of Agronomy. 18:815–819. 1926.

6781. ______. Food reserves in relation to other factors limiting the growth of grasses. Plant Physiology. 6:43–72. 1931.

6782. ______. Competitive efficiency and productivity of bluegrass (*Poa Pratensis* L.) with partial defoliation at two levels of cutting. Journal of the American Society of Agronomy. 25:328–333. 1933.

6783. Graber, L. F. and J. W. Ream. Growth of bluegrass with various defoliations and abundant nitrogen supply. Journal of the American Society of Agronomy. 23:-938–944. 1931.

6784. Grable, A. R., and D. D. Johnson. Efficiency of recovery of applied nitrate nitrogen by perennial ryegrass from different soils. Soil Science Society of America Proceedings. 24:503–507. 1960.

6785. Gradwell, M. W. The effect of grass cover on overnight heat losses from soil and some factors affecting the thermal conductivities of soils. New Zealand Journal of Science. 11(2):284–300. 1968.

6786. Grady, The supply outlook. Proceedings of the Mid-Atlantic Association of Greenskeepers Conference. pp. 20–23. 1951.

6787. Graetz, K. E. and C. H. Jent. Roadbank revolution. Soil Conservation. 28:-56–57. 1962.

6788. Graffis, D. W. Quality lawn seed. Ohio Agricultural Research and Development Center. Lawn and Ornamentals Research. 6:3–6. 1965.

6789. Graffis, H. Record attendance marks the first outdoor meet at Chicago. Golfdom. 3(9):23–25. 1929.

6790. ______. Greenkeeper's record crowd busy at Louisville meeting. Golfdom. 4(3):32–36. 1930.

6791. ______. Crowds attend Amherst confab. Golfdom. 9(4):48, 50, 52, 54. 1935.

6792. Graffis, J. Greensmen all set. Golfdom. 10(3):21–24. 1936.

6793. Graffis, H. Superintendents report heavy work schedule for fall. Golfdom. 23(9):25–27, 58. 1949.

6794. ______. Golf facilities. National Golf Foundation. Chicago. 80 pp. 1949.

6795. ______. Who plays golf today? Proceedings of Midwest Regional Turf Conference. pp. 50–52. 1964.

6796. ______. Giving golfers what they need. Golfdom. 40(7):46–48 and 70–75. 1966.

6797. ______. 40th birthday for the GCSAA. Golfdom. 40(9):44, 46, 62–70. 1966.

6798. Graffis, J. And to think it all started with $500! Golfdom. 41(2):34–35, 80–85. 1967.

6799. Graft, N. Golf with a dash of salt. Golfdom. 46(5):60–63. 1972.

6800. Grafton, B. F. Vegetative cover study for problem soils. Louisiana Polytechnic Institute and Louisana Department of Highways, BPR, HPR-1(2), State Project No. 736–00–71. 26 pp. 1968.

6801. Graham, E. R. Solving the phosphorus problem in turf. Proceedings Missouri Lawn and Turf Conference. pp. 26–27. 1963.

6802. ______. The meaning of soil tests results. Proceedings Missouri Lawn and Turf Conference. pp. 1–3. 1964.

6803. Graham, J. A. Insect pests of greens and their control. New Zealand Institute for Turf Culture Newsletter. 14:4–6. 1961.

6804. Graham, J. H., and V. G. Sprague. The effects of controlled periods on high and low humidities on the development of orchardgrass. Phytopathology. 43(11):642–643. 1953.

6805. Graham, M. D. Golf greens and lawns in East Africa. East African Agriculture and Forestry Journal. 11:94. 1945.

6806. Gramckow, J. Is your grass safe? Report, Cal-Turf Inc., Camarillo, California. Mimeo. 48 pp. 1968.

6807. Grant, J. A. The developer looks at sod. Proceedings University of Florida Turf-Grass Management Conference. 8:66–68. 1960.

6808. Grant, R. Turf nurseries establishment, maintenance and utilization. Turf Clippings. University of Massachusetts. 1(5):A-14 to A-16. 1960.

6809. Grant, R. E. Perimeter sprinkler method of watering greens. Golf Course Reporter. 30(6):46–47. 1962.

6810. Grant, W. J., and E. Epstein. Physical properties and moisture relationships of some representative Maine soil types. Maine Agricultural Experiment Station Technical Bulletin. 2:1–8. 1962.

6811. Grantham, A. E. How plant food elements function for better turf. Golfdom. 4(3):94, 96, 98, 100. 1930.

6812. ______. Functions of the three plant food elements. The National Greenkeeper. 4(3):11–12, 14, 16, 50. 1930.

6813. Grasso, A. P. Winter injury. Proceedings 1970 3-Day Turf Courses, Rutgers University. pp. 42–43. 1970.

6814. Gratz, L. O. Progress of turf research in Florida. Florida Greenkeeping Superintendents Association and the Southeastern Turf Conference Turf Management Conference. pp. 7–11. 1949.

6815. Grau, F. V. Obtaining accuracy in the application of materials to turf. USGA Green Section Bulletin. 13(1):7–16. 1933.

6816. ______. Control of crabgrass and other turf weeds with chemicals. USGA Green Section Bulletin. 13(3):47–52. 1933.

6817. ______. Drift and speed of putted ball on bents as determined by mechanical putter. USGA Green Section Bulletin. 13(3):-74–81. 1933.

6818. ______. Use of sodium chlorate and other chemicals in controlling turf weeds. USGA Green Section Bulletin. 13(6):-154–179. 1933.

6819. ______. Green section wins two year battle on crab grass. Golfdom 8(4):13–15. 1934.

6820. ______. Here's the latest on sodium chlorate. Golfdom. 10(2):53–54. 1936.

6821. ______. Turf trouble-shooting. Golfdom. 10(4):21–24. 1936.

6822. ______. Trouble shooting on eastern courses. The Greenkeeper's Reporter. 4(10):9–13. 1936.

6823. ______. Lawns. Pennsylvania Agricultural Extension Circular. 160:1–12. 1936.

6824. ______. The International Grasslands Congress. The Greenkeepers' Reporter. 5(9):7–13, 28–29, 1937.

6825. ______. Are weeds your trouble? Golfdom. 13(8):9–12. 1939.

6826. ______. Chemical weed control on lawns and sports fields. Turf Culture. 1(1):-53–60. 1939.

6827. ______. How to fight weeds. Golfdom. 15(3):56, 58, 62. 1941.

6828. ______. What research is doing to improve turf. Golfdom. 20(5):48, 50, 52. 1946.

6829. ______. Turf roundup of 1947. Golfdom. 21(10):51–52, 56, 79–82. 1947.

6830. ______. The U.S.G.A. Section—plans and progress. Parks & Recreation. 30(8):399–403. 1947.

6831. ______. Aeration and moisture relationship in turf. Golf Course Reporter. 16(2):24–25, 35, 1948.

6832. ______. Crabgrass control. Midwest Turf-News and Research. 2(3):1–2, 4. 1948.

6833. ______. What's new in turf. Southwest Turf Conference Proceedings. pp. 20–32. 1948.

6834. ______. Diseases of turf grasses and their control. Southwest Turf Conference Proceedings. pp. 64–67. 1948.

6835. ______. Control of weeds in lawns, fairways, and putting greens. Southwest Turf Conference Proceedings. pp. 75–83. 1948.

6836. ______. *Poa annua*—friend or foe? U.S.G.A. Journal and Turf Management. 1(2):13–15. 1948.

6837. ______. Let's save water. Golf Course Reporter. 17(6):5–6. 1949.

6838. ______. Things to come in turf management. Golf Course Reporter. 17(2):-5–11. 1949.

6839. ______. Tenn. conference examines southern turf problems. Golfdom. 23(2):60, 62, 64–65. 1949.

6840. ______. Turf round-up of 1949. Golfdom. 23(10):35–37, 40–41, 97–99. 1949.

6841. ______. Water conservation in turf. Proceedings of the Mid-Atlantic Association of Greenkeepers Conference. pp. 18–25. 1949.

6842. ______. New and interesting grasses. Proceedings of the Mid-Atlantic Association of Greenkeepers Conference. pp. 26–31. 1949.

6843. ______. Soil compaction and aeration. Proceedings of Midwest Regional Turf Conference. pp. 31–37. 1949.

6844. ______. Predictions for things to come in turf management. Proceedings of Midwest Regional Turf Conference. pp. 53–59. 1949.

6845. ______. Train men to replace you. Midwest Turf-News and Research. 3(2):1. 1949.

6846. ______. Turf problems in tree areas. 25th National Shade Tree Conference Proceedings. 1949.

6847. ______. *Poa annua* vs. bermudagrass. New York State Turf Association. Bulletin 4. p. 16. 1949.

6848. ______. Insect and disease control of southern grasses. Oklahoma-Texas Turf Conference Proceedings. pp. 48–50. 1949.

6849. ______. Basic causes of poor turf. The Pennsylvania State College Eighteenth Annual Turf Conference. pp. 7–15. 1949.

6850. ______. Basic principles of bentgrass management. Proceedings of the Oklahoma-Texas Turf Conference. 4:7–14. 1949.

6851. ______. Nearly everyone has crabgrass. USGA Journal and Turf Management. 2(3):25–27. 1949.

6852. ______. Turf troubles on golf courses. U.S.G.A. Journal and Turf Management. 2(5):26–27. 1949.

6853. ______. What happened to turf this summer? USGA Journal and Turf Management. 2:28–30. 1949.

6854. ______. Bentgrass in the south. USGA Journal. 2(5):30–32. 1949.

6855. ______. Report on cooperative work by USGA Green Section. Central Plains Turfgrass Conference Proceedings. pp. 30–36. 1950.

6856. ______. Water management. Central Plains Turfgrass Conference Proceedings. pp. 56–63 pp. 1950.

6857. ______. The nutrition of turf grasses. Southern California Conference on Turf Culture. pp. 59–63. 1950.

6858. ______. Turf round-up of 1950. Golfdom. 24(10):29–31, 34–35, 86–91. 1950.

6859. ______. Turf research. Greenkeeping Superintendents Association National Turf Conference. 21:99–104. 1950.

6860. ______. Soil and water relationships and their effect upon water usage. Proceedings of the Mid-Atlantic Association of Greenkeepers Conference. pp. 10–16. 1950.

6861. ______. Warm and cool-season grasses. Proceedings of the Mid-Atlantic Association of Greenkeepers Conference. pp. 37–44. 1950.

6862. ______. Turf grasses. Proceedings of Midwest Regional Turf Conference. pp. 41–46. 1950.

6863. ______. What's new in turf. Oklahoma-Texas Turf Conference Proceedings. pp. 8–15. 1950.

6864. ______. What every man should know about turf diseases. Oklahoma-Texas Turf Conference Proceedings. pp. 63–69. 1950.

6865. ______. Water use in relation to aerification. Pennsylvania State College Turfgrass Conference Proceedings. 19:39–43. 1950.

6866. ______. Turf research in the United States. Rutgers University Short Course in Turf Management. 18:13–23. 1950.

6867. ______. Proper use of water on turf. Rutgers University Short Course in Turf Management. 18:38–40. 1950.

6868. ______. American Society of Agronomy turf report. USGA Journal and Turf Management 3(2):34–35. 1950.

6869. ______. Turf round-up of 1951. Golfdom. 25(10):42–43,46–49,117–118,120–122. 1951.

6870. ______. Grasses for various purposes. Proceedings of the Mid-Atlantic Association of Greenkeepers Conference. pp. 53–61. 1951.

6871. ______. Problems in turf today. Proceedings of Midwest Regional Turf Conference. pp. 7–12. 1951.

6872. ______. Testing for better grasses. Proceedings of Midwest Regional Turf Conference. pp. 84–85. 1951.

6873. ______. Turf maintenance in the U.S. 1950 Rutgers University Short Course in Turf Management. 19:70–81. 1951.

6874. ______. Soil compaction and aeration. Southern California Conference on Turf Culture. pp. 36–39. 1951.

6875. ______. What's new in turf grasses. Southern California Conference on Turf Culture. pp. 64–67. 1951.

6876. ______. Further suggestions for research of *Poa annua*. USGA Journal and Turf Management. 4(5):30–32. 1951.

6877. ______. Turf roundup of 1952. Golfdom. 26(10):84,86–87,90–91. 1952.

6878. ______. *Poa annua*—friend or foe. Proceedings School of Soils, Fertilization & Turf Maintenance Green Section, Royal Canadian Golf Association. pp. 40–42. 1952.

6879. ______. Turf grasses we should know. Proceedings School of Soils, Fertility & Turf Mainenance Green Section, Royal Canadian Golf Association. pp. 46–48. 1952.

6880. ______. Fall renovation of backward greens and fairways. Proceedings School of Soils, Fertilization & Turf Maintenance Green Section, Royal Canadian Golf Association. pp. 82, 1952.

6881. ______. The green section expands. Southern California Turf Culture. 2(3):1. 1952.

6882. ______. Report on two improved turf grasses. USGA Journal and Turf Management. 5(3):31–32. 1952.

6883. ______. Better lawns to come. U.S.G.A. Journal and Turf Management. 5(5):32–36. 1952.

6884. ______. Report of the turfgrass committee. Agronomy Journal. 45(12):650. 1953.

6885. ______. From the USGA Green Section. Golf Course Reporter. 21(1):24–26. 1953.

6886. ______. Turf roundup of 1952. Golfdom. 27(1):52–54. 1953.

6887. ______. Turf roundup of 1952. Golfdom. 27(2):52–54,56,72–75. 1953.

6888. ______. Warm season grasses. Golfdom 27(4):92, 94,96–98. 1953.

6889. ______. Cost of turf renovation and establishment with zoysia grasses. Proceedings of the Mid-Atlantic Association of Greenkeepers Conference. pp. 21–24. 1953.

6890. ______. Turf quality. Proceedings of the Arizona Turfgrass Conference. pp. 20–24. 1954.

6891. ______. Turfgrass questions answered. Golfdom. 28(8):23–24. 1954.

6892. ______. Turfgrass questions answered. Golfdom. 28(9):50,52. 1954.

6893. ______. Turfgrass questions answered. Golfdom. 28(10):58,60,62. 1954.

6894. ______. Tough grasses for hard wear. Journal of Housing. p. 336. 1954.

6895. ______. Bermuda and zoysia grass management.—panel discussion. Proceedings of the Mid-Atlantic Association of Golf Course Superintendents Conference. pp. 5–7. 1954.

6896. ______. Grass planting- methods and devices. Proceedings of the Mid-Atlantic Association of Golf Course Superintendents Conference. pp. 28–33 1954.

6897. ______. Techniques and turf quality. Proceedings of Midwest Regional Turf Conference. pp. 14–19. 1954.

6898. ______. Athletic field reseeding. Proceedings of Midwest Regional Turf Conference. pp. 44–48. 1954.

6899. ______. Control of grain in putting greens. Oklahoma Turfgrass Conference Proceedings. pp. 8–12. 1954.

6901. ______. Turf quality. Proceedings of the Southern California Turfgrass Conference. pp. 15–19. 1954.

6902. ______. Superior putting greens. West Point Products Corporation Bulletin. 14 pp. 1954.

6903. ______. Establishment of specialized turfgrasses. Golf Course Reporter. 23(3):10–12. 1955.

6904. ______. Turfgrass questions answered. Golfdom. 29(1):36–38. 1955.

6905. ______. Turfgrass questions answered. Golfdom. 29(3):94,96,98. 1955.

6906. ______. Turfgrass questions answered. Golfdom. 29(4):81, 84,86,88. 1955.

6907. ______. Turfgrass questions answered. Golfdom. 29(6):58,60,62. 1955.

6908. ______. Turfgrass questions answered. Golfdom. 29(7):59–62. 1955.

6909. ______. Turfgrass questions answered. Golfdom. 29(8):57–58,60–61. 1955.

6910. ______. Turfgrass questions answered. Golfdom. 29(9):54,56–57. 1955.

6911. ______. Turfgrass questions answered. Golfdom. 29(10):96,98–99,102. 1955.

6912. ______. Put yourself in his place. Proceedings of Midwest Regional Turf Conference. pp. 40–44. 1955.

6913. ______. The right turfgrass for you. Rocky Mountain Regional Turfgrass Conference Proceedings. 1:1–3. 1954.

6914. ______. Better turf for recreation areas. Rutgers University Short Course in Turf Management. Vol. 23. 1 p. 1955.

6915. ______. Better turf for golf. Rutgers University Short Course in Turf Management. Vol. 23 2 pp. 1955.

6916. ______. Relation of soil texture and structure to turfgrass production. Southeastern Turfgrass Conference. 9:16–22. 1955.

6917. ______. Grau answers turfgrass questions. Golfdom. 30(1):53,56,58. 1956.

6918. ______. Grau answers turfgrass questions. Golfdom. 30(2):69–70,72. 1956.

6919. ______. Grau answers turfgrass questions. Golfdom. 30(3):106–108. 1956.

6920. ______ Grau answers turfgrass questions. Golfdom. 30(4):80,82–84. 1956.

6921. ______. Turfgrass questions answered by Grau. Golfdom. 30(5):84–87,114. 1956.

6922. ______. Turfgrass questions answered by Grau. Golfdom. 30(6):70–74. 1956.

6923. ______. Turfgrass questions answered by Grau. Golfdom. 30(7):56,60,62–64,82. 1956.

6924. ______. Turfgrass questions answered by Grau. Golfdom. 30(8):50–51,74. 1956.

6925. ______. Turfgrass questions answered by Grau. Golfdom. 30(9):58, 60–64. 1956.

6926. ______. Watering lawns. Handbook on Lawns. Brooklyn Botanic Garden. pp. 84–90. 1956.

6927. ______. Too much water? Proceedings of the 25th Annual Penn State Turfgrass Conference. pp. 42–47. 1956.

6928. ______. Handbook on lawns. Plants and Gardens. 1956.

6929. ______. New horizons for the golf course superintendent. Proceedings University of Florida Turf Management Conference. 5:58–60. 1957.

6930. ______. Soil structure and amendments. Golf Course Reporter. 25(6):14–21. 1957.

6931. ______. Factors in selecting grasses. Proceedings of Midwest Regional Turf Conference. pp. 85–88. 1957.

6932. ______. Human relations on the golf course. Proceedings Eleventh Southeastern Turfgrass Conference. pp. 13–15. 1957.

6933. ______. To topdress or not—that is the question. Golf Course Reporter. 26(3):-20–22. 1958.

6934. ______. Nitrogen materials and their utilization. Proceedings of Midwest Regional Turf Conference. pp. 12–13. 1958.

6935. ______. Water. Parks and Recreation. 41(1):12. 1958.

6936. ______. How thick should sod be cut? Warren's Turf Nursery. Palos Park, Illinois. pp. 5–6. 1959.

6937. ______. Zoysia for golf turf. Golfdom. 34(3):52–54. 1960.

6938. ______. Avoiding built-in headaches. Proceedings Fourteenth Southeastern Turfgrass Conference. pp. 12–15. 1960.

6939. ______. Even better turf needs proper water, nutrition. Golfdom. 35:45–48,-76. 1961.

6940. ______. A time to rest. Golfdom. 35:64–65. 1961.

6941. ______. Ideal fertilizer may be blend of N sources. Golfdom. 35:76–78. 1961.

6942. ______. Wanted: tougher grasses for the transition zone. Golfdom. 35:86–88,128. 1961.

6943. ______. Fairways—1940 to 1960. Proceedings of the Midwest Regional Turf Conference. pp. 18–22. 1961.

6944. ______. Modern methods of aeration and thatch removal. Park Maintenance. 14:10–13. 1961.

6945. ______. How nitrogen works. Golfdom 36(6):39–40. 1962.

6946. ______. Seedbed protection. Golfdom. 36(4):46–48,52,124. 1962.

6947. ______. Water and weeds. Oklahoma Turfgrass Conference Proceedings. pp. 7–8. 1962.

6948. ______. Nitrogen nutrition—fairways. Oklahoma Turfgrass Conference Proceedings. pp. 15–16. 1962.

6949. ______. Soil compaction and related factors. Proceedings Sixteenth Southeastern Turfgrass Conference. pp. 17–19. 1962.

6950. ______. Vegatative creeping bentgrasses. Turf Clippings University of Massachussetts. 1(7):21-A to 26-A. 1962.

6951. ______. Zoysia dissected. Central Plains Turfgrass Conference. pp. 3–4. 1962.

6952. ______. Grau's answers to turf questions. Golfdom. 37:44–46,76–77. 1963.

6953. ______. We open a new golf course. Proceedings of the Mid-Atlantic Association of Golf Course Superintendents Conference. pp. 5–9. 1963.

6954. ______. Principles involved with residual nitrogen. Proceedings of the Midwest Regional Turf Conference. pp. 49–51. 1963.

6955. ______. Roundup of technical developments in 1964. Golfdom. 38(9):78–80, 104. 1964.

6956. ______. The day's topics—questions and answers. Proceedings of the Mid-Atlantic Association of Golf Course Superintendents Conference. pp. 16–17. 1964.

6957. ______. Principals involved with residual nitrogen. University of Nebraska Turf Conference. 3 pp. 1964.

6958. ______. Water is vital Golfdom. 39(2):64–68. 1965.

6959. ______. Space and turf growth: an introduction. Proceedings of the Midwest Regional Turf Conference. pp. 6–8. 1965.

6960. ______. Protect fairways from competition. Proceedings of the Midwest Regional Turf Conference. pp. 43–44. 1965.

6961. ______. Let's talk fertilizer. Northern Ohio Turf Grass News. 7(3):2–3. 1965.

6962. ______. Grau's answers to turf questions. Golfdom. 40(4):35,38. 1966.

6963. ______. Grau's answers to turf questions. Golfdom. 40(5):22,92,94. 1966.

6964. ______. Grau's answers to turf questions. Golfdom. 40(6):20,66,68,70. 1966.

6965. ______. Grau's answers to turf questions. Golfdom. 40(8):10. 1966.

6966. ______. Grau's answers to turf questions. Golfdom. 40(9):18,20. 1966.

6967. ______. Grau's answers to turf questions. Golfdom. 40(10):10. 1966.

6968. ______. Planting techniques, continuing establishment, and early maintenance. Proceedings of the Midwest Regional Turf Conference. pp. 66–68. 1968.

6969. ______. For erosion control, 'no maintenance,' and beauty-crownvetch. Weeds, Trees, and Turf. 9(9):6–11. 1970.

6970. ______. Turf maintenance: What's ahead? Golfdom. 45(6):36–39. 1971.

6971. ______. Where we've been, where we are, where we're going. USGA Green Section Record. 9(2):2–5. 1971.

6972. ______. Does your turf need sulfur? Better Crops with Plant Food. 16(1):-22–25. 1972.

6973. ______. The importance of water management part II. Mid-Atlantic Newsletter. 23(8):3–4. 1972.

6974. ______. Progress toward better turf. Proceedings of the Midwest Regional Turf Conference. pp. 4–9. 1972.

6975. ______. Sulfur for turfgrass. Weeds, Trees and Turf. 11(2):22,48–64. 1972.

6976. Grau, F. V. and J. M. O'Donnell. Solid urea-form: preparation, properties, and performance. Agronomy Abstracts. p. 65. 1958.

6977. Grau, F. V. and M. H. Ferguson. Pointers on making good lawns. Grass. The Yearbook of Agriculture. USDA. pp. 302–307. 1948.

6978. ______. Bad news for crabgrass. Crops and Soils. 1(8):26–27. 1949.

6979. ______. Pointers on making good lawns. Leaflet No. 281 U.S. Department of Agriculture 6 pp. 1950.

6980. Grau, F. V., and A. F. Grau. Crownvetch, promising new cover crop. Crops and Soils. 4(5):22–25. 1952.

6981. ______. Crownvetch. Pennsylvania Farmer. 146(11):26–27, 35. 1952.

6982. Grau, F. V. and O J. Noer. Golf is played on grass. Grass. The Yearbook of Agriculture. USDA. pp. 324–330. 1948.

6983. Grau, F. V. and A. M. Radko. Meyer (Z-52) Zoysia. USGA Journal and Turf Management 4(6):30–31. 1951.

6984. ______. Experiences with combinations of warm-season and cool-season grasses for turf. Agronomy Abstracts. p. 40. 1952.

6985. ______. Report findings of national Merion bluegrass survey. Golfdom. 26(10):46,48,50. 1952.

6986. ______. National Merion bluegrass survey. Golf Course Reporter. 20(5):-24–28. 1952.

6987. ______. Merion bluegrass survey. U.S.G.A. Journal and Turf Management. 5(6):25–28. 1952.

6988. Grau, F. V., J. B. Page, B. Shelton, G. Jones and W. E. Zimmerman. Water in relation to physical characteristics of soil and soil fertility. Proceedings of the Annual Texas Turfgrass Conference. 9:61–66. 1954.

6989. Graulmann, H. O. Our sources of seeds of grasses and legumes. New York State Turf Association Bulletin. 68:261–263. 1961.

6990. Graves, H. A. and D. G. Hoag. Your lawn, it can be beautiful. North Dakota Agricultural Extension Circular. A244:1–6. 1956.

6991. Graves, J. E. and W. E. McMurphy. Burning and fertilization for range improvement in central Oklahoma. Journal of Range Management. 22:165–168. 1969.

6992. Graves, R. Automatic irrigation for today's golf course. A Patch of Green. Michigan and Border Cities GCSA Publication. pp. 8–12. September, 1971.

6993. Graves, R. M. Problems, schedules and costs in golf course construction. Proceedings of Arizona Turfgrass Conference. pp. 1–4. 1972.

6994. Graves, S. New water lines at Westwood Country Club. Proceedings of Midwest Regional Turf Conference. pp. 24–27. 1952.

6995. Gray, A. S. Sprinkler irrigation handbook. Rainbird Sprinkler Mfg. Co., Glendora, California. 44 pp. 1961.

6996. Gray, C. Water quality and salt problems. Proceedings Annual Texas Turfgrass Conference. 21:61–62. 1966.

6997. Gray, S. D. Need and use of potash in turf development. Golfdom. 24(3):86,88, 90. 1950.

6998. ______. The use of potash in turf development. Greenkeeping Superintendents Association National Turf Conference. 21:-35–39. 1950.

6999. ______. The use of potash in turf development. Rutgers University Short Course in Turf Management. 18:58–65. 1950.

7000. Graybill, H. B. Lawn grasses for South China. Christian College Bulletin No. 25. Canton, China. 5 pp. 1920.

7001. Gray, T. D. Making the home lawn attractive. West Virginia Agricultural Extension Service Landscape Series. 5:4.

7002. Greb, B. W. Percent soil cover by six vegetative mulches. Agronomy Journal. 59(6):610–611. 1967.

7003. Greek, H. Build a bowling green. Exposition Conference. Southern California. 5 pp. 1966.

7004. ______. Build a bowling green. The Golf Superintendent. 35(1):38, 92. 1967.

7005. ______. We built a bowling green. Park Maintenance. 21(9):8–10. 1968.

7007. Green, D. G., and J. B. Beard. Seasonal relationships between nitrogen nutrition and soluble carbohydrates in leaves of four turfgrasses. Agronomy Abstracts. p. 118. 1963.

7008. ______. Seasonal relationships between nitrogen nutrition and soluble carbohydrates in the leaves of *Agrostis palustris* Huds, and *Poa pratensis* L. Agronomy Journal. 61(1):107–111. 1969.

7009. Green, H. Methods of operation (cutting, aerifying, top-dressing, verticutting, and fertilizing) for a golf course under heavy play. Proceedings Thirteenth Southeastern Turfgrass Conference. pp. 31–32. 1959.

7010. Green, J. O. and T. A. Evans. The chemical control of grasses in Lucerne. British Weed Control Conference Proceedings. 1:269–278. 1956.

7011. Green, J. T. and R. E. Schmidt. The effects on rapid establishment and subsequent turf quality of aggressive grasses seeded with Kentucky bluegrass in three seasons and clipped at two heights. Agronomy Abstracts. p. 47. 1971.

7012. Green, J. T., and R. E. Blaser. Establishing and maintaining vegetation on steep highway slopes. Agronomy Abstracts. 2:63. 1972.

7013. Green, V. E. St. Augustinegrass. Progress by Design Sunshine State Agricultural Research Report. 8(1):37. 1963.

7014. Greenaway, T. E. and M. Budden. A discussion on the influence of relative moisture availability on the swards resulting from standard grass seed mixtures I. Mixture of the Cockle Park type. Journal of the British Grassland Society. 13(3):222–228. 1958.

7015. ______. The use of perennial ryegrass sown at one pound per acre in a standard seeds mixture. Journal of British Grassland Society. 15:235–239. 1960.

7016. Greene, F. How Prudential insures turf. Proceedings University of Florida Turfgrass Conference. 4:84–86. 1956.

7017. Greene, R. E. Virginia Short Course on Roadside Development (Ohio). 17:134–135. 1958.

7018. Greene, W. C. The scope of pesticides in highway operations. Highway Research Record No. 53. pp. 8–14. 1963.

7019. Greenfield, I. Mosses and their control in sports turf, Part II. Parks, Golf Courses & Sports Grounds. 12:482–487. 1947.

7020. ______. Controlling turf pests. Gardeners Chronicle. 141(11):292. 1957.

7021. ______. Mosses and their control in fine turf. Gardeners chronicle. 141(15):-386. 1957.

7022. ______. Turf weeds and their control Part II. Parks, Golf Courses and Sport Grounds. 23(1):29–35. 1957.

7023. ______. Turf diseases and their control. Part I. Parks, Golf Courses & Sports Grounds. 22(4):203–206. 1957.

7024. ______. Turf diseases and their control. Part II. Parks, Golf Courses and Sports Grounds. 22(5):264–269, 272. 1957.

7025. ______. Mosses and their control in sports turf. Part I. Parks, Golf Courses and Sports Grounds. 22(7):415–416. 1957.

7026. ______. Mosses and their control in sports turf. Part III. Parks, Golf Courses and Sports Grounds. 22(9):551–555. 1957.

7027. ______. Turf weeds and their control. Part I. Parks, Golf Courses and Sports Grounds. 22(12):757–758. 1957.

7028. ______. Turf pests and their control. Part I. Parks, Golf Courses & Sports Grounds. 23:272–276. 1958.

7029. ______. Turf pests and their control. Part II. Parks, Golf Courses & Sports Grounds. 23:341–345. 1958.

7030. ______. Turf pests and their control. Part III. Parks, Golf Courses & Sports Grounds. 23:417–421, 442. 1958.

7031. ______. Turf Culture. Leonard Hill Ltd., London. 364 pp. 1962.

7032. ______. Pests and diseases of turf. Pesticide Technology. 4:179–184. 1962.

7033. Greenhill, A. W. and A. C. Chibnall. The exudation of glutamine from perennial ryegrass. Biochemistry Journal 28(4):-1422–1427. 1934.

7034. Greensill, T. M. Hedges and lawns. Tropical Gardening. Frederick A. Praeger, New York. pp. 150–154. 1966.

7035. Greenway, H., and A. Rogers. Growth and ion uptake of *Agropyron elongatum* on saline substrates, as compared with a salt-tolerant variety of *Hordeum vulgare.* Plant and Soil. 18(1):21–30. 1963.

7036. Gregg, J. W. Lawn making in California. California Agricultural Experiment Station Circular. 149:1–8. 1916.

7037. Gregory, C. and J. R. Henry. Overseeding with bent helps solve Texas greens problem. Golfdom. 26(9):44, 46, 58–60. 1952.

7038. Gregory, R. P. G., and A. D. Bradshaw. Heavy metal tolerance in populations of *Agrostis tenuis* Sibth. and other grasses. The New Phythologist. 64:131–143. 1965.

7039. Greig, J. K., C. E. Long, N. W. Miles, E. B. Nilson, P. L. Roth and R. W. Campbell. Chemical weed control-Lawn and Turf. Kansas State University Agricultural Experiment Station. Bulletin 505. pp. 18–19. 1967.

7040. Gress, E. M. Preparation and care of lawns. Pennsylvania Agriculture Department Circular. 4:1–8. 1925.

7041. Grether, T. Your turfgrass headache: what variety? Parks and Recreation. 1(6):504–505. 1966.

7042. ______. Techniques of producing sprig and plugs. Proceedings GCSAA Turfgrass Conference. 38:59–61. 1967.

7043. ______. Stolons and vegetative reproduction of turfgrass. Proceedings of the Annual Northwest Turfgrass Conference. 21:59–63. 1967.

7044. Grey, E. P. Proper watering. Turf Clippings. University of Massachussetts. 2(1):1. 1966.

7045. Grieger, F. J. MH-30-ein Wachstumsregulator für gräser. Basf. Mittl. f.d. Landbau. 1965.

7046. Gries, G. A. Putting grass roots to work. Proceedings of Midwest Regional Turf Conference. pp. 32–35. 1953.

7047. Griffes, A. Selecting equipment for lawn maintenance. Proceedings University of Florida Turf-Grass Management Conference. 12:116–120. 1964.

7048. Griffin, C. W. Chemical regulations: How they will change our courses. Golfdom. 46(3):50–52, 57, 89. 1972.

7049. Griffin, H. M. Problems in building new courses and greens. Proceedings Missouri Lawn and Turf Conference. pp. 31–32. 1962.

7050. ______ Golf tour observations in 1963. Rutgers University Turfgrass Short Course. pp. 60–61. 1963.

7051. ______. Effect of tree roots on turf. USGA Journal and Turf Management. 15(5):28–30. 1962.

7052. ______. Verti-cutting and mowing. Proceedings of 1963 Turf Conference. Southern Turfgrass Association. pp. 4–6. 1963.

7053. ______Overseeding methods. Proceedings of 1963 Turf Conference. Southern Turfgrass Association. pp. 9–11. 1963.

7054. ______ Water and turf diseases. Rocky Mountain Regional Turfgrass Conference Proceedings. 9:29–31. 1962.

7055. ______. Bermudagrass in the Northeast. USGA Green Section Record. 1(4):4–5. 1963.

7056. ______. Water and turf diseases. USGA Journal and Turf Management. 15(7):23–26. 1963.

7057. ______. Winterkill on bermuda grasses. Proceedings of the Mid-Atlantic Association of Greenkeeper's Conference. p. 3. 1964.

7058. ______. Trees for golf course use. USGA Green Section Record. 1(5):1–3. 1964.

7059. ______. The individual's responsibility for golf course care. USGA Green Section Record. 2(3):12–13. 1964.

7060. ______. USGA putting green construction methods. Sixteenthth R.C.G.A. Sports Turfgrass Conference. pp. 17–21. 1965.

7061. ______. Analysis of fairway grasses. Sixteenth R.C.G.A. Sports Turfgrass Conference. pp. 23–25. 1965.

7062. ______. Recipe for good greens. USGA Green Section Record. 3(5):1–2. 1966.

7063. ______. A closer look at watering. USGA Green Section Record. 4(3):7–10. 1966.

7064. ______. Planting the golf course. USGA Green Section Record. 4(4):1–6 1966.

7065. ______. Irrigation news. Proceedings GCSAA Annual Turfgrass Conference. 38:73–75. 1967.

7066. ______. Renovation vs. rebuilding greens. USGA Green Section Record. 4(6):-12–13. 1967.

7067. ______. Putting green turf from seed. Turf Bulletin. 4(8):3–4. 1968.

7068. ______. Turf management through genetics. Turf Bulletin. 4(8):6, 11–12. 1968.

7069. ______. Soil physics and green construction. USGA Green Section Record. 5(6):9–10. 1968.

7070. ______. Putting green turf from seed. USGA Green Section Record. 5(6):19–20. 1968.

7071. ______. Management basics for bent greens in southern areas. USGA Green Section Record. 7(1):10–13. 1969.

7072. ______. Management basics for bent greens. Proceedings Fourth Annual Tennessee Turfgrass Conference. pp. 22–26. 1970.

7073. ______. Winter problems—what they look like—what to do about them. USGA Green Section Record. 8(2):2–3. 1970.

7074. ______. Winter troubles with bermudagrass. Mid-Atlantic Superintendents Conference Proceedings. pp. 9–11. 1971.

7075. ______. Streamlining the operation. USGA Green Section Record. 9(2):29–31. 1971.

7076. ______. Overseeding, 1971, to transition, 1972. USGA Green Section Record. 9(4):1–4. 1971.

7077. ______. Organization in maintenance. USGA Green Section Record. 10(2):-7–8. 1972.

7078. ______. How dependable is preemergence weed control? USGA Green Section Record. 10(3):1–3. 1972.

7079. ______. Sources and uses of soil modifiers in turf. USGA Green Section Record. 10(5):7–9. 1972.

7080. Griffin, H. M., A. Choate, R. E. Engel, and J. P. English. Concepts of a perfect putting green. USGA Green Section Record. 1(6):6–7. 1964.

7081. Griffin, J. T. Presiding remarks. Ohio Short Course on Roadside Development. 21:70–75. 1962.

7082. Griffith, D. E. Maintenance of unpaved areas. Texas Engineering Experiment Station Bulletin. 81:166–173. 1944.

7083. Griffith, E. Night turf maintenance. Lakeshore News. 4(5):2. 1972.

7084. Griffith, G., and R. J. K. Walters. The sodium and potassium content of some grass genera, species, and varieties. Journal of Agricultural Science. 67(1):81–89. 1966.

7085. Griffiths, D. J. The liability of seed crops of perennial ryegrass *(Lolium perenne)* to contamination by wind-borne pollen. Journal of Agricultural Science. 40(1):19–38. 1950.

7086. Grigsby, B. H. Growing beautiful lawns. Cooperative Extension Service, Michigan State College. 224:3–23 1941.

7087. ______. Selective control of crabgrass. Michigan Agricultural Experiment Station Bulletin. 30(4):369–373. 1948.

7088. ______. Crabgrass control experiments in Michigan. Golf Course Reporter. 18(5):20–22. 1950.

7089. ______. Control of crabgrass and other weeds in lawns. Proceedings North Central Weed Control Conference. 7:62–63. 1950.

7090. ______. Control of mossy stonecrop (*Sedum acre* L.) and certain other lawn weeds. Michigan Agricultural Experiment Station Bulletin. 33(4):326–331. 1951.

7091. ______. Use of chlordane for the control of crabgrass. Michigan Agricultural Experiment Station. Quarterly Bulletin. 34:-158–161. 1951.

7092. ______. Summary of chemical control measures for crabgrass. Proceedings of Midwest Regional Turf Conference. pp. 80–84. 1951.

7093. ______. 2, 4-D spraying more effective in low temperatures. Park Maintenance. 4(5):7–10. 1951.

7094. ______. Use of chlordane for control of crabgrass. Golf Course Reporter. 20(5):5–7. 1952.

7095. ______. Efficient weed control on today's golf course. Golf Course Reporter. 21(6):10–12. 1953.

7096. ______. Weed control. Golfdom. 27(10):45. 1953.

7097. ______. Broad-leaved weed control with 2, 4-D and related materials. Special Proceedings of the Turf Section Weed Society of America. pp. 23–28. 1956.

7098. ______. Control of chickweed in turf. North Central Weed Control Conference Proceedings. 15:37–38. 1958.

7099. Grime, J. P. and D. W. Jeffray. Seedling establishment in vertical gradients of sunlight. Journal of Ecology. 53(3):621–642. 1965.

7100. Grimm, D. G. Methods of applying maleic hydrazide. Proceedings of the Northeastern Weed Control Conference. 15:-457–463. 1961.

7102. ______. Inhibitors for economic maintenance. Ohio Short Course on Roadside Development. 22:78. 1963.

7103. Grimm, H. and J. C. Knolle. Turfgrass seed in the form of pellets and granules. Proceedings of the First International Turfgrass Research Conference. pp. 559–564. 1969.

7105. Grisez, J. P. A comparison of four methods of sampling small seeds. M. S. Thesis, Oregon State University. 1967.

7107. Grogan, A. E. What a club expects of its superintendent. USGA Green Section Record. 9(2):16–18. 1971.

7108. Gross, F. C. "Dibbler" plants stolons without loss of plan. Golfdom. 4(4):115–116. 1930.

7109. ______. Pitch holding greens. Greenkeepers Club of New England Newsletter. 4(9):4–6. 1932.

7110. Gross, E. M. The grasses of Pennsylvania. Pennsylvania Department of Agriculture General Bulletin 384. Bureau of Plant Industry Technical Series No. 2. 1924.

7111. Gross, E. R. Drainage is major turf need. Golfdom. 12(6):29–31. 1938.

7112. Gross, R. L. Home lawns. Washington State University Extension Service. 1960.

7113. Grossbard, E. New hope for disease control. Golf Course Reporter. 21(5):-24–26. 1953.

7114. Grotelueschen, R. D. Development and loss of cold resistance in timothy (*Phleum pratense* L.) and associated changes in carbohydrates and nitrogen as influenced by nitrogen and potassium fertilization. PhD Thesis, University of Wisconsin. 99 pp. 1967.

7115. Grotelueschen, R. D. and D. Smith. Carbohydrates in grasses. III. Estimations of the degree of polymerization of the fructosans in the stem bases of timothy and bromegrass near seed maturity. Crop Science. 8(2):210–212. 1968.

7116. Groves, I. W. Some common lawn mushrooms. Greenhouse Garden Grass; Canada Department of Agriculture. 4:18–22. 1964.

7117. Grun, P. Cytogenetic studies of *Poa.* I. Chromosome numbers and morphology of interspecific hybrids. American Journal of Botany. 41:671–678. 1954.

7118. Grunder, M. S. Notes; unusual inflorescence types in Italian ryegrass. Journal of the American Society of Agronomy. 40:-655–659. 1948.

7119. ______. Progress report on the pearlwort control project at the Western Washington Experiment Station. Proceedings 6th Annual Northwest Turf Conference. 6:29–32. 1952.

7120. ______. Preliminary report on Pearlwort control. New York State Turf Association Bulletin 47. p. 182. 1953.

7121. Gudauskas, R. T. Stem and crown necrosis of Coastal bermuda grass caused by *Helminthosporium spiciferum.* Plant Disease Reporter. 46(7):498–500. 1962.

7122. Gudauskas, R. T. and S. M. McCarter. Occurrence of rust on zoysia species in Alabama. The Plant Disease Reporter. 50(11):885. 1966.

7123. Gudauskas, R. T. and N. E. McGlohon. *Sclerotinia* blight of bahia grass in Alabama. The Plant Disease Reporter. 48(5):418. 1964.

7124. Gudauskas, R. T., F. J. Subirats, and J. A. Lyle. Zoysiagrass rust. Highlights of Agricultural Research. 17(4):3. 1970.

7125. Gueho, E. M. History and problems in Canadian turf. Proceedings, Northwest Turf Conference. 12:17–18. 1958.

7126. Gullakson, G., L. E. Foote, and J. A. Jackobs. Seedling vigor of *Festuca arundinacea, Panicum virgatum* and *Bothrichloa caucasia* and their response to added nutrients. Journal of Range Management. 17(4):-214–216. 1964.

7127. Gumm, G. C. Green re-construction and drainage. Proceedings of the Mid-Atlantic Association of Golf Course Superintendents Conference. p. 15. 1963.

7128. Gunary, D. and S. Larsen. The influence of method of watering on phosphate uptake by ryegrass grown in pots: effect on the L-value. Plant and Soil. 24(3):351–358. 1966.

7129. Gundell, H. C. What we have learned judging 1,000 lawns. Rocky Mountain Regional Turfgrass Conference Proceedings. 6:10–12. 1960.

7130. Gunderson, H. Pocket gopher control. Golf Course Reporter. 21(7):18–22. 1953.

7131. Gunner, H. B. Environmental control of disease—a new approach. Turf Bulletin. Massachusetts Turf and Lawn Grass Council. 3(3):8. 1966.

7132. ______. Turf treatment and the balance of nature. Turf Clippings. University of Massachusetts. 4(1):A–39 to A–40. 1969.

7133. Gunnison, O. M. Lawn care and groundcovers. Practical gardening. Doubleday and Co., Inc. New York. pp. 218–231. 1955.

7134. Guppy, J. C. Life history and behavior of the armyworm, *Pseudoletia unipunctata* (Haw.) *(Lepidoptera: Noctiudae)* in eastern Ontario. Canada Entomologist. 93(12):1141–1153. 1961.

7135. Gureshi, J. N. Relative value of zinc sulfide as a source of zinc. M.S. Thesis, University of Florida. 1971.

7136. Gurie, A. Lawns, their construction and upkeep. News Chronicle Publications, London. 72 pp. 1950.

7137. Gustafsson, A. Apomixis in higher plants. I. Mechanism of apomixis. Lund Universitets Arsskrift N. F. 42(3):1–68. 1946/1947.

7138. ______. Apomixis in higher plants. II. The casual aspect of apomixis. Lund Universitets Arsskrift N. F. 43(2):69–180. 1946/1947.

7139. ______. Apomixis in higher plants. III. Biotype and species formation. Lund Universitets Arsskrift N. F. 43(12):181–370. 1946/1947.

7140. Gutberlet, P. Preparation for a major tournament. New Zealand Institute for Turf Culture Newsletter. 65:17, 20–21. 1970.

7141. Guthrie, F. E. Ground pearls. Proceedings of the First Annual University of Florida Turfgrass Conference. 1:38. 1952.

7142. Gutberlet, P. Rehabilitation of Hutt Golf Club greens. New Zealand Institute for Turf Culture. Newsletter 51:4–6. 1967.

7143. Guyer, G. E. Current trends in turf pests and their control. Michigan Turfgrass Research Report. 1(1):7. 1963.

7144. Guyer, R. Kentucky bluegrass fairways. Proceedings, Missouri Lawn and Turf Conference. pp. 38–39. 1963.

7145. Haas, H. J., and Rogler, G. A. A technique for photographing grass roots in situ. Agronomy Journal. 45(4):173. 1953.

7146. Habeck, D. H. and L. C. Kuitert. Control of mole crickets. Sunshine State Agricultural Research Report. 9(1):11–12. 1964.

7147. Habenicht, D. Weed control in turf nurseries. Proceedings of the Midwest Regional Turf Conference. p. 28. 1960.

7148. ______. Water, fertilizer and mowing, the three essentials. Proceedings of the Midwest Regional Turf Conference. pp. 80–81. 1961.

7149. ______. Large area soil sterilization. Proceedings of the Midwest Regional Turf Conference. pp. 54–55. 1966.

7150. Hackel, E. The true grasses. Henry Holt and Company. New York. 228 pp. 1890.

7151. ______. Zur biologie der *Poa annua* L. Osterr. Bot. Zeitschr. LIV. 1904.

7152. Hacskaylo, J. Mode of action of systematic herbicides. Proceedings of the Annual Texas Turfgrass Conference. 21:37. 1966.

7154. Hadden, C. Controlling turf diseases. Proceedings First Annual Tennessee Turfgrass Conference. pp. 34–36. 1967.

7155. Hadden, W. A., D. A. Alexander, C. H. Thomas, and H. T. Barr. Herbicides for roadsides in Louisiana. Investigation of methods for controlling weeds and brush and retarding vegetative growth chemically. Louisiana State University Division of Engineering Research Bulletin No. 87. 80 pp. 1965.

7156. Hadley, C. H. and W. E. Fleming. Control of Japanese and Asiatic beetles. Greenkeepers' Reporter. 5(3):4–6, 10–11. 1937.

7157. ______. Newer insecticides for Japanese beetle control. New York State Turf Association Bulletin 18:69–70. 1950.

7158. ______. Newer insecticides for Japanese beetle control. New York State Turf Association Bulletin. 19:75–76. 1950.

7159. Hadley, F. B. Black Hawk's green making and maintenance methods. Golfdom. 1(8):5–7. 1927.

7160. Haes, E. C. M. Annual meadowgrass in turf-an appraisal. Journal of the Sports Turf Research Institute. 9(32):216–218. 1956.

7161. ______. Lawns: the problem of fibre mat. Gardeners Chronicle. 141(11):281. 1957.

7162. ______. The lawn's first feed. Gardeners Chronicle. 141(16):416. 1957.

7163. Hafenrichter, A. L. New grasses and legumes for soil and water conservation. Advances in Agronomy. 10:349–406. 1958.

7164. Hafenrichter, A. L., L. A. Mullen, and R. L. Brown. Grasses and legumes for soil conservation in the Pacific northwest. USDA Miscellaneous Publication No. 678. 56 pp. 1949.

7165. Haff, M. A reasonable program of top-dressing. Golfdom. 3(7):16. 1929.

7166. Hagan, B. Watering practices. Oklahoma Turfgrass Conference Proceedings. pp. 20–22. 1953.

7167. Hagan, R. M. Know how to water. North California Turf Conference. pp. 9–15. 1952.

7168. ______. Water—how much and when? North California Turf Conference. pp. 24–31. 1953.

7169. ______. Know how to water. Proceedings of the Southern California Turf Conference. pp. 23–30. 1952.

7170. Hagan, R. M., and J. R. Stockton. Effect of porous soil amendments on water retention characteristics of soils. USGA Journal and Turf Management. 5(1):29–31. 1952.

7171. Hagan, R. M. Know how to water. USGA Journal and Turf Management. 5(7):-26–30. 1953.

7172. ______. Water requirements of turfgrasses. Proceedings of the Annual Texas Turfgrass Conference. 8:9–20. 1954.

7173. ______. Watering lawns and turf and otherwise caring for them. Water. The Yearbook of Agriculture. USDA. pp. 462–477. 1955.

7174. ______. Water management. Golfdom. 30(6):42, 44, 46, 48. 1956.

7175. ______. Water management. Golfdom 30(7):46, 50, 52, 54. 1956.

7176. ______. Water management. The Golf Course Reporter. 24(4):5–17. 1956.

7177. ______. Water-soil-plant relations. California Agriculture. 11(4):9–12. 1957.

7178. ______. Know how to water. Florida Turf Association Bulletin. 4(2):4. 1957.

7179. ______. Water-soil-plant relations. Southern California Turfgrass Culture. 7(4):-25–30. 1957.

7180. Hagan, R. M. and M. L. Peterson. Soil moisture extraction by irrigated pasture mixtures as influenced by clipping frequency. Agronomy Journal. 45(7):288–292. 1953.

7181. Hagan, R. M., J. H. Madison, Jr., and T. K. Hodges. Soil moisture extraction by Merion Kentucky bluegrass as affected by irrigation frequency, height of mowing, and heration practices. Agronomy Abstracts. 52–70. 1960.

7182. Hagan, R. M., Y. Vaadia, and M. B. Russell. Interpretation of plant responses to soil moisture regimes. Advances in Agronomy. 11:77–98. 1959.

7184. Hager, O. B. Mulch as an aid to erosion control. Ohio Short Course on Roadside Development. 20:76–90. 1961.

7185. Haggar, R. I. The significance and control of *Poa trivialis* in ryegrass pastures. Journal of the British Grassland Society. 26(3):117–122. 1971.

7186. Hagler, T. B. Role of the extension service in turf education. Auburn University 2nd Annual Turfgrass Short Course. pp. 34–37. 1960.

7187. Haight, J. C. Presoaking and drying treatments to improve the performance of orchardgrass and bluegrass seed. M.S. Thesis, Oregon State University. 1972.

7188. Haise, H. R., W. W. Donnon, J. T. Phelan, L. F. Lawhon, and D. G. Shockley. The use of cylinder infiltrometers to determine the intake characteristics of irrigated soils. USDA Agricultural Research Service. Soil Conservation Series. 41(7):1. 1965.

7189. Håkansson, A. Die entwicklung des Embryosacks und die Befruchtung bie *Poa Alpina.* Hereditas. 29:25–61. 1943.

7190. Halcrow, J. G. Weed, worm and disease control. The Groundsman. 19(3):8–10. 1965.

7191. ______. Grass variety trials. Journal of the Sports Turf Research Institute. 41:-40–47. 1965.

7192. ______. Turf disease notes, 1965. Journal of the Sports Turf Research Institute. 41:53–58. 1965.

7193. Halisky, P. M. Fungus diséases of turf grasses. Rutgers University Turfgrass Short Course. 12 pp. 1966.

7194. Halisky, P. M. and C. R. Funk. Environmental factors affecting growth and sporulation of *Helminthosporium vagans* and its pathogenicity to *Poa pratensis.* Phytopathology. 56(11):1294–1296. 1966.

7195. ______. Stripe smut in turfgrasses. Rutgers University Short Course in Turf Management. 3 pp. 1969.

7196. ______. Stripe smut in turfgrasses. Rutgers University College of Agriculture and Environmental Science. Lawn and Utility Turf Section. pp. 58–60. 1969.

7197. Halisky, P. M. and J. L. Peterson. Occurrence of mushrooms and puffballs and their association with fairy rings in turfgrass areas of New Jersey. Turfgrass Research. New Jersey Agricultural Experiment Station. Bulletin 818. pp. 15–19. 1967.

7198. Halisky, P. M., C. R. Funk and P. L. Babinski. Control of stripe smut in Kentucky bluegrass turf with a systemic fungicide. The Plant Disease Reporter. 52(8):635–637. 1968.

7199. ______. Chemical control of stripe smut in Merion Kentucky bluegrass. Scotts Turfgrass Research Seminar. pp. 38–42. 1968.

7200. ______. Chemical control of stripe smut in Merion Kentucky bluegrass. The Plant Disease Reporter. 53(4):286–288. 1969.

7201. Halisky, P. M., C. R. Funk and S. Bachelder. Stripe smut of turf and forage grasses—its prevalence, pathogenicity and response to management practices. The Plant Disease Reporter. 50(5):294–298. 1966.

7202. ______. Stripe smut of turf and forage grasses . . . its prevalence, pathogenicity and response to management practices. Turf Bulletin. 4(1):15, 18–19. 1966.

7203. ______. Stripe smut attacks Merion bluegrass. Weeds, Trees and Turf. 5(12):-8–9. 1966.

7204. Halisky, P. M., C. R. Funk, and R. E. Engel. Occurrence and pathogenicity of *Helminthosporium sativum* in the Rutgers turf plots in 1964 and 1965. Turfgrass Research. New Jersey Agricultural Experiment Station. Bulletin 816. pp. 72–78. 1966.

7205. ______. Melting-out of Kentucky bluegrass varieties by *Helminthosporium vagans* as influenced by turf management practices. The Plant Disease Reporter. 50(9):703–706. 1966.

7206. Hall, D. L. New bermuda strains for South. Golfdom. 15(6):13–15. 1941.

7207. ______. Sodium arsenite as control for crabgrass, *Poa annua.* Golfdom. 27(5):40, 42, 93. 1953.

7208. ______. Better turf management-greens. Golf Course Reporter. 22(3):18–23. 1954.

7209. ______. The use of sodium arsenite on fairways and greens. Southeastern Turfgrass Conference. 9:51–54. 1955.

7210. ______. My thatch control program. Proceedings University of Florida Turfgrass Management Conference. 7:27–28. 1959.

7211. ______. Winter and summer greens. Golf Course Reporter. 27(7):70–71. 1959.

7213. Hall, J. M. Turf nursery production problems. II. Planting methods. University of Florida Turfgrass Conference Proceedings. 3:68. 1955.

7214. Hall, J. R. Problems in attempting to use tissue testing to determine fertilizer needs. Ohio Turfgrass Conference Proceedings. pp. 55–64. 1970.

7215. ______. The effect of phosphorus, season, and method of sampling on foliar analysis, mineral depletion, and yield of Merion Kentucky bluegrass. Ph.D Thesis, Ohio State University. 1971.

7216. ______. Turf management. Turf Bulletin (Massachusetts). 8(5):6. 1972.

7217. Hall, J. R. and R. W. Miller. The influence of phosphorus incorporation, time, and method of sampling on the chemical composition and yield of Merion Kentucky bluegrass. Agronomy Abstracts. p. 47. 1971.

7218. Hall, R. H. Southern course building, too, needs right man on job early. Golfdom. 5(5):98, 100–101. 1931.

7219. ______. Building pointers that better bermuda grass greens. Golfdom. 5(9):56, 58. 1931.

7220. Hall, T. D. and D. Moses. The fertility factor in turf production. South African Journal of Science. 27:180–201. 1931.

7221. Hall, T. D., D. Meredith, and S. M. Murray. Dry matter and protein of pastures as affected by amounts and forms of nitrogen applied. South African Journal of Science. 44:111–118. 1948.

7222. ______. Dry matter and protein of *Cynodon dactylon* as affected by amounts and forms of nitrogen applied. Better Turf Through Research. South African Turf Research Fund. pp. 29–35. 1948.

7223. Hall, T. D., D. Meredith, S. M. Murray, and R. E. Altona. The effect of fertilizers on turf grasses at the Frankenwald Botanical Research Station. Better Turf Through Research. South African Turf Research Fund. pp. 1–16. 1948.

7225. Halligan, C. P. Landscaping the home grounds. Michigan State College Co-op Extension Service. 1949.

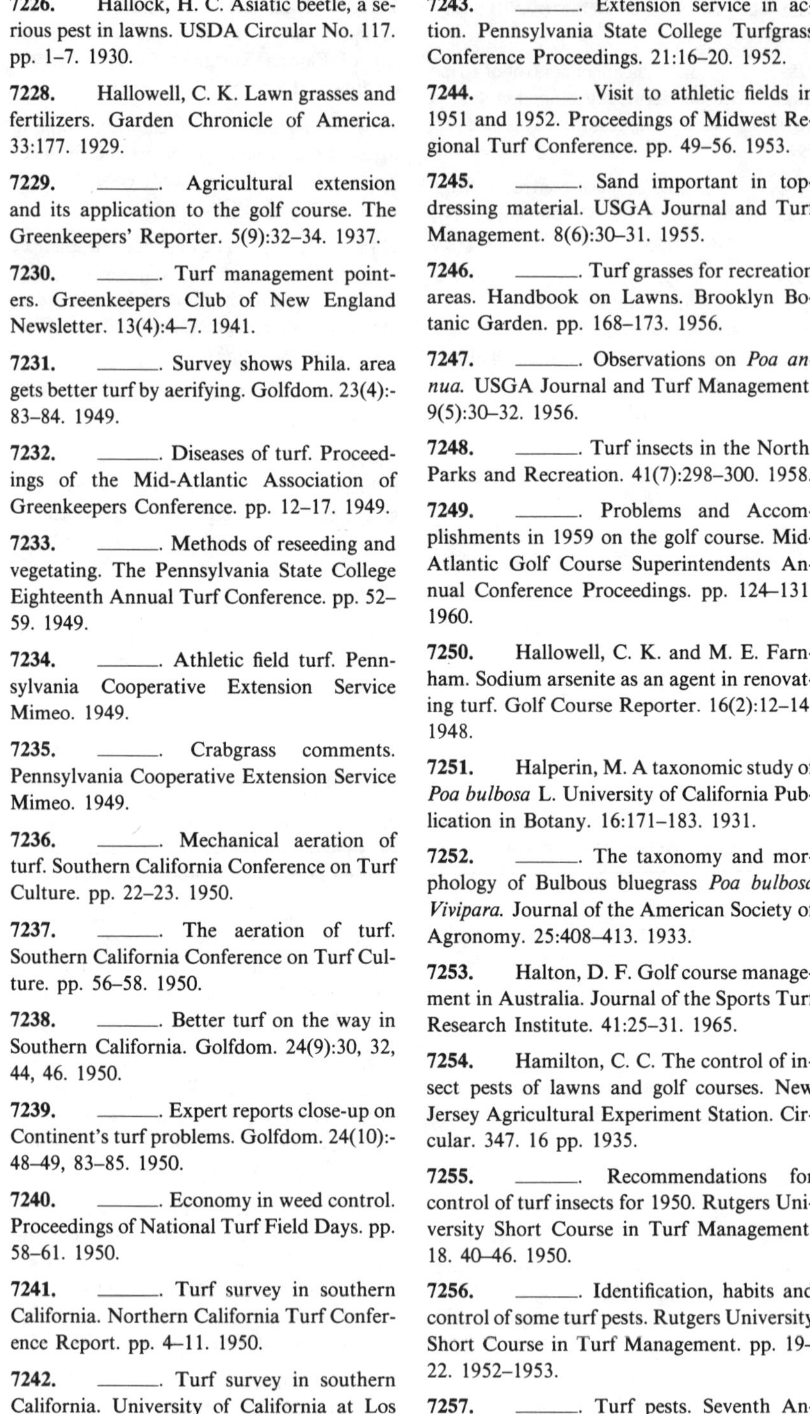

7226. Hallock, H. C. Asiatic beetle, a serious pest in lawns. USDA Circular No. 117. pp. 1–7. 1930.

7228. Hallowell, C. K. Lawn grasses and fertilizers. Garden Chronicle of America. 33:177. 1929.

7229. ______. Agricultural extension and its application to the golf course. The Greenkeepers' Reporter. 5(9):32–34. 1937.

7230. ______. Turf management pointers. Greenkeepers Club of New England Newsletter. 13(4):4–7. 1941.

7231. ______. Survey shows Phila. area gets better turf by aerifying. Golfdom. 23(4):-83–84. 1949.

7232. ______. Diseases of turf. Proceedings of the Mid-Atlantic Association of Greenkeepers Conference. pp. 12–17. 1949.

7233. ______. Methods of reseeding and vegetating. The Pennsylvania State College Eighteenth Annual Turf Conference. pp. 52–59. 1949.

7234. ______. Athletic field turf. Pennsylvania Cooperative Extension Service Mimeo. 1949.

7235. ______. Crabgrass comments. Pennsylvania Cooperative Extension Service Mimeo. 1949.

7236. ______. Mechanical aeration of turf. Southern California Conference on Turf Culture. pp. 22–23. 1950.

7237. ______. The aeration of turf. Southern California Conference on Turf Culture. pp. 56–58. 1950.

7238. ______. Better turf on the way in Southern California. Golfdom. 24(9):30, 32, 44, 46. 1950.

7239. ______. Expert reports close-up on Continent's turf problems. Golfdom. 24(10):-48–49, 83–85. 1950.

7240. ______. Economy in weed control. Proceedings of National Turf Field Days. pp. 58–61. 1950.

7241. ______. Turf survey in southern California. Northern California Turf Conference Report. pp. 4–11. 1950.

7242. ______. Turf survey in southern California. University of California at Los Angeles Publication. 1–17 pp. 1950.

7243. ______. Extension service in action. Pennsylvania State College Turfgrass Conference Proceedings. 21:16–20. 1952.

7244. ______. Visit to athletic fields in 1951 and 1952. Proceedings of Midwest Regional Turf Conference. pp. 49–56. 1953.

7245. ______. Sand important in topdressing material. USGA Journal and Turf Management. 8(6):30–31. 1955.

7246. ______. Turf grasses for recreation areas. Handbook on Lawns. Brooklyn Botanic Garden. pp. 168–173. 1956.

7247. ______. Observations on *Poa annua.* USGA Journal and Turf Management. 9(5):30–32. 1956.

7248. ______. Turf insects in the North. Parks and Recreation. 41(7):298–300. 1958.

7249. ______. Problems and Accomplishments in 1959 on the golf course. Mid-Atlantic Golf Course Superintendents Annual Conference Proceedings. pp. 124–131. 1960.

7250. Hallowell, C. K. and M. E. Farnham. Sodium arsenite as an agent in renovating turf. Golf Course Reporter. 16(2):12–14. 1948.

7251. Halperin, M. A taxonomic study of *Poa bulbosa* L. University of California Publication in Botany. 16:171–183. 1931.

7252. ______. The taxonomy and morphology of Bulbous bluegrass *Poa bulbosa Vivipara.* Journal of the American Society of Agronomy. 25:408–413. 1933.

7253. Halton, D. F. Golf course management in Australia. Journal of the Sports Turf Research Institute. 41:25–31. 1965.

7254. Hamilton, C. C. The control of insect pests of lawns and golf courses. New Jersey Agricultural Experiment Station. Circular. 347. 16 pp. 1935.

7255. ______. Recommendations for control of turf insects for 1950. Rutgers University Short Course in Turf Management. 18. 40–46. 1950.

7256. ______. Identification, habits and control of some turf pests. Rutgers University Short Course in Turf Management. pp. 19–22. 1952–1953.

7257. ______. Turf pests. Seventh Annual Sports Turfgrass Conference, Ontario

Agricultural College, Guelph. pp. 20–23. 1956.

7258. ______. Profiles of some turf grass and landscape criminals. Rutgers University Short Course in Turf Management. Vol. 27. 15 pp. 1959.

7259. Hamilton, K. C. Crabgrass control on bermudagrass. Turfgrass Research. University of Arizona. Report 203. pp. 37–39. 1961.

7260. ______. Weed control research in bermudagrass turf. Turfgrass Research, Report 212, University of Arizona. pp. 23–25. 1962.

7261. ______. Spurge control in bermudagrass. Turfgrass Research, Report 230. University of Arizona. pp. 1–2. 1965.

7262. ______. Weed control in dormant bermudagrass turf. Turfgrass Research. University of Arizona. Report 240. pp. 7–12. 1966.

7263. ______. Control of khakiweed in bermudagrass. Turfgrass Research. University of Arizona. Report 250. pp. 2–3. 1967–1968.

7264. ______. Control of wild celery and other weeds in bermudagrass. Turfgrass Research. University of Arizona. Report 250. pp. 3–4. 1967–1968.

7265. ______. Rates of MSMA for control of purple nutsedge. Turfgrass Research. University of Arizona. Report 250. pp. 5–6. 1967–68.

7266. Hamilton, K. C., and S. Heathman. Johnsongrass control in Arizona. Arizona Agricultural Extension Service and Experiment Station Bulletin A-53. 16 pp. 1968.

7267. Hamman, P. J. Developments in chinch bug control. Proceedings of the Texas Turfgrass Conference. 23:92–94. 1968.

7268. ______. Control of southern chinch bug. *Blissus insularis.* in Brazos County, Texas. Proceedings of Scotts Turfgrass Research Conference. 1:15–17. 1969.

7269. Hammer, C. L., and H. B. Tukey. Selective herbicidal action of mid-summer and fall applications of 2,4-dichlorophenoxyacetic acid. Botanical Gazette. 106(2):232–245. 1944.

7270. Hammerton, J. L. and R. J. Johnson. Experiments on sod-seeding herbicides. British Weed Control Conference Proceedings. 1:85–92. 1962.

7272. Hammond, F. Height of cut of putting greens. Greenkeepers Club of New England Newsletter. 12(10):2–4. 1940.

7273. ______. Velvet bent as a manufactured product for golf. Golfdom. 22(2):62–64. 1948.

7274. ______. Planting and care of new stolon bent greens. Golfdom. 22(4):48–50. 1948.

7275. ______. Getting greens turf that you can control. Golfdom. 22(7):29,32,77. 1948.

7276. Hammond, L. C. Soil moisture, its availability to turf. Proceedings of the University of Florida Turf-Grass Management Conference. 8:16–17. 1960.

7277. ______. Water movement in soils. Proceedings of the Florida Turfgrass Management Conference. 18:45–47. 1970.

7278. Hammer, J. E. Preparing a Southern golf course for the USGA amateur. USGA Journal and Turf Management. 1(7):-12–14. 1949.

7279. ______. Preparing your greens for winter play. USGA Journal and Turf Management. 6(5):32. 1953.

7280. Hampton, H. E. Potassium, the neglected nutrient. Proceedings of the Texas Turfgrass Conference. 19:31–36. 1964.

7281. Han, S. J. Apomictic reproduction in Kentucky bluegrass. Rutgers University Short Course in Turf Management. 2 pp. 1969.

7282. ______. Apomictic reproduction in Kentucky bluegrass. Rutgers University. College of Agriculture and Environmental Science. Lawn and Utility Turf Section. pp. 15–16. 1969.

7283. Han, S. J., and C. R. Funk. Effect of gibberellic acid, light intensity, day length, fertility level, position of flowers, temperature shock and pollen parent on the mode of reproduction in *Poa pratensis* L. Agronomy Abstracts. p. 63. 1968.

7284. Handoll, C. Grass variety trials. Journal of the Sports Turf Research Institute. 42:49–53. 1966.

7285. ______. Turf disease notes, 1966. Journal of the Sports Turf Research Institute. 42:65–68. 1966.

7286. ______. A report on grass variety trials. The Groundsman. 20(12):15–16. 1967.

7287. ______. Grass variety trials. Journal of the Sports Turf Research Institute. 43:-12–22. 1967.

7288. ______. Turf disease notes 1967. Journal of the Sports Turf Research Institute. 43:28–33. 1967.

7289. Hanes, J. K. Turf maintenance at Wappoo Links, Charleston, S. C. USGA Green Section Bulletin. 11(9):184–186. 1931.

7290. ______. Southern luxury. Golfdom. 11(3):32–34. 1937.

7291. ______. Maintaining turf in the South. The Greenkeepers' Reporter. 5(2):26–29. 1937.

7292. Hankinson, H. Seed mixture impurities show wisdom of buying right. Golfdom. 4(8):33–35. 1930.

7293. Hanley, J. H. and F. F. Weinard. The Chemical eradication of lawn weeds. American Society of Horticultural Science Proceedings. 35:845–349. 1937.

7294. ______. Chemical eradication of lawn weeds. Greenkeepers' Reporter. 6(4):-9–10, 32–33, 35. 1938.

7295. Hanna, W. J. Soil testing for turf. Rutgers University Annual Short Course in Turf Management. 19:75–77. 1952–1953.

7296. Hansen, A. A. The use of chemical weed killers on golf courses. USGA Green Section Bulletin. 1(7):128–131. 1921.

7297. ______. Bentgrasses. House and Garden. 57:184. 1930.

7298. Hansen, C. O. Control of winter annual weeds in southern turf with paraquat. Weed Science Society of America Abstracts. p. 93. 1964.

7299. Hansen, G. Re-building greens at Greenville. The National Greenkeeper. 1(9):-5–6. 1927.

7301. Hansen, L. I. Plastic coated fertilizers. Turf Clippings. University of Massachusetts. 1(8): A–44 to A–49. 1963.

7302. Hansen, M. Nitrogen losses. Proceedings of the Midwest Regional Turf Conference. pp. 59–60. 1961.

7303. Hansen, R. Turf fertilizer trials at Weihenstephan. Proceedings of the First International Turfgrass Research Conference. pp. 200–203. 1969.

7304. Hansen, R. and L. Roemer. Rasenmischungen. Richtlinien für Strassenbepflanzung. Teil 2, Köln. 1964.

7305. Hansen, R. and G. Rudge. Converting to automatic irrigation. The Golf Superintendent. 38(5):13–17, 42. 1970.

7306. Hansen, R. G., R. M. Forbes and D. M. Carlson. A review of the carbohydrate constituents of roughages. University of Illinois Agricultural Experiment Station Bulletin. 634 (N. Central Regional Pub. 88) 47 pp. 1958.

7307. Hanson, A. A. Grass varieties in the United States. USDA Agricultural Research Service Handbook No. 170. 1959.

7308. ______. Royal cape bermudagrass —a new variety for lawn use in the Imperial Valley. USDA Mimeograph. 1960.

7309. ______. Grass varieties in the United States. USDA Agriculture Handbook 170. 72 pp. 1965.

7311. Hanson, A. A., and F. V. Juska. A "progressive" mutation induced in *Poa pratensis* L. by ionizing radiation. Nature. 184(4691):1000, 1001. 1959.

7312. ______. Winter root activity in Kentucky bluegrass (*Poa pratensis* L.). Agronomy Journal. 53(6): 372–374. 1961.

7313. ______. Seedling vigor of Kentucky bluegrass seed sources. Agronomy Abstracts. 54:103. 1962.

7314. ______. Induced mutations in Kentucky bluegrass. Crop Science. 2(5):369–371. 1962.

7315. ______. The characteristics of *Poa pratensis* L. clones collected from favorable and unfavorable environements. Proceedings of the 9th International Grassland Congress (Sao Paulo, Brasil). pp. 159–161. 1962.

7316. ______. Imported Kentucky bluegrass and red fescue seed performance. Seed World. 94(6):14–15. 1964.

7317. ______. Bluegrass varieties, *Poa pratensis* L., and how they differ. Illinois Turfgrass Conference Proceedings. 7 pp. 1965.

7319. ______. Turfgrass Science. American Society of Agronomy. Monograph Series Number 14. pp. 1–715. 1969.

7320. Hanson, A. A. and V. G. Sprague. Heading of perennial grasses under greenhouse conditions. Agronomy Journal. 45(6):-248–251. 1953.

7321. Hanson, A. A., R. J. Garber, and W. M. Myers. Yields of individual and combined apomictic strains of Kentucky bluegrass (*Poa pratensis* L). Agronomy Journal. 44(3):125–132. 1952.

7322. Hanson, A. A., V. G. Sprague, and W. M. Myers. Evaluation of Kentucky bluegrass strains grown in association with white clover. Agronomy Journal. 44(7):373–376, 1952.

7323. Hanson, C. D. Chinch bug. Proceedings of the Texas Turf-grass Conference. 17:18–20. 1962.

7325. Hanson, J. B. Roots—selectors of plant nutrients. Turf Bulletin. Massachusetts Turf and Lawn Grass Council. 4(7):16–18. 1968.

7326. Hanson, J. B. and F. W. Slife, How does 2-4-D kill a plant? Illinois Research 3(3):3–4. 1961.

7327. Hansen, M. C. Physical properties of calcined clays and their utilization for rootzones. M.S. Thesis, Purdue University. 64 pp. 1962.

7328. Harban, W. S. Ridding putting greens of crab grass. USGA Green Section Bulletin. 3(5):131–132. 1923.

7329. Harban, W. S. Injuries to putting greens by careless mowing USGA Green Section Bulletin. 4(10):239–240. 1924.

7330. ______. Why some greens planted by stolen method have been unsatisfactory. USGA Green Section Bulletin. 5:170–172. 1925.

7332. Harberd, D. J. Observations on population structure and longevity of *Festuca rubra*. New Phytologist. 60:184–206. 1961.

7333. ______. Some observations on natural clones in *Festuca ovina*. New Phytologist. 61:85–100. 1962.

7334. Hard, C. G. Cultured sod production. University of Minnesota Fact Sheet. Horticulture No. 6. 1965.

7335. Harder, P. How to handle those tough shady spots. Turf Bulletin. (Massachusetts). 8(5):7. 1972.

7336. ______. 1972—a tough season. Turf Bulletin (Massachusetts). 8(5):20. 1972.

7337. Harder, P. R. and J. Troll. Performance of seven fungicides for control of snow-mold. Turf Bulletin (Massachusetts). 8(4):6–7. 1972.

7338. Hardesty, J. O., J. W. Mitchell, and P. C. Marth. Stability of 2, 4–D stored with mixed fertilizer. USGA Journal and Turf Management. 2(3):31. 1949.

7339. Hardin, E. E. Fluorescence in ryegrass certification. Weeds, Trees and Turf. 11(5):28, 52. 1972.

7340. Harding, G. F. and G. O. P. Eaton. Observations on the use of maleic hydrazide. Proceedings of the British Weed Control Conference. 1:213–218. 1954.

7341. Harding, I. T. Golf course watering. New Zealand Institute for Turf Culture Newsletter. 31:4–9. 1964.

7342. ______. Golf course irrigation. New Zealand Institute for Turf Culture Newsletter. 48:4–9. 1967.

7343. ______. Automatic watering system—new Wairakei international golf course. New Zealand Institute for Turf Culture Newsletter. 59:11–18. 1969.

7344. Harding, R. B., T. W. Embleton, W. W. Jones, and T. M. Ryan. Leaching and gaseous losses of nitrogen from some non-tilled California soils. Agronomy Journal. 55(6):515–518. 1963.

7345. Hardison, J. R. Observations on grass diseases in Kentucky September, 1942 to September, 1944 and a preliminary check list. Plant Disease Reporter. 29(3):76–85. 1945.

7346. ______. Commercial control of *Puccinia striiformis* and other rusts in seed crops of *Poa pratensis* by nickel fungicides. Phytopathology. 53:209–216. 1963.

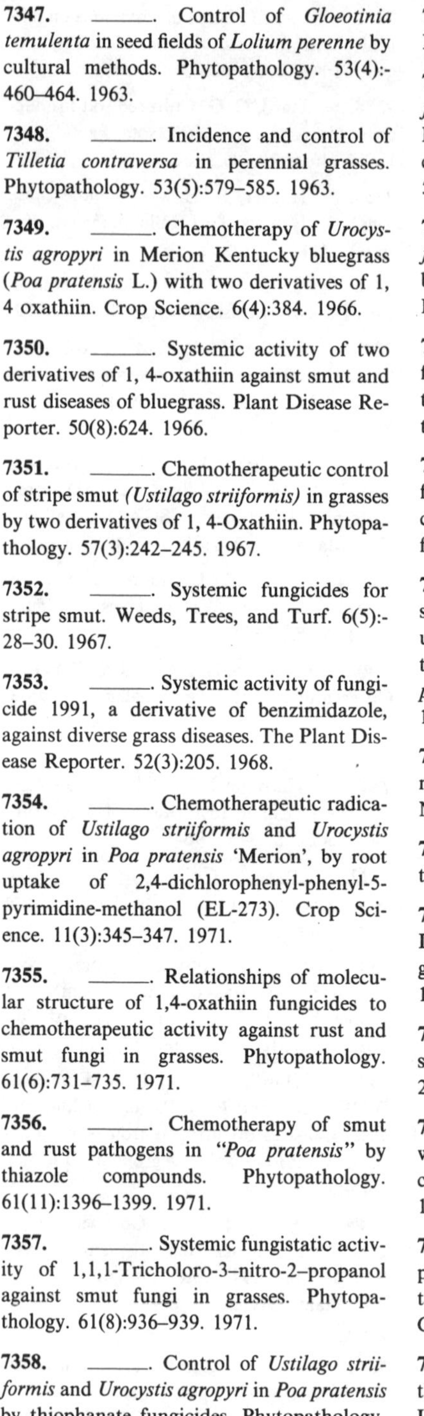

7347. ______. Control of *Gloeotinia temulenta* in seed fields of *Lolium perenne* by cultural methods. Phytopathology. 53(4):-460–464. 1963.

7348. ______. Incidence and control of *Tilletia contraversa* in perennial grasses. Phytopathology. 53(5):579–585. 1963.

7349. ______. Chemotherapy of *Urocystis agropyri* in Merion Kentucky bluegrass (*Poa pratensis* L.) with two derivatives of 1, 4 oxathiin. Crop Science. 6(4):384. 1966.

7350. ______. Systemic activity of two derivatives of 1, 4-oxathiin against smut and rust diseases of bluegrass. Plant Disease Reporter. 50(8):624. 1966.

7351. ______. Chemotherapeutic control of stripe smut *(Ustilago striiformis)* in grasses by two derivatives of 1, 4-Oxathiin. Phytopathology. 57(3):242–245. 1967.

7352. ______. Systemic fungicides for stripe smut. Weeds, Trees, and Turf. 6(5):-28–30. 1967.

7353. ______. Systemic activity of fungicide 1991, a derivative of benzimidazole, against diverse grass diseases. The Plant Disease Reporter. 52(3):205. 1968.

7354. ______. Chemotherapeutic radication of *Ustilago striiformis* and *Urocystis agropyri* in *Poa pratensis* 'Merion', by root uptake of 2,4-dichlorophenyl-phenyl-5-pyrimidine-methanol (EL-273). Crop Science. 11(3):345–347. 1971.

7355. ______. Relationships of molecular structure of 1,4-oxathiin fungicides to chemotherapeutic activity against rust and smut fungi in grasses. Phytopathology. 61(6):731–735. 1971.

7356. ______. Chemotherapy of smut and rust pathogens in "*Poa pratensis*" by thiazole compounds. Phytopathology. 61(11):1396–1399. 1971.

7357. ______. Systemic fungistatic activity of 1,1,1-Tricholoro-3–nitro-2–propanol against smut fungi in grasses. Phytopathology. 61(8):936–939. 1971.

7358. ______. Control of *Ustilago striiformis* and *Urocystis agropyri* in *Poa pratensis* by thiophanate fungicides. Phytopathology. 61(12):1462–1464. 1971.

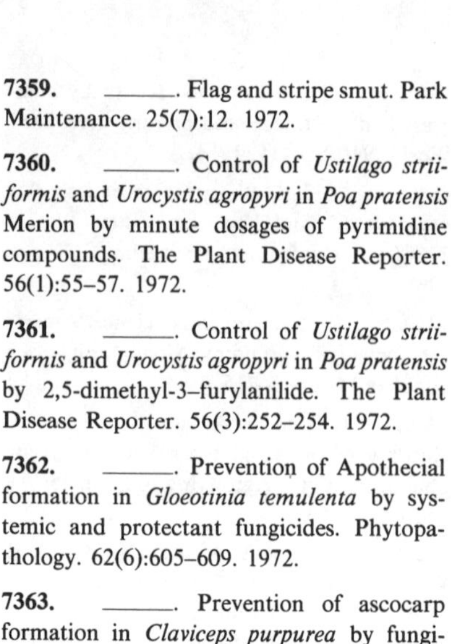

7359. ______. Flag and stripe smut. Park Maintenance. 25(7):12. 1972.

7360. ______. Control of *Ustilago striiformis* and *Urocystis agropyri* in *Poa pratensis* Merion by minute dosages of pyrimidine compounds. The Plant Disease Reporter. 56(1):55–57. 1972.

7361. ______. Control of *Ustilago striiformis* and *Urocystis agropyri* in *Poa pratensis* by 2,5-dimethyl-3–furylanilide. The Plant Disease Reporter. 56(3):252–254. 1972.

7362. ______. Prevention of Apothecial formation in *Gloeotinia temulenta* by systemic and protectant fungicides. Phytopathology. 62(6):605–609. 1972.

7363. ______. Prevention of ascocarp formation in *Claviceps purpurea* by fungicides applied over *Sclerotia* at the soil surface. Phytopathology. 62(6):609–611. 1972.

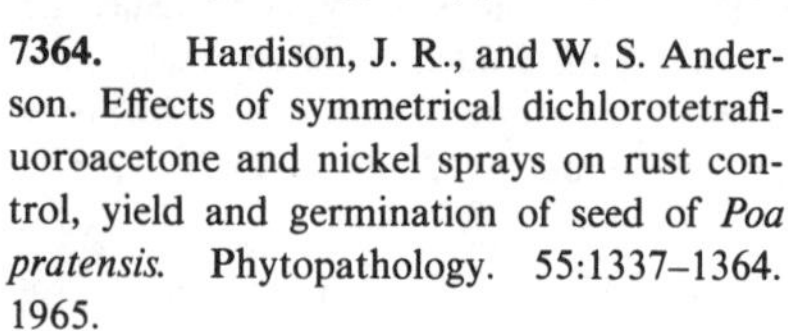

7364. Hardison, J. R., and W. S. Anderson. Effects of symmetrical dichlorotetrafluoroacetone and nickel sprays on rust control, yield and germination of seed of *Poa pratensis.* Phytopathology. 55:1337–1364. 1965.

7365. Hardt, F. M. Green section committee. Greenkeepers Club of New England Newsletter. 10(3):5–6. 1938.

7366. ______. Introducing "turf culture". Turf Culture 1(1):1–5. 1939.

7367. Hardwick, B. C. and B. Axelrod. Isolation of octopamine from annual rye grass. Plant Physiology. 44(12):1745–1746. 1969.

7368. Hardy, R. Renovation of a professional football pitch. The Groundsman. 21(7):37–38. 1968.

7369. Hardy, W. H. Weed control in fairways, tees and greens. Turf Bulletin. Massachusetts Turf & Lawn Grass Council. 2(12):-13–19. 1965.

7370. Haring, C. M. Grass and forage plant investigations. Report of the Agricultural Experiment Station of the University of California for 1921. p. 50. 1922.

7371. ______. Grass garden. Report of the Agricultural Experiment Station of the University of California for 1922. p. 70. 1923.

7372. Harlan, J. R. Development and selection of superior grasses and their relation to disease. Oklahoma Turfgrass Conference Proceedings. pp.25–27. 1953.

7373. ______. Better grasses—can they help in the fight against pests? Oklahoma Turfgrass Conference Proceedings. 9:21–27. 1954.

7374. ______. Turfgrass for the high plains. Oklahoma Turfgrass Conference Proceedings. pp.45–46. 1955.

7376. Harlan, J. R. and J. M. J. de Wet. Sources of variation in *Cynodon dactylon* (L.) Pers. Crop Science. 9(6):774–778. 1969.

7377. Harlan, J. R., and S. P. Sengupta. A cytogeographical study of the genus *Cynodon,* Rich. Agronomy Abstracts. p.7. 1966.

7378. Harlan, J. R., R. M. Ahring, and W. R. Kneebone. Grass seed production under irrigation in Oklahoma. Oklahoma Agricultural Experiment Station. Bulletin, B-481. 15pp. 1956.

7379. Harlan, J. R., J. M. J. deWet, W. W. Huffine, and J. R. Deakin. A guide to the species of *Cynodon (Gramineae).* Oklahoma State University Agricultural Experiment Station Bulletin 8–673. 1–37. 1970.

7380. Harlan, J. R., J. M. J. de Wet, K. M. Rawal, M. R. Felder, and W. L. Richardson. Cytogenetic studies in *Cynodon* L. C. Rich. *(Gramineae).* Crop Science. 19(3):288–291. 1970.

7381. Harmon, D. Let's get involved. Proceedings of the Midwest Regional Turf Conference. pp.18–20. 1972.

7382. Harms, L. Designing roadside sprinkling systems for plant survival. 28th Short Course on Roadside Development. Ohio Dept. of Highways. 28:65–68. 1969.

7383. Harold, L. L. and F. R. Dreibelbis. Evaluation of agricultural hydrology by monolith lysimeters 1944–45. USDA Technical Bulletin No. 1179. 166 pp. 1958.

7384. Harpaz, Y., L. Shanan, and N. H. Tadmor. Effects of a synthetic rubber crust mulch on the emergence and early growth of three grasses on sand dunes. Israel Journal of Agricultural Research. 15(3):149–153. 1965.

7386. Harper, H. J. The effect of natural gas on the growth of microorganisms and the accumulation of nitrogen and organic matter in the soil. Soil Science. 48:461–466. 1939.

7387. Harper, J. Research. Proceedings of National Turf Field Days. pp.20–22. 1950.

7388. ______. Tests of fairway grasses. Pennsylvania State College Turfgrass Conference Proceedings. 20:71–75. 1951.

7389. ______. Relationship of aerification, irrigation, and compaction to phosphorus, penetration, root development, and population changes in a mixed turf of permanent grasses. Ph.D. Thesis. Pennsylvania State University. 126 pp. 1952.

7390. ______. The effect of aerification on phosphorous penetration. Pennsylvania State College Turfgrass Conference Proceedings. 21:32–36. 1952.

7391. ______. Irrigation, compaction, and aeration of fairway turf. USGA Journal and Turf Management. 6(4):27–31. 1953.

7392. ______. Suggestions for maintaining established lawns in the District of Columbia and vicinity. USDA Mimeograph. Spring, 1953.

7393. ______. Suggestions for the establishment and care of Meyer zoysia-Merion bluegrass combination turf. USDA Mimeograph. 1953.

7394. ______. USDA turf research at Beltsville. Golf Course Reporter. 22(7):18–22. 1954.

7395. ______. Down with the roots. Proceedings, Annual University of Florida Turf Conference. 2:4–7. 1954.

7396. ______. Zoysia for turf: varieties and adaptations. Proceedings of the 23rd Annual Penn State Turfgrass Conference. pp.47–50. 1954.

7397. ______. Bermuda strain characteristic chart. USDA Mimeograph. 1954.

7398. ______. Control of lawn insects. USDA Mimeograph. 1954.

7399. ______. Establishment and care of Merion bluegrass lawns. USDA Mimeograph. 1954.

7400. ______. Establishment and care of Meyer zoysia lawns. USDA Mimeograph. 1954.

7401. ______. Lawn diseases. USDA Mimeograph. Spring, 1954.

7402. ______. Suggestions for maintaining turf in shaded areas. USDA Mimeograph. 1954.

7403. ______. U-3 bermudagrass. USDA Mimeograph. 1954.

7404. ______. Zoysia characteristic chart. USDA Mimeograph. 1954.

7405. ______. Turf nursery production problems. I. Soil sterilization methods. University of Florida Turf Management Conference Proceedings. 3:64–67. 1955.

7406. ______. Turf grasses and compaction. University of Florida Turfgrass Conference Proceedings. 3:101–103. 1955.

7407. ______. Warm season grasses, today—tomorrow. Golf Course Reporter. 23(2):16–22. 1955.

7408. ______. Down with the roots. Southeastern Turfgrass Conference. 9:9–15. 1955.

7409. ______. Commercial Zoysia production. Proceedings of Midwest Regional Turf Conference. pp. 47–51. 1956.

7410. ______. Seedbed sterilization. Proceedings of the 25th Annual Penn State Turfgrass Conference. pp. 36–41. 1956.

7411. ______. On the mowing of grass. Parks & Recreation. 40(4):24–25,35. 1957.

7412. ______. Soil and water requirements of good turf. Proceedings Eleventh Southeastern Turfgrass Conference. pp.1–8. 1957.

7413. ______. Soil sterilization methods. Proceedings of Midwest Regional Turf Conference. pp. 54–58. 1958.

7414. ______. Nature & man vs. turf. Parks and Recreation. 41(5):227–229. 1958.

7415. ______. Turf management under excessive rainfall conditions. Golfdom. 33:75. 1959.

7416. ______. On Eastern problems: Athletic fields. Golf Course Reporter. 28(6):-15–31. 1960.

7417. ______. Athletic field maintenance. Pennsylvania Agricultural Extension Service Leaflet. 1965.

7418. ______. Fertilization; a planned program. Proceedings of the 37th International Turfgrass Conference. pp. 57–60. 1966.

7419. ______. Soil modification. Mid-Atlantic Superintendents Conference Proceedings. pp.18–19. 1966.

7420. ______. Athletic fields—specification outline, construction, and maintenance. The Pennsylvania State University Extension Service. pp.1–19. 1967.

7421. ______. History of *Poa annua.* Turf clippings. University of Massachusetts. 2(2):A–2–9. 1967.

7422. ______. Golf course specifications and construction problems. University of Maine Turf Conference Proceedings. 6:8–15. 1968.

7423. ______. Athletic fields—specification outline, construction, and maintenance. Pennsylvania Agricultural Extension Service, U. Ed. 7–750. 1968.

7424. ______. Turfgrass establishment. The Bonnie Greensward, Philadelphia Association of Golf Course Superintendents Publication. pp.2–4. 1969.

7425. ______. The aftereffects of irrigation. Turf Clippings. University of Massachussetts. 4(1):A–40 to A–44. 1969.

7426. ______. Athletic field specifications. Turf Clippings. University of Massachussetts. 4(1):A–45 to A–51. 1969.

7427. ______. Fertilizer . . . nitrogen sources, Part 2. Grounds Maintenance. 5:70. 1970.

7428. ______. The turf extension specialist: if one teaspoon is good—two must be better. Proceedings of the 41st International Turfgrass Conference. pp.21–25. 1970.

7429. ______. Turfgrass fertilization. Lakeshore News. 2(2):11,8. 1970.

7430. ______. Soil modification for greens. Annual RCGA National Turfgrass Conference. 21:16. 1970.

7431. ______. Urea-formaldehyde as a nitrogen source. Ohio Turfgrass Conference Proceedings. pp.43–47. 1971.

7432. ______. Seeding methods. Ohio Turfgrass Conference Proceedings. pp.21–27. 1971.

7433. Harper, J. C. and M. A. Hein. Better Lawns. USDA. Home and Garden Bulletin. No.51. 32 pp. 1957.

7434. Harper, J. C., and H. B. Musser. The effects of watering and compaction on fairway turf. Pennsylvania State College Turfgrass Conference Proceedings. 19:43–52. 1950.

7436. Harper, J. C. II, M. A. Hein and F. V. Juska. Better lawns. USDA. Home and Garden Bulletin. No. 51. 32 pp. 1964.

7437. Harper, J. C., E. J. Merkel, and H. B. Musser. The effects of aerification on runoff and fertilizer penetration under various soil conditions. Agronomy Abstracts. pp. 40–41. 1952.

7438. Harper, R. D. Turf problems of parks, cemeteries and recreational areas. University of Florida Turf-Management Conference Proceedings. 3:98–100. 1955.

7439. Harper, R. S. Mulch as an aid to erosion control. Ohio Short Course on Roadside Development. 20:91–98. 1961.

7440. Harrington, H. D. and L. W. Durrell. Key to some Colorado grasses in vegetative condition. Colorado Agricultural Experiment Station Technical Bulletin 33. 86 pp. 1944.

7441. Harris, B. K. and J. J. Barry. Japanese beetle control for 1938. Greenkeepers Club of New England Newsletter. 10(9):10. 1938.

7442. Harris, D. H. Application techniques. Control of Weeds, Pests and Diseases of Cultivated Turf Proceedings. 1:30–33. 1967.

7444. Harris, D. G. and C. H. M. van Bavel. A comparison of measured and computed evapotranspiration from bermudagrass and sweet corn. Agronomy Abstracts. 50:37. 1958.

7445. Harris, E. D. Take a close look at insecticides. Sunshine State Agricultural Research Report. 7(1):20. 1962.

7446. Harris, F. S., and H. H. Yao. Effectiveness of mulches in preserving soil moisture. Journal Agricultural Research. 23:727–742. 1923.

7447. Harris, G. K. The use of Maintain® CF 125 to control the growth rate of grass and suppress weed growth. Annual RCGA National Turfgrass Conference. 21:-17–19. 1970.

7448. Harris, G. K. and D. O. Anderson. Maintain CF 125, a growth retardant for turf, vines, shrubs, and trees. North Central Weed Control Conference Proceedings. 25:100–102. 1970.

7449. Harris, G. S. Soil acidity and means of control. New Zealand Institute for Turf Culture Newsletter. 5:7. 1960.

7450. ______. Buried seeds and playing greens. New Zealand Institute for Turf Culture Newsletter. 7:6–7. 1960.

7451. ______. From seed to turf. New Zealand Institute for Turf Culture Newsletter. 9:4. 1960.

7452. ______. Grasses and greenkeeping. New Zealand Institute for Turf Culture Newsletter. 9:9. 1960.

7453. ______. From seed to turf. New Zealand Institute for Turf Culture Newsletter. 10:2. 1960.

7454. ______. The periodicity of germination in some grass species. New Zealand Journal of Agricultural Research. 4:253–260. 1961.

7455. ______. Some aspects of *Poa annua* as a turf weed. New Zealand Institute for Turf Culture Newsletter. 11:2. 1961.

7456. ______. Grasses and greenkeeping. New Zealand Institute for Turf Culture Newsletter. 11:6–7. 1961.

7457. ______. From seed to turf. New Zealand Institute for Turf Culture Newsletter. 12:2. 1961.

7458. ______. Grasses and greenkeeping. New Zealand Institute for Turf Culture Newsletter. 12:5. 1961.

7459. ______. From seed to turf. New Zealand Institute for Turf Culture Newsletter. 12:9–10. 1961.

7460. ______. From seed to turf. New Zealand Institute for Turf Culture Newsletter. 13:2. 1961.

7461. ______. The *Poa annua* problem. New Zealand Institute for Turf Culture Newsletter. 14:1–2. 1961.

7462. ______. From seed to turf. New Zealand Institute for Turf Culture Newsletter. 15:13–14. 1961.

7463. ______. From seed to turf. New Zealand Institute for Turf Culture Newsletter. 16:4. 1961.

7464. ______. Turf fertilizers. New Zealand Institute for Turf Culture Newsletter. 18:15–17. 1962.

7465. ______. Phosphatic fertilisers. New Zealand Institute for Turf Culture Newsletter. 19:17. 1962.

7466. ______. Potash fertilisers. New Zealand Institute for Turf Culture Newsletter. 21:13. 1962.

7467. ______. Minor fertiliser elements. New Zealand Institute for Turf Culture Newsletter. 21:13–14. 1962.

7468. ______. Dispersal of weed seeds. New Zealand Institute for Turf Culture Newsletter. 22:2–3. 1962.

7469. ______. Dispersal of weed seeds. New Zealand Institute for Turf Culture Newsletter. 23:17. 1963.

7470. ______. The problem of problem weeds. New Zealand Institute for Turf Culture Newsletter. 26:5–6. 1963.

7471. ______. The ecology of turf. New Zealand Institute for Turf Culture Newsletter. 37:4–5. 1965.

7472. ______. Identification of plants. New Zealand Institute for Turf Culture Newsletter. 37:6–7. 1965.

7473. ______. Research notes. New Zealand Institute for Turf Culture Newsletter. 63:20–22. 1969.

7474. ______. Research notes. New Zealand Institute for Turf Culture Newsletter. 64:18–20. 1969.

7475. ______. Control of turf weeds. New Zealand Institute for Turf Culture Newsletter. 69:15. 1970.

7476. ______. Varieties in *Cotula.* New Zealand Institute for Turf Culture Newsletter. 74:123. 1971.

7477. ______. Soil stability. New Zealand Institute for Turf Culture Newsletter. 76:185–189. 1971.

7478. ______. Items of interest from overseas research. New Zealand Institute for Turf Culture Newsletter. 76:189–191. 1971.

7479. ______. The *Poa annua* problem. New Zealand Institute for Turf Culture Newsletter. 78:54–55. 1972.

7480. ______. Use of mulches to improve seedling establishment. New Zealand Institute for Turf Culture Newsletter. 78:55,57. 1972.

7481. Harris, H. H., P. H. Schuldt and L. E. Limpel. Dimethyl 2,3,5,6—Tetra chloroterephthalate (DAC–893), a promising pre-emergence turf herbicide. North Central Weed Control Conference Proceedings. 16:-48. 1959.

7483. Harris, J. and D. S. Chamblee. Carolina lawns. North Carolina Agricultural Extension Circular. 292:1–12. 1950.

7484. ______. Carolina lawns. North Carolina Agricultural Extension Circular. 292:1–12. 1953.

7485. ______. Carolina lawns. North Carolina Agricultural Extension Circular. 292:1–16. 1957.

7486. ______. Carolina lawns. North Carolina Agricultural Extension Circular. 292:1–16. 1961.

7487. Harris, J. H. and R. L. Lovvorn. Carolina lawns. North Carolina Agricultural Extension Circular. 292:1–10. 1946.

7488. Harris, R. B. The fundamentals of golf course design. Proceedings of Midwest Regional Turf Conference. pp.32–37. 1948.

7489. ______. Design and construction —their impact on turf management. Proceedings University of Florida Turf Management Conference. 4:39–42. 1956.

7490. ______. Architectural matters affect maintenance costs. USGA Journal and Turf Management. 11(1):25–26. 1958.

7491. Harris, R. W. Overcoming staking hazards. Proceedings of the 1972 Turf and Landscape Horticulture Institute. pp. 63–65. 1972.

7492. Harrison, A. Aeration II. Getting away from the point. The Groundsman. 23(7):20–22. 1970.

7493. Harrison, C. M. Effect of cutting and fertilizer applications on grass development. Plant Physiology. 6:669–684. 1931.

7494. ______. Grass growth factors that control cutting practices. Golfdom. 7(2):49–50. 1933.

7495. ______. Greenhouse studies on growth of Kentucky bluegrass. USGA Green Section Bulletin. 13(2):23–39. 1933.

7496. ______. Response of Kentucky bluegrass to variations in temperature, light, cutting, and fertilizing. Plant Physiology. 9:-83–106. 1934.

7497. ______. Some difference in turf maintenance between the United States and the British Isles. The Greenkeepers' Reporter. 4(9):3–5. 1936.

7498. ______. Rough grasses for parks, highway, and recreational areas. The Greenkeepers' Reporter. 12(3):30–31. 1944.

7499. ______. Establishing grass seedings. Proceedings of Midwest Regional Turf Conference. pp.13–16. 1952.

7500. ______. Turfgrass mixtures. Michigan Turfgrass Report. 3(1):4. 1965.

7501. Harrison, C. M., and C. W. Hodgson. Response of certain perennial grasses to cutting treatments. Journal of the American Society of Agronomy. 31:418–430, 1939.

7502. Harrison, D. S. Irrigations systems. Proceedings, University of Florida Turfgrass Management Conference. 13:117–123. 1965.

7503. ______. What to consider when you plan irrigation systems. Weeds, Trees and Turf. 5(4):10–11 and 38–40. 1966.

7504. Harrison, J. Using iron sulphate as a weed killer. Proceedings of the Third Annual Turf Conference. Washington State College. pp.28–29. 1950.

7505. Harrison-Smith, J. Sand dune reclamation. New Zealand Journal of Forestry. 4(4):227–235. 1939.

7506. Harriss, L. M. F. Municipal park department problems. North California Turf Conference. pp.77–78. 1951.

7507. Hart, C. H. The effect of temperature and hormones of the germination and emergence of several common turfgrass seeds. M.S. Thesis, University of California, Davis. 1966.

7508. Hart, E. Sports turf grasses from Holland. Parks, Golf Courses and Sports Grounds. 29:672–678. 1964.

7509. ______. Spring on a large playing-field scheme. The Groundsman. 21(7):40–41, 49. 1968.

7510. Hart, J. E. Common sense approach to *Poa annua* control. Annual RCGA National Turfgrass Conference. 21:20–21. 1970.

7511. Hart, R. H. and D. R. Lee. Age vs. net CO_2 exchange rate of leaves of Coastal bermudagrass. Crop Science. 11(4):598–599. 1971.

7512. Hart, R. H. and W. S. McGuire. Effect of clipping on the invasion of pastures by Velvetgrass, *Holcus lanatus* L. Agronomy Journal. 56(2):187–188. 1964.

7513. Hart, R. H., G. E. Carlson, and D. E. McCloud. Cumulative effects of cutting management on forage yields and tiller densities of tall fescue and orchardgrass. Agronomy Journal. 63(6):895–898. 1971.

7514. Hart, R. H., G. E. Carlson and H. J. Retzer. Establishment of tall fescue and white clover: effects of seeding method and weather. Agronomy Journal. 60(4):385–388. 1968.

7515. Hart, R. H., W. G. Monson and R. S. Lowrey. Autumn-saved coastal bermudagrass *(Cynodon dactylon* (L.) Pers): Effects of age and fertilization on quality. Agronomy Journal. 61(6):940–941. 1969.

7516. Hart, R. H., R. H. Hughes, C. E. Lewis and W. G. Monson. Effect of nitrogen and shading on yield and quality of grasses grown under young slash pines. Agronomy Journal. 62(2):285–287. 1970.

7517. Hart, S. W. and J. A. DeFrance. Chemicals for the control of clover in lawn turf. Contribution No. 839. Rhode Island Agricultural Experiment Station. 1954.

7518. ______. Effect of maleic hydrazide on the growth of turfgrass. Golf Course Reporter. 23(7):5–7. 1955.

7519. ______. Behavior of *Zoysia japonnica* Meyer in cool season turf. USGA Journal and Turf Management. 8(2):25–32. 1955.

7520. ______. The effect of synthetic soil conditioners in turfgrass soils. The Golf Course Reporter. 24(2):5–9. 1956.

7521. Hart, W. E. Overhead irrigation pattern parameters. Agricultural Engineering. 42:354–355. 1961.

7522. Hartley, W. The global distribution of tribes of the *Gramineae* in relation to historical and environmental factors. Australian Journal of Agricultural Research. 1(4):355–373. 1950.

7523. Hartley, W. and R. J. Williams. Centres of distribution of cultivated pasture grasses and their significance for plant introduction. Proceedings of the Seventh International Grassland Conference. pp. 190–199. 1956.

7524. Hartman, W. J. Establishment of crownvetch on droughty soils. Agronomy Abstracts. 2:164.

7525. Hartmann, H. T. Precision propagation—sources of propagating material. Proceedings of Turf, Nursery, and Landscape Tree Conference. pp. 9–1 to 9–4. 1964.

7526. Hartogh, L. PO-SAN use at Oak Park Country Club. Proceedings of the Midwest Regional Turf Conference. pp. 64–65. 1972.

7527. Hartung, M. E. Chromosome numbers in *Poa, Agropyron,* and *Elymus.* American Journal of Botany. 33:516–531. 1946.

7528. Hartwell, B. L. and S. C. Damon. The persistence of lawn and other grasses as influenced especially by the effect of manures on the degree of soil acidity. Rhode Island Agricultural Experiment Station. Bulletin 170. pp. 1–28. 1917.

7529. Hartwig, H. B. Relationships between some soil measurements and the incidence of the two common *Poa*s. Journal of the American Society of Agronomy. 30:847–861. 1938.

7530. Hartzog, M. A. Maintaining a lawn. Garden time in the south. J. Horace McFarland Co. Pennsylvania. 34–37 pp. 1951.

7531. Harvey, H. W. Lawns for Georgia. Georgia Agricultural College Extension Bulletin. 324:1–19. 1927.

7533. Harvey, W. A. Chemical control of broad-leaved weeds in lawn and turf. North California Turf Conference. pp. 66–68. 1951.

7534. ______. Weeds—can we depend on chemicals alone? North California Turf Conference. pp. 11–13. 1953.

7535. ______. Chemical control of broad-leaved weeds in lawns and turf. Southern California Turf Culture. 4(1):4. 1954.

7536. ______. Outsmarting weeds. North California Turf Conference. pp. 28–30. 1954.

7537. ______. Weed control—let's watch the gallonage. Proceedings of the Southern California Turfgrass Conference. pp. 12–14. 1954.

7538. ______. The use of 2, 4–D and 2, 4, 5–T in turf. Southern California Turfgrass Culture. 6(4):6–7. 1956.

7539. Haske, J. F. How we plant and manage U–3 Bermuda at the Washingtonian Country Club. Proceedings of the Mid-Atlantic Association of Greenkeepers Conference. pp. 16–18. 1963.

7540. ______. Bermuda on our course—how it survived winter kill. Proceedings of the Mid-Atlantic Association of Golf Course Superintendents Conference. pp. 4–6. 1964.

7541. Haskell, D. Public golf courses for the future. Proceedings of the Annual Northwest Turfgrass Conference. 21:87–90. 1967.

7542. Haskell, T. J., I. B. Lykes, and W. H. Daniel. Basic grounds maintenance. Park Management Pub. pp. 1–123. 1971.

7543. Hatfield, R. M. Research at Bingley. Parks, Golf Courses and Sports Grounds. 36(10):989–994. 1971.

7544. Hatting, J. L. Some effects of herbicides or mowing on the viable production of musk thistle near maturity. M.S. Thesis, University of Nebraska. 1972.

7545. Hauser, E. W. Response of purple nutsedge to amitrol, 2, 4–D, and EPTC. Weeds. 11:251–252. 1963.

7546. ______. Nutsedge: a worldwide plague. Ohio Turfgrass Foundation Newsletter. 23:4–5. 1971.

7547. ______. Nutsedge: a worldwide plague. Weeds Today. 2(1):21, 23. 1971.

7548. Hauser, J. S. Watch out for insect damage. Golfdom. 17(2):28–31. 1943.

7549. Haven, W. D. Micronutrients spark plugs for turf. The Golf Superintendent. 37(2):17, 19. 1969.

7550. Havens, A. V. Climate and microclimate as related to the grasses. Rutgers University Turfgrass Short Course. 1 p. 1957.

7551. Havis, J. R. Maintenance of established lawns. Turf Clippings. University of Massachussetts. 1(5):A–34 to A–36. 1960.

7552. ______. A test of chemicals for crabgrass control in turf. Northeastern Weed Control Conference Proceedings. 15:294–295. 1961.

7554. ______. Comparison of chemicals for pre-emergence crabgrass control in turf. Proceedings of the Northeastern Weed Control Conference. 16:493–494. 1962.

7555. Hawes, D. T. Watering and topdressing as related to *Poa annua.* infestations. Turf Clippings, University of Massachussetts. 1(7):10–11. 1962.

7556. ______. Control of annual bluegrass. Turf Clippings-University of Massachusetts. 1(10):A5–A10. 1965.

7557. ______. Growth characteristics of 'Penncross' creeping bentgrass *(Agrostis palustris* Huds.) at four soil temperatures and five fertility regimes. Ph.D. Thesis, University of Maryland. pp. 1–124. 1972.

7558. Hawes, D. T., and J. F. Cornman. The palliative effects of cool night temperatures on the growth of annual bluegrass *(Poa annua).* Agronomy Abstracts. p. 63. 1968.

7559. Hawes, D. T., and A. M. Decker. Response of 'Penncross' bentgrass as determined by reflectance readings and rate of coverage when grown at four soil temperatures and fertilized with two nitrogen sources at three rates. Agronomy Abstracts. p. 47. 1971.

7560. Hawk, V. B. Emerald crownvetch . . . new legume fills many needs for conservation plans. Iowa Soil and Water. 6(3):10. 1962.

7561. Hawk, V. B., and D. S. Douglas. Crownvetch, new pasture legume. Soil Conservation. 27(9):206–207. 1962.

7562. Hawk, V. B., and J. M. Scholl. Seed treatment aids crownvetch seedings. Crops and Soils. 13(6):25–26. 1961.

7563. Hawk, V. B., and W. C. Sharp. Sand dune stabilization along the North Atlantic coast. Journal of Soil and Water Conservation. 22:143–146. 1967.

7564. Hawk, V. B., and W. D. Shrader. Soil factors affecting crownvetch adaptation. Journal of Soil and Water Conservation. 19:-187–190. 1964.

7565. Hawk, V. B., and C. P. Wilsie. Emerald crownvetch released by SCS—Iowa. Crops and Soils. 14(6):19. 1962.

7568. Hawthorn, R. Turf problems down under. The Groundsman. 17(2):22–26. 1963.

7569. ______. Trainee groundsman's corner—fertilizers. The Groundsman. 19(6):-10–11. 1966.

7570. ______. Trainee groundsman's corner—weed spraying. The Groundsman. 19(9):26–28. 1966.

7571. ______. Trainee groundsman's corner (top dressing). The Groundsman. 19(12):4–6. 1966.

7572. ______. Trainee groundsman's corner (wormkilling). The Groundsman. 20(2):12–14. 1966.

7573. ______. Soils and how they support plant growth. The Groundsman. 20(5):-14–15. 1967.

7574. ______. Soils their composition, texture, structure and type. The Groundsman. 20(6):12–17. 1967.

7575. ______. Soils—manures and fertilisers, need for fertilisers, principles of fertilising turf. The Groundsman. 20(8):28–29, 37. 1967.

7576. ______. Soils—top dressing: compost: farmyard manure: sewage sludge: leaf mold: peat. The Groundsman. 20(9):23. 1967.

7577. ______. The structure of the plant. The Groundsman. 20(10):12–14. 1967.

7578. ______. The structure of the plant—part 2. The Groundsman. 20(11):19–21. 1967.

7579. ______. The structure of the plant—part 3. The Groundsman. 20(12):17–19. 1967.

7580. ______. The structure of the plant—part 4. The Groundsman. 21(1):32–34. 1967.

7581. ______. The structure of the plant—part 5. The Groundsman. 21(2):28–29. 1967.

7582. ______. The structure of the plant—part 6. The Groundsman. 21(3):20–21. 1967.

7583. ______. Physiology of the plant—part 1. The Groundsman. 21(4):14–15. 1967.

7584. ______. Classification and special botany of grasses and turf weeds—part 1. The Groundsman. 21(5):20–21. 1968.

7585. ______. Classification and special botany of grasses and turf weeds—part 2. The Groundsman. 21(6):26–28, 39. 1968.

7586. ______. Classification and special botany of grasses and turf weeds. Part 3—grasses found on sports grounds. The Groundsman. 21(7):45–47. 1968.

7587. ______. Classification and special botany of grasses and turf weeds part 4—recognition of turf weeds. The Groundsman. 21(8):24–27. 1968.

7588. ______. Weed control. The Groundsman. 21(9):31, 45. 1968.

7589. ______. Tennis court maintenance. The Groundsman. 23(7):39–41. 1970.

7590. ______. Fungal diseases on turf. The Groundsman. 23(11):14–19. 1970.

7591. Hawthorn, W. Methods of sports ground irrigation. Parks, Golf Courses and Sports Grounds. 30(10):810–813. 1965.

7592. Hawtree, F. W. Experiments with methoxone. Journal of Board of Greenkeeping Research. 7(23):41–43. 1947.

7593. Hay, W. G. Lawn bowling in Southern California. Southern California Turfgrass Culture. 4(3):3. 1954.

7594. Hayashi, Y. Fertilization in golf course. K.G.U. Green Section Turf Research Bulletin. 13:67–74. 1967.

7595. Hayes, H. K., and H. L. Thomas. A selection experiment with Kentucky bluegrass. Journal of the American Society of Agronomy. 36:1001–1002. 1944.

7596. Hays, J. T. Nitrogen fertilization of turfgrasses. Hercules Agricultural Chemicals Technical Information Bulletin A1–105. 1966.

7597. ______. Solubility relationships in performance of urea-formaldehyde fertilizers. Agronomy Abstracts. p. 52. 1967.

7598. ______. Ureaforms in turfgrass fertilization. RCGA National Turfgrass Conference. pp. 13–24. 1968.

7599. Hays, J. T. and W. W. Haden. Soluble fraction of ureaforms—nitrification, leaching, and burning properties. Agronomy Abstracts. 57:45. 1965.

7600. ______. Soluble fraction of ureaforms—nitrification, leaching, and burning properties. Journal of Agricultural and Food Chemistry. 14:339. 1966.

7601. ______. Effect of structure on nitrification of urea derivatives. Agronomy Abstracts. p. 59. 1968.

7602. Hayes, R. J. Fertilization pointers. Golfdom. 6(2):45–46. 1932.

7603. ______. Fertilization. The National Greenkeeper. 6(2):11–12. 1932.

7604. Hayes, R. J., J. MacGregor, G. Sargent, W. J. Sansom. Spring rolling—when and how. The National Greenkeeper. 3(4):-29–31. 1929.

7605. Hays, W. M. Grass gardens—methods and purposes. Office of Experiment Stations, USDA. 16:1–3. 1893.

7606. Hayes, W. P. Knowing insect life histories aids in control measures. Golfdom. 7(4):21–23. 1933.

7607. ______. Insects, their habits and control. The National Greenkeeper. 7(4):8–13. 1933.

7608. Haymaker, H. H. The living plant. The Greenkeepers' Reporter. 7(2):7–8, 34–35, 39. 1939.

7609. Hayward, H. E. Saline and alkali soil-properties and management. The Greenkeepers' Reporter. 17(4):22–25. 1949.

7610. ______. Saline and alkaline soil—properties and management. Greenkeeping Superintendents Association National Turf Conference. 20:72–78. 1949.

7612. Hazlett, C. W. More about brown patch. Greenkeepers Club of New England Newsletter. 4(6):10–11. 1932.

7613. ______. Turf watering forum. The Greenkeepers' Reporter. 5(4):7–10, 24. 1937.

7614. Heald, C. M. Pathogenicity and histopathology of *Meloidogyne graminis* infecting Tifdwarf bermudagrass roots. Journal Nematology. 1(1):9–10. 1969.

7615. Heald, C. M. and G. W. Burton Effect of organic and inorganic nitrogen on nematode populations on turf The Plant Disease Reporter. 52(1):46–48. 1968.

7616. Heald, C. M. and A. M. Golden *Meloidodera charis,* a cystoid nematode, infecting St. Augustinegrass The Plant Disease Reporter. 53(7):527. 1969.

7617. Heald, C. M. and V. G. Perry. Nematodes and other pest. American Society of Agronomy Monograph Series No. 14. 1970.

7618. Heald, C. M. and H. D. Wells. Control of endo- and ecto-parasitic nematodes in turf by hot-water treatments. The Plant Disease Reporter. 51(11):905–907. 1967.

7619. Healy, M. J. Research on fungicides for turf disease control. Illinois Turfgrass Conference Proceedings. pp. 26–28. 1963.

7620. ______. Illustration of a turf grass disease study—*Helminthosporium* leaf spot of creeping bentgrass. Illinois Turfgrass Conference Proceedings. pp. 50–53. 1964.

7621. ______. Factors influencing disease development on putting green turf. Illinois Turfgrass Conference Proceedings. 6 pp. 1965.

7622. ______. Factors affecting the pathogenicity of selected fungi isolated from putting green turf Ph.D. Thesis, University of Illinois. pp. 1–59. 1967.

7623. ______. The *Helminthosporium (sativum)* infection and development on putting green turf. Rutgers University Short Course in Turf Management. 2 pp. 1969.

7624. ______. The *Helminthosporium (sativum)* infection and development on putting green turf. Rutgers University. College of Agriculture and Environmental Science. Lawn and Utility Turf Section. pp. 63–64. 1969.

7625. Healy, M. J. and M. P. Britton. The importance of guttation fluid on turf diseases. Illinois Turfgrass Conference Proceedings. pp. 40–46. 1967.

7626. ______. Infection and development of *Helminthosporium sorokinianum* in *Agrostis palustris.* Phytopathology. 58(3):-273–276. 1968.

7627. Healy, M. J., M. P. Britton, and J. D. Butler. Stripe smut damage on Pennlu creeping bentgrass. Plant Disease Reporter. 49(8):710. 1965.

7628. Healy, W. B. New Zealand soils in relation to golf greens. New Zealand Institute For Turf Culture Newsletter. 73:76–79. 1971.

7629. Hearn, J. H. *Rhizoctonia solani* Kuhn and the brown patch disease of grass. Proceedings of Texas Academy of Science. 26:41–42. 1943.

7630. Heaviland, R. J. Seeded mat solves slope erosion problem. Park Maintenance. 15(5):50–52. 1962.

7631. Hedges, C. Expanding your authority. Proceedings of the Midwest Regional Turf Conference. pp. 22–23. 1972.

7632. Hedlund, D. Applying fertilizers through irrigation systems. Turf Bulletin. Massachusetts Turf and Lawn Grass Council. 2(5):7. 1964.

7633. Heflin, W. H. What's in the bag. Proceedings University of Florida Turfgrass Management Conference. 14:43–48. 1966.

7634. Heft, F. E. Soil and water values in highway construction. Ohio Short Course on Roadside Development. 13:74–75. 1971.

7635. Heikes, P. E. Weed control for custodians and grounds keepers. Rocky Mountain Regional Turfgrass Conference. 12:44–47. 1966.

7636. Heilman, M. D., C. L. Wiegand, and C. L. Gonzalez. Sand and cotton bur mulches, bermudagrass sod, and bare soil effects on: II salt leaching. Soil Science Society of America Proceedings. 32(2):280–283. 1968.

7637. Hein, M. A. Centipede grass USDA Mimeograph. 1947.

7638. ______. Registration of varieties and strains of bermuda grass, II *Cynodon dactylon* (L) Pers. Agronomy Journal. 45(11):572–573. 1953.

7639. ______. Registration of varieties and strains of grasses Agronomy Journal. 50(7):399–401. 1958.

7640. ______. Registration of varieties and strains of bermudagrass, III. (*Cynodon dactylon* (L.) Pers.) Agronomy Journal. 53(4):276, 1961.

7642. Heiss, J. D. Man-hour costing—a system based on job hour records. Weeds, Trees, and Turf 6(9):14–16, 24. 1967.

7643. Heissner, A. and A. Henkel. Recommendations for the use of tensiometers for the estimation of sprinkler irrigation dates in field vegetable cultivation. Deutsche Gartenbau. 12:90–95. 1965.

7644. Heldreth, H. E. Safety with pesticides. USGA Journal and Turf Management. 10(4):29–32. 1957.

7645. Hellbo, E. The distinction between seeds of Italian ryegrass and perennial ryegrass and between seeds of ryegrass and meadow fescue. International Review of Agriculture. 4:155–164. 1926.

7648. Hellyer, A. G. L. Lawns and their maintenance. The Amateur Gardener. Transatlantic Arts, Inc. Florida. pp. 381–394 1964.

7649. Heming, W. E. Worm and insect control in turf. Proceedings School of Soils, Fertilization & Turf Maintenance Green Section, Royal Canadian Golf Association. pp. 56–60. 1952.

7650. Hemphill, D. D., A. D. Hibbard, and R. E. Taven. Suggestions for establishing a lawn in Missouri. Proceedings, Missouri Lawn and Turf Conference. pp. 16–18. 1960.

7651. Hemphill, D. D. Lawn and turf weed control. Proceedings, Missouri Lawn and Turf Conference. pp. 68–71. 1960.

7652. ______. Weed killers and how they act. Proceedings, Missouri Lawn & Turf Conference. pp. 20–23. 1961.

7653. ______. Preemergence control of crabgrass. North Central Weed Control Conference Proceedings. 18:85. 1961.

7654. ______. Weed control in horticultural crops turf. North Central Weed Control Conference Proceedings. 18:119–120. 1961.

7655. ______. What's new in weed control. Proceedings, Missouri Lawn and Turf Conference. pp. 34–35. 1962.

7656. ______. Broadleaved weed control in turf. Research Report North Central Weed Control Conference. 19:104. 1962.

7657. ______. Preemergence control of crabgrass. Research Report, North Central Weed Control Conference. 19:104–105. 1962.

7658. ______. What's new in weed control? Proceedings, Missouri Lawn and Turf Conference. pp. 33–34. 1963.

7659. ______. What's new in weed control. Proceedings, Missouri Lawn and Turf Conference. pp. 34–35. 1964.

7660. ______. What's new in weed control? The Golf Course Reporter. 33(3):36–37. 1965.

7661. ______. What's new in weed control. Proceedings, Missouri Lawn and Turf Conference. pp. 19–20. 1965.

7662. ______. Herbicide review. Proceedings of the Annual Missouri Lawn and Turf Conference. 7:22. 1966.

7663. Hemstreet, C. L. and F. Dorman. Reviving old putting greens. California Turfgrass Culture 14(3):20–23. 1964.

7664. ______. Reviving old putting greens. Proceedings of Turf, Nursery and Landscape Tree Conference. pp. 1–1 to 1–7. 1964.

7665. Hemwall, J. B. Theoretical consideration of soil fumigation. Phytopathology. 52(11):1108–1115. 1962.

7667. Henderlong, P. R. The turf industry in West Virginia. 1967 West Virginia Turfgrass Conference Proceedings, West Virginia Agricultural Experiment Station Miscellaneous Publication. 5:3–10. 1968.

7668. ______. Turfgrass fertilizer terminology. West Virginia Turfgrass Conference Proceedings. pp. 12–18. 1968.

7669. ______. Effect of temperature on the establishment, growth and development of turfgrasses. Ohio Turfgrass Conference Proceedings. pp. 42–44. 1969.

7670. ______. Effect of temperature on the germination and seedling growth of cool-season turfgrasses. Agronomy Abstracts. 62:-68. 1970.

7671. ______. Micronutrients in turfgrass management. Ohio Turfgrass Conference Proceedings. pp. 49–54. 1970.

7672. ______. Effect of temperature on the germination and seedling development of turfgrasses. Ohio Agricultural Research and Development Center. Turf and Landscape Research—1971. 56:31–38. 1971.

7673. Henderlong, P. R., and T. Lederer. The effect of banded fertilizer, planting depth and temperature on the establishment and seedling growth of crownvetch (*Coronilla varia* L. Cheming). Second Crownvetch Symposium. Pennsylvania State University Agronomy Mimeograph. pp. 21–22. 1968.

7674. Henderlong, P. R., D. E. Brann, and C. Veatch. Preliminary studies on the differential movement of the granular and emulsion forms of bensulide in soils. Proceedings West Virginia Academy of Science. 40:-54. 1968.

7675. Henderson, D. W., J. A. Vomocil. Water penetration of soils. California Turfgrass Culture. 7(4):31–32. 1957.

7676. Henderson, D. W., W. C. Bianchi and L. D. Doneen. Losses of ammoniacal fertilizers from sprinkler jets. USGA Journal and Turf Management. 8(3):28–30. 1955.

7677. Henderson, D. W., D. T. Bradley, and J. Jagur. Solving drainage problems at El Macero. USGA Green Section Record. 8(4):-6–10. 1970.

7678. Henderson, G. R. and C. W. Terry. Calibration of weed sprayers. New York State Turf Association Bulletin. 3:11–12. 1949.

7679. Henderson, J. R. Some important soil characteristics in relation to turf management. Proceedings of the First Annual University of Florida Turf Conference. 1:29–32. 1953.

7680. Henderson, W. J. Turfgrass diseases. Colorado State University Agricultural Extension Service Circular. 207-A. 14 pp. 1960.

7682. Hendricks, S. B. The leaf is life. Turf Bulletin. Massachusetts Turf and Lawn Grass Council. 4(5):4. 1967.

7683. Hendricks, S. B., V. K. Toole and H. A. Borthwick. Opposing actions of light in seed germination of *Poa pratensis* and *Amaranthus arenicola.* Plant Physiology. 43(12):-2023–2028. 1968.

7684. Hendrickson, B. H. Conference on roadside erosion control. Journal of Soil and Water Conservation. 16:289. 1961.

7685. Hendrix, F. F., Jr., W. A. Campbell, and J. B. Moncrief. *Pythium* species associated with golf turfgrasses in the South and Southeast. The Plant Disease Reporter. 54(5):419–421. 1970.

7686. Hendrix, F. F., and J. B. Moncrief. *Pythium* species associated with golf greens in the south. USGA Green Section. 9(3):7–9. 1971.

7687. Heng, D. A., and D. B. White. Investigations into the activity of ethrel (2-chloroethylphosphonic acid) in the growth of *Poa pratensis.* Agronomy Abstracts. p. 54. 1969.

7688. Hennessy, E. J., and E. R. Lassone. Asbestos—cement pipe. Turf Clippings. University of Massachusetts. 1(10):A21–A27. 1965.

7689. Henry, J. P. Report from the show-me state. Midwest Turf-News and Research. 2(2):3. 1948.

7690. ______. The superintendent, the green chairman, the locker room. Proceedings of Midwest Regional Turf Conference. pp. 42–46. 1952.

7691. ______. Superintendent—green committee chairman—membership: working together. USGA Journal and Turf Management. 11(2):30–32. 1958.

7692. Henry, J. R. Texas-Okla. Turf Conference sets new high in interest. Golfdom. 24(2):45, 48, 50. 1950.

7693. ______. Equipping a golf course for maintenance. Proceedings of the Texas Turfgrass Conference. 19:12–17. 1964.

7694. Henslow, G. *Poa annua* as a lawn grass. Gardener's Chronicle. 33(858):357. 1903.

7695. Henslow, T. G. W. English lawns: how they should be levelled, planted and preserved. World Today. 53:570–574. 1929.

7696. Henson, L., G. W. Stokes and C. C. Litton. Maintenance of quanity and quality of *Thielaviopsis basicola* on various crops.

Kentucky Agricultural Experiment Station Annual Report. 74:12–14. 1961.

7697. Henson, P. R. Crownvetch, a soil conserving legume and a potential pasture and hay plant. USDA, ARS Crops Research, 34–53. 9 pp. 1963.

7698. Henson, P. R., L. A. Tayman, and G. E. Carlson. Performance of crownvetch varieties and clones under severe defoliation. Second Crownvetch Symposium—Pennsylvania State University. 6:129–133. 1968.

7699. Henzell, E. F. and D. J. Oxenham. Seasonal changes in the nitrogen content of three warm-climate pasture grasses. Australian Journal of Experimental Agriculture and Animal Husbandry. 4(15):336–344. 1964.

7700. Hepworth, H. M. Recent work in controlling hard-to-kill weeds in turfgrass. Rocky Mountain Regional Turfgrass Conference. 12:9–11. 1966.

7701. Hersman, F. C. and H. Gray. Soil management for Long Island gardens and lawns. State Institute of Agriculture on Long Island. 1947.

7703. Herbel, C. H. and R. E. Sosbee. Moisture and temperature effects on emergence and initial growth of two range grasses. Agronomy Journal. 61(4):628–631. 1969.

7704. Herbert, D. A. Lawns. Gardening in Warm Climates. Angus and Robertson. London. pp. 220–224. 1952.

7705. Herbst, M. Turf grass—tomorrow's money maker. Southern Seedsman. 19(9):60–61, 65. 1956.

7706. Herlong, M. B. Trying to make bent "at home" in Florida. Golfdom. 1(5):34, 35. 1927.

7707. Hermann, M. W. Factors in sprinkler installation. Proceedings Turfgrass Sprinkler Irrigation Conference. 2 pp. 1966.

7708. Hernandez, T. J. Weed control spray techniques. Proceedings of the Annual Texas Turfgrass Conference. 22:14–19. 1967.

7709. Herr, D. E. and R. W. Miller. Lawns—grass or weeds? Ohio Report on Research and Development. 50(1):7. 1965.

7710. Herron, J. W. Control of nimblewill *(Muhlenbergia schreberi)* in bluegrass turf. North Central Weed Control Conference Proceedings. 15:37. 1958.

7711. ______. Additional observations on the control of nimblewill *(Muhlenbergia schreberi)* in bluegrass turf. Weed Society of America Abstracts. p. 57. 1961.

7712. ______. Weed control in turf. Kentucky Agricultural Experiment Station Annual Report 74:60. 1961.

7713. ______. Lawn weed control. Kentucky Agricultural Extension Circular. 577:-1–39. 1961.

7714. ______. Weed control in turf. Kentucky Agricultural Experiment Station Annual Report. 75:62–63. 1962.

7715. ______. Nimblewill in Kentucky bluegrass lawns controlled by herbicides. Kentucky Farm and Home Science. 8(2):4–5, 8. 1962.

7716. ______. Weed control in turf. Kentucky Agricultural Experiment Station Annual Report. 76:67. 1963.

7717. ______. Control of crabgrass in Kentucky bluegrass turf. Kentucky Agricultural Experiment Station Annual Report. 77:63. 1964.

7718. ______. Responses of nimblewill and Kentucky bluegrass to nutritional variables. Kentucky Agricultural Experiment Station Annual Report. 77:63. 1964.

7719. ______. Use of herbicides in establishing Bermuda grass turf. Kentucky Agricultural Experiment Station Annual Report. 77:63. 1964.

7720. ______. Preemergence (research in Kentucky bluegrass and bermudagrass) crabgrass control. The Golf Course Reporter. 33(3):20–22. 1965.

7721. Herron, J. W., T. E. Pope and E. H. New. Turf—recommended practices—Kentucky. 19th Annual Southern Weed Conference Research Report. pp. 111–112. 1966.

7722. Herron, J. W., L. Thompson and C. H. Slack. Turf—recommended practices—additions or changes—Kentucky. 24th Annual Southern Weed Science Society Research Report. p. 83. 1971.

7723. ______. Turf—recommended practices—Kentucky. 25th Annual Southern

Weed Science Society Research Report. p. 114. 1972.

7724. Hersman, F. C. and H. Gray. Soil management for Long Island gardens and lawns. State Institute of Agriculture on Long Island. pp. 1–16. 1937.

7725. Hertel, F. Rasenanlage und Pflega. Lehrmeister-Bucherei. No. 304. Minden (Westf.), Philler. 64 pp. 1954.

7726. Hessayon, D. G. Be your own lawn expert. Pan Britannica Industries. Waltham Abbey, England. 35 pp. 1961.

7727. Hessing, V. Investigations on the variability and heredity of the characters of certain species of the *Lolium.* International Institute of Agriculture. 11:318–319. 1920.

7728. Hester, J. B. Know your soil. Better Crops with Plant Food. 29(6):1–10. 1945.

7729. Hewitt, C. W. Watering golf greens and fairways in the Canterbury district. New Zealand Institute for Turf Culture Newsletter. 17:15–17. 1962.

7730. Hewlett, J. D. Response of fescue to natural moisture gradient on an artificial slope. U.S. Forest Service Southeast Forest Experiment Station Research Notes No. 152. 2 pp. 1961.

7731. Hibbard, A. D. Watering-when, how much. Proceedings, Missouri Lawn and Turf Conference. pp. 53–59. 1960.

7732. ______. You too can grow crabgrass. Proceedings, Missouri Lawn and Turf Conference. pp. 31–34. 1961.

7733. ______. It's water under the turf that counts. Proceedings, Missouri Lawn and Turf Conference. pp. 22–23. 1962.

7734. Hibbs, W. A. The dealer's responsibility to the home owner. Proceedings University of Florida Turfgrass Management Conference. 13:77–83. 1965.

7735. Hicks, D. H. and K. J. Mitchell. Flowering in pasture grasses. New Zealand Journal of Botany. 6(1):86–93. 1968.

7736. Hicks, E. A. Advancement in erosion control protection by mulching. Ohio Short Course on Roadside Development. 114–116. 1961.

7737. Hiesey, W. M. Growth and development of species and hybrids of *Poa* under controlled temperatures. American Journal of Botany. 40:205–221. 1953.

7738. Higgins, L. J. Care of the established lawn. New Hampshire Agricultural Extension Bulletin. 130:1–11. 1955.

7739. ______. Recommendations for lawn establishment. University of Maine 5th Annual Turf Management Short Course. 4 pp. 1967.

7740. Higgins, M. C. What hour should you mow? Golfdom. 12(8):31–32. 1938.

7741. ______. What time of the day is best for mowing putting green grasses. Greenkeepers Club of New England Newsletter. 10(5):10–12. 1938.

7742. Higgins, N. Promoting better turf. Proceedings University of Florida Turf Management Conference. 6:81–82. 1958.

7743. ______. The management of high school athletic fields. Proceedings University of Florida Turf-Grass Management Conference. 9:183–184. 1961.

7744. ______. Organization and administration of a school turf program. Proceedings University of Florida Turf-Grass Management Conference. 10:116–118. 1962.

7745. ______. Can schools not justify the cost of turf? Proceedings University of Florida Turfgrass Management Conference. 14:121–123. 1966.

7746. ______. Pattern for maintenance in a county-wide school system. Turfgrass Times. 2(5):1, 4, 5. 1967.

7747. Higgins, R. E. and D. Peterson. Yard and garden weed control. Idaho Cooperative Extension Service Publication No. 150. 4 pp. 1971.

7748. Hildebrand, S. Bluegrass variety evaluations. Michigan Turfgrass Report. 3(1):5–6. 1965.

7749. ______. Bluegrass blends. Michigan Turfgrass Report. 3(1):12–13. 1965.

7750. Hildreth, R. C. The key to turf disease control. Turf-Grass Times. 1(4):1, 3. 1966.

7751. ______. Preventive spray program aimed at turfgrass disease. Park Maintenance. 20(5):40–42. 1967.

7752. Hill, A. Fertilizer trials on lawns at Craibstone. Journal of the Board of Greenkeeping Research. 3(10):153–160. 1934.

7753. Hill, A. H. Evergreens on the golf course. The National Greenkeeper. 5(5):29. 1931.

7754. Hill, A. L. The lawn under your feet. Gardens and Grounds that take Care of Themselves. Prentice-Hall, Inc., New Jersey. pp. 80–92. 1958.

7755. Hill, D. D. Grass seed—production and situation. Rutgers University Short Course in Turf Management. 19:31–38. 1951.

7756. Hill, E. R. Reproductive potential of yellow nutsedge by seed. Turf Bulletin. Massachusetts Turf & Lawn Grass Council. 2(9):7–8. 1964.

7757. Hill, H. D. and H. L. Carnahan. Effects of variables in weather and their interactions on metaphase cells in the root tips of grasses. Botany Gazette. 116(1):82–86. 1954.

7758. Hill, H. P. How to calibrate turf sprayers Weeds, Trees, and Turf. 4:8–11, 28. 1965.

7759. ______. Calibrate sprayers often. Weeds, Trees and Turf. 7(3):7 (3 pp.). 1968.

7760. Hill, J. W. Safety in turfgrass maintenance. Proceedings of the Texas Turfgrass Conference. 20:9–10. 1965.

7761. Hill, L. Turfgrass research needs. Iagreen. 1(2):4–8. 1962.

7762. Hill, L. L., J. F. Cornman, and D. J. Lathwell. A comparison of several methods of measuring phosphorus in turfgrass soils with reference to the interference of arsenates. Agronomy Abstracts. 53:74. 1961.

7763. Hill, P. A. Maintaining a golf course at Salt Lake City. The Greenkeepers' Reporter. 7(2):15–16, 36–37. 1939.

7764. ______. Hard vs. soft greens. Greenkeepers' Reporter. 7(6):10. 1939.

7765. ______. Experiences with snowmold control. Greenkeepers' Reporter. 9(6):-12. 1941.

7766. ______. Wartime greenkeeping at Salt Lake Country Club. Greenkeepers' Reporter. 11(6):16. 1943.

7767. ______. Care of bluegrass. The Greenkeepers' Reporter. 12(4):13. 1944.

7768. ______. Treating dandelion and knotweed with 2, 4–D at the country club. The Greenkeepers' Reporter. 13(5):28. 1945.

7769. Hill, R. G. Pave your waterways with grass. Michigan State University Extension Bulletin No. E–457. Farm Science Series. 2 pp. 1964.

7770. Hill, T. The profitable art of gardening. Thomas Marshe, London England. 1568.

7771. Hill, W. E. and B. B. Tucker. A comparison of injected anhydrous ammonia into bermudagrass sod compared to topdressed applications of urea and ammonium nitrate. Soil Science Society of America Proceedings. 32(2):257–260. 1968.

7772. Hilliard, J. H. Photosynthesis and photorespiration in monocots differing in carbon dioxide fixation pathways: correlations of structure and function of chloroplasts and leaf microbodies. Ph.D. Thesis, University of Florida. 1971.

7773. Hilliker, F. Sod production. Turf Bulletin. Massachusetts Turf and Lawn Grass Council. 5(1):18–19. 1968.

7774. Hillman, F. H. The seeds of the bluegrasses II. Descriptions of the seeds of the commercial bluegrasses and their impurities. U.S.D.A. Bureau of Plant Industry Bulletin. 84:15–38. 1905.

7775. ______. Distinguishing the seeds of redtop and bent grasses. Association of Official Seed Analysts Proceedings. pp. 76–79. 1917.

7776. ______. Rhode Island bent seed and its substitutes in the trade. Association of Official Seed Analysts Proceedings. pp. 64–68. 1919.

7777. ______. South German mixed bent seed described. USGA Green Section Bulletin. 1(3):37–39. 1921.

7778. ______. Identifying turf-grass seed. USGA Green Section Bulletin. 10(3):-39–43. 1930.

7779. Hillis, J. C. Regulation of sodium arsenite as an injurious material. California Turfgrass Culture. 13(4):25–26. 1963.

7780. Hills, L. D. Lawns, paths, and layout. Down to Earth Gardening. Faber and Faber. London. pp. 26–45. 1967.

7781. Hilton, G. Uniformity in irrigation. Proceedings of the Midwest Regional Turf Conference. 55–56. 1970.

7782. Himmelman, B. F. Experiments on seeding and mulching for roadside erosion control. Ninth Pan American Highway Congress. Document No. 70. 21 pp. 1963.

7783. Hines, C. A., and K. A. Tannar. Michigan sod statistics. Michigan and United States Departments of Agriculture. 1971.

7784. Hines, R. P. My thatch control program. Proceedings University of Florida Turfgrass Management Conference. 7:29–30. 1959.

7785. Hinesly, T. D. Soil amendments. Illinois Turfgrass Conference Proceedings. pp. 10–12. 1963.

7786. ______. Soil water and its movement. Illinois Turfgrass Conference Proceedings. pp. 4–9. 1964.

7787. Hinman, T. P. Fertilizing bermuda grass with ammonium sulfate USGA Green Section Bulletin. 5(11):250–251. 1925.

7788. ______. Care of Bermuda putting greens. USGA Green Section Bulletin. 7(4):-77–78. 1927.

7789. ______. Double bermuda greens and their treatment. USGA Green Section Bulletin. 9(10):196–199. 1929.

7790. Hitch, P. A. and B. C. Sharman. The vascular pattern of Festucoid grass axes, with particular reference to nodal plexi. Botanical Gazette. 132(1):38–56. 1971.

7791. Hitch, P. J. Zoysia planting systems—plugging. Proceedings of the Midwest Regional Turf Conference. pp. 63–64. 1971.

7792. Hitchcock, A. S. North American species of *Agrostis.* U.S.D.A. Bureau of Plant Industry Bulletin 68. p. 68. 1905.

7793. ______. A text-book of grasses. The Macmillan Company, New York. 276 pp. 1914.

7794. ______. The genera of grasses of the United States. U.S.D.A. Bulletin No. 772. 307 pp. 1920.

7795. ______. Manual of the grasses of the United States. USDA Miscellaneous Publication No. 200. 1051 pp. 1935.

7796. ______. Manual of the grasses of the West Indies. USDA. Miscellaneous Publication. No. 243. 439 pp. 1936.

7797. Hitchcock, A. S. and A. Chase. Manual of the grasses of the United States. USDA Miscellaneous Publication No. 200. 1051 pp. 1951.

7798. Hite, B. C. Forcing the germination of bluegrass. Association of Official Seed Analysts Proceedings. pp. 53–58. 1919.

7799. Hockersmith, S. L. Chemicals cut roadside clearing costs for Lane County, Oregon. Weeds, Trees and Turf. 6(7):8–11. 1967.

7800. Hodgden, R. and C. Harms. Soil fertility levels governing bensulide phytotoxicity to *Digitaria sanguinalis.* Agronomy Abstracts. p. 39. 1966.

7801. Hodges, C. F. Current nematode—turf research at the University of Illinois. Illinois Turfgrass Conference Proceedings. pp. 41–43. 1963.

7802. ______. Etiology of stripe smut, *Ustilago striiformis* (West.) Niessl. on Merion bluegrass. *Poa pratensis.* Ph.D. Thesis, University of Illinois. 64 pp. 1967.

7803. ______. Field identification of turfgrass diseases. Ohio Turfgrass Conference Proceedings. pp. 21–25. 1969.

7804. ______. Symptomatology and histopathology of *Agrostis palustris* infected by *Ustilago striiformis* vas. *agrostidis.* Phytopathology. 59(10):1455–1457. 1969.

7805. ______. Additional varieties of *Agrostis palustris* infected by *Ustilago striiformis* var. *Agrostidis.* Plant Disease Reporter. 53(4):298–299. 1969.

7806. ______. Morphological differences in Kentucky bluegrass infected by stripe smut and flag smut. Plant Disease Reporter. 53(12):967–968. 1969.

7807. ______. Stripe smut infection, disease development, and spread. Proceedings of the Midwest Regional Turf Conference. pp. 38–40. 1970.

7808. ______. Influence of temperature on growth of stripe-smutted creeping bentgrass and on soros development of *Ustilago striiformis.* Phytopathology. 60(4):665–668. 1970.

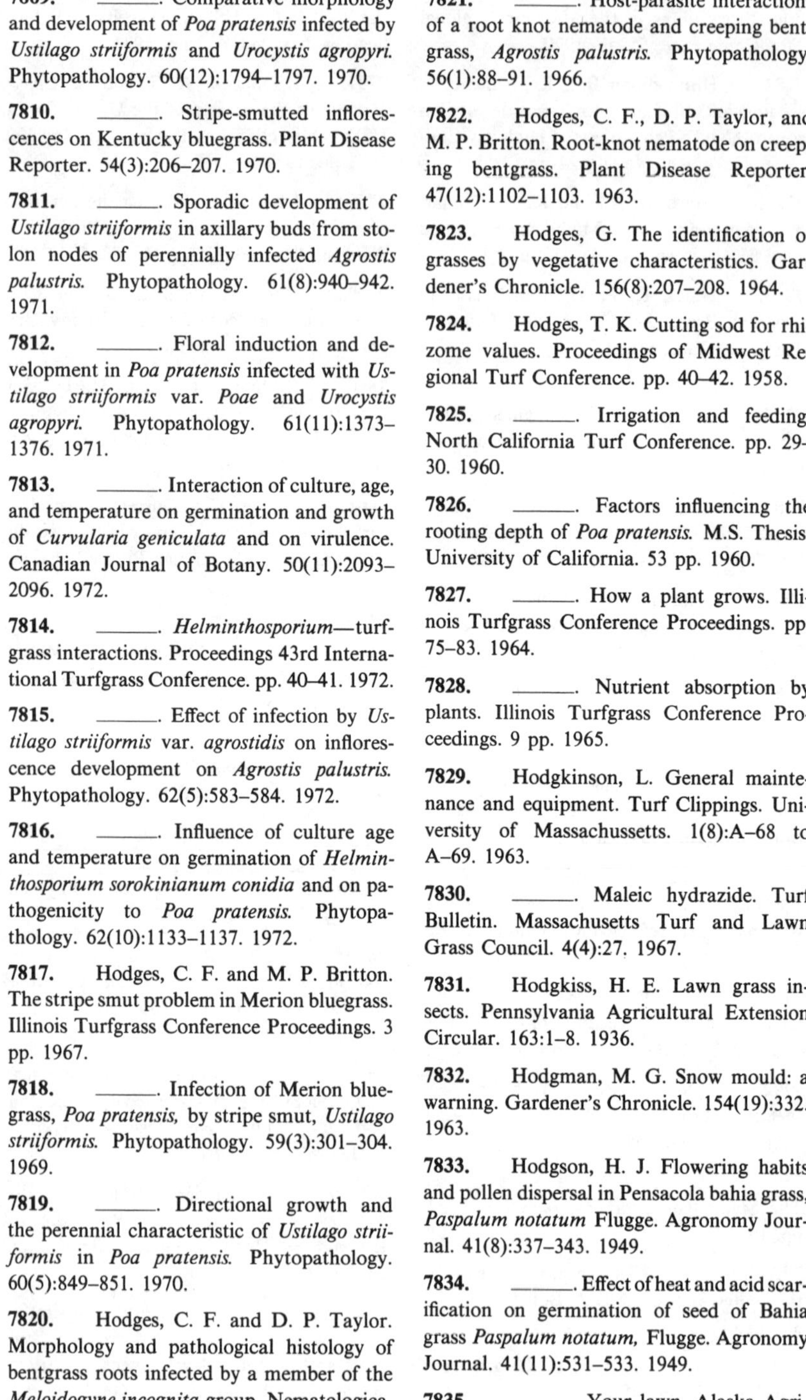

7809. ______. Comparative morphology and development of *Poa pratensis* infected by *Ustilago striiformis* and *Urocystis agropyri.* Phytopathology. 60(12):1794–1797. 1970.

7810. ______. Stripe-smutted inflorescences on Kentucky bluegrass. Plant Disease Reporter. 54(3):206–207. 1970.

7811. ______. Sporadic development of *Ustilago striiformis* in axillary buds from stolon nodes of perennially infected *Agrostis palustris.* Phytopathology. 61(8):940–942. 1971.

7812. ______. Floral induction and development in *Poa pratensis* infected with *Ustilago striiformis* var. *Poae* and *Urocystis agropyri.* Phytopathology. 61(11):1373–1376. 1971.

7813. ______. Interaction of culture, age, and temperature on germination and growth of *Curvularia geniculata* and on virulence. Canadian Journal of Botany. 50(11):2093–2096. 1972.

7814. ______. *Helminthosporium*—turfgrass interactions. Proceedings 43rd International Turfgrass Conference. pp. 40–41. 1972.

7815. ______. Effect of infection by *Ustilago striiformis* var. *agrostidis* on inflorescence development on *Agrostis palustris.* Phytopathology. 62(5):583–584. 1972.

7816. ______. Influence of culture age and temperature on germination of *Helminthosporium sorokinianum conidia* and on pathogenicity to *Poa pratensis.* Phytopathology. 62(10):1133–1137. 1972.

7817. Hodges, C. F. and M. P. Britton. The stripe smut problem in Merion bluegrass. Illinois Turfgrass Conference Proceedings. 3 pp. 1967.

7818. ______. Infection of Merion bluegrass, *Poa pratensis,* by stripe smut, *Ustilago striiformis.* Phytopathology. 59(3):301–304. 1969.

7819. ______. Directional growth and the perennial characteristic of *Ustilago striiformis* in *Poa pratensis.* Phytopathology. 60(5):849–851. 1970.

7820. Hodges, C. F. and D. P. Taylor. Morphology and pathological histology of bentgrass roots infected by a member of the *Meloidogyne incognita* group. Nematologica. 11:40. 1965.

7821. ______. Host-parasite interactions of a root knot nematode and creeping bentgrass, *Agrostis palustris.* Phytopathology. 56(1):88–91. 1966.

7822. Hodges, C. F., D. P. Taylor, and M. P. Britton. Root-knot nematode on creeping bentgrass. Plant Disease Reporter. 47(12):1102–1103. 1963.

7823. Hodges, G. The identification of grasses by vegetative characteristics. Gardener's Chronicle. 156(8):207–208. 1964.

7824. Hodges, T. K. Cutting sod for rhizome values. Proceedings of Midwest Regional Turf Conference. pp. 40–42. 1958.

7825. ______. Irrigation and feeding. North California Turf Conference. pp. 29–30. 1960.

7826. ______. Factors influencing the rooting depth of *Poa pratensis.* M.S. Thesis, University of California. 53 pp. 1960.

7827. ______. How a plant grows. Illinois Turfgrass Conference Proceedings. pp. 75–83. 1964.

7828. ______. Nutrient absorption by plants. Illinois Turfgrass Conference Proceedings. 9 pp. 1965.

7829. Hodgkinson, L. General maintenance and equipment. Turf Clippings. University of Massachussetts. 1(8):A–68 to A–69. 1963.

7830. ______. Maleic hydrazide. Turf Bulletin. Massachusetts Turf and Lawn Grass Council. 4(4):27. 1967.

7831. Hodgkiss, H. E. Lawn grass insects. Pennsylvania Agricultural Extension Circular. 163:1–8. 1936.

7832. Hodgman, M. G. Snow mould: a warning. Gardener's Chronicle. 154(19):332. 1963.

7833. Hodgson, H. J. Flowering habits and pollen dispersal in Pensacola bahia grass, *Paspalum notatum* Flugge. Agronomy Journal. 41(8):337–343. 1949.

7834. ______. Effect of heat and acid scarification on germination of seed of Bahia grass *Paspalum notatum,* Flugge. Agronomy Journal. 41(11):531–533. 1949.

7835. ______. Your lawn. Alaska Agricultural Extension Circular. 430:1–8. 1955.

7836. ______. Performance of turfgrass varieties in the subarctic. Agronomy Abstracts. 56:101. 1964.

7837. Hoeksrta, P. Water movement and freezing pressures. Soil Science Society of America Proceedings. 33(4):512–517. 1969.

7838. Hoffer, G. M. Turfgrass disease and exudated water. Mid-Atlantic Superintents Conference Proceedings. 7–8. 1969.

7840. Hoffer, G. N. Fertilizing golf greens. Better Crops with Plant Food Magazine. 29(4):9–12. 1945.

7841. ______. Clipping tests as greens fertilizing guide. Golfdom. 19(4):38, 40, 42. 1945.

7842. ______. When should golf greens be aerated? Golfdom. 19(6):44, 46–47. 1945.

7843. Hogan, D. A. Turf sprinkler system—design and materials. Proceedings 9th Annual Northwest Turf Conference. 9:16–21.

7844. ______. Turfgrass irrigation. Proceedings 16th Annual Northwest Turf Conference. 16:87–89. 1962.

7845. ______. Automatic irrigation in the West. Golf Course Reporter. 31(6):22–29. 1963.

7846. ______. The ecology of turfgrass. Proceedings of the 18th Annual Northwest Turfgrass Conference. p. 54. 1964.

7847. ______. Is automatic irrigation really necessary? Proceedings Turfgrass Sprinkler Irrigation Conference. 2 pp. 1966.

7848. ______. Designing irrigation systems for golf courses. USGA Green Section Record. 3(6):2–6. 1966.

7849. ______. Primary decisions. International Turfgrass Conference and Show. 39:56–59. 1968.

7850. Hogan, R. Water and drainage problems on turf. Southern California Conference on Turf Culture. pp. 9–17. 1951.

7852. Hojjati, S. M., R. A. McCreery, and W. E. Adams. Effects of nitrogen and potassium fertilization, irrigation, and clipping interval on chemical composition of coastal bermudagrass (*Cynodon dactylon* (L. Pers.). I. Total available carbohydrates. Agronomy Journal. 60(6):617–619. 1968.

7853. Holben, F. J. Effects of potash on turf establishment. The Pennsylvania State College Eighteenth Annual Turf Conference. pp. 96–101. 1949.

7854. ______. Potash-nitrogen fertilization of turf grasses. Pennsylvania State College Turfgrass Conference Proceedings. 20:-56–70. 1951.

7855. ______. Nitrogen-potash relationship as they affect the growth and diseases of turf grasses. Pennsylvania State College Turfgrass Conference Proceedings. 19:74–93. 1950.

7856. ______. Potash-nitrogen fertilization of fescue and bentgrass turf. Agronomy Abstracts. p. 41. 1952.

7857. ______. Potash-nitrogen fertilization of fescue and bent turf. Pennsylvania State College Turfgrass Conference Proceedings. 21:52–56. 1952.

7858. Holbrook, G. What entomology means to the greenkeeper. Greenkeepers Club of New England Newsletter. 9(9):8–10. 1937.

7859. Holbrook, M. Antitranspirants. Ground Maintenance. 4(4):30. 1969.

7860. Holcomb, G. E. and K. S. Derrick. Sad: a new disease of St. Augustine grass. Louisiana Agriculture. 15(3):10–11. 1972.

7861. Holcomb, G. E. and R. E. Motsinger. Zoysia rust in Louisiana. The Plant Disease Reporter. 51(9):726. 1967.

7862. Holcomb, G. E., K. S. Derrick, R. B. Carver, and R. W. Toler. St. Augustine decline virus found in Louisiana. The Plant Disease Reporter. 56(1):69–70. 1972.

7863. Holdane, E. S. Scots gardens in old times (1200–1800). A. MacLehose & Co., London. 243 pp. 1934.

7864. Holder, G. Peats in processing. Proceedings Fourth Annual Tennessee Turfgrass Conference. pp. 48. 1970.

7865. Holifield, E. L., and R. E. Frans. Winter weed removal from dormant turf. Proceedings of 17th Southern Weed Conference. pp. 127–131. 1964.

7866. Holland, C. G. Winter treatment of bermuda greens. USGA Green Section Bulletin. 5:249–250. 1925.

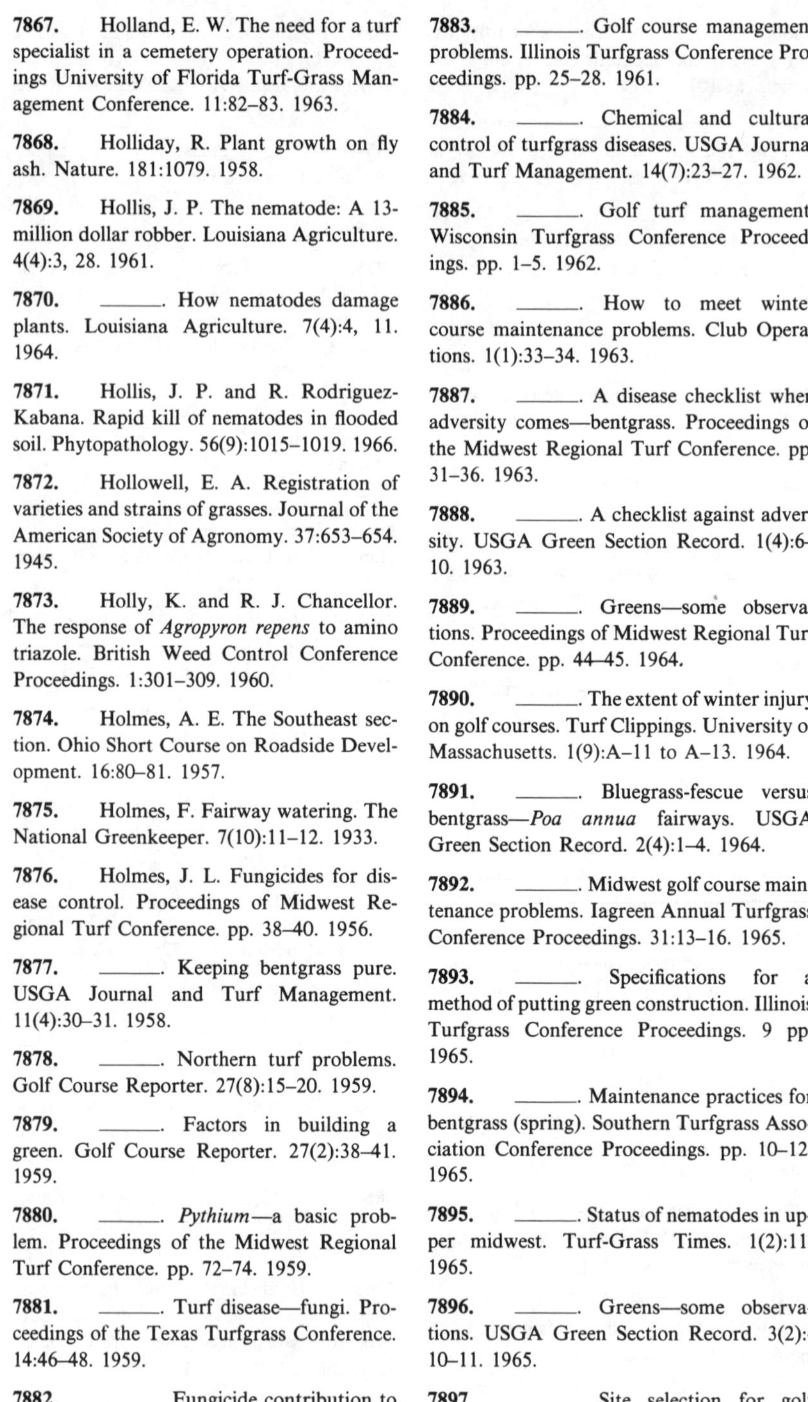

7867. Holland, E. W. The need for a turf specialist in a cemetery operation. Proceedings University of Florida Turf-Grass Management Conference. 11:82–83. 1963.

7868. Holliday, R. Plant growth on fly ash. Nature. 181:1079. 1958.

7869. Hollis, J. P. The nematode: A 13-million dollar robber. Louisiana Agriculture. 4(4):3, 28. 1961.

7870. ______. How nematodes damage plants. Louisiana Agriculture. 7(4):4, 11. 1964.

7871. Hollis, J. P. and R. Rodriguez-Kabana. Rapid kill of nematodes in flooded soil. Phytopathology. 56(9):1015–1019. 1966.

7872. Hollowell, E. A. Registration of varieties and strains of grasses. Journal of the American Society of Agronomy. 37:653–654. 1945.

7873. Holly, K. and R. J. Chancellor. The response of *Agropyron repens* to amino triazole. British Weed Control Conference Proceedings. 1:301–309. 1960.

7874. Holmes, A. E. The Southeast section. Ohio Short Course on Roadside Development. 16:80–81. 1957.

7875. Holmes, F. Fairway watering. The National Greenkeeper. 7(10):11–12. 1933.

7876. Holmes, J. L. Fungicides for disease control. Proceedings of Midwest Regional Turf Conference. pp. 38–40. 1956.

7877. ______. Keeping bentgrass pure. USGA Journal and Turf Management. 11(4):30–31. 1958.

7878. ______. Northern turf problems. Golf Course Reporter. 27(8):15–20. 1959.

7879. ______. Factors in building a green. Golf Course Reporter. 27(2):38–41. 1959.

7880. ______. *Pythium*—a basic problem. Proceedings of the Midwest Regional Turf Conference. pp. 72–74. 1959.

7881. ______. Turf disease—fungi. Proceedings of the Texas Turfgrass Conference. 14:46–48. 1959.

7882. ______. Fungicide contribution to weed control. Proceedings of the Midwest Regional Turf Conference. pp. 18–19. 1960.

7883. ______. Golf course management problems. Illinois Turfgrass Conference Proceedings. pp. 25–28. 1961.

7884. ______. Chemical and cultural control of turfgrass diseases. USGA Journal and Turf Management. 14(7):23–27. 1962.

7885. ______. Golf turf management. Wisconsin Turfgrass Conference Proceedings. pp. 1–5. 1962.

7886. ______. How to meet winter course maintenance problems. Club Operations. 1(1):33–34. 1963.

7887. ______. A disease checklist when adversity comes—bentgrass. Proceedings of the Midwest Regional Turf Conference. pp. 31–36. 1963.

7888. ______. A checklist against adversity. USGA Green Section Record. 1(4):6–10. 1963.

7889. ______. Greens—some observations. Proceedings of Midwest Regional Turf Conference. pp. 44–45. 1964.

7890. ______. The extent of winter injury on golf courses. Turf Clippings. University of Massachusetts. 1(9):A-11 to A-13. 1964.

7891. ______. Bluegrass-fescue versus bentgrass—*Poa annua* fairways. USGA Green Section Record. 2(4):1–4. 1964.

7892. ______. Midwest golf course maintenance problems. Iagreen Annual Turfgrass Conference Proceedings. 31:13–16. 1965.

7893. ______. Specifications for a method of putting green construction. Illinois Turfgrass Conference Proceedings. 9 pp. 1965.

7894. ______. Maintenance practices for bentgrass (spring). Southern Turfgrass Association Conference Proceedings. pp. 10–12. 1965.

7895. ______. Status of nematodes in upper midwest. Turf-Grass Times. 1(2):11. 1965.

7896. ______. Greens—some observations. USGA Green Section Record. 3(2):-10–11. 1965.

7897. ______. Site selection for golf courses. Illinois Turfgrass Conference Proceedings. pp. 31–35. 1966.

7898. ______. Watering systems—so what? Proceedings of the Midwest Regional Turf Conference. pp. 84–85. 1966.

7899. ______. Bluegrass—fescue vs. bentgrass—*Poa annua* fairways. Seventeenth R.C.G.A. Sports Turfgrass Conference. pp. 41–44. 1966.

7900. ______. Increases and decreases costs following fairway watering. Illinois Turfgrass Conference Proceedings. pp. 22–30. 1967.

7901. ______. Golf course irrigation needs. Sprinkler Irrigation Association Annual Technical Conference Proceedings. pp. 29–32. 1967.

7902. ______. The Green Section specifications for a putting green. Turf Clippings. University of Massachusetts. 2(2):19–25. 1967.

7903. ______. Cart paths. USGA Green Section Record. 4(5):1–5. 1967.

7904. ______. Putting green construction. USGA Green Section Record. 4(6):13–15. 1967.

7905. ______. Northern transition: winter to spring. USGA Green Section Record. 5(1):10–12. 1967.

7906. ______. Green construction—techniques and materials. USGA Green Section Record. 5(6):8–9. 1968.

7907. ______. Better drainage through slit trenches. USGA Green Section Record. 6(1):8–10. 1968.

7908. ______. Blends and mixtures of grasses for golf course turf. Ohio Turfgrass Conference Proceedings. pp. 17–20. 1969.

7909. ______. Combining herbicides to control weeds in turf. Ohio Turfgrass Conference Proceedings. p. 58. 1969.

7910. ______. Blues vs. bents for fairway turf. Turf Clippings. University of Massachussetts. 4(1):A–87 to A–93. 1969.

7911. Holmes, J. L., L. Record, and H. Griffin. Factors influencing irrigation. USGA Green Section Record. 3(6):7–9. 1966.

7912. Holmes, J. L., C. Stewart, and R. W. Willits Care and handling of golf carts. USGA Green Section Record. 1(2):3–6. 1963.

7913. Holmes, L. Agricultural chemical use on golf courses. Illinois Turfgrass Conference Proceedings. pp. 54–63. 1964.

7914. Holmes, N. H., G. E. Swailes, and G. A. Hobbs. The eriophyid mite *Aceria tulipae* (K.) *(Acarina: Eriophyidae)* and silver top in grasses. Canada Entomologist. 93:644–667. 1961.

7915. Holmes, R. L. The influence of mixed hardwood bark chips as a surfacing material for simulated recreation trails on bulk density, aeration porosity, and soil moisture content of a Southern Illinois soil. M.S. Thesis, Southern Illinois University. 1972.

7916. Holt, D. A. Diurnal variation in carbohydrate levels of selected forage crops as influenced by factors of the microenvironment. Ph.D. Thesis, Purdue University. 127 pp. 1967.

7917. Holt, D. A. and A. R. Hilst. Daily variation in carbohydrate content of selected forage crops. Agronomy Journal. 61(2):239–242. 1969.

7919. Holt, E. C. A study of creeping bentgrass for fairway uses. Ph.D. Thesis. Purdue University. 1950.

7920. ______. Research reports—Texas A&M plots. Proceedings of the Annual Texas Turfgrass Conference. 9:31–37. 1954.

7921. ______. Vegetative propagation of turf grass. Parks & Recreation. 40(6):14–15. 1957.

7922. ______. The development and characteristics of turfgrass strains. Proceedings of the Texas Turfgrass Conference. 12:-9–11. 1957.

7923. ______. Fall lawn care—in the Southwest. Golf Course Reporter. 27(7):37, 39–41. 1959.

7924. ______. Control of large brown patch on St. Augustinegrass. Golf Course Reporter. 31(5):48–50. 1963.

7925. ______. Humic acid—nitrogen ratios in bermudagrass fertilization. Agronomy Abstracts. 56:106. 1964.

7926. ______. The A B C's of better bermudagrass turf. Southern Turfgrass Association Conference Proceedings. pp. 3–4. 1964.

7927. ______. Spraying for better turf. Southern Turfgrass Association Conference Proceedings. pp. 9–10. 1964.

7928. Holt, E. C. and R. L. Davis. Two Purdue graduate students report on bent grass test. Midwest Turf News and Research. 1(3):2,4. 1947.

7929. ______. Differential responses of Arlington and Norbeck Bent grasses to kinds and rates of fertilizers. Journal of the American Society of Agronomy. 40:282–284. 1948.

7930. Holt, E. C., and R. R. Davis. Fairways with bent grasses may be next. Park Maintenance. 1(5):8–10. 1948.

7931. Holt, E. C. and J. A. Lancaster. Yield and stand survival of coastal bermudagrass as influenced by management factors. Agronomy Journal. 60(1):7–11. 1968.

7932. Holt, E. C. and J. A. Long. The use of synthetic nitrogen on turf. Proceedings of the Texas Turfgrass Conference. 13:41–45. 1958.

7933. ______. Survey of turfgrass research at Texas A&M. Proceedings of the Texas Turfgrass Conference. 14:54–56. 1959.

7934. Holt, E. C., and K. T. Payne. Variation in spreading rate and growth characteristics of creeping bentgrass seedlings. Agronomy Journal 44(2):88–90. 1952.

7935. Holt, E. C., W. W. Allen, and M. H. Ferguson. Turfgrass—maintenance costs in Texas. Texas Agricultural Experiment Station. Bulletin B–1027. 19 pp. 1964.

7936. Holt, E. C., W. W. Allen, and J. A. Long. The toxicity of soil-incorporated treatments of EPTC on nutgrass. Agronomy Abstracts. 52:70. 1960.

7937. Holt, E. C., R. C. Potts, and J. F. Fudge. Bermudagrass research in Texas. Texas Agricultural Experiment Station Circular. 129:1–25. 1951.

7938. Holyoke, V. H. Soil testing and interpretation. University of Maine Turf Conference Proceedings. 1:7 pp. 1963.

7939. ______. What happens to the nitrogen we use? University of Maine Turf Conference Proceedings. 6:48–50. 1968.

7940. Holyoke, V. and R. A. Struchtemeyer. Lawns and their care. Maine Agricultural Extension Bulletin. 495:1–15. 1962.

7941. Homan, H. J. Rebuilding a golf green. Turf Clippings. University of Massachussetts. 1(1):20–21. 1956.

7942. Hooghoudt, S. B. Tile drainage and subirrigation. Soil Science. 74:35–48. 1952.

7943. Hottenstien, W. L. Roadside erosion problems and their solution. Pennsylvania State College Turfgrass Conference Proceedings. 21:86–93. 1952.

7944. Hoover, E. R. Methods that work o.k. on my course. Golfdom. 2(6):47–51. 1928.

7945. Hoover, M. M. Native and adapted grasses for conservation of soil and moisture in the great plains and western states. USDA. Farmers' Bulletin. No. 1812. 44 pp. 1939.

7946. Hoover, M. M., J. E. Smith, Jr., A. E. Ferber, and D. R. Cornelius. Seed for regrassing great plains areas. USDA. Farmers' Bulletin. No. 1985. 37 pp. 1947.

7947. Hoover, M. M., M. A. Hein, W. A. Dayton, and C. O. Erlanson. The main grasses for farm and home. Grass. The Yearbook of Agriculture USDA. pp. 639–700. 1948.

7948. Hoover, N. K. Grading, establishing and maintaining the lawn. Approved Practices in Beautifying the Home Grounds. Interstate Printers and Publishers, Inc., Illinois. pp. 68–116. 1969.

7949. Hope, V., R. B. Rawsthorn. The water problem on golf courses. Journal of the Board of Greenkeeping Research. 4(14):207–210. 1936.

7950. Hopen, H. J. and A. J. Turgeon. Deactivation of herbicide residues for horticultural crops using activated carbon. Report From Horticulture, Vegetable Growing No. 18. 4 p. 1972.

7951. Hopen, H. J., W. E. Splittstopper, and J. D. Butler. Intra-species bentgrass selectivity of siduron. Horticultural Science Article. University of Illinois. No. 432. 1966.

7952. Hopkins, D. P. The problem of lawn weeds. Gardener's Chronicle. 157(13):-304. 1965.

7953. Hopkins, H. Variations in the growth of side-oats grama grass at Hays, Kansas, from seed produced in various parts of the great plains region. Transactions, Kansas Academy of Science. 44:86–95. 1941.

7954. Hoppe, P. E. *Pythium* species still viable after 12 years in air-dried muck soil. Phytopathology. 56(12):1411. 1966.

7955. Hopphan, C. G. Success with arsenic on 32 acres—bluegrass fairways. Proceedings of the Midwest Regional Turf Conference. pp. 28–30. 1970.

7956. Hopwood, F. B. Winter management of bowling greens and preparation for opening. New Zealand Institute for Turf Culture Newsletter. 81:157–159. 1972.

7957. Hormay, A. L. A key for identifying some important annual range grasses in the immature stage. USDA-Forest Service. Forest Research Notes. No. 26. 13 pp. 1942.

7958. Horn, A. S. Idaho lawns. Idaho Agricultural Extension Service Publication. 1966.

7959. Horn, C. "Thiosan"—a new turf fungicide. Golfdom. 16(5):13–14. 1942.

7961. Horn, G. C. What's in the fertilizer bag. Proceedings University of Florida Turf Management Conference. 6:50–54. 1958.

7962. ______. Fertilization of St. Augustine grass. Proceedings University of Florida Turfgrass Management Conference. 7:40–43. 1959.

7963. ______. Nutrition of turf grasses. Proceedings University of Florida Turfgrass Management Conference. 8:18–20. 1960.

7964. ______. Weed control in sod nursery program. Proceedings University of Florida Turfgrass Management Conference. 8:48–50. 1960.

7965. ______. Objectives of the turf research program. Proceedings University of Florida Turfgrass Management Conference. 8:140–142. 1960.

7966. ______. The effect of different rates and combinations of nitrogen, phosphorus and potash, on the yield and distance between nodes of 'Floratine' St. Augustinegrass. Proceedings University of Florida Turf Grass Management Conference. 8:150–152. 1960.

7967. ______. Evaluation and improvement of turf grasses for Florida. Proceedings University of Florida Turf Grass Management Conference. 8:156–161. 1960.

7968. ______. Effect of source of nitrogen and lime on the growth of centipedegrass. Proceedings University of Florida Turfgrass Management Conference. 8:162. 1960.

7969. ______. Chemicals control weeds in your turf. Sunshine State Agricultural Research Report. 5(3):10–11. 1960.

7970. ______. Variety studies presently under way and proposals for the future. Proceedings University of Florida Turf-Grass Management Conference. 9:123–126. 1961.

7971. Hersman, F. C. and H. Gray. Soil management for Long Island gardens and lawns. State Institute of Agriculture on Long Island. 1941.

7972. Horn, G. C. Results of research on weed control in turf. Proceedings Fifteenth Southeastern Turfgrass Conference. pp. 22–27. 1961.

7973. ______. Role of testing in turfgrass management. Florida Turf-Grass Association Bulletin, 9(2):4–7. 1962.

7974. ______. Where do we go from here? Proceedings University of Florida Turf-Grass Management Conference. 10:10–16. 1962.

7975. ______. Greens overseeding study —1962. Proceedings of University of Florida Turf-Grass Management Conference. 10:71–73. 1962.

7976. ______. Establishment and maintenance of large turf area. Soil and Crop Science Society of Florida Proceedings. 21:115–119. 1961.

7977. ______. Bermudagrass for lawns. Sunshine State Agricultural Research Report. 7(3):8–9. 1962.

7978. ______. Yellowing of turfgrass. California Turfgrass Culture. 12(3):22–24. 1963.

7979. ______. Yellowing of turfgrasses. Florida Turfgrass Association Bulletin. 10(1):1–5. 1963.

7980. ______. Which grass for what purpose? Proceedings University of Florida Turf-Grass Management Conference. 11:64–73. 1963.

7981. Watson, L. Peak season planning: baseball. Proceedings University of Florida

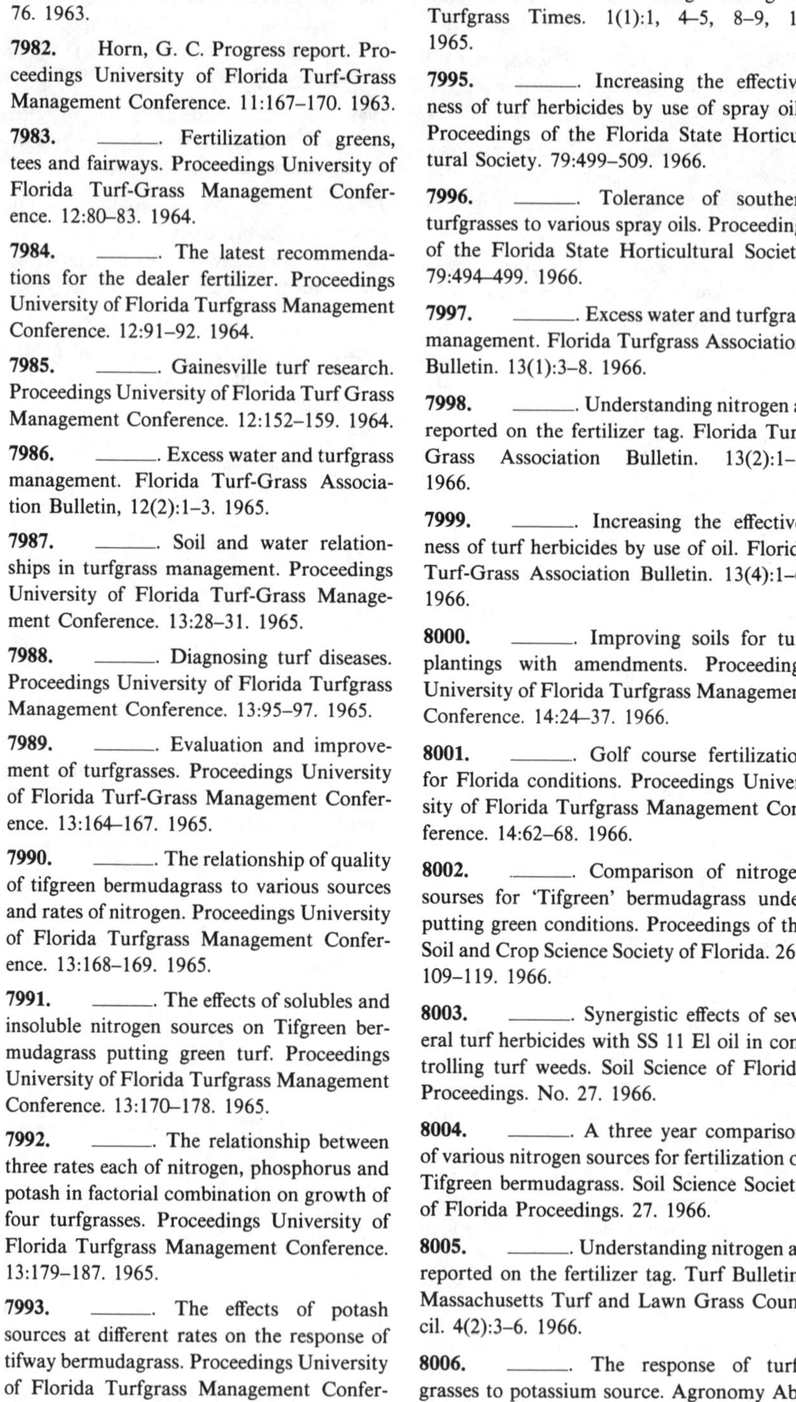

Turf-Grass Management Conference. 11:74–76. 1963.

7982. Horn, G. C. Progress report. Proceedings University of Florida Turf-Grass Management Conference. 11:167–170. 1963.

7983. ______. Fertilization of greens, tees and fairways. Proceedings University of Florida Turf-Grass Management Conference. 12:80–83. 1964.

7984. ______. The latest recommendations for the dealer fertilizer. Proceedings University of Florida Turfgrass Management Conference. 12:91–92. 1964.

7985. ______. Gainesville turf research. Proceedings University of Florida Turf Grass Management Conference. 12:152–159. 1964.

7986. ______. Excess water and turfgrass management. Florida Turf-Grass Association Bulletin, 12(2):1–3. 1965.

7987. ______. Soil and water relationships in turfgrass management. Proceedings University of Florida Turf-Grass Management Conference. 13:28–31. 1965.

7988. ______. Diagnosing turf diseases. Proceedings University of Florida Turfgrass Management Conference. 13:95–97. 1965.

7989. ______. Evaluation and improvement of turfgrasses. Proceedings University of Florida Turf-Grass Management Conference. 13:164–167. 1965.

7990. ______. The relationship of quality of tifgreen bermudagrass to various sources and rates of nitrogen. Proceedings University of Florida Turfgrass Management Conference. 13:168–169. 1965.

7991. ______. The effects of solubles and insoluble nitrogen sources on Tifgreen bermudagrass putting green turf. Proceedings University of Florida Turfgrass Management Conference. 13:170–178. 1965.

7992. ______. The relationship between three rates each of nitrogen, phosphorus and potash in factorial combination on growth of four turfgrasses. Proceedings University of Florida Turfgrass Management Conference. 13:179–187. 1965.

7993. ______. The effects of potash sources at different rates on the response of tifway bermudagrass. Proceedings University of Florida Turfgrass Management Conference. 13:188–191. 1965.

7994. ______. Overseeding winter grass. Turfgrass Times. 1(1):1, 4–5, 8–9, 19. 1965.

7995. ______. Increasing the effectiveness of turf herbicides by use of spray oils. Proceedings of the Florida State Horticultural Society. 79:499–509. 1966.

7996. ______. Tolerance of southern turfgrasses to various spray oils. Proceedings of the Florida State Horticultural Society. 79:494–499. 1966.

7997. ______. Excess water and turfgrass management. Florida Turfgrass Association. Bulletin. 13(1):3–8. 1966.

7998. ______. Understanding nitrogen as reported on the fertilizer tag. Florida Turf-Grass Association Bulletin. 13(2):1–3. 1966.

7999. ______. Increasing the effectiveness of turf herbicides by use of oil. Florida Turf-Grass Association Bulletin. 13(4):1–6. 1966.

8000. ______. Improving soils for turf plantings with amendments. Proceedings University of Florida Turfgrass Management Conference. 14:24–37. 1966.

8001. ______. Golf course fertilization for Florida conditions. Proceedings University of Florida Turfgrass Management Conference. 14:62–68. 1966.

8002. ______. Comparison of nitrogen sourses for 'Tifgreen' bermudagrass under putting green conditions. Proceedings of the Soil and Crop Science Society of Florida. 26:-109–119. 1966.

8003. ______. Synergistic effects of several turf herbicides with SS 11 El oil in controlling turf weeds. Soil Science of Florida Proceedings. No. 27. 1966.

8004. ______. A three year comparison of various nitrogen sources for fertilization of Tifgreen bermudagrass. Soil Science Society of Florida Proceedings. 27. 1966.

8005. ______. Understanding nitrogen as reported on the fertilizer tag. Turf Bulletin. Massachusetts Turf and Lawn Grass Council. 4(2):3–6. 1966.

8006. ______. The response of turfgrasses to potassium source. Agronomy Abstracts. p. 52. 1967.

8007. ______. Comparison of nitrogen sources for "Tifgreen" bermudagrass under putting green conditions. Florida Turf-Grass Association Bulletin. 14(1):1–5. 1967.

8008. ______. Facts to consider in fertilization of large turf areas. Proceedings University of Florida Turfgrass Management Conference. 15:68–71. 1967.

8009. ______. Turfgrass variety comparisons. Proceedings University of Florida Turf-Grass Management Conference. 15:91–99. 1967.

8010. ______. Comparison of several nitrogen fertilization programs for Tifgreen bermudagrass putting greens alone and when overseeded with cool season grasses. Agronomy Abstracts. p. 59. 1968.

8011. ______. Effects of various soil amendments on soil properties and growth of Tifgreen bermudagrass maintained under putting green conditions. Agronomy Abstracts. p. 59. 1968.

8013. ______. *Poa annua* in Florida turf. Proceedings University of Florida Turfgrass Management Conference. 16:42–45. 1968.

8014. ______. Research in turf at the University of Florida in Gainesville. Proceedings University of Florida Turfgrass Management Conference. 16:96–99. 1968.

8015. ______. Factors to consider when selecting a grass for turf. Florida Turf-Grass Association Bulletin. 2(3):6. 1969.

8016. ______. Results of 1969 turf research at Gainsville. Proceedings University of Florida Turf-Grass Management Conference. 17:109–113. 1969.

8018. ______. Modification of sandy soils. Proceedings of the First International Turfgrass Research Conference. pp. 151–158. 1969.

8019. ______. Potassium fertilizers for Tifway bermudagrass. Proceedings of the First International Turfgrass Research Conference. pp. 204–211. 1969.

8020. ______. Making soils tests work for you. Proceedings of Fifth Golf Turf Symposium—Milwaukee Sewerage Commission. 1970.

8021. ______. Evaluation and improvement of turfgrasses for Florida. Annual Research Report of the Institute of Food & Agricultural, Univ. of Florida. p. 109. 1969.

8022. ______. Control of weeds in warm season turfgrasses with herbicides. Annual Research Report of the Institute of Food & Agricultural Sciences, University of Florida. p. 111. 1969.

8023. ______. Fertilization of turfgrasses. Annual Research Report of the Institute of Food & Agricultural Sciences, University of Florida. p. 111. 1969.

8024. ______. Effects of fertilizers on soils and water. Proceedings of the Florida Turfgrass Management Conference. 18:24–31. 1970.

8025. ______. Evaluation and improvement of turfgrasses for Florida. Annual Research Report of the Institute of Food & Agricultural Sciences, University of Florida. p. 113. 1970.

8026. ______. Fertilization of turfgrasses. Annual Research Report of the Institute of Food & Agricultural Sciences. University of Florida. p. 114. 1970.

8027. ______. Control of weeds in warm season turfgrasses with herbicides. Annual Research Report of the Institute of Food & Agricultural Sciences, University of Florida. p. 116. 1970.

8028. ______. Greens renovation. Proceedings of the Louisiana Turfgrass Conference. 1970.

8029. ______. Seeding large turf areas. Proceedings of the Florida Turfgrass Management Conference. 19:83–98. 1971.

8030. ______. Summary of turf research conducted in Gainesville, Florida. Proceeding of the Florida Turfgrass Management Conference. 19:129–133. 1971.

8031. ______. Farewell to *Poa annua?* The Golf Superintendent. 40(8):11–16. 1972.

8032. ______. *Poa annua* control in overseeded bermudagrass greens. Proceedings 43rd International Turfgrass Conference pp. 41–44. 1972.

8033. Horn, G. C. and M. A. Brown. Report on overseeding studies. Proceedings of University of Florida Turf-Grass Management Conference. 9:139–140. 1961.

8034. Horn, G. C., and H. G. Meyers. Potassium fertilization of bermudagrass. Florida Turf Grower. 1969.

8035. ______. Nitrogen source-rate study on overseeded Tifgreen bermuda. Proceedings, Florida Turfgrass Trade Show. 7:-7–9. 1968.

8036. ______. Bahiagrass induced iron chlorosis. Florida Turfgrass Trade Show Proceedings. 7:9–11. 1968.

8037. ______. Soil amendment study putting green, progress report. University of Florida Research Plot Layout and Progress Report I. p. 1a. 1968.

8038. ______. Fertility experiment N-P-K factorial, progress report. University of Florida Research Plot Layout and Progress Report I. pp. 14a–14c. 1968.

8039. ______. Tifway (T–419) bermudagrass potassium source-rate-frequency study, progress report. University of Florida Research Plot Layout and Progress Report I. pp. 15a–15b. 1968.

8040. ______. Ormond bermudagrass nematicide tests with "on-the-market" nematicides, progress report. University of Florida Research Plot Layout and Progress Report I. p. 16a. 1968.

8041. ______. Centipedegrass evaluation of promising new nematicides for control of nematodes. University of Florida Research Plot Layout and Progress Report I. p. 17a. 1968.

8042. ______. Tifgreen (T-#328) bermudagrass nitrogen source-rate-frequency study, progress report. University of Florida Research Plot Layout and Progress Report I. pp. 19a–19b. 1968.

8043. ______. Tifdwarf bermudagrass thatch study. University of Florida Research Plot Layout and Progress Report I. pp. 25a–25b. 1968.

8044. ______. Nitrogen source-rate study on overseeded Tifgreen bermuda. Proceedings Florida Turfgrass Trade Show. 7:-7–9. 1968.

8045. ______. Research plot layout and progress report I. Turfgrass Research Unit. Department of Ornamental Horticulture. University of Florida. 1968.

8046. Horn, G. C., and W. L. Prichett. Chinch bug damage and fertilizer. Florida Turfgrass Bulletin. 9(4):3, 6–7. 1962.

8047. ______. Fertilization and turf disorders. Better Crops with Plant Food. 50(3):-22–25. 1966.

8048. ______. Role of potash in turfgrass fertilization. Florida Turf-Grass Association Bulletin. 1(2):1–3, 7–8. 1954.

8049. Horn, G. C. and G. M. Volk. Effects of ammonium sulfate and ammonium nitrate on performance of various sources of potash on 'Tifway' bermudagrass. Agronomy Abstracts. 62:69. 1970.

8050. Horn, G. C., W. L. Pritchett and J. F. Cabler. The incidence of dollar spot fungus *Sclerotinia homeocarpa* on tifway bermudagrass as affected by potash fertilization. Florida Turf-Grass Association Bulletin. 12(1):1–5. 1965.

8051. Horner, R. Sod production in Wisconsin. Wisconsin Turfgrass Conference Proceedings. 7 pp. 1965.

8052. ______. Problems in the sod growing business. Wisconsin Muck Farmers' Association Annual Meeting. University of Wisconsin 1965.

8053. ______. Sod production on muck soils in Wisconsin. Sod Producers Forum Department of Horticulture. University of Wisconsin. 1965.

8054. ______. How to reduce sod credit losses. Weeds, Trees and Turf. 5(10):20–23. 1966.

8055. Horrocks, R. D. and J. B. Washko. Studies of tiller formation in reed canarygrass (*Phalaris arundinacea* L.) and 'Climax' timothy (*Phleum pratense* L.). Crop Science. 11(1):41–45. 1971.

8056. Horton, E. C. Marketing of turfgrass sod. Turf Bulletin. Massachusetts Turf & Lawn Grass Council. 4(3):15–18. 1967.

8057. Horton, M. L., and J. T. Ritchie. Effect of compaction on soil gas composition as determined by gas chromotography. Agronomy Abstracts. 55:7. 1963.

8058. Hoshizaki, T. Nitrogen uptake and temperature response of U–3 bermudagrass. M.S. Thesis, University of California, Los Angeles. 70 pp. 1953.

8059. Hosotsuji, T. Theory of the turfgrass diseases control by chemicals. KGU Green Section Turf Research Bulletin. 19:-1–20. 1970.

8061. Hotaling, E. D. Talent scouting for committee members. USGA Green Section Record. 6(2):8–9. 1968.

8062. Hottenstein, W. L. How much do you spend on mowing? Public Works. 92(3):-121–122. 1961.

8063. ______. Common sense turf management on today's highways. Highway Research Record No. 23. pp. 66–69. 1963.

8064. ______. You can reduce roadside turf maintenance costs. Ohio Short Course on Roadside Development. 23:97–101. 1964.

8065. Houchin, A. Trees and shrubs least competitive to grasses. Oklahoma Turfgrass Conference Proceedings. pp. 5–7. 1953.

8066. Houlker, W. M. Insect pests of turf and their control. New Zealand Institute for Turf Culture Newsletter. 11:4–5. 1961.

8067. Houser, J. S. Webworms? Use lead. Golfdom. 10(3):26–27. 1936.

8068. ______. Chinch bug is tough pest. Golfdom. 10(4):69–72. 1936.

8069. ______. Sod webworms and chinch bugs. The Greenkeepers' Reporter. 4(3):6–8, 22–27. 1936.

8070. ______. Turf pests. Greenkeepers' Reporter. 6(2):14–17, 38, 40–41. 1938.

8071. ______. Control of sod web worms and chinch bugs. National Association of Greenkeepers of America Conference Proceedings. 10:100–101. 1936.

8072. ______. Sod webworms—a new pest. The National Greenkeeper. 5(9):5–10. 1931.

8074. Houston, C. E. Drainage of recreational areas. California Turfgrass Culture. 14(2):14–15. 1964.

8075. ______. Drainage of recreational areas. Proceedings of Turf, Nursery, and Landscape Tree Conference. pp. 3–1 to 3–4. 1964.

8077. Hoveland, C. S. and R. A. Burdett. How good is common bermuda? Highlights of Agricultural Research. 7(2):4. 1960.

8078. ______. Wanted: good summer perennial grasses for dairy cows. Highlights of Agricultural Research. 7(2):7. 1960.

8079. Hoveland, C. S. Gulf: improved ryegrass variety. Highlights of Agricultural Research. 9(3):9. 1962.

8080. ______. Effect of 3-indolebutyric acid on shoot development and rooting of several bermudagrasses. Agronomy Journal. 55(1):49–50. 1963.

8081. ______. Germination and seeding vigor of clover as affected by grass root extracts. Crop Science. 4(2):211–213. 1964.

8083. Hovin, A. W. Registration of six germplasm lines of Kentucky bluegrass (Reg. Nos. GP 1, GP 2, GP 3, GP 4, GP 5, and GP 6). Crop Science. 10(6):732. 1970.

8084. ______. Bulk emasculation by high temperatures in annual bluegrass *Poa annua* L. Agronomy Journal. 49(7):463. 1957.

8085. ______. Variations in annual bluegrass. Golf Course Reporter. 25(7):18–19. 1957.

8086. ______. Germination of annual bluegrass seed. Southern California Turfgrass Culture Quarterly. 7(2):13. 1957.

8087. ______. Reduction of self-pollination by high night temperature in naturally self-fertilized *Poa annua* L. Agronomy Journal. 50(7):369–371. 1958.

8088. ______. Meiotic chromosome pairing in amphihaploid *Poa annua* L. American Journal of Botany. 45:131–138. 1958.

8089. Hovland, D. Sprinkling infiltometer: an aid in evaluating roadside plots. Agronomy Journal. 58(2):242. 1966.

8090. Howard, A. The making and care of lawns in India. Agricultural Research Institute, Pusa, Bulletin No. 12:3. 1908.

8091. ______. The effect of grass on trees. Proceedings of the Royal Society of London. Series B. 97:284–321. 1925.

8092. Howard, F. L. An organic cadmium fungicide for turf disease. The Greenkeepers' Reporter. 15(2):10. 1947.

8093. ______. Turf diseases. Southern California Conference on Turf Culture. pp. 47–53. 1950.

8094. ______. Turf diseases. Northern California Turf Conference Report. pp. 24–27. 1950.

8095. ______. *Helminthosporium-Curvularia* blights of turf and their cure. Golf Course Reporter. 21(2):5–9. 1953.

8096. ______. Whats' new in turfgrass diseases and their control. Golf Course Reporter. 23(2):5–10. 1955.

8097. ______. New developments in turfgrass disease diagnosis and control. Turf Clippings, University of Massachusetts. 1(4):A–26 to A–27. 1959.

8098. Howard, F. L. and B. Champlin. Vulnerability of *Rhizoctonia solani* in relation to turf brown patch control. Phytopathology 44(9):493. 1954.

8099. Howard, F. L., and M. E. Davies. *Curvularia* 'fading-out' of turfgrasses. Phytopathology. 43(2):109. 1953.

8100. Howard, F. L., P. B. Adams and N. Jackson. Control of *Typhula* snowmold on bentgrasses. The Golf Course Reporter. 33(9):38–42. 1965.

8101. Howard, F. L., J. B. Rowell, and H. L. Keil. Fungus diseases of turf grasses. Rhode Island Agricultural Experiment Station. Bulletin. 308. 56 pp. 1951.

8102. Howard, H. L. The response of some putting green soil mixtures to compaction. M.S. Thesis, Texas A&M University. 106 pp. 1959.

8103. Howard, H. L. and M. H. Ferguson. Soil mixtures for putting greens. Agronomy Abstracts. 51:89. 1959.

8104. Howard, R. and G. L. Worf. *Helminthosporium* diseases of common turfgrasses in Wisconsin. University of Wisconsin Extension Program. 7 pp. 1972.

8105. Howarth, W. O. A synopsis of the British fescues. Botanical Society and Exchange Club of British Isles. 13:338–346. 1948.

8106. Howell, W. Spring treatment of lawns. Gardeners Chronicle. 145(12):171. 1959.

8107. ______. Turf nurseries. Gardeners Chronicle. 148(21):529. 1960.

8108. ______. More about turf nurseries. Gardeners Chronicle. 148(27):649. 1960.

8109. ______. Bowling green maintenance. Gardeners Chronicle. 149(12):257. 1961.

8110. ______. Bowling green maintenance. Gardener's Chronicle. 150(18):338. 1961.

8111. ______. Caring for the established lawn. Gardeners Chronicle. 151(9):151. 1962.

8112. ______. Spring treatment for lawns. Gardeners Chronicle. 153(12):211. 1963.

8113. ______. Impression of "weed" bowling greens in New Zealand. Parks, Golf Courses and Sports Grounds. 31(11):864–868. 1966.

8114. ______. Bowling greens in Australia. Parks, Golf Courses and Sports Grounds. 32(12):1071–1073. 1967.

8115. ______. Draining waterlogged grounds. The Groundsman. 21(8):36–37, 49. 1968.

8116. ______. Treating . . . undulating surfaces. The Groundsman. 22(8):28–31. 1969.

8117. ______. Grass on steep slopes. Parks, Golf Courses and Sports Grounds. 34(7):598–603. 1969.

8118. ______. Notes on high rates of seed sowing. Parks, Golf Courses and Sports Grounds. 36(7):668–672. 1971.

8119. ______. Turf management—a look at costs. Parks, Golf Courses and Sports Grounds. 36(11):1168–1170. 1971.

8120. Howie, J. W. Stadium turf failure licked. Park Maintenance. 7(7):7–10. 1954.

8121. Howitt, A. J. Lawn insects. Western Washington Experiment Station Turfgrass Field Day Proceedings. pp. 14–15. 1961.

8122. Howland, J. E. The vigoro lawnbook. Vigoro Incorporated, Chicago. pp. 1–14. 1970.

8123. ______. Lawn care, a consumer survey. Turf-Grass Times. 8(1):18–19. 1972.

8124. Hoyt, P. B. Fate of chlorophyll in soil. Soil Science. 111(1):49–53. 1971.

8125. Huber, D. M., G. A. Murray, and J. M. Crane. Inhibition of nitrification as a deterrent to nitrogen loss. Soil Science Society of America Proceedings. 33(6):975. 1969.

8126. Hubbard, A. F. Planting bent stolons. The National Greenkeeper. 3(7):5–6. 1929.

8127. Hubbard, C. E. Grasses. Penguin Books. 428 pp. 1954.

8128. ______. Grasses. Penguin Books Ltd., Harmondsorth, Middlesex, England. pp. 1–463. 1968.

8129. Huber, L. How I fertilize my greens. The National Greenkeeper. 4(8):16–17. 1930.

8130. ______. Nitrogen use and why. Proceedings of Midwest Regional Turf Conference. pp. 20–21. 1955.

8131. Huber, W. J. Slow starting into sod growing. Proceedings of the Midwest Regional Turf Conference. pp. 61–63. 1970.

8132. ______. Experiences in using newer grasses. Proceedings of the Midwest Regional Turf Conference. p. 71. 1971.

8133. Huberty, M. R. Soil compaction and aeration. First Annual Fall Field Day on Turf Culture. U.C.L.A. pp. 51–53. 1949.

8134. Huck, A. K. Northern golf course harnesses river for automatic irrigation. Park Maintenance. 19(2):38–42. 1966.

8135. Huckins, R. K. Principles in applying chemicals. Proceedings of the Midwest Regional Turf Conference. pp. 39–41. 1963.

8136. Huddle, C. From sand to bent greens. The National Greenkeeper. 1(4):15. 1927.

8137. Huey, P. Record keeping and budgets. Proceedings of the Texas Turfgrass Conference. 21:34–36. 1966.

8138. Huey, R., J. A. Long, and J. A. Simmons. Granular dicamba: a selective herbicide for difficult to control weeds in turfgrass. Weed Society of America Abstracts. p. 93. 1964.

8139. Huey, R. F. and R. Y. Yeh. Deactivation of bensulide treated soil by activated carbon. North Central Weed Control Conference Proceedings. 23:33. 1968.

8140. Huffaker, C. B. D. W. Ricker, and C. E. Kennett. Biological control of puncture vine. California Agriculture. 15(12):11. 1961.

8141. Huffine, W. W. Improvements in zoysiagrasses. The Golf Superintendent. 40(7):14–16. 1972.

8142. Huffine, W. W. Turf research at Oklahoma A&M College. USGA Journal and Turf Management. 8(3):25–26. 1955.

8143. ______. Turfgrass research at Oklahoma A. and M. College. Oklahoma Turfgrass Conference Proceedings. pp. 45–46. 1956.

8144. ______. Sunturf bermuda—a new grass for Oklahoma lawns. Oklahoma Agriculture Experiment Station. Bulletin B494. 7 pp. 1957.

8145. ______. Turfgrass research at Oklahoma State University. Oklahoma Turfgrass Conference Proceedings. pp. 1–2. 1957.

8146. ______. Turfgrass research at Oklahoma State University. Oklahoma Turfgrass Conference Proceedings. pp. 6–7. 1958.

8147. ______. Wear resistant turfgrass. Oklahoma Turfgrass Conference Proceedings. pp. 23–24. 1958.

8148. ______. Turfgrass research at Oklahoma State University. Oklahoma Turfgrass Conference Proceedings. pp. 37–38. 1959.

8149. ______. Field of turf research is extensive. Golf Course Reporter. 28:16–18. Spring, 1960.

8150. ______. Present day research-a study in productivity. Golfdom. 34:60–70. 1960.

8151. ______. Progress report on turfgrass management. Oklahoma Turfgrass Conference Proceedings. pp. 37–45. 1960.

8152. ______. Grasses. Turfgrass Research. Oklahoma State University. pp. 2–9. 1963.

8153. ______. The potentials of bermudagrass adaptation. Proceedings of the Texas Turfgrass Conference. 19:1. 1964.

8154. ______. Bermudagrass varieties. Proceedings of the Texas Turfgrass Conference. 19:57–59. 1964.

8155. ______. Herbicide evaluation for the control of smooth crabgrass *(Digitaria ischaemum)* and phytotoxicity determination

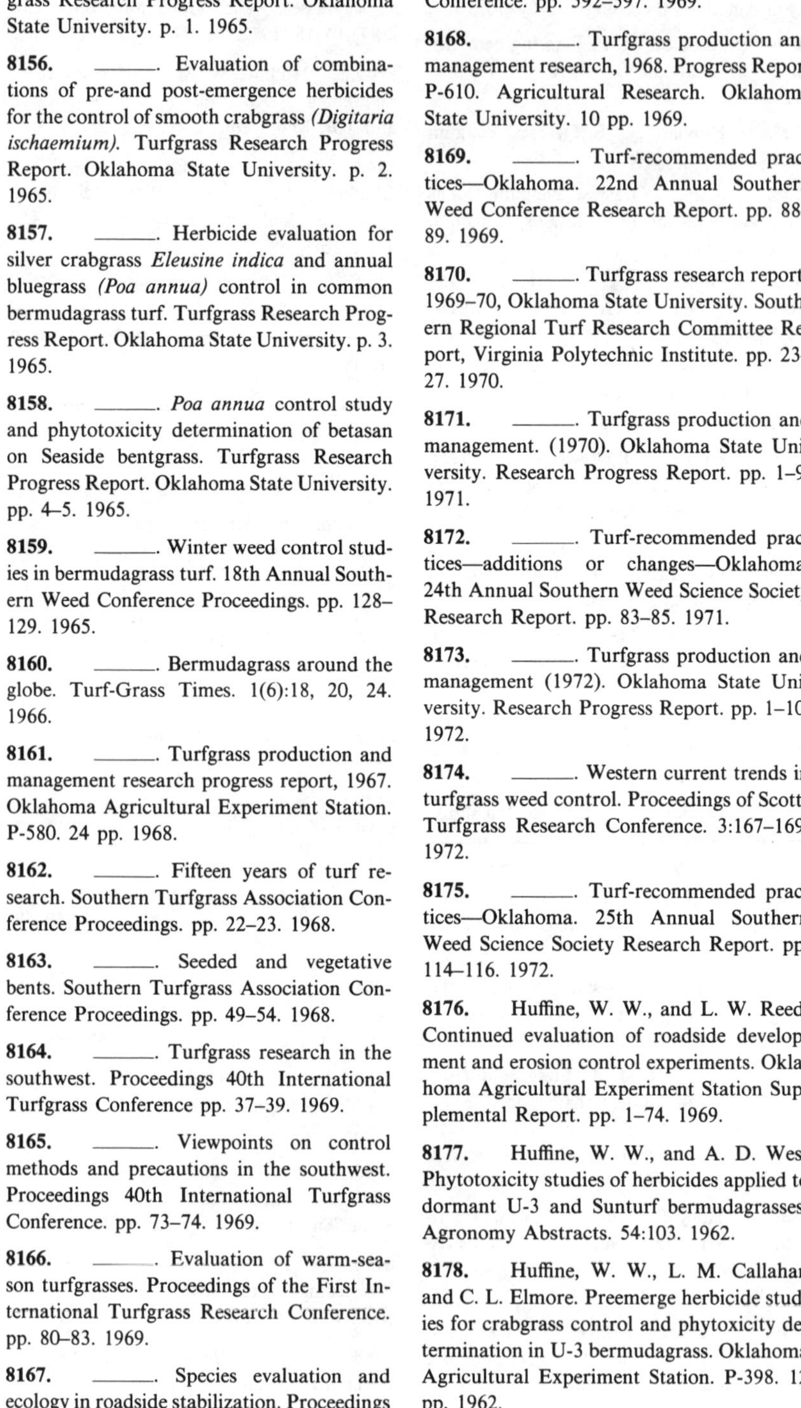

in C-7 bentgrass and Sunturf bermuda. Turfgrass Research Progress Report. Oklahoma State University. p. 1. 1965.

8156. ______. Evaluation of combinations of pre-and post-emergence herbicides for the control of smooth crabgrass *(Digitaria ischaemium).* Turfgrass Research Progress Report. Oklahoma State University. p. 2. 1965.

8157. ______. Herbicide evaluation for silver crabgrass *Eleusine indica* and annual bluegrass *(Poa annua)* control in common bermudagrass turf. Turfgrass Research Progress Report. Oklahoma State University. p. 3. 1965.

8158. ______. *Poa annua* control study and phytotoxicity determination of betasan on Seaside bentgrass. Turfgrass Research Progress Report. Oklahoma State University. pp. 4–5. 1965.

8159. ______. Winter weed control studies in bermudagrass turf. 18th Annual Southern Weed Conference Proceedings. pp. 128–129. 1965.

8160. ______. Bermudagrass around the globe. Turf-Grass Times. 1(6):18, 20, 24. 1966.

8161. ______. Turfgrass production and management research progress report, 1967. Oklahoma Agricultural Experiment Station. P-580. 24 pp. 1968.

8162. ______. Fifteen years of turf research. Southern Turfgrass Association Conference Proceedings. pp. 22–23. 1968.

8163. ______. Seeded and vegetative bents. Southern Turfgrass Association Conference Proceedings. pp. 49–54. 1968.

8164. ______. Turfgrass research in the southwest. Proceedings 40th International Turfgrass Conference pp. 37–39. 1969.

8165. ______. Viewpoints on control methods and precautions in the southwest. Proceedings 40th International Turfgrass Conference. pp. 73–74. 1969.

8166. ______. Evaluation of warm-season turfgrasses. Proceedings of the First International Turfgrass Research Conference. pp. 80–83. 1969.

8167. ______. Species evaluation and ecology in roadside stabilization. Proceedings of the First International Turfgrass Research Conference. pp. 592–597. 1969.

8168. ______. Turfgrass production and management research, 1968. Progress Report P-610. Agricultural Research. Oklahoma State University. 10 pp. 1969.

8169. ______. Turf-recommended practices—Oklahoma. 22nd Annual Southern Weed Conference Research Report. pp. 88–89. 1969.

8170. ______. Turfgrass research reports 1969–70, Oklahoma State University. Southern Regional Turf Research Committee Report, Virginia Polytechnic Institute. pp. 23–27. 1970.

8171. ______. Turfgrass production and management. (1970). Oklahoma State University. Research Progress Report. pp. 1–9. 1971.

8172. ______. Turf-recommended practices—additions or changes—Oklahoma. 24th Annual Southern Weed Science Society Research Report. pp. 83–85. 1971.

8173. ______. Turfgrass production and management (1972). Oklahoma State University. Research Progress Report. pp. 1–10. 1972.

8174. ______. Western current trends in turfgrass weed control. Proceedings of Scotts Turfgrass Research Conference. 3:167–169. 1972.

8175. ______. Turf-recommended practices—Oklahoma. 25th Annual Southern Weed Science Society Research Report. pp. 114–116. 1972.

8176. Huffine, W. W., and L. W. Reed. Continued evaluation of roadside development and erosion control experiments. Oklahoma Agricultural Experiment Station Supplemental Report. pp. 1–74. 1969.

8177. Huffine, W. W., and A. D. West Phytotoxicity studies of herbicides applied to dormant U-3 and Sunturf bermudagrasses. Agronomy Abstracts. 54:103. 1962.

8178. Huffine, W. W., L. M. Callahan and C. L. Elmore. Preemerge herbicide studies for crabgrass control and phytoxicity determination in U-3 bermudagrass. Oklahoma Agricultural Experiment Station. P-398. 12 pp. 1962.

8179. Huffine, W. W., J. L. Coltharp and L. B. Gillham. Turfgrass production and management. Oklahoma Agricultural Experiment Station Progress Report. P-632. 16 pp. 1970.

8180. Huffine, W. W., L. W. Reed, and G. W. Roach. Causes and control of soil erosion on Oklahoma highways Part I. Oklahoma Roadside Development and Erosion Control. Project No. 63–03–3. 20 pp. 1967.

8181. ______. Maintenance of vegatative ground covers on Oklahoma highways Part II. Oklahoma Roadside Development and Erosion Control. Project No. 63–03–3. 87 pp. 1967.

8182. ______. Weed control and eradication on Oklahoma highways Part III. Oklahoma Roadside Development and Erosion Control. Project No. 63–03–3. 108 pp. 1967.

8183. Huffine, W. W., R. E. Bailey, G. W. Roach and L. W. Reed. Effects of cultural practices and fertility treatments on seeded bermudagrass on a highway backslope in Oklahoma. Agronomy Abstracts. 62:73. 1970.

8185. Huffine, W. W., H. C. Young, D. F. Wadsworth, and R. V. Sturgeon. Diseases. Turfgrass Research. Oklahoma State University. pp. 10–22. 1963.

8186. Huggett, W. Producing sod for shaded areas. 42nd Annual Michigan Turfgrass Conference Proceedings. 1:119–120. 1972.

8187. Hughes, E. C. Herbicide treatments of turf. Research Report of the National Weed Committee, Western Section (Canada) 8:116–117. 1961.

8188. ______. Herbicide trials on white clover in turf. Research Report of the National Weed Committee, Western Section (Canada). 9:111–112. 1962.

8189. ______. Effect of herbicides on speedwell *(Veronica persica)* on turf. Proceedings of the 18th Annual Northwest Turfgrass Conference. pp. 51–52. 1964.

8190. ______. Effect of herbicides on established turf, Queen's Park. Proceedings of the 18th Annual Texas Turfgrass Conference. 18:53–54. 1964.

8191. Hughes, E. C., and M. Strong. Herbicide trials on speedwell *(Veronica persica)* in turfgrass. Research Report of the National Weed Committee, Western Section (Canada). p. 211. 1968.

8192. Hughes, H. D. Response of *Poa pratensis* L. to different harvest treatments measured by weight and composition of roots and forage. Report 4th International Grassland Congress. Aberystwyth, Wales. pp. 447–452. 1937.

8194. Hughes, T. Soil testing and fertilizing large areas. Illinois Turfgrass Conference Proceedings. pp. 54–57. 1969.

8196. Hughes, T. D. The effect of bulk density and soil water pressure on grass seedling emergence. M. S. Thesis, Oklahoma State University. 1966.

8197. ______. Turfgrass salt problems. Illinois Turfgrass Conference. Proceedings. pp. 7–8. 1970.

8198. ______. Slow-release nitrogen fertilizer for turf. Illinois Turfgrass Conference Proceedings. pp. 21–24. 1971.

8199. ______. Slowly soluble nitrogen fertilizers. Grounds Maintenance. 7(9):14–18. 1972.

8200. ______. Fertility study on "*Puccinellia distans.*" University of Illinois Turfgrass Field Day. p. 13. 1972.

8201. ______. Slowly soluable nitrogen on Kentucky bluegrass. University of Illinois Turfgrass Field Day. p. 26. 1972.

8202. Hughes, T. D., J. F. Stone, W. W. Huffine and J. R. Gingrich. Effect of soil bulk density and soil water pressure on emergence of grass seedlings. Agronomy Journal. 58(5):-549–553. 1966.

8203. Hull, F. H. Turf development in Florida. University of Florida Turf Management Conference Proceedings. 3:33–36. 1955.

8204. Hull, R. B. The landscape design of the golf course. Proceedings of Midwest Regional Turf Conference. pp. 88–91. 1948.

8205. ______. Good layout and design of fairways and grounds aids in golf popularity. Midwest Turf-News and Research. 2(2):1. 1948.

8206. Humbert, R. P. and F. V. Grau. Soil and turf relationships USGA Journal and Turf Management. 2(2):25–32. 1949.

8207. ______. Soil and turf relationships. Part II. USGA Journal and Turf Management. 2(3):28–29. 1949.

8208. Hume, E. P. How to have a good lawn. Vermont Agricultural Extension Circular. 121:1–15. 1951.

8209. ______. How to have a good lawn. Vermont Agricultural Extension Circular. 121:1–15. 1956.

8210. Hume, E. P. and R. H. Freyre. Propagation trials with Manila grass, *Zoysia matrella,* in Puerto Rico. Proceedings of the American Society for Horticultural Science. 55:517–518. 1950.

8211. Humphrey, W. A. A greenhouse for warm season grasses. California Turfgrass Culture. 11(2):15. 1961.

8212. ______. Improved bermudagrass. California Turfgrass Culture. 12(3):18–19. 1962.

8213. ______. Control of crabgrass in turfgrass. Southern California Turfgrass Institute Proceedings. pp. 25–26. 1963.

8214. Hunnicutt, E. A. Reducing equipment maintenance costs by using good preventative maintenance. Proceedings, Fourth Annual Tennessee Turfgrass Conference. pp. 4–8. 1970.

8215. ______. Seeding with modern equipment. Proceedings of the Midwest Regional Turf Conference. pp. 80–82. 1971.

8216. Hunt, A. C. Upgrading public turf. Proceedings of the Midwest Regional Turf Conference. 23–24. 1970.

8217. ______. Golf promotion. Proceedings of the Midwest Regional Turf Conference. pp. 28–29. 1972.

8218. Hunt, I. V. Productivity of Italian and perennial ryegrass mixtures. Journal of the British Grassland Society. 26(1):41–50. 1971.

8219. Hunt, K. W. The crisis for public recreational areas. Ohio Short Course on Roadside Development. 19:7–13. 1960.

8220. Hunter, E. J. Results of seeding rate test sections. New York State Turf Association Bulletin. 9:35. 1949.

8221. ______. Concept of sprinkler system selection. California Turfgrass Culture. 15(4):28–30. 1965.

8222. ______. Opening remarks at panel discussion—representing suppliers. Proceedings Turfgrass Sprinkler Irrigation Conference. 5:44. 1967.

8223. ______. New control systems for automatic turf irrigation. Proceedings Turfgrass Sprinkler Irrigation Conference. 6:22–28. 1968.

8224. Hunter, J. Laying down land to grass on the Clifton Park System. Annual meeting (1911) Agricultural Society of the University of Wales. Chester, England. 32 pp. 1915.

8225. Hunter, W. G. Introductory remarks: roadside cover and its control. Ohio Short Course on Roadside Development. 19:-70. 1960.

8226. Huntley, R. A. Golf course bridge construction. Turf Clippings. University of Massachussetts. 4(1):p. 2. 1969.

8227. Hurcombe, R. Chromosome studies in *Cynodon.* South African Journal of Science. 42:144–146. 1945.

8228. ______. A cytological and morphological study of cultivated *Cynodon* species. Journal of South African Botany. 13:-107–116. 1947.

8229. ______. A cytological and morphological study of cultivated *Cynodon* species. Better Turf Through Research. South African Turf Research Fund. pp. 36–47. 1948.

8230. Hurd, R. M. Grassland vegetation in the Big Horn Mountains, Wyoming. Ecology. 42:459–467. 1961.

8231. Hurley, R. Velvet bentgrass—the putter's delight. Weeds Trees and Turf. 12(1):20, 35. 1973.

8232. Hurst, H. R. Arkansas lawn weeds. University of Arkansas Agricultural Extension Service. Circular No. 528. 34 pp. 1967.

8233. ______. Turf—recommended practices—Arkansas. 22nd Annual Southern Weed Conference Research Report. pp. 84–85 1969.

8234. ______. Turf—recommended practices—additions or changes—Arkansas.

24th Annual Southern Weed Science Society Research Report. pp. 81–82. 1971.

8235. ______. Turf—recommended practices—Arkansas. 25th Annual Southern Weed Science Society Research Report. pp. 112–113. 1972.

8236. Husted, A. M. Tile heavy soils for best fairways. Midwest Turf-News and Research. 4(3):1. 1950.

8237. ______. Analyse course needs; Part II. Midwest Turf-News and Research. 4(4):4. 1950.

8238. ______. Tile heavy soils for best fairways. Midwest Regional Turf Foundation. pp. 1–3. July, 1950.

8239. ______. Husted concludes on "How" to build. Midwest Turf-News and Research. 5(1):8. 1951.

8240. Huston, W. E. Power used for pumping water. Proceedings 19th Southeastern Turfgrass Conference. pp. 26–31. 1965.

8241. Hutchinson, C. M., and C. E. Scarsbrook. Losses of ammonia from urea-treated soils. Agronomy Abstracts. 56:31. 1964.

8242. Hutchinson, F. E. Correcting compacted fairways with gypsum, limestone and surfactants. Proceedings 43rd International Turfgrass Conference. pp. 45–47. 1972.

8243. ______. Soil acidity and liming. Turf Clippings. University of Massachusetts. 2(2):A–1–2. 1967.

8245. ______. What happens to the phosphorus we use? University of Maine Turf Conference Proceedings. 6:51–54. 1968.

8246. ______. Environmental pollution from highway deicing compounds. Journal of Soil and Water Conservation. 25:144–146. 1970.

8247. ______. The importance of salt index. University of Maine Turf Conference Proceedings. 8:13–17. 1970.

8248. ______. How soil pH is affected by the fertilizer you use. Turf Bulletin. Massachusetts Turf and Lawn Grass Council. 7(3):-20–21. 1971.

8249. Hutchinson, H. G. Golf greens and greenkeeping. Country Life Ltd. London. 219 pp. 1906.

8250. Hutchinson, M. T., J. P. Reed, H. T. Streu, A. A. DiEdwardo and P. H. Schroeder. Plant parasitic nematodes of New Jersey. New Jersey Agricultural Experiment Station. Bulletin 796. 33 pp. 1961.

8251. Hutchinson, W. Handbook of grasses. Swan Sonnenschein & Co., London. 92 pp. 1895.

8252. Hutson, R. How to combat insect pests. Golfdom. 15(4):58, 60, 62. 1941.

8253. ______. How to combat insect pests. Golfdom. 15(5):17–20. 1941.

8256. Hyde, F. Present status and problems in turf development and management for public schools. Proceedings of the Texas Turfgrass Conference. 15:16–21. 1960.

8257. Hyde, R. Cool season grasses in Kansas. Kansas State University Cooperative Extension Service. Circular No. 257. 11p. 1968.

8259. Hyland, H. L. Progress report on special grass plantings on airfields. Roadside Development: Highway Research Board, pp. 29–31. 1947.

8260. ______. Progress report on special grass planting on airfields. Report of Committee on Roadside Development, Highway Research Board. 1948.

8261. Hylton, L. O., D. R. Cornelius, and A. Ulrich. Nitrogen nutrition and growth relations of tall and intermediate wheatgrasses. Agronomy Journal. 62(3):353–356. 1970.

8262. Hylton, L. O., A. Ulrich, and D. R. Correlius. Comparison of nitrogen constituents as indicators of the nitrogen status of Italian ryegrass, and relation of top to root growth. Crop Science. 5(1):21. 1965.

8263. ______. Potassium and sodium interrelations in growth and mineral content of Italian ryegrass. Agronomy Journal. 59(4):-311–315. 1967.

8264. Hylton, L. O., A. Ulrich, D. R. Cornelius, and K. Okhi. Phosphorous nutrition of Italian ryegrass relative to growth, moisture, content, and mineral constituents. Agronomy Journal. 57(5):505–508. 1965.

8265. Hylton, L. O. Jr., D. E. Williams, A. Ulrich, and O. R. Cornelius. Critical ni-

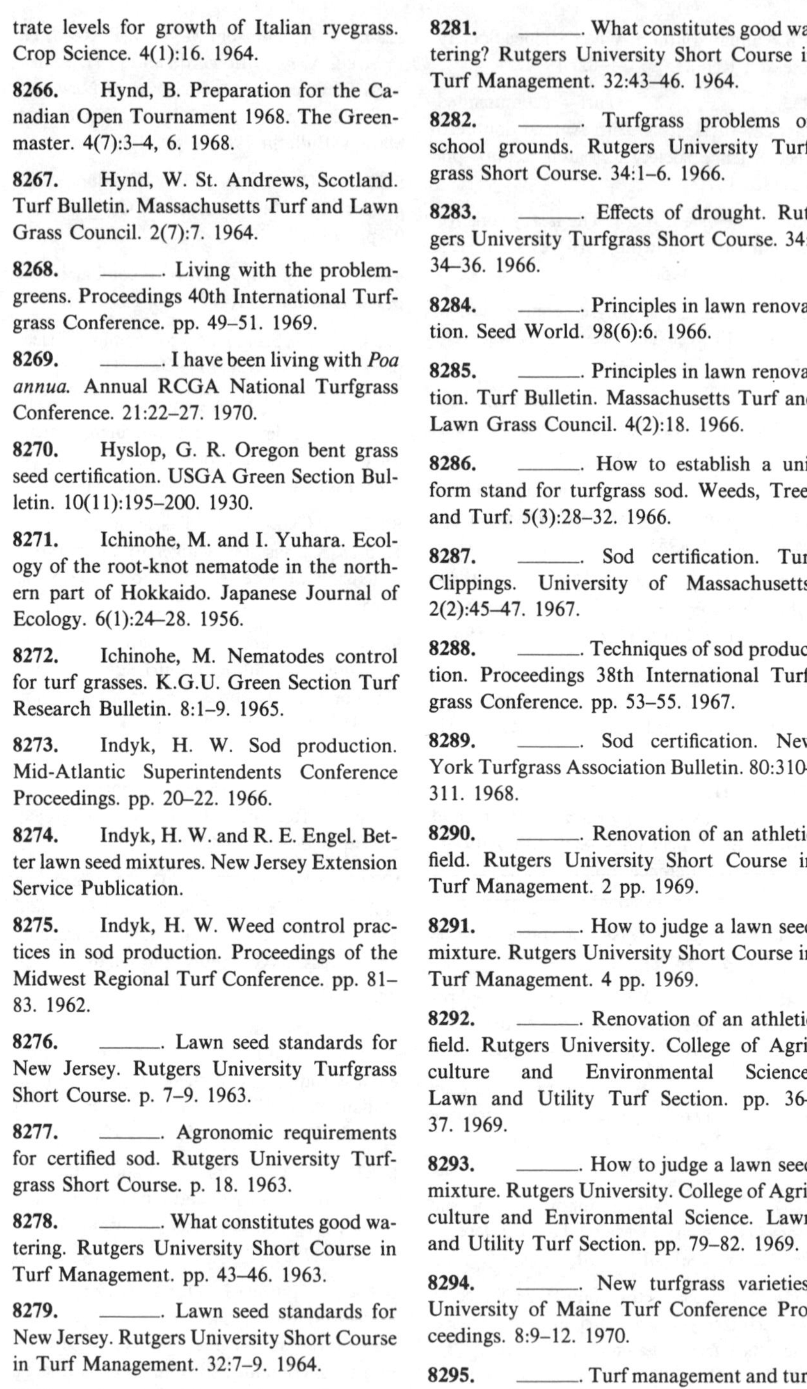

trate levels for growth of Italian ryegrass. Crop Science. 4(1):16. 1964.

8266. Hynd, B. Preparation for the Canadian Open Tournament 1968. The Greenmaster. 4(7):3–4, 6. 1968.

8267. Hynd, W. St. Andrews, Scotland. Turf Bulletin. Massachusetts Turf and Lawn Grass Council. 2(7):7. 1964.

8268. ______. Living with the problem-greens. Proceedings 40th International Turfgrass Conference. pp. 49–51. 1969.

8269. ______. I have been living with *Poa annua.* Annual RCGA National Turfgrass Conference. 21:22–27. 1970.

8270. Hyslop, G. R. Oregon bent grass seed certification. USGA Green Section Bulletin. 10(11):195–200. 1930.

8271. Ichinohe, M. and I. Yuhara. Ecology of the root-knot nematode in the northern part of Hokkaido. Japanese Journal of Ecology. 6(1):24–28. 1956.

8272. Ichinohe, M. Nematodes control for turf grasses. K.G.U. Green Section Turf Research Bulletin. 8:1–9. 1965.

8273. Indyk, H. W. Sod production. Mid-Atlantic Superintendents Conference Proceedings. pp. 20–22. 1966.

8274. Indyk, H. W. and R. E. Engel. Better lawn seed mixtures. New Jersey Extension Service Publication.

8275. Indyk, H. W. Weed control practices in sod production. Proceedings of the Midwest Regional Turf Conference. pp. 81–83. 1962.

8276. ______. Lawn seed standards for New Jersey. Rutgers University Turfgrass Short Course. p. 7–9. 1963.

8277. ______. Agronomic requirements for certified sod. Rutgers University Turfgrass Short Course. p. 18. 1963.

8278. ______. What constitutes good watering. Rutgers University Short Course in Turf Management. pp. 43–46. 1963.

8279. ______. Lawn seed standards for New Jersey. Rutgers University Short Course in Turf Management. 32:7–9. 1964.

8280. ______. Agronomic requirements for certified sod. Rutgers University Short Course in Turf Management. 32:18. 1964.

8281. ______. What constitutes good watering? Rutgers University Short Course in Turf Management. 32:43–46. 1964.

8282. ______. Turfgrass problems on school grounds. Rutgers University Turfgrass Short Course. 34:1–6. 1966.

8283. ______. Effects of drought. Rutgers University Turfgrass Short Course. 34:-34–36. 1966.

8284. ______. Principles in lawn renovation. Seed World. 98(6):6. 1966.

8285. ______. Principles in lawn renovation. Turf Bulletin. Massachusetts Turf and Lawn Grass Council. 4(2):18. 1966.

8286. ______. How to establish a uniform stand for turfgrass sod. Weeds, Trees and Turf. 5(3):28–32. 1966.

8287. ______. Sod certification. Turf Clippings. University of Massachusetts. 2(2):45–47. 1967.

8288. ______. Techniques of sod production. Proceedings 38th International Turfgrass Conference. pp. 53–55. 1967.

8289. ______. Sod certification. New York Turfgrass Association Bulletin. 80:310–311. 1968.

8290. ______. Renovation of an athletic field. Rutgers University Short Course in Turf Management. 2 pp. 1969.

8291. ______. How to judge a lawn seed mixture. Rutgers University Short Course in Turf Management. 4 pp. 1969.

8292. ______. Renovation of an athletic field. Rutgers University. College of Agriculture and Environmental Science. Lawn and Utility Turf Section. pp. 36–37. 1969.

8293. ______. How to judge a lawn seed mixture. Rutgers University. College of Agriculture and Environmental Science. Lawn and Utility Turf Section. pp. 79–82. 1969.

8294. ______. New turfgrass varieties. University of Maine Turf Conference Proceedings. 8:9–12. 1970.

8295. ______. Turf management and turf insects. Proceedings 1970 3-Day Turf Courses, Rutgers University. pp. 53–54. 1970.

8296. ______. Seedling development and sodding. Proceedings 1970 3-Day Turf Courses, Rutgers University. pp. 55–56. 1970.

8297. ______. Goosegrass and its control—the problem. Proceedings 1970 3-Day Turf Courses, Rutgers University. pp. 57–58. 1970.

8298. ______. How do we assure the customer of grass type and sod quality? Rutgers University Short Course in Turf Management Proceedings. pp. 68–70. 1971.

8299. Indyk, H. W. and R. E. Engel. Better lawn seed mixtures. New Jersey Agricultural Extension Bulletin. 357:1–8. 1961.

8300. ______. Your lawn and its care. New Jersey Agricultural Experiment Station. Extension Bulletin 362. 18 pp. 1962.

8301. Ingalls, F. Creeping bent greens at Hot Springs, Virginia. USGA Green Section Bulletin. 8(9):184–188. 1928.

8302. Inglis, H. A. Zoysia growing problems in certification. Proceedings of Midwest Regional Turf Conference. pp. 51–53. 1956.

8303. ______. The desirability of buying certified turfgrasses. Proceedings Tenth Southeastern Turfgrass Conference (10) pp. 3–6. 1956.

8304. Ingram, W. T. Golf course program planning and handling. Proceedings Annual Texas Turfgrass Conference. 21:53–54. 1966.

8305. Ingwersen, W. Making a new lawn. Gardeners Chronicle. 145(12):170. 1959.

8306. Inskeep, J. J. So you want to plant a lawn. Oregon Cooperative Extension Service Publication. 1948.

8307. Irwin, R. W. Choosing and using pumps. Seventeenth R.C.G.A. Sports Turfgrass Conference. pp. 5–7. 1966.

8308. Isaac, M. M. and J. H. Owen The gray-leaf-spot disease of St. Augustingrass. Florida Turf Association Bulletin. 4(4):4–6. 1957.

8309. Ito, S. Insects in golf turf. K.G.U. Green Section Turf Research Bulletin. 15:-1–12. 1968.

8310. Iurka, H. H. Stabilized shoulders which will support vegetation. Proceedings Highway Research Board. 26:258. 1946.

8311. ______. Progress report on stabilized turf shoulders constructed on Long Island. Report of Committee on Roadside Development, Highway Research Board. pp. 39–55. 1948.

8312. Ivimey–Cook, W. R. An account of a disease of lawns caused by a parasitic fungus. Journal of the Board of Greenkeeping Research. 5(16):18–22. 1937.

8313. Iwaniec, E. Tips on ball diamond maintenance. Park Maintenance. 21(5):22–23. 1968.

8314. Iyama, J., Y. Murata, and T. Homma. Studies on the photosynthesis of forage crops. 3. Influence of different temperature levels on diurnal changes in the photosynthesis of forage crops under constant conditions. Proceedings Crop Science Society, Japan. 33(1):25–28. 1964.

8315. Jabine, W. What constitutes breach of contract? Golfdom. 42(5):66–80. 1968.

8316. Jacklin, A. W. Merion bluegrass. Proceedings 7th Annual Northwest Turf Conference. 7:30–32. 1953.

8317. ______. An Appraisal of strains, varieties and kinds of Kentucky bluegrasses. Proceedings 15th Annual Northwest Turf Conference. 15:89–91. 1961.

8318. ______. Turf management—maintenance fertilization. Proceedings 16th Annual Northwest Turf Conference. 16:79–81. 1962.

8319. ______. An appraisal of Kentucky bluegrass varieties. 18th R. C. G. A. National Turfgrass Conference Summary. pp. 23–27. 1967.

8320. ______. New grasses for new areas. Proceedings of the Midwest Regional Turf Conference pp. 73–76. 1968.

8321. Jacklin, D. W. Introducing 0217 brand, Fylking, Kentucky bluegrass—a Kentucky bluegrass adapted to close mowing. Weeds, Trees and Turf. 6(6):27–29. 1967.

8322. ______. Production, merchandising and future plans for Fylking Kentucky bluegrass. Proceeding of the Midwest Regional Turf Conference. pp. 75–79. 1969.

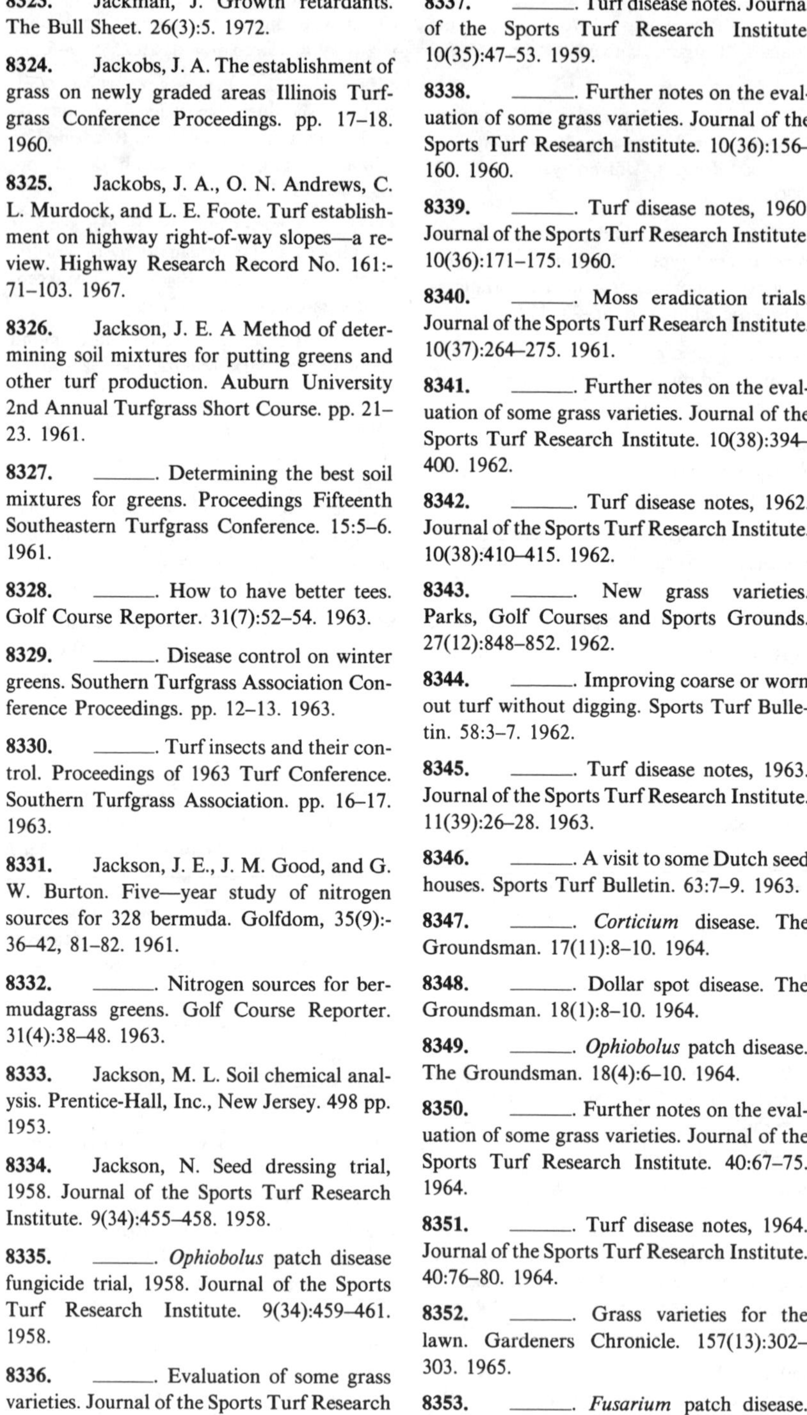

8323. Jackman, J. Growth retardants. The Bull Sheet. 26(3):5. 1972.

8324. Jackobs, J. A. The establishment of grass on newly graded areas Illinois Turfgrass Conference Proceedings. pp. 17–18. 1960.

8325. Jackobs, J. A., O. N. Andrews, C. L. Murdock, and L. E. Foote. Turf establishment on highway right-of-way slopes—a review. Highway Research Record No. 161:-71–103. 1967.

8326. Jackson, J. E. A Method of determining soil mixtures for putting greens and other turf production. Auburn University 2nd Annual Turfgrass Short Course. pp. 21–23. 1961.

8327. ______. Determining the best soil mixtures for greens. Proceedings Fifteenth Southeastern Turfgrass Conference. 15:5–6. 1961.

8328. ______. How to have better tees. Golf Course Reporter. 31(7):52–54. 1963.

8329. ______. Disease control on winter greens. Southern Turfgrass Association Conference Proceedings. pp. 12–13. 1963.

8330. ______. Turf insects and their control. Proceedings of 1963 Turf Conference. Southern Turfgrass Association. pp. 16–17. 1963.

8331. Jackson, J. E., J. M. Good, and G. W. Burton. Five—year study of nitrogen sources for 328 bermuda. Golfdom, 35(9):-36–42, 81–82. 1961.

8332. ______. Nitrogen sources for bermudagrass greens. Golf Course Reporter. 31(4):38–48. 1963.

8333. Jackson, M. L. Soil chemical analysis. Prentice-Hall, Inc., New Jersey. 498 pp. 1953.

8334. Jackson, N. Seed dressing trial, 1958. Journal of the Sports Turf Research Institute. 9(34):455–458. 1958.

8335. ______. *Ophiobolus* patch disease fungicide trial, 1958. Journal of the Sports Turf Research Institute. 9(34):459–461. 1958.

8336. ______. Evaluation of some grass varieties. Journal of the Sports Turf Research Institute. 10(35):13–28. 1959.

8337. ______. Turf disease notes. Journal of the Sports Turf Research Institute. 10(35):47–53. 1959.

8338. ______. Further notes on the evaluation of some grass varieties. Journal of the Sports Turf Research Institute. 10(36):156–160. 1960.

8339. ______. Turf disease notes, 1960. Journal of the Sports Turf Research Institute. 10(36):171–175. 1960.

8340. ______. Moss eradication trials. Journal of the Sports Turf Research Institute. 10(37):264–275. 1961.

8341. ______. Further notes on the evaluation of some grass varieties. Journal of the Sports Turf Research Institute. 10(38):394–400. 1962.

8342. ______. Turf disease notes, 1962. Journal of the Sports Turf Research Institute. 10(38):410–415. 1962.

8343. ______. New grass varieties. Parks, Golf Courses and Sports Grounds. 27(12):848–852. 1962.

8344. ______. Improving coarse or worn out turf without digging. Sports Turf Bulletin. 58:3–7. 1962.

8345. ______. Turf disease notes, 1963. Journal of the Sports Turf Research Institute. 11(39):26–28. 1963.

8346. ______. A visit to some Dutch seed houses. Sports Turf Bulletin. 63:7–9. 1963.

8347. ______. *Corticium* disease. The Groundsman. 17(11):8–10. 1964.

8348. ______. Dollar spot disease. The Groundsman. 18(1):8–10. 1964.

8349. ______. *Ophiobolus* patch disease. The Groundsman. 18(4):6–10. 1964.

8350. ______. Further notes on the evaluation of some grass varieties. Journal of the Sports Turf Research Institute. 40:67–75. 1964.

8351. ______. Turf disease notes, 1964. Journal of the Sports Turf Research Institute. 40:76–80. 1964.

8352. ______. Grass varieties for the lawn. Gardeners Chronicle. 157(13):302–303. 1965.

8353. ______. *Fusarium* patch disease. The Groundsman. 18(7):4, 34. 1965.

8354. ______. Fairy rings. The Groundsman. 18(9):18–20. 1965.

8355. ______. Miscellaneous diseases of sports turf. The Groundsman. 18(10):26. 1965.

8356. ______. Dollar spot disease and its control. Illinois Turfgrass Conference Proceedings. pp. 21–25. 1966.

8357. Jackson, N. and F. L. Howard. Fungi as agents of turfgrass disease. Journal of the Sports Turf Research Institute. 42:-9–16. 1966.

8358. Jackson, N. British and American turfgrass disease problems. Proceedings of the Midwest Regional Turf Conference. pp. 13–16. 1966.

8359. ______. Recognition and control of turfgrass diseases. Proceedings of the Midwest Regional Turf Conference. pp. 16–20. 1966.

8360. ______. British and American turfgrass disease problems. Parks, Golf Courses and Sports Grounds. 32(2):139–142. 1966.

8361. ______. Evaluation of some turfgrass fungicides—1966. Department of Plant Pathology-Entomology. Agricultural Experiment Station University of Rhode Island. 14 pp. 1966.

8362. ______. *Sclerotinia* dollar spot and snow mold. Turf Clippings. University of Massachussetts. 2(1):A–32 to A–35. 1966.

8363. ______. Winter play is important factor in injury, disease. Turf-Grass Times. 2(2):18. 1966.

8364. ______. Turfgrass disease problems in Britain and the U.S.A. Proceedings 38th International Turfgrass Conference. pp. 13–15. 1967.

8365. ______. Evaluation of turfgrass fungicides. Ohio Turfgrass Conference Proceedings. pp. 29–31. 1969.

8366. ______. Fungi as agents causing turfgrass diseases. Rutgers University Short Course in Turf Management. 2 pp. 1969.

8367. ______. Fungi as agents causing turfgrass diseases. Rutgers University. College of Agriculture and Environmental Science. Lawn and Utility Turf Section. pp. 56–57. 1969.

8368. Jackson, N. and J. M. Fenstermacher. An evaluation of some turfgrass fungicides. Park Maintenance. 23(7):12–13. 1970.

8369. Jackson, N. Evaluation of some chemicals for control of stripe smut in Kentucky bluegrass turf. The Plant Disease Reporter. 54(2):168–170. 1970.

8370. ______. The turfgrass fungicide of the future. The Golf Superintendent. 39(10):-27–28. 1971.

8371. Jackson, N. and J. M. Fenstermacher. Evaluation of turfgrass fungicides. Park Maintenance. 21(10):82–83. 1968.

8372. ______. Evaluation of some turfgrass fungicides. University of Rhode Island Agricultural Experiment Station. 17 pp. 1968.

8373. ______. *Typhula* blight; its cause, epidemiology and control. Journal of the Sports Turf Research Institute. 45:67–73. 1969.

8374. Jackson, N. and F. L. Howard Fungi as agents of turfgrass disease. Agronomy Abstracts. 57:46. 1965.

8375. ______. Disease, fungi, and turf management. The Golf Superintendent. 35(2):22–28, 51. 1967.

8376. Jackson, T. L. Oregon State fertilizer recommendations-bentgrass. Oregon State College Extension Service. FR7. 1958.

8377. Jackson, W. T. Effect of 3-amino–1, 2, 4-triayole and L-histidine on rate of elongation of root hairs of *Agrostis alba.* Weeds. 9(3):437–442. 1961.

8378. Jacob, K. D. A factor to consider in choice of fertilizer. Turfgrass Times. 3(3):1, 21. 1968.

8379. Jacob, K. D., F. E. Allison, and J. M. Braham. Chemical and biological studies with cyanamid and some of its transformation products. Journal of Agricultural Research. 28(1):37–68. 1924.

8380. Jacobs, H. L. The vitality of shade trees in relation to root environment. The National Greenkeeper. 6(4):5–10. 1932.

8381. Indyk, H. W. Fluorescence as related to ryegrass recommendations. Weeds, Trees and Turf. 11(5):14, 26, 28. 1972.

8390. Jacobson, H. G. M. What fertilizer for your lawn? Connecticut State Agricultural Experiment Station. Frontier of Plant Science. 11(1):5. 1958.

8391. Jacobson, H. G. M., E. M. Stoddard, and J. C. Schread. How good lawns grow. Connecticut Agricultural Experiment Station Circular 169. pp. 1–19. 1949.

8392. Jacobson, H. G. M. H. A. Lunt, F. W. Meyer and J. C. Schread. Lawns. Connecticut State Agricultural Experiment Station Circular. 190:1–26. 1955.

8393. Jacoby, P. W. Revegetation treatments for stand establishment on coal spoil banks. Journal of Range Management. 22:-94–97. 1969.

8394. Jacques, W. A. The effect of different rates of defoliation on the root development of certain grasses. New Zealand Journal of Science and Technology. 19(7):441–450. 1937.

8395. ______. Root development in some common New Zealand pasture plants. 9. The root replacement pattern in perennel ryegrass *(Lolium perenne).* New Zealand Journal of Science and Technology. 38A(2):160–165. 1956.

8396. ______. Secondary root hair development in grasses. The effect on plant nutrition. New Zealand Journal of Science Technology. 20:389–391. 1939.

8397. ______. Root development in some common New Zealand pasture plants. I. Perennial ryegrass *Lolium perenne.* A. Effect of time of sowing and taking a hay crop in the first harvest year. New Zealand Journal of Science and Technology. Sect. A. 22:237–247. 1941.

8398. Jacques, W. A. and B. D. Edmond. Root development in some New Zealand pasture plants. New Zealand Journal of Science and Technology. 34(3):231–248. 1952.

8399. Jacques, W. A. and R. H. Schwass. Root development in some common New Zealand pasture plants. 7. Seasonal root replacement in perennial ryegrass *Lolium perenne,* Italian ryegrass *(L. multiflorum),* and tall fescue *(Festuca arundinacea).* New Zealand Journal of Science and Technology. 37A(6):569–583. 1956.

8400. Jaffee, W. A. Introducing a new product. Proceedings of the Midwest Regional Turf Conference. pp. 42–46. 1962.

8401. ______. Using calcined clay as a soil conditioner. Turf Bulletin. Massachusetts Turf and Lawn Grass Council. 2(5):8, 11. 1964.

8402. Jagschitz, J. A. Effects of herbicides on new turf seedings. New England Agricultural Chemicals Conference and Herbicide Workshop. 1:34–36. 1954.

8403. ______. Research to rebuild and stabilize sand dunes in Rhode Island. Shore and Beach. 28:32–35. 1960.

8404. ______. Pre- and post-emergence crabgrass herbicides. New England Agricultural Chemicals Conference and herbicide workshop. 1:29–30. 1964.

8405. ______. Chemical control of spurry, carpetweed and purslane. Proceedings of the Northeastern Weed Control Conference. 20:502–505. 1966.

8406. ______. Chemical growth inhibition in turf. New York Turfgrass Association Bulletin. 78:304. 1967.

8407. ______. Effect of application date on preemergence crabgrass herbicides in turfgrass. Proceedings of the Northeastern Weed Control Conference. 21:470–477. 1967.

8408. ______. Seasonal control of hawkweed and summer control of spotted-spurge with herbicides. Proceedings of the Northeastern Weed Control Conference. 21:498–502. 1967.

8409. ______. Seasonal control of clover and broadleaf weed control in turfgrass with herbicides. Proceedings of the Northeastern Weed Control Conference. 21:508–514. 1967.

8410. Jagschitz, J. A. and A. R. Mazur. Chemical control of purslane and other broadleaf weeds in seedling turf. Proceedings of the Northeastern Weed Control Conference. 21:520–523. 1967.

8411. Jagschitz, J. A. Activated charcoal nullifies residues. New York Turfgrass Association Bulletin. 80:311–312. 1968.

8412. ______. Effectiveness of preemergence crabgrass herbicides for lawns and putting-green turf. Northeastern Weed Control Conference Proceedings. 22:384–391. 1968.

8413. ______. Use of charcoal to deactivate herbicide residues in turfgrass seedbeds. Proceedings of the Northeastern Weed Control Conference. 22:401–408. 1968.

8414. ______. Pre and postemergence chemical crabgrass control in turfgrass 1968–69. Northeastern Weed Control Conference Proceedings. 24:379–386. 1970.

8415. ______. Fall and spring use of preemergent crabgrass control chemicals in turfgrass. Proceedings of the Northeastern Weed Control Conference. p. 398–404. 1969.

8416. ______. Effects of soil-incorporated herbicides on turfgrass and weed establishment. Proceedings of the Northeastern Weed Control Conference. pp. 406–411. 1969.

8417. ______. Effect of activated charcoal on the future performance of chemicals for preemergence crabgrass control in turfgrass. Northeastern Weed Science Society Proceedings. 25:109–114. 1971.

8419. ______. Chemical control of *Poa annua* L. in turfgrass and the effect of various chemicals on seed production. Northeastern Weed Science Society Proceedings. pp. 393–400. 1970.

8420. ______. Evaluation of herbicides for pre-emergent crabgrass control. Park Maintenance. 23(7):26. 1970.

8422. ______. Response of turfgrasses and broadleaved weeds to various herbicides. Northeastern Weed Science Society Proceedings. 25:115–122. 1971.

8423. ______. Broadleaf weeds. Park Maintenance. 24(7):24. 1971.

8424. ______. Crabgrass. Park Maintenance. 24(7):25. 1971.

8425. ______. New England chemical weed control for turfgrasses. New England Weed Control Specialists—Extension Service. 4 pp. Jan. 1972.

8426. ______. Crabgrass. Park Maintenance. 25(7):18. 1972.

8427. ______. Broadleaved weeds. Park Maintenance. 25(7):20. 1972.

8428. ______. Preemergence crabgrass and goosegrass control. Park Maintenance. 25(7):20. 1972.

8429. Jagschitz, J. A., and R. S. Bell. Restoration and retention of coastal dunes with fences and vegetation. University of Rhode Island Agricultural Experiment Station Bulletin No. 382. 43 pp. 1966.

8430. ______. American beachgrass, establishment, fertilization, seeding. University of Rhode Island Agricultural Experiment Station Bulletin. 383:1–43. 1966.

8431. Jagschitz, J. A. and C. R. Skogley. Postemergence crabgrass control results for 1962 and 1963. Proceedings of the Northeastern Weed Control Conference. pp. 511–518. 1964.

8432. Jagschitz, J. A. and A. R. Mazur. Chemical control of purslane and other broadleaf weeds in seedling turf. Proceedings of Northeast Weed Control Conference. 21:-520–523. 1967.

8433. Jagschitz, J. A. and C. R. Skogley. Clover and chickweed control in lawn and fairway turf. Proceedings of the Northeastern Weed Control Conference. pp. 540–547. 1964.

8434. ______. Turfgrass response to dacthal and nitrogen. Agronomy Journal. 57(1):-35–38. 1965.

8435. ______. Chemical control of knotweed and clover in lawn turf. Proceedings of the Northeastern Weed Control Conference. 19:491–495. 1965.

8436. ______. Dicamba, mecoprop and 2, 4-D combinations for the control of clover, chickweed and dandelion in turfgrass. Proceedings of the Northeastern Weed Control Conference. 20:496–501. 1966.

8437. ______. Turfgrass response to seedbed and seedling applications of preemergence and broadleaf herbicides. Proceedings of the Northeastern Weed Control Conference. 20:554–560. 1966.

8438. Jagschitz, J. A. and R. C. Wakefield. How to build and save beaches and dunes. University of Rhode Island Marine Leaflet Series No. 4 Agricultural Experiment Station Bulletin 408. 12 pp. 1971.

8439. Jagschitz, J. A., R. C. Wakefield and A. T. Dore. Growth regulation. Park Maintenance. 24(7):22. 1971.

8440. Jagtenberg, W. D. Predicting the best time to apply nitrogen to grassland in spring. Journal of the British Grassland Society. 25(4):266–271. 1970.

8441. Jamalainen, E. A. Overwintering of *Gramineae* plants and parasitic fungi. I. *Sclerotinia borealis* Bubak and Vlengel. Mastaloust Aikakausk. 21:125–140. 1949.

8442. James, B. L. Pre-emergence treatment for control of *Poa annua* on overseeded grasses. Auburn University Turfgrass Short Course. 7:2. 1966.

8443. James, D. B. The influence of some edaphic factors on the growth and distribution of grasses. Report of Welsh Plant Breeding Station. 1960:120–124. 1961.

8444. James, E. B. Better lawns. Roy Hay Publication, Haslemere. 27 pp. 1950.

8445. James, R. Lawns, trees and shrubs in Central Africa. Purnell and Sons Ltd., Cape Town. 174 pp. 1961.

8446. Jamieson, G. L. Locate water supply. Weeds, Trees, and Turf. 8(3):8–10. 1969.

8447. Jameson, D. A., and D. L. Huss. The effect of clipping leaves and stems on number of tillers, herbage weights, root weights, and food reserves of little bluestem. Journal of Range Management. 12(3):122–126. 1959.

8448. Janson, L. E. A longer football season. The Swedish Football Association. Solna. 1967.

8449. ______. Artificial heating of sports fields. Proceedings I.A.K.S. Congress. Cologna. 1969.

8450. ______. Adequate soil type for sport turfgrasses. Proceedings of the First International Turfgrass Research Conference. pp. 142–148. 1969.

8451. ______. Theoretical investigation of artificial heating of the top soil. Proceedings of the First International Turfgrass Research Conference. pp. 243–251. 1969.

8452. ______. Theoretical investigation of artificial heating of the top soil. Weibulls Gräs Tips. December, 1971.

8453. Janson, L. and B. Langvad. Är Plastfolietäckning ett Hjälpmedel att nå Bättre Turfstandard på våra Fotballsplaner Weibulls Gräs Tips. pp. 261–265. 1966.

8454. ______. Vad är "God Matjord" till Bättre turf? Weibulls Gräs Tips. pp. 296–315. 1966.

8455. ______. Prolongation of the growing season for sport turfgrasses by means of artificial heating of the root zone. Weibulls Gräs Tips. pp. 318–354. 1967–1968.

8456. Jantti, A., and P. J. Kramer. Regrowth of pastures in relation to soil moisture and defoliation. Proceedings 7th International Grassland Congress. pp. 33–45. 1956.

8457. Jarmon, F. B. How to grow grass without pain. USGA Green Section Record. 8:9–10. 1970.

8459. Jaynes, C. Water in relation to plant growth. Proceedings of the Annual Texas Turfgrass Conference. 9:58–61. 1954.

8460. Jeannin, B. Resistance to cold in varieties of perennial forage grasses. Fourrages. 24:48–75. 1965.

8461. Jeater, R. S. L. The effect of growth-regulating weedkillers on the morphology of grasses. Journal of The British Grassland Society. 13(1):7–12. 1958.

8462. Jeater, R. S. L. and H. C. McIlvenny. The control of perennial grasses with dipyridyl herbicides. British Weed Control Conference Proceedings. 5(1):311–320. 1960.

8463. Jeffers, W. L. A quarter century of turf seed. Proceedings of the Midwest Regional Turf Conference. 4–6. 1970.

8464. Jefferson, P. Moss in lawns and sports turf. Journal of Board of Greenkeeping Research 7(23):58–63. 1947.

8466. ______. Studies of the earthworms of turf. Journal of the Sports Turf Research Institute. 9(31):6–27. 1955.

8467. ______. Studies on the earthworms of turf. Journal of the Sports Turf Research Institute. 9(32):166–179. 1956.

8468. ______. Studies on the earthworms of turf. C. Earthworms and casting. Journal of Sports Turf Research Institute. 9(34):437–452. 1958.

8469. ______. Earthworms and turf culture. Journal of the Sports Turf Research Institute. 10(37):276–289. 1961.

8470. Jefferson, R. N. Turf insect control. First Annual Fall Field Day on Turf Culture. UCLA. 1:32–33. 1949.

8471. ______. New developments in insecticides. Greenkeeping Superintendents Association National Turf Conference. 20:-78–83. 1949.

8472. ______. Turf insects. Southern California Conference on Turf Culture. pp. 7–10. 1950.

8473. Jefferson, R. N. and A. S. Deal. Dichondra pests in Southern California. California Turfgrass Culture. 14(3):17–20. 1964.

8474. ______. *Dichondra* pests in Southern California. Lasca Leaves. 14(3):67–73. 1964.

8475. Jefferson, R. N., and C. O. Eads. Control of sod webworms or lawn moths in southern California. Southern California Turf Culture. 1(1):1–2. 1951.

8476. Jefferson, R. N. and J. S. Morishita. Progress report on the bermudagrass mite and the frit fly. California Turfgrass Culture. 12(2):9–10. 1962.

8477. ______. Southern chinch bug, a new pest of turfgrass in California. California Turfgrass Culture. 18(2):10–11. 1968.

8478. Jefferson, R. N., and J. E. Swift. Control of turfgrass pests. Southern California Turfgrass Culture. 6(2):1–4. 1956.

8479. Jefferson, R. N., A. S. Deal, and S. A. Sher. Turfgrass and dichondra pests in southern California. Southern California Turfgrass Culture Quarterly. 9(2):9–15. 1959.

8480. Jefferson, R. N., I. M. Hall, and F. S. Morishita. Control of lawn moths in Southern California. Journal of Economic Entomology. 57(1):150–152. 1964.

8481. Jefferson, R. N., F. S. Morishita, A. S. Deal, and W. A. Humphrey. Look for turf pests now. California Turfgrass Culture. 17(2):9–11. 1967.

8482. Jeffords, M. K. Twenty years experience with bermudagrass turf. Florida Greenkeeping Superintendents Association and the Southeastern Turf Conference Turf Management Conference. pp. 32–35. 1949.

8483. Jeffries, C. D. Potash and plants. The Pennsylvania State College Eighteenth Annual Turf Conference. pp. 91–95. 1949.

8484. ______. The potash problem as related to turfgrass management. Agronomy Abstracts. 50:65. 1958.

8485. Jeffries, H. Bowling green construction. The Groundsman. 15(9):22–26. 1962.

8486. ______. Maintenance of the bowling green. Part 1. The Groundsman. 15(10):-10–18. 1962.

8487. ______. Maintenance of the bowling green. Part 2. The Groundsman. 15(11):-10–14. 1962.

8488. ______. Autumn work on the bowling green. The Groundsman. 22(1):62–65. 1968.

8489. ______. The bowling green—renovating a difficult surface. The Groundsman. 22(5):14–17. 1969.

8490. ______. Preparing wickets for play. The Groundsman. 22(7):36–38. 1969.

8491. ______. Bringing the bowling green into play. The Groundsman. 23(7):27, 31. 1970.

8492. Jenkin, T. J. Notes on vivipary in *Festuca ovina.* Botanical Society and Exchange Club of the British Isles. Report for 1920. 4:418–432. 1921.

8493. ______. Self-fertility in *Festuca rubra.* Welsh Plant Breeding Station. University College of Wales. Series H. No. 12. p. 160 Seasons 1921–1930.

8494. ______. The artificial hybridization of grasses. Welsh Plant Breeding Station Bulletin. Series H, No. 2. 1924.

8495. ______. Self- and cross-fertilization in *Lolium perenne* L. Journal of Genetics. 17(1):11–17. 1927.

8496. ______. Inheritance in *Lolium perenne* L. I. Seedling characters, lethal and yellow-tipped albino. Journal of Genetics. 19(3):391–402. 1928.

8497. ______. Inheritance in *Lolium perenne* L. III. Base colour factors C and R. Journal of Genetics. 22(3):389–394. 1930.

8498. ______. The method and technique of selection, breeding and strain-building in grasses. Imperial Bureau of Plant Genetics. Herbage Plants Bulletin No. 3. 1931.

8499. ______. Interspecific and intergeneric hybrids in herbage grasses. Initial crosses. Journal of Genetics. 28(2):205–264. 1933.

8500. ______. Interspecific and intergeneric hybrids in herbage grasses. V. *Lolium rigidum* Sens Ampl. with other *Lolium* species. Journal of Genetics. 52(2):252–281. 1954.

8501. ______. Interspecific and intergeneric hybrids in herbage grasses. IX. *Festuca arundinacea* with some other *Festuca* species. Journal of Genetics. 53(1):81–93. 1955.

8502. ______. Interspecific and intergeneric hybrids in herbage grasses. XV. The breeding affinities of *Festuca rubra.* Journal of Genetics. 53:125–130. 1955.

8503. Jenkins, C. M. Preparing the seed bed. The National Greenkeeper. 3(9):5–6. 1929.

8504. Jenkins, D. O. Thoughts on bowling green maintenance. The Groundsman. 21(7):34–36. 1968.

8505. Jenkins, J. C. Conditioning course with simple thrifty methods. Golfdom. 4(4):-108–110. 1930.

8506. ______. About bermuda greens. The National Greenkeeper. 7(10):5–6. 1933.

8507. Jenkins, L. The nematode situation in turf. Proceedings, Missouri Lawn and Turf Conference. p. 19. 1962.

8508. Jenkins, R. G. Cytogenetic investigations of sterility in tall fescue. M. S. Thesis, University of Missouri. 1972.

8509. Jenkins, W. R. Nematodes on turf and their control. Rutgers University short course in turf management. Vol. 28. 2 pp. 1960.

8510. Jenne, E. Steam sterilization of compost. The National Greenkeeper. 2(3):-14–17. 1928.

8511. Jennewine, W. Trimming and mowing problems in the cemetery. Proceedings University of Florida Turf Management Conference. 5:65–66. 1957.

8512. Jennings, C. Control of insects. Rhode Island Agricultural Experiment Station Miscellaneous Publication. 26:12–19. 1945.

8513. Jennings, J. L. Rhodes scale control. Golfdom. 27(10):48. 1953.

8514. Jennings, R. C. Weedkillers for use on industrial sites. Parks, Golf Courses and Sports Grounds. 24:120–126. 1961.

8515. Jenny, H. Soil backgrounds for turf. Northern California Turf Conference Report. pp. 16–19. 1950.

8516. Jensen, E. R. Turf nursery production problems. Part III—pest control. University of Florida Turf Management Conference Proceedings. 3:69–71. 1955.

8517. ______. Commercial practices in lawn establishment. Proceedings Twelfth Southeastern Turfgrass Conference. pp. 1–8. 1958.

8518. ______. Planting the new grasses on new and old golf courses. Proceedings Thirteenth Southeastern Turfgrass Conference. pp. 8–17. 1959.

8519. ______. Tifton hybrid bermudagrasses in U.S.A. KGU Green Section Turf Research Bulletin. 8:52–57. 1965.

8520. ______. Automatic machines, efficiency, good turf practices combine to overcome rising costs. Weeds, Trees and Turf. 5(7):20–22. 1966.

8521. ______. Building golf greens. Auburn University Turfgrass Short Course. 8:-16–20. 1967.

8522. ______. Tifton dwarf vs. Tifton 328 for golf greens. Southern Turfgrass Association Conference Proceedings. pp. 6–8. 1968.

8523. ______. Golf—green design and construction. Southeastern Turfgrass Conference Proceedings. 21:2–5. 1967.

8524. Jensen, H. E.; Taylor, B. B. Nevada has many areas where grass seed can be produced. Nevada Ranch & Home Review 4(4):6–7. 1968–69.

8525. Jensen, H. J. Nematodes affecting Oregon agriculture. Oregon Agricultural Experiment Station. Bulletin 579. 34 pp. 1961.

8526. Jensen, L. A. 2,4-D for weed control in lawns. North Dakota Agricultural Extension Mimeo. 4 pp.

8527. ———. Home lawns for Utah. Utah Agricultural Extension Leaflet. 1:1–12. 1955.

8528. ———. Home lawns for Utah. Utah Agricultural Extension Leaflet. 86:1–16. 1961.

8529. Jensen, M. C. Drainage of turf areas Proceedings 5th Annual Northwest Turf Conference. 5:26–28. 1951.

8530. ———. Drainage of turf areas. State College of Washington Annual Turf Conference. 4:26–28. 1951.

8531. Jensen, M. C. and J. E. Middleton. Scheduling irrigation from pan evaporation. Washington Agricultural Experiment Station. Circular 386. pp. 1–13. 1965.

8532. ———. Scheduling irrigation from pan evaporation. Washington Agricultural Experiment Stations. Circular 527. pp. 1–13. 1970.

8534. Jensen, E. R. Planting methods. Proceedings University of Florida Turfgrass Management Conference. 7:10–15. 1959.

8535. ———. Bermuda grasses. Mid-Atlantic Golf Course Superintendents Annual Conference Proceedings. pp. 109–112. 1960.

8536. ———. Maintenance methods for hybrid grasses. Proceedings of 1960 Turf Conference. Southern Turfgrass Association. pp. 19–24. 1960.

8537. ———. Observations on overseeding. Golfdom. 35(10):72,118. 1961.

8538. ———. Rebuilding gridiron turf. Proceedings University of Florida Turf-Grass Management Conference. 11:78–81. 1963.

8539. ———. New machines make fairway planting easier. Club Operations—Golf Course Section. 3(1):10–11. 1965.

8540. ———. Planting large turf areas. Proceedings University of Florida Turfgrass Management Conference. 13:130–132. 1965.

8541. ———. Selection of grasses for large turf areas: sprigging. Proceedings University of Florida Turfgrass Management Conference. 14:129–131. 1966.

8542. ———. Costs and methods of planting fairways. Proceedings First Annual Tennessee Turfgrass Conference. pp. 37–39. 1967.

8543. ———. Orange and Gator. Golf Course Reporter 31(8):12–14. 1963.

8544. Jent, C. H. Revegetating highway roadsides. Proceedings Third Annual Tennessee Turfgrass Conference. pp. 7–9. 1969.

8545. ———. Roadside revegetation and beautification for erosion control. Proceedings Fifth Annual Tennessee Turfgrass Conference. pp. 4–6. 1971.

8546. Jeppson, E. and B. Langvad. Omläggning av gräsplanen på malmö gamla idrottsplats. Weibulls Gräs Tips. pp. 103–104. 1962.

8547. Jewell, E. L. Weed green management. New Zealand Institute for Turf Culture Newsletter. 26:5. 1963.

8548. Jewett, H. H. Control of sod webworms in lawns. Kentucky Agricultural Experiment Station Bulletin. 391:89–106. 1939.

8549. Jewett, H. H., and J. T. Spencer. The plant bugs, *Miris dolobratus* L., and *Amblytylus nasutus* Kirschbaum, and their injury to Kentucky bluegrass. Journal of the American Society of Agronomy. 36:147–151. 1944.

8550. Jewiss, O. R. and M. J. Robson. Studies on the growth of ecotypes of tall fescue. Experiments in Progress, The Grassland Research Institute. Annual Report for 1960–61. 14:23–25. 1962.

8551. Jewiss, O. R., and J. Woledge. The effect of age on the rate of apparent photosynthesis in leaves of tall fescue *(F. arundinacea* Schreb.). Annals of Botany. 31(124):661–671. 1967.

8552. Jezowski, A. J. Can your golf course afford snowmobiling? The Golf Superintendent. 40(1):52–54. 1972.

8553. "Jock" Kentucky club fights brown patch and wins. Golfdom. 1(10):24–25. 1927.

8554. Johanningsmeier, E. D. Selected bent strains lose identity when they are overseeded. Golfdom. 38(5):64,116–117. 1964.

8555. ———. A look at vegetative planting material. The Golf Course Reporter. 33(2):20–26. 1965.

8556. ______. Sod production. Illinois Turfgrass Conference Proceedings. 4 pp. 1965.

8557. Johns, R. L. Planning turf facilities for public schools. Proceedings University of Florida Turf-Grass Management Conference. 7:78–80. 1959.

8558. Johnson, A. A., and S. T. Dexter. The response of quack grass to variations in height of cutting and rate of application of nitrogen. Journal of the American Society of Agronomy. 31:67–76. 1939.

8559. Johnson, A. G., M. H. Smithberg, and D. B. White. Ground covers for highway slopes: an annotated bibliography. Investigation No. 615. University of Minnesota. 104 pp. 1965.

8560. Johnson, A. G., D. B. White, and M. H. Smithberg. Development of ground covers for highway slopes. Interim Report for 1965. University of Minnesota. Miscellaneous Journal Article 1239. 87 pp. 1966.

8561. Johnson, A. G., D. B. White, M. H. Smithberg, and L. C. Snyder. Development of ground covers for highway slopes. Final Report. Investigation No. 615. University of Minnesota. 55 pp. 1971.

8563. Johnson, A. W. and W. M. Powell. Pathogenic capabilities of a ring nematode, *Criconemoides lobatam,* on various turf grasses. The Plant Disease Reporter. 52(2):-109–113. 1968.

8564. Johnson, B. J. Effects of atrazine and simazine on newly sprigged centipede and St. Augustine grasses. Agronomy Abstracts. 2:63. 1972.

8565. Johnson, C. M. Soil fumigation methods. Proceedings of 1960 Turf Conference. Southern Turfgrass Association. pp. 9–11. 1960.

8566. Johnson, C. M. and W. R. Thompson. Fall and winter seeding of lawns. Mississippi Farm Research. 24(9):4. 1961.

8567. Johnson, C. N. Considerations in the landscaping of golf courses. Mid-Atlantic Association of Golf Course Superintendents Annual Conference Proceedings. pp. 23–24. 1964.

8568. Johnson, C. P. A look at the future of spraymen. Proceedings University of Florida Turf-Grass Management Conference. 11:113–115. 1963.

8569. Johnson, D. D. The role of mineral elements in plant growth. Rocky Mountain Regional Turfgrass Conference Proceedings. 10:17–18. 1963.

8570. Johnson, E. E. Establishment and management of new bermudas for the borderline areas. Southeastern Turfgrass Conference. 9:44–48. 1955.

8571. Johnson, E. F. Cool season maintenance. National Turfgrass Conference Proceedings. 30:13. 1959.

8572. Johnson, G. Pre emerge with Balan. Proceedings of the Midwest Regional Turf Conference. 32–34. 1970.

8573. Johnson, G. Ryegrass response to nitrogen. Park Maintenance. 24(7):18. 1971.

8574. Johnson, G. V. The effects of mowing height and nitrogen fertilization of annual ryegrass on the spring recovery of bermudagrass turf. Agricultural Experiment Station Turfgrass Report 263. University of Arizona. pp. 1–4. 1970.

8575. ______. Evaluation of nitrogen fertilizers for ryegrass. Agricultural Experiment Station Turfgrass Report 263. University of Arizona. pp. 5–8. 1970.

8576. Johnson, G. V., and W. R. Kneebone. Fertilizer studies on bentgrass. Arizona Turfgrass Conference Proceedings. pp. 13–21. 1972.

8577. Johnson, H. Converting to an automatic watering system. Proceedings of the 37th International Turfgrass Conference. pp. 33–36. 1966.

8578. Johnson, H. G. Control of turf insects. Proceedings of the 5th Annual Texas Turf Conference. 6:60–67. 1951.

8579. Johnson, H. R. Lawn and turf irrigation handbook of equipment. The Golf Superintendent. 35(9):40–43. 1967.

8580. ______. Weak links in automatic irrigation. Turf-Grass Times. 2(4):12–14. 1967.

8581. ______. Preventative maintenance and service of an automatic system. Proceedings of the 41st International Turfgrass Conference. pp. 29–31. 1970.

8583. Johnson, H. W., P. G. Rothman and D. H. Bowman. Southern blight of annual ryegrass and winter oats. The Plant Disease Reporter. 49(5):408–411. 1965.

8584. Johnson, I. Practical approach to handling the power golf cart problem. Wisconsin Turfgrass Conference Proceedings. 2 pp. 1962.

8585. Johnson, J. E. Safety in the development of herbicides. Down to Earth. 27(1):-1–7. 1971.

8586. Johnson, J. M. and J. H. Madison. Evaluation of individual management practices on bentgrass. Agronomy Abstracts. p. 39. 1966.

8587. Johnson, J. P. The control of Japanese beetle grubs in turf. Greenkeepers Club of New England Newsletter. 14(4):6–7. 1942.

8588. Johnson, J. P., R. L. Beard, G. H. Plumb and M. P. Zappe. Miscellaneous insect notes. Connecticut Agricultural Experiment Station Bulletin. 488:418–421. 1944.

8589. Johnson, J. R. New technique in greens levelling. New Zealand Institute for Turf Culture Newsletter. 39:2–4. 1965.

8590. ______. Year-round greens maintenance of grass greens. New Zealand Institute for Turf Culture Newsletter. 71:49–57. 1970.

8591. Johnson, J. T. Managing bahiagrass for turf. M.S. Thesis, University of Georgia. 61 pp. 1967.

8593. Johnson, J. T. and G. W. Burton. Managing bahiagrass for turf. Agronomy Abstracts, p. 52. 1967.

8594. Johnson, M. If you want to remove leaves efficiently, here's a roundup of park equipment available. Park Maintenance. 20(9):10–14. 1967.

8595. ______. The 1968 riding mowers. Park Maintenance. 21(1):8–12. 1968.

8596. Johnson, N. C. The maintenance of putting greens. Greenkeepers' Reporter. 9(4):15–16. 1941.

8597. ______. How I manage my watered fairways. Proceedings of Midwest Regional Turf Conference. pp. 25–27. 1948.

8598. ______. Part III—using labor effectively. Proceedings of the Second Annual University of Florida Turf Conference. 2:-61–62. 1954.

8599. ______. Gene Tift. Proceedings 6th Annual University of Florida Turf Management Conference. 6:21–24. 1958.

8600. Johnson, S. W. The station forage garden. Eleventh Annual Report of the Connecticut Agricultural Experiment Station. for 1887. pp. 163–176. 1888.

8601. Johnson, T. A. Planning turf facilities for the memorial park. Proceedings University of Florida Turf-Grass Management Conference. 7:84–87. 1959.

8602. ______. Management. Proceedings University of Florida Turf-Grass Management Conference. 9:163–167. 1961.

8603. Johnson, W. H. Course construction and maintenance in southern California. The Greenkeepers' Reporter. 6(3):34–35, 37. 1938.

8604. ______. Lawn construction and maintenance. Greenkeepers' Reporter. 8(5):-13–14, 20–21. 1940.

8605. Johnston, C. H. Watering greens. New Zealand Institute for Turf Culture Newsletter. 5:4. 1960.

8606. Johnston, D. D. Water in the growth of plants. Rocky Mountain Regional Turfgrass Conference Proceedings. 9:12–14. 1962.

8607. Johnston, H. G. Insect control. Southwest Turf Conference Proceedings. pp. 51–57. 1948.

8608. Johnston, T. Golf car use and misuse. 20th Annual RCGA National Turfgrass Conference. pp. 33–34. 1969.

8609. Johnston, W. R., A. F. Pillsbury, and E. Shaw. Glass fibre filters for tile drains. California Agriculture. 17(10):8–9. 1963.

8610. Jolliff, G. D. Campground site-vegetation relationships. Ph.D. Thesis, Colorado State University. 139 pp. 1969.

8611. Jones, A. C. Installing a polythene-pipe water system. Sports Turf Bulletin. 50:-4–6. 1960.

8612. Jones, R. A. Velvet bent *(Agrostis canina)*. USGA Green Section Bulletin. 7(8):146–147. 1927.

8613. Jones, B. F., G. Barnes, and M. C. McDaniel. Insects and diseases of lawns. Arkansas Agricultural Extension Service Leaflet 414. 1971.

8614. Jones, B. K. Public golf operations in the West. Golf Course Reporter. 31(7):-26–28. 1963.

8615. Jones, B. L. and J. Amador. Downy mildew, a new disease of St. Augustine grass. The Plant Disease Reporter. 53(11):852–854. 1969.

8616. Jones, E. V. and F. Ledeboer. Lawn grasses for South Carolina. Clemson University Extension Service Circular 495. 22 pp. 1970.

8617. Jones, F. D. Pointers on how and why of 2, 4-D use. Golfdom. 20(6):38–40. 1946.

8618. Jones, G. H. The unpaved, all-weather airport. Texas Engineering Experiment Station Bulletin 81. 1944.

8619. ______. Turf grasses of the southwest and their management. Southwest Turf Conference Proceedings. pp. 43–50. 1948.

8620. Jones, G. What every turf man should know about fertilizer. Oklahoma-Texas Turf Conference Proceedings. pp. 40–44. 1950.

8621. Jones, H. Protection of our drinking water supply from contamination by sprinkler systems. Proceedings Turfgrass Sprinkler Irrigation Conference. 5 pp. 1966.

8622. Jones, J. Work on club cricket squares. The Groundsman. 23(7):24–27. 1970.

8624. Jones, J. C. and F. N. Swink. Animal damage problems on golf courses. Mid-Atlantic Association of Golf Course Superintendents Annual Conference Proceedings. pp. 9–10. 1963.

8625. Jones, J. O. Northern superintendent finds new challenges at mid-south course. Golf Course Operations. 3(4):14–15. 1965.

8626. Jones, K. The cytology of some British species of *Agrostis* and their hybrids. British Agricultural Bulletin. 5:316. 1953.

8627. ______. Species differentiation in *Agrostis.* I. Cytological relationship in *Agrostis canina* II. The significance of chromosome pairing in the tetraploid hybrids of *Agrostis canina* subsp. montana Hartmn., *A. tenuis* Sibth. and *A. stolonifera* L. III. *Agrostis gigantea* Roth and its hybrids with *A. tenuis* Sibth. and *A. stolonifera* L. Journal of Genetics. 54:370–399. 1956.

8629. Jones, L. Chickweed and clover control on our fairways at Lansing country club. Proceedings of Midwest Regional Turf Conference. pp. 92–93. 1951.

8630. ______. Control of grasses in established lucerne by paraquat. British Weed Control Conference Proceedings. 6(1):93–100. 1962.

8631. Jones, L. G. Soils in relation to growth of turf grasses. Southwest Turf Conference Proceedings. pp. 1–4. 1948.

8632. Jones, L. H. and A. V. Lewis. Weathering of fly ash. Nature. 108:400. 1960.

8633. Jones, L. R. Killing weeds with chemicals. Vermont Agricultural Experiment Station, 13th Annual Report. pp. 282–286. 1901.

8635. Jones, L. R., and Orton, W. A. Killing weeds with chemicals. Vermont Agricultural Experiment Station. 12th Annual Report. pp. 182–188. 1899.

8636. Jones, M. B. and J. E. Ruckman. Effect of particle size on long-term availability of sulfur on annual-type grasslands. Agronomy Journal. 61(6):936–939. 1969.

8637. Jones, M. D. and L. C. Newell. Size, variability, and identification of grasses pollen. Journal of the American Society of Agronomy. 40:136–143. 1948.

8638. Jones, R. F. The status of the Florida turf grass certification program. Proceedings University of Florida Turf Management Conference. 4:57–59. 1956.

8639. ______. Turf certification panel. B. What turf grass certification means to the public. Proceedings 5th Annual University of Florida Turf Management Conference. 5:31–32. 1957.

8640. ______. Trends in turf production. Proceedings University of Florida Turf Grass Management Conference. 7:34–36. 1959.

8641. ______. Fertilizers—basic chemicals. Proceedings University of Florida Turf-Grass Management Conference. 17:23–29. 1969.

8642. Jones, R. T. Good base-good green. Golfdom. 14(4):62–63. 1940.

8643. ______. Design with respect to play. USGA Journal and Turf Management. 12(2):25–27. 1959.

8644. Jönsson, H. Grass breeding, background and prospects. Weibulls Gräs Tips. pp. 9–19. 1971.

8645. Jönsson-Rose, N. Lawns and gardens. G. P. Putnam's Sons, New York. 414 pp. 1897.

8647. Joppa, L. R. and C. W. Roath. A comparison of Kenmont, Alta and other tall fescue varieties in Montana. Montana Agricultural Experiment Station Bulletin. 582. 11 p. 1964.

8648. Jordan, C. W., C. E. Evans, and R. D. Rouse. Coastal bermudagrass response to applications of P and K as related to P and K levels in the soil. Soil Science Society of America Proceedings. 30(4):477–480. 1966.

8649. Jordan, E. E. Carbohydrate production and balance in turf. Proceedings of Midwest Regional Turf Conference. pp. 26–27. 1958.

8650. ______. Leaf responses of bentgrasses. Proceedings of Midwest Regional Turf Conference. pp. 26–27. 1959.

8651. ______. The effect of environmental factors on the carbohydrate and nutrient levels of creeping bentgrass *(Agrostis palustris).* MS Thesis, Purdue University. 63 pp. 1959.

8652. Jordon, E. E. and W. H. Daniel. Carbohydrates in bentgrass leaves measure temperature influence. Agronomy Abstracts. 50–65. 1958.

8653. Jordan, J. H. Turf—basic principles of nutrition. Proceedings of the Midwest Regional Turf Conf. pp. 28–31. 1969.

8654. Jouffray, V. M. Selecting and operating spray equipment. Proceedings of the Annual Texas Turfgrass Conference. 22:47–51. 1967.

8655. Jowett, D. Populations of *Agrostis* spp. tolerant of heavy metals. Nature. 182(4638):816–817. 1958.

8656. Juchartz, D. D. How do your production costs measure up? The Sod Grower. 1(1):6. 1971.

8656a. Juchartz, D. D. See 15012.

8657. Juhren, M., W. M. Hiesey and F. W. Went. Germination and early growth of grasses in controlled conditions. Ecology 34(2):288–300. 1953.

8658. Juhren, M., W. Noble, and F. W. Went. The standarization of *Poa annua* as an indicator of smog concentrations. I. Effects of temperature, photoperiod, and light intensity during growth of the test-plants. Plant Physiology. 32:576–586. 1957.

8659. Julander, O. Drought resistance in range and pasture grasses. Plant Physiology. 20:573–599. 1945.

8660. Jungman, F. Silica and acid-detergent fiber content of five varieties of bermudagrass. M.S. Thesis, Texas A&M University. 1971.

8661. Juncker, P. H., and J. H. Madison. Soil moisture characteristics of sand-peat mixtures. Soil Science Society of America Proceedings. 31(1):5–8. 1967.

8663. Juska F. V. The response of Meyer zoysia to lime and fertilizer treatments. Agronomy Abstracts. p. 77. 1957.

8664. ______. Response of merion and common Kentucky bluegrass to height and frequency of cut. Agronomy Abstracts. 50–65. 1958.

8665. ______. Seedbed sterilants. What's New in Crops and Soils. 10(8):23–24. 1958.

8666. ______. Some effects of gibberellic acid on turfgrasses. Golf Course Reporter. 26(2):5–9. 1958.

8667. ______. Merion research observations. Golf Course Reporter. 26(5):20–21. 1958.

8668. ______. Gibberellic shows promise as regulator of turfgrass growth. Golfdom. 32(6):64–66, 86. 1958.

8669. ______. Some effects of gibberellic acid on turfgrasses. USGA Journal and Turfgrass Management. 11(3):25–28. 1958.

8670. ______. Response of Meyer zoysia to lime and fertilizer treatments. Agronomy Journal. 51(2):81–83. 1959.

8671. ______. Effects of several preemergence crabgrass chemicals on germina-

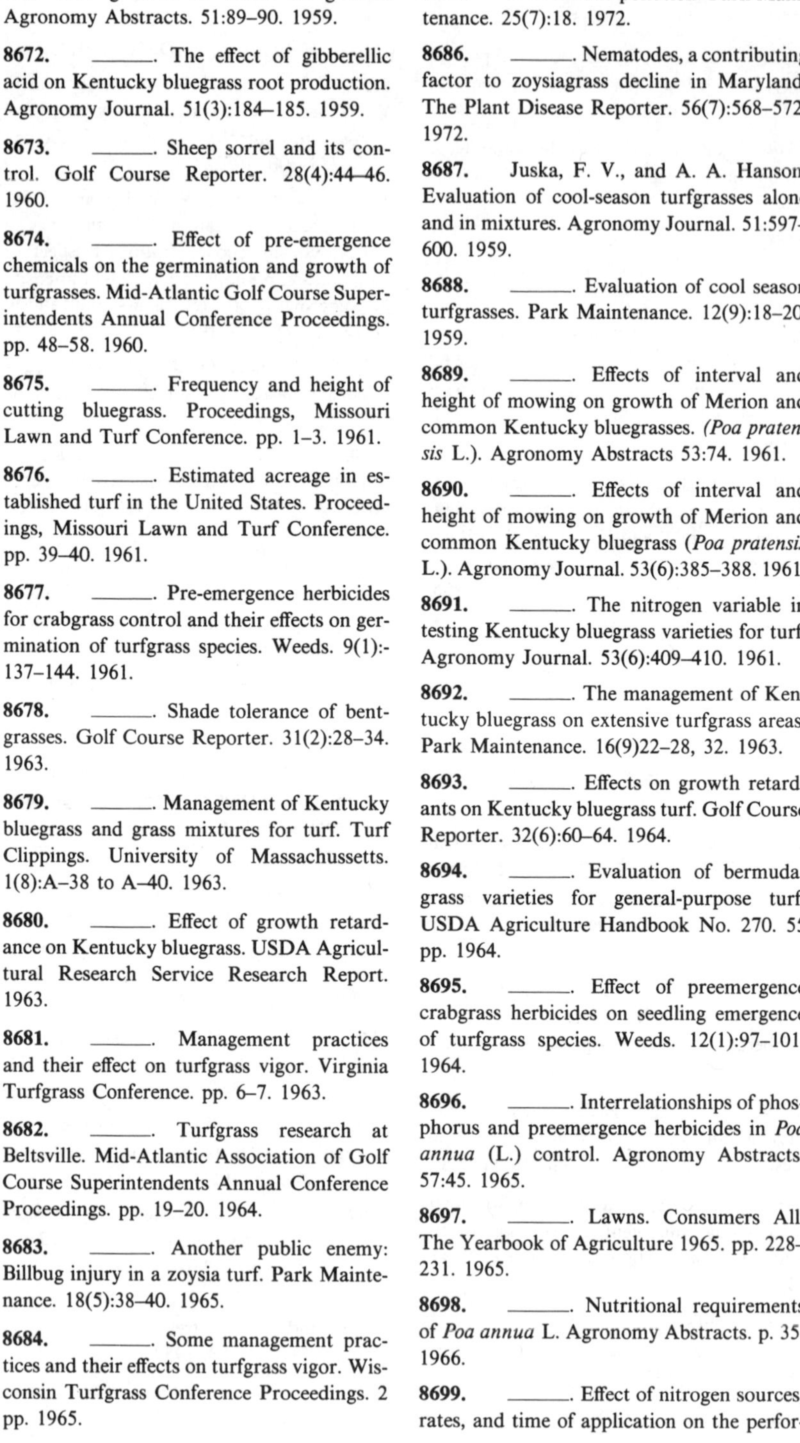

tion and growth of some turfgrasses. Agronomy Abstracts. 51:89–90. 1959.

8672. ______. The effect of gibberellic acid on Kentucky bluegrass root production. Agronomy Journal. 51(3):184–185. 1959.

8673. ______. Sheep sorrel and its control. Golf Course Reporter. 28(4):44–46. 1960.

8674. ______. Effect of pre-emergence chemicals on the germination and growth of turfgrasses. Mid-Atlantic Golf Course Superintendents Annual Conference Proceedings. pp. 48–58. 1960.

8675. ______. Frequency and height of cutting bluegrass. Proceedings, Missouri Lawn and Turf Conference. pp. 1–3. 1961.

8676. ______. Estimated acreage in established turf in the United States. Proceedings, Missouri Lawn and Turf Conference. pp. 39–40. 1961.

8677. ______. Pre-emergence herbicides for crabgrass control and their effects on germination of turfgrass species. Weeds. 9(1):-137–144. 1961.

8678. ______. Shade tolerance of bentgrasses. Golf Course Reporter. 31(2):28–34. 1963.

8679. ______. Management of Kentucky bluegrass and grass mixtures for turf. Turf Clippings. University of Massachussetts. 1(8):A–38 to A–40. 1963.

8680. ______. Effect of growth retardance on Kentucky bluegrass. USDA Agricultural Research Service Research Report. 1963.

8681. ______. Management practices and their effect on turfgrass vigor. Virginia Turfgrass Conference. pp. 6–7. 1963.

8682. ______. Turfgrass research at Beltsville. Mid-Atlantic Association of Golf Course Superintendents Annual Conference Proceedings. pp. 19–20. 1964.

8683. ______. Another public enemy: Billbug injury in a zoysia turf. Park Maintenance. 18(5):38–40. 1965.

8684. ______. Some management practices and their effects on turfgrass vigor. Wisconsin Turfgrass Conference Proceedings. 2 pp. 1965.

8685. ______. Air pollution. Park Maintenance. 25(7):18. 1972.

8686. ______. Nematodes, a contributing factor to zoysiagrass decline in Maryland. The Plant Disease Reporter. 56(7):568–572. 1972.

8687. Juska, F. V., and A. A. Hanson. Evaluation of cool-season turfgrasses alone and in mixtures. Agronomy Journal. 51:597–600. 1959.

8688. ______. Evaluation of cool season turfgrasses. Park Maintenance. 12(9):18–20. 1959.

8689. ______. Effects of interval and height of mowing on growth of Merion and common Kentucky bluegrasses. *(Poa pratensis* L.). Agronomy Abstracts 53:74. 1961.

8690. ______. Effects of interval and height of mowing on growth of Merion and common Kentucky bluegrass (*Poa pratensis* L.). Agronomy Journal. 53(6):385–388. 1961.

8691. ______. The nitrogen variable in testing Kentucky bluegrass varieties for turf. Agronomy Journal. 53(6):409–410. 1961.

8692. ______. The management of Kentucky bluegrass on extensive turfgrass areas. Park Maintenance. 16(9)22–28, 32. 1963.

8693. ______. Effects on growth retardants on Kentucky bluegrass turf. Golf Course Reporter. 32(6):60–64. 1964.

8694. ______. Evaluation of bermudagrass varieties for general-purpose turf. USDA Agriculture Handbook No. 270. 55 pp. 1964.

8695. ______. Effect of preemergence crabgrass herbicides on seedling emergence of turfgrass species. Weeds. 12(1):97–101. 1964.

8696. ______. Interrelationships of phosphorus and preemergence herbicides in *Poa annua* (L.) control. Agronomy Abstracts. 57:45. 1965.

8697. ______. Lawns. Consumers All. The Yearbook of Agriculture 1965. pp. 228–231. 1965.

8698. ______. Nutritional requirements of *Poa annua* L. Agronomy Abstracts. p. 35. 1966.

8699. ______. Effect of nitrogen sources, rates, and time of application on the performance of Kentucky bluegrass turf. Proceedings of American Society of Horticultural Science. 90:413–419. 1967.

8700. ______. Phosphorus and its relationship to turfgrasses and *Poa annua* L. California Turfgrass Culture. 17(4):27–29. 1967.

8701. ______. Factors affecting *Poa annua* L. control. The Golf Superintendent. 35(9):46–51. 1967.

8702. ______. Phosphorus and its relationship to turfgrasses and *Poa annua* L. Proceedings 38th International Turfgrass Conference. pp. 20–24. 1967.

8703. ______. Factors affecting *Poa annua* L. control. Weeds. 15(2):98–101. 1967.

8704. ______. Effect of pre-emergence and several phosphorus levels on the control of *Poa annua.* Mid-Atlantic Superintendents Conference Proceedings. pp. 19–20. 1966.

8705. ______. Nutritional requirements of *Poa annua* L. Agronomy Journal. 61(3):-466–468. 1969.

8706. ______. Effects of herbicides on the germination of some turfgrass species. Northeastern Weed Science Society Proceedings. 25:83–86. 1971.

8707. Juska, F. V. and A. W. Hovin. Preemergence herbicide effects on the growth of Newport Kentucky bluegrass *(Poa pratensis* L.) seedlings. Northeastern Weed Science Society Proceeding. pp. 387–392. 1970.

8708. ______. Preemergence herbicide effects on the growth on Newport Kentucky bluegrass. Park Maintenance. 23(7):26. 1970.

8709. Juska, F. V. and K. W. Kreitlow. Conditions affecting the development and perpetuation of zoysia rust. Plant Disease Reporter. 56(3):227–229. 1972.

8710. Juska, F. V., and J. J. Murray. Evaluation of Kentucky bluegrasses, *Poa pratensis* L., at two cutting heights and two levels of nitrogen. Agronomy Abstracts. 2:63. 1972.

8712. Juska, F. V., A. A. Hanson, and C. J. Erickson. Response of Merion and common Kentucky bluegrass to several levels of phosphorus. Agronomy Abstracts. 54:103. 1962.

8713. ______. Response of common Kentucky bluegrass and red fescue to several levels of phosphorus. Agronomy Abstracts. p. 118. 1963.

8714. ______. Effects of phosphorus and other treatments on the development of red fescue, 'Merion', and common Kentucky bluegrass. Agronomy Journal. 57(1):75–78. 1965.

8715. Juska, F. V., A. A. Hanson, and A. W. Hovin. Evaluation of tall fescue, *Festuca arundinacea* Schreb., for turf in the transitional zone. Agronomy Abstracts. p. 64. 1968.

8716. ______. Phytotoxicity of some preemergence herbicides to putting green turf. Agronomy Abstracts. p. 54. 1969.

8717. ______. Evaluation of tall fescue, *Festuca arundinacea* Schreb., for turf in the transition zone of the United States. Agronomy Journal. 61(4):625–628. 1969.

8718. ______. Kentucky 31 tall fescue—a shade tolerant turfgrass. Weeds, Trees and Turf. 8(1):34–35. 1969.

8719. ______. For winter color, overseed bermudagrass. Weeds, Trees, and Turf. 8(9):-16–17. 1969.

8720. ______. Growth response of Merion Kentucky bluegrass to fertilizer and lime treatments. Agronomy Journal. 62(1):25–27. 1970.

8721. ______. Phytotoxicity of preemergence herbicides. USGA Green Section Record. 8(5):2–6. 1970.

8722. ______. Turfgrass injury from herbicides. Park Maintenance. 24(7):24. 1971.

8723. Juska, F. V., J. Tyson, and C. M. Harrison. The competitive relationships of Merion bluegrass as influenced by various mixtures, cutting heights and levels of nitrogen. Agronomy Journal. 47(11):513–518. 1955.

8724. ______. Field studies on the establishment of Merion bluegrass in various seed mixtures. Michigan Agricultural Experiment Station. Quarterly Bulletin. 38(4):678–690. 1956.

8725. Juska, F. V., W. H. Daniel, E. C. Holt, and V. B. Youngner. Nomenclature of some plants associated with turfgrass management. Report of Turfgrass Nomenclature Committee, American Society of Agronomy Mimeo. pp. 1–21. 1961.

8726. ______. Nomenclature of some plants associated with turfgrass management. Agronomy Journal. 54:275–276. 1962.

8727. Justice, O. L. A review of literature on the use of the fluorescence test for the classification of *Lolium* species and hybrids. Association of Official Seed Analysts of North America Proceedings. 36:86–93. 1946.

8728. Kadish, V. H. Milorganite—a new fertilizer material. Industrial and Engineering Chemistry. 20(1):3. 1928.

8729. Kadowaki, H. New compounds of urea-formaldehyde condensation products. Bulletin of the Chemical Society of Japan. 11:248–261. 1936.

8730. Kaempffe, G. C. and O. R. Lunt. Availability of various fractions of urea formaldehyde. Journal of Agricultural and Food Chemistry. 15:967–971. 1967.

8731. Kaerwer, H. E. Lawn seed mixtures. Wisconsin Turfgrass Conference Proceedings. p. 1. 1963.

8732. ______. Newer grasses. Proceedings of the Midwest Regional Turf Conference. pp. 76–77. 1968.

8733. ______. Varieties and mixtures for overseeding. Proceedings of the Texas Turfgrass Conference. 23:95–98. 1968.

8734. ______. New ryegrasses for turf. Turf-Grass Times. 3(6):1, 10 & 15. 1968.

8735. ______. Choosing the grass to fit the need. Illinois Turfgrass Conference Proceedings. pp. 3–5. 1969.

8736. ______. New grasses and new combinations for winter overseedings. Arizona Turfgrass Conference Proceedings. pp. 11–13. 1972.

8737. ______. Taking the offensive against *Pythium.* The Golf Superintendent. 40(9):27–29. 1972.

8738. Kaiby, C. Nice turnout for N. J. field day. Golfdom. 11(7):42. 1937.

8739. Kaiser, W. J. Effects of light on growth and sporulation of the *Verticillium* wilt fungus. Phytopathology. 54(7):765–770. 1964.

8740. Kalitin, N. N. The measurement of the albedo of a snow cover. Monthly Weather Review, United States Weather Bureau. 58(2):59–61. 1930.

8741. Kallio, A. Chemical control of snow mold *(Sclerotinia borealis)* on four varieties of bluegrass *(Poa pratensis)* in Alaska. The Plant Disease Reporter. 50(1):69–72. 1966.

8742. Kalma, J. D. The radiation balance of a tropical pasture, II. Net all-wave radiation. Agricultural Meteorology. 10(4/5):261–275. 1972.

8743. Kalma, J. D., and R. Badham. The radiation balance of a tropical pasture, I. The reflection of short-wave radiation. Agricultural Meterology. 10(4/5):251–259. 1972.

8744. Kamm, J. A. Biology of turf insects in relation to control. Proceedings of Scotts Turfgrass Research Conference. 1:77–82. 1969.

8745. Kammeyer, K. K. How much does it cost to maintain school grounds. Exposition Conference—Southern California. 3 pp. 1966.

8746. Kamps, M. Effects of real and simulated play on newly sown turf. Proceedings of the First International Turfgrass Research Conference. pp. 118–123. 1969.

8747. Kanity, B. Resourcefulness is the key to successful turf renovation. Park Maintenance. 18(11):22–23. 1965.

8748. Kapp, H. Sawdust shows value as top-dressing humus. Golfdom. 24(8):52, 60–61. 1950.

8749. Karbassi, P., S. H. West, and L. A. Garrard. Amylolytic activity in leaves of a tropical and a temperate grass. Crop Science. 12(1):58–60. 1972.

8751. Kardos, L. T. Sewage waste water for irrigation of turf. Agronomy Abstracts. p. 54. 1969.

8752. Kramer, H. H. Morphologic and agronomic variation in *Poa pratensis* L. in relation to chromosome numbers. Journal of the American Society of Agronomy. 39:181–191. 1947.

8753. Kastl, H. J. Control of the hairy chinch bug in turf. New York Turfgrass Association Bulletin. 77:299–300. 1964.

8754. Kastner, W. Intensive fertilizing of grass playgrounds. First Czechoslovak Symposium on Sportturf Proceedings. pp. 217–222. 1969.

8755. Kates, A. Lawn weed control. Virginia Agricultural Extension Circular. 820:-1–4. 1961.

8756. Katsura, K. Control of the turfgrass diseases. KGU Green Section Turf Research Bulletin. 16:1–14. 1969.

8757. Kamon, Y. Effect of fertilizers for turfgrass growth. KGU Green Section Turf Research Bulletin. 17:49–58. 1969.

8758. ———. Effects of fertilizers for turfgrass, Part 1. KGU Green Section Turf Research Bulletin. 18:41–50. 1970.

8759. ———. Effects on the growth regulator for turfgrasses. KGU Green Section Turf Research Bulletin. 18:51–56. 1970.

8760. ———. Effects of fertilizers for turfgrass, Part 2. KGU Green Section Turf Research Bulletin. 19:57–63. 1970.

8761. ———. Research of the turfgrass variety, Part 1. KGU Green Section Turf Research Bulletin. 20:29–41. 1971.

8762. ———. Effects of fertilizers for turfgrass, Part 3. KGU Green Section Turf Research Bulletin. 21(8):39–43. 1971.

8763. ———. Effects of fertilizers for turfgrass, Part 4. KGU Green Section Turf Research Bulletin. 22(2):35–39. 1972.

8764. ———. Turf herbicide trials. KGU Green Section Turf Research Bulletin. 23:51–128. 1972.

8765. Kamon, Y., and H. Murakami. Research of the turfgrass variety, Part 2. KGU Green Section Turf Research Bulletin. 22(2):41–45. 1972.

8766. Kapusta, G. and E. C. Varsa. Nitrification inhibitors—do they work? Down to Earth. 28(1):21–23. 1972.

8767. Kaskeski, P. A. The influence of height of cut on the development of turfgrass roots. Turf Bulletin. Massachusetts Turf and Lawn Grass Council. 4(4):20. 1967.

8768. Kaufman, D. D. Persistence and degradation of commonly used turf herbicides in our environment. Proceedings of Scotts Turfgrass Research Conference. 3:93–132. 1972.

8769. Kaufman, D. D. and L. E. Williams. Effect of the soil carbon: nitrogen ratio on soil fungi. Phytopathology. 53(8):956–960. 1963.

8770. ———. Effect of mineral fertilization and soil reaction on soil fungi. Phytopathology. 54(2):134–139. 1964.

8771. Kaufman, J. M. Trends in modern turf irrigation. Sprinkler Irrigation Association Annual Technical Conference Proceedings. pp. 52–58. 1967.

8772. ———. Programming and maintenance. International Turfgrass Conference & Show. 39:77–83. 1968.

8773. Kaufman, J. E. The influence of temperature and other environmental factors on nitrate reductase activity of *Agrostis palustris* Huds. and *Cynodon dactylon* L. M.S. Thesis, Michigan State University. 43 pp. 1970.

8774. Kaufmann, J. E. and J. B. Beard. The influence of temperature and other environmental factors on nitrate reductase activity of *Agrostis palustris* Huds. Michigan Turfgrass Report. pp. 5–6. Spring, 1971.

8775. Kaufmann, J. E., J. B. Beard, and D. Penner. The influence of temperature and other environmental factors on nitrate reductase acticity of *Agrostis palustris* Huds. and *Cynodon dactylon* L. Agronomy Abstracts. 62:69. 1970.

8776. ———. The influence of temperature on nitrate reductase acticity of *Agrostis palustris* and *Cynodon dactylon.* Physiologia Plantarum. (25):378–381. 1971.

8777. Kauter, A. Contributions to the knowledge of root growth in grasses. Ber. Schweiz. Bot. Ges. 42:37–109. 1933.

8778. Kaufmann, J. E. The effect of heat stress on aspects of carbohydrate and nitrogen metabolism in *Agrostis, Cynodon,* and *Poa* species. Ph.D. Thesis. Michigan State University. 71 pp. 1973.

8779. Kearby, W. H. Biological control of insect pests. Missouri Lawn and Turf Conference Proceedings. 12:42–44. 1971.

8780. Kearns, V. E. H. Toole. Temperature and other factors affecting the germination of the seed of fescue. Compt. Ren. de l'

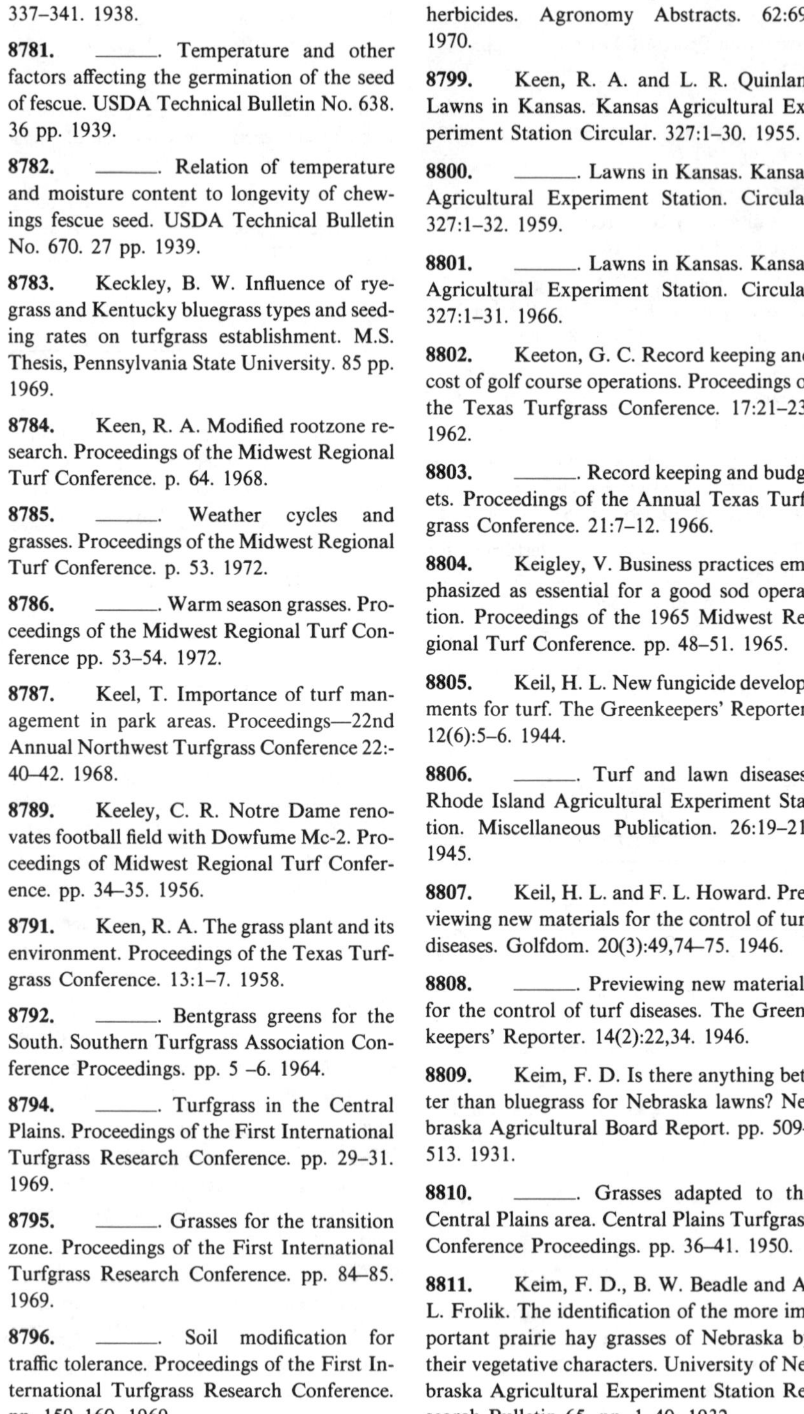

Assoc. Internatl. d'essais de Semences. 10:-337–341. 1938.

8781. ______. Temperature and other factors affecting the germination of the seed of fescue. USDA Technical Bulletin No. 638. 36 pp. 1939.

8782. ______. Relation of temperature and moisture content to longevity of chewings fescue seed. USDA Technical Bulletin No. 670. 27 pp. 1939.

8783. Keckley, B. W. Influence of ryegrass and Kentucky bluegrass types and seeding rates on turfgrass establishment. M.S. Thesis, Pennsylvania State University. 85 pp. 1969.

8784. Keen, R. A. Modified rootzone research. Proceedings of the Midwest Regional Turf Conference. p. 64. 1968.

8785. ______. Weather cycles and grasses. Proceedings of the Midwest Regional Turf Conference. p. 53. 1972.

8786. ______. Warm season grasses. Proceedings of the Midwest Regional Turf Conference pp. 53–54. 1972.

8787. Keel, T. Importance of turf management in park areas. Proceedings—22nd Annual Northwest Turfgrass Conference 22:-40–42. 1968.

8789. Keeley, C. R. Notre Dame renovates football field with Dowfume Mc-2. Proceedings of Midwest Regional Turf Conference. pp. 34–35. 1956.

8791. Keen, R. A. The grass plant and its environment. Proceedings of the Texas Turfgrass Conference. 13:1–7. 1958.

8792. ______. Bentgrass greens for the South. Southern Turfgrass Association Conference Proceedings. pp. 5 –6. 1964.

8794. ______. Turfgrass in the Central Plains. Proceedings of the First International Turfgrass Research Conference. pp. 29–31. 1969.

8795. ______. Grasses for the transition zone. Proceedings of the First International Turfgrass Research Conference. pp. 84–85. 1969.

8796. ______. Soil modification for traffic tolerance. Proceedings of the First International Turfgrass Research Conference. pp. 159–160. 1969.

8797. ______. Nitrogen fertilizers as herbicides. Agronomy Abstracts. 62:69. 1970.

8799. Keen, R. A. and L. R. Quinlan. Lawns in Kansas. Kansas Agricultural Experiment Station Circular. 327:1–30. 1955.

8800. ______. Lawns in Kansas. Kansas Agricultural Experiment Station. Circular 327:1–32. 1959.

8801. ______. Lawns in Kansas. Kansas Agricultural Experiment Station. Circular 327:1–31. 1966.

8802. Keeton, G. C. Record keeping and cost of golf course operations. Proceedings of the Texas Turfgrass Conference. 17:21–23. 1962.

8803. ______. Record keeping and budgets. Proceedings of the Annual Texas Turfgrass Conference. 21:7–12. 1966.

8804. Keigley, V. Business practices emphasized as essential for a good sod operation. Proceedings of the 1965 Midwest Regional Turf Conference. pp. 48–51. 1965.

8805. Keil, H. L. New fungicide developments for turf. The Greenkeepers' Reporter. 12(6):5–6. 1944.

8806. ______. Turf and lawn diseases. Rhode Island Agricultural Experiment Station. Miscellaneous Publication. 26:19–21. 1945.

8807. Keil, H. L. and F. L. Howard. Previewing new materials for the control of turf diseases. Golfdom. 20(3):49,74–75. 1946.

8808. ______. Previewing new materials for the control of turf diseases. The Greenkeepers' Reporter. 14(2):22,34. 1946.

8809. Keim, F. D. Is there anything better than bluegrass for Nebraska lawns? Nebraska Agricultural Board Report. pp. 509–513. 1931.

8810. ______. Grasses adapted to the Central Plains area. Central Plains Turfgrass Conference Proceedings. pp. 36–41. 1950.

8811. Keim, F. D., B. W. Beadle and A. L. Frolik. The identification of the more important prairie hay grasses of Nebraska by their vegetative characters. University of Nebraska Agricultural Experiment Station Research Bulletin 65. pp. 1–40. 1932.

8812. Keller, J. Effect of water application on soil tilth. Sprinkler Irrigation Association Annual Technical Conference Proceedings. pp. 4–14. 1967.

8813. Keller, W. Interpretation of self-fertility in grasses by frequency distributions. Journal of the American Society of Agronomy. V40:894–900. 1948.

8814. Kellerman, K. F. Tip cuttings for vegetative planting. USGA Green Section Bulletin V. 3(11):293–295. 1923.

8815. ______. Bacterial inculation useless for growing grass. USGA Green Section Bulletin. 5(7):155. 1925.

8816. Kelley, B. A turf fertilizer and care program. Proceedings of the Midwest Regional Turf Conference. pp. 63–64. 1961.

8817. Kelley, J. B. Observations of a fertilizer and grass seed salesman. Illinois Turfgrass Conference Proceedings. pp. 40–43. 1960.

8818. Kelley, A. The management of penncross bent at Bangor Municipal. University of Maine Turf Conference Proceedings. 6:22–24. 1968.

8819. Kelly, J. B. Servicing modern equipment. Proceedings of the Midwest Regional Turf Conference. pp. 58–59. 1970.

8821. Kelsheimer, E. G. Insect pests of lawns. Florida Agricultural Experiment Station Press Bulletin. 642. 4 pp. 1948.

8822. ______. Damaging insects to turf and their control. Florida Greenkeeping Superintendents Association and the Southeastern Turf Conference Turf Management Conference. pp. 36–38. 1949.

8823. ______. Control of mole-crickets. University of Florida Agricultural Experiment Stations, Circular S–15. 7 pp. 1950.

8824. ______. Insects and other pests of lawns and turf. Florida Agricultural Experiment Station Circular S42:1–11. 1952.

8825. ______. Armyworms, sod webworms, beetles, etc. Proceedings of the First Annual University of Florida Turf Conference. 1:39. 1953.

8827. ______. The hunting billbug, a serious pest of zoysia. Proceedings Florida State Horticultural Society. 69:415–418. 1956.

8828. ______. The practical use of pesticides. Sunshine State Agricultural Research Report. 12(4):11. 1967.

8829. Kelsheimer, E. G. and S. H. Kerr. Insects and other pests of lawns and turf. Florida Agricultural Experiment Station Circular. S96:1–22. 1957.

8830. Kelsheimer, E. G. and A. J. Overman. Notes on some ectoparasitic nematodes found attacking lawns in the Tampa Bay area. Proceedings Florida State Horticultural Society. 66:301–303. 1953.

8831. Kemble, A. R. and H. T. Macpherson. Liberation of amino acids in perennial ryegrass during wilting. Biochemistry Journal. 58:46–50. 1954.

8832. Kemmerer, H. R. Controlling soil pest problems before they develop. Illinois Turfgrass Conference Proceedings. pp. 10–12. 1961.

8833. ______. Effects of post-emergence herbicides on establishment of spring seeded Kentucky bluegrass. Illinois Turfgrass Conference Proceedings. pp. 11–13. 1962.

8834. ______. Mulches for roadside landscape plantings. 28th Short Course on Roadside Development. Ohio Dept. of Highways. 28:113–118. 1969.

8835. Kemmerer, H. R. and J. D. Butler. Establishing spring-seeded lawns. Illinois Research, Illinois Agricultural Experiment Station. 4:5. 1962.

8836. ______. The effect of seeding rates, fertilizers and weed control on the species establishment of several lawn grasses. Proceedings of American Society of Horticultural Science. 85:599–604. 1964.

8837. ______. The effect of seeding rates, fertility, and weed control on the spring establishment of several lawn grasses. Proceeding of the American Society for Horticultural Science. 85:599–604. 1965.

8838. Kemmerer, H. R. and F. F. Weinard. How to have an attractive lawn. Illinois Agricultural Extension Service. Circular 729. 16 pp. 1954.

8839. ______. How to have an attractive lawn. Illinois Extension Service. Circular 729. 16 pp. 1959.

8840. Kendall, K. K. Water: friend or foe? Golf Course Reporter. 25(8):20–21. 1957.

8841. Kennedy, D. Acti-dione. Oklahoma Turfgrass Conference Proceedings. pp. 29–30. 1956.

8843. Kennedy, P. B. The structure of the caryopsis of grasses with reference to their morphology and classification. USDA Division of Agrostology Bulletin. 19:1–44. 1899.

8844. ______. *Lippia* possible warm country fairway turf. Golfdom. 1(11):24–25. 1927.

8845. ______. Proliferation in *Poa bulbosa.* Journal of the American Society of Agronomy. 21:80–91. 1929.

8846. Kennedy, W. K. and M. B. Russell. Relationship of top growth, root growth, and apparent specific gravity of the soil under different clipping treatments of a Kentucky bluegrass—wild white clover pasture. Journal of the American Society of Agronomy. 40:535–540. 1948.

8847. Kennerly, A. B. Through college on grass roots. Southern Seedsman. 21(3):-34–35,42. 1958.

8848. Kinney, E. J. Steam sterilization as a possible means of controlling weeds on putting greens. USGA Green Section Bulletin. 5(10):232–234. 1925.

8849. Kinney, L. F. Trial of lawn grasses. Annual Report of the Rhode Island State Agricultural School and Experiment Station Part II. p. 156. 1891.

8850. Kenwinski, J. Shifting maintenance for play on public courses. Proceedings University of Florida Turf Management Conference. 5:44–45. 1957.

8851. Keohane, J. A. Environmental studies of *Fusarium* blight in Merion bluegrass. M.S. Thesis, University of Massachusetts. 116 pp. 1967.

8852. Keohane, J., and J. Troll. Summer herbicidal treatments on fairway turf. Turf Bulletin. Massachusetts Turf & Lawn Grass Council. 2(13):9–10. 1965.

8853. Kephart, L. W. Quack grass. USDA. Farmers' Bulletin. No. 1307. 32 pp. 1923.

8854. Kepler, B. J. Roadside equipment for economical operation. Ohio Short Course on Roadside Development. 18:77–91. 1959.

8855. Kepner, R. A., and W. E. Howard. Gopher-bait applicator. California Agriculture. 14(3):7,14. 1960.

8856. Kern, D. How to stop guessing when you buy seed. Proceedings of Southern California Turfgrass Institute. pp. 13–22. 1969.

8857. ______. How to stop guessing when you buy seed. R.C.G.A. National Turf Conference. 22:23–30. 1971.

8858. Kerr, A. Factors influencing the development of brown patch in lawns of *Sagina procumbens* L. Australian Journal of Biology. 9(3):322–338. 1956.

8859. Kerr, C. F. *Poa annua* restriction in existing turf for golf courses, athletic areas and fine lawns. Turf Clippings. University of Massachussetts. 2(1):A–9 to A–13. 1966.

8860. ______. *Poa annua*-turf enemy No. 1. Weeds Trees and Turf. 7(3):13–16,43. 1968.

8861. ______. Program for gradual removal of *Poa annua* for cool season grasses. Proceedings 1970 3–day Short Courses, Rutgers University. pp. 37–39. 1970.

8862. ______. The mode of action of arsenicals in the soil. Turf Bulletin (Massachusetts). 8(2):3–4,20–22. 1971.

8863. ______. Arsenic and its relation to the environment. Proceedings of the Midwest Regional Turf Conference. pp. 54–56. 1972.

8864. Kerr, H. D. Selective grass control with siduron. Weed Science. 17(2):181–186. 1969.

8866. Kerr, J. A. N. I. playing fields maintenance. The Groundsman. 23(7):35–36. 1970.

8867. Kerr, J. A. M., and J. H. Bailie. A note on the use of paraquat as a selective herbicide for grassland. Report of Agricultural Research North Ireland. 14(2):1–7. 1965.

8868. Kerr, S. H. Insect pests of Florida lawns. Florida Entomology Mimeo Series 55–2.

8869. ______. Insect pests of Florida lawns. Florida Entomology Mimeo Series 56–2.

8870. ______. Life history of tropical sod webworm, *Panchyzancla phaeopteralis* Guenee. Florida Entomologist. 38:3–11. 1955.

8871. ______. Reviewing turf insect research. University of Florida Turf Management Conference Proceedings. 3:29–32. 1955.

8872. ______. Insect problems—identification. University of Florida Turf-Grass Management Conference Proceedings. 3:-128–129. 1955.

8873. ______. Results with new chemicals for chinch bug control. University of Florida Turf Management Conference Proceedings. 4:87–90. 1956.

8874. ______. Chinch bug control on lawns in Florida. Journal Economic Entomology. 49(1):83–85. 1956.

8875. ______. Some fundamentals of insect life. A. The place of insects in the animal kingdom. Proceedings University of Florida Turf Management Conference. 5:23–26. 1957.

8876. Kerr, S. H., and F. A. Robinson. Progress in lawn insect research—1957. University of Florida Turf Management Conference Proceedings. 5:84–87. 1957.

8877. Kerr, S. H. Progress in insect problems. Proceedings of University of Florida Turf Management Conference. 6:96–100. 1958.

8878. ______. Turf insects problem is growing in South. Parks and Recreation. 41(7):301–303. 1958.

8879. ______. Progress in insect research on lawns—1958. Proceedings University of Florida Turfgrass Management Conference. 7:92–97. 1959.

8880. ______. Recommendations for commercial lawn spraymen. Florida Agricultural Experiment Station Circular. S121:7 pp. 1960.

8881. ______. Insect control. Proceedings of University of Florida Turf-Grass Management Conference. 8:116–118. 1960.

8882. ______. Lawn chinch bug research—1961. Proceedings of University of Florida Turf-Grass Management. Conference. 9:211–221. 1961.

8883. ______. Outlook of turfgrass insect studies in Florida. Florida Turf-Grass Association Bulletin, 9(2):2–4. 1962.

8884. ______. Bermudagrass mite developments. Florida Turfgrass Association Bulletin. 9(4):7. 1962.

8885. ______. Lawn insect studies—1962. Proceedings University of Florida Turf-Grass Management Conference. 10:-201–208. 1962.

8886. ______. Turf fertilization research. Proceedings University of Florida Turf-Grass Management Conference. 10:209–215. 1962.

8887. ______. Turf grass insects in the gulf states. Golf Course Reporter. 30(8):28–34. 1962.

8888. ______. Recommendations for commercial lawn sprayment. University of Florida Agricultural Experiment Station Circular. S121A:8 pp. 1961.

8889. ______. Mr. Big: the lawn chinch bug. Proceedings of University of Florida Turf-Grass Management Conference. 11:13–21. 1963.

8890. ______. Mr. Almost as bad: lawn caterpillars. Proceedings of University of Florida Turf-Grass Management Conference. 11:23–27. 1963.

8891. ______. Insect pests of Florida turfgrass nurseries. Proceedings of University of Florida Turf-Grass Management Conference. 11:138–140. 1963.

8892. ______. Lawn insect studies: 1963. Proceedings of University of Florida Turf-Grass Management Conference. 11:155–158. 1963.

8893. ______. Preliminary report on a billbug control test. Florida Turfgrass Association Bulletin. 11(1):5. 1964.

8894. ______. Hunting billbug control. Florida Turf-Grass Association Bulletin. 12(2):3. 1965.

8895. ______. Insect control by commercial lawn spraymen. Proceedings University of Florida Turf-Grass Management Conference. 12:112–115. 1964.

8896. ______. Lawn insect research. Proceedings University of Florida Turf-Grass Management Conference. 12:160–166. 1964.

8898. ______. Chinch bug control studies. Proceedings University Florida Turfgrass Management Conference. 13:145–146. 1965.

8899. ______. Biology of the lawn chinch bug, *Blissus insularis.* Florida Entomologist. 49(1):9–18. 1966.

8900. ______. Biology of the lawn chinch bug. Florida Turf-Grass Association Bulletin. 13(4):8. 1966.

8901. ______. Biology of the lawn chinch bug. Turf Bulletin. Massachusetts Turf & Lawn Grass Council. 4(3):23. 1967.

8902. ______. Structure of organophosphorus compounds in relation to control of the southern chinch bug. Journal of Economic Entomology. 61(2):523–525. 1968.

8903. ______. Toxicology of insecticides & miticides. Annual Research Report of the Institute of Food & Agricultural Sciences. University of Florida. p. 78. 1968.

8904. ______. Diagnosing lawn insect problems. Proceedings of the Florida Turfgrass Management Conference. 18:77–83. 1970.

8905. Kerr, S. H. and J. E. Brodgon. The bermudagrass mite. Florida Turfgrass Association Bulletin 2(2):4–5. 1969.

8906. Kerr, T. W. Lawn insect control. Rhode Island Agricultural Experiment Station. Miscellaneous Publication. 48:1–8. 1956.

8907. Keshen, A. S. Reservoirs overcome drought for New Jersey sod grower. Weeds Trees and Turf. 5(11):14–16. 1966.

8908. Kesler, C. D., R. H. Cole, and C. E. Phillips. Preemergence and postemergence crabgrass control in turfgrass. Proceedings of the Northeastern Weed Control Conference. 16:524–527. 1962.

8909. Van Keuren, R. W. Fertilization and root life. Turf Bulletin. Massachusetts Turf and Lawn Grass Council. 4(5):14–16. 1967.

8910. Khattat, F. H. Pest control and the environmental challenge. Turf-Grass Times. 8(1):1–6,20–21,24. 1972.

8911. Kidd, W. J. and H. F. Haupt. Effects of seedbed treatment on grass establishment on logging roadbeds in central Idaho. U.S. Forest Service Research Paper (Intermountain). 53:1–9. 1968.

8912. Kidwell, J., and M. Hurdzan. Pride beat the steam drill. USGA Green Section Record. 10(2):5–6. 1972.

8913. Kiellander, C. L. Studies on apospory in *Poa pratensis* L. Svensk Botanisk Tidskrift. 35:321–332. 1941.

8915. Kilian, K. C., O. J. Attoe, and L. E. Engelbert. Urea-formaldehyde as a slowly available form of nitrogen for Kentucky bluegrass. Agronomy Journal. 58(2):204–206. 1966.

8916. Killian, J. O. Planting turf. U.S. Army Crops of Engineers Manual. Em 1110–1-321. 1961.

8917. Killian, K. K. One method of laying out a golf hole. Wisconsin Turfgrass Conference Proceedings. p.1. 1963.

8918. Killick, H. J. and I. Greenfield Earthworms and their control. Part I. Parks, Golf Courses and Sports Grounds. 26(10):-707–708,729. 1961.

8919. ______. Earthworms and their control. Part II. Parks, Golf Courses and Sports Grounds. 26(11):773–776. 1961.

8920. ______. Earthworms and their control. Part III. Parks, Golf Courses and Sports Grounds. 26(12):885–890. 1961.

8921. Kilmer, V. J., and L. T. Alexander. Methods of making mechanical analyses of soils. Soil Science. 68:15–24. 1949.

8922. Kilpatrick, R. A., C. L. Mobley, and G. G. Williges. Curvularia leaf spot, a new disease of bluestem grasses. Phytopathology. 57(9):975–977. 1967.

8923. Kiltz, B. F. Military turf uses. Proceedings of Midwest Regional Turf Conference. pp. 33–34. 1957.

8924. ______. The expanding field of special purpose turf. Proceedings of the Texas Turfgrass Conference. 15:1–7. 1960.

8925. Kimball, M. H. Brown spots in your lawn. California Agricultural Experiment Station Extension Folder. 1953.

8926. ______. Question and answer clinic. North California Turf Conference. pp. 34–62. 1953.

8927. ______. Your problem clinic. Proceedings of the Southern California Turfgrass Conference. pp. 17–40. 1953.

8928. ______. Turf is big business. North California Turf Conference. pp. 37–40. 1954.

8929. ______. Turfgrass by the thousands of acres.Southern California Turfgrass Culture. 5(1):1–2. 1955.

8930. ______. The turfgrass picture in California, 1961. Proceedings Northern California Turfgrass Institute. pp. 1–5. 1961.

8931. Kimball, M. H., B. Day, and C. L. Hemstreet. Weed control adjacent to grassed areas. Southern California Turfgrass Culture. 6(4):1–2. 1956.

8932. Kinbacher, E. J. Resistance of seedlings to frost heaving injury. Agronomy Journal. 48(4):166–170. 1956.

8933. Kinbacher, E. J. and H. M. Laude. Frost heaving of seedlings in the laboratory. Agronomy Journal. 47(9):415–418. 1955.

8934. Kinch, R. C., and F. D. Keim. Eradication of bindweed in bluegrass lawns. Journal of American Society of Agronomy. 29:30–39. 1937.

8935. King, B. M. Kentucky bluegrass in Missouri. Missouri Agricultural Experiment Station Circular. 155. 11 pp. 1927.

8936. King, D. Financial benefits derived from good cemetery turf. Texas Turf Conference Proceedings. pp. 15–19. 1950.

8937. King, J. Competition between established and newly sown grass species. Journal of the British Grassland Society. 26(4):-221–230. 1971.

8938. King, J., and G. E. Davis. The effect of dalapon on the species of hill grassland. Journal of British Grassland Society. 18:52–55. 1963.

8939. King, J., and R. Goss. Velvetgrass control. Proceedings Northwest Turf Conference. 12:13–14. 1958.

8940. King, J. W. Factors affecting the heating and damage of Merion Kentucky bluegrass *(Poa pratensis* L.) sod under simulated shipping conditions. Ph.D. Thesis, Michigan State University. 161 pp. 1970.

8941. ______. Factors affecting the heating and damage of Merion Kentucky bluegrass sod under simulated shipping conditions. Michigan Turfgrass Report pp. 7–8. Summer, 1970.

8942. ______. The two-year turfgrass management program at Michigan State University. USGA Green Section Record. 8(6):-12–13. 1970.

8943. ______. Winter injury to bermudagrass. Southern Turfgrass Association Quarterly News Bulletin. 1971.

8944. King, J. W. and J. B. Beard. Soil and management factors affecting the rooting capability of organic and mineral grown sod. Agronomy Abstracts, p. 53. 1967.

8945. ______. Measuring rooting of sodded turfs. Agronomy Journal. 61(4):497–498. 1969.

8946. ______. Post harvest sod heating. Research Report 104. Michigan State University Agricultural Experiment Station. pp. 3–4. October, 1969.

8947. ______. Physiological mechanisms and cultural factors affecting Merion Kentucky bluegrass *(Poa pratensis* L.) sod heating during shipment. Agronomy Abstracts. 62:69. 1970.

8948. ______. Postharvest cultural practices affecting the rooting of Kentucky bluegrass sods grown on organic and mineral soils. Agronomy Journal. 64(3):259–262. 1972.

8949. King, J. W. and C. R. Skogley. Effect of nitrogen and phosphorus placements and rate on turfgrass establishment. Agronomy Journal. 61(1):4–6. 1969.

8950. King, L. D. The effect of varying rates of liquid sewage sludge on soil properties and yield and chemical composition of Coastal bermudagrass and rye. Ph.D. Thesis, University of Georgia. 1971.

8951. King, L. D., and H. D. Morris. Land disposal of liquid sewage sludge: I. The effect on yield, in vivo digestibility, and chemical composition of Coastal bermudagrass *(Cynodon dactylon* L. Pers.). Journal of Environmental Quality. 1(3):325–329. 1972.

8952. King, L. J., and J. A. Kramer. A review of the crabgrass, *Digitaria ischaemum* and *D. sanguinalis* with notes on their preemergence control in turf. Proceedings Northeastern Weed Control Conference. 9:359–363. 1955.

8953. King, W. R. Effective labor management on institutional grounds. Ohio Turfgrass Conference Proceedings. pp. 76–79. 1970.

8954. Kindig, E. L. How much does it cost to provide and maintain equipment needs for parks? Exposition Conference. Southern California. 3 pp. 1966.

8955. Kirby, R. S. The take-all disease of cereals and grasses caused by *Ophiobolus cariceti* (Berkeley and Broome) Saccardo. New York Agricultural Experiment Station Memoir. 88. 45 pp. 1925.

8956. Kirk, L. E. A dry-land turf grass. Turf Culture. 1(2):105–110. 1939.

8958. Kirkpatrick, S. Lawn maintenance problems.—Part IV. Selling the maintenance service. University of Florida Turf Management Conference Proceedings. 3:95–97. 1955.

8959. ______. Soluble fertilizers in the commercial spray program. Proceedings of University of Florida Turf-Grass Management Conference. 9:208–210. 1961.

8960. Kiser, C. F. Fungicides and new developments in fungicides. Proceedings of the Texas Turfgrass Conference. 20:3–4. 1965.

8961. ______. Golf course management. Proceedings Annual Texas Turfgrass Conference. 21:63. 1966.

8962. ______. Aerification of tees and greens. Proceedings of the Annual Texas Turfgrass Conference. 22:67–68. 1967.

8963. Kitashiba, M., Y. Sasada, and N. Maekubo. Winter problems on bent greens. KGU Green Section Turf Research Bulletin. 6:47–57. 1964.

8964. Kitchen, J. W. Development of park use areas on sanitary landfills. Proceedings of the 19th Annual Texas Turfgrass Conference. 19:39–42. 1964.

8965. ______. Beautification of grounds: parks, schools, industrial sites. Proceedings of the Texas Turfgrass Conference. 20:17. 1965.

8966. ______. Assessing maintenance efficiency. Grounds Maintenance 2(2):34–35. 1967.

8967. ______. Lawn edging. Grounds Maintenance. 2(6):37. 1967.

8968. ______. Effluent water for golf irrigation. Grounds Maintenance. 7(12):58,61. 1972.

8969. Kitchen, J. W. and J. D. Kretschmer. Traffic control with concrete design. Grounds Maintenance. 3(5):25–27. 1968.

8970. Kitchener, R. A. Fungous disease control. New Zealand Institute For Turf Culture Newsletter. 80:113–124. 1972.

8971. Kitching, H. W. Golf course irrigation systems operations and maintenance. Proceedings, School of Soils, Fertilization & Turf Maintenance Green Section Royal Canadian Golf Association. pp. 46–50. 1951.

8972. Kitwoski, T. L. The effects of certain growth inhibitors and growth retardants on 'Kentucky 31' tall fescue *(Festuca arundinacea* Schreb.). M.S. Thesis, Southern Illinois University. 1971.

8973. Klaucke, E. The fungus and how it works. Greenkeepers Club of New England Newsletter. 8(8):4. 1936.

8974. ______. What happens inside a grass blade. Greenkeepers Club of New England Newsletter. 8(8):6. 1936.

8975. ______. What happens inside a grass blade. Golfdom. 11(2):63–64. 1937.

8976. ______. The fungus and how it works. Golfdom. 11(4):82–83. 1937.

8977. Klebesadel, L. J. Lawn weeds in Alaska: identification, control. Alaska Agricultural Experiment Station Bulletin. 34:1–32. 1963.

8978. ______. Influence of planting date and latitudinal provenance on winter survival, heading, and seed production of bromegrass and timothy in the subarctic. Crop Science. 10(5):594–598. 1970.

8979. ______. Nyctoperiod modification during late summer and autumn affects winter survival and heading of grasses. Crop Science. 11(4):507–511. 1971.

8980. Klebesadel, L. J., A. C. Wilton, R. L. Taylor, and J. J. Koranda. Fall growth behavior and winter survival of *Festuca rubra* and *Poa pratensis* in Alaska as influenced by latitude-of-adaptation. Crop Science. 4(3):-340–342. 1964.

8981. Klecka, A. Influence of treadirg on associations of grass growth. Herbage Abstracts. 8(2):171–172. 1938.

8983. Klingman, D. Crabgrass control. Mid-Atlantic Golf Course Superintendents Annual Conference Proceedings. pp. 59–64. 1960.

8984. Klingman, G. C. Weed control in zoysia, tall fescue, and bermudagrass turf. Proceedings, Southern Weed Conference. 15:69–73. 1962.

8985. Kloch, G. O., L. Boersma, D. G. Watts, and R. H. Brooks. Drainage with perforated plastic tubing. Agronomy Journal. 61(1):56–58. 1969.

8986. Klomp, G. J. A comparison of the drought resistance of selective native and naturalized grasses. M.S. Thesis, Iowa State University. 73 pp. 1939.

8987. ______. The use of wood-chips and nitrogen fertilizer in seeding scab ridges. Journal of Range Management. 21(1):31–36. 1968.

8988. Klomp, G. J., and A. C. Hull. Effects of 2,4-D on emergence and seedling growth of range grasses. Journal of Range Management. 21(2):67–70. 1968.

8989. Klomparens, W. Something on fungi. Golf Course Reporter. 21(6):22–23. 1953.

8990. ______. Fungus diseases and their control in cool season grasses. Golf Course Reporter. 22(1):29–30. 1954.

8991. ______. Fungus diseases and their control in cool season grasses. Proceedings of the Mid-Atlantic Association of Golf Course Superintendents Conference. pp. 43–46. 1954.

8992. ______. A study of *Helminthosporium sativum,* P. K. and B. as an unreported parasite of *Agrostis palustris,* Huds. Ph.D. Thesis, Michigan State University. 1955.

8993. ______. Disease development in turfgrass. Golf Course Reporter. 23(5):24. 1955.

8994. ______. Disease development is slow. Proceedings of Midwest Regional Turf Conference. p. 10. 1955.

8995. ______. Lawn grass diseases. Handbook on Lawns. Brooklyn Botanic Garden. pp. 122–132. 1956.

8996. ______. Disease control recommendations. USGA Journal and Turf Management. 11(4):28–29. 1958.

8997. ______. Antibiotics for tree, shrub and turf control. Parks, Golf Courses and Sports Grounds. 25(2):84–86. 1959.

8998. ______. Fungus and fungicides. Proceedings 37th International Turfgrass Conference. pp. 52–54. 1966.

8999. ______. The role of industry in pesticide development. A Patch of Green. Michigan and Border Cities GCSA Publication. pp. 6–11,14. May, 1971.

9000. Klostermeyer, E. C. Lawn billbugs —a new pest of lawns in eastern Washington. Irrigation Experimental Station (Prosser) E. M. 2349. 1964.

9001. Klotz, D. D. and E. A. Seholer. Tennis court construction: the ABC's from experience. Park Maintenance. 21(10):84–89. 1968.

9003. Klute, A., and W. R. Gardner. Tensiometer response time. Soil Science. 93(3):204–207. 1962.

9004. Knake, E. L. How herbicides work. Illinois Turfgrass Conference Proceedings. pp. 18–20. 1966.

9005. Kneebone, W. R. Seeded bermudagrass lawns. Arizona Garden Guides. A.F. 954. 3 pp.

9006. ______. Notes from the bermudagrass breeding program 1965. Turfgrass Research—Arizona Agricultural Experiment Station. Report 230. pp. 3–6. 1965.

9007. ______. Root growth of bermudagrass varieties at three mowing heights in 1966. Agricultural Experiment Station Turfgrass Report 240. University of Arizona. pp. 15–17. 1966.

9008. ______. Components of growth in bermudagrass varieties under varying nitrogen regimes. Agricultural Experiment Station Turfgrass Report 263. University of Arizona. pp. 9–16. 1970.

9009. ______. Bentgrass selection program. Arizona Turfgrass Conference Proceedings. pp. 25–28. 1972.

9010. Kneebone, W. R., and J.S. Hillman. Economics of turfgrass in Arizona. Progressive Agriculture in Arizona. 21(2):3,6. 1969.

9011. Kneebone, W. R. and G. V. Johnson Progress report on the Rincon Vista turfgrass research area. Agricultural Experiment Station Turfgrass Report 263. University of Arizona. pp. 17–22. 1970.

9012. ______. Bermudagrass trials—Tucson area. Arizona Turfgrass Conference Proceedings. pp. 22–24. 1972.

9013. Kneebone, W. R., and G. L. Major Bermudagrass variety effects on winter overseedings in 1965–1966. Turfgrass Research. University of Arizona Agricultural Experiment Station. Report 240. pp. 1–3. 1966.

9014. ______. Differential survival of cool season turfgrass species overseeded on different selections of bermudagrass. Crop Science. 9(2):153–155. 1969.

9015. Kneebone, W. R. and G. L. Seitz. Fertilizer trials on bermudagrass as recreational turfgrass. Agricultural Experiment Station Turfgrass Report 257. University of Arizona. pp. 17–20. 1969.

9016. ______. Differential reactions to and recovery from drouth stress among bermudagrass selections. Agricultural Experiment Station Turfgrass Report 250. University of Arizona. pp. 7–8. 1967–68.

9017. Knierim, J. A. Soil testing for the presence of harmful nematodes. Michigan Turfgrass Research Report. 1(2):17–22. 1963.

9018. Knight, D. M. Soil studies. Parks, Golf Courses, and Sports Grounds. 36(1):-80–86. 1970.

9019. Knight, W. E. The influence of photoperiod and temperature on growth, flowering, and seed production of Dallisgrass, *Paspalum dilatatum* Poir. Agronomy Journal. 47(12):555–559. 1955.

9020. Knight, W. E. and H. W. Bennett. Preliminary report of the effect of photoperiod and temperature on the flowering and growth of several southern grasses. Agronomy Journal. 45:268–269. 1953.

9021. Knowles, R. H. Evaluation of the behaviour of turfgrass species and cultivars to variations in management practices. University of Alberta. Progress Report. 1972.

9022. Knochenhauer, W. Inwieweit sind die temperature—u. feuchtigkeits—messungen unserer. flughäfen repräsentatin? Erfahr. Ber. d. D. Flugwetterd., 9. Folge Nr. 2, 1934.

9023. Kolb, J. Fertilizer—fungicides for snow mold control. Proceedings. Ninth Annual Northwest Turf Conference. 9:pp. 9–10. 1955.

9024. Knoop, W. E. "A truly balanced fertilizer benefits turf growers . . ." Better Crops With Plant Food. 50(3):28–29. 1971.

9025. ______: Establishing an athletic field with sod or seed. Park Maintenance. 25(12):11–12. 1972.

9026. ______. Turf nutrition. Weeds, Trees and Turf. 11(2):14. 1972.

9027. Knoop, W. E. and E. C. Roberts. Correlation between macro element deficiency symptomology and chemical composition of major warm season turfgrasses. Agronomy Abstracts. 62:70. 1970.

9028. Knowles, R. P. Comparison of grasses for dryland turf. Canada Journal of Plant Science. 41:602–606. 1961.

9029. ______. The agronomists' role in highway construction. Proceedings of 1st Western Canada Roadside Development Conference. pp. 23–25. 1964.

9030. ______. Subfreezing storage of grass seeds. Agronomy Journal. 59(1):86. 1967.

9031. ______. Nonrandom pollination in polycrosses of smooth bromegrass, *Bromus inermis* Leyss. Crop Science. 9(1):58–61. 1969.

9032. Knowles, R. P. and A. N. Ghosh. Isolation requirements for smooth bromegrass. *Bromus inermis* Leyss, as determined by a genetic marker. Agronomy Journal. 60(4):371–374. 1968.

9033. Knox, G. P. Experimenting with bent. The National Greenkeeper. 1(2):16. 1927.

9034. Knutti, H. J. and M. Hidiroglou. The effect of cutting and nitrogen treatments on yield, protein content and certain morphological characteristics of timothy and smooth bromegrass. Journal of the British Grassland Society. 22(1):35–41. 1967.

9036. Koch, W. Environmental factors affecting the germination of some annual grasses. British Weed Control Conference Proceedings. 9(1):14–19. 1968.

9037. Kock. A. Bevattning an Och Bevattningsanläggningar på Sportarenor. Weibulls Gräs Tips. pp. 285–287. 1966.

9038. Kock, A., and B. Langvad. Bevattning av och bevattningsan läggningar, på sportarenor. Weibulls Gräs Tips. pp. 109–118. 1962.

9039. Koehler, G. J. Selling materials to home owners. Proceedings of the Midwest Regional Turf Conference. pp. 73–75. 1965.

9040. Koers, V. Implications of roadside beautification. Proceedings of the Midwest Regional Turf Conference. pp. 74–76. 1966.

9041. Koerwer, J. F., J. E. Gallagher and C. Stark. Summary of performance of A-820 on ornamental turfgrasses. North Central Weed Control Conference Proceedings. 26:-90–92. 1971.

9042. Kohnke, H. The space between soil particles. Proceedings of 1965 Midwest Regional Turf Conference. pp. 10–13. 1965.

9043. ______. Soil pores in golf greens. Proceedings of the Midwest Regional Turf Conference. pp. 53–54. 1968.

9044. Kohnke, H. and R. Davis. Soil structure, aeration, and drainage. Proceedings of Midwest Regional Turf Conference. pp. 7–13. 1950.

9045. Kolterman, D. W. The development and characteristics of urea-form fertilizers. Proceedings of the 25th Annual Penn State Turfgrass Conference. pp. 52–58. 1956.

9046. Kolb, J. L. The role of plant nutrients. University of Florida Turf Management Conference Proceedings. 4:20–24. 1956.

9047. ______. Let's look at the grasses. New Mexico Turfgrass Conference Proceedings. 1:4–7. 1956.

9048. ______. Let's look at the grasses. Rocky Mountain Regional Turfgrass Conference Proceedings. 3:19–21. 1956.

9049. ______. Cultural practices influencing weed control. Golf Course Reporter. 25(3):10–14. 1957.

9050. ______. Fundamentals of equipment use. Golf Course Reporter. 31(9):22–30. 1963.

9051. ______. The super's future in golf. Golfdom 41(5):28–32, 74. 1967.

9052. Kollett, J. R., and J. A. DeFrance. Some effects of gibberellic acid on various turfgrasses. Golf Course Reporter. 27(3):30–32. 1959.

9053. ______. Crabgrass control with postemergence chemical treatment. Proceedings of the Northeastern Weed Control Conference. pp. 155–159. 1959.

9054. ______. Crabgrass troubles? Try chemicals! Rhode Island Agriculture. 5(3):4. 1959.

9055. Kollett, J. R., A. J. Wisniewski, and J. A. DeFrance. The effect of ureaform fertilizers in seedbeds for turfgrass. Park Maintenance. 11(5):12–20. 1958.

9056. Kolterman, D. W. Fall fertilization—a success. Golf Course Reporter. 26(8):25–26. 1958.

9057. ______. Nitrogen fertilizations—objectives and methods. Proceedings of the Twelfth Annual Northwest Turf Conference. 12:37–41. 1958.

9058. ______. Performance of compounded complete fertilizers containing ureaform nitrogen. Agronomy Abstracts. 51:90. 1959.

9059. ______. Objectives and methods in turfgrass fertilization. Guelph Turfgrass Conference Proceedings. pp. 16–18. 1959.

9060. Komblas, K. N. Biology and control of the lawn chinch bug, *Blissus insularis.* Ph.D. Thesis, Louisiana State University. 82 p. 1962.

9061. Konieczny, E. G. Potash experiments on turf grasses. Turf Bulletin. Massachussetts Turf and Lawn Grass Council. 5(3):4–8. 1969.

9062. Kohnke, H. Infiltration and pore sizes. Proceeding of the Midwest Regional Turf Conference. pp. 8–9. 1969.

9063. Konsilapa, C. Fertility needs of Pensacola bahiagrass and *Sericea lespedeza* on a severely eroded Loring soil. M.S. Thesis, Mississippi State University. 1972.

9065. Koths, J. S. Some microbiological aspects of degradation of thatch in turf. Agronomy Abstracts. 2:63. 1972.

9066. ______. Thatch. Park Maintenance. 25(7):17. 1972.

9067. ______. Concerning biological control of thatch in turf. USGA Green Section Record. 10(3):7–10. 1972.

9068. Koshy, T. K. Breeding systems in annual bluegrass, *Poa annua* L. Crop Science. 9(1):40–43. 1969.

9069. Koval, C. F. 1972 Suggested turf insect control guide. Department of Entomology, University of Wisconsin Publication. 1972.

9070. Kovitvadhi, K., and S. H. Kerr. Artificial diet for the zoysiagrass billbug, *(Sphenophorus ventaus vestius, (Coleoptera: Curculionidae).* and notes on its biology. The Florida Entomologist. 51(4):247–250. 1968.

9071. Kozelnicky, G. M. Fairy ring. Turf-Grass Times. 3(8):1,4,5,15. 1968.

9072. ______. First report of stripe smut on bluegrass in Georgia. The Plant Disease Reporter. 53(7):580. 1969.

9073. Kozelnicky, G. M. and W. N. Garrett. The occurrence of zoysia rust in Georgia. The Plant Disease Reporter. 50(11):839. 1966.

9074. Kozelnicky, G. M. and J. B. Moncrief. The unusual occurrence of a stinkhorn fungus on golf turf. The Plant Disease Reporter. 50(11):840. 1966.

9075. Kozelnicky, G. M., F. F. Hendrix, and F. A. Pokorny. Turfgrass research reports 1969–1970, Georgia. Southern Regional Turf Research Committee Report, Virginia Polytechnic Institute. pp. 8–12. 1970.

9076. Kozlowski, T. T. Soil aeration prime factor in development of turf. Golfdom. 25(3):48–49,85–87. 1951.

9077. Kraft, J. M. and R. M. Endo. Zoospore infection of bentgrass roots by *Pythium aphanidermatum* Phytopathology. 56(2):149. 1966.

9078. Kraft, J. M., and R. M. Endo and D. C. Erwin. Infection of primary roots of bentgrass by zoospores of *Pythium aphanidermatum* Phytopathology. 57(1):86–90. 1967.

9079. Krambule, J. F. Compressed air drains irrigation systems. The Golf Superintendent. 35(8):16–18,41. 1967.

9080. Kramer, J. Lawns. Gardening and Home Landscaping Guide. Arco Publishing Co., Inc., New York. pp. 12–19. 1968.

9081. Kramer, N. W. Keeping a tight bentgrass turf. Proceedings of the Midwest Regional Turf Conference. pp. 35–37. 1964.

9082. ______. Fairway improvement—second report. Proceedings of the 1965 Midwest Regional Turf Conference. pp. 39–41. 1965.

9083. ______. Manicuring fairway turf—3rd report. Proceedings of the Midwest Regional Turf Conference. pp. 34–36. 1966.

9084. Kramer, P. J. Causes of injury to plants resulting from flooding of the soil. Plant Physiology. 26:722–736. 1951.

9085. Kralovec, R. D., and W. A. Morgan. Condensation products of urea and formaldehyde as fertilizer with controlled nitrogen availability. Journal of Agriculture and Food Chemistry. 2(2):92–95 1954.

9086. Kreitlow, K. W. Ustilago striaeformis. II. Temperature as a factor influencing development of smutted plants of *Poa pratensis* L. and germination of fresh chlamydospores. Phytopathology. 33(11):1055–1063. 1943.

9087. Kreitlow, K. W., and F. V. Juska. Susceptibility of Merion and other Kentucky bluegrass varieties to stripe smut *(Ustilago striiformis)* Agronomy Journal. 51(10):596–597. 1959.

9088. ______. Lawn diseases, how to control them. USDA. Home and Garden Bulletin. No. 61. 16 pp. 1960.

9089. ______. A comparison of fungicides applied with and without latex for controlling turf diseases. Agronomy Abstracts. p. 106. 1964.

9090. ______. A comparison of eight fungicides applied with and without latex for controlling turf diseases. The Plant Disease Reporter. 48(6):433–435. 1964.

9091. ______. Lawn diseases, how to control them. Part II. The Cemeterian. 32(6):9,10,43,44. 1968.

9092. ______. Lawn diseases, how to control them. Part III. The Cemeterian. 32(7):9,10,43,44. 1968.

9093. ______. Lawn diseases, how to control them. The Cemeterian. 32(8):46. 1968.

9094. Kreitlow, K. W., and W. M. Myers. Prevalence and distribution of stripe smut or *Poa pratensis* in some pastures of Pennsylvania. Phytopathology. 34(4):411–415. 1944.

9095. ______. Resistance to crown rust in *Festuca elatior* and *F. Elatior* var. *Arundinacea.* Phytopathology. 37(1):59–63. 1947.

9096. Kreitlow, K. W., F. V. Juska and R. T. Haard. A rust on *Zoysia japonica* new to North America. The Plant Disease Reporter. 49(3):185–186. 1965.

9097. Kreitlow, K. W., H. Sherwin and C. L. Lefebvre. Susceptibility of tall and meadow fescues to *Helminthosporium* infection. Plant Disease Reporter. 34(6):189–190. 1950.

9098. Kreiyinger, E. J. Lawns. Washington Agricultural Experiment Station Bulletin. 364:1–4. 1947.

9099. Krenek, K. Landscaping coordinated with turf. Proceedings of the Texas Turfgrass Conference. 18:24–25. 1963.

9100. Krenzer, E. G., and D. N. Moss. Carbon dioxide compensation in grasses. Crop Science. 9(5):619–621. 1969.

9101. Kresge, C. B. Bermudagrass. Maryland Agricultural Extension Service Agronomist. 1(2), 1964.

9102. Kresge, C. B., and D. P. Satchell. Gaseous loss of ammonia from nitrogen fertilizers applied to soils. Agronomy Journal. 52(2):104–107 1960.

9103. Kresge, C. B. and S. E. Younts. Effect of nitrogen source on yield and nitrogen content of bluegrass forage. Agronomy Journal. 54(2):149–152. 1962.

9104. ______. Response of orchardgrass to potassium and nitrogen fertilization on Wickham silt loam. Agronomy Journal. 55(2):161–164. 1963.

9105. Kress, A. What the contractor left me. Wisconsin Turfgrass Conference Proceedings. p. 1. 1964.

9106. Kreutzer, W. A. Ecology of soil microorganisms and its relation to turf fertilization. Rocky Mountain Regional Turfgrass Conference Proceedings. 10:38–40. 1963.

9107. Krogman, K. K. Evapotranspiration by irrigated grass as related to fertilizer. Canadian Journal of Plant Science. 47:281–287. 1967.

9108. Kruger, F. The putting greens at Olympia Fields Country Club. USGA Green Section Bulletin. 8(9):190–191. 1928.

9109. Krusberg, L. R. A new nematode in turfgrass. Weeds, Trees and Turf. 4(7):-14–15. 1965.

9110. Kubo, T. Weeds control in summer. K.G.U. Green Section Turf Research Bulletin. 4:25–40. 1963.

9111. ______. Construction of the green bed. KGU Green Section Turf Research Bulletin. 5:19–35. 1963.

9112. ______. Symposium at the 14th K. G. U. turf conference. K. G. U. Green Section Turf Research Bulletin. 15:13–28. 1968–6.

9113. Kubo, T., and N. Maekubo. Soil conditions for the seaside bent turf, Part 3. KGU Green Section Turf Research Bulletin. 4:15–18. 1963.

9114. ______. Drainage for the seaside bent turf, Part 2. KGU Green Section Turf Research Bulletin. 4:19–24. 1963.

9115. ______. Practical theory in putting green construction. KGU Green Section Turf Research Bulletin. 4:49–65. 1963.

9116. ______. Effects on the soil conditioners for zoysia turf, Part 3. KGU Green Section Turf Research Bulletin. 5:37–52. 1963.

9117. ______. Tifton hybrid bermudagrasses, how in Japan. KGU Green Section Turf Research Bulletin. 6:23–29. 1964.

9118. ______. Effects on the soil conditioners for turf, Part 5. KGU Green Section Turf Research Bulletin. 9:35–42. 1965.

9119. ______. Effects on the soil conditioners for turf, Part 6. KGU Green Section Turf Research Bulletin. 10:35–44. 1966.

9120. Kubo, T., N. Maekubo, S. Murase, and Y. Okumoto. Effects on the soil conditioners for zoysia turf, Part 4. KGU Green Section Turf Research Bulletin. 7:31–54. 1964.

9121. Kucera, C. L. Identification of grasses by vegetative characters. Proceedings, Missouri Lawn and Turf Conference. pp. 5–11. 1960.

9122. Kucera, C. L., and R. C. Dahlman. Root-rhizome relationships in fire-treated stands of big bluestem. *Andropogon gerardi* Vitman. American Midland Nature. 80(1):-268–271. 1968.

9123. Kucera, C. L., and M. Koelling. The influence of fire on composition of central Missouri prairie. American Midland Nature. 72(1):142–147. 1964.

9124. Kuck, L. E. and R. C. Tongg. Lawns and other ground covers. The Modern Tropical Garden. Tongg Publishing Co., Hawaii. pp. 151–156. 1955.

9125. Kuhn, A. O. and W. B. Kemp. Response of different strains of Kentucky bluegrass to cutting. Journal of the American Society of Agronomy. 31:892–895. 1939.

9126. Kuitert, L. C. Part IV—insects and their control. Proceedings, Second Annual University of Florida Turf Conference. 2:19–21. 1954.

9127. ______. Fundamentals of insect control. Proceedings of University of Florida Turf-Grass Management Conference. 11:8–12. 1963.

9128. Kuitert, L. C. and G. C. Nutter. Chinch bug control and subsequent renovation of St. Augustine grass lawns. Florida Agricultural Experiment Station. Circular. S50:1–10. 1952.

9129. Kulfinski, F. B. Establishment of vegetation on highway backslopes in Iowa. Iowa Highway Research Board Bulletin. 11:-1–35. 1957.

9130. Kundtz, R. C. Miami Beach parks department turf and landscape program. Proceedings University of Florida Turf-Grass Management Conference. 12:126–127. 1964.

9131. Kunkle, S. H. Effects of road salt on a Vermont stream. Highway Research Abstracts. 42(10):4. 1972.

9132. Kunze, J. R. The effect of compaction of different golf green mixtures on plant growth. M.S. Thesis, Texas A&M University. 1956.

9133. Kunze, R. J., M. H. Ferguson, and J. B. Page. The effects of compaction on golf green mixtures. USGA Journal and Turf Management. 10(6):24–27. 1957.

9134. Kurtz, K. W. Effect of nitrogen fertilization on the establishment, density, and strength of Merion Kentucky bluegrass sod grown on a mineral soil. M.S. Thesis, Western Michigan University. 45 pp. 1967.

9135. ______. Slow release nitrogen sources. Park Maintenance. 24(7):19. 1971.

9136. ______. Colorants. Park Maintenance. 24(7):23. 1971.

9137. ______. Soil amendments. Park Maintenance. 25(7):15. 1972.

9138. ______. *Poa annua.* Park Maintenance 25(7):19. 1972.

9139. Kurtz, K. and J. Van Dam. Color it green. Park Maintenance. 23(7):22–23. 1970.

9140. Kurtz, K. W., A. Mooser, and H. Mees. Evaluation of the Purr-Wick rootzone system under western semi-arid conditions. Western Landscaping News. 11(6):12–14. 1971.

9141. Kurup, K. P. Growth analysis and regrowth potential of three cool season grasses in spring. M.S. Thesis, Virginia Polytechnic Institute. 1972.

9142. Kuwabara, Y. The first seedling leaf in grass systematics. Journal of Japanese Botany. 35(5):139–145. 1960.

9143. Kuwabara, Y. Systematic and autecological studies on grasses. Advancing Frontiers of Plant Sciences. 15:77–86. 1966.

9144. Kuykendall, R. Control of coco or nut grass on Southern golf courses. USGA Green Section Bulletin. 9(12):225–226. 1929.

9145. Kyd, S. and J. W. Thomas. Control of soil insects in the lawn. Proceedings, Missouri Lawn and Turf Conference. p. 85. 1960.

9146. Lafkin, W. E. Spring lawn management. Golf and Lawn Supply Corporation. 7 pp.

9147. ______. Making the new lawn. Golf and Lawn Supply Corp. White Plains, New York. 8 pp.

9148. ______. Wartime fertilizer developments and future trends. Golfdom. 20(3):-35, 38, 69. 1946.

9149. ______. Renovating the established lawn. Golf and Lawn Supply Corp. White Plains, New York. 12 pp. 1949.

9150. ______. Crabgrass control in 1950. Rutgers University Short Course in Turf Management. 19:41–47. 1951.

9151. ______. New lawn grasses. Midwest Turf News and Research. 6(3):1,4. 1952.

9152. ______. Lafkin concludes new lawn grasses. Midwest Turf News and Research. 6(4):2–3. 1952.

9153. ______. New lawn grasses. New York State Turf Association Bulletin. 34:-131–132. 1952.

9154. ______. Athletic fields and their maintenance. New York State Turf Association Bulletin. 59:229. 1957.

9155. Laflamme, G. Traitement du sol contre la compaction des terrains de golf. M.S. Thesis, Macdonald College. 1971.

9156. LaFontaine, G. Cemetery equipment maintenance. 42nd Annual Michigan Turfgrass Conference Proceedings. 1:91–92. 1972.

9157. LaGasse, A. L. Maintenance of park turf. Texas Turf Conference Proceedings. pp. 12–14. 1950.

9158. Lagasse, R. Weed control in home lawns. Proceedings of University of Florida Turf-Grass Management Conference. 8:81–87. 1960.

9159. Lage, D. P. and E. C. Roberts. Influence of nitrogen and a calcined clay soil conditioner on development of Kentucky bluegrass turf from seed and sod. Proceedings of the Society for Horticultural Science. 84:-630–635. 1964.

9161. Lair, J. A look at the Cotton Bowl. Golf Course Reporter. 31(8):18. 1963.

9162. Laird, A. S. A study of the root systems of some important sod-forming grasses.Florida Agricultural Experiment Station Bulletin 211. 27 pp. 1930.

9163. Lake, N. Preparation and maintenance of large turf areas. Proceedings of University of Florida Turf-Grass Management Conference. 9:174–176. 1961.

9164. Lambe, R. C. How to control fairy ring. Grounds Maintenance. 1(7):8–9. 1966.

9165. Lambert, L. E. Maintaining a satisfactory *Poa annua* green. Golfdom. 26(6):43. 1952.

9166. ______. Lawns. Golf Course Reporter. 28(7):66. 1960.

9167. ______. GCSA guide for golf course construction. Golfdom. 35(4):50, 52, 92, 94. 1961.

9168. Lambert, M. Panogen turf fungicide: Morton's New chemical for lawn spraymen. Weeds and Turf. pp. 12, 17. April, 1963.

9169. Lambert, W. A. Establishment and maintenance of campus turf. Turf Clippings. University of Massachussetts. 2(1):A-51 to A-55. 1966.

9170. Lamper, J. F. and E. C. Roberts. Development of golf course turf on military land for recreational purposes. Agonomy Abstracts. 51:90. 1959.

9171. Lamson-Scribner, F. Sand-binding grasses. USDA Yearbook, 1898 pp. 405–420. 1899.

9172. Lance, P. Attack on burnout. Golfdom. 44(7):48–49. 1970.

9173. ______. Whitemarsh gives *Poa* the heave-hoa. Weeds, Trees, and Turf. 9(8):26–27. 1970.

9174. Land, H. Seeding, sodding, top dressing and contouring the putting greens. Proceedings of the 20th Annual Northwest Turfgrass Conference. pp. 82–83. 1966.

9175. Langdale, G. W., and J. R. Thomas. Soil salinity effects on absorption of nitrogen, phosphorus, and protein synthesis by coastal bermudagrass. Agronomy Journal. 63(5):708–711. 1971.

9176. Lamson-Schribner, F. Grass gardens. USDA Yearbook, 1895. pp. 301–308. 1896.

9177. Lange, A. H. Principles of selective weed control. Southern California Turfgrass Institute Proceedings. pp. 1–2. 1963.

9178. Langer, R. H. M. A study of leaf growth in timothy *(Phleum pratense).* Journal of the British Grassland Society. 9(4):-275–284. 1954.

9179. ______. Growth and nutrition of timothy *(Phleum pratense).* I. The life history of individual tillers. Annals of Applied Biology. 44(1):166–187. 1956.

9180. ______. A study of growth in swards of timothy and meadow fescue. I. Uninterrupted growth. Journal of Agricultural Science. 51(3):347–352. 1958.

9181. ______. A study of growth in swards of timothy and meadow fescue. II. The effects of cutting treatments. Journal of Agricultural Science. 52(3):273–281. 1959.

9182. ______. Tillering in herbage grasses. Herbage Abstracts. 33(3):141–148. 1963.

9183. Langer, R. H. M., and G. J. A. Ryle. Vegetative Proliferation in Herbage grasses. Journal of The British Grassland Society. 13(1):29–33. 1958.

9184. Langford, G. S. Grub control in turf. Proceedings of the Mid-Atlantic Association of Greenkeepers Conference. pp. 42–43. 1949.

9185. ______. Insecticides for grass. Proceedings of the Mid-Atlantic Association of Greenkeepers Conference. pp. 5–11. 1951.

9186. ______. Controlling troublesome insects on lawns, greens and other turfgrass areas. Virginia. Turfgrass Conference. pp. 42–46. 1963.

9187. Langford, W. R. and E. M. Evans. Summer grasses differ in their responses to nitrogen. Chilean Nitrate Farm Forum No. 55:16. 1955.

9188. Langhans, R. W. and A. Spomer. Soil moisture and aeration—the basic concept of soil. The Golf Superintendent. 35(7):-10, 12, 35. 1967.

9189. Langille, A. R. and G. W. McKee. Early growth of crownvetch under reduced light. Agronomy Journal. 62(4):552–554. 1970.

9190. Langton, A. California greens problems cover wide range. Golfdom. 4(8):-35–37. 1930.

9191. ______. East works most beneath the summer sun—but coast greens work is never done. Golfdom. 5(1):25–27. 1931.

9192. ______. Some details California is learning about watering. Golfdom. 5(4):42,-46, 48. 1931.

9193. ______. California's bermuda fairways stubbornly in command. Golfdom. 6(5):21–24. 1932.

9194. ______. Coast costs at all-time low. Golfdom. 12(10):15–18. 1938.

9195. Langton, W. E. Some ideas on brown patch. Greenkeepers Club of New England Newsletter. 3(9):2–4. 1931.

9196. ______. Vitamin B, still in test stage. Golfdom. 14(4):56, 58, 60. 1940.

9197. ______. Workers must fit their jobs. Golfdom. 14(10):25–28. 1940.

9198. Langvad, B. Gräsklippare och Klippning. Weibulls Gräs Tips. pp. 73–80. 1961.

9199. ______. Luftningsmaskiner för luftning av greens och annan turf. Weibulls Gräs Tips. pp. 81–82. 1961.

9200. ______. Orienterande gräsförsök I norrland och nord-norge. Weibulls Gräs Tips. pp. 89–95. 1962.

9201. ______*Poa Annua,* Vitgröe. Weibulls Gräs Tips. pp. 95–99. 1962.

9202. ______. Anläggning Av Grasområ den vid arlanda flygfält. Weibulls Gräs Tips. pp. 105–106. 1962.

9203. ______. Omläggning av Täby galoppbana våren 1961. Weibulls Gräs Tips. pp. 107–108. 1962.

9204. Lamson-Scribner, F. Division of agrostology. USDA Yearbook, 1897. pp. 160–175. 1898.

9205. Langvad, B. Jacobsen's F-tractor for rational turf cutting. Weibulls Gräs Tips. 8:165–168. 1964.

9206. ______. The W's—method of constructing advanced sport turf. Weibulls Gräs Tips. 8:168–174. 1964.

9207. ______. An investigation of 8 grass species: germination—time, growth and total length 20 days after sowing. Weibulls Gräs Tips. 8:186–190. 1964.

9208. ______. Our *Agrostis* species as turf-grasses. Weibulls Gräs Tips. 8:195–198. 1964.

9209. ______. Aerification of turf culture. Weibulls Gräs Tips. 8:202–203. 1964.

9210. ______. Berol snow-kill. Weibulls Gräs Tips. 8:204–205. 1964.

9211. ______. Construction and maintenance of football turf. Weibulls Gräs Tips. pp. 213–250. June, 1965.

9212. ______. Försök med Turfgräs I Stadsplanteringar 1963–1965. Weibulls Gräs Tips. 9:266–273. 1966.

9213. ______. Gräs under Alléträd. Weibulls Gräs Tips. 9:274–278. 1966.

9214. ______. Återställning av Grustäker. Weibulls Gräs Tips. 9:279–282. 1966.

9215. ______. Etablering av Gräskultur I Uppfyllda Hamnbassängen I Landskrona. Weibulls Gräs Tips. 9:283–284. 1966.

9216. ______. Jägersro Galoppbana. Weibulls Gräs Tips. 9:289–295. 1966.

9217. ______. Ball-bouncing and ball-rolling as a function of mowing height and kind of soil have been studied at Weibullsholm. Weibulls Gräs Tips. pp. 355–357. 1967–1968.

9218. ______. *Poa pratensis,* one of the main turfgrass species in Sweden. Weibulls Gräs Tips. pp. 358–370. 1967–1968.

9219. ______. Variety trials with fine leafed red fescue. Weibulls Gräs Tips. pp. 371–376. 1967–1968.

9220. ______. The Weigrass—method for construction of football-grounds in grass. Weibulls Gräs Tips. pp. 377–379. 1967–1968.

9221. ______. Result of an analyse and evaluating the turfstandard on some international football arenas. Weibulls Gräs Tips. pp. 380–387. 1967–1968.

9222. ______. Soil heating under sports turf. The Groundsman. 23(1):42–45. 1969.

9223. Langvad, B. and W. Weibull. Turfgrasses in Sweden. Proceedings of the First International Turfgrass Research Conference. p. 13. 1969.

9224. Langvad, B. Breeding and trial techniques in Sweden. Proceedings of the First International Turfgrass Research Conference. pp. 86–87. 1969.

9225. ______. Soil heating under sports turf in Sweden. Proceedings of the First International Turfgrass Research Conference. pp. 252–257. 1969.

9226. ______. Testing variety resistance of *Poa pratensis* against *Helminthosporium* spp. Proceedings of the First International Turfgrass Research Conference. pp. 362–365. 1969.

9227. ______. Turfgrass advisory services in Sweden. Proceedings of the First International Turfgrass Research Conference. p. 433. 1969.

9228. ______. Seeding techniques for establishing grass on Swedish roadsides. Proceedings of the first International Turfgrass Research Conference. pp. 580–582. 1969.

9229. ______. Vara Gronytor—anlaggning och skotsel. 184 p. 1971.

9230. Laning, E. R. and V. H. Freed. Growth inhibition of grasses. Western Weed Control Conference 155. 1952.

9231. Lanphear, F. O. The landscape can reduce pollution. Proceedings of the Midwest Regional Turf Conference. pp. 15–16. 1970.

9232. Lantz, H. L. Report of experiences and research with fine turf for 1943. Iowa State Horticultural Society. 78:215–218. 1943.

9233. ______. Turf research at Ames. Golfdom. 18(4):14–15,44. 1944.

9234. ______. Iowa conference. Golfdom. 18(4):28,30. 1944.

9235. ______. Brains and hard work bring Iowa thru tough year. Golfdom. 19(1):-32. 1945.

9236. ______. Outlines a season program for maintenance. Golfdom. 19(4):14. 1945.

9237. ______. A plan for rejuvenating run down greens. Golfdom. 19(5):22,24. 1945.

9238. ______. Bent grass trials in Iowa. Project 760, Iowa Agricultural Experiment Station Report. 6 pp. 1945.

9239. ______. Lawns without weeds. Iowa Agricultural Experiment Station Paper. 9 pp. 1945.

9240. ______. Iowa reports on summer tests of 2,4-D. Golfdom. 20(1):33,36,38,40. 1946.

9241. ______. Iowa bent trials promise better strains. Golfdom. 20(3):13–14,68–69. 1946.

9242. Lantz, H. L., L. C. Grove and E. P. Sylvester. Home lawn. Iowa Agricultural Experiment Station Bulletin. P80:645–664. 1946.

9243. Lantz, H. L. Turf garden, 1947. Iowa Greenkeepers Association. 16:2. 1947.

9244. ______. Insect and disease controls feature Iowa short course. Golfdom. 22(4):-82–84. 1948.

9245. ______. Iowa greenkeepers hold 15th annual meet at Ames. Golfdom. 23(5):-83–87. 1949.

9246. ______. Turf fungicide investigations at Iowa State College. Central Plains Turfgrass Conference Proceedings. 1:46–51. 1950.

9247. ______. Tips on application of fungicides. Golfdom. 27(8):42. 1953.

9248. ______. A management program for greens. Iowa Greenkeepers and Turf Association 20th Annual Short Course. March, 1954.

9249. Lamson-Scribner, F. Lawns and lawn making. USDA Yearbook, 1897. pp. 355–372. 1898.

9250. Lantz, H. L. Cool season grasses-bluegrass, fescue, bent. Golf Course Reporter. 23(2):32–37. 1955.

9251. ______. Kentucky bluegrass still "old reliable" in north. Golfdom. 29(7):36,-38,40,44. 1955.

9252. Lantz, H. L. and B. Taylor. Maintenance of athletic turf. Iowa State University Leaflet. 1954.

9253. Lantz, H. L., L. C. Grove, E. P. Sylwester, and A. E. Cott. The home lawn. Iowa Agricultural Experiment Station Bulletin P80. 18 pp. 1948.

9254. La Plante, M. G. A comparative cost analysis of golf course turf maintenance in Georgia. Georgia Agricultural Experiment Station Research Bulletin 108. 1972.

9255. Lapp, W. S. A study of factors affecting the growth of lawn grasses. Pennsylvania Academy of Science Proceedings. 17:-117–148. 1943.

9256. Laptev, A. A. Gazony (ustroĭstvq ukhod za nimi). Akademiia Arkitektury Ukrainskoff Ssr. Kiev. 74 pp. 1955.

9257. Large, R. L. Effect of sulfur and micronutrients on composition and yield of Midland bermudagrass. M.S. Thesis, Oklahoma State University. 31 pp. 1966.

9258. Larson, A. H. A study of some turf grasses. Greenkeepers' Reporter. 2(8–9):1–3. 1934.

9259. ______. Chemicals in weed control. The Greenkeeper's Reporter. 13(3):5–7. 1945.

9260. ______. Functions of water in plants. The Greenkeeper's Reporter. 13(2):-22–23. 1945.

9261. Larson, E. M. Utah's roadside development program. Ohio Short Course on Roadside Development. 22:30–36. 1963.

9262. Larson, K. L. Turf research at North Dakota agricultural experiment station. Scotts Turfgrass Research Seminar. p. 47. 1968.

9263. Larson, R. A. The practical approach to handling the power golf cart problem. Wisconsin Turfgrass Conference Proceedings. 3 pp. 1962.

9264. ______. The Wisconsin golf course superintendents association. Wisconsin Turfgrass Conference Proceedings. 2 pp. 1965.

9265. ______. Minor element deficiencies. Proceedings of the 37th Annual Turfgrass Conference. pp. 55–56. 1966.

9266. ______. Pebble Beach irrigation system built around plastics. The Golf Superintendent. 36(4):22,23,26. 1968.

9267. Larson, R. A. and J. R. Love. Minor element deficiency symptoms in turfgrass. Golfdom. 41(8):31–34. 1967.

9268. LaRue, C. D. The time to cut dandelions. Science. 80(2128):350. 1935.

9269. LaRue, M. E., D. R. Nielsen, and R. M. Hagan. Soil water flux below a ryegrass root zone. Agronomy Journal. 60(6):625–629. 1968.

9270. Latch, G. C. M. Control of brown patch. New Zealand Institute for Turf Culture Newsletter. 42:10–11. 1966.

9271. ______. Disease control in turf. New Zealand Institute for Turf Culture Newsletter. 53:5–7. 1968.

9272. ______. Turf diseases of bowling greens. New Zealand Institute for Turf Culture Newsletter. 56:10–11. 1968.

9273. Latham, J. M. Symposium—controlling thatch development. Part II—fertilization. University of Florida Turf Management Conference Proceedings. 3:52–54. 1955.

9274. ______. Results of the turfgrass soil fertility tests. Proceedings. Tenth Southeastern Turfgrass Conference. 10:pp. 7–16. 1956.

9275. ______. Choosing a lawn grass for the South. Southern Seedsman. 19(4):46–48,-62–63. 1956.

9276. ______. Building and planting putting greens—a summary. Proceedings Eleventh Southeastern Turfgrass Conference pp. 9–12. 1957.

9277. ______. Trends in management practices in the southeast. Proceedings of University of Florida Turf Management Conference. 6:30–34. 1958.

9278. ______. South shall rise again—with turfgrass. Golfdom. 32(5):40,77–78. 1958.

9279. ______. Area measurement and equipment calibration. Proceedings Twelfth Southeastern Turfgrass Conference. pp. 20–25. 1958.

9280. ______. Compost vs. commercial materials for topdressing. University of Florida Turf-Grass Management Conference Proceedings. 7:23–26. 1959.

9281. ______. Water movement in soils. Auburn University Annual Turfgrass Short Course. pp. 24–25. 1960.

9282. ______. Turf roundup. Rocky Mountain Regional Turfgrass Conference Proceedings. 7:33–34. 1960.

9283. ______. Turf problems and maintenance practices—past, present and future. Proceedings of Texas Turfgrass Conference. 15:52–57. 1960.

9284. ______. Comparison of water sources. USGA Journal and Turf Management. 13(1):31–32. 1960.

9285. ______. Water movement in soils. Proceedings of University of Florida Turf-Grass Management Conference. 9:41–42. 1961.

9286. ______. Turf roundup. Rocky Mountain Regional Turfgrass Conference Proceedings. 8:15–17. 1961.

9287. ______. Public relations in turf management. Proceedings of the Texas Turfgrass Conference. 16:13–15. 1961.

9288. ______. Principles and practices of overseeding. Proceedings of the Texas Turfgrass Conferece. 16:48–50. 1961.

9289. ______. Overseeding winter greens. Golf Course Reporter. 30(9):56–57. 1962.

9290. ______. Winter grass overseeding —in various southern trials. International Turf-Grass Conference Proceedings. 33:9. 1962.

9291. ______. Fertilization in relation to disease control. Proceedings of the Missouri Lawn and Turf Conference. pp. 36–37. 1962.

9292. ______. Natures sequences of weed infestations. Proceedings of the Midwest Regional Turf Conference. pp. 36–39. 1963.

9293. ______. Soil analysis interpreting analytical results and case histories. Supplement to Proceedings for Oklahoma Turfgrass Conference. pp. 5–7. 1963.

9294. ______. Nitrogen—the key to better turf. Rocky Mountain Regional Turfgrass Conference Proceedings. 10:10–11. 1963.

9295. ______. Nature's sequences of weed infestations. Southern California Turfgrass Institute Proceedings. pp. 18–21. 1963.

9296. ______. Fall preparation . . .? Proceedings of 1963 Turf Conference. Southern Turfgrass Association. pp. 1–3. 1963.

9297. ______. Aeration and spiking. Proceedings of 1963 Turf Conference. Southern Turfgrass Association pp. 7–8. 1963.

9298. ______. New developments in turfgrass management. Proceedings of the Annual Texas Turfgrass Conference. 18:1–3. 1963.

9299. ______. The role of sewage sludge. Turf Clippings. University of Massachusetts. 1(8):A–49 to A–51. 1963.

9300. ______. Some principles in the development of weed populations. Proceedings of the Texas Turfgrass Conference. 19:2–3. 1964.

9301. ______. Overseeding bermudagrass greens—the seed mixtures. Proceedings of the Texas Turfgrass Conference. 19:18–19. 1964.

9302. ______. Care of bent greens—winter maintenance. Proceedings of the Texas Turfgrass Conference. 19:24–25. 1964.

9303. ______. Turf stress—warm and hot conditions. Proceedings of the Midwest Regional Turf Conference. pp. 60–63. 1964.

9304. ______. Management problems with warm season grasses in the Missouri area. Proceedings of the Missouri Lawn and Turf Conference. pp. 4–7. 1964.

9305. ______. Keep bluegrass growing. Proceedings of the 1965 Midwest Regional Turf Conference. pp. 44–45. 1965.

9306. ______. Soil test results and interpretation. Proceedings of the 1965 Midwest Regional Turf Conference. pp. 45–46. 1965.

9307. ______. Comparison of common to other Bermudagrasses. Proceedings of the Annual Texas Turfgrass Conference. 21:31–33. 1966.

9308. ______. Nitrogen fertilization for grasses. Auburn University Annual Turfgrass Short Course. pp. 3–6. 1967.

9309. ______. Where do we go from here. Southern Turfgrass Association Conference Proceedings. pp. 35–37. 1967.

9310. ______. Bacteria and organic additions. Proceedings of the Midwest Regional Turf Conference. pp. 79–81. 1968.

9311. ______. Fertilizing bentgrass greens. Proceedings Sceond Annual Tennessee Turfgrass Conference. pp. 12–14. 1968.

9312. ______. What is turf renovation? Proceedings of the Midwest Regional Turf Conference. pp. 82–83. 1968.

9313. ______. Control and care of *Poa annua.* Rocky Mountain Regional Turfgrass Conference Proceedings. pp. 20–23. 1968.

9314. ______. The role of lime in turf management. West Virginia Turfgrass Conference Proceedings. pp. 22–23. 1968.

9315. ______. Techniques of fertilization. Florida Turf-Grass Management Conference Proceedings. 19:44–47. 1971.

9316. ______. Factors affecting soil temperature. Ohio Turfgrass Conference Proceedings. pp. 39–41. 1969.

9317. ______. Choice of turf for fairways. Rutgers University Short Course in Turf Management Proceedings. pp. 59–62. 1971.

9318. ______. Turf management and pollution. 5th Annual Tennessee Turfgrass Conference. pp. 10–11. 1971.

9319. Latta, W. M. Experiences and experiments with zoysia. Proceedings of the Annual Missouri Lawn and Turf Conference. 7:26–28. 1966.

9320. Laude, H. M. The nature of summer dormancy in perennial grasses. Botanical Gazette. 114:284–292. 1953.

9321. Laude, H. M. and B. A. Chaugle. Effect of stage of seedling development upon heat tolerance in bromegrasses. Journal of Range Management. 6(5):320–324. 1953.

9322. Laude, H. M., J. E. Shrum, Jr., and W. E. Biehler. The effect of high soil temperatures on the seedling emergence of perennial grasses. Agronomy Journal. 44(3):110–112. 1952.

9323. Lauder, B. Lightning. The Golf Superintendent. 35(5):21,23–24. 1967.

9324. Laughlin, C. W. Nitrogen sources for Tifgreen bermuda tees. Proceedings of the Mid-Atlantic Association of Golf Course Superintendents. p. 26. 1966.

9325. ______. Taking samples to determine the presence of nematodes. Golf Superintendent. 38(1):104. 1970.

9326. ______. Nematode problems associated with cool-season turfgrasses. 42nd Annual Michigan Turfgrass Conference Proceedings. 1:16–17. 1972.

9327. ______. Nematodes in Michigan turfgrasses. A Patch of Green, Michigan and Border Cities GCSA Publication. p. 8. May, 1972.

9328. ______. Taking samples to determine the presence of nematodes. A Patch of Green. Michigan and Border Cities GCSA Publication. p. 9. May, 1972.

9329. Laughlin, C. W. and J. M. Vargas. Influence of benomyl on the control of *Tylenchorhynchus dubius* with selected nonfumigant nematicides. The Plant Disease Reporter. 56(6):546–548. 1972.

9330. ______. Pathogenic potential of *Tylenchorhynchus dubius* on selected turfgrass. Journal of Nematology. 4(4):277–280. 1972.

9331. Lautz, W. Chemical control of nematodes parasitic on turf and sweet corn. Proceedings of the Florida State Horticultural Society. 71:38–40. 1958.

9332. ______. Increase of *Belonolaimus longicaudatus* on various plant species in artifically inoculated soil. Plant Disease Reporter. 43(1):48–50. 1959.

9333. Launchbaugh, J. L. Effects of early spring burning on yields of native vegetation. Journal of Range Management. 17(1):5–6. 1964.

9334. Launchbaugh, J. L. and C. E. Owensby. Seeding rate and first-year stand relationships for six native grasses. Journal of Range Management. 23:414–417. 1970.

9335. Lavender, D. Stress fertilizing, drainage, first year of a course. Golfdom. 24(4):66. 1950.

9336. ______. Turf maintenance at West Point Military Academy. Greenkeeping Superintendents Association National Turf Conference. 21:110–112. 1950.

9337. Laver, A. Brown patch caused by beetles. The National Greenkeeper. 3(8):16–17. 1929.

9339. Lawn, A. G. Gleanings from midwest regional turf foundation. Proceedings Northwest Turf Conference. 13:37–39. 1959.

9340. Law, A. G. Turfgrass varieties for eastern Washington. Proceedings 16th Annual Northwest Turf Conference. 49–51. 1962.

9341. ______. Performance of bluegrass varieties under two heights of clipping. Proceedings of the 19th Annual Northwest Turfgrass Conference. pp. 27–32. 1965.

9342. ______. Vegetative identification of grasses. Turf Management Handbook. Washington State University. pp. 14–18. 1965.

9343. ______. Performance of bluegrass varieties clipped at two heights. Weeds, Trees and Turf. 5(5):26–28. 1966.

9344. ______. Advanced training for turfgrass managers. Proceedings of the Annual Northwest Turfgrass Conference. 21:-91–101. 1967.

9345. ______. History of the Northwest Turfgrass Association. Northwest Turfgrass Topics. 9(1):4–6. 1967.

9346. Law, A. G. and J. K. Patterson. Crabgrass control trials. Proceedings 14th Annual Northwest Turf Conference. 14:15–16. 1960.

9347. Law, A. G., R. L. Goss, and J. L. Schwendiman. Registration of Cougar Kentucky bluegrass (Reg. No. 7). Crop Science. 12(2):255. 1972.

9348. Law, A. G., J. L. Schwendiman, and J. Clausen. Registration of Newport bluegrass. Crop Science. 4:115. 1964.

9349. Law, A. G., J. K. Patterson, T. J. Musik, and R. Gross. Turf research in eastern Washington. Proceedings 15th Annual Northwest Turf Conference. 15:69–72. 1961.

9350. Law, E. Everything not brown patch. Greenkeepers Club of New England Newsletter. 6(8):10. 1934.

9351. Lawrence, C. The turf program at Upjohns. Proceedings of Midwest Regional Turf Conference. pp. 17–19. 1952.

9352. Lawrence, F. H. A note on the use of *Aira caespiosa* as a hazzard on golf courses. Journal of the Board of Greenkeeping Research. 4(13):114–115. 1935.

9353. Lawrence, R. L. Florida's turf problems are increased by Rhodes scale. Golfdom. 26(10):60–61,64. 1952.

9354. Lawrence, T. The influence of fertilizer on the winter survival of intermediate wheat-grass following a long period of drought. Journal of the British Society. 18(4):292–294. 1963.

9355. Lawrence, T., and M. R. Kilcher. The effect of fourteen root extracts upon germination and seedling length of 15 plant species. Canadian Journal of Plant Science. 42(2):308–313. 1962.

9356. Lawrence, T., F. G. Warder, and R. Ashford. Effect of fertilizer nitrogen and clipping frequency on the crude protein content, crude protein yield and apparent nitrogen recovery of intermediate wheatgrass. Canadian Journal of Plant Science. 50(6):723–730. 1970.

9357. Layng, C. Landscaping sells homes. Landscape Design and Construction. 13(3):13,26. 1967.

9358. Lazanby, A. Some effects on the yields of ryegrass strains of varying the growing technique and the condition of management. Journal of British Grassland Society. 12:257–263. 1957.

9359. Leach, B. R. The Japanese beetle and its relation to golf courses. USGA Green Section Bulletin. 4(4):97–101. 1924.

9360. ______. Control of Japanese beetle in lawns. Pennsylvania Department of Agriculture Bulletin. 8(14):1–12. 1925.

9361. ______. Improvements in the method of treating golf greens for the control of the Japanese beetle. USGA Green Section Bulletin. 5(5):100–102. 1925.

9362. ______. Foreign grubs, a menace of the future. Golfdom. 1(9):14–16. 1927.

9363. ______. Foreign grubs, a menace of the future. Golfdom. 1(11):11–13. 1927.

9364. ______. The weed problem with suggestions for control USGA Green Section Bulletin. 7(11):206–209. 1927.

9365. ______. Foreign grubs, a menace of the future. Golfdom. 2(2):13–15. 1928.

9366. ______. How to grub-proof established greens. Golfdom. 2(3):19–22. 1928.

9367. ______. How to handle fairways in battle with grubs. Golfdom. 2(4):22–24. 1928.

9368. ______. How soil conditions and worms affect greens. Golfdom. 2(5):53–57. 1928.

9369. ______. Away with worms. Golfdom. 2(6):9–12. 1928.

9370. ______. Doing away with weeds. Golfdom. 2(8):12–15. 1928.

9371. ______. Why we have weeds; How we prevent 'em. Golfdom. 2(9):10–13. 1928.

9372. ______. Some questions & answers from Leach's mail. Golfdom, 2(11):31–36. 1928.

9373. ______. Controlling grubs and earthworms with Arsenate of Lead. USGA Green Section Bulletin. 8(11):218–221. 1928.

9374. ______. Divots from Leach's mailbag. Golfdom. 3(1):32–38. 1929.

9375. ______. Turf research. Golfdom. 3(3):23–25. 1929.

9376. ______. Leach's mail bag. Golfdom. 3(3):83–88. 1929.

9377. ______. Questions asked of B. R. Leach, and his answers. Golfdom. 3(4):42–46. 1929.

9378. ______. Leach's mail bag. Golfdom. 3(5):79–82. 1929.

9379. ______. Leach's mail bag. Golfdom. 3(6):58–59. 1929.

9380. ______. Divots from Leach's mailbag. Golfdom. 3(8):46–49. 1929.

9381. ______. Green section in mid-summer meets. Golfdom. 3(9):22,54–58. 1929.

9382. ______. Top-dressing preparation by the "soiling method." Golfdom. 3(9):50,-52,54. 1929.

9383. ______. Leach's mail-bag. Golfdom. 3(10):44,45,46. 1929.

9384. ______. Control of white grubs in lawns and golf courses. New Jersey Agriculture Department Circular. 163:1–13. 1929.

9385. ______. Leach answers some greenkeeping queries. Golfdom. 4(2):76,78. 1930.

9386. ______. From Leach's mail-bag. Golfdom. 4(4):117–120. 1930.

9387. ______. Green plots are questioned. Golfdom. 4(5):78,80,85–86. 1930.

9388. ______. Some divots from Leach's mail bag. Golfdom. 4(5):111–112. 1930.

9389. ______. Results show value of three phase fertilization. Golfdom. 4(7):21–23. 1930.

9390. ______. From Leach's mail-bag. Golfdom. 4(7):75. 1930.

9391. ______. Fall fairways fertilization for fall season results. Golfdom. 4(9):66,68,-70–71. 1930.

9392. ______. Out of Leach's mail-bag. Golfdom. 4(9):71–72. 1930.

9393. ______. Ants and weeds as next greens research topics. Golfdom. 5(2):108–110,112–113. 1931.

9394. ______. Greens grief shows need of revision in architecture. Golfdom. 5(11):12–15. 1931.

9395. Leach, B. R. and J. W. Lipp. A method for grub-proofing turf. USGA Green Section Bulletin. 6(2):34–39. 1926.

9396. ______. Additional experiments in grub-proofing turf. USGA Green Section Bulletin. 7(2):23–32. 1927.

9397. Leach, C. M. and M. Pierpoint. *Rhizoctonia solani* may be transmitted with seed of *Agrostis tenuis.* Plant Disease Reporter. 42(2):240. 1958.

9398. Leach, J. G., C. V. Lowther, and M. A. Ryan. Stripe smut *(Ustilage striaeformis)* in relation to bluegrass improvement. Phytopathology. 36(1):57–72. 1946.

9399. Leaman, D. E. Techniques of contract fumigation on golf greens. Golf Course Reporter. 31(6):56–59. 1963.

9400. ______. Techniques of contract fumigation on golf greens. 34th International Turf-Grass Conference Proceedings. p. 9. 1963.

9401. ______. Soil fumigation. Southern California Turfgrass Institute Proceedings. pp. 6–9. 1963.

9402. Leasure, J. K. The effects of added penetrant aids and wetting agents on the response of quackgrass *(Agropyron repens)* to Dalapon. British Weed Control Conference Proceedings. 5(1):279–286. 1960.

9403. ______. The mode of action of Dalapon. California Turfgrass Culture. 13(3):19–22. 1963.

9404. Lebeau, J. B. Pathology of winter-injured turfgrass. Agronomy Abstracts. 56:-101. 1964.

9405. ______. Control of snow mold by regulating winter soil temperature. Phytopathology. 54:693–696. 1964.

9406. ______. Pathology of winter injured grasses and legumes in Western Canada. Crop Science. 6:23–25. 1966.

9407. ______. Recent advances in controlling winter injury to turfgrass. Proceedings of the Annual Northwest Turfgrass Conference. 21:14–21. 1967.

9408. ______. Soil warming and winter survival of turfgrass. Journal of the Sports Turf Research Institute. 43:5–11. 1967.

9409. ______. Turf renovation. The Greenmaster. 5(9):16, 18. 1969.

9410. ______. Pink snow mold. Golf Superintendent. 39(9):24–28. 1971.

9411. ______. Turfgrass diseases in western Canada. Proceedings of Scotts Turfgrass Research Conference. 2:43–54. 1971.

9412. Lebeau, J. B., and M. W. Cormack. A simple method for identifying snow-mold damage on turfgrasses. Phytopathology. 46(5):298. 1956.

9413. Lebeau, J. B., and J. G. Dickson. Preliminary report on production of hydrogen cyanide by a snow mold pathogen. Phytopathology. 43(10):581–582. 1953.

9414. Lebeau, J. B. and E. J. Hawn. A simple method for control of fairy ring caused by *Marasmius oreades.* Journal of the Sports Turf Research Institute. 11(39):23–25. 1963.

9415. ______. Formation of hydrogen cyanide by the mycelial stage of a fairy ring fungus. Phytopathology. 53(12):1395–1396. 1963.

9416. Lebeau, J. B., and C. E. Logsdon. Snow mold of forage crops in Alaska and Yukon. Phytopathology. 48(3):148–150. 1958.

9417. Lebeau, J. B. and J. E. Moffatt. A suitable grass for western greens. The Greenmaster 4(1):3. 1967.

9418. Lebeau, J. B., J. E. Moffatt, and C. McCullough. Electrical heating of turfgrass in Banff. The Greenmaster. 5(2):4–6. 1969.

9419. Leben, C. and L. V. Barton. Effect of gibberellic acid on growth of Kentucky bluegrass. Science. 125:494–495. 1957.

9420. Leben, C., E. F. Alder, and A. Chichuk. Infulence of gibberellic acid on the growth of Kentucky bluegrass. Agronomy Journal, 51(2):116–117. 1959.

9421. Leber, F. El Conquistador's gamble. Golfdom. 42(4):29–30, 40. 1968.

9422. ______. A superintendent's challenge. Golfdom. 42(5):26–27, 78. 1968.

9423. Lechtenburg, V. L., D. A. Holt, and H. W. Youngberg. Diurnal variation in nonstructural carbohydrates of *Festuca arundinacea* (Schreb.) with and without N fertilizer. Agronomy Journal. 64(3):302–305. 1972.

9424. LeCroy, W. C. Characterization of zoysia through the microscope. Proceedings of the Midwest Regional Turf Conference. pp. 8–9. 1963.

9425. Ledeboer, F. B. Investigations into the nature of lawn thatch and methods for its decomposition. M.S. Thesis, University of Rhode Island. 67 pp. 1966.

9426. ______. Modern fertilizer management on fairway turf. University of Maine 5th Annual Turf Management Short Course. 2 pp. 1967.

9427. ______. Electrical soil heating studies with cool season turfgrasses. Ph.D. Thesis, 80 p. University of Rhode Island. 1969.

9428. ______. Turfgrass research reports 1970, Clemson, S. C. Southern Regional Turf Research Committee Report, Virginia Polytechnic Institute. pp. 28–31. 1970.

9429. ______. *Poa annua.* Park Maintenance. 24(7):24. 1971.

9430. ______. Effects of variable cutting on several overseeded grasses on dormant bermudagrass sod. Agronomy Abstracts. 2:-63. 1972.

9431. ______. Cool-season grasses for South Carolina piedmont lawns. Clemson University Extension Service Circular 528. pp. 1–19. 1972.

9432. ______. Overseeding establishment with various fertilizers. Park Maintenance. 25(7):14. 1972.

9433. ______. Fertilizer management of cool season grasses. Park Maintenance. 25(7):14. 1972.

9434. ______. Growth retardants. Park Maintenance. 25(7):16. 1972.

9435. ______. *Poa annua.* Park Maintenance. 25(7):18–19. 1972.

9436. Ledeboer, F. B. and C. R. Skogley. Investigations into the nature of thatch add methods for its decomposition. Agronomy Journal. 59(4):320–323. 1967.

9437. ______. Plastic screens for winter protection. The Golf Superintendent. 35(8):-22–33. 1967.

9438. ______. Effects of late fall fertilization on the performance of cool season turfgrasses. Agronomy Abstracts. 60:59–60. 1968.

9439. ______. Reducing winter damage on putting greens. USGA Green Section Record. 8(6):9–10. 1970.

9440. Ledeboer, F. B., C. G. McKiel, and C. R. Skogley. Soil heating studies with cool season turfgrasses. I. Effects of watt density, protective covers, and ambient environment on soil temperature distribution. Agronomy Journal. 63(5):677–680. 1971.

9441. Ledeboer, F. B., C. R. Skogley and C. G. McKiel. Turf response to soil heating, protective covers and nitrogen fertilization during the winter. Agronomy Abstracts. p. 70. 1970.

9442. ______. Soil heating studies with cool season turfgrasses. II. Effects of N fertilization and protective covers on performance and chlorophyll content. Agronomy Journal. 63(5):680–684. 1971.

9443. ______. Soil heating studies with cool season turfgrasses. III. Methods for the establishment of turf with seed and sod during the winter. Agronomy Journal. 63(5):-686–689. 1971.

9444. Ledig, P. Specifications for sodding, plugging, sprigging, seeding, quality. Proceedings of Southern California Turfgrass Institute. pp. 10–12. 1971.

9445. Lee, B. and J. H. Priestley. The plant cuticle. I. Its structure, distribution, and function. Annals of Botany. 38:525–545. 1924.

9446. Lee, G. A. and H. P. Alley. Weed control in lawns. Wyoming Agricultural Experiment Station Bulletin 452. 23 pp. 1966.

9447. Lee, T. H. and H. K. Lee. Studies on a new method for the fixation of a drifting sand dune. Research Report, Office of Rural Development. Suwon, 7(2):79–89. 1964.

9448. Lee, O. C. 2, 4-D proves to be effective weed killer. Midwest Turf-News and Research. 1(1):4. 1947.

9449. ______. Turf weeds and their control. Proceedings of Midwest Regional Turf Conference. pp. 77–78. 1948.

9450. ______. 2, 4-D a course aid if used with care. Midwest Turf-News and Research. 3(3):4. 1949.

9451. ______. Chemical crabgrass control. Proceedings of Midwest Regional Turf Conference. pp. 5–8. 1952.

9452. ______. Killing weeds with 2, 4-D. Purdue Agricultural Extension Service. Extension Bulletin. 389:12 pp. 1953.

9453. Lee, W. O. Effect of picloram on production and quality of seed in several grasses. Weed Science. 18(1):171–173. 1970.

9454. Lee, T. A., and R. W. Toler. St. Augustine rust in Texas. The Plant Disease Reporter. 56(7):630–632. 1972.

9455. Leech, C. S. Manurial treatment of greens. New Zealand Institute for Turf Culture Newsletter. 17:13–14. 1962.

9456. ______. Manurial treatment of Taupo greens. New Zealand Institute for Turf Culture Newsletter. 24:4–5. 1963.

9457. ______. The influence of trial plots on practical greenkeeping. New Zealand Institute for Turf Culture Newsletter. 41:7–8. 1966.

9458. Leedy, C. D. Fertilizer facts for homeowners. New Mexico State University Cooperative Extension Service Circular No. 415. 1968.

9459. ______. Control iron chlorosis, a common disease of ornamentals, lawns, trees. It makes plants unattractive, and it can kill them. New Mexico State University Cooperative Extension Service. Circular 421. 1970.

9460. Lebeau, J. B. Investigation and control of turfgrass diseases in Western Canada. C.D.A. Lethbridge. Alberta. Progress Report.

9461. Lefebvre, C. L. *Claviceps yanagawaensis* in imported seed of Japanese lawn grass. Phytopathology. 32(9):809–812. 1942.

9462. ______. Copper spot on turf grasses. Timely Turf Topics. USGA Green Section. June. p. 2. 1947.

9463. Lefebvre, C. L., F. L. Howard, and F. V. Grau. How to keep turfgrass healthy. Plant Diseases. USDA Yearbook. pp. 285–291. 1953.

9464. Leftwich, R. H. Moles in turf. Missouri Lawn and Turf Conference Proceedings. 12:45–48. 1971.

9465. Legg, D. C. Selective weedkiller for use on young turf. Journal of the Sports Turf Research Institute. 43:40–48. 1967.

9466. ______. A note on the effect of chlordane on seedling turf. Journal of the Sports Turf Research Institute. 43:59–60. 1967.

9467. ______. Comparison of various worm-killing chemicals. Journal of the Sports Turf Research Institute. 44:47–48. 1968.

9468. Leggatt, C. W. Germination of seeds of three species of *Agrostis.* Canada Journal of Research. 24:7–21. 1946.

9469. Le Grand, F. Iron chlorosis in Roselawn St. Augustine grass growing on muck soils of the Everglades. Proceedings of the Soil and Crop Science Society of Florida. 19:374–378. 1959.

9470. Lehker, G. Insect control. Proceedings of Midwest Regional Turf Conference. pp. 86–87. 1948.

9471. ______. The control of turf insects. Proceedings of Midwest Regional Turf Conference. p. 8. 1949.

9472. ______. Insects of turf. Proceedings of Midwest Regional Turf Conference. pp. 69–71. 1951.

9473. Leising, N., J. Stellrecht, and K. Freeland Training guideline for golf course worker for educable mentally handicapped adolescents. USGA Green Section Record. 4(5):8–9. 1967.

9474. Lelacheur, G. Canadian certified bent seed. USGA Green Section Bulletin. 10(11):212–213. 1930.

9475. Lemley, E. L. Motivation: how to get your people to "turn on" to work. USGA Green Section Record. 10(2):2–4. 1972.

9477. Lentz, J. W. Grass problems. The Modern Cemetery. 49(9):154. 1939.

9478. Leonard, D. E. Biosystematics of the "*Leucopterus* complex" of the genus *Blissus (Heteroptera: Lygaeidae).* Connecticut Agricultural Experiment Station Bulletin 677. 47 pp. 1966.

9479. Leonard, R. T. The influence of nitrogen fertilizer treatments on the carbohydrate reserves of timothy *(Phleum pratense* L.). M.S. Thesis, University of Rhode Island. pp. 1–57. 1967.

9480. Leonard, T. Winter grass overseeding in South Texas. Golf Course Reporter. 30(9):52–55. 1962.

9481. ______. Winter grass overseeding —on greens in south Texas. International Turf-Grass Conference Proceedings. 33:9–10. 1962.

9482. ______. Vertical cutting and aerification. Proceedings of the Texas Turfgrass Conference. 20:68–69. 1965.

9483. ______. Weed control in turfgrass. Proceedings of the Annual Texas Turfgrass Conference. 21:70–71. 1966.

9484. Leopold, A. C. The control of tillering in grasses by auxin. American Journal of Botany. 36(6):437–440. 1949.

9485. Le Roux, M. and H. Weinmann. Studies on the water relations of *Cynodon dactylon.* Better Turf Through Research. South African Turf Research Fund. pp. 52–55. 1948.

9486. Lert, P. J. Customer service—problem or opportunity? Proceedings of Turf, Nursery, and Landscape Tree Conference. pp. 13–1 to 13–3. 1964.

9487. ______. Making customer service pay—panel. Proceedings of Turf, Nursery, and Landscape Tree Conference. pp. 14–1 to 14–4. 1964.

9488. Leslie, J. K. Factors responsible for failures in the establishment of summer grasses on the black earths of the Darling Downs, Queensland. Queensland Journal of Agriculture and Animal Science. 22:17–38. 1965.

9489. Letey, J. Aeration, compaction, and drainage. California Turfgrass Culture. 11(3):17–21. 1961.

9490. Letey, J., L. H. Stolzy, and W. Morgan. Compacted golf greens respond to deep aeration, controlled irrigation; Los Angeles County tests. California Agriculture. 18:6. 1964.

9491. Letey, J. Drainage principles. California Turfgrass Culture. 15(4):25–28. 1965.

9492. ______. Consideration of soil physical properties in soil modification. Agronomy Abstracts. 60:60. 1968.

9493. ______. Modifying water for turfgrass production. Agronomy Abstracts. 61:-54. 1969.

9494. ______. Management factors affecting root behavior. Proceedings Annual Turfgrass Sprinkler Irrigation Conference. 8:30–35 1970.

9495. Letey, J., W. D. Kemper, and L. Noonan. The effect of osmotic pressure gradients on water movement in unsaturated soil. Soil Science Society of America Proceedings. 33(1):15–18. 1969.

9496. Letey, J., R. E. Pelishek, and J. Osborn. Wetting agents. California Turfgrass Culture. 12(1):3–4. 1962.

9497. Letey, J., O. R. Lunt, L. H. Stolzy, and T. E. Szuszkiewicz. Plant growth, water use and nutritional response to rhizosphere differentials of oxygen concentration. Soil Science Society of America Proceedings. 25:-183–186. 1961.

9498. Letey, J., W. C. Morgan, S. J. Richards, and N. Valoras. Physical soil amendments, soil compaction, irrigation, and wetting agents in turfgrass management. III. Effects on oxygen diffusion rate and root growth. Agronomy Journal. 58(5):531–535. 1966.

9500. Letey, J., L. H. Stolzy, O. R. Lunt, and N. Valoras. Soil oxygen and clipping height effects on the growth of Newport bluegrass. California Turfgrass Culture. 14(2):-9–12. 1964.

9501. ______. Soil oxygen and clipping height. Golf Course Reporter. 32(2):16–26. 1964.

9503. Letey, J., L. H. Stolozy, O. R. Lunt, and V. B. Youngner. Growth and nutrient uptake of Newport bluegrass as affected by soil oxygen. Plant and Soil. 20(2):-143–148. 1964.

9504. Letey, J., L. H. Stolzy, T. E. Szuszkiewicz, and N. Valoris. Soil aeration essential for maximum growth. California Agriculture. 16(3):6–7. 1962.

9505. Letey, J., N. Welch, R. E. Pelishek, and J. Osborn. Effect of wetting agents on irrigation of water repellent soils. California Turfgrass Culture. 13(1):1–2. 1963.

9507. Leukel, W. A., J. P. Camp and J. M. Coleman. Effect of frequent cutting and nitrate fertilization on the growth behavior and relative composition of pasture grasses. Florida Agricultural Experiment Station Bulletin. 269. 48 pp. 1934.

9508. Leuthold, L. D., W. A. Geyer, C. E. Long, N. W. Miles, J. K. Greig and E. B. Nilson. Chemical weed control in horticultural and forestry plants—herbicides for lawn and turf. Kansas State University Agricultural Experiment Station. Bulletin 544. pp. 12–14. 1971.

9509. Leuzinger, P., and A. J. Turgeon. Tolerance of bentgrass putting green turf to various herbicides. University of Illinois Turfgrass Field Day. pp. 11–12. 1972.

9510. Levy, E. B. New Zealand greenkeeping research. Journal of the Board of Greenkeeping Research. 2(7):258–267. 1932.

9511. ______. Some aspects of research in greenkeeping. Greenkeeper's Reporter. 9(1):24, 32–34. 1941.

9512. Levy, E. B. and W. Davies. Perennial ryegrass strain investigation. Single plant studies at the plant research station. New Zealand Journal of Agriculture. 41:147–163. 1930.

9513. Lery, B. and E. A. Madden. Weeds in lawns and greens: control with chemical sprays. New Zealand Journal of Agriculture. 42(6):406–421. 1931.

9514. Levy, E. B., W. A. Kiely, and W. M. Horton. Construction, renovation and care of the golf course. New Zealand Institute for Turf Culture. Palmerston North, New Zealand.

9515. Lewis, I. G. Strains of *Agrostis* and their relation to sports turf. Journal of the Board of Greenkeeping Research. 2(5):112–115. 1931.

9516. ______. A Greenkeeper's guide to the grasses. Journal of the Board of Greenkeeping Research. 2(7):273–281. 1932.

9517. ______. A Greenkeeper's guide to the grasses. 2. The genus Festuca. Journal of the Board of Greenkeeping Research. 3(9):-94–98. 1933.

9518. ______. A greenkeeper's guide to grasses. 3. The genus *Agrostis.* Journal of the Board of Greenkeeping Research. 3(10):148–152. 1934.

9519. ______. A greenkeeper's guide to the grasses. 4. The significance of strain and its possibilities in relation to turf improvement. Journal of the Board of Greenkeeping Research. 4(12):50–53. 1935.

9520. ______. A greenkeeper's guide to the grasses. 5. The hair grasses. Journal of the Board of Greenkeeping Research. 4(13):110–113. 1935.

9521. ______. A greenkeeper's guide to the grasses. 6. The meadow grasses *(Poa).* Journal of the Board of Greenkeeping Research. 4(14):193–197. 1936.

9522. ______. Back to better grass. Faber and Faber Limited. London. 68 pp. 1942.

9523. ______. Turf. Faber and Faber. London. 141 pp. 1948.

9524. Lewis, O. B. The use of fungicides in turf grass disease control. Proceedings of the 20th Annual Texas Turfgrass Conference. 20:1–2. 1965.

9525. Lewis, R. D. Public and private support for turfgrass research. Proceedings of the Texas Turfgrass Conference. 15:50–51. 1960.

9526. ______. The development of the turf research program at the Texas Agricultural Experiment Station. Proceedings of the Annual Texas Turfgrass Conference. 9:21–25. 1954.

9527. Lewis, R. F., and N. V. Rothwell. Implications of nucleolar differences in the root epidermis among several grass species.

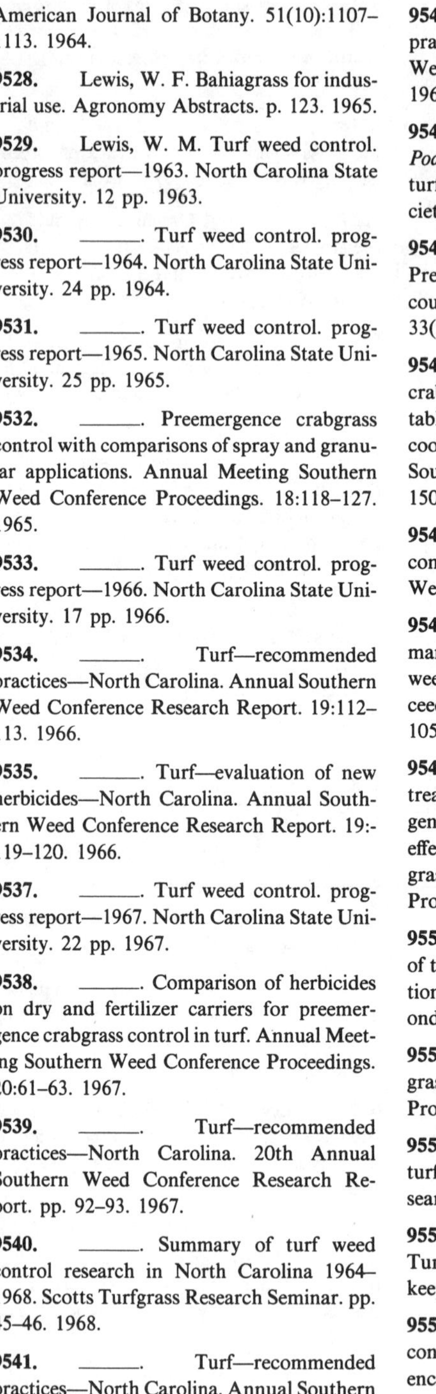

American Journal of Botany. 51(10):1107–1113. 1964.

9528. Lewis, W. F. Bahiagrass for industrial use. Agronomy Abstracts. p. 123. 1965.

9529. Lewis, W. M. Turf weed control. progress report—1963. North Carolina State University. 12 pp. 1963.

9530. ———. Turf weed control. progress report—1964. North Carolina State University. 24 pp. 1964.

9531. ———. Turf weed control. progress report—1965. North Carolina State University. 25 pp. 1965.

9532. ———. Preemergence crabgrass control with comparisons of spray and granular applications. Annual Meeting Southern Weed Conference Proceedings. 18:118–127. 1965.

9533. ———. Turf weed control. progress report—1966. North Carolina State University. 17 pp. 1966.

9534. ———. Turf—recommended practices—North Carolina. Annual Southern Weed Conference Research Report. 19:112–113. 1966.

9535. ———. Turf—evaluation of new herbicides—North Carolina. Annual Southern Weed Conference Research Report. 19:-119–120. 1966.

9537. ———. Turf weed control. progress report—1967. North Carolina State University. 22 pp. 1967.

9538. ———. Comparison of herbicides on dry and fertilizer carriers for preemergence crabgrass control in turf. Annual Meeting Southern Weed Conference Proceedings. 20:61–63. 1967.

9539. ———. Turf—recommended practices—North Carolina. 20th Annual Southern Weed Conference Research Report. pp. 92–93. 1967.

9540. ———. Summary of turf weed control research in North Carolina 1964–1968. Scotts Turfgrass Research Seminar. pp. 45–46. 1968.

9541. ———. Turf—recommended practices—North Carolina. Annual Southern Weed Conference Research Report. 22:87–88. 1969.

9542. ———. Turf—recommended practices—North Carolina. Annual Southern Weed Conference Research Report. 22:90. 1969.

9543. ———. Pre and postemergence *Poa annua* control in common bermudagrass turf. 23rd Annual Southern Weed Science Society Proceedings. p. 121. 1970.

9544. Lewis, W. M. and W. B. Gilbert. Preemergence crabgrass control in golf course turf. The Golf Course Reporter. 33(3):44, 46. 1965.

9545. ———. The effect of siduron on crabgrass and goosegrass control and the establishment of five warm-season and three cool-season turfgrasses. Annual Meeting Southern Weed Conference Proceedings. 19:-150–154. 1966.

9546. ———. Preemergence siduron controls crabgrass safely in four turfgrasses. Weeds Trees and Turf. 5(4):20, 22. 1966.

9547. Lewis, W. M., and G. C. Klingman. Three evaluation methods for taking weed control data in bermudagrass turf. Proceedings, Southern Weed Conference. 16:-105–109. 1963.

9548. Lewis, W. M., and J. P. Lilly. Retreatments of preemergence and postemergence crabgrass herbicides and their residual effects on the establishment of three turfgrasses. Annual Southern Weed Conference Proceedings. 19:161–167. 1966.

9550. Lewton-Bain, L. On the anatomy of the leaves of British grasses. The Transactions of the Linnean Society of London. Second Series. 6(7):315–360. 1904.

9551. Leyendecker, P. J. Diseases of turfgrasses. New Mexico Turfgrass Conference Proceedings. 1:23–27. 1955.

9553. Libbey, R. P. Common weeds of turf. Journal of Board of Greenkeeping Research. 5(18):211–212. 1938.

9554. ———. Establishment of Sports Turf From Seed. Journal of Board of Greenkeeping Research. 7(24):156–161. 1948.

9555. Libby, J. L. Turf and lawn pest control—1963. Wisconsin Turfgrass Conference Proceedings. pp. 1–2. 1963.

9556. Lichenstein, E. P., and J. B. Polivka. Persistence of some chlorinated hydrocarbon insecticides in turf soils. Journal of Economic Entomology. 52(2):289–293. 1959.

9557. Lidgate, H. J. Earthworms in the lawn. Gardeners Chronicle. 156(19):482. 1964.

9558. Lidgate, H. J. Lawn fertilization. Gardeners Chronicle. 157(13):303. 1965.

9559. ______. Weed control. Gardeners Chronicle. 158(8):203, 216. 1965.

9560. ______. Fertilizers for tomorrow. The Groundsman. 19(8):16–18. 1966.

9561. ______. Earthworm control with chlordane. Journal of the Sports Turf Research Institute. 42:5–8. 1966.

9562. ______. Earthworm control with chlordane. The Groundsman. 20(9):24–25. 1967.

9563. Likes, D. E. The influence of height of cut and irrigation on fairway turf grasses. M.S. Thesis, Purdue University. 1950.

9564. ______. Found: bents having disease resistance. Midwest Turf-News and Research. 4(2):3. 1950.

9565. ______. Watering fairways reported by Likes. Midwest Turf-News and Research. 4(3):1. 1950.

9566. ______. Testing fairway grasses. Proceedings of Midwest Regional Turfgrass Conference. pp. 89–90. 1951.

9567. ______. Fertilizing greens and why. Proceedings of Midwest Regional Turf Conference. pp. 18–20. 1955.

9568. ______. Using warm season grasses in Cincinnati. Proceedings of Midwest Regional Turf Conference. pp. 43–45. 1958.

9569. ______. Troubled with wilt: check pumping system. Golfdom. 33(3):54. 1959.

9570. ______. Warm season grasses. Proceedings of the Midwest Regional Turf Conference. pp. 49–51. 1959.

9571. ______. Utilizing zoysia. Proceedings of the Midwest Regional Turf Conference. pp. 35–36. 1961.

9572. ______. Holding *Poa annua* fairways. Proceedings of the 1965 Midwest Regional Turf Conference. pp. 38–39. 1965.

9573. ______. Living with *Poa annua* fairways. Proceedings 40th International Turfgrass Conference. pp. 52–53. 1969.

9574. Lighty, W. Starting a new lawn in western Oregon. USDA—Oregon State University. 2 pp. 1967.

9575. Lighty, W. and W. L. Bluhm. A look at Oregon parks—their lawns, play fields and golf courses. Proceedings, 24th Annual Northwest Turfgrass Conference. 24:-46–54. 1970.

9576. Lilly, D. M. For whom do you manage? USGA Green Section Record. 1(4):-1–4. 1963.

9577. Lilly, D. M. and J. R. Watson. Adequate equipment contributes to efficiency. USGA Journal and Turf Management. 11(1):29–31. 1958.

9578. Limpel, L. E., P. H. Schuldt, and F. Batkay. The responses of turf and certain turf weeds to Dacthal. Northeastern Weed Control Conference Proceedings. 15:296–297. 1961.

9579. Limpel, L. E., P. H. Schuldt, and D. Lamont. Preemergence control of crabgrass and other weeds in turf by DAC-893. Proceedings of the Northeastern Weed Control Conference. pp. 299. 1960.

9580. Limpel, L. E., P. H. Schuldt, and R. F. Lindemann. DAC-893, a promising new pre-emergence herbicide for use on turf. Agronomy Abstracts. 51:90. 1959.

9582. Linderman, H. O. Overseeding panel; bentgrasses. Florida Turfgrass Management Conference Proceedings. 14:73–76. 1966.

9583. Lindgren, E. Restoring turf and stopping erosion by mechanical renovation. Park Maintenance. 8(1):4–5. 1955.

9585. Lindsay, P. S. Low cost fairway renovation. Greenkeeper's Reporter. 9(1):9–10. 1941.

9586. Lindsay, W. B. Soils and sub-soils. Greenkeepers Club of New England Newsletter. 2(6):2–3. 1930.

9587. ______. Germination. Greenkeepers Club of New England Newsletter. 2(9):-2–3. 1930.

9588. ______. Soils and sub-soils. The National Greenkeeper. 4(9):28–29. 1930.

9589. ______. Soils, sub-soils and grasses. Greenkeepers Club of New England Newsletter. 12(8):4–6. 1940.

9590. Lindsay, W. L. Trace elements and chelation in fertilizers. Rocky Mountain Regional Turfgrass Conference Proceedings. 10:19–24. 1963.

9592. Lindsey, K. E., and M. L. Peterson. High temperature suppression of flowering in *Poa pratensis* L. Crop Science. 2(1):-71–74. 1962.

9593. ______. Floral induction and development in *Poa pratensis* L. Crop Science. 4:540–544. 1964.

9594. Linehan, P. A. and S. P. Mercer. The varietal purity of commercial Italian ryegrass. Proceedings of the International Seed Testing Association. 4:153–160. 1932.

9595. Lingappa, B. T. and J. L. Lockwood. Direct assay of soils for fungistasis. Phytopathology. 53(5):529–531. 1963.

9596. Linkogel, R. Robert Linkogel of Westwood Golf Club tells local practices. Midwest Regional Turf Foundation. pp. 1–2. October, 1947.

9597. Linkogel, A. How I manage my greens on aeration, irrigation and drainage. Proceedings of Midwest Regional Turf Conference. pp. 23–24. 1948.

9598. ______. Experiences with U-3 bermuda. Proceedings of Midwest Regional Turfgrass Conference. pp. 87–89. 1951.

9599. ______. Seedhead prevention on bentgrass nursery. Proceedings of the Midwest Regional Turf Conference. pp. 25–26. 1961.

9600. ______. Planting stolons on large areas. Proceedings of Midwest Regional Turf Conference. pp. 59–61. 1964.

9601. ______. Vegetative planting of grasses. Proceedings of the Midwest Regional Turf Conference. pp. 63–64. 1970.

9602. ______. Zoysia into other turf. Proceedings of the Midwest Regional Turf Conference. pp. 51–52. 1972.

9603. Lipman, C. B., and M. E. Wank. The availability of nitrogen in peat. Soil Science. 18:311–316. 1924.

9604. Lipman, J. G. Soils in relation to golf course turf. USGA Green Section Bulletin. 9(4):62–70. 1929.

9605. ______. Bacteria in the growing of turf. Golfdom. 6(2):55–57. 1932.

9606. Lipman, L. Fall fertilizing stores grass food for spring start. Golfdom. 6(9):38, 40–41. 1932.

9607. Lipman, J. G. Bacteria in the growing of turf. The National Greenkeeper. 6(7):5–8. 1932.

9608. Lipman, L. Fall fertilizing gives turf spring health it needs. Golfdom. 5(8):60, 62. 1931.

9609. Lipman, L. H. Why fall turf fertilization? Park and Cemetery. 42(7):191–192. 1932.

9610. Liptay, A. M. and H. Tiessen. Influences of polyethylene-coated paper mulch on soil environment. Journal of the American Society for Horticultural Science. 95(4):395–398. 1970.

9611. List, M. Proper use of water on greens. Golf Course Reporter. 21(6):9. 1953.

9612. Lithgow, A. V. Good seed. New Zealand Institute for Turf Culture Newsletter. 9:6–8. 1960.

9613. ______. Analysis of seed purity examination. New Zealand Institute for Turf Culture Newsletter. 10:1–2. 1960.

9614. ______. Analysis of seed testing for germination. New Zealand Institute for Turf Culture Newsletter. 11:8–9. 1961.

9615. Livingston, R. B. Turf research project established in St. Louis. Midwest Turf-News and Research. 2(4):3. 1948.

9616. ______. Turf research in Missouri. Proceedings of Midwest Regional Turf Conference. pp. 45–48. 1949.

9617. ______. U. of Mo. begins bermuda studies. Midwest Turf-News and Research. 3(4):2. 1949.

9618. ______. Bermuda grass studies in Missouri. Missouri University Mimeograph. 1949.

9619. Livingston, W. A. A nine months superintendent. Turf-Grass Times. 1(2):1, 9, 18. 1965.

9620. Lloyd, I. C. The highway and its surrounding environment. Short Course on Roadside Development (Ohio). 13:101–104. 1971.

9621. Lobb, W. R. Watering of greens. New Zealand Institute for Turf Culture Newsletter. 24:5–9. 1963.

9622. Lobenstein, C. W. Observing bluegrasses. Proceedings of the Midwest Regional Turf Conference. pp. 66–69. 1962.

9623. ______. Common Kentucky bluegrass—a composite of many types. Illinois Turfgrass Conference Proceedings. pp. 37–40. 1963.

9624. ______. How bluegrass spreads. Proceedings of the Midwest Regional Turf Conference. pp. 9–14. 1963.

9625. ______. Sod forming characteristics of Kentucky bluegrass as affected by morphological and physiological factors. Ph.D. Thesis, Purdue University. 110 pp. 1963.

9626. ______. Green grass and grass roots. Illinois Turfgrass Conference Proceedings. pp. 22–25. 1964.

9627. ______. Research for better bluegrass. Proceedings of the Midwest Regional Turf Conference. pp. 49–50. 1964.

9628. ______. Arsenic and low phosphate soils. Illinois Turfgrass Conference Proceedings. 4 pp. 1965.

9629. ______. Green grass and grass roots. Turf Bulletin. Massachusetts Turf & Lawn Grass Council. 2(11):19–20. 1965.

9630. ______. Green grass and grass roots. The Golf Superintendent. 35(1):32–34. 1967.

9631. ______. Views of turf problems in the 70's. 11th Illinois Turfgrass Conference Proceedings. pp. 14–18. 1970.

9632. ______. Zoysia at Alvamar Hills. Missouri Lawn and Turf Conference Proceedings. 11:28–30. 1970.

9633. ______. Growth habits of bluegrass. Missouri Lawn and Turf Conference Proceedings. 12:24–26. 1971.

9634. Lobenstein, C. W. and W. H. Daniel. Subjective evaluation of sod-forming characters in bluegrass. Agronomy Abstracts. 54:-103.1962.

9635. Lock, H. C. Lawn and turf culture for gardens and grounds. Surrey County Cricket Club. Wimbledon. 56 pp. 1963.

9636. ______. Pitches for cricket. The Groundsman. 23(7):23 pp. 1970.

9637. Lock, L. F., and H. V. Eck. Iron deficiency in plants: how to control it in yards and gardens. USDA. Home and Garden Bulletin. No. 102. 7 pp. 1965.

9638. Lockwood, H. Altitude is turf problem on Wyoming course. Park Maintenance. 9:14–16. 1956.

9639. Lockwood, J. L. Lysis of mycelium of plant-pathogenic fungi by natural soil. Phytopathology. 50(11):787–789. 1960.

9642. Lofgren, D. E. How to evaluate maintenance time and justify equipment cost. Grounds Maintenance. 1(5):7–9. 1966.

9643. ______. Save man hours and machinery costs. Grounds Maintenance. 1(12):-14–15. 1966.

9644. ______. Fertilizer—What's it worth? Weeds, Trees and Turf. 6(3):16–18. 1967.

9645. ______. Building maintenance into the design. Grounds Maintenance. 3(4):10–12. 1968.

9646. ______. How to justify men and salaries. Grounds Maintenance. 3(9):15–16. 1968.

9647. Loft, P. and J. Morrisey. Bullish on Baron. Weeds, Trees and Turf. 11(2):25, 33. 1972.

9648. Logan, K. T. and E. B. Peterson. A method of measuring and describing light patterns beneath the forest canopy. Canadian Department of Forestry, Forest Research Branch Publication No. 1073. 1964.

9649. Lohmeyer, W. Über die Ansaat niedrigbleibender Rasen an Strassen und Autobahnen. Natur und Landschaft. 3. 1968.

9650. Long, C. E., N. W. Miles, J. K. Greig, E. B. Nilson, W. A. Geyer and L. D. Leuthold. Chemical weed control in horticultural and forestry plants—lawn and turf. Kansas State University Agricultural Experiment Station. Bulletin 524. pp. 13–14. 1969.

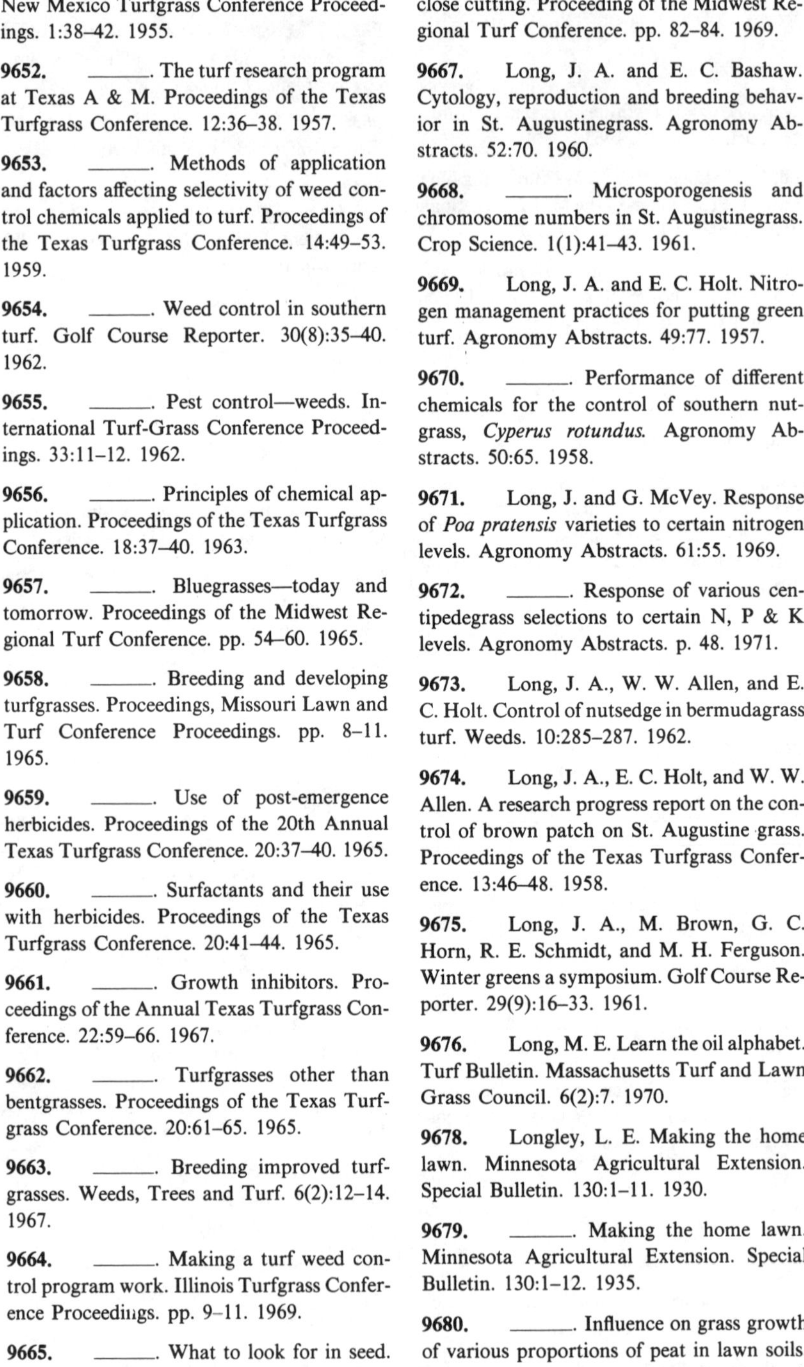

9651. Long, J. A. Weed control in turf. New Mexico Turfgrass Conference Proceedings. 1:38–42. 1955.

9652. ______. The turf research program at Texas A & M. Proceedings of the Texas Turfgrass Conference. 12:36–38. 1957.

9653. ______. Methods of application and factors affecting selectivity of weed control chemicals applied to turf. Proceedings of the Texas Turfgrass Conference. 14:49–53. 1959.

9654. ______. Weed control in southern turf. Golf Course Reporter. 30(8):35–40. 1962.

9655. ______. Pest control—weeds. International Turf-Grass Conference Proceedings. 33:11–12. 1962.

9656. ______. Principles of chemical application. Proceedings of the Texas Turfgrass Conference. 18:37–40. 1963.

9657. ______. Bluegrasses—today and tomorrow. Proceedings of the Midwest Regional Turf Conference. pp. 54–60. 1965.

9658. ______. Breeding and developing turfgrasses. Proceedings, Missouri Lawn and Turf Conference Proceedings. pp. 8–11. 1965.

9659. ______. Use of post-emergence herbicides. Proceedings of the 20th Annual Texas Turfgrass Conference. 20:37–40. 1965.

9660. ______. Surfactants and their use with herbicides. Proceedings of the Texas Turfgrass Conference. 20:41–44. 1965.

9661. ______. Growth inhibitors. Proceedings of the Annual Texas Turfgrass Conference. 22:59–66. 1967.

9662. ______. Turfgrasses other than bentgrasses. Proceedings of the Texas Turfgrass Conference. 20:61–65. 1965.

9663. ______. Breeding improved turfgrasses. Weeds, Trees and Turf. 6(2):12–14. 1967.

9664. ______. Making a turf weed control program work. Illinois Turfgrass Conference Proceedings. pp. 9–11. 1969.

9665. ______. What to look for in seed. Illinois Turfgrass Conference Proceedings. pp. 52–54. 1969.

9666. ______. Bluegrass response to close cutting. Proceeding of the Midwest Regional Turf Conference. pp. 82–84. 1969.

9667. Long, J. A. and E. C. Bashaw. Cytology, reproduction and breeding behavior in St. Augustinegrass. Agronomy Abstracts. 52:70. 1960.

9668. ______. Microsporogenesis and chromosome numbers in St. Augustinegrass. Crop Science. 1(1):41–43. 1961.

9669. Long, J. A. and E. C. Holt. Nitrogen management practices for putting green turf. Agronomy Abstracts. 49:77. 1957.

9670. ______. Performance of different chemicals for the control of southern nutgrass, *Cyperus rotundus.* Agronomy Abstracts. 50:65. 1958.

9671. Long, J. and G. McVey. Response of *Poa pratensis* varieties to certain nitrogen levels. Agronomy Abstracts. 61:55. 1969.

9672. ______. Response of various centipedegrass selections to certain N, P & K levels. Agronomy Abstracts. p. 48. 1971.

9673. Long, J. A., W. W. Allen, and E. C. Holt. Control of nutsedge in bermudagrass turf. Weeds. 10:285–287. 1962.

9674. Long, J. A., E. C. Holt, and W. W. Allen. A research progress report on the control of brown patch on St. Augustine grass. Proceedings of the Texas Turfgrass Conference. 13:46–48. 1958.

9675. Long, J. A., M. Brown, G. C. Horn, R. E. Schmidt, and M. H. Ferguson. Winter greens a symposium. Golf Course Reporter. 29(9):16–33. 1961.

9676. Long, M. E. Learn the oil alphabet. Turf Bulletin. Massachusetts Turf and Lawn Grass Council. 6(2):7. 1970.

9678. Longley, L. E. Making the home lawn. Minnesota Agricultural Extension. Special Bulletin. 130:1–11. 1930.

9679. ______. Making the home lawn. Minnesota Agricultural Extension. Special Bulletin. 130:1–12. 1935.

9680. ______. Influence on grass growth of various proportions of peat in lawn soils. Proceedings, American Society for Horticultural Science. 34:649–652. 1936.

9681. ______. Making the home lawn. Minnesota Agricultural Extension. Special Bulletin. 130:1–12. 1938.

9682. Longley, L. E. and R. A. Phillips. Making the home lawn. Minnesota Agricultural Extension Bulletin. 130:1–12. 1949.

9683. Longenecker, G. W. Pruning on the golf course. The Greenkeepers' Reporter. 6(6):5–6, 26. 1938.

9684. Longnecker, T. C. Studies on the penetration of nutrient elements and their seasonal fluctuations in grassland soil as measured by rapid chemical tests. M.S. Thesis, Rutgers University. 1937.

9685. ______. Soil and fertilizer chemistry. Southwest Turf Conference Proceedings. pp. 5–10. 1948.

9686. ______. Diagnosing turf troubles. Southwest Turf Conference Proceedings. pp. 33–42. 1948.

9687. ______. Preparation and application of top-dressing. Southwest Turf Conference Proceedings. pp. 84–90. 1948.

9688. ______. Proper diagnosis of trouble helps prevent turf failures. Golfdom. 23(5):37, 40, 94–95. 1949.

9689. ______. What every turf man should know about soil chemistry. Oklahoma-Texas Turf Conference Proceedings. pp. 44–50. 1950.

9690. ______. Lime—ageless aid to turf. Mid-Atlantic Newsletter. 24(2):4–5. 1973.

9691. Longnecker, T. C., and H. B. Sprague. Rate of penetration of lime in soils under permanent grass. Soil Science. 50:277–288. 1940.

9692. Longo, A. B. Fertilizer solution use in turf maintenance. Golfdom. 24(8):32–33, 63–65. 1950.

9693. ______. Liquid fertilization. Turf Clippings, University of Massachusetts. 1(4)-9–11. 1959.

9694. ______. The use of liquid fertilizers. Turf Clippings. University of Massachusetts. 1(9):A–3 to A–6. 1964.

9695. Loomis, R. S. Color it green. Turf Bulletin. Massachusetts Turf and Lawn Grass Council. 4(5):4–6. 1967.

9696. Loomis, W. E. The control of dandelions in lawns. Journal of Agricultural Research. 56:855–868. 1938.

9697. Loomis, W. E. and N. L. Noecker. Petroleum sprays for dandelions. Science. 83(2142):63–64. 1936.

9698. Loper, M. A review of the trace elements. Turf Bulletin. Massachusetts Turf and Lawn Council. 7(4):8–11. 1971.

9699. Lopez, R. R., A. G. Matches, and J. D. Baldridge. Vegetative development and organic reserves of tall fescue under conditions of accumulated growth. Crop Science. 7(5):409–412. 1967.

9700. Lorant, B. H. Pesticides on the national scene. Ohio Turfgrass Conference Proceedings. pp. 1–3. 1970.

9701. Lord, E. B. Preparing compost topdressing. The National Greenkeeper. 4(9):10. 1930.

9702. ______. Problems of the past season and how I solved them. Greenkeepers Club of New England Newsletter. 3(4):3. 1931.

9704. Lott, N. "Ask me another". Golfdom. 1(6):16–17. 1927.

9705. ______. "Ask me another". Golfdom. 1(7):13–14. 1927.

9706. ______. "Ask me another". Golfdom. 1(8):15–16. 1927.

9707. ______. "Ask me another". Golfdom. 1(10):26–27. 1927.

9708. ______. "Ask me another". Golfdom. 1(11):21. 1927.

9710. Lourence, F. J. Investigations of factors influencing the origin and quantity of dew which forms on a turf crop. M.S. Thesis, University of California, Davis. 58 pp. 1964.

9712. Love, J. R. Mineral deficiency symptoms in turfgrass. Golfdom. 36(9):20A–20D. 1962.

9713. ______. Mineral deficiency symptoms in turfgrass. Supplement to Proceedings for Oklahoma Turfgrass Conference. pp. 10–13. 1963.

9714. ______. Mineral deficiency symptoms on turfgrass I. Major and secondary nutrient elements. Wisconsin Academy of Science, Arts, and Letters. LI:135–140. 1963.

9715. ______. Soil physical conditions and water movement in soils. Wisconsin Turfgrass Conference Proceedings. 5 pp. 1965.

9716. ______. Salinity and its related problems in turfgrass. The Golf Superintendent. 35(6):20–21. 1967.

9717. ______. Mineral deficiency symptoms in turfgrass. RCGA National Turfgrass Conference. pp. 25–27. 1968.

9718. Lovelace, D. A., E. C. Holt, and W. B. Anderson. Nitrate and nutrient accumulation in two varieties of bermudagrass (*Cynodon dactylon* (L.) Pers.) as influenced by soil-applied fertilizer nutrients. Agronomy Journal. 60(5):551–554. 1968.

9719. Lovibond, B. Investigations on the control of leather jackets. Journal of the Board of Greenkeeping Research. 5(16):12–17. 1937.

9720. Lovitt, D. F. Certification of professional lawn spray applicators. 42nd Annual Michigan Turfgrass Conference Proceedings. 1:59–60. 1972.

9721. ______. Japanese beetle quarantine as it affects sod growers. 42nd Annual Michigan Turfgrass Conference Proceedings. 1:-128–134. 1972.

9722. Lovvorn, R. L. The effects of fertilization, species competition, and cutting treatments on the behavior of Dallis grass (*Paspalum dilatatum* Poir) and carpet grass (*Axonopus affinis* Chase). Journal of the American Society of Agronomy. 36(7):590–600. 1944.

9723. ______. The influence of lespedeza and fertilizer treatment on the behavior of dallis grass, carpet grass, and bermuda grass. Journal of the American Society of Agronomy. 36(10):791–802. 1944.

9724. ______. The effect of defoliation, soil fertility, temperature, and length of day on the growth of some perennial grasses. Journal of the American Society of Agronomy. 37(7):570–582. 1945.

9725. Low, P. The effect of wind on rotary sprinkler distribution uniformity. M.S. Thesis, University of California, Davis. 1972.

9726. Lower, J. The sod webworm problem. Missouri Lawn and Turf Conference Proceedings. 12:34–35. 1971.

9727. Lowery, J. C. Turf grass letters 1–12. Auburn University Agricultural Extension Service Mimeo.

9728. Lownie, J. D. The water problem on golf courses. Journal of the Board of Greenkeeping Research. 4(12):54–57. 1935.

9729. Lycanus, R., K. J. Mitchell, G. G. Pritchard, and D. M. Calder. Factors influencing survival of strains of ryegrass during the summer. New Zealand Journal of Agricultural Research. 3(1):185–193. 1960.

9730. Lucas, L. T., and J. C. Wells. Turfgrass disease research in North Carolina. Southern Regional Turf Research Committee Report, Virginia Polytechnic Institute. pp. 21–22. 1970.

9731. Lucas, M. The South's problem on golf greens. Golf Course Reporter. 21(1):18, 22. 1953.

9732. Lucas, M. B., Creeping bent fairways. Proceedings 40th International Turfgrass Conference. pp. 16–17. 1969.

9733. Lucas, M. B. Chemical treatment of goosegrass at the Garden City Golf Club 1966–1969. Proceedings 1970 3-Day Turf Courses, Rutgers University. pp. 35–36. 1970.

9734. ______. The calcium arsenate program at the Garden City Golf Club. Proceedings 1972 3-Day Turf Courses, Rutgers University. p. 48. 1972.

9735. Lucas, R. E. Fertilizer application methods. Michigan Turfgrass Research Report. 3(1):3–4. 1965.

9736. ______. Watering and water sources for turf. Michigan Turfgrass Research Report. 3(1):10. 1965.

9737. Lucas, R. E., P. E. Rieke, and R. S. Farnham. Peats for soil improvement and soil mixes. Michigan Cooperative Extension Bulletin No. 516. pp. 1–11. 1965.

9738. Lucks, H. W. Turf fertilizers—from plant to plant. Proceedings of the Midwest Regional Turf Conference. pp. 40–42. 1966.

9739. ______. Urea for turf. Ohio Turfgrass Conference Proceedings. pp. 53–54. 1971.

9740. Ludeke, K. L. Methods and costs of vegetative stabilization of copper mine tailing disposal berms. Arizona Turfgrass Conference Proceedings. p. 4. 1972.

9742. Ludwick, A. E. Iron and its use in turf maintenance. Annual Rocky Mountain Regional Turfgrass Conference Proceedings. 18:28–32. 1972.

9743. ______. Iron for turfgrass. Weeds, Trees and Turf. 12(1):16, 30. 1973.

9744. Ludwig, R. A. Toxin production by *Helminthosporium sativum* P. K. and B. and its significance in disease development. Canadian Journal of Botany. 35:291–303. 1957.

9745. Luekel, W. A. and J. M. Coleman. Growth behavior and maintenance of organic foods in Bahia grass. Florida Agricultural Experiment Station Bulletin. 219. 56 pp. 1930.

9746. Luginbill, P. Bionomics of the chinch bug. USDA Bulletin 1016. 14 pp. 1922.

9747. Luginbill, P. and H. R. Painter. May beetles of the United States and Canada. USDA Technical Bulletin No. 1060. 102 pp. 1953.

9749. Lukens, R. J. Turf disease control and use of fungicides. Turf Clippings. University of Massachusetts. 1(6):A33–37. 1961.

9750. ______. Control of bluegrass footrot disease with a single drench of fungicide. Phytopathology. 55(6):708. 1965.

9751. ______. Urea, an effective treatment for stripe smut on *Poa pratensis.* The Plant Disease Reporter. 49(4):361. 1965.

9752. ______. Chemical control of stripe smut. The Plant Disease Reporter. 51(5):-355–357. 1967.

9753. ______. Infection of inflorescence of *Poa pratensis* by *Helminthosporium vagans.* The Plant Disease Reporter. 51(9):752. 1967.

9754. ______. Low light intensity promotes melting out of bluegrass. Phytopathology. 58:1058. 1968.

9755. ______. Low sugar disease "melts-out" bluegrass. Turf-Grass Times. 3(5):1, 12–13. 1968.

9756. ______. *Helminthosporium (vagans)* leaf spot and melting-out in Kentucky bluegrass. Rutgers University Short Course in Turf Management. 2 pp. 1969.

9757. ______. *Helminthosporium (vagans)* leaf spot and melting-out in Kentucky bluegrass. Rutgers University. College of Agriculture and Environmental Science. Lawn and Utility Turf Section. pp. 61–62. 1969.

9758. ______. Melting-out of Kentucky bluegrass, a low sugar disease. Phytopathology. 60(8):1276–1278. 1970.

9759. ______. Melting-out of Kentucky bluegrass. Park Maintenance. 24(7):18. 1971.

9760. ______. Mode of action of the disease organism. Proceedings of Scotts Turfgrass Research Conference. 2:13–30. 1971.

9761. Lukens, R. J. and E. M. Stoddard. Diseases and other disorders of turf. Connecticut State Agricultural Experiment Station. Circular. 208:1–11. 1959.

9762. ______. Control of stripe smut on *Poa pratensis* with nabam. The Plant Disease Reporter. 44(8):672. 1960.

9763. ______. Wilt disease of golf greens and its control with nabam. Phytopathology. 51(8):577. 1961.

9764. ______. *Rhizoctonia solani* in relation to maintenance of golf courses. USGA Journal and Turf Management. 14(4):27–31. 1961.

9765. ______. Diseases and other disorders of turf. Connecticut Agricultural Experiment Station. Circular. 208:1–12. 1962.

9766. Lumpkins, G. Fertilizers, topdressing, insecticides and fungicides. Proceedings of the Midwest Regional Turf Conference. pp. 49–51. 1971.

9767. Lundqvist, A. Genetics of self-incompatibility in *Festuca pratensis* Huds. Hereditas. 41:518–520. 1955.

9768. Lundstrom, A. E. Consider maintenance first. The National Greenkeeper. 4(6):25–26. 1930.

9769. Lunt, H. A. The use of woodchips and other wood fragments as soil amendments. Connecticut Agricultural Experiment Station Bulletin. No. 593. 46 pp. 1955.

9770. ______. Improving nursery soil by addition of organic matter. Connecticut Agricultural Experiment Station Circular 219. 8 pp. 1961.

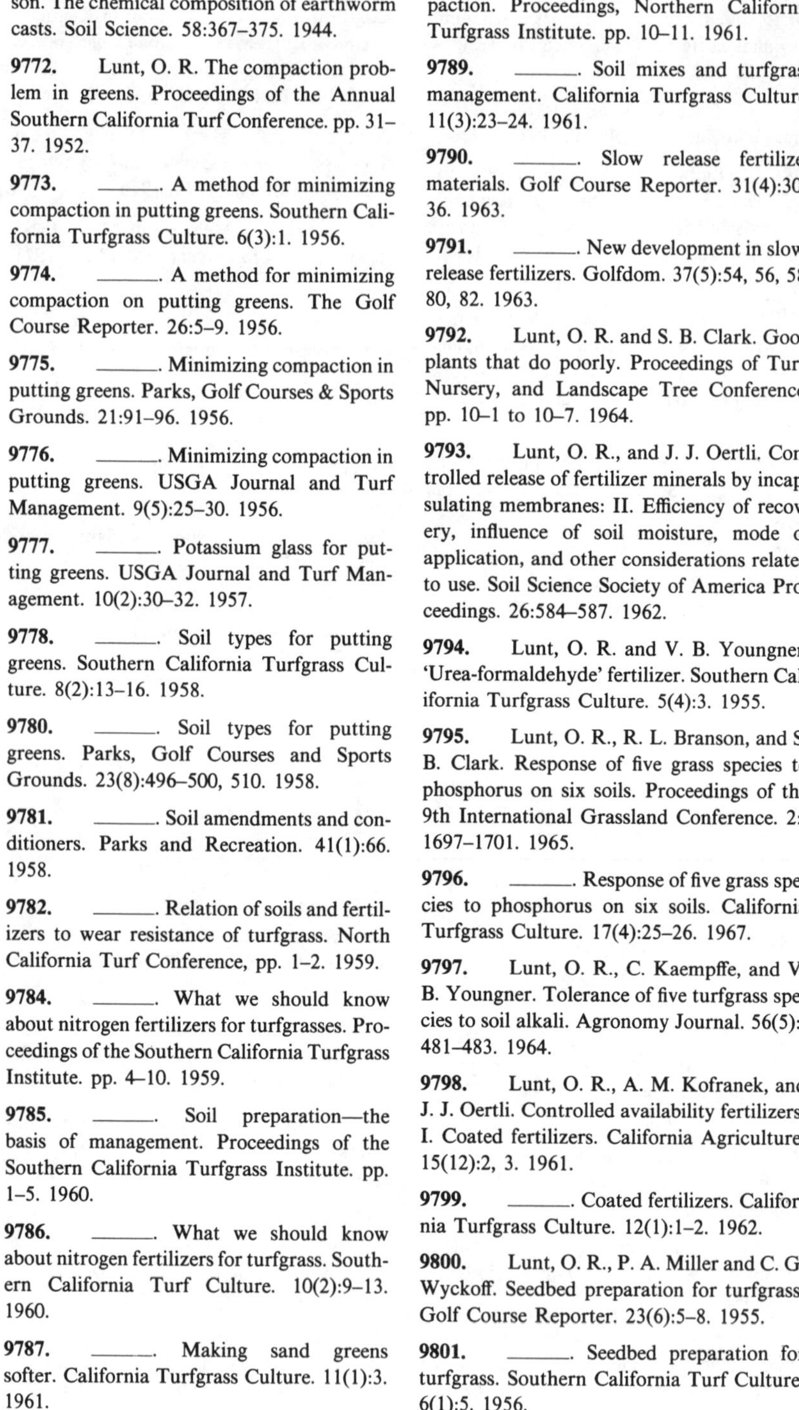

9771. Lunt, H. A., and H. G. M. Jacobson. The chemical composition of earthworm casts. Soil Science. 58:367–375. 1944.

9772. Lunt, O. R. The compaction problem in greens. Proceedings of the Annual Southern California Turf Conference. pp. 31–37. 1952.

9773. ______. A method for minimizing compaction in putting greens. Southern California Turfgrass Culture. 6(3):1. 1956.

9774. ______. A method for minimizing compaction on putting greens. The Golf Course Reporter. 26:5–9. 1956.

9775. ______. Minimizing compaction in putting greens. Parks, Golf Courses & Sports Grounds. 21:91–96. 1956.

9776. ______. Minimizing compaction in putting greens. USGA Journal and Turf Management. 9(5):25–30. 1956.

9777. ______. Potassium glass for putting greens. USGA Journal and Turf Management. 10(2):30–32. 1957.

9778. ______. Soil types for putting greens. Southern California Turfgrass Culture. 8(2):13–16. 1958.

9780. ______. Soil types for putting greens. Parks, Golf Courses and Sports Grounds. 23(8):496–500, 510. 1958.

9781. ______. Soil amendments and conditioners. Parks and Recreation. 41(1):66. 1958.

9782. ______. Relation of soils and fertilizers to wear resistance of turfgrass. North California Turf Conference, pp. 1–2. 1959.

9784. ______. What we should know about nitrogen fertilizers for turfgrasses. Proceedings of the Southern California Turfgrass Institute. pp. 4–10. 1959.

9785. ______. Soil preparation—the basis of management. Proceedings of the Southern California Turfgrass Institute. pp. 1–5. 1960.

9786. ______. What we should know about nitrogen fertilizers for turfgrass. Southern California Turf Culture. 10(2):9–13. 1960.

9787. ______. Making sand greens softer. California Turfgrass Culture. 11(1):3. 1961.

9788. ______. Grass roots and soil compaction. Proceedings, Northern California Turfgrass Institute. pp. 10–11. 1961.

9789. ______. Soil mixes and turfgrass management. California Turfgrass Culture. 11(3):23–24. 1961.

9790. ______. Slow release fertilizer materials. Golf Course Reporter. 31(4):30–36. 1963.

9791. ______. New development in slow-release fertilizers. Golfdom. 37(5):54, 56, 58, 80, 82. 1963.

9792. Lunt, O. R. and S. B. Clark. Good plants that do poorly. Proceedings of Turf, Nursery, and Landscape Tree Conference. pp. 10–1 to 10–7. 1964.

9793. Lunt, O. R., and J. J. Oertli. Controlled release of fertilizer minerals by incapsulating membranes: II. Efficiency of recovery, influence of soil moisture, mode of application, and other considerations related to use. Soil Science Society of America Proceedings. 26:584–587. 1962.

9794. Lunt, O. R. and V. B. Youngner. 'Urea-formaldehyde' fertilizer. Southern California Turfgrass Culture. 5(4):3. 1955.

9795. Lunt, O. R., R. L. Branson, and S. B. Clark. Response of five grass species to phosphorus on six soils. Proceedings of the 9th International Grassland Conference. 2:-1697–1701. 1965.

9796. ______. Response of five grass species to phosphorus on six soils. California Turfgrass Culture. 17(4):25–26. 1967.

9797. Lunt, O. R., C. Kaempffe, and V. B. Youngner. Tolerance of five turfgrass species to soil alkali. Agronomy Journal. 56(5):-481–483. 1964.

9798. Lunt, O. R., A. M. Kofranek, and J. J. Oertli. Controlled availability fertilizers. I. Coated fertilizers. California Agriculture. 15(12):2, 3. 1961.

9799. ______. Coated fertilizers. California Turfgrass Culture. 12(1):1–2. 1962.

9800. Lunt, O. R., P. A. Miller and C. G. Wyckoff. Seedbed preparation for turfgrass. Golf Course Reporter. 23(6):5–8. 1955.

9801. ______. Seedbed preparation for turfgrass. Southern California Turf Culture. 6(1):5. 1956.

9802. Lunt, O. R., J. J. Oertli and V. B. Youngner. The tolerance of some turfgrass species toward excessive boron supplies. Agronomy Abstracts. 52:71. 1960.

9803. Lunt, O. R., R. H. Sciaroni, and A. M. Kofranek. Ion exchange fertilizers and ammoniated organic matter. California Turfgrass Culture. 12(3):21–22. 1962.

9804. Lunt, O. R., F. T. Yamaguchi, and S. B. Clark. Controlled availability fertilizers. III. Metal ammonium phosphate. California Agriculture. 16(2):6–7. 1962.

9805. ______. Metal ammonium phosphates. California Turfgrass Culture. 12(2):-11, 15–16. 1962.

9806. Lunt, O. R., V. B. Youngner, and S. B. Clark. Use of coated and limited solubility fertilizers on turfgrass. Agronomy Abstracts. 53:74–75. 1961.

9807. Lunt, O. R., V. B. Youngner, and J. J. Oertli. Salinity tolerance of five turfgrass varieties. Agronomy Journal. 53(4):247–249. 1961.

9808. Lunt, O. R., V. B. Youngner, and A. H. Khadr. Critical nutrient levels in Newport bluegrass. Agronomy Abstracts. 56:106. 1964.

9809. Lunt, O. R., J. H. Madison, M. H. Kimball, and V. B. Youngner. Questions and answers. North California Turf Conference pp. 1–8. 1959.

9810. Lunt, O. R., E. M. Romney, R. L. Branson and G. V. Alexander. Potassium depletion by grass as influenced by clay and accessory minerals on eight semi-arid region soils. Agronomy Abstracts. 58:37. 1966.

9811. Lunt, O. R., J. Stark, R. H. Sciaroni, and T. Bryne. Studies of several long-lasting nitrogen sources on several floral and nursery crops and turfgrasses. California Agricultural Experiment Station Project #1469. 35 pp. 1958.

9812. Lunt, O. R., V. B. Youngner, J. J. Oertli, and S. Spaulding. Response and composition of 'Newport' Kentucky bluegrass to ratios of cations and to ratios of anions. Agronomy Abstracts. 54:104. 1962.

9813. Luscombe, H. A. Turf establishment on the Gatineau Parkway. Guelph Turf Conference Proceedings. pp. 41–43. 1959.

9814. Luttrell, E. S. A taxonomic revision of *Helminthosporium sativum* and related species. American Journal of Botany. 42:57–67. 1955.

9815. ______. *Rhizoctonia* blight of tall fescue grass. The Plant Disease Reporter. 46(9):661–664. 1962.

9816. Lutz, J. A. and C. I. Rich. The effect of soluble salts on the availability of phosphate fertilizers. Virginia Agricultural Experiment Station. Research Report 59. 32 pp. 1961.

9818. Lycklama, J. C. The absorption of ammonium and nitrate by perennial ryegrass. Acta Botanica Neerlandica. 12:361–423. 1963.

9819. Lyda, S. D., and G. D. Robinson. Soil respiratory activity and organic matter depletion in an arid Nevada soil. Soil Science Society of America Proceedings. 33(1):92–94. 1969.

9820. Lyle, J. A. Lawn grass disease control. Highlights of Agricultural Research. 14(1):14. 1967.

9821. Lyles, L., D. V. Armbrust, J. D. Dickerson, and N. P. Woodruff. Spray-on adhesives for temporary wind erosion control. Journal of Soil and Water Conservation. 24(5):190–193. 1969.

9822. Lynch, G. A. Working automatic watering system. Proceedings of the 37th International Turfgrass Conference. pp. 30–32. 1966.

9823. Lynch, R. I. *Poa annua* not a self-fertilizer. Gardener's Chronicle. 33(859):380. 1903.

9824. Lynd, J. Q. Fertilization for improved turf. Oklahoma Turfgrass Conference Proceedings. p. 5. 1959.

9825. Lynd, J. Q., C. E. Rieck, and P. W. Santelmann. Soil components determining bensulide phytotoxicity. Agronomy Journal. 58(5):508–510. 1966.

9826. Lyons, B. Golf promotion—my ideas. Proceedings of the Midwest Regional Turf Conference. 26–28. 1972.

9827. Lyons, W. How science has helped my greenkeeping. Golfdom. 21(9):57, 78. 1947.

9828. ______. Happy grass requires dolomite limestone. Park Maintenance. 4:-5–6. 1951.

9829. ______. Softening hard greens a simple, safe way. Golfdom. 26(1):35–36. 1952.

9830. ______. Nitrogen tests for turf. Golf Course Reporter. 21(4):11–12. 1953.

9831. ______. Nitrogen use and why. Proceedings of Midwest Regional Turf Conference. pp. 45–48. 1955.

9832. ______. How to make quick work of planting a nursery green. Golfdom. 30(2):-49, 52. 1956.

9833. ______. Asphalt mulch gives fine results on Akron Merion blue project. Golfdom. 33(5):59. 1959.

9834. ______. Why I seldom topdress greens. Proceedings of Midwest Regional Turf Conference. pp. 13–15. 1959.

9835. ______. The how and why of night maintenance. Midwest Regional Turf Conference Proceedings. pp. 52–54. 1969.

9836. ______. Night maintenance. Golfdom. 36(7):30. 1962.

9837. ______. Liming turfgrass. First Ohio Turfgrass Conference Proceedings. pp. 31–33. 1967.

9838. ______. Liming turfgrasses. The Golf Superintendent. 36(8):28–29. 1968.

9839. ______. Sterilizing soil with anhydrous ammonia. Proceedings of the Midwest Regional Turf Conference. pp. 29–30. 1972.

9840. Macadam, G. C. Sports ground maintenance in dry weather. Part I. Parks, Golf Courses, and Sports Grounds. 30(8):-610–612. 1965.

9841. ______. Sports ground maintenance in dry weather. Part 2. Parks, Golf Courses, and Sports Grounds. 30(9):715, 729. 1965.

9842. ______. Sports ground maintenance in dry weather. Part 3. Parks, Golf Courses and Sports Grounds. 30(10):797–798. 1965.

9843. MacAlpine, A. N. How to know grasses by their leaves. Rural Publishing Company, New York. 92 pp. 1890.

9844. Macbeth, N. Bent putting greens in California. USGA Green Section Bulletin. 8(2):58–60. 1928.

9845. McCammon, D. Control of *Poa annua* with betasan or pre-san. Proceedings of the Mid-Atlantic Association of Golf Course Superintendents. pp. 34–36. 1969.

9846. MacCurrach, A. Watering. Turf Clippings. University of Massachusetts. 1(6):14–15. 1961.

9847. MacDonald, J. Lawns, links and sportsfields. C. Scribner's Sons, New York. 77 pp. 1923.

9848. MacGregor, J. Taming the dandelion after long battle. Golfdom. 2(4):59–61. 1928.

9849. ______. Give thought to your equipment. The National Greenkeeper. 2(7):-23–24. 1928.

9850. ______. Don't despair when nature frowns. Golfdom. 3(4):32–33. 1929.

9851. ______. Dandelions and plantain eradication method. Golfdom. 3(7):58–60. 1929.

9852. ______. Weed control by use of iron sulfate. Golfdom. 3(9):28, 30. 1929.

9853. ______. The why of poor fairways. The National Greenkeeper. 4(5):10–11. 1930.

9854. ______. Irrigation. The National Greenkeeper. 5(4):20–23. 1931.

9855. ______. Golf course maintenance budgeting. The National Greenkeeper. 6(3):-5–7. 1932.

9856. ______. I keep *Poa annua.* Golfdom. 8(10):23. 1934.

9857. ______. Proper cutting height saves money and trouble. Golfdom. 18(5):46. 1944.

9858. MacKenzie, D. Soil analysis, its interpretation and value in turf production. Guelph Turfgrass Conference Proceedings. pp. 4–11. 1959.

9859. MacLean, A. W. A few thoughts on the practicing of better management, to help balance reduced budgets. Greenkeepers Club of New England Newsletter. 5(7):2–4. 1933.

9860. MacLean, N. A. Disease control on Canadian turf. Proceedings, Northwest Turf Conference. 12:15–16. 1958.

9861. ______. Soil condition and turf disease. Golf Course Reporter. 29(1):12–46. 1961.

9862. ______. Amino acid nutrition and turf fungi. Proceedings of the 18th Annual Northwest Turfgrass Conference. pp. 40–46. 1964.

9863. MacLean, A. J., B. Stone, and W. E. Cordukes. Amounts of mercury in some golf course soils. Research Branch, C.D.A., Ottawa. 1972.

9864. Macleod N. H. A comparison of liquid and solid fertilizer for turf. M. S. Thesis, University of Massachusetts. 112 pp. 1958.

9865. Macself, A. J. Grass: A new and thoroughly practical book on grass for ornamental lawns and all purposes of sports and games. C. Palmer, London. 203 pp. 1924.

9866. ______. Lawns and sports greens. W. H. and L. Collingridge Ltd., London. 133 pp. 1932.

9867. ______. Lawns and sports greens. W. H. and L. Collingridge Ltd., London. 103 pp. 1947.

9868. McAfee, J. A. Growth regulators. Proceedings of the Midwest Regional Turf Conference. p. 38. 1972.

9869. McAlister, D. F. Determination of soil drought resistance in grass seedlings. Journal of the American Society of Agronomy. 36(4):324–336. 1944.

9870. McAlister, J. Some notes on weeding and upkeep on a seaside course. Journal of the Board of Greenkeeping Research. 4(13):116–118. 1935.

9871. McAloon, J. P. Golf course irrigation in Florida. USGA Green Section Bulletin. 8(7):142–143. 1928.

9872. McAnlis, T. How to promote and not to promote golf. Proceedings of the Midwest Regional Turf Conference. pp. 23–25. 1972.

9873. ______. Percolating with Purrwick. Proceedings of the Midwest Regional Turf Conference. pp. 46–48. 1972.

9874. McAvoy, W. J. Some related aspects of life history of common chickweed *(Stellaria media).* M.S. Thesis, Rutgers University. 131 pp. 1970.

9875. McBean, G. A. An investigation of turbulence within the forest. Journal of Applied Meteorology. 7(3):410–416. 1968.

9876. McBee, G. G. Post-emergence herbicide studies on certain weeds in bermudagrass turf. Texas Agricultural Experiment Station Progress Report. PR–2408. 5 pp. 1966.

9877. ______. Effects of mowing heights on texture of bermudagrass turf. Texas A & M University, Department of Soil and Crop Science. Technical Report No. 10. 1966.

9878. ______. Studies on the association of light quality, quantity and performance of selected turfgrasses. Agronomy Abstracts. 59:53. 1967.

9879. ______. Performance of certain cool-season grasses in overseeding studies on a Tifgreen bermudagrass golf green. Texas Agricultural Experiment Station Progress Report. PR–2457. 5 pp. 1967.

9880. ______. Turf—recommended practices—Texas. Annual Southern Weed Conference Research Report. 20:91–92. 1967.

9881. ______. Association of certain variations in light quality with the performance of selected turfgrasses. Crop Science. 9(1):14–17. 1969.

9882. ______. North American turf research. International Turfgrass Conference Proceedings. 41:14–17. 1970.

9883. McBee, G. G. and E. C. Holt. Shade tolerance studies on bermudagrass and other turfgrasses. Agronomy Abstracts. 58:-35. 1966.

9884. McBee, G. G. and W. G. Menn. Relationships between total N, chlorophyll a and b, carotenoid fractions, IAA and carbohydrate fractions in six warm season turfgrasses. Agronomy Abstracts. 61:55. 1969.

9885. McBee, G. G. and L. E. Surles. Some effects of certain benzoic, phenoxyacetic and phenoxypropionic acid derivatives on St. Augustinegrass. Texas Agricultural Experiment Station Progress Report. PR–2530. 5 pp. 1968.

9886. McBee, G. G., E. C. Holt, and C. R. Brooks. Evaluation of fungicides for control of brown patch disease of St. Augustinegrass, 1963 and 1964. Texas Agricultural Experiment Station Progress Report. PR–2382. 4 pp. 1965.

9887. McBee, G. G., W. E. McCune and K. R. Beerwinkle. Effect of soil heating on winter growth and appearance of bermudagrass and St. Augustinegrass. Agronomy Journal. 60(2):228–231. 1968.

9888. McBee, G. G., W. Menn, and A. Zemanek. Evaluation of certain herbicides for selective eradication of Dallisgrass, crabgrass, and nutsedge in a bermudagrass turf. Texas Agricultural Experiment Station Progress Report. PR–2458. 6 pp. 1967.

9889. McBee, G. G., W. G. Menn and R. D. Palmer. Turf: recommended practices—Texas. Annual Southern Weed Conference Research Report. 22:90. 1969.

9890. McBeth, C. W. Tests on the susceptibility and resistance of several southern grasses to the root-knot nematode *Heterodera marioni.* Helminthological Society of Washington Proceedings. 12(2):41–44. 1945.

9891. McCain, A. H. Dichondra leafspot. California Turfgrass Culture. 17(4):26. 1967.

9892. McCain, A. H. and R. M. Endo. Turfgrass disease control. California Turfgrass Culture. 20(3):20–22. 1970.

9893. McCain, A. H. Guide to turfgrass pest control. California Agricultural Experiment Station Leaflet 209. 23 pp. 1971.

9894. McCain, A. H. and T. G. Byrne. Systemic control of blue grass rust. Turf-Grass Times. 4(2):10. 1968.

9895. McCain, A. H. and P. M. Halisky. Infection of bermudagrass by *Ustilago cynodontis.* Phytopathology. 52(8):742. 1962.

9896. McCain, A. H., T. G. Byrne, and M. R. Bell. Melting-out of bluegrass. California Turfgrass Culture. 15(4):30–31. 1965.

9897. McCall, M. A. Application of science to greenkeeping. The Greenkeepers' Reporter. 5(2):7–9, 33. 1937.

9898. ______. Bureau of plant industry welcomes turf culture. Turf Culture. 1(1):-6–9. 1939.

9899. McCallip, W. Uses of peat and muck. The National Greenkeeper. 5(2):28–29. 1931.

9900. McCallum, R. E. Automatic irrigation. Proceedings of the Turfgrass Sprinkler Irrigation Conference. 3 pp. 1966.

9901. ______. Latest irrigation installation techniques. Turf-Grass Times. 2(2):4–5, 15. 1966.

9902. McCammon, D. Automatic greens and tees—my experience as a user. Proceedings of the 1965 Midwest Regional Turf Conference. pp. 28–30. 1965.

9903. McCarter, S. M. and R. H. Littrell. Pathogenicity of *Pythium myriotylum* to several grasses and vegetable crops. Plant Disease Reporter. 52(3):179–183. 1968.

9904. McCarver, O. Lawns: new and old. Montana Agricultural Extension Folder. 79:-1–6. 1964.

9905. McCloud, D. E. Evapo-transpiration as a guide to turf irrigation. Proceedings of the Annual University of Florida Turf Conference. 2:25–29. 1954.

9906. ______. Irrigation management for turf. University of Florida Turf Management Conference Proceedings. 3:11–14. 1955.

9907. ______. Moisture and plant growth. Proceedings of the University of Florida Turf Management Conference. 4:17–19. 1956.

9908. ______. The theory of water loss. Golf Course Reporter. 27(5):18–20. 1959.

9909. ______. Water requirements for turf. Proceedings Florida Turfgrass Management Conference. 18:88–90. 1970.

9910. McClure, G. M. The soil profile. The National Greenkeeper. 2(8):29–30. 1928.

9911. ______. How I control brownpatch. The National Greenkeeper. 4(6):22–23. 1930.

9912. ______. Fertilizer in the soil. The Greenkeepers' Reporter. 4(6):6–7, 26. 1936.

9913. ______. What happens to fertilizer in the soil? National Association of Greenkeepers of America Conference Proceedings. 10:103–134. 1936.

9914. ______. Lawns; establishing a new lawn. Ohio Agricultural Extension Bulletin. 129:1–32. 1940.

9915. ______. Retail sales and customer relations. Proceedings University of Florida Turf-Grass Management Conference. 9:131–134. 1961.

9916. McClure, G. M., C. J. Willard and F. A. Welton. Lawns. Ohio Agricultural Extension Bulletin. 129:1–24. 1932.

9917. ______. Lawns. Ohio Agricultural Extension Bulletin. 129:1–24. 1935.

9918. ______. Lawns; establishing a new lawn. Ohio Agricultural Experiment Station. 129:1–32. 1937.

9919. McCollan, M. E. Possibilities of creeping bentgrass. Western Washington Agricultural Experiment Station Bulletin. 12:-26–30. 1924.

9920. McCool, M. M. and G. J. Bouyoucos. Causes and effects of soil heaving. Michigan Agricultural Experiment Station. Special Bulletin 192. 11 pp. 1929.

9921. McCormack, J. The maintenance of stolon greens. Greenkeepers Club of New England Newsletter. 1(1):2. 1929.

9922. ______. A resume of brown patch control. Greenkeepers Club of New England Newsletter. 4(9):3–4. 1932.

9923. McCown, R. L., and M. L. Peterson. Effects of low temperature and age of plant on flowering in *Lolium perenne* L. Crop Science. 4:388–391. 1964.

9924. McCoy, J. Labor relations at the Cincinnati Country Club. Proceedings of Midwest Regional Turf Conference. pp. 14–15. 1955.

9925. ______. Why and how I topdress. Proceedings of Midwest Regional Turf Conference. pp. 15–16. 1959.

9926. ______. Greens—my ideas. Proceedings of Midwest Regional Turf Conference. pp. 42–44. 1964.

9927. ______. Maintenance of Ohio State University golf courses. Greenkeepers' Reporter. 10(5):5–6. 1942.

9928. ______. Golf course maintenance at Ohio State University. Midwest Turf-News and Research. 2(2):2. 1948.

9929. McCoy, N. The action of a fungicide. Proceedings of the Annual Texas Turfgrass Conference. 23:4–7. 1968.

9930. McCoy, N. L., R. W. Toler and J. Amador. St. Augustine decline (sad)—a virus disease of St. Augustine grass. The Plant Disease Reporter. 53(12):955–958. 1969.

9931. ______. St. Augustine decline (sad)—a virus disease of St. Augustine grass. Turf Bulletin. Massachusetts Turf and Lawn Grass Council. 6(2):15–18. 1970.

9932. McCoy, R. E. A study of the etiology of spring dead spot. M.S. Thesis, Oklahoma State University. 1967.

9933. ______. 1972 *Pythium* control results in south Florida. Florida Turf. 4(6):3. 1972.

9934. ______. Spring dead spot. Florida Turfgrass Association. 5(4):3. 1972.

9935. McCrawley, R. F. Recalling the earlier zoysia. Proceedings of the Midwest Regional Turf Conference. p. 61. 1971.

9936. McCrea, C. What we do to minimize traffic injury to turf. Rutgers University Short Course in Turf Management. 2 pp. 1965.

9937. ______. The long and short of it. Golfdom. 41(9):34–36, 54. 1967.

9938. McCrea, C. and R. E. Engel. The effect of fertilizer rates and placement on turfgrass seedlings. USGA Journal and Turf Management. 12(7):28–29. 1959.

9939. McCrea, C. and E. J. Hunter. Irrigation systems—economics. USGA Green Section Record. 4(1):8–13. 1966.

9940. McCue, C. The case for forward tees. USGA Green Section Record 4(6):20. 1967.

9941. McCulley, W. Herbicides to kill weeds. Proceedings of the Annual Texas Turfgrass Conference. 21:84–87. 1966.

9942. McCullough, C. *Poa Annua* as I see it. Second Western Turf Conference at University of Alberta, Edmonton. pp. 30–33. 1953.

9943. ______. Golf green construction. Proceeding School of Soils, Fertilization & Turf Maintenance Green Section, Royal Canadian Golf Association. pp. 75–79. 1954.

9944. ______. Living with *Poa annua.* International Turf-grass Conference Proceedings. 32:19. 1961.

9945. ______. Electric greens. The Greenmaster. 3(10):1, 10, 11. 1967.

9946. ______. Electrical underground heating. 20th Annual RCGA National Turfgrass Conference. pp. 35–36. 1969.

9947. McCully, W. G. Herbicides in turfgrass management. Proceedings of the Texas Turfgrass Conference. 17:30–33. 1962.

9948. McCully, W. G. and W. J. Bowmer. Post-surface control of bermudagrass on highway shoulder pavements. Down to Earth. 23(1):13–17. 1967.

9949. McCully, W. G. Vegetation control helps Texas reduce maintenance costs. Better Roads. 38(9):19–22. 1968.

9950. McCully, W. G., and W. J. Bowmer. Promoting establishment of vegetation for erosion control. Texas Transportation Institute, Texas A&M University. Research Report Number 67–6, Study 2–18–63–67. 19 pp. 1967.

9951. McCully, W. G., W. J. Bowmer, and A. F. Wiese. Control of grasses and weeds growing in asphalt pavements. Highway Research Record No. 246. Roadside Development. pp. 50–58. 1968.

9952. McCully, W. G., E. L. Whiteley, and W. J. Bowmer. The influence of mulching and tillage on turf establishment. Agronomy Abstracts. 56:101. 1964.

9953. McCune, W. E., K. R. Beerwinkle and G. G. McBee. The effect of soil heating on winter growth and appearance of warm-season turfgrasses. Texas Agricultural Experiment Station. Progress Report PR–2360. 1–17 pp. 1965.

9954. McDermott, J. Replanting golf greens. Proceedings of Midwest Regional Turf Conference. pp. 58–59. 1964.

9955. McDill, R. L. Seeding experiments on highway backslopes. Iowa Highway Research Board Bulletin. 9:1–35. 1961.

9956. McDowell, B. Weed killing chemicals. The Modern Cemetery. 57(11):123–124. 1948.

9957. McElroy, J. J. The coordination of a program in turf culture in the university. Southern California Conference of Turf Culture. pp. 40–45. 1951.

9958. ______. Turfgrass—what of its future? North California Turf Conference. pp. 1–5. 1959.

9959. McElwee, E. W. Part I—fertilization and nutrition. Proceedings of the Second Annual University of Florida Turf Conference. pp. 10–12. 1954.

9960. ______. Better use of landscape materials on the golf course. Proceedings University of Florida Turf Management Conference. 4:43–44. 1956.

9961. ______. Landscaping parks and playgrounds for beauty and durability. Proceedings University of Florida Turf Management Conference. 6:94–95. 1958.

9962. ______. Landscaping large areas. Proceedings University of Florida Turf-Grass Management Conference. 10:122–124. 1962.

9963. McFaul, J. A. Renovating old turf with calcium cyanamid. Agri-Chem Review. 1954.

9964. ______. Renovating old turf with calcium cyanamid. New York State Turf Association Bulletin. 49:187–188. 1954.

9965. ______. Further work with cyanamid in seedbeds. New York State Turf Association Bulletin. 50:191–192. 1955.

9966. ______. Potassium cyanate controls spotted spurge. New York State Turf Association Bulletin. 52:202. 1957.

9967. McFeely, P. C. and R. S. Taylor. Some aspects of the nitrogen: water interaction on grass swards. Journal of the British Grassland Society. 25(4):261–265. 1970.

9968. McGehee, W. L. How to cultivate bluegrass lawns: discussing its enemies. Park and Cemetery. 41(6):182. 1931.

9969. McCoy, R. E., and H. C. Young. Bermudagrass thatch decomposition in relation to spring dead spot. Phytopathology. 58:401. 1968.

9970. McGeorge, W. T. Gypsum, a soil corrective and soil builder. Univ. of Arizona Agricultural Experiment Station Bulletin. 200:1–14. 1945.

9971. ______. Sulphur, a soil corrective and soil builder. University of Arizona

Agricultural Experiment Station Bulletin 201:1–20. 1945.

9972. McGinnies, W. J. Effects of moisture stress and temperature on germination of six range grasses. Agronomy Journal. 52(3):-159–162. 1960.

9973. ______. Effects of shade on the survival of crested wheatgrass seedlings. Crop Science. 6:482–484. 1966.

9974. ______. Effects of nitrogen fertilizer on an old stand of crested wheatgrass. Agronomy Journal. 60(5):560–562. 1968.

9975. ______. Effects of controlled plant spacing on growth and mortality of three range grasses. Agronomy Journal. 63(6):868–870. 1971.

9976. McGlohon, N. E. Nematode damage to turfgrasses. Auburn University Annual Turfgrass Short Course. pp. 18–20. 1961.

9977. McGregor, J. I. Problems of airfield turf. Proceedings of the 6th Annual Texas Turf Conference. pp. 48–52. 1951.

9979. McHenry, W. B. Substitute herbicides for sodium arsenite. California Turfgrass Culture. 13(4):26–28. 1963.

9980. ______. Herbicides used in turf, ornamental and non-selective weed control. Southern California Turfgrass Institute Proceedings. pp. 3–5. 1963.

9981. McIlroy, R. J. Carbohydrates of grassland herbage. Horticulture Abstracts. 37(2):79–87. 1967.

9982. McKay, A. G. Bentgrass putting greens at Chattanooga. USGA Journal and Turf Management. 6(2):25–27. 1953.

9983. ______. Converting bermuda greens to bent. Golf Course Reporter. 22(4):-10–11. 1954.

9984. ______. Bent greens o.k. in South. Golfdom. 28(5):52–53. 1954.

9985. ______. The 8-inch layer. Golfdom, 38(3):100. 1964.

9986. McKay, H. Sprinkler irrigation terminology. California Turfgrass Culture. 19(3):22–24. 1969.

9987. McKee, G. W. Penngift crownvetch. Crop Science. 2(4):356. 1962.

9988. McKee, G. W. and A. R. Langille. Effect of soil pH, drainage, and fertiiity on growth, survival, and element content of crownvetch, *Coronilla varia* L. Agronomy Journal. 59(6):533–536. 1967.

9989. ______. Germination inhibitors in crownvetch seed. Second Crownvetch Symposium, Pennsylvania State University. 6:60–62. 1968.

9990. McKee, G. W. and M. L. Risius. Varietal differences in crownvetch cotyledon size. Agronomy Journal. 62(6):711–714. 1970.

9991. McKee, W. H., R. E. Blaser, and D. G. Barkley. Mulches for steep cut slopes. Highway Research Record No. 53:35–42. 1963.

9992. McKee, W. H., R. H. Brown, and R. E. Blaser. Effect of clipping and nitrogen fertilization on yield and stands of tall fescue. Crop Science. 7(6):567–570. 1967.

9993. McKee, G. W., M. L. Risius, and A. R. Langille. Flowering of crownvetch as affected by thermo-inductive treatment, photoperiod, plant age, and genotype. Crop Science. 12(5):553–557. 1972.

9994. McKee, W. H., R. E. Blaser, C. K. Curry and R. B. Cooper. Effect of microclimate on adaptation of species along Virginia highway banks. Agronomy Abstracts. 56:-102. 1964.

9995. McKee, G. W., A. R. Langille, W. P. Ditmer, and P. K. Joo. Germination and seedling growth of 48 plant species as affected by a leachate from seeds of *Coronilla varia* L. Crop Science. 11(5):614–617. 1971.

9996. McKee, W. H., A. J. Powell, R. B. Cooper, and R. E. Blaser. Microclimate conditions on highway slope facings as related to adaptation of species. Highway Research Board. 93:38–43. 1965.

9997. McKeen, H. Thoroughness is vital in building perfect greens. Golfdom. 7(4):-16–18. 1933.

9998. ______. We changed our greens to bent without closing the course. Golfdom. 7(8):18–21. 1933.

9999. McKell, C. M. and V. B. Youngner. Carbohydrate reserves of a warm season and a cool season perennial grass in relation to temperature regimes. Agronomy Abstracts. 59:42. 1967.

10000. McKell, C. M., V. B. Youngner, F. J. Nudge, and N. J. Chatterton. Carbohydrate accumulation of Coastal bermudagrass and Kentucky bluegrass in relation to temperature regimes. Crop Science. 9(5):534–537. 1969.

10001. McKendrick, J. D. Big bluestem and indiangrass vegetative reproduction and critical levels of reserve carbohydrates and nitrogen. Ph.D. Thesis, Kansas State University. 1971.

10002. McKenzie, R. E. The ability of forage plants to survive early spring flooding. Scientific Agriculture. 31(8):358–367. 1951.

10003. McKenzie, R. E., L. J. Anderson, and D. H. Heinricks. The effect of flooding on emergence of forage crop seeds. Scientific Agriculture. 29(5):237–240. 1949.

10004. McKiel, C. G., F. B. Ledeboer, and C. R. Skogley. Soil heating studies with cool season turfgrasses. IV. Energy requirements for electric soil heating. Agronomy Journal. 63(5):689–691. 1971.

10006. McLaren, M. Whats going on in Cleveland. Midwest Turf-News and Research. 2(1):3. 1948.

10007. ______. Large scale application of DDT. Greenkeepers' Reporter. 17(3):12–13. 1949.

10008. ______. Large scale application of DDT. Greenkeeping Superintendents Association. National Turf Conference. 20:83–86. 1949.

10009. ______. Maintenance that makes a course outstanding. Golfdom. 24(4):68, 70, 103–104. 1950.

10010. ______. Irrigation and fertilization for healthy turf. Proceedings of the Midwest Regional Turf Conference. p. 18. 1956.

10011. McLean, A. Turfgrass varieties for the interior of British Columbia. Proceedings of the 18th Annual Northwest Turfgrass Conference. pp. 19–20. 1964.

10012. McLean, D. Diagnosing lawn and ornamental problems. Florida Turf-Grass Management Conference Proceedings. 19:-59–63. 1971.

10014. McLeod, G. F. and K. E. Maxwell. Experiments to control hairy chinch bug infesting turf on Long Island. Journal of Economic Entomology. 30(3):432–437. 1937.

10015. McLeod, L. B. and R. B. Carson. Influence of K on the yield and chemical composition of grasses grown in hydroponic culture with 12, 50, 75% of N as NH_4+. Agronomy Journal. 58(1):52–57. 1966.

10016. MacLeod, N. H., E. C. Roberts, and J. E. Steckel. A comparison of turfgrass responses to liquid and solid fertilizer. Agronomy Abstracts. 50:66. 1958.

10017. McLaughlin, W. T. and R. L. Brown. Controlling coastal sand dunes in the Pacific northwest. U.S.D.A. Circular No. 660. p. 46. 1942.

10018. McLoughlin, J. W. The control of colonial bentgrass in Kentucky bluegrass turf. M.S. Thesis, Oregon State University. 1969.

10019. McLoughlin, J. W., N. R. Goetze and J. A. Yungen. Selective control of colonial bentgrass in Kentucky bluegrass turf. Agronomy Abstracts. p. 70. 1970.

10020. McMaugh, P. A desiccant approach to *Poa annua* control. Journal of the Sports Turf Research Institute. 46:63–75. 1970.

10021. ______. Control of encroachment of *Agrostis* spp. swards by warm season turfgrasses. Journal Sports Turf Research Institute. 47:33–40. 1971.

10022. McMicken, C. R. Selection and maintenance of turf equipment. Golf Superintendent. 36(7):26, 27, 29. 1968.

10023. McMillen, C. L. Watering and mowing of Bahia grass. Proceedings, 17th Annual University of Florida Turf-Grass Management Conference. 17:82–87. 1969.

10024. McMillan, R. C. The effects of smoke pollution on plant life. Parks, Golf Courses and Sports Grounds. 20(3):159–163. 1954.

10025. McMurray, S. F. Panel: Weed control in large and intensive areas. Proceedings University of Florida Turfgrass Management Conference. 14:137. 1966.

10026. McNamara, J. J. Turf grasses for Pennsylvania. USGA Green Section Bulletin. 3(1):19–20. 1923.

10027. ______. Brown-patch in western Pennsylvania. The National Greenkeeper. 1(10):18. 1927.

10028. McNeely, W. H., and W. C. Morgan. Review of soil amendments. Classification and development. Turfgrass Times. 3(3):2–5, 18. 1968.

10029. ______. Review of soil amendments Part 2. Classification and development. Turfgrass Times. 3(4):2, 11–15. 1968.

10030. McNeur, A. J. Soil sterilisation. New Zealand Institute for Turf Culture Newsletter. 23:12–16. 1963.

10031. McNew, G. L. The effects of soil fertility. Plant Diseases. USDA Yearbook. pp. 100–114. 1953.

10033. McPhersone, A. Bowling greens in New Zealand. Turf for Sport. 4(1):10–13. 1962.

10034. McSloy, H. J. Principles and practices in watering. The Golf Course Reporter. 33(6):18–22. 1965.

10035. McSwain, E. Pointers on buying turfgrass seed. New Mexico Turfgrass Conference Proceedings. 1:13–15. 1955.

10036. McTaggart, A. Cricket—the end of the season. The Groundsman. 15(2):10–12. 1961.

10037. ______. Spring is coming—there is work to be done. The Groundsman. 16(7):-6–10. 1963.

10038. ______. The cricket square—getting ready for the summer. The Groundsman. 17(8):12–16. 1964.

10039. ______. Maintaining our cricket facilities. The Groundsman. 18(12):10–12. 1965.

10040. ______. Maintaining our cricket facilities. The Groundsman. 19(1):8. 1965.

10041. ______. Maintaining our cricket facilities. The Groundsman. 19(4):8–12. 1965.

10042. ______. Spring is here—work to be done. The Groundsman. 19(7):4–10, 14. 1966.

10043. ______. Laying the foundations. The Groundsman. 20(1):14–20. 1966.

10044. ______. Preparing for the season —renovation of winter playing areas. The Groundsman. 20(7):18–26. 1967.

10045. ______. Preparing for the autumn and winter. The Groundsman. 21(1):34–36, 39. 1967.

10046. ______. Laying the foundations . . . The Groundsman. 21(11):18–20, 24. 1968.

10047. ______. Food for thought. The Groundsman. 23(9):26–27. 1970.

10048. ______. Spring (1). The Groundsman. 24(7):20. 1971.

10049. McVeigh, K. J. Adjuvants with turfgrass herbicides. M.S. Thesis, Rutgers University. 1971.

10050. ______. The soil as a source of turf weeds. Rutgers University Short Course in Turf Management Proceedings. pp. 7–11. 1971.

10051. McVeigh, K. J., R. E. Engel, and R. D. Ilnicki. Results with several surfactants in combination with turfgrass herbicides. Northeastern Weed Science Society Proceedings. p. 401. 1970.

10052. ______. Effects of the addition of surfactants and vegetable-mineral oil combinations for turfgrass weed control. Northeastern Weed Science Society Proceeding. 25:146. 1971.

10053. McVey, G. R. Response of turfgrass seedlings to various phosphorus sources. Agronomy Abstracts, 59:53. 1967.

10054. ______. How seedlings respond to phosphorous. Weeds, Trees, and Turf. 7(6):18–19. 1968.

10055. ______. Fertilizer development and growth regulation. Short Course on Roadside Development (Ohio). 13:83–92. 1971.

10056. McVey, G. and J. Long. Response of *Poa pratensis* varieties to 6 Azauracil. Agronomy Abstracts. 61:55. 1969.

10057. ______. Aluminum tolerance of Windsor Kentucky bluegrass as influenced by lime and phosphorus. Agronomy Abstracts. p. 48. 1971.

10058. McVey, G. R. and E. W. Mayer. Response of 'Tifgreen' bermudagrass and

'Windsor' Kentucky bluegrass to various light spectra modifications. Agronomy Journal. 61(5):655–659. 1969.

10059. McVey, G. R. Response of Windsor Kentucky bluegrass to various potassium rates and sources. Agronomy Abstracts. 60:-60. 1968.

10060. McVey, G. R., E. W. Mayer, and J. A. Simmons. Responses of various turfgrasses to certain light spectra modifications. Proceedings of the First International Turfgrass Research Conference. pp. 264–272. 1969.

10061. McVickar, M. H. Manganese status of some important Ohio soil types and uptake of manganese by Kentucky bluegrass. Journal of the American Society of Agronomy. 34(2):123–128. 1942.

10062. McWhinnie, A. Brownpatch. The Greenkeepers' Reporter. 6(5):13–14, 35. 1938.

10063. Madison, J. H. Inside the roots. North California Turf Conference. pp. 18–22. 1954.

10064. ______. Turf invasion by weedy grasses. California Agricultural Experiment Station—California Agriculture. 12(4):11. 1958.

10065. ______. Drouth—1959. North California Turf Conference. pp. 1–7. 1959.

10066. ______. Discussion of fertilizer test plots. Southern California Turfgrass Conference Proceedings. pp. 31–32. 1959.

10067. ______. The effect of the root temperature of turfgrasses on the uptake of nitrogen as urea, ammonium, and nitrate. Agronomy Abstracts. 52:71. 1960.

10068. ______. The mowing of turfgrass I. the effect of season, interval, and height of mowing on the growth of seaside bentgrass turf. Agronomy Journal. 52(8):449–452. 1960.

10069. ______. When the well runs dry. Golf Course Reporter. 28(2):22, 24, 28–36. 1960.

10070. ______. Observations—experimental fertility plots. North California Turf Conference. pp. 35–37. 1960.

10071. ______. The ecology of turfgrass management practices in terms of competition. Agronomy Abstracts. 53:75. 1961.

10072. ______. The grass plant and its management. Proceedings Northern California Turfgrass Institute. pp. 27–31. 1961.

10073. ______. The effect of pesticides on turfgrass disease incidence. The Plant Disease Reporter. 45(11):892–893. 1961.

10074. ______. The mowing of turfgrass II. responses of three species of grass. Agronomy Journal. 54(3):250–252. 1962.

10075. ______. Mowing of turfgrass. III. The effect of rest on seaside bentgrass turf mowed daily. Agronomy Journal. 54(3):252–253. 1962.

10076. ______. Turfgrass ecology. Effects of mowing, irrigation, and nitrogen treatments of *Agrostis palustris* Huds., "Seaside" and *Agrostis tenuis* Sibth., "Highland" on population, yield, rooting, and cover. Agronomy Journal. 54(5):407–412. 1962.

10077. ______. The effect of management practices on invasion of lawn turf by bermudagrass (*Cynodon dactylon* L.) Proceedings of the American Society for Horticultural Science. 80:559–564. 1962.

10078. ______. Irrigation—systems and procedures. California Turfgrass Culture. 14(1):1–5. 1964.

10079. ______. Irrigate to survive disease. Golf Course Reporter. 32(5):16. 1964.

10080. ______. Recognizing your turf problem. Nursery Landscape Tree and Turf Proceedings. pp. 14–1 to 14–2. 1965.

10081. ______. Effect of wetting agents on water movement in the soil. Agronomy Abstracts. 58:35. 1966.

10082. ______. Optimum rates of seeding turfgrasses. Agronomy Journal. 58(4):-441–443. 1966.

10083. ______. Brown patch of turfgrass caused by *Rhizoctonia solani* kuhor. California Turfgrass Culture. 16(2):9–13. 1966.

10084. ______. Water importance and problems. International Turfgrass Conference Proceedings. 37:19–25. 1966.

10085. ______. Special soils for special turf areas. Proceedings of Turf, Landscape Tree, and Nursery Conference. pp. 1–1 to 1–4. 1966.

10086. ______. Lessons learned in automatic irrigation. USGA Green Section Record. 6(3):10–13. 1968.

10087. ______. Sands used in soil mixes. California Turfgrass Culture. 19(1):3–5. 1969.

10088. ______. Chemical pest control. California Turfgrass Culture. 19(3):19–22. 1969.

10089. ______. Chemical pest control. Golf Superintendent. 37(9):24–26, 50–53. 1969.

10090. ______. Relationships between turfgrass and soil under irrigation. Proceedings First International Turfgrass Research Conference. pp. 292–300. 1969.

10091. ______. Relationships between plants and mowing. Proceedings of the First International Turfgrass Research Conference. pp. 469–480. 1969.

10092. ______. Rooting from sod by *Poa pratensis* L. and *Agrostis tenuis* Sibth. Crop Science. 10(6):718–719. 1970.

10094. ______. Do we have a new turfgrass disease? Journal of the Sports Turf Research Institute. 46:17–21. 1970.

10095. ______. Holes in soil. Proceedings Park and Recreation Institute. 1970.

10096. ______. An appreciation of monocotyledons. Notes, Royal Botanical Garden Edinburgh. 39(2):377–390. 1970.

10097. ______. Practical turfgrass management. Van Nostrand Reinhold Company, New York. pp. 1–456. 1971.

10098. ______. Principles of Turfgrass Culture. Van Nostrand Reinhold Company, New York. 420 pp. 1971.

10100. ______. Soil-water relationships. Proceedings of the 1972 Turf and Landscape Horticulture Institute. pp. 31–34. 1972.

10101. ______. Effects of aeration, fertilization, and irrigation on turfgrass reaction to pests. Proceedings of the 1972 Turf and Landscape Horticulture Institute. pp. 46–49. 1972.

10103. Madison, J. H. and A. H. Andersen. A chlorphyll index to measure turfgrass response. Agronomy Journal. 55(5):-461–464. 1963.

10104. Madison, J. H. and W. B. Davis. Know your turfgrasses. University of California Agricultural Extension Service, Turfgrass Series. AXT–9. 8 pp. 1966.

10105. Madison, J. H., and R. M. Hagan. Extraction of soil moisture by Merion bluegrass turf, as affected by irrigation frequency, mowing height, and other cultural operations. Agronomy Journal. 54(2):157–160. 1962.

10106. Madison, J. H., and T. Kono. The growth of three turfgrass species as affected by height, frequency, and season of mowing. Agronomy Abstracts. 51:90. 1959.

10107. Madison, J. H., J. M. Johnson, and J. L. Paul. Methods for evaluating herbicide injury to turfgrasses. Agronomy Abstracts. 59:56. 1967.

10108. Madison, J. H., L. J. Petersen, and T. K. Hodges. Pink snowmold on bentgrass as affected by irrigation and fertilizers. Agronomy Journal 52(10):591–592. 1960.

10109. Madison, J. H., J. M. Johnson, W. B. Davis, and R. M. Sachs. Testing fluorine compounds for chemical mowing of turfgrass. California Agriculture. 23(8):8–10. 1969.

10110. Machielse, P. L. Greenkeeping and its problems in South Africa. Journal of the Sports Turf Research Institute. No. 44. pp. 61–65. 1968.

10111. Maekubo, N. Soil conditioner for putting greens. KGU Green Section Turf Research Bulletin. 8:60–67. 1965.

10112. ______. Effects on the soil conditioners for turf, Part 7. KGU Green Section Turf Research Bulletin. 11:41–54. 1966.

10113. ______. Effects of compaction on green bed soil, Part 2. K.G.U. Green Section Turf Research Bulletin. 11:55–66. 1966.

10114. ______. Effects on the soil conditioners for turf, Part 8. K.G.U. Green Section Turf Research Bulletin. 12:29–40. 1967.

10115. ______. Effects on the soil conditioners for turf, Part 8. K.G.U. Green Section Turf Research Bulletin. 14:23–36. 1968.

10116. ______. Effects on the soil conditioners for turf, Part 9. KGU Green Section Turf Research Bulletin. 16:39–52. 1969.

10117. ______. Effects on the soil conditioners for turf, Part 11. KGU Green Section Turf Research Bulletin. 17:37–48. 1969.

10118. ______. Effects of compaction on green bed soil, Part 3. KGU Green Section Turf Research Bulletin. 19:41–46. 1970.

10119. ______. Effects of compaction on green bed soil, Part 4. KGU Green Section Turf Research Bulletin. 20:21–28. 1971.

10120. Maekubo, N., and Y. Chibe. Effects on the light for turfgrasses. K.G.U. Green Section Turf Research Bulletin. 14:-47–50. 1968.

10121. Maekubo, N. and Y. Kamon. Trials of relaxative nitrogen fertilizers. K.G.U. Green Section Turf Research Bulletin. 14:-55–62. 1968.

10122. ______. Trials of relaxative nitrogen fertilizers, Part 2. KGU Green Section Turf Research Bulletin. 16:67–76. 1969.

10123. Magill, P. L., F. R. Holden, and C. Ackley. Air pollution handbook. McGraw-Hill Co., New York. 480 p. 1956.

10124. Maguire, J. D. and K. M. Steen. Effects of potassium nitrate on germination and respiration of dormant and nondormant Kentucky bluegrass (*Poa pratensis* L.) seed. Crop Science. 11(1):48–50. 1971.

10125. Mahdi, M. Z. The point quadrat method for analyzing the composition of turf. Southern California Turf Culture. 1(2):4. 1951.

10126. ______. Egyptian bermudagrass strain has many merits. Golfdom. 29(10):82. 1955.

10127. ______. The bermudagrass—bentgrass combination for an all-year putting or lawn bowling green. Southern California Turf Culture. 6(2):8. 1956.

10128. ______. The use of plugging for changing grasses in turf. Southern California Turf Culture. 6(3):21–23. 1956.

10129. Mahdi, Z. and V. T. Stoutemyer. A method of measurement of populations in dense turf. Agronomy Journal. 45(10):514–515. 1953.

10130. ______. The bermuda—bentgrass combination for an all-year putting green. Golf Course Reporter. 21(3):10–11. 1953.

10131. Mahdi, Z. and C. G. Wyckoff. A comparison of two methods of establishing turf from vegetative division. Golf Course Reporter. 21(6):20–21. 1953.

10132. Mahdi, Z. and V. T. Stoutemyer. The changes of populations of turf grasses by plugging. Golf Course Reporter. 21(4):22–27. 1953.

10133. Mahilum, B. C. Fate of urea and ammonium nitrate with various crops and soils. Ph.D. Thesis, Oklahoma State University. 1971.

10134. Maier, W. Untersuchungen zur frage der lichtwirkung auf die keimung einiger *Poa*-arten. Jahr bücher für wissenschaftliche Botanik. 77:321–392. 1933.

10135. Maire, R. G. How to figure your costs. Southern California Turfgrass Institute Conference Proceedings. pp. 29–30. 1959.

10136. ______. How to figure your fertilizer costs. Southern California Turfgrass Culture. 10(2):14–16. 1960.

10137. Major, H. F. Lawns and lawn making. Missouri Agricultural Experiment Station Circular. 136:1–12. 1925.

10138. ______. Development and care of lawns. Missouri Agricultural Extension Circular 204. pp. 1–12. 1939.

10139. Major, R. Seed dormancy of side-oats gramagrass, *Bouteloua curtipendula* (Michx.) Torr. Ph.D. Thesis, University of Arizona. 1972.

10140. Mrkvica, M. Possibilities of production of grass seeds suited for lawns in Czechoslovakia. First Czechoslovak Symposium on Sportturf Proceedings. pp. 231–235. 1969.

10141. Malca, I. and R. M. Endo. Identification of galactose in cultures of *Sclerotinia homeocarpa* as the factor toxic to bentgrass roots. Phytopathology. 55(7):775–780. 1965.

10142. Malca, I. M., and J. H. Owen. The gray leaf spot disease of St. Augustinegrass. Plant Disease Reporter. 41(10):871–875. 1957.

10143. Malcolm, D. R. Biology and control of the timothy mite, *Paratetranychus pratensis* (Banks). Washington Agricultural Experiment Station Technical Bulletin 17. 35 pp. 1955.

10144. Malek, R. B. Turf nematode problems. Illinois Turfgrass Conference Proceedings. pp. 11–13. 1971.

10145. Malek, R. B. and W. R. Jenkins. Aspects of the host-parasite relationships of nematodes and hairy vetch. New Jersey Agricultural Experiment Station Bulletin 813. 31 p. 1964.

10146. Malleson, G. B. Rulers of India. Akbar. Oxford at the Clarendon Press. pp. 204. 1891.

10147. Malone, C. B. History of the Peking summer palaces under the Ch'ing Dynasty. Illinois Studies in the Social Sciences Vol. XIX. Nos. 1–2. University of Illinois. pp. 247. 1934.

10148. Maloney, M. J. Promoting lawn care. Proceedings of the Midwest Regional Turf Conference. pp. 15–17. 1968.

10149. Malpass, D., J. Zoller, E. Sears, and J. Beyeht. New equipment and ideas for maintaining turfgrass areas—panel discussion. Proceedings—22nd Annual Northwest Turfgrass Conference 22:35–39. 1968.

10150. Malte, M. O. Commercial bent grasses *(Agrostis)* in Canada. National Museum of Canada, Annual Report Bulletin. 50:106–126. 1926.

10152. ______. Commercial bentgrasses *(Agrostis)* in Canada. National Museum of Canada Annual Report for 1926. 126 p. 1928.

10153. ______. Bent grasses in Canada. The National Greenkeeper. 3(4):11–17, 37. 1929.

10154. Man, Th. J. de and J. G. de Hous. The carbohydrates in grass. I. The soluble carbohydrates. Rec. Tran. Chim. 68:43–50. 1949.

10155. Manis, H. C. Insect control in turf. Proceedings of the Third Annual Turf Conference. Washington State College. pp. 25–27. 1950.

10156. ______. Insect control in turf. State College of Washington Turf Conference Proceedings. 3:25–27. 1950.

10157. Madden, E. A. Soils for playing greens and sports fields. New Zealand Institute for Turf Culture Newsletter. 5:7–8. 1960.

10158. Mann, J. D., W. B. Storey, L. S. Jordan, B. E. Day, and H. Haid. Light dependency in seed germination. Turf Bulletin. Massachusetts Turf and Lawn Grass Council. 4(1):3–4. 1966.

10159. Mann, L. D., D. D. Focht, H. A. Joseph, and L. H. Stolzy. Increased denitrification in soils by additions of sulphur as an energy source. Journal of Environmental Quality. 1(3):329–332. 1972.

10160. Macksam, W. G. Use of mass plantings in the golf course landscape. 18th Annual Rocky Mountain Regional Turfgrass Conference Proceedings. pp. 63–64. 1972.

10161. Manner, R. Finnish lawn study project. First Czechoslovak Symposium on Sportturf Proceedings. pp. 167–173. 1969.

10162. Mannering, J. V. Infiltration and soil surfaces. Proceedings of the Midwest Regional Turf Conference. pp. 13–14. 1965.

10163. ______. Infiltration and soil surface. 25th Ohio Short Course on Roadside Development. pp. 103–106. 1966.

10164. ______. Water movement and evaporation. Proceedings of the Midwest Regional Turf Conference. pp. 5–7. 1969.

10165. Mannering, J. V., and L. D. Meyer. The effects of various rates of surface mulch on infiltration and erosion. Soil Science Society of America Proceedings. 27:84–86. 1963.

10166. Madden, E. A. Garden lawns and playing greens. Whitcombe and Tombs. Christchurch. 93 pp. 1952.

10167. Mansfield, P. Watering the sward. The Groundsman. 17(8):22. 1964.

10168. ______. A practical guide to the bowling green. The Groundsman. 19(1):10–11. 1965.

10169. Mansfield, R. D. How we licked our weed problem. Golfdom. 15(9):20–23. 1941.

10170. ______. Weed control with Milarsenite. Greenkeepers Club of New England Newsletter. 14(6):4–5. 1942.

10171. Mansur, J. D. Application techniques safe for turf. New England Agricultural Chemicals Conference and Herbicide Workshop. 1:37–38. 1954.

10172. Mantell, A. Effect of irrigation frequency and nitrogen fertilization on growth and water use of a kikuyugrass lawn. (*Pennisetum clandestinum* Hochst.). Agronomy Journal. 58(6):559–561. 1966.

10173. Mantell, A. and G. Stanhill. Comparison of methods for evaluating the response of lawngrass to irrigation and nitrogen treatments. Agronomy Journal. 58(5):-465–468. 1966.

10174. Maples, F. Bermuda turf and sand greens at Pinehurst, N.C. USGA Green Section Bulletin. 11(9):182–184. 1931.

10175. ______. Development of turf at Pinehurst. Greenkeepers' Reporter. 16(1):-36–37. 1948.

10176. Maples, H. How Pinehurst prepares turf for winter play. Golfdom. 24(3):76, 78, 80. 1950.

10177. ______. Turf on courses for winter play. Greenkeeping Superintendents Association National Turf Conference. 21:61–65. 1950.

10178. Maples, H. H. Program for 12-months course care in South is outlined. Golfdom. 28(6):64, 66, 68, 81–82, 84. 1954.

10179. Maples, P. The transition period in bermuda-ryegrass greens. Proceedings. Fourteenth Southeastern Turfgrass Conference. 14:31–32. 1960.

10180. ______. A method for measuring greens. The Golf Course Reporter. 33(4):64. 1965.

10181. ______. Living with the problem —*Poa annua* in fairways. International Turfgrass Conference Proceedings. 40:67–69. 1969.

10182. ______. Basic fundamentals and maintenance practices on golf courses. Proceedings Fifth Annual Tennessee Turfgrass Conference. pp. 12–16. 1971.

10183. ______. Motivation and in-service training. USGA Green Section Record. 9(2):32. 1971.

10184. March, A. W. Turfgrass irrigation research at the University of California. California Turfgrass Culture. 20(1):1–2. 1970.

10185. Marchbanks, W. W. Limits of viability of roughpea and dallisgrass seed. Embryology of *Lathysus hirsutus* L. Ph.D. Thesis. Mississippi State College. 109 p. 1953.

10186. Madden, E. A. Turf research in New Zealand. Journal of the Sports Turf Research Institute. 10:138–145. 1960.

10187. ______. Soil compaction, causes, and effects. New Zealand Institute for Turf Culture Newsletter. 14:2–3. 1961.

10188. Marcussen, K. H. Trees and shrubs for golf courses. New Zealand Institute for Turf Culture Newsletter. 47:13–15. 1967.

10189. Margadant, W. D. Jarowisatie van weidergrassen, speciaal *Lolium perenne.* Versl. Centraal. Inst. Landb. Onderz. 39:-1951.

10190. Mariam, E. K. Taxonomy of the *Agropyron intermedium* and *Agropyron trichophorum* complex. M.S. Thesis, South Dakota State University. 1972.

10191. Marini, D. Weeds and diseases. Turf Clippings. University of Massachusetts. 1(8):A–67 to A–68. 1963.

10192. Markarian, D. Turfgrass breeding. Proceedings Northwest Turf Conference. 12:35–36. 1958.

10193. Markland, F. E. and E. C. Roberts. Influence of nitrogenous fertilizers on dollar spot incidence in Washington bentgrass. Agronomy Abstracts. p. 46. 1965.

10194. ______. Influence of varying nitrogen and potassium levels on growth and mineral composition of *Agrostis palustris* Huds. Agronomy Abstracts. 59:53. 1967.

10195. ______. Influence of nitrogen fertilizers on Washington creeping bentgrass, *Agrostis palustris* Huds. I. Growth and mineral composition. Agronomy Journal. 61(5):-698–700. 1969.

10196. Markland, F. E., E. C. Roberts and L. R. Frederick. Influence of nitrogen fertilizers on Washington creeping bentgrass, *Agrostis palustris* Huds. II. Incidence of dollar spot, *Sclerotinia homeocarpa,* infection. Agronomy Journal. 61(5):701–705. 1969.

10197. Marks, J. J. Turfgrass research reported at Michigan conference. Michigan Turfgrass Research Report. 3(1):11–14. 1968.

10198. Marlatt, G. V. Together we stand, divided . . . Golfdom. 41(5):46, 48, 76, 78. 1967.

10199. Marlatt, N. E. The interactions of microclimate, plant cover, and soil moisture content affecting evapotranspiration rates. Colorado State University Agricultural Experiment Station. Atmospheric Science Technical Paper. Report 23. 13 p. 1961.

10200. Marrese, R. J. Crabgrass control with dacthal. Proceedings 15th Annual Northwest Turf Conference. 15:73–78. 1961.

10201. Marriott, L. F. Nitrogen fertilization of perennial grasses. Pennsylvania State University Agricultural Experiment Station. Bulletin 688. 17 pp. 1961.

10202. Marsh, A. W. Water measuring and control equipment. Southern California Turfgrass Culture. 8(2):11–13. 1958.

10203. ______. How to receive the greatest benefits from turfgrass irrigation. California Turfgrass Culture. 16(4):27–29. 1966.

10204. ______. How to receive the greatest benefits from turfgrass irrigation management. Proceedings of the Turfgrass Sprinkler Irrigation Conference. 4 pp. 1966.

10205. ______. Turfgrass irrigation. Parks and Recreation. 2(1):43–44, 52–53. 1967.

10206. ______. Water distribution. Proceedings Turfgrass Sprinkler Irrigation Conference. 5:37–43. 1967.

10207. ______. Water distribution. California Turfgrass Culture. 18(1):3–5. 1968.

10208. ______. Turfgrass irrigation research at the University of California. Proceedings Annual Turfgrass Sprinkler Irrigation Conference. 7:60–63. 1969.

10209. ______. Guides for developing an irrigation program. Role of the soil moisture sensor. Turfgrass Sprinkler Irrigation Conference Proceedings. 10:42–45. 1972.

10210. ______. Drip-trickle irrigation for landscape plants. Proceedings of the 1972 Turf and Landscape Horticulture Institute. pp. 71–73. 1972.

10211. ______. The role of the soil moisture sensor. Western Landscaping News. 12:-4–8. 1972.

10212. ______. Turfgrass irrigation research at the University of California. Proceedings Annual Turfgrass Sprinkler Irrigation Conference. 6:6–9. 1968.

10213. Marsh, W. L. Landscape vocabulary. Miramar Publishing Co., Los Angeles, California. pp. 1–315. 1964.

10214. Marshall, D. S. Overcoming the Charlie Brown syndrome. USGA Green Section Record. 10(2):22–25. 1972.

10215. Marshall, G. D. Pinpointing our fertilizer problems. Southern California Turfgrass Conference Proceedings. pp. 1–2. 1959.

10216. Madden, E. A. Lawn weeds: identification and control. New Zealand Institute for Turf Culture Newsletter. 18:1–3. 1962.

10217. Marston, R. H. Building storage ponds. Rutgers University Turfgrass Short Course. 34:37–38. 1966.

10218. Marth, P. C. New developments in weed control with 2, 4-D. The Greenkeeper's Reporter. 14(5):9–12. 1946.

10219. Madden, E. A. Lawn weeds: identification and control. New Zealand Institute for Turf Culture Newsletter. 19:8–14. 1962.

10220. Marth, P. C. 2, 4-D questions answered by field and lab. tests. Golfdom. 21(9):58–60. 1947.

10221. ______. Experiments on the use of 2, 4-D for weed eradication on sod areas. The Greenkeeper's Reporter. 15(2):11–12. 1947.

10222. Marth, P. C. and J. W. Mitchell. Effect of spray mixtures containing 2, 4-Dichlorophenoxy-acetic acid, urea, and fermate on the growth of grass. Botanical Gazatte. 107(3):417–424. 1946.

10223. ______. Selective herbicidal effects of 2, 4-Dichlorphenoxyaceticacid applied to turf-in-dry-mixture with fertilizer. Botanical Gazette. 108(3):414–420. 1947.

10224. Marth, P. C., V. K. Toole, and E. H. Toole. Yield and viability of Kentucky bluegrass seed produced on sod areas treated with 2, 4-D. Journal of the American Society of Agronomy. 39(5):426–429. 1947.

10225. Martin, C. K. and A. L. Lang. Better drainage for claypan soils. Illinois Research. 2(3):5. 1960.

10226. Martin, D. Lawns for South Dakota. South Dakota University Extension Fact Sheet 354. 2 pp. 1967.

10227. Martin, D. P. The composition of turfgrass thatch and the influence of several materials to increase thatch decomposition. M.S. Thesis. Michigan State University. 42 pp. 1970.

10228. ———. The influence of temperature, cultural factors, and analytical techniques on carbohydrate levels in turfgrasses. Ph.D. Thesis, Michigan State University. 89 pp. 1972.

10229. ———. Cultural practices for low maintenance recreational areas in Michigan. 42nd Annual Michigan Turfgrass Conference Proceedings. 1:82–85. 1972.

10230. Martin, D. P., and J. B. Beard. Composition and biological degradation of turfgrass thatch. Agronomy Abstracts. p. 48. 1971.

10231. ———. Investigations of turfgrass thatch. Michigan Turfgrass Research Report. pp. 7–8. Spring, 1970.

10232. ———. An evaluation of carbohydrate extraction and analysis techniques using three turfgrasses. Agronomy Abstracts. 2:64. 1972.

10233. Martin, D. P. and J. E. Kaufmann. Ecological relationships in establishment of roadside grass communities in Michigan. Agronomy Abstracts. p. 73. 1970.

10234. Madden, E. A. *Poa annua* . . . problem weed in sports greens. The Golf Superintendent. 35(1):13–14. 1967.

10235. Martin, H. C. Turf for school and recreation fields. Part III—Maintenance. Florida Turf Management Conference Proceedings. 4:66–68. 1956.

10236. ———. Grasses and maintenance short cuts. Florida Turf Management Conference Proceedings. 6:83–87. 1958.

10237. ———. Gridirons. Proceedings of University of Florida Turf-Grass Management Conference. 8:110–111. 1960.

10238. ———. Landscaping parks and playgrounds. Proceedings of University of Florida Turf-Grass Management Conference. 9:171–173. 1961.

10239. ———. Peak season planning: gridirons. Proceedings of Florida Turf-Grass Management Conference. 11:77. 1963.

10240. ———. Fertilizing large turf areas. Proceedings of Florida Turf Grass Management Conference. 12:128–130. 1964.

10241. ———. Preplanting preparation for lawns. Proceedings, Florida Turf-Grass Management Conference. 15:88–90. 1967.

10242. Martin, J. A. What turf grass certification means to growers. Florida Turf Management Conference Proceedings. 5:30. 1957.

10243. ———. Bentgrass or annual bluegrass. Rutgers University Short Course in Turf Management. 2 pp. 1969.

10244. ———. Bentgrass or annual bluegrass. Rutgers University. College of Agriculture and Environmental Science. Lawn and Utility Turf Section. pp. 72–73. 1969.

10245. Martin, J. B. and R. E. Blaser. Interrelations of aluminum toxicity and calcium nutrition in grasses and legumes. Agronomy Abstracts. 53:75. 1961.

10246. Martin, J. D. Soil preparation and planting. Florida Turf Management Conference Proceedings. 6:88–90. 1958.

10247. Maddox, C. E. Good architecture and good construction. Proceedings of the 37th Annual Turfgrass Conference and Show. GCSAA. pp. 8–10. 1966.

10248. Martin, L. B. The turfgrass variety plots: early management. Proceedings of the Southern California Turfgrass Institute Conference. pp. 31–33. 1960.

10249. Martin, L. B. and R. J. Seibert. *Microlaena stipoides.* Southern California Turfgrass Culture 5(2):3. 1955.

10250. Martin, W. Microorganisms and nitrogen release. Golfdom. 33:58, 60, 92. 1959.

10251. ———. Fertilizers. National Turfgrass Conference Proceedings. 30:5. 1959.

10252. Martin, W. H. Soil conditioner solves compaction problem. Golfdom. 28(7):-40–41, 44, 62–66. 1954.

10253. Martin, W. P. and C. W. Volk. Soil conditioners. National Fertilizer Review. 27(4):11–13. 1952.

10254. Marzak, J. L. Chemical outlook for turf fungicides. Proceedings of Midwest Regional Turf Conference. pp. 65–68. 1951.

10255. Mascaro, C. G. St. Augustine renovation. Proceedings of Florida Turf-Grass Management Conference. 10:151–152. 1962.

10256. ______. Special equipment rental for lawn renovation. Proceedings of Florida Turf-Grass Management Conference. 11:-102–103. 1963.

10257. Mascaro, T. Improving athletic field turfgrass. Bulletin No. 2, West Point Products Corporation, West Point, Pennsylvania.

10258. ______. Soil aeration. Central Plains Turfgrass Conference Proceedings. 1:-52–55. 1950.

10259. ______. Soil and its maintenance for turf betterment. Golfdom. 24(7):40–41, 60–61. 1950.

10260. ______. Report on turf field days. Golfdom. 24(9):36, 38. 1950.

10261. ______. Better turf machinery seen in crystal ball. Midwest Turf-News and Research. 4(2):2, 3. 1950.

10262. ______. Park turf. Parks and Recreation. 34(3):11–13. 1951.

10263. ______. Park turf. Parks and Recreation. 34(4):15–16. 1951.

10264. ______. Park turf. Parks and Recreation. 34(5):14–15. 1951.

10265. ______. Park turf. Parks and Recreation. 34(6):19–20. 1951.

10266. ______. Park turf. Parks and Recreation. 34(11):7–8. 1951.

10267. ______. Benefits from aeration. Proceedings of the 6th Annual Texas Turf Conference. pp. 31–37. 1951.

10268. ______. Leveling tests on soil surfaces under turf cover. U.S. Air Force, Chanute Air Force Base. Rantoul, Illinois. 5–21. 1951.

10269. ______. Air in the soil. Golf Course Reporter. 20(1):8–11. 1952.

10270. ______. Why aerifying has become standard practice. Golfdom. 26(7):58, 60–61. 1952.

10271. ______. Physical conditions of soils in growing grasses. Proceedings of the Arizona Turfgrass Conference. pp. 13–12. 1953.

10272. ______. Times and methods of aerification. Proceedings of the Mid-Atlantic Association of Greenkeepers Conference. p. 17–20. 1953.

10273. ______. Thatch on golf greens. Proceedings 7th Annual Northwest Turf Conference. 7:5–7. 1953.

10274. ______. Soil aeration. Proceedings of School of Soils, Fertilization and Turf Maintenance. Royal Canadian Golf Association Green Section. pp. 35, 38. 1953.

10275. ______. Times and methods of aerification. Second Western Turf Conference at University of Alberta, Edmonton. pp. 34–37. 1953.

10276. ______. Handbook for new green committee chairmen. West Point Products Corporation. 1–15 pp. 1957.

10277. ______. Growing turf the hard way. Florida Turf Management Conference Proceedings. 6:35. 1958.

10278. ______. Growing turfgrass the hard way. Golfdom. 32(4):60. 1958.

10279. ______. Growing turfgrass the hard way. Proceedings Twelfth Southeastern Turfgrass Conference. pp. 9–10. 1958.

10280. ______. Why, when and how—renovation. Golf Course Reporter. 28(6):57–61. 1960.

10281. ______. Aerification an important part of good turf maintenance. Park Maintenance. 13(5):40–41. 1960.

10282. ______. Turfgrass management versus renovation. Proceedings of University of Florida Turf-Grass Management Conference. 9:73–75. 1961.

10283. ______. Renovation of large turfgrass areas and athletic fields. Proceedings of University of Florida Turf-Grass Management Conference. 9:168–170. 1961.

10284. ______. Turfgrass management versus renovation. Illinois Turfgrass Conference Proceedings. 2:40–41. 1961.

10285. ______. Mechanical aeration

and thatch control—part II. International Turf-Grass Conference Proceedings. 32:16. 1961.

10286. ______. Turfgrass management versus renovation. Proceedings Fifteenth Southeastern Turfgrass Conference. pp. 42–56. 1961.

10287. ______. Causes of compaction and wear on turfgrass areas. Proceedings of the Annual Texas Turf Conference. 16:1–2. 1961.

10288. ______. Municipal Handbook for Golf Course Committees. American Institute of Park Executives, Inc. Oglebay Park, Wheeling, West Virginia. pp. 11–22. 1962.

10289. ______. Growing grass the hard way. Proceedings of the Florida Turf-Grass Conference. 10:61–62. 1962.

10290. ______. Mechanical aeration and thatch control. Part 1: Principles. Golf Course Reporter. 30(1):82, 86, 89, 91. 1962.

10291. ______. Causes of compaction and wear on turfgrass areas. Proceedings Sixteenth Southeastern Turfgrass Conference. pp. 1–2. 1962.

10292. ______. Mechanical weed control. Proceedings of the Texas Turfgrass Conference. 17:16–17. 1962.

10293. ______. Turfgrass . . . for athletic fields, playgrounds and other recreational turfgrass areas. Turf Clippings. University of Massachussetts. 1(7):41–A to 42–A. 1962.

10294. ______. Turfgrass management with deficient rainfall. Iagreen, 30th Annual Conference Proceedings. pp. 6–8. 1963.

10295. ______. Salesmanship—your job. Proceedings of the Midwest Regional Turf Conference. pp. 4–6. 1963.

10296. ______. Water—ample and available. Proceedings of the Midwest Regional Turf Conference. pp. 41–42. 1963.

10297. ______. The proper placement of fertilizer on turfgrass areas. Rocky Mountain Regional Turfgrass Conference Proceedings. 10:12–13. 1963.

10298. ______. Meeting the golf cart problem. Proceedings 17th Southeastern Turfgrass Conference. pp. 32–39. 1963.

10299. ______. Turfgrass management with deficient rainfall. Iagreen. Iowa Turfgrass Conference Proceedings. 30:6–8. 1964.

10300. ______. Use and misuse of chemicals for weed control. Proceedings 18th Southeastern Turfgrass Conference. pp. 17–21. 1964.

10301. ______. Thatch—its development, effects and control. Proceedings of the Texas Turfgrass Conference. 19:51–56. 1964.

10302. ______. How to cure the causes of soil compaction. Golf Course Operations. 3(4):10–13, 32. 1965.

10303. ______. Thatch prevention and its control. The Golf Course Reporter. 33(7):8. 1965.

10304. ______. Meeting the golf cart problem. Sixteenth R.C.G.A. Sports Turfgrass Conference. pp. 27–32. 1965.

10305. ______. Water and traffic problems. Proceedings 19th Southeastern Turfgrass Conference. pp. 42–45. 1965.

10306. ______. 20 years of progress in turfgrass maintenance. Proceedings of the Texas Turfgrass Conference. 20:11–12. 1965.

10307. ______. Management practices. Proceedings of the Texas Turfgrass Conference. 20:13–14. 1965.

10308. ______. We need mechanization for survival. Turfgrass Times. 1(2):5, 24. 1965.

10309. ______. Tom Mascaro's guide to turfgrass renovation. Weeds, Trees, and Turf. 4(2):8–9. 1965.

10310. ______. Mechanization for survival. The Greenmaster 2(8):4. 1966.

10311. ______. Meeting the golf cart problem. Proceedings of the Mid-Atlantic Association of Golf Course Superintendents. pp. 10–12. 1966.

10312. ______. Getting through to the roots. Proceedings Missouri Lawn and Turf Conference. 7:3–4. 1966.

10313. ______. Cutting labor costs in turfgrass management. Proceedings, Florida Turf-Grass Management Conference. 15:32–137. 1967.

10315. ______. Dew is not dew. Proceedings of the Texas Turfgrass Conference. 23:-69–81. 1968.

10316. ______. Cutting labor costs in turfgrass management. Turf Clippings. University of Massachusetts. 3(3):A24–28. 1968.

10317. ______. Dew is not dew. Proceedings of the Mid-Atlantic Association of Golf Course Superintendents. pp. 5–7. 1969.

10318. ______. Dew is not dew. Proceedings of the Midwest Regional Turf Conference. pp. 60–65. 1969.

10319. ______. Dew is not dew. Turf Clippings. University of Massachussetts. 4(1):A–28 to A–35. 1969.

10320. ______. Budget for manpower. Turfgrass Times. 5(2):5. 1969.

10321. ______. Look out your windows. The Golf Superintendent. 38(9):22. 1970.

10322. ______. And a thought on golf course "laborers" . . . The Golf Superintendent. 38(9):23. 1970.

10323. ______. Dew is not dew. Proceedings Fourth Annual Tennessee Turfgrass Conference. pp. 10–18. 1970.

10324. ______. Techniques of mowing. Florida Turfgrass Management Conference Proceedings. 19:38–40. 1971.

10325. ______. Basic principles to determine aeration specifications and costs. Proceedings of Southern California Turfgrass Institute. pp. 91–94. 1971.

10326. ______. Mechanical modification of soil. Ohio Turfgrass Foundation Newsletter. 28:4–6. 1972.

10327. Mashie, E. Water—its use on turf. Golf Course Reporter. 21(5):15. 1953.

10328. Mason, H. How to have a good lawn in the South. Your Garden in the South. D. Van Nostrand Company, Inc. New Jersey. pp. 5–20. 1961.

10329. Mason, T. F. Greenkeeping on clay soil. Journal of the Board of Greenkeeping Research. 3(11):224–232. 1934.

10330. Massey, J. The grass tennis court —maintenance and equipment. The Groundsman. 21(8):21–23. 1968.

10331. Massie, L. B., H. Cole, and J. Duich. Pathogen variation in relation to disease severity and control of *Sclerotinia* dollar spot of turfgrass by fungicides. Phytopathology. 58(12):1616–1619. 1968.

10332. Masterson, P. M. Park improvement through better turf. Proceedings of the Third Annual Turf Conference, Washington State College. 3:33–36. 1950.

10333. ______. Park improvement through better turf. State College of Washington Turf Conference Proceedings. 3:33–36. 1950.

10334. Masumori, K., and N. Maekubo. Relationship with drainage and putting value (bent greens). KGU Green Section Turf Research Bulletin. 6:31–45. 1964.

10335. Matches, A. G. Influence of cutting height in darkness on measurement of energy reserves of tall fescue. Agronomy Journal. 61(6):896–898. 1969.

10336. ______. Influence of intact tillers and height of stubble on growth responses of of tall fescue *(Festuca arundinacea* Schreb.). Crop Science. 6:484–487. 1966.

10337. Maddox, W. E. Planning new turf facilities. Proceedings Midwest Regional Turf Conference. pp. 49–50. 1970.

10338. Matheson, M. Beautification of bowling greens. New Zealand Institute for Turf Culture Newsletter. 15:11–12. 1961.

10339. ______. Undesirable weeds of the bowling green. New Zealand Institute for Turf Culture Newsletter. 15:12–13. 1961.

10340. ______. Pests of the bowling green. New Zealand Institute for Turf Culture Newsletter. 15:14–15. 1961.

10341. ______. Renovation of the bowling green. New Zealand Institute for Turf Culture Newsletter. 12:2–3. 1961.

10342. ______. Weed greens. New Zealand Institute for Turf Culture Newsletter. 12:7–8. 1961.

10343. ______. Weed greens. New Zealand Institute for Turf Culture Newsletter. 13:1–2. 1961.

10344. ______. Weed greens. New Zealand Institute for Turf Culture Newsletter. 14:6–7. 1961.

10345. Mathews, F. Maintenance of new playing fields. The Groundsman. 15(10):4–8. 1962.

10346. Mathias, E. L., O. L. Bennett, G. A. Jung, and P. E. Lundberg. Effect of two growth-regulating chemicals on yield and water use of three perennial grasses. Agronomy Journal. 63(3):480–483. 1971.

10347. Maddux, L. D. Effect of fertilizer, gypsum, and herbicide on establishment and maintenance of a vegetative ground cover for erosion control on Oklahoma highways. M.S. Thesis. Oklahoma State University. 37 pp. 1967.

10348. Matkin, O. A. Liquid fertilizer injection. California Turfgrass Culture. 16(4):-31–32. 1966.

10349. Matkin, O. A. and F. H. Peterson. Automation aids golf course fertilization. Park Maintenance. 15(3):86–88. 1962.

10350. Matlock, R. S. Growing healthier plants for disease control. Oklahoma Turfgrass Conference Proceedings. pp. 46–53. 1960.

10351. Matocha, J. E. Response of Coastal bermudagrass to various sources of sulfur on a sandy soil of East Texas. Texas Agricultural Experiment Station Progress Report PR-2696. pp. 1–15. 1969.

10352. ———. Influence of sulfur sources and magnesium on forage yields of coastal bermudagrass (*Cynodon dactylon* (L.) Pers.). Agronomy Journal. 63(3):493–496. 1971.

10353. Matsuki, G. The special qualities of the diammonium phosphate. K.G.U. Green Section Turf Research Bulletin. 21(8):-15–17. 1971.

10354. Matthews, J. W. Lawn grasses on trial at Kirstenbosch. Journal of the Botanical Society of South Africa. 21. 1935.

10355. Matthews, L. J. Weed control in turf. New Zealand Institute for Turf Culture Newsletter. 5:6. 1960.

10356. Matthews, W. B. Dreams and reality in golf course design. Midwest Regional Turf Conference Proceedings. pp. 30–31. 1972.

10357. Matthysse, J. G. The control of turf insects. New York State Turf Association Bulletin 1. pp. 3–4. 1949.

10358. ———. Grub control tests and demonstration. New York State Turf Association. Bulletin 17. pp. 67–68. 1950.

10359. ———. Insect control. USGA Journal and Turf Management. 7(2):26–29. 1954.

10360. ———. Insect control on turf—1957–58. New York State Turf Association. Bulletin 57. pp. 219–222. 1957.

10361. Mattice, N. L. Look before you seed! The National Greenkeeper. 1(7):10, 23–24. 1927.

10362. ———. Arsenate of lead as a beetle, worm and weed eradicator. USGA Green Section Bulletin. 7(9):167–168. 1927.

10363. ———. Feeding versus seeding turf. USGA Green Section Bulletin. 8(2):25–26. 1928.

10364. Mattwell, M. O. Complete irrigation with central control. Golfdom. 40(8):28, 30, 62, 64, 66, 68, 70. 1966.

10365. Maude, P. F. Chromosome numbers in some British plants. New Phytologist. 39(1):17–32. 1940.

10366. Mauldin, M. P. Grass seed testing is tricky! Southern Seedsman. 14(1):42–43, 66–67. 1951.

10367. Maun, M. A., C. L. Canode, and I. D. Teare. Influence of temperature during anthesis on seed set in *Poa pratensis* L. Crop Science. 9(2):210–212. 1969.

10368. Maun, M. A., I. D. Teare, and C. L. Canode. Effect of soil temperature on the reproductive processes of Kentucky bluegrass *Poa pratensis* L. 'Newport'). Agronomy Journal. 60(6):666–668. 1968.

10369. ———. In vitro germination of Kentucky bluegrass pollen (*Poa pratensis* L. Newport). Crop Science. 9(3):389–390. 1969.

10370. Maurer, J. A Purr-Wick green. Midwest Regional Turf Conference Proceedings. 48–49 pp. 1971.

10371. ———. Purr-Wick green at Belle Meade. Proceedings Fifth Annual Tennessee Turfgrass Conference. pp. 34–35. 1971.

10372. Maxwell, F. G., J. N. Jenkins, and W. L. Parrott. Resistance of plants to insects. Advances in Agronomy. 24:187–265. 1972.

10373. Maxwell, K. E. and G. F. MacLeod. Experimental studies of the hairy chinch bug. Journal of Economic Entomology. 29(2):339–343. 1936.

10374. Maxwell, L. S. Weeds. Proceedings of Florida Turf-Grass Management Conference. 10:132–133. 1962.

10375. May, J. W. New and old chemicals for pre-emergence crabgrass control. Rocky Mountain Regional Turfgrass Conference. 12:5–6. 1966.

10376. ______. New fine-leafed grass varieties. Rocky Mountain Turfgrass Conference. 12:55–61. 1966.

10377. ______. An evaluation of nine pre-emergence herbicides for the control of annual grasses in bluegrass turf. Scotts Turfgrass Research Seminar. pp. 11–14. 1968.

10378. May, J., H. Hepworth and J. Fults. Progress on new and old chemicals for pre-emergence crabgrass control. Rocky Mountain Regional Turfgrass Conference. 12:7–9. 1966.

10379. ______. Progress report on recent work in controlling hard-to-kill weeds in turfgrass. Rocky Mountain Regional Turfgrass Conference. 12:11–12. 1966.

10380. May, L. H. The utilization of carbohydrate reserves in pasture plants after defoliation. Herbage Abstracts. 30(4):239–245. 1960.

10381. Mayo, J. P. Brownpatch at pebble beach. The National Greenkeeper. 1(8):5. 1927.

10382. Mays, W. P. and E. E. Deal. Nitrogen fertilization and cutting depth studies on tall fescue—Kentucky bluegrass sod. Agronomy Abstracts. 60:60. 1968.

10383. Mays, D. A., and E. M. Evans. Effects of variety, seeding rate, companion species, and cutting schedule on crownvetch yield. Agronomy Journal. 64(3):283–285. 1972.

10384. Mays, D. A. and G. L. Terman. Sulfur-coated urea and uncoated soluble nitrogen fertilizers for fescue forage. Agronomy Journal. 61(4):489–492. 1969.

10385. ______. Response of coastal bermudagrass to nitrogen in sulphur-coated urea, urea and ammonium nitrate. Turf Bulletin. Massachusetts Turf and Lawn Grass Council. 6(1):3–6. 1970.

10386. Mazur, R. Bioassay for bensulide, DCPA, and siduron in turfgrass. M.S. Thesis, University of Rhode Island.

10387. Maddy, J. K., and B. H. Rountree. Use, increase, and seed production of Emerald crownvetch in Iowa. Second Crown Vetch Symposium. Pennsylvania State University. pp. 73–78. 1968.

10389. Mazur, A. R. Testing for herbicide residues in soils. New York Turfgrass Association Bulletin. 84:326–327. 1969.

10390. ______. Dealing with the scars of winter. Northern Ohio Turfgrass News. 12(5):1. 1969.

10391. ______. Drainage—the key to better golf turf. USGA Green Section Record. 7(4):9–11. 1969.

10392. ______. The fate of herbicides. USGA Green Section Record. 6(4):8–9. 1968.

10393. ______. Weeds and their control. USGA Green Section Record. 7(5):1–4. 1969.

10394. Mazur, A. R., J. A. Jagschitz, and C. R. Skogley. Bioassay for bensulide, DCPA and siduron in turfgrass. Weed Science. 17(1):31–34. 1969.

10395. Mazure, A. R. Spring, a time to assess drainage. Golf Superintendent. 38(3):-61. 1970.

10396. ______. Drainage—the key to better golf turf. The Greenmaster. 6(5):6–10. 1970.

10398. ______. Golf course construction and related problems. Illinois Turfgrass Conference Proceedings. 11:3–6. 1970.

10399. ______. Winter injury. Turf Clippings, Stockbridge School Conference Proceedings. p. A3. 1970.

10400. ______. Winter protection through sound management. USGA Green Section Record. 8:8. 1970.

10401. ______. Winter injury problems. Illinois Turfgrass Conference Proceedings. pp. 25–27. 1971.

10402. Mazur, A. R., and T. D. Hughes. Effect of fungicide treatments and nitrogen form on the quality of bentgrass turf. University of Illinois Turfgrass Field Day. p. 22. 1972.

10403. Mazur, A. R. and J. A. Jagschitz. Control of dandelion and spotted-spurge in lawn turf with herbicides. Proceedings of the Northeastern Weed Control Conference. 22:-395–400. 1968.

10404. Mazur, A. R., and A. J. Turgeon. Evaluations of pre- and post-emergence herbicides for selective control of annual grasses and broadleaved weeds in turf. University of Illinois Turfgrass Field Day. pp. 7–9. 1972.

10405. Mazzeo, A. R. Wetting agents aid water penetration. The Golf Superintendent. 34(6):24, 44. 1966.

10406. Meade, J. A. Herbicides for sod field weed control. Weeds, Trees and Turf. 6(1):20–22. 1967.

10407. ______. Safety with herbicides. Proceedings 1970 3-Day Turf Courses, Rutgers University. pp. 1–3. 1970.

10408. Meade, J. A., H. W. Indyk, and R. E. Engel. Weed control in home lawns. Rutgers University Short Course in Turf Management Proceedings. pp. 39–45. 1971.

10409. Meadows, W. A. Grasses for Southern lawns—and how they are established. Seed World. 93(7):8, 10. 1963.

10410. Means, R. M. Trials of new fungicides. The Pennsylvania State College Eighteenth Annual Turf Conference. pp. 74–76. 1949.

10411. Mecheltree, W. A. Some facts about fertilizers. Rutgers University 19th Annual Short Couse in Turf Management. pp. 5–14. 1961.

10412. Mechling, P. Careful with chemicals. Proceedings of the Midwest Regional Turf Conference. pp. 23–24. 1968.

10413. Mecklenburg, R. A. Artificial versus living turf. The Golf Superintendent. 40(10):64–65. 1972.

10414. ______. Selection and maintenance of trees for turfgrass areas. 42nd Annual Michigan Turfgrass Conference Proceedings. 1:34–38. 1972.

10415. Mecklenburg, R. A., W. F. Rintelmann, D. R. Schumaier, C. VanDen-Brink, and L. Flores. The effect of plants on microclimate and noise reduction in the urban environment. HortScience. 7(1):37–39. 1972.

10418. Meggitt, W. F. Effect of pre-emergence herbicides on desirable turfgrass species. Michigan Turfgrass Research Report. 3(1):14. 1965.

10419. ______. Behavior of perennial grasses and their control. Proceedings of the Northeastern Weed Control Conference. 22:-17–18. 1968.

10420. Meiners, J. P. A turf disease research program. State College of Washington Annual Turf Conference. 4:22. 1951.

10421. ______. Results of the snowmold control experiments at Pullman and Spokane, Washington, 1951–1952. Proceedings 6th Annual Northwest Turf Conference. 6:22–23. 1952.

10422. ______. Results of the turf fungicide trials—1952–1953. Proceedings 7th Annual Northwest Turf Conference. 7:9–11. 1953.

10423. ______. Etiology and control of snow mold of turf in the Pacific northwest. Phytopathology. 45(1):59–62. 1955.

10424. Meisch, M. V. Mosquito control. Arkansas Agricultural Extension Service Leaflet 395 (Rev.) 4 pp. 1971.

10425. Meister, E. L. Selling the idea. USGA Green Section Record. 4(6):6–7. 1967.

10426. Melady, J. H. Better lawns for your home. Grosset and Dunlap. New York. 130 pp. 1952.

10427. Melkerson, E. J. Comparative performance of vegetative and seedling bluegrasses for turf. M.S. Thesis, Purdue University. 65 pp. 1963.

10428. Melville, C. M. Brown patch no danger to healthy greens. Golfdom. 1(7):37–38. 1927.

10429. ______. Humus characteristics and use in course maintenance. Golfdom. 7(6):53–55. 1933.

10430. Ménage, R. H. Soil pH. Gardeners Chronicle. 152(6):104–105. 1962.

10431. Mendenhall, C. Constructing and keeping sand greens. The National Greenkeeper. 1(12):5, 26. 1927.

10432. ______. Making compost. The National Greenkeeper. 5(4):7–8. 1931.

10433. ______. What heat taught. Golfdom. 9(5):67. 1935.

10434. ______. Our irrigation system. The Greenkeepers' Reporter. 6(3):7–9, 26. 1938.

10435. ______. Crabgrass vs. bluegrass. Greenkeeper's Reporter. 10(5):13, 33. 1942.

10436. ______. Fifty years of progress in aerating established turf. Golfdom. 23(3):56, 58. 1949.

10437. ______. Golf course landscaping. Central Plains Turfgrass Conference. 11:3. 1961.

10438. Mendenhall, C., B. Daniels, and H. Henry. The sod industry. Central Plains Turfgrass Conference. p. 4. 1963.

10439. Mendenhall, M. My experience in *Poa annua* control. Proceedings of the Midwest Regional Turf Conference. pp. 21–23. 1960.

10440. ______. *Poa annua* control. Central Plains Turfgrass Conference. 11:1–2. 1961.

10441. ______. Revising Kenwood Country Club. Proceedings of the Midwest Regional Turf Conference. pp. 10–12. 1970.

10442. Menefree, T. and J. S. Finger. Semi-sod method of planting hybrid bermudagrass. Golfdom. 33(10):68, 70. 1959.

10443. Menn, W. G. Brownpatch control. Proceedings of the Texas Turfgrass Conference. 23:19–20. 1968.

10444. ______. St. Augustinegrass attacked by SAD virus. Park Maintenance. 23(7):18. 1970.

10445. ______. Crabgrass. Park Maintenance. 24(7):25. 1971.

10446. Menn, W., and R. L. Duble. St. Augustine decline (SAD) virus. Park Maintenance. 25(7):12. 1972.

10447. ______. Growth retardants. Park Maintenance. 25(7):16. 1972.

10448. ______. Thatch. Park Maintenance. 25(7):17. 1972.

10449. Menn, W. G. and G. G. McBee. A study of certain nutritional requirements for Tifgreen bermudagrass utilizing a hydroponic design. Agronomy Abstracts. 59:54. 1967.

10450. ______. A comparison of propagation methods and effect of fertilization on rate of establishment of St. Augustine and zoysiagrasses. Texas Agricultural Experiment Station Progress Report. 2610:1–7. 1968.

10451. ______. Growth of 3 cool season grass types as affected by preemergence herbicide residues resulting from a controlled sequential leaching schedule. Agronomy Abstracts. 61:55. 1969.

10452. ______. A study of certain nutritional requirements for Tifgreen bermudagrass (*Cynodon dactylon* x *C. transvaalensis* L.) utilizing a hydroponic system. Agronomy Journal. 62(2):192–194. 1970.

10453. ______. Turfgrass research reports 1969–70, Texas A & M University. Southern Regional Turf Research Committee Report, Virginia Polytechnic Institute. pp. 41–44. 1970.

10454. ______. Grass mixtures in overseeding. Park Maintenance. 24(7):20. 1971.

10455. ______. An evaluation of various cool-season grasses and grass mixtures in overseeding a Tifgreen bermuda-grass golf green. Texas Agricultural Experiment Station Progress Report 2878. 16 pp. 1971.

10456. Menn, W. G., K. W. Brown, and J. R. Melton. Nitrate, mercury and arsenic leaching through golf green profiles. Agronomy Abstracts. 2:64. 1972.

10457. Mercurio, F. B. Department of labor workplace standards. USGA Green Section Record. 9(2):23–26. 1971.

10458. Meredith, D. Turf maintenance problems in South Africa. Journal of Board of Greenkeeping Research. 5(17):99–106. 1937.

10459. ______. The value of *Cynodon dactylon* Pers. as a pasture grass. Better Turf Through Research. South African Turf Research Fund. pp. 17–28. 1948.

10460. ______. The grasses and pastures of South Africa. Cape Times Ltd., Parow. 771 pp. 1955.

10461. Meredith, D. and R. E. Hurcombe. Growth rate studies. Better Turf

Through Research. South African Turf Research Fund. pp. 48–51. 1948.

10462. Merkel, E. Research. Proceedings of National Turf Field Day. p. 19. 1950.

10463. ______. The effect of aerification on water absorption and runoff. Pennsylvania State College Turfgrass Conference Proceedings. 21:37–41. 1952.

10464. Merkle, M. G. The use of surfactants with herbicides. Proceedings of the Annual Texas Turfgrass Conference. 22:31–32. 1967.

10465. Merrick, C. P. Pond construction and management. Proceedings of the Mid-Atlantic Association of Golf Course Superintendents Conference. pp. 13–14. 1963.

10466. Merrill, L. G. Development of resistance to insecticides. Rutgers University Short Course in Turf Management. 28:3. 1960.

10468. Merritt, M. G. Practical Lawn Care. A. T. De Lamare Company, Inc. New York. 82 pp. 1939.

10469. Meszaros, J. P. Burn thatch out. The Golf Superintendent. 35(5):51–57. 1967.

10470. Metcalf, J. I., and P. R. Henderlong. Establishment and seedling growth of Kentucky-31 tall fescue on an exposed clay subsoil as influenced by fertilization and wood by-products. Proceedings West Virginia Academy of Science. 39:146–151. 1967.

10471. Metcalf, M. M. Thin turf and luxuriant turf, their treatments and their relations to par. USGA Green Section Bulletin. 3(5):135. 1923.

10474. Metcalfe, C. R. Anatomy of the monocotyledons. I. *Gramineae.* Oxford University Press, London. 1960.

10476. Metsker, S. E. Alternative water system. The Golf Superintendent. 35(3):71–72. 1967.

10477. ______. Give your man a faster start. International Turfgrass Conference Proceedings. 38:2–3. 1967.

10478. Metzger, J. E. Fertilizers and their use. The Greenkeepers' Reporter. 7(2):-28–30, 64. 1939.

10480. Metzger, F. W. and W. W. Maines. Relation between the physical properties and chemical components of various grades of geraniol and their attractiveness to the Japanese beetle. USDA. Technical Bulletin. No. 501. 14 pp. 1935.

10481. Meusel, H. A study of wilt. Turf Clippings. University of Massachusetts. 1(8):A–28 to A–33. 1963.

10482. ______. What makes grass wilt? Golf Course Reporter. 32(3):24. 1964.

10483. ______. A study of wilt. New York Turfgrass Association Bulletin. 74:286–287. 1964.

10484. ______. Ecology of a golf course. The Golf Superintendent. 38(7):20–23. 1970.

10486. Meyer, T. E. Hydro mulching versus spot sodding for establishing bermuda grass lawns. Agronomy Abstracts. 2:165. 1972.

10487. Meyer, W. A. The nature of soil-borne diseases. Illinois Turfgrass Conference Proceedings. 47–48. 1969.

10488. ______. Systemic fungicide activity. Illinois Turfgrass Conference Proceedings. 11:32. 1970.

10489. Meyer, W. A. and J. B. Sinclair. *Pyrenochaeta terrestris,* a root pathogen on creeping bentgrass. The Plant Disease Reporter. 54(6):506–507. 1970.

10490. Meyer, W. A., J. F. Nicholson, and J. B. Sinclair. Translocation of benomyl in creeping bentgrass. Phytopathology. 61(10):1198–1200. 1971.

10491. Meyer, W. A., M. C. Shurtleff, and A. J. Turgeon. *Sclerotinia* dollar spot of turfgrasses. University of Illinois Cooperative Extension Service. Report on Plant Diseases No. 407. 3 pp. 1972.

10492. Meyers, H. Effects of various levels of nitrogen fertilization, vertical mowing intensity and frequency on Ormond bermudagrass. Proceedings of Florida Turf-Grass Management Conference. 11:48. 1963.

10494. Meyers, H. E., and R. I. Throckmorton. Some experiences with asphalt in the establishment of grasses and legumes for erosion control. Soil Science Society of America Proceedings. 6:459–461. 1941.

10495. Meyers, H. G. Effects of nitrogen levels and vertical mowing intensity and frequency on growth and chemical composition of Ormond bermudagrass. Proceedings of the Florida Turfgrass Management Conference. 12:77–79. 1964.

10496. ______. Two methods for calibration of boom sprayers. Florida Turf Grower. 1(1):1–7. 1966.

10497. ______. What the dealer needs to know about pesticides. Proceedings, Florida Turfgrass Management Conference. 14:88–90. 1966.

10498. ______. Their selection and use. Florida Turf Grower. 2(1):1–6. 1967.

10499. ______. Vertical mowing of warm-season grasses. University of Florida Extension Circular 314. pp. 8. 1967.

10500. ______. Comparison of turfgrasses for use in Florida. University of Florida Departmental Mimeograph. 12 pp. 1968.

10501. ______. How much equipment is enough? Golfdom. 42(10):57, 60, 64, 70. 1968.

10502. Meyers, H. G. and C. A. Conover. Home grounds weed control in Florida. University of Florida Departmental Mimeograph. 6 pp. 1968.

10504. Meyers, H. G. and G. C. Horn. Turfgrass fertilization. Florida Cooperative Extension Service Circular 357. 1–11 pp.

10505. ______. Construction and maintenance of football fields. Florida Turf Grower. 2. 1967.

10506. ______. Golf course fertilization. Florida Turf Grower. 2(2):1–6. 1967.

10507. ______. Selection of grasses for overseeding. Proceedings, Florida Turf-Grass Management Conference. 15:47–52. 1967.

10508. ______. Turf requirements for football fields. Southern Florist and Nurseryman. 80(33):42–50. 1967.

10509. ______. Index to the proceedings of the Florida Turfgrass Management Conference. Turfgrass Association. 32 pp. 1968.

10510. ______. Selection of cool season grass mixtures for overseeding golf course greens. Proceedings, Florida Turfgrass Management Conference. 16:33–37. 1968.

10511. ______. Bahiagrass vertical mowing. Proceedings Annual Florida Turfgrass Trade Show. 7:14–15. 1968.

10512. ______. Basic equipment requirements for various golf courses. Florida Turf Grower. 3(3):1–11. 1968.

10513. ______. Overseeding recommendations for Florida golf courses. Florida Turf Grower. 3(5):1–4. 1968.

10514. ______. Bahiagrasses—establishment and maintenance. Florida Extension Circular. 1969.

10515. ______. Maintenance fertilization (St. Augustinegrasses). Proceedings of the Florida Turf-Grass Management Conference. 17:60–62. 1969.

10516. Meyers, H. G., and C. A. Conover. Calibration of hand sprayers for weed control in small areas of turf and ornamentals. Florida Turf Grower. 4(1):1–9. 1969.

10517. Meyers, H. G., and G. C. Horn. Management considerations for a good transition from overseeded back to permanent warm season grasses. Florida Turf Grower. 4(2):1–7. 1969.

10518. ______. Turf irrigation. Florida Turf Grower. 4(3):1–5. 1969.

10519. ______. Turfgrass fertilization. Florida Turf Grower. 4(6):1–7. 1969.

10520. ______. The two-grass system in Florida. Proceedings of the First International Turfgrass Research Conference. pp. 110–117. 1969.

10521. ______. Transition from overseeded to permanent warm season grasses. Golf Superintendent. 38(1):62–65. 1970.

10522. ______. Turf irrigation. Florida Turfgrass Association. 5(1):3–5. 1972.

10523. Meyers, H. G. and J. N. Joiner. Effects of ferrous sulfate, chelated iron and versene-T levels on growth and chemical composition of centipedegrass. Proceedings of the Florida State Horticultural Society. 79:464–468. 1966.

10524. Meyers, H. G., G. C. Horn, E. O. Burt, and G. M. Whitton. Bahiagrasses for lawns. California Turfgrass Culture. 20(3):-23–24. 1970.

10525. ______. Bahiagrasses for Florida lawns. Florida Turf. 3(2):3–10. 1970.

10526. Meyers, W. M., and V. G. Sprague. Evaluation of strains of Kentucky bluegrass in association with white clover. Journal of the American Society of Agronomy. 36(12):1003. 1944.

10527. Michael, E. J. All is not bent that creeps. The National Greenkeeper. 1(4):11–12. 1927.

10528. ______. Installing watering systems. USGA Journal and Turf Management. 10(3):26–29. 1957.

10529. Michael, E. J. and J. DeBottis. First aid: for a faulty water supply. USGA Green Section Record. 7(1):5–6. 1969.

10530. Michael, P. W. and W. Reyenga. Selectivity of paraquat against an annual ryegrass in seedling mixtures with two perennial grasses and lucerne. Weed Research. 8(2):-156–158. 1968.

10531. Micheltree, W. A. Gypsum and soil management. Rutgers University Short Course in Turf Management. 18:8–13. 1950.

10532. ______. How water acts in the soil. The Golf Course Reporter. 23(4):32–34. 1955.

10533. Middleton, J. T. The taxonomy, host range, and geographic distribution of the genus *Pythium*. Torrey Botanical Club Memoirs. 20(1):1–171. 1943.

10534. Midyette, J. Checking the seeds you buy. Virginia Turfgrass Conference. pp. 16–30. 1963.

10535. Miles, D. L. Water laws and legislation affecting the turf industry. Annual Rocky Mountain Regional Turfgrass Conference Proceedings. 18:24–27. 1972.

10536. Miles, N. W., J. K. Greig, C. E. Long, E. B. Nilson, and W. A. Geyer. Chemical weed control in forestry and horticultural plants—lawn and turf. Kansas State University Agricultural Experiment Station Bulletin. 516:16–17. 1968.

10537. Miles, T. J. *Poa annua*—Chicago style. Missouri Lawn and Turf Conference Proceedings. 12:29–32. 1971.

10538. Millar, C. E. Michigan short course gives close-up on problems. Golfdom. 6(3):89–93. 1932.

10539. ______. Soils, their composition and fertility. The National Greenkeeper. 7(3):16–21. 1933.

10540. Miller, A. J. Golf course irrigation: good ideas. Weeds, Trees and Turf. 9(3):20–21. 1970.

10541. Miller, C. W. Saline soils and water problems in west Texas and Oklahoma. Oklahoma-Texas Turf Conference Proceedings. pp. 83–88. 1950.

10542. ______. Treatment of sewage sludge by composting using bacteria activators. Agronomy Abstracts. 51:91. 1959.

10543. ______. Invasion of King Ranch bluestem in lawns and turf areas on the Southwest. Agronomy Abstracts. 56:122. 1964.

10544. Miller, D. Saving irrigation at Panther Valley. Golfdom. 43(6):45, 76. 1969.

10546. Miller, F. P. The soil profile. The Golf Superintendent. 36(3):24–25. 1968.

10547. ______. Soil differences affect pipe life. Turf-Grass Times. 3(8):16. 1968.

10548. Miller, H. A. Building up run down fairways. The National Greenkeeper. 2(1):13. 1928.

10549. ______. Preventing winter kill on greens. Golfdom. 3(2):55. 1929.

10550. Miller, H. N. Part II—diseases and their control. Proceedings of the Second Annual University of Florida Turf Conference. 2:13–15. 1952.

10551. ______. Endoparasitic fungi of cyst and sting nematodes. Florida Institute of Food and Agricultural Sciences Annual Research Report. p. 118. 1970.

10552. Miller, J. F. Weed identification. Georgia Cooperative Extension Service Bulletin 632. 97 pp. 1964.

10553. ______. Weeds and their identification. Proceedings 18th Southeastern Turfgrass Conference. pp. 1–6. 1964.

10554. Miller, J. F. and W. S. Hardcastle. Turf—recommended practices—Georgia. Annual Southern Weed Conference Research Report. 22:86. 1969.

10555. Miller, J. F., and W. H. Hogan. Turf—recommended practices—Georgia.

Annual Southern Weed Conference Research Report. 19:110–111. 1966.

10556. Miller, J. R. Soil testing for turfgrasses. Annual Mid-Atlantic Golf Course Superintendent's Conference Proceedings. pp. 31–41. 1960.

10557. ______. Turf: soils and fertilizer relationships. Proceedings of the Mid-Atlantic Association of Golf Course Superintendents. p. 11. 1964.

10558. Miller, L. E. Success with arsenic on 40 acres. Proceedings of the Midwest Regional Turf Conference. pp. 26–28. 1970.

10559. ______. Which grass for Louisville?—bent. Midwest Regional Turf Conference Proceedings. pp. 65–67. 1971.

10560. Miller, M. G. Preparing for a championship. USGA Green Section Record. 4(6):4–6. 1967.

10561. Miller, M. H. Fertilizer use and pollution. RCGA National Turfgrass Conference. pp. 28–34. 1968.

10563. Miller, P. The gardeners kalendar. Bible and Crown. London. 7th ed. 355 pp. 1745.

10564. Miller, P. A. Turf fungicides. First Annual Fall Field Day on Turf Culture. (UCLA) pp. 34–36. 1949.

10565. ______. Turf disease control. Field Day on Turf Culture. (UCLA) pp. 3–6. 1950.

10566. ______. Turf diseases. Southern California Conference on Turf Culture. pp. 6–8. 1951.

10567. ______. Dollar spot control trials. Southern California Turf Culture. 2(1):4. 1952.

10568. ______. Turf fungicide trials—U.C.L.A. 1952. Southern California Turf Conference Proceedings. pp. 20–21. 1952.

10569. ______. Diseases—can we prevent or control them? North California Turf Conference. pp. 6–9. 1953.

10570. ______. Turfgrass disease control. Southern California Turf Culture. 6(1):7. 1956.

10571. ______. Turfgrass diseases. Southern California Turf Culture. 7(2):9–10. 1957.

10572. Miller, P. A. and O. R. Lunt. Turf fungicide trials—U.C.L.A. 1952. Southern California Turf Culture. 3(1):4. 1953.

10573. ______. Dollar spot control. Southern California Turf Culture. 4(2):3. 1954.

10574. Miller, P. A. and C. G. Wyckoff. Turf fungicide trials—1954. Southern California Turf Culture. 5(2):1, 4. 1955.

10575. Miller, P. A., M. E. Mathias, F. W. Roewekamp, and F. V. Grau. Trees and turf. Southern California Conference on Turf Culture. pp. 46–55. 1951.

10576. Miller, P. M. and P. E. Waggoner. Control of soil born fungi and incidence of *Pratelenchus penetrans.* Phytopathology. 52(9):926. 1962.

10577. Miller, R. T. Practical management of turf for disease control. Proceedings Second Annual Tennessee Turfgrass Conference. pp. 27–29. 1968.

10578. Miller, R. Yes, lime does have a role in turfgrass management. Lakeshore News. 4(2):11. 1972.

10579. Miller, R. A. Seed sod study. Illinois Turfgrass Conference Proceedings. 3:-39–45. 1962.

10580. ______. Bluegrass growth response to various formulations, placement and rates of plant food. Illinois Turfgrass Conference Proceedings. 4:19–22. 1963.

10581. Miller, R. K. Herbicidal effects of Picloram in two turfgrasses: metabolism and translocation. M.S. Thesis, Southern Illinois University. 26 pp. 1970.

10582. Miller, R. L. Insect control. Ohio Turfgrass Conference Proceedings. pp. 57–61. 1971.

10583. Miller, R. M. The role of ureaforms in the turf fertilizer industry. Turf Clippings. University of Massachussetts. 1(8):A–51 to A–55. 1963.

10584. Miller, R. T. Remarks by Robert T. Miller, turf specialist. Proceedings of the Midwest Regional Turf Conference. pp. 41–42. 1956.

10585. ______. Developments in fungicides and disease control. Oklahoma Turfgrass Conference Proceedings. pp. 9–11. 1958.

10586. ______. Remarks about turf fungicides. Oklahoma Turfgrass Conference Proceedings. pp. 24–25. 1956.

10587. ______. Turf fungicides in turf management. Guelph Turfgrass Conference Proceedings. pp. 28–31. 1959.

10588. ______. What is new in turfgrass disease control. Proceedings, Missouri Lawn and Turf Conference. 4:10–11. 1963.

10589. ______. Nitrogen fertilization of turfgrass. Proceedings, Missouri Lawn and Turf Conference. 4:23–25. 1963.

10590. ______. Disease control through maintenance practices. Oklahoma Turfgrass Conference Proceedings. pp. 9–12. 1963.

10591. ______. Proper use of turf fungicides. Proceedings of the Mid-Atlantic Association of Golf Course Superintendents. pp. 12–13. 1964.

10592. ______. Diseases of overseeded grasses. Proceedings of the Texas Turfgrass Conference. 19:20–21. 1964.

10593. ______. Turfgrass disease control. Proceedings of the Texas Turfgrass Conference. 19:26. 1964.

10594. ______. Disease control in turf. Sixteenth R.C.G.A. Sports Turfgrass Conference. pp. 33–35. 1965.

10596. ______. New developments in disease control in turf. Proceedings of the Annual Texas Turfgrass Conference. 22:28–30. 1967.

10597. ______. Buyer beware. International Turfgrass Conference Proceedings. 41:6–9. 1970.

10598. ______. Birth of a chemical. Annual RCGA National Turfgrass Conference. 21:28–30. 1970.

10599. ______. Birth of a chemical. Proceedings, Fourth Annual Tennessee Turfgrass Conference. pp. 19–21. 1970.

10600. ______. Diseases of turf. Florida Turfgrass Management Conference Proceedings. 18:48–51. 1970.

10601. ______. How a manufacturer looks at disease control in turf. Annual RCGA National Turfgrass Conference. 23:-47–49. 1972.

10602. ______. Programmed turf disease control. Weeds, Trees, and Turf. 11(2):16, 40–41. 1972.

10603. Miller, R. W. The thatch problem. Weeds, Trees and Turf. 4(10):8–14. 1965.

10604. ______. The effect of certain management practices on the botanical composition and winter injury to turf containing a mixture of Kentucky bluegrass (*Poa pratensis,* L.) and tall fescue (*Festuca arundinacea,* Schreb). Illinois Turfgrass Conference Proceedings. 7:39–46. 1966.

10605. ______. The effects of certain management practices on the botanical composition and winter injury to turf containing a mixture of Kentucky bluegrass and tall fescue. Ohio Agricultural Research and Development Center. Lawn and Ornamentals Research Summary No. 24. pp. 13–20. 1967.

10606. ______. Herbicides for dicot weed control in turf. Turf Talks. Scotts Marysville, Ohio. p. 3. August, 1967.

10607. ______. Thatch development and control. 1967 West Virginia Turfgrass Conference Proceedings. West Virginia Agricultural Experiment Station Miscellaneous Publication 5:41–44. 1968.

10608. ______. Plant—water relationships. West Virginia Turfgrass Conference Proceedings. pp. 23–28. 1968.

10609. ______. Weed control in turf. West Virginia Turfgrass Conference Proceedings. pp. 51–56. 1968.

10610. ______. Turfgrass conference organization. Proceedings of the First International Turfgrass Research Conference. pp. 434–436. 1969.

10611. ______. Fertilization of lawns. Ohio Agricultural Research and Development Center Research Summary 40. pp. 7–8. 1969.

10612. ______. Athletic field maintenance. Proceedings of the First International Turfgrass Research Conference. pp. 526–532. 1969.

10613. ______. A program for broadleaf weed control in turf. Ohio Turfgrass Conference Proceedings. pp. 59–61. 1969.

10614. ______. Varieties of Kentucky bluegrass. Ohio Turfgrass Foundation Newsletter. 14:1–2. 1969.

10615. ______. Tall fescue and tall fescue—bluegrass mixtures for athletic fields and other turfgrass areas. Ohio Turfgrass Conference Proceedings. pp. 9–16. 1969.

10616. ______. Bentgrasses. Turf and Ornamentals Research Summary 48. Ohio Agricultural Research and Development Center. pp. 3–6. 1970.

10617. ______. Controlling broadleaf weeds in turf. Ohio Report on Research and Development. 55(3):54–55. 1970.

10618. ______. Soil testing to determine fertilizer needs. Ohio Turfgrass Conference Proceedings. pp. 65–73. 1970.

10619. ______. Pre-emergence control of annual grasses. Ohio Turfgrass Conference Proceedings. pp. 90–96. 1970.

10620. ______. Thatch regulation. Midwest Regional Turf Conference Proceedings. pp. 82–83. 1971.

10621. ______. Using newer grasses. Midwest Regional Turf Conference Proceedings. pp. 76–80. 1971.

10622. ______. Using newer grasses. Ohio Agricultural Research and Development Center. Research Summary. 56. pp. 1–6. 1971.

10623. ______. Soil testing to determine fertilizer needs. Ohio Agricultural Research and Development Center Research Summary 56. pp. 7–14. 1971.

10624. ______. Pre-emergence control of annual grasses. Ohio Agricultural Research and Development Center Research Summary 56. pp. 17–22. 1971.

10625. ______. Thatch regulation. Ohio Agricultural Research and Development Center Research Summary 56. pp. 29–30. 1971.

10626. ______. Evaluation of Kentucky bluegrass, fine fescue and ryegrass varieties. Ohio Turfgrass Conference Proceedings. pp. 9–14. 1971.

10627. ______. Broadleaf weed control. Ohio Turfgrass Foundation Newsletter. 22:7. 1971.

10628. ______. The turfgrass industry in Ohio. Ohio Turfgrass Foundation Newsletter. 23:1–2. 1971.

10629. ______. Pre-emergence control of annual grasses. Rutgers University Short Course in Turf Management Proceedings. pp. 73–79. 1971.

10630. ______. The nature of pre-emergence turf herbicides. Rutgers University Short Course in Turf Management Proceedings. pp. 80–82. 1971.

10631. ______. Evaluation of Kentucky bluegrass, fine fescue, and ryegrass varieties. Ohio Agricultural Research and Development Center, Research Summary. 62:1–3. 1972.

10632. ______. Bentgrass varieties vary in tolerance to dicamba. Ohio Agricultural Research and Development Center, Research Summary 62. p. 11. 1972.

10633. ______. Evaluation of Kentucky bluegrass, fine fescue and ryegrass varieties. A Patch of Green. Michigan and Border Cities GCSA Publication. pp. 12–13. January, 1972.

10634. Miller, R. W. and R. R. Davis. Preemergence herbicides for crabgrass control. The Golf Course Reporter. 33(3):48–49. 1965.

10635. ______. Varieties of Kentucky bluegrass. Ohio Agricultural Research and Development Center Research Summary 6. pp. 9–11. 1965.

10636. ______. Crabgrass can be controlled. Ohio Agricultural Research and Development Center. Research Summary 6. pp. 17–19. 1965.

10637. ______. Bentgrass varieties for golf courses and lawns. Lawn and Ornamental Research—1966. Research Summary 16. Ohio Agricultural Research and Development Center. pp. 7–8. 1966.

10638. Miller, R. W. and E. W. Stroube. Weed control in turf. Turf and Ornamentals Research Summary 48. Ohio Agricultural Research and Development Center. pp. 7–14. 1970.

10639. Miller, V. Turf as a research tool. Proceedings of the American Society for Horticultural Science. Western Region Abstracts. 3:1. 1961.

10640. Miller, V. J. Temperature effect on the rate of apparent photosynthesis of Seaside bent and bermuda grass. Arizona Turf Conference Proceedings. pp. 14–15. 1959.

10641. ______. Temperature effects on the rate of apparent photosynthesis of seaside bent and bermudagrass. Proceedings of the American Society for Horticultural Science. 75:700–703. 1960.

10642. Miller, W. Bentgrasses. Lakeshore News. 2(5):4, 8, 11, 15. 1970.

10643. Miller, W. O. Recent developments with Dursban insecticide for chinch bug control. Down to Earth. 27(3):1–6. 1971.

10644. Miller, W. P. Golf course drainage. The National Greenkeeper. 2(1):20–21, 31. 1928.

10645. ______. Golf course drainage. The National Greenkeeper. 2(3):23, 24. 1928.

10646. ______. Golf course drainage. The National Greenkeeper. 2(5):29–30. 1928.

10647. ______. Golf course drainage—part V. The National Greenkeeper. 2(6):27–29. 1928.

10648. ______. Science must supply base for turf campaign. Golfdom. 3(10):49–50–51. 1929.

10649. ______. Summary of turf "eras". Golfdom. 3(11):35–37, 39. 1929.

10650. ______. Soils, drainage and their part in profitable operation. Golfdom. 4(3):-88, 90, 92. 1930.

10651. ______. Drainage and soils. The National Greenkeeper. 4(4):33–40. 1930.

10652. ______. Hoseless irrigation. The National Greenkeeper. 4(8):9–14. 1930.

10653. Miller, W. T. Which kind of pipe? cast iron. Golf Course Reporter. 32(6):34–35. 1964.

10654. Milliken, J. D. Landscape planning during club expansion. 18th R. C. G. A. National Turfgrass Conference Summary. pp. 29–33. 1967.

10655. Mills, C. B. First in lawns. Princeton University Press. 1–23 pp. 1961.

10656. Mills, H. A. The effect of pH, rate of nitrogen application and plants on ammonium volatilization. M.S. Thesis, University of Massachusetts. 1972.

10657. Mills, J. E. *Fusarium* patch on grass. Gardeners Chronicle. 151(5):88. 1962.

10658. ______. Leather jackets on turf. Gardeners Chronicle. 151(11):201. 1962.

10659. ______. Rectifying turf hollows in summer. Gardeners Chronicle. 151(21):-407. 1962.

10660. ______. Remedying wet lawns. Gardeners Chronicle. 153(8):143. 1963.

10661. ______. Some worthy grasses for lawns. Gardeners Chronicle. 153(12):211. 1963.

10662. ______. Aids to grass seeding. Gardeners Chronicle. 153(13):228. 1963.

10663. ______. Notes on turfing in spring. Gardeners Chronicle. 153(14):1963.

10664. ______. When lawn liming is justified. Gardeners Chronicle. 154(4):70. 1963.

10665. ______. Lawn grasses for various purposes. Gardeners Chronicle. 155(9):175. 1964.

10666. ______. A spring tonic for the lawn. Gardeners Chronicle. 155(11):217. 1964.

10667. ______. Mossy lawns—cause and control. Gardeners Chronicle. 155(14):297. 1964.

10668. ______. Lawn weed control. Gardeners Chronicle. 156(17):419. 1964.

10669. Mills, W. All according to the book. The Groundsman. 20(5):10–12. 1967.

10670. ______. I've got fairies at the bottom of my ground . . . The Groundsman. 21(10):14–21. 1968.

10671. ______. A method of turfing. The Groundsman. 23(7):30–31. 1970.

10672. ______. Principles of irrigation—I. The Groundsman. 23(8):28–32. 1970.

10673. ______. Principles of irrigation—II. The Groundsman. 23(9):14–16. 1970.

10674. ______. Chlordane and common sense. The Groundsman. 23(10):9–14. 1970.

10675. Mills, Z. Water sources. Turf Clippings. University of Massachussetts. 1(7):39–A to 41–A. 1962.

10676. Milne, A. Biology and ecology of the garden chafer *Phyllopertha horticola* (L.). IX. Spatial distribution. Bulletin of Entomological Research. 54:761–795. 1963.

10677. Milne, K. S. Control of some non-disease conditions in turf. New Zealand Institute for Turf Culture Newsletter. 76:177–180. 1971.

10678. Milne, W. W. Fertilizing for growth control. Proceedings of the Midwest Regional Turf Conference. pp. 62–63. 1961.

10679. Milosch, R. Labor problems—public golf course. Ohio Turfgrass Conference Proceedings. p. 80. 1970.

10680. Milthorpe, F. L., and J. D. Ivins. The growth of cereals and grasses. Butterworths, London. 359 pp. 1966.

10681. Miner, W. Specifications for sod. International Turfgrass Conference Proceedings. 38:56–57. 1967.

10682. Minton, N. A. and H. Ivey. The pseudo-root-knot nematode on Bermudagrass in Alabama. The Plant Disease Reporter. 51(2):148. 1967.

10683. Minton, W. H. Factors affecting utilization and expansion potential for ornamental plants and turf. Kentucky Agricultural Experiment Station Annual Report. 84:11. 1971.

10684. Mirza, K. and V. G. Perry. Histopathology of St. Augustinegrass roots infected by *Hypsoperine graminis* Sledge and Golden. Nematologica. 13:146–147. 1967.

10685. Mishra, S. N. and P. N. Drolsom. Evaluation of two methods of hybridization in *Bromus inermis* Leyss. Crop Science. 12(3):389–391. 1972.

10686. Mitchell, H. Getting to the roots of watering problems. Golfdom. 28(9):40–41. 1954.

10687. Mitchell, H. C. The use of water in turf culture. Greenkeepers Club of New England Newsletter. 11(2):2–3. 1939.

10688. ______. Useful fertility. Golfdom. 31:27–28. 1957.

10689. Mitchell, H. S. Bent grass for home lawn. The Greenkeepers' Reporter. 6(5):19. 1938.

10690. ______. Use of lime on golf courses. Proceedings Annual Texas Turfgrass Conference. 21:50–52. 1966.

10691. Mitchel, J. Worm control in sports turf. New Zealand Institute for Turf Culture Newsletter. 33:13–14. 1964.

10692. Mitchell, J., and R. L. Morris. Evaluation of experimental fungicides on turf, particularly against *Fusarium nivale*. Proceedings of the First International Turfgrass Research Conference. pp. 366–368. 1969.

10693. Mitchell, J. W., and P. C. Marth. Effects of 2, 4–D on the growth of grass plants. Botanical Gazette. 107(2):276–284. 1945.

10694. Mitchell, J. W., F. F. Davis, and P. C. Marth. Turf and weed control with plant growth regulators. Golfdom. 18(10):34, 36, 38. 1944.

10695. Mitchell, K. J. Influence of light and temperature on the growth of ryegrass (*Lolium* spp.). I. Pattern of vegetative development. Physiologia Plantarium. 6:21–46. 1953.

10696. ______. Influence of light and temperature on the growth of ryegrass (*Lolium* spp.). II. The control of lateral bud development. Physiologia Plantarum. 6:425–443. 1953.

10697. ______. Growth of pasture species. I. Short rotation and perennial ryegrass. New Zealand Journal of Science and Technology. Section A. 36(3):191–206. 1954.

10698. ______. Influence of light and temperature on growth of ryegrass (*Lolium* spp.). III. Pattern and rate of tissue formation. Physiologia Plantarum. 7:51–65. 1954.

10699. ______. Growth of pasture species. II. Perennial ryegrass *(Lolium perenne),* cocksfoot *(Dactylis glomerata)* and paspalum *(Paspalum dilatatum).* New Zealand Journal of Science and Technology. Section A. 37(1):-8–26. 1955.

10700. ______. Growth of pasture species under controlled environment. I. Growth at various levels of constant temperature. New Zealand Journal of Science and Technology. Section A. 38(2):203–215. 1956.

10701. Mitchell, K. J., and D. M. Calder. The light regime within pastures. New Zealand Journal of Agricultural Research. 1(1):-61–68. 1958.

10702. Mitchell, K. J., and S. T. J. Coles. Effects of defoliation and shading on short-rotation ryegrass. New Zealand Journal of Science and Technology. Section A. 36(6):-586–604. 1955.

10703. Mitchell, K. J. and J. J. Kerr. Differences in rate of use of soil moisture by stands of perennial ryegrass and white clover. Agronomy Journal. 58(1):5–9. 1966.

10704. Mitchell, K. J., and R. Lucanus. Growth of pasture species in controlled environment. II. Growth at low temperatures. New Zealand Journal of Agricultural Research. 3(4):647–655. 1960.

10705. Mitchell, K. J., and K. Soper. Effects of differences in light intensity and temperature on the anatomy and development of leaves of *Lolium perenne* and *Paspalum dilatatum.* New Zealand Journal of Agricultural Research. 1(1):1–16. 1958.

10706. Mitchell, M. L. Environmental and genetic effects on seedling vigor and seed dormancy in tall fescue. M.S. Thesis, University of Missouri. 1972.

10707. Mitchell, R. Greenkeepers query themselves. Golfdom. 14(5):2–13. 1940.

10709. Mitchell, R. A. The story of Kernwood bent. Greenkeepers Club of New England Newsletter. 1(2):2. 1929.

10710. ______. Growing velvet bent under low budget conditions. Greenkeepers Club of New England Newsletter. 10(1):8–9. 1938.

10711. ______. Velvet bents. Greenkeepers Club of New England Newsletter. 11(12):6–7. 1939.

10712. Mitchell, R. C. Canadian turf pest. The Golf Superintendent. 36(7):30–31. 1968.

10713. Mitchell, R. V. How we treat greens. Golf Course Reporter. 25(4):32. 1957.

10714. Mitchell, R. L. The winning questionnaire. The Greenkeepers' Reporter. 7(6):5. 1939.

10715. ______. Snowmobiles on the golf course, the pro's. Turf-Grass Times. 8(1):23. 1972.

10716. Mitchell, R. V. Healthy turf through fertilization and irrigation. Proceedings of the Midwest Regional Turf Conference. pp. 17–18. 1956.

10717. ______. The superintendent in the seventies. Annual RCGA National Turfgrass Conference. 23:50–55. 1972.

10718. Mitchell, S. S. Proper watering of greens and fairways. Golf Course Reporter. 21(5):12–14. 1953.

10719. Mitchell, W. The four pillars of fertility. Greenkeepers Club of New England Newsletter. 12(4):12, 14. 1940.

10720. ______. Remodelling and renovation greens. Greenkeeping Superintendents Association National Turf Conference. 21:-114–117. 1950.

10721. Mitchell, W. F. Golf course construction today. Southern Turfgrass Association Conference Proceedings. pp. 20–21. 1968.

10722. Mitchell, W. H. Influence of cutting heights, irrigation and nitrogen on the growth and persistence of orchardgrass. University of Delaware Agricultural Experiment Station Bulletin. 364. 15 pp. 1967.

10723. Mitcheltree, W. A. How to buy lime and fertilizer. Rutgers University Turfgrass Short Course. 5 pp. 1957.

10724. Mitchener, A. V. Worm and insect control. Proceedings of School of Soils, Fertilization and Turf Maintenance. Royal Canadian Golf Association. Green Section. pp. 31–34. 1953.

10725. Miyoshi, R. Mixed cultivation of turfgrasses in green. K.G.U. Green Section Turf Research Bulletin. 14:63–68. 1968.

10726. Moberg, E. L. Turfgrass cultivar identification by perioxidase isoenzyme composition. Ph.D Thesis, Pennsylvania State University. 1972.

10727. Moberg, E. L., and J. M. Duich. Identification of Kentucky bluegrass cultivars using isoenzyme techniques. Agronomy Abstracts. p. 49. 1971.

10728. Moberg, E. L., D. V. Waddington, and J. M. Duich. Evaluation of slow-release nitrogen sources on Merion Kentucky bluegrass. Soil Science Society of America Proceedings. 34(2):335–339. 1970.

10729. Mock, A. F. Lawn grasses and mixtures. Handbook on Lawns. Brooklyn Botanic Garden. pp. 110–116. 1956.

10730. ______. Careful choice required to obtain best types of grass. Park Maintenance. 10(12):22. 1957.

10731. Mock, D. Diseases of ornamentals and turfgrasses. Proceedings 16th Annual Northwest Turf Conference. 16:43–45. 1962.

10732. Mock, G. Techniques of ground spraying. Proceedings Pacific Northwest Turf Conference. 13:61–63. 1959.

10733. Mock, L. G., L. C. Erickson, R. L. Goss, B. Johnson, and D. Mock. Panel discussion of fundamentals of ground spraying. Proceedings 16th Annual Northwest Turf Conference. 16:31–46. 1962.

10734. Moe, P. G., J. V. Mannering, and C. B. Johnson. Further studies of nitrogen losses in surface runoff water on fragipan soils. Purdue Agricultural Experiment Station Research Progress Report 287. 4 pp. 1967.

10735. Moellering, W. A. County uses granular herbicide to control Canada thistles. Better Roads. 39(2):21. 1969.

10736. Moesch, R. Mechanical laying-out, care and renovation of playground and other lawns. First Czechoslovak Symposium on Sportturf Proceedings. pp. 117–128. 1969.

10737. Moffett, S. Reels versus flails and rotaries. The Bonnie Greensward. Philadelphia Association of Golf Course Superintendents Publication. p. 4. September, 1971.

10738. Mohammed, E. and J. Letey. The effect of non-ionic surfactants on seed germination, growth, and root distribution. Agronomy Abstracts. p. 70. 1970.

10739. Mohle, F. Labor saving practices and maintenance of large turf areas. Proceedings University of Florida Turf-Grass Management Conference. 9:185–186. 1961.

10741. Moldenhauer, W. C., J. Maddy, B. L. Schmidt, and W. D. Shrader. Establishing vegetation on exposed subsoil in southern Iowa and northern Missouri. USDA Agriculture Information Bulletin No. 280. 15 pp. 1964.

10742. Molenaar, A. Irrigation practices. State College of Washington Turf Conference Proceedings. 3:9–11. 1950.

10743. ______. Irrigation of turf areas. Proceedings 4th Annual Northwest Turf Conference. 5:23–25. 1951.

10744. ______. Irrigation of turf areas. State College of Washington Annual Turf Conference. 4:23–25. 1951.

10746. Molton, H. C. Maintenance of automatic sprinkler systems. Proceedings Annual Turfgrass Sprinkler Irrigation Conference. 5:59–60. 1967.

10747. Moncrief, J. B. Turf management calculations. USGA Journal and Turf Management. 10(7):24–28. 1958.

10748. ______. Pressing problems in turf research. Auburn University Annual Turfgrass Short Course. pp. 26–33. 1960.

10749. ______. Golf course maintenance. Proceedings Fourteenth Southeastern Turfgrass Conference. 14:21–24. 1960.

10750. ______. Suggestions for planning and programming of work. Proceedings Fifteenth Southeastern Turfgrass Conference. pp. 7–10. 1961.

10751. ______. How to meet winter course maintenance problems. Club Operations. 1(1):35. 1963.

10752. ______. Traffic and wear. Proceedings of Florida Turf-Grass Management Conference. 11:60–63. 1963.

10753. ______. Roads on the golf course. Proceedings 17th Southeastern Turfgrass Conference. pp. 6–14. 1963.

10754. ______. The best fairway grasses. Proceedings of Florida Turf-Grass Management Conference. 12:75–76. 1964.

10755. ______. Bent moves South. USGA Green Section Record. 2(3):1–6. 1964.

10756. ______. Overseeding. Auburn University Annual Turfgrass Short Course. pp. 5–9. 1965.

10757. ______. Types of irrigation systems and their use. Proceedings 19th Southeastern Turfgrass Conference. pp. 11–25. 1965.

10758. ______. Sources of water for irrigation. Proceedings 19th Southeastern Turfgrass Conference. pp. 32–36. 1965.

10759. ______. Mulch and soil conditioners. Proceedings of the Texas Turfgrass Conference. 20:45–47. 1965.

10760. ______. Bentgrasses—varieties, growth habits and areas of adaptation. Proceedings of the Texas Turfgrass Conference. 20:48–53. 1965.

10761. ______. Diseases of bermudagrasses. USGA Green Section Record. 3(2):-1–7. 1965.

10762. ______. Winter injury to turf. Auburn University Annual Turfgrass Short Course. pp. 24–28. 1966.

10763. ______. Public relations for the superintendent. Proceedings Florida Turfgrass Management Conference. 14:58–61. 1966.

10764. ______. Tifdwarf—bermudagrass for championship greens. Auburn University Annual Turfgrass Short Course. pp. 21–28. 1967.

10765. ______. Fertilization of greens. Proceedings First Annual Tennessee Turfgrass Conference. pp. 32–33. 1967.

10766. ______. Tifdwarf management to include insect control. Proceedings of the Annual Texas Turfgrass Conference. 23:1–3. 1968.

10767. ______. Bent varieties for Texas greens. Proceedings of the Texas Turfgrass Conference. 23:21–22. 1968.

10768. ______. Popular bermudagrass strains: requirements and peculiarities. USGA Green Section Record. 5(6):12–14. 1968.

10769. ______. Enigma of spring dead spot. USGA Green Section Record. 6(1):16–18. 1968.

10770. ______. Selecting a variety. Proceedings of the Florida Turf-Grass Management Conference. 17:41–43. 1969.

10771. ______. Automation and economics in turf management. Proceedings Third Annual Tennessee Turfgrass Conference. pp. 3–6. 1969.

10772. ______. Sources of water. USGA Green Section Record. 6(4):4–7. 1968.

10773. ______. Warm season grasses we should know about. USGA Green Section Record. 8(2):24–25. 1970.

10774. ______. 1970 down south—disaster hits bermudagrass. USGA Green Section Record. 8(6):2–5. 1970.

10775. ______. Status and future of hybrid bermudas in the south. Proceedings Fifth Annual Tennessee Turfgrass Conference. pp. 28–31. 1971.

10776. ______. Maintenance is a must. USGA Green Section Record. 9(2):33–34. 1971.

10777. ______. Cart paths and car roads can be turf savers. USGA Green Section Record. 9(5):1–5. 1971.

10778. ______. Instant bentgrass greens. USGA Green Section Record. 9(6):1–5. 1971.

10779. ______. Turfgrass management in the Argentine. USGA Green Section Record. 10(6):9–11. 1972.

10780. Moncrief, J. B. and M. H. Ferguson. Golf course ponds and lakes. USGA Journal and Turf Management. 12(6):26–28. 1959.

10781. Moncrief, J. B., C. Danner, and L. Record Roads on the golf course. USGA Green Section Record. 1(1):11–13. 1963.

10782. Moncrief, J. B., T. M. Baumgardner, P. Maples, H. Wright and C. Danner. Control of crabgrass, goosegrass, *Poa anna,* clover, sedges, spotted spurge and others. Proceedings 18th Southeastern Turfgrass Conference. pp. 28–38. 1964.

10783. Moncrief, J. B., H. Land, E. Godwin, and S. E. Clarke. What have we learned about Tifdwarf bermudagrass for golf greens? Southeastern Turfgrass Conference Proceedings. 21:13–21. 1967.

10784. Monroe, C. A., G. D. Coorts, and C. R. Skogley. Effects of nitrogen-potassium levels on the growth and chemical composition of Kentucky bluegrass. Agronomy Journal. 61(2):294–296. 1969.

10785. Monroe, J. New grass pathology study. Golfdom. 40(9):28–29. 1966.

10786. ______. Seeding greens the easy way. Golfdom. 41(9):22–24. 1967.

10787. Monro, J. P. Bowls Encyclopedia. Wilke & Co., Ltd., Melbourne, Australia. p. 295. 1953.

10788. Montanya, T. Injection systems for turf irrigation. Turfgrass Sprinkler Irrigation Conference. 9:19–23. 1971.

10789. Monteith, J. The leaf-spot disease of bluegrass. USGA Green Section Bulletin. 4(7):172–173. 1924.

10790. ______. July experiments for control of brown-patch on Arlington experimental turf garden. USGA Green Section Bulletin. 5(8):173–176. 1925.

10791. ______. Leaf-Spot of bluegrass. USGA Green Section Bulletin. 5(9):198–199. 1925.

10792. ______. August experiments for control of brown-patch at Arlington experimental turf garden USGA Green Section Bulletin. 5(9):202–203. 1925.

10793. ______. Checking the growth of algae on greens. USGA Green Section Bulletin. 5(10):218. 1925.

10794. ______. Control of turf disease with chemicals. USGA Green Section Bulletin. 5(10):219–223. 1925.

10795. ______. Control of brown-patch in turf. Phytopathology. 16(1):76. 1926.

10796. ______. The brown-patch disease of turf: its nature and control. USGA Green Section Bulletin. 6(6):127–142. 1926.

10797. ______. Corrosive sublimate as a control for brown-patch. USGA Green Section Bulletin. 6(7):151–155. 1926.

10798. ______. 1926 experiments on brown-patch control. USGA Green Section Bulletin. 6(10):221–226. 1926.

10799. ______. Observations of brown-patch control in 1926. USGA Green Section Bulletin. 6(12):261–266. 1926.

10800. ______. Can you identify brown-patch? The National Greenkeeper. 1(6):7–11. 1927.

10801. ______. When brown-patch appears. The National Greenkeeper. 1(8):18–21, 31. 1927.

10802. ______. Winter injury of turf. USGA Green Section Bulletin. 7(4):62–76. 1927.

10803. ______. Preventing snow-mold injury on greens. USGA Green Section Bulletin. 7(10):193–194. 1927.

10804. ______. 1927 experiments on brown-patch control. USGA Green Section Bulletin. 7(11):210–216. 1927.

10805. ______. Probing the disease of turfgrasses. Golfdom. 2(3):26–28. 1928.

10806. ______. Some diseases of turf grasses. The National Greenkeeper. 2(5):5–9. 1928.

10807. ______. Fall treatments for snow-mold. USGA Green Section Bulletin. 8(9):-192–193. 1928.

10808. Monteith, J., and A. S. Dahl. The control of snow-mold. USGA Green Section Bulletin. 8(10):200–204. 1928.

10809. Monteith, J. Demonstration turf gardens on golf courses. USGA Green Section Bulletin. 8(12):239–243. 1928.

10810. ______. Cultivating creeping bent a hundred years ago. USGA Green Section Bulletin. 9(1):8–15. 1929.

10811. ______. Some effects of lime and fertilizer on turf diseases. USGA Green Section Bulletin. 9(5):82–99. 1929.

10812. ______. Changing grasses on putting greens. USGA Green Section Bulletin. 9(10):176–178. 1929.

10813. ______. Demonstration turf garden reports. USGA Green Section Bulletin. 9(12):210–221. 1929.

10814. ______. The Arlington turf garden. USGA Green Section Bulletin. 8(12):-244–245. 1928.

10815. ______. Classification of redtop and the common bentgrasses. USGA Green Section Bulletin. 10(3):44–50. 1930.

10816. ______. Controlling weeds in putting greens. USGA Green Section Bulletin. 10(8):142–155. 1930.

10817. ______. Experimental results at Miami Beach, Florida. USGA Green Section Bulletin. 11(10):190–194. 1931.

10818. ______. Demonstration turf garden results: A three-year summary. USGA

Green Section Bulletin. 11(12):230–246. 1931.

10819. ______. Illustrated lecture on turf diseases. Golfdom. 6(2):49. 1932.

10820. ______. Fairway grasses. Golfdom. 6(5):79. 1932.

10821. ______. Soil acidity and lime for bent turf. USGA Green Section Bulletin. 12(5):190–195. 1932.

10822. Monteith, J. and K. Welton. Demonstration turf garden reports. USGA Green Section Bulletin 12(6):218–223. 1932.

10823. Monteith, J. A *Pythium* disease of turf. Phytopathology. 23(1):23–24. 1933.

10824. ______. Chinch bugs are old pest. Golfdom. 9(6):23–25. 1935.

10825. ______. '35 had its troubles. Golfdom. 10(2):22–25. 1936.

10826. ______. Hot or cold water? Golfdom. 10(8):38, 40–42. 1936.

10827. ______. What can we do about those weeds? Golfdom. 10(10):30–33. 1936.

10828. ______. Some greenkeeping lessons taught. National Association of Greenkeepers of America Conference Proceedings. 10:71–89. 1936.

10829. ______. Ant problem is baffling. Golfdom. 11(3):66–69. 1937.

10830. ______. Chemical control of weeds. Golfdom. 11(9):17–20. 1937.

10831. ______. Over here, over there. Golfdom. 12(2):53–57. 1938.

10832. ______. Drainage first. Golfdom. 12(3):20–23. 1938.

10833. ______. Death of Walter Harban great loss to greenkeeping. Golfdom. 12(4):-23–25. 1938.

10834. ______. 38, year of the "big rains". Golfdom. 12(10):13–15. 1938.

10835. ______. Arlington tour well attended. Golfdom. 12(10):52–53. 1938.

10836. ______. Turf unhurt by winter sports. Golfdom. 13(1):9–11. 1939.

10837. ______. Twenty years of bent. Golfdom. 13(3):17–19. 1939.

10838. ______. "Practical lawn craft" is outstanding turf text book. Golfdom. 13(5):-26–28. 1939.

10839. ______. Water according to turf's needs. Golfdom. 13(10):18–20. 1939.

10840. ______. New developments in golf turf maintenance. The Greenkeepers' Reporter. 7(3):54–57, 59, 61. 1939.

10841. ______. Experimental greens. The Greenkeepers' Reporter. 7(5):5–7. 1939.

10842. ______. New varieties of Kentucky bluegrass. Turf Culture. 1(2):97–105. 1939.

10843. Monteith, J. and J. W. Bengtson. Experiments with fertilizer on bluegrass turf. Turf Culture. 1(3):153–191. 1939.

10844. Monteith, J. Why corrugated turf? Golfdom. 14(5):15–17. 1940.

10845. ______. What war is doing to turf treatment. Golfdom. 14(16):17–19. 1940.

10846. ______. USGA reports on substitutes for mercury fungicides. Golfdom. 16(5):28, 30. 1942.

10847. ______. Turf in the national war program. Greenkeepers Club of New England Newsletter. 14(6):6–8. 1942.

10848. ______. Turf for airfields and other defense projects. Turf Culture. 2(4):-193–239. 1942.

10849. ______. Dew. Quarterly Journal of the Royal Meteorological Society. 83(357):322–341. 1957.

10850. ______. The reflection of short-wave radiation by vegetation. Quarterly Journal of the Royal Meteorological Society. 85(366):386–392. 1959.

10851. Monteith, J. and J. W. Bengston. Arsenical compounds for the control of turf weeds. Turf Culture. 1(1):10–43. 1939.

10852. Monteith, J. and A. S. Dahl. A comparison of some strains of *Rhizoctonia solani* in culture. Journal of Agricultural Research. 36:897–903. 1928.

10853. ______. Turf diseases and their control. USGA Green Section Bulletin. 12(4):87–187. 1932.

10854. Monteith, J. and A. E. Rabbitt. Killing weed seeds in soil with chloropicrin. Turf Culture. 1(1):63–79. 1939.

10855. ______. Management of park turf. Parks and Recreation. 24(8):374–382. 1941.

10856. Monteith, J., and K. Welton. Demonstration turf garden reports. USGA Green Section Bulletin. 11(6):122–133. 1931.

10857. ______. Putting tests upon bent grasses. USGA Green Section Bulletin. 12(6):224–227. 1932.

10859. ______. Use of peat and other organic materials on golf courses. USGA Green Section Bulletin. 13(4):90–110. 1933.

10860. ______. Green section to submit data on demonstration garden results. Golfdom. 8(6):16–20. 1934.

10861. ______. Fertilizers give differing results in section's test gardens. Golfdom. 8(7):12–16. 1934.

10862. ______. How demonstration gardens rated putting grasses. Golfdom. 8(8):-7–10. 1934.

10863. ______. Fairway fertilizers rated at demonstration gardens. Golfdom. 8(9):9–12. 1934.

10864. Montieth, R. E. Sources of plant food elements. Rocky Mountain Regional Turfgrass Conference Proceedings. 10:5–9. 1963.

10866. Montgomery, D. Recent experience with non-selective herbicides. Parks, Golf Courses and Sports Grounds. 23(11):-719–724. 1958.

10867. ______. The application of non-selective herbicides. Parks, Golf Courses, and Sports Grounds. 27(1):21–22. 1961.

10868. ______. Developments in the use of chemicals for weed control. The Groundsman. 22(1):41–43. 1968.

10869. Montgomery, F. H. The life span of seeds. Sixth Annual Sports Turfgrass Conference, Ontario Agricultural College, Guelph. pp. 33–36. 1955.

10870. Montgomery, F. H., and C. M. Switzer. Weed control in lawns. Ontario Agricultural College, University of Guelph and Ontario Department of Agriculture and Food Publication 529. pp. 1–39.

10871. Montgomery, M. E. Lawns and lawn making. Cornell Agricultural Extension Bulletin. 7:77–80. 1916.

10872. Montgomery, R. Progress report on rootzone research. Proceedings of the Midwest Regional Turf Conference. pp. 41–43. 1960.

10873. ______. The evaluation of calcined clay aggregates for putting green rootzones. Proceedings of the Midwest Regional Turf Conference. pp. 88–91. 1961.

10874. Moody, R. W. The living soil. New Zealand Institute for Turf Culture Newsletter. 59:7–9. 1969.

10875. Moore, D. Weed control measures in memorial parks. Proceedings of the Southern California Turfgrass Institute Conference. p. 32. 1963.

10877. Moore, D., H. B. Couch and J. R. Bloom. Influence of postinfection air temperature on *Pythium* blight of Highland bentgrass. Phytopathology. 52(9):926. 1962.

10878. Moore, G. Problems of maintaining turf around industrial grounds. Turf Clippings. University of Massachusetts. 1(9):A–22 to A–24. 1964.

10879. ______. Problems of maintaining turf around industrial grounds. Turf Bulletin. Massachusetts Turf and Lawn Grass Council. 2(7):9, 12. 1964.

10880. Moore, G. J. Maintenance at an insurance company grounds. Turf Clippings. University of Massachussetts. 1(3):17–19. 1958.

10881. Moore, G. T. Fertilizing lawns. The American Fertilizer. 62(12):34–35. 1925.

10882. Moore, H. C. Summer at Sea Island is busy time of year. Golfdom. 5(2):84, 86. 1931.

10883. ______. Planting and maintenance tips that assure results and thrift. Golfdom. 6(11):25–26. 1932.

10884. Moore, J. G. Lawns. Wisconsin Agricultural Extension Stencil Circular. 244:1–18. 1945.

10885. ______. Lawns. Wisconsin Agricultural Extension Stencil Circular. 244:1–18. 1948.

10886. Moore, L. D. Pectic and cellulolytic enzyme activity with *Pythium* ultimum-blighted Highland bentgrass. Phytopathology. 55:1069. 1965.

10887. Moore, L., and G. D. Butler. Progress report on the biological control of punc-

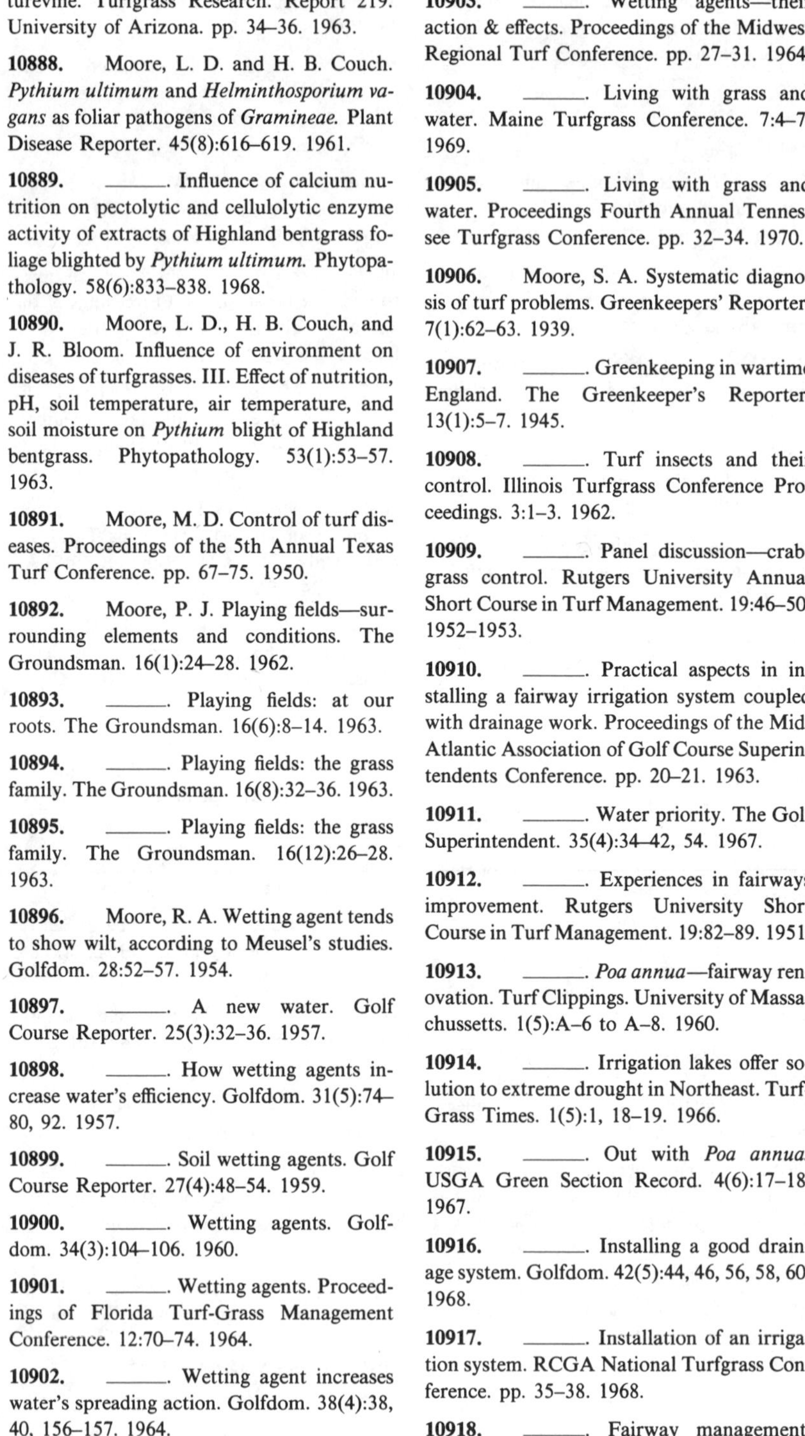

turevine. Turfgrass Research. Report 219. University of Arizona. pp. 34–36. 1963.

10888. Moore, L. D. and H. B. Couch. *Pythium ultimum* and *Helminthosporium vagans* as foliar pathogens of *Gramineae.* Plant Disease Reporter. 45(8):616–619. 1961.

10889. ______. Influence of calcium nutrition on pectolytic and cellulolytic enzyme activity of extracts of Highland bentgrass foliage blighted by *Pythium ultimum.* Phytopathology. 58(6):833–838. 1968.

10890. Moore, L. D., H. B. Couch, and J. R. Bloom. Influence of environment on diseases of turfgrasses. III. Effect of nutrition, pH, soil temperature, air temperature, and soil moisture on *Pythium* blight of Highland bentgrass. Phytopathology. 53(1):53–57. 1963.

10891. Moore, M. D. Control of turf diseases. Proceedings of the 5th Annual Texas Turf Conference. pp. 67–75. 1950.

10892. Moore, P. J. Playing fields—surrounding elements and conditions. The Groundsman. 16(1):24–28. 1962.

10893. ______. Playing fields: at our roots. The Groundsman. 16(6):8–14. 1963.

10894. ______. Playing fields: the grass family. The Groundsman. 16(8):32–36. 1963.

10895. ______. Playing fields: the grass family. The Groundsman. 16(12):26–28. 1963.

10896. Moore, R. A. Wetting agent tends to show wilt, according to Meusel's studies. Golfdom. 28:52–57. 1954.

10897. ______. A new water. Golf Course Reporter. 25(3):32–36. 1957.

10898. ______. How wetting agents increase water's efficiency. Golfdom. 31(5):74–80, 92. 1957.

10899. ______. Soil wetting agents. Golf Course Reporter. 27(4):48–54. 1959.

10900. ______. Wetting agents. Golfdom. 34(3):104–106. 1960.

10901. ______. Wetting agents. Proceedings of Florida Turf-Grass Management Conference. 12:70–74. 1964.

10902. ______. Wetting agent increases water's spreading action. Golfdom. 38(4):38, 40, 156–157. 1964.

10903. ______. Wetting agents—their action & effects. Proceedings of the Midwest Regional Turf Conference. pp. 27–31. 1964.

10904. ______. Living with grass and water. Maine Turfgrass Conference. 7:4–7. 1969.

10905. ______. Living with grass and water. Proceedings Fourth Annual Tennessee Turfgrass Conference. pp. 32–34. 1970.

10906. Moore, S. A. Systematic diagnosis of turf problems. Greenkeepers' Reporter. 7(1):62–63. 1939.

10907. ______. Greenkeeping in wartime England. The Greenkeeper's Reporter. 13(1):5–7. 1945.

10908. ______. Turf insects and their control. Illinois Turfgrass Conference Proceedings. 3:1–3. 1962.

10909. ______. Panel discussion—crabgrass control. Rutgers University Annual Short Course in Turf Management. 19:46–50. 1952–1953.

10910. ______. Practical aspects in installing a fairway irrigation system coupled with drainage work. Proceedings of the Mid-Atlantic Association of Golf Course Superintendents Conference. pp. 20–21. 1963.

10911. ______. Water priority. The Golf Superintendent. 35(4):34–42, 54. 1967.

10912. ______. Experiences in fairways improvement. Rutgers University Short Course in Turf Management. 19:82–89. 1951.

10913. ______. *Poa annua*—fairway renovation. Turf Clippings. University of Massachussetts. 1(5):A–6 to A–8. 1960.

10914. ______. Irrigation lakes offer solution to extreme drought in Northeast. Turf-Grass Times. 1(5):1, 18–19. 1966.

10915. ______. Out with *Poa annua.* USGA Green Section Record. 4(6):17–18. 1967.

10916. ______. Installing a good drainage system. Golfdom. 42(5):44, 46, 56, 58, 60. 1968.

10917. ______. Installation of an irrigation system. RCGA National Turfgrass Conference. pp. 35–38. 1968.

10918. ______. Fairway management.

RCGA National Turfgrass Conference. pp. 39–44. 1968.

10919. ______. Little things can count in tiling golf courses. USGA Green Section Record. 5(5):6–9. 1968.

10920. ______. A superintendent's thoughts on turfgrass disease. Golf Superintendent. 37(7):26–29. 1969.

10921. Moore, T. Twenty years of fairway treatment. Journal of the Board of Greenkeeping Research. 7(25):226–231. 1949.

10922. Moore, W. Stevens park plots. Proceedings of the Annual Texas Turfgrass Conference. 9:26–30. 1954.

10923. ______. Cricket ground problems. Turf for Sport. 4(1):3–7. 1962.

10924. ______. Coarse grass. Turf for Sport. 4(3):3–7. 1962.

10925. Moote, D. S. Earthworms and their effect on fine turf. Rutgers University Short Course in Turf Management. pp. 5–9. 1952–1953.

10926. ______. Earthworms and their effect on fine turf. Golf Course Reporter. 22(3):14–16. 1954.

10927. ______. Irrigation installation techniques. Golf Course Reporter. 30(6):32–33, 36–37. 1962.

10928. ______. Shall we diversify. International Turfgrass Conference Proceedings. 38:64–66. 1967.

10929. ______. Canadian turfgrass production and problems. Turf Clippings. University of Massachusetts. 3(3):A–8–12. 1968.

10930. ______. Maintaining greens in troublesome locations. The Greenmaster. 5(10):6. 1969.

10931. ______. My experience with irrigation equipment. R.C.G.A. National Turf Conference. 22:33–36. 1971.

10932. Moote, R. Landscaping golf course properties. Annual RCGA National Turfgrass Conference. 23:56–59. 1972.

10933. Moote, R. F. Green construction. Golf Course Reporter. 29(9):42–47. 1961.

10934. Morgan, A. H. Grass and man. Turf Bulletin. Massachusetts Turf & Lawn Grass Council. 2(8):3–4. 1964.

10935. Morgan, M. A., W. A. Jackson, and R. J. Volk. Nitrate absorption and assimilation in ryegrass as influenced by calcium and magnesium. Plant Physiology. 50(4):-485–490. 1972.

10936. Morgan, M. F. Lawn fertilization, principles and practice. Connecticut Agricultural Experiment Station Circular. 77:41–49. 1931.

10937. Morgan, M. F., E. M. Stoddard, and R. B. Friend. Lawn management. Connecticut Agricultural Experiment Station Circular. 113:63–70. 1936.

10938. Morgan, M. F., E. M. Stoddard, and J. P. Johnson. Turf management. Connecticut Agricultural Experiment Station Circular. 139:13–27. 1940.

10939. Morgan, P. Natural organics. Ohio Turfgrass Conference Proceedings. p. 52. 1971.

10940. Morgan, W. C. Principles for any green. Proceedings of the Midwest Regional Turf Conference. pp. 22–23. 1969.

10941. ______. Humus and sand greens —western style. Proceedings of the Midwest Regional Turf Conference. pp. 24–25. 1969.

10942. ______. Is your grass safe? Proceedings of the Midwest Regional Turf Conference. pp. 93–95. 1969.

10943. ______. Tensiometers in turfgrass. California Turf Culture. 10(4):28–29. 1960.

10944. ______. Arboretum turfgrass variety plots. Proceedings of the Southern California Turfgrass Institute Conference. pp. 28–30. 1960.

10945. ______. Water management of turfgrasses and trees. California Turfgrass Culture. 11(3):21–22. 1961.

10946. ______. Turfgrass survey of Los Angeles County. Agricultural Extension Service, University of California Mimeo. 1961.

10947. ______. Observations on turfgrass aeration and vertical-mowing. California Turfgrass Culture. 12(2):12–13. 1962.

10948. ______. Turfgrass youth educational programs. California Turfgrass Culture. 13(1):2–3. 1963.

10949. ______. Possible controls for dallisgrass and kikuyugrass in turf. Proceedings of the Southern California Turfgrass Institute Conference. pp. 27–31. 1963.

10950. ______. Turfgrass irrigation by tensiometer—controlled system. Agronomy Abstracts. 56:102. 1964.

10951. ______. Sprinkler can tests can help you. California Turfgrass Culture. 14(2):12–13. 1964.

10952. ______. Summer aeration helps turf growth. California Turfgrass Culture. 14(3):23–24. 1964.

10953. ______. Controlling weeds in *Dichondra.* Lasca Leaves. 14(3):64–65. 1964.

10954. ______. New irrigation and aerification methods. California Turfgrass Culture. 15(2):11–15. 1965.

10955. ______. Tensiometer for controlling turfgrass irrigation. The Golf Course Reporter. 33(6):10–14. 1965.

10956. ______. New method of renovating turfgrass. The Golf Course Reporter. 33(10):32, 34, 36. 1965.

10957. ______. Deep aerification for renovating turfgrass. Parks and Recreation. 48(6):378–379. 1965.

10958. ______. Tensiometers for controlling turfgrass irrigation. Parks and Recreation. 48(9):517–519. 1965.

10959. ______. Is your turfgrass problem due to soils or irrigation? California Turfgrass Culture. 16(2):14–16. 1966.

10960. ______. Turfgrass management and irrigation. Proceedings of the Turfgrass Sprinkler Irrigation Conference. 3 pp. 1966.

10961. ______. Turf-grass in Hawaii. Turf-Grass Times. 3(2):1–7. 1967.

10962. ______. Vertical mulching boasts root growth. Weeds Trees and Turf. 6(2):-20–22. 1967.

10963. ______. Effects of nutrients on the grass plants. The Golf Superintendent. 36(4):36, 37, 44, 47. 1968.

10964. ______. An approach to programming turfgrass management. Agronomy Abstracts. 61:55–56. 1969.

10965. ______. Efficiency in irrigation. Proceedings of the First International Turfgrass Research Conference. pp. 307–310. 1969.

10966. ______. Commercial advisory services. Proceedings of the First International Turfgrass Research Conference. p. 437. 1969.

10967. ______. Research review—sand—organic mixes for putting green construction. Divot News. 1970. 9(3):1. 1970.

10968. ______. Principles for any green. Turf Bulletin. Massachusetts Turf and Lawn Grass Council. 6(1):16–17. 1970.

10969. ______. Specifications for amending soils. Proceedings of Southern California Turfgrass Institute. pp. 51–60. 1971.

10970. ______. Nitrogen carriers and turfgrass disease. Divot News. 11(2):7. 1972.

10971. ______. How fertilizer moves and reacts in the soil. Divot News. 11(10):8, 9, 11. 1973.

10972. Morgan, W. C. and A. W. Marsh. Turfgrass irrigation by tensiometer controlled system. California Agriculture. pp. 4–6. 1965.

10973. Morgan, W. C. and H. H. Williams. Selective control of dallisgrass in turfgrasses in Los Angeles County. Agronomy Abstracts. 58:39. 1966.

10974. Morgan, W. C., J. Letey, and L. H. Stolzy. Turfgrass renovation by deep aerification. Agronomy Journal. 57(5):494–496. 1965.

10975. Morgan, W. C., A. Lang, C. Elmore, and C. Downing. Selective control of Kikuyugrass in turfgrasses. Agronomy Abstracts. 59:57. 1967.

10976. Morgan, W. C., J. Letey, S. J. Richards, and J. Valoras. Effects of soil amendments and irrigation on soil compactibility, water infiltration, and growth of bermuda grass. Agronomy Abstracts. p. 46. 1965.

10977. ______. Physical soil amendments, soil compaction, irrigation, and wetting agents in turfgrass management: I. Effects on compactibility, water infiltration rates, evapotranspiration, and number of irrigations. Agronomy Journal. 58(5):525–528. 1966.

10978. ______. The use of physical soil amendments, irrigation and wetting agent in turfgrass management. California Turfgrass Culture. 16(3):17. 1966.

10979. ______. Soil amendments, irrigation and wetting agents. Turf-Grass Times. 2(6):6, 16–17. 1967.

10980. Morgenweck, G. Comparative seeding rate trials in pure sowings of grasses. Pflanzenbau. 17:24–30; 33–64; 75–92. 1940.

10981. Morinaga, T. Effect of alternating temperatures upon germination of seeds. American Journal of Botany. 13(2):141–158. 1926.

10982. Morishita, F. S., R. N. Jefferson, and L. Johnston. Southern chinch bug, a new pest of St. Augustine grass in southern California. California Turfgrass Culture. 19(2):-9–10. 1969.

10983. Morishita, F. S., W. Humphrey, L. C. Johnston, and R. N. Jeffries. Control of billbugs on turf. California Turfgrass Culture. 21(2):13–14. 1971.

10984. Morley, J. Why I use charcoal. The National Greenkeeper. 1(1):15. 1927.

10985. ______. Greenkeeping yesterday and today. The National Greenkeeper. 1(2):-17–19. 1927.

10986. ______. Following through with a grass seed. The National Greenkeeper. 1(4):8–9. 1927.

10987. ______. Is *Poa annua* good or bad? The National Greenkeeper. 1(7):7–8. 1927.

10988. ______. Care of seeded greens at Youngstown, Ohio. USGA Green Section Bulletin. 8(9):188. 1928.

10989. ______. Compost and charcoal. The National Greenkeeper. 3(9):8, 10–11, 26. 1929.

10990. ______. The stimulation of plant growth by means of weak poisons. The National Greenkeeper. 6(9):12. 1932.

10991. Morozov, A. S. Storing of carbohydrates by forage grasses. Comp. Rend. Acad. Sci. U.R.S.S. 24:407–409 1939.

10992. Morre, D. L., W. R. Eisinger, and H. W. Mussell. Roadside development research—chemical weed control. Indiana State Highway Commission-Bureau of Public Roads. HPR–1(5).

10993. Morrill, D. W. Here's what you need to start a sod farm. Weeds, Trees and Turf. 8(8):30–31. 1969.

10994. Morris, H. D. Effect of burning on forage production of 'coastal' bermudagrass at varying levels of fertilization. Agronomy Journal. 60(5):518–521. 1968.

10995. Morris, O. N. The development of the clover mite, *Bryobia praetiosa, (Acarina, Tetranychidae)* in relation to the nitrogen, phosphorus and potassium nutrition of its plant host. Annals of the Entomological Society of America. 54:551–557. 1961.

10996. Morris, R. L. Control of weeds, pests and diseases of cultivated turf. Current practices in turf weed control. Proceedings of the First Symposium on the Control of Weeds, Pests and Diseases of Cultivated Turf. pp. 8–11. 1967.

10997. ______. Current practice in turf weed control. Parks, Golf courses, and Sports Grounds. 33(8):684–687. 1968.

10998. ______. Establishing grass playing surfaces. Gardeners Chronicle. 165(26):-10–13. 1969.

10999. ______. Establishing grass playing surfaces—part 2. Gardeners Chronicle. 166(1):25–26. 1969.

11000. ______. Grass playing surfaces. The Groundsman. 23(1):46–50. 1969.

11001. ______. Do we play fair with our sports turf grasses? Parks, Golf Courses, and Sports Grounds. 37(8):800–804. 1972.

11002. Morrish, R. H., and C. M. Harrison. The establishment and comparative wear resistance of various grasses and grass-legume mixtures to vehicular traffic. Journal of the American Society of Agronomy. 40(2):168–179. 1948.

11003. Morrish, R. H., A. E. Rabbitt and E. B. Cale. Airfields and flight strips. Grass. USDA Yearbook. pp. 319–323. 1948.

11004. Morrison, J. Watering the golf course. Pennsylvania State College Turfgrass Conference Proceedings. 21:125–127. 1952.

11005. Morrison, K. J. Panel—home lawns. Proceedings Northwest Turf Conference. 12:19–23. 1958.

11006. ______. Turf grass varieties. Proceedings of the 19th Annual Northwest Turfgrass Conference. pp. 24–27. 1965.

11007. ______. How a grass plant grows. Proceedings—22nd Annual Northwest Turfgrass Conference. 22:43–50. 1968.

11008. Morrison, K. J., C. B. Harston, H. H. Wolfe, D. H. Brannon and M. R. Harris. Lawns. Washington Agricultural Extension Bulletin. 482:1–15. 1953.

11009. ______. Lawns. Washington Agricultural Extension Bulletin. 482:1–15. 1957.

11010. Morrow, D. How Cal-Turf plants and grows bermuda stolons. Weeds, Trees, and Turf. 5(2):22–27. 1966.

11011. Morrow, R. Grass for player safety. Turf-Grass Times. 3(1):2, 16. 1967.

11012. Mortimer, G. B., and H. L. Ahlgren. Influence of fertilization, irrigation, and stage and height of cutting on yield and composition of Kentucky bluegrass. Journal of the American Society of Agronomy. 28(7):515–533. 1936.

11013. Morton, H. L. Application practices as a key to successful use of chemicals. Proceedings of the Texas Turfgrass Conference. 17:7–12. 1962.

11014. Morwood, W. Lawn maintenance. The Lazy Gardener's Garden Book. Doubleday and Co., Inc. New York. pp. 3–48. 1970.

11015. Moser, L. E. Rhizome and tiller development of Kentucky bluegrass (*Poa pratensis* L.) as influenced by photoperiod, vernalization, nitrogen level, growth regulators, and variety. Ph.D. Thesis, Ohio State. 159 pp. 1967.

11016. ______. Rhizome formation in Kentucky bluegrass. First Ohio Turfgrass Conference Proceedings. pp. 66–72. 1967.

11017. ______. Rhizome initiation and development of Windsor, Merion, and Delta Kentucky bluegrass. International Turfgrass Conference and Show. 39:83–85. 1968.

11018. ______. Sod development of Kentucky bluegrass. Proceedings of the First International Turfgrass Research Conference. pp. 565–571. 1969.

11019. ______. Effects of management practices on turfgrass diseases. Ohio Turfgrass Conference Proceedings. pp. 32–38. 1969.

11020. ______. True photoperiodic effects on rhizome and tiller production of four Kentucky bluegrass (*Poa pratensis* L.) varieties. Agronomy Abstracts. p. 49. 1971.

11021. Moser, L. E. and R. R. Davis. Bentgrass varieties. Ohio Agricultural Research and Development Center. Research Summary. 40. pp. 3–5. 1969.

11022. Moser, L. E., S. R. Anderson, and R. W. Miller. Rhizome and tiller development of seedling Kentucky bluegrass, *Poa pratensis* L. as influenced by photoperiod, vernalization and variety. Agronomy Abstracts. 59:54. 1967.

11023. ______. Rhizome and tiller development of Kentucky bluegrass (*Poa pratensis* L.) as influenced by photoperiod, cold treatment and variety. Agronomy Journal. 60(6):-632–635. 1968.

11024. Moses, D. and I. H. McGillivray. The relation of fertilizer treatment to soil reaction under turf. South African Journal of Science. 29:378–388. 1932.

11025. Mosher, E. The grasses of Illinois. Illinois Agricultural Experiment Station Bulletin. 205:261–425. 1918.

11026. Moss, D. N. Relation in grasses of high photosynthetic capacity and tolerance to atrazine. Crop Science. 8(6):774. 1968.

11027. Moss, D. N. and R. B. Musgrave. Photosynthesis and crop production. Advances in Agronomy. 23:317–336. 1971.

11028. Mott, G. O. Turf on stabilized granular materials. 31st Annual Convention, American Association of State Highway Officials. (Committee on Roadside Development.) pp. 1–10. 1944.

11029. ______. Bent grass, chickweed, management problems on fairways. Midwest Turf, News and Research. Introductory Issue. p. 4. 1946.

11030. ______. Growing grass under existing and made roadside conditions. Highway Research Board, Committee on Roadside Development. 1947.

11031. ______. Midwest regional turf foundation program. Greenkeepers' Reporter. 16(3):30–32. 1948.

11032. ______. Report of the Midwest Regional Turf Foundation Incorporated. Midwest Regional Turf Foundation Incorporated. pp. 1–9. 1948.

11033. ______. Soil compaction, aeration and drainage. Greenkeepers' Reporter. 17(5):28–30. 1949.

11034. ______. Curing the problems of soil compaction and drainage. Golfdom. 23(7):50, 52, 54. 1949.

11035. ______. The problem of soil compaction, aeration and drainage. Greenkeeping Superintendents Association Twentieth National Turf Conference. pp. 110–116. 1949.

11036. ______. MRTF history told by Mott. Midwest Turf-News and Research. 4(1):2, 3. 1950.

11037. ______. Soil structure, aeration, and drainage. Proceedings of the Third Annual Turf Conference. Washington State College. pp. 12–16. 1950.

11038. ______. Soil structure, aeration, and drainage. State College of Washington Turf Conference Proceedings. 3:12–16. 1950.

11039. Mount, R. F. Turf cutting. The Groundsman. 20(8):24–25. 1967.

11040. ______. Turf cutting—part 2. The Groundsman. 20(11):22–23. 1967.

11041. ______. Turf cutting. The Groundsman. 21(1):58–59. 1967.

11042. ______. Turf cutting. The Groundsman. 21(3):18–21. 1967.

11043. ______. Turf cutting during the war. The Groundsman. 21(4):18–20. 1967.

11044. Mower, R. G. Histological studies of suscept-pathogen relationships of *Helminthosporium sativum* P. K. & B., *Helminthosporium vagans* Drechsl., and *Curvularia lunata* (Wakk.) Boed. on leaves of Merion and common Kentucky bluegrass (*Poa pratensis* L.). Ph.D. Thesis, Cornell University. 150 pp. 1961.

11045. ______. Histological studies of suscept—pathogen relationships of *Helminthosporium sativum, Helminthosporium vagans* and *Curvularia lunata* on leaves of Merion and common Kentucky bluegrass. Agronomy Abstracts. 54:104. 1962.

11046. Mower, R. G. and J. F. Cornman. Selective control of *Veronica filiformis* in turf. Proceedings of the Northeastern Weed Control Conference. pp. 142–150. 1958.

11047. ______. Observations on pre-emergence and post-emergence crabgrass control; on the control of *Veronica filiformis* with endothal; and on the effectiveness of 2, 4, 5–TP in controlling a variety of turf weeds. Proceedings of the Northeastern Weed Control Conference. 13:162–171. 1959.

11048. ______. Pre-emergence and post-emergence crabgrass control. Proceedings of the Northeastern Weed Control Conference. 14:271–277. 1960.

11049. ______. Experiments in preemergence crabgrass control. Proceedings of the Northeastern Weed Control Conference. 15:-264–267. 1961.

11050. ______. Pre-emergence crabgrass control. New York Turfgrass Association Bulletin. 69:267–268. 1962.

11051. ______. Preemergence crabgrass control. Proceedings Northeastern Weed Control Conference. 16:489–492. 1962.

11052. ______. Experiments in preemergence crabgrass control. Weed Abstracts. 12(3):138. 1963.

11053. Mower, R. G. and R. L. Millar. Histological relationships of *Helminthosporium vagans, H. sativum,* and *Curvularia lunata* in leaves of 'Merion' and common Kentucky bluegrass. Phytopathology. 53(3):-351. 1963.

11054. Mracek, T. J. A highway planting program in Illinois. 23rd Short Course on Roadside Development, Ohio. pp. 79–82. 1964.

11055. Mruk, C. Fertilizing turf areas other than golf courses. Turf Clippings—University of Massachusetts. 1(10):A38–A42. 1965.

11056. Mruk, C. K. and J. A. DeFrance. A comparison of chemicals for the control of annual bluegrass (*Poa annua* L.) in lawn turf. Golf Course Reporter. 25(6):5–7. 1957.

11057. Mruk, C. K., A. J. Wisniewski, and J. A. DeFrance. A comparison of urea-formeldahyde material for turfgrass fertilization. Golf Course Reporter. 25(3):5–8. 1957.

11058. Mueller, I. M. and J. E. Weaver. Relative drought resistance of seedlings of dominant prairie grasses. Ecology. 23(4):-387–398. 1942.

11059. Mueller, K. E. Plant—water relationships. Proceedings of the 1972 Turf and Landscape Horticulture Institute. pp. 35–38. 1972.

11060. Mueller, L. When is sod ready to cut. Proceedings of the Midwest Regional Turf Conference. pp. 51–52. 1965.

11061. ______. Handling sod for maximum returns. Illinois Turfgrass Conference Proceedings. pp. 72–74. 1969.

11062. Mueller, R. C. Summary and farewell. Proceedings of the Turfgrass Sprinkler Irrigation Conference. 1 p. 1966.

11063. ______. A speaker, a listner . . . presto, communication! Proceedings Annual Turfgrass Sprinkler Irrigation Conference. 5:49–52. 1967.

11064. Mühle, E. Möglichkeiten des Pflantzenschutzes in Grassamenbau. Nachrichtenblatt für Den Deutschen Pflanzenschutzdienst. 3:150–152. 1949.

11065. Muller, E. W. and H. Porter. Use of urea—formaldehyde fertilizers when seeding on subsoil highway slopes. Highway Research Board. pp. 15–20. 1958.

11066. Muller, E. W. Trials to determine if MH–30 can be used in a roadside maintenance program in New York State. Proceedings of the Northeast Weed Control Conference. 17:401–406. 1963.

11067. Muller, J. F. The value of raw sewage sludge as fertilizer. Soil Science. 28:-423–432. 1929.

11068. Mullin, R. S. Current lawn disease control recommendations. Proceedings of University of Florida Turf-Grass Management Conference. 8:90–93. 1960.

11069. ______. Disease control recommendations for 1961–62. Proceedings of University of Florida Turf-Grass Management Conference. 9:157–160. 1961.

11070. ______. Fungus and nematode diseases—1962 University recommendations. Proceedings of Florida Turf-Grass Management Conference. 10:137–138. 1962.

11071. ______. What else can we spray? Proceedings of Florida Turf-Grass Management Conference. 11:116–118. 1963.

11072. ______. Diseases. Proceedings of the Florida Turfgrass Management Conference. 12:97–98. 1964.

11073. ______. Toxicity of fungicides. Florida Turf. 6(3):4. 1972.

11074. Mulliner, H. R. and H. W. Temple. Watering and fertilizing lawns through sprinklers. Nebraska Agricultural Extension. EC 61–717:1–11.

11075. Munn, M. T. Seed tests made at the station during 1912. New York Agricultural Experiment Station Bulletin No. 362:-137–163. 1913.

11076. ______. Spraying lawns with iron sulfate to eradicate dandelions. New York Agricultural Experiment Station Bulletin No. 466:21–59. 1919.

11077. ______. Twenty year lawn experiment. New York State Agricultural Experiment Station. Farm Research. 16:10. 1950.

11078. ______. Lawn mixtures sold in New York in 1951. New York State Turf Association. Bulletin 37. pp. 144–146. 1952.

11079. ______. Lawn mixtures sold in New York in 1951. New York State Turf Association. Bulletin 38. p. 150. 1952.

11080. Munnecke, D. E. Movement of nonvolatile, diffusible fungicides through columns of soil. Phytopathology. 51(9):593–599. 1961.

11081. Munro, W. On the identification of the grasses of Linnaeus's Herbarium. Journal of the Proceedings of the Linnean Society of Botany. 6:33–55. 1862.

11082. Munsell, R. I., and B. A. Brown. The nitrogen content of grasses as influenced by kind, frequency of application, and amount of nitrogenous fertilizer. Journal of the American Society of Agronomy. 31(5):-388–398. 1939.

11083. Müntzing, A. Apomictic and sexual seed formation in *Poa.* Hereditas. 17:-131–154. 1933.

11084. ______. Further studies on apomixis and sexuality in *Poa*. Hereditas. 26:-115–190. 1940.

11085. Munzenmaier, L. Chemical *Poa annua* control. Proceedings of the Midwest Regional Turf Conference. pp. 40–41. 1952.

11086. Murata, Y. and J. Iyama. Studies on the photosynthesis of forage crops. Proceedings of the Crop Science Society of Japan. 31(3):311–321. 1963.

11087. Murbeck, A. S. Studier öfver kritiska kärlväxtformer. De nordeuropeiska formerna of slägtet *Agrostis*. Botaniska Notiser. pp. 1–14. 1898.

11088. Murdoch, C. L. Turf research in Arkansas. Southern Turfgrass Association Conference Proceedings. pp. 29–30. 1967.

11089. Murdoch, C. L., A. E. Spooner, R. E. Frans, and T. M. Fullerton. DCPA effects on establishment and winter hardiness of bermudagrass as influenced by date of application. Agronomy Abstracts. 60:64. 1968.

11090. Murphy, G. Trench with an old chain saw. Golf Superintendent. 36(1):40. 1968.

11091. Murphy, G. M. Cost analysis—North. International Turfgrass Conference Proceedings. 39:60–61. 1968.

11092. Murphy, H. F. The control of bermuda grass through the use of chlorates. Journal of the American Society of Agronomy. 25(10):700–704. 1933.

11093. ______. Progress report on turf research at Oklahoma A & M. Oklahoma-Texas Turf Conference Proceedings. pp. 25–28. 1950.

11094. Murphy, R. P. and A. C. Arny. The emergence of grass and legume seedlings planted at different depths in five types of soil. Journal of the American Society of Agronomy. 31(1):17–28. 1939.

11095. Murphy, W. J., O. H. Fletchall, and E. J. Peters. Effect of 2,4–D and related compounds on seedling grasses. North Central Weed Control Conference Research Report. 18:75–76. 1961.

11096. Murray, C. M. Chemical weed eradication. USGA Green Section Bulletin. 7(12):226–227. 1927.

11097. ______. Turf culture. Journal of the Board of Greenkeeping Research. 1(3):-124–129. 1929–1930.

11098. ______. Greenkeeping in South Africa. South African Golf. 104 pp. 1932.

11099. Murray, H. Producing and promoting new turfgrasses. West Virginia Turfgrass Conference Proceedings. pp. 2–3. 1968.

11100. ______. Teaming up on sod growing. Midwest Regional Turf Conference Proceedings. pp. 58–60. 1972.

11101. Muse, R. R. Kentucky bluegrass melting-out fungicide trial. Ohio Agricultural Research and Development Center. Research Summary 40. pp. 17–19. 1969.

11102. ______. Techniques for application of fungicides. Ohio Turfgrass Conference Proceedings. pp. 26–28. 1969.

11103. ______. Evaluation of five chemicals for control of stripe and flag smut in Kentucky bluegrass turf. Turf and Ornamentals Research Summary 48. Ohio Agricultural Research and Development Center. pp. 15–18. 1970.

11104. ______. Evaluation of five chemicals for control of melting-out of Kentucky bluegrass. Turf and Ornamentals Research Summary 48. Ohio Agricultural Research and Development Center. pp. 19–21. 1970.

11105. ______. Snow mold diseases on bentgrasses. Turf and Ornamentals Research Summary 48. Ohio Agricultural Research and Development Center. pp. 23–25. 1970.

11106. ______. Test results show "Bromosan" effective for control of dollar spot and melting out. Park Maintenance. 23(7):13. 1970.

11107. ______. Chemical control of *Fusarium* blight of Merion Kentucky bluegrass. Ohio Agricultural Research and Development Center Research Summary 56. pp. 23–27. 1971.

11108. ______. *Fusarium*. Park Maintenance. 24(7):18. 1971.

11109. ______. *Helminthosporium vagans*. Park Maintenance. 24(7):18. 1971.

11110. ______. Stripe and flag smut in Kentucky bluegrass. Park Maintenance. 24(7):18. 1971.

11111. ______. Chemical control of *Fusarium* blight of Merion Kentucky bluegrass. The Plant Disease Reporter. 55(4):-333–335. 1971.

11112. ______. Kentucky bluegrass melting-out fungicide trial. Ohio Agricultural Research and Development Center, Research Summary 62. 13–16 pp. 1972.

11113. Muse, R. R., and H. B. Couch. Influence of environment on diseases of turfgrasses. IV. Effect of nutrition and soil moisture on corticium red thread of creeping red fescue. Phytopathology. 55(5):507–510. 1965.

11114. Muse, R. R., H. B. Couch, L. D. Moore, and B. D. Muse. Pectolytic and cellulolytic enzymes associated with *Helminthosporium* leaf spot on Kentucky bluegrass. Canadian Journal of Microbiology. 18(7):-1091–1098. 1972.

11115. Musil, A. F. Distinguishing species of *Poa* from their seed. Division of Forage Crops and Diseases, United States Bureau of Plant Industry. 10 pp. 1946.

11116. ______. Identification of crop and weed seeds. USDA Agriculture Handbook 219. 171 pp. 1963.

11117. Musser, A. M. Lawns for South Carolina. South Carolina Agricultural Extension Circular 56. 4 pp. 1923.

11118. Musser, H. B. How Penn State strives to breed ideal greens bent. Golfdom. 6(1):17–21. 1932.

11119. ______. Progress at Penn State in hunt for perfect greens grass. Golfdom. 7(5):-23–24. 1933.

11120. ______. Hunting for the perfect grass. The National Greenkeeper. 7(3):5–9. 1933.

11121. ______. As bents differ, so must care. Golfdom. 10(6):29–31. 1936.

11122. ______. To test turf under fire. Golfdom. 11(2):27–28. 1937.

11123. ______. Breeding grasses. Pennsylvania Agricultural Experiment Station Bulletin 352. p. 31. 1937.

11124. ______. Breeding grasses. Pennsylvania Agricultural Experiment Station Bulletin 367. pp. 19–20. 1938.

11125. ______. Fairways: Today's problems. Golfdom. 13(3):30, 61–64. 1939.

11126. ______. Fairways: Today's problem. Golfdom. 13(2):51–52, 54. 1939.

11127. ______. Unity needed in turf research. Golfdom. 14(7):9–11. 1940.

11128. ______. The effect of burning and various fertilizer treatments on seed production of red fescue *Festuca rubra* L. Journal of the American Society of Agronomy. 39(4):-335–340. 1947.

11129. ______. Effects of soil acidity and available phosphorus on population changes in mixed Kentucky bluegrass-bent turf. Journal of the American Society of Agronomy. 40(7):614–620. 1948.

11130. ______. Control of weeds in special purpose turf with 2,4–D. Pennsylvania Agricultural Experiment Station. Progress Report No. 1. 7 pp. 1948.

11131. ______. Control of weeds in special purpose turf with 2, 4–D. Greenkeepers' Reporter. 17(2):30–35. 1949.

11132. ______. Vegetatively propagated bent grass to become seed source. Pennsylvania Agricultural Experiment Station Bulletin 515. pp. 11–12. 1949.

11133. ______. Fall applications of 2, 4–D kill most weeds in grass. Pennsylvania Agricultural Experiment Station Bulletin 515. p. 12. 1949.

11134. ______. Tests of urea-formaldehyde formulations. The Pennsylvania State College Eighteenth Annual Turf Conference. pp. 102–107. 1949.

11135. ______. The use and misuse of water. Greenkeepers' Reporter. 18(2):5–9. 1950.

11136. ______. The use and mis-use of water on turf. Greenkeeping Superintendents Association National Turf Conference. 21:-48–53. 1950.

11137. ______. Turf management. McGraw-Hill Book Company, Inc., New York. pp. 1–354. 1950.

11138. ______. The turf program at Penn State. USGA Journal and Turf Management. 2(7):23–28. 1950.

11139. ______. Use and misuse of water. USGA Journal and Turf Management. 3(4):-30–31. 1950.

11140. ______. Weed control. Proceedings of the Mid-Atlantic Association of Greenskeepers Conference. pp. 23–31. 1951.

11141. ______. Roadside and airports. Proceedings of Midwest Regional Turf Conference. pp. 33–39. 1951.

11142. ______. Breeding turf grasses. Proceedings of Midwest Regional Turf Conference. pp. 99–103. 1951.

11143. ______. Crabgrass control—summary of results of chemical control tests. Pennsylvania State College Turfgrass Conference Proceedings. 20:101–109. 1951.

11144. ______. Water relations in turf maintenance. Proceedings of School of Soils, Fertilization, and Turf Maintenance. Green Section, Royal Canadian Golf Association. pp. 12–16. 1951.

11145. ______. Turf fertilization. Proceedings, School of Soils, Fertilization & Turf Maintenance Green Section, Royal Canadian Golf Association. pp. 41–46. 1951.

11146. ______. Turf for heavy duty. Southern California Conference on Turf Culture. pp. 18–25. 1951.

11147. ______. The weed problem in turf. Southern California Conference on Turf Culture. pp. 56–63. 1951.

11148. ______. The Pennsylvania turf program. Southern California Conference on Turf Culture. pp. 72–75. 1951.

11149. ______. Fundamentals in turf fertilization. Golf Course Reporter. 20(5):31–32. 1952.

11150. ______. Fundamentals in turf fertilization. Golf Course Reporter. 20(6):20–21. 1952.

11151. ______. Merion bluegrass, new strains of fescues and polycross bent. Pennsylvania State College Turfgrass Conference Proceedings. 21:6–16. 1952.

11152. ______. Experiments on slope control. Pennsylvania State College Turfgrass Conference Proceedings. 21:93–99. 1952.

11153. ______. New developments in soil management. Proceedings School of Soils, Fertilization & Turf Maintenance Green Section, Royal Canadian Golf Association. pp. 49–55. 1952.

11154. ______. Fundamentals of turf fertilization. Proceedings School of Soils, Fertilization & Turf Maintenance, Green Section, Royal Canadian Golf Association. pp. 86–92. 1952.

11155. ______. Cool season grasses in today's turf. Golfdom. 27(3):74, 76, 78, 100–104. 1953.

11156. ______. Grasses on your lawn for cooler regions. Flower Grower. 1953.

11157. ______. Making your lawn. Flower Grower. 1953.

11158. ______. Nitrogen fertilizers for turf. Proceedings of the Midwest Regional Turf Conference. pp. 10–12. 1953.

11159. ______. Evaluating the new turf grasses. Golfdom. 28(8):44. 1954.

11160. ______. Crabgrass control. Proceedings of the Mid-Atlantic Association of Greenkeepers Conference. pp. 38–42. 1954.

11161. ______. New grasses and their value in lawn mixtures. New York State Turf Association. Bulletin 48. pp. 183–185. 1954.

11162. Musser, H. B., W. L. Hottenstein, and J. P. Stanford. Penngift crown vetch for slope control on Pennsylvania highways. Pennsylvania State University Agricultural Experiment Station Bulletin. 576:1–21. 1954.

11163. Musser, H. B. Panel discussion on soil problems. Proceedings of the 23rd Annual Penn State Turfgrass Conference. pp. 33–35. 1954.

11164. ______. Factors involved in fertilizing golf turf. Proceedings School of Soils, Fertilization & Turf Maintenance Green Section, Royal Canadian Golf Association. pp. 44–48. 1954.

11165. ______. Evaluation of new grasses. Proceedings School of Soils, Fertilization & Turf Maintenance Green Section, Royal Canadian Golf Association. pp. 53–60. 1954.

11166. ______. The new lawn grasses. Seed World. 74(1):8, 40–43. 1954.

11167. ______. Getting the most out of fertilizer. Golf Course Reporter. 23(3):5–8. 1955.

11168. ______. How to get the most out of fertilizer. Golfdom. 29(3):52–54. 1955.

11169. ______. Principles of turfgrass management. Sixth Annual Sports Turfgrass Conference, Ontario Agricultural College, Guelph. pp. 49–55. 1955.

11170. ______. Lawns need fertilizer. Handbook on Lawns. Brooklyn Botanic Garden. pp. 91–95. 1956.

11171. ______. Nitrogen sources and use on turfgrasses. Oklahoma Turfgrass Conference Proceedings. pp. 20–23. 1956.

11172. ______. Rate of nitrogen availability from urea-formaldehyde and other nitrogen fertilizers. Proceedings of the 25th Annual Penn State Turfgrass Conference. pp. 60–67. 1956.

11173. ______. Principles of turfgrass management. Proceedings of the 25th Annual Penn State Turfgrass Conference. pp. 94–100. 1956.

11174. ______. Seeding rates of perennial grasses. Seventh Annual Sports Turfgrass Conference, Ontario Agricultural College, Guelph. pp. 27–31. 1956.

11175. ______. Influence of climatic and environmental factors in chemical weed control. Special Proceedings of the Turf Section, Weed Society of America. pp. 5–11. 1956.

11176. ______. Ten years of nitrogen studies. Proceedings of the Midwest Regional Turf Conference. pp. 6–7. 1957.

11177. ______. Nutrition is basic. Proceedings of the Midwest Regional Turf Conference. pp. 9–11. 1957.

11178. ______. Problems in growing sod. Proceedings of the Midwest Regional Turf Conference. pp. 36–38. 1957.

11179. ______. Seeding principles. Proceedings of the Midwest Regional Turf Conference. pp. 39–41. 1957.

11180. ______. Cool season grasses. Parks and Recreation. 40(5):18–19. 1957.

11181. ______. Nitrogen and turfgrasses. Parks and Recreation. 40(11):9–10. 1957.

11182. ______. Nitrogen fertilization of turfgrasses. Rutgers University Turfgrass Short Course. 5 pp. 1957.

11183. ______. Objectives and principles: fall fertilization. Golf Course Reporter. 27(7):15–18. 1959.

11184. ______. Turf annual vol. III. Park Maintenance. 12(7):21–36. 1959.

11185. ______. Studies of nitrogen sources for modern turfgrass fertilization. Guelph Turfgrass Conference Proceedings. pp. 19–26. 1959.

11186. ______. New developments in the turf world. Guelph Turfgrass Conference Proceedings. pp. 55–62. 1959.

11187. ______. New developments in the turf world. Seed World. 84(3):4–8. 1959.

11188. ______. Grasses. USGA Journal and Turf Management. 12(1):31–32. 1959.

11189. ______. How thick should sod be cut? Warren's Turf Nursery. Palos Park, Illinois. pp. 7–8. 1959.

11190. ______. Topdressing its preparation and use. Golf Course Reporter. 28(3):16, 18–22. 1960.

11191. ______. Failures in course construction result of corner cutting. Golfdom. 36(3):31–32, 112, 114, 117, 120. 1962.

11192. ______. Fertilizer use and weed control. Proceedings of the Midwest Regional Turf Conference. pp. 15–18. 1960.

11193. ______. Building new soils for turfgrass areas. Park Maintenance. 13(8):10–15. 1960.

11194. ______. Topdressing mixtures for turfgrass areas. Park Maintenance. 13(7):12–15. 1960.

11195. ______. Renovation—A standard method for improvement of turf areas. Park Maintenance. 13(9):20–22. 1960.

11196. ______. Cost relation in turfgrass production. Park Maintenance. 13(10):22–28. 1960.

11197. ______. Fertilizing turf-grass seed beds. Landscape Architecture. 51(2):-118–120. 1961.

11198. ______. Let's consider standardized greens. Golf Course Reporter. 30(4):-15–34. 1962.

11199. ______. Turf management. McGraw-Hill Book Company, Inc., New York. pp. 1–356. 1962.

11200. Musser, H. B., J. C. Harper, and J. M. Duich. Athletic fields, specification outline, construction and maintenance. Pennsylvania Agricultural Extension Service, 2–411. 1962.

11201. Musser, H. B. Modification of soils for greens construction and top dressing. Turf Clippings. University of Massachussetts. 1(7):27–A to 32–A. 1962.

11202. ______. Nitrogen—yesterday and today. Proceedings of the Midwest Regional Turf Conference. pp. 34–35. 1964.

11203. ______. Golf course construction. Seventeenth R.C.G.A. Sports Turfgrass Conference. pp. 29–31. 1966.

11204. ______. A sound putting green maintenance program. Seventeenth R.C.G.A. Sports Turfgrass Conference. pp. 33–39. 1966.

11205. ______. Soil mixing operations. Turf-Grass Times. 1(6):6–7. 1966.

11206. ______. Guide lines for setting up a sound turfgrass maintenance program. 18th R.C.G.A. National Turfgrass Conference Summary. pp. 35–43. 1967.

11207. ______. Turf management. Proceedings of the Mid-Atlantic Association of Golf Course Superintendents. pp. 13–14. 1969.

11208. Musser, H. B. and W. H. Daniel. Turf construction: Musser and Daniel make suggestions. Park Maintenance. 10:10, 10–11. 1957.

11209. Musser, H. B. and J. A. DeFrance. Greenswards in the cooler regions. Grass. USDA Yearbook. pp. 307–310. 1948.

11210. Musser, H. B. and J. M. Duich. Response of creeping bentgrass putting-green turf to urea-form compounds and other nitrogenous fertilizers. Agronomy Journal. 50(7):381–384. 1958.

11211. Musser, H. B. and J. E. Nicholas. Seed drier uses infrared electric lamps. Agricultural Engineering. 22(12):421–423. 1941.

11212. Musser, H. B., J. M. Duich, and J. C. Harper. Guide for preparation of specifications for golf course construction. Special Bulletin, Agricultural Extension Service. Pennsylvania State University. 1965.

11213. Musser, H. B., J. R. Watson, J. P. Stanford, and J. C. Harper. Urea—formaldehyde and other nitrogenous fertilizers for use on turf. Pennsylvania Agricultural Experiment Station Bulletin. 542. 14 p. 1951.

11214. Mustafa, M. A., and J. Letey. Factors influencing effectiveness of two surfactants on water-repellent soils. Turf Bulletin. Massachusetts Turf and Lawngrass Council. 7(1):21–22. 1970.

11215. ______. Effect of two nonionic surfactants on penetrability and diffusivity of soils. Soil Science. 111(2):95–100. 1971.

11216. Mutoza, E. S. California's expanding sod industry. Proceedings of Turf, Landscape Tree, and Nursery Conference. pp. 5–1 to 5–5. 1966.

11217. Muzik, T. Panel on weed control for turf areas. Northwest Turf Conference Proceedings. 11:35–36. 1957.

11218. Muzik, T. J., G. W. Luvisi, and H. J. Cruzado. A method for statistical evaluation of new herbicides. Agronomy Journal. 44(2):91–92. 1952.

11219. Myers, H. E. Soils common to central plains area, origin and structure. Central Plains Turfgrass Conference Proceedings. 1:15–18. 1950.

11220. Myers, W. M. Second generation progeny tests of the method of reproduction in Kentucky bluegrass, *Poa pratensis* L. Journal of the American Society of Agronomy. 35(5):413–419. 1943.

11222. ______. Registration of varieties and strains of fescues. Agronomy Journal. 43(5):237. 1951.

11224. ______. Registration of varieties and strains of bluegrass. Agronomy Journal. 44(3):155. 1952.

11225. Myers, W. M. and H. D. Hill. Distribution and nature of polyploidy in *Festuca eliator* L. Torrey Botanical Club Bulletin. 74(2):99–111. 1947.

11227. Myreus, A. and B. Langvad. Arbetsbeskrivning för Flygfältsarbeten. Weibulls Gräs Tips. pp. 287–289. 1966.

11228. Naegele, J. A. Grub identification and control. New York State Turf Association. Bulletin 47. pp. 179–181. 1953.

11229. Nakamura, N. Identification of turfgrass by paper chromatography. KGU Green Section Turf Research Bulletin. 19:-35–40. 1970.

11230. ———. Hentification of turfgrass by paper-chromatography, Part 2. KGU Green Section Turf Research Bulletin. 22(2):-25–32. 1972.

11231. Nakamura, N., and K. Ishizaki. Effects of the chemicals on turfgrass growth. KGU Green Section Turf Research Bulletin. 15:31–38. 1968.

11232. Nakamura, N., and S. Maekawa. Growing behavior of various turfgrasses, Part 1. KGU Green Section Turf Research Bulletin. 10:19–33. 1966.

11233. ———. Mixed cultivation of turfgrasses. K.G.U. Green Section Turf Research Bulletin. 13:45–60. 1967.

11234. Nakamura, N., and M. Sugimoto. Mixed cultivation of turfgrasses. K.G.U. Green Section Turf Research Bulletin. 14:-9–22. 1968.

11235. Nakamura, N., and M. Terabun. Day length and turfgrass growth, seed head. KGU Green Section Turf Research Bulletin. 17:31–36. 1969.

11236. Nakano, T., and N. Maekubo. Summer etiolation on zoysia green and its control. KGU Green Section Turf Research Bulletin. 10:67–71. 1966.

11237. Nash, L. B. Bowling greens. The Groundsman. 17(8):8, 10. 1964.

11238. ———. Autumn and winter work on the cricket square. The Groundsman. 18(1):4–6. 1964.

11239. ———. Just wickets. The Groundsman. 20(9):19–21. 1967.

11240. ———. Cricket square problems —IV. The Groundsman. 23(8):33–34. 1970.

11241. ———. Cricket squares. preparing the wickets. The Groundsman. 24(8):24–27. 1971.

11242. ———. Drainage problems. The Groundsman. 24(10):16–17. 1971.

11243. Nash, R. G. and D. D. Johnson. Soil texture influence on applied nitrogen recovery. Agronomy Journal. 59(3):272–275. 1967.

11244. Nash, S. H. The provision and maintenance of a parish playing field. Parks, Golf Courses and Sports Grounds. 29:320. 1964.

11245. Nashed, R. B. and R. D. Ilnicki. The fate of linuron in corn, soybean and crabgrass. Proceedings of the Northeastern Weed Control Conference. 21:564–565. 1967.

11246. Nasinec, J. Problems relating to cultivation turf playgrounds. First Czechoslovak Symposium on Sportturf Proceedings. pp. 263–272. 1969.

11247. Naughton, M. Weed control on a Washington bent nursery. Greenkeepers' Reporter. 6(2):12, 13, 26. 1938.

11248. Naylor, A. W. Effects of temperature, calcium, and arsenous acid on seedlings of *Poa pratensis.* Botanical Gazette. 101(2):-366–379. 1939.

11249. Neal, J. L., W. B. Bollen, and K. C. Lu. Influence of particle size on decomposition of red alder and douglas fir sawdust in soil. Nature. 205(4975):991–993. 1965.

11250. Neale, H. J. Report of committee on mulches and ground covers. Highway Research Abstracts. pp. 12–15. 1947.

11251. Nees, J. Timers. International Turfgrass Conference & Show. 39:68–70. 1968.

11252. Neff, P. W. and C. G. Wilson. "Scorched" earth: fairway renovation. Golf Course Reporter. 27(2):55–56. 1959.

11253. Neff, P. W. Experiences in fairway renovation, what and why! Proceedings of the Midwest Regional Turf Conference. pp. 65–67. 1959.

11254. Nehrling, H. Best lawn grass for Florida. My Garden in Florida. Vol. 1. The American Eagle. Florida. pp. 113–114. 1944.

11255. Neidlinger, T. J. *Poa annua* L.: susceptibility to several herbicides and temperature requirements for germination. M. S. Thesis, Oregon State University. 1965.

11256. Neidlinger, T. J., W. R. Furtick, and N. R. Goetze. Susceptibility of annual bluegrass and turfgrasses to bensulide and three uracil herbicides. Weed Science. 16(1):-16–18. 1968.

11257. Neill, J. C. The conversion of grass greens to *Cotula pulchella.* New Zealand Institute for Turf Culture Newsletter. 50:3–7. 1967.

11258. ______. The *Cotula pulchella* bowling green. New Zealand Institute For Turf Culture Newsletter. 77:4–11. 1972.

11259. Neilson, H., and C. Wolfrom. Fairway renovation. A Patch of Green. Michigan and Border Cities GCSA Publication. pp. 16–18. June, 1971.

11260. Neiswander, C. R. The annual white grub, *Ochrosidia villosa* Burm., in Ohio lawns. Journal of Economic Entomology. 31(3):340–344. 1938.

11261. Neller, J. R. and C. E. Hutton. Comparison of surface and subsurface placement of superphosphate on growth and uptake of phosphorus by sodded grasses. Agronomy Journal. 49(7):347–351. 1957.

11262. Nelson, A. The germination of *Poa* spp. Annals of Applied Biology. 14(2):-157–174. 1927.

11265. Nelson, L. V. Thatch build-up, management and control. Michigan Turfgrass Research Report. 3(1):8. 1965.

11266. Nelson, M. and H. B. Musser. Results of six years of tests of vegetative strains of creeping bentgrass. Proceedings of the 23rd Annual Penn State Turfgrass Conference. pp. 70–73. 1954.

11269. Nelson, R. W. Maintenance outline for upper midwest Golf Courses. Greenkeepers' Reporter. 17(6):14–15. 1949.

11270. Nelson, R. Golf courses of the future. Illinois Turfgrass Conference Proceedings. 5:39–46. 1964.

11271. Nelson, R. R., and D. M. Kline. The pathogenicity of certain species of *Helminthosporium* to species of the *Gramineae.* Plant Disease Reporter. 45(8):644–648. 1961.

11272. ______. Intraspecific variation in pathogenicity in the genus *Helminthosporium* to Gramineous species. Phytopathology. 52(10):1045–1049. 1962.

11273. ______. Evolution of sexuality and pathogenicity. III. Effects of geographic origin and host association on cross-fertility between isolates of *Helminthosporium* with similar conidial morphology. Phytopathology. 54(8):963–967. 1964.

11274. ______. Evolution of sexuality and pathogenicity. IV. Effects of geographic origin and host association on the pathogenicity of isolates of *Helminthosporium* with similar conidial morphology. Phytopathology. 54(10):1207–1209. 1964.

11275. Nelson, R. W. Watering greens with center green (sod cup) method. Golf Course Reporter. 30(6):48, 50. 1962.

11276. Nelson, S. Practical and theoretical aspects of subsurface irrigation. Ph.D. Thesis, University of California, Riverside. 1971.

11277. Nelson, W. L. Potash important for golf greens. Proceedings of the Midwest Regional Turf Conference. pp. 13–15. 1957.

11278. ______. Lime and its effects on soils and plants. You Can Grow A Good Lawn; The American Potash Institute. pp. 25–27. 1959.

11279. ______. Basic principles of potassium use on turf. Proceedings of the Midwest Regional Turf Conference. pp. 15–18. 1963.

11280. ______. Is your turf behind? Midwest Potash Newsletter. M-141. September-October. 1966.

11281. Nelson, W. R. Landscape design considerations for the golf course. Illinois Turfgrass Conference Proceedings. 4:30–36. 1963.

11282. ______. Grass in the landscape. Illinois Turfgrass Conference Proceedings. pp. 80–82. 1969.

11283. Nelson, W. R., and L. D. Baver. Movement of water through soils in relation to the nature of the pores. Soil Science Society of America Proceedings. 5:69–76. 1940.

11284. NeSmith, J. What a turfman should know about soil. Florida Turfgrass Management Conference Proceedings. 18:-63–65. 1970.

11285. Nettles, W. C., C. A. Thomas, and R. F. Nash. Lawn insects, how to control them. Clemson University Extension Service, Lawngrass Circular. 1971.

11286. Neuberger, A. Seed and seeding. USGA Green Section Record. 4(6):19–20. 1967.

11287. ______. Control versus confusion and controversy. USGA Green Section Record. 5(1):8–9. 1967.

11288. ______. Effects of watering on the grass plant and the turf. Rutgers University Short Course in Turf Management. 2 pp. 1969.

11289. ______. Effects of watering on the grass plant and the turf. Rutgers University. College of Agriculture and Environmental Science. Lawn and Utility Turf Section. pp. 10–11. 1969.

11290. New, E. Lawn care notes. Seed World. 100(7):17. 1967.

11291. Newberger, A. Power sprayers. USGA Green Section Record. 4(4):8–13. 1966.

11292. Newcomb, D. G. Big league drainage problem. Grounds Maintenance. 1(10):28–30. 1966.

11293. Newcomb, D. and G. W. Seferovich. Pebble Beach and Doral prepare for televised tournament play. Grounds Maintenance. 2(2):24–26. 1967.

11294. Newcomer, J. L. How to buy seed. Proceedings of the Mid-Atlantic Association of Golf Course Superintendents. pp. 24–26. 1964.

11295. ______. Certification of sod. International Turfgrass Conference Proceedings. 38:57–59. 1967.

11296. Newell, L. C. and F. D. Keim. Effects of mowing frequency on the yield and protein content of several grasses grown in pure stands. Nebraska Agricultural Experiment Station Research Bulletin. 150:36 pp. 1947.

11297. Newell, L. C., R. D. Staten, E. B. Jackson, and E. C. Conrad. Side-oats grama in the central Great Plains. Nebraska Agricultural Experiment Station Research Bulletin No. 207. 38 pp. 1962.

11298. Newhook, F. J. Soil fumigation. New Zealand Institute for Turf Culture Newsletter. 26:6–8. 1963.

11299. ______. Soil fumigation. New Zealand Institute for Turf Culture Newsletter. 38:8–10. 1965.

11300. ______. Soil sterilization. New Zealand Institute for Turf Culture Newsletter. 71:36–38. 1970.

11301. Newman, R. Turf weed control in Wisconsin. Wisconsin Turfgrass Conference Proceedings. 2 pp. 1965.

11302. ______. Turf weed control. Wisconsin Turfgrass Conference Proceedings. pp. 32–33. 1966.

11303. ______. Weed control in nursery sod. Illinois Turfgrass Conference Proceedings. 8:13–15. 1967.

11304. ______. Pre-emergence herbicides for turf. Super Talk 2(1):4. 1967.

11305. ______. Fertilizing small lawn areas. Illinois Turfgrass Conference Proceedings. pp. 29–31. 1969.

11306. ______. Seed—the thread of life. Illinois Turfgrass Conference Proceedings. pp. 66–67. 1969.

11307. Newbould, P., R. Taylor, and K. R. Howse. The absorption of phosphate and calcium from different depths in soil by swards of perennial ryegrass. Journal of the British Grassland Society. 26(4):201–208. 1971.

11308. Newman, R. Controlling lawn weeds. Wisconsin Agricultural Extension Service Special Circular 118. April, 1970.

11309. ______. Turfgrass research. University of Wisconsin. Research Works for Wisconsin at the Emmons Blaine Experimental Farm. Research Report 80. p. 8. 1971.

11310. ______. Turfgrass research. University of Wisconsin. Research Works for Wisconsin at the Ashland Experimental Farm. Research Report 79. p. 15–16. 1971.

11311. ______. Turfgrass research. University of Wisconsin. Research Works for Wisconsin at the Marshfield Experimental Farm. Research Report 77. p. 16. 1971.

11313. ______. Nurturing a good home lawn. University of Wisconsin Extension A1492. 1972.

11314. Newton, J. P., J. P. Craigmiles, S. V. Stacy, and J. M. Elrod. Winter lawn colorants. Georgia Agricultural Research. 3(1):-12. 1961.

11315. Newton, J. P. Turfgrass research reports 1969–70, Georgia. Southern Regional Turf Research Committee Report, Virginia Polytechnic Institute. 7 pp. 1970.

11316. Nicar, R. L. and Blaser, R. E. The use of wood cellulose mulch. American Roadbuilder. 39(3):14–16. 1962.

11317. Nicholson, H. P. Pesticides in water. Proceedings of Scotts Turfgrass Research Conference. 1:35–45. 1969.

11318. Nicholson, J. F. Tolerance of *Sclerotinia* dollar spot fungus to dyrene. Illinois Turfgrass Conference Proceedings. 11:-33. 1970.

11319. Nicholson, J. F., G. G. Gray and J. B. Sinclair. Excised grass blades for fungicidal evaluation against *Helminthosporium sorokinianum.* The Plant Disease Reporter. 55(11):959–960. 1971.

11320. Niehaus, M. H. Kentucky bluegrass varieties. Ohio Agricultural Research and Development Center. Research Summary 24. pp. 9–10. 1967.

11321. ———. Development of new bluegrass varieties. Ohio Agricultural Research and Development Center. Research Summary 24. p. 11. 1967.

11322. ———. Breeding of turfgrasses. First Ohio Turfgrass Conference Proceedings. pp. 34–38. 1967.

11323. ———. Bluegrass varieties. Ohio Agricultural Research and Development Center Research Summary 31. pp. 1–2. 1968.

11324. ———. Relative amounts of stripe and flag smut on Merion Kentucky bluegrass. The Plant Disease Reporter. 52(8):633–634. 1968.

11325. ———. Varieties and varietal development in Kentucky bluegrass. Ohio Agricultural Research and Development Center Research Summary 40. pp. 1–2. 1969.

11326. ———. Use and misuse of grass mixtures. Ohio Turfgrass Conference Proceedings. pp. 1–4. 1969.

11327. ———. Kentucky bluegrass blends. Turf and Ornamentals Research Summary 48. Ohio Agricultural Research and Development Center. pp. 1–2. 1970.

11328. ———. Kentucky bluegrass breeding. Ohio Turfgrass Foundation Newsletter. 24:3–4. 1971.

11329. ———. Evaluation of five Kentucky bluegrass varieties alone and in blends. Ohio Agricultural Research and Development Center. Research Summary 62. 5–6. 1972.

11330. ———. Effects of nitrogen fertilizer and mowing height on weed content of a Kentucky bluegrass turf. Ohio Agricultural Research and Development Center Research Summary 62. 7–9. 1972.

11331. ———. Grass selection for general purpose turf. Ohio Turfgrass Foundation Newsletter. 28:8. 1972.

11332. Niehaus, M. H. and R. R. Davis. Kentucky bluegrass varieties. Lawn and Ornamentals Research—1966. Ohio Agricultural Research and Development Center. Research Summary 16. pp. 3–5. 1966.

11333. ———. Which is the best variety? Ohio State University Experiment Station, Report on Research and Development. 54(3):42–44. 1969.

11334. ———. Kentucky bluegrass: which is the best variety? Lakeshore News. 2(2):9. 1970.

11335. Niehaus, M. H. and R. R. Davis. Kentucky bluegrass variety evaluations. Ohio State University Agricultural Experiment Station. Research Circular 177. 7 pp. 1970.

11336. Niehaus, M. H. and G. B. Triplett. Turf renovation. Ohio Agricultural Research and Development Center Research Summary 56. pp. 15–16. 1971.

11337. Nielsen, E. L. Cytology and breeding behavior of selected plants of *Poa pratensis.* Botanical Gazette. 106(4):357–382. 1945.

11338. ———. Breeding behavior and chromosome numbers in progenies from twin and triplet plants of *Poa pratensis.* Botanical Gazette. 108(1):26–40. 1946.

11339. ———. The Origin of multiple macrogametophytes in *Poa pratensis.* Botanical Gazette. 108(1):41–50. 1946.

11340. ———. Earthworms and soil fertility. Proceedings of New Zealand Grassland Association. 14:158–67. 1952.

11341. Nielsen, K. F., and R. K. Cunningham. The effects of soil temperature and form and level of nitrogen on growth and chemical composition of Italian ryegrass. Soil Science Society of America Proceedings. 28:-213–218. 1964.

11342. Nielson, E. L. and L. M. Humphrey. Grass studies. I. Chromosome numbers in certain members of the tribes *Festuceae, Hordeae, Aveneae, Agrostideae, Chlorideae, Phalarideae* and *Tripsaceae.* American Journal of Botany. 24(5):276–279. 1937.

11344. Niemczyk, H. D. Identification and life cycles of turf insects. Ohio Turfgrass Conference Proceedings. pp. 62–71. 1971.

11345. Nigh, E. L. Susceptibility of some turfgrasses in Arizona golf greens to the attack of a spiral nematode, *Helicotylenchus erythrinae.* Turfgrass Research. Report 219. University of Arizona. pp. 37–38. 1963.

11346. ———. A comparison of soil drench and subsurface irrigation for application of an organo-phosphate nematocide. Turfgrass Research Report 230. University of Arizona. pp. 24–26. 1965.

11347. ———. The influence of nematodes on winter development of overseeded annual ryegrass (*Lolium multiflorum.)* Report on Turfgrass Research, Arizona Agricultural Experiment Station. Report 240. pp. 4–6. 1966.

11348. Nighswonger, J. J. and J. C. Pair. Fertilizing lawns in Kansas. Kansas State University Cooperative Extension Service. Circular No. 391. 11 pp. 1968.

11349. ———. Fertilizing lawns in Kansas. Kansas State University Cooperative Extension Service. Circular No. 391. 11 pp. 1971.

11350. Nikola, H. C. and S. J. Toth. Establishment and maintenance of roadside vegetation. Agronomy Abstracts. p. 93. 1954.

11351. Nilsson, A. Grass species and herbs on roadside bankings. Weibulls Gräs Tips. pp. 139–151. 1963.

11354. ———. Some notes about southern types of *Festuca arundinacea* Schreb. var *Aspera* (Mutel) A.O.G. and similar types from abroad. Weibulls Gräs Tips. 8:175–185. 1964.

11355. ———. Om rödklövern, Trifolium pratense, vid vägarna i nordligare delar av Sverige. Weibulls Gräs Tips. pp. 251–258. 1965.

11356. Nilson, E. B., W. A. Geyer, J. K. Greig, L. D. Leuthold, C. E. Long, N. W. Miles, and F. D. Morrison. Chemical weed control in horticultural and forestry plants: herbicides for lawn and turf. Kansas Agricultural Experiment Station Bulletin. 551:9–10. 1972.

11357. Nilsson, A. F. Frösättningen hos ängsgröe, *Poa pratensis.* Botaniska Notiser. pp. 85–109. 1937.

11358. Nisbet, K. Saving your club money. International Turfgrass Conference Proceedings. 37:60–63. 1966.

11359. Nishimura, M. Comparative morphology and development of *Poa pratensis, Phleum pratense* and *Setaria italica.* Japanese Journal of Botany. 1:55–85. 1923.

11360. Nishihara, N. The fertilizers for old and infirm turfgrasses. KGU Green Section Turf Research Bulletin. 21(8):19–20. 1971.

11362. Nissen, O. Chromosome numbers, morphology, and fertility in *Poa pratensis* L. from southeastern Norway. Agronomy Journal, 42(3):136–144. 1950.

11363. Nittler, L. W. Seeding characteristics useful in identifying Kentucky bluegrass. Turf Bulletin. Massachusetts Turf and Lawn Grass Council. 4(1):5–6. 1966.

11364. ———. Seedling characteristics useful in identifying Kentucky bluegrass. Farm Research. 32(1):14–15. 1966.

11365. Nittler, L. W. and T. J. Kenny. Response of seedlings of *Festuca rubra* varieties to environmental conditions. Crop Science. 7(5):463–465. 1967.

11366. ———. Seedling difference among *Agrostis* species and varieties. Crop Science. 9(5):627–628. 1969.

11367. ———. Cultivar differences among calcium-deficient Kentucky bluegrass seedlings. Agronomy Journal. 64(1):73–75. 1972.

11368. ———. Distinguishing annual from perennial ryegrass. Agronomy Journal. 64(6):767–768. 1972.

11369. ______. Perennial ryegrass varietal response to maleic hydrazide. Crop Science. 12(1):117–118. 1972.

11370. Nix, H. M. Lawn problems in the Denver area. Rocky Mountain Regional Turfgrass Conference Proceedings. 7:13–15. 1960.

11371. Nicar, R. L. and R. E. Blaser. The use of wood cellulose mulch. American Road Builder. 39(3):14–16. 1962.

11372. Nixon, E. S. and C. McMillan. The role of soil in the distribution of four grass species in Texas. American Midland naturalist. 71:114–140. 1964.

11373. Noble, W. B. Sod webworm and their control in lawns and golf greens. United States Agriculture Circular. 248:1–4. 1932.

11374. ______. Sod webworms and their control. USGA Green Section Bulletin. 12(1):14–17. 1932.

11377. Noer, O. J. Activated sludge: A new source of organic nitrogen. The American Fertilizer. 62(12):24–27. 1925.

11378. ______. The use of "activated sludge" as a fertilizer for golf courses. USGA Green Section Bulletin. 5(9):203–205. 1925.

11379. ______. Activated sludge: its production, composition, and value as a fertilizer. Journal of the American Society of Agronomy. 18(11):953–962. 1926.

11380. ______. Fertilization of new fairway seedings. Golfdom. 1(6):5, 6, 7, 8. 1927.

11381. ______. The ABC of turf culture. The National Greenkeeper. 1(1):12–13. 1927.

11382. ______. The ABC of turf culture: physical properties of the soil and their effect on turf production. The National Greenkeeper. 1(2):22–25. 1927.

11383. ______. The ABC of turf culture: conducting experiments with Milorganite. The National Greenkeeper. 1(3):7–9. 1927.

11384. ______. The ABC of turf culture: Lime in sand, soil or water often overcomes acidic properties of sulfate of ammonia. The National Greenkeeper. 1(5):18, 41. 1927.

11385. ______. The ABC of turf culture: The nature of soil acidity and effect of fertilizer materials on soil reaction. The National Greenkeeper. 1(7):13–14. 1927.

11386. ______. The ABC of turf culture: Essential plant food elements and how plants feed. The National Greenkeeper. 1(8):9–10. 1927.

11387. ______. The ABC of turf culture: Soil characteristics and how plant food becomes available. The National Greenkeeper. 1(9):13–14, 35. 1927.

11388. ______. The ABC of turf culture: functions of plant elements and characteristics of various groups of fertilizer materials. The National Greenkeeper. 1(10):15–16, 29. 1927.

11389. ______. The ABC of turf culture: Composition and properties of individual fertilizer materials. The National Greenkeeper. 1(11):11–13, 32. 1927.

11390. ______. The ABC of turf culture: principles underlying the practical use of fertilizers on greens and fairways. The National Greenkeeper. 1(12):9–11, 33. 1927.

11391. ______. Valuable papers read at Green Section meeting. Golfdom. 2(2):35–39. 1928.

11392. ______. Fertilizers. Golfdom. 2(6):26–30. 1928.

11393. ______. Watch construction pitfalls. Golfdom. 2(8):16–19. 1928.

11394. ______. The ABC of turf culture. The National Greenkeeper, Inc., Cleveland, Ohio. 93 pp. 1928.

11395. ______. Physical soil factors affecting turf growth. USGA Green Section Bulletin. 8(1):6–10. 1928.

11396. ______. The nature of soil acidity and how it develops. USGA Green Section Bulletin. 8(3):46–48. 1928.

11397. ______. Effects of individual fertilizer materials on soil reaction. USGA Green Section Bulletin. 8(2):68–72. 1928.

11398. ______. Fairway fertilization. The National Greenkeeper. 3(4):20–23. 1929.

11399. ______. Soil's part in causing and correcting sick turf. Golfdom. 3(4):78–79. 1929.

11400. ______. Renewing fairways. Golfdom. 3(5):16–17. 1929.

11401. ______. Soils I have seen. The National Greenkeeper. 3(6):5–7. 1929.

11402. ______. Describes soil's part in turf maintenance. Golfdom. 4(6):23–25. 1930.

11403. ______. Feeding hungry fairways right diet for better turf. Golfdom. 4(8):17–20. 1930.

11404. ______. "Easy on high-power nitrogen" is southern winter warning. Golfdom. 5(10):18–20. 1931.

11405. ______. Fairway fertilization. The National Greenkeeper. 6(8):11–14. 1932.

11406. ______. Fall feeding of southern greens. The National Greenkeeper. 6(10):-5–6. 1932.

11407. ______. Outstanding maintenance practices of the 1932 season. Golfdom. 7(3):43–47. 1933.

11408. ______. Needs of soil determine plan of fairway fertilizing. Golfdom. 7(10):-62, 64, 66–68. 1933.

11409. ______. Maintenance practices of 1932. The National Greenkeeper. 7(3):11–15. 1933.

11410. ______. Fertilizer facts for fairway improvement. The National Greenkeeper. 7(8):5–7. 1933.

11411. ______. Physical properties of soils and their relation to turf maintenance. The National Greenkeeper. 7(9):5–8. 1933.

11412. ______. Physical properties of soils and their relation to turf maintenance. The National Greenkeeper. 7(10):7–8. 1933.

11413. ______. How to fertilize golf turf. Golfdom. 8(3):46, 48–50, 52, 54. 1934.

11414. ______. Fall is the year's best time to fertilize fairways. Golfdom. 8(8):21–22, 24. 1934.

11415. ______. Concluded notes of the Pittsburgh conference (golf course fertilization). Greenkeepers' Reporter. 2(4):1–4. 1934.

11416. ______. Fundamental principles underlying greens maintenance in the South. Greenkeeper's Reporter. 2(5):1–4. 1934.

11417. ______. Some principles of turf culture: soils and lawn grasses. The Modern Cemetery. 44(6):110–111. 1934.

11418. ______. Fall treatment of cemetery lawns to repair season's drought damage. The Modern Cemetery. 44(7):126. 1934.

11419. ______. Major greenkeeping problems of Canada. The Greenkeeper's Reporter. 3(2):13–15. 1935.

11420. ______. Have you a sound fairway program? Golfdom. 10(2):43, 46, 48, 50. 1936.

11421. ______. This matter of soil testing. Golfdom. 10(5):25–27. 1936.

11422. ______. Soil analysis. National Association of Greenkeepers of America Conference Proceedings. 10:26–48. 1936.

11423. ______. Underlying causes of turf trouble. The ABC of Turf Culture, Chapter 1, Milwaukee Sewerage Commission. 1937.

11424. ______. How grasses grow—the function of individual fertilizer elements—their use and mis-use. The ABC of Turf Culture, Chapter 2, Milwaukee Sewerage Commission. 1937.

11425. ______. Factors controlling turf management. The ABC of Turf Culture, Chapter 3, Milwaukee Sewerage Commission. 1937.

11426. ______. Soil as a medium for growth and a source of plant food. The ABC of Turf Culture, Chapter 4, Milwaukee Sewerage Commission. 1937.

11427. ______. Soil factors and their control. The ABC of Turf Culture, Chapter 5, Milwaukee Sewerage Commission. 1937.

11428. ______. Basic principles of grass fertilization. The ABC of Turf Culture, Chapter 6, Milwaukee Sewerage Commission. 1937.

11429. ______. Fertilizer tests and trials —plant nutritional requirements. The ABC of Turf Culture, Chapter 7, Milwaukee Sewerage Commission. 1937.

11430. ______. Practical aspects of fertilizer usage on fairways, cemetery lawns and parks. The A.B.C. of Turf Culture, Chapter 8, Milwaukee Sewerage Commission. 1937.

11431. ______. Fertilization of greens and related practices. The A.B.C. of Turf Culture, Chapter 9, Milwaukee Sewerage Commission. 1937.

11432. ______. Underlying causes of turf trouble. Golfdom. 11(2):21–22. 1937.

11433. ______. How grasses grow—the function of individual fertilizer elements—their use and misuse. Golfdom. 11(3):25–26. 1937.

11434. ______. Factors controlling turf management. Golfdom. 11(4):33–34. 1937.

11435. ______. Soil as a medium for growth and a source of plant food. Golfdom. 11(5):25–26. 1937.

11436. ______. Soil factors and their control. Golfdom. 11(6):21–22. 1937.

11437. ______. Basic principles of grass fertilization. Golfdom. 11(7):17–18. 1937.

11438. ______. Fertilizer tests and trials. . . . plant nutritional requirements. Golfdom. 11(8):5–6. 1937.

11439. ______. Practical aspects of fertilizer usage on fairways, cemetery lawns and park. Golfdom. 11(9):5–6. 1937.

11440. ______. Fertilization of greens and related practices. Golfdom. 11(10):25–26. 1937.

11441. ______. The season of 1937—a challenge. The Greenkeepers' Reporter. 6(1):7–8, 10. 1938.

11442. ______. Excess rain is turf menace. Golfdom. 13(1):12–14. 1939.

11443. ______. Lime's role in fine turf. Golfdom. 13(4):19–21. 1939.

11444. ______. Seeding winter greens. Golfdom. 13(10):48, 50. 1939.

11445. ______. "Winter greens" seeding methods. Golfdom. 15(10):34, 36. 1941.

11447. ______. South tests new grasses for tees, greens. Golfdom. 16(9):22–23. 1942.

11448. ______. What height of cut for fairways? Greenkeeper's Reporter. 10(1):24. 1942.

11449. ______. Winter damage to bent greens on northern courses. Greenkeeper's Reporter. 10(6):5–6, 20–21. 1942.

11450. ______. Out-smarting winter on the golf course. Golfdom. 17(1):27. 1943.

11451. ______. Greenkeeping tips. Golfdom. 17(3):28. 1943.

11452. ______. What kind of turf? Golfdom. 17(7):27, 30, 32, 34. 1943.

11453. ______. It takes the right kind of soil to grow good turf. Golfdom. 17(10):16–17. 1943.

11454. ______. Turf work guidance in Rhode Island report. Golfdom. 18(1):12–13. 1944.

11455. ______. Turf maintenance—now and later. Golfdom. 18(9):13–14, 16. 1944.

11456. ______. Postwar fairway maintenance. Golfdom. 18(10):25, 28–29. 1944.

11457. ______. Fungicides for snow mold control. The Greenkeeper's Reporter, 12(3):13–14, 24–25. 1944.

11458. ______. Yield and chemical composition of clippings from a green of Washington bent grass. Golfdom. 19(2):13–16. 1945.

11459. ______. Brynwood adopts chemical weed control program. Golfdom. 19(8):-15–16, 18. 1945.

11460. ______. How to improve postwar turf maintenance. Golfdom. 19(10):13–16, 56–58. 1945.

11461. ______. How to improve postwar turf maintenance. Golfdom. 20(1):54–58, 61. 1946.

11462. ______. How to improve postwar turf maintenance. Golfdom. 20(2):27–28, 59–61. 1946.

11463. ______. The effect of acidity on turf and the chemistry of acid soils. Golfdom. 20(6):41, 44, 56. 1946.

11464. ______. How soil acidity and related factors affect turf. Golfdom. 20(7):44, 46, 48. 1946.

11465. ______. Weed killing at Oak Ridge C. C. Golfdom. 20(8):50. 1946.

11466. ______. Practical aspects of lime usage on turf grasses. Golfdom. 20(9):15–18, 58. 1946.

11467. ______. Renovating fairways with strong weed-free turf. Golfdom. 20(10):-23–24, 74–77. 1946.

11468. ______. Care of bent grass golf greens. Golfdom. 21(2):21–22, 50, 52, 54. 1947.

11469. ______. Care of bent grass greens. Golfdom. 21(3):38, 76, 78–80. 1947.

11470. ______. Making proper topdressing for bent greens. Golfdom. 21(4):37, 97–99. 1947.

11471. ______. Topdressing and its use on bent grass greens. Golfdom. 21(5):44, 104–105. 1947.

11472. ______. Fertilizer and lime usage on bent greens. Golfdom. 21(7):52, 54, 56. 1947.

11473. ______. Fertilizer and lime usage in bent green care. Golfdom. 21(8):54, 56–59. 1947.

11474. ______. Science, mechanics and art in bent greens mowing. Golfdom. 21(10):-64, 66, 89. 1947.

11475. ______. The problem of golf turf maintenance. The Greenkeeper's Reporter. 15(1):7–8, 32. 1947.

11476. ______. 1947 was bad for turf on bent greens. Midwest Turf-News and Research. 1(4):2. 1947.

11477. ______. The elimination of ryegrass and the care of bermuda grass on greens in the South. Timely Turf Topics. USGA Green Section. May. p. 2. 1947.

11478. ______. Fertilization of bermuda greens before overseeding with ryegrass for winter play. Timely Turf Topics. USGA Green Section. September. p. 3. 1947.

11479. ______. Chlorosis: troublemaker on velvet bent greens. Golfdom. 22(2):53, 56. 1948.

11480. ______. Restoring moisture to localized dry spots. Golfdom. 22(3):65, 68. 1948.

11481. ______. Leveling bumpy peat fairways. Golfdom. 22(4):62, 90. 1948.

11482. ______. Grub identification important factor in control with DDT. Golfdom. 22(6):62, 95, 97. 1948.

11483. ______. Rolf sub-irrigator for dry spots. Golfdom. 22(9):50, 52. 1948.

11484. ______. Highlights of golf turf maintenance in 1948. Golfdom. 22(8):54–57, 90. 1948.

11485. ______. Water management. Proceedings of Midwest Regional Turf Conference. pp. 9–14. 1948.

11486. ______. Turf problems on parks, cemeteries and lawns. Proceedings of Midwest Regional Turf Conference. pp. 63–68. 1948.

11487. ______. Watering bent greens during hot weather. Midwest Turf News and Research. 2(3):2, 4. 1948.

11488. ______. Winter injury on greens and fairways. Midwest Turf-News and Research. 2(4):4. 1948.

11489. ______. The care and feeding of fairway turf with relation to the soil structure. Florida Greenkeeping Superintendents Association and the Southeastern Turf Management Conference. pp. 25–31. 1949.

11490. ______. Winter injury by snow mold prevented by fungicide. Golfdom. 23(2):56–57. 1949.

11491. ______. Controlling factors in the development of better turf. Golfdom. 23(4):-37, 40–41, 44, 94–97. 1949.

11492. ______. Developing fine turf with aid of fertilizers and chemicals. Golfdom. 23(5):52–53, 56, 58, 88–92. 1949.

11493. ______. The practical approach to fairway turf renovation. Golfdom. 23(7):-31, 34, 36, 72–77. 1949.

11494. ______. Preventing bent green damage during hot, humid weather. Golfdom. 23(8):32–33, 57, 60, 62. 1949.

11495. ______. Physical soil factors cause big turf loss in 1949. Golfdom. 23(10):-70–71, 74–75. 1949.

11496. ______. Reducing white grub damage. Greenkeepers' Reporter. 17(5):14. 1949.

11497. ______. Golf course construction in relation to efficient maintenance. Proceedings of the Mid-Atlantic Association of Greenkeepers Conference. pp. 5–11. 1949.

11498. ______. Turf problems from everywhere in kodachrome. Proceedings of Midwest Regional Turf Conference. pp. 1–7. 1949.

11499. ______. Fertilizing turf. Proceedings of Midwest Regional Turf Conference. pp. 9–12. 1949.

11500. ______. Course construction for easy maintenance. New York State Turf Association. Bulletin 4. p. 14. 1949.

11501. ______. Course construction for easy maintenance. New York State Turf Association. Bulletin 5. p. 18. 1949.

11502. ______. Course construction for easy maintenance. New York State Turf Association. Bulletin 6. p. 24. 1949.

11503. ______. Modern equipment for turf maintenance. Oklahoma—Texas Turf Conference Proceedings. pp. 15–20. 1949.

11504. ______. Fertilizing bermuda turf. Oklahoma—Texas Turf Conference Proceedings. pp. 35–41. 1949.

11505. ______. Correcting windburn injury without interrupting play. Golfdom. 24(2):60, 62. 1950.

11506. ______. Fundamental aspects of the soil as a medium for turf growth. Proceedings of the Mid-Atlantic Association of Greenkeepers Conference. pp. 5–9. 1950.

11507. ______. Turf fertilization and fertilizer materials. Proceedings of Midwest Regional Turf Conference. pp. 46–56. 1950.

11508. ______. What's new in turf. Oklahoma-Texas Turf Conference Proceedings. pp. 15–20. 1950.

11509. ______. What every man should know about turf weeds. Oklahoma-Texas Turf Conference Proceedings. pp. 56–63. 1950.

11510. ______. Presenting turf problems to the club. Rutgers University Short Course in Turf Management. 18:77–83. 1950.

11511. ______. Turf in 1949. Rutgers University Short Course in Turf Management. 18:93–98. 1950.

11512. ______. Water management. Southeastern New York Turf School. pp. 47–52. 1950.

11513. ______. Renovation of existing turf. Central Plains Turf Conference. 2:37–46. 1951.

11514. ______. Cultural practices and turf diseases. Central Plains Turfgrass Conference. 2:68–75. 1951.

11515. ______. Suggestions for early season golf turf maintenance. Golfdom. 25(1):-26–27, 46, 48, 50. 1951.

11516. ______. Suggestions for early season golf turf maintenance. Golfdom. 25(2):-54–60. 1951.

11517. ______. Maintenance of tees, roughs and traps needs attention. Golfdom. 25(5):32–34, 69–71. 1951.

11518. ______. Avoid trouble with greens by studying fertilizer needs. Golfdom. 25(6):29–33, 66–69. 1951.

11519. ______. Creeping bent fairways need rough treatment. Golfdom. 25(8):37, 74. 1951.

11520. ______. Past, present and future of turf maintenance. Golfdom. 25(10):77–81. 1951.

11521. ______. Timely topics of 1950. Proceedings of the Mid-Atlantic Association of Greenskeepers Conference. pp. 68–75. 1951.

11522. ______. Turf maintenance in wartime. Proceedings of Midwest Regional Turf Conference. pp. 12–18. 1951.

11523. ______. Chemical control, a summary. Proceedings of Midwest Regional Turf Conference. pp. 93–98. 1951.

11524. ______. Relation of fertilization, lime and other cultural practices to turf diseases. Pennsylvania State College Turfgrass Conference Proceedings. 20:41–49. 1951.

11525. ______. The nutrient requirements of turf. Southern California Conference on Turf Culture. pp. 26–35. 1951.

11526. ______. Selling a sound maintenance program. Southern California Conference on Turf Culture. pp. 68–71. 1951.

11527. ______. A Kodachrome review of turf problems and improvements in 1951. Proceedings of School of Soils, Fertilization and Turf Maintenance. Green Section, Royal Canadian Golf Association. pp. 31–39. 1951.

11528. ______. Diagnosing turf troubles. Proceedings School of Soils, Fertilization & Turf Maintenance Green Section, Royal Canadian Golf Association. pp. 53–59. 1951.

11529. ______. How management of turf influences disease incidence. Proceedings of the 6th Annual Texas Turf Conference. pp. 13–23. 1951.

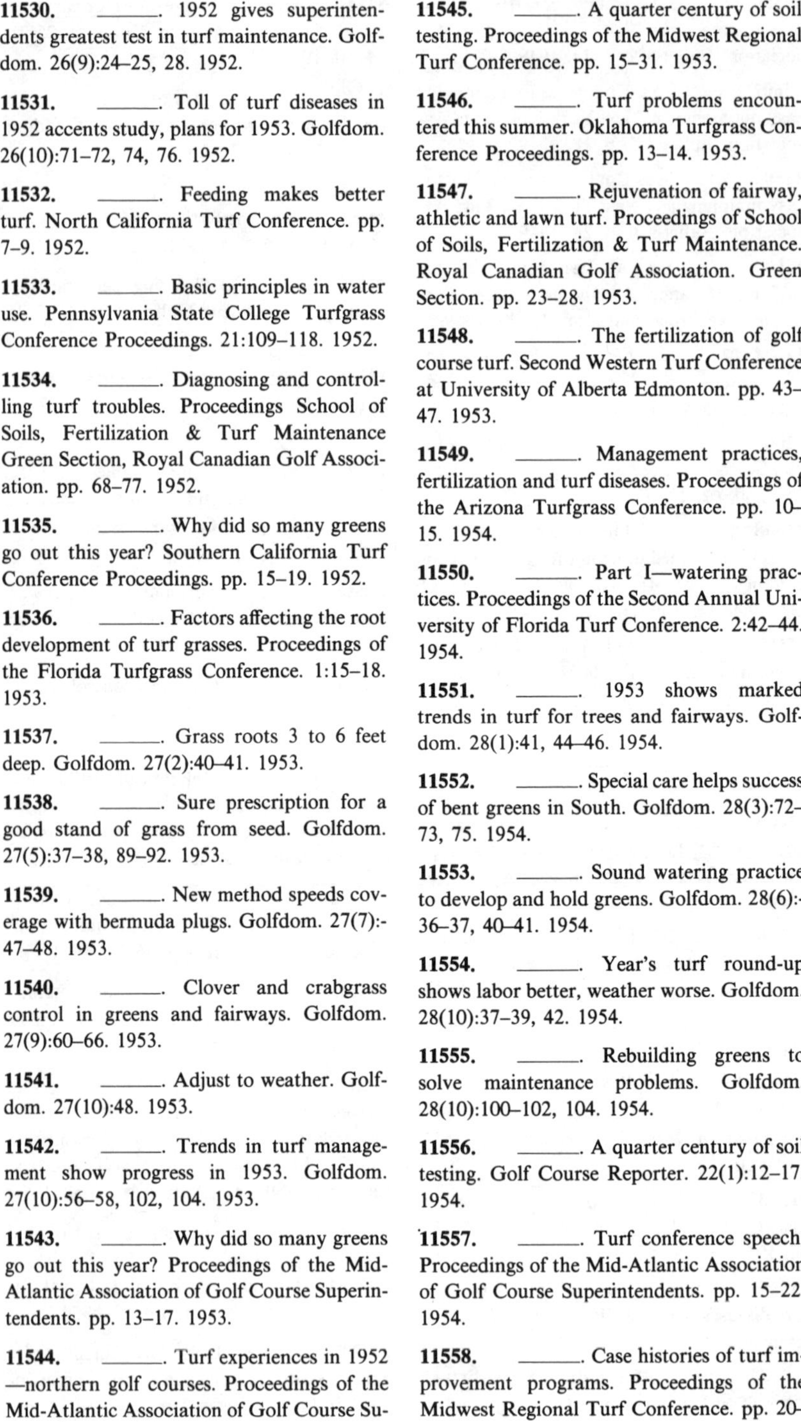

11530. ______. 1952 gives superintendents greatest test in turf maintenance. Golfdom. 26(9):24–25, 28. 1952.

11531. ______. Toll of turf diseases in 1952 accents study, plans for 1953. Golfdom. 26(10):71–72, 74, 76. 1952.

11532. ______. Feeding makes better turf. North California Turf Conference. pp. 7–9. 1952.

11533. ______. Basic principles in water use. Pennsylvania State College Turfgrass Conference Proceedings. 21:109–118. 1952.

11534. ______. Diagnosing and controlling turf troubles. Proceedings School of Soils, Fertilization & Turf Maintenance Green Section, Royal Canadian Golf Association. pp. 68–77. 1952.

11535. ______. Why did so many greens go out this year? Southern California Turf Conference Proceedings. pp. 15–19. 1952.

11536. ______. Factors affecting the root development of turf grasses. Proceedings of the Florida Turfgrass Conference. 1:15–18. 1953.

11537. ______. Grass roots 3 to 6 feet deep. Golfdom. 27(2):40–41. 1953.

11538. ______. Sure prescription for a good stand of grass from seed. Golfdom. 27(5):37–38, 89–92. 1953.

11539. ______. New method speeds coverage with bermuda plugs. Golfdom. 27(7):-47–48. 1953.

11540. ______. Clover and crabgrass control in greens and fairways. Golfdom. 27(9):60–66. 1953.

11541. ______. Adjust to weather. Golfdom. 27(10):48. 1953.

11542. ______. Trends in turf management show progress in 1953. Golfdom. 27(10):56–58, 102, 104. 1953.

11543. ______. Why did so many greens go out this year? Proceedings of the Mid-Atlantic Association of Golf Course Superintendents. pp. 13–17. 1953.

11544. ______. Turf experiences in 1952 —northern golf courses. Proceedings of the Mid-Atlantic Association of Golf Course Superintendents. pp. 24–28. 1953.

11545. ______. A quarter century of soil testing. Proceedings of the Midwest Regional Turf Conference. pp. 15–31. 1953.

11546. ______. Turf problems encountered this summer. Oklahoma Turfgrass Conference Proceedings. pp. 13–14. 1953.

11547. ______. Rejuvenation of fairway, athletic and lawn turf. Proceedings of School of Soils, Fertilization & Turf Maintenance. Royal Canadian Golf Association. Green Section. pp. 23–28. 1953.

11548. ______. The fertilization of golf course turf. Second Western Turf Conference at University of Alberta Edmonton. pp. 43–47. 1953.

11549. ______. Management practices, fertilization and turf diseases. Proceedings of the Arizona Turfgrass Conference. pp. 10–15. 1954.

11550. ______. Part I—watering practices. Proceedings of the Second Annual University of Florida Turf Conference. 2:42–44. 1954.

11551. ______. 1953 shows marked trends in turf for trees and fairways. Golfdom. 28(1):41, 44–46. 1954.

11552. ______. Special care helps success of bent greens in South. Golfdom. 28(3):72–73, 75. 1954.

11553. ______. Sound watering practice to develop and hold greens. Golfdom. 28(6):-36–37, 40–41. 1954.

11554. ______. Year's turf round-up shows labor better, weather worse. Golfdom. 28(10):37–39, 42. 1954.

11555. ______. Rebuilding greens to solve maintenance problems. Golfdom. 28(10):100–102, 104. 1954.

11556. ______. A quarter century of soil testing. Golf Course Reporter. 22(1):12–17. 1954.

11557. ______. Turf conference speech. Proceedings of the Mid-Atlantic Association of Golf Course Superintendents. pp. 15–22. 1954.

11558. ______. Case histories of turf improvement programs. Proceedings of the Midwest Regional Turf Conference. pp. 20–37. 1954.

11559. ______. Soil physics and soil fertility and their effect upon pests. Oklahoma Turfgrass Conference Proceedings. 9:13–20. 1954.

11560. ______. Turf conference speech. Proceedings of the 23rd Annual Penn State Turfgrass Conference. pp. 62–69. 1954.

11562. ______. Water in relation to the enemies of good turf weed, diseases, algae, scald. Proceedings of the Annual Texas Turfgrass Cnference. 9:67–79. 1954.

11563. ______. Symposium—troubleshooting in turf. Fertility problems—major elements. Florida Turf Management Conference Proceedings. 3:108–111. 1955.

11564. ______. Management and fertilization practices minimize disease. Golfdom. 29(3):78, 80, 82, 84. 1955.

11565. ______. U-3 bermuda ingeniously planted, proves ok at K.C. Golfdom. 29(8):36–37. 1955.

11566. ______. *Zoysia matrella* ideal facing for traps at Indian Creek. Golfdom. 29(9):24–25. 1955.

11567. ______. Turf round-up. Golfdom. 29(10):58–59, 62, 64. 1955.

11568. ______. The management of bent grass fairways. Proceedings of the Midwest Regional Turf Conference. pp. 49–52. 1955.

11569. ______. Bentgrass fairway management. Sixth Annual Sports Turfgrass Conference, Ontario Agricultural College, Guelph. pp. 28–32. 1955.

11570. ______. Management practices, fertilization, and turf diseases. Rocky Mountain Regional Turfgrass Conference Proceedings. 1:11–15. 1955.

11571. ______. Turf round-up. Golfdom. 30(1):29, 32–34, 36. 1956.

11572. ______. Fertilizer for warm season grasses. Golfdom. 30(3):98, 100, 102, 104. 1956.

11573. ______. Soil tests that tell needs of golf turf. Golfdom. 30(6):33, 36. 1956.

11574. ______. 1956 turf round-up. Golfdom. 30(10):59–60, 69–70, 76. 1956.

11575. ______. Fertilization of bermuda greens. The Golf Course Reporter. 24(4):20. 1956.

11576. ______. Turf roundup. Seventh Annual Sports Turfgrass Conference, Ontario Agricultural College, Guelph. pp. 35–40. 1956.

11577. ______. Warning on herbicides. Golfdom. 31(7):32–34. 1957.

11578. ______. The impact of cultural practices upon disease incidence on bent grasses. New Mexico Turfgrass Conference Proceedings. pp. 1–6. 1957.

11579. ______. The establishment and behavior of turf grasses. Parks and Recreation. 40(4):21–23. 1957.

11580. ______. Chemical properties of soil. Parks and Recreation. 40(8):6. 1957.

11581. ______. How chloratic grass responded quickly to iron sulphate. Golfdom. 32(7):40. 1958.

11582. ______. Technical advances which may counteract unnecessary maintenance costs. USGA Journal and Turf Management. 11(1):26–27. 1958.

11583. ______. New developments in top-dressing. Proceeding of University of Florida Turf-Grass Management Conference. 7:20–22. 1959.

11584. ______. Disaster averted where club guarded against it. Golfdom. 33(1):40–41, 71. 1959.

11585. ______. 1958 turf round-up. Proceedings Thirteenth Southeastern Turfgrass Conference. pp. 1–7. 1959.

11586. ______. What does the future hold? Proceedings Thirteenth Southeastern Turfgrass Conference. pp. 75–93. 1959.

11587. ______. Winterkill plays Havoc with greens in northern part of country. Golfdom. 33(5):29–30. 1959.

11588. ______. 3–Way aerifying improves matted greens. Golfdom. 33(6):35–36. 1959.

11589. ______. Thirty years of turfgrass soil testing. Southern California Turfgrass Institute Conference Proceedings. pp. 18–22. 1959.

11590. ______. Better bent greens fertilization and management. Turf Service Bureau, Milwaukee Sewerage Commission Bulletin No. 2. pp. 1–33. 1959.

11591. ______. Thirty years of turf grass soil testing. Southern California Turfgrass Culture. 10(1):4–6. 1960.

11592. ______. Bermuda overseeding. Golfdom. 34(1):44–46. 1960.

11593. ______. Lyons' unique stolon planting method. Golfdom. 34(5):66. 1960.

11594. ______. Air and water management for better turf. Mid-Atlantic Golf Course Superintendent's Annual Conference Proceedings. pp. 141–156. 1960.

11595. ______. Thirty years of turf grass soil testing. North California Turf Conference. pp. 18–22. 1960.

11596. ______. Thirty-five years of turf grass experience. Southeastern Turfgrass Conference. 14:1–11. 1960.

11597. ______. Nitrogen in turf production. Proceedings of University of Florida Turf-Grass Management Conference. 9:6–12. 1961.

11598. ______. Summary of 1960–61 overseeding studies. Proceedings of University of Florida Turf-Grass Management Conference. 9:84–85. 1961.

11599. ______. Much remains to be learned about herbicides. Golfdom. 35(1):60, 62, 79–80. 1961.

11600. ______. How to get deep roots. Golfdom. 35(8):40. 1961.

11601. ______. Location is factor in choice of grass selection. Golfdom. 35(10)68, 118. 1961.

11602. ______. Let's look at turfgrass. Proceedings of the Midwest Regional Turf Conference. pp. 68–70. 1961.

11603. ______. Overseeding bermuda greens for winter play. Proceedings of the Florida Turf-Grass Management Conference. 10:63–65. 1962.

11604. ______. There's sugar in that turf. Golfdom. 38(2):36, 38, 114–115. 1964.

11605. ______. Spring and winter desiccation problems. Golf Course Reporter. 30(3):60, 62, 64. 1962.

11606. ______. Winter and spring desiccation problems. International Turf-Grass Conference Proceedings. 33:5–6. 1962.

11608. ______. Six years of tests help turfmen pin down some secrets of overseeding. Golfdom. 37(9):39–40, 74–75. 1963.

11609. ______. "As O. J. sees it"—a summary. Iagreen, 30th Annual Conference Proceedings. pp. 9–10. 1963.

11610. ______. Utilization of plant nutrient elements. Supplement to Proceedings For Oklahoma Turfgrass Conference. pp. 1–4. 1963.

11611. ______. The future of turfgrass in the south. Proceedings of 1963 turf conference. Southern Turfgrass Association. pp. 21–22. 1963.

11612. ______. The transition period. Proceedings of 1963 Turf Conference. Southern Turfgrass Association. pp. 23–24. 1963.

11613. ______. Soil and leaf tissue for nitrogen. Golf Course Reporter. 32(4):36–37, 40. 1964.

11614. ______. Soil and leaf tissue tests for potassium. Golf Course Reporter. 32(6):-56–58. 1964.

11615. ______. Soil and leaf tissue tests for phosphorus. Golf Course Reporter. 32(5):63–64. 1964.

11616. ______. *Poa annua* in bentgrass greens Golf Course Reporter. 32(10):12. 1964.

11617. ______. As O. J. sees it. Iagreen. Iowa Turfgrass Conference Proceedings. 30:-9–10. 1964.

11618. ______. Diagnosing problems on golf courses. Proceedings of the Florida Turfgrass Management Conference. 13:70–74. 1965.

11619. ______. The role of sod in turfgrass culture. The Golf Course Reporter. 33(2):12–16. 1965.

11620. ______. Winter kill problems on bentgrass greens. The Golf Course Reporter. 33(3):66. 1965.

11621. ______. Bermudagrass tees. The Golf Course Reporter. 33(5):12–13. 1965.

11622. ______. Grasses for tees. The Golf Course Reporter. 33(6):48–50. 1965.

11623. ______. Winter kill. The Golf Course Reporter. 33(7):42–44. 1965.

11624. ______. *Poa annua.* The Golf Course Reporter. 33(8):46–49. 1965.

11625. ______. Overseeding bermudagrass greens. The Golf Course Reporter. 33(9):48–50. 1965.

11626. ______. Advances on golf courses in foreign countries. Proceedings 19th Southeastern Turfgrass Conference. pp. 1–10. 1965.

11627. ______. Catastrophe with a happy ending. The Golf Superintendent. 34(1):21. 1966.

11628. ______. Iron and magnesium requirements are small but vital. The Golf Superintendent. 34(2):28, 52. 1966.

11629. ______. Constant treatment brings complete eradication of sedge and pennywort in greens. The Golf Superintendent. 34(5):30. 1966.

11630. ______. Diagnosing problems on golf courses. Turf Bulletin. Massachusetts Turf and Lawn Grass Council. 3(3):18–20. 1966.

11631. Noer, O. J. and F. V. Grau. 1956 turf roundup. Golfdom. 31(1):52–53, 65–68. 1957.

11632. ______. 1957 turf roundup. Golfdom. 32(1):40–44, 68. 1958.

11633. ______. Turf roundup for 1958. Golfdom. 32(10):54–58, 106–108. 1958.

11634. ______. 1959 turf roundup. Golfdom. 33(10):48–51, 54, 96. 1959.

11635. Noer, O. J., Hamner, J. E. How much and what is cut from a Bermuda green. Golfdom 30(7):28, 32, 34. 1956.

11636. Noer, O. J. and C. G. Wilson. The role of soil tests in lawn fertilization. Handbook on Lawns. Brooklyn Botanic Garden. pp. 96–101. 1956.

11637. ______. Thirty years of soil testing of turfgrass areas. Agronomy Abstracts. 50:66. 1958.

11638. ______. Better turfgrass is through soil analysis and controlled fertility. Proceedings of the Midwest Regional Turf Conference. pp. 69–72. 1959.

11639. Noer, O. J., J. E. Hamner, and C. G. Wilson. The yield and chemical composition of clippings from a Tifgreen bermudagrass green. Agronomy Abstracts. 51:91. 1959.

11640. Noer, O. J., C. G. Wilson, and J. M. Latham. Winter grass overseeding on bermuda putting greens. Agronomy Abstracts. 52:71. 1960.

11641. ______. Winter grass overseeding on bermudagrass putting greens. Proceedings Fifteenth Southeastern Turfgrass Conference. pp. 33–41. 1961.

11642. Noer, O. J., C. Winchell, G. F. Stewart, and R. Donaldson. Principles of turfgrass fertilization. Turf Clippings, University of Massachusetts. 1(4):A–1 to A–5. 1959.

11643. Noggle, G. R. Photosynthesis as related to turf production. Proceedings of University of Florida Turf-Grass Management Conference. 8:12–15. 1960.

11644. ______. Functions of nitrogen in grass. Proceedings of University of Florida Turf-Grass Management Conference. 9:13–16. 1961.

11645. Nordan, W. W. Commercial turfgrass production. Auburn University Annual Turfgrass Short Course. 9:10–12. 1968.

11646. Norman, A. G. The composition of forage crops. I. Ryegrass (western wolths). Biochemical Journal. 30(7):1354–1362. 1936.

11647. Norman, A. G. and H. L. Richardson. The composition of forage crops. II. Ryegrass (western wolths). Changes in herbage and soil during growth. Biochemical Journal. 31:1556–1566. 1937.

11648. Norman, M. J. T., A. W. Kemp, and J. E. Taylor. Winter temperatures in long and short grass. Meteorological Magazine. 86(1,019):148–152. 1957.

11649. Norman, A. G., C. P. Wilsie, and W. G. Gaessler. The fructosan content of some grasses adapted to Iowa. Iowa State College Journal of Science. 15(3):301–305. 1941.

11650. Norris, D. M. Tree diseases. International Turfgrass Conference Proceedings. 37:13–15. 1966.

11651. North, H. F. A. Grasses found on the golf courses of R. I. and types and varieties used in the R. I. experiments. Greenkeepers Club of New England Newsletter. 5(6):-4–5. 1933.

11652. ______. Lawn seeds and seeding. Greenkeepers Club of New England Newsletter. 5(10):5–6. 1933.

11653. ______. What to do for worms? Golfdom. 9(4):59–60. 1935.

11654. ______. A co-operative study in earthworm control in Rhode Island, U.S.A. Journal of the Board of Greenkeeping Research. 4(13):101–103. 1935.

11655. ______. "Scald" and leaf spot diseases. Greenkeepers Club of New England Newsletter. 8(6):14. 1936.

11656. ______. Seed selection and buying. Golfdom. 11(4):70–72, 75–80. 1937.

11657. ______. Growing seed of golf course grasses. The Greenkeepers' Reporter. 5(6):16–18, 20, 22, 32–34, 40. 1937.

11658. ______. Growing seed of golf course grasses. National Association of Greenkeepers of America Conference Proceedings. 11:50–57. 1937.

11659. North, H. F. A. and T. E. Odland. Putting green grasses and their management. Greenkeepers Club of New England Newsletter. 6(10):5–6. 1934.

11660. ______. Seed yields of Rhode Island colonial bent (*Agrostis tenuis* sibth) as influenced by the kind of fertilizer applied. Journal of the American Society of Agronomy. 26(11):939–945. 1934.

11661. ______. Putting green grasses and their management. Rhode Island Agricultural Experiment Station Bulletin. 245. 44 pp. 1934.

11662. ______. The relative seed yields in different species and varieties. Journal of the American Society of Agronomy. 27(5):374–383. 1935.

11663. North, H. F. A. and G. A. Thompson. Investigations regarding the bluegrass webworms in turf. Greenkeepers Club of New England Newsletter. 5(5):4–6. 1933.

11664. ______. Investigations regarding the bluegrass webworms in turf. Greenkeepers Club of New England Newsletter. 5(6):-2–3. 1933.

11665. ______. Investigations regarding bluegrass webworms in turf. Journal of Economic Entomology. 26:1116–1125. 1933.

11666. North, H. F. A., T. E. Odland, and J. A. DeFrance. Lawn grasses and their management. Rhode Island Experiment Station Bulletin 264. 36 p. 1938.

11667. Norton, B. E. and J. W. McGarity. The effect of burning of native pasture on soil temperature in northern New South Wales. Journal of the British Grassland Society. 20(2):101–105. 1965.

11668. Norton, D. C. Relationship of nematodes to small grains and native grasses in north and central Texas. Plant Disease Reporter. 43(2):227–235. 1959.

11669. ______. Nematology in the north central region 1956–1966. Iowa Agricultural Experiment Station Special Report 58. 20 pp. 1968.

11670. Norton, J. B. S. Maryland grasses. Maryland Agricultural Experiment Station Bulletin. 323:251–326. 1930.

11671. Norum, E. N. A method of evaluating the adequacy and efficiency of overhead irrigation systems. American Society of Agricultural Engineering Annual Meeting Proceedings. 61:206. 1961.

11672. Nowakowski, T. Z. Effects of nitrogen fertilizers on total nitrogen, soluble nitrogen, and soluble carbohydrate content of grass. Journal of Agricultural Science. 59:-387–392. 1962.

11673. Nowakowski, T. Z. and R. K. Cunningham, K. F. Nielson. Nitrogen fractions and soluble carbohydrates in Italian ryegrass. 1. Effects of soil temperature, form and level of nitrogen. Journal of the Science of Food and Agriculture. 16:124–134. 1965.

11674. Nowakowski, T. Z., A. C. D. Newman, and A. Penn. Nitrogenous fertilizers—solids or solutions. Journal of Agricultural Science. 68(1):123–129. 1967.

11675. Nowosad, F. S., D. E. N. Swales, and W. G. Dore. The identification of certain native and naturalized hay and pasture grasses by their vegetative characters. Macdonald College, McGill University, Technical Bulletin 16. 1936.

11676. Nuessle, W. Stolonizing. International Turfgrass Conference Proceedings. 38:43–45. 1967.

11677. Nunn, W. Public relations for you. Proceedings of the 20th Annual Northwest Turfgrass Conference. pp. 3–8. 1966.

11678. Nuss, J. R. The effect of non-ionic wetting agent on rooting and root development in selected species. M. S. Thesis, Pennsylvania State University. 81 pp. 1962.

11679. Nutter, G. C. Building the new lawn. University of Florida Department of Agronomy Mimeo Series 55–2.

11680. ______. Improved bermudagrass lawns. University of Florida Department of Agronomy Mimeo Series 55–4.

11681. ______. Development and management of zoysiagrass lawns. University of Florida Department of Agronomy Mimeo Series 55–5.

11682. ______. Characteristics and management of St. Augustinegrass lawns. University of Florida Department of Agronomy Mimeo Series 55–6.

11683. ______. Characteristics and production of centipedegrass lawns. University of Florida Department of Agronomy Series 56–2.

11684. ______. Introducing—the mole drain. New York State Turf Association. Bulletin 4. p. 13. 1949.

11685. ______. Crabgrass control with potassium cyanate. New York State Turf Association. Bulletin 15. pp. 57–58. 1950.

11686. ______. The control of broad leaf weeds. Proceedings of Southeastern New York Turf School. pp. 52–58. 1950.

11687. ______. Crabgrass control. Proceedings of southeastern New York Turf School. pp. 59–63. 1950.

11688. ______. A comparison of available grasses for Florida lawns. University of Florida, Dept. of Agronomy Mimeo. 1952.

11689. ______. The turf research program in Florida. Proceedings of the University of Florida Turf Conference. 1:11–14. 1953.

11690. ______. The Florida lawn. Florida Turf Association Bulletin. 1(2):4–6. 1954.

11691. ______. Are you using topdressing as a cover-up. Florida Turf Association Bulletin. 1(2):6–7. 1954.

11692. ______. Are you considering zoysia? Florida Turf-Grass Association Bulletin. 1(4):4. 1954.

11693. ______. Searching the year's research. Proceedings of the Second Annual University of Florida Turf Conference. 2:-30–32. 1954.

11694. ______. Part III—fertilization. Proceedings of the Second Annual University of Florida Turf Conference. 2:47–51. 1954.

11695. ______. Are you using the best grass. Proceedings of the Second Annual University of Florida Turf Conference. 2:65. 1954.

11696. ______. Nematode investigations in turf. Florida Agricultural Experiment Station Annual Report. p. 58. 1955.

11697. ______. Soil sterilization—a valuable tool in turf management. Florida Turf Association Bulletin. 2(4):6–8. 1955.

11698. ______. Fertility requirements in turf production. Florida Turf Management Conference Proceedings. 3:20–24. 1955.

11699. ______. Symposium—lawn maintenance problems. Mowing and fertilization. Florida Turf Management Conference Proceedings. 3:82–91. 1955.

11700. ______. Grass is greener on the other lawn. Florida Agricultural Experiment Station Research Report. 1(4):10–11. 1956.

11701. ______. What is a grass plant? Florida Turf Management Conference Proceedings. 4:5–8. 1956.

11703. ______. Soil sterilization practices in turf. Proceedings Tenth Southeastern Turfgrass Conference. pp. 17–24. 1956.

11704. ______. The nematode outlook in turf. U.S.G.A. Journal and Turf Management. 9(4):25–31. 1956.

11705. ______. Warm season grasses for parks and playgrounds. Parks and Recreation. 40(6):12–15. 1957.

11706. ______. Soil sterilization practices in turf. USGA Journal and Turf Management. 10(2):25–30. 1957.

11707. ______. Future trends in turf grass nursery production. Florida Turf Management Conference Proceedings. 6:36–40. 1958.

11708. ______. Fertilization and mowing of lawn grasses. Florida Turf Management Conference Proceedings. 6:73–80. 1958.

11709. ______. Progress in nematode research. Florida Turf Management Conference Proceedings. 6:101–108. 1958.

11710. ______. Floratine St. Augustinegrass—a new variety for ornamental turf. Florida Turf Management Conference Proceedings. 6:118–120. 1958.

11711. ______. Nematode problems in turf. Golf Course Reporter. 26(7):5–9. 1958.

11712. ______. Turfgrass protection programs. Parks and Recreation. 41(4):184. 1958.

11713. ______. Nematodes, unseen enemy of turfgrass. Parks and Recreation. 41(9):379–385. 1958.

11714. ______. In the southeast. Golf Course Reporter. 27(7):33–35. 1959.

11715. ______. Nematicides. National Turfgrass Conference Proceedings. 30:6–7. 1959.

11716. ______. Caddies, carts and catastrophe. Proceedings of University of Florida Turf-Grass Management Conference. 8:40–47. 1960.

11717. ______. Turf grass review. Park Maintenance. 13(7):17–32. 1960.

11718. ______. Caddies, cars and catastrophe? Proceedings of the Texas Turfgrass Conference. 15:8–15. 1960.

11719. ______. The management challenge. Proceedings of University of Florida Turf-Grass Management Conference. 9:89–97. 1961.

11720. ______. The how and why of job motivation. Proceedings, Fifteenth Southeastern Turfgrass Conference. pp. 14–21. 1961.

11721. ______. Ten years of progress in turf. Proceedings of the Florida Turf-Grass Management Conference. 10:3–9. 1962.

11722. ______. Principles of weed control. Proceedings of Florida Turf-Grass Management Conference. 12:22–31. 1964.

11723. ______. Turfgrass is a four billion dollar industry. Turf-Grass Times. 1(1):1. 1965.

11724. ______. Overseeding winter grass (a panel discussion). Turf-Grass Times. 1(1):1, 4. 1965.

11725. ______. Sod production expands and mechanizes. Turf-Grass Times. 1(3):12–13, 18–19. 1966.

11726. ______. Weed control fundamentals. Turf-Grass Times. 1(4):11–13, 22. 1966.

11727. ______. Golf course operations—a changing, challenging field with a future. Turf-Grass Times. 1(6):1966. 17, 20. 1966.

11728. ______. Conditioning football fields. Turf-Grass Times. 1(6):1, 22–23. 1966.

11729. ______. Recruiting, training and keeping top quality men. Proceedings Florida Turf-Grass Management Conference. 15:19–23. 1967.

11730. ______. Habits and control of chinch bugs in turf. Turf-Grass Times. 2(5):-1–2, 10. 1967.

11731. ______. The A-B-C's of overseeding. Turf-Grass Times. 3(1):10–11. 1967.

11732. ______. Accentuate the positive. Turf Talks. Scotts Marysville, Ohio. p. 1. January, 1967.

11733. ______. Soil for turf facilities. Proceedings, University of Florida Turf-Grass Management Conference. 17:19–22. 1969.

11734. ______. Artificial turf faces credibility gap. Turf-Grass Times. 4(5):1, 6, 12–13. 1969.

11735. ______. Budgetary principles and practices. Ohio Turfgrass Conference Proceedings. pp. 74–75. 1970.

11736. ______. Artificial turf faces credibility gap. Proceedings 1970 3-Day Turf Courses, Rutgers University. pp. 44–48. 1970.

11737. ______. Grass and trees reduce noise and visual pollution. Turfgrass Times. 5(7):19. 1970.

11738. ______. Florida Turf-Grass Association 1972 membership directory. Proceedings Florida Turfgrass Trade Show. No. 11. 51 pp. 1972.

11739. ______. Returfing sewer lines. Turfgrass Times. 8(1):8–9. 1972.

11740. Nutter, G. C. and R. J. Allen. 'Floratine' St. Augustinegrass. A new variety of ornamental turf. University of Florida Agricultural Experiment Station Circular. S–123. 12 pp. 1960.

11741. Nutter, G. C. and T. F. Bryan. Vegetative propagation studies with southern turf grasses. Florida Turf Management Conference Proceedings. 5:94–98. 1957.

11742. Nutter, G. C. and J. R. Christie. Nematode investigations on turfgrasses. Agronomy Abstracts. 50:66. 1958.

11743. ______. Nematode investigations on putting green turf. Proceedings of the Florida State Horticultural Society. 71:445–449. 1958.

11744. ______. Nematode investigations on putting green turf. Oklahoma Turfgrass Conference Proceedings. pp. 39–44. 1959.

11745. ______. Nematode investigations on putting green turf. USGA Journal and Turf Management. 11(7):24–28. 1959.

11746. Nutter, G. C. and J. F. Cornman. Comparative studies with crabgrass herbicides in turf. New York State Turf Association. Bulletin 21. pp. 81–84. 1950.

11747. ______. Endothal for clover control. Golf Course Reporter. 20(5):10–12. 1952.

11748. ______. Second report on endothal for clover control. New York State Turf Association. Bulletin 35. pp. 135–136. 1952.

11749. Nutter, G. C. and E. L. Ervin. Mobility in maintenance. Turf-Grass Times. 2(3):1, 11, 20. 1967.

11750. Nutter, G. C. and G. M. Whitton. Nematode investigations on turf grasses. Florida Agricultural Experiment Station Annual Report. pp. 120–121. 1957.

11751. Nutter, G. C. and A. Witherspoon. The effectiveness of maleic hydrazide as a growth retardant on two southern turfgrasses. Special Proceedings of the Turf Section, Weed Society of America. pp. 43–60. 1956.

11752. Nutter, E. C., J. F. Cornman and S. N. Fertig. A new chemical control for clover in turf. Golfdom. 25(7):23–29. 1951.

11753. ______. A new chemical control for clover in turf. New York State Turf Association. Bulletin 26&27. pp. 103–107. 1951.

11754. Nutter, G. C., J. M. Good and J. R. Christie. Symposium—trouble shooting in turf. Nematode investigations on Florida turf. Florida Turf Management Conference Proceedings. 3:133–141. 1955.

11755. Nutter, G. C., B. B. Sumrell, and R. W. White. The double-quadrat method of measuring lateral growth of turf grasses. Agronomy Abstracts. 49:78. 1957.

11756. Nutter, G., G. Bockholt, J. Long, W. Allen, and C. Wilson. Weed control. Proceedings of Texas Turfgrass Conference. 14:-75–76. 1959.

11757. Nye, W. F. A general cemetery seed mixture. Is it possible? The Modern Cemetary. 50(2):28. 1940.

11758. Nye, W. F. and C. W. Baker. The cultural treatment of bent stolons. Greenkeepers Club of New England Newsletter. 7(6):8, 10. 1935.

11759. Nyquist, W. E. Fluroescent perennial ryegrass. Crop Science. 3(3):223–226. 1963.

11760. Nylund, R. E., and R. Stadtherr. Studies on the control of crabgrass in bluegrass lawns. Weeds. 4(2):264–274. 1956.

11761. Oakes, A. J. and W. R. Langford. Cold tolerance in *Digitaria.* Agronomy Journal. 59(4):387–388. 1967.

11762. Oakley, R. A. The behavior of Rhode Island bent redtop mixtures. USGA Green Section Bulletin. 3(8):213–215. 1923.

11763. ______. Brown-patch investigation. USGA Green Section Bulletin. 4(4):-87–92. 1924.

11764. ______. Some suggestions for beginners on the vegetative planting of creeping bent. USGA Green Section Bulletin. 4(8):-182–184. 1924.

11765. ______. Fall and winter topdressing of putting greens. USGA Green Section Bulletin. 4(10):248–250. 1924.

11766. ______. Mottled condition of bent turf. USGA Green Section Bulletin. 4(11):259. 1924.

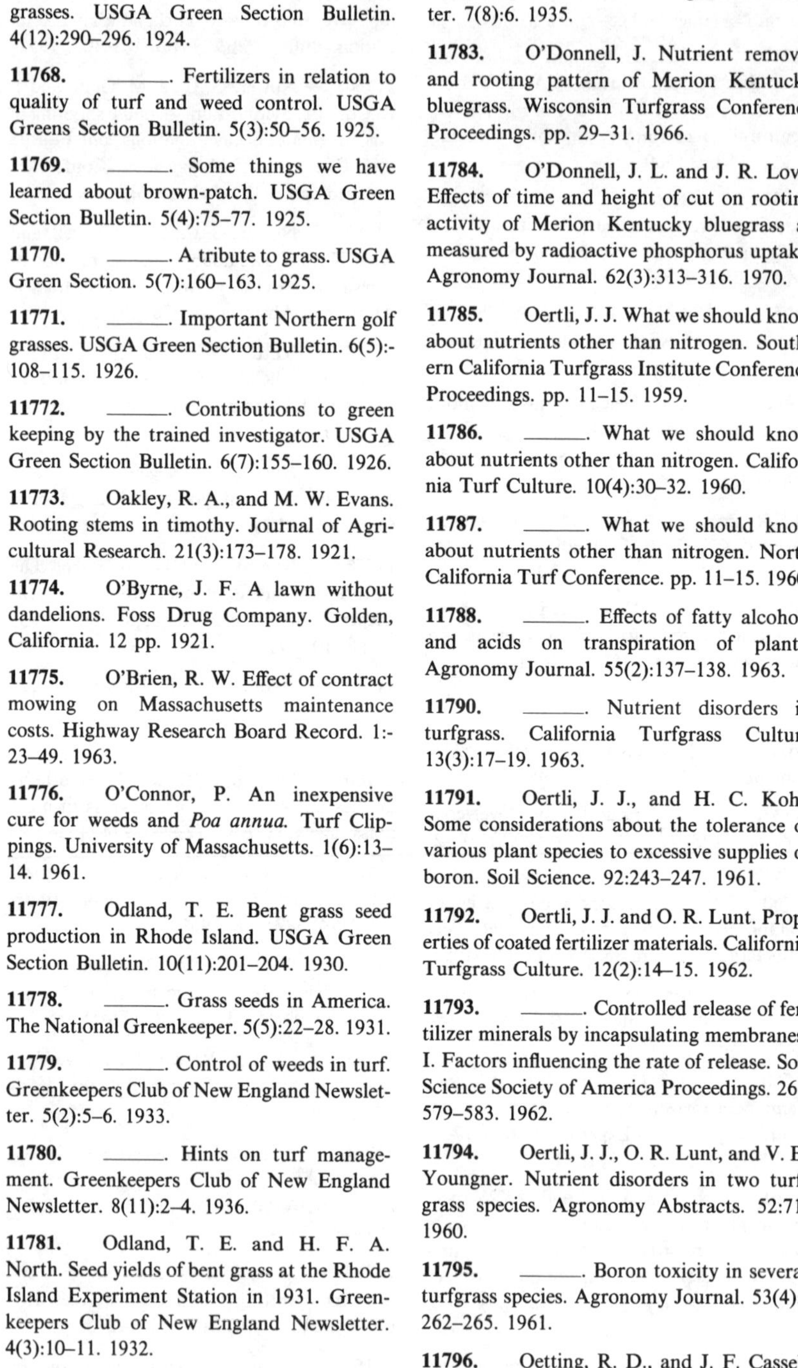

11767. ______. Important northern golf grasses. USGA Green Section Bulletin. 4(12):290–296. 1924.

11768. ______. Fertilizers in relation to quality of turf and weed control. USGA Greens Section Bulletin. 5(3):50–56. 1925.

11769. ______. Some things we have learned about brown-patch. USGA Green Section Bulletin. 5(4):75–77. 1925.

11770. ______. A tribute to grass. USGA Green Section. 5(7):160–163. 1925.

11771. ______. Important Northern golf grasses. USGA Green Section Bulletin. 6(5):-108–115. 1926.

11772. ______. Contributions to green keeping by the trained investigator. USGA Green Section Bulletin. 6(7):155–160. 1926.

11773. Oakley, R. A., and M. W. Evans. Rooting stems in timothy. Journal of Agricultural Research. 21(3):173–178. 1921.

11774. O'Byrne, J. F. A lawn without dandelions. Foss Drug Company. Golden, California. 12 pp. 1921.

11775. O'Brien, R. W. Effect of contract mowing on Massachusetts maintenance costs. Highway Research Board Record. 1:-23–49. 1963.

11776. O'Connor, P. An inexpensive cure for weeds and *Poa annua.* Turf Clippings. University of Massachusetts. 1(6):13–14. 1961.

11777. Odland, T. E. Bent grass seed production in Rhode Island. USGA Green Section Bulletin. 10(11):201–204. 1930.

11778. ______. Grass seeds in America. The National Greenkeeper. 5(5):22–28. 1931.

11779. ______. Control of weeds in turf. Greenkeepers Club of New England Newsletter. 5(2):5–6. 1933.

11780. ______. Hints on turf management. Greenkeepers Club of New England Newsletter. 8(11):2–4. 1936.

11781. Odland, T. E. and H. F. A. North. Seed yields of bent grass at the Rhode Island Experiment Station in 1931. Greenkeepers Club of New England Newsletter. 4(3):10–11. 1932.

11782. ______. The relative seed yields in different species and varieties of bentgrass. Greenkeepers Club of New England Newsletter. 7(8):6. 1935.

11783. O'Donnell, J. Nutrient removal and rooting pattern of Merion Kentucky bluegrass. Wisconsin Turfgrass Conference Proceedings. pp. 29–31. 1966.

11784. O'Donnell, J. L. and J. R. Love. Effects of time and height of cut on rooting activity of Merion Kentucky bluegrass as measured by radioactive phosphorus uptake. Agronomy Journal. 62(3):313–316. 1970.

11785. Oertli, J. J. What we should know about nutrients other than nitrogen. Southern California Turfgrass Institute Conference Proceedings. pp. 11–15. 1959.

11786. ______. What we should know about nutrients other than nitrogen. California Turf Culture. 10(4):30–32. 1960.

11787. ______. What we should know about nutrients other than nitrogen. North California Turf Conference. pp. 11–15. 1960.

11788. ______. Effects of fatty alcohols and acids on transpiration of plants. Agronomy Journal. 55(2):137–138. 1963.

11790. ______. Nutrient disorders in turfgrass. California Turfgrass Culture 13(3):17–19. 1963.

11791. Oertli, J. J., and H. C. Kohl. Some considerations about the tolerance of various plant species to excessive supplies of boron. Soil Science. 92:243–247. 1961.

11792. Oertli, J. J. and O. R. Lunt. Properties of coated fertilizer materials. California Turfgrass Culture. 12(2):14–15. 1962.

11793. ______. Controlled release of fertilizer minerals by incapsulating membranes: I. Factors influencing the rate of release. Soil Science Society of America Proceedings. 26:-579–583. 1962.

11794. Oertli, J. J., O. R. Lunt, and V. B. Youngner. Nutrient disorders in two turfgrass species. Agronomy Abstracts. 52:71. 1960.

11795. ______. Boron toxicity in several turfgrass species. Agronomy Journal. 53(4):-262–265. 1961.

11796. Oetting, R. D., and J. F. Cassel. Effects of interstate right-of-way mowing on wildlife, snow buildup, and motorists' opinions in North Dakota. A preliminary report. Highway Research Abstracts. 39(12):74. 1970.

11797. O'Halloran, T. E. Removing leaves from fairways, lawns and parks. Midwest Turf-News and Research. 2(4):1, 3. 1948.

11798. O'Hanlon, D. J. Planting U-3 bermudagrass sprigs. Golf Course Reporter. 31(6):48–49. 1963.

11799. Ohigashi, M. On turf disease. KGU Green Section Turf Research Bulletin. 7:81–84. 1964.

11800. Ohlrogge, A. J. The Purdue soil and plant tissue tests. Purdue Agricultural Experiment Station Bulletin 584. 1952.

11801. ———. Fertilizer facts and fancies. Proceedings of the Midwest Regional Turf Conference. pp. 38–42. 1954.

11802. ———. Fertilizer facts and fancies. Golf Course Reporter. 23(5):5–7. 1955.

11803. Ohlson, A. Brown patch. Greenkeepers Club of New England Newsletter. 2(3):3. 1930.

11804. Ojiimi, E. Fertilizer on the turf. KGU Green Section Turf Research Bulletin. 4:70–73. 1963.

11805. Okamura, G. T. Illustrated key to the *Lepidopterous* larvae attacking lawns in California. California Department of Agriculture Bulletin. 48(1):15–21. 1959.

11806. Okajima, H., and D. Smith. Available carbohydrate fractions in the stem bases and seed of timothy, smooth bromegrass, and several other northern grasses. Crop Science. 4:317–320. 1964.

11807. Olusuye, S. A. and C. A. Raguse. Inclined point quadrat estimation of species contributions to pasture dry matter production. Agronomy Journal. 60(4):441–442. 1968.

11808. O'Kelly, J. D. The maintenance of lawns. Landscape and Garden. 4(1):37–38. 1937.

11809. O'Kelly, W. M. A. How Butte, Montana re-built and maintains its course. Golfdom. 23(4):68, 70, 72. 1949.

11810. O'Knefski, R. The co-operative extension advisory service. Proceedings of the First International Turfgrass Research Conference. pp. 438–439. 1969.

11811. Olcott, J. B. Fine versus coarse *Agrostis.* Connecticut Agricultural Experiment Station. 11th Annual Report. pp. 177–181. 1887.

11812. ———. Grass-gardening. Connecticut Agricultural Experiment Station 14th Annual Report. pp. 162–174. 1890.

11813. ———. Talk about a grass garden. Connecticut Agricultural Report. Hartford. 26 pp. 1892.

11814. Oldale, A. Cutting costs on turf. Parks, Golf Courses and Sports Grounds. 32(2):166–168. 1966.

11815. O'Leary, P. Observations from the Warwick Country Club. Turf Clippings. University of Massachussetts. 1(1):18. 1956.

11816. ———. Winter problems at Ekwanok. Turf Clippings. University of Massachussetts. 1(5):A–8 to A–10. 1960.

11817. O'Leary, T. Brown-patch control. Greenkeepers Club of New England Newsletter. 1(3):2. 1929.

11818. Oliver, A. D. and K. N. Komblas. Controlling chinch bugs in St. Augustine grass. Louisiana Agriculture. 11(4):3, 16. 1968.

11819. Oliver, J. R. Tall fescue can be controlled. New Zealand Journal of Agriculture. 116(6):46–49. 1968.

11820. Olmsted, C. E. Growth and development in range grasses. I. Early development of *Bouteloua curtipendula* in relation to water supply. Botanical Gazette. 102(3):499–519. 1941.

11821. ———. Growth and development in range grasses. II. Early development of *Bouteloua curtipendula* as affected by drought periods. Botanical Gazette. 103(3):-531–542. 1942.

11822. ———. Growth and development in range grasses. III. Photoperiodic responses in the genus *Bouteloua.* Botanical Gazette. 105(2):165–181. 1943.

11823. ———. Growth and development in range grasses. IV. Photoperiodic responses in twelve geographic strains of side-oats grama. Botanical Gazette. 106(1):46–74. 1944.

11824. ______. Growth and development in range grasses. V. Photoperiodic responses of clonal divisions of three latitudinal strains of side-oats grama. Botanical Gazette. 106(4):382–401. 1945.

11825. Olney, A. J. Lawns. Kentucky Agricultural Extension Circular. 229:1–8. 1930.

11826. Olney, V. W. Plants need minor elements. Weeds, Trees and Turf. 5(5):18, 20. 1966.

11827. Olson, C. O. Whys and what nots of irrigation design. Proceedings of the Turfgrass Sprinkler Irrigation Conference. 5 pp. 1966.

11828. Olson, H. C. How chemicals control weeds. Proceedings 18th Southeastern Turfgrass Conference. pp. 7–13. 1964.

11829. Olson, R. V. Growth requirements. Central Plains Turfgrass Conference Proceedings. 1:19–23. 1950.

11830. Olsson, G. and B. Langvad. New methods for constructing permanent green areas and road bankings in connection with road construction. Weibulls Gräs Tips. pp. 121–138. 1963.

11831. Olton, G. S. Approaches to turfgrass insect control. Arizona Turfgrass Conference Proceedings. p. 28. 1972.

11832. O'Neil, J. B. Research and development of a pesticide. Proceedings of the Florida Turf-Grass Management Conference. 10:43–60. 1962.

11833. Ono, S., H. Nakashima, and K. Ehara. Physiological and ecological studies on the regrowth of herbage plants. 8. Effect of cutting treatments on the original tiller regrowth and new tiller development of orchardgrass. Journal of Japanese Society of Grassland Science. 14(1). 1968.

11834. O'Quinn, D. Course-owned turf nursery cuts construction, maintenance costs. Club Operations. 2(2):40–41. 1964.

11835. Orchard, A. H. Ecology and chemical control (spraying) of *Poa annua.* New Zealand Institute for Turf Culture Newsletter. 54:6–11. 1968.

11836. Orgell, W. H. Temperature relations of the microclimate. M. S. Thesis, Pennsylvania State College. 57 pp. 1952.

11837. Ormand, T. Experiences in fairway improvement. Rutgers University Short Courses in Turf Management. 19:90–91. 1951.

11838. Ormrod, D. P. Light responses of turfgrasses. Proceedings of the 18th Annual Northwest Turfgrass Conference. pp. 50–51. 1964.

11839. Orr, H. P. and E. J. Donovan. The roadside landscape. Alabama Agricultural Experiment Station. 13(3):6. 1966.

11840. Orr, C. C. and A. M. Golden. The pseudo-root-knot-nematode of turf in Texas. Plant Disease Reporter. 50(9):645. 1966.

11841. Orsenigo, J. R. Weed control. Proceedings of University of Florida Turf-Grass Management Conference. 8:124–139. 1960.

11842. ______. Weed control in the turf nursery. Proceedings of University of Florida Turf-Grass Management Conference. 9:118–122. 1961.

11843. ______. Weed control, A to Z: a primer for turf. Florida Turf Management Conference Proceedings. 10:180–184. 1962.

11844. ______. Herbicide equipment calibration. Golf Course Reporter. 31(1):26–30. 1963.

11845. ______. Application of herbicides to turf. Proceedings of Florida Turf-Grass Management Conference. 12:59–66. 1964.

11846. ______. Weed control in large and intensive areas. Proceedings Florida Turfgrass Management Conference. 14:138–140. 1966.

11847. Orton, C. R. What "dose" best for brown patch? Golfdom. 1(4):22, 23. 1927.

11848. ______. Weeds and the grass diseases on golf courses. Golfdom. 3(5):90–94. 1929.

11849. Orton, L. Control of vegetation on Oregon highways. Proceedings 7th Annual Northwest Turf Conference. 7:35–37. 1953.

11850. Orullian, G. D. Sulfur—the essential element. USGA Green Section Record. pp. 11–13. 1970.

11851. ______. Misfit items in a maintenance budget. USGA Green Section Record. 9(2):8–10. 1971.

11852. Osaka, S. Ears and etiolation on zoysia turf. KGU Green Section Turf Research Bulletin. 6:59–83. 1964.

11853. Osborn, J. F., J. Letey, and N. Valoris. Surfactant longevity and wetting characteristics. California Turfgrass Culture. 19(3):17–18. 1969.

11855. Osner, G. A. Leaf smut of timothy. Cornell University Agricultural Experiment Station Bulletin 381:186–230. 1916.

11856. Oswald, A. K., G. P. Allen, and J. G. Elliott. The growth performance of ryegrass plants obtained from long established swards improved by the use of dalapon for the selective suppression of weed grasses. British Weed Control Conference Proceedings. 10(2):506–512. 1970.

11858. Oswalt, D. T., A. R. Bertrand, and M. R. Teel. Influence of nitrogen fertilization and clipping on grass roots. Soil Science Society of America Proceedings. 23:-228–230. 1959.

11859. O'Toole, M. A. Grass production on peat soils. Journal of the British Grassland Society. 25(2):131–135. 1970.

11861. Ousley, J. E. Factors affecting sod quality. Proceedings of University of Florida Turf-Grass Management Conference. 8:53–57. 1960.

11862. ______. Insect control on large turf acreage. Florida Turf Management Conference Proceedings. 10:185–190. 1962.

11863. ______. Why I went certified. Proceedings, University of Florida Turf-Grass Management Conference. 11:133–135. 1963.

11864. ______. Insect pest control on large turf areas. Proceedings of the Florida Turfgrass Management Conference. 12:133–137. 1964.

11865. ______. The effects of turf-grass certification in Florida. The Golf Course Reporter. 33(2):42–46. 1965.

11866. ______. Selection of grasses for large turf areas: sod. Proceedings, Florida Turf-Grass Management Conference. 14:-124–125. 1966.

11867. ______. Sprigging and plugging. International Turfgrass Conference Proceedings. 38:62–63. 1967.

11868. ______. Selecting a variety of St. Augustine grass. Proceedings of the Florida Turf-Grass Management Conference. 17:55–56. 1969.

11869. Overholt V. Water management. Golf Course Reporter. 22(7):5–9. 1954.

11870. Overman, A. J. Use of nematacides on established turf. Proceedings of the Soil Science Society of Florida. 14:170–173. 1954.

11871. Overrein, L. N., and P. G. Moe. Factors affecting urea hydrolysis and ammonia volatilization in soil. Soil Science Society of America Proceedings. 31:57–61. 1967.

11872. Ovian, K. Progress through drainage. Turf Clippings. University of Massachussetts. 1(5):A–10 to A–12. 1960.

11873. ______. A question of management. Golfdom 41(4):30, 32, 94, 96. 1967.

11874. Owen, J. Maryland sod business bright. Turf-Grass Times. 1(6):10–11. 1966.

11875. Owen, J. H. Turf disease principles. Florida Turf Management Conference Proceedings. 3:25–28. 1955.

11876. ______. Symposium—trouble shooting in turf. Disease problems. Identification and control. Florida Turf Management Conference Proceedings. 3:142–145. 1955.

11877. ______. Fundamentals of turf diseases. A. Nature and cause of diseases. Florida Turf Management Conference Proceedings. 6:16–17. 1958.

11878. Owens, C. B. Sodium trichloroacetate—centipede grass killer. Weeds. 6:-174–176. 1958.

11879. Owens, O. E. Texas greens and the heat. Golf Course Reporter. 19(5):8. 1951.

11880. Owensby, C. E., G. M. Paulsen, and J. D. McKendrick. Effect of burning and clipping on big bluestem reserve carbohydrates. Journal of Range Management. 23:-358–362. 1970.

11881. Oyer, E. B. Crabgrass control in lawns. Indiana Agricultural Experiment Station Mimeo. BP51:1–2. 1952.

11882. Ozasa, S. Observation of the bermuda grass. KGU Green Section Turf Research Bulletin. 4:67–69. 1963.

11883. ______. Ears on zoysia turf. KGU Green Section Turf Research Bulletin. 9:93–95. 1965.

11884. ______. Discussion of fertilization on zoysiagrass of golf course. KGU Green Section Turf Research Bulletin. 11:-83–92. 1966.

11885. ______. Practical fertilization. K.G.U. Green Section Turf Research Bulletin. 13:75–90. 1967.

11886. Ozilins, R. The miracle of the soil. The Bull Sheet. 24(10):1. 1971.

11887. Pack, M. R. Peculiarities of New Mexico soils. New Mexico Turfgrass Conference Proceedings. 27–31 pp. 1955.

11888. Packard, E. L. Trends in car path design. Golfdom. 42(5):38–39. 1968.

11889. ______. Golf Course design principles. Illinois Turfgrass Conference Proceedings. pp. 34–40. 1969.

11890. Page, C. Lawns—the importance of initial soil preparation. Gardeners Chronicle. 163(5):21–23. 1968.

11891. ______. Lawns a selection of grasses and seed mixtures. Gardeners Chronicle. 163(6):20–23. 1968.

11892. ______. Lawns—care of young turf & annual maintenance. Gardeners Chronicle. 163(7):23–27. 1968.

11893. ______. Lawns—irrigation and renovation. Gardeners Chronicle. 163(8):21–23. 1968.

11894. Page, G. E. Soil fumigation equipment. Oregon Agricultural Experiment Station. Extension Bulletin 813. 14 p. 1963.

11895. Page, J. B. Physical soil requirements for growth of turf grasses. Proceedings of the 6th Annual Texas Turf Conference. pp. 23–31. 1951.

11897. Painter, R. H. Notes on the injury to plant cells by chinch bug feedings. Annals of the Entomology Society America. 21:232–242. 1928.

11898. Pair, C. H., W. W. Hinz, C. Reid, and K. R. Frost. Sprinkler irrigation. Sprinkler Irrigation Association, Washington, D. C. 3rd Edition. pp. 1–444. 1969.

11899. Pair, J. and R. A. Keen. Comparing percentages of green mixtures. USGA Journal and Turf Management. 15(3):26–28. 1962.

11900. Palin, R. W. Choosing the right grass for the job. The Groundsman. 15(11):-4–8. 1962.

11901. ______. Aeration and useless fibre. Turf for Sport. 4(5):10–12. 1962.

11902. Pallas, J. E., J. D. Neves, and E. R. Beaty. Light quality under saran shade cloth. Agronomy Journal. 63(4):657–658. 1971.

11903. Pallas, J. E., S. R. Wilkinson, W. G. Monson and G. W. Burton. Thermo and photoperiod effects on growth and chlorophyll concentration of *Cynodon dactylon* cultivars. Plant Physiology Abstract. 47:30. 1971.

11904. Palmer, R. D., W. G. Menn, A. C. Novosad, and J. N. Pratt. Turf—recommended practices—Texas. 25th Annual Southern Weed Science Society Research Report. pp. 116–117. 1972.

11905. Palmertree, H. D. Refertilization of established roadside slopes. Ohio Short Course on Roadside Development. 24:70–75. 1965.

11906. Palmertree, H. D. and C. Y. Ward. Mississippi turfgrass research report —1967. Southern Turfgrass Association Conference Proceedings. pp. 38–39. 1968.

11907. Palmertree, H. D., E. L. Kimbrough and C. Y. Ward. The evaluation of several sources and rate of nitrogen for fertilization of established roadside turf. Agronomy Abstracts. 58:39. 1966.

11909. Papavizas, G. C. and C. B. Davey. Saprophytic behavior of *Rhizoctonia* in soil. Phytopathology. 51(10):693–699. 1961.

11910. ______. Activity of *Rhizoctonia* in soil as affected by carbon dioxide. Phytopathology. 52(8):759–766. 1962.

11911. Parker, B. T. and C. O. Finn. Establishment of cover on poor soil and stabilization of sand through the use of vegetation mulch. Short Course on Roadside Development (Ohio). 19:80–82. 1960.

11912. Parker, C. W. A new spike roller. Greenkeepers Club of New England Newsletter. 3(2):3–4. 1931.

11913. ______. The lawn. Hale, Cushman & Flint. Boston. 118 pp. 1939.

11915. ______. Mulch use pays in modern fine turf production. Golfdom. 26(1):51–54. 1952.

11916. Parker, J. The nature of winter injury to plants. Turf Clippings. University of Massachussetts. 1(5):A–1 to A–2. 1960.

11917. Parker, J. M. and C. J. Whitfield. Ecological relationships of playa lakes in the southern great plains. Journal of the American Society of Agronomy. 33(1):125–129. 1945.

11918. Parker, J. R. Cemetery and memorial park maintenance problems. Proceedings Florida Turf-Grass Management Conference. 14:132–136. 1966.

11919. Parker, K. W. and A. W. Sampson. Influence of leafage removal on the anatomical structure of roots of *Stipa pulchra* and *Bromus hordeaceus.* Plant Physiology. 5(4):543–553. 1930.

11920. Parks, O. C., and P. R. Henderlong. Germination and seedling growth rate of ten common turfgrasses. Proceedings West Virginia Academy of Science. 39:132–140. 1967.

11921. Parks, W. L., and W. B. Fisher. Influence of soil temperature and nitrogen on ryegrass. Growth and chemical composition. Soil Science Society of America Proceedings. 22:257–259. 1958.

11928. Parnell, R. The grasses of Britain. William Blackwood and Sons, Edinburgh and London. pp. 310. 1845.

11930. Parris, G. K. Practical control of two lawn grass diseases without fungicides by removal of mower clippings. The Plant Disease Reporter. 55(9):778–779. 1971.

11931. Parrott, J. Ala.-N.W. Fla. turfmen get latest on zoysia, centipedegrass, bermudagrass field trial results. Weeds, Trees and Turf. 4(11):16–17. 1965.

11932. Parsons, J. L. and P. H. Struthers. Crownvetch in Ohio is a vigorous perennial legume. Ohio Farm and Home Research. 47:-90–91. 1962.

11933. Parsons, J. S. Fescue greens at Portland Country Club. Greenkeepers Club of New England Newsletter. 2(5):2. 1930.

11934. ______. Power cutting green mowing vs. hand mowing. Greenkeepers Club of New England Newsletter. 3(5):2–4. 1931.

11935. Parsons, M. M. PMAS on tees, my experience. Proceedings of Midwest Regional Turf Conference. pp. 78–80. 1951.

11936. Partridge, N. L. Comparative water usage and depth of rooting of some species of grass. Proceedings of the American Society for Horticultural Science. 39:426–432. 1941.

11937. Partyka, R. E. Stripe smut of Merion Kentucky bluegrass. Ohio Agricultural Research and Development Center. Research Summary No. 16. pp. 15–16. 1966.

11938. ______. Fairy rings difficult to control. Turf-Grass Times. 3(7):16. 1968.

11939. ______. Effects of soil and air temperatures on turfgrass disease development. Ohio Turfgrass Conference Proceedings. pp. 50–52. 1969.

11940. ______. Stripe smut on bluegrass. Ohio Turfgrass Foundation Newsletter. 15:-1–2. 1969.

11941. ______. Leafspot diseases on bluegrass lawns. Lakeshore News. 2(2):8. 1970.

11942. ______. Melting-out of bluegrass. Ohio Turfgrass Foundation Newsletter. 19:-5–6. 1970.

11943. ______. Disease notes. Ohio Turfgrass Foundation Newsletter. 25:3. 1971.

11944. Pass, B. C. Control of sod webworms, *Crambus teterrellus, C. trisectus,* and *C. mutabilis* in Kentucky. Journal of Economic Entomology. 59(1):19–21. 1966.

11945. Pass, B. C., R. C. Buckner, and P. R. Burrus. Differential reaction of Kentucky bluegrass strains to sod webworms. Agronomy Journal. 57(5):510–511. 1965.

11946. Pass, H. A. and B. J. Watt. Improved herbicides for weed control in turf. Proceedings of the Northeastern Weed Control Conference. 18:548–551. 1964.

11947. Pass, H. A., M. Nurse, and B. J. Watt. Weed control in turf. Proceedings of the Northeastern Weed Control Conference. 21:524–526. 1967.

11948. Patchan, G. M. Growth and development of Merion bluegrass as influenced by subsurface moisture barriers, irrigation treatment and soil mixtures. M. S. Thesis, University of Delaware. 78 pp. 1970.

11949. Pate, D. A. Weed control—modes and methods. Proceedings Second Annual Tennessee Turfgrass Conference. pp. 24–26. 1968.

11950. ______. Latest developments in weed control. Proceedings of the Texas Turfgrass Conference. 23:30–32. 1968.

11951. Patel, A. S. and J. P. Cooper. The influence of seasonal changes in light energy on leaf and tiller development in ryegrass, timothy, and meadow fescue. Journal of the British Grassland Society. 16(4):299–308. 1961.

11952. Patrick, Z. A. Phytotoxic substances associated with the decomposition in soil of plant residues. Soil Science. 111(1):-13–18. 1971.

11953. Patterson, E. Turf injections for filling depressions. Park Maintenance. 7:12–13. 1954.

11954. Patterson, J. C., and J. P. Capp. Sintered fly ash as a soil modifier. Park Maintenance. 23(7):22. 1970.

11955. Patterson, J. C., and P. R. Henderlong. Turfgrass soil modification with sintered fly ash. Proceedings of the First International Turfgrass Research Conference. pp. 161–171. 1969.

11956. Patterson, J. C., P. R. Henderlong, and L. M. Adams. Sintered fly ash as a soil modifier. Proceedings West Virginia Academy of Science. 40:151–159. 1968.

11957. Patterson, J. K. Comparative performance of the P.N.W. bluegrass selections. Proceedings Northwest Turf Conference. 12:39–41. 1958.

11958. ______. A new bluegrass variety in the making. Golf Course Reporter. 27(8):-48–49. 1959.

11959. ______. Comparative performances of bluegrasses for turf purposes. Proceedings Northwest Turf Conference. 13:79–82. 1959.

11960. Patterson, J. K. and A. G. Law. Nitrogen source test. Proceedings 14th Annual Northwest Turf Conference. 14:17–19. 1960.

11961. Pattison, E. E. Clean seeds and fewer weeds. The National Greenkeeper. 2(3):19–20. 1928.

11962. ______. Seeds for golf courses—*Agrostis vulgaris.* The National Greenkeeper. 2(5):22–23. 1928.

11963. ______. Seeds for golf courses. The National Greenkeeper. 2(6):15–16, 31. 1928.

11964. ______. Seeds for golf courses. The National Greenkeeper. 2(7):13–14. 1928.

11965. ______. Seeds for golf courses—Fescues and rye grasses. The National Greenkeeper. 2(9):22–24. 1928.

11966. ______. Grasses for Southern courses. The National Greenkeeper. 2(11):5, 6. 1928.

11967. ______. Doggone it—what is dog bent? The National Greenkeeper. 3(7):26–27. 1929.

11968. ______. Is it a racket? Greenkeepers Club of New England Newsletter. 5(5):-2–4. 1933.

11969. ______. Laboratory facts about grass and seed: selecting seed mixtures. The Modern Cemetery. 43(5):105–106. 1933.

11970. Patton, A. R. Seasonal changes in the lignin and cellulose content of some Montana grasses. Journal of Animal Science. 2(1):59–62. 1943.

11972. Paul, J. L. Reactions involving nitrogen fertilizers in soil. Proceedings of the 1972 Turf and Landscape Horticulture Institute. pp. 18–22. 1972.

11973. Paul, J. L., and J. H. Madison. Growth of 'Merion' bluegrass, *Poa pratensis* L., at different nitrogen levels, influenced by salinity and temperature. Agronomy Abstracts. 2:64. 1972.

11974. Paul, J. L., J. H. Madison, and L. Waldron. Effects of organic and inorganic amendments on the hydraulic conductivity of three sands used for turfgrass soils. Journal, Sports Turf Research Institute. 46:22–32. 1970.

11975. Paul, M. R. Fairway watering. The National Greenkeeper. 3(2):15, 42. 1929.

11976. Paulin, G. N. Soil sterilants. New Zealand Institute for Turf Culture Newsletter. 14:7–8. 1961.

11977. ———. Control of pests and diseases in turf. New Zealand Institute for Turf Culture Newsletter. 42:4–5. 1966.

11978. ———. Weed control on golf courses. New Zealand Institute for Turf Culture Newsletter. 54:5–6. 1968.

11979. Paulsen, G. M. and D. Smith. Influence of several management practices on growth characteristics and available carbohydrate content of smooth bromegrass. Agronomy Journal. 60(4):375–379. 1968.

11980. ———. Organic reserves, axillary bud activity, and herbage yields of smooth bromegrass as influenced by time of cutting, nitrogen fertilization, and shading. Crop Science. 9(5):529–534. 1969.

11981. Payne, J. D. Planting grasses vegetatively—primarily sprigging. Proceedings of University of Florida Turf-Grass Management Conference. 8:106–107. 1960.

11982. Payne, K. T. Well-organized grass projects set up at Beltsville, Penn State. Midwest Turf-News and Research. 3(2):5. 1949.

11983. ———. The turf breeding research. Proceedings of Midwest Regional Turf Conference. pp. 38–41. 1949.

11984. ———. National turf field day reported on by Payne. Midwest Turf-News and Research. 5(4):3–4. 1951.

11985. ———. Establishing bent trials at Purdue. Midwest Turf-News and Research. 6(1):1, 3. 1952.

11986. ———. The grasses and their uses. Michigan Forestry and Park Conference Proceedings. 43:18–19. 1969.

11987. ———. Developments in the ryegrasses. The Golf Superintendent. 40(7):14–16. 1972.

11988. ———. Progress in fescue varietal improvement at MSU. 42nd Annual Michigan Turfgrass Conference Proceedings. 1:7. 1972.

11989. ———. Proper selection of turfgrasses. 42nd Annual Michigan Turfgrass Conference Proceedings. 1:89–90. 1972.

11990. ———. Development of improved red fescue varieties for sod production and new Kentucky bluegrass varieties for the sod industry. 42nd Annual Michigan Turfgrass Conference Proceedings. 42(1):121–122. 1972.

11991. ———. Students—today and tomorrow. Midwest Regional Turf Conference Proceedings. pp. 9–12. 1972.

11992. ———. Selecting and improving grasses. Midwest Regional Turf Conference Proceedings. pp. 60–61. 1972.

11993. Payne, K. T. and J. M. Vargas. Improvement of turfgrass varieties. Research Report 104. Michigan State University Agricultural Experiment Station. p. 5. October, 1969.

11994. Peabody, D. V., Some promising new herbicides. Proceedings 9th Annual Northwest Turf Conference. 9:31–33. 1955.

11995. Peacock, J. F., D. M. Martin, and R. Parker. Weed control in lawns and other turf. South Dakota State University Cooperative Extension Service. F3–419. 7 pp. 1969.

11996. Pearson, G. A., and L. Bernstein. Influence of exchangeable sodium on yield and chemical composition of plants: II. Wheat, barley, oats, rice, tall fescue, and tall wheatgrass. Soil Science. 86:254–261. 1958.

11998. Peart, M. E. Chemical weed control. Seventh Annual Sports Turfgrass Conference, Ontario Agricultural College, Guelph. pp. 32–35. 1956.

12000. Peck, T. R. Effects of soil and soil mixtures on plants. Illinois Turfgrass Conference Proceedings. pp. 42–43. 1969.

12001. Peckham, R. W. Fescue rough works well to speed play. Golfdom:3(2):36. 1929.

12002. Peglau, J. T. Controlling weeds on a school ground. Proceedings of the Southern California Turfgrass Institute Conference. p. 34. 1963.

12003. Peiffer, R. A., G. W. McKee, and M. L. Risius. Germination and emergence of crownvetch as affected by seed maturity and depth of planting. Agronomy Journal. 64(6):-772–774. 1972.

12004. Pellegrino, D. The use of sod. Turf Clippings. University of Massachusetts. 1(6):A–72–75. 1961.

12005. Pellett, H. M. and E. C. Roberts. Effects of nitrogen, phosphorus and potassium on high temperature induced growth recession in Kentucky bluegrass. Agronomy Abstracts. 54:104. 1962.

12006. ______. Effects of mineral on high temperature induced growth retardation of Kentucky bluegrass. Agronomy Journal. 55(5):473–476. 1963.

12007. Pence, R. J., J. Letey, R. E. Pelishek, and J. Osborn. New aqueous resinous soil stabilizers. Florida Turfgrass Association Bulletin. 11(1):6. 1964.

12008. Pengelly, D. H. *Thymelieus lineola* (Ochs) *Lepidoptera Hesperidae* a pest of hay and pasture grasses in Southern Ontario. Proceedings of Entomology Society of Ontario. 91:189–197. 1961.

12009. Pennman, H. L. Natural evaporation from open water, bare soil, and grass. Proceedings Royal Society of London Series A. 193:120–45. 1948.

12010. Peoples, D. Soil amendments. Turf Bulletin. Massachusetts Turf and Lawn Grass Council. 4(7):19, 21–22. 1968.

12011. Peperzak, P. Correlation of selected soil indices with plant growth on highway backslopes. Iowa Highway Research Board Bulletin 10. 130 pp. 1956.

12012. Pepin, G. W. Hybridization of Kentucky bluegrass. Rutgers University short course in Turf Management. 2 pp. 1969.

12013. ______. Hybridization of Kentucky bluegrass. Rutgers University. College of Agriculture and Environmental Science. Lawn and Utility Turf Section. pp. 17–18. 1969.

12014. ______. A comparison of twenty hybrid strains of Kentucky bluegrass (*Poa pratensis* L.) with their parent varieties for a number of turf, disease, vegetative, and reproductive characteristics. M. S. Thesis, Rutgers University. 60 pp. 1970.

12015. ______. Evaluation of selected turf, reproductive, and disease response characteristics in crossed and selfed progenies of Kentucky bluegrass (*Poa pratensis* L.). Ph.D. Thesis. Rutgers University. 1971.

12016. ______. Breeding Kentucky bluegrass for powdery mildew resistance. Rutgers University Short Course in Turf Management Proceedings. pp. 52–54. 1971.

12017. Pepin, G. W. and C. R. Funk. Performance of selected intraspecific hybrids of Kentucky bluegrass (*Poa pratensis* L.). Agronomy Abstracts. p. 71. 1970.

12018. ______. Evaluation of selfed and crossed progenies of Kentucky bluegrass for turf potential. Agronomy Abstracts. p. 49. 1971.

12019. ______. Intraspecific hybridization as a method of breeding Kentucky bluegrass (*Poa pratensis* L.) for turf. Crop Science. 11(3):445–448. 1971.

12020. Pepin, G. W., C. R. Funk, and S. J. Han. Breeding turf-type Kentucky bluegrass (*Poa pratensis* L.) by intraspecific hybridization. Agronomy Abstracts. 61:56. 1969.

12021. Pepper, E. H. Nematodes associated with melting-out of turfgrass. The Plant Disease Reporter. 49(6):519–521. 1965.

12023. Pepper, J. O. Standard methods for control of turf insects. The Pennsylvania State College Eighteenth Annual Turf Conference. pp. 40–43. 1949.

12024. ______. New materials for insect control. The Pennsylvania State College Eighteenth Annual Turf Conference. pp. 77–82. 1949.

12025. ______. Control of turf insects. Pennsylvania State College Turfgrass Conference Proceedings. 21:65–67. 1952.

12026. ______. Injurious insects of turf grasses. Handbook on Lawns. Brooklyn Botanic Garden. pp. 117–121. 1956.

12027. Percival, J. Agricultural botany —theoretical and practical. Henry Holt and Company, New York. 806 pp. 1908.

12029. Perkins, A. T. Effective turfgrass weed control. University of Maine Turf Conference Proceedings. 6:16–21. 1968.

12030. ______. Soil modification research at Penn State. University of Maine Turf Conference Proceedings. 6:25–31. 1968.

12031. Perkins, A. T., J. M. Duich and D. V. Waddington. Pre and postemergence crabgrass control results for 1967 and 1968. Proceedings of the Northeastern Weed Control Conference. p. 391–397. 1969.

12032. Perkins, A. T. Effective turfgrass weed control. USGA Green Section Record. 6(1):11–15. 1968.

12033. Perkins, W. E. Maintenance of college sports fields. Greenkeepers Club of New England Newsletter. 7(7):3–4, 6, 8. 1935.

12035. Perron, W. H. Melanges a gazon. Agriculture (Montreal). 18(2):49–52. 1961.

12036. Perry, A. W. Pipe talk. International Turfgrass Conference & Show. 39:65–67. 1968.

12037. Perry, R. Symposium—lawn maintenance problems Soil preparation and planting. Florida Turf Management Conference Proceedings. 3:78–81. 1955.

12039. Perry, R. M. Standardized wear index for turfgrasses. Southern California Turfgrass Culture. 8(4):30–31. 1958.

12040. Perry, V. G. Return of nematodes following fumigation of Florida soils. Proceedings of the Florida State Horticulture Society. 66:112–113. 1953.

12041. ______. The awl nematode, *Dolichodorus heterocephalus* a devastating plant parasite. Proceedings of the Helminthological Society. 20(1):21–27. 1953.

12042. ______. A disease of Kentucky bluegrass incited by certain spiral nematodes. Phytopathology. 48(3):397. 1958.

12043. ______. Progress on nematode control. Proceedings of University of Florida Turf-Grass Management Conference. 7:101–104. 1959.

12044. ______. Nematode control. Proceedings of University of Florida Turf-Grass Management Conference. 8:122–123. 1960.

12045. ______. Nematicides and their recommended usage in turf. Proceedings of University of Florida Turf-Grass Management Conference. 9:161–162. 1961.

12046. ______. What are nematodes. Proceedings of Florida Turf-Grass Management Conference. 10:20–22. 1962.

12047. ______. Recommendations for turf nematode control. Proceedings of Florida Turf-Grass Management Conference. 11:119–120. 1963.

12048. ______. Nematode studies, north Florida. Proceedings of the Florida Turfgrass Management Conference. 12:146–147. 1964.

12049. ______. Turf nematode research-Gainsville. Proceedings of the Florida Turf-Grass Management Conference. 13:142–144. 1965.

12050. ______. Nematodes are a major nemesis to quality turf: damage costly. Turf-Grass Times. 1(2):1, 7, 8, 11. 1965.

12053. ______. Developments in nematode control. Florida Turfgrass Management Conference Proceedings. 19:118–120. 1971.

12054. Perry, V. G., and G. C. Horn. The nematode parasites of warm-season turfgrasses. Proceedings of the First International Turfgrass Research Conference. pp. 330–336. 1969.

12055. Perry, V. G. and K. M. Maur. The pseudo—root—knot nematode of turfgrasses. Florida Turf. 1(1):3, 8. 1968.

12056. ______. Pseudo root-knot nematode of turf grasses. The Golf Superintendent. 37(10):30–32. 1969.

12057. Perry, V. G., and G. C. Smart. Turf nematode problems in Florida. Florida Turf-Grass Association Bulletin. 12(2):4–6. 1965.

12058. ______. Developments in nematode control. Proceedings, Florida Turfgrass Management Conference. 15:100–101. 1967.

12059. Perry, V. G. and J. A. Winchester. Developments in nematode control. Proceedings of Florida Turf-Grass Management Conference. 17:88–90. 1969.

12060. Perry, V. G., H. M. Darling, and G. Thorne. Anatomy, taxonomy, and control of certain spiral nematodes attacking bluegrass in Wisconsin. Wisconsin Agricultural Experiment Station Research Bulletin. 24 pp. 1959.

12061. Perry, V. G., G. C. Smart, and G. C. Horn. Nematode control on golf courses by injected DBCP. Journal of Nematology. 3(4):324. 1971.

12062. Perry, V. G., J. A. Winchester, and G. C. Smart. Control of nematodes on turf. Proceedings, Florida Turfgrass Management Conference. 16:82–84. 1968.

12063. Perry, W. E. Athletic field improvement. Greenkeepers' Reporter. 17(3):-10. 1949.

12064. Persson, S. Seed production for turf areas. Weibulls Gräs Tips. pp. 20–21. 1971.

12065. Pessner, B. Solving problems on athletic turf. Proceedings Northern California Turfgrass Institute. pp. 19–20. 1961.

12066. Peto, F. H. The cytology of certain intergeneric hybrids between *Festuca* and *Lolium.* Journal of Genetics. 28(1):113–157. 1934.

12067. Peters, D. Earthworms and their control. The Groundsman. 16(8):18–24. 1963.

12068. Peters, D. B. Water use by plants. Turf Bulletin. Massachusetts Turf and Lawn Grass Council. 4(8):28–30. 1968.

12069. Peters, E. J., and S. A. Lowance. Establishment of crownvetch with herbicides. Agronomy Journal. 63(2):230–232. 1971.

12070. Peters, E. J., J. F. Stritzke, and F. S. Davis. Wild garlic its characteristics and control. Missouri Agricultural Experiment Station, Agricultural Handbook No. 298. pp. 1–22. 1965.

12071. Peters, R. A. Control of weeds in home lawns. Connecticut Agricultural College Extension Bulletin. 61–7. 1962.

12072. ______. Crabgrass—a successful weed. New England Agricultural Chemicals Conference and Herbicide Workshop. 1:25–26. 1964.

12073. Peters, R. A., H. C. Yokum, and K. C. Stevens. Observations on chemical control of crabgrass in turf (1961). Proceedings of the Northeastern Weed Control Conference. 16:519–523. 1962.

12075. Petersen, F. H. Equipment for metering liquid fertilizers. Proceedings of Turf, Tree Landscape, and Nursery Conference. pp. 16–1 to 16–3. 1966.

12076. ______. Fertilizer injection and distribution through sprinkler irrigation systems. Proceedings Annual Turfgrass Sprinkler Irrigation Conference. 6:12–17. 1968.

12077. Petersen, G. W., R. L. Cunningham, and R. P. Matelski. Moisture characteristics of Pennsylvania soils: I. Moisture retention as related to texture. Soil Science Society of America Proceedings. 32:271–275. 1968.

12078. Petersen, L. J. Patterns of turfgrass disease. California Turfgrass Culture. 11(4):30–32. 1961.

12079. ______. Patterns of turfgrass disease. Proceedings Northern California Turfgrass Institute. pp. 6–9. 1961.

12080. ______. The preventive program in controlling turf diseases. California Turfgrass Culture. 19(1):8. 1969.

12081. Peterson, D. A. Ureaform in turf management. Seventeenth R.C.G.A. Sports Turfgrass Conference. pp. 69–73. 1966.

12082. Peterson, D. R. Progress report of the pearlwot control project at the Western Washington Experiment Station. Proceedings 7th Annual Northwest Turf Conference. 7:11–15. 1953.

12083. ______. Sodium arsenite and organic mixed for pearlwort control. Golfdom. 28(5):40, 56. 1954.

12085. Peterson, L., J. H. Madison, and T. Kono. The incidence of pink snowmold on Seaside and Highland bentgrasses as influenced by irrigation practice and fertility levels. Agronomy Abstracts. 51:90–91. 1959.

12086. Peterson, M. Possibilities of reclaimed water for turf irrigation. Missouri Lawn and Turf Conference Proceedings. 12:-56–59. 1971.

12087. Peterson, M. L. Physiological response of Kentucky bluegrass to different management treatments. Ph.D. Thesis, Iowa State College. 87 pp. 1946.

12088. ______. The role of the university in California turfgrass culture. Proceedings of Turf, Nursery, and Landscape Tree Conference. pp. 5–1 to 5–4. 1964.

12089. Peterson, M. L. and W. E. Loomis. Effects of photoperiod and temperature on growth and flowering of Kentucky bluegrass. Plant Physiology. 24(1):31–43. 1949.

12090. Peterson, M. L., J. P. Cooper, and L. E. Bendixen. Thermal and photoperiodic induction of flowering in Darnel *(Lolium temulantum).* Crop Science. 1(1):17–20. 1961.

12091. Peterson, R. J. Seed production. Turf Clippings. University of Massachusetts. 3(3):A41–44. 1968.

12092. Petrie, A. H. K. and J. G. Wood. Studies on the nitrogen metabolism of plants. I. The relation between the content of proteins, amino-acids, and water in the leaves. Annals of Botany N.S. 2(5):33–60. 1938.

12093. Pettit, R. H. Insects infesting golf courses and lawns. Michigan Agricultural Extension Bulletin. 125:1–11. 1932.

12094. Petty, H. B. Insect identification and control. Illinois Turfgrass Conference Proceedings. 1:36–39. 1960.

12095. ______. Turf insects of 1961. Illinois Turfgrass Conference Proceedings. 2:-17–20. 1961.

12096. Pew, W. D. Whats in the bag. Proceedings of the Arizona Turfgrass Conference. pp. 24–27. 1954.

12097. Phelps, R. M. ABC's of course landscaping. The Golf Superintendent. 39(4):35–37. 1971.

12098. ______. Trends in building new and remodeling old golf courses. Annual Rocky Mountain Regional Turfgrass Conference Proceedings. 18:65–68. 1972.

12101. Philipson, W. R. A revision of the British species of the genus *Agrostis* Linn Journal of the Linnean Society of London. 51:73–151. 1937.

12102. Phillippe, P. M. Effects of some essential elements on the growth and development of Kentucky bluegrass *(Poa pratensis).* The Ohio State University Press. Abs. of Doctoral Dissertations. 39:295–302. 1943.

12103. Phillips, C. E. Lawns. Delaware Agricultural Extension Mimeographed Circular. 50:1–3. 1948.

12104. ______. The use of vegetative characteristics in grass identification. Proceedings of the Northeastern Weed Control Conference. 15:1–4. 1961.

12105. ______. Some grasses of the Northeast. Delaware Agricultural Experiment Station Field Manual No. 2. 77 pp. 1962.

12106. ______. Chemical control of crabgrass in lawn turf. Proceedings of the Northeastern Weed Control Conference. 17:-485–489. 1963.

12108. Phillips, H. E. Overseeding panel: ryegrass. Proceedings Florida Turf-Grass Management Conference. 14:77–78. 1966.

12109. Phillips, J. S. Drainage. Proceedings of the Mid-Atlantic Association of Golf Course Superintendents. pp. 34–37. 1954.

12110. Phillips, T. G., J. T. Sullivan, M. E. Longhlin, V. G. Sprague Chemical composition of some forage grasses. Agronomy Journal. 46(8):361–369. 1954.

12111. Phillips, W. R. Cost to maintain athletic fields. Exposition Conference, Southern California. 3 pp. 1966.

12112. Pickett, R. C. Building towards better grasses. Proceedings of the Midwest Regional Turf Conference. pp. 56–58. 1956.

12113. ______. Improving bluegrasses. Proceedings of Midwest Regional Turf Conference. pp. 31–33. 1958.

12114. Pickett, W. F. The Central Plains Turf Foundation. Golf Course Reporter. 21(5):27–28. 1953.

12115. Picot, A. J. Use for sprays on golf courses. New Zealand Institute for Turf Culture Newsletter. 48:12. 1967.

12116. Pierce, L. T. Estimating seasonal and short-term fluctuations in evapo-transpiration from meadow crops. Bulletin of the American Meteorological Society. 39(2):73–78. 1958.

12117. Pierre, W. H. Nitrogenous fertilizers and soil acidity I. Effect of various nitrogenous fertilizers on soil reaction. Journal of the American Society of Agronomy. 20(3):254. 1928.

12118. ______. The equivalent acidity or basicity of fertilizers as determined by a newly proposed method. Journal of Associa-

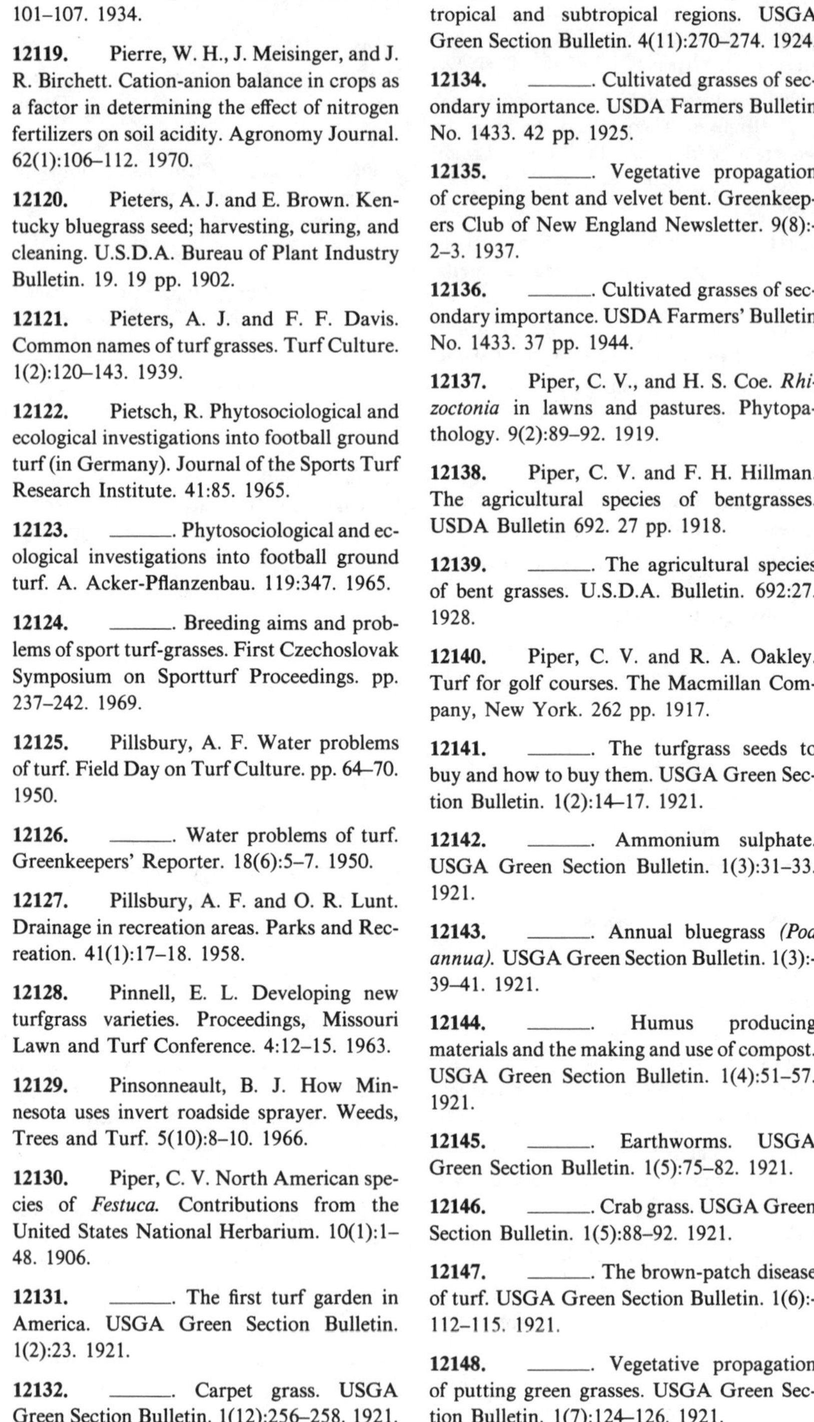

tion of Official Agricultural Chemists. 17:-101–107. 1934.

12119. Pierre, W. H., J. Meisinger, and J. R. Birchett. Cation-anion balance in crops as a factor in determining the effect of nitrogen fertilizers on soil acidity. Agronomy Journal. 62(1):106–112. 1970.

12120. Pieters, A. J. and E. Brown. Kentucky bluegrass seed; harvesting, curing, and cleaning. U.S.D.A. Bureau of Plant Industry Bulletin. 19. 19 pp. 1902.

12121. Pieters, A. J. and F. F. Davis. Common names of turf grasses. Turf Culture. 1(2):120–143. 1939.

12122. Pietsch, R. Phytosociological and ecological investigations into football ground turf (in Germany). Journal of the Sports Turf Research Institute. 41:85. 1965.

12123. ______. Phytosociological and ecological investigations into football ground turf. A. Acker-Pflanzenbau. 119:347. 1965.

12124. ______. Breeding aims and problems of sport turf-grasses. First Czechoslovak Symposium on Sportturf Proceedings. pp. 237–242. 1969.

12125. Pillsbury, A. F. Water problems of turf. Field Day on Turf Culture. pp. 64–70. 1950.

12126. ______. Water problems of turf. Greenkeepers' Reporter. 18(6):5–7. 1950.

12127. Pillsbury, A. F. and O. R. Lunt. Drainage in recreation areas. Parks and Recreation. 41(1):17–18. 1958.

12128. Pinnell, E. L. Developing new turfgrass varieties. Proceedings, Missouri Lawn and Turf Conference. 4:12–15. 1963.

12129. Pinsonneault, B. J. How Minnesota uses invert roadside sprayer. Weeds, Trees and Turf. 5(10):8–10. 1966.

12130. Piper, C. V. North American species of *Festuca.* Contributions from the United States National Herbarium. 10(1):1–48. 1906.

12131. ______. The first turf garden in America. USGA Green Section Bulletin. 1(2):23. 1921.

12132. ______. Carpet grass. USGA Green Section Bulletin. 1(12):256–258. 1921.

12133. ______. Golf course grasses in tropical and subtropical regions. USGA Green Section Bulletin. 4(11):270–274. 1924.

12134. ______. Cultivated grasses of secondary importance. USDA Farmers Bulletin No. 1433. 42 pp. 1925.

12135. ______. Vegetative propagation of creeping bent and velvet bent. Greenkeepers Club of New England Newsletter. 9(8):-2–3. 1937.

12136. ______. Cultivated grasses of secondary importance. USDA Farmers' Bulletin No. 1433. 37 pp. 1944.

12137. Piper, C. V., and H. S. Coe. *Rhizoctonia* in lawns and pastures. Phytopathology. 9(2):89–92. 1919.

12138. Piper, C. V. and F. H. Hillman. The agricultural species of bentgrasses. USDA Bulletin 692. 27 pp. 1918.

12139. ______. The agricultural species of bent grasses. U.S.D.A. Bulletin. 692:27. 1928.

12140. Piper, C. V. and R. A. Oakley. Turf for golf courses. The Macmillan Company, New York. 262 pp. 1917.

12141. ______. The turfgrass seeds to buy and how to buy them. USGA Green Section Bulletin. 1(2):14–17. 1921.

12142. ______. Ammonium sulphate. USGA Green Section Bulletin. 1(3):31–33. 1921.

12143. ______. Annual bluegrass *(Poa annua).* USGA Green Section Bulletin. 1(3):-39–41. 1921.

12144. ______. Humus producing materials and the making and use of compost. USGA Green Section Bulletin. 1(4):51–57. 1921.

12145. ______. Earthworms. USGA Green Section Bulletin. 1(5):75–82. 1921.

12146. ______. Crab grass. USGA Green Section Bulletin. 1(5):88–92. 1921.

12147. ______. The brown-patch disease of turf. USGA Green Section Bulletin. 1(6):-112–115. 1921.

12148. ______. Vegetative propagation of putting green grasses. USGA Green Section Bulletin. 1(7):124–126. 1921.

12149. ______. Turf for golf courses. The MacMillan Company, New York. pp. 1–262. 1923.

12150. ______. Canada bluegrass *(Poa compressa).* USGA Green Section Bulletin. 3(1):14. 1923.

12151. ______. Annual bluegrass *(Poa annua).* USGA Green Section Bulletin. 7(7):-128–129. 1927.

12152. Piper, C. V. and W. E. Stokes. Centipede grass. *(Eremochloa ophiuroides).* USGA Green Section Bulletin. 5(9):196–197. 1925.

12153. Piper, C. V., R. A. Oakley, and L. Carrier. Seeds and seeding for new greens and new fairways: What the Green Section recommends. USGA Green Section Bulletin. 3(6):159–161. 1923.

12154. Pirone, P. P. Diseases of turf. Proceedings of Southeastern New York Turf School. pp. 28–32. 1950.

12155. Pitblado, R. E. and L. V. Edgington. Movement of benomyl in field soils as influenced by acid surfactants. Phytopathology. 62(5):513–516. 1972.

12156. Pittuck, B. C. Grasses and forage plants. Texas Agricultural Experiment Station Bulletin No. 46:1009–1030. 1898.

12157. Plemmons, B. The ideal golf course, according to the professional. Proceedings University of Florida Turf-Grass Management Conference. 9:66–67. 1961.

12158. Plent, R. A. Experiments with creeping bent for cemetery lawns. The Modern Cemetery. 48(7):126–127. 1938.

12159. Plummer, A. P. The germination and early seedling development of twelve range grasses. Journal of the American Society of Agronomy. 35(1):19–34. 1943.

12160. Plummer, R. Construction changes give Texas good bent greens. Golfdom. 23(2):50, 52. 1949.

12161. Pocklington, T. W. The color variations of bentgrass varieties as affected by iron and magnesium. M. S. Thesis, University of Illinois. 1968.

12162. Pohjakallio, O. and S. Antila On the effect of removal of shoots on the drought resistance of red clover and timothy. Acta Agricultura Scandinavica. 5:239–244. 1955.

12163. Pohl, R. W. A taxonomic study on the grasses of Pennsylvania. The American Midland Naturalist. 38(3):513–604. 1947.

12164. Poincelot, R. P. The fundamentals of composting. The Greenmaster. 8(11):3, 5–12. 1972.

12165. Pokorny, F. A. Pine bark in the soil improves turf quality. Geoigia Agricultural Research. 11(1):5–6. 1969.

12166. ______. Growth and cold tolerance of Tifgreen bermudagrass. USGA Green Section. 9(1):9–11. 1971.

12167. Poland, T. C. and F. L. Howard. 1959 turf disease studies. Park Maintenance. 13(5):44–46. 1960.

12168. Polivka, J. B. Comparative initial effect of insecticides in control of Japanese beetle grub. Journal Economic Entomology. 43(6):936. 1950.

12169. ______. Effect of insecticides upon earthworm population. Ohio Journal of Science. 51(4):195–196. 1951.

12170. ______. The relation of soil pH to Japanese beetle larval populations. Agronomy Abstracts. p. 41. 1952.

12171. ______. Field test of insecticides for control of Japanese beetle larvae. Journal Economic Entomology. 45(2):251–254. 1952.

12172. ______. Control of the northern masked chafer with aldrin and dieldrin. Journal Economic Entomology. 45(2):347–348. 1952.

12173. ______. Residual effectiveness of some organic insecticides in control of Japanese beetle larvae. Journal Economic Entomology. 46(3):517–519. 1953.

12174. ______. Control of Japanese beetle larvae with isodrin and endrin. Journal Economic Entomology. 47(4):707. 1954.

12175. ______. Japanese beetles are now found in 56 of Ohio's counties. Ohio Farm and Home Research. 39(289):56, 61. 1954.

12176. ______. Lawn insects and their control. Pesticide News. 7:2. 1954.

12177. ______. Chlordane applications help reduce damage to bentgrass. Ohio Farm and Home Research. 40(294):43. 1955.

12178. ______. Biology and control of turf grubs. Ohio Agricultural Experiment Station Research Bulletin. 829:1–30. 1959.

12179. ______. Control of the hairy chinch bug, *Blissus leucopterus hirtus,* Mont., in Ohio. Ohio Agricultural Experiment Station Research Circular 122. 8 pp. 1963.

12180. ______. Billbug control in grasses. Ohio Lawn and Ornamental Day. pp. 14–15. 1963.

12181. ______. Effectiveness of insecticides for the control of white grubs in turf. Ohio Agricultural Research Development Center Research Circular 140. 8 pp. 1965.

12182. ______. Turf insect control. Ohio Agricultural Research and Development Center Research Summary 6. pp. 25–26. 1965.

12183. ______. Turf insect problems. Lawn and Ornamental Research—1966. Ohio Agricultural Research and Development Center. Research Summary 16. p. 11. 1966.

12184. Polivka, J. B. and T. M. Stockdale. Eliminate the mole from lawns. Ohio Agricultural Experiment Station Published Series. 26:1–3. 1961.

12185. Polon, J. A. Improvement of soil properties may help. Park Maintenance. 16(8):18–20. 1963.

12186. Ponnamperuma, F. N. The chemistry of submerged soils. Advances in Agronomy. 24:29–96. 1972.

12187. Pool, R. J. Marching with the grasses. University of Nebraska Press. Lincoln, Nebraska. 210 pp. 1948.

12188. Pooley, S. G. Use of tensiometers in turfgrass irrigation. Proceedings Annual Turfgrass Sprinkler Irrigation Conference. 6:10–11. 1968.

12189. Pollock, R. F. Care of turf for future use. Greenkeeper's Reporter. 11(2):31, 40. 1943.

12190. Poore, J. E. Rodent control. Southwest Turf Conference Proceedings. pp. 62–63. 1948.

12191. Pope, T. E. and P. Gray. Establishing and maintaining turf on Kentucky athletic fields, school grounds, and other recreational areas. University of Kentucky, Cooperative Extension Service Bulletin 609. 1966.

12192. Porter, C. D., and A. W. Selders. Selection, application techniques, and calibration of sprayers. West Virginia Turfgrass Conference Proceedings. pp. 37–49. 1968.

12193. Porter, H. L. Rhizomes in tall fescue. Agronomy Journal. 50(8):493–494. 1958.

12194. ______. Pesticides regulations in Ohio. Ohio Turfgrass Conference Proceedings. pp. 4–5. 1970.

12195. Porter, R. H. Weed control in golf greens and fairways. Greenkeepers Club of New England Newsletter. 6(7):4, 6–8, 10. 1934.

12196. ______. Diseases of golf grasses. Greenkeepers Club of New England Newsletter. 8(9):8–10. 1936.

12197. ______. Experiments with modified techniques for the determination of purity and viability of bluegrass seed, *Poa pratensis* L. Iowa Agricultural Experiment Station Research Bulletin. 235:91–111. 1938.

12198. Porterfield, H. G. Survival of buffalo grass following submersion in playas. Ecology. 26(1):98–100. 1945.

12199. Portz, H. L. Frost heaving of soil and plants. I. Incidence of frost heaving of forage plants and meteorological relationships. Agronomy Journal. 59(4):341–344. 1967.

12201. Postlethwait, S. N. Grass leaves at work. Proceedings of the Midwest Regional Turf Conference. pp. 5–8. 1954.

12202. Potatosova, E. G. Conditions of germination of the sclerotia of the fungi of the genus *Typhula.* Zashch. Rast. Moskva 4:40. 1960.

12203. Potts, R. C. Grass identification. Proceedings of the Texas Turfgrass Conference Proceedings. 12:29–31. 1957.

12204. ______. Professional training in recreation and parks. Proceedings of the Texas Turfgrass Conference. 20:24. 1965.

12206. Powell, A. J. Physiological and color aspects of cool season turfgrasses with fall and winter nitrogen fertilization. Ph.D. Thesis, Virginia Polytechnic Institute. 92 pp. 1967.

12207. ______. "Turf"—The anti-pollutant. The Bull Sheet. 24(6):5. 1970.

12208. ______. Bent roots. Golf Superintendent. 38(1):106. 1970.

12209. ______. Review of the seasonal problems. Proceedings of the Mid-Atlantic Association of Golf Course Superintendents. pp. 4–5. 1970.

12210. ______. Tall fescue management for athletic fields. Park Maintenance. 23(7):-22. 1970.

12211. ______. Accumulation of crabgrass pre-emergence herbicides in soils. Park Maintenance. 23(7):26. 1970.

12212. ______. Proper turf maintenance lessens disease severity. Turf-grass Times. 5(6):4. 1970.

12213. ______. "Turf"—The anti-pollutant. Seed World. 107(7):21. 1970.

12214. ______. Manicuring course or cost. The Bull Sheet. 24(8):5–6. 1971.

12215. ______. Control of turf weeds—control of perennial grasses and sedges. Rutgers University Short Course in Turf Management Proceedings. pp. 33–35. 1971.

12216. ______. Turf management. quackgrass (*Agropyron repens* L. Beauv.) Turf Bulletin. Massachusetts Turf and Lawn Grass Council. 7(3):14–15. 1971.

12217. ______. Turf management. A Patch of Green. Michigan and Border Cities GCSA Publication. pp. 7–11. March, 1972.

12218. Powell, A. J. and G. Bean. Turf diseases. Grounds Maintenance. 6(8):5–6. 1971.

12219. Powell, A. J. and W. H. McKee. Effect of different nitrogen sources on winter and spring response of cool season grass. Agronomy Abstracts. p. 46. 1965.

12220. Powell, A. J., R. E. Blaser, and R. E. Schmidt. Physiological and color aspects of turfgrasses with fall and winter nitrogen. Agronomy Journal. 59(4):303–307. 1967.

12221. ______. Effect of nitrogen on winter root growth of bentgrass. Agronomy Journal. 59(6):529–530. 1967.

12222. Powell, J. B. and G. W. Burton. Fragment accessory chromosomes in *Cynodon.* Agronomy Abstracts. 58:13. 1966.

12223. ______. Gamma-ray induced mutants in vegetatively propagated turf bermudagrass. Agronomy Abstracts. p. 49. 1971.

12224. Powell, J. B., and F. V. Juska. The prediction of thatch accumulation in the breeding improvement of turfgrass cultivars. Agronomy Abstracts. 2:64. 1972.

12225. Powell, J. B., I. Forbes and G. W. Burton. A *Cynodon dactylon* (L.) Pers. (bermudagrass) clone with five accessory chromosomes. Crop Science. 8(2):267–268. 1968.

12226. Powell, N. T. The role of plant-parasitic nematodes in fungus diseases. Phytopathology. 53(1):28–34. 1963.

12227. Powell, R. H. and A. W. Vink. The measurement of turf growth by photography and microscopy. The Journal of the Sports Turf Research Institute. 45:49–54. 1969.

12228. Powell, W. M. The occurrence of *Tylenchorhynchus maximus* in Georgia. Plant Disease Reporter. 48(1)70. 1964.

12229. ______. Are you sure your course is nematode-free? USGA Green Section Record. 11(1):6–8. 1973.

12230. Power, J. F., D. L. Grunes, G. A. Reichman, and W. W. Willis. Soil temperature effects on phosphorus availability. Agronomy Journal. 56(6):545–548. 1964.

12231. Power, J. F. Effect of moisture on fertilizer nitrogen immobilization in grasslands. Soil Science Society of America Proceedings. 31:223–226. 1967.

12233. Power, R. E. What golf rules affect the greenkeeper. The National Greenkeeper. 1(1):20–21. 1927.

12234. Prasad, R., C. L. Foy, and A. S. Crafts. Effects of relative humidity on absorption and translocation of foliarly applied Dalapon. Weeds. 15(2):149–156. 1967.

12235. Prasad, R., G. B. Rajale, and B. A. Lakhdive. Nitrification retarders and slow-release nitrogen fertilizers. Advances in Agronomy. 23:337–383. 1971.

12237. Pratt, H. B. Golf carts traffic control and twelve months of grass. USGA Green Section Record. 6(1):5–7. 1968.

12239. Presny, R. W. Home lawns, meeting the needs of urban clients. Wisconsin

Turfgrass Conference Proceedings. 3 pp. 1965.

12240. Pressler, J. Seeded greens at the Allegheny Country Club. USGA Green Section Bulletin. 8(9):184. 1928.

12241. Preston, J. I. The grass tennis court. Parks, Golf Courses & Sports Grounds. 20:501–504. 1955.

12242. ______. Bowling greens: construction and maintenance part I. Parks, Golf Courses & Sports Grounds. 20:640–683. 1955.

12243. ______. Bowling greens: construction and maintenance. Part II. Parks, Golf Courses & Sports Grounds. 20(11):706–708, 727. 1955.

12244. Preyde, J. M. Hako-ett Märke-ett Begrepp. Weibulls Gräs Tips. pp. 85–86. 1961.

12245. Pretty, K. M. Balanced nutrition for quality turf. R.C.G.A. National Turf Conference. 22:37–42. 1971.

12246. Price, B. Perhaps golf can foster world peace. Turf Bulletin. Massachusetts Turf & Lawn Grass Council. 4(3):28. 1967.

12247. Price, E. G. and W. W. Huffine. Effect of three growth regulants on three turf-type bermudagrasses. Agronomy Abstracts. 59:57. 1967.

12248. Pride, R. E. and A. W. Biocourt. For a better lawn. Massachusetts Agricultural Extension Leaflet. 279:1–8. 1955.

12249. Pridham, A. M. S. 2, 4–Dichlorophenoxyacetic acid reduces germination of grass seed. Proceedings of the American Society for Horticultural Science. 47:439–445. 1946.

12250. ______. The effect of 2,4–Dichlorophenoxyacetic acid applied at the time of seed germination in reducing stands of annual grasses. Proceedings of the American Society for Horticultural Science. 49:-355–358. 1947.

12251. ______. The effect of 2,4–D applied at the time of seed germination in reducing stand of annual grasses. The Greenkeepers' Reporter. 15(4):11–13. 1947.

12252. Pridham, A. M. S. and J. F. Cornman. 2,4–D and weed free lawns. Cornell Agricultural Extension Bulletin. 698:1–4. 1946.

12253. Pridham, A. M. S., P. B. Kaufman, and E. B. Wahlgren. Low pressure, low volume spray equipment for applying 2,4–D and other herbicides to turf. Northeastern Weed Control Conference Proceedings. 1949.

12254. Prince, F. S. Lawns their building and maintenance. New Hampshire Agricultural Extension Circular. 177:1–11. 1936.

12255. Prine, G. M., and G. W. Burton. The effect of nitrogen rate and clipping frequency upon the yield protein content and certain morphological characteristics of coastal bermudagrass. Agronomy Journal. 48(7):296–301. 1956.

12256. Pritchett, W. L. Fertilizer materials for turf. Florida Turf Management Conference Proceedings. 3:15–19. 1955.

12257. ______. Understanding the fertilizer tag. Florida Turf Management Conference Proceedings. 4:103–107. 1956.

12258. Pritchett, W. L., G. C. Nutter and R. W. White. The relationship of fertilization practices to soil fertility conditions under putting greens. Florida Turf Management Conference Proceedings. 5:48–54. 1957.

12259. Pritchett, W. L. Progress in fertilizer materials. Florida Turf Management Conference Proceedings. 6:113–117. 1958.

12260. ______. New fertilizer materials. Golf Course Reporter. 27(7):18–24. 1959.

12261. ______. Nitrogen alone is not enough. Proceedings of University of Florida Turf-Grass Management Conference. 9:33–40. 1961.

12262. ______. Relationship of water and turf disorders: fertilizers. Proceedings of the Florida Turfgrass Management Conference. 13:42–46. 1965.

12263. ______. Some soil-fertilizer relationships. Proceedings of the Florida Turf-Grass Management Conference. 14:38–42. 1966.

12264. Pritchett, W. L. and C. F. Eno. Is a soil nitrogen test of value in Florida? Sunshine State Agricultural Research Report. 6(2):9–10. 1961.

12265. Pritchett, W. L. and G. C. Horn. Turf fertilization research. Florida Turf Management Conference Proceedings. 10:-209–215. 1962.

12266. ______. Dry application of pesticides and fertilizers. Proceedings of Florida Turf-Grass Management Conference. 11:-121–127. 1963.

12267. ______. Research on turf fertilization. Proceedings of Florida Turf-Grass Management Conference. 11:159–163. 1963.

12268. ______. Fertilization fights turf disorders. Better Crops with Plant Food. 50(3):22–25. 1966.

12269. Pritchett, W. L. and J. Nesmith. Incorporating fertilization into an existing spraying program. Proceedings of Florida Turf-Grass Management Conference. 10:-155–159. 1962.

12270. Proctor, G. Selecting soils and fumigation. Proceedings of the 20th Annual Northwest Turfgrass Conference. pp. 81–82. 1966.

12271. Proctor, J. M. Rotary cultivation for the control of rhizomatous grass weeds. British Weed Control Conference Proceedings. 5(1):265–269. 1960.

12272. Protsenko, E. P. New case of joint infection of grasses by fungi and nematodes. Bulletin of Botanical Garden of Moscow. 29:-91–93. 1958.

12273. Pruett, L. J. Presurface applications of herbicides for highways. Down to Earth. 17(3):11–12. 1961.

12274. Pruitt, W. O. Correlation of evapotranspiration with evaporation from pans and atmometers. Correlation of climatological data with water requirements of crops 1959–60. Department of Irrigation Annual Report. University of California. Davis. pp. 29–39. 1960.

12275. ______. Evapotranspiration—a guide to irrigation. California Turfgrass Culture. 14(4):27–32. 1964.

12276. ______. Evapotranspiration—a guide to irrigation. Proceedings of Turf, Nursey, and Landscape Tree Conference. pp. 2–1 to 2–10. 1964.

12277. Pryor, M. R. The chemical control of puncture vine. California Turfgrass Culture. 13(4):29–31. 1963.

12278. Ptacek, J. J. and E. C. Roberts. Pre-emergence crabgrass control aided by Iowa State testing results. Park Maintenance. 15(4):22–28. 1962.

12279. Pumphrey, F. V. Fertilizing Kentucky bluegrass and fine fescue for seed production in Northeastern Oregon. Oregon Agricultural Experiment Station. Bulletin 601. 15 pp. 1965.

12280. Purdy, H. C. Weed control in Canada. Greenkeepers' Reporter. 9(3):19–22. 1941.

12281. ______. The arsenicals for curbing clover and weeds. The Greenkeeper's Reporter. 14(4):15–17. 1946.

12282. Pursley, W. Symposium—turf nursery production problems. Part V. Marketing and merchandising. Florida Turf Management Conference Proceedings. 3:76–77. 1955.

12283. Putnam, A. R., and S. K. Ries. Factors influencing the phytotoxicity and movement of paraquat in quackgrass. Weed Science. 16(1):80–83. 1968.

12284. Putnam, K. Fairway renovation. Northwest Turf Conference Proceedings. 11:21–24. 1957.

12285. ______. Fairway renovation at Seattle golf club. USGA Journal and Turf Management. 11(4):25–27. 1958.

12286. ______. Thoughts on disease control. Proceedings of the 20th Annual Northwest Turfgrass Conference. pp. 44–45. 1966.

12287. ______. Sub grades for putting greens. Proceedings of the 20th Annual Northwest Turfgrass Conference. p. 80. 1966.

12288. Pyenson, L. How to keep the lawn healthy. Keep Your Garden Healthy. E. P. Dutton and Co., Inc. New York. pp. 108–131. 1964.

12289. Pyle, E. J. I like velvet stolons. Golfdom. 11(8):11–14. 1937.

12290. ______. The practical application of turf research developments. Greenkeepers Club of New England Newsletter. 7(6):2–4,6. 1935.

12291. ______. Hartford Park Development's nursery of 14276 velvet bent. Greenkeepers Club of New England Newsletter. 7(11):2–4. 1935.

12292. ______. Correcting topsoil difficulties on the putting green. Greenkeepers Club of New England Newsletter. 9(2):14. 1937.

12293. Pyne, F. W. H. Some aspects of sports ground management. The Groundsman. 15(9):4–10. 1962.

12296. Quackenbush, T. H., and J. T. Phelan. Irrigation water requirement of lawns. Agronomy Abstracts. 55:132. 1963.

12297. Quaill, J. The effects of poisons, insecticides and fungicides on soil. The National Greenkeeper. 4(5):31–33. 1930.

12298. ______. How we sod greens in Pittsburgh. The National Greenkeeper. 5(1):-5–6. 1931.

12299. ______. Economy on the golf course. The National Greenkeeper. 6(4):12, 14–18. 1932.

12300. Questel, D. D. and W. G. Genung. Effect of a severe winter on survival of the recently established parasite of the rhodesgrass scale in Florida. Florida Entomologist. 44(3):115. 1961.

12301. Quinn, C. A. Types of organisms responsible for plant diseases—part 1. The Groundsman. 21(9):34–37. 1968.

12302. ______. Types of organisms responsible for plant diseases—part 2. The Groundsman. 21(10):22. 1968.

12303. ______. A general look at turf pests and their control. The Groundsman. 21(11):15–16. 1968.

12304. ______. Soil—A world within a world. The Groundsman. 21(12):24–25. 1968.

12305. ______. Inorganic fertilisers. The Groundsman. 22(2):27–28. 1968.

12306. ______. Movement of soil water. The Groundsman. 22(11):22. 1969.

12307. ______. Photosynthesis, transpiration, respiration. The Groundsman. 23(11):26. 1970.

12309. ______. Notes for the trainee groundsman. The Groundsman. 24(1):53–54. 1970.

12311. Rabbitt, A. E. Importance of fertilizer in establishing new turf. Parks and Recreation. 26(2):55–60. 1942.

12312. ______. Economies in turf maintenance through seed usage. Proceedings of National Turf Field Days. pp. 45–49. 1950.

12313. ______. Trees and shrubbery as they influence turf management. Texas Turfgrass Conference Proceedings. 13:30–35. 1958.

12314. Rabbitt, A. E. and J. W. Daniel. Pre-emergence crabgrass control on established bluegrass turf. Agronomy Abstracts. p. 71. 1960.

12315. Rachesky, S. Golf course insect pests. The Golf Superintendent. 35(10):28–35, 44. 1967.

12316. ______. Control of insects. The Golf Superintendent. 36(10):22, 23. 1968.

12317. ______. Midwest insect problems. The Bull Sheet. 24(6):3. 1970.

12319. Radcliffe, J. and W. R. Dale. *Ehrharta erecta*—a possible turf species for coastal sands. New Zealand Institute for Turf Culture Newsletter. 30:6–8. 1964.

12320. Rader, L. F., L. M. White and C. W. Whittaker. The salt index—a measure of the effect of fertilizers on the concentration of the soil solution. Soil Science. 55:201–218. 1943.

12321. Radko, A. M. *Poa annua* as a companion to warm season grasses. Golfdom. 26(4):37. 1952.

12322. ______. USGA reports findings of 1951 national crabgrass trials. Golfdom. 26(4):56. 1952.

12323. ______. What about maleic hydrazide? USGA Journal and Turf Management. 6(2):30–32. 1953.

12324. ______. Principles of turf renovation. Proceedings of the Midwest Regional Turf Conference. pp. 5–9. 1953.

12326. ______. Rates of seeding turf grasses. USGA Journal and Turf Management. 6(3):29–31. 1953.

12328. ______. Know your grasses. Proceedings of School of Soils, Fertilization and Turf Maintenance. Royal Canadian Golf Association Green Section. pp. 16–20. 1954.

12329. ______. The importance and development of turf nurseries. Proceedings of School of Soils, Fertilization and Turf Maintenance. Royal Canadian Golf Association Green Section. pp. 41–43. 1954.

12330. ______. Summer management of putting greens. USGA Journal and Turf Management. 7(2):25. 1954.

12331. ______. The danger period for putting greens. USGA Journal and Turf Management. 7(3):27–30. 1954.

12332. ______. Fairway turfgrasses in the Northeast. USGA Journal and Turf Management. 7(6):29–30. 1954.

12333. ______. Use of water on the golf course. Rutgers University Short Course in Turf Management. 23:2. 1955.

12334. ______. Zoysia seed storage and germination tests. USGA Journal and Turf Management. 8(6):25–26.

12335. ______. Fairway renovation. Golfdom. 30(4):92, 114–117. 1956.

12336. ______. Is fairway renovation paying off? The Greenkeeper's Reporter. 24:-20–24. 1956.

12337. ______. Hurricane damage in the northeast. USGA Journal and Turf Management. 9(3):13–16. 1956.

12338. ______. Grass seed. Parks and Recreation. 40(5):20–21. 1957

12339. ______. Highlights of the northeast in '56. Rutgers University Short Course in Turf Management. 2 pp. 1957.

12340. ______. Weed control. USGA Journal and Turf Management. 10(5):24–27. 1957.

12341. ______. Summary of the annual fine turfgrass conference. Turf Clippings. University of Massachusetts. 1(3):6–9. 1958.

12342. Radko, A. M., J. M. Latham, J. L. Holmes, M. H. Ferguson, and W. H. Bengeyfield. Winter 1958–59. What it did to turf. Golf Course Reporter. 27(4):20–28. 1959.

12343. Radko, A. M. Golf turf in the Northeast—1958, Part II. Rutgers University Short Course in Turf Management. 27:2. 1959.

12344. ______. Lessons learned from the 1958 season as applied to golf course maintenance. Turf Clippings, University of Massachusetts. 1(4):A–21 to A–24. 1959.

12345. ______. Renovation vs. rebuilding. USGA Journal and Turf Management. 12(1):25–27. 1959.

12346. ______. Water and golf turfgrass. USGA Open Championship Annual. pp. 42, 102. 1959.

12347. ______. Ideas, gadgets and things. Southeastern Turfgrass Conference Proceedings. 16:20–27. 1962.

12348. ______. Grasses for greens in New England and their maintenance—*Poa annua.* Turf Clippings, University of Massachusetts. 1(7):16–A to 18–A. 1962.

12349. ______. Yes, you can have a putting green lawn. USGA Open Championship Annual. pp. 80–81, 179. 1962.

12350. ______. How to meet winter course maintenance problems. Club Operations. 1(1):33. 1963.

12351. ______. Maintenance practices which will minimize or overcome harmful effects of traffic. Southeastern Turfgrass Conference Proceedings. 17:21–22. 1963.

12352. ______. Specifications for a method of putting green construction. Turf Clippings. University of Massachussetts. 1(8):A–33 to A–38. 1963.

12353. ______. A double victory over winter-spring injury. USGA Green Section Record. 1(3):8–10. 1963.

12354. ______. Eighteen alternate greens. USGA Green Section Record. 1(3):-10–11. 1963.

12355. ______. Let's look at and learn from winter injury. Golf Course Reporter. 32(9):14–18. 1964.

12356. ______. Pros and cons for bermudagrass in the Mid-Atlantic region. Proceedings of the Mid-Atlantic Association of Golf Course Superintendents. pp. 1–2. 1964.

12357. ______. Knotweed Control at Wethersfield. USGA Green Section Record. 2(1):10–11. 1964.

12358. ______. A modification for thatching and mowing units. USGA Green Section Record. 2(4):5. 1964.

12359. ______. An open championship and a problem. USGA Green Section Record. 2(5):1–3. 1965.

12360. ______. Sodding vs. stolonizing. The Golf Superintendent. 34(1):22–23. 1966.

12361. ______. Mulching stolons and seed. International Turfgrass Conference Proceedings. 37:46–48. 1966.

12362. ______. Role of minor elements in turfgrass management. Turf clippings. University of Massachusetts. 2(1):A–22 to A–26. 1966.

12363. ______. Useful tips. International Turfgrass Conference Proceedings. 38:40–41. 1967.

12364. ______. Performance of bentgrasses under varying maintenance conditions. RCGA National Turfgrass Conference. 18:45–47. 1967.

12365. ______. Recent trends in the control of *Poa annua.* RCGA National Turfgrass Conference. 18:49–50. 1967.

12366. ______. *Poa annua* panel. Turf Clippings. University of Massachusetts. 2(2):16–19. 1967.

12367. ______. *Poa annua*—Jekyll or Hyde? USGA Green Section Record 4(6):-16–17. 1967.

12368. ______. Why the nitrogen race? Northern Ohio Turfgrass News. 2(10):2–3. 1968.

12369. ______. Turf problems. Turf clippings. University of Massachusetts. 3(3):A1–2. 1968.

12370. ______. Bentgrasses for putting greens. USGA Green Section Record. 5(6):-11–12. 1968.

12371. ______. Grooming your golf course is important. USGA Green Section Record. 6(2):1–4. 1968.

12372. ______. Specifications for a method of putting green construction. West Virginia Turfgrass Conference Proceedings. pp. 32–37. 1968.

12373. ______. A method of putting green construction. New York Turfgrass Association Bulletin 83:322–323. 1969.

12374. ______. Points to ponder—desiccation. Northern Ohio Turfgrass News. 12(1):3. 1969.

12375. ______. Turf highlights of the 1968 season. 20th Annual RCGA National Turfgrass Conference. 20:37–38. 1969.

12376. ______. Summary of remarks on our film and specifications for a method of putting green construction. 20th Annual RCGA National Turfgrass Conference. 20:-39–40. 1969.

12377. ______. How important are turfgrass diseases? Their importance on golf turf. Rutgers University. College of Agriculture and Environmental Science. Lawn and Utility Turf Section. p. 69. 1969.

12378. ______. Methods of coping with winter injury. Rutgers University. College of Agriculture and Environmental Science. Lawn and Utility Turf Section. p. 70. 1969.

12379. ______. How important are turfgrass diseases? Their importance on golf turf. Rutgers University Short Course in Turf Management. 37:1. 1969.

12380. ______. Methods of coping with winter injury. Rutgers University Short Course in Turf Management. 37:1. 1969.

12381. ______. Beauty and the blast. USGA Green Section Record. 7(5):10–12. 1969.

12382. ______. Review of the Green Section research program. USGA Green Section Record. 8:1–6. 1970.

12383. ______. Some thoughts and observation on management and control of annual bluegrass. Rutgers University Short Course in Turf Management Proceedings. pp. 29–32. 1971.

12384. ______. Research stretches the budget dollar. USGA Green Section Record. 9(2):22. 1971.

12385. ______. Weed control on golf courses. 23rd Annual R.G.C.A. National Turfgrass Conference. pp. 60–61. 1972.

12386. ______. *Poa annua* maintenance —how to keep it. 42nd Annual Michigan Turfgrass Conference Proceedings. (1):43–44. 1972.

12387. ______. Fertilizer carriers—major elements. 42nd Annual Michigan Turfgrass Conference Proceedings. (1):106–109. 1972.

12388. ______. Kentucky bluegrasses in perspective for golf course use. Proceedings 1972 3–Day Turf Courses, Rutgers University. p. 53. 1972.

12389. ______. Ideas and gadgets. USGA Green Section Record. 10(2):10–14. 1972.

12390. ______. Research needs your support through National Golf Day. USGA Green Section Record. 10(3):4–6. 1972.

12392. Radko, A. M. and F. V. Grau. Operation zoysia. USGA Journal and Turf Management. 5(2):26–28. 1952.

12393. Radko, A. M. and G. C. Keeton. Minimizing effects of traffic. USGA Green Section Record. 1(2):1–3. 1963.

12394. Radko, A. M., and L. Record. Water box controls sediment in water systems. USGA Green Section Record. 1(5):13. 1964.

12395. ______. A new tee at Pine Valley. USGA Green Section Record. 1(6):11. 1964.

12396. Radko, A. M. and T. T. Taylor. Turf problems—you name it and we had it in 1959. Turf Clippings. University of Massachussetts. 1(5):A–3 to A–4. 1960.

12397. Radko, A. M. and C. G. Wilson. Problems involved in national coordinated turf trials. Agronomy Abstracts. p. 42. 1952.

12398. Radko, A. M., H. Griffin, and L. Record. Tees and the golf course. USGA Green Section Record. 2(1):1–7. 1964.

12399. Radko, A. M., L. Record, and A. Neuberger. Budget reporting. USGA Green Section Record. 4(5):9–13. 1967.

12400. Radko, A. M., H. M. Griffin, L. Record, and R. E. Harman. Winter-spring injury in the east. USGA Green Section Record. 1(2):7–13. 1963.

12401. Radko, A. M., J. B. Moncrief, L. Record, and G. B. Shuey. Putting green grasses and their management. USGA Green Section Record. 1(6):8–11. 1964.

12402. Radwony, E. L. Selecting seed for airport turfing. Airports. 10. 1946.

12403. ______. Tips for selecting airport grasses. Aviation Maintenance and Operations. p. 36. 1947.

12404. ______. The history of some grasses. Golf Course Reporter. 20(1):14–17. 1952.

12406. Radway, F. S. Bent grasses. The National Greenkeeper. 3(7):20–23. 1929.

12407. Ragland, J. L. and J. H. Byars. Effect of amount and location of calcium in the soil on its uptake by plants. Kentucky Agricultural Experiment Station Annual Report. 75:29. 1962.

12408. ______. Effect of amount and location of calcium in the soil on its uptake by plants. Kentucky Agricultural Experimental Station Annual Report. 76:19. 1963.

12409. Ragland, J. L. and H. F. Massey. Effects of amount and location of calcium in the soil on its uptake by plants. Kentucky Agricultural Experiment Station Annual Report. 74:20. 1961.

12411. Rahling, B. The successful superintendent. The Golf Superintendent. 36(2):-37, 43, 56–59. 1968.

12412. Raleigh, S. M. Crabgrass control. Pennsylvania State College Turfgrass Conference Proceedings. 19:25–27. 1950.

12413. Raleigh, S. M., T. R. Flanagan, C. Veatch. Life history studies as related to weed control in the Northeast: 4–quackgrass. Rhode Island Agricultural Experiment Station Bulletin 365. 10 pp. 1962.

12414. Ralston, D. Variable depths of rootzone materials. Proceedings of the Midwest Regional Turf Conference. pp. 65–66. 1968.

12415. ______. Rootzone observations. Proceedings of the Midwest Regional Turf Conference. pp. 15–16. 1969.

12416. ______. A study on new methods for construction of putting green rootzones. Ph.D. Thesis, Purdue University. 122 pp. 1970.

12417. ______. Purr-wick research review 1966–1970. Proceedings of the Midwest Regional Turf Conference. pp. 42–45. 1970.

12418. ______. Panel discussion on Purr-Wick. Proceedings of the Midwest Regional Turf Conference. pp. 45–48. 1970.

12419. ______. Principles in soil drainage. Proceedings of the Midwest Regional Turf Conference. pp. 37–40. 1971.

12420. ______. What you should know about drainage. Grounds Maintenance. 7(12):18–24. 1972.

12421. Ralston, D. S. and W. H. Daniel. Variation in type of material and water table depths for rootzones of sand over plastic. Agronomy Abstracts. p. 71. 1970.

12422. ______. Effect of temperatures and water table depth on the growth of creeping bentgrass roots. Agronomy Journal. 64(6):709–713. 1972.

12423. Ramlins, S. Plants resist water flow, cause mid-day wilting. Turf Bulletin. Massachusetts Turf and Lawn Grass Council. 2(5):15. 1964.

12424. Rampton, H. H. The use of morphological characters as compared with flourescence tests with ultra-violet light in classifying the rye grasses (*Lolium* spp) of western Oregon. Journal of the American Society of Agronomy. 30(11):915–922. 1938.

12425. ______. Grass and legume varieties for seed yields in Oregon. Oregon Agricultural Experiment Station. Bulletin 600. 59 pp. 1965.

12426. Rampton, H. H. and T. M. Ching. Longevity and dormancy in seeds of several cool-season grasses and legumes buried in soil. Agronomy Journal. 58(2):220–222. 1966.

12427. Randell, R. 1965 turf insects. Illinois Turfgrass Conference Proceedings. 6:-1–3. 1965.

12428. ______. Turf insects and insecticides. Illinois Turfgrass Conference Proceedings. 8:16–19. 1967.

12429. ______. What causes turf insect problems? Illinois Turfgrass Conference Proceedings. pp. 15–18. 1968.

12430. ______. What fault turf insect control? Illinois Turfgrass Conference Proceedings. p. 13. 1969.

12431. ______. Turf insects and their control. Illinois Turfgrass Conference Proceedings. pp. 8–10. 1971.

12432. ______. Effects of various pesticides on thatch accumulation in Kentucky bluegrass. University of Illinois Turfgrass Field Day. pp. 10–11. 1972.

12433. ______. Insect identification and diagnosis of injury in turf. University of Illinois Turfgrass Field Day. p. 25. 1972.

12434. Randell, R., J. D. Butler, and T. D. Hughes. The effect of pesticides on thatch accumulation and earthworm populations in 'Kentucky' bluegrass turf. Hort Science. 7(1):64–65. 1972.

12435. Randerson, D. Predicting the weather for turf. Texas Turfgrass Conference Proceedings. 23:40–50. 1968.

12436. Randolph, N. M. Proper use of insecticides for control of insects on lawn grasses. Texas Turfgrass Conference Proceedings. 21:47–49. 1966.

12437. Randolph, N. M. and P. M. Wagner. Biology and control of the fall armyworm. Texas Agricultural Experiment Station Progress Report PR–2431. 6 pp. 1966.

12438. Ranft, H. Leasing and renting equipment. Midwest Regional Turf Conference Proceedings. pp. 62–64. 1972.

12439. Rapp, W. D. Eliminating loss of sod after installation. Rutgers University. College of Agriculture and Environmental Science. Lawn and Utility Turf Section. pp. 46–48. 1969.

12440. ______. Eliminating loss of sod after installation. Rutgers University Short Course in Turf Management. 37:1–3. 1969.

12441. Rasmussen, L. W. The physiological action of 2, 4–dichlorophenoxyacetic acid on dandelion. Plant Physiology, 22:377–392. 1947.

12442. ______. Weed control in turf. Pacific Northwest Turf Conference Proceedings. 6:26–29. 1952.

12443. ______. White grub infestation at St. Paul. The Greenkeepers' Reporter. 7(1):-58. 1939.

12444. Rathjens, A. J. Experiences in fairway improvement. Rutgers University Short Course in Turf Management. 19:92–94. 1951.

12445. ______. Pin and tee placement for better turf. Rutgers University Short Course in Turf Management. p. 59. 1963.

12446. Rathmell, A. Maintenance of grass tennis courts, end of season treatment. The Groundsman. 15(2):14, 16. 1961.

12447. Ratnam, B. V. A study of some aspects of drought resistance of grasses. Ph.D. Thesis, Duke University. 90 pp. 1961.

12448. Rauser, W. E. and W. L. Crowle. Salt tolerance of Russian wild ryegrass in relation to tall wheatgrass and slender wheatgrass. Canadian Journal of Plant Science. 43(3):397–407. 1963.

12449. Rea, J. Flora, cerea, and pomona. Richard Marriot, London, England. pp. 1–239. 1665.

12450. Read, D. W. L. and R. Ashford. Effect of varying levels of soil and fertilizer phosphorus and soil temperature on the growth and nutrient content of bromegrass and reed canarygrass. Agronomy Journal. 6(6):680–682. 1968.

12451. Read, H. K. Improving turf on sandy soil. USGA Green Section Bulletin. 8(1):12–14. 1928.

12452. Ream, C. L. The war against ants. The National Greenkeeper. 1(7):9. 1927.

12453. Ream, H. Some studies on root reserves in *Poa pratensis* and *Agropyron repens.* B. S. Thesis, University of Wisconsin. 12 pp. 1930.

12454. ______. Curing drainage ills. Golfdom. 9(9):11–13. 1935.

12455. Reber, L. Herbicidal effects of Picloram on two turfgrasses: varietal tolerance, root and foliar absorption. M. S. Thesis, Southern Illinois University. 22 pp. 1970.

12456. Reber, L. J., R. K. Miller, J. A. Tweedy, and J. D. Butler. Herbicidal effects of picloram on bermudagrass. Weed Science. 19(5):521–524. 1971.

12457. Rechenthin, C. A. Elementary morphology of grass growth and how it affects utilization. Journal of Range Management. 9(4):167–170. 1956.

12458. Record, L. Green management. University of Maine Turf Conference Proceedings. 1:5 pp. 1963.

12459. ______. Water. University of Maine Turf Conference Proceedings. 1:7 pp. 1963.

12460. ______. Traffic on the golf course. New York Turfgrass Association Bulletin. 73:284. 1963.

12461. ______. Golf cars and turfgrass. Turf Clippings. University of Massachusetts. 1(9):A–42 to A–43. 1964.

12462. ______. Long term effects of herbicides. Turf Clippings. University of Massachusetts. 1(10) A10–A14. 1965.

12463. ______. Long term effects of herbicides. USGA Green Section Record. 3(3):-7–10. 1965.

12464. ______. Golf course maintenance equipment. USGA Green Section Record. 4(4):7–8. 1966.

12465. ______. Renovation—timing and nutrients. Turf Clippings. University of Massachusetts. 2(2):A–13–15. 1967.

12466. ______. Sand vs. grass. USGA Green Section Record. 4(6):21–22. 1967.

12467. ______. Fungicides—forever more? USGA Green Section Record. 5(2):-1–5. 1967.

12468. ______. Bringing greens into play. Turf Bulletin. Massachusetts Turf and Lawn Grass Council. 4(8):4–5. 1968.

12469. ______. 1967 turfgrass problems. Turf Clippings. University of Massachusetts. 3(3):3–4. 1968.

12470. ______. Bringing greens into play. USGA Green Section Record. 5(6):17–18. 1968.

12471. ______. Winter protection for automatic controllers. USGA Green Section Record. 6(3):1–2. 1968.

12472. ______. Topdressing and cultivating fine turf. Proceedings of the Midwest Regional Turf Conference. pp. 25–26. 1969.

12473. ______. The use of dicamba and MCPP for weed control in turfgrass. Ohio Turfgrass Conference Proceedings. pp. 56–58. 1969.

12474. ______. Carts and golfers today. Proceedings of the Midwest Regional Turf Conference. pp. 16–18. 1970.

12475. ______. Zoysia—A turf for transition zone fairways. USGA Green Section Record. 9(4):5–6. 1971.

12476. ______. Winter injury in the cool temperate zone. The Bull Sheet. 26(7):8–9. 1972.

12477. ______. Manpower versus mechanization. USGA Green Section Record. 10(2):15–17. 1972.

12478. ______. Updating the list for golf course maintenance equipment. USGA Green Section Record. 10(4):15–16. 1972.

12479. ______. Aerial fungicide applications? USGA Green Section Record. 10(5):-1–4. 1972.

12480. Redenbacher, O. C. Growing turf on sand. Proceedings of the Midwest Regional Turf Conference. pp. 69–72. 1966.

12481. Redman, L. Hydro-mulching zoysia. Midwest Regional Turf Conference Proceedings. pp. 64–65. 1971.

12482. ______. Selected sand and organic constructed green. Midwest Regional Turf Conference Proceedings. pp. 49–50. 1972.

12483. Reed, C. F. and R. O. Hughes. Selected weeds of the United States. U.S.-D.A. Handbook. 366:1–463. 1970.

12484. Reed, F. J. Lawns and playing fields. Faber & Faber Ltd., London. 212 pp. 1950.

12485. ______. Grass seed mixtures for sports turf. The Groundsman. 16(5):16–22. 1963.

12487. Reed, J. P., W. R. Jenkins, R. T. Guest and R. A. Davis. Soil fumigation. New Jersey Agricultural Experiment Station. Extension Bulletin 353. 8 p.

12488. Reed, L. W. A study of saline-alkali soils in Oklahoma. Oklahoma Agricultural Experiment Station Processed Series P–430. 37 pp. 1962.

12489. Reed, L. W., F. W. Roach, R. J. Schneider, N. Bhrommalee, M. D. Sinkler, and W. W. Huffine. Weed control on Oklahoma highways. Highway Research Abstracts. 39(12):74. 1970.

12490. Ree, W. O. The establishment of vegetation lined waterways. Short Course on Roadside Development (Ohio). 19:54–65. 1960.

12491. Reeder, J. R. The embryo in grass systematics. American Journal of Botany. 44(9):756–768. 1957.

12492. Rees, D. L. After the constructor —what? The National Greenkeeper. 1(11):-7–8. 1927.

12493. ______. Divot replacing, *Poa annua* greens, interest Rees in Scotland. Golfdom. 5(7):62–65. 1931.

12494. Rees, J. L. Lawns, greens, and playing fields. Angus & Robertson, Sydney, Australia. 290 pp. 1962.

12495. Rees, W. J. and G. H. Sidrak. Plant nutrition on fly-ash. Plant and Soil. 8(2):141–159. 1956.

12496. Reeves, S. A.The effect of nitrogen source and clipping on the absorption of N. P. and K by Tifgreen bermudagrass, *Cynodon dactylon* x *C. transvaalensis* L. Ph.D Thesis, Texas A&M University. 1971.

12497. Reeves, S. A., and G. G. McBee. Effects of application intervals and levels of N. P and K on cold hardiness relationships in certain warm season turfgrasses. Agronomy Abstracts. p. 64. 1968.

12498. ______. Nutritional influences on cold hardiness of St. Augustinegrass (*Stenotaphrum secundatum*). Agronomy Journal. 64(4):447–450. 1972.

12499. Reeves, S. A., G. G. McBee, and M. E. Bloodworth. Effect of N. P. and K tissue levels and late fall fertilization on the cold hardiness of Tifgreen bermudagrass (*Cynodon dactylon* x *C. transvaalensis*). Agronomy Journal. 62(5):659–662. 1970.

12500. Reeves, S. A., G. G. McBee, and H. E. Joham. Effect of repeated clipping on the absorption of N, P and K by Tifgreen bermudagrass (*Cyndon dactylon* x *C. transvaalensis* L.). Agronomy Abstracts. p. 65. 1972.

12501. Regan, J. B. The use of Dowco 221 for selective control of annual grasses in broadleaf crops and turf. Proceedings of the North Central Weed Control Conference 24:-57. 1969.

12502. Rehberg, R. Research findings on the use of Kerb for controlling *Poa annua* in turf under Florida conditions. Florida Turfgrass Management Conference Proceedings. 18:99–100. 1970.

12503. Rehling, C. J. and E. Truog. Activated sludge, Milorganite. Journal of Industrial and Engineering Chemistry. Analytical Edition. 11:281–283. 1939.

12504. ______. "Milorganite" as a source of minor nutrient elements for plants. Journal of the American Society of Agronomy. 32(11):894–906. 1940.

12505. Rei, Chuck. King Nitrohumus presents—growth control chemicals. Kellogg Supply, Inc. Bulletin. 4(1):6–10. 1970.

12506. Reichardt, K. Water infiltration into uniform and layered soils. Ph.D. Thesis. University of California, Davis. 1971.

12507. Reid, D. G. The cockchafer beetle. The Groundsman. 20(9):28. 1967.

12508. ______. Two common turf diseases. The Groundsman. 20(12):19. 1967.

12509. ______. Individual grasses—part 1 *Agrostis tenuis graminaceae.* The Groundsman. 21(7):49. 1968.

12510. ______. Individual grasses–2 *(Agrostis canina graminaceae).* The Groundsman. 21(10):25. 1968.

12511. ______. Water requirements on specialized turf areas. The Groundsman. 22(1):61. 1968.

12512. ______. Liquid feeding of specialised turf areas. The Groundsman. 22(4):22–23. 1968.

12513. ______. Sowing grass under bitumen. The Groundsman. 22(11):23. 1969.

12514. ______. Controlling leatherjackets. The Groundsman. 23(2):30. 1969.

12515. ______. How does a plant breeder develop a new strain? The Groundsman. 23(3):24. 1969.

12516. ______. Question and answer. The Groundsman. 23(6):21. 1970.

12517. ______. How to sow down a sports field. The Groundsman. 23(7):37, 39. 1970.

12518. ______. Question and answer. The Groundsman. 23(12):21. 1970.

12519. ______. History and habits of earthworms. The Groundsman. 24(3):25. 1970.

12520. ______. Question and answer. The Groundsman. 24(7):24–25. 1971.

12521. Reid, D. and M. E. Castle. The response of grass-clover and pure-grass leys to irrigation and fertilizer nitrogen treatment. 1. Irrigation effects. Journal of Agricultural Science. 54(2):185–194. 1965.

12522. Reid, G. C. Preparation and maintenance of southern winter greens. National Turfgrass Conference Proceedings. 30:11. 1959.

12523. ______. Fully automatic irrigation systems. Golf Course Reporter. 30(6):-42–45. 1962.

12524. ______. Advantages of automatic irrigation. Proceedings of the Turfgrass Sprinkler Irrigation Conference. 5:16–18. 1967.

12525. Reid, A. Soil management—preparation for planting. Northern California Turf Conference Proceedings. pp. 10–25. 1951.

12526. Reid, J. J. 2, 4–D at usual rates harmless to soil. USGA Journal and Turf Management. 6(3):32. 1953.

12527. Reid, J. A. Wetting agent use. Golf Course Reporter. 28(1):65–66. 1960.

12529. ______. My experience with wetting agents. International Turf-Grass Conference Proceedings. 32:16–17. 1961.

12530. ______. Wetting agents. Mid-Atlantic Golf Course Superintendents Annual Conference Proceedings. pp. 132–135. 1960.

12531. Reid, M. E. The effects of soil reaction upon the growth of several types of bent grasses. USGA Green Section Bulletin. 12(5):196–212. 1932.

12532. ______. Effect of variations in concentration of mineral nutrients upon the growth of several types of turf grasses. USGA Green Section Bulletin. 13(5):122–131. 1933.

12533. ______. Effects of shade on the growth of velvet bent and metropolitan creeping bent. USGA Green Section Bulletin. 13(5):131–135. 1933.

12534. Reid, R. L., E. K. Odhuba, and G. A. Jung. Evaluation of tall fescue pasture under different fertilization treatments. Agronomy Journal. 59(3):265–271. 1967.

12535. Reidy, J. J. The effects of soil oxygen concentrations on root growth. Turf Bulletin. Massachusetts Turf and Lawn Grass Council. 4(6):3–4, 18–19. 1967–1968.

12538. Reilly, D. Control of dollar spot disease on turf in New South Wales with the new systemic fungicide, Benomyl. The Journal of the Sports Turf Research Institute. 45:-63–66. 1969.

12539. Reimer, E., and A. J. Renney. Tests with ioxynil mixtures to control 4 persistent lawn weeds. Research Report of the National Weed Committee, Western Section (Canada) pp. 212. 1968.

12540. Reinecke, E. Automation in irrigation management. Southern California Turfgrass Institute Proceedings. pp. 9–12. 1960.

12541. ______. Revolution in turf irrigation. Park Maintenance. 16:28–30. 1963.

12542. Reinert, J. A. Insects in large turf areas of St. Augustinegrass and bahiagrass. Florida Turfgrass Management Conference Proceedings. 19:107–109. 1971.

12543. Reisch, K. M. Fact and fancy in fertilization. Short Course on Roadside Development (Ohio). 28:84–86. 1969.

12544. Reilly, D. Control of winter grass in "*Cynodon dactylon*" (L). Pers. turf in New South Wales with Pronamide. Journal Sports Turf Research Institute. 47:26–32. 1971.

12545. Remsberg, R. E. Studies in the genus *Typhula.* Mycologia. 32:52–96. 1940.

12546. ______. The snow molds of grains and grasses caused by *Typhula itoana* and *Typhula idahoensis.* Phytopathology. 30(2):-178–180. 1940.

12547. Renney, A. J. Preventing *Poa annua* infestations. Proceedings of the Northwest Turfgrass Conference. 18:3–5. 1964.

12548. Renney, A. J. and D. J. Omrod. Weed control related to leaf surfaces. Proceedings of the Northwest Turfgrass Conference. 20:58–64. 1966.

12549. Rennie, W. W. Fertilization principles and practices. Florida Turf Management Conference Proceedings. 6:91–93. 1958.

12550. Repin, A. Fertilizing and topdressing bent greens. Oklahoma-Texas Turf Conference Proceedings. pp. 21–24. 1949.

12551. Rettig, J. M. Basic factors to be followed when constructing course. Golfdom. 5(10):53–55. 1931.

12552. Rewinski, T. F. Growing Kentucky bluegrass fairways. Proceedings 1972 3–Day Turf Courses, Rutgers University. pp. 51–52. 1972.

12553. Reynolds, E. N. Friction loss and velocity. International Turfgrass Conference Proceedings. 37:26–29. 1966.

12554. ______. Sprinkler dirt. Proceedings of the Turfgrass Sprinkler Irrigation Conference. 3 pp. 1966.

12555. ______. Dirt—villain in the sprinkler system. Park Maintenance. 21(5):-18–20. 1968.

12556. Reynolds, G. Our turf disease control program. Proceedings of the Midwest Regional Turf Conference. pp. 49–50A. 1961.

12557. Reynolds, J. H. Carbohydrate reserve trends in orchardgrass (*Dactylis glomerata* L.) grown under different cutting frequencies and nitrogen fertilization levels. Crop Science. 9(6):720–723. 1969.

12558. Reynolds, J. H., and D. Smith. Trend of carbohydrate reserves in alfalfa, smooth bromegrass and timothy grown under various cutting schedules. Crop Science. 2(4):333–336. 1962.

12559. Rhoades, E. D. Grasses and flood survival. Agricultural Engineering. 44(1):22–23. 1963.

12560. ______. Inundation tolerance of grasses in flooded areas. Transactions of the ASAE. 7(2):164–166, 169. 1964.

12561. ______. Grass survival in flood pool areas. Journal of Soil and Water Conservation. 22(1):19–21. 1967.

12562. Rhoades, H. L. Sting and stubbyroot nematodes on St. Augustinegrass. Proceedings of the Florida Turf-Grass Management Conference. 10:28–29. 1962.

12563. ______. Effects of sting and stubby-root nematodes on St. Augustine grass. The Plant Disease Reporter. 46(6):424–427. 1962.

12564. ______. Parasitism and pathogenocity of *Trichodorus proximus* to St. Augustine grass. Plant Disease Reporter. 49(5):259–262. 1965.

12565. ______. Quality of water for irrigation. Soil Science. 113(4):277–284. 1972.

12567. Rhodemyre, S. E., H. F. Miller, and G. W. Thomas. Comparison of ammonium nitrate and urea as sources of N for orchard grass-bluegrass sod. Kentucky Agricultural Experiment Station Annual Report. 84:41. 1971.

12568. Rhodes, I. The yield, canopy structure and light interception of two ryegrass var. in mixed culture and monoculture. Journal of the British Grassland Society. 24(2):123–128. 1969.

12569. ______. The production of contrasting genotypes of perennial ryegrass (*Lolium perenne* L.) in monocultures and mixed cultures of varying complexity. Journal of the British Grassland Society. 25(4):-285–288. 1970.

12570. ______. Productivity and canopy structure of two contrasting varieties of perennial ryegrass (*Lolium perenne* L.) grown in a controlled environment. Journal of the British Grassland Society. 26(1):9–16. 1971.

12571. Rhodes, W. W. Fertilizers and fungicides: the function of soluble fertilizers and fungicide chemicals in the maintenance of putting greens. The National Greenkeeper. 1(10):9–12. 1927.

12572. Rhue, R. D. Availability and residual effects of gypsum, sulfur, and elemental sulfur on two soil series in North Carolina. M.S. Thesis, North Carolina State University. 1971.

12573. Rice, E. J. and J. A. DeFrance. Control of hawkweed in lawn turf. Golf Course Reporter. 28(5):40–43. 1960.

12574. ______. Postemergence crabgrass control with chemicals in lawn turf. Proceedings of the Northeastern Weed Control Conference. 14:284–287. 1960.

12575. Rice, E. J. and C. R. Skogley. Preemergence control of crabgrass in lawn turf. Proceedings of the Northeastern Weed Control Conference. 15:284–288. 1961.

12576. ______. The tolerance of lawn grasses to certain crabgrass herbicides. Proceedings Northeastern Weed Control Conference. 16:466–473. 1962.

12577. ______. Preemergence control of crabgrass in lawn turf. Weed Abstracts. 12(3):138. 1963.

12578. Rice, G. H. Alternative management philosophies direction vs. development. Proceedings of the 20th Annual Texas Turfgrass Conference. 20:25–31. 1965.

12580. Rich, M. C. Seedbed preparation —small or big equipment—acreage necessary. Rocky Mountain Regional Turfgrass Conference. 12:14. 1966.

12581. Richards, L. A. Soil moisture tensiometer materials and construction. Soil Science. 53:241–248. 1942.

12582. ______. Diagnosis and improvement of saline and alkali soils. U.S.D.A. Handbook. 60:1–160. 1954.

12583. Richards, L. A., C. A. Bower, and M. Fireman. Tests for salinity and sodium status of soil and irrigation water. U.S.-D.A. Circular. 982:1–19. 1956.

12584. Richards, S. J. Soil water relations. California Turfgrass Culture. 11(4):29. 1961.

12585. ______. Turf irrigation based on instruments. Proceedings of Turf, Nursery, and Landscape Tree Conference. University of California, Davis. pp. 4–1 to 4–2. 1964.

12586. ______. Water usage. California Turfgrass Culture. 18(2):11–14. 1968.

12587. ______. Water usage. International Turfgrass Conference and Show. 39:-13–18. 1968.

12588. Richards, S. J. and L. V. Weeks. Evapotranspiration for turf measured with automatic irrigation equipment. California Agriculture. 17(7):12–13. 1963.

12589. ______. Evapotranspiration for turf measured with automatic irrigation equipment. California Turfgrass Culture. 14(1):7–8. 1964.

12591. Richards, S. J., J. E. Warneke, A. W. Marsh, and F. K. Aljibury. Physical properties of soil mixes. Soil Science. 98(1):-129–132. 1964.

12592. Richardson, B. Maintenance from the professional standpoint. RCGA National Turfgrass Conference. 19:45. 1968.

12593. Richardson, E. C., and E. G. Diseker. Control of roadbank erosion in the Southern Piedmont. Agronomy Journal. 53(4):292–294. 1961.

12594. ______. Fertilized native plants promise quick and cheap roadside protection. Soil Conservation. 28:68–69. 1962.

12595. ______. Establishing and maintaining roadside cover in Georgia. Agronomy Abstracts. p. 102. 1964.

12596. ______. Establishing and maintaining roadside cover in the piedmont plateau of Georgia. Agronomy Journal. 57(6):-561–564. 1965.

12597. Richardson, E. C., E. G. Diseker, and B. H. Hendrickson. Crownvetch for highway bank stabilization in the piedmont uplands of Georgia. Agronomy Journal. 55(3):213–215. 1963.

12598. Richardson, G. Responsibilities of the professional designer. Proceedings Annual Turfgrass Sprinkler Irrigation Conference. 5:64–65. 1967.

12599. Richardson, L. T. and D. E. Munnecke. A bioassay for volatile toxicants from fungicides in soil. Phytopathology. 54(7):836–839. 1964.

12601. Richer, A. C. Correction of soil acidity and its effect on plant nutrients in the soil. Pennsylvania State Turf Conference. 18:31–39. 1949.

12602. ______. The use of tissue tests in diagnosing nutrition deficienceis. Pennsylvania State College Turfgrass Conference Proceedings. 19:94–97. 1950.

12603. ______. The use of commercial fertilizers. Pennsylvania State College Turfgrass Conference Proceedings. 21:41–47. 1952.

12604. ______. The mighty microbe in the soil. Pennsylvania State Turf Conference. 23:25–30. 1954.

12605. ______. The mighty microbe in the soil. Parks and Recreation. 40(7):17–18. 1957.

12606. Richer, A. C., J. W. White, H. B. Musser, and F. J. Holben. Comparison of various organic materials for use in construction and maintenance of golf greens. Pennsylvania Agricultural Experiment Station Progress Report No. 16. 6 pp. 1949.

12607. Richie, J. S. A grower's view of the proper use of sod. Rutgers University Short Course in Turf Management. 34:30–33. 1966.

12608. Richman, M. W. Renovating old lawns. Purdue Agriculture. 24:201. 1930.

12609. Richter, W. Über die Wirkung von wuchshemmenden Mitteln, insbesondere MH–30 auf Gräser. Z. Pfl. Krankh. Pfl. Schutz. Sonderheft. 3:347. 1965.

12611. Rickman, R. W., J. Letey, L. H. Stolzy. Compact subsoil can be harmful to plant growth. Parks and Recreation. 1(4):-334–335. 1966.

12613. Riddle, J. R. Panel discussion—turf management on roadsides. Fertilizers—their contribution toward good turf. Short Course on Roadside Development (Ohio). 15:66–71. 1956.

12614. Rider, N. E., and G. D. Robinson. A study of the transfer of heat and water vapour above a surface of short grass. Quarterly Journal of the Royal Meteorological Society. 77(333):375–401. 1951.

12615. Rieke, P. E. Selecting a fertilization program. Michigan Turfgrass Research Report. 3(1):13–14. 1965.

12616. ______. Soil mixtures and relative infiltration rates. Michigan Turfgrass Research Report. 3(1):3. 1965.

12617. ______. Selecting a turf fertilization program. Part IV. The Cemeterian. 66(8,9,10):11–12,49–50. 1966.

12618. ______. Growing sod on muck soils. Illinois Turfgrass Conference Proceedings. 7:12–17. 1966.

12619. ______. Selecting a turf fertilization program. Michigan Turfgrass Research Reports. 3(1):10–15. 1966.

12620. ______. Watch needs of irrigated turf. Better Crops With Plant Food. 52(4):11. 1968.

12621. ______. Forcing sod development. Proceedings of the Midwest Regional Turf Conference. pp. 43–47. 1968.

12622. ______. A realistic turf fertility program. Illinois Turfgrass Conference Proceedings. pp. 5–9. 1969.

12623. ______. Current fertilizer recommendations. Illinois Turfgrass Conference Proceedings. pp. 64–65. 1969.

12624. ______. Soil pH for turfgrasses. Proceedings of the First International Turfgrass Research Conference. pp. 212–220. 1969.

12625. ______. Soils and fertilizers. Michigan Forestry and Park Conference Proceedings. 43:23. 1969.

12626. ______. Grass killer. Park Maintenance. 24(7):23–24. 1971.

12627. ______. Thatch removal. Proceedings of Southern California Turfgrass Institute. pp. 95–98. 1971.

12628. ______. Turfgrass nutritional requirements. Turfgrass Sprinkler Irrigation Conference. 9:24–27. 1971.

12629. ______. Thatch Removal. A Patch of Green. Michigan and Border Cities GSCA Publication. pp. 9–14, 18. December, 1972.

12630. ______. The right amount of water-root hair viewpoint. A Patch of Green. Michigan and Border Cities GCSA Publication. pp. 10–14. July, 1972.

12631. ______. Nutrient storage and movement under turf. A Patch of Green. Michigan and Border Cities GCSA Publication. pp. 13–17. August, 1972.

12632. ______. Nitrogen studies and soil mixes. 42nd Annual Michigan Turfgrass Conference Proceedings. 1:1–6. 1972.

12633. ______. Correcting micronutrient deficiencies in turf. 42nd Annual Michigan Turfgrass Conference Proceedings. 1:110–112. 1972.

12634. ______. The right amount of water-root hair viewpoint. Midwest Regional Turf Conference Proceedings. pp. 39–41. 1972.

12635. ______. Nutrient storage and movement under turf. Midwest Regional Turf Conference Proceedings. pp. 41–44. 1972.

12636. Rieke, P. E., and J. B. Beard. Factors in sod production of Kentucky bluegrass. Proceedings of the First International Turfgrass Research Conference. pp. 514–521. 1969.

12637. Rieke, P. E., and K. R. English. Responses of Merion Kentucky bluegrass sod to nitrogen fertilization. 42nd Annual Michigan Turfgrass Conference Proceedings. 1:-113–116. 1972.

12638. Rieke, P. E. and R. E. Lucas. When, where, and how to sod for turf. Weeds, Trees, and Turf. 6(10):14–16. 1967.

12639. ______. Sodding a lawn. Michigan Turfgrass Research Report. 3(1):9–10. 1968.

12640. Rieke, P. E., J. B. Beard, and C. M. Hansen. A technique to measure sod strength for use in sod production studies. Agronomy Abstracts. p. 60. 1968.

12642. Rieke, P. E., J. B. Beard, and R. E. Lucas. Grass sod production on organic soils in Michigan. Proceedings, Third International Peat Congress. pp. 350–354. 1968.

12643. Rierson, D. The New Mexico nursery act in relation to turfgrass. New Mexico Turfgrass Conference Proceedings. pp. 3–4. 1956.

12644. Riffle, J. W. Root knot nematode on African bermudagrass in New Mexico. Plant Disease Reporter. 48(12):964–965. 1964.

12645. Riggs, R. D., J. L. Dale, and M. L. Hamblen. Reaction of Bermuda grass varieties and lines to root-knot nematodes. Phytopathology. 52(16):587–588. 1962.

12646. Riggs-Miller, T. H. Clear thinking. Golfdom. 3(8):13–16. 1929.

12647. ______. Skimpy seeding practice robs till, turf and time. Golfdom. 5(8):19–21. 1931.

12648. Riley, W. Water distribution systems. USGA Journal and Turf Management. 13(1):28. 1960.

12649. Riordan, T. Bluegrasses—aggressives and petites. Proceedings of the Midwest Regional Turf Conference. p. 24. 1966.

12650. ______. Improvement of Kentucky bluegrass through breeding and selection. Proceedings of the Midwest Regional Turf Conference. pp. 77–79. 1968.

12651. ______. Continuing bluegrass research 1968–1969. Proceedings of the Midwest Regional Turf Conference. pp. 84–85. 1969.

12652. ______. *Poa pratensis* L. (Kentucky bluegrass): breeding and cytology. Ph.D. Thesis, Purdue University. 39 pp. 1970.

12653. ______. Kentucky bluegrass—breeding and cytology. Proceedings of the Midwest Regional Turf Conference. pp. 66–67. 1970.

12654. Riordan, T. P. and W. H. Daniel. Selection of Kentucky bluegrass for roadside use. Agronomy Abstracts. p. 73. 1970.

12655. Rippey, J. Winter putting green protection. Turf-Grass Times. 3(1):9. 1967.

12656. Risius, M. L. Crownvetch breeding. Second Crownvetch Symposium. Pennsylvania State University. 6:64–66. 1968.

12657. Ritcher, P. O. Kentucky white grubs. Kentucky Agricultural Experiment Station Bulletin 401. pp. 73–157. 1940.

12658. ______. White grubs and their allies. Oregon State University Monograph Studies Entomology. 4 pp. 1966.

12659. Ritchey, G. E. and G. D. Thornton. Lawns in Florida. Florida Agricultural Experiment Station Bulletin. 518. 20 pp. 1953.

12660. Ritley, P. M. A preliminary report on nematode control in a turf maintenance program. Proceedings of the Soil Science Society of Florida. 14:174–176. 1954.

12661. Rivera, J. E. and A. A. DiEdwardo The effect of sting *(Belonolaimus longicaudatus)* and lance *(Hoplolaimus coronatus)* nematodes on bermudagrass. Florida Turfgrass Association Bulletin. 12(4):6–7. 1965.

12662. ______. The effect of sting *(Belonolaimus longicaudatus)* and lance *(Hoplolaimus coronatus)* nematodes on bermudagrass. Proceeding of University of Florida Turf-Grass Management Conference. 11:150–151. 1963.

12663. Rivers, E. D., and R. F. Shipp. Available water capacity of sandy and gravelly North Dakota soils. Soil Science. 113(2):-74–80. 1972.

12664. Roach, E. F. A survey of twelve golf courses in the Los Angeles area. First Annual Fall Field Day on Turf Culture. UCLA. 1:43–50. 1949.

12665. Roach, G. W. and W. W. Huffine. Herbicide evaluation for the selective control of sandbur in bermudagrass turf. Agronomy Abstracts. p. 57. 1967.

12667. Roberts, E. C. Relationships between turfgrass foliar and root development. II. A solution culture approach to the study of clipping and nutritional interactions in turf. Department of Horticulture Mimeograph, Iowa State University. 1959.

12668. Robbins, W. R. The use of water by plants. The Golf Course Reporter. 23(6):-24–25. 1955.

12669. ______. How plants use water. Rutgers University Short Course in Turf Management. 23:2. 1955.

12670. Robbins, W. W. Alien plants growing without cultivation in California. California Agricultural Experiment Station Bulletin. 637 128 pp. 1940.

12671. ______. Weed control in gardens and turf. Northern California Turf Conference Report. pp. 32–34. 1950.

12672. Robbins, W. W., M. K. Bellue, and W. S. Ball. Weeds of California. California State Printing Division. 547 pp. 1951.

12673. Robert, A. L. Turbulent transfer of fungus spores. Phytopathology. 52(11):-1095–1100. 1962.

12675. Roberts, E. C. The grass plant—feeding and cutting. Golf Course Reporter. 26(3):5–9. 1958.

12676. ______. Changes in turfgrass can be controlled. The Golf Course Reporter. 27(6):14,16–20. 1959.

12678. ______. Changing turfgrass communities. Park Maintenance. 12(9):10–11. 1959.

12679. ______. Turfgrass nutrition a disease control. Golf Course Reporter. 28(1):-50–52. 1960.

12681. ______. Relationship between foliar and root development of turfgrass—species and strains. Illinois Turfgrass Conference Proceedings. 1:32–35. 1960.

12682. ______. Caution on short cuts for lawns. Iowa Farm Science. 14:484–487. 1960.

12683. ______. Go, for a better lawn. Iowa Farm Science. 14:506–509. 1960.

12684. ______. Turfgrass fertilization requires programming. Proceedings, Missouri Lawn and Turf Conference. 1:24–33. 1960.

12685. ______. Soil tests—an aid to more effective turfgrass management. Proceedings, Missouri Lawn and Turf Conference. 1:34–36. 1960.

12686. ______. How to calculate the proper clipping height for turfgrass. Proceedings, Missouri Lawn and Turf Conference. 1:37–46. 1960.

12687. ______. Getting to the root of turfgrass maintenance problems. Proceedings, Missouri Lawn and Turf Conference. 1:47–52. 1960.

12688. ______. Turfgrass dormancy and arrested development. Park Maintenance. 13(10):38–43. 1960.

12689. ______. Changing turfgrass communities. Central Plains Turfgrass Conference. 11:2. 1961.

12690. ______. Weed control thru fertilization. Central Plains Turfgrass Conference. 11:2. 1961.

12691. ______. Mechanical aeration and thatch control—Part 1. International Turf-Grass Conference Proceedings. 32:15. 1961.

12692. ______. Turfgrass review—V. Park Maintenance. 14:17–32. 1961.

12693. ______. Broad-leaved weed control in turf. North Central Weed Control Conference Research Reports. 19:104–105. 1962.

12694. ______. Teaching the application of agronomic principles in turfgrass management. Agronomy Journal. 55(6):576–578. 1963.

12695. ______. Relationship between mineral nutrition of turf-grass and disease susceptibility. Golf Course Reporter. 31(5):-52–57. 1963.

12696. ______. The key to successful golf course construction. Park Maintenance. 16:-100–104. 1963.

12697. ______. Let the grass plant talk. Wisconsin Turfgrass Conference Proceedings. 3 pp. 1963.

12698. ______. Comparative value of bentgrass strains for greens. Wisconsin Turfgrass Conference Proceedings. 5 pp. 1963.

12699. ______. Turfgrass research report —1963. Iagreen. Iowa Turfgrass Conference Proceedings. 30:13–24. 1964.

12700. ______. How to sell a turf management program to a golfer. Turf Bulletin. Massachusetts Turf & Lawn Grass Council. 2(9):5–8. 1964.

12701. ______. What to expect from a nitrogen fertilizer. California Turfgrass Culture 15(1):1–5. 1965.

12702. ______. Why turfgrass responds to proper use of lime and sulfur compounds. The Golf Course Reporter. 33(4):28–50. 1965.

12703. ______. A new measurement of turfgrass response and vigor. The Golf Course Reporter. 33(8):10–20. 1965.

12704. ______. Getting to the roots of turfgrass maintenance problems. Minnesota Turfgrass Conference. 1965.

12705. ______. What to expect from a nitrogen fertilizer. Sixteenth R.C.G.A. Sports Turfgrass Conference. 16:37–46. 1965.

12706. ______. How to sell a turf management program to a golfer. Sixteenth R.C.G.A. Sports Turfgrass Conference. 16:-47–54. 1965.

12707. ______. Turf-grass varieties. Part I—northern. Turf-Grass Times. 1(2):3,6,12,-22,24. 1965.

12708. ______. Nitrogen—growth relationships in turfgrass. Agronomy Abstracts. p. 36. 1966.

12709. ______. Report, Committee on Coordination of Turf Conferences and Field Days, Division C-5. Crop Science Society of America Mimeograph. 1966.

12711. ______. Three steps to building good turf. Grounds Maintenance. 1(5):14–15. 1966.

12712. ______. Preventing winter damage to turf. Grounds Maintenance. 1(11):4–5. 1966.

12713. ______. Iowa State University program in turfgrass management teaching

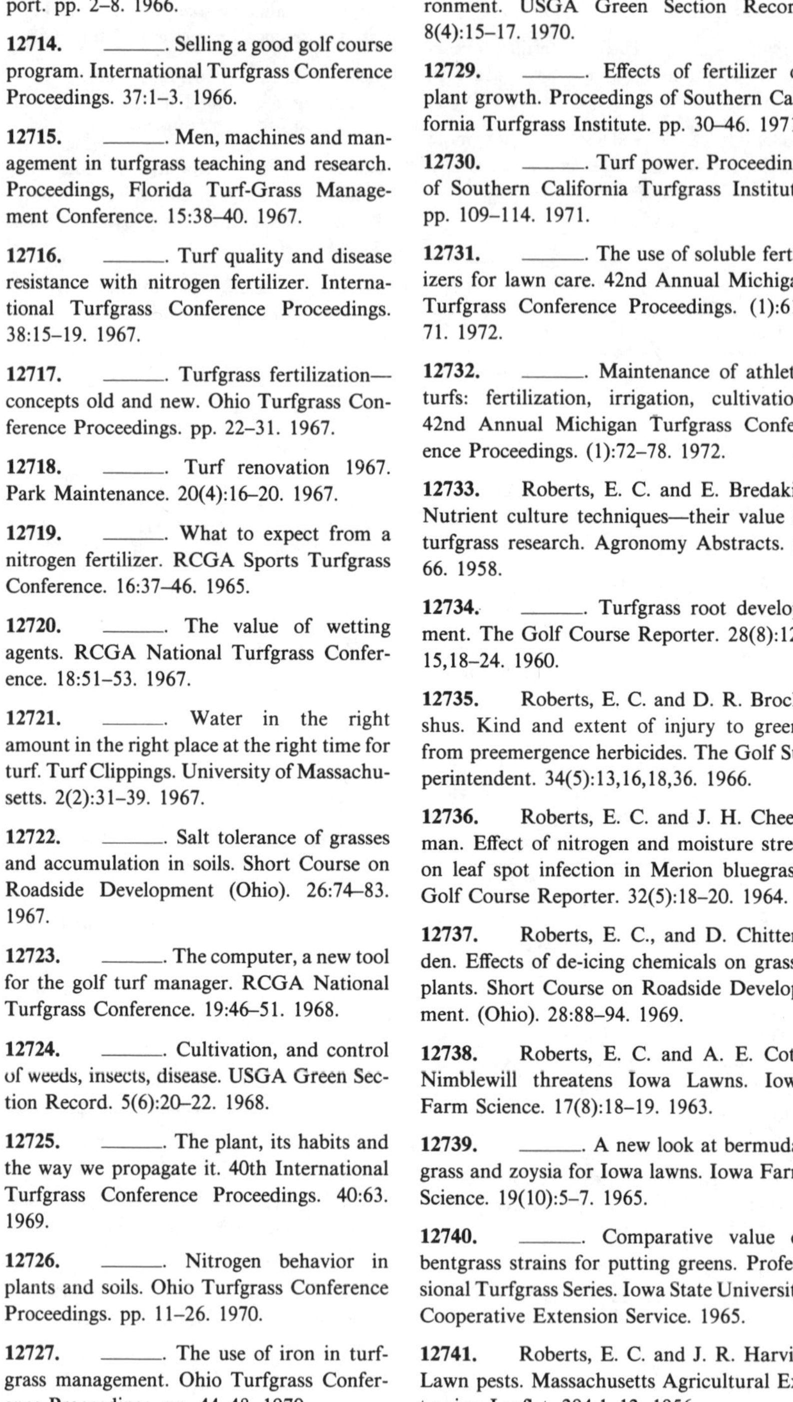

and research. Iagreen. Annual Research Report. pp. 2–8. 1966.

12714. ______. Selling a good golf course program. International Turfgrass Conference Proceedings. 37:1–3. 1966.

12715. ______. Men, machines and management in turfgrass teaching and research. Proceedings, Florida Turf-Grass Management Conference. 15:38–40. 1967.

12716. ______. Turf quality and disease resistance with nitrogen fertilizer. International Turfgrass Conference Proceedings. 38:15–19. 1967.

12717. ______. Turfgrass fertilization—concepts old and new. Ohio Turfgrass Conference Proceedings. pp. 22–31. 1967.

12718. ______. Turf renovation 1967. Park Maintenance. 20(4):16–20. 1967.

12719. ______. What to expect from a nitrogen fertilizer. RCGA Sports Turfgrass Conference. 16:37–46. 1965.

12720. ______. The value of wetting agents. RCGA National Turfgrass Conference. 18:51–53. 1967.

12721. ______. Water in the right amount in the right place at the right time for turf. Turf Clippings. University of Massachusetts. 2(2):31–39. 1967.

12722. ______. Salt tolerance of grasses and accumulation in soils. Short Course on Roadside Development (Ohio). 26:74–83. 1967.

12723. ______. The computer, a new tool for the golf turf manager. RCGA National Turfgrass Conference. 19:46–51. 1968.

12724. ______. Cultivation, and control of weeds, insects, disease. USGA Green Section Record. 5(6):20–22. 1968.

12725. ______. The plant, its habits and the way we propagate it. 40th International Turfgrass Conference Proceedings. 40:63. 1969.

12726. ______. Nitrogen behavior in plants and soils. Ohio Turfgrass Conference Proceedings. pp. 11–26. 1970.

12727. ______. The use of iron in turfgrass management. Ohio Turfgrass Conference Proceedings. pp. 44–48. 1970.

12728. ______. Plants to enhance environment. USGA Green Section Record. 8(4):15–17. 1970.

12729. ______. Effects of fertilizer on plant growth. Proceedings of Southern California Turfgrass Institute. pp. 30–46. 1971.

12730. ______. Turf power. Proceedings of Southern California Turfgrass Institute. pp. 109–114. 1971.

12731. ______. The use of soluble fertilizers for lawn care. 42nd Annual Michigan Turfgrass Conference Proceedings. (1):61–71. 1972.

12732. ______. Maintenance of athletic turfs: fertilization, irrigation, cultivation. 42nd Annual Michigan Turfgrass Conference Proceedings. (1):72–78. 1972.

12733. Roberts, E. C. and E. Bredakis. Nutrient culture techniques—their value in turfgrass research. Agronomy Abstracts. p. 66. 1958.

12734. ______. Turfgrass root development. The Golf Course Reporter. 28(8):12–15,18–24. 1960.

12735. Roberts, E. C. and D. R. Brockshus. Kind and extent of injury to greens from preemergence herbicides. The Golf Superintendent. 34(5):13,16,18,36. 1966.

12736. Roberts, E. C. and J. H. Cheesman. Effect of nitrogen and moisture stress on leaf spot infection in Merion bluegrass. Golf Course Reporter. 32(5):18–20. 1964.

12737. Roberts, E. C., and D. Chittenden. Effects of de-icing chemicals on grassy plants. Short Course on Roadside Development. (Ohio). 28:88–94. 1969.

12738. Roberts, E. C. and A. E. Cott. Nimblewill threatens Iowa Lawns. Iowa Farm Science. 17(8):18–19. 1963.

12739. ______. A new look at bermudagrass and zoysia for Iowa lawns. Iowa Farm Science. 19(10):5–7. 1965.

12740. ______. Comparative value of bentgrass strains for putting greens. Professional Turfgrass Series. Iowa State University Cooperative Extension Service. 1965.

12741. Roberts, E. C. and J. R. Harvis. Lawn pests. Massachusetts Agricultural Extension Leaflet. 294:1–12. 1956.

12742. ______. Lawn construction. Massachusetts Agricultural Extension Leaflet. 313:1–8. 1958.

12743. ______. Lawn maintenance. Massachusetts Agricultural Extension Leaflet. 312:1–4. 1959.

12744. Roberts, E. C. and D. P. Lage. Effects of an evaporation retardant, a surfactant, and an osmotic agent on foliar and root development of Kentucky bluegrass. Agronomy Journal. 56(1):71–74. 1965.

12746. Roberts, E. C. and R. Lavigne. Fungus gnats found to inhibit development of turfgrass. USGA Journal and Turf Management. 12(6):25–26. 1959.

12747. Roberts, E. C., and F. E. Markland. Nitrogen induced changes in bluegrass-red fescue turf populations. Agronomy Abstracts. p. 36. 1966.

12748. ______. Dollar spot tests yield tips. Golfdom. 40(2):38–40,42,44,46,48. 1966.

12749. Roberts, R. Irrigation today. Mid-Atlantic Superintendents Conference Proceedings. pp. 13–14. 1966.

12750. Roberts, E. C. and F. E. Markland. Effect of phosphorus levels and two growth regulators on arsenic toxicity in *Poa annua* L. Agronomy Abstracts. p. 57. 1967.

12751. ______. Fertilizing helps turf crowd out weeds. Weeds Trees and Turf. 6(3):12–14. 1967.

12752. Roberts, E. C., and H. M. Pellett. Potassium helps bluegrass face hot summer. Better Crops with Plant Food. 48(2):2–7. 1964.

12753. Roberts, E. C. and J. J. Ptacek. Pre-emergence crabgrass control. Golf Course Reporter. 30(3):18. 1962.

12754. Roberts, E. C., and E. L. Zybura. Effect of sodium chloride on grasses for roadside use. Highway Research Record. 193:-35–41. 1967.

12755. Roberts, E. C., R. C. Lambe, and A. E. Cott. Fairy rings in lawns—cause and treatment. Yard and Garden Series, Iowa State University Cooperative Extension Service PD–43. 1966.

12756. Roberts, E. C., F. E. Markland, C. E. Whitcomb. Pre-emergence crabgrass control in bentgrass. Iagreen. 31st Annual Turfgrass Conference Proceedings. p. 9. 1965.

12757. ______. Dollar spot resistance in bentgrass. Iagreen. 31st Annual Turfgrass Conference Proceedings. pp. 9–10. 1965.

12758. ______. A measurement of grass vigor. Iagreen. 31st Annual Turfgrass Conference Proceedings. pp. 10–11. 1965.

12759. ______. Wetting agents: How do they act? Iagreen. 31st Annual Turfgrass Conference Proceedings. pp. 11–12. 1965.

12760. Roberts, E. C., F. E. Markland, and H. M. Pellett. Effects of bluegrass stand and watering regime on control of crabgrass with preemergence herbicides. Weeds. 14(2):-157–161. 1966.

12761. Roberts, E. C., M. C. Shurtleff, and H. Gunderson. Stop lawn pests! Iowa Agricultural Experiment Station. Farm Science. 14:515–518. 1960.

12762. Roberts, E. C., B. S. Taylor, and A. E. Cott. Good sound sports turf is important. Iowa State University Cooperative Extension Service. 314:8. 1965.

12763. Roberts, H. M. The effect of defoliation on the seed-producing capacity of bred strains of grasses. I. Timothy and perennial ryegrass. Journal of the British Grassland Society. 13(4):255–261. 1958.

12764. Roberts, R. Irrigation techniques—automation. International Turfgrass Conference Proceedings. 38:42–43. 1967.

12765. Roberts, R. A. and I. V. Hunt. The effect of shoot cutting on the growth of root and shoot of perennial ryegrass (*Lolium perenne* L.) and of timothy (*Phleum pratense* L.). Welsh Journal of Agriculture 12:158–174. 1936.

12766. Roberts, R. H. and B. E. Struckmeyer. The effects of temperature and other environmental factors upon the photoperiodic responses of some of the higher plants. Journal of Agricultural Research. 56(9):633–677. 1938.

12767. ______. Further studies of the effects of temperature and other environmental factors upon the photoperiodic responses of plants. Journal of Agricultural Research. 59(9):699–709. 1939.

12768. Roberts, T. How to seal a leaking pond. Golf Superintendent. 38(1):44. 1970.

12769. Robertson, I. M., and A. B. Stewart. Weed eradication in lawns by chemical treatment. Journal of the Board of Greenkeeping Research. 5(18):213–216. 1938.

12770. Robertson, J. H. Effect of frequent clipping on the development of certain grass seedlings. Plant Physiology. 8(3):425–447. 1933.

12771. Robertson, W. K. Inter- and intra-stolon movement of fertilizer nutrients in St. Augustine grass as affected by moisture stress. Soil Science Society of America Proceedings. 27:385–388. 1963.

12772. Robey, M. J. Use of ion-exchange resins in fertilization of turfgrasses. Proceedings of the Midwest Regional Turf Conference. pp. 17–18. 1969.

12773. ______. Use of ion-exchange resins in fertilization of turfgrasses. Turf Bulletin. Massachusetts Turf and Lawngrass Council. 5(5):20. 1969.

12774. ______. Exchange resins as a source of nitrogen for turfgrasses. Proceedings of the Midwest Regional Turf Conference. pp. 50–51. 1970.

12775. ______. Purdue stadium maintenance program. Proceedings of the Midwest Regional Turf Conference. pp. 51–53. 1970.

12776. ______. Natural turf care costs—our records. Midwest Regional Turf Conference Proceedings. pp. 75–77. 1972.

12777. Robey, M. J. and W. Daniel. Maintenance of athletic fields. Proceedings of the Midwest Regional Turf Conference. pp. 21–27. 1971.

12778. ______. Going the extra mile in athletic field care. Proceedings of the Midwest Regional Turf Conference. pp. 31–32. 1971.

12779. Robinette, G. Traffic control with plants. Grounds Maintenance. 3(4):35–38. 1968.

12780. ______. Rating plants for traffic control. Grounds Maintenance. 3(12):25. 1968.

12781. ______. Functional uses of plant material. Parks and Recreation. 3(5):48–49. 1968.

12782. ______. The functional spectrum of plants . . . atmospheric purification. Grounds Maintenance. 4(4):70–71. 1969.

12783. Robinson, B. "Proper turf renovation methods". Central Plains Turfgrass Conference. p. 2. 1963.

12784. Robinson, B. H. Four-cycle internal combustion engines. International Turfgrass Conference and Show. 39:53–54. 1968.

12785. Robinson, B. P. Other methods of determining the nutritional requirements of turf grasses. Southern Turf Foundation Bulletin No. 1. Fall, 1960.

12786. ______. Better turf by weed control. Fifth Annual Turf Conference, Georgia Coastal Plain Experiment Station. May, 1951.

12787. ______. Some principles to follow in applying fertilizer materials to turf. Southern Turf Foundation Bulletin No. 2. Spring, 1951.

12788. ______. Good bermuda putting greens require nitrogen. Southern Turf Foundation Bulletin No. 2. 1951.

12791. ______. Southeast appraises its research plan. Golfdom. 26(3):54,96–98. 1952.

12792. ______. Stronger grasses, nitrogen, *Poa annua* answer? Golfdom. 26(7):66–67. 1952.

12793. ______. A comparison of several herbicides for weed control in turf. Proceedings Southern Weed Conference. 1952.

12794. ______. Weed control in turf. Proceedings of the Florida Turf Grass Conference. 1:19–28. 1953.

12795. ______. Recommendations for planting bermudagrass on highway projects. Mimeograph Paper No. 79. 1953.

12796. ______. Ground pearl—a soil born insect damaging Southern turf grasses. Southern Turf Foundation Bulletin No. 4. Spring, 1953.

12797. ______. The selective control of spotted spurge, *(Euphorbia supina) (E. maculata, nutans)* in close cut turf. Proceedings Southern Weed Conference. 1953.

12798. ______. Part II—weed control. Proceedings of the Second Annual University of Florida Turfgrass Conference. 2:45–46. 1954.

12799. ______. Weed control in southern turf. Golf Course Reporter. 22(2):14–19. 1954.

12800. ______. Green Section gives soil testing advice. Golfdom. 28(8):52–54. 1954.

12801. ______. Weed control in turf. Parks, Golf Courses and Sports Grounds. 19. 1954.

12802. ______. Keeping weeds out of southern turf. Southern Florist and Nurseryman. May, 1954.

12803. ______. Weed control in southern turf. Southern Turf Bulletin No. 5. Spring, 1954.

12804. ______. Golf course superintendents, professionals, green chairmen and experiment stations rate field performance of Tiffine bermudagrass. Southern Turf Foundation Bulletin No. 5. 1954.

12805. ______. Fertilizing greens, tees, and fairways. Florida Turf Management Conference Proceedings. 3:55–59. 1955.

12806. Robinson, B. P. and J. M. Latham. Tifgreen, new high-rated bermuda, is released. Golfdom. 30(4):45–46, 48. 1956.

12807. Robinson, B. P. A summary of turfgrass weed control tests. Southeastern Turfgrass Conference Proceedings. 10:41–45. 1956.

12808. ______. A summary of turfgrass weed control tests. USGA Journal and Turf Management. 9(6):26–28. 1956.

12809. ______. Major weed problems in Southern turf. Special Proceedings of the Turf Section, Weed Society of America. pp. 31–34. 1956.

12810. ______. Fertilizing warm season grasses. Golf Course Reporter. 25(1):10–17. 1957.

12811. ______. Turfgrass weed control. Southeastern Turfgrass Conference Proceedings. 11:29–31. 1957.

12812. ______. Maintenance of machinery. Southeastern Turfgrass Conference Proceedings. 13:33–35. 1959.

12813. ______. Factors to consider in sprinkler irrigated turfgrasses. Park Maintenance. 15(6):22–28. 1962.

12814. ______. Liquid injection of fertilizers. Proceedings of the 18th Annual Texas Turfgrass Conference. 18:41–43. 1963.

12815. Robinson, B. P. and G. W. Burton. Breeding bermudagrass for turf. USGA Journal and Turf Management. 3(1):25–27. 1950.

12816. ______. Turf research at the Southeastern Turf Research Center. USGA Journal and Turf Management. 5(7):24–28. 1952.

12817. ______. Tiffine (Tifton 127) bermuda is developed at Tifton. Golfdom. 27(4):48. 1953.

12818. ______. Tiffine (Tifton 127) turf bermuda grass. Southern Turf Foundation Bulletin No. 4. 1953.

12819. Robinson, B. P. and J. E. Gallagher. Weed control—a problem north and south. Parks and Recreation. 41(6):264–266. 1958.

12820. Robinson, B. P. and J. M. Latham. Tifgreen—a hybrid turf bermudagrass. Georgia Coastal Plain Experiment Station Mimeograph Series N.S. 23. 1956.

12822. ______. Tifgreen bermuda introduced. The Greenkeeper's Reporter. 24(2):-34. 1956.

12823. ______. New Tifgreen is putter's dream. Southern Seedsman. 19(9):57. 1956.

12824. ______. Tifgreen—an improved turf bermuda grass. USGA Journal and Turf Management. 9(1):26–28. 1956.

12825. Robinson, B. P. and L. W. Morgan. Ground pearl—new threat to turf. Crops and Soils. 5(9):11, 21. 1953.

12826. ______. Ground pearl damaging southern turf grasses. USGA Journal and Turf Management. 6(5):28–29. 1953.

12827. Robinson, C. Don't argue with nature. Golfdom. 10(7):19–20. 1936.

12828. Robinson, C. B. Why argue? Nature makes the choice. Greenkeepers Club of New England Newsletter. 8(5):8. 1936.

12829. Robinson, C. E. Golf and golf course conditions in Canada. Pennsylvania State Turf Conference. 25:8–12. 1956.

12830. Robinson, G. S. Diploma in turf culture. New Zealand Institute for Turf Culture Newsletter. 43:14–15. 1966.

12831. ______. Drainage problems in turf culture. New Zealand Institute for Turf Culture Newsletter. 53:13. 1968.

12832. ______. Greenkeeping problems in New Zealand. Proceedings of the First International Turfgrass Research Conference. pp. 10–12. 1969.

12833. ______. The New Zealand turf advisory service. Proceedings of the First International Turfgrass Research Conference. pp. 440–443. 1969.

12834. ______. Impressions of greenkeeping in Western U.S.A. and the United Kingdom. New Zealand Institute For Turf Culture Newsletter. 65:7–10. 1970.

12835. Robinson, J. Sprinklers. International Turfgrass Conference & Show. 39:63–65. 1968.

12836. Robinson, J. B. Soil nitrification as influenced by growth of perennial grasses. RCGA Sports Turfgrass Conference. 17:27. 1966.

12837. Robinson, P. W., and C. F. Hodges. Effect of benomyl on eradication of *Ustilago striiformis* from *Agrostis palustris* and on plant growth. Phytopathology. 62(5):-533–535. 1972.

12839. Robinson, R. R., and W. H. Pierce. Response of permanent pastures to lime and fertilizers 1930–36. West Virginia Agricultural Experiment Station Bulletin. 289. 47 pp. 1938.

12840. Robinson, R. R., V. G. Sprague, and A. G. Lueck. The effect of irrigation, nitrogen fertilization and clipping treatments on persistence of clover and on total and seasonal distribution of yields in a Kentucky bluegrass sod. Agronomy Journal. 44(5):-239–244. 1952.

12841. Robinson, W. H. Insect and mite pests of lawn and turfgrass. Virginia Polytechnic Institute and State University Cooperative Extension Service. No. 471. 8 pp. 1971.

12842. Robison, A. E. Lawn watering systems sales and experiences. Proceedings of the Midwest Regional Turf Conference. pp. 34–35. 1965.

12843. ______. Automatic sensing controllers for agriculture and turf watering. Proceedings of the Midwest Regional Turf Conference. pp. 35–36. 1965.

12844. Robson, M. J. and O. R. Jewiss. A comparison of British and North African varieties of tall fescue *(Festuca arundinacea)*. 2. Growth during winter and survival at low temperatures; 3. Effects of light, temperature and day length on relative growth rate and its components. Journal of Applied Ecology. 5(1):179–190:191–204. 1968.

12845. Rockfeller, W. J. Applying ammonium sulfate. USGA Green Section Bulletin. 5(1):3. 1925.

12846. ______. Keep the weeds out of new turf. The National Greenkeeper. 1(3):-13–15. 1927.

12847. ______. Cutting, moving, and relaying sod. USGA Green Section Bulletin. 9(8):137–139. 1929.

12848. Rockwell, F. F. Lawns. The Macmillan Company, New York. 87 pp. 1929.

12849. Rockwell, F. F. and E. C. Grayson. The complete book of lawns. The American Garden Guild and Doubleday & Company, Inc., Garden City, New York. 190 pp. 1956.

12850. Rodale, J. I. Lawns. How to Landscape Your Own Home. Rodale Books, Inc. Emmaus, Pennsylvania. pp. 579–647. 1963.

12851. Rodale, J. I. Lawn beauty the organic way. Rodale Books, Inc., Emmaus, Pa. 411 pp. 1970.

12852. Rodman, R. Problems and trends of highway turf establishment. Proceedings of the 15th Annual Texas Turfgrass Conference. 15:36–39. 1960.

12853. Roeder, F. My 1931 conditioning program dodged brown-patch. Golfdom. 5(12):52. 1931.

12854. Rogers, C. The seasonal renovation of winter games pitches. Parks, Golf Courses, and Sports Grounds. 31(7):516, 518, 534. 1966.

12855. ______. Some aspects of sports field drainage. Parks, Golf Courses, and Sports Grounds. 31(9):715–724. 1966.

12856. Rogers, C. F. The plant biochemistry of water. Greenkeeper's Reporter. 6(5):-7–10, 24–29. 1938.

12857. Rodgers, D. R. Highway erosion control. Journal of Soil and Water Conservation. 20:189–190. 1965.

12858. Rogers, P. A. Let's learn more about turfgrasses—mowing. Kellogg Supply, Inc. Bulletin. 4(1):3–6. 1970.

12859. ______. Let's learn more about turfgrasses. Kellogg Supply, Inc. Bulletin. 3(6):13–14. 1969.

12860. Rogler, G. A. Response of geographical strains of grasses to low temperature. Journal of the American Society of Agronomy. 35(7):547–559. 1943.

12861. Rogler, G. A., H. H. Rampton, and M. D. Atkins. The production of grass seeds. Seeds, Yearbook of Agriculture (U.S.-D.A.) pp. 163–171. 1961.

12862. Rohweder, D. A. What is a grass? Wisconsin Turfgrass Conference Proceedings. 4 pp. 1965.

12863. ______. Turfgrass seed. Wisconsin Turfgrass Conference Proceedings. pp. 37–45. 1966.

12864. Rolfs, P. H. Grasses and forage plants. Florida Agricultural Experiment Station Bulletin. 18. pp. 4–10. 1891.

12865. Rommell, G. J. Latest news on experimental plots at Charles River. Greenkeepers Club of New England Newsletter. 2(7):3–6. 1930.

12866. Roney, J. N. Bermudagrass insects. Arizona Turf Conference Proceedings. pp. 26–27. 1959.

12867. Roome, B. W. Management and maintenance of an industrial sports ground. Journal of the Sports Turf Research Institute. 8(30):413–422. 1954.

12868. ______. Grass cutting—some of the problems which arise. Journal of the Sports Turf Research Institute. 9(32):221–224. 1956.

12869. Rooseveare, G. M. Germany: Reseeding flooded lands. Journal of the British Grassland Society. 2(4):226–229. 1947.

12870. Root, J. Roadside mowing. Grounds Maintenance. 2(1):14–17. 1967.

12871. ______. Roadside mowing. Grounds Maintenance. 2(12):28–31. 1967.

12872. Roper, L. Hedges and lawns. Successful Town Gardening. Country Life Limited. London. pp. 84–89. 1957.

12873. Roquemore, W. A. Contract planting service. Proceedings of Florida Turf-Grass Management Conference. 10:177–179. 1962.

12874. ______. Soil fumigation. Auburn University Annual Turfgrass Short Course. pp. 22–26. 1964.

12875. ______. Weed control in turf. Auburn University Annual Turfgrass Short Course. pp. 27–37. 1964.

12876. ______. Revision and renovation of tees. Southeastern turfgrass Conference Proceedings. 20:6–8. 1966.

12877. ______. What to consider in selecting a turfgrass. Proceedings, Florida Turf Grass Management Conference. 15:75–79. 1967.

12878. Roquemore, W. A., and J. Shirley. Planting golf greens to bermudagrass. Southeastern Turfgrass Conference Proceedings. 21:6–12. 1967.

12879. Roquemore, W. A. Soil preparation and planting. Proceedings of the Florida Turf-Grass Management Conference. 17:44–48. 1969.

12880. Rosa, N. Control of yarrow in lawns. Research Report of the National Weed Committee, Eastern Section (Canada). 6:137. 1961.

12881. Rose, F. T. The Great Plains section. Short Course on Roadside Development (Ohio). 16:77–79. 1957.

12882. Rose, R. E. Modern aerification equipment and its use. RCGA National Turfgrass Conference. 18:55–56. 1967.

12883. ______. Equipment for the turfgrass industries. Northwest Turfgrass Conference Proceedings. 24:55–64. 1970.

12884. Rosell, C. H. Comparison of plant characteristics of annual ryegrass (Oregon), *Lolium multiflorum* Lam., and Linn perennial ryegrass, *Lolium perenne* L. M.S. Thesis, Oregon State University. 39 pp. 1967.

12885. Roseman, J. Turf methods that make good in Florida. Golfdom. 4(2):90, 95–96. 1930.

12886. ______. Re-turfing Florida golf courses. The National Greenkeeper. 4(2):11–15. 1930.

12888. Rosenberg, N. J. Response of plants to the physical effects of soil compaction. Advances in Agronomy. 16:181–196. 1964.

12889. Rosenquist, D. W. and D. H. Gates. Responses of four grasses at different stages of growth to various temperature regimes. Journal of Range Management. 14(4):198–202. 1961.

12890. Ross, C. G., W. R. Furtick, and L. C. Burrill. Testing seedling grass tolerance to postemergence herbicides. Western Weed Control Conference Research Program Report. pp. 64–65. 1966.

12891. Ross, R. J. The design and construction of golf courses. Parks and Recreation. 17(12):422–426. 1934.

12892. ______. The design and construction of golf courses. Parks and Recreation. 18(1):17–21. 1934.

12893. Rossi, D. A. Economic trends in golf course construction. 42nd Annual Michigan Turfgrass Conference Proceedings. 1:-51–53. 1972.

12894. ______. Trends in the golf course industry. 23rd Annual RCGA National Turfgrass Conference. pp. 62–64. 1972.

12895. Rossiter, J. Hydraulic valves and tubes. International Turfgrass Conference & Show. 39:71–73. 1968.

12896. Rossiter, R. Polyethylene covers for putting greens. Turf Clippings—University of Massachusetts. 1(10):5–6. 1965.

12897. Rost, C. O. Soil characteristics in relation to golf courses. Golfdom. 6(6):58, 60. 1932.

12898. ______. Soil and its relation to plant growth. Golfdom. 13(4):25–28. 1939.

12899. ______. The modern conception of soil and its relation to plant growth. The Greenkeepers' Reporter. 7(4):5–6, 43–45. 1939.

12901. Rothwell, D. F. and C. C. Hortenstine. Composted muncipal refuse: its effects on carbon dioxide, nitrate, fungi, and bacteria in arrendondo fine sand. Agronomy Journal. 61(6):837–840. 1969.

12903. Rouse, R. D. Soil testing and its value in a fertilizer program for turfgrass. Auburn University Annual Turfgrass Short Course. pp. 38–44. 1960.

12904. ______. The chemical side of soils. Auburn University Annual Turfgrass Short Course. pp. 12–21. 1964.

12905. Rouze, B. L. Care and management of cemetery turf. Proceedings of the 6th Annual Texas Turf Conference. pp. 78–83. 1951.

12906. Row, H. C., and J. R. Reeder. Root hair development as evidence of relationships among genera of *Gramineae.* American Journal of Botany. 44(7):596–601. 1957.

12907. Rowell, J. B. New fungicides for turf. Greenkeepers' Reporter. 16(4):22–23, 35. 1948.

12908. ______. New fungicides for turf diseases. Proceedings of Midwest Regional Turf Conference. pp. 83–85. 1948.

12909. ______. New fungicides for turf diseases. Midwest Turf-News and Research. 2(2):4. 1948.

12910. ______. Cooperative turf fungicide trials. USGA Journal and Turf Management. 3(1):31. 1950.

12911. ______. Observations on the pathogenicity of *Rhizoctonia solani* on bent grasses. Plant Disease Reporter. 35(5):240–242. 1951.

12912. ______. Brown patch observations on bentgrasses. USGA Journal and Turf Management. 4(4):28–29. 1951.

12913. Rowland, C. E. Characteristics of pipe used for sprinkler systems. California Turfgrass Culture. 16(1):5–8. 1966.

12914. ______. Updating and maintaining of old sprinkler irrigation systems. Proceedings of the Turfgrass Sprinkler Irrigation Conference. 1 p. 1966.

12915. Rowley, R. Use of methyl bromide for control of undesirable vegetation. Proceedings of the Annual Texas Turf Conference. 6:102–106. 1951.

12916. Rubins, E. J., and F. E. Bear Carbon-Nitrogen ratios in organic fertilizer materials in relation to the availability of their nitrogen. Soil Science. 54:411–423. 1942.

12917. Rudge, G. Plastic pipe. Turf Clippings. University of Massachusetts. 1(10):A27–A33. 1965.

12918. ______. Watering system. Golfdom. 41:28–29. 1967.

12919. Rudolfs, W. Experiments with common rock salt: II. Eradication of weeds and cleaning of roadsides with salt. Soil Science. 12:457–470. 1921.

12920. Ruepl, T. Water, its source, and your rights. International Turfgrass Conference Proceedings. 38:66–68. 1967.

12921. Ruf, R. H. Planting a new lawn. Nevada Agricultural Extension Circular. 123:1–7.

12922. Ruffner, J. D., and J. G. Hall. Crownvetch in West Virginia. West Virginia Agricultural Experiment Station Bulletin. 487. 19 pp. 1963.

12923. Ruelke, C. O. Unkempt bahiagrass gains a kept look. Sunshine State Agricultural Research Report. 9(3):14–15. 1964.

12924. Ruhmann, J. H. The cost of watering turf grasses. Proceedings of the Texas Turfgrass Conference. 8:6–8. 1954.

12925. ______. The cost of watering turf grasses. Proceedings of the 25th Annual Texas Turf Conference. 20:6–8. 1970.

12926. Ruhnke, G. N. Soil tests. Golfdom. 9(3):27–30. 1935.

12927. Ruhnke, G. N. Limitations in the use and interpretations of chemical tests of golf course soils. The Greenkeepers Reporter. 3(2):20–22. 1935.

12928. Rumberg, C. B. The accumulation of organic matter at the soil surface of bentgrass turf quality as affected by cultural practices. M.S. Thesis, Rutgers University. 57 pp. 1956.

12929. ______. The effect of environmental factors on the herbicidal activity and mode of action of selected arsenic compounds. Ph.D. Thesis, Rutgers University. 1958.

12930. Rumberg, C. B., R. E. Engel, and W. F. Meggitt. Effect of temperature on the herbicidal activity and translocation of arsenicals. Weeds. 8(4):582–588. 1960.

12931. Runge, G. F. Turf diseases: cause and control. The Groundsman. 15(12):6–24. 1962.

12932. ______. Turf diseases: cause and control. Park Maintenance. 15(3):76–84. 1962.

12933. Runkels, J. R. Wilt and turfgrasses. Proceedings of the 20th Annual Texas Turfgrass Conference. 20:15–16. 1965.

12934. Runnels, H. A. Fungus diseases cause unsightly lawns. Ohio Farmer. 213(10):15. 1954.

12935. ______. Turf diseases and their control. Ohio Pesticide Institute News. 7(2):-33–34. 1954.

12936. ______. Tests on dollar spot and snowmold. Golf Course Reporter. 31(5):42. 1963.

12937. ______. Diseases of turfgrasses. Lawn and Ornamental Research—1966. Ohio Agricultural Research and Development Center. Research Summary 16. pp. 13–14. 1966.

12938. ______. Turf fungicide trials Ohio Agricultural Research and Development Center. Research Summary 24. p. 35. 1967.

12939. Runnels, H. A. and J. D. Wilson. The influence of certain spray materials, herbicides, and other compounds on the desiccation of plant tissue. Ohio Agricultural Experiment Station. Bimonthly Bulletin. 19(168):104–109. 1934.

12940. Runyan, C. R. The control of crabgrass in a cemetery. Turf Culture. 1(1):-61–62. 1939.

12941. ______. Alta fescue for turf. Proceedings of Midwest Regional Turf Conference. pp. 52–54. 1948.

12942. ______. Runyan explains cemetery turf problems with traffic, new areas and interments. Midwest Turf News and Research. 3(4):1–2. 1949.

12943. ______. Cemetery turf problems,

part 2. Midwest Turf News and Research. 4(1):3–4. 1950.

12944. Rupar, R. The proper approach to buying an irrigation system. Proceedings of the Midwest Regional Turf Conference. pp. 30–31. 1966.

12945. ______. Budgeting your irrigation needs. Missouri Lawn and Turf Conference Proceedings. 6:12–14. 1965.

12946. ______. Irrigation systems for turfgrass production. Ohio Turfgrass Conference Proceedings. pp. 14–16. 1967.

12947. Rupel, T. Grass, carts and paths. Golf Course Reporter. 26(2):44–46. 1958.

12948. Russell, H. H. Report on the Green Section survey. USGA Green Section Record. 5(2):6–7. 1967.

12949. Russell, P. Chickweed control in Louisville. Proceedings of Midwest Regional Turf Conference. pp. 91–92. 1951.

12950. Russell, R. A. Correct method of lawnseed labeling in the northeastern states. Seed World. 94(2):18–20. 1964.

12951. Russell, T. E. Approaches to turfgrass disease control. Arizona Turfgrass Conference. Proceedings. pp. 28–29. 1972.

12952. Ruthven, W. H. C. Fertilizing for sod nurseries. Proceedings of the Midwest Regional Turf Conference. pp. 24–25. 1956.

12953. ______. Producing sod. Proceedings of the Midwest Regional Turf Conference. pp. 35–36. 1957.

12954. ______. Growing sod—how fast? Proceedings of the Midwest Regional Turf Conference. pp. 36–38. 1958.

12955. ______. How thick should sod be cut? Warren's Turf Nursery. Palos Park, Illinois. p. 13. 1959.

12956. Ruychaver, G. J. Turfgrass in the Netherlands. Proceedings of the First International Turfgrass Research Conference. pp. 8–9. 1969.

12957. Ryan, M., W. F. Wedin, and W. B. Bryan. Nitrate-N levels of perennial grasses as affected by time and level of nitrogen application. Agronomy Journal. 64(2):-165–168. 1972.

12958. Rydstrom, A. G. The economic value of turfgrass Colorado. Rocky Mountain Regional Turfgrass Conference Proceedings. pp. 18–21. 1964.

12959. Ryker, T. C. Materials for chemical weed control. USGA Journal and Turf Management. 2(3):30. 1949.

12960. ______. New and improved chemicals boon to turf maintenance. Golfdom. 25(2):45–46. 1951.

12961. Ryle, G. J. A. Effects of light intensity on reproduction in S.48 timothy (*Phleum pratense* L.). Nature. 191(4784):-196–197. 1961.

12962. ______. Studies in the physiology of flowering of timothy (*Phleum pratense* L.). III. Effects of shoot age and nitrogen level on the timing of inflorescence production. Annals of Botany. 27:453–465. 1963.

12963. ______. Studies in the physiology of flowering of timothy (*Phleum pratense* L.). IV. Effects of shoot age and nitrogen level on the size of the inflorescence. Annals of Botany. 27:467–479. 1963.

12964. ______. The influence of date of origin of the shoot and level of nitrogen on ear size in three perennial grasses. Annals of Applied Biology. 53:311–323. 1964.

12965. ______. A comparison of leaf and tiller growth in seven perennial grasses as influenced by nitrogen and temperature. Journal British Grassland Society. 19(3):281–290. 1964.

12966. ______. Effects of daylength and temperature on ear size in S.24 perennial ryegrass. Annals of Applied Biology. 55(1):107–114. 1965.

12967. ______. Effect of the environment on leaf growth and tillering in herbage grasses. Experiments in Progress, Grassland Research Institute. 17:31–33. 1963–64.

12968. Ryan, J. C. Practical suggestions for fighting weed pests and care of cemetery lawns. The Modern Cemetery. 43(3):56–57. 1933.

12969. Saakov, S. G. Gazony Tsvetochnoe of ormlenie. Akademia Nauk SSSR. Moskva. 156 pp. 1954.

12972. Sacamcno, C. M. Kentucky bluegrass lawns for northern Arizona. Arizona Garden Guides. A.F. 953. 1–4 pp.

12973. Sachs, R. Chemical control of plant growth and development. California Turfgrass Culture. 11(1):4–7. 1961.

12974. ______. Growth retardants. California Turfgrass Culture 15(1):5–7. 1965.

12975. ______. Growth control of landscape plants. Proceedings of the 1972 Turf and Landscape Horticulture Institute. pp. 66–70. 1972.

12976. Sachs, R. M., R. W. Kingsbury, and J. DeBie. Retardation by carboxin of low-temperature induced discoloration in zoysia and bermudagrass. Crop Science. 11(4):585–586. 1971.

12977. Saegusa, T. Distribution and detection of the soil nematodes. KGU Green Section Turf Research Bulletin. 8:10–25. 1965.

12978. ______. Control of the soil nematodes by medicines. KGU Green Section Turf Research Bulletin. 8:26–30. 1965.

12979. ______. The root nema, "Meloidogyne," control by the warm water treatment on the turfgrass. K.G.U. Green Section Turf Research Bulletin. 12:27–28. 1967.

12980. Sagar, G. R. An important factor affecting the movement of 2, 2-dichloropropionic acid (Dalapon) in experimental systems of *Agropyron repens.* British Weed Control Conference Proceedings. 5(1):271–277. 1960.

12981. St-Pierre, J. C. and M. J. Wright. Distribution of 14C photosynthates in timothy (*Phleum pratense* L.) during the vegetative stage of growth. Crop Science. 12(2):-191–194. 1972.

12982. St. Pierre, L. V. An eviction notice for *Poa annua* on fairways. USGA Green Section Record. 5(5):5–6. 1968.

12983. ______. *Poa annua* suppression at Longmeadow Country Club. Annual RCGA National Turfgrass Conference. 21:-31–32. 1970.

12984. Saladini, J. L. and F. W. Zettler. Characterization and transmissibility of sugarcane mosaic virus infecting St. Augustinegrass in Florida. S-70 Southern Region Corn Improvement Project Annual Report for 1970. 1971.

12985. ______. Survey for viral diseases of St. Augustinegrass in Florida. The Plant Disease Reporter. 56(9):822–823. 1972.

12986. ______. Characterization of strain E of sugarcane mosaic virus infecting St. Augustinegrass. The Plant Disease Reporter. 56(10):885–889. 1972.

12987. Sale, P. J. M. Changes in water and soil temperature during overhead irrigation. Weather. 20:242–245. 1965.

12988. Salinger, J. Soil sterilisation. New Zealand Institute for Turf Culture Newsletter. 17:10–13. 1962.

12989. Sampson, A. W. and A. Chase. Range grasses of California. California Agriculture Experiment Station Bulletin 430. 94 p. 1927.

12990. Sampson, A. W., A. Chase, and D. W. Hedrick. California grasslands and range forage grasses. California Agricultural Experiment Station Bulletin. 724. 130 pp. 1951.

12991. Sampson, K. The occurrence of snow mould on golf greens in Britain. Journal of the Board of Greenkeeping Research. 2(5):116–118. 1931.

12992. ______. Note on the occurrence of a new species of *Olpidium* in the root hairs of *Agrostis.* Journal of the Board of Greenkeeping Research. 3(8):32–33. 1933.

12993. Sampson, K., and J. H. Western. Diseases of British grasses and herbage legumes. Cambridge University Press. 85 pp. 1941.

12994. ______. Diseases of British grasses and herbage legumes. Cambridge University Press (British Mycological Society). 118 pp. 1954.

12995. Sams, T. Manually watered fairways. Proceedings of the Midwest Regional Turf Conference. pp. 27–28. 1965.

12996. ______. Discussion—the thinking superintendent. 42nd International Turfgrass Conference and Show Proceedings. pp. 5–6. 1971.

12997. ______. Putting zoysia into Audubon C. C. fairways. Midwest Regional Turf Conference Proceedings. p. 62. 1971.

12998. ______. Zoysia into fairways. Midwest Regional Turf Conference Proceedings. pp. 50–51. 1972.

12999. Samuels, G. The management of golfing turf on heavy soil. Journal of the Board of Greenkeeping Research. 2(7):242–248. 1932.

13000. Sanas, M. G. Lawn insect pests and diseases. Connecticut Agriculture College Extension Bulletin. 61–6:1–11. 1961.

13001. Sanday, E. Breaking through the subsoil. The Groundsman. 19(7):24, 30. 1966.

13002. Sanders, A. F. Turf compaction and maintenance of greens in Japan. Golf Course Reporter. 19(6):7–10, 22–23. 1951.

13003. ______. New turf pests. Agronomy Journal. 45(12):631–632. 1953.

13004. Sanders, L. Grass lawns . . . in Alexandria, Egypt., Royal Horticultural Society, Alexandria. pp. 37–41. 1904.

13005. Sanders, T. W. Lawns and greens: their formation and Management, Garden, tennis and croquet lawns, bowling and golf greens, cricket grounds, grass paths, etc. W. H. L. Collinridge. London. 141 pp. 1911.

13006. Sandusky, J. Comments on park planning and construction. Northwest Turfgrass Conference Proceedings. 21:29–38. 1967.

13007. Sansom, W. J. Greenkeeping in Canada—yesterday and today. The National Greenkeeper. 3(3):9–18. 1929.

13008. ______. Fall seeding helps greens. The National Greenkeeper. 3(9):12–13. 1929.

13009. Santawisuk, T. The effect of irrigation and mulch on soil surface temperature and soil moisture near the soil surface. Ph.D. Thesis, Mississippi State University. 1971.

13010. Santelmann, P. W. Chickweed control in lawns. Proceedings of the Northeastern Weed Control Conference. 13:160–161. 1959.

13011. ______. Preemergence crabgrass control in Maryland. Proceedings of the Northeastern Weed Control Conference. 15:-393–395. 1961.

13012. ______. Turf—recommended practices—Oklahoma. Annual Southern Weed Conference Research Report. 19:113–114. 1966.

13013. Santelmann, P. W. and J. A. Meade. Premergence crabgrass control in lawns. Proceedings of the Northeastern Weed Control Conference. 14:288–291. 1960.

13014. Santelmann, P. W. and R. E. Wagner. Lawn care. Maryland Agricultural Extension Bulletin. 171:1–16. 1960.

13016. Sapuncakis, M. S. Response of common purslane to dicamba treatment. Ph.D. Thesis, University of Massachusetts. 1972.

13017. Sargent, G. Selective control of weeds explained. Golfdom. 2(10):12–15. 1928.

13018. Sarsfield, A. C. Which type of irrigation system? Golf Course Reporter. 32(6):20–27. 1964.

13019. ______. How to select a sprinkler irrigation system. Grounds Maintenance. 2(12):12–14. 1967.

13020. ______. Explanation of the mechanics of automatic sprinkling. Proceedings of the Turfgrass Sprinkler Irrigation Conference. 5:7–15. 1967.

13021. ______. Eight-point check list for selecting irrigation equipment. Grounds Maintenance. 3(12):92. 1969.

13022. Sartoretto, P. A. Gibberellic acid, amazing growth stimulant. Golf Course Reporter. 25(2):40–44. 1957.

13023. ______. Fungicides and weed control. Central Plains Turfgrass Conference. 11:2–3. 1961.

13024. ______. MCPP for weed control on bentgrass. Turf Clippings. University of Massachusetts. 1(10):A1–5. 1965.

13025. ______. Keeping control. International Turfgrass Conference Proceedings. 38:3–5. 1967.

13026. ______. Arsenicals as turf herbicides—their chemistry, mode of action, volatility, and residues. Rutgers University Short Course in Turf Management Proceedings. pp. 26–28. 1971.

13027. Satchell, D. P. A basic guide to turfgrass fertilization. Weeds and Turf. pp. 8–10. April, 1963.

13028. Sauer, G. Über den einsatz chemischer mittel zur pflage von grünflächen an strasser. Die Neue Landschaft. 11:556. 1966.

13029. Saunders, J. A. A helping hand to mother nature. (Ohio) Short Course on Roadside Development. 27:58–61. 1968.

13030. Saupe, D., F. Giles, M. C. Carbonneau, and A. J. Turgeon. Establishment of various ground covers with herbicides and shredded bark. University of Illinois Turfgrass Field Day. pp. 14–16. 1972.

13031. Savage, D. A. Buffalo grass for fairways in the Plains States. USGA Green Section Bulletin. 13(5):144–149. 1933.

13032. Savage, D. A., and L. A. Jacobson. The killing effect of heat and drought on buffalo grass and blue grama grass at Hays, Kansas. Journal of the American Society of Agronomy. 27(7):566–582. 1935.

13033. Savage, S. M., J. P. Martin, and J. Letey. Contribution of some soil fungi to natural and heat-induced water repellency in sand. Soil Science Society of America Proceedings. 33(3):405–409. 1969.

13034. Sawada, T. The drainage for the golf courses. K. G. U. Green Section Turf Research Bulletin. 12:1–14. 1967.

13035. Sawhney, J. S. The structure of the rhizomes of *Agropyron repens* Beau; *Poa pratensis* L.; and *Festuca arundinancea* Schreb. variety Alta. Ph.D. Thesis, Ohio State University. 1965.

13036. Sawtelle, E. R. Water vs. mowing. Golfdom. 7(5):49–50. 1933.

13037. Sayre, J. D. The relation of hairy leaf coverings to the resistance of leaves to transpiration. Ohio Journal of Science. 20(3):55–86. 1920.

13038. Scagnetti, P. R. Labor savings through use of equipment. Annual RCGA National Turfgrass Conference. 21:33–34. 1970.

13039. Scarsbrook, C. E. Regression of nitrogen uptake on nitrogen added from four sources applied to grass. Agronomy Journal. 62(5):618–620. 1970.

13041. Scarseth, G. What plant tissue tests tell. Golfdom. 13(6):14–16. 1939.

13042. Schaaf, H. M. Phenotypic selection in crested wheatgrass. Crop Science. 8(6):643–647. 1968.

13043. Schabinger, J. E. Part III—South Florida. Proceedings, University of Florida Turf Conference. 2:39–41. 1954.

13044. ______. Symposium—controlling thatch development. Varietal differences. Florida Turf Management Conference Proceedings. 3:47–51. 1955.

13045. Schacht, F. C. Maintenance costs —intramural and athletic fields. Exposition Conference Southern California. 5 pp. 1966.

13046. ______. UCLA maintaining athletic fields . . . how much does it cost? Grounds Maintenance. 2(8):29–31. 1967.

13047. ______. General maintenance of sprinkler systems at University of California. Proceedings of the Turfgrass Sprinkler Irrigation Conference. 5:1–4. 1967.

13048. ______. Relationship of landscape construction specifications to grounds maintenance. Proceedings of Southern California Turfgrass Institute. pp. 106–108. 1971.

13049. Schacht, F. C. and E. G. Dickson. Two annual grid classics . . . demand year round maintenance. Grounds Maintenance. 3(1):11–13,39. 1968.

13050. Schade, R. O. Irrigation of golf greens. The Golf Superintendent. 35(7):29–30. 1967.

13051. Schader, D. L. Insect control in turf. Proceedings of the Midwest Regional Turf Conference. pp. 44–47. 1957.

13056. Schallock, D. A., H. W. Indyk, and R. E. Engel. Preemergence crabgrass control–1966. Rutgers University Turfgrass Short Course. 1966.

13057. Schardt, A. Brown-patch control resulting from early-morning work on greens. USGA Green Section Bulletin. 5(11):254–255. 1925.

13058. Schardt, C. A. Designing more effective sprinkler systems. Proceedings of the Turfgrass Sprinkler Irrigation Conference. 1 p. 1966.

13059. Scheibe, W. G. Management skills and records for progress in turf. Proceedings 17th Annual Texas Turfgrass Conference. 17:24–27. 1962.

13060. Scheider, F. Weeding and watering open spring session in South. Golfdom. 2(4):14. 1928.

13061. Scheibner, R. A., W. W. Gregory, and H. G. Raney. Insecticide recommendations for field corn, small grains, grain sorghum, and bluegrass. University of Kentucky Cooperative Extension Service. Publication 278–I. 5 pp. 1972.

13062. Schell, G. W. Maintaining turf for beautility. Texas Turfgrass Conference Proceedings. 22:83–85. 1967.

13063. Scherer, H. Schöner Rasen aber wie? Verlag Stichnote, Darmstadt. 159 pp. 1966.

13064. Schery, R. W. Gobs of good grass. The Lawn Institute. Marysville, Ohio. 4 pp.

13065. ______. Turfgrass cultivars. American Horticulturist. 51(2):6.

13067. ______. Plant for profit. The Lawn Institute. Marysville, Ohio. 4 pp.

13068. ______. Modern lawn maintenance. Building Maintenance and Modernization. 16(4):4.

13069. ______. Integrating grasses into the landscape. Building Operating Management. 18(2).

13070. ______. Autumn is for lawn care. The Family Handyman. 19(5):1–3.

13071. ______. Slow-release fertilizer for lawns. Part I: Lawn and garden series. Fertilizer Solutions. 15(4).

13072. ______. Try autumn for lawn renovation. Part II: Lawn and garden series. Fertilizer Solutions. 15(5).

13073. ______. Anti-pollution, ward for weeds? Part III: Lawn and garden series. Fertilizer Solutions. 15(6).

13074. ______. Season to seed, feed and weed. The Floral Magazine. 68(9):1–4.

13076. ______. A stitch in time. Flower and Garden. 13(3):1.

13077. ______. Summer suggestions for lawns. Flower and Garden. 13(6):1–2.

13078. ______. A new era dawns for bluegrass. Flower and Garden. 14(8):1–2.

13079. ______. Fescue facts fescue. Flower and Garden. 15(8).

13080. ______. The changing lawn scene. Flower and Garden. 15(11).

13082. ______. Starting a new lawn. The Lawn Institute. Marysville, Ohio. 2 pp. November 11, 1966.

13083. ______. Common sense lawn care. The Lawn Institute. Marysville, Ohio. 2 pp. November 11, 1966.

13084. ______. Live with your lawn and like it. The Lawn Institute. Marysville, Ohio. 2 pp.

13085. ______. Lawn zip and zoom. The Lawn Institute. Marysville, Ohio. 2 pp. November 11, 1966.

13086. ______. New lawngrasses and their fertilization. The Gardener. 30(4).

13088. ______. Lawns: their making and keeping. Handbook on Gardening. 8 pp.

13089. ______. New lawn seeds ready to sprout profits. Home and Garden Supply Merchandiser. 20(3):1 p.

13090. ______. A spotless summer lawn takes careful planning. Home Garden. 57(2):-1–2.

13091. ______. Lawn care starts this month. Home Garden. 57(3):1–2.

13092. ______. Lawn care now pays green dividends. Home Garden. 57(4):1–2.

13093. ______. Fescues the hard-working grasses for home lawns. The Lawn Institute. Marysville, Ohio. 2 pp.

13094. ______. A lawn you'll have time to enjoy. Home Garden. 59(3).

13095. ______. There is a difference in grass seed. The Lawn Institute. Marysville, Ohio. 2 pp.

13096. ______. Lawns. The Lawn Institute. Marysville, Ohio. 3 pp. November 11, 1966.

13097. ______. The label's the clue to lawn seed. The Lawn Institute. Marysville, Ohio. 2 pp.

13098. ______. Winter feeding of lawns. Horticulture. 47(1):1 p.

13099. ______. Lawn thatch, what it's all about. Horticulture. 47(9):1–2.

13100. ______. Spring handbook on lawns. Horticulture. 48(3).

13101. ______. Top turfgrasses. Horticulture. 49(4):4 pp.

13102. ______. Steps to assure a good lawn. The Lawn Institute. Marysville, Ohio. 2 pp. November 11, 1966.

13103. ______. Landscape turf. Landscape Industry. 14(6):2. 1969.

13104. ______. The new look in lawnscaping. Landscape Industry. 15(2):30–31. 1970.

13105. ______. Lawngrass proprietaries come of age. Landscape Industry. 17(1). 1972.

13111. ______. Quality turfgrass. The Lawn Institute. 14 pps.

13112. ______. Grasses for turf. Proceedings of the 13th Annual Meeting of the Oregon Seed Growers League. pp. 21–26.

13113. ______. Your outdoor carpet. Popular Gardening. 2 p.

13114. ______. Lawn weeds . . . don't let them swamp you. The Lawn Institute. Marysville, Ohio. 3 pp. November 11, 1966.

13115. ______. Invest now in your lawns. Resort Management. p. 4.

13116. ______. Start your lawn planning now. The Lawn Institute. Marysville, Ohio. November 11, 1966.

13117. ______. Lawns and turfs in the United States and Europe. Proceedings of the 29th Annual Meeting of the Oregon Seed Growers League. p. 9.

13118. ______. Winterseeding: are seedsmen missing a bet? Seedsmen's Digest. 1 p.

13119. ______. New look for winter turf. The Lawn Institute. Marysville Ohio. 2 pp.

13120. ______. Establishing a lawn. Southern Gardens. 7(3):1–2.

13121. ______. Fine-textured winterseeding. Southern Turf Newsletter. 13:1, 3–4.

13122. ______. The fabulous 2–4–D. The Modern Cemetery. 57(5):51–52. 1947.

13123. ______. Bluegrass and blueblood. Golf Course Reporter. 22(2):26–29. 1954.

13124. ______. Lawn climates. Handbook on Lawns. Brooklyn Botanic Garden. pp. 133. 1956.

13125. ______. Grateful for grass. Parks and Recreation. 39(3):4–6. 1956.

13126. ______. Better lawns are autumn sponsored. Flower and Gardan Magazine for Mid-America. 4 pp. August, 1957.

13127. ______. Patience pays in seeding lawns. The Green Thumb. pp. 91–92. April, 1957.

13128. ______. Here's how to build a new lawn. Horticulture. 35(8):407, 427. 1957.

13129. ______. What's ahead for better lawns. Horticulture. 35(9):452–453, 474–475. 1957.

13130. ______. Northern lawns: how to keep them green all season. Flower Grower. 2 pp. 1958.

13131. ______. Good lawn seed goes with autumn. Home Maintenance and Improvement. 2 p. Fall, 1958.

13132. ______. Lawn weed grumbles. Proceedings of the North Central Weed Control Conference. 15:38–39. 1958.

13133. ______. Balanced roadside seeding. Short Course on Roadside Development. Ohio Department of Highways. 17:79–85. 1958.

13134. ______. Have a carefree lawn. Popular Gardening. 1 p. Sept, 1958.

13135. ______. Bluegrass sprouting under stress. Agronomy Abstracts. p. 91. 1959.

13136. ______. What grass to plant. You Can Grow a Good Lawn; The American Potash Institute. pp. 12–15. 1959.

13137. ______. The red, white and blue of beauty. American Rose Magazine. 15(8):4, 5, 24. 1959.

13138. ______. Turf (preparation for summer heat). Building Maintenance and Modernization. 6(14):1–4. 1959.

13139. ______. Bluegrass' grassroots empire. Economic Botany. 13(1):75–84. 1959.

13140. ______. Let the lawngrass do your weeding. Flower and Garden Magazine. 4 p. May, 1959.

13141. ______. Beauty and the beast. The Garden Journal of the New York Botanical Garden. 9(2):47–49, 64, 67. 1959.

13142. ______. What's new in lawn building. Horticulture. 37(9):457, 484. 1959.

13143. ______. The story of bluegrass. Horticulture. 37(10):530–531. 1959.

13145. ______. Lawn facts and fancies. Popular Gardening. 2 pp. April, 1959.

13146. ______. If you care for your lawn —start now. Seed World. 84(5):31. 1959.

13147. ______. A new lawn patching method. Seed World. 84(6):28. 1959.

13148. ______. New Home—new lawn. Seed World. 84(8):24. 1959.

13149. ______. The newer way for starting lawns. Seed World. 85(3):28. 1959.

13150. ______. Planting lawnseed—or trouble? Seed World. 85(5):27. 1959.

13151. ______. Showcase for roses. American Rose Magazine. 15(19):6, 7, 26. 1960.

13152. ______. Modern power mowers. Better Building Maintenance. 4 p. July, 1960.

13153. ______. The prestige of quality turf. Concept. p. 35–43. August, 1960.

13154. ______. Lawn time coming up! Flower and Garden Magazine. 4 pp. August, 1960.

13155. ______. Quality lawn seed. The Garden Journal of the New York Botanical Garden. 10(2):59–60, 67. 1960.

13156. ______. Weeding lawns. The Garden Journal of the New York Botanical Garden. 10(3):95–97. 1960.

13157. ______. Don't let crabgrass spoil your lawn. Horticulture. 38(5):271, 285. 1960.

13158. ______. Lawn establishment and care. Missouri Botanical Garden Bulletin. 1960.

13159. ______. What's so great about grass. Proceedings, Missouri Lawn and Turf Conference. 1:1–4. 1960.

13160. ______. Lawn grasses—old and new. Proceedings, Missouri Lawn and Turf Conference. 1:12–15. 1960.

13161. ______. Turf and your park. Park Maintenance. 13(5):20–21. 1960.

13162. ______. The grass in your life. Parks and Recreation. 43(11):503–511. 1960.

13164. ______. Lawn-keeping: the lazy man's version. Popular Science Monthly. 176(6):176–177, 198–199. 1960.

13165. ______. The best turf for athletic fields. Scholastic Coach. 29(5):44, 46. 1960.

13166. ______. Lawn tending logic. Seed World. 86(8):25. 1960.

13167. ______. The cost of living lawngrass. Seed World. 86(9):24. 1960.

13168. ______. Hot weather precautions. Seed World. 87(2):19. 1960.

13169. ______. Your lawn's summer siesta is not permanent. Seed World. 87(3):22. 1960.

13170. ______. New lawns and nursegrasses. Seed World. 87(5):27. 1960.

13171. ______. No fuss with fescues. Seed World. 87(6):22. 1960.

13172. ______. The lawn makes the tree king. Trees Magazine. 4 pp. July-Aug., 1960.

13173. ______. Grasses and grass mixtures for New England lawns. Turf Clippings. University of Massachussetts. 1(5):A–29 to A–34. 1960.

13174. ______. Big bargains in turf. The American Cemetery. 34(8):29–30. 1961.

13175. ______. Lawns and roses—have needs in common. American Rose Magazine. 16(4):10, 11, 29, 30. 1961.

13176. ______. Are you ready for lawn seeding? American Rose Magazine. 16(8):8, 28. 1961.

13177. ______. Planting the new lawn. Better Building Maintenance. 4 p. April, 1961.

13178. ______. Choose lawn beauty–I. The Cemeterian. pp. 1–4. Feb., 1961.

13179. ______. Choose lawn beauty–II. The Cemeterian. 4 pp. March, 1961.

13180. ______. Fertilizing lawns in winter. Concept. p. 31–35. Jan., 1961.

13181. ______. Lawngrass or weed—choice is yours. The Gardener. 21:2. 1961.

13182. ______. Autumn lawn seed sales: yours for the promoting. Home and Garden Supply Merchandiser. 2 p. August, 1961.

13183. ______. Lawns need food too! Horticulture. 39(1):33, 49. 1961.

13184. ______. Theories about lawn care. Horticulture. 39(4):202, 227. 1961.

13185. ______. Insure lawn planting with fertilizer. The Lawn Institute. 2 pp. July, 1961.

13186. ______. Autumn lawn seeding is best. The Lawn Institute. 2 pp. July, 1961.

13187. ______. What's new for starting turf. The Lawn Institute. 2 pp. July, 1961.

13188. ______. Special lawn grasses for special uses. The Lawn Institute. 2 pp. July, 1961.

13189. ______. Ten spring lawn problems: how to solve them. The Lawn Institute. Marysville, Ohio. 2 pp. 1961.

13190. ______. The lawn book. The Macmillan Company, New York. 207 pp. 1961.

13191. ______. Quick sprouting of lawn seed. Seed World. 88(7):28. 1961.

13192. ______. Why lawn seed mixtures. Seed World. 88(8):21. 1961.

13193. ______. Fescue as a nursegrass. Seed World. 88(9):26. 1961.

13194. ______. Autumn lawn seeding is best. Seed World. 89(4):28–30. 1961.

13195. ______. Lawns need fall fertilizing. Seed World. 89(5):24. 1961.

13196. ______. What's new for starting turf. Seed World. 89(6):19. 1961.

13197. ______. Special lawn grasses for special uses. Seed World. 89(10):19. 1961.

13198. ______. Grass greets the guest. Tourist Court Journal. p. 4. 1961.

13199. ______. The lawn, 1962 model. Family Handyman. 3 p. 1962.

13200. ______. Remake your lawn in autumn. The Family Handyman. 4 p. 1962.

13201. ______. The lawn and outdoor living. The Lawn Institute. 2 pp. Feb., 1962.

13202. ______. For a good lawn—do, but don't overdo. The Lawn Institute. 2 pp. Feb., 1962.

13203. ______. Wise choice of grass seed. The Lawn Institute. 2 pp. Feb., 1962.

13204. ______. Lawn pests losing out? The Lawn Institute. 2 pp. Feb., 1962.

13205. ______. Which lawn grass varieties are out front? The Lawn Institute. 2 pp. Feb., 1962.

13206. ______. New lawns and nurse grasses. The Lawn Institute. 1 p. July, 1962.

13207. ______. Why lawn seed is sold in mixture. The Lawn Institute. 2 p. July, 1962.

13208. ______. How's your lawn I.Q.? The Lawn Institute. 2 pps. 1962.

13209. ______. Autumn lawn seeding is best. The Lawn Institute. 2 pp. July, 1962.

13210. ______. Steps in new lawn construction. Proceedings of the Midwest Regional Turf Conference. pp. 76–78. 1962.

13211. ______. Establishing and maintaining turf on highway right-of-ways. Proceedings, Missouri Lawn and Turf Conference. 3:1–2. 1962.

13212. ______. Large area seeding—a rundown on turf. Park Maintenance. 15(4):-54–58. 1962.

13213. ______. Selecting lawn grasses. T.F.H. Publications. Jersey City. 32 pp. 1962.

13214. ______. Selecting the right grass. 1962 Wisconsin Turfgrass Conference Proceedings. pp. 1–3. 1962.

13215. ______. Turf is big business. Wisconsin Turfgrass Conference Proceedings. pp. 1–3. 1962.

13216. ______. The curious case of Highland bentgrass. Garden Journal of the New York Botanical Garden. 13(5):171–173. 1963.

13217. ______. The lawn accents your landscaping. The Lawn Institute. 2 pp. Feb., 1963.

13218. ______. Start lawn repairs immediately. The Lawn Institute. 2 pp. Feb., 1963.

13219. ______. New wrinkles in lawn keeping. The Lawn Institute. 2 pp. Feb. 1963.

13220. ______. Fescues aren't fussy. The Lawn Institute. 1 p. July, 1963.

13221. ______. A million reasons for a good lawn mixture. The Lawn Institute. 1 p. July, 1963.

13222. ______. Oregon dolls the nation. The Lawn Institute. 1 p. July, 1963.

13223. ______. Highland bentgrass to the fore. The Lawn Institute. p. 1–3. July, 1963.

13224. ______. The big bluegrass mixup. The Lawn Institute. 2 pp. July, 1963.

13225. ______. Featuring fine fescues. The Lawn Institute. 2 p. July, 1963.

13226. ______. Steps for starting a lawn. The Lawn Institute. 2 p. July, 1963.

13227. ______. Lawn seed cost is minor. The Lawn Institute. 2 p. July, 1963.

13228. ______. Seed size has a bearing. The Lawn Institute. 1 p. July, 1963.

13229. ______. Lawn planting automated. The Lawn Institute. 2 p. July, 1963.

13230. ______. Lawn frills and fads. The Lawn Institute. 2 p. July, 1963.

13231. ______. Lawngrass varieties and mixtures. University of Maine Turf Conference Proceedings. 1:3 pp. 1963.

13232. ______. Quality cultivars. Proceedings, Missouri Lawn and Turf Conference. 4:16–17. 1963.

13233. ______. Why thatch? Proceedings, Missouri Lawn and Turf Conference. 4:28. 1963.

13234. ______. Winterseeding. Proceedings, Missouri Lawn and Turf Conference. 4:31. 1963.

13236. ______. The householder's guide to outdoor beauty. Pocket Books, Inc., New York. 337 pp. 1963.

13237. ______. Business opportunities in turf reseeding. Weeds and Turf. pp. 6–9, 16. September, 1963.

13238. ______. What lawn to plant where. American Nurseryman. 119(8):10, 11. 1964.

13239. ______. The grass is always greener . . . The Lawn Institute. Marysville, Ohio. 4 pp. 1964.

13240. ______. Highland bent for close-clipped turf. The Lawn Institute. 1 pp. Feb., 1964.

13241. ______. Preventing crabgrass. The Lawn Institute. 1 pp. Feb., 1964.

13242. ______. Selected bentgrass hardly a pest. The Lawn Institute. 1 pp. Feb. 1964.

13243. ______. Fine fescue, all-purpose grass. The Lawn Institute. 2 pp. Feb., 1964.

13244. ______. Annual seeding for difficult sites. The Lawn Institute. 2 pp. Feb., 1964.

13245. ______. Weeds in lawn seed. The Lawn Institute. 2 pp. Feb., 1964.

13246. ______. Warmth helps lawn sprouting. The Lawn Institute. 2 pp. Feb., 1964.

13247. ______. Seed and fertilize lawns at the same time. The Lawn Institute. 2 pp. Feb. 1964.

13248. ______. Brighten the lawn this spring. The Lawn Institute. 2 pp. Feb. 1964.

13249. ______. A lawn seed guarantee. The Lawn Institute. 2 pp. Feb. 1964.

13250. ______. New lawngrass labeling easily understood. The Lawn Institute. 2 pp. Feb. 1964.

13251. ______. Lawn renovation with chemicals. The Lawn Institute. 2 pp. Feb., 1964.

13252. ______. Kentucky bluegrass varieties. The Lawn Institute. 2 pp. Feb. 1964.

13253. ______. Kentucky bluegrass, fine fescue and thatch. The Lawn Institute. 2 p. Feb. 1964.

13254. ______. Feeding fescues. The Lawn Institute. 2 pp. Feb., 1964.

13255. ______. Ways to control lawn weeds. The Lawn and Garden Counselor. 1(1):5. 1964.

13256. ______. Spring lawn cleanup: early steps to brighter turf. The Lawn and Garden Counselor. 1(1):4. 1964.

13257. ______. The importance of quality seed. Rutgers University Short Course in Turf Management. 32:1–6. 1964.

13258. ______. The importance of quality seed. Seed World. 94(3):6–11. 1964.

13259. ______. Weeds in lawn seed. Seed World. 94(7):20. 1964.

13260. ______. Kentucky bluegrass, fine fescue and thatch. Seed World. 94(8):20. 1964.

13261. ______. Fertilize the lawn. Seed World. 95(4):20. 1964.

13262. ______. Lawn time '64. Seed World. 95(5):22. 1964.

13263. ______. Last chance for lawn weed control. Seed World. 95(6):18. 1964.

13264. ______. Mowing before winter. Seed World. 95(7):18. 1964.

13265. ______. Simplified lawn renovation. Seed World. 95(8):21. 1964.

13266. ______. Lawn seed sweepstakes. Seed World. 95(10):14–15. 1964.

13267. ______. Kentucky bluegrass. Weeds and Turf. 3(7):12–13. 1964.

13268. ______. Fine fescues. Weeds and Turf. 3(8):16–17. 1964.

13269. ______. Turfgrass portraits III: bentgrasses. Weeds and Turf. 3(9):16, 17. 1964.

13270. ______. Wintergrass. Weeds and Turf. 3(10):16–17. 1964.

13271. ______. Turfgrass portraits V: Bermudagrass. Weeds and Turf. 3(11):8, 9. 1964.

13272. ______. Turfgrass portraits. VI: Zoysia. Weeds, Trees and Turf. 3(12):12–13. 1964.

13273. ______. Lawn seed, and what's a weed. The American Horticultural Magazine. 44(2):71–83. 1965.

13274. ______. Pure grass seed. Auburn University Annual Turfgrass Short Course. pp. 1–4. 1965.

13275. ______. Maintenance of lawns. Auburn University Annual Turfgrass Short Course. pp. 10–14. 1965.

13276. ______. Start winter lawns soon. The Lawn Institute. Marysville, Ohio. 1965.

13277. ______. Steps for winter turf. The Lawn Institute. Marysville, Ohio. 1965.

13278. ______. Darker green wintergrass. The Lawn Institute. Marysville, Ohio. 1965.

13279. ______. Every man's lawn. The Lawn Institute. Marysville, Ohio. 1965.

13280. ______. Golf green quality for the lawn. The Lawn Institute. Marysville, Ohio. 1965.

13281. ______. Luxury lawns for winter. The Lawn Institute. Marysville, Ohio. 1965.

13282. ______. New way to winterseed. The Lawn Institute. Marysville, Ohio. 1965.

13283. ______. This remarkable Kentucky bluegrass. Annals of the Missouri Botanical Garden. 52(3):444–451. 1965.

13284. ______. Lawn seed without weeds. Proceedings, Missouri Lawn and Turf Conference. 6:1–2. 1965.

13285. ______. Mulches for seeding. Proceedings, Missouri Lawn and Turf Conference. 6:17–18. 1965.

13286. ______. The migration of a plant. Natural History Magazine. 74(11):40–45. 1965.

13287. ______. How to get a good buy on good seed for roadside seeding. Ohio Short Course on Roadside Development. 24:46–51. 1965.

13289. ______. Seed for sod. Parks and Recreation. 48(4):218–221. 1965.

13290. ______. How to distinguish bluegrass. Seed World. 96(4):20. 1965.

13291. ______. Spring lawn improvement. Seed World. 96(7):20. 1965.

13292. ______. Fine fescues acclaimed for lawns. Seed World. 96(8):20. 1965.

13293. ______. Highland bentgrass seed astronomical. Seed World. 97(3):29. 1965.

13294. ______. Good lawn seed sprouts fast. Seed World. 97(4):19. 1965.

13295. ______. Lawn renovation. Seed World. 97(5):20. 1965.

13296. ______. Fertilize fine fescues, bluegrass. Seed World. 97(6):22. 1965.

13297. ______. Lawn seed and lawn weeds. Seed World. 97(9):6–11. 1965.

13298. ______. August is the month for home and community lawn projects. Turf Bulletin. Massachusetts Turf and Lawn Grass Council. 2(11):9–10. 1965.

13299. ______. Bahiagrass. Weeds, Trees, and Turf. 4(1):16–17. 1965.

13300. ______. St. Augustinegrass. Weeds, Trees, and Turf. 4(3):16–17. 1965.

13301. ______. Centipedegrass. Weeds, Trees, and Turf. 4(2):16–17. 1965.

13302. ______. Air cushion mowing. Weed, Trees, and Turf. 4(9):14–15. 1965.

13303. ______. The lawn seed industry comes of age. Crops and Soils. 19(3):8–11. 1966.

13304. ______. Why not bentgrass blends? Golfdom. 40(3):90–91, 94, 96. 1966.

13305. ______. It's wintergrass seeding time again. The Lawn Institute. Marysville, Ohio. 1 p. Autumn, 1966.

13306. ______. Wintergrasses that go farther. The Lawn Institute. Marysville, Ohio. 2 pp. Autumn, 1966.

13307. ______. New winterseeding ideas for the lawn. The Lawn Institute. Marysville, Ohio. 1 p. Autumn, 1966.

13308. ______. Lawns and the water shortage. Seed World. 98(4):20. 1966.

13309. ______. Spring lawn seeding. Seed World. 98(5):22. 1966.

13310. ______. Spring lawn "do's". Seed World. 98(6):21. 1966.

13311. ______. Warmth helps lawn sprouting. Seed World. 98(8):21. 1966.

13312. ______. Top lawn grasses need little mowing. Seed World. 99(3):22. 1966.

13313. ______. Bargain time for lawns. Seed World. 99(5):21. 1966.

13314. ______. Where bargains are not bargains. Seed World. 99(8):22. 1966.

13315. ______. Seed and fertilize lawns at the same time. Seed World. 99(8):22. 1966.

13316. ______. The migration of a plant. Turf Bulletin. Massachusetts Turf & Lawn Grass Council. 3(1):5–9. 1966.

13317. ______. Good seed makes good sod. Turf Bulletin. Massachusetts Turf & Lawn Grass Council. 3(2):5–8. 1966.

13318. ______. Seed selection. Turf Bulletin. Massachusetts Turf & Lawn Grass Council. 3(2):19–20. 1966.

13319. ______. Remarkable Kentucky bluegrass. Weeds, Trees and Turf. 5(10):16–17. 1966.

13320. ______. Looking to turfgrass quality. Wisconsin Turfgrass Conference Proceedings. pp. 1–10. 1966.

13321. ______. Select seed wisely. The Golf Superintendent. 35(10):14–18. 1967.

13322. ______. Minimum maintenance turf. Illinois Turfgrass Conference Proceedings. 8:8–9. 1967.

13323. ______. Chemical lawn edging. Seed World. 100(2):19. 1967.

13324. ______. The spring lawn program. Seed World. 100(6):20. 1967.

13325. ______. Stop crabgrass. Seed World. 100(7):17. 1967.

13326. ______. Highland for lawn patterns. Seed World. 100(9):19. 1967.

13327. ______. Bluegrass in the yard by the yard. Seed World. 100(10):21. 1967.

13328. ______. Grass or ground cover. Seed World. 101(4):22. 1967.

13329. ______. Remove lawn thatch early. Seed World. 101(5):18. 1967.

13330. ______. All-American lawns. Seed World. 101(6):20. 1967.

13331. ______. Fine fescue as roadside grass. Seed World. 101(8):21. 1967.

13332. ______. Red fescue true blue. Seed World. 101(9):20. 1967.

13333. ______. Weed turf with fertilizer. Weeds Trees and Turf. 6(11):20–21. 1967.

13334. ______. Seed and feed to hex the weed. American Rose Annual. pp. 26–34. 1968.

13335. ______. Autumn lawns: up, up and away! The Floral Magazine. pp. 1–8. 1968.

13336. ______. Bluegrass/bentgrass checks *Poa annua.* The Golf Superintendent. 36(10):32–34. 1968.

13337. ______. Evaluation of turfgrass for roadsides. Short Course on Roadside Development (Ohio). 27:78–82. 1968.

13338. ______. Lawn fescues check weeds. Seed World. 102(4):16. 1968.

13339. ______. Bluegrass stands Guard. Seed World. 102(5):22. 1968.

13340. ______. Chemical lawn mowing. Seed World. 102(7):17. 1968.

13341. ______. Lawn thatch. Seed World. 102(8):21. 1968.

13342. ______. Guard against lawn weeds. Seed World. 103(7):19. 1968.

13343. ______. Mechanical renovation —one method for upgrading turf. Weeds, Trees, and Turf. 7(4):21. 1968.

13344. ______. Fylking and Tifdwarf bermuda. Weeds, Trees, and Turf. 7(11):23–25. 1968.

13345. ______. Turfgrass today. Grounds Maintenance. 3(12):44. 1968.

13346. ______. Turfgrass seed production in the U.S.A. Proceedings of the First International Turfgrass Research Conference. pp. 137–140. 1969.

13347. ______. Lawn fertilizers. Seed World. 104(4):20. 1969.

13348. ______. Spring lawn requirements. Seed World. 104(6):18. 1969.

13349. ______. Bluegrass breeding shows. Seed World. 104(7):18. 1969.

13350. ______. Good seed makes good sod. Seed World. 104(8):18. 1969.

13351. ______. Lawn seedbed important. Seed World. 105(2):20. 1969.

13352. ______. Autumn best for lawns. Seed World. 105(4):20. 1969.

13353. ______. Advantage of seed blends. Seed World. 105(6):20. 1969.

13354. ______. Winter-hardy lawns. Seed World. 105(8):19. 1969.

13355. ______. Winning turf combination: good seed, good fertilizer, and. . . . Weeds, Trees and Turf. 8(9):14–15. 1969.

13356. ______. How to turn grass into a lawn. Better Homes and Gardens. 1970.

13357. ______. Penncross. The Golf Superintendent. 38(4):18–20. 1970.

13358. ______. The essentials for roadside vegetation. 29th Ohio Short Course on Roadside Development. pp. 63–75. 1970.

13359. ______. New turfgrass varieties. Professional Turf News. Borden Greens and Fairways. 1(3):1. 1970.

13360. ______. To seed or sod? Seed World. 106(3):20. 1970.

13361. ______. Seeding spring lawns. Seed World. 106(4):20. 1970.

13362. ______. Spring lawn requirements. Seed World. 106(7):20. 1970.

13363. ______. Autumn is time to spruce up lawns. Seed World. 107(3):21. 1970.

13364. ______. Fashionable fescues. Seed World. 107(5):20. 1970.

13365. ______. Can lawns lick pollution? Seed World. 107(6):24. 1970.

13366. ______. Kentucky bluegrass: turfgrass par excellence. Weeds, Trees, and Turf. 9(1):6–7. 1970.

13367. ______. Trends in turfgrass. The American Cemetery. 44(9):38–40. 1971.

13368. ______. Perspectives on golf green fertilization. The Golf Superintendent. 39(3):26–29. 1971.

13369. ______. Lawn renovation the modern way. Home Garden. 58(5):38–39. 1971.

13370. ______. Bluegrass. Park Maintenance. 24(7):20. 1971.

13371. ______. Seed mixtures for sod. The Sod Grower. 1(4):16–17. 1971.

13372. ______. Lawns slow pollution. Turf Bulletin. Massachusetts Turf and Lawn Council. 7(4):15. 1971.

13373. ______. Fescues are shady characters. Turf Bulletin (Massachusetts). 8(1):-14. 1971.

13374. ______. Lawngrass extraordinary . . . fine fescues. Weeds, Trees and Turf. 10(1):16–18. 1971.

13375. ______. New turf grass varieties bred to resist disease. American Cemetery. 45(3):4 pps. 1972.

13376. ______. New lawn grasses applauded. The American Rose. 21(21):10, 11. 1972.

13377. ______. New lawngrass varieties. Flower and Garden. 16(11):2 pp. 1972.

13378. ______. Avoid summer brownout in lawns. The Gardener. 32(4):1. 1972.

13379. ______. A lawn you'll have time to enjoy. Home Garden. 59(3):40–41. 1972.

13380. ______. Top turfgrasses. Iowa Golf Course Superintendents Reporter. 4(11):8. 1972.

13381. ______. New grasses dramatize lawn renovation. Landscape Industry. 17(2):-26–27. 1972.

13382. ______. Environmental restrictions affect lawnseed costs. Ohio Turfgrass Foundation Newsletter. 29:1. 1972.

13383. ______. New ryegrasses better looking—harder. Ohio Turfgrass Foundation Newsletter. 30:6. 1972.

13384. ______. Of watering and lawn-grass rooting. Ohio Turfgrass Foundation Newsletter. 30:7. 1972.

13385. ______. Trends in the lawnseed trade. Seed World. 110(5):4–6. 1972.

13386. ______. Slow-release fertilizer for lawns. Turf Bulletin (Massachusetts). 8(3):-4–6. 1972.

13387. Schewndimna, J. L. Old and new grasses for turf use in the northwest. Proceedings Pacific Northwest Turf Conference, 4:-37–39. 1950.

13388. Shields, E. Golf course maintenance on fairways. Southeastern Turfgrass Conference Proceedings. 14:25–30. 1960.

13389. Schilleter, A. E. Lawns for South Carolina. Clemson Agricultural College, U.S. Dept. of Agriculture Circular 308. pp. 1–11. 1948.

13390. Schilletter, A. E. and H. A. Woodle. Lawns for South Carolina. South Carolina Agricultural Extension Circular 308:1–11. 1951.

13391. ______. Lawns for South Carolina. South Carolina Agricultural Extension Circular. 308:1–15. 1955.

13392. Schindler, H. and O. Porsch. Schlüssel zur mikroskopischen Bestimmung der Wiesengräser im blütenlosen Zustande. Verlag von Julius Springer. Wien. 31 pp. 1925.

13393. Schioler, E. Fertilization by slow release. Parks, Golf Courses, and Sports Grounds. 27(11):782, 805. 1962.

13394. Schirman, R., and K. P. Buchholtz. Influence of atrazine on control and rhizome carbohydrate reserves of quackgrass. Weeds. 14(3):233–236. 1966.

13395. Schlaack, N. F. Lawn renovation. Proceedings Florida Turf-Grass Management Conference. 14:99–103. 1966.

13396. ______. Mowing and watering of St. Augustine grass. Proceedings of Florida Turf-Grass Management Conference. 17:63–66. 1969.

13397. Schloss, I. E. Preparing the club for tournament play. Part II—The role of the tournament chairman. Florida Turf Management Conference Proceedings. 4:48–49. 1956.

13398. Schmehl, W. R. Soil phosphates. Rocky Mountain Regional Turfgrass Conference Proceedings. pp. 40–42. 1963.

13399. Schmeisser, H. Part II—West central Florida. Proceedings, University of Florida Turfgrass Conference. 2:37–38. 1954.

13400. Schmer, D. A. Carbohydrate translocation in blue grama, buffalograss and western wheatgrass as influenced by temperature and growth stage. M.S. Thesis, University of Wyoming. 1972.

13401. Schmidt, B. L. Method of controlling erosion on newly-seeded highway backslopes in Iowa. Iowa Highway Research Bulletin. 24:1–47. 1961.

13402. ______. Soil-water relationships. Ohio Agricultural Research and Development Center. Research Summary 24. pp. 21–24. 1967.

13403. Schmidt, B. L., G. S. Taylor, and R. W. Miller. Roadbank stabilization and vegetative establishment with corn steep liquor solutions and straw mulch. Agronomy Abstracts. p. 49. 1965.

13404. ______. Effect of corn steep liquor for erosion control and vegetative establishment on highway backslopes. Agronomy Journal. 61(2):214–217. 1969.

13405. Schmidt, L. Turf weed problems. State College of Washington Annual Turf Conference. 4:34. 1951.

13406. Schmidt, R. E. Overseeding winter greens in Virginia. Golf Course Reporter. 30(9):44, 46–47. 1962.

13407. ______. Winter grass overseeding —tests in Virginia. International Turf-Grass Conference Proceedings. 33:10. 1962.

13408. ______. Sensible watering of turfgrasses. Third Virginia Turfgrass Conference Proceedings. pp. 37–41. 1963.

13409. ______. The influence of night temperatures, light intensity, and nitrogen fertility on growth and physiological changes in *Agrostis* and *Cynodon* turfgrasses. Agronomy Abstracts. p. 47. 1965.

13410. ______. Some physiological responses of two grasses as influenced by temperature, light, and nitrogen fertilization. Ph.D. Thesis. Virginia Polytechnic Institute. 117 pp. 1965.

13411. ______. Environmental effects of nitrogen utilization. Agronomy Abstracts. p. 36. 1966.

13412. ______. Influence of light and temperature on turf (both warm and cool season grasses.). International Turfgrass Conference Proceedings. 37:42–45. 1966.

13413. ______. Hydraulic vegetative planting of turfgrass. The Golf Superintendent. 35(3):10, 13, 69. 1967.

13414. ______. Future turf management. The Golf Superintendent. 35(5):27–30. 1967.

13415. ______. Environmental influence on nitrogen utilization. Journal of the Sports Turf Research Institute. 43:49–58. 1967.

13416. ______. VPI's putting greens test modified soils. Weeds, Trees, and Turf. 6(2):-17–18. 1967.

13417. ______. Growing a vigorous, strong root system on cool season turfgrass. Weeds, Trees and Turf. 6(7):22–23. 1967.

13418. ______. The effect of modifying a silt loam soil on bentgrass putting turf quality. Agronomy Abstracts. p. 61. 1968.

13419. ______. Nitrogen on root growth. Mid-Atlantic Superintendents Conference Proceedings. p. 23. 1966.

13420. ______. Overseeding cool-season turfgrasses on dormant bermudagrass for winter turf. Proceedings of the First International Turfgrass Research Conference. pp. 124–126. 1969.

13421. ______. Nitrogen nutrition of turfgrasses. Proceedings of the First International Turfgrass Research Conference. pp. 191–195. 1969.

13422. ______. A sod producers two goals. Weeds, Trees and Turf. 11(1):31. 1972.

13423. Schmidt, R. E. and R. E. Blaser. Overseeding bermudagrass with cool-season grasses for winter putting turf. Agronomy Abstracts. pp. 71–72. 1960.

13424. ______. Cool season grasses for winter turf on bermuda putting greens. USGA Journal and Turf Management. 14(5):25–29. 1961.

13425. ______. Establishing winter bermuda putting turf. USGA Journal and Turf Management. 15(5):30–32. 1962.

13426. ______. Soil modification for heavily used turfgrass areas. Agronomy Abstracts. p. 54. 1967.

13427. ______. Effect of temperature, light, and nitrogen on growth and metabolism of Cohansey bentgrass (*Agrostis palustris* Huds.). Crop Science. 7(5):447–451. 1967.

13428. ______. Effect of temperature, light and nitrogen on growth and metabolism of 'Tifgreen' bermudagrass (*Cynodon* spp.). Crop Science. 9(1):5–9. 1969.

13429. Schmidt, R. E. and W. E. Chappell. Crabgrass control studies in turf. Proceedings of the Northeastern Weed Control Conference. 14:278–283. 1960.

13430. Schmidt, R. E. and H. B. Musser. Some effects of 2,4–D on turfgrass seedlings. Agronomy Abstracts. pp. 66–67. 1958.

13431. ______. Some effects of 2,4–D on turfgrass seedlings. USGA Journal and Turf Management. 11(6):29–32. 1958.

13432. Schmidt, R. E. and J. F. Shoulders. Overseeding bermudagrass with cool season grasses for winter turf. Agronomy Abstracts. p. 102. 1964.

13433. ______. Quality of cool season turfgrasses overseeded on bermudagrass for winter turf as influenced by thatch removal and nitrogen fertilization. Agronomy Abstracts. p. 71. 1970.

13434. ______. Fertilization practices and quality turf. USGA Green Section Record. 9(6):12–13. 1971.

13435. ______. Winter turf development on dormant bermudagrass as influenced by summer cultivation and winter N fertilization. Agronomy Journal. 64(4):435–437. 1972.

13436. Schmidt, R. and V. Snyder. Chelated iron and nitrogen effects on bentgrass. International Turfgrass Conference Proceedings. 43:48–49. 1972.

13437. Schmidt, R. E., R. E. Blaser, and M. T. Carter. Evaluation of turfgrasses for Virginia. Research Division—Virginia Polytechnic Institute Bulletin 12. pp. 1–16. 1967.

13438. Schmidt, R. E., J. F. Shoulders, R. E. Blaser, and A. S. Beecher. Turfgrass guide for lawns and other turf areas. Virginia Polytechnic Institute Agricultural Extension Service Circular No. 818. 11 pp. 1965.

13439. Schmitthenner, A. F. Isolation of *Pythium* from soil particles. Phytopathology. 52(11):1133–1138. 1962.

13440. Schmitz, N. Lawns. Pennsylvania Agricultural Experiment Station Circular. 143:1–10. 1931.

13441. Schmitz, G. Soil analysis specifications and interpretations. Proceedings of Southern California Turfgrass Institute. pp. 47–50. 1971.

13442. Schneider, E. Gets members help in zoysia program. Golfdom. 26(10):50. 1952.

13443. ______. Labor policies at my course. Proceedings of the Midwest Regional Turf Conference. pp. 15–16. 1955.

13444. ______. Using bermuda and zoysia. Proceedings of the Midwest Regional Turf Conference. pp. 42–43. 1958.

13445. ______. Survival of bermuda and zoysia. Proceedings of the Midwest Regional Turf Conference. pp. 51–52. 1959.

13446. ______. Starting and maintaining bermuda grass. Proceedings of the Midwest Regional Turf Conference. pp. 38–40. 1961.

13447. ______. Maintenance of U–3 bermuda fairway. Golf Course Reporter. 31(6):-40–44. 1963.

13448. ______. Keeping tight turf-bermuda grass. Proceedings of the Midwest Regional Turf Conference. pp. 39–40. 1964.

13449. ______. What is enough? Proceedings of the Midwest Regional Turf Conference. pp. 41–42. 1964.

13450. ______. Preparing for a national tournament. Proceedings of the Midwest Regional Turf Conference. pp. 36–40. 1966.

13451. ______. Report on U–3 fairways. Midwest Regional Turf Conference Proceedings. pp. 67–68. 1971.

13452. Schneider, J. Planting of slopes. Strass and Verkehr. 52(7):397–404. 1966.

13453. Schneider, V. E. and G. E. Korzan. An economic analysis of ryegrass seed. Oregon Agricultural Experiment Station. Bulletin 585. 15 pp. 1962.

13454. Schoeneweiss, D. F. Plant selection and maintenance—keys to disease control. Illinois Turfgrass Conference Proceedings. 11:27–31. 1970.

13455. Shoonover, W. R. Pre-planting considerations. Northern California Turf Conference Proceedings. pp. 5–10. 1951.

13456. Schoeneweiss, D. F. Controlling tree diseases. The Golf Superintendent. 39(4):38–43. 1971.

13457. Schoevers, T. A. C. Some observations on turf diseases in Holland. Journal of the Board of Greenkeeping Research. 5(16):23–26. 1937.

13458. Scholz, H. *Agrostis tenuis* 'Highland' bent; ein synonym der *Agrostis castellana.* Deutsche Botanische Gesellschaft. 78(9):322–325. 1965.

13459. Schoop, G., C. Brooks, G. W. Thomas, and W. W. Moschler. Seedling responses to liming, phosphorus, and available aluminum. Agronomy Abstracts. p. 91. 1959.

13460. Schoth, H. A. Seed production of turf grasses on the Pacific Coast. Turf Culture. 1(2):111–119. 1939.

13461. ______. Grass seed production on the west coast. Greenkeeping Superintendents Association Twentieth National Turf Conference. pp. 98–103. 1949.

13462. ______. Turf agronomy. Northern California Turf Conference Proceedings. pp. 26–33. 1951.

13463. ______. Turf management in western Oregon and Washington. Pacific Northwest Turf Conference. 4:15–17. 1951.

13464. ______. Turf management in Western Oregon and Washington. State College of Washington Annual Turf Conference. 4:15–17. 1951.

13465. Schoth, H. A., and M. Halperin. The distribution and adaptation of *Poa bulbosa* in the United States and in foreign countries. Journal of the American Society of Agronomy. 24(10):786–792. 1932.

13466. Schoth, H. A. and C. R. Enlow. The ryegrasses. U.S. Department of Agriculture, Bureau of Plant Industry. No. 196. 6 pp. 1940.

13467. Schread, J. C. Control of ground moles. Connecticut Agricultural Experiment Station. Special Bulletin.

13468. ______. Soil insects controlled by chlordane. Timely Turf Topics. USGA Green Section. October. p. 4. 1947.

13469. ______. Chlordane rates high in insect control tests. Golfdom. 22(3):39, 42, 43, 111. 1948.

13470. ______. Control of soil insects. Greenkeepers' Reporter. 16(1):7–10. 1948.

13472. ______. Residual activity of insecticides in control of turf insects. Journal of Economic Entomology. 42(2):383–387. 1949.

13473. ______. A new chlorinated insecticide for control of turf-inhabiting insects. Journal of Economic Entomology. 42(3):-499–502. 1949.

13474. ______. Chinch bug control in lawns. Connecticut State Agricultural Experiment Station Circular. 168:1–6. 1949.

13475. ______. Control of insects injurious to turf. Greenkeepers' Reporter. 17(4):-5–9. 1949.

13476. ______. Control of insects injurious to turf. Greenkeeping Superintendents Association Twentieth National Turf Conference. pp. 62–71. 1949.

13477. ______. A major pest of turf and its control. Parks and Recreation. 32(4):215–216. 1949.

13478. ______. Chinch bug control. USGA Journal and Turf Management. 2(4):-32. 1949.

13479. ______. Modern insecticides protect turf grasses. Crops and Soils. 3(2):18–19, 22. 1950.

13480. ______. Progress in control of new pest, the stinkworm. Golfdom. 24(6):36, 38, 40, 82–87. 1950.

13481. ______. The tropical earthworm and its control. Greenkeeping Superintendents Association National Turf Conference. 21:120–124. 1950.

13482. ______. Control of insects and other animals. Proceedings of the Mid-Atlantic Association of Greenkeepers Conference. pp. 51–58. 1950.

13483. ______. Turf insects. Proceedings of Midwest Regional Turf Conference. pp. 56–66. 1950.

13484. ______. The oriental earthworm and its control. New York State Turf Association. Bulletin 12. pp. 47–48. 1950.

13485. ______. The tropical earthworm. Rutgers University Short Course in Turf Management. 18:24–32. 1950.

13486. ______. Chemical control of turf insects. Proceedings of Southeastern New York Turf School. pp. 14–19. 1950.

13487. ______. Oriental earthworm and its control. USGA Journal and Turf Management. 3(1):32. 1950.

13488. ______. Control of the Japanese beetle and the Asiatic garden beetle. Connecticut Agricultural Experiment Station Circular 184. p. 1–10. 1953.

13489. ______. Isodrin, endrin and lindane for grub control in turf. Journal of Economic Entomology. 46(2):357–359. 1953.

13490. ______. Chinch bug control. USGA Journal and Turf Management. 6(2):-27–29. 1953.

13491. ______. Insects and their control. Proceedings of the Mid-Atlantic Association of Greenkeepers Conference. pp. 8–14. 1954.

13492. ______. Insect pests of Connecticut lawns. Connecticut Agricultural Experiment Station Circular. 212:1–10. 1960.

13493. ______. Chinch bug and its control. Connecticut Agricultural Experiment Station Circular. 223:1–4. 1963.

13494. ______. The effect of last year's weather upon this year's incidence of turf insects. Turf Clippings. University of Massachussetts. 1(8):A–1 to A–4. 1963.

13495. ______. Insect pests of Connecticut lawns. Connecticut Agricultural Experiment Station Circular 212. 1964.

13496. ______. Weather affects insects. Golf Course Reporter. 32(2):40–42, 44, 46. 1964.

13497. ______. Chinch bug and its control. Turf Bulletin. Massachusetts Turf and Lawn Grass Council. 2(6):13–14. 1964.

13498. ______. Newer insects—newer emphasis. International Turfgrass Conference Proceedings. 38:71–73. 1967.

13499. ______. Insects in turf and their control. Turf Clippings. University of Massachussetts. 4(1):A–36 to A–38. 1969.

13500. ______. Frit fly injury to putting greens. Park Maintenance. 23(7):20. 1970.

13501. ______. Sod webworms cause "moth-eaten" turf appearance. Park Maintenance. 23(7):20. 1970.

13502. ______. Turf pests. Rutgers University Short Course in Turf Management. 38:59–61. 1970.

13503. Schread, J. C. and G. C. Chapman. Control of ants in turf and soil. Greenkeeper's Reporter. 16(5):12. 1948.

13504. ______. Control of ants in turf and soil. USGA Journal and Turf Management. 2(1):31–32. 1949.

13505. Schread, J. C. and A. M. Radko. A new turfgrass insect pest? USGA Journal and Turf Management. 11(3):29–30. 1958.

13506. Schread, J. C. and A. R. Twombly. Chinch bug control 100% by chlordane emulsion. Golfdom. 24(8):54–56. 1950.

13507. ______. Control of chinch bug by chordane emulsion. New York State Turf Association. Bulletin 6. pp. 21–22. 1949.

13508. Schreiner, O., J. J. Skinner, L. C. Corbett, and F. L. Mulford. Lawn soils and lawns. USDA Bureau of Soils Bulletin 75. 55 pp. 1911.

13509. Schroder, V. N. and O. C. Rielke. Comparison of photosynthetic and respiratory rates in some Florida pasture grasses. Proceedings of the Crop and Soil Science Society of Florida. 19:365–368. 1959.

13511. Schrunk, J. F. Soil moisture relationships and designs for efficiency. Rocky Mountain Regional Turf Conference Proceedings. pp. 20–24. 1954.

13512. Schubert, O. E., C. Veatch, K. L. Carvell. Chemical weed control—suggestions. West Virginia University Agricultural Experiment Station. Current Report 50. pp. 27–30. 1967.

13513. Schuch, W. Shade problems of the sod grower. Rutgers University. College of Agriculture and Environmental Science. Lawn and Utility Turf Section. pp. 49–50. 1969.

13514. ______. Shade problems of the sod grower. Rutgers University Short Course in Turf Management. 37:1–2. 1969.

13515. Schudel, H. L. and H. H. Rampton. Home lawns for Oregon. Oregon Agricultural Experiment Station Bulletin 516:1–45. 1952.

13516. Schuder, D. L. Notes on the biology and control of sod webworms. Proceedings of the Midwest Regional Turf Conference. pp. 53–54. 1966.

13517. Schuler, S. How to make and maintain a lawn. Gardening From the Ground Up. Macmillan Co., New York. pp. 162–177. 1968.

13518. Schultheis, R. The management of cemetery turf. New York State Turf Association. Bulletin 2. pp. 5–6. 1949.

13519. Schultz, H. K. and H. K. Hayes. Artificial drought tests of some hay and pasture grasses and legumes in sod and seedling stages of growth. Journal of the American Society of Agronomy. 30(8):676–682. 1938.

13520. Schuster, J. E. Using vapam soil fumigant. Park Maintenance. 24(9):18–19. 1971.

13521. Schwabauer, R. A. The effect of soil mixture and soil cover on residual activity of herbicides measured by seedling emergence of *Poa annua* L. M.S. Thesis, Oregon State University. 1963.

13522. Schwartzbeck, R. A. Fertilizers for lawns in the winter garden area. Texas Agricultural Experiment Station Miscellaneous Publication. 174:1–3. 1956.

13523. Schwartz, P. *Poa annua* help! Northern Ohio Turfgrass News. 2(10):4. 1968.

13524. Schwartzkopf, C. Cart paths and construction. Midwest Regional Turf Conference Proceedings. pp. 66–68. 1972.

13525. ______. *Poa annua*—What to do with it. USGA Green Section Record. 10(4):-12–14. 1972.

13526. ______. Potassium, calcium, magnesium—how they relate to plant growth. USGA Green Section Record. 10(6):1–2. 1972.

13527. Schwass, R. H., and W. A. Jacques. Root development in some common New Zealand pasture plants. 8. The relationship of top growth to root growth in perennial ryegrass *(Lolium perenne),* Italian ryegrass *(L. multiflorum)* and tall fescue *(Festuca arundinacea).* New Zealand Journal of Science and Technology. Section A. 38(2):-109–119. 1956.

13528. Schweizer, E. E. and C. G. McWhorter. Surfactants: how they increase herbicide action. Weeds Trees and Turf. 4(1):8–10. 1965.

13529. Schwendiman, J. L. Old and new grasses for turf use in the northwest. State College of Washington Turf Conference Proceedings. 3:37–38. 1950.

13530. Schwendiman, J. L., and A. G. Law. Registration of Drayler bluegrass. Crop Science. 4:115–116. 1964.

13531. Schwendiman, J. L., A. L. Hafenrichter, and A. G. Law. Registration of Durar hard fescue. Crop Science. 4:114–115. 1964.

13533. Sciaroni, R. H. Fertilizer material solubility. California Turfgrass Culture. 17(1):6–7. 1967.

13534. Scobee, M. Po-San at Highland Country Club. Midwest Regional Turf Conference Proceedings. p. 66. 1972.

13535. Scobee, R. E. Fairway disease control. Proceedings of the Midwest Regional Turf Conference. pp. 27–28. 1968.

13536. Scott, B. Treats *Poa annua* before seed formation for best control. Golfdom. 26(6):60–61. 1952.

13537. Scott, D. H. Understanding turf diseases. Proceedings of the Midwest Regional Turf Conference. pp. 101–104. 1969.

13538. ______. The impact of disease. Proceedings of the Midwest Regional Turf Conference. pp. 40–41a. 1970.

13539. Scott, D. J. Seed quality and seed testing. New Zealand Institute for Turf Culture Newsletter. 81:167–170. 1972.

13540. Scott, J. C. Golf courses in southern California. Turf Clippings. University of Massachussetts. 1(3):13. 1958.

13541. Scott, O. Lawn care, building and maintaining. Scott, Marysville, Ohio. 107 pp. 1955.

13542. ______. The Seeding and Care of Golf Courses. Norman T. A. Munder and Co. Baltimore, Maryland. 55 pp. 1923.

13543. ______. Spring seeding. The National Greenkeeper. 1(3):12. 1927.

13545. Scott, O. M. The role of turfgrass in environmental pollution. Northwest Turfgrass Conference Proceedings. 24:71–72. 1970.

13546. Scott, R. Preventing crabgrass seed. U.S.G.A. Bulletin. 4(5):118–119. 1929.

13547. ______. Today's turfgrass challenges grower. Golf Course Reporter. 22(6):-5–7. 1954.

13548. Scribner, F. L. Grasses as sand and soil binders. Yearbook of the US Department of Agriculture, 1894. pp. 421–436. 1895.

13549. ______. Useful and ornamental grasses. Bulletin No. 3. Division of Agrostology. U.S.D.A. 119 pp. 1896.

13553. Sears, E. J. Warm season grasses. Proceedings of the Midwest Regional Turf Conference. pp. 47–49. 1959.

13555. Seay, W. A. Tall fescue—a progress report. Kentucky Farm and Home Science. 6(1): pp. 3–4, 8. 1960.

13556. Seeker, B. Notre Dame football thrives on fumigated soil, weed free turf. Park Maintenance. 11:6–8. 1958.

13557. Seeker, B. Roadside vegetation control and the public. Short Course on Roadside Development (Ohio). 19:87–91. 1960.

13558. Seferovich, G. H. At Arlington National Cemetery prolonged drought means new methods and materials. Grounds Maintenance. 2(1):32–35. 1967.

13559. Seitz, G. L., and W. R. Kneebone. Response to treatments for elimination of summer chlorosis in bermudagrass as measured by total chlorophyll content. Agricultural Experiment Station Turfgrass Report 257. University of Arizona. pp. 13–16. 1967.

13560. ———. Response of different bermudagrasses during summer chlorosis to iron compounds, sulfur and nitrogen. Agronomy Abstracts. p. 71. 1970.

13561. Seitz, G., R. Briggs, and G. C. Horn. Comparison of two preemergence herbicides and various depth of topdressing on germination of NK–100 ryegrass. Agronomy Abstracts. p. 50. 1971.

13562. Seitz, G. L., G. C. Horn, and G. S. Smith. Growth of three warm season turfgrasses as affected by a gradient of soil temperatures. Agronomy Abstracts. p. 65. 1972.

13563. Seitz, G. L. and G. R. McVey. Response of Windsor Kentucky bluegrass to nutrient solutions deficient in major and minor elements. Agronomy Abstracts. p. 61. 1968.

13565. Selby, A. D. and T. F. Manns. Studies in diseases of cereals and grasses. Ohio Agricultural Experiment Station Bulletin 203:187–236. 1909.

13566. Self, R. L. Turf diseases. Auburn University Annual Turfgrass Short Course. pp. 10–20. 1960.

13567. ———. Methods of grass planting. Auburn University Annual Turfgrass Short Course. pp. 38–44. 1964.

13569. Sellars, S. Greenkeeping on chalk soil. Journal of the Board of Greenkeeping Research. 3(8):23–28. 1933.

13570. Seneca, E. D. Germination response to temperature and salinity of four dune grasses from the outer banks of North Carolina. Ecology. 50(1):45–53. 1969.

13571. Seraya, G. P. Specific features of shoot formation in *Poa pratensis* L. as related to the water content of the soil. Botanische Zhurnal. 5(3):425–429. 1965.

13572. Serbousek, W. E. A new concept in *Poa annua* control. Illinois Turfgrass Conference Proceedings. pp. 45–46. 1969.

13573. Serdy, F. S. Effect of temperature and planting depth on seed germination and emergence of 28 weed species. M. S. Thesis, Pennsylvania State University. 53 pp. 1969.

13574. Seymour, C. P. and F. W. Zettler. St. Augustine decline (SAD) survey. Division of Plant Industry Biennial Report. 1970.

13575. Shackleford, T. Football fields. Central Plains Turfgrass Conference. pp. 2–3. 1963.

13576. Shadbolt, C. A., and F. L. Whiting. Urea herbicide breakdown is slow. California Agriculture. 15(11):10–11. 1961.

13577. Shaidee, G., B. E. Dahl, and R. M. Hansen. Germination and emergence of different age seeds of six grasses. Journal of Range Management. 22:240–243. 1969.

13578. Shallock, D. A. Chemicals offer control of numerous weeds. Rutgers University Short Course in Turf Management. 2 pp. 1957.

13579. Shanahan, J. Seeded bent greens at Brae Burn Country Club. USGA Green Section Bulletin. 8(9):189–190. 1928.

13580. ———. Braeburn velvet. Greenkeepers Club of New England Newsletter. 1(1):2–3. 1929.

13581. ———. Seasonable hints. Greenkeepers Club of New England Newsletter. 3(2):2. 1931.

13582. Shankley, R. From grassless mud to verdant sward. Turf for Sport. 4(4):3–5. 1962.

13583. Shannon, S. Let's build a turf. The Modern Cemetery. 61(6):183. 1951.

13584. Shantz, H. L., and R. L. Piemeisel. Fungus fairy rings in eastern Colorado and their effect on vegetation. Journal of Agricultural Research. 11(5):191–245. 1917.

13585. Sharman, B. C. Shoot apex in grasses and cereals. Nature. 149(3768):82–83. 1942.

13586. ———. Leaf and bud initiation in the *Gramineae.* Botanical Gazette. 106(3):-269–289. 1945.

13587. ———. The biology and developmental morphology of the shoot apex in the *Gramineae.* New Phytologist. 46:20–34. 1947.

13588. Sharkey, R. W. Management of various park and turf gardens. Turf Clippings. University of Massachusetts 2(2):A47–49. 1967.

13589. Sharp, C. Chemung crown vetch. Seed World. 87(5):1. 1960.

13590. Sharp, C. R. Operating and maintaining an old sprinkler system. Proceedings of the Turfgrass Sprinkler Irrigation Conference. 3 pp. 1966.

13591. ______. Hints on operating and maintaining old sprinkler systems. Park Maintenance. 21(7):14–15. 1968.

13592. Sharp, W. C. Effects of clipping and nitrogen fertilization on seed production of creeping red fescue. Agronomy Journal. 57(3):252–253. 1965.

13593. Sharrock, R. W. The control of rabbits and moles on golf courses. Journal of the Board of Greenkeeping Research. 5(17):-120–127. 1937.

13594. Sharvelle, E. G. Purdue pathologist comments on new turf disease controls. Midwest Turf-News and Research. 1(1):4. 1947.

13595. ______. Sharvelle gives latest news on "blight busters for better turf." Midwest Turf News and Research. 1(3):1–4. 1947.

13596. ______. Do turf treatments trouble turf? Midwest Turf News and Research. 2(1):1–2, 4. 1948.

13597. ______. The wheel of turf improvement. Proceedings of Midwest Regional Turf Conference. pp. 33–41. 1950.

13598. ______. How turf fungicides performed in 1949. Midwest Turf News and Research. 4(2):2. 1950.

13599. ______. What's in a name? Midwest Turf-News and Research. 4(1):6. 1950.

13600. ______. How turf fungicides performed in 1949. Midwest Turf-News and Research. 4(2):2. 1950.

13601. ______. The wheel of turf improvement. Greenkeepers' Reporter. 18(4):-5–9. 1950.

13602. ______. The 1950 fungicide trials. Proceedings of Midwest Regional Turf Conference. pp. 75–77. 1951.

13603. ______. Value of new fungicides for the prevention and cure of dollar spot disease explained. Midwest Turf News and Research. 5(1):2–4. 1951.

13604. ______. Sharvelle describes fungicide progress. Midwest Turf News and Research. 5(3):2–3. 1951.

13605. ______. Value of new fungicides for the prevention and cure of dollar spot disease explained. Midwest Turf News and Research. 5(1):2–4. 1951.

13606. ______. The wheel of turf improvement. State College of Washington Annual Turf Conference. 4:4–8. 1951.

13607. ______. Turf diseases and fungicides for 1951. State College of Washington Annual Turf Conference. 4:18–21. 1951.

13608. ______. Compatibility of turfgrass fungicides and insecticides. Texas Turfgrass Conference Proceedings. 22:72–80. 1967.

13609. ______. Compatibility of turfgrass pesticides. The Golf Superintendent. 37(7):14–17, 40. 1969.

13610. Sharvelle, E. G. and D. E. Likes. "Grease spot" suggested as name for new disease. Midwest Turf News and Research. 3(4):3. 1949.

13611. Sharvelle, E. G., and W. Skrdla. Turf diseases and their control. Proceedings of Midwest Regional Turf Conference. pp. 27–30. 1949.

13612. ______. New fungicides tested at Purdue. Midwest Turf News and Research. 3(1):1, 4. 1949.

13613. Shaw, E. J. Western fertilizer handbook. California Fertilizer Association, Sacramento, California. pp. 200. 1961.

13614. Shaw, M. S., D. J. Samborski and A. Oaks. Some effects of indoleacetic acid and maleic hydrazide on the respiration and flowering of wheat. Canadian Journal of Botany. 36(2):233–237. 1958.

13616. Shaw, W. C., C. R. Swanson, and R. L. Lovvorn. Bermudagrass and its control. U.S.D.A. Mimeograph. 1953.

13617. Shaybany, B. The anatomical and morphological effects of DCPA on seedlings of selected species of plants. Ph.D. Thesis, Utah State University. 84 pp. 1969.

13618. Sheard, R. W. Influence of defoliation and nitrogen on the development and the fructan composition of the vegetative reproductive system of timothy (*Phleum pratense,* L.). Crop Science. 8(1):55–60. 1968.

13619. ______. Relationship of carbohydrate and nitrogen compounds in the haplocorm to the growth of timothy (*Phleum pratense* L.) Crop Science. 8(6):658–660. 1968.

13620. ______. "Organics—can you afford them". 23rd Annual RCGA National Turfgrass Conference. pp. 65–66. 1972.

13621. Shearer, M. N. Principles of draining turfgrass soils. Northwest Turfgrass Conference Proceedings. 17:14–17. 1963.

13622. ______. Electrical resistance gypsum blocks for scheduling irrigations. Oregon Agricultural Experiment Station. Extension Bulletin. 810. 11 pp. 1963.

13623. Shearman, R. C. Cultural and environmental factors influencing the stomatal density and water use rate of Penncross creeping bentgrass. M.S. Thesis, Michigan State University. 57 pp. 1971.

13624. Shearman, R. C. and J. B. Beard. Factors influencing the stomatal density and water use rate of Penncross creeping bentgrass turf. Agronomy Abstracts. p. 50. 1971.

13625. ______. Stomatal density and distribution in *Agrostis* as influenced by species, cultivar, and leaf blade surface and position. Crop Science. 12(6):822–823. 1972.

13626. ______. Selection of turfgrass species for recreational areas in Michigan. 42nd Annual Michigan Turfgrass Conference Proceedings. (1):79–81. 1972.

13627. Shearman, R. C., and L. V. Nelson. An innovative approach to turfgrass extension education. Agronomy Abstracts. p. 173. 1972.

13628. Shearman, R. C., and P. E. Rieke. How to interpret soil test results for turfgrasses. 42nd Annual Michigan Turfgrass Conference Proceedings. (1):93–96. 1972.

13630. Shedley, D. G. Insect pests of lawns. Journal of Agriculture, West Australian Series. 4:507–514, 565–571. 1963.

13631. Sheehan, M. R. and J. F. Cornman. Illustrated guide to turf weeds. Part I. New York State Turf Association. Bulletin 23. pp. 89–92. 1951.

13632. ______. Illustrated guide to turf weeds. Part 2. New York State Turf Association. Bulletin 24. pp. 93–96. 1951.

13633. ______. Illustrated guide to turf weeds. Part 3. New York State Turf Association. Bulletin 24, supplement. pp. 97–98. 1951.

13634. Sheehan, T. J. Simplified soil chemistry. Florida Turf Management Conference Proceedings. 4:14–16. 1956.

13635. Shelford, V. E. An experimental and observational study of the chinch bug in relation to climate and weather. Illinois Natural History Survey Bulletin. 19:487–547. 1932.

13636. Shelley, C. H. and J. M. Duich. Effect of broadleaf herbicides on seedling turfgrasses. Proceedings of the Northeastern Weed Control Conference. 21:515–519. 1967.

13637. Shelley, W. B. Golf-course dermatitis due to thiram fungicide. Turf Bulletin. Massachusetts Turf and Lawn Grass Council. 2(7):3–5. 1964.

13638. Shelton, B. The second and third greens. Midwest Regional Turf Conference Proceedings. pp. 48–49. 1972.

13639. Shenefelt, R. D. Residual effect of chlordane on crabgrass when applied to lawns for control of sod webworm. Journal of Economic Entomology. 45(1):138, 139. 1952.

13640. Shepherd, H. R. Studies in breaking the rest period of grass plants by treatments with potassium thiocyanate and in stimulating growth with artificial light. Transactions of the Kansas Academy of Science. 41:139–149. 1938.

13641. Sheridan, J. Putting green construction. The National Greenkeeper. 3(1):-28–29. 1929.

13642. Sheridan, L. F. Winter liming. The Golf Superintendent. 35(1):36, 79. 1967.

13643. Sherlock, C. C. How to build lawns. City and suburban gardening. A. T. De La Mare Co., Inc. New York. pp. 23–30. 1928.

13644. Sherwood, F. Care of equipment can make or break budget. Golfdom. 3(6):-19–20. 1929.

13645. ______. Last acts on season's course program make or break greenkeeper. Golfdom. 3(9):26, 28. 1929.

13646. Sherwood, R. T. and C. G. Rindberg. Production of a phytotoxin by *Rhizoctonia solani.* Phytopathology. 52(6):586–587. 1962.

13647. Shewell-Cooper, W. E. The ABC of gardening. English Universities Press. London. 320 pp. 1935.

13649. Shickluna, J. C. Soil testing-the first step in efficient turfgrass production. Michigan Turfgrass Research Report. 1(2):-6–8. 1963.

13651. Shields, E. A. Bermuda greens maintenance in the South. Greenkeepers' Reporter. 18(3):5–9. 1948.

13652. ______. Seven steps to rye. Greenkeepers' Reporter. 17(5):7–9. 1949.

13653. ______. Bermuda green maintenance methods detailed. Golfdom. 22(4):68–74, 96–100. 1948.

13654. ______. Golf-course records. Southeastern Turfgrass Conference Proceedings. 13:36–38. 1959.

13655. Shields, L. R. Fertilizing turf grasses how much-when-for what reason? Golf Course Reporter. 21(2):33–40. 1953.

13656. ______. How to plan fertilizing work for best results. Golfdom. 27(6):48–49, 76–78. 1953.

13657. ______. Fall and Winter operations on the golf course. Golf Course Reporter. 31(9):14–21. 1963.

13658. ______. Bermuda grass at Woodmont. Proceedings of the Mid-Atlantic Association of Golf Course Superintendents. p. 6. 1964.

13659. ______. Trouble at Woodmont. The Golf Superintendent. 36(9):24–26, 28. 1968.

13660. Shildrick, J. P. Turfgrass variety trials in the U.K. Proceedings of the First International Turfgrass Research Conference. pp. 88–99. 1969.

13661. ______. Grass variety trials, 1969. The Journal of the Sports Turf Research Institute. 45:5–40. 1969.

13662. ______. Grass variety trials, 1970. Journal, Sports Turf Research Institute. 46:97–146. 1970.

13663. ______. Grass variety trials, 1971. Journal Sports Turf Research Institute. 47:86–128. 1971.

13664. ______. The latest developments at Bingley. Parks, Golf Courses, and Sports Grounds. 37(8):832, 834, 836. 1972.

13665. Shildrick, J. P. and R. D. C. Evans. Grass variety trials, 1968. Journal of the Sports Turf Research Institute. 44:27–39. 1968.

13666. Shiley, C. F. Practical approach to handling the power golf cart problem. Wisconsin Turfgrass Conference Proceedings. 2 pp. 1962.

13667. ______. Record keeping. Wisconsin Turfgrass Conference Proceedings. 1 p. 1964.

13668. Shim, S. Y. and S. S. Lee. Shade tolerance on forest land conserving grasses. Research Report, Office of Rural Development, Suwon. 7(2):73–78. 1964.

13669. Shimshi, D. Effect of soil moisture and phenylmercuric acetate upon stomatal aperture. Plant Physiology. 38(6):713–721. 1963.

13670. Shiotani, I. The genus of bluegrass. Proceedings of the Midwest Regional Turf Conference. pp. 52–53. 1959.

13671. Shiozaki, H. The distinctive features of the ureaform and their mixed fertilizers. KGU Green Section Turf Research Bulletin. 21(8):13–14. 1971.

13672. Shipman, R. D. and R. C. Bunker. Soil-applied herbicides in the control of temperate zone grasses, broadleaf weeds and woody plants. Proceedings of the Northeastern Weed Science Society. 25:155–156. 1971.

13673. Shirel, G. G. Preparing the air-cooled engine for winter. Grounds Maintenance, 1(11):18–19. 1966.

13674. ______. Liquid-cooled engine winterizing guide. Grounds Maintenance. 2(11):19–22. 1967.

13675. ———. Selecting shop tools and equipment. Grounds Maintenance. 3(3):21–23. 1968.

13676. Shively, S. B. and J. E. Weaver. Amount of underground plant materials in different grassland climates. Nebraska University, Department of Conservation Survey Bulletin 21. p. 68. 1939.

13677. Shoemaker, E. Golf course irrigation—1963. Proceedings of the Mid-Atlantic Association of Golf Course Superintendents Conference. pp. 11–12. 1963.

13678. ———. The value of proper moisture environment for healthy turf. Proceedings, Missouri Lawn and Turf Conference. 5:28–31. 1964.

13679. ———. A modern watering system for your golf course. Proceedings of the Midwest Regional Turf Conference. pp. 30–32. 1965.

13680. ———. Comparison of hydraulic and electric sprinkler systems. Texas Turfgrass Conference Proceedings. 22:1–6. 1967.

13681. ———. Electric valves and wire. International Turfgrass Conference & Show. 39:74–76. 1968.

13682. Shoemaker, J. S. and B. J. E. Teskey. How to make and maintain a lawn. Practical Horticulture. John Wiley and Sons, Inc. New York. 23–31 pp. 1955.

13683. Shoop, G. J. The effects of various coarse textured material and peat on the physical properties of Hagerstown soil for turfgrass production. Ph.D. Thesis, Pennsylvania State University. 225 pp. 1967.

13684. ———. Soil mixtures for golf course greens. West Virginia Turfgrass Conference Proceedings. pp. 27–33. 1967.

13685. ———. Soil mixtures for golf course greens. Proceedings of the 1967 West Virginia Turfgrass Conference. West Virginia University Agricultural Experiment Station. Miscellaneous Publication. 5:27–33. 1968.

13686. Shoop, G. J., C. R. Brooks, R. E. Blaser, G. W. Thomas. Differential responses of grasses and legumes to liming and phosphorus fertilization. Agronomy Journal. 53(2):111–115. 1961.

13688. Shoop, G. J., J. M. Duich, L. T. Kardos, and B. R. Fleming. Soil modification for turfgrass. New York Turfgrass Association Bulletin. 77:298–299. 1964.

13689. Shore, L. B. How we do it—handling of topdressing. Tennessee Turfgrass Conference Proceedings. 3:1–2. 1969.

13690. Shorter, H. H. and J. W. Thompson. Layout of playing fields and sports areas as seen through the contractors' eyes. Parks, Golf Courses, and Sports Grounds. 30(11):-862–869. 1965.

13691. Shoulders, J. F. Soils and their relationship to better grasses. Proceedings of the Mid-Atlantic Association of Golf Course Superintendents. pp. 7–10. 1964.

13692. ———. The use of test demonstrations for practical research and extension teaching. Proceedings of the First International Turfgrass Research Conference. pp. 444–446. 1969.

13693. ———. Cost factors in budgeting for sod production. Turf-grass Times. 5(2):-17. 1969.

13694. Shoulders, J. F. and R. E. Schmidt. Fertilizer programs, established bentgrass putting greens. Virginia Polytechnic Institute and State University Cooperative Extension Service. Publication 155. 2 pp. 1971.

13695. Shrader, T. Field responses of selected bermudagrass clones to foliar applications of dalapon and paraquat. M.S. Thesis, University of Arizona. 1972.

13697. Shurtleff, M. C. Brown patch of turf caused by *Rhizoctonia solani.* Thesis, University of Minnesota. 1953.

13698. ———. Susceptibility of lawn grasses to brown patch. Phytopathology. 43:-110. 1953.

13699. ———. Factors that influence *Rhizoctonia solani* to incite turf brown patch. Phytopathology. 43:484. 1953.

13700. ———. New look at brown patch. Rhode Island Agricultural Experiment Station Research. 4:42–43. 1954.

13701. ———. Control of turf brown patch. Rhode Island Agricultural Experiment Station Bulletin. 328:1–25. 1955.

13702. ———. Curvularia hits golf greens. The Golf Course Reporter. 24(4):21. 1956.

13703. ______. Disease control for lawns and fine turf. Oklahoma Turfgrass Conference Proceedings. 35–44 pp. 1956.

13704. ______. Disease control for lawns and fine turf. Proceedings of the Midwest Regional Turf Conference. pp. 70–78. 1957.

13705. ______. Control disease through good management. Golfdom. 33:100, 102. 1959.

13706. ______. Chemical control of bentgrass diseases. Illinois Turfgrass Conference Proceedings. 2:29–32. 1961.

13707. ______. Chemical control lawn grass diseases. Illinois Turfgrass Conference Proceedings. 2:33–39. 1961.

13709. ______. Turfgrass disease control. Illinois Turfgrass Conference Proceedings. 3:14–18. 1962.

13710. ______. Disease problems for the golf course superintendent. Wisconsin Turfgrass Conference Proceedings. pp. 1–2. 1962.

13711. ______. Disease control in lawns. Wisconsin Turfgrass Conference Proceedings. pp. 1–2. 1962.

13712. ______. Controlling grass diseases. Illinois Turfgrass Conference Proceedings. 4:49–52. 1963.

13713. ______. Looking behind the fungicide label. Illinois Turfgrass Conference Proceedings. 6:1–7. 1965.

13714. ______. Pesticide compatibilities. Illinois Turfgrass Conference Proceedings. 7:1–7. 1966.

13715. ______. How to control plant diseases in home and garden. Iowa State University Press. 649 pp. 1966.

13716. ______. *Rhizoctonia* brown patch and *Pythium* disease. Turf Clippings. University of Massachussetts. 2(1):A–27 to A–32. 1966.

13717. ______. Pesticide application do's and dont's. Grounds Maintenance. 2(5):30–35. 1967.

13718. ______. The billion dollar pest plant-feeding nematodes. Grounds Maintenance. 2(8):24–28. 1967.

13719. ______. Buying and stocking fungicides. Grounds Maintenance. 2(9):27–31. 1967.

13720. ______. Pesticide compatibility. Turf Bulletin. Massachusetts Turf and Lawn Grass Council. 4(3):3–4, 23. 1967.

13721. ______. Nematode/soil pest control guide. Grounds Maintenance. 3(3):41–46. 1968.

13722. ______. A fungicide inventory for the turf manager. Illinois Turfgrass Conference Proceedings. pp. 44–49. 1968.

13723. ______. What's new with bentgrass diseases. Proceedings of the Midwest Regional Turf Conference. pp. 105–107. 1969.

13724. ______. Turf ornamental bed weed control guide. Grounds Maintenance. 5(5):24–34. 1970.

13725. ______. New disease resistant turf varieties. Grounds Maintenance. 5(6):-18–21. 1970.

13726. ______. Changing the environment to reduce turf diseases. Illinois Turfgrass Conference Proceedings. 11:19–21. 1970.

13727. Shurtleff, M. C. and M. P. Britton. Slime molds. Report on Plant Diseases, University of Illinois. Report No. 401. pp. 1–2. 1962.

13728. ______. Turfgrass disease control. University of Illinois Cooperative Extension Service. Report on Plant Diseases. 402:-1–5. 1963.

13729. ______. Turfgrass disease control. University of Illinois Cooperative Extension Service. Report on Plant Disease. 402:-1–6. 1972.

13730. Shurtleff, M. C. and J. D. Butler. Disease control—yes or no? Illinois Turfgrass Conference Proceedings. pp. 11–13. 1969.

13731. ______. Current fungicide recommendations. Illinois Turfgrass Conference Proceedings. pp. 68–71. 1969.

13732. Shurtleff, M. C., and F. L. Howard. 1953 turf fungicide trials in Rhode Island. Golf Course Reporter. 22(4):5–9. 1954.

13733. Shurtleff, M. C., and A. J. Turgeon. Slime molds. University of Illinois Cooperative Extension Service. Report on Plant Disease. 401:1–2. 1972.

13734. ______. Turfgrass disease control. University of Illinois Cooperative Extension Service. Report on Plant Disease. 402:-1–5. 1972.

13735. ______. Fairy rings. University of Illinois Cooperative Extension Service. Report on Plant Disease. 403:1–2. 1972.

13736. ______. Snow molds. University of Illinois Cooperative Extension Service. Report on Plant Diseases. 404:1–3. 1972.

13737. ______. *Helminthosporium* leaf, crown, and root diseases of lawn grasses. University of Illinois Cooperative Extension Service. Report on Plant Diseases No. 405. 5 pp. 1972.

13738. ______. Powdery mildew of bluegrasses. University of Illinois Cooperative Extension Service. Report on Plant Diseases No. 406. 3 pp. 1972.

13739. Shurtleff, M. C., M. P. Britton, and J. D. Butler. Fairy rings. University of Illinois Cooperative Extension Service. Report on Plant Diseases. 403:1–3. 1964.

13740. ______. Snow molds. University of Illinois Cooperative Extension Service. Report on Plant Diseases. 404:1–4.

13743. Shurtleff, M. C., E. E. Burns, and A. J. Turgeon. Recommendations for the control of diseases of turfgrasses. University of Illinois Cooperative Extension Service. Report on Plant Diseases No. 400. 13 pp. 1972.

13744. Shurtleff, M. C., H. D. Wells, and T. E. Freeman. Declare war on turf disease. Parks and Recreation. 41(5):230–232. 1958.

13745. Shurtleff, M. C., T. H. Bower, E. E. Burns, and A. J. Turgeon. Leaf smuts of turfgrasses. University of Illinois Cooperative Extension Service. Report on Plant Disease. 409:1–5. 1972.

13746. Sidle, R. C. Evaluation of a turfgrass-soil system to utilize and purify municipal waste water. M. S. Thesis, University of Arizona. 1972.

13747. Sidle, R. C., and G. V. Johnson. Use and purification of sewage effluent by soil-turfgrass systems. Agronomy Abstracts. p. 187. 1972.

13748. Siebenthaler, J. Landscaping and maintenance of turf on industrial sites. Proceedings of the Florida Turfgrass Management Conference. 12:131–132. 1964.

13749. Siefert, W. B. Some common lawn weeds and how to control them. Illinois Turfgrass Conference Proceedings. pp. 32–33. 1969.

13750. Sieling, D. The role of phosphorous in turf production. Greenkeeping Superintendents Association National Turf Conferences. 21:31–34. 1950.

13751. Siems, H. B. For better lawns and gardens; a practical guide for home gardeners. Swift and Company. Chicago. 58 pp. 1931.

13752. ______. Fertility and fertilizers. The National Greenkeeper. 6(8):15–19. 1932.

13753. Sigalov, B. I. Dekorativnye gazony. Minsterstvo Kommunal 'Nogo Khoziaĭstva RSFR. Moskva. 62 pp. 1955.

13754. Silker, T. H. Effect of clipping upon the forage production, root development, establishment, and subsequent drought resistance of western and crested wheatgrass seedling. M. S. Thesis, Iowa State College. 69 pp. 1941.

13755. Sill, W. H., and R. J. Chin. Kentucky bluegrass, *Poa pratensis* L., a new host of the Bromegrass mosaic virus in nature. Plant Disease Reporter. 43(1):85. 1959.

13756. Silva, J. A. Liquid vs. solid fertilizers. Weeds, Trees and Turf. 5(3):8–10, 16. 1966.

13757. Silvar, R. Scorched earth at Knickerbocker. U.S.G.A. Green Section Record 4(6):19. 1967.

13758. Silven, B. C. Don't get caught short. Golf Course Reporter. 26(5):8–9. 1958.

13759. Siler, T. McKay, he brought bent greens to Tennessee. Golfdom. 31(8):46–50. 1957.

13760. Silvester, G. Weed and grass control. New Zealand Institute for Turf Culture Newsletter. 42:5–6. 1966.

13761. Silveus, W. A. Texas grasses—classification and description of grasses. Published by W. A. Silveus. 782 pp. 1933.

13762. Sim, J. Parks are for people. Northwest Turfgrass Conference Proceedings. 24:17–20. 1970.

13763. Simmons, J. A. Turf is big business. Rocky Mountain Regional Turfgrass Conference Proceedings. pp. 5–10. 1961.

13764. ______. Keeping pace. Rocky Mountain Regional Turfgrass Conference. 12:33–39. 1966.

13765. ______. Turfgrass research—an industrial approach. Turf Clippings. University of Massachusetts. 3(3):A16–23. 1968.

13767. Simmons, J. A. and E. O. Burt. Tolerance of seedling and established turfgrasses to bandane and chlordane. Proceedings North Central Weed Control Conference. 19:51. 1962.

13768. Simmons, J. A. and J. A. DeFrance. The effectiveness of chemicals for the control of mouse-ear chickweed in turf. Proceedings of the Northeastern Weed Control Conference. No. 792. 1952.

13770. ______. Studies with endothal for clover control in turf. Proceedings, 7th Annual Northeastern Weed Control Conference. pp. 251–253. 1953.

13771. ______. Phenyl mercurials effective on crabgrass, tests reveal. Park Maintenance. 6(9):16–17. 1953.

13772. ______. Chemicals for the control of crabgrass in putting-green turf. Proceedings, 7th Annual Northeastern Weed Control Conference. pp. 255–262. 1953.

13773. Simmons, J. A., and R. Huey. The response of Kentucky bluegrass to single and repeat applications of chlordane and polychlorodicyclopentadiene. Weed Society of America Abstracts. p. 94. 1964.

13774. Simons, A. B. Nitrate nitrogen accumulation in orchardgrass (*Dactylis glomerata* L.) as influenced by soil temperature, light, and nitrogen supply. M. S. Thesis, University of Maryland. 1967.

13775. Simpson, A. G. W. Selection of grass seeds. The Groundsman. 16(2):14–18. 1962.

13776. ______. Ureaform nitrogen fertilisers and chlorinated hydrocarbons. The Groundsman. 16(8):38, 40. 1963.

13777. ______. Watering, and some of its myths. The Groundsman. 16(10):18. 1963.

13778. ______. Old and modern seed mixtures. The Groundsman. 17(1):24–28. 1963.

13779. ______. Organic chemical weedkillers. The Groundsman. 17(2):10–14. 1963.

13780. ______. Van Engelens Dutch grass strains. The Groundsman. 17(4):23–25. 1963.

13781. ______. The weed control problem explained. The Groundsman. 17(5):20, 22. 1964.

13782. ______. The weed control problem explained. The Groundsman. 17(6):18–22. 1964.

13783. ______. Soil indicator plants. The Groundsman. 17(7):12, 16. 1964.

13784. ______. Trace elements their functions and deficiences. The Groundsman. 19(10):22. 1966.

13785. ______. Trace elements or micronutrients. The Groundsman. 19(11):10–12. 1966.

13786. ______. Trace elements of micronutrients. The Groundsman. 20(1):22–28. 1966.

13787. ______. The maintenance of hockey pitches. The Groundsman. 20(7):29, 38. 1967.

13788. ______. Maintenance of a hockey pitch. The Groundsman. 21(2):43–45. 1967.

13789. ______. Maintenance of a hockey pitch. The Groundsman. 21(3):24–25. 1967.

13790. ______. Maintenance of a soccer pitch—part 1. The Groundsman. 21(5):33–34. 1968.

13791. ______. Maintenance of a soccer pitch—part 2. The Groundsman. 21(6):35–37. 1968.

13792. ______. Renovation of a soccer pitch. The Groundsman. 21(8):43–45. 1968.

13793. Simpson, B. Soil analysis. The Groundsman. 19(6):6–8. 1966.

13794. ______. Diploids—triploids—polyploids etc. The Groundsman. 19(8):12–14. 1966.

13795. Simpson, D. M. H., and S. W. Melsted. Gaseous ammonia losses from urea solutions applied as a foliar spray to various grass sods. Soil Science Society of America Proceedings. 26:186–189. 1962.

13796. Simpson, I. B. Possible damage to greens by nematodes. New Zealand Institute for Turf Culture Newsletter. 48:12–14. 1967.

13797. Simpson, S. L. and C. Y. Ward. Manufactured mulches compared with grain straw for mulching roadside seedings. Agronomy Abstracts. p. 103. 1964.

13798. Simpson, T. Golf architecture in Europe and America—a comparison. The National Greenkeeper. 5(12):9–12. 1931.

13800. Sincerbeau, R. A. Operation municipal, provides lots of golf for Flint. Golf Course Reporter. 27(3):54–57. 1959.

13801. ______. Adequate records for good control and budgeting. International Turfgrass Conference and Show. 39:40–45. 1968.

13802. Singh, D. N. Classification of *Gramineae* in relation to cytology. Advancing Frontiers of Plant Sciences. 17:197–203. 1966.

13803. Singh, R. K. N. and R. W. Campbell. Herbicides on bluegrass. Weeds. 13(2):-170–171. 1965.

13804. Singh, N. and R. Kumar. Some effects of weed competition and herbicide residues on growth and development of bluegrass (*Poa pratensis* L.). Dissertation Abstracts. 25(3):1454. 1964.

13805. Singh, R. S. and J. E. Mitchell. A selective method for isolation and measuring the population of *Pythium* in soil. Phytopathology. 51(7):440–444. 1961.

13807. Singleton, J. T. Automatic irrigation in the East. Golf Course Reporter. 31(6):31–36. 1963.

13808. ______. The golf industry's new professional. Turf Clippings. University of Massachusetts. 1(10):A45–A48. 1965.

13809. Singley, J. E. Water quality and quantity. Florida Turfgrass Management Conference Proceedings. 18:19–23. 1970.

13810. Sinha, R. D., J. A. Jackobs, L. E. Foote, and C. N. Hittle. The influence of rates and time of application of organic and inorganic nitrogen on the maintenance of sod on highway slopes. Agronomy Abstracts. p. 104. 1962.

13811. Sinninger, J. C. Turf management for Purdue University football stadium and practice fields. Proceedings of the Midwest Regional Turf Conference. pp. 95–97. 1969.

13813. Skaggs, E. *Poa annua* and crabgrass control with calcium arsenate. Proceedings of the Midwest Regional Turf Conference. pp. 58–59. 1959.

13814. Skakala, E. Problems of playground and park lawns in Czechoslovakia and our experiences. First Czechoslovak Symposium on Sportturf Proceedings. pp. 105–115. 1969.

13815. Skaptason, J. S. Synergism from phenoxy, propionic, and benzoic acid herbicide mixtures. Proceedings of the North Central Weed Control Conference. 24:58–61. 1969.

13816. Skillman, E. F. Weed killing by flame method ground thawing. The Modern Cemetery. 55(1):147–148. 1945.

13817. Skinner, G. A. Hypo syringe and gasoline deal death to dandelions. Golfdom. 8(6):25–26. 1934.

13818. Skirde, W. MH–30-ein rasenhemnastoff? Die neue Landschaft. 10:368. 1965.

13819. ______. The selection of grasses. Garten und Landschaft. 77(2):41–43. 1967.

13820. ______. Artenkombinationen und Sortenfragen beim Aufbau von Mischungen für Zier—und Gebrauchsrasen. Das Gartenamt. p. 104. 1968.

13821. ______. Ergebnisse aus dem Trackensommer 1967 für Rasenpflege und Rasengräserzuchtung. Rasen und Rasengräser. 2:21. 1968.

13822. ______. The situation of turfgrass research for sportsfields in the German Federal Republic. First Czechoslovak Symposium on Sportturf Proceedings. pp. 137–156. 1969.

13823. ______. The world assortment of the lawn grasses. First Czechoslovak Symposium on Sportturf Proceedings. pp. 259–262. 1969.

13824. ______. Reaction of turfgrasses to watering. Proceedings of the First International Turfgrass Research Conference. pp. 311–322. 1969.

13825. ______. The development, present position and future objectives of turf research in Giessen. Journal, Sports Turf Research Institute. 46:33–45. 1970.

13826. ______. Results of salt tolerance tests with different grass varieties. Rasen-Turf-Gazon. 1:12–14. 1970.

13827. Skogley, C. R. Grasses and seed mixtures for lawn turf. Rhode Island Extension Service Bulletin. 178:1–8.

13828. ______. Transforming poor turf to good turf. Rutgers University Short Course in Turf Management. 27:2. 1959.

13829. ______. Making your new lawn. Rhode Island Agriculture. 6(4):6–7. 1960.

13830. ______. Lawn maintenance. Rutgers University Short Course in Turf Management. 28:1–2. 1960.

13831. ______. Grasses for lawn and utility turf. Rutgers University Short Course in Turf Management. 28:1–3. 1960.

13832. ______. The effect of zytron on seedling turfgrasses. Proceedings of the Northeastern Weed Control Conference. 15:-258–263. 1961.

13833. ______. Lawn weed control. Rhode Island Agriculture. 7(4):4. 1961.

13834. ______. Building a new lawn. Rhode Island Agricultural Extension Bulletin 183. 10 pp. 1962.

13835. ______. The establishment and care of lawns. University of Maine Turf Conference Proceedings. 1:5 pp. 1963.

13836. ______. Chemical weed control. University of Maine Turf Conference Proceedings. 1:12 pp. 1963.

13837. ______. Turfgrass nutrition and management for crabgrass control. New England Agricultural Chemicals Conference and Herbicide Workshop. 1:27–28. 1964.

13838. ______. New URI grass varieties. Rhode Island Agriculture. 10(4). pp. 3–4. 1964.

13839. ______. Winter play on golf greens. The Golf Course Reporter. 33(10):-22–26. 1965.

13840. ______. Turf annual. Park Maintenance. 18(7):17–44. 1965.

13841. ______. Letter. The Golf Superintendent. 34(10):14, 16. 1966.

13842. ______. Turfgrass fertilizer research at the Rhode Island Agricultural Experiment Station. Journal of the Sports Turf Research Institute. 43:34–39. 1967.

13843. ______. Turfgrass research report. Scotts Turfgrass Research Seminar. pp. 52–57. 1968.

13844. ______. Turf research abroad. Turf Clippings. University of Massachusetts. 3(3):A13–14. 1968.

13845. ______. Turfgrass research in the northeast. International Turfgrass Conference Proceedings. 40:19–21. 1969.

13846. ______. Viewpoints on control methods and precautions—northeast. International Turfgrass Conference Proceedings. 40:57–58. 1969.

13847. ______. Controlling annual bluegrass through management and chemicals. University of Maine Turf Conference Proceedings. 7:8–10. 1969.

13848. ______. A look at new turf grasses for the Northeast. University of Maine Turf Conference Proceedings. 7:20–21. 1969.

13849. ______. Turning green grass into greenbacks. Rhode Island Agriculture. 15(2):4–5. 1969.

13850. ______. Artificial turf versus heated turf. Rhode Island Agriculture. 15(4):4–6. 1969.

13851. ______. Turf research at University of Rhode Island. Proceedings of the Mid-Atlantic Association of Golf Course Superintendents. pp. 26–29. 1970.

13852. ______. Highlights of our turfgrass research program. Annual RCGA National Turfgrass Conference. 21:35–37. 1970.

13853. ______. New developments in bentgrass. The Golf Superintendent. 39(10):-30–32. 1971.

13854. Skogley, C. R., and D. T. Duff. Bluegrass varieties evaluated at Univ. of Rhode Island. Park Maintenance. 23(7):17. 1970.

13855. ______. Plastic screens for winter protection. Park Maintenance. 23(7):23. 1970.

13856. Skogley, C. R. and R. E. Engel. Better lawn seed mixtures. New Jersey Agricultural Extension Bulletin. 318:1–8. 1959.

13857. ______. Lawn care. New Jersey Agricultural Extension Bulletin. 320:1–15. 1959.

13858. Skogley, C. R. and J. A. Jagschitz. The effect of various preemergence crabgrass herbicides on turfgrass seed and seedlings. Proceedings of the Northeastern Weed Control Conference. 18:523–529. 1964.

13859. ______. Chemical crabgrass control in turfgrass. The Golf Course Reporter. 33(3):14–16. 1965.

13860. ______. Clover, chickweed and dandelion control with herbicides in lawn and golf course turf. Proceedings of the Northeastern Weed Control Conference. 19:-500–507. 1965.

13861. ______. Chemical control of crabgrass and spotted spurge in turfgrass. Proceedings of the Northeastern Weed Control Conference. 20:531–536. 1966.

13862. Skogley, C. R. and J. W. King. Controlled release nitrogen fertilization of turfgrass. Agronomy Journal. 60(1):61–64. 1968.

13863. Skogley, C. R. and F. B. Ledeboer. Evaluation of several Kentucky bluegrass and red fescue strains maintained as lawn turf under three levels of fertility. Agronomy Journal. 60(1):47–49. 1968.

13864. Skogley, C. R., J. A. Jagschitz, and V. A. Gibeault. Early and mid-season chemical control of knotweed in turfgrass. Proceedings of the Northeastern Weed Control Conference. 20:486–489. 1966.

13865. Skoss, J. D. Types of herbicides and their uses. First Annual Fall Field Day on Turf Culture. UCLA. 1:20–27. 1949.

13866. ______. The control of *Poa annua* (annual bluegrass) in putting greens. Southern California Turf Culture. 1(4):1. 1951.

13867. ______. Weed control in *Dichondra.* Southern California Turf Culture. 7(1):-5–6. 1957.

13868. Skrdla, W. Turf aggregates under test in replacing hard surfacing by Purdue University Agronomists. Midwest Turf News and Research. 3(1):1, 4. 1949.

13869. Skroch, W. A. and T. J. Monaco. Glueing techniques used for solid field fumigation. Down to Earth. 26(1):5–6. 1970.

13870. Slana, L. and A. Boyle. Resistance of bermudagrass (*Cynodon* spp.) to *Helminthosporium cynodontis* Marignoni. Turfgrass Research Report, Arizona Agricultural Experiment Station. 219:39–41. 1963.

13871. Slawson, H. H. New control measures reduce brown patch. Park Maintenance. 7:52–53. 1954.

13872. ______. Eliminating unsightly damage to lawns by European beetle. Park Maintenance. 8(4):31. 1955.

13873. Sledge, E. B. Studies on *Meloidogyne* sp. on grass. 23rd Biennial Report, State Plant Board of Florida. 2(14):108–110. 1960.

13874. ______. Preliminary report on a *Meloidogyne* sp. parasite of grass in Florida. The Plant Disease Reporter. 46(1):52–54. 1962.

13875. Sledge, E. B. and A. M. Golden. *Hypsoperine graminis (Nematoda: Heteroderidae),* a new genus and species of plant-parasitic nematode. Proceedings of the Helminthological Society. 31(1):83–88. 1962.

13876. Slife, F. W. Weed control in lawns. Illinois Turfgrass Conference Proceedings. 1:24–26. 1960.

13877. ______. Weed control in turf. Illinois Turfgrass Conference Proceedings. 2:-3–5. 1961.

13878. ______. Weed control in turf. Illinois Turfgrass Conference Proceedings. 3:-26–28. 1962.

13879. ______. Industrial weed control. Grounds Maintenance. 2(3):52. 1967.

13880. ______. Deactivation of herbicides in soils. Illinois Turfgrass Conference Proceedings. p. 7. 1971.

13881. Slife, F. W. and J. D. Butler. Weed control in turf. Illinois Turfgrass Conference Proceedings. 4:29. 1963.

13882. ______. Weed control in turf. Illinois Turfgrass Conference Proceedings. 5:-47–49. 1964.

13883. ______. Weed control in turf. Illinois Turfgrass Conference Proceedings. 6:-1–3. 1965.

13884. Sloan, M. J. Soil insecticides. Oklahoma Turfgrass Conference Proceedings. 1–3 pp. 1953.

13885. Sloan, R. E. Repairing golf fairways. Parks and Recreation. 19(9):351. 1936.

13886. Slykhuis, J. T. An international survey for virus diseases of grasses. F.A.O. Plant Protection Bulletin. 10:1–16. 1962.

13887. Small, W. A. Spring dead spot of bermuda controlled by fungicidal treatment of the root-zone. Agronomy Abstracts. p. 106. 1964.

13888. ______. Application of soil drench fungicides to large turf areas. Agronomy Abstracts. p. 57. 1967.

13889. ______. Spring deadspot of bermuda. Southern Turfgrass Association Conference Proceedings. pp. 24. 1968.

13890. ______. Disease and insect control. Southern Turfgrass Association Conference Proceedings. pp. 42–43. 1968.

13891. Small, W. A., N. Jackson, and W. C. Stienestra. Mercurial fungicides in the golf course use pattern. Agronomy Abstracts. p. 50. 1971.

13892. Smalley, R. R. Soil amendments for putting greens. Golf Course Reporter. 27(7):50–51. 1959.

13893. ______. Watering practices. Proceedings of University of Florida Turf-Grass Management Conference. 7:53–55. 1959.

13894. ______. Soils and soil amendments in turf production. Proceedings of University of Florida Turf-Grass Management Conference. 8:6–11. 1960.

13895. ______. How the turf research program in South Florida will help the sod growers. Proceedings of University of Florida Turf-Grass Management Conference. 8:51–52. 1960.

13896. ______. Two-year summary of putting green soil amendment study. Proceedings of University of Florida Turf-Grass Management Conference. 9:68–72. 1961.

13897. ______. Translocation of nitrogen, phosphorus, potassium, calcium, and magnesium in "Floratine" St. Augustinegrass. Proceedings of University of Florida Turf-Grass Management Conference. 9:101–105. 1961.

13898. ______. The turf research program in South Florida. Proceedings of University of Florida Turf-Grass Management Conference. 9:233–236. 1961.

13899. ______. Overseeding greens in southeast Florida. Proceedings of Florida Turf-Grass Management Conference. 10:66–70. 1962.

13900. ______. Mowing heights for St. Augustinegrass and Pensacola bahiagrass. Proceedings of Florida Turf-Grass Management Conference. 10:107–109. 1962.

13901. ______. Turf research in South Florida in 1961–62. Proceedings of Florida Turf-Grass Management Conference. 10:-216–227. 1962.

13902. Smalley, R. and G. C. Horn. Soil amendment study for putting greens. Proceedings of University of Florida Turf-Grass Management Conference. 8:143–149. 1960.

13903. ______. Nutrient element translocation study in 'Floratine' St. Augustine grass. Proceedings of University of Florida Turf-Grass Management Conference. 8:153–161. 1960.

13904. ______. A method to study the effects of translocation on the growth of stoloniferous grasses. Agronomy Abstracts. p. 105. 1962.

13905. Smalley, R. R. and W. L. Pritchett. Soil amendments for putting greens. Golf Course Reporter. 30(4):37–53. 1962.

13906. Smalley, R. R., W. L. Pritchett, and L. C. Hammond. Effects of four soil amendments on some physical properties of putting green soils. Agronomy Abstracts. p. 75. 1961.

13907. ______. Effects of four amendments on soil physical properties and on yield and quality of putting greens. Agronomy Journal. 54(5):393–395. 1962.

13908. Smart, D. C. Use the right grass seed. The Groundsman. 22(12):30. 1969.

13909. Smart, G. C. Plant nematode problems on turfgrasses. Annual Research Report of the Institute of Food & Agricul-

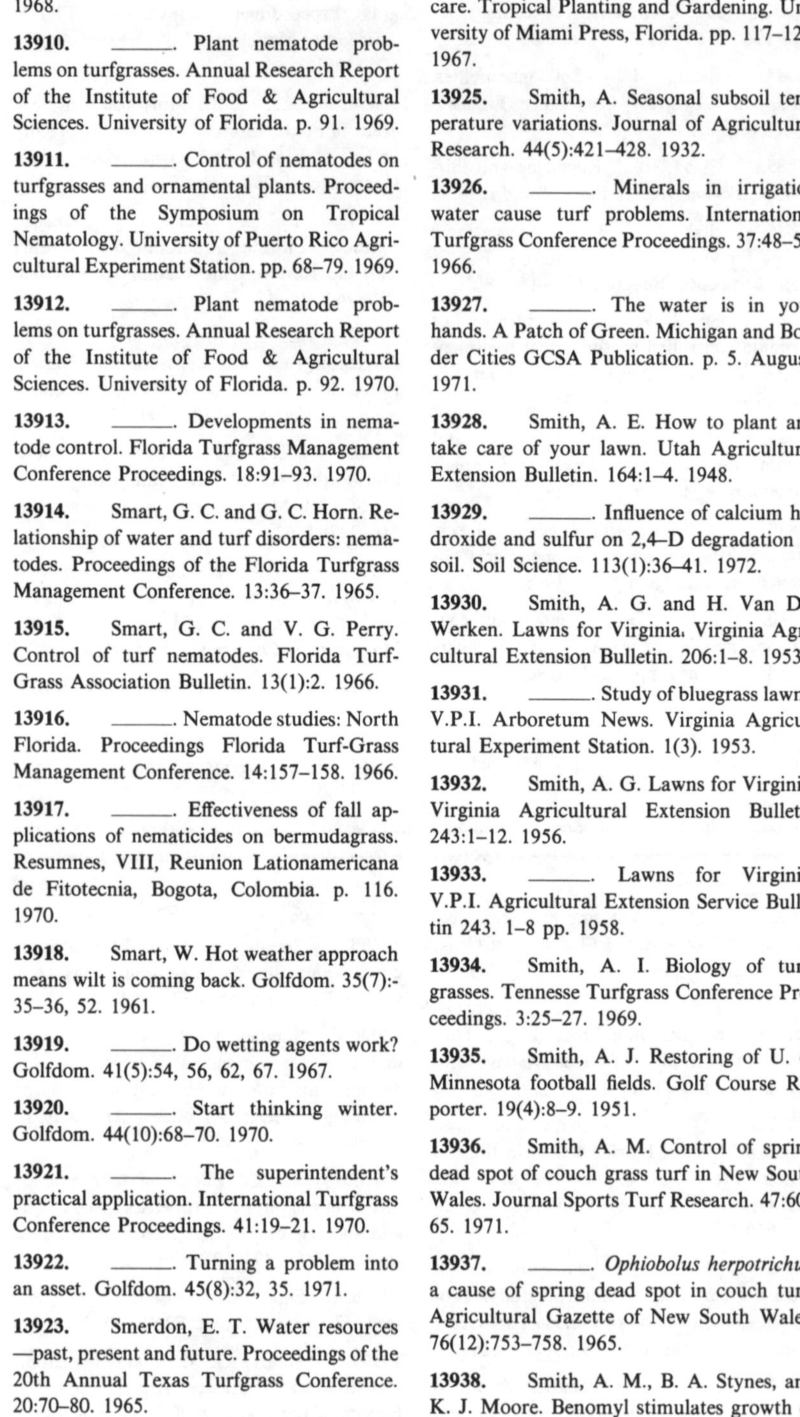

tural Sciences. Univ. of Florida. pp. 78–79. 1968.

13910. ______. Plant nematode problems on turfgrasses. Annual Research Report of the Institute of Food & Agricultural Sciences. University of Florida. p. 91. 1969.

13911. ______. Control of nematodes on turfgrasses and ornamental plants. Proceedings of the Symposium on Tropical Nematology. University of Puerto Rico Agricultural Experiment Station. pp. 68–79. 1969.

13912. ______. Plant nematode problems on turfgrasses. Annual Research Report of the Institute of Food & Agricultural Sciences. University of Florida. p. 92. 1970.

13913. ______. Developments in nematode control. Florida Turfgrass Management Conference Proceedings. 18:91–93. 1970.

13914. Smart, G. C. and G. C. Horn. Relationship of water and turf disorders: nematodes. Proceedings of the Florida Turfgrass Management Conference. 13:36–37. 1965.

13915. Smart, G. C. and V. G. Perry. Control of turf nematodes. Florida Turf-Grass Association Bulletin. 13(1):2. 1966.

13916. ______. Nematode studies: North Florida. Proceedings Florida Turf-Grass Management Conference. 14:157–158. 1966.

13917. ______. Effectiveness of fall applications of nematicides on bermudagrass. Resumnes, VIII, Reunion Lationamericana de Fitotecnia, Bogota, Colombia. p. 116. 1970.

13918. Smart, W. Hot weather approach means wilt is coming back. Golfdom. 35(7):-35–36, 52. 1961.

13919. ______. Do wetting agents work? Golfdom. 41(5):54, 56, 62, 67. 1967.

13920. ______. Start thinking winter. Golfdom. 44(10):68–70. 1970.

13921. ______. The superintendent's practical application. International Turfgrass Conference Proceedings. 41:19–21. 1970.

13922. ______. Turning a problem into an asset. Golfdom. 45(8):32, 35. 1971.

13923. Smerdon, E. T. Water resources —past, present and future. Proceedings of the 20th Annual Texas Turfgrass Conference. 20:70–80. 1965.

13924. Smiley, N. Lawn grasses and their care. Tropical Planting and Gardening. University of Miami Press, Florida. pp. 117–128. 1967.

13925. Smith, A. Seasonal subsoil temperature variations. Journal of Agricultural Research. 44(5):421–428. 1932.

13926. ______. Minerals in irrigation water cause turf problems. International Turfgrass Conference Proceedings. 37:48–51. 1966.

13927. ______. The water is in your hands. A Patch of Green. Michigan and Border Cities GCSA Publication. p. 5. August, 1971.

13928. Smith, A. E. How to plant and take care of your lawn. Utah Agricultural Extension Bulletin. 164:1–4. 1948.

13929. ______. Influence of calcium hydroxide and sulfur on 2,4–D degradation in soil. Soil Science. 113(1):36–41. 1972.

13930. Smith, A. G. and H. Van De-Werken. Lawns for Virginia. Virginia Agricultural Extension Bulletin. 206:1–8. 1953.

13931. ______. Study of bluegrass lawns. V.P.I. Arboretum News. Virginia Agricultural Experiment Station. 1(3). 1953.

13932. Smith, A. G. Lawns for Virginia. Virginia Agricultural Extension Bulletin 243:1–12. 1956.

13933. ______. Lawns for Virginia. V.P.I. Agricultural Extension Service Bulletin 243. 1–8 pp. 1958.

13934. Smith, A. I. Biology of turfgrasses. Tennesse Turfgrass Conference Proceedings. 3:25–27. 1969.

13935. Smith, A. J. Restoring of U. of Minnesota football fields. Golf Course Reporter. 19(4):8–9. 1951.

13936. Smith, A. M. Control of spring dead spot of couch grass turf in New South Wales. Journal Sports Turf Research. 47:60–65. 1971.

13937. ______. *Ophiobolus herpotrichus,* a cause of spring dead spot in couch turf. Agricultural Gazette of New South Wales. 76(12):753–758. 1965.

13938. Smith, A. M., B. A. Stynes, and K. J. Moore. Benomyl stimulates growth of a basidiomycete on turf. The Plant Disease Reporter. 54(9):774–775. 1970.

13939. Smith, B. Cost to maintain Dodger Stadium turf. Exposition Conference. Southern California. 1 p. 1966.

13940. Smith, C. Value of a survey of the sod industry. Proceedings, of University of Florida Turf-Grass Management Conference. 8:58–60. 1960.

13941. Smith, C. B. Trace elements. Pennsylvania State College Turfgrass Conference Proceedings. 21:47–52. 1952.

13942. Smith, C. N. New approaches and trends in insect control. Proceedings of Florida Turf-Grass Management Conference. 11:34–40. 1963.

13943. ______. Plans for turf marketing study. Proceedings of Florida Turf-Grass Management Conference. 11:144–146. 1963.

13944. Smith, D. Keep bent greens great year-round in Arizona. Golfdom. 27(6):36–37. 1953.

13945. ______. Organizing young workers. Proceedings of the Midwest Regional Turf Conference. pp. 19–21. 1965.

13946. ______. Winter injury and killing of turf plants. Wisconsin Turfgrass Conference Proceedings. pp. 11–18. 1966.

13947. ______. Carbohydrates in grasses. II. Sugar and fructosan composition of the stem bases of bromegrass and timothy at several growth stages and in different plant parts at anthesis. Crop Science. 7:62–67. 1967.

13948. ______. Carbohydrates in grasses. IV. Influence of temperature on the sugar and fructosan composition of timothy plant parts at anthesis. Crop Science. 8(3):-331–334. 1968.

13949. ______. How to promote golf in 1972. Midwest Regional Turf Conference Proceedings. pp. 25–26. 1972.

13950. Smith, D., and R. D. Groteluesc-hen. Carbohydrates in grasses. I. Sugar and fructosan composition of the stem bases of several northern—adapted grasses at seed maturity. Crop Science. 6:263–266. 1966.

13951. Smith, D. and O. R. Jewiss. Effects of temperature and nitrogen supply on the growth of timothy (*Phleum pratense* L.). Annals of Applied Biology. 58(1):145–157. 1966.

13952. Smith, D. C. Pollination and seed formation in grasses. Journal of Agricultural Research. 68(2):79–95. 1944.

13953. ______. Progress in grass breeding. Advances in Agronomy. 8:127–162. 1956.

13954. ______. Turf for roadsides and rough areas. Wisconsin Turfgrass Conference Proceedings. 5 pp. 1965.

13955. Smith, D. C. and E. L. Nielsen. Morphological variation in *Poa pratensis* L. as related to subsequent breeding behavior. Journal of the American Society of Agronomy. 37(12):1033–1040. 1945.

13956. ______. Comparative breeding behavior of progenies from enclosed and open-pollinated panieles of *Poa pratensis* L. Journal of the American Society of Agronomy. 38(9):804–809. 1946.

13957. ______. Comparisons of clonal isolations of *Poa pratensis* L. from good and poor pastures for vigor, variability, and disease reactions. Agronomy Journal. 43(5):-214–218. 1951.

13958. Smith, D. C., E. L. Nielsen, and H. L. Ahlgren. Variation in ecotypes of *Poa pratensis.* Botanical Gazette. 108(2):143–166. 1946.

13959. Smith, D. H. Effect of fumigants on the soil status and plant uptake of certain elements. Soil Science Society of America Proceedings. 27:538–541. 1963.

13960. Smith, A. L., and R. H. Knowles. The effect of environment on the growth and developmental behaviour of four creeping bentgrass strains. Masters' Thesis. University of Alberta. Edmonton, Alberta. Canada.

13962. Smith, F. G. A method of leveling depressions in turf. Journal of the Board of Greenkeeping Research. 7(26):342–343. 1950.

13963. Smith, F. H. and F. B. Ledeboer. Controlling turfgrasses diseases. Clemson University Extension Service, Lawn Grass Circular. Supplement 2. 1971.

13964. Smith, F. W. Fertilization. Central Plains Turfgrass Conference Proceedings. 1:24–29. 1950.

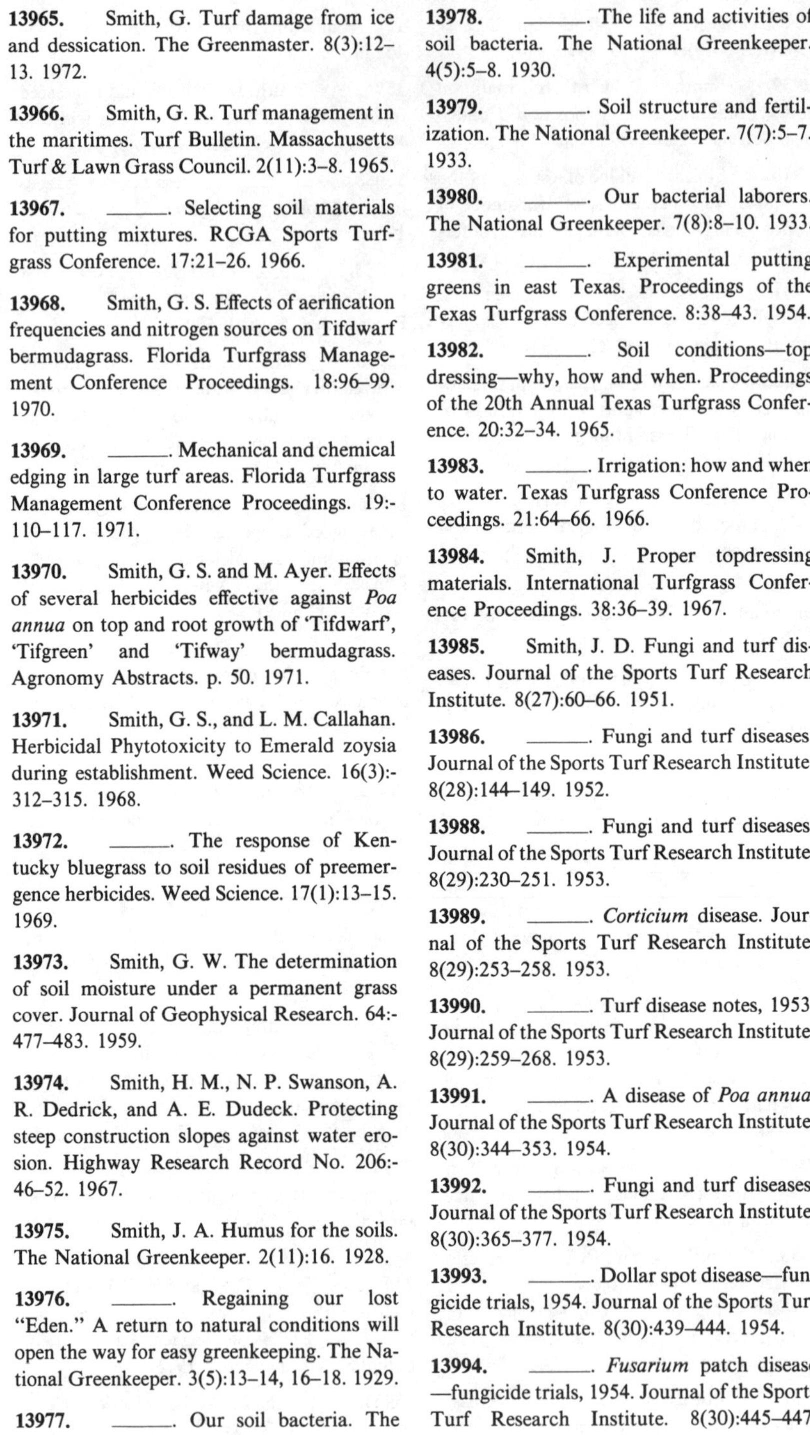

13965. Smith, G. Turf damage from ice and dessication. The Greenmaster. 8(3):12–13. 1972.

13966. Smith, G. R. Turf management in the maritimes. Turf Bulletin. Massachusetts Turf & Lawn Grass Council. 2(11):3–8. 1965.

13967. ______. Selecting soil materials for putting mixtures. RCGA Sports Turfgrass Conference. 17:21–26. 1966.

13968. Smith, G. S. Effects of aerification frequencies and nitrogen sources on Tifdwarf bermudagrass. Florida Turfgrass Management Conference Proceedings. 18:96–99. 1970.

13969. ______. Mechanical and chemical edging in large turf areas. Florida Turfgrass Management Conference Proceedings. 19:-110–117. 1971.

13970. Smith, G. S. and M. Ayer. Effects of several herbicides effective against *Poa annua* on top and root growth of 'Tifdwarf', 'Tifgreen' and 'Tifway' bermudagrass. Agronomy Abstracts. p. 50. 1971.

13971. Smith, G. S., and L. M. Callahan. Herbicidal Phytotoxicity to Emerald zoysia during establishment. Weed Science. 16(3):-312–315. 1968.

13972. ______. The response of Kentucky bluegrass to soil residues of preemergence herbicides. Weed Science. 17(1):13–15. 1969.

13973. Smith, G. W. The determination of soil moisture under a permanent grass cover. Journal of Geophysical Research. 64:-477–483. 1959.

13974. Smith, H. M., N. P. Swanson, A. R. Dedrick, and A. E. Dudeck. Protecting steep construction slopes against water erosion. Highway Research Record No. 206:-46–52. 1967.

13975. Smith, J. A. Humus for the soils. The National Greenkeeper. 2(11):16. 1928.

13976. ______. Regaining our lost "Eden." A return to natural conditions will open the way for easy greenkeeping. The National Greenkeeper. 3(5):13–14, 16–18. 1929.

13977. ______. Our soil bacteria. The National Greenkeeper. 4(1):5–9. 1930.

13978. ______. The life and activities of soil bacteria. The National Greenkeeper. 4(5):5–8. 1930.

13979. ______. Soil structure and fertilization. The National Greenkeeper. 7(7):5–7. 1933.

13980. ______. Our bacterial laborers. The National Greenkeeper. 7(8):8–10. 1933.

13981. ______. Experimental putting greens in east Texas. Proceedings of the Texas Turfgrass Conference. 8:38–43. 1954.

13982. ______. Soil conditions—top dressing—why, how and when. Proceedings of the 20th Annual Texas Turfgrass Conference. 20:32–34. 1965.

13983. ______. Irrigation: how and when to water. Texas Turfgrass Conference Proceedings. 21:64–66. 1966.

13984. Smith, J. Proper topdressing materials. International Turfgrass Conference Proceedings. 38:36–39. 1967.

13985. Smith, J. D. Fungi and turf diseases. Journal of the Sports Turf Research Institute. 8(27):60–66. 1951.

13986. ______. Fungi and turf diseases. Journal of the Sports Turf Research Institute. 8(28):144–149. 1952.

13988. ______. Fungi and turf diseases. Journal of the Sports Turf Research Institute. 8(29):230–251. 1953.

13989. ______. *Corticium* disease. Journal of the Sports Turf Research Institute. 8(29):253–258. 1953.

13990. ______. Turf disease notes, 1953. Journal of the Sports Turf Research Institute. 8(29):259–268. 1953.

13991. ______. A disease of *Poa annua.* Journal of the Sports Turf Research Institute. 8(30):344–353. 1954.

13992. ______. Fungi and turf diseases. Journal of the Sports Turf Research Institute. 8(30):365–377. 1954.

13993. ______. Dollar spot disease—fungicide trials, 1954. Journal of the Sports Turf Research Institute. 8(30):439–444. 1954.

13994. ______. *Fusarium* patch disease—fungicide trials, 1954. Journal of the Sports Turf Research Institute. 8(30):445–447. 1954.

13996. ______. Fungi and turf diseases. Journal of the Sports Turf Research Institute. 9(31):35–59. 1955.

13997. ______. Turf disease notes 1955. Journal of the Sports Turf Research Institute. 9(31):60–75. 1955.

13998. ______. Fungi and turf diseases. Journal of the Sports Turf Research Institute. 9(32):180–202. 1956.

13999. ______. The use of griseofulvin against dollar spot and *Fusarium* patch disease of turf. Journal of the Sports Turf Research Institute. 9(32):203–209. 1956.

14000. ______. Dollar spot trials, 1956. Journal of the Sports Turf Research Institute. 9(32):235–243. 1956.

14001. ______. Seed dressing trials, 1956. Journal of the Sports Turf Research Institute. 9(32):244–250. 1956.

14002. ______. *Ophiobolus* patch disease. Parks, Golf Courses, and Sports Grounds. 21(7):431–432. 1956.

14003. ______. Turfgrasses for the north. Northwest Turfgrass Conference Proceedings. 23:35–40. 1969.

14004. ______. Overwintering diseases of turfgrasses. Northwest Turfgrass Conference Proceedings. 23:65–78. 1969.

14005. ______. Powdery mildew on bluegrass cultivates and selections. Canada Agriculture Research Station Report. 1971.

14006. ______. *Phleospora* stem eyespot of fescues in Oregon and the *Didymella* perfect stage of the pathogen. The Plant Disease Reporter. 55(1):63–67. 1971.

14007. ______. Fungi and turf diseases. Journal of the Sports Turf Research Institute. 9(33):324–352. 1957.

14008. ______. Cadmium chloride/urea for dollar spot control. Journal of the Sports Turf Research Institute. 9(33):355–359. 1957.

14009. ______. *Fusarium* patch disease fungicide trials, 1957. Journal of the Sports Turf Research Institute. 9(33):360–363. 1957.

14010. ______. A new fungicide formulation for *Fusarium* patch disease control. Journal of the Sports Turf Research Institute. 9(33):364–366. 1957.

14011. ______. Seed dressing trial, 1957. Journal of the Sports Turf Research Institute. 9(33):369–372. 1957.

14012. ______. The effect of species and varieties of grasses on turf diseases. Journal of the Sports Turf Research Institute. 9(34):-462–466. 1958.

14013. ______. The effect of lime application on the occurrence of *Fusarium* patch disease on a forced *Poa annua* turf. Journal of the Sports Turf Research Institute. 9(34):-467–470. 1958.

14014. ______. Turf diseases in the north of Scotland. Journal of the Sports Turf Research Institute. 10(35):42–46. 1959.

14017. Smith, J. D., and E. C. M. Haes. Fungicide dressings for lawn grass seed. Gardeners Chronicle. 141(14):360. 1957.

14018. Smith, J. D., and N. Jackson. Fungal diseases of turf grasses. Partridge Printers Limited, England. 97 pp. 1965.

14020. Smith, L. A. Measuring courses accurately. USGA Green Section Record, 5(1):1–4. 1967.

14023. Smith, M., H. Suzuki, and M. Malina. Development of analytical procedure for the analysis of *Dicamba metabolite.* Journal of Association of Official Agricultural Chemists. 48:1164–1169. 1965.

14024. Smith, N. A. *Helminthosporium*-scourge of the grass family. Michigan Turfgrass Research Report. 1(1):12. 1963.

14025. ______. Control of turfgrass diseases. Michigan Turfgrass Research Report. 3(1):6–7. 1965.

14026. Smith, N. A. and G. Guyer. Chemical control of Kentucky bluegrass leafspot caused by *Helminthosporium vagans.* Quarterly Bulletin, Michigan State University. 44(2):226–229. 1961.

14027. Smith, N. R. Micro-organisms of the soil. Golfdom. 11(4):23–26. 1937.

14028. ______. Soil organisms in relation to turf. The Greenkeepers' Reporter. 5(7):-3–6, 12–13, 1937.

14029. ______. Soil organisms in relation to golf turf. National Association of Greenkeepers of America Conference Proceedings. 11:39–40. 1937.

14030. Smith, P. M. Lawns for South Carolina. South Carolina Agricultural Extension Circular. 308:1–21. 1960.

14031. Smith, P. W. Lawns from turf. Landscape and Garden. 3(1):51–52. 1936.

14032. ———. The planning, construction and maintenance of playing fields. Oxford University Press. 224 pp. 1950.

14033. Smith, R. C. *Nomophila noctuella* as a grass and alfalfa pest in Kansas *(Lepidoptera, Pyralididae).* Journal of the Kansas Entomological Society. 15(1):25–34. 1942.

14034. Smith, R. H. Insects of interest. The Greenkeepers' Reporter. 6(5):15–16, 33. 1938.

14035. Smith, R. S. Using selective weedkiller on the lawn. Gardeners Chronicle. 145(24):405. 1959.

14036. ———. Summer care of lawns. Gardeners Chronicle. 146(2–3):27. 1959.

14037. ———. Spring work on lawns. Gardeners Chronicle. 147(11):152, 156. 1960.

14038. ———. Fertilizers for the lawn. Gardeners Chronicle. 147(13):180. 1960.

14039. ———. Watering lawns. Gardeners Chronicle. 147(17):297. 1960.

14040. ———. Lawn grasses. Gardeners Chronicle. 148(10):247. 1960.

14041. ———. Dryness on lawns. Gardeners Chronicle. 150(10):171. 1961.

14042. ———. Moss on lawns. Gardeners Chronicle. 150(15):269. 1961.

14044. Smith, S. M. New lawns—autumn treatment. Gardeners Chronicle. 158(13):298. 1965.

14045. Smith, T. Turf management vs. turf renovation. Proceedings of the Midwest Regional Turf Conference. pp. 50A–53. 1961.

14046. Smith, W. Superintendent helps nature take its course. Grounds Maintenance. 1(5):10–13. 1966.

14047. Smith, W. D. Silvex for chickweed control. North Central Weed Control Conference Proceedings. 17:23. 1960.

14048. Smith, W. F. Studies on fall *Panicum* and its response to the triazine herbicides atrazine and simazine. M. S. Thesis, Rutgers University. 1972.

14049. Smith, W. L. Basal plant density guide to protect highways-other slopes. Soil Conservation. 28(3):58–59. 1962.

14050. Smith, Y. What's new in fertilizers. Texas Turfgrass Conference Proceedings. 21:21–26. 1966.

14051. Smoliak, S. and A. Johnston. Germination and early growth of grasses at four root-zone temperatures. Canadian Journal of Plant Science. 48(2):119–127. 1968.

14052. Smolik, J. D., and R. B. Malek. *Tylenchorhynchus nudus* and other nematodes associated with Kentucky bluegrass turf in South Dakota. The Plant Disease Reporter. 56(10):898–900. 1972.

14054. Sneep, J., B. H. Olfhoff, and J. K. Groenewolt. Rassenlijst. Instituut voor Rassenonderzoek van Landbouwgewassen. 332 pp. 1965.

14055. ———. Rassenlijst. Instituut voor Rassenonderzoek van Landbouwgewassen. 336 pp. 1966.

14056. Sneep, J., B. H. Olfhoff, and J. A. Hogen. Rassenlijst. Instituut voor Rassenonderzoek van Landbouwgewassen. 336 pp. 1967.

14057. ———. Rassenlijst. Instituut voor Rassenonderzoek van Landbouwgewassen. 328 pp. 1968.

14058. ———. Rassenlijst. Instituut voor Rassenonderzoek van Landbouwgewassen. 328 pp. 1969.

14060. ———. Rassenlijst. Instituut voor Rassenonderzoek van Landbouwgewassen. 320 pp. 1971.

14061. Snodsmith, R. L. *Poa annua.* Illinois Turfgrass Conference Proceedings. 4:-13–15. 1963.

14063. Snyder, A. A. Golf course maintenance in the desert. Golf Course Reporter. 31(7)36–42. 1963.

14064. ———. Ridding greens of frost. The Golf Superintendent. 34(2):24. 1966.

14065. Snyder, D. The finishing touch. USGA Green Section Record. 4(6):23–24. 1967.

14066. Snyder, G. H. Fertilization of turfgrasses. Annual Research Report of the Institute of Food & Agricultural Sciences, University of Florida. p. 167. 1969.

14067. ______. Two types of Bahiagrass yellowing. Proceedings of Florida Turf Grass Management Conference. 17:101–104. 1969.

14068. ______. Soil water repellency. Proceedings, University of Florida Turf-Grass Management Conference. 17:105–106. 1969.

14069. ______. Fertilization of turf-grasses. Annual Research Report of the Institute of Food & Agricultural Sciences. University of Florida. p. 175. 1970.

14070. ______. Fertilization of turf through the irrigation system. Florida Turf-grass Management Conference Proceedings. 18:66–72. 1970.

14071. ______. Soils related turf research at the Ft. Lauderdale research center. Florida Turfgrass Management Conference Proceedings. 19:123–124. 1971.

14072. Snyder, L. C. and R. C. Rose. Home lawn. Minnesota Agricultural Extension Folder. 165:1–8. 1953.

14073. Snyder, R. How to make an enduring lawn. The Complete Book for Gardeners. D. Van Nostrand Co., Inc. New Jersey. 43–61 pp. 1964.

14074. Snyder, V. Effects of chelated iron and nitrogen fertilization on the physiology and growth of creeping bentgrass. M. S. Thesis, Virginia Polytechnic Institute. 1972.

14075. Snyder, V., and R. E. Schmidt. Nitrogen and chelated iron fertilization of Penncross bentgrass (*Agrostis palustris* Hudson). Agronomy Abstracts. p. 65. 1972.

14076. Snyder, W. E. Quackgrass control in waste areas. New York State Turf Association. Bulletin 18. p. 72. 1950.

14078. Solon, E., and A. J. Turgeon. Studies on vegetative establishment of Kentucky bluegrass. University of Illinois Turf-grass Field Day. pp. 6–7. 1972.

14079. ______. Control of weedy perenial grasses. University of Illinois Turf-grass Field Day. pp. 20–21. 1972.

14080. Sommers, R. Firm greens: best for you and the course. USGA Green Section Journal and Turfgrass Management. 19(1). 1966.

14081. Solly, C. Perfect turf; how to plant a lawn and maintain a perfect turf in the Pacific Northwest. Cecil Solly Garden Notebook Series, Seattle. 32 pp. 1948.

14082. Soper, D. Special weed problems. Proceedings of the First Symposium on the Control of Weed, Pests and Diseases of Cultivated Turf. pp. 12–16. 1967.

14083. ______. Special weed problems. The Groundsman. 21(11):25–27. 1968.

14084. ______. The role of the hydroxybenzonitriles as selective weed-killers in sports turf. Proceedings of the First International Turfgrass Research Conference. pp. 401–411. 1969.

14085. Soper, K. The anatomy of the vegetative shoot of *Paspalum dilatatum* Poir. New Zealand Journal of Science and Technology. Section A. 37(6):600–605. 1956.

14086. ______. Effects of flowering on the root system and summer survival of rye-grass. New Zealand Journal of Agricultural Research. 1(3):329–340. 1958.

14087. Soper, K., and K. J. Mitchell. The developmental anatomy of perennial ryegrass (*Lolium perenne* L.). New Zealand Journal of Science and Technology. Section A. 37(6):-484–504. 1956.

14089. Sosebee, R. E. and H. H. Wiebe. Effect of water stress and clipping on photosynthate translocation in two grasses. Agronomy Journal. 63(1):14–17. 1971.

14090. Sotari, A. M. Effects of various rates and combination of N, P, K, and cutting height on the development of rhizome, root, total available carbohydrate, and foliage composition of *Poa pratensis* L. Merion grown on Houghton muck. Ph.D. Thesis, Michigan State University. 127 pp. 1967.

14091. Sousa, S. Public golf courses—with a difference. Parks and Recreation. 4(5):49–50. 1969.

14092. Southards, C. J. The pseudo-root-knot nematode of bermuda grass in Tennessee. The Plant Disease Reporter. 51(6):455. 1967.

14093. ______. Nematodes in turf. Proceedings of the Tennessee Turfgrass Conference. 2:30–31. 1968.

14094. Southwood, T. R. E., and W. F. Jepson. The productivity of grasslands in England for *Oscinella frit* (L.) *(Chloropidae)* and other stem-boring *Diptera*. Bulletin of Entomological Research. 53:395–407. 1962.

14095. Spangler, W. A. Training a good foreman. The Cemeterian. 66(4):21–22, 27. 1966.

14096. Spanis, W. C., D. E. Munnecke, and R. A. Solberg. Biological breakdown of two organic mercurial fungicides. Phytopathology. 52(5):455–462. 1962.

14097. Sparks, D. Sand greens—their construction and care. The National Greenkeeper. 3(1):25–26. 1929.

14098. ______. Sand greens in Oklahoma. The National Greenkeeper. 5(4):34–35. 1931.

14099. Sparrow, G. N. Principles of irrigation. Southeastern Turfgrass Conference Proceedings. 14:16–20. 1960.

14100. Spaulding, S. Prostrate birdsfoot trefoil—a turf for difficult sites. California Turfgrass Culture. 10(4):25–26. 1960.

14101. ______. Seen from the rough. Divot News. 10(5):2. 1971.

14102. Spaulding, S. and V. B. Youngner. The influence of various environments on the growth of *Lotis tenuis,* (narrowleaf birdsfoot trefoil). Agronomy Abstracts. pp. 91–92. 1959.

14103. ______. Evaluation of bluegrass cultivars for turf by various methods. Agronomy Abstracts. p. 64. 1968.

14104. Spaulding, T. Profile of a rolling course. The Golf Superintendent. 36(9):14–16, 18, 47. 1968.

14105. Speelman, C. W. Trends in irrigation. Tennessee Turfgrass Conference Proceedings. 3:32–35. 1969.

14106. ______. Irrigation system of the future. Florida Turfgrass Management Conference Proceedings. 18:58–62. 1970.

14107. Speir, W. H., E. H. Stewart, and E. O. Burt. Moisture retention, movement, measurement & availability to plant in Florida soils. Annual Research Report of the Institute of Food & Agricultural Sciences. University of Florida. p. 185. 1968.

14108. Spencer, G. Surveying technique for turf areas. Proceedings of Midwest Regional Turf Conference. pp. 15–21. 1949.

14109. Spencer, J. T. Seed production of Kentucky-31 fescue and orchard grass as influenced by rate of planting, nitrogen fertilization and management. Kentucky Agricultural Experiment Station. Bulletin 554. 18 pp. 1950.

14110. Spencer, J. T., and E. N. Fergus. Floret and seed types in Kentucky bluegrass in relation to yield and quality of seed. Journal of the American Society of Agronomy. 34(11):1035–1041. 1942.

14111. Spencer, J. T., H. H. Jewett, and E. N. Fergus. Seed production of Kentucky bluegrass as influenced by insects, fertilizers, and sod management. Kentucky Agricultural Experiment Station. Bulletin 535. 44 pp. 1949.

14112. Sperandio, A. J. What about top dressing? Greenkeepers Club of New England Newsletter. 12(4):4–6. 1940.

14113. Sperandio, A. J. Business management of disease control. Greenkeepers Club of New England Newsletter. 13(5):6–10. 1941.

14114. Sperry, T. M. Root systems in Illinois prairie. Ecology. 16(2):178–202. 1935.

14115. Spinelli, J. Irrigation inspector. Proceedings of the Turfgrass Sprinkler Irrigation Conference. 2 pp. 1966.

14116. Spink, W. T. and J. R. Dogger. Chemical control of the ground pearl, *Eumargarodes laingi.* Journal of Economic Entomology. 54(3):423–424. 1961.

14117. Starks, K. J. and R. Thurston. Silver top of bluegrass. Journal of Economic Entomology. 55(6):865–867. 1962.

14118. Spiro, D. A. Urea leaching in a sandy soil. M. S. Thesis, University of Arizona. 1972.

14119. Splittstoesser, W. E., and H. J. Hopen. Response of bentgrass to siduron. Weeds. 15(1):82–83. 1967.

14120. ______. Root growth inhibition by siduron and its relief by kinetin. Physiologia. Plantarum. 23(5):964–970. 1970.

14121. Splechtner, F. Studien über die Blüh—und Befruch-tungsverhaltnisse einiger Klone und Populationen von *Agrostis stolonifera* L. Angewandte Botanik. 4:250–256. 1922.

14123. Spomer, A. and R. W. Langhans. Soil moisture and aeration. Part II. The Golf Superintendent. 36(6):16–22. 1968.

14124. ______. Soil moisture and aeration. Part III. The Golf Superintendent. 37(6):16–22. 1969.

14125. Sprogell, F. T. Organic matter helps to rebuild depleted soil. Golfdom. 38(6):34. 1964.

14127. Sprague, H. B. Fertilizer experiments at New Brunswick (N.J.) summarized. Golfdom 3(6):61–62. 1929.

14128. ______. Turf experiments in New Jersey. The National Greenkeeper. 3(12):5–12. 1929.

14129. ______. Turf experiments at the New Jersey State Station. USGA Green Section Bulletin. 8(12):251–252. 1928.

14130. ______. How and why of water's effect on golf course grasses. Golfdom. 5(3):-34–37. 1931.

14131. ______. How and why of water's effect on golf course grasses. Golfdom. 5(4):-98, 100, 102, 104. 1931.

14132. ______. Some water relations of turf plants. The National Greenkeeper. 5(3):-16–28. 1931.

14133. ______. Soil conditions and root development. Golfdom. 6(2):53–55. 1932.

14134. ______. How study of root system tells story of soil. Golfdom. 6(3):68, 71–72, 74, 76. 1932.

14135. ______. Soil conditions and root development. The National Greenkeeper. 6(5):5–8, 10–13, 30. 1932.

14136. ______. Recent turf experiments in New Jersey. Greenkeepers Club of New England Newsletter. 5(4):2–3. 1933.

14137. ______. Root development of perennial grasses and its relation to soil conditions. Soil Science. 36:189–209. 1933.

14138. ______. Notes for your lawn loving club members. Greenkeepers' Reporter. 264:29–30. 1934.

14139. ______. Organic materials for soil improvement. Greenkeepers Club of New England Newsletter. 6(3):6–8. 1934.

14140. ______. Commercial fertilizers for lawns. Greenkeepers Club of New England Newsletter. 6(4):6–10. 1934.

14141. ______. Controlling crab grass on lawns. Greenkeepers Club of New England Newsletter. 6(7):3–4. 1934.

14142. ______. Utilization of nutrients by Colonial bent *(Agrostis tenuis)* and Kentucky bluegrass *(Poa pratensis)*. Greenkeepers Club of New England Newsletter. 6(8):-3–7. 1934.

14143. ______. Planting new lawns in late August or September. Greenkeepers Club of New England Newsletter. 6(9):3–4. 1934.

14144. ______. Successful lawns on shaded areas. Greenkeepers Club of New England Newsletter. 6(9):4, 6. 1934.

14145. ______. Repair lawn injuries in early autumn. Greenkeepers Club of New England Newsletter. 6(9):6–7. 1934.

14146. ______. Liming lawn soils. Greenkeepers Club of New England Newsletter. 6(12):5–6. 1934.

14147. ______. Lime acid lawns in winter or early spring. Greenkeepers Club of New England Newsletter. 6(12):8. 1934.

14148. ______. Summary of experiments on utilization of nutrients by colonial bent and Kentucky bluegrass. Greenkeeper's Reporter. 2(8–9):19–20. 1934.

14149. ______. Utilization of nutrients by colonial bent, *(Agrostis tenuis)* and Kentucky bluegrass, *(Poa pratensis)*. New Jersey Agricultural Experiment Station. Bulletin 570. 16 pp. 1934.

14150. ______. Crabgrass control on lawns. New Jersey Agricultural Experiment Station Circular 354. 4 p. 1935.

14151. ______. Spring care of established lawns. Greenkeepers Club of New England Newsletter. 7(4):10. 1935.

14152. ______. Making temporary lawns. Greenkeepers Club of New England Newsletter. 7(4):10, 12. 1935.

14153. ______. Plant new lawns in late August or September. Greenkeepers Club of New England Newsletter. 7(9):3. 1935.

14154. ______. Green lawns on terrace slopes. Greenkeepers Club of New England Newsletter. 7(9):3–4. 1935.

14155. ______. Successful lawns on shaded areas. Greenkeepers Club of New England Newsletter. 7(9):4–5. 1935.

14156. ______. Roots matter most. Golfdom. 10(4):27–28. 1936.

14157. ______. Rolling and top-dressing the lawn. Greenkeepers Club of New England Newsletter. 8(2):8. 1936.

14158. ______. Soil water and its relation to the grass plant. Greenkeepers Club of New England Newsletter. 8(8):2–3. 1936.

14159. ______. Summary of the weed problem on turf. Greenkeepers Club of New England Newsletter. 8(8):4–6. 1936.

14160. ______. The relation of root growth to the vigor of turf grasses. The Greenkeeper's Reporter. 4(2):5–6, 22. 1936.

14161. ______. Root development and grasses. National Association of Greenkeepers of America Conference Proceedings. 10:-4–26. 1936.

14162. ______. Liming lawn soils. New Jersey Agricultural Experiment Station. Circular 362. 4 p. 1936.

14163. ______. Feeding turf grasses on lawns, parks, and recreation fields. New Jersey Agricultural Experiment Station Circular 365. 4 p. 1936.

14164. ______. Brown patch on lawns can be prevented by the timely use of mercury compounds. E. I. duPont de Nemours & Co. Agriculture Newsletter. 4(9):127. 1936.

14165. ______. Soil water and the grass plant. Golfdom. 11(2):59. 1937.

14166. ______. Weed problem of turf. Golfdom. 11(2):60–62. 1937.

14167. ______. Changing the soil structure. Golfdom. 11(2):64–65. 1937.

14168. ______. Some lawn information. Greenkeepers Club of New England Newsletter. 9(7):5–6. 1937.

14169. ______. Lime acid lawns in winter or early spring. Greenkeepers Club of New England Newsletter. 9(12):5. 1937.

14170. Sprague, H. B. and G. W. Burton. Annual bluegrass (*Poa annua* L.) and its requirements for growth. New Jersey Agricultural Experiment Station Bulletin 630. 24 pp. 1937.

14171. Sprague, H. B. Use your watering system right. Golfdom. 12(10):25–28. 1938.

14172. ______. Turf field day at the New Jersey Agricultural Experiment Station. Greenkeepers Club of New England Newsletter. 11(9):4–6. 1939.

14173. ______. Velvet bent grass for putting greens and other fine turf. Greenkeepers Club of New England Newsletter. 11(9):6, 8–9. 1939.

14174. ______. Better lawns for homes and parks. Whittlesey House, McGraw-Hill Book Company, Inc. New York. 205 pp. 1940.

14175. ______. The story of Raritan velvet bent grass. Greenkeepers Club of New England Newsletter. 13(4):9–10. 1941.

14176. ______. Better lawns. Doubleday, Garden City. 205 pp. 1945.

14177. ______. Organic materials for soil improvement. The Greenkeeper's Reporter. 13(4):14–32. 1945.

14178. ______. Drainage and soil aeration for greens. Timely Turf Topics. USGA Green Section. September. p. 2. 1947.

14179. ______. Aeration of fine turf. Southwest Turf Conference Proceedings. pp. 68–74. 1948.

14180. ______. What every turf man should know about watering. Oklahoma—Texas Turf Conference Proceedings. pp. 50–56. 1950.

14181. ______. Improvement of fairways without a watering system. Proceedings of the 5th Annual Texas Turf Conference. 6:-44–50. 1951.

14182. ______. The expanding field of special purpose turf. Pennsylvania State Turf Conference. 23:7–11. 1954.

14183. ______. The expanding field of

special turf. Golf Course Reporter. 23(1):-9–12. 1955.

14184. ______. Turf Management Handbook. The Interstate Printers & Publishers, Inc., Danville, Illinois. 253 pp. 1970.

14185. Sprague, H. B. and E. E. Evaul. Experiments with turf grasses in New Jersey. New Jersey Agricultural Experiment Station. Bulletin 497. 55 pp. 1930.

14186. Sprague, H. B., and J. F. Marrero. The effect of various sources of organic matter on the properties of soils as determined by physical measurements and plant growth. Soil Science, 32:35–49. 1931.

14187. ______. Further studies on the value of various types of organic matter for improving the physical condition of soils for plant growth. Soil Science. 34:197–208. 1932.

14188. Sprague, M. A. Principles of renovation. Rutgers University Short Course in Turf Management. 18:86–89. 1950.

14189. Sprague, R. Diseases of cereals and grasses in North America. The Ronald Press Co., New York. 538 pp. 1950.

14190. Sprague, V. G. Germination of freshly harvested seeds of several *Poa* species and of *Dactylis glomerata.* Journal of the American Society of Agronomy. 32(9):715–721. 1940.

14191. ______. The effects of temperature and day length on seedling emergence and early growth of several pasture species. Soil Science Society of America Proceedings. 8:287–294. 1943.

14192. ______. The relation of supplementary light and soil fertility to heading in the greenhouse of several perennial forage grasses. Journal of the American Society of Agronomy. 40(2):144–154. 1948.

14193. ______. Distribution of atmospheric moisture in the microclimate above a grass sod. Agronomy Journal. 47(12):551–559. 1955.

14194. Sprague, V. G. and L. F. Graber. The utilization of water by alfalfa *(Medicago sativa)* and by bluegrass *(Poa pratensis)* in relation to managerial treatments. Journal of the American Society of Agronomy. 30(12):-986–997. 1938.

14195. Sprague, V. G. and J. T. Sullivan. Reserve carbohydrates in orchard grass clipped periodically. Plant Physiology. 25(1):92–102. 1950.

14196. Sprague, V. G., A. V. Havens, A. M. Decker, and K. E. Varney. Air temperatures in the microclimate at four latitudes in the northeastern United States. Agronomy Journal. 47(1):42–44. 1955.

14197. Sprague, V. G., H. Neuberger, W. H. Orgell, and A. V. Dodd. Air temperature distribution in the microclimatic layer. Agronomy Journal. 46(3):105–108. 1954.

14198. Springer, D. K., J. D. Burns, H. A. Fibourg, and K. E. Graetz. Roadside revegetation and beautification in Tennessee. University of Tennessee SP 162. 22 pp. 1967.

14199. Spurway, C. H. Soil reaction (pH) preferences of plants. Michigan Agricultural Experiment Station Special Bulletin. 36 pp. 1941.

14200. Stadtherr, R. J. and L. C. Snyder. Home lawn. Minnesota Agricultural Extension Folder. 165:1–16. 1955.

14201. Stadtherr, R. J. Home lawn. Minnesota Agricultural Extension Folder. 165:-1–15. 1958.

14202. ______. Home lawn. Minnesota Agricultural Extension Folder. 165:1–20. 1960.

14203. ______. Studies on the use of arsenicals for crabgrass control in turf. Ph.D. Thesis, University of Minnesota. 1963.

14204. Stahl, J. L. Lawns. Western Washington Agricultural Experiment Station Bulletin. 8:7–8. 1920.

14205. ______. Renewing the lawn. Western Washington Agricultural Experiment Station. 9:18–19. 1921.

14206. Stählin, A. Annual meadow grass, "*Poa annua*" as a lawngrass. Garten und Landschaft. 77(2):44–45. 1967.

14207. Stakman, E. C. and F. J. Piemeisel. Biologic forms of *Puccinia graminis* on cereals and grasses. Journal of Agricultural Research. 10(9):429–496. 1917.

14208. Stamen, T. On turf and crabgrass. Turf Bulletin. Massachusetts Turf and Lawn Grass Council. 2(5):8–11. 1964.

14209. Stamm, R. H. Fast seeding and mulching. Proceedings of the Midwest Regional Turf Conference. pp. 72–74. 1966.

14210. Standifer, L. Purple nutsedge: World's worst weed? Louisiana Agriculture. 14(3):12–13. 1971.

14211. Standish, J. D. The golf course, the greenkeeper and the player. Proceedings of Midwest Regional Turf Conference. pp. 3–7. 1950.

14212. Stanford, J. P. Research. Proceedings of National Turf Field Days. pp. 22–24. 1950.

14213. ______. Tests of fairway grasses. Pennsylvania State College Turfgrass Conference Proceedings. 20:75–79. 1951.

14214. Stanford, J. P., and H. B. Musser. Availability of nitrogen from urea-form and other nitrogenous materials. Pennsylvania State College Turfgrass Conference Proceedings. 19:62–73. 1950.

14215. Stangel, H. Methylene ureas. Turf clippings. University of Massachussetts. 1(8):A–42 to A–44. 1963.

14216. Stanley, R. L., E. R. Beaty and J. D. Powell. Effect of clipping height on forage distribution and regrowth on Pensacola bahiagrass. Agronomy Journal. 59(2):185–186. 1967.

14218. Stapledon, R. G. Germination of indigenous grass and clover seeds. Journal of the Ministry of Agriculture. 29(2):118–125. 1922.

14219. ______. The seasonal productivity of herbage grasses. Welch Plant Breeding Station Bulletin Series H. No. 3. 1924.

14224. Stark, A. L. Lawn weed control. Utah State University Extension Leaflet No. 144. 1969.

14225. Stärk, E. The Stärk AWeS sports lawn. First Czechoslovak Symposium on Sportturf Proceedings. pp. 45–50. 1969.

14226. Stark, J. Use of injurious materials requires permit. Southern California Turfgrass Culture. 6(2):6. 1956.

14227. ______. Problems faced by cemeteries in fertilization program. Southern California Turfgrass Institute Proceedings. p. 3. 1959.

14229. Stark, R. H., A. L. Hafenrichter, and W. A. Moss. Adaptation of grasses for soil and water conservation at high altitudes. Agronomy Journal. 42(3):124–127. 1950.

14230. Starkey, R. L. Relations of microrganisms to control of thatch in turf. Golf Course Reporter. 21(7):9–14. 1953.

14231. ______. Relations of microorganisms to control of thatch. Golfdom. 27(5):76–78, 80. 1953.

14232. ______. Soil miroorganism the dynamic phase of the soil. Golf Course Reporter. 22(4):14–16. 1954.

14233. Starks, K. J. Insects attacking grasses. Kentucky Agricultural Experiment Station Annual Report. 73:55–56. 1960.

14234. ______. Insect pests of lawns. Kentucky Agricultural Extension Circular. 570:1–15. 1960.

14235. Starks, K. J., and R. Thurston. Control of plant bugs and other insects on Kentucky bluegrass *(Poa pratensis)* grown for seed. Journal of Economic Entomology. 55(6):993–997. 1962.

14236. Stark, N. Review of highway planting, information appropriate to Nevada. University of Nevada Bulletin B–7. 209 pp. 1966.

14240. Staten, R. D. The anatomy of the grass plant. Texas Turfgrass Conference Proceedings. 21:99–101. 1966.

14241. Stebbins, G. L. Cytogenetics and the evolution of the grass family. American Journal of Botany. 43(10):890–905. 1956.

14242. ______. Taxonomy and the evolution of genera, with special reference to the family *Gramineae.* Evolution. 10:235–245. 1956.

14243. Stebbins, G. L. and B. Crampton. A suggested revision of the grass genera of temperate North America. Recent Advances in Botany. pp. 133–145. 1961.

14244. Steckel, J. E. Fertilizing and liming. Turf Clippings. University of Massachussetts. 1(5):A–28 to A–29. 1960.

14245. ______. Soil reaction to arsenical compounds. Turf Clippings. University of Massachusetts. 1(6):A–45–48. 1961.

14246. Steel, J. B. Proper top dressing materials and mixtures. Second Western Turf

Conference at University of Alberta, Edmonton. pp. 37–42. 1953.

14247. ______. Cool season maintenance. National Turfgrass Conference Proceedings. 30:14. 1959.

14248. ______. Golf course maintenance in Manitoba. Guelph Turf Conference. Royal Canadian Golf Association Green Section. pp. 44–49. 1959.

14249. ______. Topdressing. Part I. The Greenmaster 4(5):4–6. 1968.

14250. ______. Top dressing. The Greenmaster. 4(6):12, 14. 1968.

14251. ______. The techniques of preparing and applying top dressing. RCGA National Turfgrass Conference. 19:52–55. 1968.

14252. ______. An unpleasant Halloween surprise in the Winnipeg area. The Greenmaster. 8(3):9–10. 1972.

14253. Steen, E. and Lenander, S. Grassörter för Grönytor. 1932.

14254. Steffek, E. F. How to have a good lawn. Gardening: The Easy Way. Holt, Rinehart and Winston. New York. pp. 23–33. 1961.

14255. Steiner, W. W. Recent development in soil erosion practices and materials. Roadside Development, Highway Research Board. 654:1–416. 1948.

14256. Steiniger, E. B. 22 yrs. progress aerifying turf. Golfdom. 25(10):64–69. 1951.

14257. Steiniger, E. Cool season maintenance. National Turfgrass Conference Proceedings. 30:13. 1959.

14258. Steiniger, E. R. Water distribution systems. USGA Journal and Turf Management. 13(1):25–26. 1960.

14259. ______. The story of Cohansey. USGA Green Section Record. 6(3):3–7. 1968.

14260. ______. The story of Cohansey. California Turfgrass Culture. 19(4):31–32. 1969.

14261. Stelling, A. C. Specifications and use of sod. Rutgers University Turfgrass Short Course. 6 pp. 1966.

14262. Stent, S. M. South African species of *Cynodon.* Bothalia. 2(1):6. 1927.

14263. Stephen, A. My experience with fertilizers. The National Greenkeeper. 6(9):-5–6. 1932.

14264. Stephens, E. R. Preparing the club for tournament play. Part IV. The role of the State Golf Association. Florida Turf Management Conference Proceedings. 4:52–53. 1956.

14266. Stephens, J. L. A report on plant introduction. Southeastern Turfgrass Conference Proceedings. 10:25. 1956.

14267. Stephenson, R. B. Sterilization technique for grass seeds. Plant Physiology. 17:324–325. 1942.

14268. Stermer, R. A. A fast method for determining grass seed purity. Seed World. 96(4):10. 1965.

14269. Stevens, O. A. The number and weight of seeds produced by weeds. American Journal of Botany. 19(9):784–794. 1932.

14270. ______. Weed development notes. North Dakota Agricultural Experiment Station Research Report No. 1. pp. 6–21. 1960.

14271. Stevens, W. J. Lawns. Agricultural and Horticultural Association, Limited. London. 20 pp. 1908.

14274. Stevenson, T. Lawn guide. Robert B. Luce, Inc. Washington, D. C. 76 pp. 1965.

14276. Stevenson, T. M. and W. J. White. Root fibre production of some perennial grasses. Scientific Agriculture. 22(2):-108–118. 1941.

14277. Stevenson, W. R. and G. L. Worf. Powdery mildew of ornamentals and turf. University of Wisconsin College of Agriculture and Life Sciences Cooperative Extension Programs. No. 2404. 2 pp. 1972.

14278. Stewart, C. E. Fairway watering benefits show need of more study. Golfdom. 22(1)28–29. 1948.

14279. ______. Irrigation systems. Proceedings of Midwest Regional Turf Conference. pp. 21–22. 1948.

14280. ______. The design and installation of golf course irrigation systems. Pennsylvania State College Turfgrass Conference Proceedings. 21:119–125. 1952.

14281. ______. Golf course irrigation. Golfdom. 32(8):27–28, 67. 1958.

14282. ______. Golf course irrigation. Golfdom. 32(10):74, 76, 78. 1958.

14283. ______. Irrigation for turf. Proceedings of the Midwest Regional Turf Conference. pp. 78–82. 1958.

14284. Stewart, C. E. and J. P. McBride. Automatic irrigation. The Golf Superintendent. 34(2):12–14, 48. 1966.

14285. Stewart, C. W. Nitrogen materials and their utilization. Proceedings of the Midwest Regional Turf Conference. pp. 9–11. 1957.

14286. Stewart, E. H., E. O. Burt and R. R. Smalley. Subirrigation of turf. Turf Bulletin. Massachusetts Turf and Lawn Grass Council. 3(3):21–22. 1966.

14287. ______. Subirrigation of turf. Proceedings of the Florida Turfgrass Management Conference. 13:153–159. 1965.

14288. Stewart, F. C. Turfgrass in Colorado. Rocky Mountain Regional Turfgrass Conference Proceedings. pp. 13–16. 1963.

14289. ______. The management aids of turfgrass irrigation. Sprinkler Irrigation Association Open Technical Conference Proceedings. pp. 73–76. 1963.

14290. ______. Introduction to sodding program. Rocky Mountain Regional Turfgrass Conference. 12:13. 1966.

14291. ______. Panel—questions and answers. Rocky Mountain Regional Turfgrass Conference. 12:22–25. 1966.

14292. Stewart, G. F. Establishing, maintaining, and selling sod for turf areas in New England. Turf Clippings. University of Massachusetts. 1(9):A–20 to A–22. 1964.

14293. ______. Post management of sod. Turf Clippings. University of Massachusetts. 2(2):44–45. 1967.

14294. Stewart, P. M. Well built bunkers reduce upkeep. National Greenkeeper. 1(3):-10–11. 1927.

14295. Stewart, P. Golf layouts. The National Greenkeeper. 4(7):5–6. 1930.

14296. Stewart, V. I. It's all in the soil. The Groundsman. 24(2):22–24 pp. 1970.

14297. ______. Getting off the matt. Parks, Golf Courses, and Sports Grounds. 37(8):784, 787–788. 1972.

14298. Stewart, V. I. and W. A. Adams. County cricket wickets. Journal of the Sports Turf Research Institute. 44:49–60. 1968.

14299. ______. Soil factors affecting the control of pace on cricket pitches. Proceedings of the First International Turfgrass Research Conference. pp. 533–546. 1969.

14300. Stewart, W. My trail to Hillcrest. The National Greenkeeper. 1(1):18–19. 1927.

14301. Stewart, W. W. Putting greens must be good. Greenkeepers Club of New England Newsletter. 7(7):10. 1935.

14302. Stienstra, W. C. Gray snow mold. Golf Superintendent. 39(9):24–28. 1971.

14303. Stiles, W. and T. E. Williams. The response of a rye grass/white clover sward to various irrigation regimes. Journal Agricultural Science. 65(3):351–364. 1965.

14304. Stimpson, E. Introducing the stimp. Golfdom. 11(2):40–41, 44. 1937.

14306. Stiteler, H. Football turf from a coach's point of view. Texas Turf Conference Proceedings. 5:6–9. 1950.

14307. Stith, W. Care of harvested grass. International Turfgrass Conference Proceedings. 38:62. 1967.

14308. Stitt, L. L. Mode of action, movement, and hazards of preemergence herbicides. Proceedings of the 19th Annual Texas Turfgrass Conference. 19:4–7. 1964.

14309. ______. Weed control in turfgrasses. Proceedings of the 19th Annual Texas Turfgrass Conference. 19:43–47. 1964.

14310. Stockdill, S. M. J. Treatment of weed greens. New Zealand Institute for Turf Culture Newsletter. 16:11–12. 1961.

14311. Stoddard, E. M. and R. J. Lukens. Chemotherapy breaks par. Frontiers of Plant Science. Connecticut Agricultural Experiment Station. p. 6. November, 1959.

14312. ______. Chemotherapy breaks par. California Turf Culture. 10(4):27. 1960.

14314. Stoddard, G. Spraying methods and chemical combinations for greens and fairways, bent greens in the west. International Turfgrass Conference Proceedings. 40:17–18. 1969.

14315. Stoddard, G. E. Make time study analysis basis for improved budgeting and efficiency. The Golf Superintendent. 34(6):-20, 22. 1966.

14316. Stoddard, G. S. Programming the work at Irvine Coast Country Club. Proceedings of the Turfgrass Sprinkler Irrigation Conference. 3 pp. 1966.

14317. ———. The game of sales. Proceedings Annual Turfgrass Sprinkler Irrigation Conference. 5:61–63. 1967.

14318. Stoddart, J. L. An assessment of (2–chloroethyl) trimethylammonium chloride as a potential aid to grass-seed production. Journal British Grassland Society. 19(4):373–375. 1964.

14319. Stoddart, L. A. Osmotic pressure and water content of prairie plants. Plant Physiology. 10(4):661–680. 1935.

14320. ———. How long do roots of grasses live? Science. 81(2109):544. 1935.

14321. Stodola, H. W. Municipal course maintenance. The National Greenkeeper. 7(4):14–17, 26. 1933.

14322. Stoesz, A. D., and R. L. Brown. Stabilizing sand dunes. Soil. USDA Yearbook of Agriculture. 1957. pp. 321–326.

14323. Stoin, H. R. Effects of nitrogen nutrition and temperature on the growth, carbohydrate content, and nitrogen metabolism of cool-season grasses. Ph.D. Thesis, Michigan State University. 66 pp. 1968.

14324. Stoin, H. R., and J. B. Beard. The effects of high temperature on the soluble nitrogen fraction of Kentucky bluegrass (*Poa pratensis* L.). Agronomy Abstracts. p. 36. 1966.

14326. Stokes, W. E. Lawn grass studies. Annual Report of the Florida Agricultural Experiment Station for 1922. p. 38R. 1922.

14327. ———. Florida turf work. Florida Agricultural Experiment Station Bulletin Annual Report. pp. 31–45. 1923.

14328. ———. Lawns in Florida. Florida Agricultural Experiment Station. Press Bulletin. 389:2. 1926.

14329. Stolz, E. Pipe for irrigation systems. Proceedings of the Midwest Regional Turf Conference. pp. 27–30. 1966.

14330. Stoltz, L. P. Weed control in horticultural crops. Kentucky Agricultural Experiment Station. Annual Report 78. p. 63. 1965.

14331. Stolzy, L. H., J. Letey, T. E. Szuszkiewicz, and O. R. Lunt. Root growth and diffusion rates as functions of oxygen concentration. Soil Science Society of America Proceedings. 25:463–467. 1961.

14332. Stone, J. F. Soil structure. Oklahoma Turfgrass Conference Proceedings. pp. 1–4. 1959.

14333. Stone, P. C. Lawn insects. Proceedings, Missouri Lawn and Turf Conference. 1:82–84. 1960.

14334. ———. Lawn pests. Proceedings, Missouri Lawn & Turf Conference. 2:8–9. 1961.

14335. Stone, R. J. Simulation modeling of highway maintenance operations applied to roadside mowing. Highway Research Abstracts. 42(12):78. 1972.

14336. Stone, W. New greens—heavy play—drought—clover—but we licked 'em all. Golfdom. 15(7):12–14. 1941.

14337. Story, W. A Purr-Wick green. Midwest Regional Turf Conference Proceedings. pp. 47–48. 1971.

14338. Stott, L. G. Treatments for the sod web worm. Greenkeepers Club of New England Newsletter. 10(3):12. 1938.

14339. Stottlemyer, W. and R. Bailey. Unique approaches to weed control. Proceedings of Scotts Turfgrass Research Conference. 3:75–91. 1972.

14340. Stoutemyer, V. T. Many vital course jobs can be tackled in winter. Golfdom. 8(1):34, 36. 1934.

14341. ———. A grass of possible value for dry or sandy fairways. Greenkeepers Club of New England Newsletter. 7(11):6. 1935.

14342. ———. Turf culture from an ecological viewpoint. The Greenkeepers' Reporter. 6(1):11–14, 34, 36, 38, 40. 1938.

14343. ———. Grass variety and turf management studies. First Annual Fall Field Day on Turf Culture. UCLA. 1:37–42. 1949.

14344. ———. Research and extension turf projects on a regional basis. Greenkeepers' Reporter. 17(5):21–23. 1949.

14345. ______. Variety testing. Field Day on Turf Culture. pp. 24–27. 1950.

14346. ______. The experimental turf program in southern California. Northern California Turf Conference Report. pp. 12–15. 1950.

14347. ______. Let's first understand bermudagrass. Golf Life. 1951.

14348. ______. New ideas in turf culture. Golf Life. 1951.

14349. ______. Turf grasses and turf management. North California Turf Conference Proceedings. pp. 73–75. 1951.

14350. ______. Turf grasses in California. Southern California Conference on Turf Culture. pp. 1–2. 1951.

14351. ______. Mowing grass is big business. Golf Life. 1952.

14352. ______. The turf program at Los Angeles. Southern California Turf Conference Proceedings. pp. 5–7. 1952.

14353. ______. The influence of management on turf composition. Southern California Turf Conference Proceedings, pp. 44–48. 1952.

14354. ______. Grass combinations for turfs. California Agriculture. 7(12):9–10. 1953.

14355. ______. Bermuda-bentgrass mixture. California Agriculture. 7(11):13. 1953.

14356. ______. Evaluations of fescues and bluegrasses. Southern California Turf Culture. 3(1):3. 1953.

14357. ______. Merion bluegrass in California. Southern California Turf Culture. 3(2):1–3. 1953.

14358. ______. The possibilities of sedges as turf. Southern California Turf Culture. 3(2):4. 1953.

14359. ______. The possibility of sedges as turf. Golf Course Reporter. 21(5):22–23. 1953.

14360. ______. Unconventional ideas in turf culture. Golf Life. 1953.

14361. ______. Zoysia is strong, weed resistant. Golf Life. 1953.

14362. ______. Annual bluegrass and its value in turf. Golf Life. 1953.

14363. ______. Zoysia seeding for western turf. Golf Life. 1953.

14365. ______. Select the right grass. North California Turf Conference Proceedings. pp. 18–23. 1953.

14366. ______. Unconventional ideas in turf culture. Southern California Turfgrass Conference Proceedings. pp. 5–8. 1953.

14367. ______. Plugs to change turf. California Agriculture. 8(2):5–6. 1954.

14368. ______. Annual bluegrass as a cool season grass for bermudagrass mixtures. Southern California Turf Culture. 4(1):1–2. 1954.

14369. ______. The rotary mower in California. Southern California Turf Culture 4(2):1–2. 1954.

14370. ______. Turfgrasses for sports areas. Golf Life. 1954.

14371. ______. How to choose turfgrasses. Western Feed and Seed. California. 1954.

14372. ______. Problems of mowing the warm season stoloniferous grasses. Southern California Turfgrass Culture. 5(4):4. 1955.

14373. ______. Problem of mowing the warm season stoloniferous grasses. The Greenkeeper's Reporter. 24:31–32. 1956.

14374. ______. Newport Kentucky bluegrass. California Turfgrass Culture. 10(2):16. 1960.

14375. Stoutemyer, V. T. and P. A. Miller. Evaluation of bentgrass strains for bowling and putting green turf. Southern California Turf Culture 3(3):4. 1953.

14376. Stoutemyer, V. T. and F. B. Smith. The effects of sodium chloride on some turf plants and soils. Journal of the American Society of Agronomy. 28(1):16–23. 1936.

14377. Stower, J. S. The value of irrigation for parks and sports grounds. Parks, Golf Courses & Sports Grounds. 24(1):22–23. 1958.

14378. ______. The value of irrigation for parks and sports grounds. Parks, Golf Courses & Sports Grounds. 24(3):162–163, 171. 1958.

14379. ______. The value of irrigation for parks and sports grounds. Parks, Golf Courses & Sports Grounds. 24(4):238–239. 1958.

14380. Strand, D. Renovation of turf. Greenkeepers' Reporter. 17(3)18–19, 33. 1949.

14381. ______. Renovation of turf. Greenkeeping Superintendents Association Twentieth National Turf Conference. pp. 104–107. 1949.

14382. Straub, C. Sod is for the pro's. The Farm Quarterly. 20(4):62–65, 122–125. 1965–66.

14383. Street, J. R. The effect of nitrogen source, rate, and time on the growth and chemical composition of tall fescue. M.S. Thesis, Ohio State University. 1971.

14384. Street, O. E. Weed-free seedbeds —sterilants. Rutgers University Short Course in Turf Management Proceedings. pp. 36–38. 1971.

14385. Streu, H. T. Some effects of pesticides in the turfgrass ecosystem. Scotts Turfgrass Research Seminar. pp. 43–44. 1968.

14386. ______. Some cumulative effects of pesticides in the turfgrass ecosystem. Proceedings of Scotts Turfgrass Research Conference. 1:53–64. 1969.

14387. ______. Some effects of the annual application of pesticides to turfgrass. USGA Green Section Record. 8(2):21. 1970.

14388. Streu, H. T. and C. Cruz. Control of the hairy chinch bug in turfgrass in the northeast with Dursban insecticide. Down to Earth. 28(1):1–4. 1972.

14389. Streu, H. T. and L. M. Vasvary. Sod webworm control trials. Turfgrass Research. New Jersey Agricultural Experiment Station Bulletin 816. pp. 83–84. 1966.

14390. ______. Pesticide activity and growth response effects in turfgrass. New Jersey Academy Science Bulletin. 11:17–21. 1966.

14391. ______. Control of the hairy chinch bug, *Blissus hirtus* Mont. in New Jersey. New Jersey Agricultural Experiment Station Bulletin. 816:78–82. 1966.

14393. ______. The nematocidal activity of some insecticides in turfgrass. Turfgrass Research, New Jersey Agricultural Experiment Station Bulletin 818. pp. 77–93. 1967.

14394. Streets, R. B. Turf diseases in southern Arizona. Proceedings of the Annual Arizona Turf Conference. pp. 30–32. 1953.

14396. Stringfellow, T. L. Biology and control of insects & related pests of turfgrasses. Annual Research Report of the Institute of Food & Agricultural Sciences. University of Florida. pp. 184. 1968.

14397. ______. Chinch bug control: where do we go from here. Florida Turf. 1(5):3–4. 1968.

14398. ______. Turfgrass insect research in Florida. Proceedings of Scotts Turfgrass Research Conference. 1:19–34. 1969.

14399. ______. Development in Florida turfgrass insect control, 1969. Proceedings of Florida Turf-Grass Management Conference. 17:94–100. 1969.

14400. Stringfellow, T. and J. S. Roussel. Chinch bug control in St. Augustine lawns. Louisiana Agriculture. 3(3):3, 16. 1960.

14401. Strobel, J. Turfgrass. Florida Turfgrass Management Conference Proceedings. 19:19–28. 1971.

14402. Stroehlein, J. L. Fertilization of two varieties of bermuda grass. Report on Turfgrass Research, Arizona Agricultural Experiment Station. 212:12–14. 1962.

14403. ______. Fertilization of two varieties of bermudagrass. Report on Turfgrass Research, Arizona Agricultural Experiment Station. 219:1–2. 1963.

14404. ______. Fertilizer studies on common bermudagrass. Turfgrass Research. University of Arizona Agricultural Experiment Station. Report 240. pp. 18–19. 1966.

14405. ______. The use of phosphorus on bermudagrass. Turfgrass Research. University of Arizona Agricultural Experiment Station. Report 250. pp. 9–10. 1967–1968.

14406. Stroehlein, J. L., P. R. Ogden, and B. Billy. Time of fertilizer application on desert grasslands. Journal of Range Management. 1968. 21(2):86–89.

14407. Strome, I. R. Preventing winter kill on greens. Golfdom. 15(10):21–23. 1941.

14408. Strong, L. A fairway renovation program. Rutgers University Short Course in Turf Management. 18:90–92. 1950.

14409. ______. Experiences in fairway improvement. Rutgers University Short Course in Turf Management. 19:94–95. 1951.

14410. Strong, L. A. Insects cannot win. The Greenkeepers' Reporter. 7(3):7–8, 28–29. 1939.

14411. Strong, L. J. From foreman to superintendent. The Golf Course Reporter. 33(1):28, 32, 34. 1965.

14412. Strong, W. C. Sprinkler irrigation manual. General Sprinkler Corporation. 1972.

14413. Stroube, E. W. Controlling weeds in turf. Ohio Agricultural Research and Development Center. Research Summary 24. pp. 25–29. 1967.

14414. ______. Controlling weeds in turf. Ohio Agricultural Research and Development Center. Research Summary 31. pp. 3–9. 1968.

14415. ______. Broadleaf weed control in turf. Ohio Turfgrass Conference Proceedings. pp. 53–56. 1969.

14416. ______. Controlling weeds in turf. Ohio Agricultural Research and Development Center. Research Summary 40. pp. 9–15. 1969.

14418. Struble, F. B. The little but mighty nematode. Oklahoma Turfgrass Conference Proceedings. 59–61 pp. 1960.

14419. Struchtmeyer, R. Soil requirements for turf. University of Maine Turf Conference Proceedings. 1:3 pp. 1963.

14420. Stuart, D. W. The production of grass seed for amenity turf in Oregon. Journal of the Sports Turf Research Institute. 44:-41–46. 1968.

14421. Stuckey, I. H. Seasonal growth of grass roots. American Journal of Botany. 28(6):486–491. 1941.

14423. ______. Influence of soil temperature on development of colonial bentgrass. Plant Physiology. 17:116–122. 1942.

14424. Stuckey, I. H. and W. G. Banfield. The morphological variations and the occurrence of aneuploids in some species of *Agrostis* in Rhode Island. American Journal of Botany. 33(3):185–190. 1946.

14425. Stufflebaum, J. From seed to sod farming. Grounds Maintenance. 7(5):22–23. 1972.

14426. Sturgeon, R. V. Control of algae on bentgrass greens with a coordination product of zinc ion and maneb. USGA Green Section Record. 2(5):6–7. 1965.

14427. Sturkie, D. G. Control of weeds in lawns with calcium cyanamid. Journal of the American Society of Agronomy. 25(1):-82–84. 1933.

14428. ______. Control of weeds in lawns with calcium cyanamid. Journal of the American Society of Agronomy. 29(10):803–808. 1937.

14429. ______. New lawn grass for the south. Southern Agriculture. 74(10):24. 1944.

14430. ______. Fairway and lawn maintenance. The Greenkeeper's Reporter. 15(3):-15–16. 1947.

14431. ______. Controlling crabgrass in lawns. Alabama Agricultural Experiment Station. Highlights of Agricultural Research. 10(2):12. 1963.

14432. ______. Mulches and land preparation in establishing roadside vegetation. Agronomy Abstracts. p. 103. 1964.

14433. ______. Controlling annual bluegrass in lawns. Alabama Agricultural Experiment Station. Highlights of Agricultural Research. 11(3):6. 1964.

14434. ______. Controlling broadleaf winter weeds. Alabama Agricultural Experiment Station. Highlights of Agricultural Research. 12(3):8. 1965.

14435. ______. Tour of turf research at Auburn University. Auburn University Annual Turfgrass Short Course. pp. 20–23. 1966.

14436. ______. Turf—recommended practices—Alabama. Annual Southern Weed Conference Research Report. 19:108–109. 1966.

14437. ______. Controlling nutgrass (nutsedge) in lawns. Alabama Agricultural

Experiment Station. Highlights of Agricultural Research. 14(1):4–5. 1967.

14438. Sturkie, D. G., and H. S. Fisher. The planting and maintenance of lawns. Alabama Agricultural Experiment Station. Circular 85. 20 pp. 1942.

14439. ______. The planting and maintenance of lawns. Alabama Agricultural Experiment Station. Circular 85. 20 pp. 1950.

14440. Sturkie, D. G., and R. D. Rouse. Response of zoysia and Tiflawn bermuda to P and K. Agronomy Abstracts. p. 54. 1967.

14441. ______. Zoysia and Tiflawn bermuda grasses, growth and composition. As affected by phosphorus and potassium. Auburn University Annual Turfgrass Short Course. pp. 7–15. 1967.

14442. Stuurman, E., and W. Versteeg. The construction of sportsgrounds on artificially drained soils in the Netherlands. First Czechoslovak Symposium on Sportturfs Proceedings. pp. 87–104. 1969.

14443. Subirats, F. J. and R. L. Self. *Fusarium* blight of centipede grass. The Plant Disease Reporter. 56(1):42–44. 1972.

14444. Sudell, R. Lawns. Landscape Gardening. Ward, Lock & Co., Ltd. London. pp. 325–338. 1933.

14445. Suholet, D. Designing trails compatible within the highway right of ways. Short Course on Roadside Development (Ohio). 13:105–109. 1971.

14446. Sullivan, E. F. Effects of soil reaction, clipping height, and nitrogen fertilization on the productivity of Kentucky bluegrass sod transplants in pot culture. Agronomy Journal. 54(3):261–263. 1962.

14447. Sullivan, E. H. The importance of public relations to golf and sports clubs. Journal of the Sports Turf Research Institute. 11(39):19–22. 1963.

14448. Sullivan, J. T. and R. J. Garber. Chemical composition of pasture plants. Pennsylvania State College. School of Agriculture. Agricultural Experiment Station Bulletin. 489. pp. 1–61. 1947.

14449. Sullivan, J. T. and V. G. Sprague. Composition of the roots and stubble of perennial ryegrass following partial defoliation. Plant Physiology. 18(4):656–670. 1943.

14450. ______. The effect of temperature and growth on the composition of the stubble and roots of perennial ryegrass. Plant Physiology. 24(4):706–719. 1949.

14451. ______. Reserve carbohydrates in orchardgrass cut for hay. Plant Physiology. 1953. 28(2):304–313.

14452. Sullivan, J. T., T. G. Phillips, M. E. Loughlin, and V. G. Sprague. Chemical composition of some foliage grasses. II. successive cuttings during the growing season. Agronomy Journal. 48(1):11–14. 1956.

14453. Sullivan, L. J. Why low phosphorus and higher potassium. Turf Clippings. University of Massachussetts. 1(8):A–55 to A–59. 1963.

14454. Sumner, D. C. and K. E. Lindsey. The use of field maturity data to establish optimum harvest period for Merion bluegrass seed production. Agronomy Journal. 54(5):-416–418. 1962.

14455. Sumner, D. C. and M. D. Miller. Grass seed production. California Agricultural Extension Service. Circular 155. 22 pp. 1949.

14456. Sumner, D. C., J. R. Goss, and B. R. Houston. Merion bluegrass seed production. California Agricultural Experiment Station. Extension Circular 470. 27 pp. 1958.

14457. Sumner, D. C., R. M. Hagan and D. S. Mikkelsen. Merion bluegrass seed production. USGA Journal and Turf Management. 8(1):27–32. 1955.

14458. Sumner, D. R. Nematodes in bluegrass. The Plant Disease Reporter. 51(6):457–460. 1967.

14459. Sund, J. M., E. L. Nielsen, and H. L. Ahlgren. Response of Kentucky bluegrass (*Poa pratensis* L.) strains to fertility and management. Wisconsin Agricultural Experiment Station Research Report 20. 1–28 pp. 1965.

14460. Suominen, O. Susceptibility of stands to devastation by snow—An investigation into snow devastation in southern Finland in winter 1958–1959. Silva Fennica. 112(5):35. 1963.

14462. Sutton, M. A. F. Golf courses: design, construction, and upkeep. Sutton and Sons Ltd., Pub., Reading, England. 192 pp. 1950.

14463. ______. Earthworms in sports turf. Turf for Sport. 4(2):13. 1962.

14464. ______. The use of the brush on turf. Turf for Sport. 4(3):10–12. 1962.

14465. ______. Nature's influence on grasses. Turf for Sport. 4(4):6–7. 1962.

14466. ______. Lawn and sports grounds. Sutton. Reading, England. 248 pp. 1962.

14467. Sutton, M. A. F., T. F. N. Alexander, and F. C. West. A study of the growth of grass in "surface—stabilised" soil. Sutton & Sons, Ltd. 22 pp.

14468. Sutton, M. H. F. Garden lawns, tennis lawns, putting greens, cricket grounds. Simkin, Marshall, Hamilton, Kent and Co. Ltd. London. 34 pp. 1899.

14469. ______. The Laying Out and Upkeep of Golf Courses and Putting Greens. Simpkin, Marshall, Hamilton, Kent, and Co. Ltd. 47 pp. 1908.

14470. ______. The Book of the Links—a Symposium on Golf. W. H. Smith and Son. London. 212 pp. 1912.

14471. ______. Notes on British grasses. The National Greenkeeper. 3(3):19–24. 1929.

14472. Sutton, R. T. The agronomist and the highway roadside. Ohio Short Course on Roadside Development. 21:64–69. 1962.

14473. Suzuki, M. Behavior of long-chain Fructosan in the basal top of timothy as influenced by N, P, and K, and defoliation. Crop Science. 11(5):632–635. 1971.

14474. Svehla, F. Cultivation by discing. Greenkeeper's Reporter. 10(6):16–17. 1942.

14475. Svetlik, V. Possibility of cultivation and utilization of grass species for lawns. First Czechoslovak Symposium on Sportturf Proceedings. pp. 243–251. 1969.

14476. Swank, G. Fungicides for the control of turf diseases. Proceedings of the Midwest Regional Turf Conference. pp. 42–44. 1956.

14477. Swann, C. W. and K. P. Buchholtz. Control and carbohydrate reserves of quackgrass as influenced by uracil herbicides. Weeds. 14(2):103–105. 1966.

14478. Swanson, N. P. and A. R. Dedrick, and A. E. Dudeck. Protecting steep construction slopes against water erosion. I. Effects of selected mulches on seed, fertilizer and soil loss. Agronomy Abstracts. p. 40. 1966.

14479. ______. Protecting steep construction slopes against water erosion. Part I. Nebraska Agricultural Experiment Station. Progress Report. pp. 1–47. 1966.

14480. ______. Protecting steep fill slopes against water erosion. Agronomy Abstracts. p. 55. 1967.

14481. ______. Protecting steep construction slopes against water erosion. Highway Research Record No. 206. pp. 46–52. 1967.

14482. Swartz, W. E., and L. T. Kardos. Effects of compaction on physical properties of sand-soil-peat mixtures at various moisture contents. Agronomy Journal. 55(1):7–10. 1963.

14483. Sweetman, H. L. Ants. Turf Bulletin. Massachusetts Turf & Lawn Grass Council. 2(8):5–6. 1964.

14484. Swift, F. C. Sod webworms and lawn moths. New Jersey Agricultural Extension Leaflet. 310:1–2. 1962.

14485. ______. Chinch bugs. New Jersey Agricultural Extension Leaflet. 319:1–2. 1962.

14486. Swift, R. W., W. H. James, L. F. Marcy, R. F. Elliot, V. F. Smith, and H. Higbee. Monthly yields and composition of herbage composed of Kentucky bluegrass, *Poa pratensis* L., and White Clover, *Trifolium repens* L., as affected by fertilizer treatments. Journal of the American Society of Agronomy. 40(12):1051–1060. 1948.

14487. Switzer, C. M. Chemical control of weeds in turf. Research Report of the National Weed Committee, Eastern Section (Canada). 6:137–139. 1961.

14488. ______. Residual effects of some herbicides used for control of crabgrass in turf. North Central Weed Control Conference Research Report. 18:92–93. 1961.

14489. ______. Chemical control of turf weeds. Research Report of the National Weed Committe, Eastern Section (Canada). 7:107–108. 1962.

14490. ______. Effects of turf weed herbicides on a variety of weed species. Research Report of the National Weed Committee, Eastern Section (Canada). 7:108–110. 1962.

14491. ______. Experiments on the chemical control of crabgrass in lawn turf. Proceedings of the Northeastern Weed Control Conference. 16:536–542. 1962.

14492. ______. Effect of tordon on turfweeds. Research Report of the National Weed Committee, Eastern Section (Canada). pp. 125. 1964.

14493. ______. Granular herbicide-fertilizer mixture application to wet and dry turf. Research Report of the National Weed Committee, Eastern Section (Canada). pp. 125. 1964.

14494. ______. Effects of various mixtures of 2,4–D and dicamba on turf weeds. Research Report of the National Weed Committee, Eastern Section (Canada). pp. 154. 1965.

14495. ______. Control of turf weeds with herbicides. Sixteenth R.C.G.A. Sports Turfgrass Conference. 16:55–56. 1965.

14496. ______. Weed control. The Greenmaster 3(12):4, 6–9. 1967.

14497. ______. Herbicides stop growth of crabgrass seedlings. Weeds, Trees, and Turf. 6(5):31. 1967.

14498. ______. Weed control for 1968. RCGA National Turfgrass Conference. 19:-56–58. 1968.

14499. ______. Turfgrass research in Canada. Proceedings of the First International Turfgrass Research Conference. pp. 2–3. 1969.

14500. ______. Control of broadleaf weeds in turf. Proceedings of the First International Turfgrass Research Conference. pp. 412–416. 1969.

14501. ______. Highlights of the First International Turfgrass Conference. Annual RCGA National Turfgrass Conference. 21:-38–39. 1970.

14502. ______. Northern current trends in turfgrass weed control. Proceedings of Scotts Turfgrass Research Conference. 3:-161–166. 1972.

14504. Sykes, G. F., H. Bracewell, and V. Proctor. The water problem on golf courses. Journal of the Board of Greenkeeping Research. 5(16):27–33. 1937.

14505. Sylvester, E. P. Weed control in gardens and lawns. Transactions of the State Horticultural Society of Iowa. pp. 216–224. 1947.

14506. Sylvester, G. Turf management on the Tauranga golf course. New Zealand Institute for Turf Culture Newsletter. 17:17–18. 1962.

14507. Sylvester, J. How we saved the turf at North Hempstead. Golfdom. 32(6):46, 88. 1958.

14508. ______. Wetting agent keeps "*Poa annua*" turf healthy. Club Operations. 3(1):G–24–G–25. 1965.

14509. Tabor, P. Natural reseeding of bahia grass after a sod is plowed. Agronomy Journal. 41(12):585. 1949.

14510. ______. Some observations of bahiagrass for soil conservation in the southeastern United States. Agronomy Journal. 42(7):362–364. 1950.

14511. ______. Permanent cover for road cuts and similar conditions by secondary succession. Agronomy Journal. 54(2):-179. 1962.

14512. Tadge, C. H. From *Poa annua* to bluegrass. Turf Clippings. University of Massachusetts. 2(2):A–10–13. 1967.

14513. ______. Machinery and timing in renovation—bluegrass. Proceedings of the Midwest Regional Turf Conference. pp. 31–33. 1968.

14514. ______. Successful control in practice fairways. International Turfgrass Conference Proceedings. 40:55–56. 1969.

14515. ______. The Purr-wick system—our experiences. Proceedings of the Midwest Regional Turf Conference. pp. 48–50. 1970.

14516. Tadmor, N. H., and Y. Cohen. Root elongation in the preemergence stage of Mediterranean grasses and legumes. Crop Science. 8(4):416–419. 1968.

14518. Takematsu, T. Theory and practice of weed control on turf. KGU Green

Section Turf Research Bulletin. 17:1–16. 1969.

14519. Talbert, T. J. and E. M. Brown. Lawn culture in Missouri. Missouri Agricultural Experiment Station Circular. 322:1–11. 1948.

14520. Taliaferro, C. M., D. B. Leuck and M. W. Stimmann. Tolerance of *Cynodon* clones to phytotoxemia caused by the two-line spittlebug. Crop Science. 9(6):765–766. 1969.

14521. Talley, J. Green fairways but dormant turf. USGA Green Section Record. 7(5):5–7. 1969.

14522. Tally, R. Modern school ground maintenance. Proceedings of the Florida Turfgrass Management Conference. 12:123–141. 1964.

14524. Tanler, B. 60 years' sprinker know-how. Golfdom. 41(2):36, 38–39, 101, 103. 1967.

14525. Tanler, W. Two greens are better than one. Golfdom. 41(5):42–44, 72. 1967.

14526. Tanner, J. W. Roots underground agents. Turf Bulletin. Massachusetts Turf and Lawn Grass Council. 4(6):11–13. 1967.

14527. ______. Roots underground agents. The Greenmaster. 4(3):4–7, 9. 1968.

14528. Tarjan, A. C. Rejuvenation of nematized centipedegrass turf with chemical drenches. Proceedings of the Florida State Horticultural Society. 77:456–461. 1964.

14529. Tarjan, A. C., and P. C. Cheo. Reduction of root-parasitic nematode populations in established bent grass turf by use of chemical drenches. Phytopathology. 45(6):-30. 1955.

14530. Tarjan, A. C., and M. H. Ferguson. Observation of nematodes in yellow tuft of bentgrass. USGA Journal and Turf Management. 4(2):28–30. 1951.

14531. Tarjan, A. C., and S. W. Hart. Occurrence of yellow tuft of bentgrass in Rhode Island. Plant Disease Reporter. 39(2):185. 1955.

14532. Tarleton, D. Species for overseeding. USGA Green Section Record. 5(6):14–15. 1968.

14533. Tashiro, H. Bluegrass billbug is a serious pest. Park Maintenance: 23(7):20. 1970.

14534. ______. The grub complex: recognition, biology, and control. Rutgers University Short Course in Turf Management. 38:62–64. 1970.

14535. Tashiro, H., and K. E. Personius. Changes in billbug and chafer controls. New York Turfgrass Association Bulletin. 86:335–336. 1970.

14536. Tasugi, H. On the physiology of *Typhula graminum* Karst. Journal of the Tokyo Agricultural Experiment Station. 2(4):443–458. 1935.

14537. Tate, H. F. and S. Fazio. Lawns for Arizona. Arizona Agricultural Extension Circular. 135:1–20. 1957.

14538. ______. Lawns for Arizona. Arizona Agricultural Extension Bulletin. A6:1–20. 1960.

14539. ______. Lawns for Arizona. University of Arizona Cooperative Extension Service Bulletin A–6. 1965.

14540. Tate, H. F. and J. S. Folkner. Turf on large recreation and play areas. Arizona Cooperative Extension Service Bulletin A–48. 1966.

14541. Tate, H. F., S. Fazio, J. N. Roney, and A. Boyle. Lawns for Arizona. University of Arizona Cooperative Extension Service and Agricultural Experiment Station. Bulletin A–6. 1968.

14542. Tateoka, T. On the systematic significance of starch grains in *Poaceae.* Journal of Japanese Botany. 29(11):341–347. 1954.

14543. Tatge, J. How John Verdier builds sand dunes. Park Maintenance. 15(3):-10–17. 1962.

14544. Taven, R. Zoysia. Proceedings, Missouri Lawn and Turf Conference. 1:20–23. 1960.

14545. ______. A simple key with descriptions of common lawn weeds. Proceedings, Missouri Lawn and Turf Conference. 1:60–67. 1960.

14546. ______. Lawn diseases. Proceedings, Missouri Lawn and Turf Conference. 1:72–81. 1960.

14547. ______. Moles and their control. Proceedings, Missouri Lawn and Turf Conference. 1:86–87. 1960.

14549. Taylor, A. A study of wilting conditions in southwest England. Journal of the British Grassland Society. 18(4):318–322. 1963.

14550. Taylor, A. D. Landscape construction notes III. Landscape Architecture. 12(1):278–291. 1922.

14551. ______. Landscape construction notes. XIV. Landscape Architecture. 15(3):-198–202. 1924.

14552. ______. Landscape construction notes. XV. Landscape Architecture. 15(4):-279–289. 1925.

14553. ______. Landscape construction notes. XX. Landscape Architecture. 17(2):-128–142. 1927.

14554. ______. Further notes on maintenance of bowling greens. Landscape Architecture. 18(4):320–321. 1928.

14555. Taylor, B. Tips on greens program. Golfdom. 28(4):64, 66. 1954.

14556. Taylor, B. B., A. H. Furrer, Jr., R. W. Duell, and R. D. Ilnicki. Control of bermudagrass by chemical and cultural methods. Proceedings of the Northeastern Weed Control Conference. 21:303–306. 1967.

14557. Taylor, B. S. Common sense facts about watering. Golf Course Reporter. 21(5):16–20. 1953.

14558. ______. Better turf management —greens. Golf Course Reporter. 22(4):20–21. 1954.

14559. ______. Green maintenance from a to z. Golf Course Reporter. 30(5):60–63. 1962.

14560. Taylor, B. S. and E. Roberts. Athletic fields . . . speaking from the Midwest. Golf Course Reporter. 28(6):48–51. 1960.

14561. Taylor, D. K. Turfgrass variety trials. Research Station Report, Canada Department of Agriculture, Agassiz, British Columbia. pp. 1–13. 1971.

14562. ______. Turfgrass varieties for the future. Northwest Turfgrass Conference Proceedings. 25:39–48. 1971.

14564. Taylor, D. P. Nematodes in grasses. Illinois Turfgrass Conference Proceedings. 3:7–10. 1962.

14565. Taylor, D. P., M. P. Britton, and H. C. Hechler. Occurrence of plant parasitic nematodes in Illinois golf greens. The Plant Disease Reporter. 47(2):134–135. 1963.

14566. Taylor, G. H. Mechanical aids to fine turf. Gardeners Chronicle. 158(8):206–207. 1965.

14567. Taylor, G. R. Burying cable in turf. The Groundsman. 23(5):30. 1970.

14568. Taylor, H. R. Golf course management techniques around the world. International Turfgrass Conference Proceedings. 38:5–12. 1967.

14569. Taylor, J. C. and J. S. Shoemaker. Lawns. Ontario Agriculture Department Bulletin. 448:5–42. 1952.

14571. Taylor, M. We're winning our crabgrass fight. Golfdom. 14(2):15–16. 1940.

14572. ______. Sodium arsenite gave us a 98% crabgrass kill. Golfdom. 15(2):23–24. 1941.

14573. ______. Turf maintenance below the arctic circle. The Golf Superintendent. 36(3):36, 37, 43. 1968.

14574. Taylor, R. Black mountain tests fertilizers and bentgrasses. Weeds, Trees, and Turf. 9(4):24–27. 1970.

14576. Taylor, T. H. and W. C. Templeton. Tiller and leaf behavior of orchardgrass (*Dactylis glomerata* L.) in a broadcast planting. Agronomy Journal. 58(2):189–192. 1966.

14577. ______. Quantity and quality of late summer and autumn produced Kentucky bluegrass and tall fescue herbage. Kentucky Agricultural Experiment Station. Annual Report 83. pp. 32–33. 1970.

14578. ______. Quality and quantity of late-summer and autumn-produced Kentucky bluegrass and tall fescue herbage. Kentucky Agricultural Experiment Station Annual Report. Vol. 84. pp. 30–31. 1971.

14579. Taylor, T. H., J. P. Cooper, and K. J. Treharne. Growth response of orchardgrass (*Dactylis glomerata* L.) to different light and temperatures environments. I. Leaf development and senescence. Crop Science. 8(4):437–440. 1968.

14587. Taylor, T. H., W. C. Templeton, and R. E. Sigatus. Evaluation of turf-type bermuda grass. Kentucky Agricultural Experiment Station. Annual Report 77. p. 22. 1964.

14594. Taylor, T. T. Turfgrass—its development and progress. USGA Journal and Turf Management. 10(5):28–32. 1957.

14595. ______. Golf turf in the Northeast—1958, Part I. Rutgers University Short Course in Turf Management. 27:2. 1959.

14596. ______. The time factor in remodeling. USGA Journal and Turf Management. 12(2):30–32. 1959.

14597. Teare, I. D., M. A. Maun, and C. L. Canode. Viability of Kentucky bluegrass pollen (*Poa pratensis* L. 'Newport') as influenced by collection time and temperature. Agronomy Journal. 62(4):515–516. 1970.

14598. Teeguarden, J. O. Planning, executing, and maintaining the cemetery beautiful. The Cemeterian. 66(4):19–20, 29–30. 1966.

14599. Teel, M. R. Basics in plant physiology. Proceedings of the Midwest Regional Turf Conference. pp. 19–22. 1964.

14600. ______. Plant carbohydrate must balance nitrogen. Proceedings of the Midwest Regional Turf Conference. pp. 39–40. 1955.

14601. Tegner, R. F. Pesky weeds licked as roadside problem. Soil Conservation. 28(3):65–66. 1962.

14602. Telford, H. S. Turf insects in the Pacific Northwest. Pacific Northwest Turf Conference Proceedings. 6:34–35. 1952.

14603. ______. Insect control on turf. Pacific Northwest Turf Conference Proceedings. 7:7–8. 1953.

14604. Templeton, W. C. Some effects of temperature and light on growth and flowering of tall fescue (*Festuca arundinacae* Schreb.). Ph.D. Thesis, Purdue University. 1960.

14605. Templeton, W. E., C. F. Buck, and N. W. Bradley. Renovated Kentucky bluegrass and supplementary pastures for steers. University of Kentucky Agricultural Experiment Station. Bulletin 709. 1–19 pp. 1970.

14606. Templeton, W. C., G. O. Mott and R. J. Bula. Some effects of temperature and light on growth and flowering of tall fescue, *Festuca arundinacea* Schreb. Crop Science. 1(3):216–219. 1961.

14607. Templeton, W. C., T. H. Taylor, J. R. Todd. Comparative ecological and agronomic behavior of orchardgrass and tall fescue. University of Kentucky Agricultural Experiment Station. Bulletin 699. 18 pp. 1965.

14611. Teng, J. I. The effect of night temperatures and potassium fertilization on iron chlorosis of centipede. Florida Turfgrass Association Bulletin. 11(1):1–3. 1964.

14612. Teng, J. I. and W. L. Pritchett. Effects of season, night temperature, and potassium on the absorption and translocation of iron in centipede grass (*Eramochloa ophluroides* [Munro] Hock). Botanical Gazette. 131(4):272–276. 1970.

14613. Terell, E. E. Taxonomic implications of genetics in ryegrass *(Lolium)*. Botanical Review. 32(2):138–164. 1966.

14614. ______. Meadow fescue: *Festuca elatior* L. or *F. pratensis* Hudson? Brittonia. 19(2):129–132. 1967.

14615. Terry, C. W. Low pressure spraying equipment. New York State Turf Association. Bulletin 3. pp. 9–10. 1949.

14616. ______. Tips on weed sprayer design and operation. New York State Turf Association. Bulletin 44. pp. 173–174. 1953.

14617. Tervet, I. W. Turf injuries in Minnessota. Greenkeeper's Reporter. 9:40. 1941.

14619. Terzis, A. Turfgrass its contribution to the environment. The Greenmaster. 7(9):21–22. 1971.

14620. Tessman, G. F. Minnesota highway maintenance costs. Minnesota Department of Highways. 51 pp. 1970.

14622. Thames, W. Mole-cricket control. Florida Greenkeeping Superintendents Association and the Southeastern Turf Management Conference. pp. 20–24. 1949.

14623. Therkildson, W. F. Soil must be built right for the permanent golf course. Golfdom. 8(10):25–28. 1934.

14624. Thirumalachar, M. J., and J. G. Dickson. Spore germination, cultural characters, and cytology of varieties of *Ustilago striiformis* and the reaction of hosts. Phytopathology. 43(9):527–535. 1953.

14625. Thomas, A. S. The uses of *Paspalum notatum* in Uganda. East African Agricultural Journal. 7:236. 1942.

14626. Thomas, B. and F. E. Moon. A preliminary study of the effects of manurial treatment, and of age, on the carotene-content of grass. Empiracal Journal of Experimental Agriculture. 6:235–245. 1938.

14627. Thomas, C. E. A summary of some experiments on weed control. Journal of the Board of Greenkeeping Research. 7(23):44–48. 1947.

14628. Thomas, C. H., L. C. Standifer, and W. K. Porter. Easy lawn edging with oil. Louisiana Agriculture. 5(4):10–11. 1962.

14629. Thomas, F. H. Management of organic soils for sod production. Proceedings Florida Turf-Grass Management Conference. 14:149–152. 1966.

14630. Thomas, F. H. and C. C. Hortenstine. Fertility studies with grasses grown on organic soils. Proceedings of University of Florida Turf-Grass Management Conference. 9:106–114. 1961.

14631. Thomas, G. C. Golf architecture in America: Its strategy and construction. Times-Mirror Press. Los Angeles, Cal. 342 pp. 1927.

14632. Thomas, G. W. Pests of lawn and turf. Proceedings, Missouri Lawn and Turf Conference. 2:10–12. 1961.

14633. ______. The sod webworm problem. Proceedings, Missouri Lawn and Turf Conference. 4:20–22. 1963.

14634. ______. Controlling cutworms. Proceedings, Missouri Lawn and Turf Conference. 4:29–30. 1963.

14635. Thomas, H. L. Park Kentucky bluegrass. Minnesota Farm and Home Science. 17:(1)6, 19. 1959.

14636. ______. Kentucky bluegrass seed production in Minnesota. Proceedings of the Midwest Regional Turf Conference. pp. 36–38. 1960.

14637. Thomas, H. L., and H. K. Hayes. A selection experiment with Kentucky bluegrass. Journal of the American Society of Agronomy. 39(3):192–197. 1947.

14638. Thomas, J. E. June beetle, reconditioning and drainage tips offered. Golfdom. 22(6):56–57, 60. 1948.

14639. ______. Southern turf maintenance. Greenkeepers' Reporter. 17(2):16–17. 1949.

14640. ______. The control of earthworms and water. Greenkeepers' Reporter. 18(1):7–8. 1950.

14641. ______. Aerification is a must. USGA Journal of Turf Management. 5:30–31. 1952.

14642. ______. Labor relations. Proceedings of the Mid-Atlantic Association of Golf Course Superintendents. pp. 17–19. 1964.

14643. Thomas, J. R., and R. V. Frakes. Clonal and progeny evaluations in two populations of tall fescue (*Festuca arundinacea* Schreb.). Crop Science. 7:55–58. 1967.

14644. Thomas, L. K. Road salt (sodium chloride) injury to Kentucky bluegrass. Highway Research Record No. 161:116–120. 1967.

14645. Thomas, L. K., and G. A. Bean. Winter rock salt injury to turf. Turf Bulletin. Massachusetts Turf and Lawn Grass Council. 2(13):11–13. 1965.

14646. Thomas, P. The importance of turf in landscape development. Oklahoma-Texas Turf Conference Proceedings. pp. 31–33. 1950.

14647. Thomas, P. A. Dursban insecticide for the professional pest control operator. Down To Earth. 25(3):26–33. 1969.

14648. Thomas, R. J. Sound problem solving. Proceedings of 15th Annual Texas Turfgrass Conference. 15:67–71. 1960.

14649. ______. Work smarter—it's easier. Iagreen, 30th Annual Turfgrass Conference proceedings. p. 1. 1963.

14650. ______. Where-o-wear. Proceedings of the Florida Turf-Grass Management Conference. 13:127–129. 1965.

14651. ______. What's the best mowing speed. The Golf Superintendent. 34(2):24–26. 1966.

14652. ______. Manicuring turf. Texas Turfgrass Conference Proceedings. 21:42–43. 1966.

14653. ______. Where-o-wear. Turf Bulletin. Massachusetts Turf and Lawn Grass Council. 3(3):23–24. 1966.

14654. ______. Where-o-wear. Wisconsin Turfgrass Conference Proceedings. pp. 46–50. 1966.

14655. ______. Levels of maintenance. International Turfgrass Conference and show. 39:47–48. 1968.

14656. ______. Equipment for all purposes and its care. RCGA National Turfgrass Conference. 19:59. 1968.

14657. ______. Reducing maintenance costs is basic to budgeting. Turfgrass Times. 5(2):10–15. 1969.

14658. ______. Expanding horizons for equipment. Proceedings of the Midwest Regional Turf Conference. pp. 68–70. 1970.

14659. ______. Reducing maintenance costs. Tennessee Turfgrass Conference Proceedings. 4:1–3. 1970.

14660. ______. Progress through mechanization on golf courses. USGA Green Section Record. 10(2):18–21. 1972.

14661. ______. The influence of seed weight on seedling vigor in *Lolium perenne.* Annals of Botany. 30:111–121. 1966.

14662. Thomas, R. P. Soil physics. Proceedings of the Mid-Atlantic Association of Greenskeepers Conference. pp. 32–41. 1949.

14663. Thomason, I. J., and J. G. Dickson. Influence of soil temperature on seedling blight of smooth bromegrass. Phytopathology. 50(1):1–7. 1960.

14664. Thompson, C. E. Bents in the South. Turf Clippings. University of Massachussetts. 1(5):19. 1960.

14666. Thompson, H. Turf insect lab. Central Plains Turfgrass Conference. p. 2. 1963.

14667. Thompson, H. E. Buffalograss sod webworm. Turf-Grass Times. 2(5):7. 1967.

14668. ______. Sod webworm and billbug research studies. Proceedings of Scotts Turfgrass Research Conference. 1:83–88. 1969.

14669. Thompson, J. T. Chemical weed control in turf. Southeastern Turfgrass Conference Proceedings. 18:14–16. 1964.

14670. Thompson, J. T., and W. S. Hardcastle. Control of crab and dallisgrass in narrow leaf turf. Southern Weed Conference Proceedings. 16:115. 1963.

14671. Thompson, R. Thatch control in bermudas and zoysias. Proceedings of the Tennessee Turfgrass Conference. 2:22–23. 1968.

14672. Thompson, T. Buyer beware. International Turfgrass Conference Proceedings. 41:9–10. 1970.

14673. Thompson, T. W. Golf course administration. RCGA Sports Turfgrass Conference. 17:45–47. 1966.

14674. ______. Highlights of metropolitan Toronto's golf facility operations. Annual RCGA National Turfgrass Conference. 21:-40–41. 1970.

14675. Thompson, W. R. The traffic problem and some thoughts about traffic control. Southeastern Turfgrass Conference Proceedings. 17:1–2. 1963.

14676. ______. Fertilization of golf green. Southern Turfgrass Association Conference Proceedings. pp. 14–15. 1963.

14677. ______. Progress report on turfgrass research at Mississippi State University. Southern Turfgrass Association Conference Proceedings. pp. 18–20. 1963.

14678. ______. Mowing and fertilization. Mississippi Agricultural Experiment Station Turfgrass Mimeo Series No. 8. 1964.

14679. ______. Insect control in turf. Mississippi Agricultural Experiment Station Turfgrass Mimeo Series No. 12. 1964.

14680. ______. Sand trap construction and maintenance. Southern Turfgrass Association Conference Proceedings. pp. 11–12. 1964.

14681. ______. Turfgrass research at Mississippi State University. Southern Turfgrass Association Conference Proceedings. pp. 19–21. 1964.

14682. ______. Management of bermudagrass greens. Auburn University Annual Turfgrass Short Course. pp. 20–21. 1965.

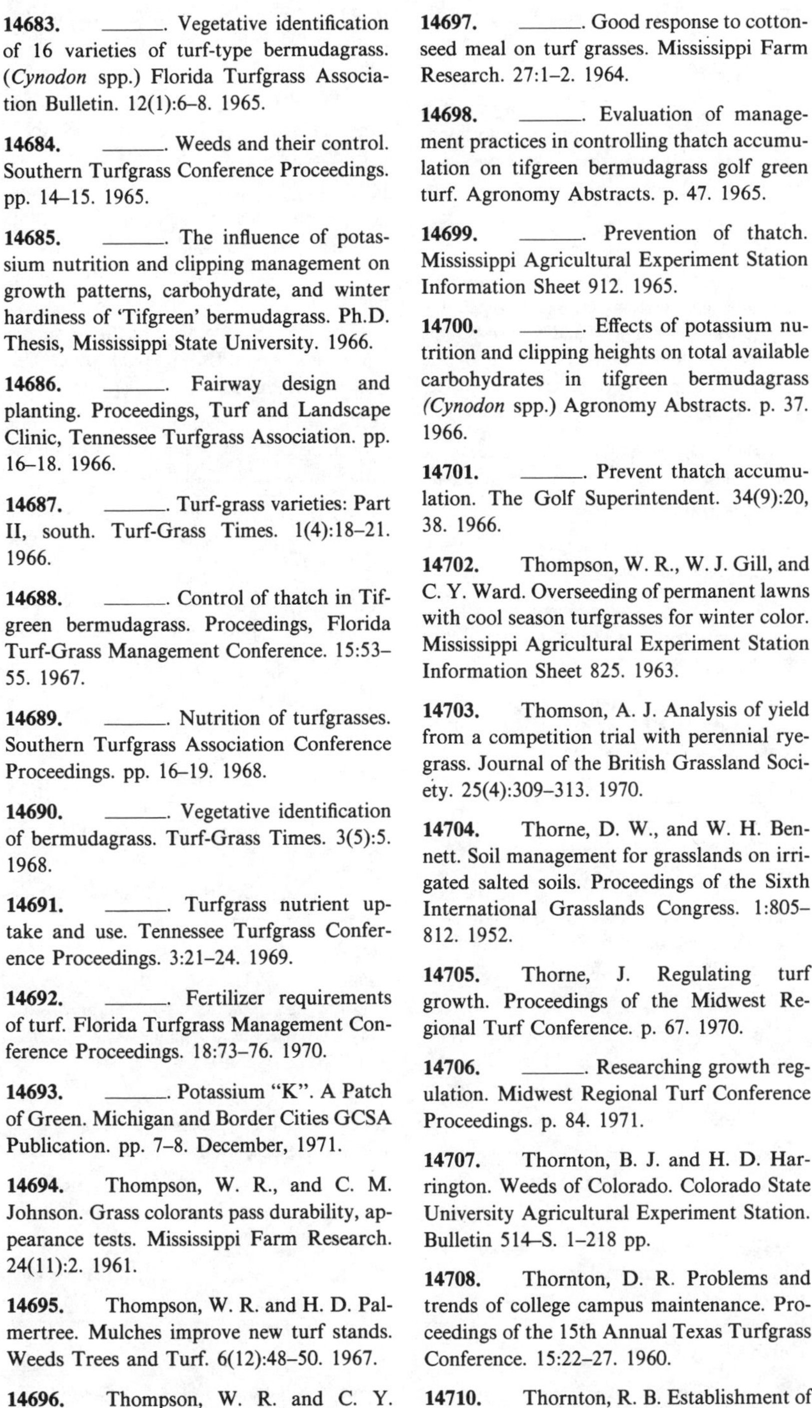

14683. ______. Vegetative identification of 16 varieties of turf-type bermudagrass. (*Cynodon* spp.) Florida Turfgrass Association Bulletin. 12(1):6–8. 1965.

14684. ______. Weeds and their control. Southern Turfgrass Conference Proceedings. pp. 14–15. 1965.

14685. ______. The influence of potassium nutrition and clipping management on growth patterns, carbohydrate, and winter hardiness of 'Tifgreen' bermudagrass. Ph.D. Thesis, Mississippi State University. 1966.

14686. ______. Fairway design and planting. Proceedings, Turf and Landscape Clinic, Tennessee Turfgrass Association. pp. 16–18. 1966.

14687. ______. Turf-grass varieties: Part II, south. Turf-Grass Times. 1(4):18–21. 1966.

14688. ______. Control of thatch in Tifgreen bermudagrass. Proceedings, Florida Turf-Grass Management Conference. 15:53–55. 1967.

14689. ______. Nutrition of turfgrasses. Southern Turfgrass Association Conference Proceedings. pp. 16–19. 1968.

14690. ______. Vegetative identification of bermudagrass. Turf-Grass Times. 3(5):5. 1968.

14691. ______. Turfgrass nutrient uptake and use. Tennessee Turfgrass Conference Proceedings. 3:21–24. 1969.

14692. ______. Fertilizer requirements of turf. Florida Turfgrass Management Conference Proceedings. 18:73–76. 1970.

14693. ______. Potassium "K". A Patch of Green. Michigan and Border Cities GCSA Publication. pp. 7–8. December, 1971.

14694. Thompson, W. R., and C. M. Johnson. Grass colorants pass durability, appearance tests. Mississippi Farm Research. 24(11):2. 1961.

14695. Thompson, W. R. and H. D. Palmertree. Mulches improve new turf stands. Weeds Trees and Turf. 6(12):48–50. 1967.

14696. Thompson, W. R. and C. Y. Ward. Summer turf may be set in winter. Mississippi Farm Research. 26:6–7. 1963.

14697. ______. Good response to cottonseed meal on turf grasses. Mississippi Farm Research. 27:1–2. 1964.

14698. ______. Evaluation of management practices in controlling thatch accumulation on tifgreen bermudagrass golf green turf. Agronomy Abstracts. p. 47. 1965.

14699. ______. Prevention of thatch. Mississippi Agricultural Experiment Station Information Sheet 912. 1965.

14700. ______. Effects of potassium nutrition and clipping heights on total available carbohydrates in tifgreen bermudagrass (*Cynodon* spp.) Agronomy Abstracts. p. 37. 1966.

14701. ______. Prevent thatch accumulation. The Golf Superintendent. 34(9):20, 38. 1966.

14702. Thompson, W. R., W. J. Gill, and C. Y. Ward. Overseeding of permanent lawns with cool season turfgrasses for winter color. Mississippi Agricultural Experiment Station Information Sheet 825. 1963.

14703. Thomson, A. J. Analysis of yield from a competition trial with perennial ryegrass. Journal of the British Grassland Society. 25(4):309–313. 1970.

14704. Thorne, D. W., and W. H. Bennett. Soil management for grasslands on irrigated salted soils. Proceedings of the Sixth International Grasslands Congress. 1:805–812. 1952.

14705. Thorne, J. Regulating turf growth. Proceedings of the Midwest Regional Turf Conference. p. 67. 1970.

14706. ______. Researching growth regulation. Midwest Regional Turf Conference Proceedings. p. 84. 1971.

14707. Thornton, B. J. and H. D. Harrington. Weeds of Colorado. Colorado State University Agricultural Experiment Station. Bulletin 514–S. 1–218 pp.

14708. Thornton, D. R. Problems and trends of college campus maintenance. Proceedings of the 15th Annual Texas Turfgrass Conference. 15:22–27. 1960.

14710. Thornton, R. B. Establishment of vegetation on subsoils. Highway Research Record. 93:31–37. 1965.

14711. ______. Herbicides to kill weeds. Texas Turfgrass Conference Proceedings. 21:77–83. 1966.

14712. Throm, E. L. How to grow the best lawn and garden in your neighborhood; a complete guide to gardening and landscaping. Popular Mechanics, Chicago. 176 pps. 1951.

14713. Thurman, P. C. and F. A. Pokorny. The relationship of several amended soils and compaction rates on vegetative growth, root development and cold resistance of 'Tifgreen' bermudagrass. Journal of the American Society for Horticultural Science. 94(5):463–465. 1969.

14714. Thurston, H. W. Cadmium is base of new method of dollar spot control. Golfdom. 22(6):70–71, 92–93. 1948.

14715. ______. A catalog of turf diseases. Greenkeepers' Reporter. 17(4):14–15. 1949.

14716. ______. A catalogue of turf diseases. New York State Turf Association. Bulletin 2. pp. 7–8. 1949.

14717. ______. Standard methods for control of turf diseases. Pennsylvania State Turf Conference. 18:44–47. 1949.

14718. ______. Control of disease of turf. Proceedings of the Mid-Atlantic Association of Greenkeepers Conference. pp. 48–51. 1950.

14719. ______. Summary of national turf fungicide trials in 1949. Pennsylvania State College Turfgrass Conference Proceedings. 19:97–100. 1950.

14720. ______. Dollarspot control at the Philadelphia Country Club 1950. Pennsylvania State College Turfgrass Conference Proceedings. 20:31–32. 1951.

14721. ______. Report on turf fungicide tests. Pennsylvania State College Turfgrass Conference Proceedings. 21:60–76. 1952.

14722. Tiaranan, N. Influence of lime, inoculum, and molybdenum pelleting of legume seed on germination, growth, and nitrogen content of crownvetch. M.S. Thesis, University of Kentucky. 1971.

14723. Tiedjens, V. Understanding the use of lime in the soil. Greenkeepers' Reporter. 17(6):7–9. 1949.

14724. Tiemeier, O. Birds vs. spraying. Central Plains Turfgrass Conference. 11:2. 1961.

14725. Timm, G. Beiträge zur biologie und systematica von *Poa annua* L. Z. Acker a. Pflbau. 122(3):267. 1965.

14726. Timmerman, J. W. Thatch and mat control: a yearly operation. The Bonnie Greensward. Philadelphia Association of Golf Course Superintendents Publication. p. 4. July, 1969.

14727. ______. A look at turf problems around the region. University of Maine Turf Conference Proceedings. 7:11–13. 1969.

14728. ______. Bringing new greens into play. University of Maine Turf Conference Proceedings. 7:22–25. 1969.

14729. ______. The art and science of greenskeeping. Northern Ohio Turfgrass News. 12(1):4. 1969.

14730. ______. Thatch and mat control: A yearly operation. Northern Ohio Turfgrass News. 12(4):1, 3. 1969.

14731. ______. The golf course and ecology. USGA Green Section Record. 8(4):1–5. 1970.

14732. ______. Green belt planting. A Patch of Green. Michigan and Border Cities GCSA Publication, pp. 13–14. February, 1972.

14733. Timmons, F. L. New herbicides for noncrop areas. Weeds Trees and Turf. 6(1):9–11. 1967.

14734. Tincker, M. A. H. The effect of length of day upon the growth and reproduction of some economic plants. Annals of Botany. 39:721–754. 1925.

14735. Tinney, F. W. Cytology of parthenogensis in *Poa pratensis.* Journal of Agricultural Research. 60(5):351–360. 1940.

14737. Tissot, A. N. Chinch bugs. Proceedings University of Florida Turf Conference. 1:38. 1952.

14738. Tobey, G. B. Critique: regional highway design competition. Short Course on Roadside Development (Ohio). 13:22–45. 1971.

14739. Tod, H. Moss Control—A new approach. Gardeners Chronicle. 158(8):205. 1965.

14740. Todd, E. H. Sugarcane mosaic on St. Augustine grass in Florida. The Plant Disease Reporter. 48(6):442. 1964.

14741. Toler, R. W. St. Augustine decline (SAD)—a new lawngrass disease. Proceedings of Scotts Turfgrass Research Conference. 1971. 2:55–66.

14742. Toler, R. W., N. L. McCoy, and J. Amador. A new mosaic disease of St. Augustinegrass. Phytopathology. 59(2):118. 1969.

14743. Tolhurst, D. A plan for all seasons. Golfdom 41(1):31–32, 98, 100, 102–104, 106–108. 1967.

14744. Tolin, B. Experiences in weed control in parks. Southern California Turfgrass Institute Proceedings. p. 33. 1963.

14745. Toma, G. Keeping stadium turf playable and pleasing. Missouri Lawn and Turf Conference Proceedings. 8:5–9. 1967.

14746. ______. Professional stadium and turf use. Proceedings of the Midwest Regional Turf Conference. pp. 9–11. 1968.

14747. ______. Talking turf—Fylking bluegrass. Grounds Maintenance. 6(6):8–11. 1971.

14748. ______. Talking turf—Pennstar bluegrass. Grounds Maintenance. 6(7):6–7. 1971.

14749. ______. The fine fescues—creeping and chewings. Grounds Maintenance. 7(1):6–7. 1972.

14750. ______. The ryegrasses. Grounds Maintenance. 7(6):8. 1972.

14751. Tomasello, R. P. Symposium—lawn maintenance problems. Pest control. Florida Turf Management Conference Proceedings. 3:92–94. 1955.

14752. ______. Costing a job. Proceedings of the Florida Turf-Grass Management Conference. 14:118–120. 1966.

14754. Tomonaga, M. Tour to Tifton, the center of Tifton hybrid bermudagrasses. KGU Green Section Turf Research Bulletin. 7:75–78. 1964.

14755. Toogood, E. K. Toogood's treatise on lawns, cricket Grounds, etc. Toogood and Sons. Southhampton. 19 pp. 1900.

14756. Toogood, J. A. Golf soil characteristics. Second Western Turf Conference at University of Alberta, Edmonton. pp. 5–11. 1953.

14757. Toole, E. H. Problems of germinating the various bluegrasses. Seed World. 14(3):23–30. 1923.

14758. Toole, E. H. and V. K. Toole. Germination of seed of goosegrass, *Eleusine indica.* Journal of the American Society of Agronomy. 32(4):320–321. 1940.

14759. ______. Progress of germination of seed of *Digitaria* as influenced by germination temperature and other factors. Journal of Agricultural Research. 63(2):65–90. 1941.

14760. Toole, V. K. Factors affecting the germination of bulblets of bulbous bluegrass, *Poa bulbosa.* Journal of the American Society of Agronomy. 33(10):1037–1045. 1941.

14761. Toole, V. K. and H. A. Borthwick. Effect of light, temperature, and their interactions on germination of seeds of Kentucky bluegrass (*Poa pratensis* L.). Journal of the American Society for Horticultural Science. 96(3):301–304. 1971.

14762. Toomey, H. C. Metropolitan bent at Marble Hall. USGA Green Section Bulletin. 7(8):147–149. 1927.

14763. Topp, T. E. Automatic irrigation in the east. The Golf Course Reporter. 33(6):-24–26. 1965.

14765. Torstensson, G. Influence of the interval of time between cuts and of the height of stubble on yield and root development in grasses. Herbage Abstracts. 8(4):420. 1938.

14766. ______. Influence of the interval of time between cuts and height of stubble on yield and root development in grasses. Medd. Svenska Betes-o. Vallforer No. 5. pp. 1–37. 1938.

14767. Tovey, R. A method for measuring water intake rate into soil by sprinkler design. Sprinkler Irrigation Association Open Technical Conference Proceedings. pp. 109–118. 1963.

14768. Tovey, R., J. S. Spencer, and D. C. Muckel. Turfgrass evapotranspiration. Agronomy Journal. 61(6):863–867. 1969.

14769. Tower, R. All-Year turf at Tampa, Florida. USGA Green Section Bulletin. 11(10):194–198. 1931.

14770. Tower, R., and T. J. Lundy. Dixie experts give tips on bermuda turf. Golfdom 4(2):64, 66. 1930.

14771. Townsend, R. B. A look at the Rose Bowl. Golf Course Reporter. 31(8):20–21. 1963.

14772. Townsend, R. R. One aspect of mechanical treatment of greens. New Zealand Institute for Turf Culture Newsletter. 41:10–11. 1966.

14773. Trask, A. D. Inhibitors for economic maintenance. 21st Short Course on Roadside Development, Ohio. pp. 98–101. 1962.

14775. Treacy, R. W. Woodmont bent raking tool ends green misery. Golfdom. 5(4):106. 1931.

14776. Treat, C. E. Browsing in brownpatch. Greenkeepers Club of New England Newsletter. 1(3):2. 1929.

14777. Tregillus, C. A. Rhode Island bent as a putting green turf. USGA Green Section Bulletin. 6(6):143–144. 1926.

14778. ______. Servicing the putting green. Golfdom. 1(4):10–12. 1927.

14779. ______. Some reasons and remedies for poor greens. Golfdom 1(5):13–14. 1927.

14780. ______. Mid-summer pointers on maintenance. Golfdom. 1(6):9–10. 1927.

14781. ______. Compost characteristics and its preparation. Golfdom. 1(7):15–17. 1927.

14782. ______. Canadian courses and maintenance problems. The National Greenkeeper. 2(4):13–16. 1928.

14783. ______. How Canada fights weeds. The National Greenkeeper. 2(8):18. 1928.

14784. ______. Conditions which influence the growth of turf. USGA Green Section. 8(3):37–42. 1928.

14785. ______. Soil conditioning. Golfdom. 3(7):11–13. 1929.

14786. ______. The new experimental turf garden in Chicago. USGA Green Section Bulletin. 9(3):47–49. 1929.

14787. ______. My maintenance methods. Golfdom. 10(3):15–18. 1936.

14788. Tregillus, C. A. and N. C. Johnson. Fairway watering. Greenkeeper's Reporter. 10(3):20–24, 29. 1942.

14789. Treharne, K. J., J. P. Cooper, and T. H. Taylor. Growth response of orchardgrass (*Dactylis glomerata* L.) to different light and temperature environments. II. Leaf age and photosynthetic activity. Crop Science. 8(4):441–445. 1968.

14790. Trew, E. M. Home lawns. Texas Agricultural Extension Bulletin 203. 14 pp. 1960.

14791. ______. Home lawns. Texas Agricultural Extension Service Bulletin 203. 1962.

14792. Trew, E. M. and J. Long. Chemical weed control in lawns. Texas Agricultural Extension Leaflet. 425:1–10. 1959.

14793. Triebelhorn, H. L. Opening remarks at panel discussion—representing suppliers. Proceedings Turfgrass Sprinkler Irrigation Conference. 5:46. 1967.

14794. Triplett, G. B., and R. R. Davis. Controlling broadleaf weeds in lawns. Ohio Agricultural Research and Development Center. Research Summary 6. pp. 21–23. 1965.

14795. ______. Spot treatment for perennial grass weeds. Ohio Agr. Research and Development Center. Research Summary 16. pp. 9–10. 1966.

14796. ______. Reseeding weedy turf. Ohio Agricultural Research and Development Center. Summary No. 24. pp. 31–33. 1967.

14797. Trlica, M. J., and J. L. Schuster. Effects of fire on grasses of the Texas high plains. Journal of Range Management. 22:-329–333. 1969.

14798. Trogdon, W. O. Turfgrass nutrition and fertilizer use. Proceedings, 16th Annual Texas Turf Conference. 16:42–47. 1961.

14799. ______. Turf-grass nutrition and fertilizer use. Golf Course Reporter. 30(10):-18–22. 1962.

14800. ______. A guide to the use of fertilizers. Golfdom. 36(4):74–78. 1962.

14801. ______. Turf-grass nutrition and fertilizer use. International Turf-Grass Conference Proceedings. 33:5. 1962.

14802. ______. The role of lime in turfgrass management. Proceedings, 17th Annual Texas Turf Conference. 17:28–29. 1962.

14803. Troll, J. The constant battle. Turf Clippings. University of Massachussetts. 1(3):13–14. 1958.

14804. ______. Review of seasons pests. Turf Clippings, University of Massachusetts. 1(7):A–1 to A–3. 1962.

14805. ______. Snow mold. Massachusetts Turf and Lawn Grass Council. 2(5):16. 1964.

14806. Troll, J., S. E. Robbins, A. Brewer, R. W. Sharkey, E. J. Pyle, O. Capizzi, and V. Taricano. How to grow grass on a limited budget. Turf Clippings. University of Massachusetts. pp. A6–A11. 1959.

14807. Troll, J. Spring lawn construction. Turf Bulletin. Massachusetts Turf and Lawn Grass Council. 4(3):22–23. 1967.

14808. ______. Early spring lawn advice. Turf Bulletin. Massachusetts Turf and Lawn Grass Council. 4(3):27. 1967.

14809. ______. Lawn renovation. Turf Bulletin. Massachusetts Turf and Lawn Grass Council. 4(5):10. 1967.

14810. ______. Performance of two fungicides for the control of snow mold. Turf Bulletin. Massachusetts Turf and Lawn Grass Council. 4(8):7–8. 1968.

14811. ______. Comparison of several fertilizer salts and their use on Penncross creeping bentgrass top growth. Turf Bulletin. Massachusetts Turf and Lawn Council. 7(4):-5–7. 1971.

14812. ______. Thatch and its control. Turf Bulletin. Massachusetts Turf and Lawn Council. 7(4):14. 1971.

14813. ______. Kentucky bluegrass variety trials. Turf Bulletin (Massachusetts). 8(5):10–14. 1972.

14814. Troll, J., and R. Healy. Fungicide trials for the control of turf diseases infecting velvet bentgrass, Merion bluegrass and annual bluegrass—creeping bent mixture. Turf Bulletin. Massachusetts Turf and Lawn Grass Council. 4(3):8. 1967.

14815. Troll, J., and J. Keohane. Fungicide trials for control of dollar spot. Turf Bulletin. Massachusetts Turf & Lawn Grass Council. 2(13):5. 1965.

14816. Troll, J., and R. A. Rohde. Pathogenicity of the nematodes *Pratylenchus penetrans* and *Tylenchorynchus claytoni* on turfgrasses. Phytopathology. 55:1285. 1965.

14817. ______. Pathogenicity of *Pratylenchus penetrans* and *Tylenchorhynchus claytoni* on turfgrasses. Phytopathology. 56(9):995–998. 1966.

14818. ______. The effects of nematocides on turfgrass growth. The Plant Disease Reporter. 50(7):489–492. 1966.

14819. ______. The effects of nematocides on turfgrass growth. Turf Bulletin. Massachusetts Turf and Lawn Grass Council. 4(1):7–9. 1966.

14820. ______. Nematocide tests on established lawn turf. Turf Bulletin. Massachusetts Turf and Lawn Grass Council. 4(3):18. 1967.

14821. Troll, J. and A. C. Tarjan. Root parasitic nematodes in golf course greens. Crop Life. Bulletin 840. 1954.

14822. ______. Widespread occurrence of root parasitic nematodes in golf course greens in Rhode Island. Plant Disease Reporter. 38(5):342–344. 1954.

14823. Troll, J., and J. Zak. Preemergence control of crabgrass. Turf Bulletin. Massachusetts Turf & Lawn Grass Council. 2(13):6. 1965.

14824. Troll, J., J. Zak, and D. Waddington. Crabgrass control. Massachusetts Agricultural Extension Publication. 383:1–4. 1962.

14825. ______. Preemergence control of crabgrass with chemicals. Proceedings of the Northeastern Weed Control Conference. 16:-484–487. 1962.

14826. ______. Toxicity of preemergence crabgrass killers to some basic grasses. Proceedings of the Northeastern Weed Control Conference. 16:488. 1962.

14827. ______. Crabgrass control. Massachusetts Turf and Lawn Grass Council. 2(6):2, 14. 1964.

14828. Troop, J. Grasses of Indiana. Indiana Agricultural Experiment Station. Bulletin 29 Purdue University. 44 pp. 1889.

14829. Troughton, A. Studies on the roots and storage organs of herbage plants. Journal of the British Grasslands Society. 6:-197–206. 1951.

14830. ______. The application of the allometric formula to the study of the relationship between the roots and shoots of young grass plants. Agricultural Progress. 30(1):59–65. 1955.

14831. ______. Cessation of tillering in young grass plants. Nature. 176:514. 1955.

14832. ______. Studies on the growth of young grass plants with special reference to the relationship between the shoot and root systems. Journal of the British Grassland Society. 11:56–65. 1956.

14833. ______. The underground organs of herbage grasses. Bulletin No. 44. Commonwealth Bureau of Pasture and Field Research, Welsh Plant Breeding Station. 163 pp. 1957.

14834. ______. Growth correlations between the roots and shoots of grass plants. Proceedings, Eighth International Grassland Congress. 8:280–283. 1960.

14835. ______. Further studies on the relationship between shoot and root systems of grasses. Journal of British Grassland Society. 15(1):41–47. 1960.

14836. ______. The effect of photoperiod and temperature on the relationship between the root and shoot systems of *Lolium perenne.* Journal British Grassland Society. 16(4):291–295. 1961.

14837. Troutman, B. C., and J. A. Jagschitz. Evaluation of chemicals for crabgrass control in turfgrass—1970. Northeastern Weed Science Society Proceedings. 25: p. 91–95. 1971.

14838. ______. Effects of preemergent herbicides on development and rooting of Kentucky bluegrass sod. Agronomy Abstracts. p. 50. 1971.

14839. ______. Evaluation of chemicals for crabgrass control in turfgrass—1970. Proceedings of the Northeastern Weed Science Society. 25:91–95. 1971.

14840. True, L. Establishment and care of hybrid bermudagrass lawns. Arizona Garden Guides. A. F. 953. 1–4 pp.

14841. Truex, P. Lawns. The City Gardener. A. A. Knopf. New York. 214–216 pp. 1964.

14845. Truog, E. Soil reaction influence on availability of plant nutrients. Soil Science Society of America Proceedings. 11:305–308. 1946.

14846. Tucker, M. C., and J. L. Dale. Rust on zoysia in Arkansas. The Plant Disease Reporter. 51(10):893. 1967.

14847. Tucker, W. H. Greens subsoil. Golfdom. 6(4):93–94. 1932.

14848. ______. Soil must "breathe." Golfdom. 7(6):11–12. 1933.

14849. ______. Grass vs. turf. Golfdom. 7(8):34–36. 1933.

14850. Tufts, L. Producing turf on poor land at Pinehurst, North Carolina. USGA Green Section Bulletin. 1(12):254–258. 1921.

14851. Tufts, R. S. Planning of golf course features. USGA Green Section Record. 1(1):6–9. 1963.

14852. Tuite, J. The isolation and growth of fungi that cause plant diseases. Proceedings of the Midwest Regional Turf Conference. pp. 20–23. 1963.

14853. Tull, A. Golf course design. Golf Course Reporter. 25(5):24–25. 1957.

14854. Tullis, E. C. Covered smut of crabgrass. The Plant Disease Reporter. 46(1):64. 1962.

14855. Tulloch, A. Winter and spring conditions 1936–37. The Greenkeepers' Reporter. 6(3):10–13. 1938.

14856. Tuppen, S. Heres "how" from Florida! The National Greenkeeper. 1(2):13–14. 1927.

14857. Turcotte, P. A case for wetting agents. Golfdom. 42(10):68, 100–101, 104. 1968.

14858. Turgeon, A. J. Turfgrass weed control. Michigan Forestry and Park Conference Proceedings. 43:26. 1969.

14859. ______. The *Poa annua* problem. Illinois Turfgrass Conference Proceedings. pp. 5–6. 1971.

14860. ______. The role of 7-oxabicyclo (2.2.1) heptane-2.3-dicarboxylic acid (endothall) in annual bluegrass (*Poa annua* L.) control in turf. Ph.D. Thesis. Michigan State University. 101 pp. 1971.

14861. ______. Broadleaved weed control in turf. Michigan Turfgrass Research Report. p. 9. Spring, 1971.

14862. ______. How to use the metric system. The Golf Superintendent. 40(4):51–52. 1972.

14863. ______. A GM primer on good weed control methods. Grounds Maintenance. 7(12):44–46. 1972.

14864. ______. Weed control in turf. Twenty-Fourth Illinois Custom Spray Operators Training School. 154–156 pp. 1972.

14865. ______. Mowing your lawn. University of Illinois Agricultural Cooperative Extension Service Circular 1050. 4 pp. 1972.

14866. ______. Studies on the control of annual bluegrass in closely clipped Kentucky bluegrass turf. University of Illinois Turfgrass Field Day. pp. 18–20. 1972.

14867. ______. Studies on the control of annual bluegrass with endothall. 42nd Annual Michigan Turfgrass Conference Proceedings. 1:30–33. 1972.

14868. ______. Research in *Poa annua* control. 42nd Annual Michigan Turfgrass Conference Proceedings. 1:45–50. 1972.

14869. Turgeon, A. J. and R. L. Courson. Steps to a better lawn. Turfgrass Management Slide Series, University of Illinois. 1:13 pp. 1972.

14870. ______. Lawn weeds: identification and control. Turfgrass Management Slide Series No. 2. University of Illinois. 8 pp. 1972.

14871. Turgeon, A. J., and T. D. Hughes. The future of our turf program. The Bull Sheet. 25(7):5. 1971.

14872. ______. The future of our turf program. The Bull Sheet. 26(6):11. 1972.

14873. ______. Fertilizer recommendations for turf. Horticulture series H–690, University of Illinois. 4 pp. 1972.

14874. Turgeon, A. J. and A. R. Mazur. Lawn establishment. University of Illinois Agricultural Cooperative Extension Service Circular 1066. 8 p. 1972.

14875. Turgeon, A. J. and W. F. Meggitt. Turfgrass weed control. Michigan State University Agricultural Experiment Station. Research Report 104. pp. 5–6. 1969.

14876. ______. Chemical control of creeping speedwell. Weeds, Trees, and Turf. 9(7):22–23. 1970.

14877. ______. Lawn weed control. Michigan State University Extension Service. Farm Science Series. Bulletin E-653. 4 pp. 1969.

14878. ______. Role of endothall in the control of annual bluegrass. Proceedings of the Northeastern Weed Science Society. 25:-399. 1971.

14879. ______. A small-plot sprayer. Weed Science. 19(3):245–247. 1971.

14880. Turgeon, A. J., and M. C. Shurtleff. Turfgrass varietal evaluation. University of Illinois Turfgrass Field Day. pp. 4–6. 1972.

14881. Turgeon, A. J., T. D. Hughes, J. D. Butler. Thatch accumulation in bluegrass after applying preemergence herbicides two years. Illinois Turfgrass Conference Proceedings. pp. 19–20. 1971.

14882. Turgeon, A. J., W. F. Meggitt and D. Penner. Effects of endothall on annual bluegrass and two turfgrass species. North Central Weed Control Conference Proceedings. 26:90. 1971.

14883. ______. Role of endothall in the control of annual bluegrass in turf. Weed Science. 20(6):562–565. 1972.

14884. Turgeon, A. J., D. Penner, and W. Meggitt. Absorption, translocation and metabolism of endothall by three turfgrass species. Weed Science Society of America. pp. 3–4. 1972.

14885. ______. Selectivity of endothall in turf. Weed Science. 20(6):557–561. 1972.

14886. Turk, F. M. Common disease of turf in eastern Canada and their control. Guelph Turf Conference. Royal Canadian

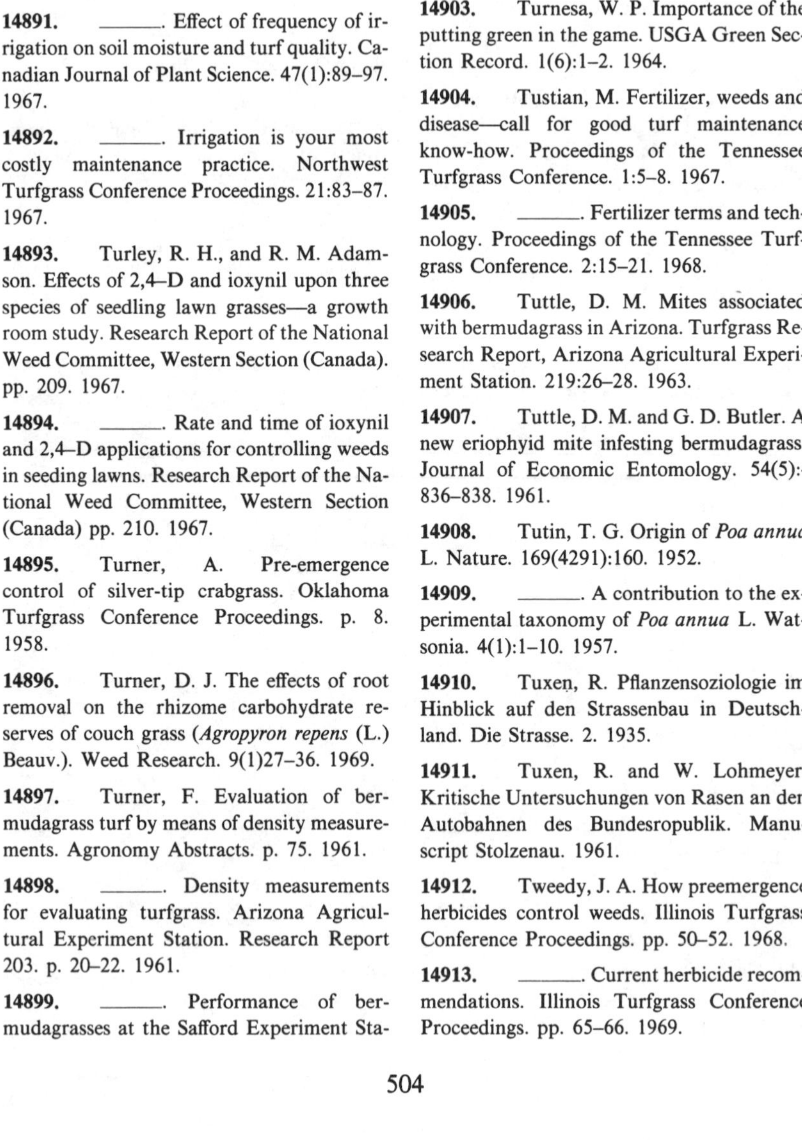

Golf Association Green Section. pp. 50–54. 1959.

14887. Turk, L. M. Soil germs—their role in composts and special fertilizers. Golfdom. 15(7):26–32. 1941.

14888. ______. Functions of the microbial population. Golfdom. 15(8):15–16. 1941.

14889. ______. Soil germs, their role in compost and special fertilizers. Greenkeeper's Reporter. 9(2):21–49. 1941.

14890. Turley, R. H. Irrigation needs of sportsgrass turf. Proceedings of the Northwest Turfgrass Conference. 18:26–32. 1964.

14891. ______. Effect of frequency of irrigation on soil moisture and turf quality. Canadian Journal of Plant Science. 47(1):89–97. 1967.

14892. ______. Irrigation is your most costly maintenance practice. Northwest Turfgrass Conference Proceedings. 21:83–87. 1967.

14893. Turley, R. H., and R. M. Adamson. Effects of 2,4–D and ioxynil upon three species of seedling lawn grasses—a growth room study. Research Report of the National Weed Committee, Western Section (Canada). pp. 209. 1967.

14894. ______. Rate and time of ioxynil and 2,4–D applications for controlling weeds in seeding lawns. Research Report of the National Weed Committee, Western Section (Canada) pp. 210. 1967.

14895. Turner, A. Pre-emergence control of silver-tip crabgrass. Oklahoma Turfgrass Conference Proceedings. p. 8. 1958.

14896. Turner, D. J. The effects of root removal on the rhizome carbohydrate reserves of couch grass (*Agropyron repens* (L.) Beauv.). Weed Research. 9(1)27–36. 1969.

14897. Turner, F. Evaluation of bermudagrass turf by means of density measurements. Agronomy Abstracts. p. 75. 1961.

14898. ______. Density measurements for evaluating turfgrass. Arizona Agricultural Experiment Station. Research Report 203. p. 20–22. 1961.

14899. ______. Performance of bermudagrasses at the Safford Experiment Station. Turfgrass Research, Arizona Agricultural Experiment Station Report. 219:42. 1963.

14900. ______. Turfgrass management under saline conditions Safford Experiment Station 1965. Turfgrass Research—University of Arizona Agricultural Experiment Station. Report 230. pp. 27–29. 1965.

14901. Turner, K. A consultants' views. Turf Bulletin. Massachusetts Turf & Lawn Grass Council. 2(8):6. 1964.

14902. ______. Turf diseases—prevention and control. University of Maine Turf Conference Proceedings. 8:3–5. 1970.

14903. Turnesa, W. P. Importance of the putting green in the game. USGA Green Section Record. 1(6):1–2. 1964.

14904. Tustian, M. Fertilizer, weeds and disease—call for good turf maintenance know-how. Proceedings of the Tennessee Turfgrass Conference. 1:5–8. 1967.

14905. ______. Fertilizer terms and technology. Proceedings of the Tennessee Turfgrass Conference. 2:15–21. 1968.

14906. Tuttle, D. M. Mites associated with bermudagrass in Arizona. Turfgrass Research Report, Arizona Agricultural Experiment Station. 219:26–28. 1963.

14907. Tuttle, D. M. and G. D. Butler. A new eriophyid mite infesting bermudagrass. Journal of Economic Entomology. 54(5):-836–838. 1961.

14908. Tutin, T. G. Origin of *Poa annua* L. Nature. 169(4291):160. 1952.

14909. ______. A contribution to the experimental taxonomy of *Poa annua* L. Watsonia. 4(1):1–10. 1957.

14910. Tuxen, R. Pflanzensoziologie im Hinblick auf den Strassenbau in Deutschland. Die Strasse. 2. 1935.

14911. Tuxen, R. and W. Lohmeyer. Kritische Untersuchungen von Rasen an den Autobahnen des Bundesropublik. Manuscript Stolzenau. 1961.

14912. Tweedy, J. A. How preemergence herbicides control weeds. Illinois Turfgrass Conference Proceedings. pp. 50–52. 1968.

14913. ______. Current herbicide recommendations. Illinois Turfgrass Conference Proceedings. pp. 65–66. 1969.

14914. Twombly, A. R. Emergency aerification. New York State Turf Association. Bulletin 7. pp. 25–26. 1949.

14915. ______. Emergency aerification. Greenkeepers' Reporter. 18(1):20. 1950.

14916. ______. Reduces *Poa annua* in greens. Golfdom. 26(7):67–69. 1952.

14917. ______. Putting green renovation. New York State Turf Association. Bulletin 62. pp. 239–242. 1958.

14918. Tyldesley, S. D. New techniques and sprays. The Groundsman. 17(11):16, 18. 1964.

14919. Tyler, K. B., and F. E. Broadbent. Nitrogen uptake by ryegrass from three tagged fertilizers. Soil Science Society America Proceedings. 22:231–234. 1958.

14920. Tyson, J. The putting green. Michigan State University, Soil Science Department. 4 pp.

14921. ______. Fertilizer chart. The Greenkeepers' Reporter. 2(4):12–13. 1934.

14922. ______. Management of bentgrass lawns. Michigan Agricultural Experiment Station Bulletin. 156:18. 1936.

14923. ______. Snowmold injury to bentgrasses. Michigan Agricultural Experiment Station Quarterly Bulletin. 19(2):87–92. 1936.

14924. ______. Golf course soils. The Greenkeepers' Reporter. 5(2):14–15, 30–32. 1937.

14926. ______. Michigan State short course. The Greenkeepers' Reporter. 6(2):-45–47. 1938.

14927. ______. Watch drainage as turf problem source. Golfdom. 20(3):53, 56–57. 1946.

14928. ______. Dilution chart to 2,4 dichlorophenoxyacetic acid to be used for killing weeds in turf. The Greenkeeper's Reporter. 14(3):14–15. 1946.

14929. ______. Importance of water and air drainage. Greenkeepers' Reporter. 16(3):-22–23, 41. 1948.

14930. ______. A sound fertilizer program for turf. Proceedings of Midwest Regional Turf Conference. pp. 92–93. 1948.

14931. ______. Making a new seeding. Proceedings of Midwest Regional Turf Conference. pp. 94–97. 1948.

14932. ______. Turf research in Michigan. Proceedings of Midwest Regional Turf Conference. pp. 49–52. 1949.

14933. ______. Turf research in Michigan. Midwest Turf News and Research. 3(2):-3–4. 1949.

14934. ______. Selection of grasses and turf maintenance. The Modern Cemetery. 61(2):139–140. 1950.

14935. ______. Golf soil classification and management principles. Sports Turfgrass Conference. Royal Canadian Golf Association Green Section. pp. 5–10. 1955.

14936. ______. Principles of turf fertilization. Sports Turfgrass Conference. Royal Canadian Golf Association Green Section. pp. 20–26. 1955.

14937. ______. Principles of turf fertilization. The Golf Course Reporter. 24:14–17. 1956.

14938. ______. Making a new lawn. Michigan Agricultural Extension Folder. F211:1–6. 1956.

14939. ______. Care of an established lawn. Michigan Agricultural Extension Folder. F212:1–8. 1956.

14940. ______. The effect of seeding mixture on establishment of fairway turf. Sports Turfgrass Conference. Royal Canadian Golf Association Green Section. pp. 13–18. 1956.

14941. ______. Making a new lawn. Michigan Agricultural Extension Folder. F211:1–8. 1958.

14942. ______. Care of an established lawn. Michigan Agricultural Extension Folder. F212:1–8. 1960.

14943. ______. Making a new lawn. Michigan State University Cooperative Extension Service Folder. F–211. 1960.

14944. ______. The basic soil requirements for turf. 1962 Wisconsin Turfgrass Conference Proceedings. pp. 1–2. 1962.

14945. ______. Principles to consider in selecting the right soil for a sod farm. 1962 Wisconsin Turfgrass Conference Proceedings. pp. 1–2. 1962.

14946. Tyson, J., and E. A. Finney. Progress report on study of turf growth on soil mixtures available for highway shoulder construction in Michigan. Highway Research Board, Commission on Roadside Development, 27th Annual Meeting. pp. 63–82. 1947.

14947. ______. Soil mixtures available for highway shoulder construction in Michigan. Report of Committee on Roadside Development, Highway Research Board. 63–82. 1948.

14948. Tyson, J. and B. Grigsby. Growing beautiful lawns. Michigan Extension Bulletin. 224. 1952.

14949. Ueno, M. and K. Yoshihara. Spring and summer root growth of some temperate-region grasses and summer root growth of tropical grasses. Journal of the British Grassland Society. 22(2):148–152. 1967.

14950. Uhland, R. E. Controlling small gullies by bluegrass sod. U.S.D.A. Leaflet. 82:1–4. 1931.

14951. Umeda, Y. Green maintenance plan of the Simonoseki Golf Club. KGU Green Section Turf Research Bulletin. 5:93–103. 1963.

14952. ______. On the pre-emergence treatments of zoysia turf seeds. KGU Green Section Turf Research Bulletin. 5:119–122. 1963.

14953. Underwood, J. K. Progress report on the new turf area. Tennessee Farm & Home Scientific Progress Report. 25:4–5. 1958.

14954. Underwood, J. K., F. C. Galle. Tennessee lawns, planting and care. Tennessee Agricultural Extension Publication. 326:-1–24. 1951.

14955. Underwood, J. K. Rust on Merion bluegrass. Golf Course Reporter. 32(5):-22. 1964.

14956. ______. Tennessee lawns. University of Tennessee Agricultural Extension Service Bulletin 326. 1964.

14957. Underwood, J. New slant on the mod sod. Sports Illustrated. 1971.

14958. Unegami, K. Characteristics and how to use the IB-fertilizer. KGU Green Section Turf Research Bulletin. 21(8):11–12. 1971.

14959. Ungar, I. A. Species-soil relationships on the Great Salt Plains of North Oklahoma. American Midland Naturalist. 80(2):-392–406. 1968.

14960. Ungar, I. A., W. Hogan, and M. McClelland. Plant communities of saline soils at Lincoln, Nebraska. American Midland Naturalist. 82(2):564–577. 1969.

14961. Unglaub, H. The water requirements of *"Poa pratensis."* Pflanzenbau. 15:-360–370. 1939.

14962. Uoti, J. M. Flowering and tillering of meadow fescue seedlings under controlled environmental conditions. M.S. Thesis, Purdue University. 1972.

14963. Updegraff, W. E. Proper watering pays dividends. Golf Course Reporter. 21(5):20. 1953.

14964. Ushioda, T. Greens maintenance and the CDU. KGU Green Section Turf Research Bulletin. 21(8):21–23. 1971.

14965. Vaartnou, H. Colonial bentgrass on the West coast. Proceedings of the Northwest Turfgrass Conference. 18:21. 1964.

14966. ______. Responses of five genotypes of *Agrostis* L. to variations in environment. Ph.D. Thesis, Oregon State University. 149 pp. 1966.

14968. Vaartnou, H., and C. R. Elliott. Snowmolds on lawns and lawngrasses in northwest Canada. The Plant Disease Reporter. 53(11):891–894. 1969.

14969. Vadala, B. Calcium arsenate use at Metropolis Country Club. Proceedings 1972 3-Day Turf Courses, Rutgers University. pp. 49–50. 1972.

14970. Valentine, G. H. Seeds—facts and fancy. Midwest Regional Turf Conference Proceedings. pp. 73–74. 1971.

14971. Valentine, J. Controlling fairway weeds with sulphate of ammonia. USGA Green Section Bulletin. 8(6):122–123. 1928.

14972. ______. Sodding a putting green. The National Greenkeeper. 3(4):24. 1929.

14973. ______. Efficiency is keynote of better course management. Golfdom. 21(10):68, 70. 1947.

14974. Valoras, N., W. C. Morgan, and J. Letey. Physical soil amendments, soil compaction, irrigation, and wetting agents in turfgrass management: II. Effects on top growth, salinity, and minerals in the tissue. Agronomy Journal. 58(5):528–531. 1966.

14975. Valoras, N., J. Letey, and J. F. Osborn. Adsorption on nonionic surfactants by soil materials. Soil Science Society of America Proceedings. 33(3):345–348. 1969.

14976. Van Bavel, C. H. M. and D. G. Harris. Evapotranspiration rates from bermudagrass and corn at Raleigh, North Carolina. Agronomy Journal. 54(4):319–322. 1962.

14977. Vance, A. M. and B. A. App. Lawn insects, how to control them. USDA Home and Garden Bulletin No. 53. 24 pp. 1956.

14978. Van Cleef, C. Grass problems of the park superintendent. Proceedings of the University of Florida Turf Conference. 1:10. 1953.

14979. Van Dam, J. Ryegrass. Park Maintenance. 24(7):19. 1971.

14980. ______. *Poa annua.* Park Maintenance. 24(7):24–25. 1971.

14981. ______. Crabgrass. Park Maintenance. 24(7):25. 1971.

14982. ______. Why the need for specifications. Proceedings of Southern California Turfgrass Institute. pp. 1–3. 1971.

14983. ______. The economics of overseeding and colorizing dormant Bermudagrass. California Turfgrass Culture. 22(4):-26–27. 1972.

14984. ______. The effect of management practices on weed invasion. Proceedings of the 1972 Turf and Landscape Horticulture Institute. pp. 53–59. 1972.

14985. Van Dam, J., and K. Kurtz. Overseed or colorize. Grounds Maintenance. 7(9):42–44. 1972.

14986. Vandecaveye, S. C. The present fertilizer situation. State College of Washington Annual Turf Conference. 4:9. 1951.

14987. ______. The use of commercial fertilizers on turf grasses. New Mexico Turfgrass Conference Proceedings. 14–18. 1956.

14988. VandenBerg, G. E., A. W. Cooper, A. E. Erickson, and W. M. Carleton. Soil pressure distribution under tractor and implement traffic. Agricultural Engineering. 38(12):854, 855, 859. 1957.

14989. Vanden Born, W. H. The effect of dicamba and Picloram on quackgrass, bromegrass and Kentucky bluegrass. Weeds. 13:309–312. 1965.

14990. van der Horst, J. P. Advisory work in the Netherlands. Proceedings of the First International Turfgrass Research Conference. p. 432. 1969.

14991. ______. Turfgrass management in the Netherlands. Proceedings of the First International Turfgrass Research Conference. pp. 522–525. 1969.

14992. ______. Sports turf research in the Netherlands. Journal of the Sports Turf Research Institute. 46:46–57. 1970.

14993. Van Dersal, W. R. The ecology of a lawn. Ecology. 17(3):515–527. 1936.

14994. Van Gorder, E. W. Keeping our fairways green. The National Greenkeeper. 1(12):7–8. 1927.

14995. Van Gundy, S. D., L. H. Stolzy, T. E. Szuszkiewicz, and R. L. Rackham. Influence of oxygen supply on survival of plant parasitic nematodes in soil. Phytopathology. 52(7):628–632. 1962.

14996. Van Horn, G. A. Penn State speaker sees big turf demands ahead. Golfdom. 34(4):72. 1960.

14997. ______. Crabgrass control varies. Parks and Recreation. 46(2):71–85. 1963.

14998. Van Keuren, R. W. Fertilization and root life. Turf Bulletin. Massachusetts Turf and Lawn Grass Council. 4(5):14–16. 1967.

14999. ______. Crownvetch research in Ohio. Second Crownvetch Symposium, Pennsylvania State University. 6:134–138. 1968.

15000. Van Luijk, A. Antagonism between various microorganisms and different species of the genus *Pythium* parasitizing upon grasses and lucerne. Mededelingen Phytopathologisch Laboratorium "Willie Commelin Scholten." 14:43–82. 1938.

15001. Van Emden, H. F. A technique for the marking and recovery of turf samples in stem borer investigations. Entomology, Experimental and Applied. 6:194–198. 1963.

15003. Van Schilfgaarde, J., and R. E. Williamson. Studies of crop response to drainage. I. Growth chambers. Transactions of the ASAE. 8(1):94–97. 1965.

15004. Van Scoyoc, G. E. Diazinon adsorption by Carlisle muck, Toledo silty clay, Wauseon sandy loam, and Ciro clay soils as related to various soil properties. M.S. Thesis, Ohio State University. 1971.

15005. Van Slijken, A. Significance of sowing depth (Dutch). Sports Turf Research Institute. Journal of the Sports Turf Research Institute. 41:85. 1965.

15006. Van Slijken, A. I. and I. A. Andries. Semis d'herbages et de gazons Quelques considération sur la densité de semis et la levée. Centre National de Recherches Herbagères et Fourragères—1re Section Subventionné par l'Institut pour l'Encouragement de la Recherche Scientifique dans l'Industrie et l'Agriculture (I.R.S.I.A.) 16(2):219–232. 1963.

15007. Van Weerdt, L. G., W. Birchfield, and R. P. Esser. Observations on some subtropical plant parasitic nematodes in Florida. Proceedings of the Soil and Crop Science Society of Florida. 19:443–451. 1960.

15008. Vargas, J. M. Evaluation of the systemic fungicides. Michigan State University Agricultural Experiment Station. Research Report 104. p. 7. 1969.

15009. ______. Systemic fungicides for the control of powdery mildew. Michigan Forestry and Park Conference Proceedings. 43:26. 1969.

15010. ______. Report on *Helminthosporium*. Michigan Turfgrass Research Report. pp. 6. 1970.

15011. ______. Current turf disease control research. Illinois Turfgrass Conference Proceedings. pp. 14–15. 1971.

15012. Juchartz, D. D. Control of *Fusarium* blight on Merion Kentucky bluegrass. The Sod Grower. 1(1):16. 1971.

15013. Vargas, J. M. Controlling turf diseases with systemic fungicides. Grounds Maintenance. 7(7):41–44. 1972.

15014. ______. Turf disease control guide. Grounds Maintenance. 7(12):32–33, 38–43. 1972.

15015. ______. Evaluation of four systemic fungicides for control of stripe smut in Merion Kentucky bluegrass turf. The Plant Disease Reporter. 56(4):334–336. 1972.

15016. Vargas, J. M. and J. B. Beard. Snow mold. Michigan State University Agricultural Experiment Station. Research Report 104. p. 6. 1969.

15017. ______. *Typhula* snow mold control. Michigan Turfgrass Research Report. pp. 4–6. Winter, 1970.

15018. ______. Chloroneb, a new fungicide for the control of *Typhula* blight. The Plant Disease Reporter. 54(12):1075–1077. 1970.

15019. ______. *Typhula* blight. Park Maintenance. 24(7):18. 1971.

15020. ______. Comparison of application dates for the control of *Typhula* blight. The Plant Disease Reporter. 55(12):1118–1119. 1971.

15021. Vargas, J. M. and R. Detweiler. Control of powdery mildew on Merion Kentucky bluegrass. 42nd Annual Michigan Turfgrass Conference Proceedings. 1:13–14. 1972.

15022. ______. *Sclerotinia* dollar spot control. 42nd Annual Michigan Turfgrass Conference Proceedings. 1:15. 1972.

15023. Vargas, J. M., and C. W. Laughlin. The role of *Tylenchorhynchus dubius* in the development of *Fusarium* blight of Merion Kentucky bluegrass. Phytopathology. 62(11):1311–1314. 1972.

15024. ______. Benomyl for the control of *Fusarium* blight of Merion Kentucky bluegrass. The Plant Disease Reporter. 55(2):-167–170. 1971.

15025. ______. Benomyl for the control of *Fusarium* blight of "Merion" Kentucky bluegrass. Turf Bulletin. Massachusetts Turf and Lawn Council. 7(4):17–18. 1971.

15026. ______. The role of *Tylenchorhynchus dubius* in the development of

Fusarium blight. 42nd Annual Michigan Turfgrass Conference Proceedings. 1:8. 1972.

15027. Vargas, J. M., A. L. Anderson and P. E. Rieke *Fusarium* blight. Michigan State University Agricultural Experiment Station. Research Report 104. 6 pp. 1969.

15028. Vargas, J. M., J. B. Beard, and R. Detweiler. *Typhula* blight (gray snowmold) control. 42nd Annual Michigan Turfgrass Conference Proceedings. 1:9–12. 1972.

15029. Vargas, J., J. B. Beard, and K. T. Payne. Snow mold. Park Maintenance. 25(7):12. 1972.

15030. ______. Comparative incidence of *Typhula* blight and *Fusarium* patch on 56 Kentucky bluegrass cultivars. The Plant Disease Reporter. 56(1):32–34. 1972.

15031. Vargas, J. M., C. W. Laughlin, and R. L. Shearman. *Fusarium* blight. Park Maintenance. 24(7):18. 1971.

15032. Varner, R. W., M. B. Weed and H. L. Ploeg. A new herbicide for the selective control of annual seedling weed grasses in turf and crops. Proceedings of the Northeastern Weed Control Conference. p. 520–527. 1965.

15033. Vaughn, J. R. Control of turf diseases in Michigan. Proceedings of Midwest Regional Turf Conference. pp. 72–75. 1951.

15034. ______. Prevention and cure in halting of dollar spot. Golfdom. 27(5):82. 1953.

15035. ______. Turf diseases. Proceedings of the Mid-Atlantic Association of Golf Course Superintendents. pp. 11–13. 1953.

15036. Vaughn, J. R. and W. Klomparens. Drugs on the green. Golf Course Reporter. 20(2):5–7. 1952.

15037. ______. Control of *Helminthosporium* or melting-out. New York State Turf Association. Bulletin 34. pp. 133–134. 1952.

15038. Veatch, C. L., and P. Tabor. Basal seeding of road cut slopes. Journal of Soil and Water Conservation. 16:184. 1961.

15039. Veatch, C., O. E. Schubert, and K. L. Carvell. Weed control—1960 suggestions. Turf and Lawn. West Virginia University Agricultural Experiment Station. Circular 108. pp. 10–11. 1960.

15040. ______. Weed control—1962–1963 suggestions. Turf and lawn. West Virginia University Agricultural Experiment Station. Current Report 34. pp. 12–14. 1962.

15041. Vegiard, H. What I've learned about crested wheat grass. Golfdom. 15(8):-13–14. 1941.

15042. Venable, R. T. Problems in operation. Texas Turfgrass Conference Proceedings. 21:17–20. 1966.

15043. Vengris, J. Lawns—basic factors, construction and maintenance of fine turf areas. Thomson Publications, Davis, California. pp. 1–229. 1969.

15044. Vengris, J., E. R. Hill, and D. L. Field. Clipping and regrowth of barnyardgrass. Crop Science. 6:342–344. 1966.

15045. Verghese, K. G., R. E. Hanes, L. W. Zelazny, and R. E. Blaser. Sodium chloride uptake in grasses as influenced by fertility interaction. Roadside Development and Maintenance. Highway Research Board. No. 335. pp. 13–15. 1970.

15046. Vezina, P. E. and D. W. K. Boulter. The spectral composition of near ultraviolet and visible radiation beneath forest canopies. Canadian Journal of Botany. 44(9):1267–1284. 1966.

15047. Vezina, P. E. and G. Pech. Solar radiation beneath conifer canopies in relation to crown closure. Forest Science. 10(4):443–451. 1964.

15048. Viergever, R. L. The costs of mowing. Northern California Turfgrass Institute Proceedings. pp. 32–34. 1961.

15049. ______. Summary of proceedings 32nd International Turfgrass Conference and Show. Northern California Turfgrass Institute Proceedings. pp. 40–41. 1961.

15050. ______. The modern golf course superintendent. Thomson Publications, Fresno, Ca. pp. 1–106. 1970.

15051. Vigliotti, V. J. Spray equipment for the golf course. Proceedings of the Florida Turfgrass Management Conference. 13:65–69. 1965.

15052. Villaveces, J. W. Allergenic plants and pollens. Proceedings of the 1972

Turf and Landscape Horticulture Institute. pp. 80–81. 1972.

15053. Viltos, A. J. How research lead to weed control with CRAG 1. Golfdom. 29(6):56. 1955.

15054. Vinall, H. N. and M. A. Hein. Breeding miscellaneous grasses. USDA Yearbook. pp. 1032–1102. 1937.

15055. Vinall, H. N. and H. L. Westover. Bulbous bluegrass, *Poa bulbosa.* Journal of the American Society of Agronomy. 20(4):-394–399. 1928.

15056. Vincente-Chandler, J., R. W. Pearson, F. Abruña, and S. Silva. Potassium fertilization of intensively managed grasses-under humid tropical conditions. Agronomy Journal. 54(5):450–453. 1963.

15057. Virgin, H. I. Light-induced unfolding of the grass leaf. Physiologia Plantarum. 15:380–389. 1962.

15058. Virtuoso, A. P. Financing the remodeling job. USGA Journal and Turf Management. 12(2):29–30. 1959.

15059. Voight, J. E. Turf in Wisconsin parks and institution. Wisconsin Turfgrass Conference Proceedings. pp. 1–5. 1965.

15060. Volk, G. M. Nitrogen sources for maintenance of turf grasses. Florida Turf-Grass Association Bulletin. 1(3):4–5,8. 1954.

15061. ______. Nitrogen sources for maintenance of turf grasses. The Golf Course Reporter. 22(8):5–8. 1954.

15062. ______. Volatile loss of ammonia following surface application of urea to turf or bare soils. Agronomy Journal. 5(12):746–749. 1957.

15064. ______. The fate of surface applied nitrogen. Proceedings of University of Florida Turf-Grass Management Conference. 9:25–32. 1961.

15065. ______. What is Ureaform fertilizer nitrogen? Sunshine State Agricultural Research Report. 9(3):22–23. 1963.

15067. ______. Liquid versus dry fertilizers for turf. Proceedings Florida Turfgrass Management Conference. 14:52–57. 1966.

15068. ______. Efficiency of fertilizer urea as affected by method of application, soil moisture, and lime. Agronomy Journal. 58(3):249–252. 1966.

15069. ______. Fertilization of turfgrasses. Annual Research Report of the Institute of Food & Agricultural Sciences University of Florida. pp. 115; 1968.

15070. ______. Fertilization of turfgrasses. Annual Research Report of the Institute of Food & Agricultural Sciences. University of Florida. pp. 123–124. 1969.

15071. ______. Fertilization of turfgrasses. Annual Research Report of the Institute of Food & Agricultural Sciences. University of Florida. p. 129. 1970.

15072. ______. Compressibility of turf as a measure of grass growth and thatch development on bermudagrass greens. Agronomy Journal. 64(4):503–506. 1972.

15073. Volk, G. M. and G. C. Horn. Response of tifgreen bermudagrass to soluble and slowly available nitrogen sources as measured by visual ratings and turf weights. Proceedings Florida Turfgrass Management Conference. 13:147–152. 1965.

15074. ______. Nitrogen requirements of turf. Florida Turfgrass Management Conference Proceedings. 18:84–87. 1970.

15075. ______. Response of Tifway bermudagrass to sulfur on sandy soils. Agronomy Journal. 64(3):359–361. 1972.

15076. Volk, N. J. Work director tells of foundation start at October field day. Midwest Turf-News and Research. 1(1):2. 1947.

15077. ______. Research director reports. Midwest Turf-News and Research. 2(1):1 and 4. 1948.

15079. Volkman, C. M. Lawn seed chart and guide for building lawns. C. M. Volkman and Company. San Francisco. 6 pp. 1950.

15080. Voltz, C. W. Which kind of pipe? steel—cement. Golf Course Reporter. 32(6):-48. 1964.

15081. von Hofsten, C. G. Vosst kan man hålla nere vitklövern. Weibulls Gräs Tips. pp. 101–102. March, 1962.

15082. Voorhees, E. B. The cost of available nitrogen. New Jersey Agricultural Experiment Station Publication. 8 pp.

15083. Voorhees, E. B., J. H. Gehrs, and E. Davenport. Soil fertility and how to maintain it. The Complete Book of Garden Magic. Tudor Publishing Co. pp. 16–27. 1948.

15084. Vorst, J. J. Effects of certain management practices on winter injury to turf containing a mixture of Kentucky bluegrass (*Poa pratensis* L.) and tall fescue (*Festuca arundinacea* Schreb.) M.S. Thesis, Ohio State University. 39 pp. 1966.

15085. Vos, H., and W. Scheijgrond. Varieties and mixtures for sports turf and lawns in the Netherlands. Proceedings of the First International Turfgrass Research Conference. pp. 34–44. 1969.

15086. Vose, P. B. Nutritional response and shoot root ratio as factors in the composition and yield of genotypes of perennial ryegrass, *Lolium perenne* L. Annals of Botany. 26:425–437. 1962.

15087. Vose, R. H. Science wages webworm turf war. Golfdom. 6(8):26–28. 1932.

15088. Voss, R. L. Improving soils for different turf uses. Weeds, Trees and Turf. 5(6):22. 1966.

15089. Voykin, P. Mechanization. The Golf Superintendent. 38(7):28–30. 1970.

15090. ______. The President's message. The Bull Sheet. 26(2):1–2. 1972.

15091. ______. Over-grooming is overspending. Midwest Regional Turf Conference Proceedings. pp. 35–38. 1972.

15092. de Vries, D. M. Methods of determining the botanical composition of hay fields and pastures. Report of the Fourth International Grassland Congress. pp. 474–480. 1937.

15093. Vukolov, V. Prazske okrasne a hristove travniky. Vytiskla Statni Tiskarna. Praze. 17 pp. 1939.

15094. Waddington, D. V. Soil compaction. Turf Clippings. University of Massachussetts. 1(7):32–A to 36–A. 1962.

15095. ______. Soil modification and results of further testing. Turf Clippings. University of Massachusetts. 2(2):25–30. 1967.

15096. ______. Soil modification research at Penn State. Agronomy Abstracts. p. 61. 1968.

15097. ______. Effects of soil drainage on the growth of crownvetch. Second Crownvetch Symposium, Pennsylvania State University. 6:44–47. 1968.

15098. ______. Soil modification research. New York Turfgrass Association Bulletin. 82:317–319. 1968.

15099. ______. Soil modification research. RCGA National Turfgrass Conference. 19:60–63. 1968.

15100. ______. Controlled—release nitrogen studies. West Virginia Turfgrass Conference Proceedings. pp. 19–21. 1968.

15101. ______. Particle size and pore size relationships in soils. West Virginia Turfgrass Conference Proceedings. pp. 29–32. 1968.

15102. ______. Soil fertility research. Proceedings of the Mid-Atlantic Association of Golf Course Superintendents. pp. 17–19. 1971.

15103. ______. Soil amendments. Ohio Turfgrass Conference Proceedings. pp. 1–6. 1971.

15104. ______. Natural organic sources of nitrogen. Ohio Turfgrass Conference Proceedings. pp. 38–42. 1971.

15105. Waddington, D. V. and J. H. Baker. Influence of soil aeration on the growth and chemical composition of three grass species. Agronomy Journal. 57(3):253–258. 1965.

15108. Waddington, D. V. and E. L. Moberg. Turfgrass fertilization with isobutylidene diurea (IBDU). Agronomy Abstracts. p. 51. 1971.

15109. Waddington, D. V. Influence of soil aeration on the growth of three grass species. Ph.D. Thesis, University of Massachusetts. 1964.

15110. Waddington, D. V., J. M. Duich, and E. L. Moberg. Lawn fertilizer test. Pennsylvania State University Agricultural Experiment Station Progress Report 296. 58 p. 1969.

15111. ______. Evaluation of fertilizers containing composted refuse. Pennsylvania State University, Agricultural Experiment Station, Progress Report 327. 1972.

15112. Waddington, D. V., J. M. Duich, and T. L. Zimmerman. Golf course, athletic

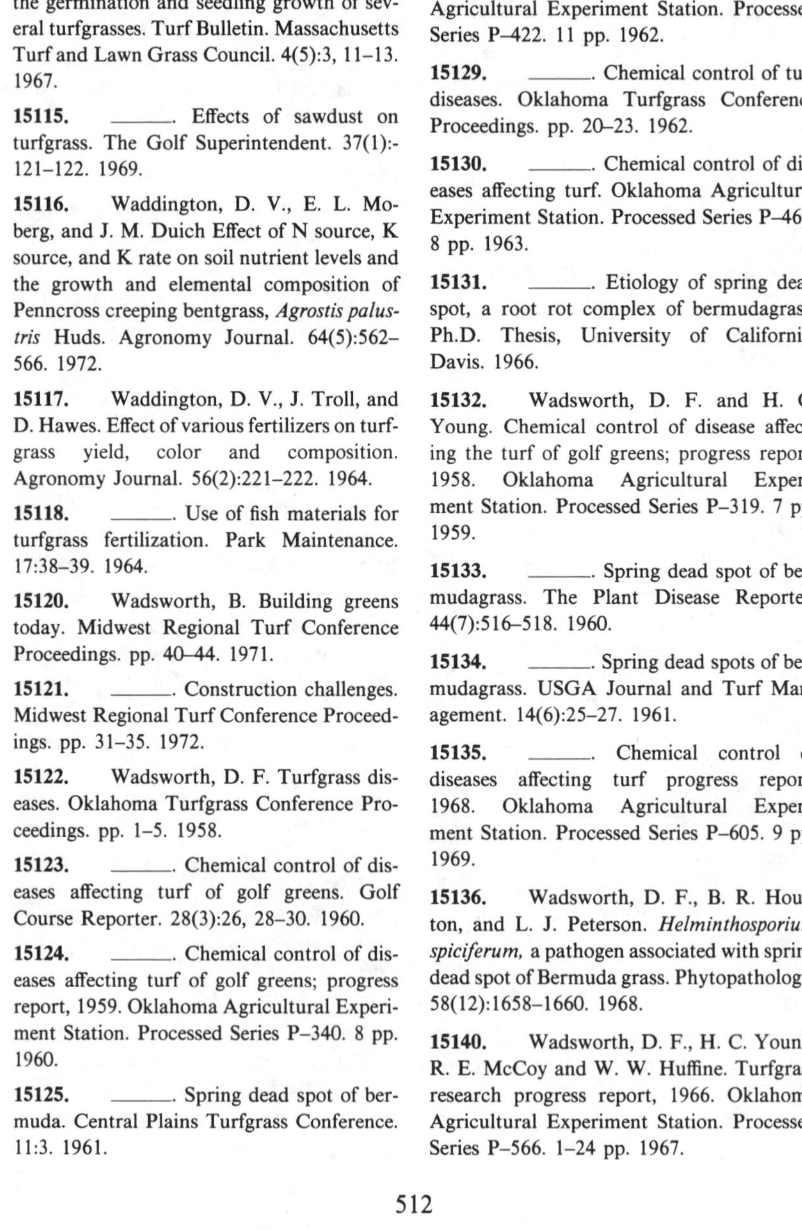

field managers helped by soil modification data. Pennsylvania State University Agricultural Experiment Station Bulletin 763. 80–81 pp. 1968–69.

15113. Waddington, D. V., W. C. Lincoln, and J. Troll. Effect of sawdust on the germination and seedling growth of several turfgrasses. Agronomy Journal. 59(2):137–139. 1967.

15114. ______. The effect of sawdust on the germination and seedling growth of several turfgrasses. Turf Bulletin. Massachusetts Turf and Lawn Grass Council. 4(5):3, 11–13. 1967.

15115. ______. Effects of sawdust on turfgrass. The Golf Superintendent. 37(1):-121–122. 1969.

15116. Waddington, D. V., E. L. Moberg, and J. M. Duich Effect of N source, K source, and K rate on soil nutrient levels and the growth and elemental composition of Penncross creeping bentgrass, *Agrostis palustris* Huds. Agronomy Journal. 64(5):562–566. 1972.

15117. Waddington, D. V., J. Troll, and D. Hawes. Effect of various fertilizers on turfgrass yield, color and composition. Agronomy Journal. 56(2):221–222. 1964.

15118. ______. Use of fish materials for turfgrass fertilization. Park Maintenance. 17:38–39. 1964.

15120. Wadsworth, B. Building greens today. Midwest Regional Turf Conference Proceedings. pp. 40–44. 1971.

15121. ______. Construction challenges. Midwest Regional Turf Conference Proceedings. pp. 31–35. 1972.

15122. Wadsworth, D. F. Turfgrass diseases. Oklahoma Turfgrass Conference Proceedings. pp. 1–5. 1958.

15123. ______. Chemical control of diseases affecting turf of golf greens. Golf Course Reporter. 28(3):26, 28–30. 1960.

15124. ______. Chemical control of diseases affecting turf of golf greens; progress report, 1959. Oklahoma Agricultural Experiment Station. Processed Series P–340. 8 pp. 1960.

15125. ______. Spring dead spot of bermuda. Central Plains Turfgrass Conference. 11:3. 1961.

15126. ______. Chemical control of diseases affecting turf on golf greens. Oklahoma Agricultural Experiment Station. Processed Series P–379. 10 pp. 1961.

15127. ______. Results of chemical drenches in the control of spring dead spot of Bermuda grass. Phytopathology. 51(9):646. 1961.

15128. ______. Chemical control of diseases affecting turf on golf greens. Oklahoma Agricultural Experiment Station. Processed Series P–422. 11 pp. 1962.

15129. ______. Chemical control of turf diseases. Oklahoma Turfgrass Conference Proceedings. pp. 20–23. 1962.

15130. ______. Chemical control of diseases affecting turf. Oklahoma Agricultural Experiment Station. Processed Series P–462. 8 pp. 1963.

15131. ______. Etiology of spring dead spot, a root rot complex of bermudagrass. Ph.D. Thesis, University of California, Davis. 1966.

15132. Wadsworth, D. F. and H. C. Young. Chemical control of disease affecting the turf of golf greens; progress report, 1958. Oklahoma Agricultural Experiment Station. Processed Series P–319. 7 pp. 1959.

15133. ______. Spring dead spot of bermudagrass. The Plant Disease Reporter. 44(7):516–518. 1960.

15134. ______. Spring dead spots of bermudagrass. USGA Journal and Turf Management. 14(6):25–27. 1961.

15135. ______. Chemical control of diseases affecting turf progress report, 1968. Oklahoma Agricultural Experiment Station. Processed Series P–605. 9 pp. 1969.

15136. Wadsworth, D. F., B. R. Houston, and L. J. Peterson. *Helminthosporium spiciferum,* a pathogen associated with spring dead spot of Bermuda grass. Phytopathology. 58(12):1658–1660. 1968.

15140. Wadsworth, D. F., H. C. Young, R. E. McCoy and W. W. Huffine. Turfgrass research progress report, 1966. Oklahoma Agricultural Experiment Station. Processed Series P–566. 1–24 pp. 1967.

15143. Wagner, R. E. Role of potassium in turf grass management. Turf Clippings. University of Massachussetts. 2(1):A–16 to A–22. 1966.

15144. ______. Role of potassium in turfgrass management. Wisconsin Turfgrass Conference Proceedings. pp. 19–28. 1966.

15145. ______. The role of potassium in the metabolism of turfgrasses. Agronomy Abstracts. p. 55. 1967.

15146. ______. Grass beauty is more than blade deep. Better Crops With Plant Food. 54(1):28–29. 1970.

15147. Wagoner, C. A. Cost of renovating greens. University of California Turf, Landscape Tree, and Nursery Conference Proceedings. pp. 6–7 to 6–8. 1966.

15148. ______. What's your line in irrigation. USGA Green Section Record 5(2):-12–13. 1967.

15149. ______. Certification for GCSAA members. USGA Green Section Record. 9(5):6–7. 1971.

15150. ______. Certified golf course superintendent. What does it mean? Arizona Turfgrass Conference Proceedings. pp. 5–9. 1972.

15151. Waite, R. and J. Boyd. The water-soluble carbohydrates of grasses. I. Changes occurring during the normal life-cycle. Journal of the Science of Food and Agriculture. 4:197–204. 1953.

15152. ______. The water-soluble carbohydrates of grasses. II. Grasses cut at grazing height several times during the growing season. Journal of the Science of Food and Agriculture. 4:257–261. 1953.

15153. Waite, R. and A. R. N. Garrod. The structural carbohydrates of grasses. Journal of the Science of Food and Agriculture. 10:308–317. 1959.

15154. ______. The comprehensive analysis of grasses. Journal of the Science of Food and Agriculture. 10:317–326. 1959.

15155. Wakefield, R. C. Nitrogen, key to grass growth. Rhode Island Agriculture. 8(3):4. 1962.

15156. ______. Finding where the grass is greener. Rhode Island Agriculture. 13(1):-7–8. 1967.

15157. Wakefield, R. C., and A. J. Clapham. Management of turfgrass treated with maleic hydrazide. Highway Research Record No. 246. Roadside Development. pp. 36–43. 1968.

15158. Wakefield, R. C., and A. T. Dore. Rhode Island roadside research. Short Course on Roadside Development (Ohio). 13:63–68. 1971.

15160. Waldrep, T. W. and J. F. Freeman. Herbicides for nimblewill in Kentucky bluegrass pasture. Weeds. 12:317–318. 1964.

15161. Walejko, R. N., J. W. Pendleton, G. Tenpas, R. Rand, and W. Paulson. Effect of snowmobile traffic on established stands of nonforest vegetation. Agronomy Abstracts. p. 166. 1972.

15162. Wallace, F. Green section plans to extend research team-work. Golfdom. 18(8):13–14. 1944.

15164. Walker, C. Renovation of deteriorated turf. New Zealand Institute for Turf Culture Newsletter. 5:1–2. 1960.

15165. ______. Defects in greens management and their remedies. New Zealand Institute for Turf Culture Newsletter. 5:3–4. 1960.

15166. ______. Renovation and care of the bowling green. New Zealand Institute for Turf Culture Newsletter. 7:1–2. 1960.

15167. ______. Seasonal notes. New Zealand Institute for Turf Culture Newsletter. 9:5–6. 1960.

15168. ______. Research notes. New Zealand Institute for Turf Culture Newsletter. 9:8. 1960.

15169. ______. Seasonal notes. New Zealand Institute for Turf Culture Newsletter. 10:3–5. 1960.

15170. ______. Soil conditioning for greens renovation. New Zealand Institute for Turf Culture Newsletter. 10:10–11. 1960.

15171. ______. Seasonal notes. New Zealand Institute for Turf Culture Newsletter. 11:9–11. 1961.

15172. ______. Winter playing fields. New Zealand Institute for Turf Culture Newsletter. 13:4–6. 1961.

15173. ______. Summer sports areas. New Zealand Institute for Turf Culture Newsletter. 13:6–9. 1961.

15174. ______. Some aspects of green mis-management. New Zealand Institute for Turf Culture Newsletter. 14:3–4. 1961.

15175. ______. Seasonal notes. New Zealand Institute for Turf Culture Newsletter. 14:10–13. 1961.

15176. ______. Summer watering. New Zealand Institute for Turf Culture Newsletter. 16:2–3. 1961.

15177. ______. Seasonal notes. New Zealand Institute for Turf Culture Newsletter. 16:5–6. 1961.

15178. ______. Bitumastic sealing of turf. New Zealand Institute for Turf Culture Newsletter. 16:10–11. 1961.

15179. ______. Influence of acidity on sports turf texture. New Zealand Institute for Turf Culture Newsletter. 18:18–20. 1962.

15180. ______. Some impressions of Australian sports areas and practices. New Zealand Institute for Turf Culture Newsletter. 19:1–4. 1962.

15181. ______. Points in weed spraying. New Zealand Institute for Turf Culture Newsletter. 20:6–8. 1962.

15182. ______. "Worms, fish manure, sawdust" for rugby grounds. New Zealand Institute for Turf Culture Newsletter. 20:9–10. 1962.

15183. ______. Seasonal notes. New Zealand Institute for Turf Culture Newsletter. 21:6–8. 1962.

15184. ______. At what height do you mow your golf greens? New Zealand Institute for Turf Culture Newsletter. 21:9. 1962.

15185. ______. Use of water. New Zealand Institute for Turf Culture Newsletter. 22:4–5. 1962.

15186. ______. Seasonal notes. New Zealand Institute for Turf Culture Newsletter. 22:6–7. 1962.

15187. ______. Fertilizers for turf. New Zealand Institute for Turf Culture Newsletter. 22:8–12. 1962.

15188. ______. New bowling greens from old. New Zealand Institute for Turf Culture Newsletter. 23:2–7. 1963.

15189. ______. Golf green renovation. New Zealand Institute for Turf Culture Newsletter. 23:7–8. 1963.

15190. ______. Manurial treatment of greens. New Zealand Institute for Turf Culture Newsletter. 23:8–9. 1963.

15191. ______. Seasonal notes. New Zealand Institute for Turf Culture Newsletter. 23:9–11. 1963.

15192. ______. Winter management of rugby grounds. New Zealand Institute for Turf Culture Newsletter. 24:2–4. 1963.

15193. ______. Turf management. New Zealand Institute for Turf Culture Newsletter. 25:4–5. 1963.

15194. ______. Seasonal notes. New Zealand Institute for Turf Culture Newsletter. 25:9–12. 1963.

15195. ______. Fine turf playing areas (bowls, golf, cricket wickets, croquet, tennis, etc.). New Zealand Institute for Turf Culture Newsletter. 27:8–10. 1963.

15196. ______. Off-season management of bowling greens. New Zealand Institute for Turf Culture Newsletter. 27:12–13. 1963.

15197. ______. Soil acidity in greenkeeping. New Zealand Institute for Turf Culture Newsletter. 29:2–3. 1964.

15198. ______. Recent developments in lawn bowling establishment. New Zealand Institute for Turf Culture Newsletter. 1964. 29:6–10. 1964.

15199. ______. Colour effect on temperatures under rubber bowls mats. New Zealand Institute for Turf Culture Newsletter. 29:10–11. 1964.

15200. ______. Weed control. New Zealand Institute for Turf Culture Newsletter. 30:11–13. 1964.

15201. ______. Soil acidity correction. New Zealand Institute for Turf Culture Newsletter. 30:13–14. 1964.

15202. ______. Lawns and the home. New Zealand Institute for Turf Culture Newsletter. 31:13–15. 1964.

15203. ______. Stock problems on golf greens. New Zealand Institute for Turf Culture Newsletter. 32:2–3. 1964.

15204. ______. Rates of seeding. New Zealand Institute for Turf Culture Newsletter. 32:6–7. 1964.

15205. ______. Kikuyu grass on golf greens. New Zealand Institute for Turf Culture Newsletter. 32:7–8. 1964.

15206. ______. Seasonal notes: winter playing fields, racecourses, fine turf areas. New Zealand Institute for Turf Culture Newsletter. 33:3–7. 1964.

15207. ______. The acid theory in sports turf management. New Zealand Institute for Turf Culture Newsletter. 33:7–11. 1964.

15208. ______. Winter manuring of sports turf. New Zealand Institute for Turf Culture Newsletter. 33:12–13. 1964.

15209. ______. Current research at Milson Experimental area. New Zealand Institute for Turf Culture Newsletter. 34:2–6. 1964.

15210. ______. Seasonal notes: fine turf areas, winter sports areas, race-courses. New Zealand Institute for Turf Culture Newsletter. 34:6–8. 1964.

15211. ______. "Weed" greens. New Zealand Institute for Turf Culture Newsletter. 34:11–13. 1964.

15212. ______. Plastic covers for winter sports areas. New Zealand Institute for Turf Culture Newsletter. 34:14. 1964.

15213. ______. New bowling greens from old. New Zealand Institute for Turf Culture Newsletter. 35:2–6. 1965.

15214. ______. Seasonal notes: fine turf areas, winter sports areas, soil tests. New Zealand Institute for Turf Culture Newsletter. 35:6–9. 1965.

15215. ______. Keeping abreast of research. New Zealand Institute for Turf Culture Newsletter. 35:9–10. 1965.

15216. ______. Seasonal notes: fine turf areas, winter sports areas, race-courses. New Zealand Institute for Turf Culture Newsletter. 36:2–4. 1965.

15217. ______. The importance of phosphates in turf thrift. New Zealand Institute for Turf Culture Newsletter. 36:4–6. 1965.

15218. ______. Consolidation and compaction. New Zealand Institute for Turf Culture Newsletter. 36:7–9. 1965.

15219. ______. Common defects in greens management. New Zealand Institute for Turf Culture Newsletter. 37:5–6. 1965.

15220. ______. Manurial treatment of racecourses. New Zealand Institute for Turf Culture Newsletter. 37:8. 1965.

15221. ______. Management of winter sports areas. New Zealand Institute for Turf Culture Newsletter. 37:9–11. 1965.

15222. ______. Seasonal notes. New Zealand Institute for Turf Culture Newsletter. 37:12–13. 1965.

15223. ______. Renewal of golf greens. New Zealand Institute for Turf Culture Newsletter. 37:14–15. 1965.

15224. ______. Seasonal notes. New Zealand Institute for Turf Culture Newsletter. 38:10–12. 1965.

15225. ______. Have we the answer to *Paspalum?* New Zealand Institute for Turf Culture Newsletter. 39:4–5. 1965.

15226. ______. Importance of fertilizer balance. New Zealand Institute for Turf Culture Newsletter. 39:6–7. 1965.

15227. ______. Seasonal notes: winter sports grounds, race-courses, fine turf playing areas. New Zealand Institute for Turf Culture Newsletter. 39:7–11. 1965.

15228. ______. Watering of greens. New Zealand Institute for Turf Culture Newsletter. 39:11–12. 1965.

15229. ______. *Cotula* bowling greens in the North Island. New Zealand Institute for Turf Culture Newsletter. 39:12–13. 1965.

15230. ______. Mole draining on golf greens. New Zealand Institute for Turf Culture Newsletter. 39:13–14. 1965.

15231. ______. Experiment with strains of *Cynodon.* New Zealand Institute for Turf Culture Newsletter. 40:11. 1965.

15232. ______. The influence of trial plots on practical greenkeeping. New Zealand Institute for Turf Culture Newsletter. 41:7–8. 1966.

15233. ______. Seasonal notes: fine turf areas, winter playing areas, race-courses. New Zealand Institute for Turf Culture Newsletter. 41:2–5. 1966.

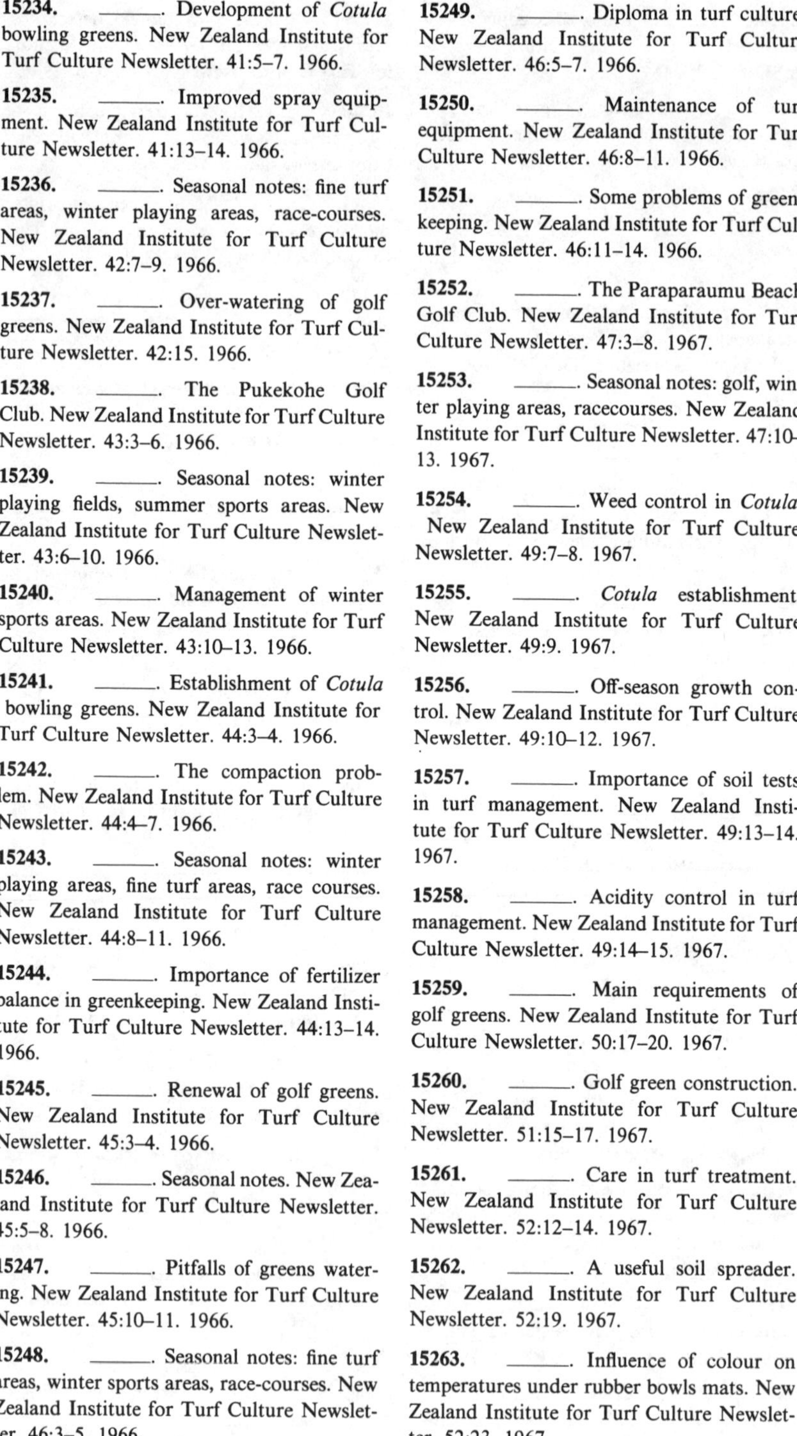

15234. ______. Development of *Cotula* bowling greens. New Zealand Institute for Turf Culture Newsletter. 41:5–7. 1966.

15235. ______. Improved spray equipment. New Zealand Institute for Turf Culture Newsletter. 41:13–14. 1966.

15236. ______. Seasonal notes: fine turf areas, winter playing areas, race-courses. New Zealand Institute for Turf Culture Newsletter. 42:7–9. 1966.

15237. ______. Over-watering of golf greens. New Zealand Institute for Turf Culture Newsletter. 42:15. 1966.

15238. ______. The Pukekohe Golf Club. New Zealand Institute for Turf Culture Newsletter. 43:3–6. 1966.

15239. ______. Seasonal notes: winter playing fields, summer sports areas. New Zealand Institute for Turf Culture Newsletter. 43:6–10. 1966.

15240. ______. Management of winter sports areas. New Zealand Institute for Turf Culture Newsletter. 43:10–13. 1966.

15241. ______. Establishment of *Cotula* bowling greens. New Zealand Institute for Turf Culture Newsletter. 44:3–4. 1966.

15242. ______. The compaction problem. New Zealand Institute for Turf Culture Newsletter. 44:4–7. 1966.

15243. ______. Seasonal notes: winter playing areas, fine turf areas, race courses. New Zealand Institute for Turf Culture Newsletter. 44:8–11. 1966.

15244. ______. Importance of fertilizer balance in greenkeeping. New Zealand Institute for Turf Culture Newsletter. 44:13–14. 1966.

15245. ______. Renewal of golf greens. New Zealand Institute for Turf Culture Newsletter. 45:3–4. 1966.

15246. ______. Seasonal notes. New Zealand Institute for Turf Culture Newsletter. 45:5–8. 1966.

15247. ______. Pitfalls of greens watering. New Zealand Institute for Turf Culture Newsletter. 45:10–11. 1966.

15248. ______. Seasonal notes: fine turf areas, winter sports areas, race-courses. New Zealand Institute for Turf Culture Newsletter. 46:3–5. 1966.

15249. ______. Diploma in turf culture. New Zealand Institute for Turf Culture Newsletter. 46:5–7. 1966.

15250. ______. Maintenance of turf equipment. New Zealand Institute for Turf Culture Newsletter. 46:8–11. 1966.

15251. ______. Some problems of greenkeeping. New Zealand Institute for Turf Culture Newsletter. 46:11–14. 1966.

15252. ______. The Paraparaumu Beach Golf Club. New Zealand Institute for Turf Culture Newsletter. 47:3–8. 1967.

15253. ______. Seasonal notes: golf, winter playing areas, racecourses. New Zealand Institute for Turf Culture Newsletter. 47:10–13. 1967.

15254. ______. Weed control in *Cotula.* New Zealand Institute for Turf Culture Newsletter. 49:7–8. 1967.

15255. ______. *Cotula* establishment. New Zealand Institute for Turf Culture Newsletter. 49:9. 1967.

15256. ______. Off-season growth control. New Zealand Institute for Turf Culture Newsletter. 49:10–12. 1967.

15257. ______. Importance of soil tests in turf management. New Zealand Institute for Turf Culture Newsletter. 49:13–14. 1967.

15258. ______. Acidity control in turf management. New Zealand Institute for Turf Culture Newsletter. 49:14–15. 1967.

15259. ______. Main requirements of golf greens. New Zealand Institute for Turf Culture Newsletter. 50:17–20. 1967.

15260. ______. Golf green construction. New Zealand Institute for Turf Culture Newsletter. 51:15–17. 1967.

15261. ______. Care in turf treatment. New Zealand Institute for Turf Culture Newsletter. 52:12–14. 1967.

15262. ______. A useful soil spreader. New Zealand Institute for Turf Culture Newsletter. 52:19. 1967.

15263. ______. Influence of colour on temperatures under rubber bowls mats. New Zealand Institute for Turf Culture Newsletter. 52:23. 1967.

15264. ______. Basic principles in greenkeeping. New Zealand Institute for Turf Culture Newsletter. 53:3–4. 1968.

15265. ______. Effects of mowing height on turf formation. New Zealand Institute for Turf Culture Newsletter. 53:14–17. 1968.

15266. ______. Establishing a home lawn. New Zealand Institute for Turf Culture Newsletter. 53:18–19. 1968.

15267. ______. Seasonal notes. New Zealand Institute for Turf Culture Newsletter. 53:21–22. 1968.

15268. ______. Seasonal notes. New Zealand Institute for Turf Culture Newsletter. 54:11–15. 1968.

15269. ______. Bromacil on *Cotula.* New Zealand Institute for Turf Culture Newsletter. 54:17. 1968.

15270. ______. Importance of balanced nutrition. New Zealand Institute for Turf Culture Newsletter. 54:20–21. 1968.

15271. ______. Turf management observations. New Zealand Institute for Turf Culture Newsletter. 55:3–7. 1968.

15272. ______. Fine turf sports areas. New Zealand Institute for Turf Culture Newsletter. 55:10–14. 1968.

15273. ______. Compaction and its effects on turf. New Zealand Institute for Turf Culture Newsletter. 56:20–21. 1968.

15274. ______. Aids to greenkeeping. New Zealand Institute for Turf Culture Newsletter. 57:9–10. 1968.

15275. Paulin, G. N. Control of grass weeds in fine turf. New Zealand Institute for Turf Culture Newsletter. 57:23–25. 1968.

15276. Walker, C. Auckland bowling greens. New Zealand Institute for Turf Culture Newsletter. 59:3–4. 1969.

15277. ______. Application of spray materials. New Zealand Institute for Turf Culture Newsletter. 59:5–6. 1969.

15278. ______. N. Z. golf courses. New Zealand Institute for Turf Culture Newsletter. 60:3–5. 1969.

15279. ______. Grooming of greens. New Zealand Institute for Turf Culture Newsletter. 60:6–7. 1969.

15280. ______. Seasonal notes. New Zealand Institute for Turf Culture Newsletter. 60:9–15. 1969.

15281. ______. *Poa annua* destruction. New Zealand Institute for Turf Culture Newsletter. 60:17–18. 1969.

15282. ______. Balanced fertility. New Zealand Institute for Turf Culture Newsletter. 60:18–19. 1969.

15283. ______. *Poa annua* control. New Zealand Institute for Turf Culture Newsletter. 61:5–7. 1969.

15284. ______. Fine turf sports areas. New Zealand Institute for Turf Culture Newsletter. 61:11–15. 1969.

15285. ______. Control of *Poa annua* in Australia. New Zealand Institute for Turf Culture Newsletter. 62:5–9. 1969.

15286. ______. Function of rollers on sports fields. New Zealand Institute for Turf Culture Newsletter. 62:10–11. 1969.

15287. ______. Seasonal notes. New Zealand Institute for Turf Culture Newsletter. 62:21–28. 1969.

15288. ______. Impressions of Australian sports areas. New Zealand Institute for Turf Culture Newsletter. 62 Supplement:1–24. 1969.

15289. ______. Golf course progress. New Zealand Institute for Turf Culture Newsletter. 63:3–8. 1969.

15290. ______. Fine turf playing areas. New Zealand Institute for Turf Culture Newsletter. 63:12–15. 1969.

15291. ______. Renovation of sod-bound greens. New Zealand Institute for Turf Culture Newsletter. 63:17. 1969.

15292. ______. An efficient sod cutter. New Zealand Institute for Turf Culture Newsletter. 64. 7–9. 1969.

15293. ______. Control of coarse grasses in fine turf. New Zealand Institute for Turf Culture Newsletter. 64:12. 1969.

15294. ______. Seasonal notes. New Zealand Institute for Turf Culture Newsletter. 64:23–27. 1969.

15295. ______. Fine turf areas, seasonal notes. New Zealand Institute For Turfculture Newsletter. 65:28–33. 1970.

15296. ______. Fine turf areas, seasonal notes. New Zealand Institute For Turf Culture Newsletter. 66:9–12. 1970.

15297. ______. Establishment of greens from turf. New Zealand Institute For Turf Culture Newsletter. 66:13, 15. 1970.

15298. ______. Recent developments in greenkeeping equipment. New Zealand Institute For Turf Culture Newsletter. 66:16–24. 1970.

15299. ______. *Cotula* establishment and management. New Zealand Institute For Turf Culture Newsletter. 66:25, 27–29. 1970.

15300. ______. Elimination of coarse grasses from golf greens. New Zealand Institute for Turf Culture Newsletter. 66:32–33. 1970.

15301. ______. Fine sports turf areas. New Zealand Institute for Turf Culture Newsletter. 67:15, 18–19. 1970.

15302. ______. A mud bath for bowling greens. New Zealand Institute For Turf Culture Newsletter. 68:15. 1970.

15303. ______. Seasonal notes. New Zealand Institute For Turf Culture Newsletter. 68:18–19, 21–25. 1970.

15304. ______. Current turf research in N.S.W. New Zealand Institute For Turf Culture Newsletter. 69:7–8. 1970.

15305. ______. Seasonal notes fine turf area. New Zealand Institute For Turf Culture Newsletter. 69:18–24. 1970.

15306. ______. Progress at the northern bowling club. New Zealand Institute For Turf Culture Newsletter. 70:4–9. 1970.

15307. ______. Conversion of grass bowling greens to *Cotula.* New Zealand Institute For Turf Culture Newsletter. 70:15, 18. 1970.

15308. ______. Seasonal notes fine turf areas. New Zealand Institute for Turf Culture Newsletter. Vol. 70:22–27. 1970.

15309. ______. Seasonal notes fine turf areas. New Zealand Institute for Turf Culture Newsletter. 72:63–67. 1970.

15310. ______. Modern greenkeeping equipment. New Zealand Institute for Turf Culture Newsletter. 72:58–59. 1971.

15311. ______. Fine turf sports areas. New Zealand Institute For Turf Culture Newsletter. 73:91–95. 1971.

15312. ______. Modern greenkeeping equipment. New Zealand Institute For Turf Culture Newsletter. 73:97. 1971.

15313. ______. Fine turf areas. New Zealand Institute For Turf Culture Newsletter. 74:115–122. 1971.

15314. ______. Seasonal notes fine turf areas. New Zealand Institute For Turf Culture Newsletter. 75:159–165. 1971.

15315. ______. Seasonal notes fine turf areas. New Zealand Institute for Turf Culture Newsletter. 76:192–198. 1971.

15316. ______. Turf culture. Simon Printing Co., Ltd. New Zealand. pp. 1–352. 1971.

15317. ______. Fine turf areas. New Zealand Institute For Turf Culture Newsletter. 77:20–23. 1972.

15318. ______. Modifications to greenkeeping equipment. New Zealand Institute for Turf Culture Newsletter. 78:40–41, 43. 1972.

15319. ______. Balanced fertility. New Zealand Institute for Turf Culture Newsletter. 78:43, 45–46. 1972.

15320. ______. Triplex putting green mowers. New Zealand Institute for Turf Culture Newsletter. 78:49, 51. 1972.

15321. ______. Observations on overseas bowling greens. New Zealand Institute for Turf Culture Newsletter. 80:108–112. 1972.

15322. ______. Fine turf areas. New Zealand Institute for Turf Culture Newsletter. 80:125–137. 1972.

15323. ______. Fine turf areas. New Zealand Institute for Turf Culture Newsletter. 81:171–178. 1972.

15325. Walker, R. T. Trends in highway seeding operations. Highway Research News. 12:67–73. 1964.

15326. Walker, W. H. and C. Y. Ward. Phytotoxicity of preemergence herbicides on overseeded bermudagrass turf. Agronomy Abstracts. p. 72. 1970.

15327. Walker, W. M. and J. Pesek. Chemical composition of Kentucky bluegrass as a function of applied nitrogen, phosphorus, and potassium. Agronomy Journal. 55(3):247–250. 1963.

15328. ______. Yield of Kentucky bluegrass *(Poa pratensis)* as a function of its percentage of nitrogen, phosphorus, and potassium. Agronomy Journal. 59(1):44–47. 1967.

15329. Wallace, A. T., G. B. Killinger, R. W. Bledsoe, and D. B. Duncan. Design, analysis and results of an experiment on response of pangolagrass and Pensacola Bahiagrass to time, rate and source of nitrogen. Florida Agricultural Experiment Station Bulletin 581. 1957.

15330. Wallace, C. A. Crownvetch for spoilbank reclamation and grading. Second Crownvetch Symposium, Pennsylvania State University. 6:79–82. 1968.

15331. Wallace, E. and W. M. Davidson. Protection against false claims for fungicides and insecticides. Turf Culture. 2(4):244–246. 1942.

15333. Wallner, W. E. Turfgrass insect control. Michigan Turfgrass Research Report. 3(1):9. 1965.

15334. ______. Turfgrass insect control. 42nd Annual Michigan Turfgrass Conference Proceedings. 1:54–58. 1972.

15335. Walls, I. G. The maintenance of turf. Gardeners Chronicle. 159(13):295. 1966.

15336. ______. Acid mat of turf. Gardeners Chronicle. 160(12):10. 1966.

15337. Walsh, L. M. Sources of nitrogen fertilizer. Wisconsin Turfgrass Conference Proceedings. 2 pp. 1964.

15338. Walsh, L. M. and D. R. Keeney. The pollution problem (understanding the nitrogen cycle). The Greenmaster. 6(9):6–9. 1970.

15339. Walsh, S. Sprinkler irrigation for roadside vegetation in urban areas. Highway Research News. 16:21–22. 1964.

15341. Walter, R. J. Which kind of pipe? P.V.C. Golf Course Reporter. 32(6):42, 44, 46. 1964.

15342. Walton, R. Athletic tracks: water requirements. Parks, Golf Courses, and Sports Grounds. 32(8):691–692. 1967.

15343. ______. Irrigation on composite surfaces. Parks, Golf Courses, & Sports Grounds. 33(3):227–230. 1967.

15344. ______. Irrigation—facts and fallacies. The Groundsman. 21(5):27–30, 36. 1968.

15345. Walton, W. R. The southern green June beetle as a pest on golf links. USGA Green Section Bulletin. 1(4):60–63. 1921.

15346. ______. The changa or West Indian mole cricket as a pest on golf courses. USGA Green Section Bulletin. 1(6):104–106. 1921.

15347. ______. The control of white grubs on golf links. USGA Green Section Bulletin. 1(9):174–177. 1921.

15348. ______. Cutworms on golf greens. USGA Green Section Bulletin. 9(9):-156–157. 1929.

15349. Ward, C. Y. Progress report on turf research at Mississippi State University. Southern Turfgrass Association Conference Proceedings. pp. 18–21. 1965.

15350. ______. Nitrogen uptake and assimilation. Agronomy Abstracts. p. 37. 1966.

15351. ______. What is grass chemically. Proceedings of the Midwest Regional Turf Conference. pp. 62–67. 1966.

15352. ______. Sod production in the south. Proceedings of the Midwest Regional Turf Conference. pp. 82–84. 1966.

15353. ______. Turf research in Mississippi. Proceedings Southeastern Highway Officials. pp. 20–23. 1967.

15354. ______. Winter injury to turf. Southern Turfgrass Association Conference Proceedings. pp. 21–23. 1967.

15355. ______. Turf research at Mississippi State University. Southern Turfgrass Association Conference Proceedings. pp. 31–32. 1967.

15356. ______. Preemergence treatment of *Poa annua* on golf greens. Auburn University Annual Turfgrass Short Course. 9:13–15. 1968.

15357. ______. Soils—their role in turf production and management. Southern Turfgrass Association Conference Proceedings. pp. 25–30. 1968.

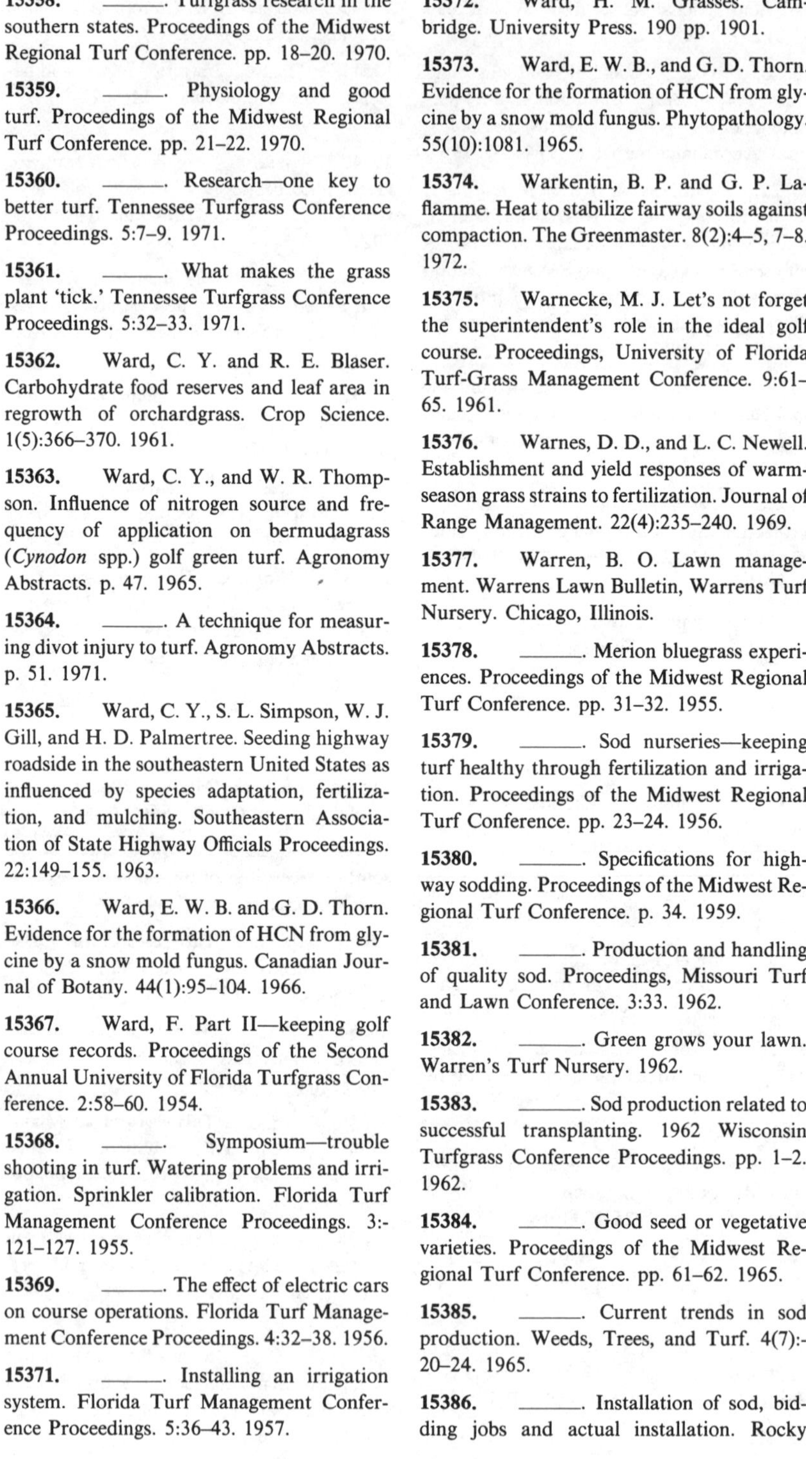

15358. ______. Turfgrass research in the southern states. Proceedings of the Midwest Regional Turf Conference. pp. 18–20. 1970.

15359. ______. Physiology and good turf. Proceedings of the Midwest Regional Turf Conference. pp. 21–22. 1970.

15360. ______. Research—one key to better turf. Tennessee Turfgrass Conference Proceedings. 5:7–9. 1971.

15361. ______. What makes the grass plant 'tick.' Tennessee Turfgrass Conference Proceedings. 5:32–33. 1971.

15362. Ward, C. Y. and R. E. Blaser. Carbohydrate food reserves and leaf area in regrowth of orchardgrass. Crop Science. 1(5):366–370. 1961.

15363. Ward, C. Y., and W. R. Thompson. Influence of nitrogen source and frequency of application on bermudagrass (*Cynodon* spp.) golf green turf. Agronomy Abstracts. p. 47. 1965.

15364. ______. A technique for measuring divot injury to turf. Agronomy Abstracts. p. 51. 1971.

15365. Ward, C. Y., S. L. Simpson, W. J. Gill, and H. D. Palmertree. Seeding highway roadside in the southeastern United States as influenced by species adaptation, fertilization, and mulching. Southeastern Association of State Highway Officials Proceedings. 22:149–155. 1963.

15366. Ward, E. W. B. and G. D. Thorn. Evidence for the formation of HCN from glycine by a snow mold fungus. Canadian Journal of Botany. 44(1):95–104. 1966.

15367. Ward, F. Part II—keeping golf course records. Proceedings of the Second Annual University of Florida Turfgrass Conference. 2:58–60. 1954.

15368. ______. Symposium—trouble shooting in turf. Watering problems and irrigation. Sprinkler calibration. Florida Turf Management Conference Proceedings. 3:-121–127. 1955.

15369. ______. The effect of electric cars on course operations. Florida Turf Management Conference Proceedings. 4:32–38. 1956.

15371. ______. Installing an irrigation system. Florida Turf Management Conference Proceedings. 5:36–43. 1957.

15372. Ward, H. M. Grasses. Cambridge. University Press. 190 pp. 1901.

15373. Ward, E. W. B., and G. D. Thorn. Evidence for the formation of HCN from glycine by a snow mold fungus. Phytopathology. 55(10):1081. 1965.

15374. Warkentin, B. P. and G. P. Laflamme. Heat to stabilize fairway soils against compaction. The Greenmaster. 8(2):4–5, 7–8. 1972.

15375. Warnecke, M. J. Let's not forget the superintendent's role in the ideal golf course. Proceedings, University of Florida Turf-Grass Management Conference. 9:61–65. 1961.

15376. Warnes, D. D., and L. C. Newell. Establishment and yield responses of warm-season grass strains to fertilization. Journal of Range Management. 22(4):235–240. 1969.

15377. Warren, B. O. Lawn management. Warrens Lawn Bulletin, Warrens Turf Nursery. Chicago, Illinois.

15378. ______. Merion bluegrass experiences. Proceedings of the Midwest Regional Turf Conference. pp. 31–32. 1955.

15379. ______. Sod nurseries—keeping turf healthy through fertilization and irrigation. Proceedings of the Midwest Regional Turf Conference. pp. 23–24. 1956.

15380. ______. Specifications for highway sodding. Proceedings of the Midwest Regional Turf Conference. p. 34. 1959.

15381. ______. Production and handling of quality sod. Proceedings, Missouri Turf and Lawn Conference. 3:33. 1962.

15382. ______. Green grows your lawn. Warren's Turf Nursery. 1962.

15383. ______. Sod production related to successful transplanting. 1962 Wisconsin Turfgrass Conference Proceedings. pp. 1–2. 1962.

15384. ______. Good seed or vegetative varieties. Proceedings of the Midwest Regional Turf Conference. pp. 61–62. 1965.

15385. ______. Current trends in sod production. Weeds, Trees, and Turf. 4(7):-20–24. 1965.

15386. ______. Installation of sod, bidding jobs and actual installation. Rocky

Mountain Regional Turfgrass Conference. 12:26–33. 1966.

15387. ______. The business of sod installation—estimating, bidding and installing. Turf-Grass Times. 2(1):9–11, 21. 1966.

15388. ______. The sod industry. Wisconsin Turfgrass Conference Proceedings. pp. 51–52. 1966.

15389. ______. Merits of vegetative establishment. International Turfgrass Conference Proceedings. 38:52–53. 1967.

15390. ______. My experience with bluegrass varieties. Ohio Turfgrass Conference Proceedings. pp. 47–50. 1967.

15391. ______. Growing and distribution of sod. Turf Clippings. University of Massachusetts. 2(2):43–44. 1967.

15392. ______. The future of the sod industry. Seed World. 103(5):8–9, 20. 1968.

15393. ______. Producing quality sod. Illinois Turfgrass Conference Proceedings. pp. 76–77. 1969.

15394. ______. Vegetative planting of grasses—1970. Proceedings of the Midwest Regional Turf Conference. p. 65. 1970.

15395. ______. Productions and plans for Warren's A–20 bluegrass. Proceedings of the Midwest Regional Turf Conference. pp. 81–82. 1969.

15396. ______. Experiences with retail and contract users of sod. Rutgers University Short Course in Turf Management. 38:31–32. 1970.

15397. ______. Sodding techniques. 12th Illinois Turfgrass Conference Proceedings. p. 28. 1971.

15398. ______. Plugging and sodding vegetative bluegrass. Midwest Regional Turf Conference Proceedings. pp. 72–73. 1971.

15399. ______. Establishing bluegrass by vegetative methods. Missouri Lawn and Turf Conference Proceedings. 12:26–27. 1971.

15400. ______. Vegetative propagation of Kentucky bluegrass. Rocky Mountain Regional Turfgrass Conference Proceedings. 18:33–34. 1972.

15401. ______. Recent trends in sod production. Rocky Mountain Regional Turfgrass Conference Proceedings. 18:61–62. 1972.

15402. Warren, B. and D. Habenicht. Highway sodding tests and results. Proceedings of the Midwest Regional Turf Conference. pp. 28–29. 1959.

15403. Warren, J. T. Research in turf management. Gardeners Chronicle. 153(25):-440–441. 1963.

15404. Warren, L. O. and J. E. Roberts. A Hesperiid, at *Alopedes campestris* (BDV.) as a pest of bermuda grass pastures. Journal of the Kansas Entomological Society. 29(4):-139–141. 1956.

15405. Warren, R. Weed control on highway shoulders, fence rows, and ditchbanks. Oregon State University Agricultural Extension Service. 2 pp. 1970.

15406. Warren, R. M. Sod grower associations a review and development. Proceedings of the Midwest Regional Turf Conference. pp. 56–58. 1966.

15407. ______. How sod should be handled in a garden center. Seed World. 99(4):20. 1966.

15408. ______. What good is a sod growers association? Weeds, Trees and Turf. 5(5):-32–34, 38–39. 1966.

15409. Warren, W. H. Bake oven soil sterilization. Parks and Recreation. 24(9):-410–413. 1941.

15410. Warrick, G. C. Turf grasses. Gardeners Chronicle. 146(25):338–339. 1959.

15411. ______. Turf grasses. Gardeners Chronicle. 147(12):162–163. 1960.

15412. ______. Turf grasses. Gardeners Chronicle. 147(24):486–487. 1960.

15413. ______. Know your grasses. The Groundsman. 17(1):22, 24. 1963.

15414. ______. Some notes on recently introduced cultivars of lawn and turf grasses. The Groundsman. 19(5):34–35. 1966.

15415. Wascom, B. W. and W. A. Young. Turf—recommended practices—Louisiana. Annual Southern Weed Conference Research Report. 22:86–87. 1969.

15416. Wasmuth, A. G. The control of broadleaved weeds in sports turf with a mixture of ioxynil and mecoprop (MCPP). New Zealand Institute For Turf Culture Newsletter. 74:129–130. 1971.

15417. Waterhouse, F. L. Humidity and temperature in grass microclimates with reference to insolation. Nature. 166(4214):232–233. 1950.

15418. ______. Microclimatological profiles in grass cover in relation to biological problems. Quarterly Journal of the Royal Meteorological Society. 81(347):63–71. 1955.

15419. Waters, D. F. Soil testing for golf courses. New Zealand Institute for Turf Culture Newsletter. 11:3. 1961.

15420. ______. The value of complete soil tests. New Zealand Institute for Turf Culture Newsletter. 25:7–9. 1963.

15421. Waters, H. A. New methods of application of 2, 4–D. Greenkeeper's Reporter. 16(5):5–7. 1948.

15422. ______. Promising new chemicals. Greenkeepers' Reporter. 16(4):30–31. 1948.

15423. ______. New methods of application of 2, 4–D. Proceedings of Midwest Regional Turf Conference. pp. 73–76. 1948.

15424. ______. Promising new chemicals. Proceedings of Midwest Regional Turf Conference. pp. 79–82. 1948.

15425. Watkin, E. M. and G. R. Sagar. Residual activity of paraquat in soils. Weed Research. 11(1):1–11. 1971.

15426. ______. Residual activity of paraquat in soils. Weed Research. 11(4):247–256. 1971.

15427. Watkins, H. How to produce commercial sod. Kentucky Cooperative Extension Service Publication. 10–72. 3 pp.

15428. ______. Herbicide research and finesse. Proceedings of the Midwest Regional Turf Conference. pp. 35–36. 1968.

15430. Watkins, J. A., and M. E. Snoddy. Turf irrigation manual. Telsco Industries, Dallas, Texas. 1965.

15431. Watkins, J. M. The growth habits and chemical composition of bromegrass as affected by different environmental conditions. Journal American Society Agronomy. 32(7):527–538. 1940.

15432. Watkins, J. M., G. W. Conrey, and M. W. Evans. The distribution of Canada bluegrass and Kentucky bluegrass as related to some ecological factors. Journal of the American Society of Agronomy. 32(9):726–728. 1940.

15433. Watschke, T. L. Physiological responses of turfgrasses to high temperature stress. Ph.D. Thesis, Virginia Polytechnic Institute. 1971.

15434. Watschke, T. L. and R. E. Schmidt. Responses of some Kentucky bluegrass cultivars to high temperature and nitrogen fertility. Agronomy Abstracts. p. 56. 1969.

15435. ______. Performance of some Kentucky bluegrasses under high temperatures. Proceedings of the First International Turfgrass Research Conference. pp. 258–259. 1969.

15436. ______. Photosynthesis and respiration in Kentucky bluegrasses *(Poa pratensis* L.). Agronomy Abstracts. p. 51. 1971.

15437. Watschke, T. L., R. E. Schmidt, and R. E. Blaser. Responses of some Kentucky bluegrasses to high temperature and nitrogen fertility. Crop Science. 10(4):372–376. 1970.

15438. Watschke, T. L., R. E. Schmidt, E. W. Carson, and R. E. Blaser. Some metabolic phenomena of Kentucky bluegrass under high temperature. Crop Science. 12(1):-87–90. 1972.

15439. Watson, A. J., and J. K. Leasure. A promising new herbicide for use on turf. Agronomy Abstracts. p. 92. 1959.

15440. Watson, C. E. Turfgrasses and their adaptation to New Mexico. New Mexico Turfgrass Conference Proceedings. pp. 9–13. 1955.

15441. ______. General observations made on turf during the summer of 1956. New Mexico Turfgrass Conference Proceedings. pp. 1–3. 1956.

15442. ______. Turfgrass studies in New Mexico. Third Annual New Mexico Turfgrass Conference. Proceedings. pp. 14–15. 1957.

15443. Watson, C. K. Trends in modern turf irrigation. Southern Turfgrass Association Conference Proceedings. pp. 9–15. 1968.

15444. ______. New concepts in irrigation. Proceedings of the Midwest Regional Turf Conference. pp. 66–68. 1969.

15445. Watson, D. J. Three "turfeteers" leadway to contract maintenance. Turf-Grass Times. 8(2):22–24. 1972.

15446. Watson, D. P. Anatomical modification of velvet bentgrass *(Agrostis canina* L.) caused by soil treatment with 2, 4–dichlorophenoxyacetic acid. American Journal of Botany. 37(6):424–431. 1950.

15447. ______. Beautiful home grounds —through methods simplied for suburbanites. Home and Family Series Extension Bulletin 425. Michigan State University. 1963.

15448. Watson, E. B. Buying fertilisers. The Groundsman. 21(4):21–22. 1967.

15449. ______. Fertilisers for sports turf. The Groundsman. 22(9):14–19. 1969.

15450. ______. New pesticides. The Groundsman. 23(6):27. 1970.

15451. ______. Weed control and conservation. The Groundsman. 24(7):48 p. 1971.

15452. Watson, G. H. In Birmingham, they have a 12-month job. Golfdom. 13(2):-15–16. 1939.

15453. Watson, J. H. Plant and weed identification. Mississippi Cooperative Extension Service Publication 553. 1–4 pp. 1966.

15455. Watson, J. R. Southwest turf men meet. Golfdom. 21(3):82, 84–85. 1947.

15456. ______. Progress report on irrigation and compaction experiment. Pennsylvania State Turf Conference. 18:83–90. 1949.

15457. ______. Irrigation and compaction on established fairway turf. Ph.D. Thesis, Pennsylvania State University. 1950.

15458. ______. Effects of irrigation and compaction on established fairway turf. Rutgers University Short Course in Turf Management. 18:33–37. 1950.

15459. ______. Irrigation and compaction on established fairway turf. USGA Journal and Turf Management. 3(4):25–28. 1950.

15460. ______. Fertilization of turf. Proceedings of the 5th Annual Texas Turf Conference. pp. 86–93. 1951.

15461. ______. Turf management. Proceedings of the Annual Arizona Turf Conference. pp. 21–28. 1953.

15462. ______. Rye-bermuda transition. Golfdom. 27(10):46–47. 1953.

15463. ______. Soil moisture relations under turf. Proceedings of the Midwest Regional Turf Conference. pp. 35–42. 1953.

15464. ______. Water—Its relation to plant and root development. Oklahoma Turfgrass Conference Proceedings. 4–5 pp. 1953.

15465. ______. Water, weeds and waste. Golf Course Reporter. 22(6):10–13. 1954.

15466. ______. Water, weeds waste the maintenance budget. Golfdom. 28(2):54, 56, 78–79. 1954.

15467. ______. Water, weeds and waste. Oklahoma Turfgrass Conference Proceedings. 28–34 pp. 1954.

15468. ______. Soils—modification can be dangerous. Southern California Turfgrass Conference Proceedings. pp. 20–28. 1954.

15469. ______. Soil characteristics affecting root development. Florida Turf Management Conference Proceedings. 3:5–10. 1955.

15470. ______. Turfgrass in the South and borderline areas. Golf Course Reporter. 23(1):20–27. 1955.

15471. ______. Nutrient absorption by plants. Proceedings of the Midwest Regional Turf Conference. pp. 7–9. 1955.

15472. ______. Watering practices. New Mexico Turfgrass Conference Proceedings. 19–22 pp. 1955.

15473. ______. Changing your soil. New Mexico Turfgrass Conference Proceedings. 31–38 pp. 1955.

15474. ______. Soil moisture relations under turf. Sports Turfgrass Conference. Royal Canadian Golf Association Green Section. pp. 42–49. 1955.

15475. ______. Water, weeds, and waste. Rutgers University Short Course in Turf Management. 23:5. 1955.

15476. ______. Soil moisture relations under turfgrass. Southeastern Turfgrass Conference. 9:23–33. 1955.

15477. ______. Snow mold control. Golfdom. 30(5):40, 42. 1956.

15478. ______. Changing your soil. The Golf Course Reporter. 24(1):5–9. 1956.

15479. ______. Snowmold control. The Golf Course Reporter. 24(3):30–31. 1956.

15480. ______. The physiological characteristics of grasses. Oklahoma Turfgrass Conference Proceedings. 12–19 pp. 1956.

15481. ______. Vital: turfgrass fertilization. Park Maintenance. 9:44–46. 1956.

15482. ______. The influence of cultural practices in weed control. Parks and Recreation. 39(9):6–7. 1956.

15483. ______. Snowmold control. Pennsylvania State Turf Conference. 25:15–17. 1956.

15484. ______. Factors influencing the use of cool and warm season turfgrasses. Pennsylvania State Turf Conference. 25:89–93. 1956.

15485. ______. Snowmold control. Sports Turfgrass Conference. Royal Canadian Golf Association Green Section. pp. 24–26. 1956.

15486. ______. Renovation and management of athletic field turfgrass. Toro Manufacturing Corporation Leaflet. 1956.

15487. ______. The influence of cultural practices in weed control. Special Proceedings of the Turf Section Weed Society of America. pp. 35–42. 1956.

15488. ______. Fundamentals of nutrient absorption. Florida Turf Management Conference Proceedings. 5:15–19. 1957.

15489. ______. Turfgrass management problems under excessive rainfall. Golf Course Reporter. 25(8):15–16. 1957.

15490. ______. Protection from winterkill. Golfdom. 31(9):33, 60. 1957.

15491. ______. What you can do to minimize winterkill. Golfdom. 31(8):66–67. 1957.

15492. ______. New approach to reducing compaction in putting turf. Golfdom. 31(4):84, 86. 1957.

15493. ______. On the mowing of grass. New Mexico Turfgrass Conference Proceedings. pp.6–10. 1957.

15494. ______. Choosing a grass for your park. Parks and Recreation. 40(5):16–17. 1957.

15495. ______. The origin and development of soils. Parks and Recreation. 40(7):-13–15. 1957.

15496. ______. Some fundamental aspects of grass management. Texas Turfgrass Conference Proceedings. 12:1–8. 1957.

15497. ______. The chinch bug on St. Augustine grass. Florida Agricultural Experiment Station Bulletin 519. 1958.

15498. ______. South converting greens to fine-leaf bermuda. Golfdom. 32(4):64, 113. 1958.

15499. ______. Turfgrass maintenance. Oklahoma Turfgrass Conference Proceedings. pp. 19–22. 1958.

15500. ______. The physiological characteristics of grasses in relation to turfgrass management. Oklahoma Turfgrass Conference Proceedings. pp. 29–35. 1958.

15501. ______. Some basic soil considerations. Texas Turfgrass Conference Proceedings. 13:8–15. 1958.

15502. ______. Turfgrass engineering. Arizona Turf Conference Proceedings. pp. 22–25. 1959.

15503. ______. Physiology of grasses in relation to turfgrass management. Proceedings of the Midwest Regional Turf Conference. pp. 35–38. 1959.

15503a. ______. Principles of water management. Golf Course Reporter. 27(4):-44–48. 1959.

15504. ______. On the mowing of grass. Proceedings of the Midwest Regional Turf Conference. pp. 38–42. 1959.

15505. ______. Soil characteristics affecting root development. Rocky Mountain Regional Turfgrass Conference Proceedings. pp. 37–41. 1959.

15506. ______. Protecting golf greens against winterkill. 14th Annual Pacific Northwest Turf Conference. 14:37–40. 1960.

15507. ______. Water and its proper use. Southern Turfgrass Association Conference Proceedings. pp. 14–18. 1960.

15508. ______. Liming, fertilizing and watering fairways. Southern Turfgrass Association Conference Proceedings. pp. 25–29. 1960.

15509. ______. Tests on leaf removal and other lawn practices. Rutgers University Short Course in Turf Management. 28:1–5. 1960.

15510. ______. Water management practices on turf areas. Turf Clippings. University of Massachusetts. 1(5): A–18 to A–22. 1960.

15511. ______. Specific care of dormant turf—Northern grasses. International Turf-Grass Conference Proceedings. 32: 17–18. 1961.

15512. ______. Patterns of mowing. Northern California Turfgrass Institute Proceedings. pp. 35–39. 1961.

15514. ______. Some soil physical effects of traffic. Proceedings of the 16th Annual Texas Turf Conference. 16: 1–9. 1961.

15515. ______. Use of covers for plant protection. Proceedings of the 16th Annual Texas Turf Conference. 16:35–41. 1961.

15516. ______. Protecting golf greens against winterkill. Proceedings of University of Florida Turf-Grass Management Conference. 9:76–83. 1961.

15517. ______. Patterns of mowing. California Turfgrass Culture. 12(4):27–29. 1962.

15518. ______. The nature and prevention of winter injury. Golf Course Reporter. 30(9):22–28. 1962.

15519. ______. Protection of greens from winterkill. Iagreen. 1(2):9–14. 1962.

15520. ______. Putting the course to bed for the winter. International Turf-Grass Conference Proceedings. 33:8. 1962.

15521. ______. Managing athletic turfgrass areas. Proceedings of the Midwest Regional Turf Conference. pp. 87–89. 1962.

15522. ______. What is adequate lawn turf fertilization. Proceedings of the Midwest Regional Turf Conference. pp. 90–91. 1962.

15523. ______. Concepts of turfgrass watering. New Mexico Turfgrass Conference Proceedings. pp. 4–10. 1962.

15524. ______. Effect of cultural practices on weed invasion and control. Oklahoma Turfgrass Conference Proceedings. pp. 1–6. 1962.

15525. ______. Weed control through fertilization athletic fields and lawns. Oklahoma Turfgrass Conference Proceedings. p. 14. 1962.

15526. ______. Some soil physical effects of traffic. Southeastern Turfgrass Conference Proceedings. 16:3–16. 1962.

15527. ______. Snowmold and winter protection of golf greens. 1962 Wisconsin Turfgrass Conference Proceedings. pp. 1–4. 1962.

15528. ______. Turfgrass management with excessive rainfall. Iagreen, 30th Annual Conference Proceedings. pp. 2–5. 1963.

15529. ______. Use and misuse of water. Oklahoma Turfgrass Conference Proceedings. pp. 1–4. 1963.

15530. ______. Patterns of mowing. Park Maintenance. 16:32–33. 1963.

15531. ______. Mowing practices—agronomic principles. Proceedings of the 18th Annual Texas Turfgrass Conference. 18:4–7. 1963.

15532. ______. Methods of minimizing winter damage. Agronomy Abstracts. p. 103. 1964.

15533. ______. Communications: from the superintendent to club officers. Golf Course Reporter. 32(10): pp. 16–18, 20, 22, 24. 1964.

15534. ______. Turfgrass management with excessive rainfall. Iagreen. Iowa Turfgrass Conference Proceedings. 30:2–5. 1964.

15535. ______. Mowing, an ecological factor. Proceedings of the Northwest Turfgrass Conference. 18:22–25. 1964.

15536. ______. Frost—its effects and prevention. Proceedings of the 19th Annual Texas Turfgrass Conference. 19:8–11. 1964.

15537. ______. Turf—the integrator of space and water. Proceedings of the Midwest Regional Turf Conference. pp. 17–18. 1965.

15538. ______. Economical automatic lawn watering systems. Proceedings of the Midwest Regional Turf Conference. pp. 32–34. 1965.

15539. ______. Turf renovation. Proceedings of the Midwest Regional Turf Conference. pp. 47–48. 1965.

15540. ______. Mowing practices—agronomic principles. Oklahoma Turfgrass Conference. 1965.

15541. ______. Why topdress. Southern Turfgrass Association Conference Proceedings. pp. 8–9. 1965.

15542. ______. Methods of minimizing winter damage. USGA Green Section Record. 2(5):13. 1965.

15543. ______. Winter protection of greens. Proceedings of the Mid-Atlantic Association of Golf Course Superintendents. pp. 26–27. 1966.

15544. ______. Efficiency through long-range planning. Proceedings Missouri Lawn and Turf Conference. 7:7–10. 1966.

15545. ______. Frost protection. Proceedings of the Northwest Turfgrass Conference. 20:68–74. 1966.

15546. ______. Turfgrass and the weather. Texas Turfgrass Conference Proceedings. 21:72–76. 1966.

15547. ______. Water requirements as a function of clipping height and frequency. Proceedings of the Turfgrass Sprinkler Irrigation Conference. 6 pp. 1966.

15548. ______. Frost: its effects and prevention. Turf-Grass Times. 2(1):12–13. 1966.

15549. ______. Water requirements as a function of clipping height and frequency. California Turfgrass Culture. 17(1):1–3. 1967.

15550. ______. Peat classifications. California Turfgrass Culture. 17(3):21–24. 1967.

15551. ______. Mowing theory and practices. 18th Annual Central Plains Turfgrass Conference. 1967.

15552. ______. Peat classifications. International Turfgrass Conference Proceedings. 38:45–49. 1967.

15553. ______. Equipment for the future—mechanical and mental. Missouri Lawn and Turf Conference Proceedings. 8:1–4. 1967.

15554. ______. Using equipment effectively. Missouri Lawn and Turf Conference Proceedings. 8:42–45. 1967.

15555. ______. Small area irrigation systems. Ohio Turfgrass Conference Proceedings. pp. 10–14. 1967.

15556. ______. Care of turf on football fields. Texas Turfgrass Conference Proceedings. 22:7–13. 1967.

15557. ______. Cutting labor costs in turf management. Texas Turfgrass Conference Proceedings. 22:20–25. 1967.

15558. ______. Watering practices as a function of clipping height and frequency. Weeds, Trees, and Turf. 6(6):10–13. 1967.

15559. ______. Blankets to protect golf greens against winter injury. Agronomy Abstracts. p. 61. 1968.

15560. ______. Peat and organic additives. Proceedings of the Midwest Regional Turf Conference. pp. 55–57. 1968.

15561. ______. Watering greens effectively—a review. Proceedings of the Midwest Regional Turf Conference. pp. 72–73. 1968.

15562. ______. Theory and practices of mowing. Northwest Turfgrass Topics. 10(1):1, 4, 7. 1968.

15563. ______. Mowing-irrigation relationships. Parks, Golf Courses, and Sports Grounds. 33(9):733–738. 1968.

15564. ______. Turfgrass culture on American athletic fields. Parks, Golf Courses, and Sports Grounds. 33(12):1040–1045. 1968.

15565. ______. Fundamentals of mowing turfgrass. Proceedings of the Tennessee Turfgrass Conference. 2:6–9. 1968.

15566. ______. Small area irrigation systems. Weeds, Trees and Turf. 7(5):10–15. 1968.

15567. Watson, J. R. and E. A. Hunnicutt. Turf equipment and its use. Illinois Turfgrass Conference Proceedings. pp. 16–18. 1969.

15568. ______. Equipment to reduce maintenance costs. Illinois Turfgrass Conference Proceedings. pp. 59–62. 1969.

15569. Watson, J. R. Prevention and control of desiccation on golf greens. Proceedings of the First International Turfgrass Research Conference. pp. 301–306. 1969.

15570. ______. Mowing practices. Proceedings of the First International Turfgrass Research Conference. pp. 454–463. 1969.

15571. ______. Winter protection of greens. 20th Annual RCGA National Turfgrass Conference. 20:41–45. 1969.

15572. ______. Effects of cultural practice in relation to microclimate and thatch. Northwest Turfgrass Conference Proceedings. 23:56–64. 1969.

15573. ______. Effective mowing techniques. Southeastern Turfgrass Conference Proceedings. 23:19–26. 1969.

15574. ______. The why and how of mowing—reels, rotaries and vertical mowers. Southeastern Turfgrass Conference Proceedings. 23:27–34. 1969.

15575. ______. Characteristics of grasses as related to the science of mowing. Weeds Trees and Turf. 8(6):22–25. 1969.

15576. ______. Techniques of watering. Florida Turfgrass Management Conference Proceedings. 19:48–52. 1971.

15577. ______. Soluble forms of nitrogen. Ohio Turfgrass Conference Proceedings. pp. 33–37. 1971.

15578. ______. Watering and mowing practices are related. A Patch of Green. Michigan and Border Cities GCSA Publication. p. 8. August, 1971.

15579. ______. Care and feeding of athletic fields. Park Maintenance. 24(8):10–12. 1971.

15580. ______. Tomorrow is the day you should have planned yesterday. USGA Green Section Record. 9(2):12–15. 1971.

15581. ______. Increasing efficiency through selection of adequate equipment. Arizona Turfgrass Conference Proceedings. pp. 29–33. 1972.

15582. ______. Protecting golf greens against winter injury. The Golf Superintendent. 40(9):22–25. 1972.

15583. ______. Anatomical characteristics of grasses as related to mowing practices. Ohio Turfgrass Foundation Newsletter. 28:-6–8. 1972.

15584. Watson, J. R. and H. E. Bratley. Chinch bug on St. Augustine grass lawns. Florida Agricultural Experiment Station Press Bulletin. 409:2. 1929.

15585. Watson, J. R. and E. D. Cook. Chemical control of crabgrass in special purpose turf. Texas Agricultural Experiment Station Progress Report. 145:1–3. 1952.

15586. Watson, J. R. and A. W. Crain. The home lawn . . . good turf for utility and beauty. Texas Agricultural Experiment Station Bulletin. 747. 22 pp. 1952.

15587. ______. Home lawn, good turf for quality and beauty. Texas Agricultural Extension Bulletin. 203:1–22. 1953.

15588. Watson, J. R., and E. A. Hunnicutt. Budget for new equipment. Turfgrass Times. 5(2):20–21. 1969.

15589. Watson, J. R. and J. L. Kolb. Snowmold control. New York State Turf Association. Bulletin 53. pp. 204–206. 1955.

15590. ______. Snowmold control. Golfdom. 30(10):88, 90, 92, 94–96. 1956.

15591. ______. Snowmold control. The Golf Course Reporter. 24(7):5–10. 1956.

15592. ______. Snowmold control. USGA Journal and Turf Management. 10(6):27–32. 1957.

15593. Watson, J. R. and L. Wicklund. Plastic covers protect greens from winter damage. Golf Course Reporter. 30(9):30–32, 36–38. 1962.

15594. Watson, J. R., H. E. Kroll, and L. Wicklund. Protecting golf greens against winterkill. Agronomy Abstracts. p. 72. 1960.

15595. ______. Protecting golf greens against winterkill. Golf Course Reporter. 28(7):10–16. 1960.

15596. Watson, J. R., J. R. Skidgel, and M. T. Elstad. Putting the course "to bed" for the winter. Golf Course Reporter. 30(9):13–20. 1962.

15597. Watson, J. R., H. Joham, C. Jaynes, and E. Staten. Water relation to plant growth. Proceedings of the Texas Turfgrass Conference. 8:50–58. 1954.

15598. Watson, J. R., A. W. Crain, L. Howard, J. Holmes, and W. L. Clark. Building or renovating turf areas. Texas Turfgrass Conference Proceedings. 14:77–78. 1959.

15599. Watson, L. Thatch control in turf grasses. Proceedings of University of Florida

Turf-Grass Management Conference. 8:78–80. 1960.

15600. ______. Peak season planning: baseball. Proceedings of Florida Turf-Grass Management Conference. 11:74–76. 1963.

15601. ______. Thatch control. Proceedings of Florida Turf-Grass Management Conference. 11:98–101. 1963.

15602. Watson, L. E. Diagnosing lawn problems: fertilizers. Proceedings of Florida Turfgrass Management Conference. 13:102–104. 1965.

15604. Watson, S. A. and C. W. Stewart. Improved turf from corn gluten and corn hulls. Golf Course Reporter. 26(4):5–8. 1958.

15605. Watson, S. H., and F. Fuss. Erosion control on dams and levees. Oklahoma—Texas Turf Conference Proceedings. 101–104 pp. 1950.

15606. Watson, W. *Poa annua* as a lawn grass. Gardener's Chronicle. 33(859):380. 1903.

15607. Waugh, F. A. The lawn. Everybody's Garden. Orange Judd Publ. Co., Inc. New York. pp. 46–59. 1930.

15608. Way, W. A. Successful lawns. University of Vermont Extension Service. 15 pp.

15609. ______. A better lawn in '63. Vermont Farm and Home Science. 5(2):3–4. 1962.

15610. ______. Statement of basic philosophy regarding the use of nitrogen on lawn grasses. University of Vermont Agricultural Extension Service. p. 1. 1966.

15611. ______. Good turf: best for good skiing. Park Maintenance. 21(11):12–13. 1968.

15613. Wayland, J. H. Clinical handbook on economic poisons. U. S. Department of Health Education and Welfare, Health Service Publication. 475:144. 1963.

15614. Wayell, C. G. Control of weeds in turf. Research Report of the National Weed Committee, Eastern Section (Canada). 6:144. 1961.

15615. Wear, J. I. Nutrient elements in plants and soils. Auburn University Annual Turfgrass Short Course. pp. 6–9. 1960.

15616. ______. Minor elements for turf. Auburn University Annual Turfgrass Short Course. pp. 36–37. 1960.

15617. Weathers, L. G. A mosaic virus disease of *Dichondra.* California Turfgrass Culture. 22(3):24. 1972.

15618. Weaver, B. Cites arsenate control of webworm menace. Golfdom. 9(7):21. 1935.

15620. Weaver, J. E. The wonderful prairie sod. Journal of Range Management. 1963. 16(4):165–171.

15621. Weaver, J. E. and F. W. Albertson. Resurvey of grasses, forbs, and underground plant parts at the end of the great drought. Ecological Monographs. 13(1):63–117. 1943.

15623. Weaver, J. E. and E. Zink. Extent and longevity of the seminal roots of certain grasses. Plant Physiology. 20:359–379. 1945.

15624. ______. Length of life of roots of ten species of perennial range and pasture grasses. Plant Physiology. 21(2):201–217. 1946.

15625. Weaver, J. E. Root development of field crops. McGraw-Hill Book Company, Inc. New York. 291 p. 1926.

15626. Weaver, R. J. Water usage of certain native grasses in prairie and pasture. Ecology. 22:175–192. 1941.

15627. Webb, T. Policy for releasing new turf grasses. Proceedings, of University of Florida Turf-Grass Management Conference. 8:65. 1960.

15628. Webber, E. R. Inhibiting grass growth with maleic hydrazide. Parks, Golf Courses, and Sports Grounds. 20(1):23–27. 1954.

15629. Webber, L. R. Water movement in soil. RCGA National Turfgrass Conference. 18:65–70. 1967.

15630. Weber, G. F. Brown patch of lawns and golf greens and its control. Florida Agricultural Experiment Station. Press Bulletin 437. 2 pp. 1931.

15632. Webster, G. T. and R. C. Buckner. Cytology and agronomic performance of *Lolium-Festuca* hybrid derivatives. Crop Science. 11(1):109–112. 1971.

15633. Webster, F. M. The chinch bug. Farmers' Bulletin No. 657. 28 pp. 1915.

15636. Webster, J. E., G. Shryock, and P. Cox. The carbohydrate composition of two species of grama grasses. Oklahoma Agricultural Experiment Station Technical Bulletin T–104. 14 pp. 1963.

15637. Wedge, S. Wilt damage on bent greens. Golf Course Reporter. 27(4):38–39. 1959.

15638. Weed, M. B. Success with Tupersan® in seeding turfgrasses. Proceedings Missouri Lawn and Turf Conference. 7:21. 1966.

15639. Weed, M. B., I. J. Belasco, and H. L. Ploeg. Further studies with siduron for the selective control of annual grass weeds in turf. Weed Society of America Abstracts. p. 75. 1966.

15641. Weeks, M. C. How much does it cost to maintain neighborhood vs. large parks? Exposition Conference. Southern California. 6 pp. 1966.

15642. Weibull, G. Den gröna matten; en bok em gräs för grönytor, gräsmattens anläggning och vrd. Norstedt. Stockholm. 95 pp. 1962.

15644. Weihing, J. L. Control of lawn diseases in Nebraska. Nebraska Agricultural Extension Service. EC 58–1818:1–16.

15645. ______. Turfgrass disease control. University of Nebraska Turf Conference. 2:1. 1964.

15646. ______. Common diseases of bermudagrass and bentgrass and their control. Texas Turfgrass Conference Proceedings. 23:33–39. 1968.

15647. Weihing, J. L. and M. C. Shurtleff. Lawn diseases in the midwest. Nebraska Extension Service, North Central Regional Extension Publication No. 12. 1–19 pp. 1961.

15648. Weihing, J. L., S. G. Jenson, and R. I. Hamilton. *Helminthosporium sativum* a destructive pathogen of bluegrass. Phytopathology. 47(12):744–746. 1957.

15649. Weihing, J. L., M. C. Shurtleff, and R. E. Partyka. Lawn diseases in the midwest. North Central Regional Extension Publication No. 12. University of Nebraska. 20 pp. 1970.

15650. Weihing, R. M. Growth of ryegrass as influenced by temperature and solar radiation. Agronomy Journal. 55(6):519–521. 1963.

15651. Weill, K. G. Your greensmower and its care. Southern Turfgrass Association Conference Proceedings. pp. 13–15. 1964.

15652. ______. Preventive maintenance on small one-cylinder air cooled engine. International Turfgrass Conference and Show. 39:48–53. 1968.

15653. Weinard, F. F. Soil testing facilities at the University of Illinois. Illinois Turfgrass Conference Proceedings. 2:15–16. 1961.

15654. Weinbrenn, C. Investigations into the germination of *Cynodon dactylon* seed. Better turf Through Research. South African Turf Research Fund. pp. 76–85. 1948.

15655. Weinmann, H. Underground development and reserves of grasses. British Grassland Society Journal 3:115–140. 1948.

15656. ______. Carbohydrate reserves in grasses. Proceedings of the 6th International Grassland Congress. 1:655–660. 1952.

15657. Weinmann, H. and E. P. Goldsmith. Underground reserves of *Cynodon dactylon.* Better Turf Through Research. South African Turf Research Fund. pp. 56–75. 1948.

15658. Weinmann, H. and L. Reinhold. Reserve carbohydrates in South African grasses. Journal of South African Botany. 12:57–73. 1946.

15659. Weintraub, F. C. Grasses introduced into the United States. USDA Forest Service. Agriculture Handbook 58. 79 pp. 1953.

15660. Weintraub, R. L. and L. Price. Developmental physiology of the grass seedling. II. Inhibition of mesocotyl elongation in various grasses by red and by violet light. Smithsonian Miscellaneous Collections. 106(21):1–15. 1947.

15661. Weisner, M. and L. A. Kanipe. Delayed germination of *Lolium* multiflorum-common ryegrass. Proceedings of the Association of Official Seed Analysts. 41:86–88. 1951.

15662. Weiss, P. E. New approach to control of crabgrass and *Poa annua.* Golfdom. 25(8):44, 46. 1951.

15663. ______. An inexpensive method of crabgrass control. Greenkeepers' Reporter. 19(1):5–6. 1951.

15664. ______. A new approach to crabgrass and *Poa annua* control. Pennsylvania State College Turfgrass Conference Proceedings. 20:99–101. 1951.

15665. ______. Thatch in fairway turf. Golfdom. 27(7):63–66. 1953.

15666. ______. Some experiences with sodium arsenite. Rutgers University Short Course in Turf Management. pp. 32–34. 1952–1953.

15667. ______. Budgeting and planning for the golf course. Golfdom. 41(10):32–36. 1967.

15668. Weldon, M. D. Methods of lawn improvement. Nebraska Agricultural Extension Service. EC 126:1–8. 1947.

15669. ______. Soil preparation for seeding to turf. Central Plains Turf Conference. 2:25–30. 1951.

15670. Wellhausen, E. J., K. W. Kreitlow, and J. G. Leach. Observations on the prevalence and economic importance of stripe smut *(Ustilago striaeformis)* on bluegrass. Plant Disease Reporter. 27:23–24. 1943.

15671. Wellhausen, H. W. Dallis and bahia grass. Arkansas Cooperative Extension Leaflet 332. 1972.

15672. Wells, H. D. Results of turf disease survey and control studies. Southeastern Turfgrass Conference Proceedings. pp. 26–40. 1956.

15674. ______. Southern turfgrass disease control. Southeastern Turfgrass Conference Proceedings. pp. 16–28. 1957.

15675. ______. Southern turfgrass diseases and their control. Southeastern Turfgrass Conference Proceedings. 12:26–29. 1958.

15676. ______. Panel—Diseases of winter grasses used for golf turf. Proceedings of University of Florida Turf-Grass Management Conference. 7:33. 1959.

15677. ______. Southern turf problems. Golf Course Reporter. 27(8):20–23. 1959.

15678. ______. Preventing and controlling turf diseases. Southern Turfgrass Association Conference Proceedings. pp. 12–13. 1960.

15679. ______. Diseases of Southern turfgrasses. Auburn University Annual Turfgrass Short Course pp. 5–11. 1961.

15680. ______. Cottony blight disease. Golf Course Reporter. 30(5):33–39. 1962.

15681. ______. Pest control—cottony blight disease. International Turfgrass Conference Proceedings. 33:10. 1962.

15682. ______. Year-around disease control on southern grasses. Southeastern Turfgrass Conference Proceedings. 16:34–37. 1962.

15683. ______. Georgia turfgrass diseases and their control. Georgia University Agricultural Experiment Stations. Circular N.S. 39. 1963.

15684. ______. Chloroneb, a foliage fungicide for control of cottony blight of ryegrass. The Plant Disease Reporter. 53(7):-528–529. 1969.

15685. ______. Disease and pest control. Southeastern Turfgrass Conference. 23:35–43. 1969.

15686. Wells, H. D. and C. J. Hearn. Southern turfgrass diseases and their control. Georgia Agricultural Experiment Station Leaflet NS. 16:1–4. 1957.

15687. Wells, H. D., and G. M. Kozelnicky. Disease control on golf greens. Southeastern Turfgrass Conference Proceedings. 21:38–45. 1967.

15688. Wells, H. D., and J. F. McGill. NK-37 bermudagrass is highly susceptible to *Helminthosporium stenospilum.* Agronomy Journal. 51(10):625. 1969.

15689. Wells, H. D., and B. P. Robinson. Cottony blight of ryegrass caused by *Pythium aphanidermatum.* Phytopathology. 44:509–510. 1954.

15690. ______. Important diseases of ryegrass greens. USGA Journal and Turf Management. 7(5):25–27. 1954.

15691. Wells, H. D., B. P. Robinson, and J. M. Latham. Diseases of southern turfgrass and their control. USGA Journal and Turf Management. 9(7):26–30. 1957.

15693. Wells, J. C. and H. R. Garriss. Controlling lawn grass diseases. North Carolina Agricultural Extension Folder. 135. 4 pp. 1963.

15694. Wells, K. L. and G. Armstrong. Nitrogen topdressing of cool-season grasses. Kentucky Agricultural Experiment Station. Annual Report 84. p. 107. 1971.

15695. Wells, N. M. Roadside vegetation cover research. Landscape Bureau. New York State Department of Public Works. pp. 39–42. 1955.

15696. Welton, F. A. Sodium chlorate as a lawn weed killer. Agricultural Experiment Station Bimonthly Bulletin 141. pp. 188–190. 1929.

15697. ______. Nitrogen carriers for turf grasses. Ohio Agricultural Experiment Station Bulletin 497. pp. 37–40. 1932.

15698. ______. Soil reaction not an efficient method by which to control some lawn weeds. Ohio Agricultural Experiment Station Bulletin 497. pp. 40–41. 1932.

15699. ______. Crabgrass controlled by shading. Ohio Agricultural Experiment Station Bulletin. 516. pp. 30–31. 1933.

15700. ______. Control of two lawn weeds—yarrow and creeping buttercup. Ohio Agricultural Experiment Station Bulletin 548. pp. 29–31. 1935.

15701. ______. Side lines in artificial watering of turf. Ohio Agricultural Experiment Station Bulletin 561. pp. 32–34. 1936.

15702. ______. A weed-free seedbed for lawns. Ohio Agricultural Experiment Station Bulletin 579. pp. 28–30. 1937.

15703. Welton, F. A., and J. C. Carroll. Renovation of an old lawn. Journal of American Society of Agronomy. 26(6):486–491. 1934.

15704. ______. Crabgrass in relation to arsenicals. Journal of the American Society of Agronomy. 30(10):816–826. 1938.

15705. ______. Lawn experiments. Ohio Agricultural Experiment Station. Bulletin 613. 43 pp. 1940.

15706. ______. Control of lawn weeds and the renovation of lawns. Ohio Agricultural Experiment Station Bulletin. 619. 85 pp. 1941.

15707. ______. Lead arsenate for the control of crabgrass. Journal of American Society of Agronomy. 39(6):513–521. 1947.

15708. Welton, F. A. and R. M. Salter. Better lawns. Ohio Agricultural Experiment Station Special Circular 18. 16 pp. 1929.

15709. ______. Maintenance of lawn grass. Ohio Agricultural Experiment Station Bulletin 446:44–46. 1930.

15710. Welton, F. A. and J. D. Wilson. Water-supplying power of the soil under different species of grass and with different rates of water applications. Plant Physiology. 6(3):485–493. 1931.

15711. ______. Comparative rates of water loss from soil, turf, and water surfaces. Ohio Agricultural Experiment Station Bimonthly Bulletin. 190:13–16. 1938.

15712. Welton, F. A., J. C. Carroll, and J. D. Wilson. Artificial watering of lawn grass. Ecology. 15(4):380–387. 1934.

15713. ______. Artificial watering of lawn grass. USGA Journal and Turf Management. 3(5):31–32. 1950.

15714. Welton, K. Golf course water supply. USGA Green Section Bulletin. 8(7):-133–135. 1928.

15715. ______. Rebuilding the putting green. USGA Green Section Bulletin. 9(8):-142–151. 1929.

15716. ______. Clues to turf miseries of 1931 make greensmen deep thinkers. Golfdom. 5(10):9–12. 1931.

15717. ______. What '31 greenkeeping taught greensmen to plan for '32. Golfdom. 6(1):22–26. 1932.

15718. ______. Soil structure of greens. Golfdom. 6(2):59–60. 1932.

15719. ______. War against usual summer turf troubles being waged. Golfdom. 6(7):11–16. 1932.

15720. ______. Soil structure of putting greens. The National Greenkeeper. 6(4):19–23. 1932.

15721. ______. Structural requisites of putting green soil. USGA Green Section Bulletin. 12(2):29–37. 1932.

15722. ______. Arlington putting grass plots appraised by Nation's pro stars. Golfdom. 7(4):28–30, 32–33. 1933.

15723. ______. Survey of 1933 maintenance gives economy lessons Golfdom. 7(10):28, 31–33, 36. 1933.

15724. ______. Fertilization of fairways: some experimental results. USGA Green Section Bulletin. 13(6):183–199. 1933.

15725. ______. When and how spiking improves your putting greens. Golfdom. 8(10):21–23. 1934.

15726. ______. The path to perfect fairways. Golfdom. 9(7):18–21. 1935.

15727. ______. The path to perfect fairways. Golfdom. 9(8):13–16. 1935.

15728. ______. Fairway fertilizing. The Greenkeeper's Reporter. 3(2):6–9. 1935.

15729. ______. Fairway fertilizing. The Greenkeepers' Reporter. 3(3):14–17. 1935.

15730. ______. Source and cure of course drainage problems. Golfdom. 20(6):21–22, 70–72. 1946.

15731. ______. Some thoughts on putting green drainage. Proceedings of Midwest Regional Turf Conference. pp. 15–20. 1948.

15732. ______. Putting green drainage important. Midwest Turf-News and Research. 2(1):3–4. 1948.

15733. ______. How soil structure helps putting green drainage. Golfdom. 23(4):54, 56–57, 89–93. 1949.

15734. Wendt, C. W. Results from surface applications of an anionic on soil moisture, cotton yield, and bermudagrass growth during 1966. Texas Agricultural Experiment Station. Progress Report PR–3080. pp. 1–7. 1972.

15736. Wene, G. P. Flea beetle damage to *Dichondra.* Turfgrass Research. University of Arizona Agricultural Experiment Station. Report 250. p. 20. 1967–1968.

15737. ______. Control of granulate cutworms in *Dichondra* lawns. Turfgrass Research. University of Arizona Agricultural Experiment Station. Report 263. pp. 23–26. 1970.

15738. Wene, G. P. Control of green June beetle larvae. Turfgrass Research. Arizona Agricultural Experiment Station. Turfgrass Report 263. pp. 27–28. 1970.

15739. ______. Ground pearl damage to Tifgreen: a research report USGA Green Section Record. 9(4):7–10. 1971.

15740. Wene, G. R. and P. Sexton. Control of three insect pests of *Dichondra* lawns. Turfgrass Research. University of Arizona Agricultural Experiment Station. Report 257. pp. 9–12. 1969.

15741. Wene, G. P. and L. F. True. Ground pearl control—progress report for 1970. Turfgrass Research. Arizona Agricultural Experiment Station. Turfgrass Report 263. pp. 29–36. 1970.

15742. Wene, G. P., L. F. True and G. L. Seitz. The ecology and control of ground pearls. Turfgrass Research. University of Arizona Agricultural Experiment Station. Report 250. pp. 11–19. 1967–1968.

15743. Wene, G. P., L. F. True and P. Sexton. Ground pearl control—progress report for 1969. Turfgrass Research. University of Arizona Agricultural Experiment Station. Report 257. pp. 1–8. 1969.

15744. ______. Ground pearls still a problem in Arizona. Park Maintenance. 23(7):20–21. 1970.

15746. Wenger, O. E. Comparative inhibition of grasses and trees with maleic hydrazide (slo-gro) and maleic hydrazide plus adjuvant (Royal slo-gro) Northeastern Weed Science Society Proceedings. 24:279–280. 1970.

15749. Wentworth, S. W. Making the lawn. New Mexico Agricultural Extension Farm Courier. 8:10–11. 1920.

15751. Werminghausen, B. Welche bedeutung hat Styromull in Landschafts-gartenbau. Neue Landschaft. 10(7):275. 1965.

15752. ______. Styromull/styropar für den bau von sportanlagen und gehwegen. Neue Landschaft. 12(9):472. 1967.

15753. ______. Neue, Möglichkeiten der bodenver besserung bei der anlage von Rasensportflächen. Sportstättenbau und Bäderanlagen. 2(2):230. 1968.

15754. ______. Cellular polystyrene in the preparation of grass playing fields. Proceedings of the First International Turfgrass Research Conference. pp. 172–176.

15755. Werner, I. *Agrostis tenuis* in the forest province. Weibulls Gräs Tips. VII:198–201. May, 1964.

15756. Wernham, C. C. The disease control without mercurials. Greenkeepers Club of New England Newsletter. 14(4):8–11. 1942.

15757. ———. Turf disease control without mercurials Greenkeeper's Reporter. 10(2):9–10. 1942.

15758. Wernham, C. C., and R. S. Kirby. A new turf disease Phytopathology. 31:24. 1941.

15759. ———. Prevention of turf diseases under war conditions. Greenkeeper's Reporter. 11(4):14–15, 26–27. 1943.

15760. Wessel, R. D., and J. B. Polivka. Soil pH in relation to Japanese beetle population. Journal Economic Entomology. 45(4):-733–735. 1952.

15761. West, E. Diseases. Proceedings of the Florida Turf Conference. 1:33–34. 1953.

15762. ———. Why a plant disease. Proceedings of the Second Annual University of Florida Turfgrass Conference. 2:8–9. 1954.

15763. ———. Weed problems—identification. Florida Turf Management Conference Proceedings. 3:146–149. 1955.

15764. West, G. C. Humus and peat. Greenkeepers Club of New England Newsletter. 2(9):3, 6. 1930.

15765. ———. New Jersey field day. Greenkeepers Club of New England Newsletter. 3(6):4–6. 1931.

15766. West, G. M. Aeration no. 1 priority. New Zealand Institute for Turf Culture Newsletter. 59:23–25. 1969.

15767. West, J. R. How to adjust granular spreaders with V-shaped hoppers. Weeds, Trees and Turf. 5(7):13, 36. 1966.

15768. West, S. H. Water functions and requirements in turfgrasses. Proceedings Florida Turfgrass Management Conference. 13:32–35. 1965.

15769. West, S. R. How water affects plant life. Weeds, Trees and Turf. 5(4):12–14. 1966.

15770. Wester, H. V., and E. E. Cohen. Salt damage to vegetation in the Washington D. C. area during the 1966–67 winter. Plant Disease Reporter. 52:350–354. 1968.

15771. Westermeier, L. J. What is maximum lawn care? Proceedings of the Midwest Regional Turf Conference. pp. 18–20. 1968.

15772. Westfall, N. Keeping the golf course in play. International Turfgrass Conference Proceedings. 37:4–6. 1966.

15773. Westfall, R. T. and G. R. McVey. Spectrophotometric determination of turf color under field conditions. Agronomy Abstracts. p. 55. 1967.

15774. Westfall, R. T., and J. A. Simmons. Germination and seedling development of Windsor Kentucky bluegrass as influenced by phosphorus and other nutrients. Agronomy Abstracts. p. 52. 1971.

15775. Westner, R. Greens mowing procedure. Turf Clippings, University of Massachusetts. 1(7):9–10. 1962.

15776. Weston, T. A. Want a lawn like a putting green? American Home. Hercules Powder Company. 6 pp. 1960.

15777. Westover, H. L. Milorganite—an activated sludge. USGA Green Section Bulletin. 7(9):168–170. 1927.

15778. ———. Miscellaneous fertilizers. USGA Green Section Bulletin. 7(10):186–190. 1927.

15779. Westover, H. L. and C. R. Enlow. Planting and care of lawns. Farmers Bulletin No. 1677. U.S.D.A. 18 pp. 1931.

15780. Westover, H. L. and O. B. Fitts. *Poa bulbosa.* USGA Green Section Bulletin. 7(4):78–82. 1927.

15781. Whaley, J. W., and H. M. Taylor. The relationship between structure and fungicidal activity of pyridine alkane and carbinol compounds as turf fungicides. Phytopathology. 60(5):771–778. 1970.

15782. Whalley, R. D. B., C. M. McKell, and L. R. Green. Seedling vigor and early nonphotosynthetic stage of seedling growth in grasses. Crop Science. 6:147–150. 1966.

15783. Wheeler, E. H. Hastening a reduction in Japanese beetle populations with milky disease. Turf Bulletin. Massachusetts

Turf & Lawn Grass Council. 2(11):13–16. 1965.

15784. ______. Chaos in pesticide names. Turf Bulletin. Massachusetts Turf and Lawn Grass Council. 4(1):10–11. 1966.

15785. ______. Pesticide names—guidelines for their use in communicating to your audience. Turf Bulletin. Massachusetts Turf and Lawn Grass Council. 4(3):26–27. 1967.

15786. Wheeler, H. J. and J. A. Tillinghast. Quantities of nitrogen for grass. Rhode Island Agricultural Experiment Station Bulletin 57. 17 pp. 1899.

15787. ______. Effect of liming upon the relative yields and durability of grass and weeds. Rhode Island Agricultural Experiment Station Bulletin 66. 1900.

15788. Wheeler, J. Salinity tolerance of turfgrass. Turf Bulletin. Massachusetts Turf and Lawngrass Council. 5(3):19–22. 1969.

15789. Wheeler, W. H. Seeding and feeding with compressed air. The Golf Superintendent. 36(10):24. 1968.

15790. Wheeting, L. C. Soil alkali on turf areas. State College of Washington Turf Conference Proceedings. 3:17–19. 1950.

15791. Whitcomb, C. E. and E. C. Roberts. Turfgrass growth with wetter water. The Golf Superintendent. 35(1):24, 26, 28, 30. 1967.

15792. ______. Effects of surfactants on growth of turfgrasses. American Society for Horticultural Science Proceedings. 90:420–426. 1967.

15793. Whitcomb, C. E. Grass and tree root relationships. Proceedings, Florida Turfgrass Management Conference. 16:46. 1968.

15794. ______. Root competition between trees and turf. International Turfgrass Conference and Show. 39:18–20. 1968.

15795. ______. Influence of tree root competition on growth response of four cool season turfgrasses. Agronomy Journal. 64(3):355–359. 1972.

15796. ______. When trees compete with turfgrass. The Golf Superintendent. 40(3):-30–32. 1972.

15797. Whitcomb, L. S. How to calibrate hand-carried truck-mounted granular spreaders. Weeds, Trees and Turf. 5(7):12, 26. 1966.

15798. Whitcomb, W. D. Turf injury by a manure beetle. Greenkeepers Club of New England Newsletter. 9(8):8, 10. 1937.

15799. White, D. B. Common questions on turf. Seed World. 94(12):20. 1964.

15800. ______. Chemical regulation of growth in turfgrasses. Proceedings of the First International Turfgrass Research Conference. pp. 481–492. 1969.

15801. ______. The home lawn. University of Minnesota Agricultural Extension Service Extension Bulletin 366. 15pp. 1971.

15802. White, D. D. Fescues for the future. The Golf Superintendent. 39(10):30–32. 1971.

15803. White, D. B., and T. B. Bailey. Vegetation, maintenance practices, programs, and equipment on Minnesota highways. University of Minnesota Department of Horticulture Science and Minnesota Department of Highways Investigation No. 619. 69pp. 1969.

15804. White, D., J. M. Macgregor, and H. Johnson. Home lawn. Minnesota Agricultural Extension Folder. 165:1–10. 1963.

15805. White, J. When to water? Golfdom. 12(5):22–24. 1938.

15806. ______. Putting greens and the time for watering. Greenkeepers Club of New England Newsletter. 10(6):4, 6–8. 1938.

15807. White, J. H. Pests of turf and their control. Proceedings of the First Symposium on the Control of Weeds, Pests and Diseases of Cultivated Turf. pp. 25–29. 1967.

15808. White, J. L. The particles of soils —clays. Proceedings of the Midwest Regional Turf Conference. pp. 8–10. 1965.

15809. ______. Clays and their actions. Proceedings of the Midwest Regional Turf Conference. pp. 10–11. 1969.

15810. White, J. W. How mercury, lead arsenate control nitrification. Golfdom. 5(5):-38–40. 1931.

15811. ______. Effect of mercury compounds and arsenate of lead on soil nitrification. The National Greenkeeper. 5(4):26–30. 1931.

15812. ______. Soil teems with life, so culture practices are complicated. Golfdom 8(5):22–23. 1934.

15813. ______. Soil teems with life. Golfdom. 11(5):27–29. 1937.

15814. ______. Fertilizing fine turf. Pennsylvania Agricultural Experiment Station Bulletin. 382. p. 21. 1939.

15815. White, J. W. and H. B. Musser. Fertilization of fine turf. Pennsylvania Agricultural Experiment Station Bulletin. 352:29. 1937.

15816. White, J. W., F. J. Holben, and C. D. Jeffries. Growth of turf grasses and weeds in relation to soil acidity. Pennsylvania Agricultural Experiment Station. 43rd Annual Report, Bulletin 258. pp. 18–19. 1930.

15817. White, L. W. and W. H. Bowles. Practical groundsmanship. English University Press. 258 pp. 1952.

15818. White, P. A comparison. Turf Clippings. University of Massachussetts. 2(1):3–5. 1966.

15819. White, R. Putting green maintenance at Wykagyl. USGA Green Section Bulletin. 8(9) 182–183. 1928.

15821. White, R. W. Symposium—trouble shooting in turf. Watering problems and irrigation—watering maladjustments. Florida Turf Management Conference Proceedings. 3:118–120. 1955.

15822. ______. How grass produces food. Florida Turf Management Conference Proceedings. 4:9–10. 1956.

15823. ______. Turf for school and recreation fields. Part I—Grasses. Florida Turf Management Conference Proceedings. 4:60–63. 1956.

15824. ______. Part II. Fundamentals of nutrition and fertilization. Florida Turf Management Conference Proceedings. 5:20–22. 1957.

15825. ______. Fertilizing for production. Florida Turf Management Conference Proceedings. 6:55–57. 1958.

15826. ______. Selection and establishment of grasses. Florida Turf Management Conference Proceedings. 1958. 6:70–72.

15827. ______. Production problems encountered in a large turf nursery. Proceedings University of Florida Turf-Grass Management Conference. 9:99–100. 1961.

15828. ______. Ten years of growth and service—Florida Turf-Grass Association. Florida Turf-Grass Association Bulletin. 9(2):1, 7. 1962.

15829. ______. Diagnosing lawn problems. Proceedings of Florida Turf-Grass Management Conference. 10:143–147. 1962.

15830. ______. Thatch problems. Proceedings of Florida Turf-Grass Management Conference. 10:175–176. 1962.

15831. ______. Diagnosing lawn problems. Proceedings of Florida Turf-Grass Management Conference. 11:131–132. 1963.

15832. ______. Control of broadleaf weeds in Florida turfgrasses. Proceedings of Florida Turfgrass Management Conference. 12:54–58. 1964.

15833. ______. How to diagnose turfgrass problems. Weeds, Trees and Turf. 4(4):-16–23. 1965.

15834. ______. How to diagnose turfgrass problems, part II. Weeds, Trees and Turf. 4(5):18–21. 1965.

15835. ______. Relating the problem to the grass. Proceedings of the Florida Turfgrass-Management Conference. 13:84–88. 1965.

15836. ______. Typical symptoms and causes of lawn problems. Florida Turf 1(3):-6–7. 1968.

15837. ______. Southern turfgrass production and problems. Turf Clippings. University of Massachusetts. 3(3):A5–7. 1968.

15838. ______. Grasses—what they are. Proceedings of the Florida Turf-Grass Management Conference. 17:36–40. 1969.

15839. White, R. W., and G. C. Nutter. Yield versus qualitative evaluations for inter and intra variety comparisons in turf research. Agronomy Abstracts. p. 78. 1957.

15840. White, R. W., W. L. Pritchett and G. C. Nutter. Effect and rate of frequency of fertilization on the year-round performance of Bayshore and Everglades 1 bermudagrass greens. Florida Turf Management Conference Proceedings. 5:55–57. 1957.

15841. White, R. W., S. H. Kerr, T. E. Freeman, G. M. Whitton and A. G. Witherspoon. Pest control panel. Florida Turf Management Conference Proceedings. 6:58–61. 1958.

15842. White-Stevens, R. A perspective on pesticides. USGA Green Section Record. 10(4):17–21. 1972.

15843. White, W. J. and W. H. Horner. The winter survival of grass and legume plants in fall sown plots. Scientific Agriculture. 23(7):399–408. 1943.

15844. Whitehead, S. B. Garden lawns. W & G Foyle Ltd. London. 96pp. 1955.

15845. Whitely, E. L. Surfactants. Texas Turfgrass Conference Proceedings. 21:3–4. 1966.

15846. ______. Water—why and when to irrigate. Texas Turfgrass Conference Proceedings. 22:39–42. 1967.

15847. Whitlock, L. T. Planting composition for the golf course. Illinois Turfgrass Conference Proceedings. 7:26–27. 1966.

15848. Whitman, W. C. Seasonal changes in bound water content of some prairie grasses. Botanical Gazette. 103(1):38–63. 1941.

15849. Whitney, C. M. Lawns. The Bermuda Garden. The Garden Club of Bermuda. Bermuda. pp. 16–18. 1955.

15850. Whitt, D. M. The role of bluegrass in the conservation of the soil and its fertility. Soil Science Society of America Proceedings. 6:309–311. 1941.

15851. ______. Environmental benefits of vegetation. Short Course on Roadside Development (Ohio). 13:59–62. 1971.

15852. Whittet, J. B. Kikuyugrass *(Pennisetum clandestinum)* Chiov. New South Wales Department of Agriculture, Numbered Leaflet. 1946.

15853. Whitton, G. M. Aspects of the nematode problem. Florida Turf Management Conference Proceedings. 4:99–102. 1956.

15854. ______. Weed control. Proceedings of Florida Turf-Grass Management Conference. 10:139–140. 1962.

15855. ______. Trouble shooting lawns. Proceedings of Florida Turf-Grass Management Conference. 11:84–88. 1963.

15856. ______. Diagnosing lawn problems: nematodes. Proceedings of the Florida Turfgrass Management Conference. 13:100–101. 1965.

15857. ______. Trouble shooting ornamentals and turf. Proceedings of Florida Turfgrass Management Conference. 14:91–92. 1966.

15858. ______. Bahia grass. Florida Turf. 1(2):1, 4. 1968.

15859. ______. Thatching of St. Augustine. Florida Turf. 1(5):6. 1968.

15860. Whitton, G. and G. C. Nutter. Progress in nematode research—1957. Florida Turf Management Conference Proceedings. 5:91–93. 1957.

15861. Wiant, H. V. The concentration of carbon dioxide at some forest microsites. Journal of Forestry. 62(11):817–819. 1964.

15862. Wick and McCloud. Observations on turf. Professional Turf News. Borden Greens and Fairways. 1(3):2. 1970.

15863. Wickham, V. Bag cart traffic is course wear problem. Golfdom. 20(4):33, 36, 64. 1946.

15864. ______. Municipal golf course: organizing and operating guide. National Golf Foundation, Inc. 120 pp. 1955.

15865. Widdowson, A. The maintenance and upkeep of a cricket ground. Journal of Board of Greenkeeping Research. 5(16):51–55. 1937.

15866. Wiegand, C. L., M. D. Heilman, and W. A. Swanson. Sand and cotton bur mulches, bermudagrass sod and bare soil effects on: I. Evaporation suppression. Soil Science Society of America Proceedings. 32(1):276–283. 1968.

15867. Wierenga, P. J., R. M. Hagan and E. J. Gregory. Effects of irrigation water temperature on soil temperature. Agronomy Journal. 63(1):33–36. 1971.

15868. Wiersma, D. Water is basic. Proceedings of the Midwest Regional Turf Conference. pp. 15–17. 1957.

15869. ______. Soil moisture storage and delivery. Proceedings of the Midwest Regional Turf Conference. pp. 15–16. 1965.

15870. Wiese, A. F. Herbicides for beginners. Weeds Trees and Turf. 9(2):6–8. 1970.

15871. Wiese, R. A. Topsoil for your lawn do you need it? 1962 Wisconsin Turfgrass Conference Proceedings. p. 1. 1962.

15872. ______. Fertilizer and fertilizer materials. Wisconsin Turfgrass Conference Proceedings. 2pp. 1963.

15873. ______. Soil fertility—the element nitrogen. Wisconsin Turfgrass Conference Proceedings. 3pp. 1965.

15874. Wiesner, L. E. and D. F. Grabe. Effect of temperature preconditioning and cultivar on ryegrass (*Lolium* sp.) seed dormancy. Crop Science. 12(6):760–764. 1972.

15876. Wilcoxson, R. D., and H. L. Thomas. Studies on blue grass diseases at Minnesota, 1959–1965. Agronomy Abstracts. p. 47. 1965.

15877. Wilcox, A. T. Some recommendations on 2, 4–D. Parks and Recreation. 30(6):281–282. 1947.

15878. Wilcox, H. Safe athletic fields. American School Board Journal. 1964.

15879. ______. Safer athletic fields. Athletic Journal. 1965.

15880. Wilcox, L. V. Agricultural uses of reclaimed sewage effluent. Sewage Works Journal. 20:24–35. 1948.

15881. ______. The quality of water for irrigation use. USDA Technical Bulletin 962. 1948.

15882. ______. Determining the quality of irrigation water. Agricultural Information Bulletin. 197. 6pp. 1958.

15885. Wilder, R. Some observations on turf surfaces. Parks and Recreation. 19(5):-144–146. 1936.

15886. Wildman, W. E. What on earth is soil? Proceedings of the 1972 Turf and Landscape Horticulture Institute. pp. 7–10. 1972.

15887. Wildermuth, P. Economics of turf disease control. Proceedings, Missouri Lawn and Turf Conference. 5:19–24. 1964.

15889. Wildman, W. In appreciation of clay. The Golf Superintendent. 35(9):9, 31d. 1967.

15890. Wiley, R. H. Thatch, its cause and control. Rocky Mountain Regional Turfgrass Conference Proceedings. pp. 21–25. 1961.

15891. ______. Thatch control. 15th Annual Pacific Northwest Turf Conference. 15:-81–85. 1961.

15892. ______. Thatch, its causes and control. Proceedings of Florida Turf-Grass Management Conference. 10:98–100. 1962.

15893. ______. Weed control through renovation. Iagreen. 1(2):22–23. 1962.

15894. ______. Aerification—principles and practices. New Mexico Turfgrass Conference Proceedings. pp. 13–16. 1962.

15895. ______. Aerification—principles and purpose. 16th Annual Pacific Northwest Turf Conference. 16:91–93. 1962.

15896. ______. Aerification principles and purpose. Rocky Mountain Regional Turfgrass Conference Proceedings. pp. 22–24. 1962.

15897. ______. Thatch causes and removal. University of Maine turf Conference Proceedings. 1:9 pp. 1963.

15898. Wilhelm, R. A. Turf research at Marysville. RCGA National Turfgrass Conference. 21:42–43. 1970.

15899. Wilkie, W. J. Happy irrigation systems. Ohio Turfgrass Conference Proceedings. pp. 16–21. 1967.

15900. ______. Automatic irrigation. Proceedings of the Midwest Regional Turf Conference. pp. 68–70. 1969.

15901. ______. Automatic irrigation and disease control. The Golf Superintendent. 38(4):22–23. 1970.

15902. ______. Wilkie's wisdom on irrigation. Lakeshore News. 2(4):12. 1970.

15903. ______. Wilkie's wisdom on irrigation. Lakeshore News. 2(8):6. 1970.

15904. ______. Wilkie's wisdom on irrigation. Lakeshore News. 3(3):9, 12. 1971.

15905. Wilkie, W. J. What is automatic irrigation. Ohio Turfgrass Conference Proceedings. pp. 81–86. 1970.

15906. Wilkins, F. S. Effect of overgrazing on Kentucky bluegrass under conditions of extreme drouth. Journal of American Society of Agronomy. 27(2):159. 1935.

15907. Wilkins, J. R. Sod production—germination to sod—fertilizer and irrigation. Rocky Mountain Turfgrass Conference. 12:-15–17. 1966.

15908. Wilkinson, A. T. Leatherjackets: new pest for golf greens. USGA Green Section Record. 6(1):20–21. 1968.

15909. Wilkinson, J. F. The effects of fall fertilization on the cold resistance, color, and growth of Kentucky bluegrass. M. S. Thesis. University of Rhode Island. 46pp. 1971.

15910. Wilkinson, J. F., and J. B. Beard. Electrophoretic identification of *Agrostis palustris* and *Poa pratensis* cultivars. Agronomy Abstracts. p. 65. 1972.

15911. ______. Electrophoretic identification of *Agrostis palustris* and *Poa pratensis* cultivars. Crop Science. 12(6):833–834. 1972.

15912. Wilkinson, J. F., and D. T. Duff. Rooting of *Poa annua* L., *Poa pratensis* L., and *Agrostis palustris* Huds. at three soil bulk densities. Agronomy Journal. 64(1):66–68. 1972.

15913. ______. Effects of fall fertilization on cold resistance, color, and growth of Kentucky bluegrass. Agronomy Journal. 64(3):-345–348. 1972.

15914. Wilkinson, S. R., W. E. Adams, and W. A. Jackson. Chemical composition and in vitro digestibility of vertical layers of Coastal bermudagrass (*Cynodon dactylon* L.). Agronomy Journal. 62(1):39–43. 1970.

15915. Wilkinson, S. R., R. N. Dawson, W. E. Adams, and W. A. Jackson. Changes in growth and chemical composition of crownvetch with maturity. Second Crownvetch Symposium. The Pennsylvania State University. 6:140–149. 1968.

15916. Wilkinson, S. R., L. F. Welch, G. A. Hillsman and W. A. Jackson. Compatibility of tall fescue and coastal bermudagrass as affected by nitrogen fertilization and height of clip. Agronomy Journal. 60(4):359–362. 1968.

15917. Willard, C. J. Lawn grasses and lawns. Ohio Agricultural Extension Crop Talk. 37:4. 1926.

15918. Willard, C. J. and G. M. McClure. The quantitative development of tops and roots in bluegrass with an improved method of obtaining root yields. Journal of American Society of Agronomy. 24(7):509–514. 1932.

15919. Willard, C. J. and V. H. Ries. Your lawn. Ohio Agricultural Extension Bulletin. 271:1–8. 1946.

15920. Willard, C. J. and E. D. Witman. Treatment of broad leaved weeds with 2, 4–D. Proceedings of the North Central Weed Control Conference. 3:71–77. 1946.

15921. Willard, C. J., V. H. Ries, and R. H. Davis. Success with your lawn depends on soil and mowing. Ohio Agricultural Experiment Station. 271:1–8. 1954.

15922. ______. Your lawn. Ohio Agricultural Experiment Station. Bulliten No. 271. p. 1–8. 1956.

15923. Willard, C. J. and V. H. Ries. Your lawn. Ohio Agriculture Extension Service Bulletin 271. 1946.

15924. Willhite, F. M., A. R. Grable, and N. K. Rouse. Interaction of nitrogen and soil moisture on the production and persistence of timothy in lysimeters. Agronomy Journal. 57(5):479–481. 1965.

15925. Williams, A. S. Turfgrass diseases and factors influencing their control. Third Virginia Turfgrass Conference Proceedings. pp. 8–13. 1963.

15926. ______. Effect of nematocides on bermudagrass putting greens. Virginia Turfgrass Conference Proceedings. 8:125–127. 1967.

15927. ______. Effect of nematicides on bermudagrass putting greens. Results of 1967 Research Program for Control of Weeds and Diseases of Turfgrasses and Ornamentals. Virginia Polytechnic Institute, Department of Plant Pathology and Physiology Information Note 101–A. pp. 126–127. 1968.

15928. Williams, A. S., and R. E. Schmidt. Studies on dollar spot and melting out. Golf Course Reporter. 31(5):36–40. 1963.

15929. Williams, C. B. How to secure better lawns in North Carolina. North Carolina Agricultural Extension Circular. 28:1–8. 1916.

15930. ______. Better lawns in North Carolina. North Carolina Agricultural Extension Circular. 189:1–8. 1931.

15931. ______. The farm grasses of Ohio. Ohio Agricultural Experiment Station Bulletin 225. pp. 151–174. 1911.

15932. ______. Lawn and golf course problems being studied. Forty Sixth Annual Report of the Ohio Agricultural Experiment Station for 1926–27. Bulletin 417. pp. 18–20. 1928.

15933. Williams, D. A. Grass in soil and water conservation. Turf Bulletin. Massachusetts Turf and Lawn Grass Council. 3(2):-11–12, 18–19. 1966.

15935. Williams, H. H. A study of landscaping in Negro communities of the Southeastern States. Journal of Negro Education. 15(4):628. 1946.

15936. ______. New opportunities for garden supply dealers. Proceedings of Florida Turf-Grass Management Conference. 10:129–131. 1962.

15937. ______. Physiology and morphology of *Dichondra* as related to cultural practices. Lasca Leaves. 14(3):54–63. 1964.

15938. ______. Control of lawn, flower, and shrub insect pests. Proceedings of the Tennessee Turfgrass Conference. 1:11–15. 1967.

15939. ______. Electricity in climate control for winter-green bermudagrass. California Turfgrass Culture. 19(4):28–30. 1969.

15940. Williams, H. Operation green carpet. Proceedings of the First International Turfgrass Research Conference. pp. 447–450. 1969.

15941. Williams, H. R. A new approach to sports turf. Parks, Golf Courses, and Sports Grounds. 23(6):366–368. 1958.

15942. Williams, J. L., O. C. Lee, and G. F. Warren. Weeding with chemicals. Purdue University Cooperative Extension Service 1D–1. 19 pp. 1965.

15943. Williams, M. The moisture content of grass seed in relation to drying and storage. Welsh Journal of Agriculture. 14:-213–232. 1938.

15944. Williams, P. C. Grasses for the cemetery lawn. Park and Cemetery. 40(8):-214–215. 1930.

15945. ______. Grasses for the cemetery lawn. Park and Cemetery. 40(10):265–266. 1930.

15946. ______. Seed vs. stolons. Parks and Recreation. 14(5):263–267. 1931.

15947. ______. Classification and selection of grasses and seeds for cemetery lawn making. The Modern Cemetery. 43(8):172–173. 1933.

15948. ______. The water problem on golf courses. Journal of the Board of Greenkeeping Research. 3(11):207–219. 1934.

15949. ______. New slants on lawn seedings. The Modern Cemetery. 47(8):167. 1937.

15950. Williams, R. D. Depth of sowing grass and clover seeds. Journal of the Ministry of Agriculture. 29(2):132–137. 1922.

15951. ______. Assimilation and translocation in perennial grasses. Annals of Botany. 28:419–426. 1964.

15953. Williams, R. M. Beverly Country Club man applies 2, 4-D with new perfected fan type spray head. Midwest Turf-News and Research. 1(4):1–3. 1947.

15954. ______. Nitrogen use for good golf course turf. Golf Course Reporter. 23(5):12–13. 1955.

15955. ______. Nitrogen use and why. Proceedings of the Midwest Regional Turf Conference. pp. 17–18. 1955.

15956. ______. Keeping healthy turf through fertilization and irrigation. Proceedings of the Midwest Regional Turf Conference. pp. 19–21. 1956.

15957. ______. Planning (long range). USGA Journal and Turf Management. 11(2):25–26. 1958.

15958. ______. Mechanical and chemical management of fairways. Golf Course Reporter. 27(6):26–32. 1959.

15959. ______. Mechanical and chemical control of grasses in fairways. Proceedings of the Midwest Regional Turf Conference. pp. 42–45. 1959.

15960. ______. Fairway maintenance. Golfdom. 34(5):38–113. 1960.

15961. ______. Selective disease control on fairways for the sixties. Proceedings of the Midwest Regional Turf Conference. pp. 41–43. 1961.

15963. ______. Spell out what you need —tips on budgeting: course superintendent. Golfdom. 40(10):30–31. 1966.

15964. Williams, B. Five playing surfaces. The Golf Superintendent. 34(9):42. 1966.

15965. ______. Greens mowing not as easy as it looks. The Bull Sheet. 26(2):5–6. 1972.

15966. Williams, S. Making cotton seed hull greens at Parris Island Golfdom. 2(6):30. 1928.

15967. Williams, T. G. Lawns. Georgia Agricultural College Extension Circular. 380:1–6. 1954.

15968. ______. Lawns. Georgia Agriculture College Extension Circular. 380:1–8. 1957.

15969. ______. Lawns. Georgia Agriculture College Extension Circular. 380:1–12. 1962.

15970. Williamson, J. What years have taught me about practical maintenance. Golfdom. 5(5):112, 117–120. 1931.

15971. ______. Rebuilding and resodding of putting greens and tees. The National Greenkeeper. 6(6):9–15. 1932.

15972. Williamson, R. E. Root aeration and fescue growth. Plant Physiology. 38(supplement). p. 49. 1963.

15973. Williamson, R. E., and C. R. Willey. Effect of depth of water table on yield of tall fescue. Agronomy Journal. 56(6):585–588. 1964.

15974. Willis, A. J. Methods of weed control and use of growth retarding substances—Part 1. Parks, Golf Courses, and Sports Grounds. 30(8):636, 638. 1965.

15975. ______. Methods of weed control and the use of growth retarding substances—Part 2. Parks, Golf Courses, and Sports Grounds. 30(9):733–736, 740. 1965.

15976. ______. Road verges, experiments on the chemical control of grass and weeds. Parks, Golf Courses, and Sports Grounds. 35(4):341–349. 1970.

15978. Wilcox, M. and G. C. Horn. New herbicides in turf. Proceedings of University of Florida Turf-Grass Management Conference. 9:226–232. 1961.

15979. Wilkinson, A. E. The encyclopedia of trees, shrubs, vines and lawns for the home garden. The Blackiston Company. Philadelphia. 486pp. 1946.

15980. Williams, A. S., and C. W. Laughlin. Occurrence of *Hypsoperine graminis* in Virginia and additions to the host range. The Plant Disease Reporter. 52(2):-162–163. 1968.

15981. Williams, J. T. Athletic field management. Turf Clippings. University of Massachussetts. 2(1):A–56 to A–60. 1966.

15982. Williams, R. Observation on *Poa annua* trouble in fairways. Golfdom. 27(8):-48. 1953.

15983. Williams, R. M. Fertilizer, water control to keep turf healthy. Golfdom. 30(4):-74, 76. 1956.

15984. Wilman, D. The effect of nitrogenous fertilizer on the rate of growth of Italian ryegrass 2. Growth up to 10 weeks. Dry-matter yield and digestibility. Journal of the British Grassland Society. 25(2):154–161. 1970.

15985. Wilman, D. The effect of nitrogenous fertilizer on the rate of growth of Italian ryegrass. 3. Growth up to 10 weeks; nitrogen content and yield. Journal of the British Grassland Society. 25(3):242–245. 1970.

15986. ______. The effect of nitrogenous fertilizer on the rate of growth of Italian ryegrass. 4. Residual effects. Journal of the British Grassland Society. 25(4):303–308. 1970.

15987. Wilson, A. University support of the turfgrass industry. Florida Turf-Grass Association Bulletin. 9(2):1, 6. 1962.

15988. ______. 1962 Lawn fertilization recommendations. Proceedings of University of Florida Turf-Grass Management Conference. 10:141–142. 1962.

15989. Wilson, A. D. Killing chickweed with arsenite of soda. USGA Green Section Bulletin. 1(7):126–128. 1921.

15990. ______. Fighting the white grub at Merion. USGA Green Section Bulletin. 1(11):231–235. 1921.

15991. ______. Fertilizing fairways with ammonium sulfate. USGA Green Section Bulletin. 5(10):231–232. 1925.

15992. Wilson, A. M. and G. A. Harris. Hexose-, inositol-, and nucleoside phosphate esters in germinating seeds of crested wheatgrass. Plant Physiology. 41(9):1416–1419. 1966.

15993. ______. Phosphorylation in crested wheatgrass seeds at low water potentials. Plant Physiology. 43(1):61–65. 1968.

15994. Wilson, A. M. Amylase synthesis and stability in crested wheatgrass seeds at low water potentials. Plant Physiology. 48(5):541–546. 1971.

15995. Wilson, C. G. One man's methods. USGA Journal and Turf Management. 2(4):25–30. 1949.

15996. ______. Good turf is not an accident. North California Turf Conference. pp. 5–7. 1952.

15997. ______. Soil management after planting. Northern California Turf Conference Proceedings. pp. 41–46. 1951.

15998. ______. Extension looks at turf. Proceedings of the Midwest Regional Turf Conference. pp. 46–49. 1952.

15999. ______. You can't afford to be without a turf nursery. Pacific Northwest Turf Conference Proceedings. 6:24–26. 1952.

16000. ______. Turf for athletic fields and playgrounds. Southern California Turf Conference Proceedings. pp. 41–43. 1952.

16001. ______. Water management in relation to deeper roots. Proceedings of the Arizona Turfgrass Conference. pp. 7–13. 1953.

16002. ______. Seedbed preparation—is the effort worthwhile? North California Turf Conference Proceedings pp. 14–18. 1953.

16003. ______. Water management. Pacific Northwest Turf Conference Proceedings. 7:15–19. 1953.

16004. ______. Thatch and mat control for better turf. Southern California Turfgrass Conference Proceedings. pp. 13–16. 1953.

16005. ______. Matted greens contribute to poorer golf. USGA Journal and Turf Management. 6(1):25–28. 1953.

16006. ______. Be careful with organic fertilizers containing urea. USGA Journal and Turf Management. 7(3):25–26. 1954.

16007. ______. Turf for the West. USGA Journal and Turf Management. 7(1):27–31. 1954.

16008. ______. Geography influences turfgrass adaptation in West. USGA and Turf Management. 7(6):25–27. 1954.

16009. ______. Building a putting green soil. Florida Turf Management Conference Proceedings. 3:41–43. 1955.

16010. ______. Fundamentals of bentgrass maintenance. New Mexico Turfgrass Conference Proceedings. 15–18 pp. 1955.

16011. ______. Fundamentals of bentgrass maintenance. 9th Annual Pacific Northwest Turf Conference Proceedings. 9:-27–31. 1955.

16012. ______. Nutrition, chemistry, and plant growth. Oklahoma Turfgrass Conference Proceedings. 76–83. pp. 1955.

16013. ______. Nutrient insurance for healthy turf. Proceedings of the Midwest Regional Turf Conference. pp. 11–17. 1956.

16014. ______. Chemical properties of the soil. Florida Turf Management Conference Proceedings. 5:5–7. 1957.

16015. ______. Maintaining aprons-observations. Golf Course Reporter. 25(2):-24–25. 1957.

16016. ______. Would use same methods for care of collars, greens. Golfdom. 31(6):46, 48. 1957.

16017. ______. Water is basic. Proceedings of the Midwest Regional Turf Conference. pp. 17–19. 1957.

16018. ______. Maintaining aprons, observations. Proceedings of the Midwest Regional Turf Conference. pp. 52–53. 1957.

16019. ______. Soil preparation before seeding. Parks and Recreation. 40(8):10–11. 1957.

16020. ______. Rates and timing of fertilization. Parks and Recreation. 40(11):7–9. 1957.

16021. ______. Nitrogen materials and their utilization. Proceedings of the Midwest Regional Turf Conference. pp. 5–8. 1958.

16022. ______. Producing better turfs. Arizona Turf Conference Proceedings. pp. 3–6. 1959.

16023. ______. Producing better turfs. Pacific Northwest Turf Conference. 13:71–73. 1959.

16024. ______. Producing better turfs. Rocky Mountain Regional Turfgrass Conference Proceedings. pp. 31–33. 1959.

16025. ______. How thick should sod be cut? Warren's Turf Nursery. Palos Park, Illinois. p. 12. 1959.

16026. ______. Overseeding for winter color. Proceedings of University of Florida Turf-Grass Management Conference. 8:99. 1960.

16027. ______. Athletic fields. Central Plains Turfgrass Conference. 11:3. 1961.

16028. Wilson, C. G., O. J. Noer and J. M. Latham. Winter grass overseeding on Bermuda grass putting greens. Southeastern Turfgrass Conference Proceedings. 15:33–41. 1961.

16029. Wilson, C. G. Poor root system softens turfgrass for the big kill. Golfdom. 36(10):52–54, 126–127. 1962.

16030. ______. Turfgrass review. Park Maintenance. 15(7):17–40. 1962.

16031. ______. Chemicals in a coordinated management program. Proceedings of the 17th Annual Texas Turf Conference. 17:1–6. 1962.

16032. ______. Latest look at overseeding. Proceedings University of Florida Turf-Grass Management Conference. 11:49–55. 1963.

16033. ______. How not to apply chemicals. Proceedings of the Mid-Atlantic Association of Golf Course Superintendents Conference. p. 4. 1963.

16034. ______. How not to apply chemicals. New York State Turf Association Bulletin. 75:291–292. 1964.

16035. ______. Maintaining bermuda greens in the spring. Southern Turfgrass Association Conference Proceedings. p. 6. 1965.

16036. ______. Maintaining bermuda greens in the summer. Southern Turfgrass Association Conference Proceedings. p. 7. 1965.

16037. ______. Maintaining bent greens in fall and winter. Southern Turfgrass Association Conference Proceedings. p. 13. 1965.

16038. ______. Bentgrass for greens as affected by fertilizer, water and aeration. Wisconsin Turfgrass Conference Proceedings. 3 pp. 1965.

16039. ______. Few cheers for that year! Golfdom. 40(1):32–34, 90, 92, 94. 1966.

16040. ______. Plastic mulch aids germination and resists soils erosion in early spring seeding. The Golf Superintendent. 34(5):28. 1966.

16041. ______. Physiological drouth—as influenced by fertilizer salts. Proceedings of the 20th Annual Northwest Turfgrass Conference. pp. 48–52. 1966.

16042. ______. The correct sand for putting greens. California Turfgrass Culture. 18(4): 31–32. 1968.

16043. ______. The correct sand for putting green construction and topdressing. Southern Turfgrass Association Conference Proceedings. pp. 31–32. 1968.

16044. ______. The correct sand for putting greens. USGA Green Section Record. 6(3):8–9. 1968.

16045. ______. The correct sand for putting greens. The Golf Superintendent. 37(1):-52, 53, 62. 1969.

16046. ______. Overseeding bermuda greens. International Turfgrass Conference Proceedings. 40:43–47. 1969.

16047. ______. Challenge of the seventies. Missouri Lawn and Turf Conference Proceedings. 11:48–53. 1970.

16048. ______. Soil mixtures and drainage for putting greens. New York Turfgrass Association Bulletin. 88:342–344. 1971.

16049. Wilson, C. G. and F. V. Grau. Merion (B–27) bluegrass. USGA Journal and Turf Management. 3(1):27–29. 1950.

16050. ______. 1951 national cooperative turf fungicide trials. Golf Course Reporter. 20(2):8–13. 1952.

16051. ______. 1951 National cooperative turf fungicide trials. Proceedings of the Midwest Regional Turf Conference. pp. 28–31. 1952.

16052. ______. National cooperative turf fungicide trials. USGA Journal and Turf Management. 5(3):25–30. 1952.

16053. Wilson, C. G., J. M. Latham, and R. J. Welch. Winter injury. Milwaukee Milorganite Bulletin. 5:1–26. 1966.

16054. Wilson, C. G., P. Dye, G. W. Burton, and G. Armstrong. Revision of fairway and rough designs. Southeastern Turfgrass Conference Proceedings. 20:9–10. 1966.

16055. Wilson, C. M. Grass and people. University of Florida Press. Tallahassee, Florida. 233 pp. 1961.

16056. Wilson, D. B. Seedling growth of two grasses at different soil temperatures and under different types of competition. Advancing Frontiers of Plant Sciences. 1:211–218. 1962.

16057. ______. Effects of light intensity and clipping on herbage yields. Canadian Journal of Plant Science. 42(2):270–275. 1962.

16058. Wilson, E. M., W. J. Hughes, and R. H. Schieferstein. SD11831, 4-(methylsulfonyl)-2, 6-dinitro-N, N-dipropylaniline a new turf herbicide. Proceedings of the Northeastern Weed Control Conference. 20:527–530. 1966.

16059. Wilson, F. L. Identification of turf insects. Proceedings of University of Florida Turf-Grass Management Conference. 8:21–23. 1960.

16060. ______. Comparison of lawn grasses for Florida. Florida Agricultural Extension Circular. 210:1–7. 1961.

16061. ______. A comparison of several hose-on sprayers. Proceedings University of Florida Turf-Grass Management Conference. 9:151–153. 1961.

16062. ______. Spray penetration of St. Augustinegrass lawns. Proceedings University of Florida Turf-Grass Management Conference. 9:237–238. 1961.

16063. Wilson, F. H. Changing fescue greens to bent. Greenkeepers Club of New England Newsletter. 1(1):3–4. 1929.

16064. ______. Demonstration turf gardens. Greenkeepers Club of New England Newsletter. 1(2):4. 1929.

16065. ______. Demonstration turf gardens. Greenkeepers Club of New England Newsletter. 1(3):4. 1929.

16066. ______. The demonstration turf garden at the Charles River Country Club. Greenkeepers Club of New England Newsletter. 1(7):3. 1929.

16067. ______. The demonstration turf gardens at the Charles River Country Club. Greenkeepers Club of New England Newsletter. 2(10):2. 1930.

16068. ______. Demonstration turf gardens. Greenkeepers Club of New England Newsletter. 3(7):4. 1931.

16069. ______. Demonstration grass gardens. Greenkeepers Club of New England Newsletter. 4(4):2–3. 1932.

16070. ______. White grubs. Greenkeepers Club of New England Newsletter. 4(10):-3–4. 1932.

16071. ______. Spring fertilization of turf. Greenkeepers Club of New England Newsletter. 7(3):3–4. 1935.

16072. ______. How experiment work helps the greenkeepers. Greenkeepers Club of New England Newsletter. 8(4):6, 8, 10. 1936.

16073. ______. The demonstration turf garden at the Charles River Country Club. Greenkeepers Club of New England Newsletter. 8(5):3–4. 1936.

16074. ______. Fairways. Greenkeepers Club of New England Newsletter. 12(9):2–5. 1940.

16075. Wilson, H. I. Controlling crab grass. USGA Green Section Bulletin. 5(4):91. 1925.

16076. Wilson, H. K. Control of noxious plants. The Botanical Review. 10(5):279–326. 1944.

16077. Wilson, J. Soil management—post planting. Northern California Turf Conference Proceedings. pp. 46–65. 1951.

16078. ______. Crownvetch in the Great Plains. Second Crownvetch Symposium, Pennsylvania State University. 6:67–72. 1968.

16079. Wilson, J. B. Insect control in turf. West Virginia Turfgrass Conference Proceedings. pp. 57–62. 1968.

16080. Wilson, J. D. The measurement and interpretation of the water-supplying power of the soil with special reference to lawn grasses and some other plants. Plant Physiology. 2(4):385–440. 1927.

16082. Wilson, J. D. and B. E. Livingston. Wilting and withering of grasses in greenhouse cultures as related to water-supplying power of the soil. Plant Physiology. 7(1):1–34. 1932.

16085. Wilson, J. D. and F. A. Welton. The use of an evaporation index in watering lawns. Ohio Agricultural Experiment Station Bimonthly Bulletin 174. 1935.

16086. Wilson, J. K. The nature and reaction of water from hydathodes. Cornell University Agricultural Experiment Station Memoirs 65. 11 pp. 1923.

16089. Wilson, P. H. Preparing lawn and garden tools for spring. Rhode Island Agriculture. 8(2):3. 1962.

16090. Wilson, T. E. and S. Scanlon. Sewage effluent: a coming answer to irrigation problems? Grounds Maintenance. 3(7):-23–26. 1968.

16091. Wilson, T. F. Turf wear and renovation in the public park. Florida Turf Management Conference Proceedings. 5:67–68. 1957.

16092. Wilson, W. H. The team approach to corridor evaluation. Short Course on Roadside Development (Ohio). 13:19–21. 1971.

16093. Wiltbank, W. J. Let's educate the public to proper turf management. New Mexico Turfgrass Conference Proceedings. pp. 7–9. 1956.

16094. ______. Management, the key to a beautiful lawn. New Mexico Agricultural Extension Newsletter. 38:7–8. 1958.

16095. ______. Fertilizing established lawns. New Mexico Agricultural Extension Circular. 295:1–7. 1958.

16096. Wilton, A. C., E. Wiseman, and J. J. Murray. Chromsome and genetic constancy in a *Poa pratensis* L. cultivar. Crop Science. 12(6):736–738. 1972.

16097. Wilton, A. C., J. J. Murray, H. E. Heggestad, and F. V. Juska Tolerance and susceptibility of Kentucky bluegrass *(Poa pratensis* L.) cultivars to air pollution: in the field and in an ozone chamber. Journal of Environmental Quality. 1(1):112–114. 1972.

16098. Wiltse, M. G. A new herbicide for turf—zytron. Proceedings of the Northeastern Weed Control Conference. 14:292–298. 1960.

16099. Winchester, J. A. Nematodes and their control in turf grass. Florida Everglades Experimental Plantation Field Laboratory Mimeograph Report. 63–1:1–2. 1963.

16100. ______. Evaluation of nematocide treatments on turfgrass in south Florida. Florida Everglades Experimental Plantation Field Laboratory Mimeograph Report. 64–18:1–2. 1964.

16101. ______. Nematode research: South Florida. Proceedings of the Florida Turfgrass Management Conference. 12:148–151. 1964.

16102. ______. Nematode studies: South Florida. Proceedings of the Florida Turfgrass Management Conference. 13:139–141. 1965.

16103. ______. Turfgrass nematode control in South Florida. Proceedings Florida Turfgrass Management Conference. 14:153–156. 1966.

16105. Winchester, J. A., and E. O. Burt. The effect and control of sting nematodes on Ormond bermuda grass. The Plant Disease Reporter. 48(8):625–628. 1964.

16106. ______. Turfgrass gets help. Sunshine State Agricultural Research Report. 10(4):18–20. 1965.

16107. Wingert, J. B. Lawn building—maintenance—and renovation. Iowa Agricultural Extension Circular 242:1–14. 1937.

16109. Winston, J. L., and J. R. Hardin. The irrigation system and the use of soluble fertilizers. USGA Green Section Record. 9(5):8–10. 1971.

16110. Winton, T. Building golf courses sensibly. The National Greenkeeper. 5(5):16–21, 42. 1931.

16112. Wise, L. N. The lawn book. W. R. Thompson Company. State College, Mississippi. 250 pp. 1961.

16113. ______. A decade of turf-grass progress in the South. International Turf-Grass Conference Proceedings. 33:8–9. 1962.

16114. ______. Lawn grasses for the South. Seed World. 90(6):18–19. 1962.

16115. ______. The bermudagrasses. Seed World. 90(8):20–21. 1962.

16116. ______. Establishment and management of bermudagrass. Seed World. 90(10):21–22. 1962.

16117. ______. Zoysiagrasses for Southern Lawns. Seed World. 91(1):17. 1962.

16118. ______. Zoysiagrasses for Southern lawns. Seed World. 91(3):24–25. 1962.

16119. ______. Winter lawns in the South. Seed World. 91(5):20. 1962.

16120. ______. More on winter lawns. Seed World. 91(9):30. 1962.

16121. ______. "Painted" lawns. Seed World. 92(1):24. 1963.

16122. Wise, L. N. and C. M. Johnson. Painted lawns given winter test. Mississippi Farm Research. 22(11):3. 1959.

16123. Wisniewski, A. J., and J. A. DeFrance. Results of urea formaldehyde fertilization on lawn and fairway turf. Agronomy Abstracts. p. 79. 1957.

16124. ______. Clover in lawns can be controlled. Rhode Island Agriculture. 3(3):-6–7. 1957.

16125. Wisniewski, A. J., J. A. DeFrance, and J. R. Kollett. Results of ureaform fertilization on lawn and fairway turf. Agronomy Journal. 50(10):575–576. 1958.

16126. Wit, F. Hybrids of ryegrasses and meadow fescue and their value for grass breeding. Euphytica. 8(1):1–12. 1959.

16127. Witherspoon, A. The development and function of the root system. Florida Turf Management Conference Proceedings. 4:11–13. 1956.

16128. ______. Turf for school and recreation fields. Planting and establishment. Florida Turf Management Conference Proceedings. 4:64–65. 1956.

16129. ______. Fundamentals of mowing. A. Mowing physiology. Florida Turf Management Conference Proceedings. 6:4–6. 1958.

16130. ______. Propagation of turfgrasses pre-planting preparation. Proceedings of University of Florida Turf-Grass Management Conference. 7:8–9. 1959.

16132. Witteveen, G. The golf superintendent and his public relations. 20th Annual RCGA National Turfgrass Conference. 20:-46–49. 1969.

16133. ______. Trends in fairway alignment and mowing patterns. 20th Annual RCGA National Turfgrass Conference. 20:-50–52. 1969.

16134. Wittwer, S. H. and M. J. Bukovac. Gibberellin and higher plants. V. Promotion of growth in grass at low temperatures. Michigan Agricultural Experiment Station Quarterly Bulletin. 39(4):682–686. 1957.

16135. Wittwer, S. W. Foliar application of nutrients. Turf Bulletin. Massachusetts Turf and Lawn Grass Council. 4(6):8–10. 1967.

16136. Witty, P. M. The uses of a water dispersible plastic as an aid in park maintenance. Proceedings of the Florida Parks Institute. 4:1–7. 1953.

16137. White, D. B., and T. B. Bailey. Vegetation maintenance practices, programs, and equipment on Minnesota highways. United States Department of Transportation Bureau of Public Roads, Minnesota Department of Highways. 69 pp. 1968.

16138. Woerhle, T. Seeding a new course. Golf Course Reporter. 26(2):24. 1958.

16139. ______. Ice-sheet damage in your future? Keep soil porous to avoid it. Golfdom. 37(10):50, 52. 1963.

16140. ______. Ice sheet damage. Golf Course Reporter. 31(2)22–26. 1963.

16141. ______. Ice sheet damage in the Midwest. 34th International Turf-Grass Conference Proceedings. pp. 3. 1963.

16142. ______. Informing golfers when troubles occur. Proceedings of the Midwest Regional Turf Conference. pp. 21–23. 1965.

16143. ______. Improving drainage at Beverly country club. International Turfgrass Conference Proceedings. 37:11–12. 1966.

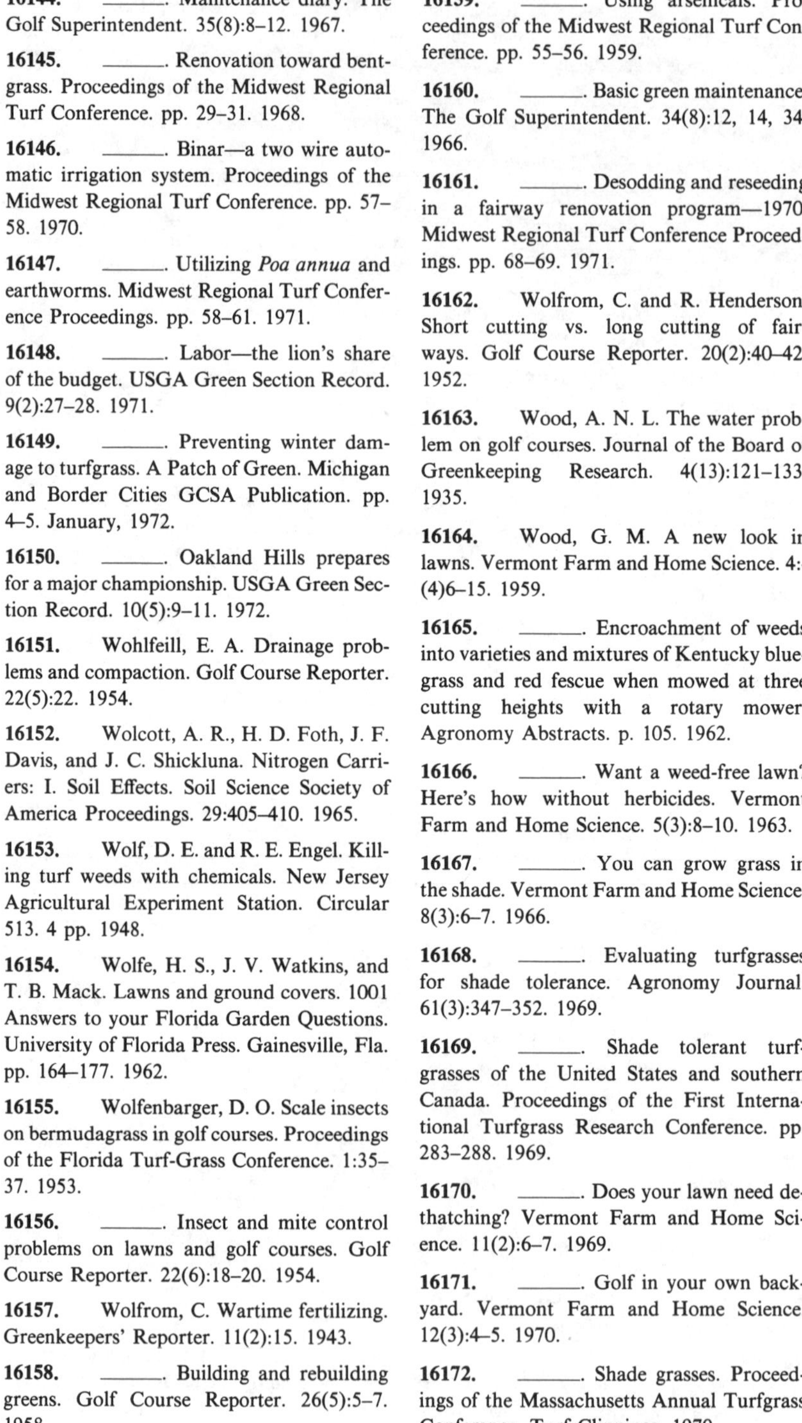

16144. ______. Maintenance diary. The Golf Superintendent. 35(8):8–12. 1967.

16145. ______. Renovation toward bentgrass. Proceedings of the Midwest Regional Turf Conference. pp. 29–31. 1968.

16146. ______. Binar—a two wire automatic irrigation system. Proceedings of the Midwest Regional Turf Conference. pp. 57–58. 1970.

16147. ______. Utilizing *Poa annua* and earthworms. Midwest Regional Turf Conference Proceedings. pp. 58–61. 1971.

16148. ______. Labor—the lion's share of the budget. USGA Green Section Record. 9(2):27–28. 1971.

16149. ______. Preventing winter damage to turfgrass. A Patch of Green. Michigan and Border Cities GCSA Publication. pp. 4–5. January, 1972.

16150. ______. Oakland Hills prepares for a major championship. USGA Green Section Record. 10(5):9–11. 1972.

16151. Wohlfeill, E. A. Drainage problems and compaction. Golf Course Reporter. 22(5):22. 1954.

16152. Wolcott, A. R., H. D. Foth, J. F. Davis, and J. C. Shickluna. Nitrogen Carriers: I. Soil Effects. Soil Science Society of America Proceedings. 29:405–410. 1965.

16153. Wolf, D. E. and R. E. Engel. Killing turf weeds with chemicals. New Jersey Agricultural Experiment Station. Circular 513. 4 pp. 1948.

16154. Wolfe, H. S., J. V. Watkins, and T. B. Mack. Lawns and ground covers. 1001 Answers to your Florida Garden Questions. University of Florida Press. Gainesville, Fla. pp. 164–177. 1962.

16155. Wolfenbarger, D. O. Scale insects on bermudagrass in golf courses. Proceedings of the Florida Turf-Grass Conference. 1:35–37. 1953.

16156. ______. Insect and mite control problems on lawns and golf courses. Golf Course Reporter. 22(6):18–20. 1954.

16157. Wolfrom, C. Wartime fertilizing. Greenkeepers' Reporter. 11(2):15. 1943.

16158. ______. Building and rebuilding greens. Golf Course Reporter. 26(5):5–7. 1958.

16159. ______. Using arsenicals. Proceedings of the Midwest Regional Turf Conference. pp. 55–56. 1959.

16160. ______. Basic green maintenance. The Golf Superintendent. 34(8):12, 14, 34. 1966.

16161. ______. Desodding and reseeding in a fairway renovation program—1970. Midwest Regional Turf Conference Proceedings. pp. 68–69. 1971.

16162. Wolfrom, C. and R. Henderson. Short cutting vs. long cutting of fairways. Golf Course Reporter. 20(2):40–42. 1952.

16163. Wood, A. N. L. The water problem on golf courses. Journal of the Board of Greenkeeping Research. 4(13):121–133. 1935.

16164. Wood, G. M. A new look in lawns. Vermont Farm and Home Science. 4:-(4)6–15. 1959.

16165. ______. Encroachment of weeds into varieties and mixtures of Kentucky bluegrass and red fescue when mowed at three cutting heights with a rotary mower. Agronomy Abstracts. p. 105. 1962.

16166. ______. Want a weed-free lawn? Here's how without herbicides. Vermont Farm and Home Science. 5(3):8–10. 1963.

16167. ______. You can grow grass in the shade. Vermont Farm and Home Science. 8(3):6–7. 1966.

16168. ______. Evaluating turfgrasses for shade tolerance. Agronomy Journal. 61(3):347–352. 1969.

16169. ______. Shade tolerant turfgrasses of the United States and southern Canada. Proceedings of the First International Turfgrass Research Conference. pp. 283–288. 1969.

16170. ______. Does your lawn need dethatching? Vermont Farm and Home Science. 11(2):6–7. 1969.

16171. ______. Golf in your own backyard. Vermont Farm and Home Science. 12(3):4–5. 1970.

16172. ______. Shade grasses. Proceedings of the Massachusetts Annual Turfgrass Conference. Turf Clippings. 1970.

16173. ______. Color infrared photography: technique and use in turfgrass research. Agronomy Abstracts. p. 52. 1971.

16174. ______. Better lawns. Vermont Farm and Home Science. 13(3):6–7. 1971.

16175. ______. Photographing the invisible world of infrared. Vermont Farm and Home Science. 14(1):7–8. 1971.

16176. ______. Mowing your lawn for the manicured look. Vermont Farm and Home Science. 1971.

16177. ______. Instant lawns—a dream come true. Vermont Farm and Home Science. 14(3):9, 11. 1972.

16178. Wood, G. M. and H. E. Buckland. Survival of turfgrass seedlings subjected to induced drouth stress. Agronomy Journal. 58(1):19–23. 1966.

16179. Wood, G. M. and J. A. Burke. Effect of cutting height and turf density of Merion, Park, Delta, Newport, and common Kentucky bluegrass. Crop Science. 1(5):317–318. 1961.

16180. Wood, G. M. and M. J. Hurdzen. Evaluating turfgrasses for shade tolerance. Agronomy Abstracts. p. 55. 1967.

16181. Wood, G. M. and P. A. Kingsbury. Seedling emergence and survival of several cool season grasses subjected to induced drouth stress. Agronomy Abstracts. p. 56. 1969.

16182. Wood, G. M., and P. A. Kingsbury. Emergence and survival of cool season grasses under drouth stress. Agronomy Journal. 63(6):949–951. 1971.

16183. Wood, G. M., and A. G. Law. Evaluating Kentucky bluegrass cultivars for wear tolerance. Agronomy Abstracts. p. 65. 1972.

16184. Wood, W. C. Sod tips: hot weather shipping and vacuum cooling. Turf-Grass Times. 1(4):7. 1966.

16185. Wood, W. E. Golf shoe spikes—who needs them? USGA Green Section Record. 9(5):11–13. 1971.

16186. Wood, W. L. Seeding and maintaining winter grass greens. The Greenkeeper's Reporter. 15(4):7–8. 1947.

16187. ______. Maintaining improved bermudagrass tees. Proceedings of the Second Annual University of Florida Turf Conference. 2:63–64. 1954.

16188. ______. Bermuda fairways made good. Golfdom. 28(10):108, 110. 1954.

16189. ______. Bermuda grass the year around in South Florida. Florida Turf Management Conference Proceedings. 3:44–46. 1955.

16190. ______. Shifting maintenance for play on private courses. Florida Turf Management Conference Proceedings. 5:46–47. 1957.

16191. Wood, W. W. The economics of turfgrass sprinkler irrigation. Proceedings of the Turfgrass Sprinkler Irrigation Conference. 4 pp. 1966.

16193. ______. The economics of turfgrass sprinkler irrigation. California Turfgrass Culture. 17(2):15–16. 1967.

16194. ______. The economics of turfgrass sprinkler irrigation. Park Maintenance. 20(7):8–11. 1967.

16195. ______. The economics of alternative sprinkler irrigation systems. Proceedings of the Turfgrass Sprinkler Irrigation Conference. 5:19–27. 1967.

16196. ______. How much must be spent for irrigation or other operations? Proceedings Annual Turfgrass Sprinkler Irrigation Conference. 8:4–9. 1970.

16197. ______. Cost budget. Proceedings of Southern California Turfgrass Institute. pp. 102–103. 1971.

16198. Woodforde, A. H. The inheritance of a substance in the roots of seedling hybrid derivatives of *Lolium perenne* L.X *Lolium multiflorum* Lam. causing a fluorescence reaction visible in filter-paper by screened ultra-violet light. The Journal of the Linnean Society of London. 50:141–150. 1935.

16199. Woodhouse, J. Public school grounds. Turf Clippings. University of Massachusetts. 1(4)12–15. 1959.

16200. ______. How sod is grown in Canada. The Golf Course Reporter. 33(2):-48–50. 1965.

16202. Woodhouse, W. W. Long-term fertility requirements of coastal bermuda. II. Nitrogen, phosphorus, and lime. Agronomy Journal. 61(2):251–256. 1969.

16203. ______. Long-term fertility requirements of coastal bermudagrass. III. Sulphur. Agronomy Journal. 61(5):705–708. 1969.

16204. Woodhouse, W. W. and R. E. Hanes. Dune stabilization with vegetation on the outer banks of North Carolina. Soils Information Series 8, Dept. of Soil Science, North Carolina State University. 1966.

16205. Woodle, H. A. Lawns for South Carolina. South Carolina Agricultural Extension Circular. 308:1–16. 1957.

16206. Woodruff, C. M. Fundamentals in soil physics. Missouri Lawn and Turf Conference Proceedings. 8:14–16. 1967.

16207. Woodruff, J. M. and R. E. Blaser. Establishing crown vetch on steep acid slopes in Virginia. Roadside Development and Maintenance; Highway Research Board. pp. 19–28. 1970.

16208. Woods, C. *Pythium* control on southern turf. Turf-Grass Times. 3(1):17. 1967.

16209. ______. "Fertilization" cuts labor costs. Turf-Grass Times. 3(6):1, 12. 1968.

16210. Woolhouse, A. R. Fungicide trials 1969. The Journal of the Sports Turf Research Institute. 45:55–61. 1969.

16211. ______. Fungicide trials 1970. Journal of the Sports Turf Research Institute. 46:5–13. 1970.

16212. ______. Fungicide trials, 1971. Journal Sports Turf Research Institute. 47:-41–47. 1971.

16213. Woolhouse, A. R. and J. P. Shildrick. The control of annual meadowgrass in fine turf. Journal Sports Turf Research Institute. 47:9–25. 1971.

16214. Woodward, G. O. Sprinkler irrigation. Sprinkler Irrigation Association, Washington, D. C. pp. 377. 1959.

16215. Woodward, R. T. Woodward's book on horticulture. Boston. 74pp. 1897.

16216. Woolson, E. A. The chemistry and toxicity of arsenic in soil. Ph.D. Thesis, University of Maryland. 98pp. 1969.

16217. Worf, G. L. High temperature diseases in Wisconsin turf. Wisconsin Turfgrass Conference Proceedings. 2pp. 1965.

16218. ______. Turf diseases and fungicides. Wisconsin Turfgrass Conference Proceedings. pp. 34–36. 1966.

16219. ______. Leaf spot and melting out of bluegrass. Super Talk 2(1):5. 1967.

16220. ______. Snow mold. Park Maintenance. 25(7):12–13. 1971.

16221. ______. Water and disease development. University of Wisconsin Area Turf Conference. 2pp. 1972.

16222. ______. New disease situations affecting turf in Wisconsin. University of Wisconsin Area Turf Conference. 3pp. 1972.

16223. Wort, D. J. Minor element nutrition of turf grass. Proceedings of the Northwest Turfgrass Conference. 18:47–49. 1964.

16224. Worthington, C. C. Spiking helps. Golfdom. 9(8):29–30. 1935.

16225. Worthington, E. H. Fairway watering from the mower manufacturer's viewpoint. The National Greenkeeper. 7(3):10, 26. 1933.

16226. Wozniak, W. The simultaneous aeration and ammonia fertilization of lawns. First Czechoslovak Symposium on Sportturf Proceedings. pp. 183–187. 1969.

16228. Wright, C. E. A preliminary examination of the differential reaction of perennial and Italian ryegrass cultivars to grass-killing herbicides. British Weed Control Conference Proceedings. 9(1):477–483. 1968.

16229. Wright, D. E. Automatic irrigation in the midwest. The Golf Course Reporter. 33(6):28–29. 1965.

16230. ______. How to get maximum use of water with automatic irrigation. The Golf Superintendent. 34(5):20. 1966.

16231. ______. Using automatic irrigation systems on need. Proceedings of the Midwest Regional Turf Conference. pp. 32–33. 1966.

16232. ______. Mist blower vs. boom sprayer. Golfdom 41(4):48, 50. 1967.

16233. ______. Trends in modern turf irrigation. Proceedings of the Tennessee Turfgrass Conference. 1:22–27. 1967.

16234. ______. Tips on installing an automatic irrigation system. Proceedings of the Tennessee Turfgrass Conference. 2:10–11. 1968.

16235. ______. Seeding bluegrass in the summer. Missouri Lawn and Turf Conference Proceedings. 12:28–29. 1971.

16236. Wright, D., D. Pate, R. Miller, S. Frederiksen and L. Callahan. Summary of panel discussion on management of fine turfgrasses. Proceedings of the Tennessee Turfgrass Conference. 1:9–10. 1967.

16237. Wright, F. G. Maintenance of turf on football and athletic fields. Texas Turf Conference Proceedings. 5:9–11. 1950.

16238. Wright, H. Fairway maintenance. Southeastern Turfgrass Conference Proceedings. 13:39–44. 1959.

16239. ______. The average day at peachtree. Southeastern Turfgrass Conference Proceedings. 15:11–13. 1961.

16240. ______. Winter grass overseeding in Florida. Golf Course Reporter. 30(9):50–52. 1962.

16241. ______. Winter grass over-seeding—on greens in Atlanta. International Turf-Grass Conference Proceedings. 33:10. 1962. 10. 1962.

16242. Wright, J. L. Turf on stabilized granular materials. American Association of State Highway Officials. 10pp. 1944.

16243. ______. Seeding slopes along Connecticut's roadways. Journal of the New York Botanical Garden. 50(593):113–114. 1949.

16244. ______. Panel discussion—uses and availability of grasses for roadside improvement projects. Short Course on Roadside Development (Ohio). 16:73–76. 1957.

16245. Wright, L. N. Drouth tolerance evaluation among range grass genera, species, and accessions of three species using program-controlled environment. Crops Research Division, USDA (University of Arizona.) Report. pp 165–169.

16246. ______. Drought tolerance program controlled environment evaluation among range grass genera and species. Crop Science. 4:472–474. 1964.

16250. Wright, L. N., and H. B. Musser. Tests of new Strains of grasses. Pennsylvania State College Turfgrass Conference Proceedings. 19:15–25. 1950.

16252. Wright, N. Research. Proceedings of National Turf Field Days. pp. 18–19. 1950.

16253. ______. Grasses for economical maintenance. Proceedings of National Turf Field Days. pp. 52–56. 1950.

16254. Wright, W. Construction of playing fields by controlled tipping. Parks, Golf Courses, and Sports Grounds. 31(8):632–638. 1966.

16255. Wright, W. H. Turf grass seeds. The Greenkeepers' Reporter. 3(2):17–18. 1935.

16256. Wurster, M. J., L. D. Kamstra, and J. G. Ross. Evaluation of cool season grass species and varieties using *in vivo* and *in vitro* techniques. Agronomy Journal. 63(2):241–245. 1971.

16257. Wycherley, P. R. Temperature and photoperiod in relation to flowering in three perennial grass species. Mededelingen Landbouwhgeschool Wageningen. 52:75–92. 1952.

16258. ______. Vegetative proliferation of floral spikelets in British grasses. Annals of Botany. 18:119–127. 1954.

16259. Wyckoff, C. G. Tests with CMU weed and grass killer. Southern California Turf Culture 4(1):3. 1954.

16260. Wyckoff, C. G. and V. T. Stoutemyer. The bahiagrasses. Southern California Turf Culture 4(2):4. 1954.

16261. ______. Evaluation of bermudagrass strains. Southern California Turf Culture 4(3):2–4. 1954.

16262. Wyckoff, C. G. The vertical mowing of grass. Southern California Turfgrass Culture 4(4):3–4. 1954.

16263. ______. Zoysias as turfgrasses for southern California. Southern California Turfgrass Culture. 5(3):1, 4. 1955.

16264. ______. The vertical mowing of grass. Parks and Recreation. 38(3):26–27. 1955.

16265. Wyllie, J. A. Golf carts. 23rd Annual RCGA National Turfgrass Conference. pp. 67–71. 1972.

16266. Wyrill, J. B. Effect of burning on soil chemical and physical properties of loamy upland bluestem range. M. S. Thesis, Kansas State University. 1971.

16267. Wyllie, T. D. What's in the picture for turf disease research? Proceedings Missouri Lawn and Turf Conference. 7:13–15. 1966.

16268. Wyllie, T. D. and O. H. Calvert. Turfgrass diseases. Proceedings, Missouri Lawn and Turf Conference. 2:12–20. 1961.

16269. Wyrick, R. F. Story of complete lawn rebuilding at Forest Lawn. The Modern Cemetery. 46(6):118–119. 1936.

16270. ______. Aftermath of the drouth. The Modern Cemetery. 49(9):146–147. 1939.

16271. Yabuki, K. The carbon dioxide environment for plant, Part 1. KGU Green Section Turf Research Bulletin. 10:1–17. 1966.

16272. ______. Micro-climates on golf courses. K.G.U. Green Section Turf Research Bulletin. 11:1–14. 1966.

16273. Yager, L. A. Lawns for Montana. Montana Agricultural Extension Bulletin. 282:1–23. 1955.

16274. Yahner, J. E. Soils—their development and adaptation to suburban uses. Proceedings of the Midwest Regional Turf Conference. pp. 50–51. 1968.

16275. Yamaguchi, M. On the relaxative nitrogen fertilizers. K.G.U. Green Section Turf Research Bulletin. 13. 61–66. 1967.

16276. ______. Practical application of the new fertilizer materials. KGU Green Section Turf Research Bulletin. 21(8):1–8. 1971.

16277. Yamamoto, S., and N. Maekubo. Reports of examination on green construction at Katayamazu Golf Club. KGU Green Section Turf Research Bulletin. 10:55–61. 1966.

16278. Yamanouchi, H. Theory and practice of fertilizers on turf. KGU Green Section Turf Research Bulletin. 18:1–20. 1970.

16279. Yarrow, J. R. The case for turf fields. Airports. pp. 14–16. 1945.

16281. Yarwood, C. E. Powdery mildews. The Botanical Review. 23(4):235–300. 1957.

16282. Yarwood, C. E., S. Sidky, M. Cohen, and V. Santilli. Temperature relations of powdery mildews. Hilgardia. 22(17):603–622. 1954.

16283. Yates, M. E., and W. A. Jacques. Root development of some common New Zealand pasture plants. VI. Importance of various roots, particularly the seminal roots of perennial ryegrass *(Lolium perenne.).* New Zealand Journal Science and Technology. Section A. 34(3):249–257. 1953.

16284. Yeatts, J. Fertility problems. Auburn University Annual Turfgrass Short Course. 9:8–10. 1968.

16285. Yee, J. Y., and K. S. Love. Nitrification of urea-formaldehyde reaction products. Soil Science Society of America Proceedings. 11:389–392. 1946.

16286. Yemm, E. W. and A. J. Willis. The effects of maleic hydrazide and 2, 4-dichlorophenoxyacetic acid on roadside vegetation. Weed Research. 2:24–40. 1962.

16287. Yesberger, E. F. Public golf operations in the East. Golf Course Reporter. 31(7)21–25. 1963.

16288. Yoder, E. J. Turf investigations for airports and highways. Purdue Engineering Bulletin No. 81. pp. 66–68. 1953.

16289. Yoshikawa, I. Physiological and ecological studies on turf diseases, Part 8. K.G.U. Green Section Turf Research Bulletin. 14:37–46. 1968.

16290. ______. The golf courses of Japan. Proceedings of the First International Turfgrass Research Conference. p. 7. 1969.

16291. ______. Physiological and ecological studies on turf diseases, Part 10. K.G.U. Green Section Turf Research Bulletin. 19:-47–56. 1970.

16292. Yoshikawa, I., and R. Asakura. Physiological and ecological studies on turf diseases. Part 5—Effects on some fungicides for *rhizoctonia* brown patch on Seaside bentgrass. KGU Green Section Turf Research Bulletin. 5:53–87. 1963.

16293. ______. Turf diseases, Part 1. KGU Green Section Turf Research Bulletin. 7. 57–72. 1964.

16294. ______. Physiological and ecological studies on turf diseases (Part 6). KGU Green Section Turf Research Bulletin. 8:33–49. 1965.

16295. ______. Turf diseases, Part 3. KGU Green Section Turf Research Bulletin. 10:47–54. 1966.

16296. ______. Physiological and ecological studies on turf diseases, part 7. K.G.U. Green Section Bulletin. 11:67–78. 1966.

16297. Yoshikawa, I. and M. Komatsu. Durability on the turf fungicides. K.G.U. Green Section Turf Research Bulletin. 14:-51–54. 1968.

16298. ______. Physiological and ecological studies on turf diseases, Part 9. KGU Green Section Turf Research Bulletin. 16:-53–66. 1969.

16299. Young, C. B. Growing grass in a tough area. Rocky Mountain Regional Turfgrass Conference Proceedings. pp. 5–7. 1956.

16300. Young, H. C. and D. F. Wadsworth. Chemical control of diseases affecting turf. Oklahoma Agricultural Experiment Station. Processed Series P–581. 17 pp. 1968.

16301. Young, H. C., R. V. Sturgeon, J. M. Vargas, and R. E. McCoy. Spring dead spot of bermudagrass. Oklahoma State University Progress Report. Disease Control Part II. pp. 1–7. 1965.

16302. ______. Dollar spot on bermudagrass. Oklahoma State University Progress Report. Disease Control Part II. pp. 7–9. 1965.

16303. ______. Dollar spot on bentgrass. Oklahoma State University Progress Report. Disease Control Part II. pp. 9–13. 1965.

16304. ______. Algae on bentgrass. Oklahoma State University Progress Report. Disease Control Part II. pp. 15–18. 1965.

16305. ______. *Pythium* disease on bentgrass. Oklahoma State University Progress Report. Disease Control Part II. pp. 18–20. 1965.

16307. Young, N. M. P. Peat—its practical value as a soil improver. The Groundsman. 17(10):16–20. 1964.

16308. Young, O. W. Fairway improvement program at the Moraine country club. Proceedings of the Midwest Regional Turf Conference. pp. 52–53. 1955.

16309. ______. Maintaining aprons around greens. Proceedings of the Midwest Regional Turf Conference. pp. 54–55. 1957.

16310. ______. Better lawns and turf. Orville W. Young. Dayton, Ohio. 62 pp.

16311. Young, P. R. Caring for a lawn. Elementary Lessons in Gardening. The National Garden Institute. Ohio. pp. 95–98.

16312. Young, V. H. and A. M. Somerville. Nematode problem in turf. Golf Course Reporter. 25(5):16, 19–20. 1957.

16313. Young, W. A., and B. W. Wascom. Turf—evaluation of new herbicides—Louisiana. Annual Southern Weed Conference Research Report. 22:92–93. 1969.

16314. Young, W. C. Report on turf grasses and legumes and turf establishment. Roadside Development Publication 222. pp. 27–29. 1952.

16315. ______. Ecology of roadside treatment. Journal of Soil and Water Conservation. 23(2):47–50. 1968.

16316. ______. Ecology of roadside treatment. Short Course on Roadside Development (Ohio). 26:48–55. 1967.

16317. Youngberg, H. W. Diurnal trends in nitrogenous constituents of selected forage species. Ph.D. Thesis, Purdue University. 88 pp. 1970.

16318. Youngman, W. H. Systemics, a new tool. Golf Superintendent. 37(9):28–37. 1969.

16319. Youngner, V. B. The control of *Poa annua* (annual bluegrass) in putting greens. Southern California Turfgrass Culture. 1(4):27–29. 1951.

16320. ______. Turfgrass research at U.C.L.A. Golf Course Reporter. 23(8):12–15. 1955.

16321. ______. Weed control by turfgrass management. California Turfgrass Culture. 6(4):7–8. 1956.

16322. ______. Evaluation of new bermudagrass species and strains. Southern California Turf Culture. 6(2):5–6. 1956.

16323. ______. Fine-leaved fescues as turfgrasses in southern California. Southern California Turf Culture. 7(1):7–8. 1957.

16324. ______. Turfgrass seed mixtures. Southern California Turf Culture. 7(2):14. 1957.

16325. ______. Turfgrass seed guide. Southern California Turf Culture. 7(2):11. 1957.

16326. ______. The turf-forming bluegrass. Southern California Turf Culture. 7(3):18–20. 1957.

16327. ______. Growth of U-3 bermudagrass under controlled temperature and light. Agronomy Abstracts. p. 67. 1958.

16328. ______. Kikuyugrass, *Pennisetum clandestinum,* and its control. Southern California Turf Culture. 8(1):1–4. 1958.

16329. ______. Gibberellic acid on zoysia grasses. Southern California Turf Culture. 8(1):5–6. 1958.

16330. ______. Management of bentgrass putting greens in the west. Southern California Turf Culture. 8(3):17–18. 1958.

16331. ______. Bermudagrasses for turf in the Southwest. Southern California Turf Culture. 8(3):21–23. 1958.

16332. ______. Tall fescue-Pensacola bahiagrass combination. Southern California Turf Culture 8(3):24. 1958.

16333. ______. The turfgrass seed mat Southern California Turf Culture. 8(4):32. 1958.

16334. ______. Kikuyugrass and its control. Golf Course Reporter. 26(1):5–7. 1958.

16335. ______. Management of bentgrass putting greens in the west. Golf Course Reporter. 26(7):26–28. 1958.

16336. ______. Green colorant applications to dormant grasses. Park Maintenance. 11:68–69. 1958.

16337. ______. Studies on wear resistance of turfgrasses. Agronomy Abstracts. p. 92. 1959.

16338. ______. Growth of U-3 bermudagrass under various day and night temperatures and light intensities. Agronomy Journal. 51(9):557–559. 1959.

16339. ______. Environmental factors affecting bermuda grass growth and dormancy. Arizona Turf Conference Proceedings. pp. 9–11. 1959.

16340. ______. Outline of turfgrasse research programs at the University of California, Los Angeles. Arizona Turf Conference Proceedings. pp.12–13. 1959.

16341. ______. Effects of winter applications of gibberellic acid on bermuda and zoysia turf. Southern California Turf Culture. 9(1):7. 1959.

16342. ______. Environmental factors affecting bermudagrass growth and dormancy. Southern California Turf Culture. 9(4):25–26. 1959.

16343. ______. The control of *Poa annua,* annual bluegrass in putting greens. Southern California Turf Culture. 9(4):27–29. 1959.

16344. ______. On the Pacific coast. Golf Course Reporter. 27(7):41–43. 1959.

16345. ______. Ecological studies of *Poa annua* in turfgrasses. Journal of the British Grasslands Society. 14(4):233–237. 1959.

16346. ______. Wear resistance of turfgrass. Northern California Turf Conference Proceedings. pp. 1–3. 1959.

16347. ______. The tolerance of turfgrass. Parks and Recreation. 42(7):308–309. 1959.

16348. ______. Fertilizer recommendations for turfgrasses. Southern California Turfgrass Culture. 9(2):16. 1959.

16349. ______. Environmental control of initiation of the inflorescence, reproductive structures, and proliferations in *Poa bulbosa.* American Journal of Botany. 47(9):753–758. 1960.

16350. ______. Growth and flowering of Zoysia species in response to various temperatures, photoperiods and light intensities. Agronomy Abstracts. p. 72. 1960.

16352. ______. Climate and growth of turfgrasses. California Turf Culture. 10(3):-23–24. 1960.

16353. ______. Heat, light, growth. Golf Course Reporter. 28(1):58, 60. 1960.

16354. ______. Temperature and light in growth of turf. Golfdom. 35(4):70–110. 1960.

16355. ______. Dovetailing turfgrass fertilization with other management practices. Northern California Turf Conference Proceedings. pp. 27–28. 1960.

16356. ______. Management of new turfgrass varieties. Southern California Turfgrass Institute Proceedings. pp. 6–8. 1960.

16357. ______. Accelerated wear tests on turfgrasses. Agronomy Journal. 53(4):217–218. 1961.

16358. ______. Turfgrass seed mixtures for fairway and park turf. California Turfgrass Culture. 11(2):16. 1961.

16359. ______. Growth and flowering of *Zoysia* species in response to temperatures, photoperiods, and light intensities. Crop Science. 1(2):91–93. 1961.

16360. ______. Population-density studies on cool-season turfgrasses grown in a subtropical climate. Journal of the British Grassland Society. 16(3):222–225. 1961.

16361. ______. Which is the best grass? Northern California Turfgrass Institute Proceedings. pp. 16–18. 1961.

16362. ______. Observations on the ecology and morphology of *Pennisetum clandestinum.* Phyton. 16(1):77–84. 1961.

16363. ______. Low temperature induced male sterility in male-fertile *Pennisetum clandestinum.* Science. 133(3452):-577–578. 1961.

16364. ______. Winter survival of *Digitaria sanguinalis* in subtropical climates. Weeds. 9(4):654–655. 1961.

16365. ______. Wear resistance of cool season turfgrasses. effects of previous mowing practices. Agronomy Journal. 54(2):198–199. 1962.

16366. Youngner, V. B., J. H. Madison, M. H. Kimball, W. B. Davis. Climatic zones for turfgrass in California. California Agriculture. 16(7):2–4. 1962.

16367. Youngner, V. B. Life cycle of crabgrass in California. California Turfgrass Culture. 12(2):13–14. 1962.

16368. ______. Which is the best turfgrass? California Turfgrass Culture. 12(4):-30–31. 1962.

16369. ______. Which is the best turfgrass. Park Maintenance. 15(3):94–95. 1962.

16370. ______. The effects of traffic on turfgrass. California Turfgrass Culture. 13(4):28–29. 1963.

16371. ______. Turf fertilization program. California Turfgrass Culture. 13(4):-31–32. 1963.

16372. ______. What makes plants respond? Golfdom. 37(4):64, 66, 150–152. 1963.

16373. ______. What makes plants respond. 34th International Turf-Grass Conference Proceedings. pp. 2. 1963.

16374. ______. Which is the best turf? Parks and Recreation. 46(4):202–203. 1963.

16375. ______. Control of some common turfgrass weeds. Southern California Turfgrass Institute Proceedings. pp. 22–24. 1963.

16376. ______. Growing turf in shaded areas. Western Landscape News. 3:4–15. 1963.

16377. ______. Turfgrasses on heavy traffic areas. Western Landscaping News. 3. 1963.

16378. ______. Bermudas, are they your turfgrass answer? University of California Turf, Nursery and Landscape Tree Conference Proceedings. pp. 6–1 to 6–3. 1964.

16379. ______. Turf fertilization. Parks and Recreation. 47(3):118–119. 1964.

16380. ______. A report on playground turf. Western Landscaping News. 4(9). 1964.

16381. ______. Fall and winter turf care. Western Landscaping News. 4(11):1964.

16383. ______. Annual bluegrass, *Poa annua.* California Turfgrass Culture 15(2):-15–16. 1965.

16384. ______. Preemergence weed control in turf. The Golf Course Reporter. 33(3):32–34. 1965.

16385. ______. Turf annual —Volume VIII, 1964. Park Maintenance. 18:17–40. 1965.

16386. ______. A report on wear resistance of turf. Parks and Recreation. 48(4):-264–265. 1965.

16387. ______. Turf and its maintenance. Western Landscaping News. 5(3). 1965.

16388. ______. *Dichondra;* past, present and future. California Turfgrass Culture. 16(3):21–23. 1966.

16389. ______. Santa Ana, a new turf bermudagrass for California. California Turfgrass Culture. 16(3):23–24. 1966.

16390. ______. Some problems in herbicide application. California Turfgrass Culture. 16(4):25–27. 1966.

16391. ______. Salinity tolerance and your turfgrass species. University of California Agricultural Extension Service Turf, Landscape Tree, and Nursery Conference Proceedings. pp. 4–1–4–3. 1966.

16392. ______. Response of plants to their environment. California Turfgrass Culture. 17(1):4–6. 1967.

16393. ______. Turfgrass adaptation in California. California Turfgrass Culture. 17(2):13–14. 1967.

16394. ______. Santa Ana—a new vegetatively propagated turf bermudagrass developed for California. Weeds Trees and Turf. 6(4):34–36. 1967.

16395. ______. Vertical mowing—aerification—and *Poa annua* invasion. California Turfgrass Culture. 18(1):6. 1968.

16396. ______. Renovation of old bermudagrass turf with calcium cyanamide. California Turfgrass Culture. 18(4):28–29. 1968.

16397. ______. Winter turf maintenance. California Turfgrass Culture. 18(4):29–30. 1968.

16398. ______. Vertical mowing—aerification and *Poa annua* invasion. Florida Turf. 1(1):1, 6–7. 1968.

16399. ______. The effects of temperature and light on vegetative growth. International Turfgrass Conference and Show. 39:-10–12. 1968.

16400. ______. Vertical mowing, aerification, and *Poa annua.* New York Turfgrass Association Bulletin. 81:315–316. 1968.

16401. ______. Fertilizing western lawns and turfs. Plant Food Review. No. 2. pp. 10–11. 1968.

16402. ______. A review of recent turfgrass research in southern California. California Turfgrass Culture. 19(1):6–7. 1969.

16403. ______. Playground turf. California Turfgrass Culture. 19(2):15–16. 1969.

16404. ______. Turfgrass research in the west. International Turfgrass Conference Proceedings. 40:40–43. 1969.

16405. ______. *Poa annua:* viewpoints on control methods and precautions in the west. International Turfgrass Conference Proceedings. 40:74–75. 1969.

16406. ______. Turfgrass varieties and irrigation practices. Proceedings Annual Turfgrass Sprinkler Irrigation Conference. 7:56–59. 1969.

16407. ______. Turfgrass varieties and irrigation practices. California Turfgrass Culture. 20(1):3–4. 1970.

16408. ______. Turfgrass varieties and irrigation practices. Golf Superintendent. 38(1):66, 68. 1970.

16409. ______. Turfgrass varieties and irrigation practices. Northwest Turfgrass Topics. 12(1):3–4. 1970.

16410. ______. Artificial turf. Proceedings Annual Turfgrass Sprinkler Irrigation Conference. 8:1–3. 1970.

16411. ______. Bermudagrass. Park Maintenance. 24(7):20. 1971.

16412. ______. Bluegrass. Park Maintenance. 24(7):21. 1971.

16413. Youngner, V. B., V. A. Gibeault, and J. R. Breece. Turf bermuda grasses. California Turfgrass Culture. 22(1):1–3. 1972.

16414. Youngner, V. B. Effects of mowing on turfgrass reaction to pests. Proceedings of the 1972 Turf and Landscape Horticulture Institute. pp. 39–45. 1972.

16415. ______. Ecological forces affecting weeds and their control. Proceeding of Scotts Turfgrass Research Conference. 3:1–26. 1972.

16416. Youngner, V. B. and T. Fuchigami. Trials of selective herbicides for crabgrass control—1955. Southern California Turf Culture. 6(1):6, 8. 1956.

16417. ______. Control of crabgrass with chemicals. Southern California Turf Culture. 6(4):4–5. 1956.

16418. ______. Colorants for dormant bermuda and other subtropical grasses. Landscaping. 4(1):8. 1958.

16419. ______. Why turfgrass aerification practices pay. Landscaping. 4(4):4, 7, 13. 1958.

16420. ______. Colorants for dormant bermuda and other subtropical grasses. Southern California Turfgrass Culture. 8(1):-7–8. 1958.

16421. ______. Aerification or cultivation of established turfgrasses. Southern California Turfgrass Culture. 8(2):9–10. 1958.

16422. ______. The control of crabgrass in established turfgrasses. Southern California Turf Culture. 8(4):29. 1958.

16423. Youngner, V. B. and V. A. Gibeault. Turfgrasses in man's environment. Turf-grass Times. 7(3):6, 14, 26. 1971.

16424. Youngner, V. B., and J. R. Goodin. Control of *Pennisetum clandestinum,* Kikuyugrass. Weeds. 9(2):238–242. 1961.

16425. Youngner, V. B. and M. H. Kimball. Zoysiagrass for lawns. California Turfgrass Culture. 12(3):23–24. 1962.

16426. Youngner, V. B., and J. Latting. Identification of turfgrasses by vegetative morphology. California Turf Culture. 10(3):-17–21. 1960.

16427. Youngner, V. B. and O. R. Lunt. Managing greens for hot weather survival. Southern California Turf Culture. 8(4):25–27. 1958.

16428. ______. Salinity tolerance of bermudagrass strains and varieties. Agronomy Abstracts. p. 103. 1964.

16429. ______. Salinity effects on roots and tops of bermudagrass. Journal of the British Grassland Society. 22(4):257–259. 1967.

16430. Youngner, V. B. and F. Nudge. Growth and carbohydrate storage of three *Poa pratensis* strains as influenced by temperature. Agronomy Abstracts. p. 56. 1967.

16431. ______. Root growth, top growth and carbohydrate reserves of *Cynodon dactylon* (L.) Pers. as affected by salinity and clipping. Agronomy Abstracts. p. 61. 1968.

16432. ______. Chemical control of annual bluegrass as related to vertical mowing. California Turfgrass Culture. 18(3):17–22. 1968.

16433. ______. Growth and carbohydrate storage of three *Poa pratensis* L. strains as influenced by temperature. Crop Science. 8(4):455–457. 1968.

16434. ______. Chemical control of annual bluegrass as related to vertical mowing. Northern Ohio Turfgrass News. 2(9):1, 3. 1968.

16435. ______. Leaf emergence and tillering rates of three Kentucky bluegrass cultivars. Agronomy Abstracts. p. 56. 1969.

16436. ______. Turf density and carbohydrate reserves of five Kentucky bluegrass cultivars grown in three climate zones. Agronomy Abstracts. p. 72. 1970.

16437. Youngner, V. B. and S. Spaulding. Growth, flowering and seed development of *Dichondra repens* as affected by various environmental factors. Agronomy Abstracts. p. 105. 1962.

16438. ______. *Dichondra* in California. Lasca Leaves. 14(3):51–53. 1964.

16439. Youngner, V. B., and W. B. Tavener. Weedfree turfgrass seedbeds. Southern California Turf Culture. 6(4):3, 8. 1956.

16440. ______. Calcium cyanimid fertilization of bermudagrass turf. Agronomy Abstracts. p. 79. 1957.

16441. Youngner, V. B., V. A. Gibeault, and K. Mueller. St. Augustinegrass for turf. California Turfgrass Culture. 22(3):17–18. 1972.

16442. Youngner, V. B., O. R. Lunt and F. Nudge. Salinity tolerance of seven varieties of creeping bentgrass, *Agrostis palustris* Huds. Agronomy Journal. 59(4):335–336. 1967.

16443. Youngner, V. B., O. R. Lunt, and S. E. Spaulding. A miniature solution culture system for turfgrass studies. Agronomy Abstracts. p. 75. 1961.

16444. Youngner, V. B., F. J. Nudge and S. Spaulding. Flowering of *Dichondra* in response to temperature and daylength. American Journal of Botany. 55(7):762–766. 1968.

16445. Youngner, V. B., J. H. Madison, and W. B. Davis. Which is the best turfgrass? University of California Agricultural Extension Service Turfgrass Series. AXT–227. 2 pp. 1966.

16446. Youngner, V. B., F. Nudge, and O. R. Lunt. Salinity tolerance of creeping bentgrass *(Agrostis palustris* Huds). Agronomy Abstracts. p. 48. 1965.

16447. Youngner, V. B., W. W. Wright, and E. Zimmerman. Kikuyugrass—its management and control. California Turfgrass Culture. 21(1):1–3. 1971.

16448. Youngner, V. B., J. H. Madison, M. H. Kimball and W. B. Davis. Climatic zones for turfgrass in California. California Turfgrass Culture. 12(4):25–27. 1962.

16449. Zahnley, J. W. Turf grass experiments in Kansas. USGA Green Section Bulletin. 7(9):179–182. 1927.

16450. ______. Weed control for turf areas. Central Plains Turfgrass Conference Proceedings. 1:80–84. 1950.

16451. Zahnley, J. W., and F. L. Duley. The effect of nitrogenous fertilizers on the growth of lawn grasses. Journal of American Society of Agronomy 26(3):231–234. 1934.

16452. Zahnley, J. W. and L. R. Quinlan. Lawns in Kansas. Kansas Agricultural Experiment Station. Bulletin 267. 32 pp. 1934.

16453. Zak, J. M. Use of maleic hydrazide for growth suppression of highway turf. Turf Clippings. University of Massachusetts. 1(10):A43–A45. 1965.

16454. ______. Controlling drifting sand dunes on Cape Cod. Massachusetts Agricultural Experiment Station Bulletin. 563. 15 pp. 1967.

16455. ______. Crownvetch—one answer to those problem maintenance areas. Turf Bulletin (Massachusetts). 8(5):8. 1972.

16456. Zak, J. M. and E. J. Bredakis. Dune stabilization at Provincetown. Agronomy Abstracts. p. 104. 1964.

16457. ______. Sand dune erosion control at Provincetown, Mass. Agronomy Abstracts. p. 126. 1965.

16458. ______. Establishment and management of roadside vegetative cover in Massachusetts. Massachusetts Agricultural Experiment Station. Bulletin 562. 28 p. 1967.

16459. ______. Use of maleic hydrazide for growth suppression of highway turf. Turf Bulletin. Massachusetts Turf and Lawn Grass Council. 4(5):17, 19–20, 25. 1967.

16460. Zak, J. M. and P. A. Kaskeski. "Maintain" as a growth retardant. Turf Bulletin (Massachusetts). 8(1):5–6. 1971.

16461. Zak, J. M., and P. A. Kaskeski. Crownvetch, an adaptable ground cover for Massachusetts roadsides. Highway Research Abstracts. 42(10):17. 1972.

16462. Zak, J. M., and J. F. Kelly. Results assessed of ten-year program of Massachusetts roadside development. Highway Research News. 48:47–51. 1972.

16464. Zanoni, L. J. Factors which influence the levels of soluble carbohydrate reserves of cool season turfgrasses. University of Massachusetts. 99 pp. 1967.

16465. Zanoni, L. J., L. F. Michelson, and W. G. Colby. Factors affecting the soluble carbohydrate reserves of cool season turfgrasses. Agronomy Abstracts. p. 56. 1967.

16466. Zanoni, L. J., L. F. Michelson, W. G. Colby, and M. Drake. Factors affecting carbohydrate reserves of cool season turfgrasses. Agronomy Journal. 61(2):195–198. 1969.

16467. Zedler, J. and O. L. Loucks. Differential burning response of *Poa pratensis* fields and *Andropogon scoparius* prairies in central Wisconsin. American Midland Naturalist. 81(2):341–352. 1969.

16468. Zeman, L. Better turf and garden. Borden, Inc., Chemical Division Publication. 1969.

16469. Zick, W. H. A new ally in the war against weeds. Parks and Recreation. 2(4):-32–33. 1967.

16470. Ziegler, G. A. Home lawns. Wisconsin Agricultural Extension Circular. 445. p. 1–12. 1953.

16471. ______. Home lawns. Wisconsin Agricultural Extension Circular 445:1–8. 1958.

16472. ______. Home lawns. University of Wisconsin Extension Service Circular 445. 8 pp. 1961.

16473. Zimmerman, H. Getting the work done. Midwest Regional Turf Conference Proceedings. pp. 44–46. 1972.

16474. Zimmerman, M. Reviewing turf tractors. Grounds Maintenance. 1(8):28–31. 1966.

16475. ______. Selecting a self-propelled mower. Grounds Maintenance. 2(2):13–15. 1967.

16476. ______. Selecting a self-propelled mower. Grounds Maintenance. 2(12):19–21. 1967.

16477. ______. Tires for turf. Grounds Maintenance. 2(5):21. 1967.

16478. ______. Super-sized mowers. Grounds Maintenance. 2(12):24–26. 1967.

16479. ______. How to select a compact tractor. Grounds Maintenance. 2(12):33–35. 1967.

16480. ______. Tractors á la carte. Grounds Maintenance. 2(12):43–46. 1967.

16481. ______. Reviewing turf tractors. Grounds Maintenance. 2(12):48–51. 1967.

16482. ______. Selecting gang-type reel mowers. Grounds Maintenance. 3(4):17–20. 1968.

16483. ______. Reviewing flail mowers. Grounds Maintenance. 3(5):35–39. 1968.

16484. ______. Selecting a rotary mower. Grounds Maintenance. 3(6):16–20. 1968.

16485. ______. Reviewing cutter bar mowers. Grounds Maintenance. 3(7):14–17. 1968.

16486. ______. Understanding the basic fertilizer spreader: spreading relationships. Grounds Maintenance. 4(4):18–20, 22, 85. 1969.

16487. ______. Grounds conditioner—retrievers . . . how they operate; what they do. Grounds Maintenance. 4(8):12–14. 1969.

16488. Zimmerman, T. L. and D. V. Waddington. Fertility levels of physically amended soils as affected by amount and kind of amendment, compaction and aerification. Agronomy Abstracts. p. 62. 1968.

16489. Zimmerman, T. L., D. V. Waddington, and J. M. Duich. Effect of amendment, compaction, soil depth, and time on the physical properties of soil mixtures. Agronomy Abstracts. p. 52. 1971.

16490. Zimmerman, W. E. Experiments with potassium cyanate to control crabgrass in turf. Greenkeepers' Reporter. 18(3):5–8. 1950.

16491. ______. Potassium cyanate passes crabgrass control tests. Golfdom. 24(8):40, 61–62. 1950.

16492. ______. What's new in turf weed control and seed bed preparation. Proceedings of the 6th Annual Texas Turf Conference. pp. 88–92. 1951.

16493. ______. Test PC wet, dry and with sludge for weed control. Golfdom. 26(6):62, 64, 66. 1952.

16494. ______. Crabgrass dies with wet or dry PC applications. Park Maintenance. 5:10–12. 1952.

16495. ______. Growing and maintaining better turf with calcium cyanamide. Parks and Recreation. 36(9):7, 28. 1953.

16496. ______. What's new in turf weed control and seed bed preparation. Proceedings of School of Soils, Fertilization and Turf Maintenance. Royal Canadian Golf Association. Green Section. pp. 92–102. 1952.

16497. Zink, C. J. Laying up your machinery. The National Greenkeeper. 2(11):-19. 1928.

16498. Zoller, J. A. Disease control at Eugene Country Club. Proceedings of the 20th Annual Northwest Turfgrass Conference. pp. 45–46. 1966.

16499. Zolman, V. Atomic turf maintenance. The Golf Superintendent. 35(3):60, 63–64. 1967.

16500. Zolman, V. J. The problem of contaminated water. Turfgrass Times. 3(5):4, 8, 14, 21. 1968.

16501. ______. Soil testing from the golf course superintendents' standpoint. The Greenmaster. 6(9):9–11. 1970.

16502. ______. The problem of contaminated water. The Greenmaster. 7(6):6–9. 1971.

16503. ______. New philosophy of approach to turf management on golf courses. The Greenmaster. 7(9):3–4. 1971.

16504. ______. New philosophy of approach to turf management on golf courses. A Patch of Green. Michigan and Border Cities GCSA Publication. pp. 8–12. December, 1971.

16505. Zontek, S. J. A guide to turfgrass fungicides for the 1970's. USGA Green Section Record. 10(4):1–7. 1972.

16506. Zukel. J. W. Progress report on use of maleic hydrazide for grass inhibition on highway areas. Roadside Development Publication 222. pp. 30–35. 1952.

16507. ______. Report on use of maleic hydrazide for temporary growth inhibition of grass. Highway Research Board, Washington, D. C. 1953.

16508. ______. Use of inhibitors. Short Course on Roadside Development (Ohio). 19:85–86. 1960.

16509. ______. A literature summary on maleic hydrazide, 1957–1963. United States Rubber, Naugatuck Chemical Division Report. 111 pp. 1963.

16510. Zukel, J. W., and C. O. Eddy. Present use of herbicides on highway areas. Weeds. 6(1):61–63. 1958.

16511. Zummo, N., and A. G. Plakidas. Brown patch of St. Augustine grass. Plant Disease Reporter. 42(10):1141–1147. 1958.

16512. Zunt, R. Browns, Indians to run on Merion blue. The Golf Course Reporter. 33(2):54–55. 1965.

16513. Zuroweste, R. Zoysia seed germination. Missouri Lawn & Turf Conference Proceedings. 12:18–19. 1971.

16514. Zybura, E. L., and E. C. Roberts. Comparison of foliar and root development of ten coarse grasses for roadside use. Agronomy Abstracts. p. 49. 1965.

SUBJECT INDEX

Absorption, nutrient, **2747**

ABS pipe **14329**

Acapulcograss, **12133**

Acarina order (see Mites)

Aceria neocynodomis (see Bermudagrass mite)

(Acetate) phenylmercury (see PMA)

Achillea millefolium (see Yarrow)

Acidity, soil (see Soil reaction)

Acme velvet bentgrass, **302, 11661, 11665, 16489**

Acroloplus popeanellus (see Sod webworm)

Acroylonitrile-butadiese-styrene pipe (see ABS pipe)

Actidione® (see Cyclohexamide)

Actinomycetes, **12604, 14889**

Activated carbon
  herbicide deactivation, **66, 3489, 7950, 8139**

Activated charcoal
  application, **8411**

Activated charcoal
  herbicide deactivation, **8411, 8413, 8417, 13852:** bensulide, **2906, 2908**

Activated charcoal
  soil modification, **4507**

Activated sewage sludge (see Sewage sludge, activated)

Activity index, **10589**

Adaptation, **310, 390, 1429, 1800, 2100, 2991, 5802, 13934, 15494, 16007, 16008**

Adaptation
  environmental effects, **3870, 16373**

Adaptation
  roadsides, **6035**

Adaptation
  shade, **1668, 2600**

Adaptation
  soil, **606, 2735, 3158, 3159**

Adaptation
  structural characteristics, **5813**

Adaptation
  wet sites, **5018**

Adelphi Kentucky bluegrass, **2208, 6330, 7287, 14813**

Adjuvants (see Surfactant)

Adorno Kentucky bluegrass, **9218**

Adventitious roots, **5646**

Advisory service, turf (see also Education, turf)
  commercial (USA), **10966**

Advisory service, turf
  cooperative extension: (see Education, turf)

Advisory service, turf
  Netherlands, **14990**

Advisory service, turf
  New England, **12833**

Advisory service, turf
  Sweden, **9227**

Aeration, soil, **18, 846, 5790, 5978, 6597, 7231, 7842, 9076, 9788, 10269, 10326, 15503**

Aeration, soil
  advantages, **5789, 9297**

Aeration, soil
  effects, **10267, 15766**

Aeration, soil
  effects of: compaction, **5356, 11144, 11153, 13683, 16489;** soil amendments, **15112;** soil mix, **11605, 13683;** soil moisture, **6831;** soil texture, **5356**

Aeration, soil
  effects on: root growth, **3299, 3948, 15086;** root-shoot ratio, **15086;** shoot growth, **3299, 9504, 15480;** thatching, **10285, 15894;** tillering, **15086;** water use rate, **7181**

Aeration, soil
  factors affecting, **11038, 14179, 15480, 15500**

Aeration, soil
  measurement, **7842, 16489**

Aeration, soil
  soil layering problems, **3301**

Aerial pesticide applications, (see Pesticide, application: aerial)

Aerification (see Cultivation)

African bermudagrass
  plant description, **16413**

African bermudagrass
  root knot nematode, **12644**

Agarious aeruginosus, **6508**

Agarious arvensis, **6508**

Agarious furfuraceus, **6508**

Agarious geotrupus, **6508**

Agarious rudus, **6508**

Agarious species (see Fairy ring)

Age
  leaf physiology, **3367**

Agio red fescue, **7287**

Agrillon, **7520**

Agrinite,® **1470**

Agrinite®
  composting, **4848**

Agrinite®
  evaluation, **11213, 15118**

Agropyron cristatum (see Fairway wheatgrass)

Agropyron desertorum (see Crested wheatgrass)

Agropyron intermedium (see Intermediate wheatgrass)

Agropyron repens (see Quackgrass)

Agropyron smithii (see Western wheatgrass)

Agropyron species
polyembryony, **4950**

Agropyron species
taxonomy, **10190**

Agropyron trachycaulum (see Slender wheatgrass)

Agrostis alba (see Redtop)

Agrostis canina (see Velvet bentgrass)

Agrostis capillaris (see Colonial bentgrass)

Agrostis castellana (see also Highland Colonial bentgrass), **13458**

Agrostis gigantea, **2284**

Agrostis hybrids, **3152, 3159**

Agrostis palustris (see Creeping bentgrass)

Agrostis species, **11811, 12139, 13320**

Agrostis species
adaptation, **12101**

Agrostis species
description, **7792, 11087, 12138, 14966, 15755:** chromosome number, **8627;** stomatal distribution, **13625**

Agrostis species
heavy metal toxicity, **8655**

Agrostis species
seed germination, **4272, 9468**

Agrostis species
seed identification, **7775, 12138**

Agrostis species
seed production, **11778**

Agrostis species
taxonomy, **10815, 12101, 13458**

Agrostis stolonifera (see also Creeping bentgrass), **3152, 3159, 12101, 14121**

Agrostis tenuis (see Colonial bentgrass)

Agrostis vulgaris (see Colonial bentgrass)

AI (see Activity index)

Aira caryophyllea (see also Hairgrass, silvery), **9520**

Aira praecox (see also Hairgrass, early), **9520**

Airfield
construction, **728, 783, 802, 803, 942, 1912**

Airfield
culture, **741, 3146, 6839, 8616, 9202, 9977, 10847, 10848, 11003, 11141, 16279:** leveling tests, **10268**

Airfield
establishment, **741, 841, 2761, 3146, 3586, 10848, 11003, 12525**

Airfield
grasses used, **395, 709, 2354, 3146, 10848:** cool season, **783, 942, 11003;** evaluation, **8259, 8260, 11454;** sandy sites, **2761;** selection criteria, **12402, 12403;** Sweden, **11227;** warm season, **11003**

Airfield
stabilized surfaces: evaluation, **11028, 13868, 14946, 16288**

Airfield
turf survey, **2854**

Air movement (see Wind)

A–10 Kentucky bluegrass, **1639, 3656, 6330, 14813**

A–20 Kentucky bluegrass, **1967, 3656, 6294, 6451, 8319**

A–20 Kentucky bluegrass
adaptation, **6315, 10614, 10633**

A–20 Kentucky bluegrass
description, **6298, 15395**

A–20 Kentucky bluegrass
evaluation, **6330, 10622, 10626, 11186, 11323, 11325**

A–34 Kentucky bluegrass, **2100, 2101, 3656, 6294, 6451**

A–34 Kentucky bluegrass
adaptation, **6298, 6315**

A–34 Kentucky bluegrass
evaluation, **6330, 14813**

Akton®
billbug control, **10983**

Akton®
sod webworm control, **14398**

Akton®
Southern chinch bug control, **7268, 10982**

Albedo, **249, 8743, 10850**

Albedo
diurnal, **8743**

Albedo
effects of: grass cover, **8743;** snow cover, **8740**

Aldicarb
ground pearl control, **15739**

Aldrin
grub control, **12181**

Aldrin
insect control, **9467, 13483**

Aldrin
Japanese beetle control, **7158, 12178**

Aldrin
June beetle control, **12178**

Aldrin
Northern masked chafer control, **12172, 12178**

Aldrin
wireworm control, **6071**

Alfalfa
roadside use, **248, 9129**

Alfalfa meal
evaluation, **6790**

Algae, **562, 665, 864, 917, 2262, 4581, 6952, 12604, 13703, 14889, 15674, 16403**

Algae
chemical control, **2262, 10793, 13703**: Dithane M–45 ®, **14426;** evaluation, **1700, 2172, 6190, 6197, 6630, 14426;** Fore®, **16208;** neburon, **6631**

Algae
control, **1028, 1274, 3997, 10677, 11476, 11567**

Alkaligrass, **3670**

Alkaline soil, **1051**

Alkaline soil
causes, **15790**

Alkaline soil
correction, **1026, 2617, 9797, 10541, 15790**

Alkaline soil
effects, **2350**

Alkaline soil
effects on: nutrient availability, **2350, 9797;** shoot growth, **9797;** weed invasion, **11666**

Alkaline soil
plant symptoms, **15790**

Alkali soils, **3185, 6262, 7610, 12488**

Alkaloids
in tall fescue, **6464**

Allantoin, **2334**

Allergenic plants
grasses, **15052**

Allium canadense (see Wild onion)

Allium vineale (see Wild garlic)

Allolobophora terrestris, **8469**

Allolobophora tuberculata, **8469**

Alsike clover
roadside use, **9129**

Alta tall fescue, **95, 866, 888, 908, 977, 6862, 6875, 7309, 8647, 9245, 11165, 11186, 14349, 14356**

Alta tall fescue
chemical composition, **12110, 14452**

Alta tall fescue
description, **7892**

Alta tall fescue
use, **873, 936, 12941**

Alternaria leaf spot
chemical control, **5405, 9891**

Alternate green, **2778, 5106, 5820**

Alternate green
culture, **5851**

Alternate green
establishment, **5851, 11555**

Alternate surfaces, **6520**

Aluminum
toxicity: correction, **10057;** seedling, **13459;** species susceptibility, **6506, 10245**

Aluminum pipe, **6426**

Aluminum sulfate
soil reaction effect, **3001**

Aluminum sulfate
weed control, **11666, 15701**

Amaranthus species (see Pigweed)

Amendment, soil (see Soil Amendment)

American beachgrass
culture, **2299, 3372, 7563, 8430**

American beachgrass
description: cytology, **3836**

American beachgrass
establishment, **3371, 8430:** fertilizer effects, **2300**

American beachgrass
use: erosion control, **3370;** sand dune stabilization, **1700, 7563, 8429, 14322**

American beachgrass
vegetative propagation, **2300**

American dunegrass, **3370, 3371, 3372**

American Sod Producers Association, **1824, 1830, 1929**

Amiben
red sorrel control, **3666a, 4563**

Amide
metabolism, **2556**

Amide content
factors affecting, **2944, 14323**

Amino acid
metabolism, **97**

Amino acid content
environmental effects, **2434, 14324**

Amino acid content
nutrient effects, **9861**

4-Amino pyrimidine nucleosides, **6237**

3-amino-1, 2, 4-triazole (see Amitrole)

Amitrole, **1551**

Amitrole
nutsedge control, **7545**

Amitrole
plant effects, **7873, 8377**

Amitrole
quackgrass control, **1238, 7873**

Ammonia
effects of: soil reaction, **13411, 14142**

Ammonia
toxicity, **4120, 14136**

Ammonia
volatilization: factors affecting, **10656, 11871, 13795;** liquid fertilization, **7676;** urea, **1804**

Ammonium
absorption: roots, **9818, 10067**

Ammonium chloride, **1555, 5636**

Ammonium magnesium phosphate
evaluation, **16275**

Ammonium nitrate, **756, 1470, 1546, 1555, 2725, 2811, 4646, 4647, 7202, 9390, 16021**

Ammonium nitrate
coated, **9793, 11793**

Ammonium nitrate
effects on: growth, **4942, 4943;**

nematodes, **11745;** soil acidity, **12, 13039, 15064**

Ammonium nitrate
evaluation, **5917, 6790, 8019, 8049, 8754, 11185, 11213, 11674, 11905, 11907, 12220, 12265, 12567, 14402, 14403**

Ammonium nitrate
leaching loss, **15064**

Ammonium nitrate
nitrogen efficiency, **13039, 15064**

Ammonium nitrate
soil relationships, **10133**

Ammonium nitrate
storage hazards, **2323**

Ammonium nitrate
volatilization loss, **5064**

Ammonium phosphate, **2811, 5634, 9790, 9805**

Ammonium phosphate
effects on: rooting, **5679;** soil reaction, **11397**

Ammonium phosphate
evaluation, **3130, 10861, 15697**

Ammonium phosphate
solubility, **9805**

Ammonium salts
effects, **4055**

Ammonium sulfate, **128, 309, 375, 483, 1470, 1546, 1555, 1777, 1803, 2257, 2811, 2941, 2945, 2946, 3001, 3206, 3462, 4098, 4896, 5634, 5678, 5683, 7787, 9804, 9958, 10863**

Ammonium sulfate
application method, **12845, 15591**

Ammonium sulfate
brown patch control, **11817**

Ammonium sulfate
effects on: assimilation, **5321;** earthworms, **2172, 8469;** *Fusarium* patch, **14004;** growth, **4942, 4943, 4960, 5679;** moss, **2172;** nematode control, **14071;** soil reaction, **12, 1485, 2172, 3001, 7223, 7464, 11024, 11384, 11397**

Ammonium sulfate
evaluation, **3130, 4650, 5636, 5637, 5638, 6790, 7220, 7222, 7223, 8019, 8049, 8699, 8754, 9045, 10066, 10861, 10863, 11134, 11145, 11176, 11185, 11666, 11674, 14148, 14402, 14403, 15118, 15697, 15709, 15787, 15815**

Ammonium sulfate
foliar burn potential, **14780**

Ammonium sulfate
guttation effects, **7033**

Ammonium sulfate
leaching loss, **15064**

Ammonium sulfate
nitrogen efficiency, **15066**

Ammonium sulfate
Ophiobolus patch control, **4592, 6763**

Ammonium sulfate
use, **7752, 12142:** composting, **4848, 11454**

Ammonium sulfate
volatilization loss, **15062, 15064**

Ammonium sulfate
weed control, **483, 723, 2172, 4725, 4760, 7752, 9370, 14971:** annual bluegrass, **13536;** clover, **2172, 2943, 6904, 11661;** crabgrass, **5555;** dandelion, **15706**

Ammonium thichloracetate
weed control, **15424**

Ammonium thiocyanate
seedbed weed control, **4901**

Ammophilia arenaria (see European beachgrass)

Ammophilia breviligulata (see American beachgrass)

Amphimallon majales (see European chafer)

Amylolytic activity
factors affecting, **8749**

Anaerobic microorganisms (see Microorganisms)

Anatomy, **5832, 5866**

Anatomy
book, **2244**

Anatomy
grass: book, **9843, 10474**

Anatomy
leaf, **9550**

Andrin
grub control, **12174, 13489**

Andropogan gerardi (see Bluestem)

Andropogon ischaemum (see Yellow bluestemweed)

Andropogon scoparius (see Little Bluestem)

Anguina agrostis (see Bentgrass nematode)

Anguina graminis, **6608**

Anhauser Kentucky bluegrass, **6306**

Anhydrous ammonia
soil sterilization, **9389, 9839**

Anhydrous ammonia
weed control, **1993, 8797**

Anilazine, **3257**

Anilazine
dollar spot control, **7285**

Anilazine
Fusarium patch control, **7192, 7285, 16212**

Anilazine
Helminthosporium species control, **1545, 11101, 14026, 14996**

Anilazine
Ophiobolus patch control, **7285**

Animal grazing
golf course, **714**

Animal pests, **432, 8624, 13593**

Animal show ring, **1095**

Animal tankage, **15118**

Anion exchange resin
fertilization, **12773**

Annual bluegrass, **141, 154, 535, 1091, 1390, 2464, 4138, 5513, 5896, 5897, 6485, 6836, 6840, 6876, 6966, 7151, 7247, 7479, 11666, 12151, 14471, 16426**

Annual bluegrass
adaptation, **2463, 2626, 2653, 3387, 3723, 6131, 6133, 7160, 11624, 12725:** high temperature stress, **2607, 5942;** ice cover tolerance, **2559, 2636;** light, **6654, 14170;** low temperature stress, **2566, 2570, 2636, 2702, 9408;** smog tolerance, **4802, 8658;** soil moisture level, **4581, 6654, 14984;** soil reaction, **483, 4768;** submersion tolerance, **2700, 2701;** temperature, **2621**

Annual bluegrass
arsenic toxicity: soil phosphorus effect, **2463, 8860**

Annual bluegrass
biological control, **14868**

Annual bluegrass
breeding, **15912**

Annual bluegrass
chemical control, **1639, 2067, 2163, 2394, 2442, 2463, 3440, 3510, 3520, 3611a, 3697a, 4059, 4140, 4440, 4445, 5449, 6102, 6136, 6652, 6667, 6955, 7556, 9172, 9339, 9540, 10539, 10629, 11835, 12029, 12032, 12544, 13523, 15304, 16319, 16343:** ammonium sulfate, **13536;** application time, **1782, 6133;** arsenicals, **1493, 1967, 4392, 4394, 4398, 4399, 4469, 4478, 4513, 4521, 6145, 6146, 6147, 6153, 7955, 8859, 10440;** arsenic-phosphorus interaction, **1689, 2069, 3728, 8701, 8703;** benefin, **5632, 8572;** bensulide, **5632, 8158, 9845, 10020, 15281, 15283, 15285, 16432, 16434;** in bentgrass, **1871, 5184, 5531, 8161, 8171, 8179;** in bermudagrass, **1782, 1871, 1967, 2100, 2647, 2894, 2908, 3517, 3521, 3522, 4016, 4064, 5381, 6381, 6573, 7175, 8027, 8031, 8161, 8171, 8179, 9138, 9543, 12544, 25356;** calcium arsenate, **8861, 9173, 9734, 10439, 10558, 12982, 12983, 13813, 14512, 14514, 14969;** calcium cyanamid, **5632;** copper thiocyanate, **1551;** DCPA, **4935, 9580;** endothall, **2672, 2682, 10020, 14860, 14867, 14878, 14882, 14883, 15281, 15283, 15285;** evaluation, **67, 1700, 2012, 2170, 2617, 2633, 2649, 2902, 3478, 3480, 3781, 4018, 4065, 4366, 4406, 4470, 4504, 4788, 4789, 4895, 5065, 5184, 5381, 5464, 5467, 5468, 5479, 5527, 5529, 5530, 5571, 5632, 6487, 6577, 6580, 6637, 6653, 6654, 6658, 6685, 6686, 8074, 8151, 8157, 8161, 8168, 8419, 8696, 8701, 8703, 9435, 9533, 9537, 9543, 10020, 10619, 10624, 11056, 11085, 11255, 11256, 12544, 14433, 14866, 15140, 16213, 16343;** formaldehyde, **5632;** general discussion, **139, 1270, 2209, 2464, 3728, 4270, 4385, 4442, 4456, 4494, 4499, 4511, 4512, 4544, 5445, 6129, 6131, 6133, 6134, 6372, 6587, 6715, 8165, 8442, 9083, 9313, 12365, 12383, 13846, 13847, 14082, 14083, 14859, 16405;** in Kentucky bluegrass, **4789, 5381, 14980;** Kerb, **3521, 3522, 3525, 8173, 12502;** lead arsenate, **327, 4411, 4827, 6629, 6790, 7510, 9385, 10234, 11616, 14170, 16160;** maleic hydrazide, **5479, 5610;** metham, **5632;** methods, **4269, 13525, 14868;** methyl bromide, **5632;** neburon, **4429, 4478, 5632, 6626;** phosphorus effects, **1700, 8696, 8700;** Posan®, **6690, 13534;** pre-emergence, **2070, 3477, 3479;** residual activity, **13521;** review, **8013;** seed head inhibition, **208, 6683, 12779;** sodium arsenite, **10782, 15662, 15664, 15666, 16159;** soil reaction effects, **1700, 8703;** terbutol, **5632;** vertical mowing effect, **16434;** winter overseeding, **2100, 2919, 9429, 15326**

Annual bluegrass
competitive ability, **3035, 3723**

Annual bluegrass
control, **141, 1365, 3878, 4368, 4417, 5437, 6922, 6983, 7247, 12366, 12458, 16398, 4478, 6485, 6847:** fairway, **10181, 14513, 15090, 16145**

Annual bluegrass
crown injury: low temperature, **2561**

Annual bluegrass
cultural control, **2164, 2499, 5449, 6685, 6686, 7125, 8269, 8738, 12547, 13336, 13525, 13847, 14859, 14916**

Annual bluegrass
culture, **2464, 2626, 2653, 2654, 3873, 4237, 4478, 7421, 8269, 9313, 9572, 9942, 9944, 10243, 10244, 10537, 11624, 12366, 12367, 12383, 12386, 13523, 15719, 16383:** cutting height, **3037, 4657, 6654, 16345;** disease control, **3873;** fairway, **9573, 16147;** fertilization, **2463, 5451, 8698, 8705;** green, **8268, 9165, 9856, 12348;** irrigation practices, **2463, 5973, 16345;** wetting agent, **14508**

Annual bluegrass
description, **1781, 2626, 2643, 2654, 2673, 4008, 4392, 5315, 6133, 6487, 6490, 7160, 7421, 7947, 8013, 8085, 9944, 12143, 12547, 12725, 14170, 14725, 14859, 14909, 15410, 16383:** annual vs. perennial types, **2654, 8088, 14909, 16345;** growth habit, **14170;** morphology, **3002, 6494;** rooting, **2680, 3037, 14161, 14170;** seedling development, **8658;** Sweden, **9201**

Annual bluegrass
diseases, **14061:** anthracnose,

8351, 13991; *Fusarium* patch, **4768;** *Helminthosporium* species, **637, 15758;** *Pythium* blight, **6171;** stripe smut, **4714**

Annual bluegrass
dissemination, **2653**

Annual bluegrass
distribution, **7421, 12725, 14206**

Annual bluegrass
flowering, **4018, 14170, 16383:** environmental effects, **8658**

Annual bluegrass
grass seed contaminant, **1700**

Annual bluegrass
growth: environmental effects, **2624, 4146, 4147, 6654, 7556, 7558;** factors affecting, **5538;** soil effects, **6654, 7421**

Annual bluegrass
identification, **14061**

Annual bluegrass
insect pests: turfgrass weevil, **3633a, 3636a, 4146, 4147**

Annual bluegrass
invasion, **1, 679, 2653, 5681, 14170:** bentgrass cultivar susceptibility, **1547, 2654, 4646;** clipping removal, **5902;** cultural factors affecting, **6878, 7555, 14916, 16395;** cutting height, **1547, 4646, 5498, 16345;** fertility, **14170;** species competition effect, **13336, 14170;** sulfur, **2668;** topdressing, **5523, 7555;** vertical mowing, **16345, 16395**

Annual bluegrass
origin, **7421, 14908, 14909**

Annual bluegrass
seed: soil content, **12547;** viability, **9068**

Annual bluegrass
seed germination, **8086, 8658:** factors affecting, **4018, 5495, 9036, 11255, 12725**

Annual bluegrass
seed head: chemical inhibition, **6134, 6135, 6686, 7526, 12794**

Annual bluegrass
seed production, **7450, 7455, 7461, 12547**

Annual bluegrass
shoot growth: seasonal variation, **3035**

Annual bluegrass
strains: herbicide selectivity, **2682, 14860**

Annual bluegrass
taxonomy, **14725, 14909**

Annual bluegrass
use, **14362:** greens, **9856, 12493;** lawn, **7694, 15606;** winter polystand, **1507, 12321**

Annual bluegrass
weed problem, **4799, 8860, 12367:** fairways, **10915, 15982**

Annual chickweed
chemical control, **2728**

Annual dropseed
use, **14341**

Annual meadowgrass (see Annual bluegrass)

Annual ryegrass (see Italian ryegrass)

Annual weedy grass
chemical control: **3608a, 4502, 4544, 14082;** evaluation, **3509, 3665a, 8182**

Annual white grub, **11260**

Anomala orientalis (see Oriental beetle)

Anthemis nobilis (see Camomile)

Anthracnose, **140, 1523, 6733, 8337, 8351, 13565, 13991**

Anthracnose
chemical control, **140**

Antibiotics
disease control, **3277, 8997**

Antitranspirant, **1700, 4585, 7859, 10084, 11788**

Antitranspirant
effects on: leaf temperature, **4583**

Antitranspirant
monomolecular layers, **1687, 2282, 2292**

Antitranspirant
physiological effects, **4066, 4584, 6341, 11788**

Antitranspirant
stomatal inhibitors, **1542, 4582, 4583**: PMA, **1549**

Antonina graminis (see Rhodesgrass scale)

Ants, **17, 432, 581, 3623, 4562, 7029, 7258, 7606, 8670, 9393, 13502**

Ants
chemical control, **404, 542, 652, 768, 798, 857, 860, 1054, 2172, 2260, 4158, 4616, 5295, 6803, 7255, 7607, 8066, 8253, 8578, 8607, 9393, 10359, 10724, 10829, 11661, 12452, 13473, 13482, 13483, 14483, 15334:** chlordane, **13468, 13470, 13491, 13503, 13504;** DDT, **791**

Aphids, **1143**

Apical dominance, **10696**

Apomixis, **7137, 7138, 11083, 11084**

Apomixis
Kentucky bluegrass, **83, 5182, 7281, 16096**

Approaches, green:
culture, **6665, 12360**

Apron, **1198, 5318, 16016**

Apron
construction, **5241**

Apron
culture, **1509, 6527, 6829, 16015, 16018, 16309:** cutting height, **11474**

Apron
grasses used, **1113**

Aqua Humus®, **14402, 14403**

Aquatic weeds
chemical control, **1274, 1715**

Aradin, **13776**

Arboretum Kentucky bluegrass, **1473, 3656, 7309, 11187**

Arboretum Kentucky bluegrass
evaluation, **6306, 6330, 8317, 10635, 11186**

Architecture
golf course, **2484, 2784, 4062, 4063, 4815, 12696, 13798**

Arcocladium cuspidatum, **7026**

Arctared red fescue, **2612**

Argentine bahiagrass, **2346, 10524, 10525, 15858**

Argentine bahiagrass
fertilization, **8014**

Argentine bahiagrass
use, **16514**

Argentine stem weevil, **7253**

Arida velvet bentgrass, **7191, 8336**

Arista Kentucky bluegrass, **6306, 8350, 9218, 14813**

Arlington creeping bentgrass, **742, 757, 866, 977, 989, 993, 3058, 6557, 6950, 7309, 7928, 11235, 12698, 14638**

Arlington creeping bentgrass
adaptation, **6870, 9408**

Arlington creeping bentgrass
disease susceptibility, **854, 9564, 12837**

Arlington creeping bentgrass
evaluation, **920, 9233, 9245, 10616, 10622, 10760, 11031, 11232, 11266, 16489**

Arlington creeping bentgrass
nutrient defiency, **7929**

Arlington creeping bentgrass
use, **789, 815, 854**

Arlington turf garden, **9898, 14594**

Arlington turf garden
field day, **10835**

Arlington turf garden
history, **10814**

Armyworm, **545, 690, 1570, 1613, 3623, 4611, 4612, 7134, 8607, 8825**

Armyworm
chemical control, **640, 1626, 5294, 5295, 8829, 9873, 12816:** evaluation, **2172, 14235**

Armyworm
description, **8829, 12315**

Armyworm, fall, **12437**

Arsenates, organic (see Organic arsenicals)

Arsenic
carriers, **4435**

Arsenic
foliar absorption, **4425**

Arsenic
mode of action, **8862, 12929**

Arsenic
phosphorus interaction, **2100, 3722, 3725, 3728, 4406, 6578, 7762, 8074, 8863, 9628, 12626, 12750, 14245**

Arsenic
plant content, **13707**

Arsenic
soil analysis, **2100, 3722, 6150, 6151, 6152, 6153**

Arsenic
soil content, **3722, 13707:** vertical movement, **6153, 10456**

Arsenic
soil relationships, **12750, 16216**

Arsenicals, **8768, 13026**

Arsenicals
annual bluegrass control, **1639, 4392, 4394, 4398, 4399, 4440, 4469, 4499, 4504, 4511, 4513, 4539, 6102, 6145, 6146, 6147, 6153, 7955, 8859:** evaluation, **4406, 10624**

Arsenicals
application timing, **12281**

Arsenicals
crabgrass control, **1231, 1290, 1441:** evaluation, **3687a, 14203, 15704**

Arsenicals
foliar burn, **4425**

Arsenicals
Japanese beetle control, **5987**

Arsenicals
Paspalum control, **15225**

Arsenicals
weed control, **3354, 4434, 4435, 4436, 4521, 9364, 10828, 10830:** factors affecting, **8863, 12281;** history, **9979**

Arsenic toxicity, **3722, 3879, 3880, 4234, 4434, 4469, 16216**

Arsenic toxicity
environmental factors affecting, **12929**

Arsenic toxicity
factors affecting, **3725, 3728, 4398, 4399, 10851**

Arsenic toxicity
roots, **4425, 12750**

Arsenic toxicity
shoots, **3722, 6150, 12750**

Arsenic toxicity
soil factors affecting, **3722, 4234:** soil reaction, **3722, 3725, 3726**

Arsenic toxicity
species variability, **3722**

Artificial heating (see Soil warming)

Artificial turf (see Synthetic turf)

ASA C–5 Division, **6868**

Asbestos cement pipe, **7688, 12036, 12913, 14329**

Ascochyta leaf spot, **2098, 3128**

Asiatic garden beetle, **414, 573, 657, 5983, 7156, 7226**

Asiatic garden beetle
chemical control, **5984, 5989, 13488**

Asparagine
temperature response, **2557, 2694, 2697**

Aspergillus sydow
soil water repellency effect, **13033**

Asphalt
herbicide incorporation, **5111**

Asphalt
mulch, **2667, 2768, 9833, 9952, 13401, 13797**

Asphalt
mulch tie-down, **1479, 2432, 3794, 10759**

Asphalt
species tolerance, **2768, 6539**

Asphalt
temperature effect, **10413**

Asphalt barrier
soil modification, **1747, 1780**

Aspon®
Southern chinch bug control, **7268**

Astoria colonial bentgrass, **347, 742, 757, 2304, 6640, 7309, 11661, 12007, 12698, 13238, 13462**

Astoria colonial bentgrass
disease control, **24, 977**

Astoria colonial bentgrass
evaluation, **10616, 10622, 10760, 11021, 11186:** disease susceptibility, **9564, 14923**

Astoria colonial bentgrass
fertilization, **4894**

Atalopedea campestris (see Skipper, field)

Athletic field (see Sports field)

Atlas Kentucky bluegrass, **9218, 11363**

Atmospheric carbon dioxide, **15861**

Atmospheric desiccation
species tolerance, **3719**

Atmospheric pollution (see Pollution, atmospheric)

Atmospheric water vapor
effects on: herbicide effectiveness, **12234**

Atmospheric water vapor
factors affecting, **9022, 15417**

Atmospheric water vapor
modification, **1943**

Atmospheric water vapor
seed viability effects, **3664a, 6393**

Atmospheric water vapor
variations, **14319:** diurnal, **10849, 14193;** vertical, **9022, 12614, 14193, 15417, 15418**

Atrazine, **3502, 8182**

Atrazine
in bermudagrass, **93**

Atrazine
carbohydrate reserve effects, **13394**

Atrazine
crabgrass control, **8178**

Atrazine
fall *Panicum* control, **14048**

Atrazine
quackgrass control, **13394**

Atrazine
roadside soil sterilant, **87**

Atrazine
soil persistence, **2279, 3394, 5930, 10451**

Atrazine
species selectivity, **3502, 3529:** zoysiagrass, **2203, 5563, 5564**

Atrazine
weed control: in centipedegrass, **8564;** in St. Augustinegrass, **8564, 11841**

Austin leveler, **1537**

Australia
golf course culture, **7253**

Auxin
tillering effect, **9484**

Availability index, **9085**

Awl nematode, **11743, 11744, 11745, 12057**

Awl nematode
parasitic effects, **12041, 12050**

Axonopus, **2932**

Axonopus affinis (see Carpetgrass)

Axonopus compressus (see Carpetgrass)

Azak® (see Terbutol)

6–Azuracil
growth regulator, **10056**

B–995, **15800**

B–995
on bermudagrass, **1871, 8161**

B–995
evaluation, **8759, 11231, 12247**

Bacillus popilliae (see Milky disease)

Backafall tall fescue, **9212, 11354**

Bacteria, **7573, 9605, 12604, 13703, 13977, 13978, 14889**

Bacteria
effects, **8815, 9607, 13977**

Bacteria
factors affecting, **9607, 12297**

Bacteria
in soil, **9605**

Bacteria
topdressing source, **13976**

Bahiagrass, **2376, 4243, 12877, 12923, 13299, 14687, 15358, 15671**

Bahiagrass
adaptation, **958, 2377, 3553, 3676, 8009, 8021, 12133, 15054**

Bahiagrass
breeding, **3553, 3584, 6046**

Bahiagrass
cultivar, **2376, 2377, 13299:** evaluation, **5120, 8009, 8591, 16514;** *Pythium* susceptibility, **6207**

Bahiagrass
culture, **10514, 10525, 15858, 16260:** fertilization, **5335, 5651, 6061, 9063; iron chlorosis, 8036, 14067;** irrigation, **5651, 10023;** mowing, **958, 8593, 10023;** vertical mowing, **10511**

Bahiagrass
description, **3534, 3553, 8009,**

10525, 15858: carbohydrate reserves, 5328, 5336

Bahiagrass
dollar spot disease, 6171, 7123

Bahiagrass
establishment, 2380, 10514

Bahiagrass
herbicide tolerance, 7995

Bahiagrass
nematode pests, 3116

Bahiagrass
propagation, 3543, 14509

Bahiagrass
seed germination: scarification, 7834

Bahiagrass
seed head chemical control, 3510, 6184

Bahiagrass
sod production, 1831

Bahiagrass
uses, 2376, 3553, 14510: East Africa, 14625

Baits
mechanical applicator, 2856

Balan® (see Benefin)

Ball bounce
on cricket wicket, 14298

Ball bounce
factors affecting, 4532, 9217

Ball marks
factors affecting, 4515, 4532, 10828

Ball marks
repair, 1802

Ball roll
factors affecting, 1636, 10334: bentgrass cultivar variation, 6817, 9381; mowing, 924, 6817, 9217; soil mix, 4532, 9217

Ball roll
measurement, 385, 14304

Bandane® (see Polychlorodicyclopentadiene)

Barbula convoluta, 2961, 7026, 8464

Barbula falax, 1092, 2961

Barbula unguiculata, 2961, 7026

Barenza chewings fescue, 7284

Barenza Kentucky bluegrass, 8350, 15414

Barenza sheep fescue, 2650, 7287

Barenza velvet bentgrass, 8336, 8341

Bargena red fescue, 7287

Bark, wood
amendment, 2043, 3046, 12165, 14713

Bark, wood
mulch, 3046

Bark, wood
soil decomposition, 172

Barnyardgrass
chemical control, 4396, 10377

Barnyardgrass
light quality effect, 5240

Baron Kentucky bluegrass, 2100, 9647, 13370

Baseball field
construction: state bulletin, 7420, 7423

Baseball field
culture, 1236, 4124, 4130, 7981, 8313, 15600

Baseball field
design, 7416

Baseball field
establishment, 1226, 4124, 4130

Baseball field
pitching mound construction, 2002

Basic slag
phosphorus source, 5684

Baygon® (see Propoxur)

Bayshore bermudagrass, 1153, 2372, 7309, 10768

Bayshore bermudagrass
culture, 8599, 15840

Bayshore bermudagrass
evaluation, 10301, 11882

Bayshore bermudagrass
uses, 8599, 13553

Beachgrass, 7947, 9171

Beachgrass
establishment, 9204

Beachgrass
sand dune stabilization, 9171, 16456

Beaumont Kentucky bluegrass, 11363

Bees, 9186

Bees
chemical control, 12316

Beetles, 8825

Bellis perennis (see English daisey)

Bellvue Kentucky bluegrass, 6322, 6330

Belonolaimus (see Sting nematode)

Belturf Kentucky bluegrass, 2027, 6322

Belturf Kentucky bluegrass
evaluation, 6330, 11325, 14813

Belturf Kentucky bluegrass
ozone injury, 16097

Benefin, 5350, 8412, 8572, 14518

Benefin
annual bluegrass control, 1967, 2070, 6487, 8031, 8168, 8572, 9533, 9537: on bermudagrass, 1871; evaluation, 5632, 8419, 10624; winter overseeding, 2311, 2312

Benefin
crabgrass control, 1700, 1782, 2027, 4139, 4141, 5185, 5192, 5193, 5199, 5200, 5383, 5549, 8701, 9531, 9533, 9537, 9544, 10619, 12031, 13861, 14839: evaluation, 7661, 8407, 8414, 14837

Benefin
degradation, 8768

Benefin
goosegrass control, **9733**

Benefin
residual phytotoxicity, **10451**

Benefin
selectivity, **2100, 8706, 8707:** on bermudagrass, **2100, 2310, 13970;** on Kentucky bluegrass cultivars, **2633**

Benomyl, **2027, 7353, 13723**

Benomyl
brown patch control, **6601, 15135**

Benomyl
dollar spot control, **2673, 3103, 4203, 6601, 12357, 12538, 15022, 15135, 16212**

Benomyl
flag smut control, **11103**

Benomyl
Fusarium blight control, **2100, 2667, 2672, 11108, 11111, 15012, 15024, 15025, 15031:** evaluation, **2170, 6764, 11107**

Benomyl
Fusarium patch control, **6755, 6756, 16211, 16212**

Benomyl
powdery mildew control, **15021**

Benomyl
red thread control, **6601, 12357, 16212**

Benomyl
resistant fungi evaluation, **13938**

Benomyl
snowmold control, **7068, 14810**

Benomyl
soil movement: surfactants effect, **12155**

Benomyl
stripe smut control, **1985, 4051, 7195, 7196, 7199, 7200, 8369, 11103, 12837, 15015**

Benomyl
stunt nematode control, **9329**

Benomyl
Typhula blight control, **8373**

Benomyl
uptake, **10490**

Bensulide, **2236, 4945, 7659, 7674, 8412, 9825, 13881, 13882**

Bensulide
annual bluegrass control, **67, 1700, 1967, 2070, 2902, 2918, 2919, 4018, 5184, 5381, 5571, 6653, 8168, 8171, 8179, 9533, 9537, 9845, 15140, 16213, 16432, 16434;** evaluation, **5632, 8157, 8158, 8419, 10020, 10624**

Bensulide
bioassay, **10386**

Bensulide
buckhorn plaintain control, **2904**

Bensulide
crabgrass control, **1700, 1782, 1871, 2027, 2916, 3701, 5185, 5199, 5205, 5383, 5543, 5545, 5549, 5561, 8168, 9529, 9530, 9531, 9533, 9537, 9544, 9548, 10375, 10377, 10378, 10404, 10619, 12031, 13859, 14823, 14837, 14839:** evaluation, **7661, 8156, 8407, 8414, 8415, 10636, 14497**

Bensulide
deactivation: activated carbon, **8139;** activated charcoal, **2906, 8417;** seedbed preparation, **2898**

Bensulide
goosegrass control, **2900, 7659, 7661, 8157**

Bensulide
phytotoxic effects, **2916, 10394**

Bensulide
residual effect, **2916, 9825, 10451**

Bensulide
selectivity, **2902, 7880, 8706, 8707, 13858:** bermudagrass, **2310, 4794;** creeping bentgrass, **8158, 8722;** *Dichondra,* **2236;** Kentucky bluegrass, **66**

Bentgrass, **351, 5770, 5977, 10642, 12139, 15413**

Bentgrass
adaptation, **310, 2581, 5820, 6854, 11468, 12828, 15054, 16007, 16366:** soil, **606, 867, 5310**

Bentgrass
classification, **10815**

Bentgrass
cultivar, **310, 2129:** disease susceptibility, **61, 1545, 2676;** evaluation, **1469, 3592a, 5453, 5771, 8294;** genetic variation, **3154;** herbicide selectivity, **2319, 7951;** low temperature hardiness, **2577, 2578, 2591, 2605;** shade adaptation, **1547**

Bentgrass
culture, **4677, 5692, 7071, 13375, 16010, 16011:** fertilization, **2007, 2760, 4896, 5183, 5636, 8576;** lawn, **5691, 14922**

Bentgrass
description, **4845, 12828:** root growth, **2553, 2555, 2695, 14161**

Bentgrass
diseases, **3111, 4050, 4052, 5089, 13706, 15646, 15672**

Bentgrass
establishment: vegetative, **296, 3051, 3053, 8126**

Bentgrass
evaluation, **5165, 6345, 6419, 10857, 12364, 15722, 16064**

Bentgrass
genetics, **3152, 3154**

Bentgrass
identification: cultivar, **385;** seedling, **2666**

Bentgrass
pesticide selectivity, **806, 976, 1000, 2173**

Bentgrass
purity, **8554**

Bentgrass
seed certification, **8270**

Bentgrass
seed production, **5300, 7776, 9474, 10150, 10152, 11777**

Bentgrass
turfgrass community compatibility, **11666**

Bentgrass
uses, **7706, 9582, 12007, 14664:** fairway, **7918, 10559;** green, **297, 565, 962, 4572, 5162, 8792, 11469, 11659;** lawn, **5785, 5887, 7297**

Bentgrass, weed
chemical control, **1493, 1572, 1579, 3668, 4646**

Bentgrass, weed
invasion, **4634**

Bentgrass nematode, **2242, 4222**

Bentgrass, South German mixed (see South German mixed bentgrass)

Bentonite clay
pond sealing, **12768**

Benzimidazole fungicides, **6599, 6601**

Benzyladenine
sod heating control, **8940, 8947**

Berkshiregrass, **1214**

Bermudagrass, **3776, 5913, 6091, 8160, 9101, 12121, 12877, 13271, 14327, 16322**

Bermudagrass
adaptation, **310, 2377, 3539, 3553, 3676, 4607, 4721, 4801, 5483, 5793, 5802, 6895, 7376, 7937, 8009, 8153, 8694, 9307, 12133, 15054, 16007, 16366, 16413:** low temperature, **74, 1078, 1685, 12499;** low temperature kill, **960, 1275, 10774;** shade, **3592;** soil reaction, **958, 1315, 11024;** temperature, **8058, 16342, 16413;** winter injury, **143, 1514, 1565, 5858, 7074, 10762, 11633**

Bermudagrass
breeding, **3538, 3549, 3553, 3555, 3580, 3586, 3611, 8166, 10775, 12223, 14754**

Bermudagrass
chemical composition, **30, 3593, 9100, 14556**

Bermudagrass
color retention, winter: plastic covers, **2399;** soil warming, **2399, 2401, 2403**

Bermudagrass
cultivars, **1153, 1327, 4426, 7206, 7926, 8459, 8519, 9117, 9662, 16413:** bermudagrass mite susceptibility, **1700, 14899, 14907;** chemical composition, **8600, 9100, 9884;** chlorophyl content, **9884, 13560;** description, **5273, 13725, 14687, 14690, 15441;** disease susceptibility, **1487, 2398, 6160, 6207, 14906;** drought tolerance, **9016;** evaluation, **870, 892, 1012, 1489, 1639, 2398, 2402, 2606, 2951, 3123, 3507, 3583, 5225, 5226, 7223, 7397, 7922, 7967, 7989, 8009, 8021, 8154, 8694, 8761, 9006, 9568, 9618, 10461, 10922, 11882, 12114, 12806, 12820, 12824, 13044, 13981, 14587, 14899, 16261, 16331;** herbicide selectivity, **1871, 3005, 4011, 14309;** iron chlorosis proneness, **13560;** lateral spreading rate, **12824;** leaf texture, **7922, 12824;** low temperature hardiness, **1472, 2566, 5236;** nutritional requirements, **5274;** oil tolerance, **7996;** root variability, **2606;** salinity tolerance, **16428, 16429;** seed head formation variability, **7922;** shade adaptation, **9883;** spring green-up rate, **7922, 13445, 14899;** thatching tendency, **7922;** vegetative identification, **14683, 14690;** wear tolerance, **3594, 16347**

Bermudagrass
culture, **3710, 4078, 4426, 4801, 5327, 6895, 8181, 8183, 8212, 8519, 8536, 8570, 9304, 10174, 12816, 14681, 14770, 15358, 16115, 16189, 16378:** cutting height, **131, 958, 1700, 7933, 9007, 16320;** fertilization, **30, 132, 3547, 3570, 4032, 4787, 7925, 7937, 8034, 8173, 8757, 8886, 9008, 9012, 9015, 10452, 10459, 11504, 12265, 12267, 12788, 14404, 14405, 15075, 15363, 16413;** green, **303, 349, 2813, 7787, 7788, 13651;** irrigation, **2887, 2939, 5651, 16413;** lawn, **266, 5914, 11680;** liming, **15, 29;** liquid sewage sludge, **8951;** mowing, **2049, 2939, 15657, 16413;** nitrogen fertilization, **40, 41, 5651, 5917, 15355;** thatch control, **1871, 2614, 8173, 15355;** weed control, **1151, 2894, 3514, 6104;** winter overseeding, **3515, 8719**

Bermudagrass
description, **3553, 3579, 4009, 5053, 5145, 5327, 7376, 7947, 8228, 8694, 14347, 16115:** chromosome number, **8227, 8228, 12222;** discoloration, **2334, 12976, 13559, 16339, 16342, 16352**

Bermudagrass
diseases, **1345, 1776, 2286, 2744, 3808, 3938, 4331, 4335, 5652, 5922, 6164, 6203, 15646, 15672:** dollar spot, **15129, 15130, 16300;** *Helminthosporium* species, **6160, 6177, 6182, 6203, 10761;** spring dead spot, **6122, 13889, 13936, 15133, 15134**

Bermudagrass
environmental effects, **3329, 6386, 7636:** light, **9881, 16342, 16413**

Bermudagrass
establishment, **2310, 4426, 6541, 6941, 8570, 12795, 16115:** seed, **720, 3102, 9005;** vegetative, **1623, 3816, 10126**

Bermudagrass
herbicide selectivity, **45, 232,**

2899, 3071, 4061, 7995, 8177, 12456

Bermudagrass
pests: bermudagrass mite, **1512, 3625, 3627, 3630, 3631, 3632, 3633, 3637, 3638, 3639, 3640, 3643, 4612, 12866;** insects, **1512, 2744, 14520, 14668, 15404;** nematodes, **2756, 5014, 6607, 9332, 12645, 14092, 15926;** rhodesgrass scale, **3628, 12866, 13003, 16155**

Bermudagrass
physiological responses, **3790, 5349, 6057**

Bermudagrass
polystands, **2400, 2523:** with bentgrass, **10725, 11233**

Bermudagrass
root growth: cultural factors affecting, **2310, 2907, 8080, 9007;** environmental factors affecting, **2069, 3486, 3488**

Bermudagrass
seed germination, **544, 3388, 7618, 15654**

Bermudagrass
spring green-up, **8574**

Bermudagrass
uses, **2369, 3547, 3553, 5473, 8183, 12356, 13658, 13981:** fairway, **13, 3585, 9193, 9304, 9568;** lawn, **4426, 12739;** tee, **11621, 16187**

Bermudagrass
wear tolerance: culture, **3594**

Bermudagrass
winter injury: prevention, **2678, 2739, 5590, 6516**

Bermudagrass, weed
chemical control, **1027, 2867, 6080, 6083, 7655, 10021, 13616:** evaluation, **1548, 8182, 13695, 14309**

Bermudagrass, weed
cultural control, **2158, 14556**

Bermudagrass, weed
invasion: effect of cultural practices, **10064, 10077**

Bermudagrass mite, **1512, 1779, 3291, 3294, 3627, 3629, 3632, 3637, 4780, 7914, 8905**

Bermudagrass mite
bermudagrass cultivar susceptibility, **3625, 3632, 3642, 14907**

Bermudagrass mite
chemical control, **3630, 3633, 3640, 8164, 8476, 8884:** diazinon, **3639, 3642, 3643;** evaluation, **1490, 1639, 1700, 3283, 3290, 3292, 3631, 3638, 3639, 3643, 8885, 8896, 14907**

Bermudagrass mite
description, **4268, 4779, 8476, 8905, 14907**

Bermudagrass mite
injury symptoms, **4268, 8481**

Bermudagrass scale, **3291, 3623, 3624, 4333, 4780, 5253, 16155**

Betasan® (see Bensulide)

Big-eyed bug, **3675a**

Biljart hard fescue, **2649, 7269**

Billbug, **1217, 1572, 3042, 3127, 3285, 3623, 4780, 8878, 9000, 11344**

Billbug
chemical control, **1570, 1779, 8893, 10156:** evaluation, **1639, 8683, 8879, 8896, 12180**

Billbug
description, **4779, 8478, 8479, 8481, 8683, 12315**

Billbug
injury symptoms, **8904**

Billbug
life history, **8744, 9070**

Billbug, hunting (see Hunting billbug)

Billbug, Phoenix (see Phoenix billbug)

Bindweed
chemical control, **1763, 8934**

Birds, **549, 7548**

Birdsfoot trefoil, **4731, 7027, 14100**

Birdsfoot trefoil
adaptation, **14100, 14102**

Birdsfoot trefoil
roadside use, **5159, 15158:** evaluation, **9129**

Bird's nest fungi, **3128**

Birka Kentucky bluegrass, **9218**

2,2-bis(p-methoxyphenyl)-1,1,1-trichlorothane (see Methoxychlor)

Bitter blue St. Augustinegrass, **7309, 11740**

Bitumen
soil modification, **4756**

Bitumen emulsion
mulch, **255**

Black beetle
chemical control, **2172, 6803, 7253**

Black medic
chemical control, **10379**

Blast furnace slag
soil amendment, **5167, 13683, 13685, 16488, 16489**

Blends, **4652, 6296, 13232, 13353**
Kentucky bluegrass cultivars, **1489, 1639, 1700, 1967, 2027, 2100, 6322, 6330:** evaluation, **2583, 2603, 10626, 11327, 11329;** sod strength, **2687, 6313**

Blind seed disease
chemical control, **7347, 7362**

Blissus hirtus (see Chinchbug, hairy)

Blissus insularis (see Southern chinch bug)

Blissus leucopterus (see Chinch bug)

Blister smut, **5941**

Blood, dried (see Dried blood)

Blue grama, **2768, 2772, 8810**
adaptation, **2770, 2771, 11823, 13032, 15848**

Bluegrass, **606, 11770**
breeding, **84, 2027, 3867, 13670**

Bluegrass billbug, **5937, 13502**
chemical control, **5937, 14534, 14535:** evaluation, **2027, 14533**

Bluegrass webworm, **78, 411**
chemical control, **11661, 11665**

Bluestem, **76, 2875, 3771**

Boar bentgrass, **8350**

Boer lovegrass, **828**

Boletus erythropus, **6508**

Bone meal, **309, 1558, 5634, 5678, 5684**
evaluation, **2172, 5636, 6790, 10861, 10863**

Bonnieblue Kentucky bluegrass, **16326**

Book
anatomy, **2244, 13392, 15372:** monocotyledons, **9843, 10474**

Book
atmospheric pollution, **10123**

Book
chromosome numbers, **4577**

Book
cricket ground culture: English, **13005, 14468, 14755**

Book
development, **2244**

Book
ecology, **3860**

Book
equipment, **7031**

Book
fertilizer handbook, **13613**

Book
golf course, **288, 6744**

Book
golf course architecture, **8249, 14462, 14469, 14631**

Book
golf course construction, **5882, 14462, 14631**: New Zealand, **9514**

Book
golf course culture, **696, 2528, 4295, 5722, 6598, 8249, 9847, 11394, 11469, 12140, 12149, 13542, 14462**: English, **14470;** New Zealand, **9514**

Book
golf course establishment, **13542**

Book
golf course management, **15050**

Book
grass, **12027, 12187, 16055**: English, **8251**

Book
grass identification, **9843, 15372**

Book
green culture, **9866, 9867**: English, **13005, 14468**

Book
ground covers, **7133**

Book
grounds culture, **7542, 15817**

Book
growth patterns, **2244**

Book
growth regulators, plant, **2296**

Book
herbicide, **2297**

Book
irrigation system, **6995, 11898, 15430, 16214:** design, **2180, 14412**

Book
lawn, **592, 1063, 1116, 1173, 1456, 2442, 2530, 2843, 5991, 7034**

Book
lawn culture, **2364, 2383, 2442, 2445, 3227, 3369, 3684a, 3949, 4096, 4097, 4295, 4744, 4753, 4979, 4981, 5697, 5698, 5744, 5745, 5754, 6005, 7133, 7136, 8444, 9523, 9847, 9865, 9867, 10426, 10468, 11913, 12484, 12494, 12848, 12849, 13190, 13236, 13541, 13647, 14073, 14081, 14174, 14176, 14184, 14274, 14466, 14712, 15043, 15607, 15844, 15979, 16112, 16154, 16215, 16310, 16311**: Central Africa, **8445;** English, **7780, 9522, 9653, 13005, 14271, 14468, 14755;** Germany, **13063;** organic, **12851;** review, **4972;** tropical regions, **13924**

Book
lawn establishment, **2443, 2444, 2445, 3684a, 4744, 4753, 4979, 4981, 5044, 5744, 5745, 6005, 7136, 9523, 11913, 12484, 12494, 12849, 13190, 13541, 13647, 15979, 16154, 16215, 16310, 16311**: English, **7780, 8224, 9522**

Book
morphology, **2243, 2244, 7150, 7793**

Book
nematodes, **6609**

Book
nutrient deficiencies, **2548**

Book
polo field culture, **4295**

Book
rhizome, **14830**

Book
roots, **14833, 15625**

Book
salinity, **1265, 12582**

Book
seed, **1442, 1456**

Book
sodic soils, **12582**

Book
soil chemical analysis, **8333**

Book
sports field construction, **14032**

Book
sports field culture, **2529, 5754, 9847, 9865, 9866, 9867, 14032, 14184, 14466**: Germany, **13063**

Book
taxonomy, grasses, **6771, 8127, 8128**

Book
tennis court culture: English, **13005, 14468**

Book
turfgrass culture, **1430, 2425, 2688, 4007, 4295, 4554, 5326, 7031, 7319, 10097, 10098, 11137, 11199, 14032, 14184, 15316, 16112**: English, **5743, 10838;** South Africa, **10460;** Sweden, **9229**

Book
turfgrass diseases, **1009, 4173, 12993, 12994, 14018, 14189**

Book
turfgrass establishment, **4007, 5325, 7031**: South Africa, **10460**

Book
turfgrass pests, **6005, 7031**

Book
turfgrass reviews, **2808**

Book
turfgrass science, **2688, 7319, 10097, 10098, 11137**

Book
weed control, **1456, 3683**

Borax
snowmold control, **5781**

Borax
weed control, **859, 10866**

Bordeaux mixture, **570, 666, 1036, 2815**
brown patch control, **3708, 12137, 12147**

Boreal red fescue, **2612, 5363**

Bore colonial bentgrass, **9208, 9212, 9213, 15755**

Boron
carriers, **1546, 9698**

Boron
deficiency symptoms, **9267, 10963, 11790**

Boron
growth effects, **4807, 5856, 11795**

Boron
nutrition, **7671, 11785**

Boron
toxicity, **1454, 3184, 3185, 7868, 9802, 11786, 11791:** effect of mowing, **9802, 11795;** species tolerance, **9802, 11791, 11795;** symptoms, **11791, 11795**

Botanical composition, **3323, 11024**

Bouteloua curtipendula (see Sideoats grama)

Bouteloua gracilis (see Blue grama)

Bouyoucos moisture blocks, **2454, 2516**

Bowling green, **4697, 7593, 10787**

Bowling green
construction, **568, 1030, 5912, 7003, 7004, 7005, 8114, 8485, 10332, 10333, 12242, 14551**

Bowling green
culture, **568, 823, 1032, 3106, 3463, 3703, 3796, 4309, 5912, 8019, 8110, 8504, 10042, 10960, 11237, 14554, 15265**: Australia, **8114, 15180, 15288;** *Cotula* species, **10344, 15211, 15234;** England, **6529, 8486, 8487, 12243, 15321;** fall, **1004, 1097, 1100, 1338, 1709, 8488, 10168;** mudbath, **15322;** New Zealand, **15167, 15169, 15173, 15175, 15177, 15183, 15186, 15194, 15210, 15214, 15216, 15222, 15224, 15227, 15233, 15239, 15243, 15246, 15248, 15267, 15268, 15271, 15272, 15280, 15284, 15287, 15290, 15294, 15295, 15296, 15303, 15305, 15308, 15309, 15311, 15313, 15314, 15315, 15322;** Rhodesia, **15321;** spring, **1071, 1132, 1177, 1775, 8491;** topdressing, **1482, 2263;** weed control, **10339, 15254;** winter, **1021, 1398, 1866, 7956, 15196**

Bowling green
diseases, **9272**

Bowling green
establishment, **568, 3106, 7005, 8110, 8485, 12242, 15213, 15309, 15918**: *Cotula,* **15234, 15241, 15255, 15276**

Bowling green
irrigation system, **3704**

Bowling green
landscaping, **10338**

Bowling green
leveling: Austin leveler, **15188**

Bowling green
maintenance costs, **1494**

Bowling green
pests: earthworms, **10340**

Bowling green
renovation, **1538, 1799, 5019, 8489, 10341, 10669, 14310, 15166:** to *Cotula,* **11257, 15307;** New Zealand, **15188, 15191, 15213, 15236, 15253**

Bowling green
rubber mat color: temperature effects, **1540, 15199, 15263**

Bowling green
species used, **1030, 1257, 4746, 8113, 12485, 15198**: *Cotula,* **3859, 10342, 15211, 15229, 15234;** *Dichondra,* **15211;** pearlwort, **1180;** starweed, **10343, 15211**

BPA, **2237**

Brabantia chewings fescue, **8343**

Brabantia Kentucky bluegrass, **15414**

Brabantia red fescue
evaluation, **8341**

Brabantia sheep fescue
evaluation, **8341**

Brachythecium rutabulum, **1092, 7026**

Bradley bermudagrass, **10461**

Bradysia impatiens (see Fungus gnat)

Brassica kaber (see Wild mustard)

Breeding, **207, 945, 1495, 3531, 3556, 3568, 3573, 3609, 3908, 3909, 3939, 3940, 5172, 5179, 5273, 6292, 6297, 6299, 6325, 6833, 7584, 9519, 9658, 9663, 11187, 11992, 13349, 15054, 16372**

Breeding
annual bluegrass, **8084, 9068, 9823**

Breeding
apomixis, **3584, 7282, 10192, 11083, 11084**: Kentucky bluegrass, **6291, 7281**

Breeding
asexual reproduction, **3375**

Breeding
bahiagrass, **3543, 3544, 3553, 3584, 3609**

Breeding
bentgrass, **4599, 11118, 11119, 11983**

Breeding
bermudagrass, **2397, 3538, 3549, 3553, 3555, 3580, 3586, 3605, 3611, 8166, 12815, 12816, 14754**

Breeding
bluegrass, **2027, 5575, 7117, 13670**

Breeding
carpetgrass, **3553**

Breeding
colonial bentgrass, **5122, 5123**

Breeding
creeping bentgrass, **304, 5165**

Breeding
crested wheatgrass, **4592, 4951, 13042**

Breeding
cross-pollination factors, **6725, 9823**

Breeding
crown vetch, **3915, 3916, 12656**

Breeding
cytogenetic studies, **7117, 8626, 15632**

Breeding
dallisgrass, **3553, 3589**

Breeding
disease resistance, **2819, 5164, 7372, 12016, 15876**

Breeding
emasculation: high temperature treatment, **8084**

Breeding
fertility: evaluation, **4599**

Breeding
Festuca-Lolium hybrids, **4276**

Breeding
history, **13953**

Breeding
hybridization, **3867, 4340, 4953, 6311, 8494, 10192, 12013, 15054:** bermudagrass, **7376, 7380**; Italian ryegrass-tall fescue, **3415, 3426, 3428, 3430, 3433, 3434, 3435**; Kentucky bluegrass, **6311, 6325, 12012, 12019**; Kentucky bluegrass-Canada bluegrass, **3240, 4336**; *Lolium-Festuca,* **15632**; perennial ryegrass-fescue hybrids, **3415, 3677a**

Breeding
hybrids: *Agrostis,* **8626**; *Festuca* species, **16126**; *Lolium* species, **16126**

Breeding
isolation distance, **7085**

Breeding
Italian ryegrass, **3553**

Breeding
Kentucky bluegrass, **61, 2031, 2208, 2847, 2848, 2849, 2852, 3418, 3420, 3427, 3429, 3431, 3432, 3553, 4553, 4490, 5158, 6293, 6312, 7283, 7314, 7317, 7321, 7322, 7595, 9657, 10427, 10842, 11220, 11321, 11322, 11328, 11958, 12014, 12015, 12017, 12113, 12645, 12650, 12651, 12652, 12653, 13954, 13955, 13958**

Breeding
kikuyugrass: induced sterility, **16363**

Breeding
methods, **61, 2038, 3416, 3588, 3607, 3609, 4592, 5575, 6043, 6319, 6325, 8498, 10192, 11328, 11983, 13955, 13957, 14643**

Breeding
mutation: irradiation, **7311, 7314, 12223**

Breeding
Paspalum species, **3494**

Breeding
perennial ryegrass, **6300, 8497, 14613**

Breeding
pollen quality, **5123, 14597**

Breeding
procedure, **3939, 3940, 4553, 7283, 7333, 9031, 11120, 11142, 13953, 16250**

Breeding
quantitative inheritance, **3558, 3561**

Breeding
red fescue, **2633, 2649, 8644, 11988, 11990, 11993, 16252**

Breeding
research summary, **6294, 12112**: Czechoslovakia, **14475**; Germany, **5591, 12124**; Netherlands, **5599, 8346**; Sweden, **1737, 1930, 8644, 9224**

Breeding
rough bluegrass, **5002**

Breeding
ryegrass, **3907, 3919, 8500, 9512**

Breeding
St. Augustinegrass, **3553, 8166, 9667**

Breeding
saltgrass, **5120**

Breeding
self-fertility: species evaluation, **5123, 8813**

Breeding
self-incompatability, **3605, 9767**

Breeding
sexual reproduction, **3375**

Breeding
tall fescue, **3416, 3417, 3419, 3423, 3424, 3428, 3553, 3564, 13555, 14643**

Breeding
timothy, **8644**

Breeding
velvet bentgrass, **4913, 14175**

Breeding
warm season turfgrasses, **3551, 3553, 5116, 5120, 8166**

Breeding
zoysiagrass, **3553, 6042, 6043**

Bridges
golf course, **3401**

Broadleaf plantain, **748, 4730**

Broadleaf weeds, **4345, 5903**

Broadleaf weeds
chemical control, **811, 1376, 2910, 4136, 4544, 4858, 5676, 6357, 6360, 7089, 7533, 7535, 8152, 8427, 9941, 10627, 11047, 12029, 12032, 12501, 13114, 13512, 13672, 13749, 13858, 13882, 14082, 14434, 14495, 14794, 14861, 14913, 15039, 15040, 15416**: application timing, **1700, 8433**; 2, 4–D, **799, 7097, 8617, 11095, 11686, 15920**; evaluation, **1639, 1782, 3780, 4640, 4669, 4847, 5382, 5732, 5733, 7656, 8173, 8182, 8423, 8432, 9465, 9531, 9533, 9537, 10404, 12693, 12808, 13636, 13860, 14500, 15832, 15978**

Broadleaf weed
control, **774, 800, 801, 1689, 2132, 4805, 10613, 14415**

Bromacil
annual bluegrass control, **6487, 11256**

Bromacil
on *Cotula,* **15269, 15277**

Bromacil
weed control, **8182, 13636**

Bromegrass
roadside use, **10233**

Bromegrass mosaic virus, **13755**

Bromosan, **11106**

Bromoxynil, **1797, 14084**

Bromoxynil
broadleaf weed control, **2178, 5382, 8410, 9465**

Bromoxynil
degradation, **8768**

Bromoxynil
selectivity, **5382, 14084**

Bromus inermis (see Smooth brome)

Bromus species
hybridization, **10685**

Brown bentgrass (see Colonial bentgrass)

Brown patch, **185, 315, 436, 438, 440, 599, 604, 608, 644, 953, 1017, 2264, 2265, 2738, 2839, 3252, 3470, 3672a, 4713, 5399, 6158, 6159, 6199, 7884, 9271, 9272, 9764, 10796, 10828, 11494, 13646, 13697, 13700, 14394, 15716, 16489**

Brown patch
adapted tolerance: fungicides, **5384**

Brown patch
chemical control, **20, 24, 433, 435, 584, 1487, 1590, 2264, 2279, 3041, 3070, 3604a, 4360, 4677, 4683, 6114, 6132, 6174, 6177, 6179, 6571, 6614, 6748, 6834, 8059, 8096, 8164, 8553, 8807, 9195, 9233, 9463, 9702, 10027, 10083, 10381, 10443, 10790, 10792, 10794, 10795, 10833, 10846, 10891, 11763, 11769, 11847, 11876, 12571, 12631, 13598, 13612, 13703, 13716, 14717, 14721, 14886, 15014, 15630, 15679, 15759, 15781**: Bordeaux mixture, **3708, 12137**; evaluation, **799, 905, 1545, 1639, 1700, 2172, 2326, 2328, 2609, 3249, 3253, 3260, 3597a, 3602a, 3605a, 3650, 4209, 4679, 4680, 4681, 4682, 4690, 4692, 4693, 6566, 6567, 6601, 7619, 7924, 8098, 8185, 8371, 9270, 9886, 10410, 10796, 10797, 10799, 10801, 10804, 11531, 11661, 12167, 12910, 13600, 13603, 13701, 13732, 13871, 14719, 15013, 15122, 15123, 15124, 15126, 15128, 15132, 15135, 15140, 16050, 16052, 16068, 16291, 16292, 16300, 16511**; mercury, **311, 2344, 11661, 13701**; nabam, **9764, 14311, 14312**; St. Augustinegrass, **168, 1545, 1700, 7933, 9674**

Brown patch
control, **431, 547, 549, 639, 718, 724, 871, 886, 1028, 1121, 4685, 5417, 6745, 9911, 10428, 10853, 14776**

Brown patch
on cool season turfgrasses: bentgrass cultivar susceptibility, **338, 854, 9564**; ryegrass, **676, 729**; tall fescue, **174, 2286**

Brown patch
cultural control, **316, 6132, 9922, 11769, 11817, 12196, 12631, 12853, 13057, 13703, 13716, 15646**: lime, **6864, 9375**

Brown patch
cultural factors affecting, **1700, 9922, 10062, 10801, 11763**: fertilization, **2162, 4169, 4170, 4171, 4681, 11803, 12196**; irrigation, **600, 4317, 5959**; mowing, **9195, 10083, 12911, 12912, 13649**; nitrogen, **975, 1273, 2997, 2998, 4319, 4361, 5395, 5467, 10443, 12716, 12719**; phosphorus, **1273**; potassium, **1273, 4840, 6705, 6708**

Brown patch
description, **4977, 6164, 10761, 12147, 13701, 14716, 15630**

Brown patch
environmental factors affecting, **8970, 10083, 10801, 13716**: atmospheric water vapor, **4318, 7612, 8858, 9195,**

13699; light, 10800; temperature, 4318, 4320, 4977, 4980, 5402, 6191, 6793, 7612, 8858, 9892, 10800, 11939, 12196, 13699, 15014; water, 564, 2997, 2998, 4318, 4319, 7612, 9195, 10443, 12196, 12911, 13699

Brown patch
factors affecting, 3777, 6790, 9815, 10073, 12147, 15723: guttation, 12911, 12912

Brown patch
injury symptoms, 5417, 6132, 6161, 6571, 7154, 7193, 9463, 9764, 9892, 10083, 10443, 10800, 10805, 10853, 10891, 11071, 11763, 11848, 11876, 12078, 12137, 12196, 12556, 12631, 12911, 13703, 13716, 14886, 15630, 15646, 15678, 15679, 16511

Brown patch
Japan, 6258, 11799

Brown patch
seed transmission, 9397

Brown patch
soil factors affecting, 2385; soil reaction, 1273, 2997, 2998

Brown patch
species susceptibility, 5417, 9815, 12137, 13698

Brown patch
on warm season turfgrasses, 6205, 7629: bermudagrass, 2286; St. Augustinegrass, 167, 16511

Browntop bentgrass (see Colonial bentgrass)

Brush
winter protection, 341

Brushing, 270, 547, 834, 4765, 5626, 6526, 6532, 14464
equipment, 6101

Bryobia praetiosa (see Clover mite)

Bryum argenteum, 7026

Bryum capillare, 7026

Bryum species (see also Moss), 2033

Buchloe dactyloides (see Buffalograss)

Buckhorn plantain, 748, 4730, 4755
chemical control, 759, 15706: evaluation, 2901, 5603, 8852, 9580, 11131

Budget, 5288, 8137

Budget
cost accounting, 14315, 16197

Budget
golf course, 1628, 1743, 2338, 2807, 2959, 3342, 3395, 3578a, 5724, 7763, 8803, 9855, 11735, 12399, 13801, 15588, 15667, 15957

Budget
preparation, 3802, 8187, 15963

Buffalograss, 8810, 16489

Buffalograss
adaption, 1686, 11917, 13031: environmental, 377, 12198, 13032

Buffalograss
culture, 8181

Buffalograss
description, 7947

Buffalograss
fairway uses, 326, 13031

Buffalograss
propagation, 561, 13031

Bulbous bluegrass, 322, 1393, 3711, 5898, 13465, 15780

Bulbous bluegrass
adaptation, 13465, 15055

Bulbous bluegrass
description, 7251, 7252, 7947, 8845, 14760, 15055, 16326

Bulbous bluegrass
use: winter overseeding, 15055, 15780

Bulbous buttercup, 7027

Bulk density (see Soil bulk density)

Bulletin, state
disease control, 4047, 4048

Bulletin, state
grasses, 7164, 8299, 13549, 14828

Bulletin, state
green, 6505

Bulletin, state
lawn culture, 3661, 3679, 3996, 4128, 4164, 4342, 4343, 5354, 7433, 7436, 7483, 7484, 7485, 7486, 7487, 7940, 8300, 8391, 8392, 8799, 8800, 8801, 8838, 8839, 9242, 9253, 9678, 9679, 9681, 9682, 9914, 9916, 9917, 9918, 10936, 10937, 10938, 11008, 11009, 12254, 12659, 13515, 14438, 14439, 16452

Bulletin, state
lawn diseases, 8101, 9088, 9761, 9765

Bulletin, state
lawn establishment, 3888, 4127, 4163, 4342, 4343, 6979, 7433, 7436, 7483, 7484, 7485, 7486, 7487, 7940, 8392, 8799, 8800, 8801, 8838, 8839, 9242, 9253, 9678, 9679, 9681, 9682, 9914, 9916, 9917, 9918, 10137, 10138, 11008, 11009, 12254, 12659, 12921, 13515, 13834, 14438, 14439, 14840, 16452

Bulletin, state
lawn insects, 8250, 8821, 8829

Bulletin, state
weed control, 5354, 6104, 6224, 8755, 9452, 14877, 15706

Bulletin, state
weeds, 3641, 5971

Burning, 229, 230, 4580, 6991

Burning
bermudagrass greens, 3114

Burning
effects, 11667, 14797: carbohydrate reserves, 11880; nutrition, 5338; polystand composition, 9123; root growth,

6780, 9122; seed production, 3537, 5362, 5650, 11128; seed stalks, 5338; shoot growth, 6780, 9333, 10994; soil chemistry, 16266; soil moisture, 229, 2875, 5338; soil physical properties, 16266; soil temperature, 5338

Burning
weed control, 294, 699, 13816

Burning tree bermudagrass, 11232

Burr clover, 14309

Burrowing nematode, 10551

Buttercup, creeping (see Creeping buttercup)

Byrum species, 1646

Byrum agenteum (see also Moss), 8464

Byrum capillare (see Moss)

Cacodylic acid, 3655, 5578

Cacodylic acid
Kentucky bluegrass selectivity, 15160

Cacodylic acid
nimblewill control, 15160

Caddy Kentucky bluegrass, 13780

Cadmium compounds, 905

Cadmium compounds
brown patch control, 4681, 14719, 16292

Cadmium compounds
copper spot control, 2329, 2330, 7390, 9245, 12907

Cadmium compounds
crabgrass control, 7390

Cadmium compounds
dollar spot control, 806, 1248, 2330, 8185, 9245, 13605, 14720: evaluation, 7192, 8351, 9244, 9246, 10568, 12907, 14714, 15355; isolate susceptibility variation, 10331

Cadmium compounds
Fusarium patch control, 6762, 9245

Cadmium compounds
red thread control, 12907

Cadmium compounds
snow mold control, 5923, 10422

Cadmium compounds
soil movement, 13891

Cadmium compounds
Typhula blight control, 21, 2633, 7337, 8100, 8373

Calcined clay, 4533, 8400, 8401

Calcined clay
soil amendment, 1687, 4551, 7327, 8400, 12010: effects, 8401, 9498, 10028, 14974; evaluation, 4466, 4505, 4702, 4704, 5167, 7327, 8018, 9159, 10873, 10974, 10976, 10977, 10978, 11605, 13683, 13907, 15096, 15112

Calcium, 6674, 9808, 10963, 11433, 11786, 13526, 14148

Calcium
deficiency, 1488, 10449, 15912

Calcium
deficiency symptoms, 9712, 9717, 10963, 11790, 12362, 15912

Calcium
effects on: *Pythium* blight, 10877, 10890; root growth, 12532, 13897; shoot growth, 5856, 12532; soil chemistry, 2449; stolen growth, 13897

Calcium
soil relationships, 9698

Calcium
sources, 10864

Calcium
translocation, 6503, 12771

Calcium
uptake: factors affecting, 11307, 12407, 12408, 12409

Calcium arsenate, 1349, 5551

Calcium arsenate
annual bluegrass control, 2463, 4434, 4442, 4445, 5571, 6487, 6576, 8861, 9173, 9339, 10558, 12983, 13813, 14512, 14514, 14866: evaluation, 3724, 8696; fairway, 5974, 9172, 9734, 14969

Calcium arsenate
crabgrass control, 1474, 1477, 1493, 1782, 3169, 3353, 3481, 3993, 4427, 4428, 4436, 5161, 5188, 5550, 5559, 5561, 5565, 6252, 6368, 6379, 6380, 6710, 7260, 8151, 11048, 11050, 11051, 13877, 14825: evaluation, 4422, 5479, 7658, 7661, 8407, 10636, 12278, 12314, 12753, 12760, 13803, 14488, 15704

Calcium arsenate
earthworm control, 1793, 5609, 8919

Calcium arsenate
goosegrass control, 9733

Calcium arsenate
pearlwort control, 5609

Calcium arsenate
selectivity, 2100, 4153, 5609, 9628: creeping bentgrass, 8722; evaluation, 3724, 8706, 8707, 14488; Kentucky bluegrass, 13803; seedling, 8695

Calcium arsenate
soil sterilant, 8182

Calcium arsenate
weed control: evaluation, 8412, 8908, 9578, 9579

Calcium carbonate, 309, 5634
evaluation, 3001, 5636, 11248

Calcium chlorate
bermudagrass control, 11092

Calcium chloride
deicing, 3165

Calcium cyanamide, 1892, 5683, 6574, 7413, 8379, 8665, 11697

Calcium cyanamide
annual bluegrass control, 5632

Calcium cyanamide
ant control, 4616

Calcium cyanamide
compost: weed seed control, **4848**

Calcium cyanamide
fumigant, **288, 6637, 8832**

Calcium cyanamide
nitrogen carrier, **6595**

Calcium cyanamide
selectivity: bermudagrass, **16123**

Calcium cyanamide
use, **16439, 16496:** composting, **11454, 16495;** renovation, **9663, 9964, 9965;** seedbed weed control, **993, 1027, 4901, 15701, 16495, 19496**

Calcium cyanamide
weed control, **14427, 14428, 16396:** evaluation, **8797, 14428**

Calcium methyl arsenate
weed control, **8908**

Calcium nitrate, **15, 1546, 2944, 2945, 2946, 5634**
evaluation, **4943, 5636, 8754, 14402, 14403, 15697, 15787**

Calcium phosphate
soil reaction effect, **11024**

Calcium propyl arsenate
crabgrass control, **1493, 12753**

Calcium propyl arsenate
Typhula blight control, **4209**

Calendra venatus vestita (see Hunting billbug)

Calibration
area method, **10180**

Calibration
equipment, **9050, 9779**

Calibration
fertilizer spreader, **10747, 15767, 15797**

Calibration
sprayer, **5765, 7678, 7708, 9050, 10747, 11844, 11845, 12192**

California method
soil modification, **16048**

Calo-Clor® (see Mercury, inorganic)

Calomel (see Mercury, inorganic)

Calonectria draminicola (see *Fusarium* patch)

Calvin cycle species
description, **3447, 4271, 7772**

Cambridge Kentucky bluegrass, **8343**
evaluation, **7191, 8336, 8350**

Camomile, **4739, 5695**

Campground
maintenance, **8610**

Campus Kentucky bluegrass, **8341, 8343, 13780**
evaluation, **6306, 7191, 8338, 9218, 10622, 11186, 14813**

Campylopus flexusus, **7026**

Canada bluegrass, **1393, 9521, 11767, 11771, 15432**

Canada bluegrass
adaptation, **12150, 15054:** soil, **7529**

Canada bluegrass
cultivars, **2650, 5313**

Canada bluegrass
description, **4080, 5315, 5671, 7947, 12150, 16326**

Canada bluegrass
environmental factors affecting, **3329, 5674**

Canada bluegrass
mineral composition, **6041**

Canada bluegrass
seed, **202, 11964**

Canada bluegrass
seed germination, **203, 204:** factors affecting, **205**

Canada bluegrass
uses, **2023, 5315**

Canada thistle
chemical control, **10735**

Canadian golf course, **1726**

Capsella bursa-pastoris (see Sheperdspurse)

Captafol, **3252**
Typhula blight control, **8373**

Captan
brown patch control, **4690**

Captan
Helminthosporium leaf spot control, **4167**

Carat hard fescue, **13780**

Carbaryl, **2026, 2477, 3745, 5528**

Carbaryl
armyworm control, **12437**

Carbaryl
billbug control, **10983**

Carbaryl
chinch bug control, **8881**

Carbaryl
cutworm control, **13234**

Carbaryl
earthworm control, **10691**

Carbaryl
hairy chinch bug control, **12179, 14391**

Carbaryl
insect control: evaluation, **9467, 12437**

Carbaryl
nematode control, **14393**

Carbaryl
sod webworm control, **12428**

Carbofuran
southern chinch bug control, **14399**

Carbofuran
white grub control, **15740**

Carbohydrate
analytical procedures, **3587, 10228, 11446**

Carbohydrate
extraction procedures, **3493, 10228, 10232, 13950, 15154**

Carbohydrate
synthesis, **3492, 4265, 5769**

Carbohydrate
translocation, **6057, 12981, 13400, 15951:** factors affecting, **14089**

Carbohydrate reserves, **91, 9981, 10001, 10991, 16414, 16436**

Carbohydrate reserves
cultural factors affecting, **4039, 4416, 15359:** cutting height, **5700, 7931, 8675, 10228, 10232, 14700, 15655, 15657, 16414;** growth regulators, **2940, 3364;** herbicides, **3623a, 12441, 13394, 14896;** irrigation, **13824;** mowing, **2295, 5032, 10380, 11880, 14195, 14473, 15044;** mowing frequency, **3445, 3850, 5307, 7852, 7931, 9507, 9745, 9992, 11979, 12558, 15655, 15656, 15657, 16414;** nitrogen, **40, 41, 90, 2006, 2295, 2564, 2566, 2574, 2704, 2977, 2982, 3364, 3582, 3720, 3850, 5233, 5235, 5307, 7007, 7008, 7852, 9423, 9479, 9992, 11672, 11673, 11973, 11979, 11980, 12220, 12534, 13410, 13427, 13428, 13448, 14075, 14090, 14195, 14325, 14451, 14473, 14600, 15044, 15437, 15656, 15657, 16464, 16465, 16466;** nutrition, **5336, 7917, 14075;** phosphorus, **14090, 14473, 15657;** potassium, **4265, 5307, 7852, 14090, 14473, 14685, 14700, 16466**

Carbohydrate reserves
diurnal variation, **7916, 9423, 15151**

Carbohydrate reserves
effects of: growth stage, **3492, 11806, 11980, 12534, 13947, 13950, 15152;** melting out, **9760;** sod heating, **8940;** tillering, **14576, 15362**

Carbohydrate reserves
effects on: growth, **2850, 4588, 4589, 6781;** heat tolerance, **8659, 15435**

Carbohydrate reserves
environmental factors affecting, **2981, 3488, 4039:** day length, **2295, 7917, 12089;** light intensity, **90, 2295, 3582, 3850, 5328, 5336, 11980, 13410, 13427, 13428;** soil water, **2363, 3364, 3365, 7852;** temperature, **88, 90, 2062, 2248, 2295, 2362, 2363, 2614, 2707, 2977, 3364, 3365, 3850, 5150, 5333, 5336, 8050, 9999, 10000, 10228, 11673, 13409, 13410, 13427, 13428, 13448, 13951, 14323, 14450, 15437, 15438, 16399, 16414, 16430, 16433, 16465, 16466**

Carbohydrate reserves
factors affecting, **3695, 5334, 7916, 11880**

Carbohydrate reserves
level: Kentucky bluegrass cultivar, **15436, 16436;** in rhizomes and stolons, **4837, 14896;** in roots, **2062, 2772, 14195, 14449, 14700;** in shoots, **14195, 14449;** species variation, **4, 2566, 3493, 9999, 12453, 15153, 16466**

Carbohydrate reserves
plant tissue distribution, **10228, 12220, 13448, 13947, 16465**

Carbohydrate reserves
qualitative characterization, **4837, 7115, 7306, 9999, 10154, 15658**

Carbohydrate reserves
seasonal variation, **10228, 11806, 12220, 15151, 15153, 15636, 15656, 15657, 16412, 16464, 16465**

Carbon (see Activated carbon)

Carbon bisulphide (see Carbon disulfide)

Carbon dioxide
diurnal variation, **16271**

Carbon dioxide
effects of: tree shade, **5654**

Carbon dioxide
effects on: seed germination, **3821**

Carbon dioxide
role in sod heating, **8940**

Carbon dioxide
seasonal variation, **16271**

Carbon dioxide
vertical variation, **16271**

Carbon dioxide, soil
effects on: *Rhizoctonia solani*, **11910**

Carbon disulfide
ant control, **542, 4616**

Carbon disulfide
crayfish control, **581**

Carbon-nitrogen ratio
effects on: fungi, **8769**

Carbon-nitrogen ratio
organic fertilizers, **12916**

Carbon-nitrogen ratio
in thatch layers, **10227**

Carbophenothion
chinch bug control, **7268, 8753, 8879, 12179, 14391, 14399**

Carbophenothion
sod webworm control, **1779, 14389**

Carbowax®
pesticide application: 2–4, D, **758, 763**

Carboxin, **2681**

Carboxin
flag smut control, **7355**

Carboxin
retardation of low temperature discoloration, **2681, 12976**

Carboxin
rust control, **7355**

Carboxin
sod webworm control, **11944**

Carboxin
stripe smut control, **7355**

Carduus nutans (see Thistle, musk)

Career sheep fescue, **8343, 13780**

Carotene, **592, 9884, 14626**

Car path (see Golf car, path)

Car path
golf course, **12947**

Carpetgrass, **2877, 4243, 12132**

Carpetgrass
adaptation, **310, 920, 3553, 12132, 12133, 15054:** soil, **958**

Carpetgrass
breeding, **3553**

Carpetgrass
chemical control, **4207**

Carpetgrass
culture, **958, 2974**

Carpetgrass
description, **3553, 3579, 7947, 14327**

Carpetgrass
use, **3546, 3553**

Carpetweed
chemical control, **1700, 8405, 8410, 8416**

Caryopsis
structure, **8843**

Cascade chewings fescue, **4894**

Casoron® (see Dichlobenil)

Castings, earthworm (see Earthworm)

Cast iron pipe, **12036, 12913, 14329**

Castor pomace, **1488, 1546, 3206**
evaluation, **3205, 9045, 10066, 15118**

Cat, **2237**

Caterpillar, **3294, 3399**
chemical control, **3290, 3292, 3293, 8890**

Cation-anion ratio
shoot growth effects, **9812**

Cation exchange capacity, **6092, 11284, 16014**

Cation exchange capacity
calcium effects, **14376**

Cation exchange capacity
effects on: bensulide activity, **9825**

Cation exchange capacity
improvement: ion exchange resins, **12772**

Catsear, potted
chemical control, **4207, 4733**

CCC, **1550, 2100, 3567a, 3569a, 3570, 8164, 15800, 16252**

CCC
on bermudagrass, **1871, 8161**

CCC
growth inhibition: evaluation, **4017, 8171, 8759, 9661, 12247, 14318, 16256**

CCC
Kentucky bluegrass phytotoxicity, **8693**

C1–C19 creeping bentgrass mix, **800, 920, 992, 993, 3057, 3058, 4646, 6939, 11634**
evaluation, **14349, 14365**

C–52 creeping bentgrass, **742, 757, 989, 3057, 3058, 7309, 11165, 12698**

C–52 creeping bentgrass
disease susceptibility, **854, 9564**

C–52 creeping bentgrass
evaluation, **854, 5781, 9245, 10616, 10622, 10760, 11031, 11232, 11266, 14349, 14365**

C–52 creeping bentgrass
uses, **789, 815**

CDAA
annual bluegrass control, **6573**

C–4 dicarboxylic acid cycle species
description, **3447, 3791, 4271, 5306, 7772**

CDU
fertilizer evaluation, **14964, 16276**

Cell division
factors affecting, **7757**

Cellular polystyrene
soil modification, **15754**

Cellulase
thatch decomposition effects, **10230**

Cellulose, **7306**

Cellulose
effects of: plant maturity, **11970**

Cellulose
species evaluation, **10227, 16256**

Cellulose
temperature effects, **14450**

Cemetery
culture, **2587, 2588, 2992, 3107, 4022, 4347, 4348, 4963, 5093, 5094, 5523, 7867, 8601, 8936, 9477, 9968, 10739, 11417, 11487, 11528, 11780, 11918, 12667, 12905, 12942, 13064, 13518, 13558, 14934:** fertilization, **3348, 9609, 11430, 11780, 12549, 14227;** mowing, **1740, 8511;** weed control, **10875, 12968, 14744**

Cemetery
equipment, **4022**

Cemetery
establishment, **3107, 10236, 12943, 13583, 15947, 15949**

Cemetery
grasses used, **3107, 6931, 11780, 12942, 13518:** cool region, **1417, 11757, 12158, 14934, 15944, 15945, 15947;** warm region, **10236**

Cemetery
irrigation system, **674**

Cemetery
management, **2960, 14598:** cost analysis, **4099, 4590**

Cemetery
renovation, **11418, 16269, 16270**

Cenchrus pauciflorus (see Sandbur)

Centers of distribution
cool season turfgrasses, **7523**

Centers of distribution
warm season turfgrasses, **7523**

Centipedegrass, **706, 4243, 6513, 7637, 9662, 10773, 11254, 12877, 14326, 14327, 15358**

Centipedegrass
adaptation, **2377, 3539, 3545, 3676, 8009, 12133:** soil, **958**

Centipedegrass
cultivars, **14687**

Centipedegrass
culture, **2372, 8564, 11683:** cutting height, **958, 2181;** fertilization, **843, 7968, 8038, 8886, 9672, 12265, 12267;** nitrogen fertilization, **843, 3570**

Centipedegrass
description, **7947, 12152, 13301**

Centipedegrass
disease: *Fusarium* blight, **14443**

Centipedegrass
establishment: vegetative, **8564**

Centipedegrass
herbicide tolerance, **7995, 15978**

Centipedegrass
iron chlorosis: control, **3386**

Centipedegrass
pests: nematodes, **258, 6607, 8563**

Centipedegrass
seed production, **842, 958**

Centipedegrass
uses, **809, 862, 12152**

Centipedegrass, weed
chemical control: TCA, **11878**

Centipedegrass decline, **5120**

Central Plains Turf Foundation, **12114**

Cerastium semidecandrum (see Seaside chickweed)

Cerastium vulgatum (see Common chickweed)

Ceratodon purpureus, **1092, 1148, 7026, 8464, 14042**

Ceratodon species (see Moss)

Cercospora fusimaculans (see *Cercospora* leaf spot)

Cercospora leaf spot, **6166**

Certification
seed (see Seed, certification)

Certification
spray applicators, **8303, 9720**

Certification
vegetative, **6044, 8303:** sod, **1736, 8280, 11295, 11863;** warm season species, **1806, 8280, 8638, 8639, 10242, 12259**

Chafer, **7030**

Chafer, northern masked (see Northern masked chafer)

Channel (see Ditch)

Charcoal (see also Activated charcoal), **637**

Charcoal
effects on: herbicides, **8426, 13851**

Charcoal
soil amendment, **733, 738:** evaluation, **11153**

Charcoal
use: greens, **10985, 10989**

C–26 hard fescue (see Biljart hard fescue)

Charming sheep fescue, **13780**

Chelated iron, **4074, 9803**

Chelating agents, **9590**

Chemical composition (see also Mineral composition), **5710, 15657**

Chemical composition
bermudagrass, **1782, 8660, 11639, 15914**

Chemical composition
crownvetch, **15915**

Chemical composition
effects of: cutting frequency, **14452;** micronutrients, **9257;** nitrogen, **2247, 2251, 3554, 6603, 9718, 14383;** phosphorus, **7215, 12450;** plant maturity effect, **6603, 12110;** potassium, **10015, 15056;** sulphur, **9257**

Chemical composition
environmental effects, **5330, 6052, 15105**

Chemical composition
seasonal variation, **2251, 7215, 15636**

Chemical composition
species variability, **2249, 2747, 14448**

Chemical composition
thatch, **10230**

Chemical mowing (see Growth regulators)

Chemung crownvetch, **6032, 9988, 13589**

Chewings fescue, **977, 2129, 3714, 6085, 13079, 13268, 13374, 14471, 16489**

Chewings fescue
adaptation, **331, 6870, 12328**

Chewings fescue
cultivar, **2566, 9340, 13376, 13725, 13823:** dollar spot susceptibility, **8336, 8338;** evaluation, **2631, 2673, 2684, 2693, 5007, 5313, 5316, 5320, 5776, 6879, 7284, 7287, 8336, 8338, 8341, 8350, 10631, 13661, 13665, 14561;** evaluation—England, **13662;** evaluation—Sweden, **9219;** green-up evaluation, **2566;** red thread susceptibility, **3341, 8336;** shade adaptation, **2204;** winter overseeding, **10455**

Chewings fescue
culture, **14749**

Chewings fescue
description, **1332, 4008, 5679, 9517**

Chewings fescue
disease control, **20, 24**

Chewings fescue
herbicide selectivity, **2172**

Chewings fescue
seed production, **1194, 1333**

Chewings fescue
seed viability: environmental factors affecting, **6084, 6087, 6393, 8782**

Chewings fescue
uses, **4747**

Chewings fescue
vegetative identification, **15412**

Chickweed, **369, 4737**

Chickweed
chemical control, **1760, 2100, 2728, 4149, 4396, 4844, 5355, 6357, 6650, 15039, 15040:** dicamba, **13024**; evaluation, **1700, 3356, 3358, 5500, 6376, 7098, 8161, 8422, 8433, 13768**; on greens, **348, 1871**; lead arsenate, **9377, 9378, 11666**; MCPP, **3757, 13024**; silvex, **14047**; sodium arsenite, **923, 11666, 15989**

Chickweed
cultural control, **9702**

Chiggers, **1024**

Chinch bug, **308, 489, 595, 599, 602, 662, 745, 760, 1521, 1570, 1571, 1953, 3285, 3294, 4611, 4612, 4834, 7323, 8878, 8889, 8900, 8901, 9060, 9186, 9746, 11344, 11897, 12542, 14486, 14737, 15633**

Chinch bug
biological control, **8882, 8885**

Chinch bug
chemical control, **567, 1217, 4060, 4971, 5294, 5295, 7323, 8068, 8071, 8250, 8578, 8829, 8871, 8880, 8883, 8887, 8889, 8895, 9128, 10359, 10643, 11818, 13470, 13475, 13482, 13483, 13498, 14751, 15841:** evaluation, **1548, 1639, 3283, 3289, 3293, 3612a, 5297, 5298, 8477, 8873, 8874, 8876, 8877, 8879, 8881, 8882, 8885, 8892, 8896, 8898, 11730, 13473, 13478, 13901, 14400, 16156**; state bulletin, **13474, 13493**

Chinch bug
control, **796, 1315, 1764, 5924, 5925, 8882, 9060, 10824, 11730**

Chinch bug
description, **3675a, 5294, 5295, 8477, 8829, 8889, 10824, 11730, 11864, 13497**

Chinch bug
environmental effects, **13494, 13497, 13635**

Chinch bug
fertilization effects, **8046, 8047, 12265, 12268**

Chinch bug
injury symptoms, **8830, 8872, 8889, 8904, 9128, 10824**

Chinch bug
on St. Augustinegrass, **1490, 15497, 15504**

Chinch bug, common, **9478**

Chinch bug, hairy, **17, 625, 7258, 8670, 9478, 13496**

Chinch bug, hairy
chemical control, **637, 4158, 7255, 8069, 8753, 10319, 12179, 13490, 13497:** carbaryl, **12179**; carbophenylthion, **12179**; chlordane, **13491, 13506, 13507**; DDT, **12179**; diazenon, **12179**; DMPA, **12179**; Dursban®, **14388**; evaluation, **8753, 10014, 10373, 12179, 14386, 14391**

Chinch bug, hairy
description, **8069, 13479, 13490**

Chinch bug, hairy
species susceptibility, **10014**

Chinch bug, southern (see Southern chinch bug)

Chipmunks, **4306**

Chlorate
herbicide, **1069**

Chlordane, **857, 5323, 5467, 9467, 9578, 9579, 10674, 12024, 13776**

Chlordane
ant control, **806, 4616, 13468, 13470, 13491, 13503, 13504**

Chlordane
caterpillar control, **3399**

Chlordane
chinch bug control, **13470, 13473, 13478**

Chlordane
crabgrass control, **1027, 1441, 1493, 1782, 4376, 4378, 4387, 4427, 4435, 5188, 5205, 5207, 5264, 5265, 5550, 5551, 5559, 5569, 5570, 6368, 6710, 7094, 9529, 9530, 9531, 11048, 11049, 11051, 12575, 13011, 13429, 13639, 13859, 14825, 14895:** evaluation, **5479, 6270, 7091, 7655, 7658, 7661, 12278, 12314, 12753, 12760**

Chlordane
cutworm control, **12177, 13234, 13491**

Chlordane
earthworm control, **1793, 7572, 8919, 9562, 14640:** evaluation, **8920, 9486, 9561**

Chlordane
effects on: thatch, **12434**

Chlordane
European chafer control, **6387**

Chlordane
goosegrass control, **5468, 5537, 6284, 6286**

Chlordane
grub control, **12171, 12181, 13468, 15740**

Chlordane
hairy chinch bug control, **13479, 13491, 13506, 13507, 14391**

Chlordane
insect control, **16, 806, 920, 4070, 6848, 10155, 13470, 13483**

Chlordane
Japanese beetle control, **5985, 5986, 7157, 12168, 12178, 13469**

Chlordane
Northern mask chafer control, **12178**

Chlordane
Ophiobolus patch control, **6763**

Chlordane
pearlwort control, **12082**

Chlordane
phytotoxicity, **3745, 4435,**

5537, 6440: chewings fescue, **6544;** colonial bentgrass, **6544;** evaluation, **6545, 8695, 9486, 12576, 13767, 14826;** Kentucky bluegrass, **6544, 13773**

Chlordane
sod webworm control, **8472, 13491:** evaluation, **12177, 14389**

Chlordane
soil persistence, **6276, 13472**

Chlordane
wireworm control, **6071**

Chlordane-fertilizer mixtures, **4070**

Chlorea®
soil sterilant, **8182**

Chlorflurenol, **216, 2100, 3020, 5046, 7447**

Chlorflurenol
growth inhibition: on bermudagrass, **9434, 10447;** evaluation, **4017, 4997, 5360, 6686, 7447, 7448, 8171, 10109, 15451, 16461;** on roadsides, **215, 1055, 5047, 15158**

Chlorflurenol
phytotoxicity, **216, 8422**

Chlorflurenol
weed control, **215, 8422**

Chloride
effects, **3930**

Chloride
soil level, **8246**

Chloride
tissue content, **3932, 15645**

Chloride
tolerance: species evaluation, **3930, 3934**

Chloride
uptake: factors affecting, **3932, 3934, 3935**

Chlorine
nutrition, **7671, 11785**

Chlorine
phytoxicity, **8758**

Chloris verticillata (see Windmillgrass)

2-chloro-4,6-bix(ethylamino)-striazine (see Simazine)

2-chloro-4-(ethylamino)-6-(isopropylamino)-s-triazine (see Atrazine)

2-chloroethyl phosphonic acid (see Ethrel)

2-chloroethyl-trimethyl-ammonium chloride (see CCC)

Chloro IPC® (see Chlorpropham)

Chloroneb
flag smut control, **11103**

Chloroneb
Pythium blight control, **6116, 15684**

Chloroneb
stripe smut control, **9752, 11103**

Chloroneb
Typhula blight control, **2633, 8373, 9933, 15017, 15018, 15019, 15020**

2-[(4-chloro-*O*-tolyl)oxyl] propionic acid (see MCPP)

Chlorophyll, **5769, 8124, 16338**

Chlorophyll
content: species variation, **3195, 3311, 9884**

Chlorophyll
factors affecting, **13559, 14789:** cultural, **9442, 10074, 10103, 10173, 13559, 14075, 15909;** environmental, **11903, 16338**

Chlorophyll content
gibberellin effects, **2940**

Chlorophyll index, **10103**

Chloropicrin, **9800, 10854, 11697, 13724**

Chloropicrin
nematode control, **12978**

Chloropicrin
soil sterilization, **8832**

Chloropicrin
use: compost weed control, **4848, 11454**

Chloropicrin
weed control, **636**

Chloroplast, **7772**

Chlorothalonil, **1776, 2027, 2787, 3257**

Chlorothalonil
brown patch control, **2787, 15140**

Chlorothalonil
dollar spot control, **2787, 3103, 4203, 12357, 14814, 14815, 15355**

Chlorothalonil
Fusarium blight control, **2787, 6764**

Chlorothalonil
Fusarium patch control, **2787, 7192**

Chlorothalonil
Helminthosporium leaf spot control, **2757, 2787, 11104**

Chlorothalonil
melting out control, **2787, 4203**

Chlorothalonil
Pythium blight control, **15135**

Chlorothalonil
rust control, **2757**

Chlorothalonil
snowmold control, **2787, 7068, 14810**

Chlorpropham
annual bluegrass control, **4398, 4406, 4434, 4442, 4445**

Chlorpropham
crabgrass control, **4906**

Chromosome number, **5653, 6269, 7757, 8499, 8752, 10365, 11342, 16126**

Chromosome number
Agropyron species, **7527, 8627, 11342**

Chromosome number
Agrostis species, **2284, 8626, 14424**

Chromosome number
book, **4577**

Chromosome number
Cynodon species, **7377, 7380, 8229, 12222, 12225**

Chromosome number
Festuca species, **8501**

Chromosome number
Italian ryegrass, **11342, 14613**

Chromosome number
Kentucky bluegrass, **7527, 8752, 11083, 11084, 11338, 11362, 12113, 12654, 16096**

Chromosome number
Lolium-Festuca hybrids, **15632**

Chromosome number
meadow fescue, **11225, 11342**

Chromosome number
perennial ryegrass, **11342, 14613**

Chromosome number
Poa species, **2258, 3373, 7117, 7527, 8088, 13670**

Chromosome number
redtop, **11342, 14424**

Chromosome number
St. Augustinegrass, **9667, 9668**

Chromosome number
tall fescue, **4275, 11225**

Chromosome number
zoysiagrass, **6043**

C I (see Chlorophyll index)

Cicada killer, **1570, 7548**

Cicadellidae family (see Leafhopper)

CIPC (see Chlorpropham)

Circumnutational growth, **1904, 5951**

Cirsium arvense (see Creeping thistle)

C–1 Kentucky bluegrass (see Newport Kentucky bluegrass)

Classification, grass, **86, 7584, 8843, 12121**
cytological, **13802**

Clatsop red fescue, **7309, 16323**

Claveria vermicularis, **6508**

Claviceps purpurea (see Ergot)

Clay, **2418, 4103, 4288, 4754, 15357, 15808, 15809, 15889**
soil amendment, **11605**

Click beetle (see Wireworm)

Climate, **12435, 13676**

Clippings
for mulching, **122, 14509**

Clippings
nutrient content: bentgrass, **11458;** bermudagrass, **11639, 12261**

Clippings
nutrient removal: evaluation, **6656, 11783**

Clipping removal, **61, 337, 743, 2566, 5902, 15509, 15826**

Clipping removal
appearance effects, **2517**

Clipping removal
effects on: annual bluegrass invasion, **5902;** disease development, **186;** gray leaf spot control, **11930;** potassium level, **6648, 6651;** rust control, **11930;** shoot growth, **15705, 15709;** thatch, **2603, 2707;** *Typhula* blight incidence, **2699**

Clipping removal
nutritional effects, **2100, 11604, 15509**

Clipping return
nutritional effects, **11438, 15074**

Clipping utilization, **2649**

Clipping utilization
Cal-turf® method, **4019**

Clipping utilization
pellitizing, **1958, 2170, 2649, 2672, 2715**

Clitocybe gigantea, **2508**

Cloud effects, **1594**

Clover
chemical control, **3452, 3948, 4284, 5449, 6887, 9388, 11540, 13024:** ammonium sulfate, **2172, 11661;** endothall, **3982, 4150, 11747, 11752;** evaluation, **2633, 3618a, 5190, 5982, 7517, 8433; 2, 4,5–T, 4151, 4369, 4395**

Clover
cultural control, **835, 1274, 5449**

Clover
invasion: soil factors affecting, **2172, 11666**

Clover
turf use, **7452**

Clover mite, **1570, 4780, 10995**
chemical control, 14386

Clover weevil, **13498**

Clover, white (see White clover)

CMA, **2172**

CMA
crabgrass control, **9531, 9533**

CMA
dallisgrass control, **9531, 9533**

CMA
sandbur control, **8161, 12665, 15140**

CMPP (see MCPP)

Coastal bermudagrass, **3571, 3572, 3696, 3791, 8078**

Coastal bermudagrass
adaptation, **28, 3572**

Coastal bermudagrass
chemical composition, **3582, 6503, 7515, 7852**

Coastal bermudagrass
cultural factors affecting: mowing, **3593, 3845, 7931;** nutrition, **3593, 3606, 8648**

Coastal bermudagrass
disease: *Helminthosporium* species, **7121**

Coastal bermudagrass
environmental factors affecting: light, **3582, 7516**

Coastal bermudagrass
establishment: sprigging, **2731**

Coastal bermudagrass
water use rate, **3581, 5055, 5056**

Coastal panicgrass
use: sand dunes, **1700**

Coated fertilizers (see Fertilizer, coated)

Cocoa hulls, **637**

Cocoa hulls
nitrogen carrier, **15815**

Cocoa shells
soil amendment, **235, 11153**

Cogongrass, **4967**

Cohansey creeping bentgrass, **742, 757, 992, 3123, 6892, 6939, 6950, 7309, 10767, 11165, 12698, 14259, 14260, 14638**

Cohansey creeping bentgrass
description, **10637, 14259**

Cohansey creeping bentgrass
evaluation, **8791, 9564, 10616, 10622, 10760, 11021, 11232, 11266**

Cohansey creeping bentgrass
fairway use, **789, 815**

Cold stress (see Low temperature stress)

Coleoptile, **3377**

Coleorhiza, seed, **6007, 11359**

Collar, putting green (see Apron)

College grounds
culture, **4108**

Colletotrichum graminicola (see Anthracnose)

Colliery wastes
sports field use, **3622**

Collins creeping bentgrass, **989, 6557, 7309, 11232, 12698**
evaluation, **9233, 11266**

Colloidal phosphate
soil amendment, **1879, 7987, 8018, 8037, 11605, 13896, 13902, 13906, 13907**

Collybia species (see Fairy ring)

Colonial bentgrass, **527, 2284, 3713, 3775, 5661, 11767, 11771, 12101, 13269, 13853, 14777, 15755**

Colonial bentgrass
adaptation, **3150, 3153, 3156, 4581, 5483, 7038**

Colonial bentgrass
breeding, **912, 3156, 3159, 5122, 8627, 14965**

Colonial bentgrass
cultivars, **4483, 10760, 13823, 13848, 14777:** annual bluegrass invasion susceptibility, **5498;** description, **1685, 5273, 8163, 9208, 13376;** evaluation, **1471, 3459, 5313, 5316, 5320, 5443, 5498, 6879, 7284, 8336, 8338, 8350, 8761, 9238, 10616, 10621, 10622, 10813, 10818, 10822, 10856, 10862, 11187, 11661, 12757, 13661, 13662, 13665, 14561, 16069;** winter overseeding evaluation, **10455**

Colonial bentgrass
culture, **8341, 11021, 12547:** cutting height, **1778, 5498;** fertilization, **8376, 14149**

Colonial bentgrass
description, **1329, 3152, 3159, 4008, 5315, 5679, 7947, 9515, 10153, 12509, 14424, 14965**

Colonial bentgrass
diseases, **20, 11661:** fairy ring, **5919;** *Fusarium* patch—cultivar susceptibility, **6758;** *Pythium* blight—cultivar susceptibility, **6207;** *Typhula* blight—cultivar susceptibility, **11105**

Colonial bentgrass
herbicide selectivity, **2172, 3620a, 3622a, 3623a:** seedling, **6629, 13430**

Colonial bentgrass
pest: bluegrass webworm—cultivar susceptibility, **11665**

Colonial bentgrass
seed, **1194, 1333**

Colonial bentgrass
uses, **5315, 7910, 12509**: Sweden, **15755**

Colonial bentgrass, weed
chemical control, **6486, 10018, 10019**

Colorants, **1209, 1781, 2027, 13556**

Colorants
application, **1766, 1767, 4795, 4800, 11314, 14694, 16121, 16122, 16336**

Colorants
cost analysis, **4795, 4800, 14983, 14985**

Colorants
effects on: winter survival, **186**

Colorants
evaluation, **8173, 9136, 9139, 11314, 14694, 16122**

Colorants
types, **1680, 4795, 16122:** dyes, **643, 4795;** evaluation, **1700, 2100, 16418, 16420;** pigments, **4795**

Colorants
use, **14983, 16121:** golf course, **61, 14521**

Color, turfgrass (see Turfgrass color)

Coltsfoot, **3881**

Columbia creeping bentgrass, **301, 302, 326, 352, 10862, 11661, 16489**

Combing, **4765**

Combi perennial ryegrass, **7191**

Common bermudagrass, **3571, 8077, 11936, 13238, 14899, 16413**

Common bermudagrass
adaptation, **960, 3581, 7977**

Common bermudagrass
culture, **3910, 7977, 9267**

Common bermudagrass
disease: spring dead spot, **15140**

Common bermudagrass
roadside use, **9952, 12595**

Common carpetgrass (see Carpetgrass)

Common chickweed, **369, 614, 9874, 15706**
chemical control, **3697a, 3698a, 4661, 7090, 8159, 9580, 12949**: evaluation, **3657a, 6375, 9578, 9579, 13010**

Common erodium, **4738**

Common sorrel (see Sorrel, common)

Communications, **2871, 9287, 11063, 15533**

Community (see Turfgrass community)

Compaction, **99, 101, 102, 103, 112, 117, 164, 984, 1029, 2953, 4373, 5755, 6634, 6649, 9788, 9958, 10287, 10302, 11033, 11034, 11163, 15094, 15514**

Compaction
causes, **3390, 3604, 6351, 6843, 10187, 10289, 10291, 12460, 12888, 15094, 16183**

Compaction
correction, **831, 6351, 6874, 6949, 8242, 11144, 11153, 12611, 13683, 15242, 15273**

Compaction
effects, **2063, 3929, 6949, 7391, 8057, 11135, 11144, 11153, 11506, 12888, 13683, 15218, 15273, 15458, 15459**: evaluation, **10118, 10119, 15457, 16488**; green, **5789, 10113, 13002**

Compaction
effects on: bulk density, **3926, 3929, 10968, 11153**; infiltration, **102, 5365, 5366, 6865, 7675, 9772, 11144, 14482, 15096, 15098, 15112, 16489**; low temperature kill, **14713**; oxygen diffusion rate, **9501, 9498, 10974, 16489**; percolation, **3926, 3929, 13683**; root growth, **148, 2680, 3929, 7389, 7421, 10974, 10976, 12165, 12166, 12611, 14713**; run-off, **100, 102, 108, 11144, 11153**; shoot growth, **7434, 10976, 12166, 12611, 12888, 13425, 14713**; soil physical properties, **3929, 14482, 16489**; soil porosity, **102, 5169, 6676, 6865, 14482, 15526**; species composition, **7387, 7434**; thatch, **13418**; weed invasion, **7434, 15458**

Compaction
evaluation, **6637, 9155, 10462**

Compaction
factors affecting, **104, 109, 7406**: irrigation practices, **937, 6843, 9772, 15457**; soil amendment, **8011, 10977, 12166, 14988**; soil mix, **8102, 9132, 9133, 9774, 9775, 9776, 10113, 10976, 13683, 15456**; soil texture, **3007, 5872, 6476, 8133, 9772**

Compaction
prevention, **3926, 7406, 9774, 9775, 15094**

Compaction
simulation: equipment, **6637, 6714**

Compaction
species tolerance, **6843, 8981, 16361, 16368, 16369, 16372**

Companion grass, **13170, 13193**

Compatibility
polystand, **6090**

Compensation point
Kentucky bluegrass cultivars, **15435, 15436, 15438**

Compensation point
species evaluation, **9100**

Competition, **1, 7011**

Competition
clover invasion, **51, 60, 7322**

Competition
cultural effects, **3035, 7512**

Competition
disease effects, **6321**

Competition
growth effects, **6402, 7185**

Competition
monostand: seeding rate effects, **10082**

Competition
polystand, **59, 4262, 4596, 5475, 5593, 7185, 8791, 8937**

Competition
seedling, **3821, 3832, 8937, 16056**

Competition
soil effects, **7529**

Complete fertilizer, **6509**

Components of turfgrass quality (see Turfgrass quality, components)

Compost
green use, **2172, 5611, 5681, 5682**

Compost
soil amendment, **5642, 9199, 10114, 12901**

Compost
weed source, **385**

Composted refuse
fertilizer evaluation, **15111**

Composting, **218, 361, 562, 627, 637, 1128, 3647a, 4905, 5394, 5634, 5636, 6790, 10989, 11454, 13978, 15815**

Composting
materials used, **11454, 12144, 16495**

Composting
procedure, **235, 382, 10432, 12144, 12164**

Composting
weed control, **4848, 4854, 4861, 4870, 11454, 16495**

Compressed air
seeding method, **15789**

Computer
golf course use, **12723**

Concrete-grass combinations, **2102**

Conference, turfgrass, **1212, 1290, 1413, 1458, 3472, 3947, 3950, 3951, 3985, 5831, 6791, 6956, 9244, 10197, 11617, 12114, 12341, 12709, 14926**
Florida: proceedings index, **10509**

Conferences, turfgrass
GCSAA, **990, 1011, 1061, 1112, 1158, 15049**

Conferences, turfgrass
Midwest Regional, **814, 852, 853, 881, 882, 883, 902, 929, 930, 969, 970, 1230, 2835, 4359**

Conferences, turfgrass
organization, **10610**

Congressional creeping bentgrass, **742, 757, 866, 989, 993, 1967, 3058, 6950, 7309, 10637, 11165, 12698**

Congressional creeping bentgrass
disease susceptibility, **854, 9564**

Congressional creeping bentgrass
evaluation, **920, 9233, 9245, 9408, 10616, 10622, 10760, 11021, 11232, 11266**

Congressional creeping bentgrass
uses, **789, 815, 854**

Conservation, **7163**

Conservation, soil (see Soil conservation)

Conservation, water
grasses used, **14229, 15933**

Construction (see also Establishment), **9631, 11890, 13066, 15502**

Construction
airport, **1912**

Construction
apron, **5241**

Construction
bowling green, **568, 7004, 7005, 14551**

Construction
cricket wicket, **5257**

Construction
golf course, **192, 586, 3469, 3661a, 3953, 3957, 4455, 4820, 5266, 5624, 6907, 6993, 8237, 9167, 9421, 10247, 10398, 10441, 11191, 11809, 12376, 12551, 12696, 16110, 16473**: costs, **5928, 6993, 7127**

Construction
green, **191, 3650a, 3676, 3953, 4067, 4298, 4574, 4914, 5241, 5243, 5245, 5251, 5805, 5810, 5811, 5825, 5868, 6001, 6547, 6561, 6917, 7069, 7127, 7219, 7904, 7906, 7941, 8521, 8642, 9011, 9943, 9985, 10933, 11198, 12372, 13641, 14728, 15120, 15260, 16009**: Japan, **9115, 9199**

Construction
measurement equipment, **14108**

Construction
Purr-Wick system, **10370, 12418, 13638, 14337, 14515**

Construction
specifications, **1637, 6671, 8315, 9167, 12372**

Construction
sports field, **1637, 4080, 4757, 4927, 5630, 6018, 6144, 6149, 6632, 6711, 10293, 10505, 13690, 14560, 16254**: Europe, **5625, 14442**

Construction
tee, **12395, 12398**

Construction
tennis court, **9001**

Contract
golf course construction, **8315**

Contract maintenance, **5208, 5212, 5390, 15445**

Convolvulus arvensis (see Bindweed)

Cool season turfgrasses, **278, 280, 420, 4039, 6838, 6842, 8014, 8096, 8735, 9251, 11180, 11467, 12007, 13345**

Cool season turfgrasses
adaptation, **95, 598, 606, 5620, 7980, 9028, 11003, 15483, 16172**: California, **8927, 16366, 16393, 16448**; dryland, **5699, 9028**; Michigan, **2571, 2618**

Cool season turfgrasses
cultivars, **1867, 5314, 11574, 13075, 13112**

Cool season turfgrasses
culture, **13375**

Cool season turfgrasses
description, **5259, 6271, 10730, 13238, 13334, 13376, 13831**

Cool season turfgrasses
development, **5786**

Cool season turfgrasses
evaluation, **3304, 11155, 11812**

Cool season turfgrasses
uses, **2371, 3029, 6535, 7041, 7163, 11331, 13380, 13387**

Cool season turfgrasses
world distribution, **7522, 7523**

Cooperative Extension Service (see Education, turf)

Coordination product of zinc ion and maneb (see Mancozeb)

Copper, **9698, 11786**

Copper
deficiency symptoms, **9267**

Copper
nutrition, **1488, 2351, 7671, 11785, 14630**

Copper
toxicity, **8760**

Copper fungicides, **570, 666**

Copper pipe, **12913**

Copper spot, **1017, 1590, 12931**

Copper spot
chemical control, **1487, 2331, 2332, 4677, 4683, 4685, 6748, 9245, 9462, 9463**: evaluation, **799, 1545, 2326, 2328, 2329, 2330, 2333, 4679, 4680, 4682, 4689, 4692, 4693, 4695, 4696, 5766, 7390, 12907, 16050, 16052**

Copper spot
cultural factors affecting: fertilization, **5439, 7390**

Copper spot
environmental factors affecting: temperature, **9462, 11939**

Copper spot
symptoms, **7193, 9462, 9463**

Copper thiocyanate
annual bluegrass control, **1551**

Coring, **891, 921, 925, 946, 951, 975, 983, 985, 1019, 1176, 1423, 2152, 5727, 6528, 7474, 9482, 9958, 10258, 10270, 10325, 10462**

Coring
cost, **10335**

Coring
effects on: dry spots, **5051;** fertilizer penetration, **7437, 11153;** oxygen diffusion rate, **9501;** root growth, **7389, 11153;** run-off water, **7437, 11153;** shoot density, **10071, 10072;** turfgrass community, **7389;** water infiltration, **2673, 2684, 10974, 15112;** wilting tendency, **10072**

Coring
equipment, **1865, 10270, 10281**

Coring
golf course, **5278, 6893, 14643**

Coring
greens, **5728, 6892, 11588:** winter overseeding effects, **13433**

Coring
thatch control, **1700, 2614, 2615, 2869, 5523, 10290, 14688, 15355**

Coring, deep, **1639, 3702, 10957, 10962, 10974**

Cork cells, leaf, **4595**

Corm (see Haplocorm)

Corn beetle
chemical control, **1626**

Corncob mulch, **2667**

Cornfield ant, **13473**

Corn gluten meal, **6595**

Corn gluten meal
nitrogen source, **6574, 6579, 14285, 15604**

Corn gluten meal
soil amendment, **14285**

Corn spurrey
chemical control, **1700**

Corn stunt virus, **1611**

Coronilla varia (see Crown vetch)

Corrosive sublimate (see Mercury, inorganic)

Corticium fuciforme (see Red thread)

Cost
cemetery culture, **4099, 4590**

Cost
coring, **10325**

Cost
disease control: mercury, **10845**

Cost
football field culture, **12776**

Cost
golf course construction, **1966, 8814**

Cost
golf course culture, **1784, 2789, 3065, 3066, 3067, 4232, 5057, 5282, 5739, 6592, 7693, 7900, 9254, 12399, 15147**

Cost
golf course renovation, **2789, 6889**

Cost
irrigation, **5870, 7176, 7900, 12924, 12925, 14892**

Cost
irrigation system, **1918, 2831:** installation, **10757, 10917**

Cost
maintenance (see Maintenance costs)

Cost
mowing, **1315, 3066, 11775, 15048, 15512, 16510**

Cost
nitrogen carrier, **15082**

Cost
renovation: financing, **5285**

Cost
roadside culture, **1621, 8182, 11775, 14620, 16510**

Cost
sod harvesting, **2316, 11814**

Cost
sports field culture, **12111, 13045, 13046, 13939**

Cost
turfgrass culture, **1663, 1719, 1939, 1946, 2608, 5168, 7935, 8119**

Cost analysis
bowling green: construction, **7003**

Cost analysis
colorants, **14983, 14985**

Cost analysis
equipment, **8954, 9642, 9643**

Cost analysis
fertilizer, **10135, 10136**

Cost analysis
golf car, **16265**

Cost analysis
golf course, **3086, 6551, 8802, 11358, 14787**

Cost analysis
irrigation system, **3087, 5270, 11091, 14279, 16195**

Cost analysis
park culture, **15641**

Cost analysis
renovation: greens, **5340, 5341, 15147**

Cost analysis
sod production, **8656, 13693**

Cost analysis
turfgrass culture: labor, **10316, 17001**

Cost analysis
winter overseeding, **14983, 14985**

Cotton bur ash
potassium source, **8049**

Cotton fiber seed mat (see Seed mat)

Cottonseed hull green construction, **317, 15966**

Cottonseed meal, **1488, 2257, 4896**

Cottonseed meal
composting, **11454**

Cottonseed meal
evaluation, **6790, 11661, 11905, 14697, 14923, 15697**

Cottonseed meal
fertilization, **1639, 11389**

Cottony blight (see *Pythium* blight)

Cotula species
bowling green, **10342, 15211, 15229, 15234**

Cotula species
culture, **1257, 2172, 3859, 7476, 10344, 15266**

Cotula species
establishment, **15214, 15295, 15296, 15299, 15303, 15307, 15317**

Cotula species
New Zealand, **11258, 15299, 15306, 15315, 15317**

Cotula species
weed control, **15254, 15261, 15277**

Cotula, weed
chemical control, **5762**

Couchgrass (see Bermudagrass)

Cougar Kentucky bluegrass, **1950, 2027, 2611, 6637, 7202, 9347, 9349, 10622, 10635, 11186, 11323, 14813**
evaluation, **1778, 6306, 6309, 6330, 6712, 8317**

Covers
use with: soil warming, **9427**

Covers, winter protection (see Winter protection covers)

Crabgrass, **333, 402, 523, 547, 686, 699, 896, 966, 1297, 1477, 2229, 3682a, 4624, 6276, 14854, 15662, 15706, 16367**

Crabgrass
chemical control, **22, 523, 858, 993, 1027, 1193, 1217, 1270, 1344, 1441, 1612, 1620, 1689, 1759, 1840, 2066, 2100, 2167, 2394, 2411, 2468, 2469, 2729, 3503, 3600a, 3604a, 3682a, 3824, 3974, 3990, 4059, 4132, 4134, 4136, 4344, 4353, 4360, 4361, 4387, 4402, 4414, 4480, 4544, 4791, 4796, 4843, 4847, 4852, 4859, 4863, 4912, 4942, 5447, 5454, 5455, 5462, 5471, 5480, 5496, 5501, 5502, 5504, 6357, 6360, 6366, 6370, 6636, 6667, 6818, 6819, 6851, 7089, 7092, 7712, 7714, 7716, 7717, 8146, 8152, 8213, 8428, 8952, 9054, 9150, 9339, 10634, 10782, 10909, 11140, 11304, 11540, 12029, 12146, 12794, 12816, 13056, 13114, 13157, 13204, 13241, 13867, 14208, 14308, 14330, 14495, 14997, 15039, 15040, 15706, 16384, 16397, 16496:** application timing, **1629, 5161, 5187, 5481, 5560, 5561, 5565, 5567, 5569, 5570, 6380, 8415**; in bentgrass, **2895, 2908**; in bermudagrass, **1871, 2100, 8701, 9888, 14837, 14981**; calcium arsenate, **3169, 3481, 15704**; chlordane, **7091, 14895**; evaluation, **98, 1074, 1302, 1465, 1474, 1493, 1700, 2327, 2730, 2904, 2912, 2913, 3359, 3653a, 3662, 3780, 3781, 3993, 4376, 4378, 4396, 4422, 4427, 4428, 4435, 4436, 4454, 4637, 4640, 4646, 4674, 4680, 4682, 4788, 4789, 4857, 4887, 4890, 4906, 4907, 4910, 4938, 5156, 5161, 5185, 5186, 5188, 5192, 5193, 5199, 5200, 5205, 5207, 5264, 5381, 5383, 5436, 5444, 5467, 5479, 5481, 5515, 5524, 5526, 5535, 5536, 5537, 5543, 5545, 5546, 5549, 5550, 5554, 5556, 5557, 5558, 5559, 5561, 5565, 5566, 5594, 5688, 5892, 6063, 6064, 6103, 6104, 6252, 6270, 6275, 6276, 6286, 6331, 6343, 6352, 6358, 6368, 6374, 6377, 6378, 6379, 6380, 6580, 6637, 6710, 6816, 7087, 7088, 7094, 7260, 7390, 7481, 7552, 7554, 7653, 7654, 7655, 7657, 7658, 7659, 7660, 7661, 7720, 8148, 8151, 8156, 8168, 8178, 8414, 8420, 8424, 8677, 8908, 8983, 9041, 9346, 9349, 9451, 9529, 9530, 9531, 9532, 9533, 9537, 9538, 9544, 9548, 10375, 10377, 10378, 10404, 10445, 10619, 10636, 11047, 11048, 11049, 11050, 11051, 11160, 11302, 11454, 11687, 11746, 11760, 11881, 11939, 12031, 12032, 12073, 12106, 12211, 12278, 12314, 12322, 12574, 12575, 12577, 12693, 12753, 12756, 12760, 12808, 13011, 13013, 13429, 13769, 13803, 13843, 13859, 13861, 13877, 13878, 13971, 14203, 14431, 14488, 14491, 14497, 14670, 14823, 14825, 14827, 14839, 14866, 15439, 15585, 15978, 16416, 16417, 16422**; factors affecting, **5555, 15707**; in Kentucky bluegrass, **2027, 4139, 4141**; lead arsenate, **3353, 5355, 11666, 13017, 15704, 15707**; PMA, **916, 998, 4853, 4909, 5792, 11143, 13771, 13772**; post-emergence, **195, 1551, 1733, 3360, 4421, 4877, 8155, 8404, 9053**; potassium cyanate, **916, 941, 2727, 5792, 11143, 11685, 12412, 16490, 16491, 16493, 16494**; pre-emergence, **63, 65, 68, 69, 70, 71, 72, 195, 836, 1231, 1522, 1639, 1782, 2072, 2692, 2916, 3687a, 3765, 4135, 5551, 8404, 8407, 8412, 8415, 8431, 9578, 9579, 9580**; residual effectiveness, **1689, 14488**; siduron, **9545, 9546**; sodium arsenite, **1666, 5792, 7175, 11153, 12940, 14571, 14572, 15662, 15663, 15664, 16153**; state bulletin, **5552, 6332, 14824**

Crabgrass
control, **313, 523, 613, 703, 896, 897, 916, 959, 1122, 1167, 1200, 1466, 2357, 4670, 4908, 5501, 6274, 6832, 6840, 7235, 14804:** history, **4858, 5502**

Crabgrass
cultural control, **294, 334, 367, 529, 1164, 1551, 2066, 2138, 2164, 4414, 5502, 5731, 5787, 6978, 7265, 12195, 13157, 13546, 13837, 14150, 14172, 14827, 15699, 15706**

Crabgrass
invasion, **7434:** cultural factors affecting—irrigation, **10064, 15701;** cultural influences, **4414, 6352, 7732, 8213;** cultural influences—cutting height, **686, 4634, 4646, 4651, 4657, 4674, 6305, 6306, 6307, 9565, 10064;** cultural influences—fertilization, **2650, 4891, 6305, 6307, 6308**

Crabgrass
seed dormancy, **6478, 6479**

Crabgrass
seed germination, **4414, 6477, 6479, 12072:** factors affecting, **6478, 14759;** seasonal variation, **8407**

Crabgrass
seed head control: chemical, **208, 13546;** cultural, **16075**

Crabgrass
seed production, **5594**

Crabgrass, large, **5240, 8952, 12072, 12146, 16364**

Crabgrass, large
chemical control, **5265, 12930**

Crabgrass, large
description, **8952**

Crabgrass, smooth (see Smooth crabgrass)

Crag 531®
brown patch control, **4681**

Crag 531®
copper spot control, **7390**

Crab 531®
dollar spot control, **14720**

Crambus teterrellus (see Bluegrass webworm)

Crane fly, **1020, 1131, 1250, 7029, 15908**

Crane fly
chemical control, **4732, 4763, 4787, 7020, 10658, 10712, 12514, 15807, 15908**

Crane fly
control, **4727, 9719, 10712, 10893, 12303**

Crane fly
life history, **4727, 5709, 10712**

Crayfish, **581**

Credo crested dog's-tail, **7287**

Creeping bentgrass, **351, 2284, 2450, 6950, 9919, 11266, 11771, 12101, 12406, 13269, 13853**

Creeping bentgrass
adaptation, **5002, 5483, 9009, 10755, 11151, 12827**

Creeping bentgrass
cultivars, **302, 908, 2572, 4483, 5854, 10760, 11542, 11571, 11576, 12007, 12328, 13823:** ball roll evaluation, **6817;** brown patch susceptibility, **1639, 9564;** description, **2451, 3649, 3663, 5273, 7934, 8163, 9258, 12161, 12698, 13367;** development, **9009, 11123, 11125, 11132, 12699, 15912;** dollar spot susceptibility, **1547, 4053, 5498;** establishment rate, **2560;** evaluation, **304, 742, 757, 789, 815, 989, 1012, 1489, 1639, 1685, 1967, 2453, 2564, 2566, 2574, 2583, 2584, 2585, 2592, 2603, 2617, 2631, 2650, 2673, 2698, 2704, 2706, 2707, 4663, 5313, 5316, 5320, 5443, 5781, 6318, 6345, 6557, 6559, 6700, 6879, 7918, 7930, 8761, 8765, 9233, 9236, 9238, 9241, 9245, 10455, 10621, 10622, 10813, 10818, 10822, 10856, 10862, 11021, 11031, 11122, 11165, 11187, 11266, 11661, 12740, 13662, 14259, 14260, 14375, 14574, 16069, 16489;** *Fusarium* patch susceptibility, **6758;** ice cover tolerance, **2581;** identification, **410, 15910, 15911;** low temperature hardiness, **1489, 2594, 9408;** origin, **6950, 14259, 14260;** post-emergence herbicide tolerance, **789, 815, 8722, 10632, 12735;** pre-emergence herbicide tolerance, **2100, 12756;** *Pythium* blight susceptibility, **6207;** salinity tolerance, **2608, 16446;** shade adaptation, **8678;** snow mold susceptibility, **1690, 3111, 11490, 14923;** spring green-up evaluation, **2566;** stripe smut susceptibility, **6445;** thatching tendency, **2706, 6513;** *Typhula* blight susceptibility, **2566, 2592, 2595, 2620, 2689, 11105;** weed invasion proneness, **4646, 5498;** winter desiccation tolerance, **1489, 9233;** winter discoloration, **2560, 2698, 10616;** yellow tuft susceptibility, **2566**

Creeping bentgrass
culture, **375, 2597, 2684, 3663, 5855, 6850, 10755, 10810, 11121, 11758:** cutting height, **1778, 5467, 5498;** fertilization, **1635, 2811, 4619, 4620, 7557, 11121**

Creeping bentgrass
description, **2284, 4008, 5315, 10153, 15411:** cytology, **3837, 8627**

Creeping bentgrass
diseases, **388, 3262, 3616, 11661:** *Helminthosporium* leaf spot, **7204, 7620, 7623, 7626;** striped smut, **7804, 7807, 7808, 7811;** *Typhula* blight, **6318, 8100**

Creeping bentgrass
establishment, **375, 10082, 11758, 11764**

Creeping bentgrass
mat formation, **1557, 1600**

Creeping bentgrass
pests: nematodes, **7820, 7821, 14565**

Creeping bentgrass
root growth: environmental factors effecting, **2552, 2696, 2963**

Creeping bentgrass
selectivity, herbicide, **94, 3622a, 3623a, 8158**

Creeping bentgrass
shoot growth: environmental factors affecting, **13960**

Creeping bentgrass
uses, **3663, 4746, 5315, 7908, 10233, 12158:** fairway, **789, 815, 6569, 7910;** green, **1635, 2465, 4568, 9984, 11552, 12401, 13759;** winter overseeding, **10455, 13423**

Creeping bentgrass, weed
chemical control, **3761, 4608**

Creeping bentgrass, weed
cultural control, **5510**

Creeping buttercup, **445, 7027**
control, **6650, 15700**

Creeping charlie (see Ground ivy)

Creeping cinquefoil, **4741**

Creeping hairbell
chemical control, **7700, 10379**

Creeping red fescue (see Red fescue)

Creeping speedwell (see Speedwell, creeping)

Creeping thistle, **3881, 7027**

Crested dog's-tail, **1554, 2187, 2650, 7286, 14471**

Crested dog's-tail
cultivar evaluation, **7284, 13661, 13662, 13663**

Crested dog's-tail
description, **4009, 15410**

Crested dog's-tail
evaluation, **7287, 8336**

Crested wheatgrass, **2988**

Crested wheatgrass
adaptation, **8956, 15054**

Crested wheatgrass
breeding, **4951**

Crested wheatgrass
culture: fertilization, **2928, 9974**

Crested wheatgrass
description, **7947, 8956**

Crested wheatgrass
establishment, **2339, 2988**

Crested wheatgrass
fairway use, **15041**

Cricket field
culture, **256, 2133, 5256, 5972, 9636**: English, **10923, 13005, 14468, 14755**

Crickets
chemical control, **6066**

Cricket wicket, **11239**

Cricket wicket
culture, **1033, 1139, 1249, 1398, 1586, 1882, 2861, 4309, 5256, 5972, 10038, 10039, 10040, 10041, 10042, 10043, 10044, 10045, 10046, 13001**: Australia, **15288;** England, **8622, 11240;** fall, **1004, 1097, 1100, 3140, 10036;** New Zealand, **15167, 15169, 15171, 15173, 15175, 15177, 15183, 15206, 15210, 15214, 15216, 15222, 15224, 15227, 15233, 15236, 15239, 15243, 15246, 15248, 15287, 15290, 15294, 15296, 15303, 15308, 15309, 15313, 15314, 15315, 15322;** spring, **1071, 1088, 1177, 3139, 11241**

Criconemoides (see Ring nematode)

Criconemoides ornatus, **5757**

Croquet court
culture, **1775, 1795**: New Zealand, **15167, 15169, 15175, 15206, 15214, 15216, 15233, 15246, 15267, 15268, 15280, 15287, 15290, 15296, 15305, 15308, 15309, 15311, 15313, 15314, 15315, 15317**

Cross pollination
species evaluation, **6725, 8495, 8500, 13952**

Crotonyliden diurea
nitrogen carrier, **16275**

Crown development
Kentucky bluegrass cultivars, **5646, 9634**

Crown height
cutting height tolerance, **3178, 9634**

Crown rust, **2819, 8351**

Crownvetch, **2409, 3214, 5110, 6940, 6980, 6981, 7567, 7697, 11932, 12922, 14999, 15330, 16455**

Crownvetch
adaptation, **6969, 7564, 9189:** soil, **5717, 9988, 15097**

Crownvetch
breeding, **3915, 3916, 12656**

Crownvetch
chemical composition, **15915**

Crownvetch
cultivars: evaluation, **5108, 5109, 5124, 5125, 6032, 7698, 9988, 9990, 10383;** shade adaptation evaluation, **9189**

Crownvetch
culture: fertilization, **5127, 7012;** liming, **14722;** weed control, **2838**

Crownvetch
description, **6969, 9993, 12922**

Crownvetch
establishment, **975, 1856, 4832, 4965, 5269, 16207:** allelopathy, **2873, 2876, 9995;** companion grasses, **1853, 4965, 5716;** evaluation, **12003, 12597;** factors affecting, **5716, 6032, 7564, 9988, 14722;** innoculum effects, **7652, 14722;** liming, **5716, 5717, 7524;** mulch evaluation, **5090;** roadside slopes, **2092, 2093;** seeding rate, **7524;** weed control, **5359, 12069**

Crownvetch
roadside use, **907, 936, 1982, 5159, 7012, 9129, 12596, 12597, 12857, 14212, 16178, 16461**

Crownvetch
seed production, **6427**

Crownvetch
seed quality, **5022**

Crownvetch
seed scarification, **3189, 3190**

Crownvetch
soil stabilization: evaluation, **12922, 14212**

Crusting, soil, **3220, 6222, 10162**

Cudweed
chemical control, **4207**

Cultivar, **13065, 13848**

Cultivar
description, **13377:** handbook, **2200, 7307**

Cultivar
descriptive list: Netherlands, **14054, 14055, 14056, 14057, 14058, 14060**

Cultivar
evaluation, **1497, 2184, 6099, 9224, 9658, 11333, 14345:** methods, **126, 4498, 6441, 11159**

Cultivar
development, **1532, 1714, 8320, 11186, 11322, 12515, 13105:** methods, **11120, 12128**

Cultivar
identification, **241:** disc gel electrophoresis, **15910, 15911;** Kentucky bluegrass, **4339;** paper chromatography techniques, **11229, 11230;** peroxidase isoenzymes, **10726, 10727**

Cultivar
release procedures, **15627**

Cultivation, **826, 1047, 1654, 1947, 2458, 2645, 4145, 4405, 5442, 5450, 5523, 6597, 6874, 7492, 8962, 9209, 10042, 10259, 10271, 10272, 10275, 10302, 11033, 11038, 11495, 12691, 12882, 12883, 15101, 15894, 16419**

Cultivation
compaction correction, **6843, 9489, 15218**

Cultivation
deep: green, **5050, 9490, 10954, 10956**

Cultivation
dual purpose fertilization: evaluation, **16226**

Cultivation
effects, **1492, 3588a, 6597, 7231, 7391, 10101, 10285, 10274, 10299, 10326, 10947, 11037, 11901, 12883, 14179, 15766, 16419, 16421**

Cultivation
effects on: aeration, **4300, 5970, 9076;** annual bluegrass invasion, **16395;** dollar spot, **5523;** fertilizer penetration, **104, 109, 7390;** infiltration, **5523, 6865, 10463;** runoff, **108, 10463**

Cultivation
equipment, **2005, 4484, 6844, 15895, 15896**: England, **12516, 14566;** golf course, **9199, 14660;** Sweden, **9209**

Cultivation
evaluation, **5441, 15069**

Cultivation
history, **10436, 14256**

Cultivation
principles, **10286, 13968, 15895, 15896**

Cultivation
thatch control, **5505, 14698**

Cultivation
timing, **5272, 8962, 10275, 10952, 14914, 14915**

Cultivation
types, **2645, 3674, 5272, 6637, 6944, 7236, 7474, 14474**

Cultivation
uses, **8962:** cricket wicket, **13001;** fairway, **831, 15959;** golf course, **3063, 7238, 11484;** green, **6863, 10182, 12331, 14772;** sports field, **2134, 15564**

Cultural practices
timeliness, **1083**

Cultural system
programming, **10964**

Culture, turfgrass (see Turfgrass culture)

Cumberland red fescue, **8338, 8341, 8350**

Cup setting, **541, 1181, 6893, 9705, 10009, 12724**
winter, **563, 1129, 1337**

Curly dock (see Dock, curly)

Curvularia leaf spot, **8922**

Curvularia lunata, **2755, 11044, 11045, 11053**

Curvularia robusta (see *Curvularia* leaf spot)

Curvularia species, **993, 1002, 1590, 2534, 2755, 3332, 6729, 13702**

Cushion (see Mat)

Cuticle, **3002, 9445**

Cutter bar mowers (see Sicklebar mower)

Cutting frequency (see Mowing frequency)

Cutting height, **337, 356, 716, 744, 1137, 1550, 2019, 7052, 7411, 7497, 8974, 9666, 11448, 12858, 15493, 15504, 15531, 15535**

Cutting height
effects, **131, 3308, 7494, 8773, 10076, 10324, 12765, 15168, 15265**

Cutting height
effects on: annual bluegrass invasion, **1547, 3035, 4646, 4657, 5498, 16345;** atmospheric environment, **9994, 11648, 15417;** ball bounce, **9217;** ball roll, **924, 9217;** bermudagrass, **1700, 10064;** carbohydrate reserves, **2552,**

7931, 8675, 10228, 10232, 14700, 15657; chemical composition, **5700, 9034, 10076**; clover invasion, **835, 4634**; crabgrass invasion, **4634, 4646, 6305, 6306, 6307, 10064**; creeping bentgrass, **4634, 5467**; crown development, **9634**; disease development, **6709, 7191, 7201, 8357, 10083**; divot recovery, **15364**; earthworms, **5902**; establishment, **2381, 2479, 2609, 6111, 6435, 7011, 8791**; *Helminthosporium* leaf spot, **6306, 11104**; impact absorption, **6806**; Kentucky bluegrass, **2517, 4644**; leaf development, **3308, 9877, 16435**; low temperature kill, **563, 590, 2705, 10604, 10605, 10615**; melting out, **7205, 9758**; mowing frequency, **10228**; polystand composition, **4630, 4631, 5562, 7191, 8717, 10605**; rhizome growth, **6442, 7493, 8710, 9125, 9622, 9634, 14090, 15657, 16179**; root growth, **797, 2606, 2479, 2552, 3035, 3200, 4258, 4633, 6628, 8192, 8398, 8664, 8675, 8689, 8690, 8710, 8767, 9125, 9162, 9341, 9343, 9501, 10072, 10076, 10091, 11007, 11783, 11784, 11858, 12697, 12734, 12765, 14090, 14134, 14135, 14137, 14161, 14765, 14766, 15657, 16179, 16431**; ryegrass persistence, **6307**; shear strength, sod, **6806**; shoot density, **2603, 2699, 6306, 6442, 6712, 8456, 10071, 10072, 10076, 10615, 12676, 15265, 16179**; shoot growth, **2429, 2733, 3035, 3200, 3308, 4578, 5700, 6628, 6717, 6782, 7496, 7513, 7931, 8192, 8398, 8447, 8640, 8675, 9007, 9125, 9178, 9500, 10068, 10072, 10074, 10076, 10091, 10105, 10106, 10335, 10526, 11012, 11783, 12697, 12765, 12840, 13900, 14134, 14446, 14765, 14766, 15705, 16057, 16179, 16431**; sod heating, **8940, 8947**; sod strength, **2170, 2630, 2633, 2649, 2672, 2704, 14090**; soil warming, **2615**; spring green-up rate, **1700, 8574, 14900**; stomatal density, **13623**; stress tolerance, **866, 2706, 6306, 8659, 10605**; tall fescue, **10604**; thatch development, **2603, 6713, 14900**; tillering, **3037, 7493, 8055, 8675, 9034, 9622, 10336, 12765, 16435**; *Typhula* blight, **2699, 11105**; verdure, **10076**; water use rate, **2667, 7181, 10703, 13623, 13624, 15549, 15558, 15711**; wear tolerance, **9782, 16386**; weed invasion, **686, 744, 1422, 4632, 4634, 4646, 5498, 6308, 6309, 6317, 6637, 6713, 8724, 10064, 10622, 11126, 11330, 12840, 13900, 16165**

Cutting height
factors affecting, **15562, 15565, 15570, 15573, 15575, 15583, 16129**

Cutting height
fairway, **654, 9563, 9857, 11126, 11516, 16162**

Cutting height
green, **834, 1154, 3463, 11503, 15184, 15965**

Cutting height
lawn, **1372**

Cutting height
roadside, **1479**

Cutting height
selection criteria, **12686**

Cutting height
species tolerance, **3178, 4634, 4653, 5498, 9563, 16320, 16261, 16368**: evaluation, **3459, 9430, 11296**

Cutting height
sports field, **1682, 3459**

Cutting height
zoysiagrass, **1492, 2609**

Cutworm, **545, 690, 2027, 3042, 3623, 4611, 4836, 7030, 8607, 8670, 10248, 11344, 13494, 13502, 14634**
chemical control, **625, 640, 1079, 1274, 1639, 2112, 4834, 8473, 8578, 9472, 10724, 13483, 14634, 15334, 15348**: chlordane, **12177, 13491**

Cutworm
description, **4779, 8473, 8478, 8479**

Cutworm, granulate
chemical control, **15737**

Cyano (methylmercuril) guanidine (see also Mercury, organic), **2633**

Cycloheximide, **2834, 3277**

Cycloheximide
copper spot control, **7390**

Cycloheximide
disease control, **8841, 11531**

Cycloheximide
dollar spot control, **10568, 10574, 15033, 15036**

Cycloheximide
Helminthosporium leaf spot control, **4167, 11104**

Cycloheximide
melting out control, **14026, 15033, 15036**

Cyclocephala borealis (see Northern masked chafer)

Cyclocephala species, **9337**

Cycocel® (see CCC)

Cygon® (see Dimethoate)

Cyndon species, **14262, 15231**

Cyndon species
chromosome number, **8229**

Cyndon species
taxonomy, **7379, 8229**

Cynodon dactylon (see also Common bermudagrass), **7379, 8229**

Cynodon incompletus var. *hirsutus* (see also Bradley bermudagrass), **7379**

Cynodon x *magennisii* (see also Magennis bermudagrass), **7379**

Cynosurus cristatus (see Crested dog's-tail)

Cyperus esculentus (see Yellow nutsedge)

Cyperus gracilis, **14349**

Cyperus rotundus (see Purple nutsedge)

Cyst nematode, **3397, 5011, 5014, 6337, 8525, 10551**

Cyst nematode
biological control, **5012**

Cyst nematode
chemical control, **5013**

Cyst nematode
description, **5009, 12057**

Cyst nematode
pathogenicity, **12050, 16101**

Cyst nematode
on St. Augustinegrass, **1648, 7616**

Cytology, **3836, 3837**

Cytology
Agrostis species, **8627**

Cytology
Festuca species, **3384, 8501, 8502, 12066**

Cytology
Poa species, **62, 84, 3374, 8913, 11337, 12652, 14735**

Cytology
Stenotaphrum species, **9667, 9668**

2,4–D, **751, 772, 806, 855, 859, 863, 865, 1940, 2237, 3389, 4154, 4851, 5615, 9956, 10996, 13122, 13779, 14518**

2,4–D
application, **3174, 15421:** carbowax, **758, 763;** methods, **781, 2446, 2448, 14928, 15423, 15953;** rates, **1010, 11130;** timing, **777, 779, 11131, 11133**

2,4–D
bindweed control, **6500, 7269**

2,4–D
broadleaf weed control, **70, 885, 2914, 5197, 5434, 7097, 10627, 11131, 11686, 13860, 14500, 15081, 15920:** evaluation, **5601, 5602, 8433, 8435, 8436, 11095, 12693**

2,4–D
catsear control, **4207**

2,4–D
clover control, **766, 5603**

2,4–D
dandelion control, **4809, 5603, 11046, 12249, 12441**

2,4–D
Dichondra control, **6344**

2,4–D
effectiveness: environmental effects, **778, 7093, 10220, 11130;** seasonal variation, **778, 780, 13430**

2,4–D
effects, **1655, 3620a, 10224, 12251, 12441**

2,4–D
effects on: grass morphology, **8461, 15446;** shoot growth, **8988, 10222, 10693, 13958**

2,4–D
English daisy control, **5603**

2,4–D
fertilizer mixtures, **795, 10218, 13958**

2,4–D
formulation, **310, 776, 799, 4010, 4263, 11130, 11131**

2,4–D
injury symptoms, **3704a, 7269**

2,4–D
mode of action, **7093, 7269, 7326, 10218**

2,4–D
nutgrass control, **3466**

2,4–D
nutsedge control, **7545**

2,4–D
onehunga control, **2172**

2,4–D
pearlwort control, **7120, 12082**

2,4–D
plantain control, **2901, 5603, 11046, 12249**

2,4–D
selectivity, **874, 3498, 3620a, 5382:** bentgrass, **94, 3237, 3595a, 3620a, 11031;** bentgrass cultivars, **789, 815, 2319, 6346;** broadleaf species, **848, 4805;** seedling, **3540, 8988, 10693, 12249, 13430, 13431;** seedling species, **1290, 11095, 13430, 14893;** species variation, **775, 7269, 9885, 10218**

2,4–D
soil persistence, **10220, 12526, 13929**

2,4–D
uses: golf course, **9450, 11452;** lawn, **8526, 12252;** roadside, **213, 214**

2,4–D
weed control, **774, 2726, 3940, 4263, 4607, 4608, 5434, 5595, 6367, 7535, 7538, 7768, 8617, 9240, 9448, 9449, 9452, 9499, 9876, 10218, 10220, 10221, 10606, 11130, 11133, 12250, 13512, 14928, 15877, 16153:** evaluation, **4607, 4755, 5302, 5382, 5732, 5733, 7022, 8432, 11947, 12808, 14894;** lawn bulletin, **55, 56**

2,4–D-dicamba combination, **1639, 1700, 1782, 2027, 2100, 2890, 3089, 3361, 8437**

2,4–D-dicamba combination
broadleaf weed control, **2889, 4809, 7659, 7661, 8405, 8408, 8422, 14494, 15978**

2,4–D-dicamba-MCPP combination, **8422, 8436**

2,4–D-dicamba-silvex combination, **8422**

2,4–D-MCPP combination, **2100, 8422, 8436, 8437**
broadleaf weed control, **8405, 8408**

2,4–D-silvex combination, **2100, 4837, 8422**

broadleaf weed control, **8405, 8408**

Daconil 2787® (see Chlorothalonil)

Dacthal® (see DCPA)

Dactylis glomerata (see Orchardgrass)

Dagger nematode, **5009, 5011, 11696, 11742**
incidence: species evaluation, **6607, 11668, 14052**

Dahlgren creeping bentgrass, **945, 6858, 6870, 7309**

Daisey, English (see English daisey)

Dalapon, **1312, 1551, 2320, 3655a, 5578, 8665, 11994, 12234, 13779**

Dalapon
adjuvant effects, **9402**

Dalapon
bentgrass control, **5677, 6244**

Dalapon
bermudagrass control, **13695**

Dalapon
crabgrass control, **6374**

Dalapon
degradation, **8768**

Dalapon
effects on: polystand composition, **8938**

Dalapon
kikuyugrass control, **16334**

Dalapon
mode of action, **9403**

Dalapon
perennial grass control, **5367, 7010, 8182**

Dalapon
quackgrass control, **3679a, 12216, 12980**

Dalapon
soil fumigation, **87, 2867**

Dalapon
tall fescue control, **2903**

Dalapon
weed control, **11856, 12808, 16320**

Dallisgrass, **3553, 8078, 15671**

Dallisgrass
adaptation, **3553, 5056, 9091, 15054**

Dallisgrass
chemical control, **1196, 1222, 1620, 6470:** in bermudagrass, **3003, 4207, 9888;** DSMA, **9652, 10973;** evaluation, **1782, 3003, 6245, 7933, 9537, 10949, 10973, 14670**

Dallisgrass
description, **3553, 3588, 7947, 10185, 14085**

Damping-off diseases, **937, 1141, 5417, 6739, 7192**
chemical control, **2520, 4685, 5417, 5617, 16212:** seed treatment, **14017**

Dandelion, **594, 3881, 5498, 11076, 15706**

Dandelion
chemical control, **446, 594, 623, 1761, 4267, 5355, 5603, 6224, 7294:** 2,4–D, **5595, 5603, 7768, 11046, 12249;** evaluation, **1700, 3618a, 3662, 4809, 8171, 8416, 8422, 8433, 8435, 8436, 8852, 10403, 13860, 15706;** iron sulfate, **9848, 10076**

Dandelion
control, **354, 372, 396, 617, 759, 761, 9268, 9696, 9697, 9851, 11774, 13817, 15706**

Dasanit® (see Fensulfothion)

Dasas rough bluegrass, **7287, 9218**

Dawson chewings fescue, **1170, 1554, 8343**
evaluation, **7284, 8338, 8341, 8350, 9219**

Day length, **11838**

Day length
developmental response, **3897, 11823, 11822, 16392:** leaf, **5646, 8658, 12967, 14606, 16359**

Day length
effects, **169, 3623a, 8739, 11903, 16359, 16373**

Day length
effects on: carbohydrate reserves, **2295, 7917, 12089;** seed germination, **11262;** temperature, **8785, 12089**

Day length
flowering response, **9593, 11822, 11823, 11824, 12089, 12766, 12767, 16258, 16392:** development, **152, 153, 2271, 2275, 3669a, 3896, 3897, 3898, 3899, 3900, 3902, 3904, 3906, 5664, 5666, 6400, 7735, 9019, 9020, 9183, 11235, 12966, 14192, 14604, 16257, 16346, 16444;** induction, **3669a, 5663, 11297, 12090, 12962, 14734, 16350, 16359**

Day length
growth response, **5674, 11822, 11823, 12766, 12767, 16392;** habit, **635, 5669:** rhizome, **2142, 10022, 11015, 11016, 11020, 11022, 11023, 16359, 16399;** root, **9724, 12089, 14836, 16359;** root-shoot ratio, **11297, 14834, 14836;** seedling, **14191;** shoot, **5666, 8550, 8657, 8658, 9178, 9724, 11235, 11297, 14604, 14836, 16359;** stolon, **16399, 16359**

Day length
leaf development: shoot density, **800, 12089;** tillering, **2295, 3897, 6402, 10020, 10696, 11015, 11020, 11023, 12967, 14606, 16399**

Dazomet, **1306, 1892, 3923, 5632, 6637, 8665, 8768, 8832, 8881, 8882, 8892, 10030, 11976, 12179, 12988, 13724**
soil fumigation, **2880, 3509**

DBCP (see Dibromochloropropane)

DCPA, **1441, 1967, 2010, 2027, 2237, 2902, 2918, 2919, 4935, 5571, 5915, 6653, 6654, 6658, 8031, 8151, 8768, 10386, 11049, 11051, 12073, 12106,**

12575, 12735, 13011, 13861, 14491, 14825, 14839

DCPA
annual bluegrass control, **2312, 6637, 8157, 8419, 8696, 9850, 10624**

DCPA
charcoal deactivation, **8417**

DCPA
chickweed control, **8416, 9850**

DCPA
crabgrass control, **1477, 1493, 1551, 1700, 1782, 2904, 4139, 5185, 5188, 5192, 5193, 5205, 5385, 5483, 5543, 5545, 5550, 5561, 5565, 6380, 6379, 6380, 6170, 7260, 7552, 8151, 8168, 8178, 9346, 9529, 9530, 9531, 9533, 9537, 10375, 10377, 10378, 10404, 10619, 11050, 11824, 12031, 13859, 14823, 14827, 16384:** evaluation, **5479, 7655, 7658, 8156, 8407, 8414, 8415, 9580, 10636, 12278, 12753, 12756, 12760, 13803, 14488**

DCPA
creeping speedwell control, **1872, 1916, 2015**

DCPA
effects on: growth, **2899, 2907, 6266, 10394, 11089, 12735;** low temperature kill, **6266, 11089;** species composition, **8343**

DCPA
goosegrass control, **2900, 5537, 8157, 9733**

DCPA
nimblewill control, **7655, 7658**

DCPA
phytotoxicity, **2899, 2902, 2907, 10619, 11052, 11089, 12375, 14826**

DCPA
selectivity, **2127:** evaluation, **5537, 6440, 6637, 8796, 8797, 9349, 10624, 14488;** seedling, **8695, 12699, 13617;** species evaluation, **4794, 8415, 9580;** bentgrass, **2908, 8722;** Kentucky bluegrass, **12760, 13803**

DCPA
soil persistence, **3394, 8768, 10451**

DCPA
weed control, **6637, 7261, 8412, 8908, 9349, 9580, 12314, 15978**

D–D®
nematode control, **12978, 16106**

DDT, **786, 798, 2109, 3284, 10008**

DDT
ant control, **791**

DDT
chinch bug control, **8876, 12179, 13473, 13478, 14400**

DDT
effect on: earthworms, **12169**

DDT
grub control, **6387, 12171, 12178, 12181**

DDT
insect control, **16, 4836, 10155, 14235**

DDT
Japanese beetle control, **844, 5986, 10007, 10008, 13475:** evaluation, **7157, 12168, 12178**

DDT
sod webworm control, **8472, 8480**

Debris removal
equipment, **16487**

Deep coring (see Coring, deep)

Deficiency symptom, nutrient (see Nutrient deficiency, symptoms)

Defoliation (see Mowing)

Defurarin urea
Nitrogen carrier, **16275**

Dehulling, seed (see Seed germination, dehulling effects)

Deicing (see also Salt, deicing)
roadside salinity problems, **1921, 1967, 3165, 9131, 12722, 14644**

Delft Kentucky bluegrass, **5781, 6306, 6307, 6309, 6330, 9218, 9226, 10622, 10626, 11186**

Delta Kentucky bluegrass, **1473, 1685, 3656, 4957, 6734, 6879, 7202, 7309, 8343, 11151, 11165, 11187, 13462**

Delta Kentucky bluegrass
disease susceptibility, **2546, 3259**

Delta Kentucky bluegrass
evaluation, **6306, 6307, 6330, 6712, 8317, 10622, 10626, 10635, 11186, 14813**

Demosan® (see Chloroneb)

Denitrification, **2308, 10159, 11972**

Densitometer
turfgrass quality evaluation, **14898**

Densitometer
vertical shoot growth measurement, **14897**

Density, shoot (see Shoot density)

Depressions, soil
correction, **10659, 11953, 13962**

Dermatogen, **13586**

Derris
earthworm control, **7572**

Deschampsia caspitosa (see Hairgrass, tufted)

Deschampsia flexuosa (see Hairgrass, wavy)

Desert saltgrass, **5113**
salinity tolerance, **5115**

Desiccation, **188, 1341, 2577, 2578, 2591, 2605**
factors affecting, **1341, 2818, 13436**

Desiccation, atmospheric (see Atmospheric dessication)

Desiccation, winter (see Winter dessication)

Design
golf course, **3964, 4819, 8643, 8917, 12891, 12892, 14853, 16110:** book, **14479;** remodeling, **3958**

Design
irrigation system, **3627a, 4617, 10927, 13018**

Design
minimizing maintenance costs, **2504**

Dethatching (see Thatch, control)

Development, **5668, 5832, 5866, 10096, 11322, 12862, 13400, 13585, 14831**

Development
book, **2244, 10680**

Development
factors affecting, **10695, 14087, 15145**

Devil's paintbrush, **702**

Dew, **1585, 9710, 10317, 10319, 10323, 10849**

Dew
beneficial effects, **10315, 10318**

Dew
control, **799**

Dew
factors affecting, **10318, 10846**

Dew
removal, **13057, 15597**

Dew point, **14193**

Dexon®
Pythium blight control, **2536, 9933, 15680**

Diammonium phosphate, **10355, 13039**

Diazinon, **15005**

Diazinon
bermudagrass control, **1700, 1779, 3639, 14907**

Diazinon
billbug control, **10983, 14533**

Diazinon
chinch bug control, **8873, 8877, 8881, 8892, 14400:** hairy, **8753, 12179, 14391;** Southern, **4782, 10982**

Diazinon
cutworm control, **13234**

Diazinon
flea beetle control, **15470**

Diazinon
frit fly control, **1779, 4322, 13500**

Diazinon
ground pearl control, **15739, 15743**

Diazinon
nematode control, **14393, 14528, 16106**

Diazinon
rhodesgrass scale control, **14398**

Diazinon
sod webworm control, **1779, 8480, 11944, 12428, 14389, 14633**

Diazinon
turfgrass weevil control, **3628a, 3631a, 3634a**

Diazinon
white grub control, **15470**

1,2 dibromo-3-chloropropane (see Dibromochloropropane)

Dibromochloropropane, **2279**
nematode control, **8040, 11744, 12053, 12058, 12061, 12062, 12978, 16106:** evaluation, **11709, 11743**

3,5-dibromo-4-hydroxybenzonitrile (see Bromoxynil)

Dicamba, **1551, 1579, 1580, 1653, 1797, 1967, 3274, 3704a, 3767, 4148, 4279, 5197, 5302, 5504, 8181, 8768, 10996, 12473, 14023**

Dicamba
broadleaf weed control, **2890, 4646, 8410, 10379, 10403, 10404, 10627, 13860:** evaluation, **2178, 3666, 7658, 8405, 8410, 8433, 12693, 13016**

Dicamba
chickweed control, **1871, 2908, 8436, 13024**

Dicamba
henbit control, **1871, 14309**

Dicamba
knotweed control, **1639, 1700, 4675, 5982, 13024, 13864, 16469:** evaluation, **7655, 8435**

Dicamba
perennial grass control, **9537, 14989, 15160**

Dicamba
persistence, **190, 8768**

Dicamba
phytotoxicity, **5382, 5982, 8433, 9885, 16469**

Dicamba
selectivity, **2914, 4805:** bentgrass, **2173, 2608, 5500, 10632;** evaluation, **4156, 8433;** Kentucky bluegrass, **2908, 15160;** seedling, **8437**

Dicamba
weed control, **3665a, 6673, 6684, 6724, 8138, 9876, 10606, 13024, 13512, 13881, 13882:** evaluation, **4156, 5382, 8182, 8432, 11947**

Dicamba
white clover control, **2901, 2908, 6267, 9530, 9533, 9537, 13024:** evaluation, **4809, 8435, 8436**

Dicamba—MCPA combination, **9465**

Dicamba—MCPP combination, **3361, 8436**

Dichlobenil
annual bluegrass control, **1967, 4016, 4018, 6654, 6658, 9138**

Dichlobenil
evaluation, **8182, 9530, 15978**

Dichloral urea
crabgrass control, **4378**

2,4-dichloro-6-o-chloro-anilino-s-triazine (see Anilazine)

1,4-dichloro-2,5-dimethoxybenzene (see Chloroneb)

Dichlorophen
dollar spot control, **12357**

Dichlorophen
red thread control, **16212**

2,4-dichlorophenoxyacetic acid (see 2,4–D)

(2,4—dichlorophenyl)-phenyl-5 -pyrimidine-methanol, **7354**

Dichloropropene—dichloropropane (see D–D)

2,2-dichloropropionic acid and sodium 2,2-dichloropropionate (see Dalapon)

Dichlorotetra fluroacetone
rust control, **7364**

Dichondra, **711, 15937, 16320, 16438**

Dichondra
adaptation, **1078, 16366, 16437**

Dichondra
culture, **2290, 9197, 15937, 16388:** weed control, **1551, 10953**

Dichondra
description, **16388, 16438:** flowering, **15937, 16437, 16444**

Dichondra
diseases, **9958, 15617**: *Alternaria* leaf spot, **5405, 9891**

Dichondra
establishment, **2290, 8926**

Dichondra
pests, **8473, 8474, 15737:** cutworm, **8473, 8474;** flea beetle, **8473, 8474, 8481, 15736, 15740;** mite, **8473, 8474**

Dichondra
uses, **1027:** lawn, **2290, 16388**

Dichondra species (see Dichondra)

Dichondra, weed
chemical control: in bentgrass, **6344**

Dickinson, Lawrence S., **3951**

Dicranella varia, **8464**

Dieldrin, **1639**

Dieldrin
grub control, **12181, 15740**

Dieldrin
insect control, **9467, 13234, 13483, 14235**

Dieldrin
Japanese beetle control, **7158, 12178**

Dieldrin
northern masked chafer control, **12172, 12178**

Dieldrin
spring dead spot control, **8185, 15127**

Dieldrin
wireworm control, **6071**

O,O–diethyl *O*–(2-isopropyl-4-methyl-6-pyrimidinyl) phosphorothioate (see Diazinon)

O,O-diethyl *O*-(3,5,6-trichloro-2-pyridyl) phosphorothioate (see Dursban®)

Difolatan (see Captafol)

Digested sewage sludge (see Sewage sludge, digested)

Digitaria ischaemum (see Smooth crabgrass)

Digitaria sanguinalis (see Crabgrass, large)

5,6—Dihydro-2-methyl-1,4–3 carboxyanilide (see Carboxin)

O,O-diisopropyl phosphorodithioate *S*-ester with *N*-(2-mercaptoethyl) benzenesulfonamide (see Bensulide)

Dilophus species (see Fever fly)

Dimethoate
flea beetle control, **15740**

1,1'dimethyl 4,4'bipyridinium (see Paraquat)

O,O-dimethyl dithiophosphate of diethyl mercaptosuccinate (see Malathion)

Dimethyl 2,3,5,6-tetrachloroterephthalate (see DCPA)

Dimethyl (2,2,2,-trichloro-1-hydroxyethyl) phosphonate (see Trichlorofon)

Dimethylsulfoxide (see DMSO)

Dinitro compounds
weed control, **859**

Dinitro (1-methyl heptyl) phenyl crotonate (see Dinocap)

Dinoben®
crabgrass control, **6378**

Dinocap
powdery mildew control, **1545**

Dioctadecyl dimethyl ammonium chloride, **18**

Diphenamid
annual bluegrass control, **2919, 9533, 9537**

Diphenamid
residual phytotoxicity, **10451**

Diphenatrile
crabgrass control, **1493, 5207, 5481, 5559, 8178, 13877**

Dipropalin
crabgrass control, **6380, 13877**

Diquot, **3513, 3520, 4954, 5033**

Disc gel electrophoresis
cultivar identification, **15910, 15911**

Discoloration (see Low temperature discoloration)

Disease, **182, 183, 194, 196, 200, 388, 431, 872, 1044, 1101, 1487, 1683, 1708, 1884, 1977, 2174, 3226, 3247, 3738, 5378, 5638, 6124, 6258, 6741, 6752, 6955, 7032, 7401, 7881, 8101, 8360, 8364, 8993, 8994, 9551, 10805, 10806, 10811, 10819, 12079, 12932, 13457, 13744, 14715, 14803, 15762, 16217, 16222**

Disease
bentgrass: chemical control, **1677**

Disease
book, **1009, 4173, 12993, 12994, 14018, 14189**

Disease
bulletin, **272, 1161, 3069, 3248**

Disease
causal organisms, **4294, 10094, 13703**

Disease
cultural effects, **1317, 1639, 3256, 5398, 5465, 6127, 6733, 7803, 8093, 9551, 10094, 10920, 11578, 12145, 13537, 14901, 15014:** clipping, **186;** cutting height, **7191, 8357;** fertilization, **5374, 5395, 5396, 6647, 6654, 6732, 9291, 10811, 11524;** irrigation, **4031, 5412, 5959, 6558, 9861, 10078, 10079, 10101, 10108, 10571, 11019, 11524, 11529, 12721, 13537, 15925;** liming, **11524, 11661;** mowing, **5412, 8357, 10571, 11019, 11524, 13537, 15925;** nitrogen, **182, 3799, 3804, 3805, 4111, 4112, 4114, 5395, 6198, 6906, 8357, 12701, 12716, 12719;** nutrition, **1290, 4179, 4182, 4198, 4199, 6655, 6702, 6975, 9749, 9861, 10031, 10101, 10108, 10196, 10571, 11019, 11113, 11529, 12268, 12695, 12699, 12705, 13537, 15925;** potassium, **1932, 2162, 5395, 6703, 6705, 9061;** thatch, **188, 4031, 5412, 9861, 11019, 13537**

Disease
development, **3665, 3805, 5400, 5403, 6191, 8312, 8364, 8375, 9406, 12078, 12079**

Disease
distribution, **6728, 6737, 6739, 6769, 8101, 8358**

Disease
effects of: guttation fluid, **2607, 3665, 5403, 5404, 5408, 5410, 7621, 7622, 7625, 8093, 8094, 8357, 10315, 10317, 10318, 10319, 10323, 13723, 15901**

Disease
effects on: polystand composition, **6321;** weed invasion, **6309**

Disease
England, **5638, 7023, 7590, 8345, 8358**

Disease
environmental effects, **187, 188, 189, 4171, 5829, 6864, 7803, 7887, 8991, 9861, 9892, 10565, 10566, 10920, 11578, 11877, 12145, 13537, 15014, 16289, 16296:** drought, **5414, 5415;** temperature, **5402, 5456, 6127, 6739, 9861, 11875, 11939, 12467, 13538, 13726;** water, **6123, 6127, 6558, 7054, 7056, 11113, 11875, 13538, 16221;** wind, **683**

Disease
evaluation techniques, **1145, 2114**

Disease
factors affecting, **185, 3258, 5397, 5417, 5486, 6191, 8375, 11114**

Disease
golf course, **1365, 5325, 11549, 12379**

Disease
identification, **272, 1161, 4174, 4181, 4687, 4688, 6117, 6119, 6132, 6864, 7620, 7803, 8097, 9686, 10806, 12377, 14012, 15672, 15674, 15675:** key, **15759;** mycelium key, **8359;** spore key, **8359**

Disease
Japan, **6258, 11799, 16293, 16294**

Disease
of Kentucky bluegrass, **184, 3242**

Disease
lawn, **1188, 3617, 6734, 8995, 12934, 14546:** state bulletin, **3128, 6188, 6195, 7680, 8806, 13000, 15647, 15649, 15683**

Disease
research, **2114, 6158, 6741**

Disease
resistance: breeding, **912, 15876**

Disease
soil effects, **188, 1287, 9861:** soil moisture, **4182, 4198, 4199;** soil reaction, **4179, 8357, 8375, 11661**

Disease
susceptibility, **4042:** species evaluation, **4180, 4199, 5399, 9892, 14012, 15672, 15674, 15675, 16361, 16369, 16372**

Disease
symptoms, **3251, 4716, 5399, 6119, 6731, 7803, 7988, 8101, 9892**

Disease
on warm season turfgrasses, **161, 6199, 10550, 14394, 15691**

Disease control, **23, 166, 380, 682, 1523, 2329, 2330, 2423, 3228, 3257, 3263, 4175, 4183, 4184, 4686, 4687, 6115, 6161, 6202, 6735, 6769, 7024, 7113, 7154, 7190, 7692, 7750, 8097, 8756, 8997, 9860, 10577, 10587, 10593, 10596, 10597, 10731, 12907, 12932, 12935, 13023, 13604, 13607, 13710, 13712, 13715, 13743, 13744, 14716, 16267, 16268**

Disease control
bulletin, **6138, 13728, 13729, 13734, 13743**

Disease control
chemical, **817, 3671, 4170, 4171, 4174, 4674, 6114, 6127, 6132, 6204, 6736, 6751, 6757, 6834, 6864, 7232, 7353, 7884, 8059, 8092, 8329, 8359, 8807, 8808, 8903, 8970, 9460, 9892, 10089, 10566, 10577, 10584, 10585, 10588, 10591, 10594, 10600, 10602, 10996, 11070, 11977, 12080, 12908, 12909, 13535, 13595, 13596, 13709, 13722, 14476, 14718, 15645, 15678, 15679, 15685, 15756, 15757, 15759, 16218:** economics, **10845, 15887;** evaluation,

8371, **8805**; latex additive, **9089**, **9090**; recommendations, **2583**, **4180**, **4199**, **4716**, **6116**, **6165**, **6731**, **8996**, **13706**, **13707**, **13731**, **14025**, **14902**, **15675**, **15682**, **15687**, **15925**

Disease control
cultural, **1308**, **3263**, **3448**, **3603a**, **3786**, **4196**, **4716**, **5416**, **5465**, **5622**, **6731**, **6736**, **6738**, **6948**, **7131**, **8990**, **9749**, **9892**, **10350**, **10569**, **10591**, **10594**, **10600**, **10853**, **11207**, **11514**, **11559**, **11564**, **11570**, **12212**, **12675**, **13705**, **13706**, **13709**, **13726**, **13730**, **14113**, **15645**, **15646**, **15925**, **16050**

Disease control
evaluation, **5176**, **5189**, **6745**, **16298**

Disease control
fairway, **5740**, **15959**

Disease control
history, **4193**, **4195**, **5888**, **10853**

Disease control
lawn, **6734**, **9091**, **9092**, **9093**, **9820**, **11068**, **13704**, **13711**

Disease control
New Zealand, **2950**, **3226**

Disease control
preventive, **1197**, **1199**, **2157**, **3673a**, **4859**, **6114**, **6116**, **7751**, **7887**, **16236**

Disease control
principles, **6132**, **8991**, **10089**

Disease control
resistant species, **7373**, **10569**

Disease control
state bulletin, **2039**, **4047**, **4048**, **4204**, **4208**, **5761**, **6217**, **6218**, **6219**, **8613**, **13963**, **15644**, **15683**, **15686**, **15693**

Disease control
USA survey, **6745**

Disease control
warm season turfgrass, **10550**, **11069**, **15691**

Disease control
winter overseeding, **9301**, **15676**

Disodium methanearsonate (see DSMA)

Distichlis strichta (see Desert saltgrass)

Disulfoton, **15742**

Disulfoton
ground pearl control, **15744**

Disulfoton
hunting billbug control, **8894**

Di-syston® (see Disulfoton)

Ditch, **2504**, **13547**
erosion control, **1479**, **2298**

2,6-di-tert-butyl-*p*-tolyl-methylcarbamate (see Terbutol)

Dithane M–45®
algae control, **14426**

Dithane M–45®
melting-out control, **7619**

Ditylenchus graminophilus, **6608**, **8337**

Ditylenchus radicicola, **6608**, **8337**

Diurnal variation
atmospheric, **16271**

Diurnal variation
plant constituents, **7916**, **8651**, **8773**, **16317**

Diurnal variation
plant osmotic pressure, **14319**

Diuron, **3394**, **8182**

Diuron
algae control, **6630**

Diuron
annual bluegrass control, **9533**, **9537**

Diuron
crabgrass control, **7260**, **8178**

Diuron
velvetgrass control, **8939**

Divot
recovery: cultural effects, **343**, **15355**, **15364**
species effects, **866**, **875**, **15355**, **15364**

Divot
repair, **1465**, **5900**, **12493**, **15355**

Divot
simulation apparatus, **15364**

DMA (see DSMA)

DMPA, **4794**, **8768**, **9349**, **10200**

DMPA
annual bluegrass control, **67**, **1700**, **4018**, **5571**, **6487**, **6653**, **6654**, **6658**, **8151**, **9533**: evaluation, **6637**, **8696**, **11255**

DMPA
crabgrass control, **1782**, **2904**, **4139**, **5161**, **5188**, **5205**, **5207**, **5481**, **5537**, **5559**, **5561**, **6368**, **6379**, **6380**, **7260**, **7552**, **7554**, **8151**, **8168**, **8178**, **9529**, **9530**, **9531**, **9533**, **9548**, **10375**, **10378**, **11048**, **11049**, **11050**, **11051**, **12073**, **12106**, **12575**, **13011**, **13859**, **13861**, **13877**, **14491**, **14823**, **14825**, **14827**, **16098**, **16384**: evaluation, **5479**, **7655**, **7658**, **7659**, **8407**, **8415**, **9349**, **10200**, **10636**, **12278**, **12314**, **12753**, **12756**, **12760**, **13803**, **14488**

DMPA
growth effects, **6486**, **6495**

DMPA
nimblewill control, **4646**, **7715**, **15160**

DMPA
phytotoxicity, **4153**, **8722**, **10619**, **11052**, **12735**, **13832**, **14826**

DMPA
selectivity, **2908**, **4794**, **5537**, **6440**, **6637**, **9349**, **9578**, **9579**, **10624**, **14488**: Kentucky bluegrass, **12760**, **13803**, **15160**; seedling, **8695**, **12699**

DMPA
weed control, **6486**, **8189**, **8412**, **8435**, **8908**, **9578**, **9579**, **15439**, **15978**, **16098**

DMSO, **15800**
fungicide effectiveness, **2535**

DMTT (see Dazomet)

Dock, common, **4742**

Dock, curly, **4742**

Dodecenylsuccinic acid
antitranspirant, **4583**

Dog's-tail, crested (see Crested dog's-tail)

Dolichodorus (see Awl nematode)

Dollar spot, **210, 315, 604, 608, 834, 953, 1017, 1048, 1094, 1101, 1141, 1977, 2817, 2839, 3252, 4053, 5399, 5421, 6159, 6199, 7884, 10491, 10796, 13566, 13703, 15723**

Dollar spot,
bentgrass susceptibility: cultivar evaluation, **388, 854, 1547, 4050, 4052, 4646, 4840, 6318, 9564, 10564, 12938,**

Dollar spot
on bahiagrass, **2346, 7123**

Dollar spot
on bermudagrass, **2346, 15129, 15130,**

Dollar spot
chemical control, **20, 584, 727, 1253, 1487, 1590, 2633, 3070, 4360, 4677, 4683, 4858, 6114, 6132, 6173, 6174, 6179, 6216, 6748, 6834, 8164, 8807, 9463, 10564, 10570, 10573, 10790, 10792, 10794, 10795, 10846, 10891, 11106, 11661, 12937, 12938, 13598, 13612, 13703, 14717, 14721, 14886, 15011, 15013, 15014, 15033, 15034, 15036, 15759, 15781:** benomyl, **2673, 15022**; cadmium compounds, **806, 1248, 9244, 9245, 15355**; chlorothalonil, **14814, 15355**

Dollar spot
chemical control: evaluation, **799, 905, 1545, 1639, 1700, 1776, 2027, 2100, 2326, 2327, 2328, 2329, 2330, 2331, 2332, 2333, 2631, 3103, 3260, 3597a, 4050, 4052, 4194, 4203, 4206, 4209, 4679, 4684, 4691, 4693, 4694, 4695, 4696, 5766, 6180, 6184, 6601, 7192, 7285, 8096, 8185, 8351, 8356, 8371, 9246, 10410, 10567, 10568, 10572, 10574, 10797, 10798, 11661, 12167, 12357, 12538, 12907, 12910, 12936, 13600, 13603, 13605, 13611, 13993, 13996, 13999, 14000, 14008, 14714, 14719, 14720, 14815, 15037, 15122, 15123, 15124, 15126, 15128, 15129, 15130, 15132, 15135, 15140, 15928, 16050, 16052, 16212, 16300, 16302, 16303**

Dollar spot
chemically resistant races, **4043, 8356, 11318**

Dollar spot
control, **547, 641, 718, 724, 762, 1028, 1115, 1248, 4685, 5417, 6745, 8348, 8362, 10853**

Dollar spot
cultural control, **806, 3070, 6132**

Dollar spot
cultural effects, **4201, 5498, 5523, 7855:** activated sewage sludge, **5467, 12757**; nitrogen, **975, 1690, 5395, 5406, 5407, 5523, 6167, 6168, 6200, 6205, 7855, 7857, 10193, 10495, 10568, 10572, 11560, 12695, 12716, 12717, 12719, 12757, 16020**; nitrogen carrier, **4114, 8019, 10193, 10196, 10970, 12701, 12748, 12757, 15928**; nutrition, **4170, 4201, 4361, 6848, 8348, 12757, 13996, 14000, 15014**; potassium, **2162, 6705, 6708, 7857, 8019, 8047, 8050, 12268**

Dollar spot
description, **5708, 6164, 10761, 14716**

Dollar spot
England, **7192, 8337, 8342, 12931**

Dollar spot
environmental effects, **8362, 9892, 13996:** temperature, **5402, 6162, 6173, 6739, 11939**

Dollar spot
isolates, **4043, 6163, 8356, 10331, 11318**

Dollar spot
phytotoxin: roots effects, **5403, 5421, 5422**

Dollar spot
soil moisture effects, **4171, 4182, 4201**

Dollar spot
species susceptibility, **352, 729, 5417**

Dollar spot
symptoms, **5417, 6132, 6161, 6173, 7154, 7193, 8348, 8362, 9463, 9892, 10800, 10853, 10891, 11071, 11848, 11876, 12078, 12556, 13996, 14886, 15646, 15679**

Dolomitic limestone, **3001, 9828, 10690**

Domed stadium, **1723, 1776, 2225, 10060**

Dormancy, **9052, 13640, 14190**

Dormancy, seed (see Seed, dormancy)

Dormancy, summer (see Summer dormancy)

Dormancy, winter (see Winter dormancy)

Dormant seeding (see Seeding, dormant)

Dowfume® (see Methyl bromide)

Downy brome
chemical control, **3671a**

Downy mildew, **4334, 8615**

Drainage, **99, 541, 1246, 2857, 3099, 4826, 5239, 5701, 6649, 6918, 7111, 7850, 8074, 8530, 9044, 10650, 11034, 11432, 12109, 12126, 12520, 12831, 14929**

Drainage
effects, **2828, 3299, 4319, 10334, 10391, 10651, 11037**

Drainage
effects on: winter injury, **563, 10802**

Drainage
factors affecting, **6860, 7986, 8075, 9491, 12125, 13621, 14927, 15455**

Drainage
fairway, **1328, 8236, 8238, 15959**

Drainage
golf course, **407, 1219, 4165, 4821, 10396, 10644, 10645, 10646, 10647, 10916, 11033, 11035, 14638, 16143**

Drainage
greens, **818, 2306, 5243, 5251, 5425, 5470, 5789, 6561, 7677, 7889, 9244, 9997, 10009, 11090, 11500, 14178, 15723, 15731, 15732, 16048**

Drainage
installation, **1601, 2426, 5239, 5470, 7677, 10916, 14550**

Drainage
methods, **4706, 8115, 8529, 10391, 10395, 12419, 12420, 12454, 14550, 14640**

Drainage
mole drain, **4728, 8115**

Drainage
principles, **4706, 9491, 12420, 13621, 14550**

Drainage
problems, **3301, 5967, 6821, 12454**

Drainage
slit trench (see Slit trench)

Drainage
sports field, **378, 1561, 1601, 11292, 12855, 14745**

Drainage
subsoiling, **2191**

Drainage
subsurface, **642, 1047, 1710, 2336, 2426, 4165, 4706, 6663, 6850, 7677, 8238, 10645, 11468, 11872, 12127, 12419, 12420, 12999, 14178, 14848, 15730, 15731:** design, **1710, 3852, 5239, 6615, 8985, 10911, 10916;** golf course, **1660, 10832, 13034, 13885;** green, **4363, 7237, 11500, 15733;** perforated pipe, **5262;** tile drain, **579, 655, 677, 901, 1219, 1246, 2426, 2483, 3827, 5290, 5470, 6615, 7942, 8074, 8529, 8609, 9997, 10225, 10650**

Drainage
surface, **2, 224, 323, 562, 563, 693, 2336, 4165, 5141, 6850, 10645, 10647, 11468, 12127, 12419, 12420, 12999, 13034, 15730, 15731:** green, **9115, 11500**

Drainage channel
erosion control, **2056**

Drain tile, **1710, 3827, 4706, 6663**

Drain tile
design, **2336, 6663, 10646, 15730, 15731**

Drain tile
fairway, **8238, 12359**

Drain tile
installation, **6663, 7677, 8075, 10646, 10919, 11872, 12359**

Drain tile
types, **5262, 8985, 10647, 12420**

Dricanum scoparium, **7026**

Dried blood, **1556, 4768, 5634, 5638**
evaluation, **2172, 5636, 5637, 15787**

Drought, **1142, 8283, 10065, 10069** (see also Water stress)

Drought
effects, **3771, 4960, 5415:** soil mix, **13894, 13896**

Drought hardiness, **3720**
factors affecting, **3720, 16406**

Drought, physiological (see Physiological drought)

Drought recovery
Kentucky bluegrass: cultivar evaluation, **2592, 2706, 2707, 6304**

Drought recovery
red fescue: cultivar evaluation, **2592, 2598, 2706, 2707**

Drought stress
evaluation methods, **3927, 3936**

Drought tolerance, **12447, 15597**

Drought tolerance
bermudagrass: cultivar evaluation, **9016**

Drought tolerance
cultural effects, **4768, 9840, 10299, 11605, 14074, 16408, 16409:** cutting height, **61, 6306, 12162, 13754;** nitrogen, **6306, 6307, 8699, 14074;** soil reaction, **1304, 4768, 5468, 5634, 5636**

Drought tolerance
effects of: rooting, **3563, 3577, 4104**

Drought tolerance
Kentucky bluegrass: cultivar evaluation, **6449**

Drought tolerance
red fescue: cultivar evaluation, **2592, 2598, 2706**

Drought tolerance
seedling, **3194, 16181, 16182:** species evaluation, **16178, 16246**

Drought tolerance
species evaluation, **912, 1149, 2339, 3720, 8986, 9869, 10065, 11058, 11064, 13519, 14997, 15621, 16245, 16361, 16368, 16369, 16406, 16408, 16409**

Dryland turf
grasses used, **9028**

Dry matter (see Shoot growth)

Dry spots
control, **7663, 7664**

Dry spots, localized (see Localized dry spots)

DSMA, **1196, 1620, 1733, 2027, 4968, 5102, 11631, 14518, 15978**

DSMA
broadleaf weed control, **12573, 12665**

DSMA
crabgrass control, **1493, 1551, 2692, 4396, 4421, 4429, 6358, 6374, 6904, 9529, 9531, 9533, 9548, 11047, 12574, 12930, 14837, 14839:** evaluation, **3653, 8155, 8156, 8414, 8431, 9053, 9733, 13803**

DSMA
dallisgrass control, **3003, 4207, 7933, 9531, 9533, 9537, 10973**

DSMA
mode of action, **5103**

DSMA
perennial grass control, **8182, 9673, 16334**

DSMA
selectivity, **3653a, 4396, 13803**

DSMA
weed control, **4264, 4404, 6361, 7933, 8169, 8172, 8175, 8836, 8908, 11599, 12115**

Dunes, sand (see Sand dune stabilization)

Durar hard fescue, **1656, 2650, 9340**

Duraturf red fescue, **1489, 4709, 7309**

Dursban®, **14647**

Dursban®
billbug control, **10983**

Dursban®
chinch bug control, **7268, 10643, 14388, 14647**

Dursban®
rhodesgrass scale control, **14398**

Dursban®
selectivity: bentgrass, **3797**

Dursban®
turfgrass weevil control, **3628a, 3631a, 3634a**

Dust control
turfgrass function, **16423**

Dwarf bunt
chemical control, **7348**

Dyes (see Colorants)

Dyfonate®
rhodesgrass scale control, **14398**

Dyfonate®
southern chinch bug control, **14399**

Dyfonte®
billbug control, **10983**

Dylox® (see Trichlorofon)

Dyrene®
dollar spot control, **3103, 8185, 15128**

Dyrene®
dollar spot resistance, **11318**

Dyrene®
melting-out control, **7619**

Dyrene®
red thread control, **12357**

Earthworm, **17, 1146, 1483, 1793, 2055, 5647, 5648, 7030, 7258, 8918, 9368, 10925, 12145, 12519, 14463, 14889**

Earthworm
beneficial effects, **10926, 13922, 16147**

Earthworm
castings, **8468, 9771**

Earthworm
chemical control, **1612, 2260, 2344, 2435, 4750, 4769, 5609, 5617, 5711, 7572, 7649, 8066, 8109, 8919, 9369, 9388, 9557, 10359, 10691, 10724, 12067, 12169, 12182, 12303, 13482, 13483, 13484, 13485, 13487, 13502, 14008, 15807:** chlordane, **9486, 9561, 9562, 14640;** evaluation, **2172, 4732, 4762, 5631, 8920, 9395, 9467, 9561, 11653, 11654, 12145, 13480;** lead arsenate, **325, 366, 4764, 6848, 9373, 9561, 11666, 12169, 14128**

Earthworm
control, **180, 397, 483, 581, 653, 860, 1483, 1602, 1845, 2034, 2822, 7190, 8469, 10340, 11666:** greens, **314, 430**

Earthworm
cultural effects, **5902, 8469, 14297:** fertilization, **5636, 8469, 11340;** forking, **5634, 5636;** nitrogen carrier, **2172, 5634, 5636, 8466, 8469**

Earthworm
description, **8466, 12145, 13484, 13485, 13487**

Earthworm
effects on: thatch, **2055, 12432, 12434**

Earthworm
factors affecting, **5649, 5902:** soil reaction, **2172, 5634, 5636, 8467, 8468, 8469**

Earthworm
quantity, **8466, 10925, 10926**

Earthworm, tropical
chemical control, **13475, 13481**

Earwigs
chemical control, **3291**

Echinochloa crusgalli (see Barnyardgrass)

Ecology
book, **3860**

Economics
chemical disease control, **15887**

Economics
drainage system: subsurface, **2426**

Economics
establishment, **11196, 12312**

Economics
golf course: construction, **5928, 15058;** management, **12299**

Economics
irrigation system, **1663, 1742, 16194**

Economics
sod production, **2120**

Economics
turfgrass culture, **11196**

Economic poisons
handbook, **15613**

EDB (see Ethylene dibromide)

Edging, **1951**

Edging
equipment, **4970**

Edging
herbicide oils, 14628

Education, turf, **142, 787, 1673, 2641, 5820, 6871, 9344, 11732, 16093**

Education, turf
Arizona, **6073**

Education, turf
California, **9957, 14344**

Education, turf
Cooperative Extention Service, **2633, 2717, 6844, 6871, 7186, 7229, 7243, 10966, 11810, 12239, 13627, 14344:** demonstration plots, **7243, 13692**

Education, turf
Czechoslovakia, **3455**

Education, turf
England, **1136, 1144, 5629, 6533**

Education, turf
Florida, **11721**

Education, turf
Germany, **3021**

Education, turf
Massachusetts, **1291, 2956**

Education, turf
New Zealand Institute for Turf Culture, **12830, 15249**

Education, turf
Operation Green Carpet: California, **15940**

Education, turf
Pennsylvania, **4126**

Education, turf
Purdue, **4371, 6148, 6578**

Education, turf
research personnel, **6844, 6858**

Education, turf
Technical training program: Michigan, **2617, 2633, 8942**

Education, turf
training, **1814, 6845, 9505, 12694**

Education, turf
university, **1822, 1825, 1828, 1829, 11991, 12088**

Ehrharta erecta, **12319**

Elastomeric polymer mulch, **2420, 2579, 2593, 5910, 12596, 13797**

Elateridae family (see Wireworm)

Electrical cable
underground placement, **14567**

Electrical resistance moisture sensors, **10202, 13622**

Elemental sulfur, **1803, 12572**

Eleusine indica (see Goosegrass)

Embryo, seed, **7189, 12491**

Embryo, seed
development, **11337, 11339, 11359**

Emerald creeping bentgrass, **1171, 1789**

Emerald crownvetch, **6032, 7560, 7565, 9988, 10387**

Emerald zoysiagrass, **3123, 6049, 6050, 6142, 7309, 8563**

Emerald zoysiagrass
adaptation, **4409**

Emerald zoysiagrass
description, **4401, 11232**

Emerald zoysiagrass
fertilization, **8016, 8038**

Employee
Department of Labor standards, **10457**

Employee
motivation, **4040, 6076, 9475, 10183, 11720**

Employee
relations: golf course superintendent, **8912, 8961, 10322**

Employee
training, **11729**

Endothall, **5479, 5615, 8435, 14860, 14883**

Endothall
absorption, **14885**

Endothall
annual bluegrass control, **67, 2633, 2672, 2682, 4018, 5381, 5464, 5467, 5468, 5527, 5529, 5531, 14866, 14867, 14878, 14882, 14883, 15281, 15283, 15285, 16123**:
evaluation, **5530, 10020, 14860**

Endothall
clover control, **2870, 3982, 4150, 11747, 11752**

Endothall
creeping speedwell control, **1221, 1235, 1493, 2633, 3999, 8189, 11046, 11047, 14574**

Endothall
kikuyugrass control, **16334**

Endothall
mode of action, **14860, 14884**

Endothall
physiological effects, **14860, 14885**

Endothall
red sorrel control, **3666a**

Endothall
selectivity, **11046, 14860, 14867, 14885**

Endothall
white clover control, **933, 7655, 11748, 13770**

Endrin
grub control, **12178, 12181**

Engine
maintenance, **1678, 5388, 6399, 12784, 13673, 14648, 14654, 15652:** manual, **1946**

Engine
operation, **6399**

Engine
selection, **1681, 5640**

Engine
winterizing, **13674**

English daisy, **4733, 7027**

English daisy
chemical control, **36, 5063, 6650, 6667**

English ryegrass (see Perennial ryegrass)

Ensign meadow fescue, **7309**

Entyloma crastophilum (see Blister smut)

Environment, **1883**

Environment
disease development affects, **189, 11578**

Environment
modification, **1943, 4530**

Environment
plant response, **5813, 11425, 16392**

Environmental quality, **3176, 4259, 4260, 8246, 9318, 10484, 16047**

Environmental quality
effects of: pesticides, **2109, 4044, 4045, 8744, 9700, 11317, 15842;** turfgrasses, **2036, 2137, 2441, 11737, 12782, 13339, 13545, 14619, 15851, 16423;**
turfgrass culture, **2684, 3670, 12207, 13372**

Environmental quality
lawn, **12213, 13365**

Environmental quality
ornamental plant effects, **9231, 12728, 12781**

Epiblast, seed, **3377, 6007, 11359**

Epidermis, **3002, 4595, 12101**

Epsom salts (see Magnesium sulfate)

EPTC
purple nutsedge control, **7545, 9670**

EPTC
weed control, **1967, 7536, 8412, 14518**

Equipment, **1106, 1983, 2456, 2457, 2459, 2461, 2462, 2938, 3749, 5932, 6002, 8579, 8855, 10203, 11749, 11912, 12244, 14108, 14775, 15262, 15580**

Equipment
Austin leveller, **1537, 15188**

Equipment
book, **7031**

Equipment
budgeting, **15588**

Equipment
calibration, **7758, 7759, 9050, 9279**

Equipment
cemetery, **4022, 10739**

Equipment
costs, **5946, 8954, 9642, 9643**

Equipment
cultivation, **1405, 6521, 6944, 9199, 9209, 12883, 14256, 14660, 15895, 15896, 16421**

Equipment
debris pick-up, **1614, 8594, 11797, 16487**

Equipment
edgers, **4022, 4970**

Equipment
efficiency, **13038, 14656, 14659**

Equipment
establishment, **5932, 8215, 11830, 12580**:
vegetative planters, **8520, 8539, 12996, 16456**

Equipment
fertilizer spreaders, **1979, 3682, 16486**

Equipment
future products, **10261, 12347, 14658, 15553**

Equipment
golf course, **43, 221, 1409, 1743, 3643a, 3750, 3954, 9577, 10149, 12389, 14660, 15089, 15288;** inventory, **7693, 10512, 12464, 12478;**
New Zealand, **15274, 15298, 15310, 15312**

Equipment
green, **257, 15318**

Equipment
history, **324, 6796, 14256, 14660**

Equipment
lawn culture, **4937, 7047, 13229, 16089**

Equipment
maintenance, **321, 541, 1711, 3313, 3676a, 3731, 5221, 5385, 5386, 5387, 5945, 8819, 9156, 9849, 10776, 12812, 13644, 13675, 14653, 14654, 14655, 14656, 14660, 15250, 16497**:
preventive, **2413, 8214, 10022, 14650;**
small engine, **3703a, 5388, 15652**

Equipment
mowers, **2456, 2457, 2459, 2461, 2462, 3749, 4022, 5946, 6838, 7052, 8595, 9198, 11586, 12358, 14369, 15517, 15568, 15803**:
green, **3863, 14775, 15320, 15651;**
maintenance, **3238, 3239, 6471**

Equipment
needs, **9642, 10308**

Equipment
operation, **4108, 9050, 11503, 14369, 15554, 15567**

Equipment
park, **3854, 8954, 13588**

Equipment
records, **5945, 13059**

Equipment
rental, **3732, 10256, 12438**

Equipment
replacement, **5168**

Equipment
roadside, **1018, 8854, 15695, 16137**

Equipment
selection, **1267, 5945, 9156, 9577, 10022, 15568, 15580, 15581**

Equipment
sod, **2316, 11725, 15292**

Equipment
sports field, **2325, 13790**

Equipment
sprayer, **1351, 2456, 2457, 2459, 2461, 2462, 2482, 3660, 4046, 5221, 7758, 7759, 11291, 11465, 15051, 15235**: types, **7369, 11586, 12129, 14615, 15421, 16232**

Equipment
tire selection, **16477**

Equipment
vertical mower, **16487**

Equipment
wear simulator, **13663, 14653**

Eremochloa ophiuroides (see Centipedegrass)

Ergot
chemical control, **7363**

Ergot
seed setting, **3536**

Erika chewings fescue, **9219**

Eriophyid mite (see Bermudagrass mite)

Erosion, **3446, 6946, 8180**

Erosion
soil, **18, 5021**

Erosion control, **3164, 4095, 7630, 9821, 12007, 15605**

Erosion control
methods, **2059, 3446, 3465, 3467, 7782, 8089, 8179, 9821, 12007, 14255**

Erosion control
mulch (see also Mulch), **79, 1605, 2432, 3265, 3467, 10165, 10494, 13403, 14481, 16040**

Erosion control
mulch evaluation, **1479, 1645, 2579, 2593, 4838, 5133, 5312, 6515, 7782, 8180, 12490, 13401, 13403, 13974, 14478, 14480**

Erosion control
roadside, **2056, 2058, 2971, 4026, 4095, 4105, 4829, 6033, 6037, 6038, 7081, 7684, 7782, 7943, 9950, 10347, 12593, 13401**

Erosion control
vegetative, **228, 2818, 3370, 8180, 9950, 14950, 16423**

Erysiphe graminis (see Powdery mildew)

Essential elements, **7671, 10478, 11386, 11787, 14921, 15615, 16013**

Essential elements
carriers, **8641, 11387**

Essential elements
deficiency symptoms (see Nutrient deficiency, symptoms)

Essential elements
function, **3933, 4922, 8641, 8653, 9046, 14691**

Establishment, **1228, 1311, 2445, 3164, 3535, 3773, 4118, 4875, 5507, 5511, 5796, 6484, 6623, 6671, 6903, 6968, 7498, 7769, 8286, 8430, 9262, 10741, 11196, 11579, 12711, 12873, 14931, 16002**

Establishment
airfield, **741, 2761, 3146, 3586a, 12525**

Establishment
bermudagrass, **2310, 2380, 5098, 6541, 10442, 16115**

Establishment
book, **5326, 7031, 10460**

Establishment
bowling green, **568, 3106, 7005, 8485**

Establishment
bulletin, **839, 3106**

Establishment
cemetery, **10236, 13583, 15947**

Establishment
competition, **2647, 3831, 7011, 8783**

Establishment
cool season species, **2416, 7399, 13289**

Establishment
on copper mine tailings, **9740**

Establishment
costs, **1120, 1375**

Establishment
creeping bentgrass: cultivar evaluation, **2560**

Establishment
cricket wicket, **5257**

Establishment
crownvetch, **4832, 5359, 7564, 9988, 12069, 12597**

Establishment
cultural effects, **341, 2445, 12338, 13459**: fertilization, **794, 2980, 5958, 6905, 7126, 7162, 7460, 9055, 10618, 10741, 11197, 12904, 13185, 13247, 14931**; fertilization evaluation, **8836, 8949, 10580, 15376, 15705**; irrigation, **2018, 2084, 13210**; mowing, **2381, 3457, 6435, 8791, 13210, 13754**; nitrogen fertilization, **2381, 6111, 6435, 7853, 8987**; phosphorus, **441, 13459, 14066**

Establishment
effects of: hexaoctadecanol, **181, 2282**

Establishment
environmental effects, **3770, 6111, 6435, 6436**

Establishment
factors affecting, **2606, 3175, 4593, 6239, 6265, 9488**

Establishment
fairway, **389, 8542, 12392, 14430**

Establishment
on fly ash, **3203**

Establishment
golf course, **288, 472, 565, 586, 1625, 4817, 4823, 5926, 11809, 12551, 12696**

Establishment
green, **1584, 2500, 3056, 3462, 4571, 4914, 7159, 7219, 10786, 14728, 15260**: seeding, **298, 7067, 7070**; stolonizing, **296, 300, 2800, 3052, 3054**

Establishment
Kentucky bluegrass: cultivar evaluation, **2560, 2630**

Establishment
large turfgrass areas, **741, 3044, 8029, 8540**

Establishment
lawn, **282, 392, 474, 532, 939, 2213, 2214, 2220, 2226, 2227, 2317, 3016, 3095, 3350, 3619, 3661, 3666, 3925, 4093, 4297, 4665, 4736, 4758, 4864, 6011, 6977, 7695, 7948, 7976, 8090, 8296, 8517, 8835, 10662, 11157, 11208, 12638, 13128, 13137, 13142, 13185, 13247, 13829, 14073, 15826**; book, **1116, 2443, 2444, 5044, 13541, 13647, 15979:** bulletin, **284, 287, 1001, 1063, 3105, 3110, 9147, 13158, 15779;** state bulletin, **1301, 2153, 2390, 2512, 2513, 2712, 2759, 3677, 3846, 4086, 4087, 4088, 4089, 4090, 4091, 4228, 4229, 4274, 4306, 4558, 4559, 4560, 4841, 4982, 4994, 4995, 5080, 5369, 5370, 5389, 5516, 5517, 5520, 5522, 5541, 5553, 5586, 6424, 7036, 8306, 8916, 9574, 10871, 10884, 10885, 10937, 10938, 11679, 12191, 12742, 13438, 13857, 13928, 14537, 14538, 14539, 14541, 14874, 14938, 14939, 14941, 14943, 15708, 15923, 15929, 15930, 16107, 16470, 16471, 16472;** warm regions, **1102, 13280, 14430**

Establishment
manilagrass, **1315, 3812**

Establishment
method, **1018, 3009, 3784, 5822, 6697, 8393, 8534, 9228, 10786, 12312, 13212, 13351**

Establishment
mulch effects (see also Mulch, evaluation), **2975, 6111, 6456, 6539, 7384, 8987, 10494, 12593**

Establishment
park, **2628, 6604, 10236, 13814**

Establishment
pest control, **11870**

Establishment
polyethylene cover, **2076, 3276**

Establishment
rate: species variability, **1700, 4715, 4900, 6111, 6238**

Establishment
roadside, **246, 247, 1068, 1859, 1863, 1877, 2964, 2966, 3208, 5159, 6038, 6414, 6512, 8117, 8302, 8325, 8544, 8911, 9228, 9813, 10347, 11350, 12795, 15695, 16315:** evaluation, **2057, 2734, 14644;** fertilization, **2671, 2970, 2985, 3729, 4026, 4301, 5275, 6039, 6231, 7012;** hydraulic seeding, **3684, 3686, 3687;** liming, **2985, 4301;** method, **1018, 1738, 2967, 2980, 4105, 8179, 11830, 15325, 16243;** method evaluation, **1018, 8179, 11830;** mulch (see also Mulch, evaluation), **2432, 5275, 8393;** mulch evaluation, **12596, 13797, 15365;** seeding rate evaluation, **9129, 11830;** slopes, **1703, 3692, 5132, 13452;** species used, **76, 245, 246, 247, 3730, 4041, 6009**

Establishment
St. Augustinegrass, **3529, 4328**

Establishment
on sand, **4079, 8429, 12480**

Establishment
seedbed preparation, **110, 1479, 2380, 5485, 5511, 5958, 6896, 7457, 8503, 9785, 9801, 12580, 12711, 12879, 13351, 13567, 15204, 15218, 15705, 16492, 16496**

Establishment
seeding (see also Seeding), **423, 2380, 5485, 5702, 6896, 7270, 7499, 7739, 8215, 8324, 10662, 11538, 13908, 14553, 14931, 16128;** depth, **2270, 8029, 10082, 11094, 15005;** methods, **1174, 12513, 13187;** rate, **3646, 3666, 4093, 4973, 8783, 11002, 12326, 12647, 15204;** rate evaluation, **3207, 8029, 9334, 12311;** time, **329, 405, 424, 463, 533, 541, 626, 701, 1160, 2431, 3010, 3207, 3646, 3666, 4864, 4973, 5076, 5511, 8566, 8837, 12311, 13174, 13543, 14185, 15705, 16235, 16458**

Establishment
seed mat (see Seed mat)

Establishment
seed mixture, **3207, 3694, 3976, 4761, 7498, 8783**

Establishment
seed versus vegetative, **3468, 6420, 9159, 10579, 15946**

Establishment
on slopes, **228, 3076, 8117**

Establishment
sports field, **1038, 1042, 3460, 4757, 4927, 6018, 6144, 6149, 6632, 10505, 12517, 13165, 14560**: Europe, **1935, 8455, 10998, 13582;** state bulletin, **7420, 7423, 12191**

Establishment
stabilized soil, **3585a, 3586a, 7126**

Establishment
Sweden, **2915, 9214, 9215**

Establishment
vegetative, **422, 1410, 2193, 6435, 6436, 6541, 7921, 8791, 9601, 11741, 11867, 12148, 12879, 15389, 16128**: Kentucky bluegrass, **14078, 15384, 15394, 15398, 15399, 15400;** method, **6896, 8539, 13413, 15394;** plugging (see also Plugging), **5019, 6248, 6896, 7921, 10126, 10131, 10132, 11539, 11867, 12996, 12998, 13567;** sodding (see also Sod transplanting), **2159, 3059, 4163, 5703, 6028, 6248, 6887, 6896, 7921, 10663, 12004, 12439, 12639, 13567,**

14290; sprigging (see also Sprigging), **1191, 1623, 3815, 6248, 6896, 7921, 10131, 11798, 12878, 13567**; stolonizing (see also Stolonizing), **2798, 7043, 8126, 9832, 11010, 11676, 11764, 11985, 12135, 12481, 12878, 14553**

Establishment
  warm season species, **1967, 2609, 8166**

Establishment
  weed control, **34, 1493, 3529, 4911, 8836, 8837, 10579, 12846, 13210, 15638**: 2,4–D, **1290, 3540**; post-emergence, **425, 8833**; pre-emergence, **2310, 3005, 4153, 5098**; seedling selectivity, **64, 65, 68, 1493, 5563, 5564**

Establishment
  zoysiagrass, **1102, 5573, 6141, 6563, 7400, 9602, 14363**

Ethephon (see Ethrel®)

Ethion
  chinch bug control, **4971, 8882**

Ethion
  hairy chinch bug control, **8753, 14391**

Ethion
  nematode control, **14393**

Ethion
  sod webworm control, **1779, 11944, 12428, 14389**

Ethion
  southern chinch bug control, **7268, 10982**

5-ethoxy-3-trichloromethyl-1,2, 4-thiadiazole (see Koban®)

Ethrel®, **7687, 9419, 15800**

Ethylene dibromide, **1232, 12978**

Ethylene level
  sod heating effects, **8940**

(*O*-ethyl *S,S*-dipropyl phosphorodithioate (see Mocap®)

Euphorbia supina (see Spurge, prostrate)

Euphorbia virgata (see Leafy spurge)

Eurhynchium proelongum, **2961, 7026**

European beachgrass, **3370, 3371, 3372, 14322**

European chafer, **1808, 6387, 6388, 13498, 14535**

European chafer
  chemical control, **6387, 13872, 14534, 14535**

European leaf mite, **1105**

European skipper, **2273**

Evaluation, turfgrass
  methods, **2114, 4498, 6441, 6833**: infared photography, **16173**; weed control research, **9547**

Evansville creeping bentgrass, **1489, 1967, 2566, 4461**
  evaluation, **10616, 10622, 10760, 11021**

Evaporation, **3220, 3221, 6075, 6492**
  environmental factors affecting, **1594, 4929**

Evapotranspiration, **3473, 12009, 12275**

Evapotranspiration
  bermudagrass, **5050, 7444, 14976**

Evapotranspiration
  cultural effects, **9107, 9905**

Evapotranspiration
  factors affecting, **75, 3413, 5867, 9908, 10199, 12276**

Evapotranspiration
  measurement, **12116, 12274, 12588**

Evapotranspiration
  rate, **7276, 9621, 10078, 10522, 12275, 12589, 14768, 15869**

Evapotranspiration
  rate evaluation, **7986, 12587, 14976**

Evapotranspiration
  seasonal variation, **10522, 16080**

Evapotranspiration
  soil effects, **146, 10977, 10979**

Evapotranspiration
  soil moisture effects, **2825, 5056, 5349**

Evapotranspiration rate
  water table depth effects, **12422, 14396**

Everglades bermudagrass, **1489, 2372, 4075, 7309, 9958, 10768, 12820, 14401, 16261**

Everglades bermudagrass
  adaptation, **3658a, 7977**

Everglades bermudagrass
  culture, **3344, 7977, 15840**

Everglades bermudagrass
  description, **3658a, 16331**

Everglades bermudagrass
  evaluation, **1182, 8154, 14365, 14906, 16320**

Evergreen timothy, **8343, 9213**
  evaluation, **1639, 7191, 8341, 9212**

Evolution of turfgrasses, **14241**

Excelsior blanket
  winter protection, **2623, 2675, 15559**

Excelsior mulch, **2667, 2874, 6010, 14695**

Excelsior mulch
  erosion control, **6716**: evaluation, **2734**

Excelsior mulch
  evaluation, **5129, 6515, 14432**

Exchangeable-sodium percentage, **11996**

Exeter colonial bentgrass, **1547, 1639, 2611, 6294, 12007, 13834, 15156**
  evaluation, **6287, 10616, 10622, 10760, 11021**

Expanded shale
  soil amendment, **13418, 13425**

Extension Service (see Education, turf)

Extension, turfgrass (see also Education, turf), **13627, 14344, 15998**

Exudation, **7838**

Exudation
content, **10315, 10318**

Exudation
pathogen invasion, **5404, 7622, 10318, 13723**

Exudation
removal, **10315**

Fairway, **830, 6815, 11126**

Fairway
annual bluegrass control, **6102, 7955, 9082, 10181, 10558, 10915, 12444, 12982, 14409, 14512:** calcium arsenate, **5974, 9173, 9734, 14969**

Fairway
construction, **5216, 15995**

Fairway
cool season turfgrasses used, **306, 312, 352, 3672, 4349, 5624, 5775, 9317, 11507, 14185, 14926, 15041, 16358:** bentgrasses, **860, 5163, 7910, 7918, 9564, 10559, 11031, 11568;** evaluation, **10813, 10818, 10822, 10856, 14213, 16250;** Kentucky bluegrass, **2388, 3673, 4459, 4470, 4471, 4482, 6327, 7144, 7910, 12522**

Fairway
crabgrass control, **2892, 3170, 3223**

Fairway
culture, **218, 457, 481, 577, 800, 914, 1328, 1359, 1374, 1465, 1791, 2182, 2280, 3170, 3861, 3968, 4237, 4349, 4470, 4482, 5195, 5900, 6829, 6891, 6943, 6960, 7061, 7144, 7391, 7539, 7899, 7910, 8597, 9573, 9853, 10009, 10181, 10286, 10435, 10558, 10918, 10921, 11029, 11125, 11126, 11403, 11409, 11410, 11456, 11462, 11481, 11491, 11492, 11528, 11568, 11569, 11634, 12999, 13239, 13388, 13446, 13447, 14045, 14248, 14785, 15726, 15728, 15958, 15960, 15995, 16054, 16074, 16133:** annual bluegrass, **1507, 7891, 9572, 16147;** costs, **2789, 3065, 3067, 6889, 7900;** cultivation, **831, 5278, 6893, 14474, 16238;** cutting height, **654, 924, 5446, 7510, 9305, 9563, 9857, 11126, 11448, 11516, 16074, 16162;** England, **1244, 5624, 6527;** fertilization, **327, 344, 541, 1053, 1671, 3067, 5248, 5394, 5585, 5726, 5880, 6595, 9335, 9391, 9426, 9596, 10548, 10856, 10863, 10918, 11183, 11383, 11390, 11398, 11400, 11403, 11405, 11410, 11414, 11420, 11430, 11462, 11489, 11492, 11498, 13852, 15508, 15591, 15724, 15726, 15729, 15958, 15959, 15983, 16238;** irrigation, **2281, 3306, 3438, 4100, 4356, 4812, 5283, 7875, 7900, 8597, 9563, 9565, 9596, 10718, 10742, 10910, 11407, 11409, 11975, 12995, 13448, 14278, 14557, 14788, 14994, 15457, 15959, 16074, 16225;** liming, **816, 15508, 16238;** mowing, **3067, 3443, 4356, 10918, 12371, 13448, 15959, 16238;** nitrogen fertilization, **4650, 6574, 6948;** overseeding, **560, 15959;** thatch control, **2869, 13448;** warm regions, **2485, 2486, 14430;** winter overseeding, **3213**

Fairway
design, **4455, 13686**

Fairway
disease control, **5740, 13535, 15959, 15961**

Fairway
diseases, **1207, 5025**

Fairway
drainage, **901, 1328, 8236, 10919, 11493, 15959**

Fairway
establishment, **389, 5241, 8542, 11380, 12392, 14430, 15728:** seeding, **4809, 11538;** stolonizing, **7539, 11676**

Fairway
grasses used, **799, 805, 1374, 1700, 4629, 4768, 5162, 5473, 5585, 6910, 6925, 6942, 6982, 7061, 7689, 7891, 7899, 8542, 8844, 9251, 9566, 10011, 10820, 11651, 12141, 12153, 12332, 14341:** evaluation, **6345, 9615, 16073**

Fairway
insect control, **2822, 5740, 10918, 15959**

Fairway
renovation, **350, 625, 805, 1013, 1282, 1285, 1374, 1465, 2758, 3119, 3875, 4471, 4627, 4827, 5734, 6394, 6793, 6880, 6889, 6891, 6952, 7209, 7233, 7278, 8242, 8629, 8747, 9081, 9082, 9083, 9409, 9583, 9585, 9732, 10282, 10435, 10469, 10912, 10913, 11252, 11253, 11259, 11467, 11493, 11513, 11632, 11837, 12284, 12285, 12335, 12336, 12444, 12451, 12465, 12996, 13757, 14181, 14408, 14409, 14512, 15662, 15726, 15727, 15893, 16161, 16188, 16308:** annual bluegrass control, **5218, 9172, 14513, 15090, 16145**

Fairway
seed mixtures used, **10361, 12485, 14940**

Fairway
warm season turfgrasses used, **312, 566, 10754, 10817:** bermudagrass, **13, 3585, 3607, 3608, 9193, 9278, 9304, 9568, 11551, 11554, 13446, 13448, 13451;** buffalograss, **326, 13031;** zoysiagrass, **6562, 6563, 7791, 12475, 12997, 12998, 13442**

Fairway
weed control, **923, 1384, 2608, 2865, 3453, 3875, 4813, 5262, 8629, 10169, 10694, 11459, 11491, 11493, 11527, 11540,**

11631, 11848, 15959: chemical, **7369, 16159**

Fairway wheatgrass, **2092, 2093, 2770**

Fairy ring, **185, 663, 918, 1141, 1192, 1487, 1523, 3603a, 4185, 5399, 5417, 5955, 6114, 6199, 6734, 6739, 6759, 9415, 10761, 11542, 11560, 13566, 13584, 13735, 13739, 16293**

Fairy ring
causal organisms, **13584, 14007**

Fairy ring
chemical control, **6179, 6728, 6730, 6748, 12755:** evaluation, **1545, 1639, 2684, 6727, 6767, 14007**

Fairy ring
control, **137, 1172, 2266, 3671, 4093, 4292, 5417, 6728, 6742, 6745, 6759, 6768, 8354, 9071, 9164, 9411, 9414, 10670, 11938, 13997, 14007**

Fairy ring
description, **5708, 6508, 6768, 7197, 8354, 9071, 11938**

Fairy ring
England, **8337, 8339, 12931**

Fairy ring
factors affecting, **6508, 6727, 13584**

Fairy ring
nitrogen effects, **2699, 6508, 9414**

Fairy ring
symptoms, **5417, 6132, 7193, 8354, 9463, 9892, 10853, 13584, 13703, 14007, 15646, 15679**

Fall armyworm (see Armyworm, fall)

Fall fescue, **16366**

Fall panicum
chemical control, **14048**

Fat hen, **4742**

FB–137 bermudagrass, **1639, 9662**
shade adaptation, **1735, 1778, 9878, 9883**

FC13521 manilagrass, **7309**

Feltia subterranea (see Cutworm, granulate)

Fenac
crabgrass control, **6368, 6378**

Fenac
red sorrel control, **3666a**

Fenac
weed control, **8182**

Fensulfothion
nematode control, **8040, 12058, 12062, 14393**

Fensulfothion
southern chinch bug control, **14399**

Fenthion
sod webworm control, **11944**

Ferrous ammonium sulfate, **2941, 3001, 9958**

Ferrous sulfate, **2776, 2942, 4725, 4760, 4786, 5634, 5670, 11581**

Ferrous sulfate
effects, **1485, 5679, 8469**

Ferrous sulfate
evaluation, **5636, 13522**

Ferrous sulfate
fertilization, **993, 3386**

Ferrous sulfate
moss control, **2961, 6630**

Ferrous sulfate
weed control, **360, 401, 483, 4267, 4768, 7220, 9851, 9852, 11096:** dandelion, **9848, 11076;** pearlwort, **2482, 7504**

Fertility (see Fertilization)

Fertilization, **102, 448, 453, 528, 675, 1166, 1947, 2127, 2386, 2632, 2740, 2776, 2827, 2972, 3337, 3349, 3352, 3969, 3998, 4032, 4033, 4160, 5073, 5074, 5317, 5471, 5604, 5678, 5705, 5850, 5905, 6022, 6346, 6503, 6582, 6593, 6617, 6732, 6831, 6857, 6906, 6921, 6922, 6965, 6991, 7429, 7474, 7575, 7929, 7983, 7984, 8318, 8817, 9433, 9626, 9631, 9644, 9686, 9824, 10047, 10504, 11055, 11177, 11182, 11428, 11429, 11432, 11437, 11438, 11549, 11572, 12897, 13842, 14799, 14937, 14987, 15083, 15499, 16226, 16397**

Fertilization
bahiagrass, **6061, 15329**

Fertilization
balance, **15282, 15319**

Fertilization
bermudagrass, **132, 1053, 3570, 4787, 7925, 8886, 9274, 11575**

Fertilization
cemetery, **9069, 11430**

Fertilization
cool season turfgrasses, **2300, 3372, 4273, 8376, 10623**

Fertilization
disease development effects, **5374, 5395, 6647, 7202, 9291, 9749, 10031, 10108, 10811, 11524, 11564, 12699, 12717:** *Ophiobolus* patch, **6637, 6647, 6651, 6654, 6660, 6694, 6733;** red thread, **2162, 6733, 6746**

Fertilization
effects, **102, 3302, 4305, 5484, 5499, 7800, 7966, 8046, 8770, 9107, 9273, 9274, 11340, 14192**

Fertilization
effects of: ion exchange resins, **12772, 12773, 12774**

Fertilization
effects on: chemical composition, **2250, 5144, 9507, 14626;** nutrient availability, **6659, 7992;** nutrient level, **6651, 7929, 7978, 12498, 15327;** polystand composition, **3158, 6422, 11024, 12839;** root growth, **2007, 2760, 3204, 6637, 8705, 8909, 9162, 9724, 14998, 15918;** seedling growth, **7126, 10470, 11383;** shoot density, **4894, 6025, 12676;** shoot growth, **2974, 5577, 7966, 8705, 9107, 9438, 9722, 9723, 9724, 10201,**

11024, 14149, 15328, 15376, 15909, 15918, 16451; soil reaction, **7985, 7992, 12258**; turfgrass quality, **4894, 11024**; winter injury, **563, 9354, 15909**

Fertilization
establishment, **441, 1231, 2745, 2976, 2980, 4974, 5275, 6939, 7460, 14244, 15376**: evaluation, **8836, 8837, 8949**

Fertilization
factors affecting, **102, 11489, 11604, 11698, 12684, 12717**

Fertilization
fairway, **327, 344, 1053, 5585, 5880, 9335, 11400, 11405, 11408, 11420, 11430, 11489, 15729, 15959**

Fertilization
fall, **664, 701, 2610, 2625, 5726, 9606, 15909, 15913**: evaluation, **9438, 12219, 15913**; low temperature hardiness affects, **2008, 12498, 12499**

Fertilization
golf course, **562, 697, 717, 739, 800, 2920, 3066, 4129, 4920, 5173, 5806, 5877, 6552, 6774, 6915, 7290, 7594, 10506, 11164, 11167, 11415, 11548, 11884, 13656, 13979, 15954, 16278**

Fertilization
green, **25, 254, 270, 455, 555, 823, 1053, 2271, 5880, 6347, 7841, 8129, 9311, 9456, 9567, 10765, 11431, 11575, 11590, 13368, 14185, 14964**

Fertilization
Kentucky bluegrass, **3591a, 6509, 15850**

Fertilization
lawn, **336, 368, 371, 492, 669, 904, 1159, 2027, 2219, 2223, 2590, 3086, 3688a, 3778, 4430, 4985, 5179, 10611, 10881, 11170, 12037, 13074, 13183, 13347, 16095**: state bulletin, **1480, 9458, 14873**

Fertilization
liquid versus granular, **6646, 13756**

Fertilization
nitrogen, **2007, 3280, 4113, 4645, 4647, 5469, 6594, 9057**

Fertilization
nitrogen-potassium ratio: shoot growth effects, **7857, 11524**

Fertilization
park, **6662, 11430, 12625**

Fertilization
phosphorus, **2404, 6801**

Fertilization
potassium, **3340, 4038, 4265, 6997**

Fertilization
practices, **448, 1434, 2617, 2633, 2777, 4033, 6347, 6857, 7418, 7480, 7962, 9059, 9309, 9315, 10678, 11145, 11154, 11163, 11171, 11192, 11297, 11405, 11504, 11507, 11563, 11570, 11596, 11610, 11708, 11801, 11885, 12037, 12543, 12623, 12635, 12717, 13027, 13161, 13434, 13655, 14163, 14263, 14689, 14692, 14800, 14904, 14936, 15060, 15074, 15187, 15460, 15481, 15840, 16020, 16284, 16348, 16355, 16379**

Fertilization
principles, **3977, 8926, 11149, 11150, 11183, 11437, 11532, 14936, 15061, 15983**

Fertilization
program, **2583, 5634, 5636, 6666, 7220**

Fertilization
program selection, **2776, 3995, 5484, 9784, 12612, 12615, 12619, 12628**

Fertilization
rates, **2976, 3349, 5577, 6025, 6027, 7290, 10618, 10843, 11192, 13655, 13656, 15460, 15824, 15840, 16355**

Fertilization
roadside, **1018, 1055, 2980, 4266, 4301, 4431, 4446, 6033, 7012, 8183, 12613, 13358, 15158**

Fertilization
seed production, **4897, 5656, 11660, 12279**

Fertilization
sod production, **2116, 2649, 14630**

Fertilization
soil fertility, **3352, 3391, 10719, 15083**

Fertilization
sports field, **6662, 8754, 10215**

Fertilization
timing, **399, 688, 2006, 2073, 2973, 4790, 5451, 5499, 6182, 9438, 9608, 11192, 13655, 13656, 15110, 15729, 15824, 16020, 16071**: evaluation, **6509, 7932, 14406, 15709**

Fertilization
tissue nutrient content, **7841, 14486**

Fertilization
warm season turfgrasses, **132, 9959, 10519, 11694, 12810, 14798**

Fertilization
weed control effects, **1434, 3785, 15482, 15727**

Fertilization
weed invasion, **1304, 6305, 10843, 11192, 11768, 12622, 12676, 12705, 12717, 12726, 12751, 12840, 13333, 13355, 14128, 14984, 15728**

Fertilization
winter, **2610, 2625, 13098, 15909, 16397**

Fertilizer, **496, 721, 1424, 1558, 1644, 2723, 3345, 3984, 4429, 4660, 5804, 5847, 5856, 6255, 6641, 6839, 6955, 6970, 7228, 7569, 7961, 8030, 8194, 8247, 8641, 8817, 9148, 9560, 9644, 9738, 9804, 10411, 10561, 11360, 11586, 11802, 12096, 12261, 12684, 13175, 13964, 14050, 14986, 15872**

Fertilizer
analysis, **403, 2723, 6672, 7633, 7671, 8620, 9389, 9738, 11433, 11666, 11802, 12257, 14050**

Fertilizer
application, **1671, 1781, 1979, 2108, 2352, 4943, 4974, 5466, 5492, 5969, 6815, 8181, 11479, 12787, 13795**: irrigation injection, **1549, 1769, 2832, 3060, 3528, 5376, 10135, 11074, 12814**; methods, **1700, 1750, 2704, 2723, 6231, 9735, 11398, 12266, 12571, 15824**

Fertilizer
availability, **3856, 4991**

Fertilizer
carriers, **1639, 1739, 3094, 3337, 3346, 3348, 3349, 4921, 4924, 5720, 5721, 12257, 16123**

Fertilizer
coated, **2855, 4326, 5503, 9793, 9798, 9799, 9806, 11792, 11793**: plastic, **1488, 1529, 1546, 1639, 2100, 2209, 7301**; urea, **2094, 2725, 3347, 5198, 11907**

Fertilizer
cost, **3066, 10135, 10136, 10723, 15448**

Fertilizer
effects, **3300, 8181, 10811, 11168, 12729**

Fertilizer
effects on: soil reaction, **5969, 8024, 8243, 8248, 11385, 11397, 11586, 12118**

Fertilizer
efficiency, **975, 13795**

Fertilizer
evaluation, **2100, 4880, 5179, 5735, 7303, 8757, 14128, 15110, 15111**

Fertilizer
foliar burn, **4481, 6661, 7301, 8247, 9735, 12262, 12571, 12712, 12717, 14811, 16041**: evaluation, **2583, 10728, 15110, 15111**

Fertilizer
foliar uptake, **2832, 16135**

Fertilizer
formulation, **1245, 1342, 1650, 2723, 3060, 9685, 9864, 10016**

Fertilizer
handbook, **13613**

Fertilizer
labeling, **129, 1527, 1568, 1576, 4324, 8005, 9644**

Fertilizer
mixed, **11473, 11972, 12257, 12603, 14905**

Fertilizer
nitrogen, **1555, 3856, 5073, 5074, 5735, 12081**

Fertilizer
nitrogen carriers, **2724, 4943, 5183, 7961, 8390**

Fertilizer
pesticide combinations, **1522, 1650, 1967, 3147, 12266, 14493**

Fertilizer
placement, **2706, 6028, 9938, 10297**

Fertilizer
rates, **2051, 3346, 5856, 8181, 12266**

Fertilizer
ratio, **1650, 1819, 4840, 5484, 5869, 5969, 6660, 6672, 6999, 7961, 7998, 8181, 8620, 10723, 11192, 11473, 12265, 12603, 13522, 14453, 15226, 15244, 15270**

Fertilizer
release rate, **2723, 4326, 9792, 9793, 11793, 12387**: slow, **2075, 8198, 9135, 9790, 9791, 13393**

Fertilizer
salt index, **3340, 4520, 9308, 10315, 12320, 15788, 16041**: evaluation, **8247, 8378, 10317, 10319**

Fertilizer
seed combinations, **947**

Fertilizer
selection criteria, **934, 2405, 5426, 6060, 11168**

Fertilizer
soil relationships, **7437, 9912, 9913, 10971, 12387**

Fertilizer
terminology, **454, 7668, 12387, 15577**

Fertilizer
types, **2632, 3955, 4000, 4098, 4429, 4550, 4856, 4879, 4923, 4985, 4998, 5023, 6469, 7569, 7671, 7998, 8926, 8927, 8959, 9685, 9692, 10478, 10538, 11055, 11392, 11493, 11507, 12305, 12387, 12543, 13183, 13752, 14552, 15117, 15187, 15449, 15615, 15778, 16006**: evaluation, **3678, 5439, 7495, 10070, 10813, 10817, 10818, 10822, 10856, 12865, 14127, 14404, 15117, 15724, 16066, 16067, 16069, 16073**

Fertilizer
use, **823, 3267, 10478, 10561, 12603, 14801, 16276**

Fertilizer
water solubility, **1739, 3337, 6380, 6988, 12259, 13533**

Fertilizer spreaders, **1979, 16486**

Ferulic acid
thatch decomposition effects, **10230**

Festuca arundinacea var. *asperia,* **11354**

Festuca capillata (see Hair fescue)

Festuca elatior (see Meadow fescue)

Festuca fallax (see Chewings fescue)

Festuca-lolium hybrids (see *Lolium-festuca* hybrids)

Festuca ovina (see Sheep fescue)

Festuca ovina var. *duriuscula* (see Hard fescue)

Festuca pratensis (see Meadow fescue)

Festuca rubra (see Red fescue)

Festuca rubra var. *commutata* (see Chewings fescue)

Festuca rubra var. *fallax* (see Chewings fescue)

Festuca species, **606, 3028, 3031, 12828**

Festuca species
chromosome number, **8501, 8502**

Festuca species
description, **4085, 8105, 12828**

Festuca species
genetics, **8499**

Festuca species
taxonomy, **12130**

Festuceae, **7522**

Festucoideae, **3378, 14241**

Fever fly, **1140, 4727, 7029**

Fiber (see Thatch)

Fiberglass mat
winter protection, **1781**

Field bindweed
chemical control, **6500**

Field day, turf, **512, 559, 613, 626, 866, 873, 888, 919, 952, 4659, 10260, 11984**

Field day, turf
American Sod Producers Association, **1929**

Field day, turf
Arlington turf garden, **10835**

Field day, turf
Michigan, **2565, 2574, 2575, 2583, 2584, 2592, 2603, 2616, 2631, 2632, 2650, 2673, 2684:** sod production, **1830, 2630, 2672**

Field day, turf
New Jersey, **1732, 5431, 8738, 10260, 15765**

Field day, turf
Ohio, **1432, 1572**

Field day, turf
Purdue, **932, 1016, 1118, 1162, 4521**

Field day, turf
Rhode Island, **1878, 1970, 2113, 2179**

Field day, turf
St. Louis, **1413, 1459**

Field day, turf
state, **480, 1735, 1993**

Field hockey field (see Hockey field)

Field skipper (see Skipper, field)

Fiery skipper (see Skipper, fiery)

Filter screens, irrigation, **12394**

Fire (see Burning)

Fire ant
chemical control, **4060**

Fired clay aggregate
soil amendment, **1879, 8037, 13685, 13906, 16488, 16489**

Fish guano, **4740**

Fish meal, **15118**

Flag smut, **7807, 11324**

Flag smut
chemical control, **7349, 7350, 7352, 7359, 11103:** evaluation, **7354, 7355, 7357, 7358, 7360, 7361, 11110**

Flag smut
effects, **7806, 7809, 7812**

Flag smut
effects on: morphology, **7806, 7809**

Flail mower (see Vertical mowing)

Flaming (see Burning)

Flawn (see Manilagrass)

Flea
chemical control, **3291**

Flea beetle, **3627, 4780**

Flea beetle
chemical control, **1779, 15740**

Flea beetle
description, **4779, 8473, 8481**

Fliorin (see Creeping bentgrass)

Flooding, **2, 2253, 6556, 8115, 12869**

Flooding
effects, **1967, 2617, 3269, 12721**

Flooding
golf course, **4961, 4962, 6556**

Flooding
species tolerance, **1811, 5931, 6386:** evaluation, **2617, 2707, 12559, 12560, 12561**

Flooding
temperature effects, **2617, 2707, 5931**

Flood irrigation, **847**

Flood lighting (see Night illumination)

Floral induction, **7735, 9592**

Floral induction
day length effects, **3669a, 6400, 12962, 14734**

Floral induction
factors affecting, **5664, 9593, 12963**

Floral induction
species variability, **3906, 5364**

Floral induction
temperature effects, **3669a, 6400, 12090**

Floral initiation, **5663, 6400**

Floral initiation
day length effects, **11297, 12090, 16350, 16359**

Floral initiation
temperature effects, **6400, 9668, 16349, 16350**

Floratine St. Augustinegrass, **4073, 4074, 4075, 7966, 8038, 11740, 12259, 14401**

Floraturf bermudagrass, **3504, 3515, 3519, 8164**

Florida – 20 (see Floratine St. Augustinegrass)

Florida bermudagrass, **10461**

Florida rust resistant ryegrass, **3894**

Florida Turfgrass Association, **11738, 15828**

Flossmore creeping bentgrass, **11661**

Flower development, **2424, 3072, 3900, 5259, 5646, 6442, 9993, 10895, 12962, 12964, 14576**

Flower development
day length effects, **3669a, 6400, 11235, 12966**

Flower development
factors affecting, **9593, 12961, 14835**

Flower development
nitrogen effects, **12962, 12963, 12964**

Flower development
temperature effects, **3669a, 6400, 10368, 12966**

Flower development
zoysiagrass, **11852, 11883**

Flowering, **2771, 6610, 7118, 7580, 7833, 12101**

Flowering
cultural effects, **8978, 12765, 14086, 14192**

Flowering
day length effects, **152, 153, 2275, 2771, 3896, 3897, 3898, 3899, 3900, 3902, 3904, 3906, 5664, 7735, 9019, 9020, 9183, 14192, 14604, 16257, 16258, 16444**

Flowering
day length-temperature interaction effects, **9593, 12089**

Flowering
effects, **7810, 9923**

Flowering
environmental effects, **7085, 7320, 8979**

Flowering
factors affecting, **12089, 14962**

Flowering
growth regulator effects, **14318, 16459**

Flowering
light intensity effects, **2770, 14192**

Flowering
pollination, **2741, 2812, 7580**

Flowering
rooting effects, **2771, 14086**

Flowering
temperature effects, **2275, 3896, 3897, 3899, 3902, 3904, 3906, 5664, 7320, 7735, 7737, 9019, 9592, 9923, 14604, 16257, 16258, 16444**

Fluorescence test
identification: *Lolium* species, **3917, 5277, 6300, 7339, 8381, 8727, 12424, 16198**

Fluoride, **2679**
crabgrass control, **5524**

Fluorodifen
rough bluegrass control, **2949**

Fluorophenoxyocetic acid
seed head repression, **208**

Fluorophenoxyacetic acid
weed control, **1270**

Fly ash, **3137, 7868, 8632**

Fly ash
effects, **3203, 9313, 11956**

Fly ash
nutrient analysis, **7868, 11956**

Fly ash
properties, **3913, 11955**

Fly ash
soil amendment, **1777, 2027, 3202, 3210, 11954, 11955, 12495**

Fly ash
use, **3210, 3913, 4956**

Fogger
types, **1942**

Foliar burn, **1304, 15110, 15111** (see also Physiological drought)

Foliar feeding, **1015, 1245, 2832, 5608, 5889, 35732**

Football field, **1786, 10942, 14182, 14306**

Football field
construction, **4124, 7420, 7423, 10505**

Football field
culture, **239, 240, 256, 1031, 1185, 1191, 1255, 1993, 4124, 4467, 4496, 4917, 8543, 9161, 10237, 10239, 10332, 10333, 10505, 10508, 11728, 12033, 12065, 12775, 12776, 12777, 13049, 13575, 13811, 14306, 14771, 15556, 16327:** fall, **1004, 1100:** spring, **1072, 1088, 1138, 1177**

Football field
establishment, **240, 1902, 4124, 10505, 12778**

Football field
frost protection, **1135, 1243**

Football field
grasses used, **1639, 10604**

Football field
renovation, **239, 1031, 1114, 1133, 1993, 2408, 8538, 8543, 8789, 10612, 12065, 13935**

Football field
soil modification, **1902, 4468, 4496, 4531, 16327**

Foot-printing (see Wilt)

Fore®
algae control, **6197**

Fore®
disease control, **3103, 4203, 4591**

Forking, **303, 738, 826, 1176, 4734, 5272, 5634, 5636, 6101, 6528**

Formaldehyde, **5632, 9800**

Formalin (see Formaldehyde)

Formica (see Ants)

Foxtail, **538**
chemical control, **6331, 10619**

Freeway (see Roadside)

Freezing
soil, **2828, 7837**

Freezing injury (see Low temperature stress)

Frit fly, **1490, 1570, 1779, 2027, 2744, 4240, 4322, 4780, 10248, 12315, 13494, 13498, 13502, 13505**

Frit fly
chemical control, **8476, 14063:** evaluation, **4322, 13500**

Frit fly
description, **127, 4779, 8476**

Frit fly
distribution, **8481, 14094**

Frost
desiccation, **15571**

Frost
effects, **15548**

Frost
injury, **1597, 15582**

Frost heaving, **1006, 4833, 8933, 9920, 12199, 15518**

Frost heaving
establishment effects, **2925, 3175**

Frost heaving
greens, **609**

Frost heaving
mechanism, **3085, 9920**

Frost heaving
prevention, **2925, 3175, 9920**

Frost heaving
seedling injury, **2925, 8932, 8933**

Frost protection, **15546, 15571, 15582**

Frost protection
methods, **2201, 15548:** irrigation, **12813, 14064**

Frost protection
removal, **1050:** syringing, **10931**

Frost protection
sports field, **1552, 2183**

Fructosan, **2245, 7306, 13619**

Fructosan
content: species variation, **2245, 4837, 11649, 11806, 12110**

Fructosan
cultural factors affecting: fertilization, **14473, 16466**; mowing, **12557, 14195, 14473**; nitrogen, **2245, 9423, 12557, 14451, 14473**

Fructosan
diurnal variation, **15151**

Fructosan
extraction techniques, **7115**

Fructosan
factors effecting, **15152:** plant maturity, **11646, 11647, 13947, 15152**; temperature, **10000, 14450**

Fructosan
plant part distribution, **13947, 14449**

Fructosan
seasonal variation, **2245**

Fructose
diurnal variation, **8651**

Fructose
factors affecting, **2552:** temperature, **8651, 8652**

Fumigation, **1060, 1493, 8665, 9399, 12040**

Fumigation
materials used, **6637, 9401, 10638, 11706, 12487, 13724**

Fumigation
methods, **8848, 9399, 9401, 12487, 12874**

Fumigation
soil (see Soil fumigation)

Fumigation
uses, **1900, 13556**

Fungi, **5258, 6735, 8375, 8973, 8989, 8990, 9388, 12604, 13703, 14852, 14889, 15035**

Fungi
benomyl resistance, **13938**

Fungi
biology, **13985, 13986**

Fungi
causal agents: diseases, **6735, 8357, 8366, 8367, 8374**

Fungi
characteristics, **4712, 6132, 11877, 12301, 13566**

Fungi
classification, **12302**

Fungi
dissemination, **1308, 1317:** methods, **9388, 9760**

Fungi
environmental factors affecting, **5639, 6739, 8739, 8769, 8770, 8776**

Fungi
growth, **9760, 9861, 11877, 13890, 14852:** factors affecting, **9862, 10853**

Fungi
identification key, **4291, 8976, 14189**

Fungi
nematode interaction, **12226, 12272**

Fungi
penetration, **9760**

Fungi
physiological relationships, **16289, 16296**

Fungi
spores (see Spore)

Fungi
toxin production, **9744**

Fungicide, **4183, 4686, 5820, 6170, 6752, 6753, 6786, 7879, 8370, 8960, 8998, 9929, 10587, 10588, 11080, 12599, 12907, 13599, 13607, 13704, 13713, 13728, 13729, 13734, 13744, 15028, 15781, 16218, 16277, 16505**

Fungicide
application, **649, 710, 1639, 4174, 4884, 8093, 8960, 9246, 10828, 12467, 13566, 13703:** calibration, **6246**; helicopter, **12479**; procedures, **6751, 8970, 9247, 9750, 10804, 10853, 11102**

Fungicide
broad spectrum, **1077, 1081, 1545**

Fungicide
cadmium compounds, **8092**

Fungicide
compatability, **12467, 13608, 13609, 13717, 14902**

Fungicide
development, **6126, 6738, 10601, 13713, 16505**

Fungicide
disease control, **6751, 10585, 10586, 13602, 13722**

Fungicide
effectiveness: factors affecting, **1639, 6254, 13566, 16277**; pathogen variation effects, **10331**; polyethylene cover effects, **2607**

Fungicide
effects on: nematode population, **10576**; shoot growth, **2603**; soil microbiology, **3922**; weed control, **7882**

Fungicide
evaluation, **3923, 4204, 4684, 4691, 4694, 8368, 8372, 8805, 16051:** brown patch control, **1677**; on cool season turfgrasses, **8361**; dollar spot control, **1677, 9246, 14719**; leaf spot control, **1677**; melting out control, **9750, 11112**; techniques, **8365, 10692, 11319**

Fungicide
history, **6126**

Fungicide
human toxicity, **11073, 13637**

Fungicide
latex additive effects, **9089, 9090**

Fungicide
mixtures, **1700, 6745, 16505**

Fungicide
phytotoxicity, **3604a, 6751**: evaluation, **3923, 11847, 12167**

Fungicide
seed treatment, **2520, 2521, 2522, 14001, 14011**

Fungicide
selection, **3257, 10597, 13719**

Fungicide
systemic (see Systemic fungicide)

Fungicide
types, **8970, 9749, 9929, 10254, 12145, 12908, 13594, 13595, 13602, 13611, 13719**

Fungicide
use, **6744, 6747, 6748, 6749, 9524, 9749, 10602, 12286, 13731, 14902**

Fungistasis, soil
assay, **9595**

Fungus gnat, **12746**

Furadan® (see Carbofuran)

Fusa Kentucky bluegrass, **9218**

Fusarium blight, **1610, 1846, 1958, 2537, 2538, 2539, 2540, 2541, 2542, 2649, 3255, 8351, 12218, 13736, 13740**

Fusarium blight
causal agents, **4191, 4192**

Fusarium blight
chemical control, **2537, 2540, 4191, 4192, 15011, 15014:** benomyl, **11108, 15012, 15025, 15031**; evaluation, **2100, 2170, 2547, 2633, 2672, 4310, 6764, 8059, 11107, 11111, 15013, 15024**; nemeticides, **15026**

Fusarium blight
on cool season grasses, **2540**

Fusarium blight
on cool season turfgrasses: Kentucky bluegrass cultivars, **2540, 4192, 4197**

Fusarium blight
cultural control, **2537, 11942:** irrigation, **2027, 2539, 2541**

Fusarium blight
description, **2536, 2539, 4176, 4177, 4191, 4192, 4197, 8355, 14443**

Fusarium blight
environmental factors affecting, **2540, 4311, 8851:** soil moisture, **2027, 2542, 2543, 4178, 4197**; temperature, **4191, 11939**

Fusarium blight
Japan, **6258**

Fusarium blight
nematode interaction, **15023, 15026**

Fusarium blight
nutritional effects, **4176, 4178, 4191**

Fusarium blight
species susceptibility, **2537, 4191, 4197**

Fusarium blight
on warm season turfgrasses: bermudagrass, **2827**; centipedegrass, **4191, 14443**; zoysiagrass, **2540, 2755, 4330**

Fusarium nivale (see also *Fusarium* patch), **9861**

Fusarium oxysporum
on Japanese lawngrass, **2755**

Fusarium patch, **499, 1055, 1101, 1141, 1260, 1446, 1977, 2135, 2814, 2815, 3251, 3252, 3271, 3272, 4315, 6699, 6729, 6734, 6769, 7832, 7884, 7894, 8345, 9271, 9272, 12508, 13990, 14014, 14968, 15016, 15477**

Fusarium patch
chemical control, **1208, 1253, 1274, 1281, 1518, 2927, 5271, 5619, 5759, 6114, 6650, 6731, 6732, 6733, 6746, 6747, 6750, 6754, 6757, 9410, 12631, 14010, 15011, 15014, 15483, 15485, 15589:** evaluation, **1545, 2100, 2667, 3253, 4321, 6667, 6727, 6730, 6755, 6756, 6762, 6765, 7192, 8337, 8339, 8342, 11661, 13994, 13998, 13999, 14009, 15590, 16210, 16211, 16212**

Fusarium patch
control, **1036, 1124, 1134, 1647, 5417, 6728, 6740, 6742, 6745, 8353, 9405**

Fusarium patch
on cool season turfgrasses, **4768, 5717:** creeping bentgrass cultivars, **4321, 6730, 6758**; Kentucky bluegrass cultivars, **15029, 15030**

Fusarium patch
cultural control, **6132, 6730, 7193, 8970, 12631**

Fusarium patch
cultural factors affecting, **13660, 15589:** fertilization, **6647, 6732, 6746, 7285, 10108, 14004**; irrigation, **10108**; lime, **483, 14004, 14013**

Fusarium patch
description, **4321, 5271, 5417, 5619, 5708, 6132, 7193, 8353, 9410, 9892, 10657, 12078, 12556, 12631, 12991, 13998**

Fusarium patch
England, **7192, 7288, 8351**

Fusarium patch
environmental factors affecting, **4321, 6739, 9892, 10423, 10657:** temperature, **5402, 6739, 7814, 9405, 11939, 13998, 14004**

Fusarium patch
Japan, **6258, 11799, 16293**

Fusarium patch
nitrogen effects, **1777, 4768, 5395, 5637, 6652, 6679, 6702, 6706, 12085, 14014**

Fusarium patch
potassium effects, **2162, 6679, 6705, 6706, 6708**

Fusarium patch
sulfur effects, **6706**

Fusarium patch
on warm season turfgrasses, **2755**

Fusarium roseum (see also *Fusarium* blight), **13565**

Fusarium solani
on Japanese lawngrass, **2755**

Fusarium species, **201, 2321, 2617**
on seeds, **4049**

Fusarium tricinotum (see *Fusarium* patch)

Fylking Kentucky bluegrass, **1843, 1967, 2027, 6294, 6315, 8319, 8320, 8322, 13344, 14747**

Fylking Kentucky bluegrass
adaptation, **3932, 6298, 16430**

Fylking Kentucky bluegrass
description, **5314, 6298, 8321**

Fulking Kentucky bluegrass
evaluation, **5781, 6330, 7287, 8321, 10626, 11186, 11325, 11329, 14813**

Galactose
root phytotoxicity, **5419**

Galaxy Kentucky bluegrass, **6330**

Galechoma hederacea (see Ground ivy)

Gall midges, **1289, 2429, 2430**

Galvanized steel pipe, **14328**

Garbage compost
soil amendment, 235

Garden center
sod marketing, **6154, 15396, 15407**

Garden chafer, **10676, 15807**

Garden store, **7734, 15936**

Garden store
customer relations, **9039**

Garden store
merchandizing, **3683, 9039, 9915**

Garden store
sod marketing, **6154, 11061, 15396, 15407**

Gardens, turf, **9176, 9204**

Gardona®
flea beetle control, **15736**

Garlic, wild (see Wild garlic)

Gasoline
dandelion control, **13817**

Gasoline
injury symptoms, **2673**

Geary Kentucky bluegrass, **8317, 14813**

Genera
taxonomy, **7794, 14243**

Genetics
Agrostis species, **3152, 3154**

Genetics
leaf development, **5309**

Genetics
Poa species, **3870, 3872**

Gene tift bermudagrass (see Bayshore bermudagrass)

Geocoris bullatus (see Big-eyed bug)

Geotropic response
rhizome, **5952**

Geraniol
Japanese beetle control, **10480**

Germander speedwell, **4743**

Germination, seed (see Seed germination)

Giant bermudagrass
cultural control, **3910**

Gibberellin, **1240, 12973, 12974**

Gibberellin
effects on, **2433, 5756, 9052, 12750:** carbohydrate reserves, **2940**; chlorophyll content, **2940**; root growth, **8672, 12750, 16329**; seed germination, **206, 2475, 3685, 8666, 8669, 9052**; shoot growth, **2940, 4155, 8669, 8672, 9052, 9419, 9420, 11231, 13022, 16329, 16341**; spring green-up, **1216, 9419, 16134**; stolon growth, **8666**; winter growth, **2940, 9052**; zoysiagrass, **1271**

Glass fiber filter
tile drainage, **8609**

Glass fiber mat
waterway evaluation, **1479, 12490**

Glass fiber mulch
evaluation, **2667, 5042, 5152, 6515, 13797, 14432**

Glass frit, potassium, **9777, 9790**

Glenbar®
crabgrass control, **5200**

Gloecoercospora sorghi (see Copper spot)

Gloeotinia temulenta (see Blind seed disease)

Glomules, **4563**

Glumes
seed germination effects, **203**

Glutamine
content: seasonal variation, **2557**; species variability, **2556**

Glutamine
disease development effects, **7621**

Glutamine
exudation, **4305, 7033**

Glutamine
growth stoppage alleviation, **3338**

Glutamine
temperature effects, **2557, 2694, 2697, 8778**

Glycoluril
nitrogen carrier, **2725, 16275**

Gnaphalium spp. (see Cudweed)

Gnat, **1406**

Goar tall fescue, **977, 7309, 8647, 11165, 11186, 14356, 14365**

Golf, **3826, 6501**

Golf
future, **5281, 5284**

Golf
growth trends, **5286, 5287, 6795**

Golf
history, **3718, 6798, 12829**

Golf
promotion, **8217, 9826, 9872, 13949**

Golf car, **11716, 11718, 12947**

Golf car
costs, **5138, 7912, 16265**

Golf car
effects: on turfgrass culture, **3167, 10304, 13666, 16190**

Golf car
operation, **1421, 8608, 13666, 15369**

Golf car
ownership, **7903, 7912, 16265**

Golf car
path, **7903, 13524:** construction, **1720, 5845, 7903, 10777, 12237, 13524**; design, **11888**; materials used, **5845, 10752, 10753**; traffic control, **12237, 13666**

Golf car
problems, **5138, 8608, 10277, 10304, 10311, 12460, 12474, 16265:** solutions, **10298, 10311**

Golf car
safety, **7912**

Golf car
selection criteria, **16265**

Golf car
turfgrass effects, **1421, 1720, 1730, 11716, 12461, 15369**

Golf car
use survey, **2792**

Golf cart, **1071, 1324**

Golf cart
effects, **11716, 15863**

Golf cart
management, **8584, 9263**

Golf course, **847, 2489, 5282, 6568, 6794, 7059, 10771, 11585, 12233, 14020, 15278, 15533**

Golf course
architecture, **2484, 2784, 4062, 4063, 4815, 12696, 13798, 14462, 14631**

Golf course
bridges, **3401, 8826**

Golf course
budget, **1628, 1743, 2338, 2807, 2959, 3342, 3395, 3578a, 5288, 5724, 7763, 8803, 9855, 11735, 11851, 12399, 13801, 15667, 15957, 15963, 16148**

Golf course
clubhouse grounds, **6610, 1683, 10321, 10654**

Golf course
construction, **151, 192, 264, 472, 586, 1699, 1917, 2484, 2784, 2797, 3469, 3953, 3954, 3957, 4012, 4455, 4814, 5266, 5282, 5401, 5624, 6907, 6920, 6953, 6964, 6993, 7218, 7422, 8237, 8239, 8603, 9421, 10247, 10337, 10356, 10398, 10441, 11191, 11203, 11393, 11809, 12376, 12551, 12696, 12893, 15370, 16110, 16138, 16473:** book, **5882, 9514, 14462, 14631**; contract, **3661a, 8315**; costs, **1267, 1966, 4820, 5928, 6993**; specifications, **7422, 9167, 11212**; trends, **5287, 12894**

Golf course
contract maintenance, **2796**

Golf course
cool season turfgrasses used, **391, 4455, 7241, 4908, 11767, 11771, 13318**

Golf course
costs, **4814, 6592, 7693, 8802, 11358, 12214, 14787**

Golf course
culture, **163, 220, 261, 288, 423, 458, 460, 588, 714, 737, 739, 740, 792, 860, 887, 983, 1035, 1347, 1938, 1992, 2050, 2104, 2209, 2254, 2345, 2353, 2489, 2804, 2933, 2948, 3090, 3124, 2161, 3643a, 3646a, 3650a, 3675, 3750, 3858, 3874, 4255, 4330, 4347, 4354, 4367, 4375, 4391, 4487, 4809, 4811, 4814, 4825, 4993, 5016, 5299, 5318, 5579, 5803, 5809, 5859, 5905, 5927, 6003, 6339, 6772, 6821, 6822, 6858, 6869, 6870, 6873, 6877, 6885, 6894, 6915, 7009, 7230, 7239, 7249, 7289, 7291, 7510, 7763, 7766, 7883, 7885, 7888, 7892, 7944, 8269, 8457, 8518, 8603, 8850, 9236, 9277, 9422, 9707, 9927, 9928, 10010, 10178, 10182, 10286, 10471, 10527, 10649,**

10688, 10882, 10985, 11167, 11407, 11411, 11443, 11451, 11455, 11475, 11484, 11499, 11525, 11526, 11530, 11531, 11544, 11556, 11602, 11604, 11631, 11633, 12363, 12375, 12646, 13414, 13540, 13547, 13597, 14104, 14316, 14506, 14507, 14556, 14625, 14652, 14769, 14787, 14850, 14856, 14973, 15375, 15580, 15717, 15723, 15818, 15957, 15970, 16144, 16239, 16287, 16499, 16503: aerial application, **1750, 1920**; after construction, **12492**; Argentine, **10779**; Australia, **243, 7253, 15288**; book, **282, 696, 2528, 4295, 4469, 5722, 6498, 8249, 9514, 9847, 11394, 12140, 12149, 13542, 14462, 14470**; Canada, **10929, 12829, 13966, 14674, 14782**; cool region, **8571, 11269, 12343, 14595**; costs, **223, 1226, 1269, 1784, 2608, 2789, 2791, 4232, 5057, 5282, 5739, 7693, 9254, 12399, 12958**; cultivation, **52, 3063, 5820, 7238, 10436, 11484**; England, **2531, 6459, 6534, 6773, 9870, 10831, 10907, 13841, 14470**; environmental factors affecting, **3144, 16272**; Europe, **1258, 1322, 5049, 5760**; excess water problems, **14171, 15489, 15805**; fall, **950, 1004, 1100, 1331, 2920, 5801, 6468, 6793, 13645, 13657, 15596**; fertilization, **562, 697, 717, 1836, 2172, 2920, 3346, 3450, 3646a, 3648, 3740, 4129, 4131, 4920, 2998, 5104, 4173, 5806, 6552, 6774, 6811, 7230, 7290, 7595, 7602, 7603, 8001, 9606, 10506, 10688, 11097, 11164, 11167, 11183, 11413, 11415, 11453, 11499, 11738, 11884, 13979, 14574, 14677, 14930, 15954, 16278**; history, **11520, 14594**; international, **2778, 10779, 11626, 14568, 15180**; irrigation, **345, 580, 713, 3642a, 4822, 6257, 7342, 7613, 8269, 8278, 8840, 9871, 10010, 10716, 11533, 12459, 14280, 15956**; irrigation practices, **1838, 5963, 9192, 10828, 10839, 11136, 12346, 14171, 15466, 15805**; Japan, **2778, 5274, 5401, 11884, 16290**; liquid fertilization, **5909, 9693**; Mexico, **6546, 7239**; mowing, **1938, 15964**; New Zealand, **9514, 15173, 15175, 15194, 15210, 15214, 15216, 15222, 15224, 15233, 15238, 15252, 15267, 15271, 15272, 15293, 15295, 15303**; night programs, **7083, 9835, 9836**; problems, **1559, 5998, 6863, 9283, 9638, 10006, 10278, 10279, 10930, 11419, 11441, 11442, 11486, 11495, 11498, 11508, 11509, 11527, 11530, 11531, 11534, 11631, 11633, 11634, 12344, 14901, 15716**; public course, **14321, 15995**; Scotland, **3644a, 5049, 5372, 6618**; soil management, **6799, 10329, 11453, 14623, 14935**; South Africa, **10362, 11098**; spring, **1088, 1386, 1444, 1775, 2145, 4214, 11516, 12342, 13060**; summer, **876, 949, 1394, 3649a, 6066, 9235, 9850, 10433, 10825, 11542, 11554, 11571, 15719**; topdressing, **6100, 6283**; trends, **5863, 9298**; USA, **2531, 6584, 7239, 8482, 9194, 14063, 14314, 14573, 15452**; warm climates, **868, 2207, 8624, 9353, 13553, 14639**; wartime, **6459, 11522, 12189**; winter, **1398, 1866, 3798, 4214, 4576, 5797, 6301, 7886, 9191, 10176, 10751, 12342, 12350, 13647, 13920, 16029**; winter preparation, **10400, 10929, 15520**

Golf course
cultural systems, **135, 199, 316, 1578, 3582a, 6775, 9691, 16504**

Golf course
design, **472, 473, 1622, 1721, 1924, 2742, 2797, 3958, 3959, 3961, 3962, 3963, 3964, 4012, 4455, 4819, 5282, 6093, 6143, 7488, 7541, 8239, 8249, 8643, 8917, 10247, 10356, 10398, 10721, 11270, 11889, 12098, 12157, 12891, 12892, 14091, 14295, 14469, 14851, 14853, 15502, 16110:** cultural considerations, **6624, 7049, 7490, 9768, 11497, 11500, 11501, 11596, 11889**

Golf course
development, **5286, 5287, 9170**

Golf course
diseases, **3252, 11549, 12379**

Golf course
disease control, **5624, 11514**

Golf course
drainage, **316, 407, 579, 1219, 4165, 4821, 5026, 6793, 7230, 10396, 10644, 10645, 10646, 10647, 11033, 11035, 12359, 14638, 15730, 16143:** subsurface, **2483, 10832, 13034**; surface, **1660, 5141, 13034**

Golf course
environmental quality, **7913, 10484, 14342**

Golf course
equipment, **43, 221, 321, 1267, 1743, 1997, 3006, 3750, 9577, 10149, 10308, 10310, 10776, 12477, 14660, 15089:** inventory, **3171, 3643a, 3646a, 7693, 10501, 10512, 12464, 12478**; New Zealand, **15298, 15310, 15312**

Golf course
establishment, **288, 290, 472, 565, 578, 586, 588, 1917, 4817, 4823, 4934, 5926, 6799, 6932, 9105, 9638, 11809, 11915, 12551, 12647, 12696, 13542, 14336, 16138:** methods, **2268, 3883, 11834**

Golf course
financing, **1443, 1874, 5281, 5282, 12893, 12894, 15058**

Golf course
future, **5281, 5284, 11270, 11727**

Golf course
grasses used, **3644a, 4663, 4810, 5312, 5859, 6013, 6020, 6879, 9250, 10026, 11188, 11452, 11551, 11611, 12827, 14359, 14370, 14849, 15470**

Golf course
grooming, **10009, 10321, 12371**

Golf course
growth, **3404, 6798**

Golf course
hazards, **6458, 12592**

Golf course
history, **732, 6798**

Golf course
irrigation system, **345, 1443, 1743, 2831, 3097, 3098, 3746, 3747, 3877, 4822, 4940, 6257, 7848, 8812, 10528, 10540, 12918, 13678:** installation, **10434, 10528, 16138**

Golf course
labor, **1510, 1743, 9197, 10322, 11542, 11567, 13945, 14787, 16148**: cost reduction, **3400, 10313, 10316, 13038**; relations, **2959, 3125, 6157, 6932, 9924, 10679, 13443**; training, **2175, 9473, 11720**

Golf course
landscaping, **2487, 2497, 3638a, 3681a, 3960, 4824, 5096, 5814, 6610, 7064, 7488, 7753, 8204, 8205, 8567, 9960, 10437, 10654, 10932, 11281, 12097, 12728, 14732, 15847**

Golf course
lighting, **1812, 1876, 3884, 4116, 6395**

Golf course
management, **264, 1268, 1403, 1774, 2467, 5036, 7075, 7107, 7690, 10214, 10288, 11791, 12204, 14340, 14673, 15050, 15375, 15864:** economics, **1743, 3802, 6551, 9859, 12299**

Golf course
municipal: culture, **3956, 8614, 12894, 13800, 14091**

Golf course
operation, **1467, 5287, 11727:** off-season, **1566, 13657**

Golf course
overseeding, **1035, 13237, 15091**

Golf course
ownership: trends, **2027, 5281, 5284**

Golf course
pests, **1054, 1626, 3250, 4562, 5624, 8309, 9359, 12093, 13476, 15345, 15346, 15990**

Golf course
pollution, **9318, 9863**

Golf course
pond maintenance, **10780**

Golf course
problems, **1624, 2176, 3166, 4803, 5860, 6873, 7050, 7883, 9282, 9286, 10298, 11035, 11506, 11510, 11511, 11521, 11533, 11543, 11557, 12209, 12337, 12339, 12369, 12396, 12469, 13414, 14650, 14727, 14850, 16039, 16047, 16142:** diagnosis, **7888, 11618, 11630**; regional, **3402, 5812, 7336, 14782, 15289**; seasonal, **4961, 5325, 6556, 10441, 11511, 11546, 12342, 16039**

Golf course
programming, **8304, 10750, 14316**

Golf course
public, **4117, 5286, 7541, 10679, 16287**

Golf course
public relations, **12714, 14447**

Golf course
rebuilding, **192, 1721, 1820, 3962, 5928, 9937, 10425, 10648, 10649, 11558, 11889, 12098, 12345, 14065, 14596, 15058**

Golf course
records, **1672, 2789, 3121, 4816, 5838, 13667, 15367**

Golf course
record keeping, **7642, 8802, 8803, 9855, 15580**

Golf course
renovation, **377, 1233, 2872, 3957, 3959, 3962, 5026, 5028, 5219, 5280, 5875, 6394, 9033, 12345, 14380, 14381**

Golf course
roads, **5845, 10753**

Golf course
site selection, **4815, 4818, 5282, 7541, 7897**

Golf course
ski program, **14743**

Golf course
snowmobiles, **1937, 5936, 8552, 10715**

Golf course
soils, **9588, 12897, 12898, 14924**

Golf course
speeding up play, **1622, 3404**

Golf course
survey, **1721, 1743, 1658, 1864, 1981, 2089, 4698, 4701, 5284, 5624, 12246**

Golf course
synthetic turf, **3219**

Golf course
tournament preparation, **1391, 2210, 2476, 2783, 5154, 6382, 7278, 13397, 13450, 14264, 16144, 16150:** culture, **5817, 7140, 8266, 10560, 11293**

Golf course
traffic control, **5837**

Golf course
traffic effects, **1391, 3161, 3801**

Golf course
tree, **383, 5862, 7058, 7064, 9683, 10188, 13456**

Golf course
warm season turfgrasses used, **3607, 3611, 4455, 8518, 11884, 12133:** zoysiagrass, **3115, 3127, 6143, 9935**

Golf course
water management, **3303, 6852, 10911, 14130**

Golf course
weed control, **1995, 2387, 2388, 3354, 3876, 5624, 6372, 7095, 9110, 9870, 10827, 11453, 11577, 11592, 11978, 12340, 12385, 12983, 14496**

Golf course superintendent, **3134, 7381, 9576, 9619, 10717, 13025**

Golf course superintendent
benefits survey, **4390, 4403**

Golf course superintendent
certification, **5319, 10707, 15149, 15150**

Golf course superintendent
club manager relations, **3173, 10190, 11873**

Golf course superintendent
club relations, **2773**

Golf course superintendent
communications, **12700, 12706, 16142**

Golf course superintendent
computer use, **12723**

Golf course superintendent
employee relations, **6342, 8961, 9197, 10279, 13945, 15772**

Golf course superintendent
future, **3134, 9051, 10717, 11727**

Golf course superintendent
golf promoter, **8217, 9826, 9872**

Golf course superintendent
golf pro relations, **5037, 10198**

Golf course superintendent
golf rules affecting, **12233**

Golf course superintendent
greens chairman relationship, **5036, 5804, 6912, 7690, 7691**

Golf course superintendent
professional development, **2793, 5038, 5217, 5319, 6912**

Golf course superintendent
public relations, **10763, 16132**

Golf course superintendent
qualifications, **6929, 10714, 15150**

Golf course superintendent
responsibility, **3661a, 4238, 5154, 5319, 7107, 7631, 9576, 10214, 10717, 10928**

Golf course superintendent
salary, **1745, 3497, 4390, 4403, 9051**

Golf course superintendent
salesmanship, **10295, 12700, 12706, 12714**

Golf course superintendent
system analysis method: for golf course, **3582a**

Golf course superintendent
training, **3629a, 9380, 14300, 14411**

Golf Course Superintendents Association of America, **142, 14594**

Golf Course Superintendents Association of America
annual conference, **990, 1011, 1013, 1061, 1112, 1158, 2870, 6792**

Golf Course Superintendents Association of America
history, **320, 847, 922, 1675, 1751, 6997**

Golf Course Superintendents Association of America
local chapters, **9264**

Golf Course Superintendents Association of America
membership, **1464, 15149**

Golf Kentucky bluegrass, **7191, 9218**

Golf putting green (see Green)

Golfrood chewings fescue, **2566, 8343**
evaluation, **2204, 7508, 8336, 8338, 8341, 8342, 8350, 9219**

Golf tournament (see Golf course, tournament preparation)

Goosegrass, **469**

Goosegrass
chemical control, **1639, 1700, 2066, 2071, 4396, 4480, 5480, 6357, 6918, 6921, 8145, 8146, 8297**: in bermudagrass, **2892, 4207**; evaluation, **2900, 3780, 4788, 4789, 5468, 5479, 5512, 5513, 5528, 5534, 5537, 5549, 5688, 6284, 6286, 6580, 7659, 7661, 8157, 9545, 9546, 9579, 9733, 10619, 13971**

Goosegrass
cultural control, **2066**

Goosegrass
seed germination: factors affecting, **6285, 14758**

Gopher
control, **4109, 4835:** baits, **2856**

Gopher
bait: application equipment, **8855**

Grading
sod, **2302**

Grain, **526, 6899, 10285**
control, **4765, 5962, 6899, 9482, 10075**

Gramineae (see *Poaceae*)

Grass, **4723, 7705, 12404**

Grass
adaptation, **2748, 15054**

Grass
book, **2425, 10680, 12027, 12187, 16055:** development, **10680**; English, **8251**

Grass
description, **4093, 8461, 11701, 14240:** pollen grain, **6461**; state bulletin, **14828**; USDA bulletin, **7164**

Grass
identification (see Identification, grass)

Grass
introduced to USA: bulletin, **15659**

Grass
uses, **10934:** soil conservation, **2818, 7164, 7945**

Grass handbook
taxonomy, **8127, 8128**

Grass manual, **2526, 2866, 2993, 3016, 3490, 3787, 5520, 7945, 7946**

Grass manual
Agrostis species: United States, **7792**

Grass manual
California, **12670, 12989, 12990**

Grass manual
cool season species, **2878**

Grass manual
England, **8251, 11928, 15372**

Grass manual
German, **7150**

Grass manual
Illinois, **11025**

Grass manual
India, **3064**

Grass manual
Kansas, **6257**

Grass manual
Kenya, **3038**

Grass manual
Maryland, **11670**

Grass manual
Ohio, **15931**

Grass manual
Oklahoma, **5750**

Grass manual
Pennsylvania, **7110, 12163**

Grass manual
South Africa, **10460**

Grass manual
Texas, **12156, 13761**

Grass manual
USA, **7793, 7794**

Grass manual
warm season species, **2877**

Grass manual
Wisconsin, **5738**

Grass manual
Wyoming, **2749**

Gray leaf spot, **6172, 6199, 13566, 15691**

Gray leaf spot
chemical control, **6159, 6174, 6176, 6177, 6201, 11876:** evaluation, **1639, 4782, 6165, 6180, 6184, 6189, 6190**

Gray leaf spot
control: clipping removal, **11930**

Gray leaf spot
cultural factors affecting, **4782**

Gray leaf spot
environmental factors affecting, **4782**

Gray leaf spot
injury symptoms, **15674**

Gray leaf spot
magnesium effects, **13897, 13904**

Gray leaf spot
susceptible species, **2348, 8308**

Gray leaf spot
symptoms, **6161, 6176, 8308, 10142, 11071, 11876**

Gray snow mold (see *Typhula* blight)

Grease spot disease (see *Pythium* species)

Green, **2237, 6505, 14903**

Green
algae control, **10793**

Green
annual bluegrass: control, **2499, 2647, 3879, 5681, 6983, 12458, 13866**; chemical control, **2070, 10439, 11835, 16319, 16343**

Green
area determination, **6815, 10188**

Green
ball marks, **1802, 10828**

Green
ball roll (see Ball roll)

Green
compaction effects, **10118, 10119**

Green
construction, **191, 1043, 1113, 1157, 1378, 1401, 1423, 1584, 1627, 1699, 1927, 1960, 1993, 2306, 2500, 3056, 3650a, 3676, 3953, 4067, 4298, 4306, 4574, 4703, 4914, 5216, 5241, 5243, 5245, 5247, 5251, 5805, 5810, 5811, 5825, 5836, 5868, 5895, 6001, 6547, 6561, 6917, 7069, 7127, 7159, 7218, 7219, 7237, 7299, 7488, 7893, 7902, 7904, 7906, 7941, 8506, 8521, 8642, 9011, 9167, 9943, 9985, 10329, 10749, 10933, 11198, 12372, 12428, 12886, 13641, 14728, 15120, 15260, 15288, 15705, 15966, 15971, 15995, 16009:** cost, **1267, 7127, 8814**; Japan, **9115, 9199**

Green
contours, **5245, 5246**

Green
cool season turfgrasses used, **312, 5163, 5624, 9844, 10961, 14128, 14185:** bentgrass, **297, 1357, 8792, 10767, 10856, 12401, 14728**; creeping bentgrass, **8152, 8301, 12370, 14375**

Green
cotton seed hull, **317, 15966**

Green
crabgrass control, **313, 7328, 4839**

Green
cultivar evaluation, **4768, 14375**

Green
culture, **50, 128, 314, 318, 326, 341, 430, 577, 793, 1465, 1628, 1635, 1652, 2013, 2280, 2552, 2684, 2785, 3106, 3645a, 3777, 3813, 4078, 4100, 4293, 4568, 4574, 4575, 4720, 4876, 5017, 5246, 5660, 6000, 6466, 6649, 6682, 6850, 6902, 6921, 6924, 6925, 7071, 7072, 7109, 7159, 7208, 7219, 7275, 7289, 7663, 7763, 7764, 7784, 7889, 8268, 8301, 8505, 8506, 8536, 8547, 8596, 8818, 9108, 9237, 9244, 9296, 9705,**

9706, 9921, 9926, 10166, 10713, 10749, 10828, 10960, 10986, 10988, 11204, 11460, 11484, 11505, 11560, 11590, 11638, 11879, 11933, 12240, 12349, 12401, 12458, 12834, 12885, 12886, 12999, 13007, 13057, 13569, 13579, 13651, 13944, 13976, 14247, 14248, 14555, 14558, 14682, 14729, 14769, 14770, 14772, 14778, 14920, 15288, 15717, 15819, 15885, 15995, 16037, 16038, 16151, 16160, 16330: acid soil theory, **15207**; Africa, **6805, 10110**; bentgrass, **11468, 11469, 16037**; bermudagrass, **292, 303, 349, 457, 2813, 3114, 5250, 5858, 6958, 7787, 7788, 13651, 13653, 16035**; book, **1288, 8249, 9866, 12494, 13005, 14468**; coring, **1405, 2951, 3674, 5728, 11588**; cost analysis, **25, 2789, 3086, 15147**; cultivation, **826, 2597, 2645, 2955, 3588a, 5272, 5623, 5624, 6863, 6893, 6925, 7842, 9199, 9597, 10182, 12231, 12691, 12714, 14558, 14775, 14915, 15725, 16224, 16330**; cutting height, **1154, 3463, 7272, 7510, 11474, 14778, 15184**; deep coring, **9490, 10957, 10974**; England, **5624, 6527, 13005, 14468**; evaluation, **2172, 5681, 8586**; fertilization, **25, 254, 455, 823, 1053, 1342, 1539, 2271, 2597, 4261, 4855, 5249, 5394, 5726, 5880, 6347, 6856, 7072, 7840, 7841, 7894, 7983, 8007, 8129, 9056, 9236, 9311, 9387, 9456, 9567, 10765, 11277, 11383, 11390, 11431, 11440, 11472, 11515, 11518, 11575, 11590, 12258, 12401, 12550, 12788, 13368, 13694, 13966, 14679, 14964, 15108, 15190, 15232, 15349, 15419, 15723, 16157, 16330, 16427**; fertilizer evaluation, **4347, 4880, 10813, 10817, 10818, 10822, 10856, 14185**; history, **11520**; irrigation, **475, 1277, 2281, 2471, 2887, 3443, 4212, 4236, 4296, 4492, 4573, 5050, 5304, 7072, 7341, 7729, 7764, 8605, 9597, 9611, 9621, 9846, 10686, 10718, 11440, 11487, 11553, 12529, 13050, 14557, 14778, 15228, 15237, 15247, 15561, 15806, 16330**; Japan, **8963, 13002, 14951**; liming, **816, 11472**; mowing, **25, 299, 834, 1154, 1249, 2175, 2597, 3680, 3680a, 3753, 4236, 7072, 7329, 7740, 7741, 11934, 14778, 15775, 15965**; mowing frequency, **7740, 10075, 14778**; New Zealand, **8590, 15169, 15171, 15177, 15195, 15206, 15214, 15215, 15227, 15236, 15239, 15243, 15246, 15248, 15251, 15253, 15259, 15264, 15268, 15279, 15280, 15284, 15287, 15296, 15303, 15305, 15308, 15309, 15311, 15313, 15314, 15317, 15322, 15323**; nitrogen fertilization, **4840, 5917, 6574, 7787, 8002, 9784, 9827, 11440, 11473, 12220, 12368, 16236**; post-establishment, **291, 341, 4915, 12468, 12470, 14728**; problems, **11529, 15165, 15174, 15203, 15219, 15251**; spring, **827, 1071, 1177, 7905, 11515, 11612, 16035**; summer, **418, 832, 9350, 10825, 11494, 11535, 12330, 12331, 14780, 16036, 16427**; survey, **4622, 6505, 12664**; thatch control, **1104, 2165, 14671**; topdressing, **218, 341, 455, 483, 2263, 2805, 3443, 3567, 5303, 5965, 6280, 6282, 6940, 7165, 9174, 9687, 9829, 9834, 9925, 10182, 11470, 11515, 11765, 12468, 12550, 13982, 14249, 14250, 14251, 14770, 14778, 15170, 16160**; USA, **4569, 6644, 9248, 16335**; vertical mowing, **752, 773, 4236, 4300, 11560**; warm regions, **2491, 4571, 11416, 16010**; winter, **4280, 9288, 9302, 12522, 16037**

Green
cup placement, **3145, 12445**

Green
design, **2500, 2795, 3659a, 4703, 5251, 5266, 5289, 5833, 5868, 5883, 7489, 9276, 10720, 10933, 11501:** cultural considerations, **5289, 7049**

Green
diseases, **140, 1365, 6741, 12664, 15682, 15687**

Green
drainage, **306, 818, 3777, 4298, 5245, 5251, 5470, 5967, 6561, 6829, 7127, 7677, 7889, 7896, 9244, 9335, 9997, 10009, 10334, 14178, 14558, 14640, 14927, 15731, 15732, 16048, 16151:** drain types, **10919, 11090, 15230**; subsurface, **11500, 14848, 15733**; surface, **9115, 9982, 11500**

Green
equipment, **257, 15318**

Green
establishment, **1584, 1870, 2500, 3051, 3053, 3056, 3106, 3275, 3462, 4571, 4914, 6682, 7159, 7219, 8136, 8152, 9199, 9276, 11815, 12291, 12878, 14728, 15260, 15297, 15705:** seed versus vegetative, **1422, 3468, 6482, 15946**; seeding, **298, 2573, 4726, 7067, 7070, 9174, 10786, 11538, 13357**; sodding, **307, 7275, 12298, 12847, 14972, 15386, 15387, 15971**; stolonizing, **2800, 3052, 3054, 3055, 3710, 3712, 4306, 4914, 4915, 5308, 5964, 7274, 8814, 11593, 11676, 12135, 12289**; vegetative, **296, 300, 2573, 10833, 12148, 12360**

Green
fumigation, **1224, 5308, 9399**

Green
grain correction, **526, 6053, 6899**

Green
grasses used, **352, 1288, 2465, 3673a, 4574, 4726, 5162, 6905, 6917, 6919, 6982, 7456, 9417, 10011, 10725, 10837,**

11419, 11933, 12141, 12153, 13819: annual bluegrass, **4100, 9165, 9856, 11616, 12348**; bentgrass, **565, 4572, 10127, 10130, 11659**; bentgrass cultivar evaluation, **757, 3123, 12740**; bermudagrass, **7219, 10127, 10130, 11585, 11632**; evaluation, **1622, 4759, 5155, 5473, 10841, 11651, 11661, 16067, 16069, 16073**; warm season, **566, 962, 2123, 10783**

Green
home lawn, **3641a, 6908, 12349, 16171**

Green
insect control, **3292, 3293, 4056**

Green
irrigation system, **4552, 6809, 13677, 13678**

Green
leveling, **2307, 8589**

Green
mat, **3978, 3979, 3981**

Green
mowers, **4564, 7329, 15320**

Green
nutrient deficiencies, **2356, 7549**

Green
overseeding, **128, 2794, 3443, 3515, 3520, 4567, 5136, 5142, 7211, 7279, 11442, 13008, 16063:** grasses used, **2495, 2794, 4575, 5121**

Green
pests, **12664, 15347, 15908:** nematodes, **13796, 14821, 15926, 15927**

Green
problems, **1206, 2834, 4703, 6966, 7399, 9706, 11476, 11562, 12832, 13659, 14779, 15862, 16299**

Green
quality, **830, 7080, 10363, 14080, 14301**

Green
rebuilding, **11555, 12420, 16158**

Green
renovation, **568, 1072, 1099, 1281, 1285, 1538, 2955, 3701, 3702, 4067, 4812, 5050, 5106, 5308, 6394, 6839, 6880, 6942, 7142, 7278, 7663, 7664, 8028, 8518, 9376, 9954, 9983, 9998, 10282, 10720, 10815, 11555, 12292, 12847, 13002, 13536, 13944, 14638, 14917, 15189, 15245, 15498:** bentgrass conversion, **9983, 9984, 10778, 11552, 11633, 12160, 13759**; cost analysis, **5340, 5341, 15147**; New Zealand, **15223, 15224, 15291**; plugging, **980, 5375**

Green
renovation vs. rebuilding, **7066, 11776**

Green
soil amendment, **9386, 13892**; sand, **10087, 16042, 16044, 16045**

Green
soil characteristics, **4622, 6428, 6519**

Green
soil mix, **475, 1627, 2043, 2500, 2996, 5247, 5251, 5811, 5830, 5848, 5872, 5876, 5879, 5881, 6024, 6410, 6411, 6547, 7062, 7628, 7879, 7894, 8326, 8327, 8523, 8642, 9044, 9133, 9368, 9778, 9780, 9789, 9829, 9985, 9997, 10157, 10940, 10941, 10967, 11201, 11034, 11501, 11555, 12270, 12292, 12414, 13889, 13896, 13966, 13967, 14780, 15492, 15718, 15720, 15721, 16048, 16206:** analysis, **8206, 8207, 12664**; compaction effects, **8102, 9132**; evaluation, **2603, 2631, 3589a, 4551, 5805, 5894, 8130, 9776, 11899, 12412, 12606, 13418, 13683, 13684, 13905, 15096, 15112**; preparation, **11203, 15705**

Green
soil modification, **562, 2254, 4519, 5244, 5825, 5881, 7430, 9111, 9773, 9775, 12412, 13896, 16048:** Purr-wick, **9766, 10370, 10371, 13638, 14337**; sub-base, **6668, 12287, 14847**; USGA, **1401, 1627, 5861, 12373**

Green
soil porosity, **4623, 4625, 9043**

Green
soil reaction, **391, 9455**

Green
soil types, **3464, 8631**

Green
soil warming, **2607**

Green
traffic injury, **1352, 3145, 3148**

Green
warm season turfgrasses used, **7994, 10961, 15205:** bermudagrass, **3598, 3601, 3607, 3608, 8152, 13981**

Green
water management, **6004, 6841**

Green
weed control, **295, 3876, 4839, 6347, 6480, 6483, 7072, 7470, 8848, 10816, 11540, 11848, 14309, 15275, 15300:** chemical, **3237, 7209, 7369, 9513, 14783**

Green
weed problems, **1151, 3100, 6909, 6910, 6911**

Green
winter injury, **1348, 2106**

Green
winter overseeding, **2491, 2493, 5137, 7975, 9675, 9879, 10177, 11608, 11641, 11724:** annual bluegrass control, **2918, 2919:** method, **6524, 7053, 10179, 13425, 15462**

Green
winter protection, **2739, 7866:** covers, **2051, 2148, 12896, 15595**

Green
winter traffic effects, **609, 1337, 2125, 4978, 11006, 13839**

Green, alternate, **2780, 5308, 12354, 14525**

Green, alternate
winter, **1729, 2125**

Green earthworms, **1147**

Green, sand (see Sand green)

Green chairman, **5036, 5804, 6912, 10276**

Green committee, **4539, 8061, 10288**

Green Section, USGA (see United States Golf Association Green Section)

Grooving, **5978, 6940**

Grooving
thatch control effects, **2615, 5523**

Ground corn cobs
mulch, **13797**

Ground covers, **2060, 2501, 8181, 13328**

Ground covers
book, **7133**

Ground covers
establishment, **13030**

Ground covers
fertilization, **6027, 8181**

Ground covers
species used, **3857:** golf course, **5312**

Ground covers
uses, **4161:** roadside, **8559, 8560, 8561**

Ground covers
warm climate, **4948**

Ground ivy, **393, 15706**

Ground ivy
chemical control, **15696**

Ground limestone (see Limestone)

Ground mole (see Mole)

Ground pearls, **3291, 3294, 3623, 3624, 5253, 7141, 11559, 12796, 12826, 14405**

Ground pearls
chemical control, **1315, 1967, 2027, 5295, 14116, 15739, 15741, 15742, 15743, 15744**

Ground pearls
description, **5295, 8479, 12825, 15739**

Ground pearls
life history, **15739, 15741, 15743**

Grounds
culture, **2004, 5209:** book, **7542, 15817**

Groundsel, **3881**

Ground squirrels, **860**

Ground squirrels
chemical control, **4836**

Growing point (see Stem apex)

Growth, **2233, 2990, 3673, 3849, 3851, 4922, 5668, 11424, 12227, 12862**

Growth
cultural effects, **4766, 16352:** nutritional, **41, 4265, 7557, 8569, 9324**

Growth
environmental effects, **5667, 6457, 6824, 7471, 11038, 16352:** light, **3809, 5667, 6055, 6056, 16372**; soil, **6457, 15480**; temperature, **5667, 6055, 6056, 7557, 8058, 15500, 16372**; water, **8606**

Growth
factors affecting, **46, 47, 3363, 3550, 3575, 3849, 3851, 4720, 11381, 14784:** wetting agent, **5423**

Growth
morphology, **5673**

Growth
physiology, **2990, 4934, 7608**

Growth
process, **4423, 4924**

Growth
seasonal pattern, **2233**

Growth
tillering, **14831**

Growth habit
cultivar variation, **11232**

Growth habit
cultural effects, **14440, 15583**

Growth habit
environmental effects: light, **635, 6443, 11365, 15431**; temperature, **11365**

Growth habit
evaluation: double quadrate method, **11755**

Growth habit
species variation, **9633, 11366**

Growth inhibitor
on Kentucky bluegrass, **4015, 4017, 8693**

Growth pattern
book, **2244**

Growth pattern
seasonal variation, **4594**

Growth regulation, **4784, 10056, 12505**

Growth regulation
endogenous, **5317**

Growth regulator, **2684, 3570a, 3576a, 4449, 9868, 13340, 14705, 14706**

Growth regulator
on bermudagrass, **1871, 2027, 3576a, 4017, 8161, 10447**

Growth regulator
book, **2296**

Growth regulator
CCC (see CCC)

Growth regulator
chlorflurenol (see Chlorflurenol)

Growth regulator
on creeping bentgrass, **2343**

Growth regulator
effects, **7507, 11015**

Growth regulator
evaluation, **1055, 2100, 2592, 2671, 3020, 3567a, 3569a, 5047, 5358, 5360, 5574, 6079,**

6686, 7155, 8151, 8171, 8179, 8439, 8680, 8759, 8972, 9230, 9661, 12247, 15800: on cool season species, **10109**: on warm season species, **10109**

Growth regulator
maleic hydrazide (see Maleic hydrazide)

Growth regulator
Phosphon® (see Phosphon®)

Growth regulator
types, **1109, 12973, 12974**: evaluation, **1550, 1593, 4017, 4997, 5568**

Growth regulator
use, **3020, 8323, 9661, 12973**: roadside, **1055, 2671, 3033, 6072, 7155, 9949**

Grub, **17, 160, 547, 581, 651, 2016, 3291, 3623, 4836, 8588, 8607, 8878, 9362, 9363, 9708, 10908, 11344, 11496, 12542, 12657, 12658**

Grub
chemical control, **160, 573, 625, 1204, 1612, 2260, 2328, 2435, 3292, 4834, 4835, 5294, 5295, 5983, 7020, 7156, 7256, 7607, 8066, 8250, 8670, 8829, 8880, 8887, 8888, 9184, 9873, 10156, 10358, 10359, 10360, 11228, 13476, 13482, 15334, 15345, 15347, 15738, 15740, 15841, 15990**: DDT, **6803, 14638**: evaluation, **1548, 2172, 7255, 9395, 9396, 11482, 12171, 12181, 13468, 13489**; lead arsenate, **366, 2322, 9363, 9365, 9367, 9373, 9376, 9392, 12443, 15798, 16070**; state bulletin, **9384**

Grub
control, **1028, 1766, 7258, 10582, 10893**

Grub
description, **4779, 4834, 5294, 5295, 7256, 8066, 8478, 8479, 8607, 8829, 11228, 12315, 12657, 16070**

Grub
identification key, **12657**

Grub
injury symptoms, **6389, 7156, 7255, 7256, 8250, 8872, 10156, 15334**

Grub
life history, **8250, 9363, 12657**

Gryllotalpidae species (see Mole cricket)

Guanidine
nitrogen carrier, **16275**

Guano, Peruvian, **5634, 5636**

Guano, phosphatic, **5684**

Guanyl urea
nitrogen carrier, **16275**

Guard cells, **3379**

Gulf Italian ryegrass, **7309, 8079**

Gullaker Kentucky bluegrass, **9218**

Guttation fluid
chemical composition, **4304, 4305, 6565, 7033, 10319, 10323**

Guttation fluid
effects, **10323, 10565**: on disease development, **2607, 5403, 5408, 5410, 5411, 5413, 5418, 5420, 7621, 7625, 8357, 8515, 10315, 10317, 10319, 10323, 12912, 15901**

Guttation fluid
pesticide effects, **4304**

Guttation fluid
toxicity, **4303**

Gypsum, **816, 1019, 1029, 1803, 2149, 8181, 12572**

Gypsum
compaction effects, **8242**

Gypsum
irrigation water additive, **2309**

Gypsum
salinity effects, **7636**

Gypsum
soil amendment, **1056, 9970**

Gypsum
soil conditioner, **1182, 9970, 10531, 11163**

Gypsum
soil reaction effects, **11397**

Gypsum
soil structure effects, **9970**

Hair fescue, **3837, 8502**

Hairgrass, early, **9520**

Hairgrass, silvery, **9520**

Hairgrass, tufted, **9352, 9520**

Hairgrass, wavy, **4761, 9520, 15412**

Hairy chinch bug (see Chinch bug, hairy)

Hairy vetch
roadside use, **9129**

Haks-beard, **4733**

Hall's bermudagrass, **8229, 10461**

Handbook
cultivar description, **2200, 7307**

Handbook
disease control, **6138**

Handbook
economic poisons, **15613**

Handbook
golf course management, **1774**

Handbook
green committee chairman, **10276**

Handbook
herbicides, **1821**

Handbook
lawn culture, **2914**

Handbook
vegetative identification, **9342**

Handbook
weeds: California, **12672**

Handbook
weed control, **6138**

Haplocorm, **5666, 11359, 13618**

Hard fescue, **3776, 11965, 14471, 15412**

Hard fescue
cultivar evaluation, **8350, 13661, 13665**

Hardiness, heat (see Heat stress, hardiness)

Hardiness, low temperature (see Low temperature stress, hardiness)

Harvester ant, **5253**

Harvesting, sod (see Sod harvesting)

Hawkweed
chemical control, **2889, 8408, 12573**

Hawkweed, mouse ear, **3881**

Hay
mulch, **2667, 3794, 9952:** evaluation, **1479, 14432**; waterway, **12490**

Healall, **400, 4737, 15706**

Heat
nematode control, **13721**

Heat dissipation
turfgrass vs. artificial turf, **10415**

Heating cables (see Soil warming, electric)

Heating, sod (see Sod heating)

Heat stress, **1492, 2607, 2624, 2643**

Heat stress
effects: growth, **2624, 12889**; metabolic, **2566, 8778, 8785, 15435**

Heat stress
factors affecting, **75, 8659, 9569**

Heat stress
hardiness, **8659:** Kentucky bluegrass cultivar, **6449, 15436**; nitrogen effects, **1488, 1923, 12005**; phosphorus effects, **1688, 12005**; potassium effects, **1688, 1923, 3720, 12005**; species evaluation, **2607, 3720, 8659, 16368, 16369, 16372**

Heat stress
injury symptoms, **5942**

Heat stress
mechanisms, **2607, 2614, 2621, 2649**

Heat stress
protection, **2556, 2621, 2624, 2643**

Heat stress
seedling stem girdling, **3076**

Heat stress
selection program, **9009**

Heaving, frost (see Frost heaving)

Heavy metal
phytotoxicity, **7038, 8655**

Heidimij timothy, **7191, 8336, 8338, 8341**

Height of cut (see Cutting height)

Helicopter spraying, **5252, 12479**

Helicotylenchus (see Spiral nematode)

Helicotylenchus pseudorobustus, **5757, 14393**

Helicotylenchus species, **11669**

Helminthosporium blight, **4190**

Helminthosporium blight
tall fescue susceptibility: cultivar evaluation, **9097**

Helminthosporium cynodontis (see *Helminthosporium* leaf blotch)

Helminthosporium dictyoides (see also *Helminthosporium* blight), **2534, 2545, 2546**

Helminthosporium erythrospilum (see Red leaf spot)

Helminthosporium giganteum (see Zonate eyespot)

Helminthosporium leaf blotch, **5399, 5417**

Helminthosporium leaf blotch
bermudagrass susceptibility: cultivar evaluation, **14906**

Helminthosporium leaf blotch
chemical control, **1639, 1776, 3130, 4679, 5417, 6182, 16050, 16052**

Helminthosporium leaf blotch
symptoms, **5417, 9892**

Helminthosporium leaf spot, **185, 608, 658, 2037, 2107, 3251, 3252, 3255, 5399, 6159, 6324, 6834, 7884, 9756, 11560, 13566**

Helminthosporium leaf spot
chemical control, **997, 1700, 4168, 5417, 6114, 6174, 6177, 6179, 6748, 10789, 15674, 15781**: evaluation, **186, 1639, 3260, 3597a, 3650, 4054, 4167, 4205, 4206, 6601, 11101, 11104, 11319, 14996**

Helminthosporium leaf spot
cultural effects, **564, 1690, 11019, 12938**: cutting height, **6306, 11104, 16219**; nitrogen, **1690, 2545, 3803, 5652, 6306, 7814, 8699, 12716, 12736, 16219**; potassium **8047, 12268**

Helminthosporium leaf spot
development, **4167, 7623, 7626**

Helminthosporium leaf spot
environmental effects, **9892**: temperature, **7814, 11939**; water, **564, 3803, 5414, 12736, 12938**

Helminthosporium leaf spot
guttation effects, **5413, 5418, 7624**

Helminthosporium leaf spot
innoculation techniques, **7626**

Helminthosporium leaf spot
Kentucky bluegrass susceptibility: cultivar evaluation, **61, 186, 2100, 2673, 2704, 2706, 4515, 4534, 4538, 5509, 6451, 7550, 11941, 11959, 14562**

Helminthosporium leaf spot
red fescue susceptibility: cultivar evaluation, **2633**

Helminthosporium leaf spot
susceptible grasses, **5417, 11272**

Helminthosporium leaf spot
symptoms, **2100, 4167, 5086, 5087, 5089, 5417, 6160, 6161, 6164, 7154, 7624, 8095, 9892, 10789, 10791, 10853, 15674, 15678**

Helminthosporium netblotch (see *Helminthosporium* blight)

Helminthosporium sativum, **2545, 2546, 3062, 3820, 5052, 8992, 9744, 11044, 11045**

Helminthosporium sativum
chemical control, **3820, 15648**

Helminthosporium sativum
pathogenicity: Kentucky bluegrass, **11053**

Helminthosporium sativum
symptoms, **15648**

Helminthosporium sativum
taxonomic revision: *Helminthosporium sorokinianum,* **9814**

Helminthosporium sorokinianum (see also *Helminthosporium* leaf spot), **7816**

Helminthosporium species, **637, 2052, 2222, 4685, 5399, 5893, 6199, 8104, 8337, 13737, 13997, 14024, 15758**

Helminthosporium species
chemical control, **20, 22, 1208, 1487, 1590, 1776, 6216**: evaluation, **1545, 2757, 12167, 14814, 15672**

Helminthosporium species
on cool season turfgrasses, **7204, 15010**

Helminthosporium species
cultural control, **1781, 15646**

Helminthosporium species
cultural effects, **1700, 4031, 7855, 13824**

Helminthosporium species
environmental effects, **2545, 2546, 6212, 6213, 6739, 15648**

Helminthosporium species
innoculation procedures, **7121**

Helminthosporium species
isolate pathogenicity, **11272, 11273, 11274**

Helminthosporium species
Kentucky bluegrass susceptibility: cultivar evaluation, **2564**

Helminthosporium species
species susceptibility, **5893, 11271**

Helminthosporium species
symptoms, **9814, 15646**

Helminthosporium species
tall fescue susceptibility: cultivar evaluation, **9097**

Helminthosporium speciferium, **6203, 15136**

Helminthosporium stenospilum, **15688**

Helminthosporium tetramera
on Japanese lawngrass, **2755**

Helminthosporium triseptatum, **2534**

Helminthosporium vagans (see also Melting out), **5087, 11044, 11045, 11064**

Helminthosporium vagans
pathogenicity: Kentucky bluegrass, **11053**

Hemicellulose, **7306, 10227**

Hemicycliophora (see Sheath nematode)

Henbit, **536**

Henbit
chemical control, **1871, 8159**: evaluation, **1700, 3657a, 8161, 13010, 14309**

Heptachlor, **13776**

Heptachlor
grub control, **6071, 12178, 12181**

Heraf perennial ryegrass, **7191, 8336, 8338, 8350, 15414**

Herbicide, **1419, 1706, 1821, 2297, 3497, 3518, 4059, 4115, 4452, 4770, 5615, 5718, 5719, 5992, 7651, 7652, 9259, 9947, 10407, 10868, 11756, 11994, 13779, 14496, 15422, 15870, 16450**

Herbicide
activated charcoal effects, **3489, 7950, 8413, 8426, 13851, 13852**

Herbicide
annual bluegrass control, **4065, 5381, 8182, 15326**

Herbicide
application, **87, 1438, 1645, 1759, 1782, 3136, 3510, 3704a, 3868, 6481, 7369, 7570, 9653, 10171, 10392, 11845, 12253, 12280, 13056, 14733, 14918, 15502, 15974, 16390**: factors affecting, **3174, 5111, 15181**; low gallonage, **15421, 15423**; methods, **4884, 5221, 6818, 7537, 11013, 12385, 16492**; rate, **5221, 15181, 15975**; rate calculation, **6246, 6249, 11686**; safety, **1560, 5587, 8585, 9686, 10407, 11846, 14498**; timing, **71, 72, 4809, 7655, 11686, 12875, 13836, 14413, 14414, 14416, 15181**

Herbicide
bioassay evaluation, **10386**

Herbicide
broadleaf weed control, **1437, 2172, 4136, 4809, 8182, 8422, 15502**

Herbicide
carrier evaluation, **9538**

Herbicide
common names, **10619**

Herbicide
compatability, **6273, 13609**

Herbicide
contact, **4855, 9259, 9980, 13865**

Herbicide
crabgrass control, **71, 1522, 1759, 2468, 2469, 4132, 4136, 5502, 5844, 8695, 11304, 12278**

Herbicide
degradation, **8768, 10392, 13576, 13880, 15870**

Herbicide
effectiveness, **3518, 6077, 12930**: factors affecting, **71, 7093, 8702, 11013, 12462, 12463, 12548, 12760, 12807, 12875, 16390**

Herbicide
effects on, **4223, 4831, 6265, 6440, 10619, 14881**: rhizomes, **6440, 6448**; root growth, **3611, 3616, 3616a, 5533, 7078, 8031, 8161, 8708, 13972**; shoot growth, **5533, 6265, 8031, 8708**

Herbicide
evaluation, **2897, 9764, 11218, 14489, 14490**

Herbicide
fertilizer combination, **1522, 10222, 13958**

Herbicide
formulation, **1466, 1782, 2905, 5561, 8435, 14498, 15502**

Herbicide
growth inhibitor combination, **15975, 15976**

Herbicide
mixtures, **5184, 5226, 5526, 7909, 8462, 9876, 13815**

Herbicide
mode of action, **530, 2239, 3762, 4604, 4931, 6365, 7078, 7152, 9004, 11828, 13836, 14308, 14339**

Herbicide
movement, **4027, 6082, 8768**

Herbicide
nonselective, **3505, 3509, 3513, 3841, 10866, 10867**

Herbicide
oil effects, **2633, 7995, 7999, 8003**

Herbicide
persistance, **5380, 8168**

Herbicide
phytotoxicity, **3602a, 3604a, 3619a, 3625a, 5542, 12463**: on bentgrass, **5184, 5188, 5204, 8151, 8703, 8716, 9509**; on bermudagrass, **5065, 5225, 7999, 8022, 8161, 8178, 16514**; evaluation, **2617, 2633, 2673, 2898, 3610a, 3615a, 5226, 5381, 5383, 5557, 6448, 7972, 7999, 8031, 8168, 8852, 10107, 10418, 10445, 11049, 11051, 11052, 11256, 11760, 11824, 12576, 12735, 13972, 14084, 14826, 14839, 14863, 15140**; on Kentucky bluegrass, **5156, 5185, 5188, 5204**; ornamentals, **2239, 3704a**; on red fescue, **5156, 5185, 5188, 5204**; on ryegrass, **16228**; on St. Augustinegrass, **7999, 9885**; on warm season turfgrasses, **5225, 7969, 7999, 13971**; seedling evaluation, **9548**

Herbicide
postemergence evaluation, **3505, 3509, 3655, 4346, 4536, 8893, 9659, 12890**

Herbicide
preemergence, **3598a, 4536, 5488, 6369, 7078, 10630, 14912**: effects, **1377, 3527, 5065, 5532, 14838**; evaluation, **3505, 3509, 3655, 8671, 8706, 8721**; evaluation techniques, **3764, 3766**; phytotoxicity, **2583, 2603, 3614a, 3782, 6379, 14838**; seed germination effects, **3527, 8671, 8677**; selectivity, **1639, 2899, 3667a, 4011, 4153, 5098, 6096, 6098, 8412, 14952**

Herbicide
residual effects, **3598a, 3600a, 3602a, 8182, 8412, 10451, 13521**

Herbicide
selectivity, **1551, 1639, 2027, 2100, 2239, 2250, 2909, 3518, 3599a, 4812, 4841, 5504, 5844, 8695, 9177, 9653, 9980, 10393, 12890, 13865, 14498, 15870, 15974:** bermudagrass, **232, 4011, 13970**; cool season turfgrasses, **63, 65, 68, 71, 3616a, 3667a, 6098, 8701**; evaluation, **2100, 2931, 3599a, 8407, 8416, 8419, 8437, 8721, 12760, 15160**; Kentucky bluegrass seedlings, **64, 65, 68, 3762, 3763, 3768, 6098, 12760, 13803, 13804**; warm season turfgrasses, **33, 3508, 3511**; winter overseeding, **13561, 15326**

Herbicide
soil accumulation, **4931, 10389, 12211**

Herbicide
spray drift, **5751, 15870, 16390**

Herbicide
storage, **898, 10407**

Herbicide
surfactant effects, **2027, 4244, 10049, 10051, 10052, 10464, 13528**

Herbicide
synergism, **6273, 13858**

Herbicide
systemic, **7152**

Herbicide
toxicity, **3598a, 5225, 12463**

Herbicide
translocation, **9980, 10393, 12930, 13865**

Herbicide
types, **3500, 3892, 9483, 9980, 10393, 11726, 11828, 11949, 12671, 13865, 14733, 15870**

Herbicide
uptake, **4931, 12462, 14498, 15428, 15974**

Herbicide
use, **4771, 8402, 10300, 11577, 14226, 16510**

Herbicide
weed control, **9259, 9535, 11523, 12959, 15502, 16313:** recommendation, **3596a, 3601a, 3621a, 6362, 14711**

Heterodera species, **3397, 5014**

Heteronychus sanctaehelenae (see Black beetle)

Hexadecanol, **1549**

Hexadecanol
effects, **2282, 12744**

Hexa-octadecanol mixture
effects: establishment, **181, 2282**; water use rate, **2292**

Hexamine, **2725**

Hieracium pilosella (see Hawkweed)

Highland colonial bentgrass, **742, 757, 972, 987, 1685, 2129, 4878, 6870, 6879, 7309, 11661, 11665, 12698, 13216, 13238, 13462**

Highland colonial bentgrass
adaptation, **9213, 13223**

Highland colonial bentgrass
culture, **4592, 4894, 13223**

Highland colonial bentgrass
description, **7670, 12007, 13216, 13223, 13242**

Highland colonial bentgrass
evaluation, **9212, 9564, 10616, 10760, 10862, 11021, 11186, 11666, 14365**

Highland colonial bentgrass
in polystands, **1778**

Highland colonial bentgrass
taxonomy, **13458**

Highland colonial bentgrass
uses, **13223:** lawn, **13240, 13293, 13326**

Highland colonial bentgrass
weed invasion, **1700**

Highlight chewings fescue, **1700, 1789, 1974, 1998, 6294, 6315, 13780, 15414**

Highlight chewings fescue
adaptation, **1778, 2204**

Highlight chewings fescue
evaluation, **7284, 7508, 8338, 8341, 8350, 9219**

High temperature stress (see Heat stress)

Highway (see Roadside)

History, **5695, 10146**
cool season turfgrasses, **11812**

History
disease control, **2837, 4195, 5888**

History
equipment, **6796, 10270**

History
golf course culture, **11630, 16050**

History
sod production, **15388**

History
sod transplanting, **12449**

History
turf development, **5696, 10147, 10563**

History
turfgrass culture, **419, 6943, 7760, 7770, 12404**

Hockey field
culture, **256, 1031, 1177, 1187, 1249, 1682, 2186, 13787, 13788, 13789:** fall, **1004, 1046, 1100**; winter, **1191, 1398**

Hockey field
renovation, **1031, 1682**

Holcus lanatus (see also Velvetgrass), **483, 4768**

Holfior colonial bentgrass, **1700, 6294, 15414**

Holfior colonial bentgrass
description, **6315, 12007**

Holfior colonial bentgrass
evaluation, **7284, 8336, 8338, 8350, 10616, 10622, 10760**

Home lawn (see Lawn)

Hoof and horn meal, **1556, 5634**

Hoof and horn meal
evaluation, **5636, 5637, 5638, 15118**

Hoplolaimus (see Lance nematode)

Hoplolaimus galeatus, **5757**

Horay plantain, **4730**

Horizontal sub-coring, **2948**

Hormone (see Growth regulator)

Horse jumping
turf effects, **1592**

Horse racing track
culture, **1769, 1775, 1792, 1866**

Hose
dragging (see Dew, removal)

Hot water
nematode control, **1899**

Humidity (see Atmospheric water vapor)

Humus, **9310, 10429**

Hunsabelle Soma Kentucky bluegrass, **9218**

Hunting billbug
chemical control, **4240, 8827, 8894:** evaluation, **10983, 14668**

Hunting billbug
description, **8827, 10983**

Hunting billbug
injury symptoms, **8827**

Hurricane, flooding, **12337**

Hybridization
bluegrass, **3869, 4337, 4338**

Hybridization
Bromus species, **10685**

Hybridization
intergeneric, **8499, 8501, 8502, 12066**

Hybridization
intraspecific, **4340, 8499, 8501, 8502, 12020**

Hybridization
Kentucky bluegrass, **4340, 12014, 12015, 12017, 12018, 12020**

Hybridization
methods, **8494**

Hydathode, **16086**

Hydrated lime, **6790, 9380**

Hydraulic conductivity, **9269, 13906, 13907**

Hydraulic fluid
injury symptoms, **2673**

Hydrofertilizing
roadsides, **3686**

Hydrogen cyanide
toxicity: from *Marasmius oreades,* **5920, 5921**

Hydromulching, **1768, 1941, 2081, 2267, 3467, 3693, 10486, 10759, 14209**

Hydrophobic soils, **9493, 13033, 14068**

Hydrocotyle sibthorpioides (see Pennywort, lawn)

Hydrophobic soil
wetting agent effects, **9493, 9496**

Hydroplanting (see also Hydroseeding), **3883, 12481, 13413, 13567, 14209**

Hydroseeder, **6414**

Hydroseeding, **1768, 1880, 2081, 2267, 2765, 3300, 3686, 5933, 5935, 6968, 7432, 14209**

Hydroseeding
golf course, **2268**

Hydroseeding
green, **6942, 10786**

Hydroseeding
roadside, **1787, 2764, 3684, 3687, 4102, 5932, 9129**

Hydroxybenzonitride
weed control, **4068**

Hydroxydimethylarsine acid (see Cacodylic acid)

Hydroxymercurichlorophenols
brown patch control, **9702**

Hydroxymercurichlorophenols
dollar spot control, **8185**

Hygrophrous species (see also Fairy ring) **6508**

Hylephila phyleus (see Skipper, fiery)

Hyloconium squarrosum, **1092**

Hyperodes bonariensis (see Argentine stem weevil)

Hyperodes species (see Turfgrass weevil)

Hypnum cupressiforme, **1092, 1148, 7026, 8464, 14042**

Hypnum peat, **8786, 15552**

Hypnum species, **1646, 2033**

Hypochoeris radicata (see Catsear, potted)

Hypodermis, **13586**

Hypsoperine graminis, **2756, 9109, 13875**

IBDU, **2027, 2100, 4534, 4537, 4543, 13386**

IBDU
characteristics, **4543, 14958**

IBDU
evaluation, **4486, 5198, 8201, 15108, 16275**

Ice cover, **2558, 2622, 2643, 2689, 6226, 7894, 10836, 14855, 16053, 16141**

Ice cover
effects, **2624, 10802, 13965, 16140**

Ice cover
injury, **1781, 2562, 2567, 2577, 2578, 2586, 2591, 10390, 11844**

Ice cover
removal, **1355, 1543, 1553**

Ice cover
species tolerance, **2559, 2566, 2567, 2570, 2577, 2578, 2582, 2586, 2591, 11844**

Ice rink, **553, 668, 10836**

Identification, grass, **1911, 1926, 3823, 4008, 4009, 6911, 11368, 14545**

Identification, grass
cultivar: disc gel electrophoresis, **15910, 15911**; creeping bentgrass, **410, 2666**; Kentucky bluegrass, **241, 4339**; seedling characteristics, **11363**

Identification, grass
grass manual, **7795, 7797, 9843**

Identification, grass
grass seed manual, **15372**

Identification, grass
key, **5459, 7150, 13761:** fescues, **8105**

Identification, grass
leaf, **271**

Identification, grass
morphology, **2820**

Identification, grass
seed, **7778:** key, **11116**; *Poa* species, **7774, 11115**; ryegrass, **7645**

Identification, grass
seedling: Kentucky bluegrass cultivars, **11364**

Identification, grass
turfgrass species, **12203**

Identification, grass
vegetative, **421, 459, 495, 1524, 2524, 2666, 2993, 3707, 3920, 4006, 4595, 5315, 5459, 7472, 7509, 7823, 7957, 9121, 9516, 15410, 15411, 15412, 16426:** book, **15372**; handbook, **9342**; Kentucky bluegrass, **13290**; key, **2820, 3865, 3866, 6272, 6273, 7440, 7957, 8811, 12104, 12105, 14690**; manual, **11675**

Identification, grass
vegetative key: for bermudagrass cultivars, **14683**

Identification, grass
weed, **1636, 4730, 15453**

Identification, grass
Zoysia species: paper chromatography, **11230**

Identification, insect, **18059**

Illahee red fescue, **95, 785, 866, 972, 7309, 9152, 11165, 11186, 11222, 13445, 16323**

Illahee red fescue
evaluation, **4709, 8341, 8350, 9219**

Imbibition, seed, **12101**

Impact energy absorption
factors affecting, **11011**

Impervious soil layer (see Soil layering)

Inclined point quadrant
polystand composition, **11807**

Indiangrass, **76, 10001**

Indigofera neglecta
overseeding: grasses used, **3507**

Indoleacetic acid
effects, **2731, 5756, 13614**

3–Indolebutyric acid
effects, **8080**

Induction, floral (see Floral induction)

Industrial grounds
culture, **2427, 3095, 5210, 8513, 10878, 10879, 10880, 13748, 14046**

Industrial grounds
establishment, **9351**

Industrial grounds
grasses used, **6931, 9351**

Infiltration, soil, **115, 9062**

Infiltration, soil
effects of: compaction, **102, 5365, 5366, 6865, 7675, 11144, 14482, 15096, 15098, 15112, 16489**; coring, **2673, 2684, 10974, 15112**; cultivation, **3702, 5523, 10463**; fertilization, **102**; mulch, **122, 3701, 10162, 10165**; slope, **5211**; soil amendment, **10977, 14482, 15098, 15112**; soil layering, **12506**; soil mix, **2631, 2707, 12030, 12421, 15095, 15096, 15098, 15099**; soil texture, **102, 10163, 10899**; surface crusting, **10162, 10163**; water application rate, **6865**; wetting agent, **9496, 9505, 11214**

Infiltration, soil
evaluation, **14767**

Infiltration, soil
factors affecting, **5523, 6492, 6493, 7675, 9062, 10100, 10162, 10899, 15501**

Infiltrometer, **7188**

Inflorescence (see also Flowering), **7585, 9753, 14240**

Inflorescence
development, **3896, 3897, 3898, 5665, 11359**

Influorescence smut, **9895**

Infrared photography
turfgrass evaluation, **2114, 16173, 16175**

Initiation, floral (see Floral initiation)

Injectors, fertilizer, **10349, 12075, 12814**

Inoculum
crownvetch seed, **14722**

Inorganic fertilizer (see Nitrogen carrier, inorganic)

Inorganic mercury (see Mercury, inorganic)

Insect, **194, 196, 412, 656, 3222, 4610, 4611, 4612, 4613, 4614, 4780, 5253, 5763, 7028, 7257, 8222, 8252, 8473, 8871, 8891, 12183, 12317, 12429, 13051, 14034, 14333, 14334, 14602, 14632, 14666**

Insect
anatomy, **4918, 8875**

Insect
attractants, **8910**

Insect
classification, **1612, 4056**

Insect
description, **4603, 4835, 5715, 8479, 8875, 11864, 12315, 12433**

Insect
environmental effects, **11559, 13494, 13496**

Insect
factors affecting, **10101**

Insect
identification, **1569, 1570, 8872, 11344, 12094, 18059**

Insect
infestation: pyrethrum test, **8478, 8479**

Insect
lawn, **3617, 7398, 12026, 13630:** state bulletin, **8824, 8868, 8869, 12841, 13000, 13492, 14234**

Insect
repellents, **8910**

Insect
resistance, **10372**

Insect control, **16, 381, 1569, 1570, 3228, 3396, 3882, 5105, 5740, 7248, 7649, 8253, 9127, 9186, 9555, 10466, 10582, 11831, 12024, 12931, 13475, 13884, 14410, 15581, 15807, 16079**

Insect control
biological, **346, 5764, 8779, 8910, 13942**

Insect control
chemical, **1119, 2205, 3287, 4159, 4603, 4722, 4781, 5644, 6803, 7020, 7143, 7548, 7607, 8330, 8478, 8470, 8479, 8578, 8887, 8895, 8927, 9145, 9470, 9471, 10088, 10155, 10357, 10360, 10538, 11977, 12025, 12094, 12182, 12427, 12430, 12431, 13051, 13470, 13483, 13486, 13491, 13498, 13942, 14603, 15938:** chlordane, **6848, 13470**; evaluation, **4253, 4325**

Insect control
cultural, **5622, 8295, 8910, 13942**

Insect control
fairway, **5740, 15959**

Insect control
golf course, **8309, 12093, 13476**

Insect control
horomal, **8910**

Insect control
lawn, **1581, 5254, 6536, 8121, 12176, 13061, 14679:** state bulletin, **2061, 7831, 8906, 11285, 12093, 13495**

Insect control
microbial, **8910**

Insect control
principles, **3285, 8910, 10088, 10089**

Insect control
state bulletin, **8613, 9069, 14977**

Insect control
warm region, **9126, 11862**

Insecticide, **4612, 4613, 5105, 7445, 7649, 8471, 9186, 9471**

Insecticide
application, **2205, 6246, 9127:** cumulative effects, **12178, 14386**; methods, **5764, 9361, 10155, 10359**; safety precautions, **11864, 12315**

Insecticide
broad spectrum, **1835**

Insecticide
compatability, **12467, 13609, 13717**

Insecticide
insect control, **12431, 13469, 14410**

Insecticide
insect resistance, **10466**

Insecticide
mammalian toxicity, **1758, 1762, 4930, 8471**

Insecticide
persistence evaluation, **9556, 13472**

Insecticide
phytotoxicity evaluation, **12428**

Insecticide
shoot growth effects, **14386, 14390**

Insecticide
thatch effects, **12432, 12434**

Insecticide
toxicity, **3745, 8903, 10497**

Insecticide
types, **1284, 9185, 10497, 13406**

Insecticide
use, **11287, 11864**

Institutional grounds
culture, **1785, 2763, 6564, 12191, 14708**

Insulation, temperature (see Temperature, insulation)

Intergeneric hybridization (see Hybridization, intergeneric)

Intermediate wheatgrass, **7947, 9129**

International Turfgrass Research Conference, **6681, 14501**

Internode, **5646**

Internode
length: factors affecting, **5646, 11719, 16359**

Inversion, temperature (see Temperature, inversion)

Invert emulsions, **5751**

Ion exchange resins
use in fertilization, **12772, 12774**

Ionopus rebriceps, **3652a**

Ioxynil, **1797**

Ioxynil
phytotoxicity, **14084**

Ioxynil
selectivity, **33, 14893**

Ioxynil
weed control evaluation, **9465, 12539, 13636, 14084, 14894**

IPC® (see Propham)

Iron, **4055, 10963, 11433, 13785, 14075**

Iron
application rate, **2156**

Iron
availability, **2156, 7979, 12727**

Iron
carrier, **2156, 2776, 7978, 9803, 12727, 16379:** evaluation, **1488, 13522, 13560, 14069**

Iron
deficiency, **1029, 7979, 9637, 9742, 11567:** correction, **993, 1948, 7978, 7979, 9637, 9742, 9743, 11479, 11567, 15616**; symptoms (see Iron chlorosis)

Iron
effects on: desiccation, **13436, 14074, 14075**; root growth, **13436, 14075**; shoot growth, **4807, 10523, 13436, 14075**; turfgrass color, **12161, 14075**; turfgrass quality, **13436, 14075**

Iron
nutrition, **242, 2146, 2156, 11572, 14440, 14611, 14630**

Iron
soil relationships, **2146, 6863, 12727**

Iron
soil test, **4830**

Iron
uptake and translocation, **14612**

Iron chelates, **1546, 1755, 13522**

Iron chlorosis, **185, 1639, 5082, 11554, 11584, 12727**

Iron chlorosis
correction, **7978, 11581, 11628**

Iron chlorosis
factors affecting, **14440, 14611**

Iron chlorosis
symptoms, **242, 1948, 2156, 7978, 7979, 9267, 9637, 9698, 9742, 9743, 9803, 10963, 11628, 11786, 11790, 11826, 12727**

Iron chlorosis
warm season turfgrasses, **9459, 9469, 12267:** bahiagrass, **8036, 14067**

Iron sulfate (see Ferrous sulfate)

Irrigation, **547, 674, 747, 937, 2337, 3473, 3829, 4212, 7173, 7378, 7613, 7911, 8579, 15339, 15443**

Irrigation
costs, **1742, 7176, 12924, 12925, 13036, 14892, 16194, 16196**

Irrigation
effects, **4944, 7063, 7241, 9565, 11288, 12624, 12699, 14860, 15457**

Irrigation
effects on: chlorophyll content, **10076, 10173**; disease development, **600, 3786, 4317, 7425, 9565, 10079, 10108, 11524, 12085, 12721, 13824**;

Fusarium blight, **2541, 2542, 2543**; nutrients, **7128, 7182, 7825**; plant responses, **7425, 13623, 13824**; red fescue, **4653, 4657**; root growth, **6432, 7174, 10072, 10076, 10079, 10172, 15712**; shoot density, **10071, 10072, 10073, 10076, 12703, 12751**; shoot growth, **2516, 9967, 10072, 10076, 10105, 10172, 10722, 11012, 12521, 12840, 13425, 14303, 14890, 15712**; soil physical properties, **7850, 8812, 13425**; soil temperature, **12987, 13009**; temperature, **4944, 10415**; turfgrass community, **4657, 6490, 15456**; weed invasion, **835, 4653, 6867, 9565, 10064, 11135, 12721, 12751, 12840, 13824, 14984, 15456, 15458, 15467, 15475, 15482, 15701**: weed invasion—annual bluegrass, **7555, 14788**

Irrigation
fairway, **3438, 4812, 5283, 9563, 15457, 15757**

Irrigation
golf course, **713, 6301, 10010, 13808**

Irrigation
green, **7729, 9380, 13050**

Irrigation
lawn, **856, 1742, 2510, 6926, 11074**

Irrigation
principles, **5474, 8926, 10743, 13402, 14099**

Irrigation
program development, **6493, 10209**

Irrigation
research methods, **4257**

Irrigation
salinity problems, **3572a**

Irrigation
water quality, **1203, 2583, 3303, 6261, 6996, 7610, 8927, 8968, 10541, 10746, 12262, 12394, 12565, 12721, 12737, 13926, 13927, 15185, 15443, 15788, 15881, 15882, 16500**

Irrigation
water source, **1203, 2301, 4455, 7341, 7343, 8134, 9284, 9736, 10529, 10675, 10757, 10758, 10772, 10914, 10917, 11869, 12648, 12721, 12920, 14377, 14379, 14504, 15371, 15714, 15948, 16163**: sewage effluent, **8751, 8968, 10544, 12086, 16090**

Irrigation
water temperature, **1700, 2681, 4318, 10826, 12987, 14089**

Irrigation practices **149, 604, 638, 975, 1019, 1026, 1040, 1050, 1189, 1286, 1293, 1295, 1296, 1305, 1639, 1643, 1947, 1967, 2147, 2515, 2516, 2954, 3088, 3413, 3991, 4476, 4990, 5153, 5476, 5477, 5489, 5798, 6531, 6840, 6856, 6939, 7063, 7166, 7171, 7174, 7175, 7176, 7389, 7613, 7731, 7733, 7844, 8178, 8281, 8840, 8927, 9906, 9958, 10065, 10069, 10167, 10205, 10327, 10518, 10672, 10673, 10718, 10742, 10744, 10757, 10931, 10960, 11062, 11144, 11373, 11407, 11550, 11570, 12813, 12945, 13408, 13777, 13893, 14280, 14287, 14289, 14377, 14378, 14963, 15185, 15464, 15467, 15472, 15475, 15558, 15569, 15597, 15821, 15983, 16001, 16003, 16017, 16077, 16196**

Irrigation practices
application methods, **5064, 15566**

Irrigation practices
application rate, **1700, 4566, 4946, 7173, 8278, 8926, 10204, 10205, 10945, 10960, 11135, 11139, 13938, 14099, 15507, 15510, 15523, 15529, 15547, 15563, 15846**

Irrigation practices
application uniformity, **10205, 10206, 10207, 12125, 12126, 13511, 14099, 15368, 15443, 15569**: assessment methods, **10206, 10207**

Irrigation practices
evaluation, **2678, 14890**

Irrigation practices
factors affecting, **7986, 10203, 10977, 12459, 15465, 15578**: cultural, **6973, 7341, 13036, 14180, 14892, 15465, 15510, 15558, 15563, 16409**; environmental, **14180, 15465, 15503a, 15507, 15510, 15523**; soil, **5069, 7172, 7179, 15523**

Irrigation practices
fairway, **4100, 11409, 14278, 15959, 16225**

Irrigation practices
frequency, **4946, 6522, 7167, 7168, 7169, 7172, 7173, 8178, 10034, 10522, 10687, 10945, 10965, 15176, 15507, 15510, 15523, 15529, 15549, 16003**: effects, **10101, 11059, 14819, 14860**; evapotranspiration effects, **9905, 12275, 12276, 14488**; factors affecting, **4566, 8278, 10078, 12459, 12586, 13938, 15472, 15503, 15563**; pan evaporation relationship, **8531, 8532**; plant responses, **149, 10071, 10072, 10076, 10105, 10172, 10173, 10482, 13624, 13625**; soil texture effects, **7167, 7168, 7173**; water use rate effects, **2677, 4246, 7181, 10172, 13623, 13624, 16085**

Irrigation practices
golf course, **345, 1838, 4822, 5797, 5963, 6257, 6958, 9192, 10828, 10839, 11136, 11594, 12333, 12346, 14171, 15466, 15805, 16196**

Irrigation practices
green, **1277, 4296, 4573, 5050, 10686, 11553, 15800**

Irrigation practices
quantity applied, **149, 2516, 4317, 4476, 4566, 4946, 5069, 6867, 7044, 7167, 7168, 7169, 7172, 8178, 8275, 10184,**

10204, 10327, 10687, 10945, 11135, 11139, 11485, 12721, 14280, 14557, 14788, 15176, 15228, 15503a, 15507, 15510, 15523, 15529, 15547, 15549, 15555, 15563, 15712, 15713, 16003: measurement techniques, **10202**

Irrigation practices
sports field, **7591, 14287**

Irrigation practices
timing, **1277, 4317, 4992, 7172, 8278, 9846, 10034, 10204, 11485, 12721, 13020, 14557, 15176, 15228, 15247, 15846:** tensiometer, **10208, 10212, 10943, 10958, 10972, 10976, 12188, 12584**

Irrigation system, **1019, 1501, 2459, 2532, 3171, 3218, 3314, 3409, 3848, 4617, 5477, 6970, 7065, 7944, 8134, 9037, 10673, 13898, 14104, 14171, 15547, 15902, 15903, 15904**

Irrigation system
automatic, **147, 1294, 1526, 1591, 1622, 1967, 1989, 2809, 3090, 3097, 3098, 3407, 3642a, 3643a, 3853, 3877, 4004, 4058, 4246, 4932, 5029, 5222, 5224, 5376, 5980, 6095, 6320, 7305, 7343, 7845, 7900, 8577, 8580, 8772, 9822, 9900, 9902, 9939, 10364, 10686, 10757, 12523, 12541, 12749, 12764, 12945, 13018, 13020, 13680, 13807, 14105, 14106, 14284, 14524, 14763, 15371, 15443, 15444, 15538, 15576, 15905, 16146, 16229, 16231, 16233, 16234:** advantages, **6992, 7847, 12524, 14284, 15900**; maintenance, **8581, 8772, 10746**; problems, **8580, 15042**

Irrigation system
book, **2180, 11898, 15430, 16214**

Irrigation system
bowling green, **3704**

Irrigation system
components, **8, 3407, 3742**

Irrigation system
controls, **1967, 2454, 3381, 8223, 9037, 12471, 12895, 14106, 15900:** electrical, **1748, 12523, 13680, 13681, 16146**; hydraulic, **1748, 12523, 13680**; installation, **5645, 12895**; types, **8223, 11251, 12895, 13020**

Irrigation system
costs, **6, 7, 1526, 1918, 3087, 7502, 7503, 10742, 16193**

Irrigation system
design, **6, 7, 147, 580, 1526, 1783, 3088, 3409, 3412, 3613, 3627a, 3703, 3746, 3747, 3829, 4002, 4617, 5029, 5062, 5069, 5222, 5267, 5870, 5871, 6522, 6620, 6621, 7173, 7305, 7382, 7781, 7843, 7844, 7848, 7849, 7949, 8580, 8971, 9822, 9854, 10078, 10652, 10927, 11827, 11975, 12555, 12648, 12946, 13018, 13047, 13058, 14258, 14280, 14281, 14282, 14287, 14504, 14763, 14793, 15342, 15555, 15576, 15899, 15948, 15995, 16163, 16229:** book, **2180, 14412, 15430**; golf course, **7175, 10528, 14994**; green, **6809, 7175, 7342, 7343, 11275, 13677**; problems, **10204, 15042**; professional, **6619, 12598, 13808**; sprinklers, **1844, 13050**

Irrigation system
distribution lines, **752, 1213, 5870, 6994, 7898, 10547, 11827, 12056, 12553, 12917, 14280, 14281, 14378, 16229:** asbestos-cement pipe, **5040, 7688**; cost, **14279, 14280**; installation, **8611, 9266, 9901**; plastic pipe, **3333, 3576a, 9266, 12917**; polyethylene pipe, **5292, 8611**; P.V.C. pipe, **5292, 12917, 14763, 15341**; selection, **3142, 3853, 12036**; types, **6426, 7843, 10653, 12036, 12913, 14329, 15080**

Irrigation system
economics, **1663, 1664, 16191, 16194**

Irrigation system
equipment, **8579, 10203**

Irrigation system
fertilizer injection, **1549, 2507, 2832, 3528, 3600, 6695, 7676, 7825, 10204, 10205, 10348, 10349, 11074, 12076, 12512, 14070, 16109, 16209:** equipment, **5376, 10788, 12076**; methods, **6267, 7632, 10788, 12076**

Irrigation system
golf course, **345, 1743, 1917, 1918, 3098, 3171, 3877, 4822, 4940, 6257, 7949, 8812, 9728, 9871, 12918, 13678, 15714**

Irrigation system
installation, **10, 1725, 5292, 5645, 5870, 6621, 7305, 7707, 7849, 7949, 8580, 10652, 10910, 10917, 10927, 11827, 14115, 14287, 14504, 14763, 15148, 15371, 15899, 16163, 16234:** cost, **2831, 7900, 10757, 10917, 16195**; golf course, **10434, 10528, 16138**; specifications, **1632, 1712, 2044**

Irrigation system
lawn, **3830, 4999, 5059, 5293, 11893, 15538, 15566**

Irrigation system
maintenance, **4946, 5292, 12914, 13047, 13590, 13591**

Irrigation system
manual, **3407, 3409, 3853, 4004, 5063, 5980, 7900, 9939, 10757, 12995**

Irrigation system
manual vs. automatic: cost analysis, **5270, 11091**

Irrigation system
moisture-sensing devices, **10202, 10204, 10205, 10209, 12585, 12843, 13622:** tensiometer, **9498, 10184, 10208, 10211, 10212, 10943, 10950, 10954, 10955, 10958, 10972, 10976, 10977, 12188, 12586, 12587, 12630, 15569**

Irrigation system
new developments, **14524, 15444**

Irrigation system
operating cost, **7845, 9939, 14284, 16195**

Irrigation system
operating pressure, **3408, 3411, 12553, 13050, 14329, 14377, 15343, 15344**

Irrigation system
operation, **3829, 6488, 7844, 8580, 10931, 13590, 13591:** cost, **2831, 7900, 16193**

Irrigation system
oscillating spray line, **14378**

Irrigation system
problems, **10084, 12554, 12555**

Irrigation system
programming, **8772**

Irrigation system
protective devices, **3835, 8621**

Irrigation system
pump, **3382, 5222, 5870, 7502, 7503, 7843, 8307, 8971, 10538, 12076, 14994, 15371, 16234:** power source, **7502, 8240, 15371**

Irrigation system
purchasing, **2412, 12944**

Irrigation system
quick coupling, **9939, 14258**

Irrigation system
race track, **1769, 5376**

Irrigation system
selection, **6621, 8221, 12946, 13021**

Irrigation system
semi-automatic, **2396, 3087, 3406, 3407, 3853, 9939, 10476, 10757**

Irrigation system
sod production, **1919, 5062, 6243**

Irrigation system
specifications, **4003, 4004, 8222**

Irrigation system
sports field, **7591**

Irrigation system
sprinkler, **3829, 4257, 5213, 6622**

Irrigation system
sprinkler head: selection, **6522, 10652, 14106, 14377, 14763, 15343, 15443, 16233**; spacing, **1844, 3410, 3829, 7382, 7781, 14317**; types, **1788, 7314, 7843, 9854, 12835**

Irrigation system
sub-irrigation, **1605, 2722, 2881, 3613, 4552, 5304, 7942, 14286, 14287, 15576**

Irrigation system
terminology, **1898, 3407, 9986**

Irrigation system
traveling sprinklers, **7175, 7875, 14378**

Irrigation system
trends, **8771, 14105**

Irrigation system
types, **8, 2406, 2831, 3306, 3407, 3827, 4036, 4100, 4257, 5060, 5292, 7342, 7502, 7503, 7521, 7843, 7898, 9038, 9854, 10023, 10210, 11671, 12541, 12813, 13018, 13019, 13677, 13678, 13679, 14379, 15555, 16195**

Irrigation system
use, **1698, 5871, 10686, 10757, 12813, 13384**

Irrigation system
valves: types, **7843, 13020**

Irrigation system
water distribution, **3408, 3411, 3829, 3835, 4246, 7173**

Irrigation system
winter drainage, **3383, 9079, 15443, 16233**

Isobutyldiene, **8198**

o-isopropoxyphenyl methylcarbamate (see Propoxur)

Isopropyl carbavilate (see Propham)

Italian ryegrass, **2342, 9332, 11368, 11767, 11771**

Italian ryegrass
adaptation, **2253, 3553**

Italian ryegrass
breeding, **3415, 3553**

Italian ryegrass
chemical control, **5328, 10530**

Italian ryegrass
culture, **5675, 6181, 6307:** nutrition, **6307, 8263, 8264, 8265, 8575**

Italian ryegrass
description, **1606, 3198, 3553, 3908, 3937, 4009, 5675, 6289, 7118, 7947, 12859, 12884, 13466**

Italian ryegrass
diseases, **2348, 8583:** *Pythium* blight, **6116, 6181, 6201**

Italian ryegrass
polystand compatibility, **6307, 7011**

Italian ryegrass
seed, **11965, 13453, 15661, 15874**

Italian ryegrass
uses, **3553, 6289, 7291**

Italian ryegrass-tall fescue hybrid
breeding, **3415, 3426, 3428, 3430, 3433, 3434, 3435**

Italian ryegrass-tall fescue hybrid
chemical composition, **3430, 3434, 3618**

Jamestown chewings fescue, **1547, 2612, 6294, 9430, 15156**

Japanese beetle, **224, 573, 607, 609, 612, 657, 3191, 7156, 7258, 9359, 11559, 13494, 13496**

Japanese beetle
biological control, **607, 610, 715, 753, 3192, 3887, 4001, 6548, 13483, 15783**

Japanese beetle
chemical control, **4158, 5662, 9354, 9361, 10358, 10360, 11228, 13477, 13488, 13491:** DDT, **10007, 12178, 13475**;

evaluation, **5985, 5986, 5987, 7157, 7158, 8587, 10480, 11482, 12168, 12173, 12174, 12178, 13469, 13472, 13473**; state bulletin, **9360**

Japanese beetle
control, **346, 645, 770, 844, 1028, 1570, 1766, 5988, 5989, 7441, 10582**

Japanese beetle
description, **5986, 6074, 7256, 12317**

Japanese beetle
dissemination, **412, 601**

Japanese beetle
distribution, **12175, 12178**

Japanese beetle
effects of: soil reaction, **12170, 15760**

Japanese beetle
quarantine: for sod production, **9721**

Japanese clover
chemical control, **6667**

Japanese lawngrass, **695, 782, 875, 2755, 6142, 9461, 16118, 16263**

Javagrass, **12133**

Johnsongrass, **3553, 3645**

Johnsongrass, weed
chemical control, **1551, 7266, 8182**

Johnsongrass, weed
control, **1025, 7303**

Johnsongrass, weed
cultural control, **7266**

June beetle, **7258, 9749**

June beetle
chemical control, **1152, 12178, 12181**

June beetle, Southern, **667, 719**

Junegrass (see Kentucky bluegrass)

Jute net
ditch bottom stabilization, **1479**

Jute net mulch, **2579, 2593, 2667, 2975, 5108, 6010**

Jute net mulch
erosion control, **2216, 3265, 6716**

Jute net mulch
evaluation, **1479, 6515, 8834**

Kaolinite clay, **2470**

Karathane® (see Dinocap)

Kenblue Kentucky bluegrass, **2612, 3431, 6294, 6298, 6315, 10633, 16097, 16179**

Kenblue Kentucky bluegrass
evaluation, **6330, 10626, 11186, 11325, 11329, 14813**

Kenblue Kentucky bluegrass
nitrogen fertilization, **14577, 14578**

Kenmont tall fescue, **8647**

Kentucky bluegrass, **76, 3497, 3775, 4049, 4460, 9521, 9623, 10233, 11666, 11767, 11771, 13139, 13267, 13773, 14471, 15432**

Kentucky bluegrass
adaptation, **310, 2100, 3387, 3553, 3716, 3928, 4384, 4601, 5228, 5483, 6314, 11151, 12328, 12827, 12828, 13123, 13316, 14003, 15054, 16007, 16326, 16366:** drought, **6306, 6449, 15906, 16178**; ice cover tolerance, **2559, 2852**; light, **10058, 16168**; shade, **2204, 2569, 2580, 2600, 2640**; soil, **867, 7529**; temperature, **2570, 2706, 6306, 8979, 8980, 15435, 15436**; water, **13308**

Kentucky bluegrass
blend, **2583, 2603, 6296, 6313, 6314, 6330:** evaluation, **2632, 2658, 2704, 6328, 6329, 7749, 10626, 11327, 11329**; sod strength evaluation, **2630, 2672**

Kentucky bluegrass
breeding, **62, 2208, 2852, 3374, 3418, 3420, 3427, 3429, 3431, 3432, 3533, 3553, 4553, 6293, 7314, 10427, 11322, 12014, 12015, 12113, 12652, 12654, 14829, 15912:** apomixis, **83, 5182, 7281, 16096**; hybridization, **12015, 12018, 12019, 12020**

Kentucky bluegrass
carbohydrate reserves, **3330, 7917, 12453:** cultivar evaluation, **15434, 15436, 15438, 16436**

Kentucky bluegrass
chemical composition, **58, 3330, 6041, 7214, 10061, 12110, 14452, 15434, 15705, 15912**

Kentucky bluegrass
cultivars, **2129, 2571, 2618, 3659, 6290, 6295, 6302, 6585, 8319, 9340, 9657, 10614, 11006, 11320, 11332, 12007, 13160, 13224, 13232, 13238, 13252, 13267, 13320, 13359, 13366, 13823, 13848, 14970, 15436, 15438:** compensation points, **15435, 15436, 15438**; description, **2518, 3656, 5273, 6316, 10635, 13367, 13376, 13725**; development, **4233, 8320, 11123, 11124, 11325**; evaluation, **61, 1471, 1473, 1489, 1639, 1967, 2027, 2100, 2564, 2566, 2574, 2575, 2576, 2583, 2584, 2589, 2592, 2598, 2603, 2616, 2617, 2631, 2632, 2650, 2672, 2673, 2684, 2698, 2704, 2706, 2707, 3421, 3425, 3432, 3672, 3673, 4447, 4450, 4538, 4644, 4646, 4672, 5001, 5007, 5225, 5226, 5313, 5320, 5766, 5776, 5781, 5916, 6304, 6306, 6310, 6317, 6320, 6328, 6330, 6626, 6712, 6879, 7191, 7287, 7315, 7316, 7317, 7748, 7836, 8294, 8317, 8321, 8336, 8338, 8341, 8350, 8685, 8691, 9218, 9343, 10376, 10621, 10622, 10626, 10631, 11186, 11323, 11325, 11329, 11334, 11335, 11631, 11959, 11990, 12087, 13437, 13661, 13662, 13663, 13665, 13822, 13852, 13854, 13863, 14103, 14561, 14562, 14813, 14880, 15390, 16179, 16183, 16412**; identifi-

cation, **241, 4339, 15910, 15911**; selection, **3672, 10842**

Kentucky bluegrass
culture, **58, 3928, 4155, 4470, 4578, 7767, 8679, 8692, 8935, 9666, 9968, 10054, 13078, 13123, 13366, 13375:** cutting height, **2077, 4636, 4644, 5062, 5077, 6317, 6717, 6782, 7496, 8664, 8675, 8689, 8692, 9305, 9666, 12632**; evaluation, **7495, 13319, 14459**; fertilization, **58, 1962, 3307, 3590a, 3591**a, **4784, 5669, 7718, 8692, 10201, 14199**; golf course, **4349, 6327**; mowing frequency, **3330, 6781, 6783, 7501, 8664, 8689**; nitrogen fertilization, **2064, 2631, 2673, 3721, 4110, 4644, 5127, 5183, 5580, 6317, 6717, 7496, 9671, 12632**; phosphorus fertilization, **675, 8712, 8713**; winter overseeding, **10455**

Kentucky bluegrass
description, **1387, 2566, 3553, 3928, 4008, 5315, 5646, 5671, 7947, 8752, 11359, 12828, 13283, 13316, 13366, 14735, 15410, 16326:** chromosome number, **3373, 12113, 12654**; cytology, **62, 2258, 3374, 3837, 8913, 11337, 12652**; flowering, **2258, 5669, 9592, 9593, 12014, 12089**; leaf, **5669, 16435**; rhizomes, **58, 1905, 3330, 3931, 5669, 5950, 9622, 9633, 11015, 11016, 11017, 11018, 13035, 13327**; root growth, **3330, 5669, 7826, 11783**; sod formation, **9627**; tillering, **9633, 11015, 11020, 11359, 16435**

Kentucky bluegrass
development, **5669, 11339**

Kentucky bluegrass
diseases, **184, 2064, 3242, 5919, 5941, 7696, 13755, 15672:** brown patch, **10073**; dollar spot, cultivar evaluation, **4053, 4201, 6330**; flag smut, **7806, 13723**; *Fusarium* blight, **4192, 15030**; *Fusarium* patch, **12832**; *Helminthosporium* leaf spot, **2017, 2107, 3671, 4167, 4168, 4205, 4206, 5087, 9756, 10791, 11941,** cultivar evaluation, **61, 186, 1776, 2100, 2673, 2704, 2706, 4515, 4534, 5509, 6306, 6309, 6330, 6457, 7192, 8336, 10622, 10626, 11323, 13725, 13822, 14562**; *Helminthosporium* species, cultivar evaluation, **2545, 2546, 2566, 9226, 11045**; melting out, **5373, 6317, 7194, 7205, 7345, 9753, 15648,** cultivar evaluation, **6290, 6328, 11019, 14562;** powdery mildew, **7345, 12016,** cultivar evaluation, **61, 13725, 14005**; *Pythium* blight, cultivar evaluation, **6207**; rust, **3243, 3259, 3671, 3705, 7345, 7346, 7364, 14955,** cultivar evaluation, **3387, 3671, 6290**; *Septoria* leaf spot, cultivar evaluation, **1473, 6446, 13725**; silver top, **7914, 14233**; stripe smut, **3671, 4714, 5509, 6317, 6453, 7195, 7345, 7806, 7807, 7810, 9086, 9094, 9762, 11940, 13723, 15670,** cultivar evaluation, **6290, 6306, 6328, 6330, 6450, 7193, 7196, 7202, 10622, 10626, 11323**; *Typhula* blight, **15030**

Kentucky bluegrass
environmental effects, **3329, 5646, 16326:** light, **5674, 7496, 8657**; moisture, **3330, 3936, 6449**; temperature, **2027, 2077, 3330, 3936, 6449, 7496, 8657, 16430**

Kentucky bluegrass
establishment: cultivar evaluation, **2560, 2566, 2630, 4632, 6306, 13663**; seeding rate, **10082**

Kentucky bluegrass
fungus-nematode complex, **12021**

Kentucky bluegrass
herbicide selectivity, **3653a, 3762, 3763, 3768, 6098, 8695, 13430, 13773, 13803, 13804**

Kentucky bluegrass
history, **3716, 13143, 13316, 13366**

Kentucky bluegrass
identification: vegetative, **11363, 13290**

Kentucky bluegrass
lawn culture: state bulletin, **12972**

Kentucky bluegrass
nutrition requirements, **4783, 12102**

Kentucky bluegrass
origin, **13286, 13316**

Kentucky bluegrass
pests, **1425, 7914, 8549:** nematodes, **7801, 12042, 12060, 14052, 14458**; root knot nematode, **1641, 6444**; sod webworm, **2407, 3432, 3436, 3665, 11945**

Kentucky bluegrass
polystands, **2523**

Kentucky bluegrass
propagation: vegetative, **14078, 15384, 15394, 15398, 15399, 15400**

Kentucky bluegrass
reproduction, **7283, 11357**

Kentucky bluegrass
rhizome growth, **1489, 3772, 4444, 5953, 5954, 9627:** cultivar evaluation, **9624, 11020**

Kentucky bluegrass
root growth, **624, 5538, 7312, 14134, 14161**

Kentucky bluegrass
seed, **3668a, 11964, 13283:** development, **202, 3214**; fungal isolation, **4049**

Kentucky bluegrass
seed germination, **4272, 14757:** environmental effects, **2473, 3327, 7683**; factors affecting, **3327, 4925**

Kentucky bluegrass
seed production, **624, 1105,**

1515, 2258, 3331, 12120, 13283, 14459

Kentucky bluegrass selections: evaluation, **6319, 6320, 7321, 7322, 13958, 14637**

Kentucky bluegrass shoot density: cultivar evaluation, **6290, 11323, 12758, 14103, 16436**

Kentucky bluegrass shoot growth: cultivar evaluation, **15438**

Kentucky bluegrass sod strength: cultivar evaluation, **2630, 2672**

Kentucky bluegrass transplant rooting, **2673**

Kentucky bluegrass uses, **3553, 3672, 5315, 9251, 15053:** fairway, **3672, 4349, 4459, 4470, 4482, 7144, 7910, 12388, 12552**; lawn, **6290, 13931**

Kentucky bluegrass water use rate, **14961**

Kentucky bluegrass wear tolerance: cultivar evaluation, **3117, 16183**

Kentucky bluegrass weed control, **4157, 6107, 13512**

Kentucky bluegrass weed invasion: cultivar evaluation, **11959**; cultural factors affecting, **6308, 11323, 13804**

Kentucky **31** tall fescue, **4, 3618, 5226, 5768, 6862, 6875, 7309, 8647, 11165, 11186, 14356**

Kentucky **31** tall fescue adaptation, **1686, 5314, 8717,** 8718, **12007, 13555**

Kentucky **31** tall fescue culture, **8715:** nitrogen fertilization, **14577, 14578, 15694**; sports field, **12210**

Kentucky **31** tall fescue establishment, **3655, 7670, 8173**

Kentucky **31** tall fescue evaluation, **7670, 8791, 14349**

Kentucky **31** tall fescue uses, **2092, 2966, 8717**

Kentucky **31** tall fescue, weed chemical control, **2903, 3657**

Kenwell tall fescue, **3426, 3618**

Kerb® annual bluegrass control, **3525, 4016, 8027, 8031, 8173, 9138, 12502:** in bermudagrass, **3521, 3522**

Kerb® species selectivity, **3521, 3525, 8173, 13970**

Kernwood velvet bentgrass, **724, 7273, 7309, 10709, 10711, 10760, 11661, 11665, 11666, 11778, 12865**

Kerosene grub control, **15347**

Kerosene injury symptoms, **2673**

Kerosene sod webworm control, **15087**

Kerosene weed control, **623, 7293**

Khaki weed chemical control, **7263**

Kikuyugrass, **15852**

Kikuyugrass adaptation, **5305**

Kikuyugrass chemical control, **1493, 7238, 10975, 16402, 16447:** evaluation, **6250, 10949, 10975, 16328, 16334, 16424**; siduron, **10021, 15304**

Kikuyugrass culture, **7220, 16447:** flowering control evaluation, **6610, 16424**

Kikuyugrass description, **5305, 6418, 16328, 16363, 16447**

Kikuyugrass use: green, **15205**

Kikuyugrass, weed, **193**

Kikuyugrass, weed control, **6251**

Kikuyugrass, weed cultural control, **16447**

Kingstown velvet bentgrass, **1609, 1639, 2612, 6294, 10616, 10760, 12007, 13838, 15156**

Kingstown velvet bentgrass adaptation, **6315, 8231**

Kingstown velvet bentgrass culture, **8231**

King timothy, **1789, 8343**

King timothy evaluation, **7191, 8336, 8338, 8341**

Kinins, **12973, 14120**

Knavel, **486**

Knitting (see Transplant rooting, sod)

Knotweed, **451, 5546**

Knotweed chemical control, **1274, 1343, 1700, 2027, 3697a, 7090, 7716:** dicamba, **4524, 7655, 13024, 16469**; evaluation, **1700, 4646, 4675, 5982, 6331, 8435, 12357, 13024, 13864**

Knotweed, prostrate, **4742**

Koban® compatibility, **3594a**

Koban® dollar spot control, **2787**

Koban® *Pythium* blight control, **6116, 6201, 9933, 15135, 15582**

Korean lawngrass (see Japanese lawngrass)

Korean lespedeza, **9129**

Korean velvetgrass (see Mascarenegrass)

Korlan® (see Ronnel)

Krilium, **957, 973, 1013, 1029**

Krilium evaluation, **2303, 7520**

Krilium
soil conditioner, **957, 973, 1013, 3143, 3476, 4363, 4372, 8120, 9776, 10252**

Kroma-chlor®
dollar spot control, **15140**

Kromad®
Helminthosporium leaf spot control, **4167**

Kyllinga brevifolia, **14349**

Labeling
seed, **10534, 14773, 16255**

Labor
budget: golf course, **16148**

Labor
cost justification, **9643, 9646**

Labor
cost reduction, **3400, 10313, 10316, 12477, 13038, 14315, 15557, 17001**

Labor
Department of Labor standards, **10457**

Labor
golf course, **11542, 14315**

Labor
management, **6076, 6342, 6560, 8598, 8953, 10320, 14642:** golf course, **3125, 9924, 13443, 14787**

Labor
need justification, **9643, 9646**

Labor
problems: golf course, **10679, 11567**

Labor
sources: for golf course, **16148**

Lacrosse field (see Sports field)

LAI (see Leaf area index)

Lake, **2986**

Lake
construction, **4775**

Lake
irrigation, **4775, 4934**

Lamium amplexicaule (see Henbit)

Lamora perennial ryegrass, **6499**

Lance nematode, **5011, 5014, 6606, 11696, 11742, 11743, 11744, 11745, 12059, 12661**

Lance nematode
chemical control, **13913**

Lance nematode
description, **5009, 12057**

Lance nematode
effects on: warm season species, **11750, 12662**

Lance nematode
incidence: survey, **6607, 14052**

Lance nematode
parasitic effects, **12050, 12661**

Lance nematode
pathogenicity, **16101**

Lancoshire red fescue, **8350**

Land
reclamation: golf course, **4810**; recreation, **3622**

Landfills
park conversion, **8964**

Landrin®
billbug control, **10983**

Land rolling (see Rolling)

Landscape
culture, **5908, 10210, 12975**

Landscape
design, **8965, 9645, 13048**

Landscape
terminology, **2060, 10213**

Landscaping, **3024, 5725, 9099, 13067, 13069, 14646**

Landscaping
golf course, **2487, 2497, 3638a, 4824, 5814, 6110, 7064, 8567, 9960, 10160, 10437, 10932, 12097, 14732, 15847**

Landscaping
lawn, **2743, 7225, 9962**

Landscaping
park, **9961, 10238**

Landscaping
pollution control, **9231**

Large animal pests, **432**

Large crabgrass (see Crabgrass, large)

Large turfgrass areas
culture, **3755, 4984, 5019, 5938, 7016, 11846, 13062:** edging, **13969**; fertilization, **8008, 10240**

Large turfgrass areas
establishment, **8029, 8540, 9163**

Large turfgrass areas
grass selection, **8541, 11866**

Large turfgrass areas
renovation, **5907, 8216**

Latex mulch, **2874**

Lawn, **967, 3662a, 3700a, 7863, 8123, 10660, 13217, 13260, 14146**

Lawn
book, **2442, 2530, 2843, 5991, 6005, 7034**

Lawn
bulletin, **585, 1850, 1851, 8122, 9149**

Lawn
construction, **487, 6059, 8604, 11890, 14553, 14807**

Lawn
cool season turfgrasses used, **3844, 3973, 4640, 4869, 4975, 5775, 6640, 9249, 10727, 11156, 11161, 11166, 13082, 13085, 13088, 13096, 13101, 13104, 13116, 13173, 13188, 13197, 13205, 13210, 13214, 13231, 13332, 13381, 13831, 14128, 14185, 14552, 15079, 15085, 15606, 15917:** annual bluegrass, **7694, 15606**; bentgrass, **1652, 5785, 10689, 11209, 13240, 13293, 13326**; England, **10661, 10665, 11891, 14040, 15606**; fescues, **11209, 13171, 13292, 13364**; Kentucky bluegrass, **4388, 4419, 11209, 13173, 13931**; red fescue, **13093, 13173, 13220, 13225, 13243**; selection criteria, **533, 13116, 13203, 13212, 13289**

Lawn
culture, 222, 277, 376, 474, 516, 532, 589, 788, 845, 1008, 1130, 1155, 1313, 1323, 1476, 1533, 1850, 1954, 2083, 2085, 2086, 2139, 2215, 2366, 2379, 2428, 2517, 2596, 3036, 3095, 3108, 3109, 3126, 3135, 3350, 3857, 3952, 3984, 4093, 4297, 4379, 4395, 4432, 4557, 4602, 4626, 4665, 4670, 4736, 4758, 4898, 5023, 5072, 5160, 5357, 5478, 5576, 5639, 5968, 6537, 6633, 6883, 6928, 7086, 7129, 7424, 7463, 7530, 7551, 7648, 7726, 7739, 7829, 7923, 7948, 7976, 8111, 8604, 8645, 9080, 10148, 10736, 11005, 11209, 11370, 11714, 11808, 12682, 12683, 13067, 13068, 13078, 13080, 13082, 13083, 13084, 13088, 13091, 13092, 13094, 13102, 13104, 13111, 13113, 13114, 13125, 13129, 13134, 13137, 13139, 13141, 13151, 13153, 13154, 13162, 13164, 13166, 13172, 13178, 13179, 13184, 13201, 13219, 13230, 13253, 13275, 13330, 13356, 13830, 13835, 14138, 14141, 14144, 14157, 14168, 14841, 14869, 15167, 15171, 15173, 15175, 15194, 15609, 15771, 15776, 15799, 16344, 16381, 16387, 16468; bentgrass, 375, 5691, 14922; bermudagrass, 5914, 10077; book, 1116, 1173, 1481, 2364, 2383, 2442, 2445, 2914, 3227, 3369, 3945, 5697, 5698, 5754, 6005, 7133, 7136, 8444, 8445, 9523, 9653, 9847, 9865, 9867, 10328, 10426, 10468, 11014, 11913, 12288, 12484, 12494, 12848, 12849, 12850, 12872, 13063, 13190, 13236, 13517, 13541, 13647, 13924, 14073, 14081, 14174, 14176, 14184, 14254, 14274, 14466, 14712, 15045, 15607, 15844, 15849, 15979, 16112, 16154, 16215, 16310, 16311; bulletin, 260, 263, 266, 281, 282, 283, 285, 287, 409, 509, 510, 784, 804, 810, 820, 869, 910, 938, 1001, 1023, 1057, 1063, 1418, 1536, 1581, 1588, 1603, 1630, 1741, 2318, 3104, 3110, 3160, 3921, 4308, 8122, 13158, 13751, 14569, 15377, 15382, 15779; cool region, 1433, 13130, 13379; crabgrass control, 13325, 14208; cutting height, 468, 1372, 6633, 11708, 12037, 14168; edging, 8967, 13323; England, 7695, 10666, 11892, 14036, 14037, 14041, 14044, 14271; (England) book, 7780, 9522, 13005, 14468, 14755; environmental effects, 576, 13124; Europe, 13063, 13117; fall, 671, 746, 851, 911, 1952, 2631, 3692a, 3968, 3989, 3992, 4865, 4874, 4987, 7923, 13070, 13126, 13264, 13312, 13335, 13351, 13363, 14145; fertilization, 52, 309, 337, 368, 371, 399, 492, 515, 669, 904, 1159, 1480, 1641, 2027, 2087, 2223, 3036, 3086, 3135, 3619, 3688a, 3692a, 4430, 4985, 5248, 5705, 6641, 7162, 8927, 9458, 9558, 10515, 10881, 10936, 11170, 11305, 11348, 11349, 11708, 12037, 13027, 13058, 13074, 13146, 13168, 13175, 13180, 13183, 13185, 13195, 13254, 13261, 13262, 13275, 13296, 13298, 13347, 13355, 14038, 14140, 14678, 14873, 15522, 15610, 15705, 15988, 16095, 16123; industrial grounds, 2427, 2428, 10166; irrigation, 630, 747, 856, 2510, 3036, 3991, 4058, 6926, 7173, 11074, 11893, 14039, 14168, 15566; liming, 309, 517, 10664, 11278, 14169; mowing, 616, 3619, 3689a, 13275, 14678, 14865, 15921, 16174, 16176; mowing frequency, 11708, 12037; new developments, 13085, 15335; New Zealand, 15206, 15233, 15236, 15239, 15246, 15272, 15280, 15284, 15287, 15290, 15294, 15296, 15303, 15305, 15308, 15309, 15311, 15313, 15314, 15315, 15317, 15322; overseeding, 13237, 13244, 13298; resort lawns, 13115, 13198; soil management, 2549, 3699a, 5261, 15088, 15921; spring, 353, 394, 444, 521, 629, 633, 767, 769, 893, 964, 1177, 1320, 1775, 2037, 2166, 2217, 3970, 4873, 8106, 8112, 9146, 10666, 11290, 12248, 13076, 13100, 13146, 13189, 13218, 13256, 13291, 13310, 13324, 13348, 13362, 14037, 14151, 14808; state bulletin, 14, 54, 57, 822, 880, 968, 1062, 1066, 1067, 1299, 1383, 1541, 1697, 1773, 1852, 1969, 2047, 2317, 2390, 2391, 2392, 2393, 2395, 2511, 2512, 2513, 2514, 2519, 2713, 2714, 2759, 2766, 2767, 2921, 3000, 3393, 3394, 3593a, 3677, 3806, 3807, 3846, 3907, 3965, 3966, 3986, 3988, 3996, 4086, 4087, 4088, 4089, 4090, 4091, 4137, 4160, 4164, 4177, 4228, 4229, 4306, 4342, 4343, 4558, 4559, 4560, 4641, 4648, 4671, 4673, 4841, 4975, 4982, 4994, 4995, 5078, 5079, 5081, 5354, 5368, 5369, 5370, 5371, 5389, 5516, 5586, 5746, 5749, 6424, 6635, 6719, 6720, 6823, 6990, 7112, 7392, 7433, 7436, 7483, 7484, 7485, 7486, 7487, 7531, 7738, 7940, 7958, 8208, 8209, 8300, 8391, 8392, 8527, 8528, 8799, 8800, 8801, 8838, 8839, 9098, 9242, 9253, 9458, 9678, 9679, 9681, 9682, 9904, 9914, 9916, 9917, 9918, 10137, 10138, 10226, 10871, 10884, 10936, 10937, 10938, 11008, 11009, 11117, 11313, 11825, 12103, 12248, 12254, 12659, 12743, 12972, 13014, 13389, 13390, 13391, 13438, 13440, 13515, 13857, 13928, 13930, 13932, 13933, 14030, 14072, 14200, 14201, 14202, 14206, 14328, 14438, 14439, 14519, 14537, 14538, 14539, 14541, 14790, 14791, 14840, 14873, 14942, 14948, 14954, 14956, 15447, 15586, 15587, 15608, 15708, 15801, 15804, 15919, 15922, 15923, 15967, 15968,

15969, 16273, 16452, 16470, 16471, 16472; summer, 398, 399, 1256, 1395, 13077, 13090, 13138, 13169, 14036; timing, 14146, 14147; top-dressing, 406, 485, 518, 14157; USA, 6640, 9124, 9166, 13117, 14184; warm regions, 1102, 3541, 3565, 5045, 9727, 14430, 16094; winter, 633, 878, 991, 3695a, 5693, 13058, 13180, 14696; world regions, 42, 1840, 7704, 8090, 8445, 13181, 13753

Lawn
disease control, 3228, 6734, 11068, 13704, 13707, 13711, 14873, 15644

Lawn
diseases, 576, 3617, 6639, 6741, 8312, 8697, 8806, 8995, 14546: snow mold, 928, 3686a, 3693a, 14968; state bulletin, 3069, 3128, 3248, 6188, 8101, 9088, 9761, 9765, 14873, 15644, 15647, 15649

Lawn
equipment, 3732, 7047, 12037

Lawn
establishment, 52, 392, 474, 532, 629, 939, 1850, 1955, 2213, 2214, 2220, 2226, 2227, 2317, 2366, 3044, 3095, 3350, 3619, 3661, 3857, 4093, 4297, 4407, 4665, 4735, 4736, 4758, 4864, 4868, 4898, 5072, 5393, 5639, 5702, 5703, 6011, 6977, 7650, 7948, 7976, 8296, 8305, 8517, 8645, 8697, 8835, 9124, 9249, 11157, 11208, 11209, 11690, 11714, 12037, 12667, 13082, 13084, 13088, 13102, 13128, 13137, 13142, 13148, 13166, 13176, 13177, 13185, 13196, 13206, 13210, 13226, 13229, 13280, 13355, 13835, 13892, 14073, 14143, 14153, 15266, 15826, 16344: book, 1116, 2442, 2443, 2444, 5744, 5745, 6005, 7136, 8224, 9523, 11913, 12288, 12484, 12494, 12849, 12850, 13190, 13517, 13541, 13643, 13647, 13682, 15979, 16154, 16215, 16310, 16311; bulletin, 282, 284, 287, 820, 822, 1001, 1063, 3105, 3110, 6979, 9147, 13158, 15779; cost, 13167; England, 7695, 14044: book, 7780, 9522, 12484, 14444; practices, 596, 927, 2139, 2374, 7739, 11197, 13147, 13149, 13202, 13247, 14154; seedbed preparation, 4983, 5076, 10241; seeding, 2199, 2378, 2379, 5472, 9005, 10662, 13083, 13127, 13191, 13194, 13314, 14553, 15799; seed versus vegetative, 2366, 13360; shade, 522, 14155; soil aspects, 572, 4037, 13508; state bulletin, 1301, 2153, 2390, 2512, 2513, 2712, 2759, 3677, 3846, 3888, 4086, 4087, 4088, 4089, 4090, 4091, 4127, 4274, 4306, 4342, 4343, 4558, 4559, 4560, 4676, 4841, 4982, 4994, 4995, 5080, 5369, 5370, 5389, 5520, 5522, 5541, 5553, 5586, 6424, 7001, 7036, 7433, 7436, 7483, 7484, 7485, 7486, 7487, 7940, 8306, 8392, 8799, 8800, 8801, 8838, 8839, 9242, 9253, 9574, 9678, 9679, 9681, 9682, 9914, 9916, 9917, 9918, 10137, 10138, 10871, 10884, 10885, 10937, 10938, 11008, 11009, 11679, 12254, 12659, 12742, 12921, 13438, 13515, 13834, 13928, 14437, 14840, 14874, 14938, 14939, 14941, 14943, 14954, 14956, 15708, 15801, 15804, 15923, 15929, 15930, 16107, 16452, 16470, 16471, 16472 timing, 471, 537, 615, 618, 3666, 7739, 8566, 11652, 13141; fall, 851, 3925, 13170, 13174, 13186, 13208, 13209, 13262, 13313, 13363, 14153; spring, 13309, 13311, 13361, 14807; vegetative, 2212, 7701, 7724, 7971, 10409, 12638, 12639, 14553; warm regions, 4328, 13120, 14430, 15749; world regions, 7704, 8090, 9124, 12494, 15202, 15214

Lawn
grasses used, 589, 2354, 2428, 3317, 3660a, 3685a, 3696a, 3983, 3987, 3989, 4093, 4602, 4629, 4747, 5023, 5267, 5354, 5704, 5747, 6099, 6883, 7228, 7374, 8144, 8352, 8616, 8809, 8926, 9431, 10011, 13160, 13162, 13819, 14366, 15266: world regions, 42, 5357, 9200

Lawn
insects, 3042, 3294, 3617, 4060, 6059, 8697, 8878, 12026, 13630, 14333, 14334, 14632: state bulletin, 8250, 8821, 8829, 8868, 8869, 14486

Lawn
insect control, 1581, 1612, 3228, 3296, 5254, 6536, 8121, 12176: state bulletin, 2061, 3296, 7831, 8512, 8906, 12093, 13495

Lawn
irrigation system, 3830, 12842, 15538

Lawn
landscaping, 2743, 7225, 9357, 13103

Lawn
moss control, 2987, 10667

Lawn
organic culture, book, 12851

Lawn
pests, 1300, 3399, 6005, 12761, 12826, 15856: small animals, 470

Lawn
pest control, 3288, 3289, 14751: state bulletin, 3286, 12741

Lawn
problems, 524, 631, 634, 879, 927, 3350, 3674a, 8925, 10012, 10191, 11005, 11486, 13189, 13378, 13566, 14041, 15835, 15836: diagnosis, 13566, 15602, 15829, 15831, 15833, 15835, 15855, 15856, 15857

Lawn
renovation, 49, 1435, 1550,

1714, 1834, 2366, 2380, 2442, 2505, 4093, 4306, 4410, 4758, 6633, 6977, 8284, 8285, 9128, 10736, 11208, 11843, 12608, 13072, 13200, 13265, 13295, 13343, 13369, 13381, 13395, 14205, 14809, 15703: bulletin, **9149, 15668, 16107**; chemical, **1572, 2867, 13251**

Lawn
seed mixtures, **275, 2618, 4655, 5461, 5519, 5956, 8220, 8291, 10729, 11652, 13111, 13173, 13192**

Lawn
seed selection, **3844, 13150, 13385**

Lawn
state bulletin, **3661, 3679, 8616, 9431**

Lawn
temporary, **14152, 14168**

Lawn
warm season turfgrasses used, **809, 1383, 2366, 3546, 3578, 3579, 3607a, 3608a, 7994, 9249, 9275, 10500, 11166, 11688, 11700, 12877, 13088, 13096, 13101, 13116, 13129:** bahiagrass, **2376, 10524**; bermudagrass, **7977, 8152**; evaluation, **4601, 10409, 15826**; zoysiagrass, **1633, 4409, 4413, 8152, 16425**

Lawn
weeds, **5957, 6008, 7651, 7709, 13182:** state bulletin, **5255, 5971, 11308**

Lawn
weed control, **26, 895, 3619, 3690a, 4158, 4986, 6642, 6643, 8425, 9508, 9650, 10408, 10502, 10668, 12769, 13255, 13263, 13833, 14505:** bulletin, **250, 1562, 1959, 9446, 10870, 14224**; chemical, **3451, 4843, 9513, 13156, 13876**; cultural, **1659, 1851, 3608a, 9239, 13140, 13749, 14035, 16166**; state bulletin, **1229, 1771, 6224, 7713, 7747, 8755, 9452, 10536, 11356, 11995, 12071, 14792, 14870, 14877, 15942**

Lawn
winter overseeding, **10409, 13237, 14702**

Lawn bowling court (see Bowling green)

Lawn care service, **5576, 8816, 8958**

Lawn tennis court (see Tennis court)

Lawn turf (see Lawn)

Layering, soil (see Soil layering)

Leaching
factors affecting, **7344**

Leaching
nitrogen carriers, **2830**

Leaching
soil nutrients, **9684, 11972, 12262, 12263, 12631**

Lead
phytotoxicity, **3150, 3156**

Lead arsenate, **16, 325, 603, 6790, 9372, 9374, 9379**

Lead arsenate
annual bluegrass control, **327, 4399, 4406, 4411, 4442, 4445, 4827, 6487, 6576, 6790, 9385, 10234, 11584, 11616, 16160:** evaluation, **8419, 11056**

Lead arsenate
application, **750, 9377**

Lead arsenate
crabgrass control, **836, 3353, 3993, 4427, 4436, 5550, 5551, 6276, 6368, 11048, 11049, 15704, 15707:** evaluation, **4422, 7658, 11666, 12760**

Lead aresnate
earthworm control, **325, 366, 1793, 4762, 4764, 6790, 6848, 8919, 9369, 9373, 11653, 11654, 12169, 14128:** evaluation, **4732, 9395, 9561, 11666**

Lead arsenate
effects on: growth, **4766, 6629, 9396**; nitrification, **15810, 15811, 15816**; seed germination, **623, 4766**

Lead arsenate
grub control, **366, 5983, 7156, 9365, 9366, 9367, 9373, 9376, 9392, 9395, 9396, 11260, 12171, 12443, 15347, 15798, 16070**

Lead arsenate
insect control, **625, 2322, 4763, 12178**

Lead arsenate
Japanese beetle control, **5662, 5986, 8587, 12168, 12178**

Lead arsenate
selectivity, **2100, 8695, 8706, 8707, 8722**

Lead arsenate
sod webworm control, **4835, 8067, 11661, 11663, 11664, 11665, 11666**

Lead arsenate
weed control, **1551, 4839, 11629, 11666, 12808, 13017**

Leaf, **8974**

Leaf
age effects, **3367, 14579, 14789**

Leaf
anatomy, **271, 3073, 3376, 4006, 4085, 4595, 5317, 5947, 7585, 9550, 10705, 12101, 12201, 14085, 14087, 14240:** book, **13392, 15372**

Leaf
appearance rate, **3900, 10695, 10697, 10700, 10702, 10704, 14579:** environmental effects, **9178, 12965, 14606**; factors affecting, **3897, 12965, 16435**; seasonal variation, **4594, 11951**

Leaf
area, **3311, 11951:** cultural effects, **3308, 12965, 14661**; environmental effects, **3309, 3311, 3312, 12965**

Leaf
composition, **7699, 15351**

Leaf
development, **2752, 3073,**

3377, 3905, 5309, 5646, 5669, 6442, 9142, 10705, 12965, 13586, 13587, 14085, 14087, 14576, 14579

Leaf
folding, **5317, 15057**

Leaf
function, **7585, 7682, 12201**

Leaf
growth, **385, 2752, 4588, 4589, 10704**

Leaf
length, **3072, 3073, 5646, 10060, 10700, 10702, 10704, 10705, 11366, 14085, 14087:** day length effects, **5646, 8658, 14606, 16359**; temperature effects, **3072, 5646, 8658, 12965**

Leaf
morphology, **3072**

Leaf
rolling, **5317**

Leaf
temperature, **2231, 3335, 4583**

Leaf
tensile strength: potassium effects, **12247**

Leaf
texture, **3072, 3073, 5646, 14085, 14087:** environmental effects, **8658, 10700, 10702, 10704, 10705**; environmental effects—temperature, **2552, 2614, 8658, 12965, 14606**; species variation, **11366, 16369, 16372**

Leaf
thickness, **2231, 10705, 14085, 14087**

Leaf
width (see Leaf, texture)

Leaf area index, **4, 9180, 12569, 14703**

Leafhopper, **3627, 8478, 9186**
chemical control, **5295, 14235, 15334**

Leaf smut, **4711, 13745**

Leaf smut
on timothy, **11855**

Leaf spot, *Helminthosporium* (see *Helminthosporium* leaf spot)

Leaf, tree
removal, **339, 627, 704, 11797**

Leafy spurge
chemical control, **2436**

Leatherjackets (see Crane fly)

Legumes, **5095**

Legumes
use: roadside, **245, 9129**

Lepidopterous species, **11805**

Lepiota (see Fairy ring)

Lesion nematode, **137, 2241, 5009, 5011, 6337, 6607, 8525, 10551, 12057, 12229**

Lesion nematode
effects on: root growth, **14816, 14817**; shoot growth, **14817**

Lesion nematode
occurrance, **11668, 14052**

Lesion nematode
pathogenicity, **14817**

Lespedeza, **9063, 13459**

Lespedeza cuneate (see Sericea lespedeza)

Lespedeza stipulacea (see Korean lespedeza)

Leveling
depressions (see Depressions, soil)

Level, surveying, **569**

Library, personal, **437, 541**

Lichens, **1251, 1646**

Light, **5841, 6739**

Light
effects, **3488, 13412, 13640, 13774, 15650:** carbohydrate reserves, **5328, 5336**; seed germination, **205, 2674, 3327, 3821, 3822**; weed control, **11175**

Light
interception: factors affecting, **3308, 14703**

Light
penetration, **4**

Light
reflection, **10173**

Light
transmission: tree canopy, **85**

Light duration (see Day length)

Lighting, night (see Night illumination)

Light intensity
effects, **8173, 10120, 16373, 16392**

Light intensity
effects on: carbohydrate reserves, **90, 2295, 2946, 13401, 13427, 13428**; chemical composition, **2946, 3582, 6052**; crabgrass control, **15699**; establishment, **6435, 7099, 9973**; flowering, **13585, 14192**; growth, **3595, 6055, 6056, 11365, 13409, 16350, 16372**; leaf area, **2533, 3311**; low temperature discoloration, **16327, 16350, 16354**; melting out, **9754**; nitrate reductase, **8773, 8785**; photosynthesis, **131, 6052, 13410, 13428**; respiration, **13410, 13428**; root growth, **10698, 14835, 16168, 16169, 16180, 16350, 16399**; root-shoot ratio, **14834**; seed germination, **10134, 14761**; shoot growth, **89, 90, 2533, 2666, 2770, 2945, 2946, 3582, 7496, 8657, 8658, 10697, 10698, 14835, 16057, 16168, 16180, 16327**; stomata, **8658, 13623, 13624**; tillering, **2295, 2533, 8055, 10076, 12961**; vegetative development, **10695, 10705, 14579**; water use rate, **2677, 13623, 13624**; weed invasion, **3648**

Light intensity
factors affecting, **10701, 11838**

Light intensity
growth responses: species variation, **5675, 16180**

Light intensity
physiological responses, **2677, 2946, 10482, 13409, 16338**

Light intensity
seasonal variation, **2821**

Light intensity
shade effects, **233, 4121, 15046**

Light intensity
vertical variation, **10703**

Lightning
damage, **1321, 9323**

Lightning
golf course protection, **1901, 9323**

Light quality
effects of: domed stadium, **10060**; plastic screen, **11902**; tree shade, **4121, 5654, 5657, 5658, 6443, 9881, 15046**

Light quality
effects on: fungi, **8739**; large crabgrass, **5240**; plant development, **9878, 15057, 15660**; seed germination, **7683**; shoot density, **1744, 9881, 10060**; shoot growth, **1744, 2225, 2666, 9881, 10058, 10060**; turfgrass color, **10058, 10060**; turfgrass quality, **1744**

Light quality
factors affecting, **11838**

Light saturation
leaf age effects, **3367**

Lignified redwood
soil amendment, **1700, 9498, 14974:** evaluation, **10974, 10976, 10977, 10978**

Lignin, **11970**

Lignin
content: species evaluation, **10227, 10230, 16256**

Lignin
effects on: thatching, **2649, 10230**

Ligule
species variation, **4595**

Lime, **3819**

Lime
cost, **10723**

Lime
selection criteria, **2405**

Lime
soil effects, **5467, 11397**

Limestone, **8242, 12601, 14466**

Limestone
calcitic, **10690**

Limestone
dolomitic (see Dolomitic limestone)

Liming, **155, 511, 562, 613, 829, 1700, 1772, 2035, 2972, 6839, 6952, 6955, 9314, 9375, 9828, 9837, 10863, 11438, 11443, 11548, 11556, 14172, 14244, 14723, 14802, 15201, 15723**

Liming
application procedures, **593, 3321, 6967**

Liming
effects on, **15, 357, 358, 1399, 2172, 2356, 5636, 8243, 9690, 9691, 10059, 11278, 12263, 12531, 13642:** disease development, **9375, 11661, 14004, 14013**; drought tolerance, **5468, 5636**; earthworms, **5636, 5902, 8469**; moss, **5636**; nitrification, **15810, 15816**; shoot density, **9691, 12676**; shoot growth, **10245, 12531, 13686, 14440, 15787**; soil reaction, **9691, 11024**; thatch, **1175, 2615, 4905, 5523**; weed invasion, **5636, 7223**

Liming
at establishment, **4301, 7524, 13459**

Liming
evaluation, **5636, 7223, 11666**

Liming
golf course, **816, 1837, 11443, 11573**

Liming
lawn, **10664, 14146, 14147, 14162, 14169**

Liming
materials, **29, 816, 2415, 9690, 10578, 10618, 10690, 10723, 11463, 11466, 12601, 12702, 12805, 13526, 15508**

Liming
practices, **800, 2415, 9838, 10578, 10690, 10821, 11384, 12601, 13434, 13642, 15508**

Liming
rate, **15, 29, 816, 1233, 3321, 10623, 11439, 11473, 11538, 11548, 12702, 12805, 12810, 14146**

Liming
species response, **958, 10245**

Liming
timing, **2615, 9838, 13642**

Lindane
hairy chinch bug control, **12179**

Lindane
wireworm control, **6071**

Linn perennial ryegrass, **6387**

Linuron, **11245**

Lippia
fairway use, **8844**

Liquid fertilization (see also Soil drench), **6646, 8950, 9692, 9958, 10348, 12217, 12259, 12269, 12731, 13756**

Liquid fertilization
advantages, **5909, 6695, 12260**

Liquid fertilization
ammonia losses, **7676**

Liquid fertilization
application method, **10348, 12731:** irrigation system, **6267, 10349, 12814, 16109**

Liquid fertilization
application rates, **1156, 7632, 12731**

Liquid fertilization
corrosion problems, **12269**

Liquid fertilization
cost, **12731**

Liquid fertilization
foliar burn, **10016, 12269**

Liquid fertilization
mixtures, **12260, 12269**

Liquid fertilization
practices, **9692, 12512, 12904, 14070**

Liquid fertilization
types, **8950, 11674, 11802, 15067**

Liquid fertilization
use, **9693, 12731**

Literature
summary: research, **935, 944**; roadside, **1368, 1631**; turfgrass, **1996**; water use rate, **3230**

Littering
roadside, **134**

Little barley
chemical control, **93**

Little bluestem (see also Bluestem), **76, 9129**

Localized dry spot, **1304, 6905, 10959, 11503**

Localized dry spot
correction, **5051, 10897, 11442, 11480, 11483, 11498:** cultivation, **731, 4734**; evaluation, **2673, 2684**; wetting agent, **6637, 10405, 10898**

Localized dry spot
soil fungi relationships, **13033**

Lolium (see also Ryegrasses), **12066**

Lolium-festuca hybrids
evaluation, **4276, 15632**

Lolium mottle virus, **2187**

Lolium multiflorum (see Italian ryegrass)

Lolium perenne (see Perennial ryegrass)

Lolium species
genetics, **7727, 8499**

Lolium species
identification: fluorescence, **8727**

Lolium species
reproduction, **3917**

Lovegrass, **828, 3194, 12595**

Low temperature *basidiomycete* (see Winter crown rot)

Low temperature discoloration, **14075, 16361**
factors affecting, **16350, 16351:** nitrogen, **12497, 14075, 16354**

Low temperature discoloration
mechanism, **2334, 16354, 16359**

Low temperature discoloration
prevention: soil warming, **2615**

Low temperature discoloration
retardation: Carboxin, **2681, 12976**

Low temperature stress, **2622, 2639, 2643, 5236, 15661**

Low temperature stress
effects on: flowering, **9923**; seedling survival, **12860**

Low temperature stress
evaluation methods, **3927, 3931, 3936**

Low temperature stress
factors affecting, **724, 2624, 5227, 10604, 12476**

Low temperature stress
hardening: protein changes, **4605, 4606, 5236**

Low temperature stress
hardiness, **74, 13946:** cultural factors affecting, **5227, 14685**; nitrogen-potassium balance effects, **2603, 6514**; factors affecting, **14173, 14713**; fall fertilization, **2499, 5779, 12498, 15909, 15913**; herbicide effects, **4794, 11089**; nutritional effects, **2678, 6516, 6517**; potassium effects, **2499, 12497, 14440, 14685**; phosphorus effects, **2499, 12497**; seasonal variability, **2594**

Low temperature stress
injury, **188, 427, 563, 693, 2586, 2690, 5779, 5864, 5893, 6228, 10401, 10774, 10802, 13946, 15545:** causes, **2558, 2702, 15548, 15569**; cutting height effects, **2705, 2706, 10615**; fertilization effects, **2705, 4894, 6514**; ice sheet associations, **2106, 6228**; nitrogen effects, **2705, 5779, 10604, 15084, 15909**

Low temperature stress
injury symptoms, **2562, 2691**

Low temperature stress
protection, **323, 341, 427, 566, 642, 655, 960, 1007, 2622, 2624, 2639, 2643, 2651, 2691, 5590, 8211, 15511:** protective cover evaluation, **2499, 2623, 2675, 3721, 12265, 12497**

Low temperature stress
species tolerance, **1639, 1700, 1778, 2561, 2566, 2577, 2578, 2586, 2591, 2594, 2598, 2605, 2620, 2636, 2639, 2689, 2691, 2702, 2836, 3720, 5227, 8460, 9408, 10774, 11761, 16368, 16369, 16372**

Lucerne moth, **4780, 14033**

Lucerne moth
description, **4779, 8473, 8478, 14033**

Lycoperdon (see Fairy ring)

Lypiagrass, **319**

Lysimachia nummularia (see Moneywort)

Lysimeter, **7383**

Magennis bermudagrass, **10461**

Magnesium, **5850, 11433, 11786, 12161, 12362**

Magnesium
carrier, **2776, 10352, 10864, 11628, 13526**

Magnesium
deficiency symptoms, **8758, 9712, 9717, 10449, 11628, 11790**

Magnesium
effects on: gray leaf spot, **13897, 13904**; root growth, **8758, 8763, 12532**; shoot growth, **5856, 8758, 8763, 10352, 10449, 12532**

Magnesium
nutrition, **8762, 9812, 13526, 14148**

Magnesium
soil relationship, **11628, 16488**

Magnesium oxide, **8762, 8763**

Magnesium sulfate, **2776**

Magnetometer
water location, **8446**

Magnolia annual ryegrass
crown rust resistance, **2819**

Maintain CF 125® (see Chlorflurenol)

Maintenance building, **3313**
golf course, **6002**

Maintenance costs
bowling green, **1494**

Maintenance costs
effects of: golf course design, **7490**

Maintenance costs
golf course, **1266**

Maintenance costs
Nebraska, **1939**

Maintenance costs
New Jersey, **1111**

Maintenance costs
operational efficiencies, **8966, 14657**

Maintenance costs
survey: Texas, **1604**

Maintenance costs
turfgrass industry, **1120, 1375**

Maize dwarf mosaic virus
on St. Augustinegrass, **4329**

Maize dwarf mosaic virus
species susceptibility, **6054**

Makari-kavi grass, **4020**

Malachite green, **643, 1036, 2815**

Maladera castanoa (see Asiatic garden beetle)

Malathion
flea beetle control, **15740**

Malathion
ground pearl control, **14116**

Malathion
rhodesgrass scale control, **14398**

Maleic hydrazide, **212, 1003, 1045, 1080, 1550, 1593, 2100, 2324, 3020, 3843, 4892, 5046, 5518, 6015, 6031, 6081, 7045, 7100, 7340, 7518, 7850, 8406, 10091, 12974, 13779, 13818**

Maleic hydrazide
annual bluegrass control, **5479, 5530, 8419**

Maleic hydrazide
application, **2718, 6031, 8406**

Maleic hydrazide
application method, **7100, 8406, 16506**

Maleic hydrazide
crabgrass control, **3972, 4906**

Maleic hydrazide
effectiveness: factors affecting, **15746, 16508**

Maleic hydrazide
effects, **3843, 12750**

Maleic hydrazide
effects on: bermudagrass, **1871, 3567a, 3569a, 10447**; flowering, **6030, 16459**; growth, **3843, 4892, 5518**; polystand composition, **16286**; shoot growth, **7340, 7518, 12323, 15800, 16286, 16459**

Maleic hydrazide
evaluation, **213, 2826, 4302, 5568, 5606, 5610, 5615, 5904, 6686, 9661, 12247, 15157, 16509**

Maleic hydrazide
growth inhibition, **1022, 4015, 5574, 11369:** evaluation, **4017, 4888, 4997, 5358, 5360, 5904, 6030, 6652, 11066, 12323, 15628, 16453, 16458, 16459**; on warm season grasses, **3515, 4283, 11751**

Maleic hydrazide
herbicide combination: evaluation, **15975, 15976**

Maleic hydrazide
nimblewill control, **7711**

Maleic hydrazide
physiological effects, **3364, 13614**

Maleic hydrazide
phytotoxicity, **213, 1080, 5606, 7340, 7518, 8693**

Maleic hydrazide
uses, **3840, 5606, 5610, 12609:** roadside, **213, 215, 974, 2717, 2718, 3045, 3769, 6029, 6072, 7012, 7102, 11066, 14773**; roadside-evaluation, **213, 1055, 5047, 15158, 16506, 16507, 16508**; winter overseeding, **136, 144, 1639, 5139, 6014, 6015**

Maleic hydrazide-chlorfluorenol combination
growth inhibition, **4015**

Mallow, common, **672**

Malva Neglecta (see Mallow, common)

MAMA, **1620**

MAMA
crabgrass control, **1493, 1551, 1733, 2692, 4429, 11047, 12574, 14491:** evaluation, **3653, 3653a, 8155, 8431, 9053, 13803**

MAMA
dallisgrass control, **4207, 7933, 9531, 9533, 9537**

MAMA
hawkweed control, **12573**

MAMA
physiological effects, **5099, 5102**

MAMA
purple nutsedge control, **5741, 9673**

MAMA
St. Augustinegrass control, **3071**

MAMA
sandbur control, **1871, 8161, 12665, 15140**

MAMA
selectivity: Kentucky bluegrass, **3653a, 13803**

Mammalian toxicity
pesticides, **1607, 8471**

Management, turf, **2549, 8602, 12578, 12715, 14649**

Management, turf
golf course, **11719:** club manager-superintendent, **77**; efficiency, **7075**; green committee, **10288**; on reduced budget, **9859**

Management, turf
labor efficiency, **8598**

Management, turf
park, **6551**

Management, turf
record keeping, **13059**

Management, turf
sod production, **15827**

Mancozeb, **3257**
Fusarium patch control, **7192**

Maneb, **4592**
Helminthosporium leaf spot control, **11104**

Manganese, **4719, 10061, 11786**

Manganese
deficiency symptoms, **9267, 9698**

Manganese
nutrition, **2351, 4807, 7671, 11785**

Manganese
soil relationships, **10061, 14630**

Manganous ethylenebisdithiccarbamate (see Maneb)

Manhattan perennial ryegrass, **2027, 2611, 2670, 6691**
description, **6298, 6315, 6499, 6691**

Manilagrass, **695, 724, 749, 765, 782, 1123, 3811, 6050, 9151, 11163, 16118**

Manilagrass
adaptation, **3812, 4093, 11692, 16263, 16350**

Manilagrass
cultivar: evaluation, **8761, 8765**; paper chromatography identification, **11229**

Manilagrass
culture, **958, 3812, 5274, 11692**

Manilagrass
description, **11587, 11692, 16263**

Manilagrass
establishment, **1315, 2365, 3812, 8210, 11692**

Manilagrass
uses: green, **2778**; trap facing, **11566**

Manual
engine maintainence, **1946**

Manual
small tractor maintainence, **1889**

Manual, grass, **7795, 7796, 7797, 7945, 7946, 12134, 12136**

Manure, **309, 386, 14132**

Manure
evaluation, **6790, 10863, 11666**

Manure
nutrient composition, **11389**

Manure
soil amendment, **9800, 14131**

Manure
weed seed source, **365**

Marasmius oreades, **2508, 6508**

Marasmius oreades
chemical control, **9414**

Marasmius oreades
hydrogen cyanide production, **9415**

Marasmius oreades
injury causes, **5920, 5921**

Marasmius oreades
root penetration, **5919**

Marasmius species (see Fairy ring)

Margarodes species (see Ground pearls)

Marketing
seed, **2374, 2375**

Marketing
sod, **2123, 8056**

Marmor gramias (see Bromegrass mosiac virus)

Mascarenegrass, **695, 6050, 7396, 16118, 16263**

Mat, **1557, 3981, 5852, 5878, 6908, 16005**

Mat
causes, **3978, 4405, 5852**

Mat
control, **3979, 4405, 5852, 6920, 14112, 14726, 14730, 16005:** topdressing, **3981**

Mat
description, **14726, 14730**

Mat
nutrient uptake, **12500**

Mat
renovation, **1557, 1600**

Mat, rubber
for bowling green, **15263**

Maturation
factors affecting, **10082, 13951**

May beetle, **573, 12507**

Mayetiola species (see Gall midges)

MCP (see MCPA)

MCPA, **5615, 5617, 10996**
weed control, **2172, 5603, 8461**

MCPA—dicamba combination (see Dicamba—MCPA combination)

MCPP, **1579, 1639, 4755, 5615, 12473, 13779, 14518**

MCPP
broadleaf weed control, **3618a, 4805, 5197, 8405, 8433, 10627**

MCPP
chickweed control, **3618a, 3757, 8436, 13024**

MCPP
clover control, **1493, 3618, 5190, 5982, 13024**

MCPP
knotweed control, **1493, 1700, 8435, 13024**

MCPP
phytotoxicity, **5190, 9885**

MCPP
selectivity: bentgrass, **1700, 2566, 2608, 5500**; seedling, **8437**

MCPP
use, **1689, 12473**

MCPP
weed control, **7022, 9876, 10355, 11947, 13024, 13882**

MCPP
white clover control, **1689, 2566, 4809, 8435, 8436, 9533**

MCPP—dicamba combination (see Dicamba—MCPP combination)

Meadow fescue, **977, 3714, 7286, 8171, 14614, 15802**

Meadow fescue
adaptation, **4601**

Meadow fescue
cultivars, **7284**

Meadow fescue
description, **1685, 4008, 4277, 7947, 9180, 14242:** cytology, **3836, 3837, 8501, 11225**

Meadow fescue
diseases, **9095, 9097**

Meadow fescue
seed, **11965:** germination, **8781**

Meadow fescue
seedling development, **14962**

Meadowgrass (see Bluegrass)

Meadow plant bug, **8549, 14235**
chemical control, **14235**

Mechanical analysis, soil (see Soil analysis, physical: mechanical)

Mechanization
golf course, **10308, 10310**

Mecopex® (see MCPP)

Mecoprop (see MCPP)

Medicago (see Alfalfa)

Medicago luoulina (see Black medic)

Medic, black (see Black medic)

Mediterranean fruit fly
sod shipment, **6234**

Meiosis, **8627**

Melle perennial ryegrass, **7191, 8350**

Meloidogyne (see Root-knot nematode)

Meloidogyne incognita, **3193**

Melting out, **1002, 2534, 2545, 2546, 4188, 5399, 6258, 8355, 9760**

Melting out
chemical control, **3671, 8095, 9755, 11109, 13703, 13732, 15014, 15759, 15928, 16498:** cyclohexamide, **15033, 15036**; evaluation, **2027, 2100, 2196, 3253, 4203, 4209, 7619, 9750, 9896, 11106, 11112, 12357, 14026**; PMA, **15033, 15037**

Melting out
cultural control, **6132, 9896**

Melting out
cultural factors affecting: mowing, **7205, 9755, 9758**; nutritional, **5373, 9755**

Melting out
environmental factors affecting, **7194, 9757, 9892:** light intensity, **9754, 9755, 9758**

Melting out
incidence: sugar content effects, **9754, 9758, 9759, 9760**

Melting out
Kentucky bluegrass susceptibility: cultivar evaluation, **6290, 6310, 6317, 6320, 6328, 7193, 7194, 7205, 9755, 9896, 11019, 13663, 14562**

Melting out
nematode complex, **12021**

Melting out
polystands, **6323**

Melting out
species susceptibility: evaluation, **2698, 10888**

Melting out
symptoms, **2100, 6132, 7193, 8095, 8099, 9463, 9892, 10853, 11942, 12078, 12556, 14716, 15480**

Memmi®
dollar spot control, **15140**

Mercuric chloride (see Mercury, inorganic)

Mercurous chloride + mercuric chloride (see Mercury, inorganic)

Mercury
soil content: golf course, **9863**

Mercury
vertical soil movement, **10456, 13891**

Mercury fungicides, **638, 659, 666, 724, 905, 1253, 2834**

Mercury fungicides
application, **531, 550**

Mercury fungicides
brown patch control, **311, 435, 5961, 6566, 6567, 8553, 11661**

Mercury fungicides
dollar spot control, **2330, 5961, 10804, 11661**

Mercury fungicides
earthworm control, **2344, 12145**

Mercury fungicides
effects on: nitrification, **15810, 15811, 15816**

Mercury fungicides
Fusarium patch control, **6762, 6765, 11661**

Mercury fungicides
moss control, **2961, 2962, 8340**

Mercury fungicides
phytotoxicity, **1590**

Mercury fungicides
red thread control, **6755**

Mercury fungicides
safety, **2027**

Mercury fungicides
snow mold control, **590, 627, 3111, 4315, 4316, 7765**

Mercury fungicides
Typhula blight control, **21, 8373**

Mercury, inorganic, **14096, 16291**

Mercury, inorganic
brown patch control, **4681, 14719:** evaluation, **10410, 10797, 10799, 12167, 13071, 15123, 16292**

Mercury, inorganic
copper spot control, **7390**

Mercury, inorganic
dollar spot control, **10568, 10574, 13605:** evaluation, **8351, 9246, 10331, 10410, 10797, 10798, 14714, 15123**

Mercury, inorganic
earthworm control, **9369, 11653**

Mercury, inorganic
fairy ring control, **9414**

Mercury, inorganic
snow mold control, **5781, 5923, 10422, 10802, 14923, 15475,** 15591, **15592**

Mercury, inorganic
Typhula blight control, **2633, 2717, 8100, 15017**

Mercury, organic, **9168**

Mercury, organic
brown patch control, **10799, 16292**

Mercury, organic
copper spot control, **2329, 2330**

Mercury, organic
snow mold control, **5923**

Merion Kentucky bluegrass, **95, 866, 873, 888, 889, 890, 905, 908, 937, 972, 977, 992, 1078, 1473, 1685, 1700, 1776, 2027, 2304, 3656, 3658a, 4666, 4667, 4668, 5070, 5438, 5458, 6840, 6842, 6862, 6869, 6875, 6879, 6882, 6963, 6987, 7202, 7309, 7914, 8319, 8343, 9151, 9153, 9245, 9251, 9671, 11165, 11187, 11363, 11631, 13238, 13462, 16049, 16164, 16179**

Merion Kentucky bluegrass
adaptation, **2589, 2700, 2701, 3978, 4388, 4447, 5314, 5748, 7181, 10614, 10633, 11151, 12007, 16430**

Merion Kentucky bluegrass
bentgrass invasion, **806**

Merion Kentucky bluegrass
breeding, **5158, 5182**

Merion Kentucky bluegrass
carbohydrate reserves: factors effecting, **7008**

Merion Kentucky bluegrass
culture, **2517, 6872, 6985, 7399, 8692, 14357:** cutting height, **6986, 8690, 8723, 16360**; fertilization, **3243, 3912, 4636, 4639, 4664, 6986, 8720, 8723, 12622**; mowing, **8690**

Merion Kentucky bluegrass
description, **3978, 4384, 5314, 8316, 10022, 11023, 11224, 14357, 16049, 16435**

Merion Kentucky bluegrass
diseases, **2546, 4419, 6452, 9226:** control, **20, 24, 2547, 3243, 4051, 4310**; flag smut, **7349, 7355, 7357, 7358, 7360, 7361, 7809, 7812, 9751, 9752, 11324**; *Fusarium* blight, **1111, 2537, 2547, 4310, 4311**; *Fusarium* blight-stylet nematode interaction, **15023**; rust, **1076, 1487, 2870, 3243, 3244, 3245, 4166, 4168, 7346, 7357, 7364**; stripe smut, **2862, 4051, 4653, 7198, 7199, 7200, 7203, 7351, 7355, 7356, 7357, 7358, 7360, 7361, 7809, 7812, 7817, 7818, 7819, 8369, 9072, 9087, 9751, 9752, 11324, 11937, 15015**; *Typhula* blight, **8741**

Merion Kentucky bluegrass
disease incidence: factors affecting, **3803, 3805**

Merion Kentucky bluegrass
effects of: growth inhibitor, **5574**; minor elements, **4807, 9267**

Merion Kentucky bluegrass
environmental factors affecting, **2700, 4806, 7181**

Merion Kentucky bluegrass
establishment, **3646, 4419, 7399, 7670:** seeding rate, **3646, 6985**

Merion Kentucky bluegrass
evaluation, **6306, 6307, 6309, 6330, 6626, 6637, 6712, 7191, 8317, 8336, 8341, 9212, 9213, 9218, 9349, 10622, 10626, 10635, 11186, 11323, 11325, 11329, 14103, 14349, 14813, 16320**

Merion Kentucky bluegrass
ozone injury, **16097**

Merion Kentucky bluegrass
PMA injury, **997**

Merion Kentucky bluegrass
root growth: factors effecting, **4777, 4797**

Merion Kentucky bluegrass
seed: fungal isolations, **4049**

Merion Kentucky bluegrass
seed production, **14456**

Merion Kentucky bluegrass
thatch: factors affecting, **4143**

Merion Kentucky bluegrass
transplant rooting: factors affecting, **5232, 5234, 8948**

Merion Kentucky bluegrass
uses, **7249, 8926, 15378, 16512:** lawn, **4388, 4419**; in mixtures, **6986, 8724**; tee, **6909, 6917**

Mesocotyl, seed
elongation, **15660**

Mesophyll tissue, **3002**

Methabenzthiazuron
annual bluegrass control, **3440, 16213**

Methabenzthiazuron
rough bluegrass control, **2949, 3440**

Metham (see SMDC)

Methin®
crabgrass control, **5156**

Methoxychlor
Japanese beetle control, **7158, 12173**

Methoxychlor
toxicity, **3745**

2-methoxy-3,6 dichorobenzoic acid (see Dicamba)

Methyl arsine oxide, **22**
disease control, **1590**

Methyl bromide, **958, 1493, 1892, 3389, 7410, 7413, 8665, 8768, 8832, 8931, 9800, 11697, 12771, 13724**

Methyl bromide
fairy ring control, **6728**

Methyl bromide
nematode control, **12978**

Methyl bromide
soil fumigation, **2880, 3509, 4407, 4587, 5352, 6349, 7149, 8832, 9400, 11976, 12874, 12976:** methods, **8565, 8789, 10030, 11298, 12415**

Methyl bromide
use, **16439:** sports field, **1114, 1900**

Methyl bromide
weed control, **978, 5632, 6349, 7655, 9670**

Methyl-1-(butylcarbamoyl)-2-benzimidazole-carbamate (see Benomyl)

Methyl 2-chloro-9-hydroxyflorene-9-carboxylate (see Chlorflurenol)

2-Methyl-4-chloro phenoxyacetic, **811**

1-(2-methylcyclohexyl)-3-phenylurea (see Siduron)

4-(Methylsulfony)-2, 6-dinitro-N, N-dipropylaniline
weed control, **13864**

Metric system
use, **14862**

Metropolitan creeping bentgrass, **301, 302, 388, 591, 742, 757, 989, 2453, 3713, 7309, 9258, 9844, 10837, 10860, 11419, 11666, 12698, 12865**

Metropolitan creeping bentgrass
evaluation, **9233, 9408, 10862, 11031, 16489:** disease susceptibility, **9564, 14923**

Metropolitan creeping bentgrass
uses: fairway, **789, 815, 14762**; green, **854**

Meyer zoysiagrass, **866, 873, 888, 945, 992, 993, 4628, 6050, 6142, 6562, 6840, 6858, 6869, 6875, 6876, 6882, 7309, 7396, 7407, 8791, 9153, 11165, 13238**

Meyer zoysiagrass
adaptation, **1073, 1364, 1404, 1633, 4401, 4409, 6554, 7519, 12475, 13445**

Meyer zoysiagrass
culture: fertilization, **8663, 8670**; soil reaction, **8670**

Meyer zoysiagrass
diseases: rust, **6186, 7861, 9096, 14846**

Meyer zoysiagrass
establishment, **6435, 10450:** sprigging, **9632**; stolonizing, **9632**

Meyer zoysiagrass
pest: billbug, **8683**

Meyer zoysiagrass
uses, **5970, 6923, 13444**

Mice, **4306**

Michigan Sod Strength Test, **1958, 9134, 12640**

Microclimate
effects on: establishment, **3770**

Microclimate
golf course, **2237, 16272**

Microclimate
roadside slope: exposure effects, **1068, 9996**

Microenvironment, **2991, 6230, 7850**

Microenvironment
factors affecting, **14003, 15572**

Microenvironment
modification, **2291, 4535**

Microlaena stipoides
description, **10249**

Micronutrients, **242, 1948, 2352, 2356, 7575, 13784, 13785, 13786, 16013**

Micronutrients
availability: factors effecting, **2888, 13941**

Micronutrients
carriers, **7671, 10864, 12504, 12633, 14692**

Micronutrients
deficiencies, **1700, 2356, 2833, 7549, 9590, 9717, 11787, 16223**

Micronutrients
deficiency symptoms, **7467, 7671, 9267, 9698, 12362, 13941, 14692**

Micronutrients
effects on: chemical composition, **9257**; shoot growth, **4783, 9257**

Micronutrients
function, **3933, 7467, 12362, 14691, 16223**

Micronutrients
requirements: Kentucky bluegrass, **4784**

Micronutrients
toxicity, **13941**

Microorganism activity
effects of: pesticides, **3580a, 3922, 5915, 7132**

Microorganism activity
environmental factors affecting, **14889**

Microorganism activity
factors affecting, **3580a, 6676, 13634, 14232, 14889:** soil reaction, **10227, 14027**

Microorganism activity
nitrogen release, **7132, 13634, 14027**

Microorganisms, soil, **114, 201, 2155, 9310, 12605, 13980, 14028, 14887, 15812**

Microorganisms, soil
antagonistic reactions, **2155**

Microorganisms, soil
effects on: nitrogen accumulation, **7386**; ureaformaldehyde, **6263**

Microorganisms, soil
plant nutrient release, **2155**

Microorganisms, soil
role, **9106, 10250, 14027, 14889**

Microorganisms, soil
thatch decomposition, **9067, 10227, 10231**

Microorganisms, soil
types, **9106, 12604**

Micropore packet
fertilization, **2108**

Midland bermudagrass, **3493, 3574, 5145, 7638**

Midway bermudagrass, **5236, 12007**

Midwest Regional Turf Foundation, **899, 903, 1065, 1117, 1298, 1427, 1428, 3122, 11031, 11036, 15077**

Midwest Regional Turf Foundation
activities, **4443, 11032, 15076**

Midwest Regional Turf Foundation
grants, **1535, 1589, 1634**

Midwest Regional Turf Foundation
membership, **1535, 1589, 1634, 4363**

Midwest zoysiagrass, **1639, 1778, 3694a, 4462, 4472, 6287**

Midwest zoysiagrass
adaptation, **1635, 12007**

Midwest zoysiagrass
establishment, **10450**

Milarsenite®, **261, 2388, 4847, 10170, 11459, 11534**

Milcyanate®
crabgrass control, **4395, 4890**

Mildew (see Powdery mildew)

Military grounds
culture, **741, 8923, 8924**: mowing, **2754**

Military grounds
establishment, **741**

Milk purseline
chemical control, **8171**

Milkweed
chemical control, **1700**

Milky disease
Japanese beetle control, **3887, 4001, 15783**

Millipede, **8888, 9186**

Millipede
chemical control, **3291**

Milorganite®, **262, 269, 406, 1470, 1488, 1546, 1639, 1777, 2027, 2293, 3205, 3206, 8728, 12503, 15777, 16021**

Milorganite®
composting, **4848**

Milorganite®
effects on: dollar spot, **1690**

Milorganite®
evaluation, **5917, 11176, 11383, 14402, 14403, 14923, 15110, 15118, 15697**

Milorganite®
historical, **11383**

Milorganite®
micronutrient source, **12504**

Mineral composition (see also Chemical composition)
effects of: fertilization, **9027, 14090**; mowing frequency, **12500**

Mineral composition
species variation, **3635, 7828, 11458, 12500, 14440**

Mining bee
chemical control, **15807**

Miris dolobratus (see Meadow plant bug)

Mites, **2866, 8342, 14906**

Mites
chemical control, **1810, 16156**

Mites
description, **8473, 8479**

Mites
injury symptoms, **8904**

Mites
state bulletin, **12841**

Miticides, **1810**

Mitosis, **3378, 7582**

Mixtures, seed (see Seed mixtures)

Mocap®
nematode control, **8040, 12062**

Mocap®
southern chinch bug control, **14399**

Moisture (see Soil water)

Moisture stress (see Water stress)

Mole, **432, 449, 581, 860, 906, 9464, 14547**

Mole
chemical control, **4836, 6460, 9472, 12182**

Mole
control, **449, 452, 4964, 8624, 8670, 9464, 13467, 13593, 14547**: state bulletin, **12184**

Mole cricket, **678, 734, 741, 1570, 3294, 8878, 11559, 12542**

Mole cricket
chemical control, **3283, 3290, 3292, 3297, 7146, 8330, 8823, 8829, 8887, 8888, 8895, 14622, 15841**

Mole cricket
control, **684, 1217**

Mole cricket
description, **8823, 8829**

Mole cricket
injury symptoms, **8904**

Mole cricket, West Indian (see West Indian mole cricket)

Mole drain, **11684, 15230**

Mole, star-nosed (see Star-nosed mole)

Mollugo verticillata (see Carpetweed)

Molybdenum, **6626, 7671, 11785, 11786**
deficiency symptoms, **9267, 9698**

Mondograss, **1205**

Moneywort, **670, 15706**

Monoammonium methanearsonate (see MAMA)

Monoammonium phosphate, **5636**

Monobor-chlorate
Johnsongrass control, **8182**

Monocotyledons
anatomy, **7577**

Monocotyledons
development, **10096**

Monomolecular antitranspirant layer (see Antitranspirant, monomolecular layers)

Monosodium methanearsonate (see MAMA)

Monostand community
competition, **14832**

Monuron **16259**

Monuron
degradation rate, **13576**

Monuron
soil sterilant, **8182, 10866**

Morley, John, **1751**

Morphology
book, **2244, 7150, 7793**

Morphology, grass, **3384, 4008, 4009, 5673, 8843, 12862**
shoot apex, **13585**

Mosquito
chemical control, **10424, 10724**

Moss, **359, 685, 1035, 1092, 1148, 1646, 2033, 7019, 8464, 14042**

Moss
causes, **10667, 14042**

Moss
chemical control, **2111, 2987, 4749, 7019, 7021, 7026, 12518, 14739:** evaluation, **6630, 8340, 15706**

Moss
control, **1376, 1646, 2961, 2962, 4864, 5617, 10677, 14042**

Moss
cultural control, **2172, 3619, 7021, 8106, 15210**

Moss
description, **7021, 7025, 8464**

Moss
factors affecting, **5636, 8464, 15924:** ammonium sulfate, **2172**; soil reaction, **2172, 5636**

Moss peat, **490**

Mossy stonecrop
chemical control, **7090**

Mott hammer knife, **1108**

Mound building ant, **7649, 13473**

Mound building prairie ant
chemical control, **3396**

Mouse ear chickweed, **369, 614, 4737, 15706**

Mouse ear chickweed
chemical control, **3697a, 6667, 7090:** evaluation, **3618a, 5732, 5733, 6375, 6376, 6543, 6626, 8416, 8436, 13860**

Mower, **3749, 9198, 14656, 15512, 15517**

Mower
adjustment, **3238, 11474, 15651**

Mower
description, **2456, 2457, 2459, 2461, 2462**

Mower
design considerations, **1956, 2049**

Mower
maintenance, **1319, 1574, 1971, 2716, 3238, 3239, 3731, 5946, 6471, 15512:**
sharpening, **1326, 6471**

Mower
operation, **1289, 2935, 3238, 3863, 4327, 5945, 10737, 13059, 15504, 15530, 15531, 15562:** cost, **5946**

Mower
records, **4564, 13059**

Mower
safety, **3238**

Mower
selection, **1971, 5640, 15530, 15568, 15583, 16476, 16482:** cost analysis, **10737**

Mower
storage, **1319**

Mower
types, **342, 1108, 1639, 1757, 2049, 2829, 2935, 3457, 8595, 9205, 11708, 13152, 13302, 14369, 15493, 15504, 15512, 15517, 15568, 15570, 15574, 15575, 15583, 16478, 16482, 16483, 16485:** comparisons, **10737, 16475**; green, **3863, 15320, 15651**; reel versus rotary, **2699**; roadside, **4211, 15803**; self-propelled, **16475, 16476**

Mowing, **374, 1137, 1186, 1249, 1550, 1740, 1947, 2829, 3680a, 5626, 6525, 7741, 8974, 8975, 12858, 13754, 14351, 15256, 15540**

Mowing
bermudagrass, **3910, 14372**

Mowing
cost, **25, 1315, 3066, 5946, 8062, 13036, 15048, 15512**

Mowing
effects, **3457, 10849, 14685, 15073, 15570, 16414**

Mowing
effects on: ball roll, **6817**; boron toxicity, **9802**; carbohydrate reserves, **2295, 5032, 10380, 11880, 12981, 14685, 14896, 16414**; disease, **8350, 12912**; polystand composition, **7220**; root growth, **2924, 8394, 8397, 8398, 10380,**

11919, 13754; shoot growth, **123, 2752, 2924, 3079, 3278, 3739, 4278, 4588, 5032, 5331, 6779, 8398, 14685**; tillering, **2295, 10697, 11833, 15362**

Mowing
efficiency, **14656**

Mowing
equipment (see Mower)

Mowing
fairway, **15504, 16133**

Mowing
green, **25, 299, 1154, 1249, 4236, 11934, 15775, 15965**

Mowing
hand versus power, **3753, 11934**

Mowing
height (see Cutting height)

Mowing
lawn, **3689a, 14865, 16174, 16176**

Mowing
pattern, **10324, 15512, 15517, 15965, 16133**

Mowing
practices, **1315, 10324, 11474, 12347, 15493, 15530, 15535, 15562, 15563, 15565, 15570, 15573, 15575, 15578, 15583, 15775, 16129, 16225**

Mowing
principles, **7052, 7411, 15531, 15551**

Mowing
problems, **12868, 14372, 14373**

Mowing
quality: mower type, **2583, 2699, 3457**

Mowing
roadside, **1018, 1068, 8062, 11796, 12870, 12871, 14335**

Mowing
speed, **10324, 14651**

Mowing
time of day, **1700, 7741**

Mowing
wash-board effect, **10844, 15565, 15583**

Mowing frequency, **356, 1186, 1460, 2019, 3459, 7052, 7411, 10076, 12858, 15493, 15504, 15531, 15535**

Mowing frequency
effects, **6472, 10076, 11474, 12765, 15168, 15657**

Mowing frequency
effects on: brown patch, **10083**; carbohydrate reserves, **3445, 5307, 7582, 7931, 8675, 9745, 9992, 12557, 12558, 15657**; chemical composition, **5361, 5700, 9507, 9745, 10076, 12500**; establishment, **2381**; grain, **10075**; irrigation practices, **15558**; nitrogen removal, **6781**; polystand composition, **5361**; protein content, **9034, 9356**; root growth, **797, 5681, 6472, 6781, 7931, 8398, 8664, 8675, 8690, 8846, 9724, 10072, 10076, 10091, 12765, 12770, 14765, 14766, 15657**; shoot density, **8675, 9034, 10071, 10072, 10076, 12765**; shoot growth, **3318, 5361, 5700, 6227, 6472, 6782, 7513, 7931, 8398, 8690, 8846, 9034, 9181, 9724, 9745, 9992, 10068, 10072, 10075, 10076, 10091, 10106, 10383, 11296, 12255, 12557, 12568, 12569, 12765, 12770, 14765, 14766**; sod strength, **2630, 2633, 2672**; soil moisture, **6472, 7180**; water use rate, **15549**

Mowing frequency
factors affecting, **10228, 10324, 12686, 15562, 15565, 15570, 15573, 15575, 15583, 16129**

Mowing frequency
green, **834, 7740**

Mowing frequency
species tolerance, **3459, 6781, 16372**

Mowrah meal
earthworm control, **7572, 9369, 11653, 12145**

MSMA
crabgrass control, **8155, 9531, 9533**

MSMA
kikuyugrass control, **10975**

MSMA
purple nutsedge control, **7265**

MSMA
sandbur control, **8161, 12665, 15140**

MSMA
selective herbicide, **4061**

MSMA
weed control, **8169, 8172, 8175**

MSMA
white clover control, **9537**

MSMA
yellow nutsedge control, **5237, 5238**

Muck soil
soil amendment, **386**

Muhlenvergia schrebari (see Nimblewill)

Mulch, **11915**

Mulch
application, **704, 3187, 5934, 7446, 11250, 13285, 14695**: equipment, **5932, 5933, 5934**

Mulch
effects, **1068, 3736, 11629, 12367**

Mulch
effects on: compaction, **9610**; frost heaving, **2925**; infiltration, **7184, 10163**

Mulch
erosion control, **18, 5132, 7081, 7736, 9991, 13974, 16040**: evaluation, **1479, 2340, 5042, 5108, 5109, 5124, 5125, 5133, 6034, 6515, 6716, 7184, 8180, 10494, 13403, 16458**

Mulch
establishment, **596, 999, 3075, 6034, 6111, 6456, 7484, 9950,**

12593, 13149, 16458: evaluation, **2420, 5021, 5108, 5109, 5124, 5125, 5133, 6515, 13404, 16454**

Mulch
evaluation, **2298, 2419, 2566, 2579, 2593, 2667, 2671, 2874, 2968, 2975, 3187, 3689, 4838, 5021, 5128, 5129, 5131, 5133, 5134, 5276, 6515, 6518, 6716, 7184, 7446, 10741, 12596, 13401, 13404, 13797, 15365, 16454, 16458**

Mulch
microenvironment effects, **2291:** soil moisture, **2246, 2291, 2420, 2667, 3050, 5134, 7184, 7446, 9610, 15695**; soil temperature, **2246, 2291, 2420, 2667, 5108, 7184, 9610, 13009, 13401**

Mulch
roadside, **2764, 2984, 7081:** establishment, **5130, 5275, 15365**; evaluation, **2058, 7782, 13401, 13797, 14432, 14479**

Mulch
sand dune stabilization, **5278**

Mulch
types, **1531, 2081, 3046, 9821, 13403:** asphalt, **999, 10494**; bituminous material, **255, 6010, 12367, 15178**; elastomeric, **5910, 7184**; evaluation, **122, 2419, 6946, 8834, 14478, 14480**; glass fiber mat, **5152**; plastic, **11629, 16040**; polyethylene coated paper, **9610; sawdust, 171, 2420**; straw (see Straw mulch); synthetic rubber, **7384**; wood cellulose fiber, **8215**; wood chips, **8987**

Mulch
winter protection, **1552, 10759**

Mulching (see Mulch, application)

Muriate of potash (see Potassium chloride)

Mushrooms, **7116, 11064, 12931**

Mushroom soil, **637, 14132**
soil amendment, **235, 11153, 14131**

Musk erodium, **4738**

Mylone® (see Dazomet)

Nabam, **3923, 9764**

Nabam
brown patch control, **14311, 14312**

Nabam
Rhizoctonia species control, **9763**

Nabam
spring dead spot control, **13888, 13936**

Nabam
striped smut control, **9762**

1–naphthyl–N–methylcarbamate (see Carbaryl)

Napiergrass, **3553**

Narragansett creeping bentgrass, **11661**

National Association of Greenskeepers of America
(see Golf Course Superintendents Association of America)

National Golf Day
research support, **12390**

National Golf Week, **1452**

Natrin®
goosegrass control, **5528**

Natural organic fertilizer (see Nitrogen carrier, natural organic)

Natural selection, **3385**

1–n–butyl–3–(3,4–dichlorophenyl)–1–methylurea
crabgrass control, **1122**

N–butyl–N–ethyl–trifluoro–2,6–dinitro-p-toluidine (see Benefin)

N-dimethyl aminosuccinamic acid (see B–995)

N(1, 1–dimethylpropynyl)–3,5–dichlorobenzamide (see Pronamide)

Neburon, **8768, 13576**

Neburon
algea control, **6630**

Neburon
annual bluegrass control, **4429, 4442, 4445, 4478, 6573, 6576:** evaluation, **5632, 6626, 8419, 11056**

Neburon
annual weedy grass control, **3665a**

Neburon
chickweed control, **4661, 6626**

Neburon
crabgrass control, **6358, 13429**

Neburon
goosegrass control, **6286**

Neburon
pearlwort control, **6626, 6628**

Neburon
weed control, **6631, 15978**

Needle ice, **3175**

Nemafene® (see D-D®)

Nemagon® (see Dibromochloropropane)

Nematicide, **596, 1126, 1217, 1350, 2241, 2756, 2999, 3385, 3449, 3583a, 3602a, 8096, 13721, 13915, 14418**

Nematicide
application, **598, 11715:** methods, **11346, 12061, 13912**

Nematicide
effects on: root growth, **14818, 14819**; shoot growth, **14818, 14819, 14820**

Nematicide
evaluation, **3281, 8686, 9331, 10551, 12978, 13910, 13912, 13913, 13917, 14528, 14529, 15926, 15927, 16103, 16106**

Nematicide
nematode control evaluation, **1700, 6337, 8040, 14818, 14819, 14820, 16105**

Nematicide
phytotoxicity, **2787, 3833**

Nematicide
use, **8272, 12045**

Nematode, **185, 1201, 1217, 1290, 1353, 1548, 1608, 2241, 2756, 2999, 5820, 7617, 7869, 8507, 8509, 10145, 11704, 12050, 12229, 12604, 13718, 14804, 14889, 16312**

Nematode
book, **6609**

Nematode
characteristics, **12046, 12050, 14393, 16100**

Nematode
distribution, **3250, 5011, 11072, 11709, 11754, 12049, 14564, 14565, 14821, 14822, 15860, 16101, 16293:** Northern USA, **2672, 7895, 9326, 9327, 11669, 14565, 14822**; survey, **5641, 6606, 6607, 8250, 11696, 11742, 12229, 14052**; warm regions, **3834, 11713, 12043, 15007**

Nematode
effects of: nitrogen carrier, **7615, 11743, 11744, 11745, 12043, 14071**

Nematode
England, **8337, 15807**

Nematode
factors affecting, **1399, 2717, 11347, 13914, 14995:** fungicides, **10576, 14071**

Nematode
fungal interaction (see Fungi, nematode interaction)

Nematode
injury symptoms, **5736, 7870, 8479, 9326, 9976, 10144, 11715, 12050, 12054, 13796, 15480, 15674, 15853**

Nematode
kinds, **137, 6608, 8250, 9327, 12054, 12057, 14418, 15480, 15853**

Nematode
melting out complex, **12021**

Nematode
parasitic effects, **2999, 12021, 12050, 12054, 14418, 16101**

Nematode
sod shipment regulations, **5008**

Nematode
soil analysis, **11711, 12977**

Nematode
soil sampling, **9017, 9325, 9328, 15853**

Nematode
yellow tuft association, **14530**

Nematode control, **137, 1232, 1366, 8509, 11704, 11870, 12044, 13721, 16099, 16312**

Nematode control
biological, **1544**

Nematode control
chemical, **2241, 2999, 3449, 3583a, 4223, 4971, 5010, 5736, 8041, 8272, 8830, 9976, 10144, 11070, 11346, 12047, 12048, 12049, 12054, 12059, 13915, 13916, 14093, 16101, 16102:** dibromochloropropane, **11709, 11743, 12053, 12061**; evaluation, **1490, 1639, 1779, 2756, 3281, 5013, 5757, 8040, 9331, 11717, 11744, 11745, 11752, 11918, 12058, 12062, 12660, 12978, 13909, 13910, 13911, 13912, 13913, 14528, 14529, 16106**; fumigation, **597, 12487, 13721**

Nematode control
flooding, **7871**

Nematode control
hot water treatment, **1899, 7618, 13721**

Neoapectana glasseri
Japanese beetle control, **6548**

Net assimilation, **10698, 13409**

Net blotch (see *Helminthosporium* blight)

Newport Kentucky bluegrass, **1370, 1385, 1473, 1685, 3274, 3656, 7202, 7309, 8343, 9958, 11187, 11363, 12007, 14374, 16179**

Newport Kentucky bluegrass
adaptation: temperature, **237, 16430**

Newport Kentucky bluegrass
culture, **4054, 8692**

Newport Kentucky bluegrass
description, **337, 6089, 16435**

Newport Kentucky bluegrass
disease susceptibility, **2546, 3259**

Newport Kentucky bluegrass
establishment, **1420**

Newport Kentucky bluegrass
evaluation, **4422, 6307, 6309, 6330, 6626, 6712, 8317, 9218, 10622, 10626, 10635, 11186, 11323, 14813**

Newport Kentucky bluegrass
nematode susceptibility, **1641**

Newport Kentucky bluegrass
seed production, **5650**

Newport Kentucky bluegrass
winter overseeding, **9879**

New Zealand bentgrass (see Colonial bentgrass)

New Zealand browntop bentgrass, **2274**

New Zealand chewings fescue, **2274, 3776, 11933**

New Zealand Institute for Turf Culture, **3941, 12830, 15249**

Night
turfgrass maintainence, **9835, 9836**

Night illumination, **3884, 5068, 9309**
golf course, **1812, 1876, 3884, 4116, 4307, 5067, 6395**

Night lighting (see Night illumination)

Nike Kentucky bluegrass, **9218**

Nimblewill, **484, 1477, 2037, 7718, 12738**

Nimblewill
chemical control, **1493, 1551, 3655, 3691a, 7710, 7715, 7716, 13132, 13204:** DCPA, **7655, 7658**; DMPA, **1689**; evaluation, **3656a, 4646, 7711, 15160**

Nimisilia creeping bentgrass, **1220, 1639, 2566**
evaluation, **10616, 10622, 10760, 11021**

Nitralin
crabgrass control, **9537**

Nitra-shell, **1555**

Nitrate, **1655, 2946, 4285**

Nitrate
absorption, **9818, 10935**

Nitrate
assimilation: factors influencing, **10935**

Nitrate
content: factors affecting, **5581, 9718, 11673, 13774**; temperature effects, **2750, 5215, 11673, 13774**

Nitrate
salinity effects, **345**

Nitrate
shoot growth effects, **2945**

Nitrate
soil relationships, **2308, 10456**

Nitrate
testing, **3196**

Nitrate
water quality, **472**

Nitrate of ammonia (see Ammonium nitrate)

Nitrate of lime (see Calcium nitrate)

Nitrate of potash (see Potassium nitrate)

Nitrate reductase
diurnal variation, **8773**

Nitrate reductase
factors affecting, **8773, 8774, 8785:** temperature, **2649, 8773, 8774, 8776, 8785**

Nitrate reductase
species variation, **3035, 8776**

Nitrate of soda (see Sodium nitrate)

Nitrification, **5588, 11972**

Nitrification
effects, **9085, 12836**

Nitrification
effects of: lead arsenate, **15810, 15816**; liming, **15810, 15816**; mercury, inorganic, **15810, 15811, 15816**

Nitrification
factors affecting, **238, 4831, 7998, 12297, 12726**

Nitrification
inhibitors, **8128, 8766, 12235, 14403**

Nitrification
nitrogen carriers, **8128, 12259**

Nitro-chalk, **1555, 4768, 5634, 5636, 5683**

Nitroform® (see Ureaformaldehyde)

Nitrogen, **6945, 10734, 13175, 13411**

Nitrogen
absorption, **12496, 13415**

Nitrogen
accumulation, **4110, 4286, 6502, 6504**

Nitrogen
as ammonia: effects, **11341**

Nitrogen
assimilation, **13415, 15350**

Nitrogen
availability, **3205, 6945, 7963, 8006, 8515, 8730, 9085, 9603, 12916, 14904**

Nitrogen
carriers (see Nitrogen carrier)

Nitrogen
deficiency symptoms, **2655, 6465, 8758, 9712, 9717, 10449, 10452, 10963, 11790, 12701, 12705, 12716, 12717, 12719, 12726**

Nitrogen
disease effects, **182, 975, 1487, 2064, 2699, 3799, 3804, 3805, 5395, 5396, 6198, 6205, 6508, 6679, 6704, 7205, 8350, 9414:** brown patch, **2997, 2998, 4169, 4840, 5467, 12196**; dollar spot, **5406, 6167, 6168, 6200, 6205, 7855, 7857, 10193, 10495, 10568, 10572, 11560, 12757, 16020**; *Fusarium* blight, **2539, 5637**; *Fusarium* patch, **4768, 6652, 6679, 12085**; gray leaf spot, **6168, 6183, 6205**; *Helminthosporium* leaf spot, **1690, 2545, 5652, 6306, 7814, 7855, 8699, 12736**; *Ophiobolus* patch, **2609, 6704**; red thread, **6647, 6679, 6728, 6733, 6766**; rust, **1487, 12719**; snow mold, **1470, 4316, 12160, 14923**; stripe smut, **6329, 7203**

Nitrogen
effects, **4840, 8331, 9485, 11341, 12760, 13436**

Nitrogen
effects on: amide content, **2944, 14323**; carbohydrate reserves, **40, 41, 90, 2245, 2295, 2566, 2574, 2704, 2946, 2977, 2982, 3364, 3720, 5235, 5307, 7007, 7008, 7114, 7852, 9423, 9479, 9992, 11672, 11673, 11973, 11980, 12220, 12557, 13410, 13427, 13428, 13948, 14075, 14090, 14195, 14323, 14451, 14600, 14896, 15437, 15657, 16464, 16465**; chemical composition, **2247, 2251, 2946, 3554, 6603, 7084, 7515, 9718, 14090**; chinch bug damage, **8046, 8047, 12265**; chlorophyll, **10076, 10173**; cool season turfgrasses, **952, 4634, 4646, 4653, 6307, 10604**; crabgrass invasion, **4891, 6306, 6307**; divot recovery, **15355, 15364**; dollar spot, **5523**; drought hardiness, **3720, 6306, 6307, 8699, 11973**; earthworms, **5636, 5902**; environmental stress hardiness, **12701, 12719, 12726, 15435, 15909**; establishment, **6435, 7853, 10001**; flower development, **12962, 12963, 12964**; haplocorm development, **13618**; heat hardiness, **1488, 1688, 1923, 3720, 6320, 12005**; low temperature color reten-

tion, **12497, 12499, 14075, 16354**; low temperature hardiness, **2499, 2705, 3720, 3721, 7114, 12497**; low temperature kill, **5779, 10604, 15084**; nutrient uptake, **2499**; polystand composition, **952, 5636, 10605, 12719, 12747**; polystand composition-Kentucky bluegrass-red fescue, **1688, 4646, 4657**; protein content, **2946, 9356, 10459, 11673, 14323**; puffiness, **5499**; rhizome growth, **5581, 6442, 8710, 9134, 11015, 12637, 14090, 15657**; root growth, **1304, 2064, 2717, 3074, 3200, 4619, 4620, 4732, 6432, 6628, 6712, 7221, 7222, 7223, 7312, 7495, 7496, 8262, 8265, 8667, 8670, 8710, 8758, 9159, 10072, 10076, 10172, 10194, 10382, 10449, 11858, 11905, 12532, 12675, 12701, 12734, 13419, 13421, 13428, 13623, 13813, 14075, 14090, 14161, 14323, 14830, 14832, 15086, 15437, 15657, 15774**; root-shoot ratio, **6712, 8262, 11907, 15086**; seed production, **12279**; shoot density, **4840, 6306, 6442, 6712, 7559, 8434, 8699, 9134, 10071, 10072, 10076, 10173, 10615, 12703, 12751, 12757, 13623, 15729**; shoot growth, **41, 90, 2672, 2732, 2944, 2946, 3200, 3275, 3279, 3482, 3554, 3890, 4278, 4619, 5469, 5571, 5581, 5856, 6434, 6594, 6628, 6717, 6783, 6784, 7221, 7222, 7223, 7495, 7496, 7515, 7516, 7557, 7699, 7771, 7857, 7931, 8192, 8261, 8262, 8265, 8576, 8667, 8670, 8710, 8758, 8949, 9008, 9103, 9104, 9134, 9159, 9442, 9718, 9967, 9974, 10072, 10076, 10129, 10172, 10194, 10195, 10201, 10382, 10384, 11012, 11524, 11783, 11858, 11921, 11980, 12006, 12220, 12255, 12532, 12557, 12637, 12697, 12736, 12752, 12757, 12840, 13428, 13619, 13623, 13862, 13951, 14074, 14075, 14148, 14214, 14323, 14446, 14628, 14811, 14830, 14832, 15086, 15116, 15155, 15786, 15984, 15985, 15986, 16202**; sod formation, **10382**; sod heating, **8940, 8947**; sod strength, **2630, 2633, 2704, 2707, 2717, 5581**; soil reaction, **6666, 6674, 9274, 10385, 16202**; spring green-up, **8574, 12497, 12499, 16354**; succulence, **10076, 11973**; thatch, **5498, 5523, 6713**; tillering, **2295, 5646, 8055, 9992, 11015, 11980**; tissue nitrogen content, **2825, 5899, 7699, 8261, 8778, 9027, 9507, 11082, 11672, 12726, 12957, 12967, 14450, 14607, 15985, 16317**; transplant sod rooting, **5233, 5235, 5581**; turfgrass color, **4840, 7559, 8575, 9008, 12220, 12757, 13813, 14103**; turfgrass quality, **2617, 2706, 2982, 9134, 10173, 13436, 14075**; verdure, **10076**; water use rate, **10172, 13623, 15710**; wear tolerance, **9782**; weed invasion, **2136, 2617, 2631, 2633, 2941, 2942, 4634, 4657, 4840, 5636, 6309, 6637, 6713, 11330, 12719, 12747, 12751, 13813, 15729**; white clover, **4634, 4657, 15697**; wilt, **10482**; winter injury, **9354, 10605, 14075**

Nitrogen
efficiency, **3268, 5637**

Nitrogen
immobilization: soil moisture effects, **12231**

Nitrogen
leaching, **2684, 3206, 11972, 12635, 14905, 15064**

Nitrogen
metabolism, **6237, 6575, 8831:** temperature effects, **2694, 2697, 5215, 14323, 14324**

Nitrogen
mineralization, **3946, 10250**

Nitrogen
movement, soil: nitrate levels, **2673**

Nitrogen
nutrition, **2686, 2978, 3298, 4251, 4448, 6802, 6811, 6812, 8130, 9812, 11433, 11644, 11785, 12102, 12719, 13620, 14148:** developmental response, **4840, 12726, 12965**; effects, **5646, 8773, 9026, 12705, 12719**; physiological responses—photosynthesis, **12220, 13410, 13428**; physiological responses—respiration, **12220, 13410, 13428**; turfgrass responses, **9294, 12708, 13421**

Nitrogen
phytotoxicity, **4218**

Nitrogen
recovery, **2724, 6784, 7939, 9356, 9784, 9967, 10728, 14919**

Nitrogen
role, **5299, 6465, 10963, 11388, 11433**

Nitrogen
soil relationships, **170, 2978, 3266, 3269, 12631, 12635, 15338, 15873**

Nitrogen
soil test, **9830, 12264**

Nitrogen
species requirement, **12628, 13628, 16361, 16368, 16372**

Nitrogen
translocation, **6503, 13904**

Nitrogen
uptake, **2928, 4110, 6504, 7855, 8058, 10067, 13411:** carrier effects, **2606, 6454, 10067**; environmental factors affecting, **10067, 13411, 15437**

Nitrogen
volatilization, **7302, 9102**

Nitrogen carrier, **414, 675, 2006, 2724, 3298, 3337, 4113, 4261, 4856, 4934, 5469, 5503, 5683, 6941, 6954, 6961, 7427, 7464, 7575, 7962, 9057, 9790, 10133, 10589, 10864, 11145,**

11154, 11158, 11181, 11202, 11243, 11388, 11392, 11472, 11597, 11674, 12096, 12256, 12260, 12263, 12603, 12631, 12684, 12701, 12904, 13434, 13964, 14323, 15060, 15061, 15067, 15074, 15082, 15337, 15481, 15824, 15872, 15955, 16021, 16371, 16379

Nitrogen carrier
ammonium versus nitrate, **2617, 9831**

Nitrogen carrier
analysis, **11389, 12619**

Nitrogen carrier
application: timing, **4943, 8332**

Nitrogen carrier
characteristics, **5484, 8199, 9784, 12305**

Nitrogen carrier
disease incidence, **4111, 4112, 4114, 7202, 7285, 16021:** dollar spot, **8019, 10193, 10196, 10970, 12701, 12748, 12757, 15928**; *Fusarium* patch, **6647, 7285, 12085**; snowmold, **1470, 14923**

Nitrogen carrier
effects, **3001, 5321, 5636, 10385, 11454, 12265**

Nitrogen carrier
effects on: chinch bug damage, **7984, 8886, 12268**; earthworms, **5634, 5636, 8466**; leaching, **2830, 3206, 10456, 15064**; nematodes, **7615, 11709, 11743, 11744, 11745**; nitrate accumulation, **4285, 4286**; nitrogen availability, **3856, 7598, 11182, 12916**; nitrogen recovery, **238, 2606, 9784, 10728, 14919**; nitrogen release, **4486, 5547, 11210**; nutrient availability, **4991, 7991, 8024, 16152**; nutrient content, **11921**; root growth, **5679, 7493, 8720, 11905, 12697, 14137**; shoot density, **8332, 8699, 15729**; shoot growth, **4448, 4639, 5180, 5181, 5183, 6454, 6594, 7771, 7925, 7985, 8720, 9103, 9324, 9786, 9902, 10195, 10384, 10385, 10722, 10728, 11210, 11960, 12748, 13862, 14142, 14214, 14628, 14811, 15075, 15102, 15110, 15118**; soil nutrient level, **15116**; soil reaction, **2574, 2830, 5636, 7220, 7972, 7991, 8024, 9784, 9786, 10024, 11454, 11666, 11972, 12117, 12499, 13752, 15064, 15697, 16152, 16451**; tissue analysis, **4639, 11082, 11673, 13862**; turfgrass color, **8575, 15118**; turfgrass quality, **2706, 4550, 8332, 10402**; volatilization, **7344, 9102, 15062, 15064**; weed invasion, **2650, 5634, 15729, 15787**

Nitrogen carrier
efficiency evaluation, **4647, 4650, 5198, 13039, 15064, 15118**

Nitrogen carrier
evaluation, **483, 821, 843, 979, 1470, 1488, 1546, 1688, 1777, 2027, 2592, 2606, 2616, 2617, 2632, 2633, 2707, 2725, 2855, 3001, 3528, 4422, 4448, 4645, 4646, 4647, 4650, 4768, 4881, 4896, 4943, 5073, 5074, 5101, 5183, 5198, 5230, 5467, 5468, 5616, 5617, 5633, 5634, 5636, 5637, 5638, 5735, 5781, 5917, 6509, 6574, 6579, 6627, 6790, 7222, 7223, 7303, 7932, 8010, 8035, 8042, 8044, 8049, 8331, 8573, 9045, 9669, 9811, 10066, 10196, 10863, 10970, 11057, 11134, 11171, 11172, 11176, 11185, 11213, 11666, 11960, 12219, 12220, 12265, 12496, 12567, 12701, 12705, 12717, 12719, 13968, 14127, 14148, 14383, 15073, 15104, 15108, 15110, 15118, 15329, 15363, 15577, 15697, 15705, 15709, 15729, 15814, 15815, 16275, 16451, 16489:** on bermudagrass, **2608, 7991, 8004, 8007, 10459, 14402**; for greens, **8002, 10861, 11383**; Japan, **10121, 10122, 11803**; on Kentucky bluegrass, **2631, 2650, 2673**; puffiness, **5499**; roadside, **2094, 7012, 11905, 11907, 12596, 13813**

Nitrogen carrier
foliar burn evaluation, **1304, 10728**

Nitrogen carrier
inorganic, **1555, 6469, 13620**

Nitrogen carrier
natural organic, **427, 707, 1488, 7285, 8699, 10939, 11907, 15104**

Nitrogen carrier
nitrification evaluation, **238, 5588, 9085, 12259**

Nitrogen carrier
organic, **697, 1556, 5636, 6469, 9831, 11642, 12043, 12916, 13898**

Nitrogen carrier
residual effects, **4650, 15064**

Nitrogen carrier
salt index, **9784**

Nitrogen carrier
slow release, **2100, 9630, 10728, 12235, 13071, 15100**

Nitrogen carrier
synthetic inorganic, **238, 1125, 1209, 1304, 1555, 2941, 3132, 3856, 4943, 6469, 12567, 13620, 16006**

Nitrogen carrier
types, **2973, 3998, 15778**

Nitrogen cycle, **7939, 14936, 15338, 15955**

Nitrogen fertilization, **2978, 4645, 5820, 6022, 9630, 10251, 10589, 11150, 11154, 11181, 11439, 11597, 12635, 15508, 15610, 16371**

Nitrogen fertilization
application, **6434, 9831:** frequency, **9669, 10382, 11082, 15363**

Nitrogen fertilization
effects, **7241, 7856, 9294**

Nitrogen fertilization
evaluation, **4646, 6579, 9974, 15709**

Nitrogen fertilization
golf course, **1836, 6948**

Nitrogen fertilization
green, **5917, 9827, 12368**

Nitrogen fertilization
program, **2824, 5633, 5637, 8010, 9308, 9786**

Nitrogen fertilization
rate, **2725, 6962, 8692:** effects, **6655, 7855, 16203**; evaluation, **8042, 10843**

Nitrogen fertilization
sod production, **9134**

Nitrogen fertilization
timing, **2006, 3280, 4650, 5335, 5779, 5917, 8440, 8692, 12220:** effects, **5899, 7925, 9441, 12957**; evaluation, **5147, 5235, 8331, 8699, 10195, 10384, 11213, 12219, 14383, 15075, 15108, 15110, 15697, 15814, 15815**

Nitrogen fertilization
warm season turfgrasses, **7991, 9187, 15355**

Nitrogen fixation, **5588**

Nitrogen nutrition (see Nitrogen, nutrition)

Nitrolime, **2172**

NJE-P–27 (see Galaxy Kentucky bluegrass)

NJE-P–56 (see Adelphi Kentucky bluegrass)

NK–100 perennial ryegrass, **2069, 6294, 7011, 8732, 8734**
description, **6298, 6499**

NK–200 perennial ryegrass, **6499**

Noer soil profile sampler, **985, 1492**

Noise abatement, **4106, 9231**

Noise abatement
roadside, **2315**

Noise abatement
turfgrass function, **11737**

Nomenclature, **476, 6542**
turfgrass terms, **8725, 8726**

Nomophila noctuello (see Lucerne moth)

No-mow bermudagrass (see FB–137 bermudagrass)

Nonselective herbicide (see Herbicide, nonselective)

Norbeck creeping bentgrass, **7309, 7928, 7929, 12698**

Norbeck creeping bentgrass
evaluation, **9233, 11031**

Norbeck creeping bentgrass
use: fairway, **789, 815**

Nordenej chewings fescue, **8343**

Norderney red fescue, **8336, 8338, 8341, 8350**

Norlea perennial ryegrass, **1489, 1685, 2566, 3112, 6294, 7309**

Norlea perennial ryegrass
adaptation, **5314, 9213, 12007**

Norlea perennial ryegrass
description, **6298, 6499**

Norlea perennial ryegrass
evaluation, **6287, 6307, 6309, 7287, 8350**

Norlea perennial ryegrass
rust disease, **1547**

Northern masked chafer
chemical control, **12172, 12178, 12181**

Northern masked chafer
description, **7256, 12178**

Northland creeping bentgrass, **1489, 2607, 9408**

Northwest Turf Association
history, **8345**

North woods creeping bentgrass, **514**

Nozzles (see Sprinkler head)

N-(trichloromethylmercapto)-4–cyclohexene-1,2–dicarboximide (see Captan)

Nucleoli, **3378, 9527**

Nudwarf Kentucky bluegrass, **12007**
evaluation, **6330, 10622, 10626, 10635**

Nugget Kentucky bluegrass, **2100, 2612, 6451**

Nugget Kentucky bluegrass
evaluation, **9218, 10626, 14813**

Nugget Kentucky bluegrass
shade adaptation, **2204**

Nursegrass (see Companion grass)

Nursery, retail
customer service, **9486, 9487**

Nursery, stolon (see Stolon Nursery)

Nursery, turf, **547, 961, 981, 983, 1288, 1327, 1667, 5106, 6923, 8847, 12329, 15999**

Nursery, turf
bentgrass: seed head prevention, **9599**

Nursery, turf
culture, **6568, 6808, 7877, 8107, 8108, 10710**

Nursery, turf
establishment, **6568, 6808, 7213, 12329:** stolonizing, **6346, 9832, 12135**

Nursery, turf
golf course, **11555, 11584, 13758**

Nursery, turf
green, **428, 1408, 6570**

Nursery, turf
pest control, **8516, 8891**

Nursery, turf
propagation: vegetative, **7525**

Nursery, turf
soil sterilization methods, **7405**

Nursery, turf
use, **6568, 15999**

Nursery, turf
weed control, **3596, 11247**

Nutgrass
chemical control, **1620, 3466, 4059:** evaluation, **2160, 7536, 10739**

Nutgrass
propagation, **4773**

Nutrient, **15615**

Nutrient
availability, **2973, 11387:** soil reaction effects, **7671, 8243, 8248, 11573, 12601, 12624, 12702, 14845**

Nutrient
excess: diagnosis, **15602, 15856**

Nutrient
plant content (see Mineral composition)

Nutrient
removal: clipping evaluation, **6656, 11783**

Nutrient
requirements, **11525:** evaluation, **7728, 9590, 12785**

Nutrient
role, **8569, 15351**

Nutrient
translocation, **13897, 13903**

Nutrient
uptake, **2747, 3224, 7325, 7828, 10874, 15471, 15488:** factors affecting, **107, 2499, 3850, 5788, 12496, 12500, 12771, 15471**; salinity effects, **7035, 9175**; soil depth effects, **6430, 6434**

Nutrient culture
research technique, **12733**

Nutrient deficiency, **1583, 2548, 13563**

Nutrient deficiency
diagnosis, **11794, 15602:** tissue test, **12602**

Nutrient deficiency
factors affecting, **13897, 13903**

Nutrient deficiency
micronutrients, **9265**

Nutrient deficiency
symptoms, **2655, 9514, 9712, 9713, 10449, 10452, 10963**

Nutrition, **178, 3157, 4247, 4463, 4660, 6582, 6617, 7963, 8653, 11177, 11424, 11829, 12261, 12309, 12628, 14799, 16012, 16077**

Nutrition
cation-anion ratios, **9812**

Nutrition
effects, **439, 5336, 6517, 13897**

Nutrition
effects on: chemical composition, **3606, 8265, 9027**; disease proneness, **1290, 4179, 4182, 4198, 5373, 6702, 8348**

Nutrition
species adaptation, **7473**

Nutrition
warm season grasses, **9959, 14798**

Nutritional balance, **581, 5788, 6707, 9027, 10055, 12247, 15270**

Nutsedge, **7547**
control, **1782, 7546, 9144, 9888**

Nutsedge, purple (see Purple nutsedge)

Nutsedge, yellow (see Yellow nutsedge)

Nuttall alkaligrass
salt tolerance, **8197**

Oasis chewings fescue, **8343, 13780**

Oasis chewings fescue
evaluation, **8338, 8341, 8350, 9219**

Oats
roadside establishment, **9129**

Ochrosidia dillosa (see Annual White Grub)

1,2,4,5,6,7,8,8,-octachloro--2,3,-3a,4,7,7a–hexahydro–4,7–methanoindene (see Chlordane)

Octadecanol (see Hexa-octadecanol mixture)

Octopamine
in Italian ryegrass, **7367**

Odonaspis ruthae (see Bermudagrass scale)

Oils, **9, 9676**

Oils
herbicide combinations: synergistic effects, **8003, 8171**

Oils
herbicide effectiveness, **7999**

Oils
injury symptoms, **2673**

Oils
lawn edging, **14628**

Oils
phytotoxicity: species tolerance, **7996**

Oils
phytotoxicity evaluation, **8179**

Oil-wax surfactant
evaporation reduction, **6075**

Oklawn centipedegrass, **9662**

Olcott Turf Garden, **11813, 12131**

Old Orchard® creeping bentgrass (see C–52 creeping bentgrass)

Olds red fescue, **7309, 9219**

Oligochaeta (see Earthworm)

Oligosaccharide
species variability, **2566**

Olpidium agrostis, **4732, 12992**

Olpidium brassicae, **3262**

Olpidium species
on bermudagrass, **4335**

Onehunga weed
chemical control, **2172**

Onion, wild (see Wild onion)

Opal velvet bentgrass, **8341, 8350**

Ophiobolus cariceti (see Take-all disease)

Ophiobolus graminis (see *Ophiobolus* patch)

Ophiobolus herpotrichus (see also Spring dead spot), **13937**

Ophiobolus patch, **1037, 1101, 1141, 1261, 1440, 1977, 6650, 6743, 13990, 13997, 14014**

Ophiobolus patch
chemical control, **6746, 6748, 6750, 7288:** evaluation, **4591, 4592, 6733, 7285, 8335, 16210**

Ophiobolus patch
control, **1475, 6666, 6740, 6745, 6763, 8349**

Ophiobolus patch
cultural effects, **13998:** fertilization, **6637, 6647, 6651, 6654, 6660, 6694, 6733**; nutrition, **1777, 2609, 6702, 6704**; phosphorus, **2609, 6704**; potassium, **2609, 6703, 6704, 6708**

Ophiobolus patch
England, **7192, 8337, 8339, 8342**

Ophiobolus patch
environmental effects, **6739, 13998**

Ophiobolus patch
soil effects, **14002:** soil reaction, **6674, 6704, 8349**

Ophiobolus patch
symptoms, **6760, 6761, 8349, 13998, 14002**

Ophiopogon species (see Mondograss)

Opizia stolonifera (see Acapulcograss)

Orchardgrass, **574, 3422, 3553, 3836**

Orchardgrass
culture, **2725, 10722**

Orchardgrass
uses, **3553, 10233**

Organic acids
factors affecting, **2946**

Organic amendment (see Soil amendment, organic)

Organic arsenicals, **8155, 12808**

Organic fertilizer (see Nitrogen carrier, organic)

Organic matter, **1516, 2779, 4289, 4586, 5891, 6411, 6689, 7679, 9310**

Organic matter
decomposition, **2272, 3046, 14230**

Organic matter
description, **3046, 3336, 4289, 5975**

Organic matter
effects on: soil physical properties, **9819, 14186, 14187**

Organic matter
factors affecting, **102, 4941**

Organic matter
soil effects, **6689, 13508, 14125, 14232**

Organic matter
types, **14177, 14186, 14187**

Organic matter
water retention, **4289, 6411**

Organic soil, **3651a, 4718**

Organic soil
sod production, **14629**

Organization
planning, **3639a**

Organizational structure, **5621**

Organizational structure
golf course, **12204, 15533**

Oriental beetle, **657, 3264, 6233, 7156, 7256, 7258**

Oriental garden beetle, **7258**

Ormond bermudagrass, **1489, 1547, 1639, 4075, 7309, 14401, 16105**

Ormond bermudagrass
adaptation, **7977**

Ormond bermudagrass
culture, **7977, 10492**

Ormond bermudagrass
description, **8212, 11232, 15442, 16378**

Ormond bermudagrass
evaluation, **8154, 11232, 11882, 14402, 14403,**

Ornamental grasses
bulletin, **13549**

Orthocide 406® (see Captan)

Oryzalin
crabgrass control, **14981**

Oscinella frit (see Frit fly)

Osmotic pressure, **9485, 14319**

Overhead sprinkler system (see Irrigation system, types)

Overseeding, **3487, 5065, 6540, 7432**

Overseeding
annual bluegrass control, **2647**

Overseeding
fairway, **560, 5318, 15959**

Overseeding
green, **128, 2794, 3443, 3520, 5136, 5142, 6015, 7279, 10836, 13008**

Overseeding
lawn, **13237, 13348**

Overseeding
practices, **587, 7037, 7211, 9432**

Overseeding
timing, **692, 2794, 13008**

Overseeding
turfgrasses used, **3520, 5121, 5142, 7291:** creeping bentgrass, **7037, 7211**

Overseeding
winter (see Winter overseeding)

7–oxabicyclo (2.2.1.) heptane–2,3–dicarboxylic acid (see Endothall)

Oxalis stricta (see Woodsorrel, yellow)

Oxamide
nitrogen carrier, **2725, 16275**

Oxathin
stripe rust control, **9894**

Oxygen
soil: effects, **9489, 9497, 9500, 9503, 14995**; factors affecting, **2294, 6661, 9498**; root growth effects, **2293, 9503, 12535, 14331**; shoot growth effects, **9503, 9497, 15105**

Ozone, **2679**

Ozone
Kentucky bluegrass susceptibility: cultivar evaluation, **8685, 16097**

Ozone
species tolerance, **3217**

Palause Kentucky bluegrass, **14813**

PAN (see Peroxyacetyl nitrate)

Pan evaporation
irrigation scheduling use, **8531, 8532**

Pangolagrass, **3553, 3581**

Paniceae, **7522**

Panicoideae, **14241**

Panicum capillare (see Witchgrass)

Panicum dichotomiflorum (see Fall panicum)

Panicum virgatum (see Switchgrass)

Panogen® (see Cyano(methylmercuril)guanidine)

Paper chromatography
cultivar identification, **11229**

Paper net mulch (see Woven paper net mulch)

paraDichlorobenzene
mole control, **6460**

Paraguay bahiagrass
adaptation, **3539**

Paraguay bahiagrass
description, **10524, 10525, 15858**

Paraquat, **3513, 3516, 3520, 3655, 5033, 5578, 7298, 7865, 8630, 8768, 8867, 12283, 14896**

Paraquat
annual grass control, **7298, 7865, 8179, 10530**

Paraquat
on bermudagrass, **45, 93, 13695**

Paraquat
phytotoxicity, **4341, 4954, 12283**

Paraquat
soil residual, **15425, 15462**

Paratetranychus pratensis (see Timothy mite)

Parathion, **3284, 4221**

Parathion
chinch bug control, **8873, 8877, 8882, 8892**

Parathion,
insect control, **12437, 13472, 13483, 14398**

Parathion
Japanese beetle control, **12173, 13472**

Park, **1698, 2753, 2937, 5592, 9130, 9575, 13762**

Park
construction, **8964, 13006**

Park,
culture, **2627, 4347, 4774, 5377, 8787, 9157, 10262, 10263, 10264, 10265, 10266, 10332, 10333, 10855, 12667, 13161, 13588, 13814, 15059:** cost analysis, **15641**; fertilization, **11430, 12549, 12625, 13161**; problems, **7506, 10024, 11486**; weed control, **14309, 14858**

Park
equipment, **3854, 13588**

Park
establishment, **2628, 6604, 10236, 13814**

Park
landscaping, **9961, 10238**

Park
renovation, **16091**

Park
turfgrasses used, **621, 2354, 3317, 4029, 4161, 4162, 6604, 13814, 13819, 14355, 14978:** cool season, **10332, 10333, 11986, 15059, 16358**; warm season, **10236, 10238, 11705**

Park Kentucky bluegrass, **1473, 2027, 2589, 3656, 4447, 7202, 7309, 7670, 11187, 11363, 12007, 13238, 14635, 16179**

Park Kentucky bluegrass
diseases, **1776, 3259:** *Helminthosporium* leaf spot susceptibility, **2546, 9226**

Park Kentucky bluegrass
evaluation, **6306, 6330, 6626, 6712, 8317, 9218, 10622, 10626, 10635, 11186, 11323, 14813**

Parthenogenesis
Kentucky bluegrass, **14735**

Parzate® (see Nabam)

Paspalum conjugatum (see Sourgrass)

Paspalum dilatatum (see Dallisgrass)

Paspalum notatum (see Bahiagrass)

Paspalum species, **3534**

Patents
turfgrass cultivars, **2452**

Path
golf car (see Golf car, path)

PAT System
soil modification, **2100, 4528, 4531, 4540, 4548**

Pattern, mowing (see Mowing, pattern)

PAX®
crabgrass control, **8148, 8151, 8178**

3–(p-chlorophenyl)–1, 1–dimethylurea (see Monuron)

PCNB
brown patch control, **168, 1545, 1700, 9886, 16511**

PCNB
disease control, **2196, 11103**

PCNB
dollar spot control, **7192, 12357**

PCNB
stripe smut control, **1985, 7195, 7196, 7200, 11103**

p-dimethylaminobenzene diazo sodium sulfonate (see Dexon ®)

Pearl millet, **3553**

Pearlwort, **1180, 4737**

Pearlwort
chemical control, **2482, 5602, 5609, 6667, 7504, 7537, 11629:** evaluation, **2303, 7119, 7120, 12082, 12083**; neburon, **6626, 6628**

Pearlwort
cultural control, **2303, 9383**

Pearlwort
factors affecting, **5634, 5636**

Pearlwort, birdseye, **1019**

Peat, **122, 237, 289, 490, 637, 4716, 15550**

Peat
decomposition, **637, 2308**

Peat
effects, **1879, 8037:** soil physical properties, **10857, 10859**

Peat
nitrogen availability, **9603**

Peat
soil amendment, **235, 386, 1546, 2996, 4842, 5805, 9199, 9680, 9737, 10029, 12010, 16307, 16488:** effects, **9498, 14974**; evaluation, **4702, 4704, 5167, 6412, 8018, 9680, 10974, 10977, 10978, 11153, 11605, 13686, 13896, 13902, 13906, 13907, 14131**

Peat
types, **145, 235, 490, 2779, 3034, 7864, 9737, 10859, 14139, 14177, 15103, 15550, 15552, 15560, 15764**

Peat humus, **7864, 9899, 10029, 10859, 12304, 13975, 15550, 15552, 15560, 15764**

Peat moss, **7864**

Peat moss
soil amendment evaluation, **10112, 10114, 10976, 14131**

Peat soil, **11859, 15560**

Peat, sphagnum (see Sphagnum peat)

Pebulate
annual bluegrass control, **4018**

Pectinase
thatch decomposition effects, **10230**

Pelliculari filamentosa (see Brown patch)

Pelo perennial ryegrass, **1396, 6294, 8732, 8734**

Pelo perennial ryegrass
description, **6298, 6499**

Pelo perennial ryegrass
establishment, **7011, 7670**

Pelo perennial ryegrass
evaluation, **7191, 7287, 7508, 8336, 8338, 8350**

Peltigera canina (see Lichen)

Penetrability, soil
factors affecting, **13864, 13907**

Penicillum nigricans
soil water repellancy effects, **13033**

Penncross creeping bentgrass, **1218, 1489, 1574, 1789, 4389, 4666, 5165, 5781, 6892, 6939, 7309, 9152, 9153, 10767, 11165, 11574, 12007, 12698, 13238, 13357**

Penncross creeping bentgrass
adaptation, **4400, 5314, 6585, 7639**

Penncross creeping bentgrass
culture, **2007, 2029, 2872, 6964, 8818, 9430**

Penncross creeping bentgrass
description, **2069, 4400, 5165, 10637, 11232, 13357**

Penncross creeping bentgrass
evaluation, **2030, 7670, 8791, 10616, 10760, 11021, 11186, 14349, 14365**

Penncross creeping bentgrass
herbicide selectivity, **2069, 3610a**

Penncross creeping bentgrass
uses, **2028, 2872**: winter overseeding, **2670, 9879**

Pennfine perennial ryegrass, **2211, 2670, 5175, 5191, 6499**

Penngift crownvetch, **6032, 6963, 9988, 11162**

Penngift crownvetch
establishment, **5157, 6969, 11162**

Penngift crownvetch
uses, **6962, 6969**

Pennisetum clandestinum (see Kikuyugrass)

Pennlawn red fescue, **975, 1052, 1547, 1700, 4666, 5539, 7309, 9879, 11186, 11631, 16323**

Pennlawn red fescue
adaptation, **2589, 7639:** drought tolerance, **1778, 2589** ; submersion tolerance, **2700, 2701**

Pennlawn red fescue
disease: red thread, **11113**

Pennlawn red fescue
evaluation, **4709, 6307, 6309, 6637, 7670, 8341, 8350, 9219, 9349**

Pennlu creeping bentgrass, **993, 1052, 3123, 7309, 10622, 10760, 11165, 11232**

Pennlu creeping bentgrass
adaptation, **7639, 9408**

Pennlu creeping bentgrass
disease: stripe smut, **7351, 7627**

Pennpar creeping bentgrass, **6294**

Pennpar creeping bentgrass
evaluation, **10616, 10622, 11021**

Pennstar Kentucky bluegrass, **1473, 1700, 1776, 2566, 3944, 5174, 7202, 14748**

Pennstar Kentucky bluegrass
adaptation, **1778, 6298, 6315, 10633:** drought tolerance, **1778, 2589**

Pennstar Kentucky bluegrass
evaluation, **6307, 6309, 6330, 9218, 10622, 10626, 11323, 11325, 11329, 14813**

Pennywort, lawn, **725**

Pennywort, lawn
control, **755, 11629**

Pensacola bahiagrass, **2931, 3539, 3571, 5120, 8078, 12596**

Pensacola bahiagrass
breeding, **3544, 3609**

Pensacola bahiagrass
cultural effects, **14216:** cutting height, **2733, 3504, 14216**; fertilization, **2732, 15329**

Pensacola bahiagrass
description, **7833, 10524, 10525, 15858**

Pensacola bahiagrass
uses, **16314, 16514**

Pensacola bahiagrass
water use rate, **3581, 5056**

Pentachloronitrobenzene (see PCNB)

Peppergrass, **520**

Perched water table, **10100**

Percolation (see Soil water, percolation)

Perennial grasses, **9179, 14835**

Perennial grasses
chemical control, **3655, 3658, 6206, 10419, 12215**

Perennial ryegrass, **4009, 7286, 7339, 10189, 11767, 11771, 13269, 13908, 14471**

Perennial ryegrass
adaptation, **5483, 6499, 8760, 13383:** light, **90, 5675, 6055, 6056**; temperature, **88, 90, 3905, 6055, 6056, 6499**

Perennial ryegrass
breeding, **8495, 8496, 8502**

Perennial ryegrass
chemical composition, **7084, 14449**

Perennial ryegrass
cultivars, **3905, 6289, 6295, 6499, 10621, 11367, 11587, 13367, 13823, 14750:** description, **6316, 8734, 13376**; evaluation, **1471, 2211, 2560, 2566, 2574, 2583, 2603, 2617, 2631, 2632, 2658, 2673, 2684, 2698, 2704, 2706, 2707, 3459, 5313, 5316, 5320, 6310, 6323, 7191, 7284, 7287, 8294, 8338, 8341, 8350, 10622, 10631, 13660, 13661, 13662, 13822, 14561, 14562, 14979, 15874**

Perennial ryegrass
culture, **6307, 6398, 6499:** fertilization, **4227, 4273**; nitrogen nutrition, **90, 6307**

Perennial ryegrass
description, **1396, 1606, 2211, 2232, 2342, 3198, 3895, 3899, 3902, 3908, 3932, 5315, 5673, 5675, 6289, 6499, 7947, 8381, 8495, 11368, 11759, 12859, 12884, 13466, 14087, 14242, 15410:** rooting, **6431, 8395, 8398, 8399, 16283**; shoot apex, **3897, 3898**

Perennial ryegrass
diseases: blind seed disease, **7347, 7362**; ergot, **7363**; red thread susceptibility, **8336, 8337, 14562**

Perennial ryegrass
establishment, **2270, 2416**

Perennial ryegrass
exudate: glutamine, **4305, 7033**

Perennial ryegrass
herbicide selectivity, **2320, 8695**

Perennial ryegrass
low temperature hardiness: cultivar evaluation, **2566, 2684, 2706**

Perennial ryegrass
polystand compatability, **14750**

Perennial ryegrass
seed, **2232, 11965, 13453, 15874**

Perennial ryegrass
uses, **4747, 5315, 5704, 6289, 14750**

Perennial ryegrass
winter overseeding: cultivar evaluation, **2100, 2211, 6496, 10455, 13423**

Perennial ryegrass x meadow fescue hybrid
breeding, **3677a**

Perlite
fertilizer carrier, **2042**

Perlite
soil amendment, **9199, 12010:** evaluation, **4704, 5332, 10112, 10114, 13902, 15096, 15112**

Perlite
water retention effects, **7170**

Per-lome®
soil amendment evaluation, **5167, 13683, 13685, 16488, 16489**

Peroxyacetyl nitrate, **2679**

Personnel
golf course, **1743, 6932:** students, **6157**; training guidelines, **9743**

Pest, **4615, 12761**

Pest
book, **7031**

Pest control, **1842, 9631**

Pest control
biological, **6268**

Pest control
chemical: principles, **10088**

Pest control
state bulletin, **9893, 12741**

Pesticide, **1617, 3282, 5380, 8149, 12960, 14672, 15331, 15450**

Pesticide
antidotes, **3284**

Pesticide
application, **1445, 1451, 2150, 3501, 3748, 5220, 5492, 5840, 6128, 6815, 7442, 8135, 9656, 10733, 13714, 13717, 16031, 16034:** aerial, **1671, 1750, 1920**; cumulative effects, **14385, 14386, 14387**; methods, **6467, 12192, 12266, 16033**

Pesticide
common names, **15784, 15785**

Pesticide
compatibility, **1340, 3594a, 3653, 10584, 12467, 13608, 13609, 13714, 13717, 13720**

Pesticide
degradation, **133, 2155, 5380**

Pesticide
development, **3620, 3621, 8999, 10598, 10599, 11832:** cost, **3620, 3621**

Pesticide
effects on, **4304, 7132, 10073:** environmental quality, **4044, 4045, 8910, 11317, 14385, 15842**; shoot growth, **2617, 2707**

Pesticide
mixtures, **1340, 12266, 13714**

Pesticide
persistance, **1360, 5296, 5380, 6473**

Pesticide
regulations, **2786, 3295, 7048, 9700, 12194**

Pesticide
safety, **1505, 3282, 3284, 3945, 5853, 5865, 7644, 10412, 12315, 14724, 15334**

Pesticide
toxicity, **1674, 3594a, 3945, 5347, 5348, 14390:** mammalian, **1360, 1607, 1674, 3620, 3621, 3745, 4930, 4955, 10497**

Pesticide
use, **4539, 5463, 5853, 7018, 7428, 8828, 15842**

Petrobia latens, **8342**

pH (see Soil reaction)

Phenoxy herbicides, **916, 1653, 3619a**

Phenoxy herbicides
persistence, **190**

Phenyl mercury acetate (see PMA)

Pheretima hupeiensis (see Earthworms)

Philaenus leucopthalmas (see Two-lined spittlebug)

Phleum nodosum (see Timothy)

Phleum pratense (see Timothy)

Phleospora idahoensis (see Stem eyespot)

Phoenix billbug
chemical control, **10983**

Pholia nutans, **2961**

Phorate
chinch bug control, **8873, 8876**

Phorate
ground pearl control, **15739**

Phorate
hunting billbug control, **8894**

Phosphon®, **1550, 3570a, 9661, 15800**

Phosphon®
on bermudagrass, **1871, 8161**

Phosphon®
phytotoxicity, **8693**

Phosphorus, **867, 3569, 3740, 3893, 5850, 6655, 6909, 7465, 11433, 11438, 11787, 12247, 14441, 14453**

Phosphorus
arsenic interaction, **2100, 3344, 3722, 3724, 3728, 4406, 6758, 7762, 8074, 12626, 14245**

Phosphorus
availability: factors affecting, **8515, 9816, 12230**; soil reaction effects, **3391, 8245, 9816**

Phosphorus
carriers, **2260, 3337, 3722, 5684, 5869, 6776, 7465, 7575, 10864, 11388, 11389, 11392, 11472, 11786, 12256, 12603, 13964, 15778, 15824:** evaluation, **2974, 14066, 14905**

Phosphorus
deficiency, **2655, 4418, 10449:** symptoms, **2974, 6465, 8758, 9712, 9717, 10452, 10963, 11790, 14440**

Phosphorus
disease effects, **6704, 11490, 11661**

Phosphorus
effects on, **874, 2088, 3591a, 3727, 4840, 5636, 7223, 8046, 8620, 9795, 11129, 13459, 13750:** annual bluegrass, **6686, 8696, 8701**; carbohydrate reserves, **14090, 15657**; chemical composition, **7217, 12450, 14090**; heat hardiness, **1688, 12005**; herbicide effectiveness, **8700, 8702**; iron chlorosis, **14440**; low temperature hardiness, **2705, 12497, 12499**; nutrient availability, **2888, 7993, 10059**; rhizome growth, **14090, 15657**; root growth, **4620, 7223, 8670, 8700, 8702, 8712, 8713, 8714, 8758, 12532, 12734, 14090, 15657**; seedling growth, **10054, 10055, 15774**; on shoot growth, **4797, 5856, 7217, 7223, 8264, 8648, 8670, 8700, 8702, 8713, 8714, 8758, 8949, 9796, 12532, 12752, 13686, 14376, 14440, 14441, 15657, 16202**

Phosphorus
nutrition, **675, 1639, 1700, 1777, 2404, 3155, 3727, 4251, 5869, 6801, 6811, 6812, 11785, 12102, 12261, 14148**

Phosphorus
role, **5869, 6465, 9026, 10963, 11388**

Phosphorus
root toxicity, **4797**

Phosphorus
soil fixation, **8245, 11556**

Phosphorus
soil leaching, **2684, 3339, 12635**

Phosphorus
soil levels, survey, **4520**

Phosphorus
soil movement, **3391, 5467**

Phosphorus
soil penetration: cultivation effects, **7389, 7390, 11153**

Phosphorus
soil relationships, **2414, 7390, 8245, 12631, 13398**

Phosphorus
soil test, **6802, 7762**

Phosphorus
translocation, **6503, 12771, 13904**

Phosphorus
uptake, **11261, 12496:** factors affecting, **7128, 8264, 11261, 11307**

Phosphorus fertilization, **2027, 2776, 5906, 6651, 6666, 6812, 10623, 11149, 11786, 12635, 13398, 15217**

Phosphorus fertilization
application rate, **8702, 8949, 11261, 11439, 12532, 14441**

Photography
turfgrass growth measurement, **12227**

Photoperiod (see Day length)

Photorespiration, **15435**

Photorespiration
C_3–C_4 plants, **3447**

Photorespiration
species variation **3366**

Photosynthesis, **2614, 7583, 7682, 9695, 11026, 11027, 11643, 12307, 15822**

Photosynthesis
cultural effects, **131, 15500:** nitrogen, **12220, 13410, 13427, 13428**

Photosynthesis
effects of: leaf age, **3367, 8551, 14789**

Photosynthesis
efficiency, **2234, 11026:** C_3–C_4 plants, **3447**

Photosynthesis
environmental effects, **6457:** light intensity, **131, 6052, 13428**; temperature, **2614, 5150, 6052, 8314, 10228, 10640, 11086, 11936, 13410, 13427, 13428, 14789, 15435, 16399**

Photosynthesis
factors affecting, **7511, 10640, 11086, 13410, 13427, 14789, 15480, 15496**

Photosynthesis
herbicide effects, **13669, 14860**

Photosynthesis
Kentucky bluegrass cultivars, **15436, 15438**

Photosynthesis
warm season turfgrasses, **10640, 13509:** bermudagrass, **3790, 3791**

Phyiiopertha horticola (see Garden chafer)

Phyllophaga species (see also June beetle), **9749**

Physarium cinereum (see Slime mold)

Physiological drought, **12939**

Physiological drought
fertilizer effects, **5179, 5637, 16041**

Physiological drought
prevention, **1700**

Phytochrome, **1649**

Phytochrome
Kentucky bluegrass seed, **14761**

Phytomer, **5646**

Phytophagus mites, **2866**

Phytotoxicity, **2069, 2876, 7996**

Phytotoxicity
effects of: plant extract, **3691, 8081,**

Phytotoxicity
hydrogen cyanide, **9415**

Phytotoxicity
nitrogen, **4218, 4219, 4220**

Phytotoxins, **10141, 11952, 13646**

Picloram, **1797, 10581, 10996**

Picloram
bermudagrass: evaluation, **12456**

Picloram
seed germination effects, **9453**

Picloram
selectivity, **12455**

Picloram
weed control, **1700, 6500, 8189, 9530, 13512, 14989:** evaluation, **8182, 8432, 14492**

Picolinic acid, **1639, 8435**

Pigweed, **8410**

Pillbug, **3042**

Pillbug
chemical control, **1847, 4060**

Pine needles, **563**

Pine needles
mulch, **122, 3046, 14432**

Pink patch (see Red thread)

Pink snow mold (see *Fusarium* patch)

Pin nematode, **1690, 4217, 11668, 14052**

Pipe, perforated (see Drainage, subsurface)

Piper velvet bentgrass, **724, 4840, 4842, 4852, 4859, 10711, 11666**

Piricularia grisea (see also Gray leaf spot), **10142**

Plagiotropic growth, **5952**

Planavin® (see Nitralin)

Plantago lanceolata (see Buckhorn plantain)

Plantago major (see Broadleaf plantain)

Plantain, **332, 15706**

Plantain
broadleaf (see Broadleaf plantain)

Plantain
buckhorn (see Buckhorn plantain)

Plantain
chemical control **446, 4267, 15706:** 2,4–D evaluation, **11046, 12249**; evaluation, **8410, 8435, 8852, 11131**

Plantain
control, **340, 9851**

Plant hormone, **632**

Plant vitamins (see also Vitamins), **632**

Plant water relations (see also Water deficits), **2604, 2652, 10608, 10672, 12668, 12669, 12933, 14123, 14131, 14132, 16017**

Plastic coated fertilizer (see Fertilizer, coated)

Plastic pipe, **1213, 3333, 3576a, 12913, 14329**

Plastic screen
light quality effects, **11902**

Plastic screen
low temperature color retention, **2399**

Plastic screen
winter protection, **1967, 2027, 2100, 2623, 2675, 9437, 9439, 12655, 13852, 13855, 15559**

Plexiglas sheet
type, **1818**

Plug
production, **7042**

Plugging (see also Establishment, vegetative), **948, 961, 980, 2609, 6248, 6955, 9601, 10131, 10132, 11867, 12996, 12998, 13567, 14367**

Plugging
equipment, **3162**

Plugging
evaluation, **1700, 11741**

Plugging
methods, **11539, 16320**

Plugging
rate of spread, **10126, 14367**

Plugging
specifications, **9444**

PMA, **3223, 8768**

PMA
antitranspirant evaluation, **4582, 4583, 4585**

PMA
brown patch control, **4681, 14719, 15123, 16292**

PMA
crabgrass control, **920, 976, 993, 998, 1000, 1073, 3993, 4376, 4378, 4387, 4396, 4402, 4852, 4857, 4858, 4859, 4863, 4890, 4891, 4899, 4907, 4909, 4910, 4938, 5156, 5444, 5524, 5557, 5892, 6358, 7390, 9451, 10909, 11143, 11160, 11746, 11760, 12412, 12574, 13861, 14839:** evaluation, **3653a, 4853, 4862, 4906, 6270, 6352, 9053, 9733, 12322, 12907, 13769, 13771, 13772**

PMA
disease control, **6728, 7390, 8059, 16291**

PMA
dollar spot control, **4858, 8185, 10568, 10574, 12907, 13605:** evaluation, **9246, 14714, 15123**

PMA
effects, **10483, 12434, 13669**

PMA
fairy ring control, **1545, 6728**

PMA
Fusarium patch control, **6728, 6764, 7192**

PMA
melting out control, **15033, 15037**

PMA
selectivity, **976, 1000, 3653a**

PMA
snow mold control, **2633, 10422, 15475, 15591, 15592**

PMA
stomate effects, **1549, 10481, 13669**

PMA
weed control, **4858, 4901, 8908, 11629, 11935, 12573, 12808**

Poa annua (see Annual bluegrass)

Poa annua var. *annua,* **6490**

Poa annua var. *reptans,* **6490**

Poa bulbosa (see Bulbous bluegrass)

Poaceae, **14542**

Poa compressa (see Canada bluegrass)

Poa nemoralis (see Wood bluegrass)

Poa species (see also Bluegrasses)

Poa species
chromosome number, **3373, 13670**

Poa species
description, **3869**

Poa species
genetics, **3869, 3872**

Poa species
seed germination, **3328**

Poa species
seed identification, **3328, 7774, 11115**

Poa trivialis (see Rough bluegrass)

Pocket gopher (see also Gopher)

Pocket gopher
chemical control, **7130**

Pohlia nutans, **1092, 7026**

Point-quadrat method
turf composition, **10125**

Poison
information centers, **1276, 1607**

Poison ivy, **619**

Poison ivy
control, **555**

Polar chewings fescue, **4709, 7284, 8350, 9212, 9213, 9219**

Pollen, **7833**

Pollen
description, **6461, 8637**

Pollen
germination, **10369, 14597**

Pollen
size: species evaluation, **8637**

Pollination, **2741, 2812**

Pollination
bentgrass, **4845**

Pollination
Kentucky bluegrass, **11357**

Pollination
perennial ryegrass, **8495**

Pollination
red fescue, **8493**

Pollution, **9318, 10561**

Pollution
atmospheric, **1756, 1967, 2235, 4802, 9231:** book, **10123**; effects, **3216, 3744**; injury symptoms, **2679, 16097**

Polo field
culture, **1796;** book, **4295**

Polychlorodicyclopentadiene, **2027, 4279**

Polychlorodicyclopentadiene
annual bluegrass control, **8151, 8157, 10624**

Polychlorodicyclopentadiene
crabgrass control, **1474, 1493, 1580, 1700, 1782, 5192, 5193, 5199, 5205, 5207, 5481, 5543, 5561, 7260, 9529, 9530, 9531, 9533, 9544, 10377, 13859, 13861, 14839:** evaluation, **5479, 7655, 7661, 8156, 8407, 48414, 8415, 10619, 10636, 12278, 12753, 13803, 14837**

Polychlorodicyclopentadiene
dollar spot control, **2904**

Polychlorodicyclopentadiene
goosegrass control, **5537, 8157**

Polychlorodicyclopentadiene
residual phytotoxicity, **3765, 10451**

Polychlorodicyclopentadiene
selectivity, **1551, 5537, 6440, 8412, 8706, 10624, 13773, 13803**

Polychlorodicyclopentadiene
spotted spurge control, **14839**

Polychlorodicyclopentadiene
weed control evaluation, **7659, 8412, 10619, 12760, 13767, 13858, 15978**

Polyembryony
Agropyron species, **4950**

Polyethylene barrier
green construction, **1378**

Polyethylene coated paper
mulch evaluation, **9610**

Polyethylene cover, **4556**

Polyethylene cover
breaking winter dormancy, **15511**

Polyethylene cover
desiccation protection, **12655, 15506, 15511, 15569, 15571**

Polyethylene cover
effects, **2607, 3487**

Polyethylene cover
for establishment, **2076, 3275, 3276, 8211, 13147, 13401**

Polyethylene cover
soil warming effects, **4545, 9225**

Polyethylene cover
winter protection, **1465, 1492, 1639, 1781, 1967, 2623, 8211, 9407, 9408, 12896, 15212, 15542:** evaluation, **5774, 5781, 15516, 15519, 15593, 15594, 15595**

Polyethylene glycol
evaluation, **10081**

Polyfilm
reclamation, **3885**

Polygonum aviculars (see Knotweed, Prostrate)

Polymer mulch (see Elastomeric polymer mulch)

Polymyxa graminis, **3262, 4335**

Polyploidy, **3836, 3837, 8499, 11225, 13794**

Polystand, **4651, 5194, 6535, 6984, 48230**

Polystand
annual bluegrass: warm season species, **12321, 14368, 16320**

Polystand
benefits, **2580, 4842**

Polystand
bentgrass: cool season species, **7286, 8849, 11762**

Polystand
bentgrass-bermudagrass, **11233, 11234, 14354, 14355, 14365, 16320:** green, **10127, 10130, 10725**

Polystand
browntop-chewings fescue, **7458**

Polystand
competition, **2835, 3695, 4634, 5593, 6307**

Polystand
composition, **8687, 8688, 11326:** determination methods, **10125, 11807, 15092;** evaluation, **5583, 14832, 14993;** factors affecting, **3784, 6328, 11129, 12122, 14353**

Polystand
cool-warm season turfgrasses, **875, 1012, 6984, 16320**

Polystand
creeping bentgrass, **13304, 14365**

Polystand
with crownvetch, **5157, 11162**

Polystand
cultural effects, **5510, 14353:** cutting height, **4630, 4631, 4634, 4636, 5562, 6305, 6398, 7191, 7425, 8717, 10605, 15916**; fertilization, **6305, 6422, 7220, 12839**; irrigation, **12521, 14303**; nitrogen, **2684, 3482, 4636, 4652, 10605, 10615, 12747, 15916**

Polystand
effects, **7270, 8723, 12568**

Polystand
effects of: soil reaction, **6422, 9528, 11129, 12839**

Polystand
effects on: shoot growth, **8723, 12569, 14703**

Polystand
environmental effects: light intensity, **16057**; water, **4652, 7014, 7425, 15459**

Polystand
establishment method, **3694, 3784**

Polystand
evaluation, **2566, 2583, 2584, 2592, 2603, 2616, 2632, 2650, 2698, 4651, 6323, 8667, 8724, 12227**

Polystand
factors affecting, **6321, 7015, 8434, 8938, 10615, 15459**

Polystand
fairway, **16066:** bentgrass-annual bluegrass, **7891, 7899**; Kentucky bluegrass-red fescue, **7891, 7899**

Polystand
Italian ryegrass-perennial ryegrass, **8218**

Polystand
Kentucky bluegrass-bentgrass, **259, 867, 8687, 11129, 11666**

Polystand
Kentucky bluegrass-bermudagrass, **875, 14354**

Polystand
Kentucky bluegrass blend evaluation, **6329, 8687, 10615**

Polystand
Kentucky bluegrass-perennial ryegrass: competition, **2647, 6307**

Polystand
Kentucky bluegrass-red fescue, **1688, 1700, 4644, 4649, 4653, 4657, 7500, 8687, 8723:** evaluation, **2617, 2707, 4651, 6307, 7891, 8724**; nitrogen effects, **4636, 12747**; sod strength evaluation, **2630, 2672**

Polystand
Kentucky bluegrass-tall fescue, **5146, 10605**

Polystand
Kentucky bluegrass-warm season species, **6497**

Polystand
Kentucky bluegrass-white clover, **8849, 10526**

Polystand
Kentucky bluegrass-zoysiagrass, **875, 948, 6554, 6882, 7393**

Polystand
with legumes: evaluation, **9722, 9723**

Polystand
Perennial ryegrass-rough bluegrass, **7185**

Polystand
ryegrass, **5157, 6398, 7015**

Polystand
secession, **8167, 8746, 9129, 10233**

Polystand
tall fescue-bahiagrass, **16332**

Polystand
tall fescue-bermudagrass, **2380, 15916**

Polystand
tall fescue-redtop, **2985**

Polystand
winter overseeding evaluation, **5583**

Polystand
with zoysiagrass, **6861, 7519**

Polytrias praemorsa (see Javagrass)

Polytrichum juniperinum, **7026**

Polytrichum species (see also Moss)

Polytrichum species, **1148, 2033, 14042**

Polyvinyl acrylic
colorant, **61, 186**

Polyvinyl chloride pipe (see PVC pipe)

Pond
construction, **10214, 10465**

Pond
maintenance, **10465, 10780**

Pond
sealing, **10529, 12768**

Pond
weed control, **10780**

Popillia japonica (see Japanese beetle)

Pop-up sprinkler head (see Sprinkler head, types: rotary pop-up)

Porcupinegrass, **76**

Pore space, soil, **6676, 9042, 9043, 11895, 12419, 15463, 15468, 15474, 15476, 15505, 15537**

Pore space, soil
effects of: compaction, **102, 6676, 6865, 14482, 15094, 15526**; irrigation practices, **13425**; organic matter, **4625**; soil amendment, **7987, 8011, 9199, 10114, 14482**; soil mix, **5830, 10873, 13907**; soil texture, **102,** 14482

Pore space, soil
effects on: soil water movement, **9043, 9062, 11283, 11703**; turfgrasses, **13906**

Pore space, soil
factors affecting, **102, 15501**

Po-San®
annual bluegrass control, **6136, 6312, 6690, 13534**

Po-San®
seed head inhibition: annual bluegrass, **7526**

Postemergence herbicide (see Herbicide, postemergence)

Potassium, **2776, 3201, 3450, 3740, 5850, 6655, 6939, 7466, 8483, 9808, 11433, 11787**

Potassium
availability, **4284, 9061**

Potassium
carriers, **1029, 2260, 3211, 4520, 5685, 6975, 7575, 8019, 8034, 10864, 11392, 11524, 11786, 12256, 12603, 13526, 13964, 14905, 15116, 15778, 15824:** effects, **7993, 8006,**

8048; evaluation, **4038, 6513, 8019, 8039, 8049, 9777, 10059, 12261**; fritted potassium, **1488**

Potassium
deficiency, **2655, 3340, 4418, 5869, 10449:** symptoms, **2974, 6465, 8758, 9061, 9712, 9717, 10452, 10963, 11790**

Potassium
disease effects, **1936, 2162, 4840, 5396, 5869, 6508, 6679, 6703, 6704, 6705, 6707, 6708, 9026, 9061, 12160, 14692:** dollar spot, **7857, 8019, 8047, 8050**; *Fusarium* patch, **2162, 6679**; *Helminthosporium* leaf spot, **5652, 8047, 12268**

Potassium
effects on, **3591a, 3727, 4840, 6077, 7084, 7853, 7855, 7993, 8046, 14440, 14612, 15116, 15145, 15146:** carbohydrate reserves, **5307, 7114, 7852, 14090, 14685, 14700**; chemical composition, **10015, 14090, 15056**; environmental stress hardiness, **3340, 5869, 15145**; heat hardiness, **1688, 1923, 12005**; low temperature hardiness, **6514, 6516, 7114, 12497, 12499, 14440, 14685**; root growth, **7223, 8758, 10194, 12532, 14090**; shoot growth, **5856, 7223, 7857, 8263, 8648, 8670, 8758, 9104, 10059, 10194, 10784, 11524, 12532, 12752, 14440, 14441, 14685, 15056**; tensile strength, **3912**; on turgor, **4265**; wear tolerance, **1936**

Potassium
factors affecting, **28, 6655, 12620**

Potassium
leaching, **12635**

Potassium
nutrition, **252, 937, 975, 1639, 1932, 1936, 1945, 3727, 4251, 4378, 4646, 6811, 6812, 7280, 10015, 11280, 11785, 12005, 12102, 12247, 15144**

Potassium
plant content, **7084, 8263**

Potassium
role, **4520, 5869, 6465, 8048, 9024, 9061, 10963, 11279, 11388, 13526, 14693**

Potassium
soil level, **2707, 4520, 6648, 6651, 6657**

Potassium
soil relationships, **1945, 2478, 3322, 3391, 9061, 11524, 12631**

Potassium
soil test, **6802, 9810**

Potassium
translocation, **6503, 13904**

Potassium
uptake, **3201, 7855, 12496**

Potassium carbonate, **8019**

Potassium carbonate
evaluation, **8049, 12261**

Potassium chloride, **3307, 7220**

Potassium chloride
effects, **6998, 11024**

Potassium chloride
evaluation, **2172, 7223, 8019, 8049, 12261**

Potassium cyanate, **993, 8768**

Potassium cyanate
crabgrass control, **916, 920, 941, 1073, 2411, 2727, 4376, 4387, 4396, 4402, 4890, 5156, 5524, 5555, 5557, 5892, 6358, 11143, 11160, 11746, 12412, 14491, 16490, 16491:** evaluation, **4906, 6270, 6352, 16493, 16494**

Potassium cyanate
weed control, **2726, 9966, 12808, 16493**

Potassium fertilization, **3341, 3591a, 4265, 6651, 6997, 6999, 7280, 8048, 8484, 9024, 10623, 11150, 11277, 11438, 11786, 14453, 14693**

Potassium fertilization
application, **6666, 10059:** rate, **8039, 14441**

Potassium fertilization
bermudagrass, **30, 8028**

Potassium fertilization
effects, **4620, 7856, 14611**

Potassium magnesium sulfate, **8049, 9808**

Potassium nitrate, **4378, 4529**

Potassium nitrate
effects on: seed germination, **204, 205, 10134, 11262**

Potassium nitrate
evaluation, **8019, 8049, 12261**

Potassium permanganate
earthworm control, **2435, 4754**

Potassium permanganate
moss control, **2961**

Potassium sulfate, **5321, 5634, 5678**

Potassium sulfate
evaluation, **5636, 8019, 8049, 12261**

Potassium thiocyanate
dormancy effects, **13640**

Pottia truncata, **7026, 8464**

Poultry manure, **5634, 5636, 5686, 10861, 11389**

Powdery mildew, **185, 1590, 3795, 6452, 12931, 13738, 14014, 16281**

Powdery mildew
chemical control, **1509, 6747, 11943, 15011, 15014:** evaluation, **1545, 14277**; systemic fungicides, **15013, 15021**

Powdery mildew
control, **6745, 16281**

Powdery mildew
environmental effects, **6443:** temperature, **11939, 16282**

Powdery mildew
on Kentucky bluegrass: cultivar susceptibility, **61, 6290, 14005**

Powdery mildew
species susceptibility: evaluation, **2698**

Powdery mildew
symptoms, **7193, 10853, 13703, 16281**

Prairie dropseed, **76**

Pramitol® (see Prometone)

Prato Kentucky bluegrass, **1700, 1789, 2612, 3656, 8343, 8732, 12007, 15414**

Prato Kentucky bluegrass
evaluation, **6330, 7191, 7508, 8336, 8341, 8350, 9218, 9226, 10622, 10626, 10635, 11323, 11325, 14103, 14813**

Pratylenchus species (see Lesion nematode)

Preemergence herbicide (see Herbicide, preemergence)

Preforan® (see Fluorodifen)

Pregermination, seed, **2988, 7187, 11631, 12338, 15654**

Pre-San® (see Bensulide)

Prescription Athletic Turf Method (see PAT System)

Presoaking seed (see Pregermination, seed)

Preventol® (see Dichlorophen)

Primary root, **5646, 16283**

Primary root
development, **15623**

Primo Kentucky bluegrass, **7287, 9212, 9213, 9218, 9226, 14813**

Prince Edward Island bentgrass (see Colonial bentgrass)

Problem diagnosis, **9686, 9688, 10778, 10906, 15833**

Processed tankage (see Tankage, processed)

Professional development, **2796, 2958**

Professional lawn care (see Lawn care service)

Program certification, **4071, 4072, 4075, 4076, 4077**

Prometone
soil sterilant, **8182**

Pronamide
annual bluegrass control, **5381, 12544**

Propagation (see Establishment)

Propham
weed control, **86, 807, 13866**

Propoxur
rhodesgrass scale control, **14398**

Prosapia bicincta (see Spittlebug)

Prosapia bicincta (see Two-lined spittlebug)

Prostrate spurge (see Spurge, prostrate)

Protective covers (see also Winter protection covers), **2561, 9441, 9442**

Protein content
cultural effects: nitrogen, **2946, 7222, 11673, 14323**

Protein content
environmental effects: light, **2946**; moisture stress, **2434, 12092**; temperature, **4605, 4606, 8778, 14323**

Protein content
seasonal variability, **5236, 11296**

Protein extraction
method, **15910, 15911**

Prunella vulgaris (see Healall)

Psalliota species (see Fairy ring)

Pseudaletia unipuncta (see Armyworm)

Pseudo root-knot nematode, **10684, 11669, 12055, 13916, 15988**

Pseudo root-knot nematode
chemical control, **12056**

Pseudo root-knot nematode
distribution, **10682, 11840, 14092, 15988**

Pseudo root-knot nematode
injury symptoms, **12055, 12056**

Pubescence, **13037**

Public relations, **11677**

Public relations
golf course maintainence, **80, 9287**

Puccinellia airoides (see Nuttall alkaligrass)

Puccinellia distans, **3185, 8200**

Puccinia coronata (see Crown rust)

Puccinia graminin (see Stem rust)

Puccinia zoysiae (see also Zoysiagrass rust), **2347**

Puffiness, **4852, 5499, 5962**

Pumice
soil amendment, **4702, 7170**

Pump, irrigation
vertical turbine, **3093**

Puncturevine
biological control: weevil, **3634, 3644, 8140, 10887**

Puncturevine
chemical control, **12277**

Puraturf® (see Cadmium compounds)

Purple nutsedge, **7546, 14210**

Purple nutsedge
chemical control: in bermudagrass, **5741, 14435**; evaluation, **7545, 9670, 14437**; organic arsenicals, **5099, 5102, 7265, 9673**

Purr-Wick system, **1961, 2027, 2100, 2885, 4501, 4509, 4512, 4514, 4517, 4519, 4523, 9766, 12417, 12422, 16048**

Purr-Wick system
construction, **4512, 4517, 4527, 9873, 12418, 14515**: cost, **9873, 10371**; green, **10370, 10371, 13638, 14337**

Purr-Wick system
evaluation, **9140, 12412, 12421**

Purr-Wick system
specifications, **4512, 4517, 10371**

Purslane, **507**

Purslane
chemical control, **1700:** evaluation, **4646, 8405, 8410, 8432, 13016**

Purslane speedwell (see Speedwell)

Putting green (see Green)

Putting quality
evaluation, **10334, 10857, 15722**

PVC pipe, **1294, 12036, 12917, 14329, 14763, 15341, 16234**

Pyrenochaeta terrestris
on creeping bentgrass, **10489**

Pyrimidine compounds
smut control, **7360**

Pyrethrum, **625, 798, 3745**

Pyrethrum
ant control, **542**

Pyrethrum
sod webworm control, **11664, 12897**

Pythium aphanidermatum (see *Pythium* blight)

Pythium blight, **555, 608, 646, 1315, 1843, 2544, 2839, 5025, 6194, 6199, 7880, 7884, 11576, 11799, 12931, 15373**

Pythium blight
on bentgrass, **9077, 16305**

Pythium blight
calcium level effects, **10877, 10886, 10890**

Pythium blight
chemical control, **61, 1487, 2536, 4677, 6114, 6174, 6177, 6179, 6215, 6216, 6513, 6748, 7880, 8096, 8185, 8783, 12631, 13716, 13723, 15014, 15674, 15680, 15684, 16208:** evaluation, **186, 1903, 1967, 2172, 2609, 2787, 3597a, 6162, 6165, 6171, 6175, 6180, 6184, 6187, 6190, 6192, 6193, 6198, 6209, 6210, 6214, 8059, 9933, 15135, 15672, 15680, 15681**

Pythium blight
cultural control, **6132, 6215, 12631, 13703, 13716, 15646, 15689**

Pythium blight
cultural effects, **4170, 6205, 16236**

Pythium blight
description, **6164, 15690**

Pythium blight
environmental effects, **6848, 13716:** temperature, **564, 5402, 6132, 6162, 6169, 6191, 6211, 10877, 10890, 11939**; water, **564, 4182, 10890**

Pythium blight
factors affecting, **6184**

Pythium blight
species susceptibility: evaluation, **5417, 6162, 6207, 6208, 10888**

Pythium blight
symptoms, **2536, 5417, 6132, 6161, 6215, 7193, 8996, 9892, 10805, 10823, 10853, 11071, 12078, 12556, 12631, 13610, 13703, 13716, 15646, 15679, 15680, 15689**

Pythium blight
on warm season turfgrasses, **6162, 7686**

Pythium myriotylum
species susceptibility: annual ryegrass, **9903**

Pythium species, **201, 2321, 5417, 10533, 15000**

Pythium species
description, **7685, 8059, 10533**

Pythium species
soil population, **13439, 13805**

Pythium species
species susceptibility, **7685, 7686**

Pythium species
viability, **7954**

Pythium ultimum (see also *Pythium* blight), **10889**

Quackgrass, **464, 8853, 15706**

Quackgrass
chemical control, **1782, 7873, 8462, 14076**; dalapon, **3679a, 6244, 12216, 12271**; evaluation, **807, 2684, 3405, 13394, 14477, 14989**

Quackgrass
control, **1381, 4959, 8853, 12271**

Quackgrass
cultural effects, **4959, 8558**

Quackgrass
description, **5315, 8853, 12216, 12413**

Quackgrass
fairway culture, **306**

Race course
culture, **15220:** Australia, **15288**; New Zealand, **15206, 15214, 15216, 15233, 15246, 15248, 15268, 15284, 15287, 15296, 15303, 15308, 15309, 15314, 15322**

Race course
grasses used: Sweden, **9203, 9216**

Race course
irrigation system, **5376**

Radopholus (see Burrowing nematode)

Ragwort, **3881**

Rain
artificially induced, **1272**

Rain
effects on, **224, 1753:** spore dissemination, **12673**; turfgrass culture, **7415, 15528**; world species distribution, **7522**

Rain
effects of: topography, **5339**

Rainier red fescue, **7309, 11113, 13462, 16323**

Ranunculus bulbosus (see Bulbous buttercup)

Ranunculus repens (see Creeping buttercup)

Raritan velvet bentgrass, **977, 5453, 7309, 10760, 14173**

Raritan velvet bentgrass
description, **5538, 14175**

Ratio, fertilizer (see Fertilizer ratio)

Rebuilding
golf course, **12345:** economics, **5928**; time schedule, **14596**

Records, **1411, 8137, 8966**

Records
equipment repair, **13059**

Records
equipment use, **2413**

Records
golf course, **1510, 1672, 2789, 3121, 5838, 7642, 8802, 8803, 9619, 13654, 13667, 15367**

Records
labor, **2413, 7642**

Records
mowers, **4564, 13059**

Records
types, **2460, 8137, 13801:** golf course, **5838**

Recreational areas
conservation, **8219**

Recreational areas
planning, **1619**

Recreational areas
soils, **6664**

Recreational turfs
culture, **1670, 4785, 6914, 7438, 10229, 16380:** bulletin, **14540**; fertilization, **6662, 8754**

Recreational turfs
turfgrasses used, **7246, 13626**

Recuperative potential
species variation, **16369, 16372**

Red clover, **4731, 9129**

Red fescue, **3714, 3776, 7332, 11767, 11771, 13079, 13268, 13374, 14471, 15412, 15802, 16323**

Red fescue
adaptation, **30, 2566, 4601, 5483, 11151, 12328, 12827, 13220, 13243, 14003:** moisture, **7730**; shade, **2569, 2580, 2600, 2640**

Red fescue
breeding, **2649, 8502, 16252**

Red fescue
cultivars, **2129, 2518, 2560, 6288, 9340, 9968, 10621, 11006, 12007, 13093, 13160, 13359, 13367, 13725, 13823, 14749:** cutting height tolerance, **5539**; dollar spot susceptibility, **8336, 8341**; evaluation, **1471, 1489, 1685, 2564, 2566, 2574, 2575, 2576, 2583, 2584, 2589, 2592, 2598, 2603, 2616, 2617, 2631, 2650, 2673, 2684, 2698, 2704, 2706, 2707, 3459, 4644, 4709, 5007, 5313, 5320, 5539, 5776, 6320, 6879, 7191, 7284, 7287, 7316, 7748, 7836, 8171, 8294, 8336, 8338, 9219, 10376, 10622, 10631, 12758, 13661, 13662, 13665, 13863, 14561, 14562**; low temperature hardiness, **1700, 2706, 8979, 8980**; *Pythium* blight susceptibility, **6207**; red thread susceptibility, **8336, 14562**; seedling drought tolerance, **16178, 16181**; shade adaptation, **2204**; weed invasion susceptibility, **5539**

Red fescue
culture, **13376, 14749:** cutting height, **5539, 12632**; fairway, **306**; fertilization, **2631, 2673, 4639, 4646, 4657, 5183, 8713, 12632, 13254**; irrigation, **4644, 4657**

Red fescue
description, **1334, 3384, 4008, 5315, 7332, 7947:** cytology, **3384, 3836, 8501**; pollination, **8493**; rooting depth, **14161**

Red fescue
diseases: fairy ring, **5919**; stem eye spot, **14006**

Red fescue
establishment, **2560, 7011, 13430, 16181**

Red fescue
preemergence herbicide selectivity, **8695, 10451**

Red fescue
seed germination, **3685, 3691, 8781**

Red fescue
seed production, **727, 861, 4767, 13592**

Red fescue
seed source evaluation, **119, 4709**

Red fescue
uses, **2761, 4746, 4747, 5315:** lawn, **6288, 13093, 13171, 13220, 13225, 13292, 13364**; roadside, **907, 936, 10233, 13331**; winter overseeding, **10455, 13423, 13432**

Red fescue
vegetative identification, **15412**

Red harvester ant, **1054**

Red leaf spot, **3255, 4186**

Red sorrel (see Sorrel, red)

Red thread, **497, 1037, 1101, 1977, 2130, 2261, 2816, 5597, 5598, 6727, 6729, 6734, 7285, 8342, 8347, 9271, 9272, 12508, 12907, 13990, 14014**

Red thread
on bermudagrass, **5922**

Red thread
chemical control, **1253, 2331, 5618, 5708, 6746, 6747, 9245, 9463, 12631, 15014:** evaluation, **1195, 2172, 5598, 6601, 6667, 6755, 6766, 7288, 8059, 8339, 13989, 13992, 16210, 16211, 16212**

Red thread
control, **724, 1036, 5417, 6728, 6740, 6742, 6745**

Red thread
on cool season turfgrasses, **13989:** red fescue cultivars,

14562; ryegrass cultivars, **8337, 14562**

Red thread
cultural control, **6728, 12631**

Red thread
cultural factors affecting: cutting height, **6709:** fertilization, **2162, 6732, 6746**

Red thread
description, **5618, 5708**

Red thread
environmental factors affecting, **8970, 13992:** soil moisture, **4182, 6739, 11113**; temperature, **5042, 6739**

Red thread
factors affecting: amino acid variations, **9861:** nitrogen, **1273, 6647, 6679, 6709, 6733, 6766, 13989**; nutrition, **6702, 11113**; phosphorus, **6679, 6709**; potassium, **6679, 6705, 6708, 6709, 6733**

Red thread
injury symptoms, **5417, 5598, 7193, 9463, 9892, 12078, 12631, 13992**

Red thread
susceptible species, **5417, 5598**

Redtop, **3713, 3775, 11661, 11767, 11771, 12406, 12864**

Redtop
adaptation, **310, 5483, 14003, 15054**

Redtop
culture: nitrogen, **4646**

Redtop
description, **1685, 3837, 5315, 9518, 14424**

Redtop
establishment, **513:** competition, **7011**; factors affecting, **13459**

Redtop
polystand compatability, **298, 1700, 4657**

Redtop
uses, **5315, 10233, 13423**

Redtop, weed
invasion: effects, **4634**

Reed-sedge peat, **7864, 15550, 15552, 15560**
soil amendment, **5742, 10029**

Reel mower
evaluation, **3457**

Reel mower
types, **16482**

Reestablishment, **2685**
football field, **240**

Reflectance spectrophotometer
turfgrass color evaluation, **2923**

Registration
bahiagrass, **7639**

Registration
bermudagrass, **7638, 7640**

Registration
bromegrass, **7639**

Registration
creeping bentgrass, **7639**

Registration
drayler upland bluegrass, **13530**

Registration
durar hard fescue, **13531**

Registration
grama grasses, **7639**

Registration
Kentucky bluegrass: germ plasm, **8083:** Merion, **11224**; Newport, **9348**

Registration
Penngift crownvetch, **9987**

Registration
red fescue, **5363, 7639:** Illahee, **11222**

Relative humidity (see Atmospheric water vapor)

Release rate (see Fertilizer, release rate)

Remote sensing, **2283**

Renovation, **982, 1280, 2172, 2685, 4495, 4597, 5694, 6639, 8747, 9312, 10255, 10309, 11336, 11666, 12718, 12783, 13828, 14605, 15164, 15598, 16002**

Renovation
bowling green, **1537, 1799, 8489, 10341, 14310, 15166:** England, **10669**; New Zealand, **15188, 15191, 15213, 15236, 15253**

Renovation
calcium cyanamid use, **9963, 9964, 9965**

Renovation
cemetery, **16269, 16270**

Renovation
cricket wicket, **1097, 1799, 3141, 10037, 11238**

Renovation
deep coring effects, **10957**

Renovation
fairway, **350, 805, 1013, 1282, 1285, 1374, 1465, 3119, 3875, 4471, 4627, 4827, 5734, 6394, 6793, 6880, 6891, 6952, 7233, 7278, 8629, 8747, 9081, 9083, 9409, 9583, 9585, 9732, 10282, 10435, 10469, 10912, 10913, 11252, 11259, 11467, 11493, 11513, 11534, 11837, 12284, 12335, 12336, 12444, 12465, 13757, 14408, 14409, 14512, 15662, 15726, 15727, 15893, 16161:** annual bluegrass control, **5218, 9172, 14513, 15090, 16145**; to bermudagrass, **16182**; cost, **6889**; sodding, **12285**; timing, **12465**

Renovation
football field, **1031, 1133, 1993, 2408, 8538, 8789, 10621, 12065**: fumigation, **13556**

Renovation
fumigation use, **1060**

Renovation
golf course, **377, 1233, 2872, 3957, 3959, 3962, 5026, 5219, 5280, 5875, 8875, 9033, 12345, 14380, 14381:** costs, **5285**

Renovation
green, **1072, 1099, 1285, 1538,**

3701, 3702, 4067, 4812, 5106, 5308, 5680, 6394, 6839, 6880, 6942, 7142, 7278, 7663, 7664, 8518, 9376, 9954, 9983, 9998, 10282, 10720, 11555, 11776, 12292, 13536, 14638, 14917, 15189, 15245: bentgrass conversion, 12160; cost analysis, 2789, 5340, 5341; New Zealand, 15223, 15224, 15291; to Tifgreen bermudagrass, 15498

Renovation
hockey field, 1031, 1682

Renovation
lawn, 49, 335, 1435, 1550, 1834, 2380, 3350, 4306, 4758, 6633, 6977, 8285, 10736, 11208, 13072, 13265, 13295, 13343, 13369, 13381, 13395, 14205, 14809, 15703: bulletin, 9149; chemical, 1572, 13251; cool regions, 2505, 11893, 12608; state bulletin, 15668, 16107

Renovation
methyl bromide use, 1114

Renovation
park, 16091

Renovation
principles, 12324, 14188

Renovation
procedures, 8344, 11195, 11547, 15538

Renovation
rugby field, 1031, 1090

Renovation
sand trap, 3743

Renovation
soccer field, 13792

Renovation
sodium arsenite use, 7250

Renovation
sports field, 1042, 1325, 1392, 1592, 1848, 1900, 1902, 2014, 2758, 4125, 4453, 6027, 6898, 7368, 8120, 8290, 8292, 8816, 10044, 10280, 10283, 11146, 12063, 12732, 12854, 15486, 10293: New Zealand, 15182, 15183, 15227

Renovation
tee, 1972, 12398, 12876

Renovation
tennis court, 1799, 1978

Reproduction
asexual, 6303, 10894

Reproduction
sexual, 6303, 10895

Reproduction
vegetative, 7582

Reptans red fescue, 9213
evaluation, 4709, 7287, 9212

Research
coordinated regional experiments, 328

Research
for extension teaching, 13692

Research methods
roadside, 6040

Research methods
solution culture, 12733, 16443

Research plots
field, 540

Research, turfgrass, 525, 944, 2369, 2619, 4370, 4465, 4549, 5807, 6871, 6877, 8150, 9511, 10748, 13601, 14344, 16306

Research, turfgrass
Alabama, 4966

Research, turfgrass
application, 7846, 9897, 12290, 16072

Research, turfgrass
approaches, 1881, 10639

Research, turfgrass
Arkansas, 11088

Research, turfgrass
benefits, 12384

Research, turfgrass
breeding: New Jersey, 6299

Research, turfgrass
California, 3678, 3715, 4700, 7238, 7370, 7371, 9957, 10248, 10944, 14344, 14345, 14346, 14352, 16340, 16402

Research, turfgrass
Canada, 3112, 3113, 3772, 5097, 5311, 5781, 14499

Research, turfgrass
Connecticut, 8600, 11813

Research, turfgrass
contributions, 53, 2105, 6828, 11184, 11582, 11722, 13840, 16030, 16385

Research, turfgrass
Czechoslovakia, 3457

Research, turfgrass
England, 175, 384, 442, 1086

Research, turfgrass
Europe, 13844

Research, turfgrass
financial sources, 5786: National golf day, 12390

Research, turfgrass
Finland, 10161

Research, turfgrass
Florida, 1059, 2353, 2355, 3512, 5584, 6814, 8045, 8203, 11689, 11693, 11721, 13895, 13901, 14401, 15987

Research, turfgrass
Georgia, 3485, 3610, 9075, 11315

Research, turfgrass
Germany, 7478, 13821, 13822, 13825

Research, turfgrass
golf course, 10833

Research, turfgrass
green culture, 9511, 10785

Research, turfgrass
history, 53, 6950, 6971, 7905, 8149, 9898, 14594: disease control, 2837

Research, turfgrass
Illinois, 14871, 14872

Research, turfgrass
Indiana, 900, 971, 4355, 4474

Research, turfgrass
international review, 2648

Research, turfgrass
Iowa, 9232, 9342, 12713

Research, turfgrass
Kansas, 3654A, 8791, 12114, 16489

Research, turfgrass
Massachusetts, **1150**

Research, turfgrass
Michigan, **2629, 14932, 14933:** sod production, **2170**

Research, turfgrass
Milson Experimental Area, **15209**

Research, turfgrass
Mississippi, **4057, 15355**

Research, turfgrass
Missouri, **9616**

Research, turfgrass
needs, **2599, 2806, 4370, 7761, 9958, 10748, 11127**

Research, turfgrass
Netherlands, **14992**

Research, turfgrass
New Jersey, **994, 5430, 5432, 5490, 5538, 14129**

Research, turfgrass
New York, **11077**

Research, turfgrass
New Zealand, **571, 2172, 7473, 9510, 10186**

Research, turfgrass
North Carolina, **9730**

Research, turfgrass
Ohio, **2024, 4646, 15708, 15932**

Research, turfgrass
Oklahoma, **8142, 8143, 8145, 8146, 8162, 8175, 11093**

Research, turfgrass
Olcott Turf Garden, **12131**

Research, turfgrass
O.M. Scott Company, **13765, 15898**

Research, turfgrass
Pennsylvania, **11138, 11148, 11982**

Research, turfgrass
Rhode Island, **724, 988, 4859, 6421, 13842, 13843**

Research, turfgrass
roadside, **995, 4281:** Mississippi, **15353**; Nebraska, **5114, 5126, 5132**; Rhode Island, **15158**

Research, turfgrass
South Africa, **10354**

Research, turfgrass
South Carolina, **9428**

Research, turfgrass
Sports Turf Research Institute, **4720, 4724, 7543, 15403**

Research, turfgrass
Sweden, **9223**

Research, turfgrass
Tennessee, **3607, 5979, 14953**

Research, turfgrass
Texas, **1713, 5800, 5925, 7933, 9526, 9692, 10453**

Research, turfgrass
USA, **787, 5835, 6859, 9882, 15810:** Central Plains, **9223**; national coordination, **12397**; Pacific Northwest, **6667, 6677**; Southeast, **6511, 12791**; Southern, **15360**; university, **124, 125, 5916**

Research, turfgrass
United States Department of Agriculture, **7394, 8682, 11982**

Research, turfgrass
USGA Green Section, **2774, 5791, 5794, 5799, 9381, 12382:** demonstration turf garden, **10809, 10813, 10818, 10822, 10856, 14786**

Research, turfgrass
Washington, **6626, 6637, 9349, 10420**

Research, turfgrass
weed control, **9511:** evaluation methods, **9547**

Research, turfgrass
Wisconsin, **11309, 11310, 11311**

Reserve carbohydrates (see Carbohydrate reserves)

Residual effect
nitrogen carriers, **15064**

Resiliency
soil amendment effects, **9199**

Resort lawn
culture, **13115, 13198**

Respiration, **2614, 7583, 12307**

Respiration
factors affecting: growth inhibitors, **13614**; herbicides, **12441, 14860**; light intensity, **13410, 13428**; nitrogen, **12220, 13410, 13427, 13428**; temperature, **8778, 10228, 11086, 13409, 13410, 13427, 13428, 15434, 15435**; wind, **3759**

Respiration, dark
factors affecting: temperature, **12220**

Respiration inhibitor
effects on: sod heating, **8947**

Respiration rate
diurnal changes, **11086**

Respiration rate
Kentucky bluegrass cultivar evaluation, **15436, 15438**

Respiration rate
warm season species evaluation, **13509**

Revere creeping bentgrass, **302**

Rhizoctonia solani (see also Brown patch), **5034, 10083**

Rhizoctonia solani
effects of: carbon dioxide soil levels, **11910**

Rhizoctonia solani
fungal growth: temperature response, **10852**

Rhizoctonia solani
on Japanese lawngrass, **2755**

Rhizoctonia species, **201, 3271, 3272**

Rhizoctonia species
effects on: root growth, **9763**

Rhizoctonia species
soil population, **2321, 11909**

Rhizome, **5672, 15620**

Rhizome
anatomy, **5954, 13035:** *Agrostis* species, **12101**

Rhizome
development, **1492, 1904, 1905, 1910, 5646, 5952, 6442, 9627, 12457, 13586:** environmental factors affecting, **5674, 11015, 11020**; factors affecting, **5672, 11016**

Rhizome
emergence, **5952:** factors affecting, **1492, 5646**

Rhizome
initiation, **4444, 5953, 11017, 11018:** cultural factors affecting, **9134**; environmental factors affecting, **10022, 11016**; seasonal variation, **5646**

Rhizome
morphology, **5954, 13035**

Rhizome
number: herbicide effects, **6448**; vernalization effects, **10022, 11016**

Rhizome
research review: book, **14833**

Rhizome
soil distribution: Kentucky bluegrass, **4444, 8649**

Rhizome growth, **5646, 5950, 5953, 9624, 9627**

Rhizome growth
circumnutational, **5951**

Rhizome growth
cultural factors affecting: cutting height, **7493, 8710, 9125, 9622, 9634, 14090, 15657, 16179**; mowing, **11018, 15657**; nutritional, **4960, 10195, 11018**

Rhizome growth
environmental factors affecting, **2142, 4960:** day length, **10022, 11016, 11023, 16359, 16399**; light intensity, **6443, 11018, 16350**; temperature, **11018, 16350**

Rhizome growth
factors affecting, **3772, 11017, 14896:** burning, **9122**; herbicides, **6440, 6448**; nitrogen, **5581, 6442, 14090, 14896, 15657**; phosphorus, **14090, 15657**; potassium, **14090**; vernalization, **11016, 11023**

Rhizome growth
Kentucky bluegrass: cultivar variation, **9634, 11020**

Rhode Island bentgrass (see Colonial bentgrass)

Rhode Island bentgrass
root growth, **14134**

Rhode Island bentgrass
seed, **11962**

Rhodesgrass scale, **987, 1639, 2842, 3628, 3645, 3758, 4611, 5253, 5795, 7692, 9353, 11818, 12542, 13003**

Rhodesgrass scale
biological control, **3645, 3758, 12300, 16155**

Rhodesgrass scale
chemical control, **2736, 3283, 3290, 3292, 8887, 11599, 14396, 16155, 16156:** evaluation, **3758, 14398**

Rhodesgrass scale
control, **3758, 8513**

Rhodesgrass scale
injury symptoms, **8513, 8904, 13003**

Ribonuclease
fungal parasitism, **2840**

Ribwort plantain
chemical control, **4760**

Right-of-way
public utilities: turf requirements, **2854**

Ring nematode, **137, 5011, 5099, 8563, 8830, 11742, 11743, 11744, 11745, 12050, 13916**

Ring nematode
incidence survey, **6607**

Ring nematode
on Kentucky bluegrass, **14052**

Ring nematode
on warm season turfgrasses, **11750:** centipedegrass, **258**

Roadside, **2854, 3030, 3188, 3351, 4025, 8219**

Roadside
chemical growth regulator: evaluation, **1055, 2671, 7155, 15158**; maleic hydrazide, **974, 2717, 2718, 3045, 3769, 7012, 16453, 16458, 16506, 16507, 16508**

Roadside
chemical growth retardation, **213, 214, 215, 1593, 3033, 6072, 9949, 14773**

Roadside
culture, **1068, 1314, 2720, 2721, 2947, 2971, 3398, 3688, 4024, 4027, 4235, 6415, 7081, 8063, 8545, 10847, 11030, 11141, 11350, 13029, 13211, 16462:** cool humid regions, **15695, 16137**; costs, **8064, 8182, 14620, 16510**; cost reduction, **1621**; design effects, **2285**; English, **1873**; equipment, **1018, 1068, 2721, 4211, 8854, 15695**; evaluation, **995, 1018, 8181, 10347**; fertilization, **1018, 2092, 2093, 2094, 2671, 2734, 2745, 2965, 2967, 2984, 3209, 3688, 4025, 4204, 4266, 4431, 4446, 5108, 5109, 6025, 6027, 6231, 6232, 8181, 11905, 12613, 12954, 13813, 15803, 16458**; fertilization—application methods, **4027, 6232**; fertilization evaluation, **1055, 6033**; Germany, **3013, 9649, 13028, 14910, 14911**; herbicide application safety, **87, 2720, 5587, 5751, 7018**; irrigation, **15339**; mowing, **797, 1018, 1068, 1479, 4025, 4027, 8064, 11796, 12595, 12870, 12871, 14335, 15803**; mowing contract, **11775**; mowing costs, **3398, 8062, 16910**; native grasses, **76**; nitrogen carrier evaluation, **11065, 11907**; soil sterilization, **87, 3841, 3842, 4302, 5119, 12754**; warm regions, **2926**

Roadside
deicing: effects, **1921, 1967, 9131**; pollution, **8246**; salinity problem, **3165, 3669, 12722**;

species tolerance, **1686, 2048, 14644**

Roadside
design, **1068, 6036**

Roadside
development, **1684, 2719, 5279, 9261:** literature review, **1631**

Roadside
drainage channel: erosion control, **2056, 3465**

Roadside
ecology, **3760, 16315**

Roadside
environmental control, **2315, 2506, 7634**

Roadside
erosion control, **2058, 4829, 5783, 6033, 6037, 6038, 7684, 7943, 12593:** fertilization effects, **6027, 7081**; ground covers, **10347, 12857**; methods, **4026, 4105**; mulches, **1605, 2340, 5042, 7081, 14479**

Roadside
establishment, **246, 247, 841, 1068, 1877, 2964, 2966, 3688, 4638, 5132, 5159, 6038, 6413, 6414, 6512, 6787, 8544, 8545, 9029, 11350, 11849, 13211, 14198, 16315:** basal seeding, **15038**; cool regions, **15695**; equipment, **8854**; erosion control, **14472**; evaluation, **1479, 2057, 2633, 2734, 14710**; factors affecting, **9950, 10347**; fertilization, **2671, 2745, 2970, 2979, 2985, 4026, 4301, 5108, 5109, 5124, 5125, 5275, 6039, 6231, 6232, 6515, 6716, 13358, 15365**; fertilizer evaluation, **1055, 2671, 7012, 8180, 15158**; hydromulching, **3693**; hydroseeding, **1768, 2764, 3684, 3686, 3687, 4102, 5932, 9129**; liming, **2979, 2985, 4301**; methods, **2971, 4105, 5124, 5125, 6040, 9228, 15325**; methods evaluation, **995, 1018, 8179, 9129, 9955, 11830;** mulches, **1436, 1531, 2432, 2764, 2984, 5130, 5275**; mulch evaluation, **2671, 7782, 8180, 12596, 13797, 14432, 15365**; nitrogen effects, **3729, 5112, 5127**; research summary, **8089, 8325**; on sand, **2717**; secondary succession, **14511**; seeding methods, **1703, 1738, 2671, 2980, 7782, 16243**; seeding rate, **2671, 2734, 2764, 11830**; slope, **1703, 3692, 5112, 5127, 13452, 14049**; sodding, **1436, 2967, 14261, 15402**; soil preparation, **1479, 2734, 3209, 3774, 8180, 8911, 12596, 14432**; species evaluation, **245, 3730, 5716, 6009, 9950**; on subsoils, **1859, 6716**; timing, **2671, 3208, 11152, 16458**; warm regions, **1863, 9952, 12595, 12852**; warm season species, **3132, 4041, 12795**

Roadside
grasses used, **1234, 1436, 2354, 2734, 2965, 2984, 3023, 3032, 3729, 4250, 6033, 6035, 6931, 7874, 8167, 12011, 13337:** cool regions, **248, 253, 1018, 1068, 1965, 4415, 4638, 5107, 6716, 9261, 11152, 13331, 13358, 14472, 15695, 16244, 16314**; cool regions-evaluation, **995, 1479, 5108, 5109, 5124, 5125, 16514**; establishment, **3208, 3209, 6039**; evaluation, **1854, 1860, 1862, 2092, 2093, 2340, 2764, 2966, 5159, 8167, 9129, 10233, 12595, 13954, 14212, 15158**; Germany, **2037, 13825**; legume-grass mixture, **2967, 5095**; native, **76**; seed mixtures, **1858, 2671, 2970, 3012, 3022, 3025, 16458**; semi-arid regions, **12881**; Sweden, **11351, 11830**; Virginia, **12881**; warm regions, **1857, 2979, 3102, 6800, 8183, 9952, 12795**; warm region evaluation, **1861, 5108, 5109, 5124, 5125, 6515, 12596, 14472, 15365**

Roadside
ground covers, **8559, 8560, 8561:** crownvetch, **936, 1982, 5108, 5109, 5124, 5125, 5716, 12597, 12857, 16462**

Roadside
landscaping, **2506, 5279, 6416, 9040, 11054, 11839:** mulches, **8834**; species used, **8225, 14236, 16458**

Roadside
littering, **134**

Roadside
microenvironment, **1068, 9620:** slopes, **5127, 9996**

Roadside
native grasses: natural succession, **16316**

Roadside
planning, **3234, 6070, 6223, 14738, 16492**

Roadside
renovation, **2967:** crownvetch, **7012**; Sericea lespideza, **7012**

Roadside
research methods, **6040**

Roadside
seeding, **3133, 3774**

Roadside
trail design, **14445**

Roadside
turf acreage, **3690**

Roadside
vegetative control: chemical, **4025, 4027, 4204, 5108**

Roadside
weed control, **87, 213, 1018, 1575, 1700, 1717, 1826, 1832, 1833, 1933, 1934, 3654, 3660, 3752, 4235, 5090, 5111, 6051, 7155, 7799, 8182, 9948, 9951, 11849, 12129, 12273, 12489, 12919, 14601, 15405:** evaluation, **4302, 4967, 10735, 10992, 15976**

Roadside
wild flowers: species comparison, **11351, 11355**; Sweden, **11351, 11355**

Roadway, turfed
grasses used, **16242**

Roadway, turfed
stabilized soil (see also Stabilized soil), **2864, 4084, 6383, 7082, 12007:** construction, **6383, 10753, 10777, 15374**; evaluation, **4778, 8310, 8311, 11028, 14946, 14947, 16288**

Rock phosphate, **3339, 7220**

Rolling, **394, 767, 2128, 6531, 7604**

Rolling
after frost heaving, **14157**

Rolling
green, **341**

Rolling
sports field, **15286**

Rolling
spring, **353, 681**

Rolling
timing, **1431, 7604**

Ronnel
chinch bug control, **8877, 8879**

Root, **14133, 16283**

Root
book, **15625**

Root
branching: species variation, **15623**

Root
competition, **59**

Root
fluorescence: *Lolium* identification, **16198**

Root
functions, **7577, 7585, 10986, 14526, 16127:** nutrient uptake, **7828, 15474, 15476**; uptake, **10063, 14133, 15469**; water uptake, **5392, 15474, 15476**

Root
measurement methods, **7145**

Root
morphology, **6722:** root knot nematode effects, **7820**

Root
number, **15624**

Root
phytotoxicity, **59:** nitrogen, **4120**

Root
research review: book, **14833**

Root
sampling methods, **15918**

Root
tip degeneration causes, **5409, 5411**

Root anatomy, **5392, 7577, 7585, 14087, 14526, 14527**

Root anatomy
Agrostis species, **12101**

Root anatomy
mowing frequency effects, **11919**

Root depth, **1492, 11537, 11600, 11784, 14134, 14137, 14829, 15912**
species evaluation, **6492, 6493, 11936, 14135, 14161, 14276, 15623**

Root development, **6722, 8399, 11359, 16127**

Root development
cultural factors affecting: defoliation, **3079**

Root development
environmental factors affecting, **6112:** light, **3486, 3488**; temperature, **3486, 3488, 14156**

Root development
factors affecting, **6549, 8397, 14133, 14156**

Root development
3-indolebutyric acid effects, **8080**

Root development
interspecific competition effects, **3695**

Root development
soil factors affecting: soil moisture, **5054, 14156**

Root development
species evaluation, **5646, 6549**

Root epidermis
nucleolar differences: species evaluation, **9527**

Root extracts
effects on: seed germination, **9355**

Root growth, **624, 6065, 6616, 8777, 9626, 14135, 14992**

Root growth
chemical stimulation, **6637**

Root growth
cultural factors affecting, **179, 2062, 10063, 11536, 12687:** cultivation, **7384, 7389, 11153, 11600**; cutting height, **2381, 2479, 2552, 2606, 3035, 3200, 4588, 4633, 4777, 5960, 7493, 7496, 8192, 8394, 8397, 8398, 8675, 8690, 8710, 9162, 9341, 9343, 9501, 10072, 10076, 10380, 11007, 11783, 11784, 11858, 12675, 12697, 12734, 12765, 13754, 14090, 14134, 14135, 14137, 14161, 14765, 14766, 15657, 16179, 16431**; fertilization, **2760, 3204, 4635, 6637, 8705, 9162, 9724, 12208, 12681, 14998, 15655, 15918, 16283**; irrigation, **2516, 6432, 7174, 7389, 9494, 10079, 10979**; irrigation frequency, **10072, 10076, 10172**; liming, **12531**; mowing, **2924, 4258, 4635, 12681, 15655**; mowing frequency, **2381, 4777, 5681, 7501, 7931, 8664, 8675, 8690, 8846, 9724, 10072, 10076, 10091, 12765, 12770, 14765, 15657**; pesticide, **9764, 10990**; soil warming, **4545**

Root growth
effects of: calcium, **12532, 13897**; carbohydrate reserves, **2551, 2772**; diseases, **5403, 5421, 9763**; flowering, **14086**; galactose, **5419**; gibberellin, **8672, 16329**; hexadecanol, **12744**; iron, **13436, 14075**; magnesium, **8758, 8763, 12532**; nematicides, **11347, 14819**; nematodes, **6437,**

11345, 12041; nitrogen, **1304, 1688, 2064, 2717, 3200, 4620, 4732, 5679, 5960, 6432, 6712, 7221, 7222, 7223, 7312, 7495, 7496, 8262, 8265, 8667, 8670, 8758, 9159, 10072, 10076, 10172, 10194, 10382, 10449, 11858, 11905, 12221, 12532, 12675, 12697, 12701, 12734, 13419, 13421, 13428, 13623, 13813, 14075, 14090, 14161, 14323, 14830, 14832, 15086, 15657**; nitrogen carriers, **5679, 8720, 11905, 14137**; phosphorus, **4620, 7223, 8700, 8702, 8712, 8713, 8714, 8758, 12532, 12734, 14090, 15657**; polystand, **8723**; potassium, **4620, 7223, 8758, 10194, 12532, 12734, 14090**; shoot density, **9975, 14832**; shoot growth, **3563, 14086, 14834, 15086**; sulfur, **12532**; tree roots, **15796**; wetting agent, **5419, 10738, 11678**

Root growth
effects on: burning, **9122**

Root growth
environmental effects, **179, 2062, 11536, 13676:** day length, **9724, 12089, 16359**; light intensity, **10698, 12208, 14835, 16168, 16169, 16180, 16350, 16399**; shading, **10702, 12533**; temperature, **2550, 2553, 2554, 2555, 2556, 2695, 2696, 3035, 4578, 7312, 7495, 7670, 9303, 9724, 10698, 11341, 12208, 12421, 12422, 12681, 12889, 13409, 13427, 13562, 14051, 14137, 14161, 14323, 14423, 14450, 14836, 15437, 15655, 16350, 16354, 16399, 16414**; water, **2339, 3563, 12208, 15655**

Root growth
factors affecting, **482, 2062, 2554, 4416, 6065, 6792, 7046, 7395, 7408, 7826, 7953, 9604, 9629, 9630, 10532, 10959, 11395, 12634, 12704, 12734, 12813, 13417, 14136, 14160, 14161, 14516, 14527, 15006**

Root growth
herbicide effects, **2310, 2908, 3611a, 7078, 8161, 8708**: 2,4–D, **3595a, 3620a**; DCPA, **2907, 11089**; DMPA, **6486, 6495**; evaluation, **1871, 2893, 3595a, 3620a, 5533, 10394, 12750, 13970, 13972**; siduron, **8864, 10394, 14119**

Root growth
measurement, **3235, 3562, 4258, 4777, 9162**

Root growth
seasonal variation, **1492, 2176, 2552, 2696, 5960, 6431, 8398, 8399, 11784, 14161:** evaluation, **12221, 14421, 14829**; species effects, **14949**

Root growth
sod transplanting, **2668, 2669**

Root growth
soil effects, **4119, 8846, 9494, 12208, 12422, 14135, 14161, 15505, 15537:** aeration, **3299, 4623, 9494, 12681, 15086, 15469**; bulk density, **5148, 15912**; compaction, **148, 5442, 7389, 10976, 10979, 12165, 12166, 14713**; excess water, **660, 3299, 12176**; mechanical resistance, **2421**; oxygen, **9503, 12535, 14331**; oxygen diffusion rate, **9489, 9498, 9500, 9501, 12422, 15105**; salinity, **16429**; soil amendment, **9494, 9498, 10114**; soil modification, **9133, 10112, 11605**; soil reaction, **4578, 7495, 8698, 8705, 10245, 11166, 11464, 12531, 14135, 14998**; water level, **2293, 2823, 4581, 5474, 6433, 6676, 7179, 7182, 10899, 12421, 14137, 14835, 15469**

Root growth
species variation, **624, 2680, 5960:** cool season turfgrasses, **3037**; warm season turfgrasses, **3571, 9162, 13562**

Root growth
winter overseeding, **15676**

Root hair
development, **6722, 11359, 12906:** factors affecting, **3943, 8396**

Root hair
growth: factors affecting, **11359, 12630**

Root hair
length, **8377, 11359**

Root hair
species variation, **15623**

Root initiation, **8649, 11359**
from sod, **4444**

Root-knot nematode, **2922, 5011, 5642, 8271, 8525, 10551, 12057, 13873**

Root-knot nematode
on bermudagrass, **12979:** cultivar susceptibility, **12644, 12645**

Root-knot nematode
control: fumigation, **12040**; warm water treatment, **12979**

Root-knot nematode
on creeping bentgrass, **7801, 7822**

Root-knot nematode
description, **5009, 7614, 10684, 13874**

Root-knot nematode
distribution, **5643**

Root-knot nematode
effects on: roots, **6437, 7820**

Root-knot nematode
host range, **4969, 5643, 6444, 9890, 13874, 16101**

Root-knot nematode
injury symptoms, **7821**

Root-knot nematode
on Kentucky bluegrass, **1641:** cultivar susceptibility, **1641**

Root-knot nematode
on warm season species, **11750, 16106**

Root lesion nematode, **12050**

Root longevity, **3756, 14320, 15624**
species evaluation, **15623**

Root maturation, **14423**

Root-shoot ratio, **13527, 14137, 14835**

Root-shoot ratio
cultural factors affecting: nitrogen, **6712, 11907, 15086**

Root-shoot ratio
factors affecting, **9724, 9975, 15086:** day length, **11297**; flowering, **2771**; light intensity, **10699, 10702, 12089**; soil, **14149, 15086**; temperature, **12089, 14836**

Root-shoot ratio
species variation, **14135**

Root system, **13566, 14114**

Root system
classification: annual-perennial, **8399, 14421**

Root system
size, **4922, 4924**

Roseland St. Augustinegrass, **11740, 13898**

Rotary mower, **955, 3457, 16484**

Rotary scarification (see Vertical mowing)

Rotary sprinkler head (see also Sprinkler head)
wind effects, **9725**

Rotary tiller, **12244**

Rotenone
earthworm control, **10691**

Rotenone
sod webworm control, **11664**

Rough, **830**

Rough
cool season turfgrasses used, **14185:** fescues, **1278, 3714, 12001**

Rough
culture, **5723, 6829, 11517, 16054**: English, **6527**

Rough
grasses used, **6891, 11651**

Rough
warm season turfgrasses used, **3607, 3608**

Rough bluegrass, **894, 3776, 9521, 11767, 11771, 13269, 14471**

Rough bluegrass
adaptation, **3387:** shade, **331, 1489, 2569, 2580, 2640**

Rough bluegrass
breeding, **5002**

Rough bluegrass
cultivar evaluation, **5313, 5316, 5320, 13663**

Rough bluegrass
description, **1388, 4008, 7947, 15410, 16326**

Rough bluegrass
establishment: competition, **3821**

Rough bluegrass
seed, **11964**

Rough bluegrass
seed contaminant, **3442**

Rough bluegrass
seed germination, **3441, 3821**

Rough bluegrass
uses, **4747:** winter overseeding, **1367, 2493, 2494, 2496, 2670, 9879, 13432**

Rough bluegrass, weed
chemical control, **2949:** methabenzthiazuron, **3440;** paraquat, **8630;** in perennial ryegrass, **2949**

Rough bluegrass, weed
cultural control, **3439**

Roughstalk bluegrass (see Rough bluegrass)

Roughstalk meadowgrass (see Rough bluegrass)

Royal Cape bermudagrass, **1472, 1489, 7308, 8229, 16320, 16331, 16413**
evaluation, **10461, 14906**

Ruby red fescue, **1891, 2204, 2612, 6294, 6315, 8732**

Rugby field
culture, **1007, 1031, 1249, 1255, 1503, 2124, 3049:** fall, **1046, 1100;** New Zealand, **15192, 15194;** spring, **1069, 1088, 1138, 1177;** winter, **1398**

Rugby field
drainage: subsurface, **3049**

Rugby field
renovation, **1031, 1090**

Rumex acetosella (see Sorrel, red)

Rumex crispus (see Dock, curly)

Runoff, **10959, 11153**

Runoff
effects of: compaction, **100, 102, 108, 11144, 11153;** cultivation, **7437, 10463, 11153;** mulch, **122, 2432;** slope, **5021, 5211;** soil texture, **18, 102**

Runoff water
effects of: turfgrass density, **11153**

Rust, **1076, 3243, 3245, 3251, 5399, 6258, 11064, 14207**

Rust
chemical control, **159, 1105, 2609, 3705, 4166, 4168, 4221, 6114, 6174, 6179, 6748, 7350, 8096, 15674:** evaluation, **2757, 6184, 7346, 7364**

Rust
control, **4685, 5417, 6745**

Rust
on cool season turfgrasses, **1473, 6891, 14955**: Kentucky bluegrass cultivars, **3387, 6290, 6891**

Rust
cultural control, **3671, 11930**

Rust
cultural factors affecting, **1690, 1700, 10105:** nitrogen, **1487, 12695, 12716, 12717, 12719**

Rust
environmental factors affecting, **14207:** temperature, **11939**

Rust
factors affecting, **2851, 9073**

Rust
injury symptoms, **5417, 6132, 6161, 7154, 9454, 9892, 10853, 12078, 13703, 15674**

Rust
species susceptibility, **5417, 9095**

Rust
on warm season turfgrasses, **6205:** zoysiagrass, **1639, 6186, 7861, 9073;** zoysiagrass cultivars, **8709**

Rust, stem (see Stem rust)

Rutting, soil, **4643**
green, **1190**

Ryegrass, **4732**

Ryegrass
adaptation, **2382, 9279, 11587, 16366**

Ryegrass
breeding, **3907, 8495, 8500, 9512**

Ryegrass
chemical composition, **3635, 11646, 11647**

Ryegrass
cultivar evaluation, **126**

Ryegrass
description, **5309, 5392**

Ryegrass
diseases, **729, 15690**: *Pythium* blight, **6169, 6180, 15689, 15690**

Ryegrass
establishment rate, **8783, 11587**

Ryegrass
identification, **6086, 12424**

Ryegrass
nitrogen metabolism, **97**

Ryegrass
in polystands, **4644**

Ryegrass
seed purity, **9594**

Ryegrass
uses: overseeding, **4567;** roadside slope, **10233;** winter overseeding, **1367, 2494, 11587, 13432**

Ryegrass blast, **3741**

Sabadilla, **796**

SADV (see St. Augustinegrass decline virus)

Safety
impact absorption, **6806**

Safety
pesticides, **1560**

Safety
shear strength: factors affecting, **6806**

Safety
turfgrass, **7760**

Sagina procumbins (see Pearlwort, birdseye)

St. Andrews golf course, **3646a**

St. Andrews golf course
culture, **3643a, 3648a, 6773, 8267**

St. Andrews golf course
description, **3643a, 8267**

St. Augustine decline virus, **7862, 7866, 9931, 13574, 14741**

St. Augustine decline virus
on St. Augustinegrass, **2027, 2197**

St. Augustine decline virus
St. Augustinegrass resistance, **10444, 10446**

St. Augustine decline virus
species susceptibility, **9930, 9931, 14741**

St. Augustine decline virus
symptoms, **6204, 9930, 9931, 14741, 14742**

St. Augustinegrass, **3579, 4243, 6513, 7013, 12877, 13300, 14327, 15358, 16441**

St. Augustinegrass
adaptation, **958, 3539, 3553, 3676, 8009, 10773, 12133, 16366:** low temperature hardiness, **12497, 12498;** shade, **3592**

St. Augustinegrass
breeding, **3553**

St. Augustinegrass
chemical control, **3071**

St. Augustinegrass
cultivars, **3507, 11740, 11868:** chinch bug susceptibility, **1490, 13898;** evaluation, **7970, 7989, 8009, 11740, 13898, 13901, 14687;** *Pythium* blight susceptibility, **6207**

St. Augustinegrass
culture, **165, 4245, 11682, 13396:** cutting height, **958, 3504, 7933;** fertilization, **2027, 7962, 8886, 10515, 12265, 12267, 12498, 13522;** thatch control, **15859**

St. Augustinegrass
description, **3553, 7947, 9667, 11232:** chromosome number, **9667, 9668**

St. Augustinegrass
diseases, **4329, 8615, 12985, 15672:** brown patch, **167, 168, 7924, 9886, 16511**: *Cercospora* leaf spot, **6166;** gray leaf spot, **4782, 6168, 6176, 6183, 6189, 8308, 10142, 15761;** rust, **9454;** SADV, **2027, 2646, 7862, 9930, 9931;** sugarcane mosaic virus, **3, 6184, 12986, 14740**

St. Augustinegrass
establishment, **4328, 10450:** weed control, **3529, 8564**

St. Augustinegrass
herbicide tolerance, **7995, 15978**

St. Augustinegrass
insect pests: chinch bug, **3612, 8883, 15497, 15584;** Southern chinch bug, **4782, 7267, 14398**

St. Augustinegrass
iron chlorosis, **9469**

St. Augustinegrass
nematodes, **5014, 5015, 6607:** cyst, **1648, 7616;** lance, **6606;** ring, **8563;** root-knot, **10684, 12056;** sting, **12563;** stubby-root, **12563, 12654**

St. Augustinegrass
renovation, **10255**

St. Augustinegrass
uses, **3548, 3553**

108–1 St. Augustinegrass
chinch bug tolerance, **3520**

St. Ives Research Station
research, **6824**

Salad burnet, **4741**

Salary
golf course superintendent, **1743, 3497**

Saline-sodic soils, **3184, 7610**

Saline soils (see also Salinity, soil), **1051, 3091, 7609, 7610, 10541, 11887, 12488, 15788**

Salinity
irrigation water, **1203, 1780, 6996, 15882**

Salinity, soil, **173, 3182, 3185, 3572a, 7692**

Salinity, soil
book, **1265**

Salinity, soil
control, **6261, 7610**

Salinity, soil
correction, **1491, 7636:** book, **12582**

Salinity, soil
diagnosis: book, **12582**

Salinity, soil
effects, **6669, 9807, 12737, 15788**

Salinity, soil
effects of: gypsum, **7636;** irrigation water, **6261;** mulches, **3736**

Salinity, soil
effects on: nutrient uptake, **7035, 9175;** root growth, **12737, 16429, 16431;** root-shoot ratio, **16429;** seed germination, **2313, 2314, 2359;** shoot growth, **3092, 4949, 7035, 9175, 9807, 9816, 12737, 16429, 16431, 16442;** turfgrass community, **14959, 14960;** turfgrass culture, **2844, 2845, 6799**

Salinity, soil
factors affecting, **3935, 11059**

Salinity, soil
injury symptoms, **9716**

Salinity, soil
roadside, **3669**

Salinity, soil
soil test, **10541**

Salinity, soil
species tolerance, **1454, 1921, 2048, 2846, 3182, 3184, 3572a, 3825, 4123, 4949, 6278, 6498, 6499, 7609, 7610, 9716, 12448, 12737, 13570, 13826, 14704, 15788, 16361, 16368, 16369, 16372, 16402, 16404:** bermudagrass cultivar, **16391, 16428, 16429;** creeping bentgrass cultivar, **2608, 16391, 16442, 16446;** evaluation, **1489, 1700, 2844, 2845, 9807, 12722, 13826, 16391, 16514;** saltgrass, **5124, 5125**

Salt
deicing, **1921, 3670:** effects, **12737, 15770;** injury prevention, **15776;** turfgrass injury, **14645**

Saltgrass
breeding, **5120**

Saltgrass
culture: roadside, **5124, 5125**

Salt index, **3340**

Sand, **637, 15357**

Sand
effects on: infiltration rate, **7419, 14482, 15098**

Sand
properties, **4288, 9778, 10087:** particle size, **27, 2882, 3301, 13688, 16044, 16045;** porosity, **2882, 10087, 14482**

Sand
soil amendment, **2996, 3587a, 5805, 9776, 11974, 16488:** evaluation, **2883, 4702, 4708, 5365, 5366, 10111, 10114, 11153, 13418, 13425, 13683, 13685, 15096, 15112, 16489**

Sand
soil modification, **2885, 12480, 13688, 15103, 16043:** green, **5245, 9773, 10087, 16042, 16043, 16044**

Sand
for sports field, **27, 2884, 2886**

Sand
in topdressing, **7245**

Sandbur
chemical control, **1782, 8164, 8182:** evaluation, **1700, 5265, 6331, 7933, 8161, 8182, 12665, 15140**

Sand dropseed
use: roadside, **9129**

Sand dune stabilization, **2864, 7563, 12480, 14543, 16462**

Sand dune stabilization
artificial barriers, **14322**

Sand dune stabilization
bulletins, **10017**

Sand dune stabilization
establishment, **1700, 4079, 14322:** American beachgrass, **16454**

Sand dune stabilization
methods, **7505, 8438, 9447, 16456, 16457**

Sand dune stabilization
mulch evaluation, **5278, 11911**

Sand dune stabilization
species used, **1700, 5278, 7563, 8429, 9171, 13548, 14322, 16454, 16456, 16457**

Sand dune stabilization
vegetative establishment: method evaluation, **8403, 11911, 16204**

Sand green, **14098**

Sand green
construction, **10431, 14097**

Sand green
culture, **10174, 10431, 14097**

Sand lovegrass
salt tolerance, **1686**

Sand trap
construction, **7218, 14294, 14680**

Sand trap
design, **5868, 7489**

Sand trap
drainage, **579, 12381, 12420**

Sand trap
facing: manilagrass, **11566**

Sand trap
maintenance, **1279, 5723, 5943, 6527, 11517, 12381, 12466, 14680**

Sand trap
renovation, **3743**

Sand trap
sand type, **1267, 12381, 12466**

Sand trap
weed control, **1976, 1995, 3523, 4867**

Sand trap rake, **3749**
power, **2948**

Santa Ana bermudagrass, **1778, 2100, 2611, 8761, 16389, 16394**

Santa Ana bermudagrass
adaptation, **16411, 16413, 16431**

Santa Ana bermudagrass
culture, **16389**

Saran shade® (see Plastic screen)

Sawdust, **2975, 10029, 15560**

Sawdust
chemical composition, **5720**

Sawdust
effects, **15115**

Sawdust
effects on: impact energy absorption, **11011;** seed germination, **2606, 15113, 15114;** seedling growth, **10470, 15113, 15114**

Sawdust
fertilizer carrier, **5720, 5721**

Sawdust
mulch, **171, 12596**

Sawdust
soil amendment, **171, 235, 920, 1777, 2230, 2606, 3046, 3567, 5720, 6689, 9137, 9720, 10028, 11249, 13902, 15103**

Sawdust
topdressing: organic matter source, **3569, 8748**

Sawdust
types, **15114**

Scald, **224, 608, 687, 864, 1050, 7056, 9394, 10811, 11034, 11495, 14617, 15597**

Scald
causes, **4886, 10811, 11440**

Scald
correction, **587, 816**

Scald
prevention, **4886, 11655**

Scald
symptoms, **11440, 11655**

Scale leaf
Agrostis species, **12101**

Scalping, **329, 716**

Scapteriscus acletus, **7146**

Scapteriscus vicinus, **7146**

Scarification, rotary (see Vertical mowing)

Scarification, seed (see Seed, scarification)

Sceempter perennial ryegrass, **7508, 8338**

Sceempter red fescue, **15414**

S. 59 chewings fescue, **5948**

School grounds, **7744, 7745, 8557**

School grounds
construction, **8282**

School grounds
culture, **4166, 4224, 5143, 7509, 9169, 10235, 14522, 15224, 16199**: New Zealand, **15246, 15287, 15296, 15305, 15308, 15309, 15314, 15315;** warm regions, **4947, 8256**

School grounds
establishment, **8256, 8282, 9169, 16128**

School grounds
grasses used, **6589, 15823**

School grounds
irrigation system, **13047**

School grounds
management, **7746, 8953**

School grounds
weed control, **12002**

Scleroderma species (see Fairy ring)

Sclerotinia borealis, **8441**

Sclerotinia homeocarpa (see also Dollar spot), **2817, 4042, 5419**

Scum (see Algae)

Scythe, hand
evaluation, **3457**

Sea erodium, **4738**

Sea serpent
fairway irrigation, **6796**

Seaside chickweed, **1336**

Seaside creeping bentgrass, **301, 347, 352, 491, 742, 757, 972, 977, 3713, 6879, 7309, 9844, 10767, 10837, 11666, 11778, 12406, 12698, 13238, 13462**

Seaside creeping bentgrass
adaptation, **5314, 6585:** soil, **2608, 4881**

Seaside creeping bentgrass
culture, **4169, 9113, 9114, 10068**

Seaside creeping bentgrass
description, **9515, 14134**

Seaside creeping bentgrass
diseases, **3650, 7619, 7815, 9564, 14923:** brown patch, **4169, 15135, 15140, 16300;** dollar spot, **4206, 5406, 5421, 5422, 15135, 15140, 16300;** *Pythium* blight, **9077, 9078**

Seaside creeping bentgrass
disease control, **20, 24, 4206**

Seaside creeping bentgrass
evaluation, **10616, 10760, 11021, 11186, 14349**

Seaside creeping bentgrass
micronutrient deficiency symptoms, **9267**

Seaside creeping bentgrass
photosynthetic rate, **11936**

Seaside creeping bentgrass
uses: green, **854, 1357, 5262, 6053;** overseeding, **5136, 5142, 7037;** winter overseeding, **2493, 2496**

Seaside *Paspalum,* **3504**

Seasonal variation
carbohydrate reserves, **10228, 12220, 15657, 16464, 16465**

Seasonal variation
fructosan content, **2245**

Seasonal variation
glutamine content, **2557**

Seasonal variation
leaf appearance rate, **11951**

Seasonal variation
leaf area, **11951**

Seasonal variation
light intensity, **2821**

Seasonal variation
low temperature hardiness, **2594**

Seasonal variation
root growth, **2552, 2696, 8398, 8399, 11784, 14949**

Seasonal variation
seed germination, **2952**

Seasonal variation
shoot density, **12751, 14103**

Seasonal variation
shoot growth, **2234, 3310, 3783, 11783**

Seasonal variation
silvex selectivity, **3623a**

Seasonal variation
sod heating, **8940**

Seasonal variation
soil nitrate level, **5581**

Seasonal variation
soil reaction: soil test, **4060**

Seasonal variation
soil temperature, **3080, 3081**

Seasonal variation
temperature, **2481**

Seasonal variation
tillering, **11951, 14576**

Seasonal variation
transplant sod rooting, **2687**

Seasonal variation
turfgrass community composition, **2523**

Sedge
chemical control, **3523, 12215, 12799, 12808:** in bermudagrass, **12807**

Sedge
control, **1196, 3505**

Sedge
uses: golf course, **14359;** lawn, **14358**

Sedge peat, **490, 5611**

Sedimentary peat, **490, 6689, 10029, 15560**

Seed, **44, 2995, 3078, 3082, 3326, 6778**

Seed
book, **1442**

Seed
certification, **3734, 8270, 12338**

Seed
classification, **5782**

Seed
cleaning: flame treatment, **3442**

Seed
development, **83, 202, 3377, 7581, 10894, 11116, 11306, 15993**: Kentucky bluegrass, **3241;** perennial ryegrass, **2232**

Seed
diseases, **720, 965, 4049, 9397**

Seed
dispersal, **44, 7580**

Seed
dormancy, **2952, 3194, 6478, 10139, 10706:** germination inhibitor, **5758;** species variation, **4021, 15874**

Seed
identification, **408, 6094, 7778, 11115**: *Agrostis* species, **7775, 7777, 12101, 12138;** annual bluegrass, **9068;** key, **11116;** manual, **15372;** ryegrass, **7645**

Seed
labeling, **1242, 2224, 3734, 10035, 10534, 10730, 11294, 12950, 13097, 13222, 13250, 13258, 13273, 13287, 13320, 16255**

Seed
laws, **1242, 1714, 9665**

Seed
marketing, **286, 13182:** warm season, **2374, 2375**

Seed
maturity: effects, **12003**

Seed
number, **2195, 4973:** live seed calculation, **6777;** mixtures, **7451, 13306;** species variability, **6777, 12324, 13097, 16325**

Seed
pregerminated, **2989, 7187, 15654**

Seed
purchasing, **494, 498, 560, 1599, 2195, 8856, 11656, 12141, 13287:** selection criteria, **1956**

Seed
purity, **447, 4976, 6788, 9594, 9613, 9665, 11294, 11969, 12863, 13155, 13274, 13284, 13320:** analysis techniques, **5277, 9613, 12197, 14268;** inert matter, **2994, 6777, 10361, 13257, 13318, 13321;** labeling, **13097;** other crop seed, **5600, 6777, 13321, 13420;** for sod production, **5600, 13317;** specifications, **2195;** weed seed, **3735, 5600, 6777, 11961, 12547, 13116, 13245, 13259, 13274, 13297, 13321, 13420**

Seed
quality, **1554, 1984, 2994, 3733, 3734, 3735, 4230, 5600, 5782, 6583, 6586, 6788, 6959,**

7292, 8276, 8279, 9612, 9665, 10534, 10730, 11968, 11969, 12338, 12863, 13095, 13131, 13150, 13155, 13249, 13258, 13282, 13318, 13334, 13350, 13536, 14110, 16255: green, **4726;** mechanical, **13257;** sod production, **4451, 4776;** weed control, **13273, 13289**

Seed
quality versus cost, **13095, 13221, 13222, 13227, 13306**

Seed
scarification, **3189, 3190, 3533:** acid, **3388, 7834, 10981;** heat, **7834;** mechanical, **6048, 15654**

Seed
selection, **2020, 3844, 13089, 13318, 13321**

Seed
size, **4976, 6094, 13220:** effects, **4593**

Seed
source, **849, 3011, 13222:** effects, **7953, 13135**

Seed
storage, **2474, 6084, 6087, 6088, 12338**

Seed
supply, **721, 794, 1085, 1211, 1333, 1356, 1414, 1453, 1886, 2370, 13385**

Seed
treatment, **6239, 7453, 7562, 10891, 12338, 14305:** germination effects, **4267, 4424, 6239;** fungicides, **937, 965, 2520, 2521, 2522, 14001**: *Pythium* blight, **14017, 15582;** sterilization, **4267**

Seed
viability, **6088, 10003, 10869:** atmospheric moisture effects, **3664a, 6393;** factors affecting, **2474, 3300, 6409, 10224;** species variation, **12426, 13577;** temperature effects, **3664a, 6409, 9030**

Seed
weight, **4973, 4976:** effects, **2270, 14516, 14661, 15782**

Seedbed
fertilization, **6939:** evaluation, **9938, 12311;** species evaluation, **8837, 10450**

Seedbed
fertilizer placement evaluation, **1055, 9938**

Seedbed
fumigation, **9800, 14384**

Seedbed
soil preparation, **5511, 7432, 12711, 13351, 15669, 16019**

Seedbed
weed control, **2898, 4854, 4861, 4870, 4904, 8402, 8837:** evaluation, **4901, 4903, 15701**

Seed coat, **3194**

Seeder (see Seeding equipment)

Seed-fertilizer mixtures, **947**

Seed germination, **2195, 4290**

Seed germination
Agrostis species, **9468, 12101**

Seed germination
crabgrass, **6478**

Seed germination
crownvetch, **9986, 9995, 14722**

Seed germination
dehulling effects, **544**

Seed germination
effects on: seedling growth, **4936**

Seed germination
factors affecting, **2876, 3802, 6048, 6417, 6478, 7581, 7798, 9587, 9995, 13294, 13321, 14190, 14722, 16513:** carbon dioxide, **3821;** day length, **8657, 11262;** drought, **16181;** drying rate, **3668a, 11211;** fertilizer, **3302;** gibberellin, **206, 2475, 7507, 8666a, 8668, 8669, 9036, 9052;** herbicides, **623, 3722, 4766, 5323, 8671, 8674, 8677, 9453;** light, 205, **2473, 2674, 3327, 3821, 3822, 4925, 6285, 6417, 8781, 10981;** light intensity, **10134, 14761;** light quality, **7683, 10158;** monomoleular films, **181, 2282;** oxygen, **2674;** planting depth, **6048;** plastic mulch, **16040;** potassium nitrate, **205, 4273, 4925, 8781, 10124, 10134, 10981, 11262;** pre-chilling, **4925, 8781;** presoaking, **3822;** root extracts, **8081, 9355;** sawdust phytotoxicity, **2606, 15113, 15114** seed maturity, **3664a, 4925, 6409, 12003, 13577;** seed source, **13135;** seed sterilization, **4267;** seed treatment, **4424, 6239, 14001, 14011;** soil salinity, **2313, 2314, 2359, 12448, 13570;** storage conditions, **2952, 9030, 14190;** temperature, **205, 1855, 2674, 3035, 3327, 3821, 3822, 4957, 5495, 6112, 6285, 6417, 7507, 7669, 7670, 7672, 8086, 8271, 8657, 8781, 8782, 9036,** 9972, 10134, 10981, 12159, 12334, 12889, 13246, 13570, 14051, 14130, 14190, 14759, 15661, 15843; thermoperiodism, **11262, 14761;** thiamine, **47;** water, **2674, 3327, 4957, 8782, 9036, 9972, 15995;** wetting agent, **5423, 10738**

Seed germination
inhibitors, **9986, 12794:** glume constituents, **73, 203**

Seed germination
Italian ryegrass, **15661**

Seed germination
physiological reactions, **7827, 10124, 15992, 15995**

Seed germination
Poa species, **203, 204, 3328, 7798, 14757**

Seed germination
process, **44, 2674, 7585, 11306, 11359**

Seed germination
rate, **2994, 4898, 8029, 11920:** species variation, **81, 2952, 4638, 7670, 9207, 11920, 14218, 16325**

Seed germination
scarification effects (see also Seed, scarification), **3533**

Seed germination
seasonal variation, **2952, 7454**

Seed germination
species minimums, **2674**

Seed germination
testing, **2192, 9614, 12197**

Seed germination
zoysiagrass, **12334, 16513**

Seed head formation, **8593, 15676**

Seed head formation
chemical control, **208, 13534**

Seed head formation
effects of: fertilization, **9274**; soil mix, **8018, 11605, 13896**; temperature, **3035**

Seed head formation
effects on: sod heating, **8940**

Seeding (see also Establishment, seeding), **11179, 12711, 13074**

Seeding
bermudagrass, **720**

Seeding
depth, **720, 2270, 15005**: evaluation, **8029, 11094**; seedling emergence effects, **10082, 12003, 12159, 13573**; species variation, **10082, 15950**; weed effects, **13573**

Seeding
equipment, **7432**

Seeding
fertilization timing, **13074**

Seeding
fertilizer placement, **947**

Seeding
methods, **1738, 2980, 3009, 5485, 7432, 7459, 12312, 14931**: compressed air, **15789**; roadside, **2980, 7782**

Seeding
rate, **794, 837, 937, 1073, 1781, 8118, 11286, 15204, 15209**: effects, **6111, 8783, 10082**; evaluation, **2172, 4596, 6625, 8029, 9334, 10980, 12311, 15705**; factors affecting, **14931**; heaving effects, **3175**; roadside, **9129**; shoot growth effects, **6090, 10383**; sod production, **2170**; species variation, **8837, 11174, 16325**; winter overseeding, **13406**

Seeding
soil preparation, **9785, 12525, 13445, 15669, 16002, 16019**

Seeding
specifications, **9444**

Seeding
time, **290, 370, 373, 1184, 1734, 1909, 2431, 11286, 14185, 14931**: evaluation, **3010, 6238, 7011, 8397, 9159, 12311, 15705**

Seeding, dormant, **1807, 5269**

Seedling, **13127, 14087**

Seedling
competition, **16056**: polystand, **3821, 3832**

Seedling
culture, **3236, 6489, 13141**: fertilization, **6489, 7126, 7462, 9785, 9950, 10470, 10580, 11380, 11390, 12747, 15774**; irrigation, **6489, 13384**; mowing, **7462, 13128, 13142**; weed control, **2672, 7462**

Seedling
development, **2952, 9142, 11359**: *Agrostis* species, **12101**; annual bluegrass, **8658**

Seedling
drought tolerance, **3194**: species evaluation, **9869, 16246**

Seedling
emergence, **2674, 7507**: drought effects, **16181, 16182**; effect of 2,4–D, **8988, 10693**; seeding depth effects, **12003, 12159, 13573**; seed maturity effects, **12003, 13577**; seed treatment effects, **6239, 8334**; seed weight effects, **14516**; soil crusting effects, **6222, 8196, 8202**; temperature effects, **7507, 9322, 14191**

Seedling
emergence rate: species variation, **4902, 6305, 6307**

Seedling
frost heaving, **8932**

Seedling
growth habit: environmental effects, **11365**

Seedling
herbicide toxicity, **2672, 3527, 3782, 6220, 6629, 8031, 10394, 12699, 13636, 13858**: 2,4–D, **8988, 13430, 13431**

Seedling
identification: Kentucky bluegrass cultivars, **11364**; perennial ryegrass flouresce, **11759**

Seedling growth, **2970, 4902, 5108, 5109**

Seedling growth
creeping bentgrass: cultivar evaluation, **7934**

Seedling growth
effects of: day length, **14191**; environmental stress, **9321, 12860, 15843, 16182**; light intensity, **7099, 9973**; phosphorus, **10053, 15774**; root extracts, **8081, 9355**; sawdust, **15113, 15114**; seed age, **2988, 9321**; soil amendment, **10470**; soil moisture, **3075, 7703, 16182**; temperature, **3075, 4028, 7670, 7672, 7703, 12860, 14191**; tree root competition, **15796**

Seedling growth
factors affecting, **2988, 3075, 3691, 4936, 5717, 7313, 9995, 10706, 14516, 15782**

Seedling growth
physiology, **7827**

Seedling growth
rate: cultivar evaluation, **2560, 8836**; species variation, **2750, 6032, 6307, 7313, 7670, 7672, 9207, 11920**

Seed mat, **156, 1174, 1292, 1310, 1492, 7630, 16333**
evaluation, **1687, 13212, 16333**

Seed mixtures, **589, 598, 622, 837, 1379, 2184, 2525, 3014, 3015, 3017, 3177, 3681, 3976, 3983, 4652, 5194, 5267, 5475, 7292, 7453, 10615, 11286, 12141, 13095, 16324**

Seed mixtures
advantages, **2580, 13207**

Seed mixtures
Canada, **3112**

Seed mixtures
cemetery, **11757**

Seed mixtures
cool region, **1433, 1734, 8731, 12863, 13214:** state bulletin, **13827, 13856**

Seed mixtures
England, **1379, 6094, 7191, 13778**

Seed mixtures
evaluation, **4878, 4902, 16360**

Seed mixtures
Germany, **5345**

Seed mixtures
golf course, **4654:** fairway, **4656, 10361, 14940, 16358**; green, **11762, 11961**

Seed mixtures
lawn, **275, 305, 330, 331, 363, 364, 972, 4654, 4655, 5956, 8220, 8274, 8276, 8291, 11078, 11079, 11652, 13173, 13192:** cool regions, **4656, 4869, 5461, 5519, 8279**

Seed mixtures
Mid-Atlantic states, **2976**

Seed mixtures
Netherlands, **14992**

Seed mixtures
Oregon, **6581**

Seed mixtures
park, **16358**

Seed mixtures
quality, **4726, 11968**

Seed mixtures
roadside, **2671, 2966, 2969, 2970, 3012, 3022, 3025, 5095, 16458:** evaluation, **1858, 9129**

Seed mixtures
selection, **1127, 2983, 5540:** criteria, **5509, 11969, 12485;** lawn, **2527, 2618, 13222**

Seed mixtures
sod production, **13371**

Seed mixtures
sports field, **1238, 3459**

Seed mixtures
state bulletin, **8299, 13438**

Seed mixtures
subsequent species composition, **8687, 8688, 10615**

Seed mixtures
Sweden, **9200, 9212**

Seed mixtures
temporary, **11326**

Seed mixtures
warm regions, **2373, 2378**

Seed mixtures
Washington, **9340**

Seed mixtures
winter overseeding, **9301, 10455, 11640**

Seed pellets, **7103**

Seed production, **415, 493, 501, 705, 1517, 2341, 2368, 3663a, 6692, 6989, 7085, 7755, 8463, 8524, 11657, 11658, 12861, 13303, 13371, 13420, 13461, 13764**

Seed production
American beachgrass, **8430**

Seed production
bentgrass, **434, 1194, 11656, 11658, 11662, 11777, 11781, 11782, 11962, 11963, 12425, 13460:** in Canada, **9474;** in Germany, **5300**

Seed production
buffalograss, **561**

Seed production
burning regulations, **13382**

Seed production
centipedegrass, **842, 958, 3545**

Seed production
chewings fescue, **1194, 9517, 11656, 12425, 13460**

Seed production
crownvetch, **6427, 10387**

Seed production
cultural practices, **3545, 12091, 12763, 14109, 14111, 14455, 14456:** burning, **3537, 3810, 5362, 5650, 11128;** cultivation, **3663a**; fertilization, **3537, 5650, 5656, 11128, 11660, 12279, 14109;** insect control, **4253;** irrigation, **7378, 12425, 14457;** weed control, **3439, 3596a, 3671a, 6221, 9453, 10224**

Seed production
Czechoslovakia, **10140, 11246**

Seed production
Dichondra, **16438**

Seed production
effects of: density, **5650, 6065;** gapping, **3663a**; planting date, **6065, 8978;** row spacing, **12425**

Seed production
environmental factors affecting, **6393, 9019, 14111, 14456:** temperature, **6393, 9019**

Seed production
establishment, **14109, 14455**

Seed production
harvesting, **12091, 14455, 14456**: Kentucky bluegrass, **11656**

Seed production
history, **1816, 7755, 8463**

Seed production
Italian ryegrass, **12425, 13453**

Seed production
Kentucky bluegrass, **82, 624, 1105, 1515, 8935, 11658, 12120, 12425, 14109, 14111, 14454, 14636:** cultivars, **4447, 8316, 11959, 14457;** in Minnesota, **14636**

Seed production
Oregon, **12091, 13460, 14420**

Seed production
perennial ryegrass, **12425, 13453**

Seed production
pests: gall midges, **2429;** grass seed nematode, **8525;** plant bug, **8549;** rust, **7346, 14456;** silver top, **7914**

Seed production
processing, **15943:** drying, **15943**

Seed production
purity, **3939, 3940:** isolation distance, **9032**

Seed production
red fescue, **727, 861, 4767, 11128, 12425**

Seed production
redtop, **513**

Seed production
species variability, **11778**

Seed production
Sweden, **12064**

Seed production
tall fescue, **12425**

Seed production
velvet bentgrass, **724, 4846, 4897**

Seed production
yield, **11656, 12425**

Seed setting, **11337, 11357**
factors affecting, **3536, 10367, 13952**

Seed testing, **5, 605, 1984, 3331, 8857, 10366, 11075, 12197, 13536**

Seed testing
germination, **2192**

Seed testing
handbook, **954**

Seed testing
international procedures, **1691**

Seed testing
official procedures: U.S., **1618**

Seed testing
sampling procedures, **7105**

Seed testing
West Germany, **5346**

Seepage
drainage, **6615**

Selectivity (see Herbicide, selectivity)

Self pollination
species evaluation, **13952**

Semesan® (see Hydroxymercurichlorophenols)

Seminal root (see Primary root)

Septoria leaf spot, **6446, 11943**

Sericea lespedeza, **3730, 12596**
roadside use, **7012**

Sevin® (see Carbaryl)

Sewage effluent, **13747**
uses, **15880, 16090:** cost analysis, **8968;** irrigation, **8751, 10544, 16090**

Sewage, liquid, **8950, 8951**

Sewage sludge, **234, 5686, 6922, 8950, 11067**

Sewage sludge
activated, **234, 1488, 1556, 1843, 2100, 2811, 4646, 4647, 4896, 5179, 5499, 9299, 9790, 11172, 11377:** application, **11378;** composting, **11454;** disease effects, **5467, 9299, 10196, 12757;** evaluation, **4650, 5198, 5230, 5781, 6509, 6574, 6579, 6595, 8002, 10066, 10861, 10863, 11057, 11134, 11145, 11185, 11213, 11666, 11905, 15108;** nematode effects, **9299, 11745;** nutrient content, **11379, 11389;** processing, **4248, 11379**

Sewage sludge
digested: soil amendment, **5742**

Sewage sludge
processing, **4081, 10542**

Sewage sludge
soil amendment, **234**

Shade (see also Light), **3648, 5939**

Shade
adaptation, **1639:** cool season turfgrasses, **2566, 2707, 5004, 6499, 15705, 16169;** cool season turfgrasses-bentgrass cultivar evaluation, **1547, 8678;** disease, **1668, 2600;** factors affecting, **5006, 8166;** mechanisms, **2177, 2569, 2580, 2601, 2602, 2640, 7099;** mixtures used, **4864;** species tolerance, **448, 1058, 1827, 2562, 2569, 2580, 2602, 2640, 3590, 3809, 5003, 7099, 13668, 16361, 16368, 16369, 16372, 16460;** species tolerance evaluation, **1735, 2100, 2204, 2601, 2698, 5006, 6443, 8718, 9213, 15795, 16168, 16172;** warm season turfgrasses, **1778, 6499, 8166, 9883, 11906**

Shade
disease problems, **6443, 9758, 9760**

Shade
environmental effects, **2569, 2601, 2602, 2640, 3577a, 5003, 5004:** carbon dioxide level, **5654, 15861;** light intensity, **233, 1530, 4121, 5655, 15046, 15407;** light penetration, **85, 4312, 9648;** light quality, **2288, 2289, 3199, 4121, 5654, 5657, 5658, 6443, 9878, 9881, 15046;** soil moisture, **16080;** sunflects, **5655;** temperature, **4579, 8678, 9973**

Shade
tree maintenance, **698, 812**

Shade
turfgrass culture, **504, 812, 1064, 1478, 1827, 2228, 2602, 3701a, 4264, 4357, 5460, 5507, 5509, 6846, 7335, 7402, 10575, 13172, 13513, 14144, 16167, 16376:** environmental factors affecting, **4264;** fertilization, **448, 967, 7516, 15793;** growth regulators, **3570a;** mowing, **2100;** soil management, **505, 506**

Shade
turfgrass establishment, **2609, 5509, 14155:** seeding, **5507, 7099;** vegetative, **5507, 6436, 9443, 13514**

Shade
turfgrass response, **3591, 3891, 6443, 16169:** carbohydrate reserves, **11980;** environmental stress hardiness, **5004;** growth habit, **6443, 15431;** root growth, **10702, 12533;** root/shoot ratio, **10699, 10702;** shoot density, **3591, 6443;** shoot growth, **3809, 6439, 10702, 11980, 12533, 15795, 16168, 16169;** tillering, **10696, 10697, 10699, 10702, 11980;** vegetative development, **3891, 6443, 10699, 10705**

Shale
properties, **3622**

Shatter cultivation, **2948**

Shear strength, sod (see Sod shear strength)

Sheath nematode, **5011**

Sheep fescue, **3776, 6870, 7333, 11767, 11771, 14471**

Sheep fescue
adaptation, **2942**

Sheep fescue
breeding, **8502**

Sheep fescue
cultivars, **13823:** evaluation, **5313, 7287, 8341, 8350, 13661, 13662, 13665**

Sheep fescue
description, **1335, 4008, 5679, 7333, 7947, 8492, 15412:** cytology, **3836**

Sheep fescue
seed, **11965**

Sheep fescue
uses, **1278, 12001**

Sheep sorrel (see Sorrel, sheep)

Sheperdspurse, **488, 9553**

Sherman big bluegrass, **7309**

Shipment, sod (see Sod shipping)

Shoe soles
effects on: green, **12460**

Shoe soles
types, **12369:** effects, **5845;** wear effects, **866, 5816, 5818, 5824, 5827**

Shoe spikes
turfgrass injury, **16185**

Shoot
anatomy, **7577, 7579**

Shoot
development, **11359, 12457, 13571**

Shoot
morphology, **7579, 13586**

Shoot apex, **3896**

Shoot apex
anatomy, **13586**

Shoot apex
development, **3380, 3897, 3900, 13585, 13587**

Shoot apex
environmental effects, **3897**

Shoot apex
morphology, **13585**

Shoot density, **1686, 2452, 9258, 11153, 13319**

Shoot density
creeping bentgrass: cultivar evaluation, **2564, 2585, 2617, 2704, 2706, 2707**

Shoot density
cultural factors affecting: cultivation, **10071, 10072;** cutting height, **2381, 2603, 6442, 6712, 10071, 10072, 10076, 10615, 12676, 15265, 16179;** fertilization, **12676, 15724;** irrigation, **10071, 10072, 10076, 10173, 12703;** liming, **9691, 11666, 12676;** mowing, **3457;** mowing frequency, **10071, 10072, 10076;** nitrogen carrier, **8699, 15729;** nitrogen fertilization, **1688, 4840, 6306, 6442, 6712, 7559, 9134, 10071, 10072, 10076, 10129, 10615, 12703, 12751, 12758, 13623, 15729**

Shoot density
effects of: weed invasion, **12751**

Shoot density
effects on: root growth, **9975, 14830, 14832;** shoot growth, **14830, 14832**

Shoot density
environmental factors affecting, **12089, 12758:** light intensity, **3591, 6443, 10076;** light quality, **1744, 9881, 10060;** temperature, **7559, 12089, 16430, 16433**

Shoot density
herbicide phytotoxicity, **2893, 12703, 12758**

Shoot density
Kentucky bluegrass: cultivar evaluation, **2564, 2617, 2630, 2658, 2704, 2706, 2707, 6290, 6328, 16436**

Shoot density
measurement method, **519, 2451, 2453, 10129**

Shoot density
perennial ryegrass: cultivar evaluation, **2560, 2704, 2706**

Shoot density
red fescue: cultivar evaluation, **2704, 2706, 2707, 14261**

Shoot density
seasonal variation, **12751, 12758, 14103**

Shoot density
species variation, **12703, 12758**

Shoot density
tall fescue: cultivar evaluation, **2704, 2706**

Shoot growth, **5329, 11635**

Shoot growth
cultural factors affecting: clipping removal, **15709;** cutting height, **2479, 2733, 3308, 4578, 5700, 6628, 7513, 7931, 8192, 8398, 8456, 8675, 8690, 8710, 9007, 9034, 9125, 9178, 9500, 10068, 10072, 10074, 10076, 10105, 10106, 10335, 10526, 10722, 11012, 11604, 11783, 12697, 12765, 12840,**

13900, 14134, 14446, 14765, 14766, 15705, 16179, 16431; fertilization, **2363, 2974, 3606, 4227, 5144, 5577, 7966, 8705, 9107, 9438, 9722, 9723, 9724, 10201, 11024, 12568, 14149, 14405, 15117, 15328, 15376, 15909, 15913, 15918;** hexa-octadecanol, **181, 2282, 12744;** irrigation, **2516, 3890, 9967, 10722, 11012, 12521, 12703, 12840, 13425, 14303, 14890, 14974;** irrigation frequency, **10072, 10076, 10105, 10172, 14891;** liming, **10245, 12531, 13686, 14440, 15787;** mowing, **123, 2850, 2924, 3079, 3278, 3739, 4278 , 5032, 5331, 8398, 12681, 14685;** mowing frequency, **3318, 5361, 5700, 6227, 7501, 7513, 7931, 8398, 8447, 8690, 8846, 9034, 9181, 9358, 9724, 9745, 9992, 10068, 10072, 10075, 10076, 10091, 10106, 11296, 12255, 12557, 12568, 12569, 12765, 12770, 14607, 14765;** soil warming, **9442, 9953;** wetting agent, **10738, 15792**

Shoot growth
effects of: aluminium, **6506;** boron, **5856, 11795;** burning, **9333, 10994;** calcium, **5856, 12532;** compaction, **10974, 10976, 12166, 13425, 14713;** carbohydrate reserves, **91, 2772, 2850, 13619;** establishment, **3784, 7514;** Ethrel®, **7687, 15800;** fungicides, **2603;** gibberillin, **2940, 8669, 8672, 9052, 9419, 9420, 13022, 16329, 16341;** iron, **10523, 13436, 14075;** leaf area, **3311, 3312;** magnesium, **5856, 8758, 10449, 12532;** magnesium carriers, **8163, 10352;** maleic hydrazide, **7518, 12323, 15800, 16286, 16459;** micronutrients, **4783, 9257;** nematicides, **14819, 14820;** pesticides, **2617, 2707, 14386;** nitrogen, **90, 2300, 2672, 2732, 2944, 2945, 2946, 3275, 3554, 3890, 4278, 4840, 5581, 5856, 6628, 6783, 7221, 7222, 7223, 7495, 7496, 7515, 7516, 7699, 7857, 7931, 8192, 8261, 8262, 8265, 8576, 8667,** nitrogen (continued), **8670, 8758, 8949, 9008, 9104, 9134, 9159, 9442, 9718, 9808, 9967, 9974, 9992, 10072, 10076, 10172, 10194, 10201, 10382, 10384, 10784, 11012, 11524, 11783, 11858, 11921, 11980, 12006, 12220, 12255, 12532, 12557, 12637, 12697, 12736, 12752, 12757, 12840, 13619, 13623, 13862, 13951, 14074, 14075, 14148, 14214, 14323, 14446, 14811, 14830, 14832, 15086, 15116, 15155, 15437, 15786, 15984, 15985, 15986, 16202;** nitrogen carriers, **6454, 7771, 7985, 8720, 9103, 9786, 10195, 10384, 10385, 10728, 11067, 11210, 11960, 12748, 13862, 14214, 14811, 15075, 15102, 15118, 15787;** phosphorus, **5856, 7215, 7217, 7223, 8648, 8700, 8702, 8714, 8758, 8949, 9796, 11261, 12532, 12752, 13686, 14376, 14441, 15657, 16202;** polystand, **8723, 12569, 14703;** potassium, **5856, 7223, 7857, 8648, 8758, 10059, 10194, 10784, 11524, 12532, 12752, 14440, 14441, 14685, 15056, 15116;** protective cover, **9442;** root growth, **3563, 14086, 14834, 15086;** root/shoot ratio, **15086;** seeding rate, **6090, 10383;** stunt nematode, **9326;** soil factors, **4949, 5056;** sulfur, **8758, 9257, 12532, 15075, 16203;** sulfur carriers, **10352;** tillering, **8447, 10336;** tree root competition, **15795, 15796**

Shoot growth
effects on: antitranspirants, **11788;** flowering, **2771;** smog injury, **8658**

Shoot growth
environmental factors affecting: day length, **8550, 8657, 8658, 9178, 9724, 11235, 11297, 14604, 16359;** light intensity, **89, 90, 2533, 2666, 2770, 2945, 2946, 3595, 7496, 8657, 10697, 10698, 10702, 11980, 12533, 14835, 15650, 15795, 16057, 16168, 16180, 16338;** light quality, **1744, 2666, 9881, 10058, 10060;** temperature, **88, 90, 2234, 2360, 2361, 2362, 2363, 2614, 2617, 2707, 2944, 3035, 3365, 4578, 5150, 5330, 7495, 7496, 7737, 8550, 8649, 8651, 8657, 8658, 8778, 9178, 9303, 9442, 9724, 10000, 10228, 10697, 10698, 10700, 10704, 11673, 11921, 12005, 12006, 12889, 13409, 13427, 13428, 13562, 13951, 14323, 14423, 14450, 14604, 14836, 15437, 15438, 15650, 16338, 16350, 16354, 16359, 16414, 16430**

Shoot growth
factors affecting, **5646, 7953, 8749, 9358, 9812, 14661, 14832**

Shoot growth
herbicide effects, **5533, 8708, 13970, 15645:** arsenicals, **3722, 3880, 9628, 12750;** bensulide, **10394;** 2,4–D, **10222, 10693, 13958;** DCPA, **10394;** DMPA, **6495;** siduron, **8864, 10394, 14119**

Shoot growth
seasonal variation, **2234, 3310, 3783, 5646, 7215, 9181, 11783, 13527, 14219**

Shoot growth
seedling, **2750, 2970, 5108, 5109**

Shoot growth
soil factors affecting, **13906, 13907, 14132, 14186:** oxygen, **9497, 9503, 15105;** salinity, **3092, 7035, 9175, 9807, 9816, 12737, 16429, 16431, 16442;** sodium, **11996;** soil amendment, **9199, 10114;** soil mix, **9133, 10112, 11605, 13894, 13896, 13906, 13907;** soil reaction, **1666, 4578, 7495,**

8705, 9797, 12531, 12681, 14446; water, **2363, 3299, 3365, 5931, 7177, 7179, 7182, 8456, 9485, 11973, 12736, 14835, 15972;** water table, **15003, 15924, 15973**

Shoot growth
species and cultivar variation, **2249, 2560, 2747, 9141, 11232, 12703**

Showering (see Syringing)

Shredded bark
mulch, **6010**

Shredded bark
soil amendment, **9769**

Sickle bar mower
evaluation, **3457, 16485**

Sideoats grama, **76, 11297**

Sideoats grama
cultivars, **11297**

Sideoats grama
culture: nitrogen fertilization, **11297**

Sideoats grama
environmental factors affecting: day length, **11822, 11823;** light, **11824;** water, **11820, 11821**

Sideoats grama
establishment, **2786**

Sideoats grama
roadside use, **9129**

Sideoats grama
seed dormancy, **10134**

Siduron, **4926, 6096, 8768, 10386**

Siduron
annual bluegrass control, **5184, 10624, 15639**

Siduron
bermudagrass control, **10021, 10778**

Siduron
crabgrass control, **1700, 1782, 2027, 2904, 4141, 5066, 5185, 5199, 5200, 5535, 5545, 5549, 9530, 9531, 9545, 9546, 10619, 12031, 13859, 14823, 14837, 14839:** evaluation, **5066, 5536, 7659, 7661, 8407, 8414, 8415, 10636**

Siduron
deactivation: activated charcoal, **8417**

Siduron
effects on: respiration, **14119;** root growth, **5066, 8864, 10394, 14119, 14120;** shoot growth, **8864, 10394, 14119, 14120**

Siduron
goosegrass control, **9545, 9546**

Siduron
kikuyugrass control, **10021, 15304**

Siduron
mouse ear chickweed control, **8416**

Siduron
selectivity, **5382, 9546, 10619:** bentgrass, **1700, 5066, 8722;** bentgrass cultivars, **7951;** evaluation, **6096, 8707, 10624;** seedling, **6220, 8437, 8864, 9545**

Siduron
spotted spurge control, **13861**

Siduron
weed control, **13882, 15032, 15638, 15639:** evaluation, **5382, 8412, 8864**

Silica cells
species variation, **4595**

Silica content
grasses, **5048, 8660**

Silvertop, **14117, 14233**

Silver weed, **4741**

Silvex, **1493, 5197, 14518**

Silvex
bentgrass control, **3622a, 4646**

Silvex
broadleaf weed control, **2914, 4805, 10627, 13512, 13860:** evaluation, **2172, 5479, 8405, 8433, 11047**

Silvex
catsear control, **4207**

Silvex
chickweed control, **13010, 14047**

Silvex
effects on: carbohydrate reserves, **3623a**; colonial bentgrass root growth, **3620a**

Silvex
henbit control, **13010, 14309**

Silvex
phytotoxicity, **3619a:** factors affecting, **3622a, 3623a**; species tolerance, **8433**

Silvex
selectivity: bentgrass, **2608, 3595, 3622a, 5500;** seasonal variation, **3623;** seedlings, **8437**

Silvex
spotted spurge control, **8408**

Silvex
white clover control, **2901, 8435, 9533**

Silvex
yarrow control, **11592**

Simazine, **1169, 1309, 3502, 13779**

Simazine
annual bluegrass control, **9533, 9537**

Simazine
bermudagrass control, **14309**

Simazine
crabgrass control, **8151, 8178, 9529**

Simazine
evaluation, **8182, 10866, 15978**

Simazine
fall *Panicum* control, **14048**

Simazine
phytotoxicity: zoysiagrass, **5863**

Simazine
residual phytotoxicity, **10451**

Simazine
roadside soil sterilant, **87**

Simazine
species tolerance, **2320, 3502, 3529**

Simazine
vegetative establishment: bermudagrass, **4794**

Simazine
weed control: in centipedegrass, **8564;** in St. Augustinegrass, **8564, 11841**

Sinbar® (see Terbacil)

Sindone®
annual bluegrass control, **8168, 9537**

Sindone®
crabgrass control, **5688, 9533, 9537, 10377**

Sindone®
goosegrass control, **5688**

Sioux red fescue, **8341, 8350**

Size
golf course: California, **4698, 4701;** Europe, **5624**

Size
golf course construction, **12893**

Size
sod industry: Michigan, **2629;** USA, **1704, 1990, 2041**

Size
turf: California, **8928, 8930, 15940;** Colorado, **12958;** Florida, **14401;** Los Angeles County, **2860, 10946;** Nebraska, **1939, 1999, 9118;** New Jersey, **1111;** Ohio, **10628;** Pennsylvania, **1702, 2608, 3077;** Southern California, **7242;** Southern Florida, **13898;** Texas, **5844;** United States, **6844, 8676, 11723;** Washington, **6680, 6718;** West Virginia, **7667**

Size
turfgrass industry, **1120, 1375**

Skandia Kentucky bluegrass, **9218, 9229**

Skating rinks, **3695**

S--21 Kentucky bluegrass, **6306, 8317, 14813**

Skipper, **8478**

Skipper
Essex, **3403, 12008**

Skipper
field, **15404**

Skipper
fiery, **3042, 4779, 4780, 8478**

Ski slopes, **553, 668, 15611**

Skunks, **4306**

Slag
soil amendment, **15096, 15112**

Slag meal, **3307**

Sleet
lethal effects, **2570**

Slender wheatgrass, **8810**
adaptation, **1686, 15054**

Slicing, **6521, 7474**

Slime mold, **1028, 2099, 3603a, 4189, 6748, 12931, 13566, 13727, 13733, 15674**

Slime mold
chemical control, **2172, 6748**

Slime mold
control, **4685, 10677**

Slime mold
symptoms, **6161, 10853, 15646**

Slit trench, **2161, 7907, 11090**

Slit trench
green drainage, **11090**

Slit trench
installation, **7907, 12420, 16143**

Slope
effects on: establishment, **3076;** run-off, **5211;** shoot growth, **2824**

Slope
orientation: microclimate effects, **75, 936, 3075, 9996, 16080;** temperature variations, **2824, 9994**

Slope
stabilization: methods, **1703, 8393, 13452, 14481;** mulch evaluation, **4838, 5131, 9991, 13974;** Penngift crown vetch, **5157, 11162;** roadside, **14049;** vegetative, **8117**

Sloughgrass, **76**

Slugs, **9186**
control, **1025**

Slush problems
winter injury, **2582**

Small animals
chemical control, **12190**

Small brown patch (see Dollar spot)

Smargd creeping bentgrass, **9213**

SMDC, **1060, 1227, 1493, 1892, 3923, 7413, 8665, 8768, 8832, 8931, 10030, 11994, 13520, 13724**

SMDC
annual bluegrass control, **5632**

SMDC
fumigant, **1224, 6637, 13520, 16320**

SMDC
kikuyugrass control, **16334**

SMDC
nematode control, **12978**

SMDC
purple nutsedge control, **9670**

SMDC
soil fumigation, **1224, 2867, 2880**

SMDC
soil sterilization, **7149, 11976, 12988**

SMDC
use, **13520, 16439**

S.53 meadow fescue, **7284, 8338, 8350**

Smog, **1028**

Smog
injury effects, **8658**

Smog
injury symptoms, **3002, 8658**

Smog
species susceptibility: annual bluegrass, **3002**

Smooth brome, **19, 4104, 14663**
roadside use, **9129**

Smooth crabgrass, **8952, 12072, 12146**

Smooth crabgrass
chemical control, **8161, 8171**

Smooth crabgrass
seed germination, **8952**

Smoothstalk meadowgrass (see Kentucky bluegrass)

Smut (see also Stripe smut and Leaf smut), **3886**

Smut
chemical control, **6748**

Snails, **9186**
chemical control, **2269**

Snow, **14855**

Snow
effects on: winter protection, **2559, 2566, 2570, 2582, 4556**

Snow
removal, **563, 693, 1552, 4556, 4576:** green, **5039, 11620, 14252;** methods, **9210;** soil warming, **4545**

Snow fence
sand dune stabilization, **14543**

Snowmobile
effects on: winter injury, **1746, 8552, 15161**

Snowmobile
on golf course, **1937:** advantages, **10715;** damage, **5936**

Snow mold (see also *Fusarium* patch and *Typhula* blight), **185, 209, 539, 563, 590, 608, 627, 647, 680, 691, 726, 735, 1017, 4313, 4315, 4316, 4713, 9416, 10802, 11490, 12546, 12931, 14804, 15016, 16053**

Snow mold
bentgrass cultivar susceptibility, **1545, 1690**

Snow mold
chemical control, **1487, 1590, 1842, 5039, 6121, 7765, 9023, 9411, 10802, 10891, 11574, 14805, 14886, 15527:** benomyl, **14810;** cadmium compounds, **10808;** daconil, **2787;** evaluation, **3111, 3260, 5773, 5781, 5923, 6336, 7068, 10421, 10422, 10423, 11457, 14923, 15475, 15591, 15592, 16220;** mercurials, **10803, 10807, 10808**

Snow mold
control, **2957, 10853, 11490**

Snow mold
cultural control, **2221, 3693a, 4956, 14252**

Snow mold
effects of: nitrogen, **1470, 4316, 5395, 11490, 14923;** nitrogen carrier, **1470, 14923;** phosphorus, **11490;** potassium, **11490;** soil temperature, **9406**

Snow mold
hydrogen cyanide producation, **9406, 9413, 15373**

Snow mold
identification: hydrogen cyanide test, **9411, 9412**

Snow mold
injury symptoms, **10853, 10891, 13703**

Snow mold
species susceptibility, **4316, 14460**

Snow thrower
selection, **5640**

Soccer field
construction, **1262, 4927:** state bulletin, **7420, 7423**

Soccer field
culture, **1046, 1088, 1255, 1398:** cultivation, **13791;** mowing, **1249;** soil modification, **9211;** soil warming, **1801, 4927, 8448**

Soccer field
establishment, **4927**

Soccer field
grasses used, **9211, 13790**

Soccer field
renovation, **13792**

Sod
development, **1426, 11007**

Sod certification, **1736, 4252, 8277, 8280, 11295**

Sod certification
benefits, **8287, 8289**

Sod certification
Florida, **6236, 8638, 11863, 11865**

Sod certification
Maryland, **11874**

Sod certification
New Jersey, **8287, 8289**

Sod certification
problems, **8287, 8289**

Sod certification
retail level, **6235**

Sod certification
warm season species, **1806, 8302**

Sodco Kentucky bluegrass, **1778, 2027, 2100, 4489, 4510, 6298, 6451, 6474**

Sodco Kentucky bluegrass
adaptation, **4534, 6315**

Sodco Kentucky bluegrass
evaluation, **4522, 6330, 11186, 14813**

Sod cooling (see Sod shipping)

Sod cutworm, **17**

Sodding (see Sod transplanting and Establishment, vegetative)

Sodding
advantages, **14261, 14290**

Sod formation
factors affecting, **9627, 10382**

Sod Growers Association
development, **15406**

Sod Growers Association of Mid-America, **15408**

Sod handling (see also Sod harvesting), **1922, 1994, 2046, 2316**

Sod handling
methods, **2041, 2737**

Sod harvesting (see also Sod handling), **1781, 1990, 2316, 2709, 2711, 4437, 11041, 11042, 11043, 11060**

Sod harvesting
equipment, **1823, 1925, 4793, 15292**

Sod harvesting
for green, **307**

Sod harvesting
methods, **2737, 14382**

Sod harvesting
thickness, **1363, 1492, 2668, 4444, 8649, 14291, 15402:** factors affecting, **4438, 4745, 4883, 6936, 11189, 12955, 16025;** sod shearing effects, **2669;** sod strength effects, **10382;** transplant rooting effects, **1958**

Sod heating, **8946, 16184**

Sod heating
causes, **1958, 2649, 8940**

Sod heating
effects of: carbon dioxide level, **8940;** ethylene level, **8940;** N^6 benzyl adenine, **8940, 8947;** oxygen level, **8940**

Sod heating
effects on: carbohydrate reserves, **1801;** transplant rooting, **8940, 8947**

Sod heating
factors affecting, **2630, 2633, 2672, 8940, 8941:** cutting height, **8940, 8947;** diurnal harvest time, **8940;** nitrogen fertilization, **8940, 8947;** seed head production, **8940**

Sod heating
lethal temperature, **8940**

Sod heating
prevention, **1958, 2170, 2649:** vacuum cooling, **16184**

Sod heating
seasonal variation, **8940**

Sodic soils, **11887**
book, **12582**

Sod industry
survey, **1662, 1990**

Sod installation (see Sod transplanting)

Sodium, **2845**

Sodium
effects on: growth, **3737, 8263;** nutrient uptake, **2350;** seed germination, **2350;** tissue composition, **8263**

Sodium
plant content, **9797, 15645:** factors affecting, **7084**

Sodium
soil levels, **3183, 8246, 14376**

Sodium
species tolerance, **3737, 3825, 6278, 9797, 14376, 15645**

Sodium arsenite, **661, 920, 1013, 2834, 5529, 7779, 10851**

Sodium arsenite
annual bluegrass control, **2463, 4399, 5464, 5527, 5530, 5531, 7175, 9339, 15662, 15664, 15666, 16159**

Sodium arsenite
chickweed control, **11666, 12949, 15989**

Sodium arsenite
clover control, **15664**

Sodium arsenite
crabgrass control, **916, 4376, 4378, 4387, 4938, 5444, 5524, 5557, 7175, 9150, 10909, 11143, 11160, 12940, 14571, 14572, 15663, 16153:** evaluation, **4906, 6352, 11454, 11666**

Sodium arsenite
knotweed control, **12357**

Sodium arsenite
pearlwort control, **2303, 7119, 7120, 12082, 12083**

Sodium arsenite
renovation: fairway, **11253**

Sodium arsenite
use, **6835, 11247:** fairway renovation, **7209;** fairway weed control, **6880, 11459, 16159;** green, **7209;** seedbed preparation, **11584**

Sodium arsenite
weed control, **923, 2751, 4839, 4843, 7250, 10851, 11599, 12280:** evaluation, **5479, 10851, 12808**

Sodium arsenoacetate
crabgrass control, **4906**

Sodium borate (see Borax)

Sodium cacodylate
annual bluegrass control, **4018**

Sodium carbonate
irrigation water: compaction effects, **3303**

Sodium chlorate, **450**

Sodium chlorate
bermudagrass control, **11092**

Sodium chlorate
bindweed control, **8934**

Sodium chlorate
crabgrass control, **699, 700, 6818, 6819, 6820**

Sodium chlorate
ground ivy control, **15696**

Sodium chlorate
weed control, **724, 859, 4839, 4843, 6818, 15703**

Sodium chloride, **15645**

Sodium chloride
deicing, **3165**

Sodium chloride
phytotoxicity, **14645, 15645:** roadside, **12754, 14644**

Sodium cyanide
white grub control, **15347, 15990**

Sodium fluoride
crabgrass control, **702**

Sodium methyldithiocarbamate (see SMDC)

Sodium molybdate, **1841**

Sodium nitrate, **309, 1470, 1555, 2942, 4896, 5321, 5634, 5679**

Sodium nitrate
effects on: dollar spot, **12757**

Sodium nitrate
evaluation, **5636, 6790, 7220, 10861, 11666, 11674, 15709, 15786, 15787**

Sodium nitrate
soil reaction effects, **15, 11024**

Sodium pentachlorphenate
moss control, **7142**

Sodium pentachlorphenate
weed control, **15424**

Sod marketing, **1988, 2123, 3584a, 4451, 8056, 8804, 11707, 12282**

Sod marketing
nematode problem, **5008**

Sod marketing
price, **2119**

Sod marketing
retailing, **11061:** garden centers, **15396;** nurserymen, **6154**

Sod marketing
survey, **2041, 13943**

Sod production, **1534, 1722, 2032, 2046, 2121, 2703, 2709, 2711, 3162, 3584a, 4152, 4458, 6140, 8640, 9137, 10993, 11100, 11178, 11619, 11645, 13317, 13764, 16177**

Sod production
accounting system, **2115**

Sod production
aquatic, **2103, 2206**

Sod production
Atlantic coast, **3163**

Sod production
bulletin, **265, 7334, 15427**

Sod production
California, **11216**

Sod production
Canada, **12953, 12954**

Sod production
Central USA, **10438**

Sod production
clipping utilization (see Clipping utilization)

Sod production
cultural practices, **1530, 1824, 1915, 1919, 1925, 1928, 1988, 4152, 7148, 8131, 8273, 8288, 11042, 11060, 12607, 12621, 14292, 14382, 14425, 15291, 15827, 15837, 15907:** cool regions, **2642, 8051, 12618, 15378;** fertilization, **1967, 2649, 2672, 5580, 9134, 12636, 12637, 12952, 14090, 14630, 15379, 15825, 15907;** irrigation, **5062, 8907, 12636, 15379, 15907;** irrigation system, **1919, 6243;** mineral soils, **13422;** mowing, **7773;** organic soils, **8053, 12618, 14629, 14630;** pre-transplanting, **15397;** rolling, **12636;** warm regions, **1831, 7409, 11861, 11862;** weed control, **2672, 3503, 7147, 7409, 7964, 7965, 8275, 10406, 11303, 12636**

Sod production
economics, **2120, 2122, 8052:** cost analysis, **8656, 13693, 14291;** credit losses, **8054**

Sod production
economic trends, **5944**

Sod production
effects on: sod transplanting, **15388**

Sod production
equipment, **3839, 11725, 12580:** flotation tires, **1928**

Sod production
establishment, **1661, 1716, 4152, 4798, 7773, 8286, 12636:** fertilization, **1958, 2116;** seedbed preparation, **8273, 12580;** seeding, **8273, 12636;** seeding rate, **1958, 2170;** seeding time, **1958, 2170, 2649, 9134;** vegetative, **1915, 7409**

Sod production
grasses used, **1990, 7025, 11990, 12636, 15837:** cool season, **2703, 6474, 13422, 15378;** Kentucky bluegrass blends, **6313, 6314;** shade mixture, **8186;** warm season, **1831, 7409, 15352**

Sod production
harvesting: palletizing, **2117**

Sod production
history, **8556, 15388:** England, **11039, 11040**

Sod production
Maryland, **1716, 11874**

Sod production
Ontario, **16200**

Sod production
overseeding, **6540**

Sod production
pests, **9721, 15837**

Sod production
pest control, **1217, 2672, 11862, 15841**

Sod production
Rhode Island, **13849**

Sod production
seed specifications, **4776, 5600**

Sod production
site selection, **7773, 14945, 15800**

Sod production
size: California, **11216;** Florida, **3225, 13940;** Maryland, **2202, 4793;** Michigan, **2629, 7783;** Ohio, **10628;** Pennsylvania, **3077**

Sod production
subsidence, soil, **1958, 2630, 2649**

Sod production
trends, **2140, 8556, 11707, 11725, 13764, 15385, 15392, 15401**

Sod production
winter injury, **1958, 1991, 2634**

Sod quality, **6277, 8298, 8804, 10681, 11619, 13317, 15393**

Sod quality
grading, **198, 14261**

Sod quality
roadside specifications, **14261**

Sod research, **1958, 2170, 2649, 2708**

Sod rooting (see Transplant rooting)

Sod shear strength
factors affecting, **1442, 2669, 6806**

Sod shear strength
measurement technique, **2669**

Sod shipment
insect regulations: state, **6234**

Sod shipping (see also Sod heating), **1994, 2711**

Sod shipping
cooling, **1573, 1770:** vacuum, **15291**

Sod shipping
inspection requirements: state, **6234**

Sod storage
factors affecting, **8940**

Sod strength (see also Michigan Sod Strength Test)

Sod strength
blends: Kentucky bluegrass, **2630, 2633, 2672, 2687**

Sod strength
effects of: cutting height, **2170, 2630, 2633, 2649, 2672, 2704, 14090;** mowing frequency, **2630, 2633, 2649, 2672;** nitrogen, **2630, 2633, 2672, 2704, 2707, 2717, 5581, 12637;** preemergent herbicide, **14838**

Sod strength
factors affecting, **1824**

Sod strength
Kentucky bluegrass: cultivar evaluation, **2630, 2633, 2672, 2687**

Sod strength
measurement technique, **2717, 12640**

Sod strength
polystand: Kentucky bluegrass-red fescue, **2630, 2633, 2672, 2717**

Sod strength
species variation, **2649**

Sod tamper, **620**

Sod transplanting, **1369, 1639, 1722, 2212, 2711, 3059, 3487, 5506, 6248, 12004, 12638, 13567, 15383, 15387**

Sod transplanting
baseball field, **1226**

Sod transplanting
on concrete, **1693**

Sod transplanting
drainage problems, **3698**

Sod transplanting
equipment, **2082**

Sod transplanting
erosion control: gullies, **14950**

Sod transplanting
football field, **1902**

Sod transplanting
green, **7275, 12298, 15387**

Sod transplanting
history, **12449**

Sod transplanting
job bidding, **15386, 15387**

Sod transplanting
lawn, **4758, 15387**

Sod transplanting
nitrogen effects, **2100, 5235**

Sod transplanting
post-transplant care, **1679, 3444, 7701, 7724, 7971, 12439, 12440, 12607, 14291, 14293**

Sod transplanting
roadside, **15402**

Sod transplanting
rooting (see Transplant rooting)

Sod transplanting
in shade, **13513, 13514**

Sod transplanting
soil preparation, **2045, 2154, 5075, 15386:** state bulletin, **1968**

Sod transplanting
species adaptation, **2154**

Sod transplanting
specifications, **2045, 2141, 2154, 9444:** state bulletin, **1968**

Sod transplanting
techniques, **2710, 2737, 3444, 12639, 15386**: England, **10671, 14031**

Sod transplanting
timing, **9159, 10663**

Sod webworm, **17, 466, 689, 1425, 1953, 1986, 2027, 2053, 2407, 3042, 3285, 3612a, 3623, 4611, 4612, 4780, 5582, 7258, 7606, 7858, 8670, 8825, 8878, 9186, 11344, 11663, 12542, 13496, 13502, 14034**

Sod webworm
chemical control, **625, 1274, 2407, 3283, 3504, 3595, 3612a, 3858, 4060, 4158, 4834, 4836, 5295, 7607, 8069, 8071, 8250, 8253, 8472, 8475, 8578, 8588, 8829, 9726, 9873, 10156, 10359, 11374, 12095, 12427, 13499, 13516, 14396, 14751, 15087, 15334, 15618:** chlordane, **12177, 13491;** evaluation, **1779, 2614, 3068, 8480, 8548, 11663, 11664, 11944, 12428, 14389, 14398, 14399, 14633;** lead arsenate, **4835, 8067, 8072, 11666, 14338**

Sod webworm
control, **551, 637, 650, 1028, 1570, 1849, 3612a, 10582, 11373**

Sod webworm
description, **4779, 4834, 4835, 5295, 7858, 8069, 8072, 8607, 8829, 8890, 11374, 12315, 14633, 15087, 15334**

Sod webworm
environmental effects, **13494**

Sod webworm
injury symptoms, **2603, 8870, 8890, 10155, 10156, 11663, 12095, 13501, 14338, 14667**

Sod webworm
Kentucky bluegrass: cultivar susceptibility, **3436, 11945**

Sod webworm
life cycle, **8069, 8250, 8475,**

8548, 8744, 8870, 12427, 13516, 14033

Sod webworm
state bulletin, **14486**

Sod webworm
on warm season turfgrasses, **3612a, 14667**

Soft cranesbill, **4738**

Soil, **18, 96, 99, 105, 111, 113, 116, 177, 219, 461, 1315, 1587, 2259, 2828, 5589, 5836, 6385, 6839, 9788, 10539, 11219, 11307, 11426, 11427, 11733, 11886, 12309, 13979, 13980, 14756, 14987, 14994, 15461, 15468, 15473, 15478**

Soil
chemical properties, **3392, 3616, 3933, 9913, 11580**

Soil
components, **9770, 10557, 10968, 13508, 14332, 15537, 15886:** air, **3933, 6661, 9188, 9489, 10100, 10267, 10269, 10651, 11037, 15480, 15496, 15500, 15501;** biological, **9818, 10874;** mineral, **5188, 13634;** organic, **3792, 10859, 11435, 12304, 13634, 14125, 15468, 15501, 16014;** water, **3933, 9188, 9489, 10100, 11485, 13402**

Soil
for cricket wicket, **14296**

Soil
effects, **3365, 8443, 11435**

Soil
effects of: traffic, **8057, 8241, 15514**

Soil
formation, **226, 7573, 9689, 15495**

Soil
freezing: refrigerant system, **8455**

Soil
for golf courses, **12898, 14924**

Soil
management, **2546, 5261, 10095, 13445, 14935, 15997, 16077**

Soil
mechanical resistance: root growth, **2421**

Soil
nitrate accumulation, **4285, 4286**

Soil
physical properties, **3933, 4704, 6410, 6411, 9715, 11401, 11402, 11411, 11412, 11703, 11895, 14419, 15357, 15501, 15505:** effects on growth, **9604, 11395;** freezing effects, **7837;** irrigation effects, **8812;** organic matter effects, **10859, 14186, 14187;** salt effects, **12737;** traffic effects, **10968, 14882, 15526**

Soil
salinity (see Salinity, soil)

Soil
sub-soil, **9589, 9856**

Soil
topsoil (see Topsoil)

Soil acidity (see also Soil reaction), **15615**

Soil acidity
correction, **1484, 1485, 4287, 15201**

Soil acidity
effects of: nitrogen carriers, **15064**

Soil acidity
effects on: polystand composition, **11129;** thatch, **2172**

Soil aeration (see Aeration, soil)

Soil amendment, **3180, 3181, 3587a, 4533, 6058, 6930, 8926, 9781, 10759, 11193, 12010, 12185, 13445, 16130**

Soil amendment
calcined clay (see Calcined clay)

Soil amendment
composting, **12901**

Soil amendment
effects, **1879, 7785, 8443, 10029**

Soil amendment
effects on: compaction, **8000, 8011, 10977, 12166;** evapotranspiration, **10977;** impact absorption, **6806, 9199;** infiltration, **10977, 15112;** pore space, **7987, 8000, 9199, 10114, 15112;** root growth, **8000, 9494, 10114;** shoot growth, **2063, 8000, 9199, 10114, 14132;** soil water retention, **7170, 7987, 15112**

Soil amendment
evaluation, **4702, 4704, 4708, 5167, 8000, 8011, 8016, 8037, 9769, 10029, 10112, 10115, 10116, 10977, 10979, 13425, 13894, 13902, 13906, 15112**: Japan, **9116, 9118, 9120, 9199, 10111, 10117**

Soil amendment
expanded shale (see Expanded shale)

Soil amendment
fly ash (see Fly ash)

Soil amendment
green, **9386, 13685, 13905, 16489**

Soil amendment
gypsum (see also Gypsum), **1056, 9970**

Soil amendment
microorganism source, **2155**

Soil amendment
organic materials, **1700, 4586, 9770, 9899, 10028, 10029:** evaluation, **637, 12606, 14132;** water retention effects, **14132, 14134**

Soil amendment
peat (see Peat)

Soil amendment
sawdust (see Sawdust)

Soil amendment
topdressing, **10974**

Soil amendment
types, **5873, 6024, 7079, 8000, 8133, 10028, 11974, 13892**

Soil amendment
uses, **7079, 8000, 10028, 10029, 10969, 13684**

Soil amendment
vermiculite (see Vermiculite)

Soil analysis (see also Soil test)
chemical, **9858, 11422, 11638, 13793:** arsenic (see Arsenic, soil analysis); book, **8333**

Soil analysis
nematode (see Nematode, soil analysis)

Soil analysis
physical, **1567, 6645:** hydrometer, **3083, 3084;** mechanical, **8921, 10271, 12664, 13691;** Sweden, **8454**

Soil bulk density
compaction effects, **5169, 11153**

Soil bulk density
effects on: root growth, **5148, 15912;** seedling emergence, **8196;** shoot growth, **13907**

Soil carbon dioxide (see Carbon dioxide, soil)

Soil classification, **11435, 14935**
7th approximation, **1400**

Soil compaction (see Compaction)

Soil conditioning, **106, 986, 993, 1019, 1710, 3143, 4380, 5755, 6403, 6893, 6988, 9781, 10253, 13445**

Soil conditioning
effects, **6403, 7520**

Soil conditioning
effects on: root growth, **7520, 9494;** seedling growth, **9801**

Soil conditioning
evaluation, **1879, 4704, 6338, 7520, 10029**

Soil conditioning
fairway, **14785**

Soil conditioning
gypsum (see Gypsum)

Soil conditioning
krilium (see Krilium)

Soil conditioning
sulfur (see Sulfur)

Soil conservation, **3446**
grasses used, **7163, 7945, 14229, 14510, 15850, 15933**

Soil crusting (see Crusting, soil)

Soil cultivation (see also Cultivation), **4034, 4145, 6887, 6905**

Soil drench (see also Liquid fertilization), **1202, 3060, 3573a, 3600, 3975, 9694**

Soil drench
effects on: irrigation system, **3600**

Soil drench
fertilizer application: injection equipment, **3682;** methods, **2507, 3573a;** sod production, **1967**

Soil drought, **16181**

Soil erosion (see Erosion)

Soil fertility (see Fertilization)

Soil fumigation, **1168, 5353, 5990, 6638, 8927, 8931, 9800, 10030**

Soil fumigation
chloropicrin (see Chloropicrin)

Soil fumigation
dazomet (see Dazomet)

Soil fumigation
effects on: nutrient uptake, **12771**

Soil fumigation
effectiveness: factors affecting, **5767, 7665**

Soil fumigation
equipment: state bulletin, **2730**

Soil fumigation
greens, **1227, 9400**

Soil fumigation
methods, **3885, 4407, 5767, 8565, 11299, 15233**

Soil fumigation
methyl bromide (see Methyl bromide)

Soil fumigation
SMDC (see SMDC)

Soil fumigation
types, **1168, 9800**

Soil fumigation
Vorlex® (see Vorlex®)

Soil fungi
effects on: localized dry spots, **13033**

Soil fungi
populations, **201**

Soil heaving (see Frost heaving)

Soil infiltration (see Infiltration, soil)

Soil layering, **3299, 5891, 12506**

Soil microorganisms (see Microorganisms, soil)

Soil mix, **385, 4705, 5810, 5830, 5878, 6634, 10085, 11733, 16130**

Soil mix
composition, **5243, 5245, 8661, 14482, 15099, 15889**

Soil mix
effects, **6476, 12000, 14713, 15711, 15889**

Soil mix
effects on: aeration, **11605, 13683;** ball bouncing, **9217;** ball roll, **9217;** compaction proneness, **9132, 9133, 9772, 9774, 9776, 10113, 10976, 13683;** drought stress, **8018, 11605, 13896;** hydraulic conductivity, **13907;** infiltration rate, **2631, 2707, 12030, 15095, 15096, 15098, 15099;** penetrability, **13894, 13907;** percolation rate, **13683, 13894, 15095, 15098;** pore space, **10873, 13907;** root growth, **9133, 10112, 11359, 11605, 15676;** seed head formation, **8018, 11605, 13896, 15676;** shoot growth, **9133, 10112, 11605, 13894, 13896, 13906, 13907;** soil water retention, **8661, 11605, 13683, 13894, 13902;** turfgrass quality, **11664, 13896, 13907**

Soil mix
evaluation, **4551, 4702, 5171, 5742, 5772, 6412, 8102, 8784, 8786, 10114, 10115, 10872, 11948, 12421, 13416, 13425**: Japan, **9116, 9118, 9120, 9199, 10111**

Soil mix
green, **475, 1062, 2996, 3589a, 5243, 5251, 5811, 5830, 5848, 5872, 5876, 5879, 5881, 5885, 5894, 6024, 6410, 6411, 7879, 8103, 8206, 8207, 8326, 8327, 8523, 9111, 9133, 9778, 9780, 9789, 9829, 9997, 10157, 10197, 10940, 11034, 11203, 11555, 12292, 12414, 12616, 13966, 13967, 14780, 15357, 15492, 15718, 15721, 16206:** evaluation, **2603, 2631, 5805, 7933, 9132, 9776, 10116, 11899, 12412, 13418, 13683, 13684, 13685, 13905, 15096, 15112, 16489;** New Zealand, **7628;** organic amendment evaluation, **9680, 9737, 12606**

Soil mix
mixing procedures, **1550, 1927, 11194, 11203, 11205**

Soil mix
physical properties, **5894, 8661, 12591**

Soil mix
sports field, **8450, 10157**: Netherlands, **14442**

Soil mix
stabilized soil, **14947**

Soil mix
Sweden, **8454**

Soil mix
topdressing, **6893, 11194, 11583**

Soil modification, **1967, 3183, 3616, 5810, 6634, 7419, 9492, 10090, 10969, 11193, 12185, 13691, 15473, 15478, 16077, 16307**

Soil modification
asphalt barrier (see Asphalt barrier)

Soil modification
complete: California Method (see California Method); PAT System (see PAT System); Purr-Wick System (see Purr-Wick System); USGA Green Section Method (see USGA Green Section Method), **7902, 16048**

Soil modification
depth, **4707, 13907**

Soil modification
effects, **4707, 9774, 13688**

Soil modification
evaluation, **1780, 5167, 5206, 5366, 5635, 8784, 9800**

Soil modification
football field, **1902**

Soil modification
greens, **562, 1960, 2043, 5244, 5881, 7430, 9111, 9775:** evaluation, **12412, 13896**

Soil modification
materials used, **4707, 5873, 5981, 6689, 7079, 8786, 10967, 10978, 11201, 11954, 11955, 12032, 13416, 13967, 14139, 14177, 15098, 15099, 15103, 15754**

Soil modification
methods, **4488, 4508, 4527, 4707, 15112**

Soil modification
partial, **4328, 4525, 4707, 7430, 10978, 11201, 12451, 15468:** for clay soils, **10859;** deep coring, **2027, 10962;** vertical slits, **2189**

Soil modification
of sandy soils: evaluation, **2883, 7430, 8018, 12451, 16130**

Soil modification
soccer field, **9211**

Soil nutrient retention (see also Fertilization), **4101, 4287, 5788, 12899**

Soil organic matter (see Organic matter)

Soil organisms (see also Microorganisms, soil), **2055, 7573, 14029**

Soil oxygen (see Oxygen, soil)

Soil pore space (see Pore space, soil)

Soil preparation
for establishment, **578, 9785, 10241, 15669:** sports field, **2188**

Soil preparation
for sod transplanting, **2045:** state bulletin, **1968**

Soil profile, **10546, 12899, 15886**

Soil reaction, **593, 816, 3392, 3740, 7449, 7679, 9686, 10430, 11396, 11443, 14723, 14802**

Soil reaction
acidity (see Soil acidity)

Soil reaction
correction, **2065, 3180, 3181, 5604, 12601, 15179, 15258:** aluminum sulfate, **3001;** liming, **969, 3321, 4867, 11397;** sulfur, **2617, 11397, 12624**

Soil reaction
effects, **724, 1304, 2449, 3461, 3821, 7574, 9457, 9689, 11436, 12624, 12702, 14136, 15179**

Soil reaction
effects of: ammonium sulfate, **2172, 7223, 12142;** fertilization, **7985, 7992, 11586, 12258;** fertilizers, **483, 8248, 11397;** gypsum, **11397;** nitrogen, **6666, 6674, 9274, 16202;** nitrogen carriers, **12, 2830, 6674, 7220, 7598, 7991, 7992, 8024, 9784, 9786, 10024, 10385, 11454, 11666, 12117, 15697, 16152, 16451;** potassium, **7993, 8048;** root-shoot ratio, **14149**

Soil reaction
effects on: annual bluegrass, **4768, 6685;** arsenic toxicity, **3722, 3725, 3726;** bentgrass, **2811, 7574;** clover, **2172, 11666;** disease development,

483, 2997, 2998, 4179, 6674, 6704, 7285, 8357, 8375, 8770, 11661; drought tolerance, 1304, 5634, 5636; earthworms, 1483, 2172, 8467, 8468, 8469; growth, 8670, 8714, 12702; herbicide effectiveness, 3623a, 9825; moss, 2172; nutrient availability, 840, 3391, 4284, 4287, 7671, 8243, 8248, 9816, 11573, 12624; nutrition, 11385, 11436, 11464, 12601, 12702; organic matter, 7983, 11463; pests, 15760; polystand composition, 6422, 11372, 12839; root growth, 4578, 7495, 8698, 8705, 10245, 11666, 12531, 14135, 14998; shoot growth, 1666, 4578, 5717, 7495, 8705, 8720, 11666, 12531, 14446; soil nitrogen relationships, 3206, 4286, 9085; weed control, 483, 15698; weed invasion, 4768, 11666, 14993, 15787

Soil reaction
factors affecting, 7983, 11396, 11463, 12702

Soil reaction
indicator plants, 13783

Soil reaction
seasonal variation, 4060

Soil reaction
species adaptation, 391, 867, 1364, 7529, 7574, 10821, 11464, 12624, 14199, 14993; evaluation, 7473, 10245

Soil salinity (see Salinity, soil)

Soil sampling, 1145, 1288, 1315, 3091, 3615, 9858

Soil sampling
procedures, 3215, 5901

Soil sampling
timing, 3215

Soil set®
mulch, 7184

Soil solution, 11387

Soil stability, 7477

Soil stabilization (see Roadway, turfed)

Soil sterilization, 1069, 1168, 1217, 4154, 5308, 5353, 6083, 7410, 7413, 8182, 8931, 11300, 11574, 11697, 11703, 11706, 11998, 14384

Soil sterilization
anhydrous ammonia (see Anhydrous ammonia)

Soil sterilization
annual bluegrass control, 5632

Soil sterilization
asphalt impregnation, 3101

Soil sterilization
chloropicrin (see Chloropicrin)

Soil sterilization
dazomet (see Dazomet)

Soil sterilization
methods, 4587, 4871, 7149, 7413, 10030

Soil sterilization
methyl bromide (see Methyl bromide)

Soil sterilization
on roadside, 87, 214, 3842, 4302, 5119

Soil sterilization
SMDC (see SMDC)

Soil sterilization
steam (see Steam)

Soil sterilization
sterilant types, 1892, 2880, 4234, 6083, 8832, 11697, 11976, 12988, 16439

Soil sterilization
topdressing, 4849, 4850, 12794

Soil structure, 107, 575, 2054, 2953, 3587a, 4118, 5891, 6930, 7574, 10959, 11037, 11382

Soil structure
effects, 122, 2155, 6915, 6988, 9044, 12125, 14332, 15468, 15731

Soil structure
effects of: drainage, 9018; fertilization, 102; gypsum, 9970; root growth, 4119, 8846; sulfur, 9971

Soil structure
effects on: infiltration, 10163; pore space, 9044, 14662

Soil structure
factors affecting: organic matter, 10859, 15357

Soil structure
greens, 14848, 15721

Soil structure
improvement, 11382, 12125, 12126, 14167, 15731

Soil survey
manual, 943, 1506

Soil temperature, 15503

Soil temperature
diurnal variation, 14089

Soil temperature
effects of: color, 7559, 9316; irrigation, 12987, 13009, 14089; mulch, 2246, 2291, 2420, 2874, 5108, 13401; soil warming, 4555, 9440, 9953

Soil temperature
effects on: growth, 15500; root growth, 9443, 11341, 14423, 16399, 16414; shoot density, 7559, 15866; shoot growth, 9442, 11341, 11921, 14423

Soil temperature
factors affecting, 1564, 9316, 9994

Soil temperature
plant effects, 9316, 12230, 14051, 15480, 15496

Soil temperature
seasonal variation, 3080, 3081, 13925

Soil temperature
vertical variation, 3080, 3081, 6785

Soil test, 556, 562, 1210, 1233, 1586, 1805, 1949, 2503, 3091, 3571a, 4129, 4306, 4323, 5427, 6650, 6821, 7214, 8020, 9293, 10556, 10623, 11163,

11421, 11573, 11613, 11636, 11637, 12625, 12903, 12927, 15257

Soil test
arsenic (see also Arsenic, soil analysis), **2100, 6145, 6146, 6147:** methods, **3722, 6153**

Soil test
book, **8333**

Soil test
factors affecting, **4282, 12620, 13649, 14441, 15116**

Soil test
golf course, **3889, 4131, 16499, 16501**

Soil test
greens: survey, **6428, 10649**

Soil test
history, **236, 11589**

Soil test
interpretation, **6802, 7938, 7973, 8001, 9306, 10618, 11421, 12926, 13441, 13628:** fertilizer recommendations, **2616, 2673, 10618, 12619, 12903, 13628**

Soil test
iron, **4830**

Soil test
nitrate, **2170, 5581**

Soil test
nutrients, **2617, 2707, 2776, 4420, 7295, 7938, 11545, 15420:** nitrogen carrier effects, **15116, 16152;** survey, **1449, 4418, 4491, 4520, 11545, 16499**

Soil test
nitrogen, **9830, 12264**

Soil test
phosphorus, **1259, 4491, 11615**

Soil test
potassium, **4491, 9810, 11614, 13649**

Soil test
procedures, **2616, 2673, 5604, 11556, 11573, 11591, 11595**

Soil test
Purdue method, **11800**

Soil test
sampling, **556, 985, 7295, 7938, 7973, 8194, 8001, 9306, 10618, 11545, 12926, 13649:** procedures, **6550, 11518, 11556**

Soil test
soil reaction, **2035, 7938, 10430, 11545, 11591, 12624, 15419, 15420, 16014:** survey, **4420, 4491**

Soil test
soluble salts, **11591**

Soil texture, **575, 3587a, 4288, 5891, 7574, 7679, 9910, 10959, 11284, 11382, 12800, 13508, 15101, 15468, 15886**

Soil texture
effects of: irrigation practices, **7171, 10522;** soil reaction, **15179**

Soil texture
effects on: compaction proneness, **3007, 5872, 6476, 15549;** disease development, **1287;** infiltration, **3099, 10163;** soil water availability, **6492, 6493, 12663;** water retention, **1869, 6810, 10644, 12077**

Soil texture
plant effects, **1442, 3722, 11243, 12422**

Soil texture
pore space, **102, 5171, 5356, 10164, 10259, 14662, 15549**

Soil texture
soil effects, **102, 146, 3099, 6476, 6915**

Soil texture
soil water relations, **4165, 10164, 13508, 14662, 15629, 16206**

Soil type, **4288, 7728, 8515, 16274**

Soil type
effects on: arsenic toxicity, **3726, 4234**

Soil type
plant effects, **5231, 6806**

Soil type
soil effects, **3270, 6810, 7169**

Soil warming, **1049, 1135, 1263, 1639, 1724, 8452, 9407, 13852**

Soil warming
bermudagrass, **1550, 2399, 2401, 2403**

Soil warming
design, **1700, 2439, 2615**

Soil warming
effects of: cutting height, **2615;** protective covers, **4545, 4547, 4555, 8455, 9225, 9427, 9440;** snow cover, **4555**

Soil warming
effects on: chlorophyll content, **2403, 9442;** establishment, **9443;** root growth, **4545, 4546, 4547, 9443;** shoot growth, **4546, 9441, 9442, 9953;** soil temperature, **2437, 4547, 4555, 9440, 9887, 9953;** winter crown rot, **9404, 9408**

Soil warming
electric, **926, 2438, 4477, 4495, 4500, 4555, 5628, 9222:** cable, **4546, 4555, 15939;** cable depth, **4547, 9887;** design, **2437, 9440;** evaluation, **4479, 4556, 5607, 5614, 8451, 9408, 9427;** green, **2607, 9418, 9445, 9946;** installation, **2437, 5607, 8455, 15939;** sports field, **6144, 6149, 8455**

Soil warming
energy requirements, **9440, 9953, 10004**

Soil warming
hot air, **2025, 5291, 8455**

Soil warming
hot water, **8455**

Soil warming
installation, **1330, 1781, 1786, 2439, 2440, 4545, 9953**

Soil warming
plant effects, **1700, 9887, 15582**

Soil warming
soccer field, **1801, 4927, 8448**

Soil warming
sports field, **1243, 1552, 2440, 8449, 13850**: Sweden, **8454, 9225**

Soil warming
types, **1967, 4545, 8455, 13851**

Soil water, **120, 121, 148, 407, 456, 1019, 3651a, 5790, 7170, 7997, 10090, 11829, 12333, 14124, 15467, 16001**

Soil water
availability, **6407, 7276:** soil texture effects, **6492, 14336**

Soil water
classes, **3814, 10644, 11436, 11485, 11512, 12419, 13511, 14936, 15463, 15476**

Soil water
determination methods, **3358, 10209, 13973**

Soil water
effects of: irrigation, **14891;** mowing, **6472, 16080;** mulch, **2246, 2291, 2420, 2667, 2874, 5134, 7446, 9610, 13009, 15695;** soil reaction, **9691, 14136;** soil type, **5474, 6810**

Soil water
effects on: aeration, **5931, 6831;** carbohydrate reserves, **3364, 3365, 7852;** compaction proneness, **15456;** disease development, **1690, 2542, 2997, 2998, 4182, 4198, 15438;** evapotranspiration, **2825, 5056;** fertilization practices, **7997, 9102, 12231;** herbicide effectiveness, **3623a, 3722, 12760, 15127;** impact absorption, **6806;** mushrooms, **11064;** polystand composition, **3179, 7014, 7387, 7434;** root growth, **2823, 4581, 5054, 6433, 6676, 7179, 7182, 10899, 14137, 14156, 14835, 15469;** seed germination, **9036, 9972, 15943;** shoot growth, **2363, 3365, 4806, 5056, 5931, 6430, 6433, 6434, 7177, 7179, 7182, 8456, 14835, 15972;** water use rate, **5056, 6433, 13623;** wear tolerance, **16386;** weed invasion, **7434, 15459**

Soil water
factors affecting, **2875, 6139, 7177, 9621, 9907, 11153, 11959, 13914, 15866, 16080**

Soil water
movement, **115, 118, 119, 150, 1520, 2410, 3387, 3814, 4565, 4699, 6404, 6405, 6406, 6408, 7277, 7786, 9285, 9495, 9715, 10090, 10164, 10532, 12306, 13511, 14124, 15463, 15474, 15476, 15505, 15629, 15868:** factors affecting, **3751, 9269, 9281, 10305, 11283, 15791**

Soil water
percolation, **15501:** cultural factors affecting, **13425, 13683;** soil mix effects, **13683, 13894, 15095, 15098, 15099**

Soil water
plant effects, **564, 3075, 7054, 8606, 11820, 12634, 12771, 13623, 14158, 14165, 14834**

Soil water
retention, **118, 120, 7733, 10069, 10090, 10532, 11144, 11153, 12415, 13402, 14124, 14158:** factors affecting, **12630, 12634, 14165;** soil amendment effects, **7170, 7987, 14132, 15112;** soil mix effects, **11605, 13683, 13894, 13902;** texture effects, **12077, 15869**

Soil water
saturated, **150, 7997:** effects, **10395, 11401**

Soil water
seasonal variability, **14319**

Soil water
turf effects, **2389**

Solar radiation, **8742**

Solution culture
methods, **12667, 16443**

Soma Kentucky bluegrass, **9218**

Sorghestrum nutens (see Indiangrass)

Sorrel, common, **4742**

Sorrel, red, **4742**
chemical control, **3666a, 6221**

Sorrel, sheep, **462, 15698**
chemical control, **4646, 6333, 8673**

Sourgrass, **12133**

South Dakota Certified Kentucky bluegrass, **6330, 10626, 11186**

Southern blight
incidence: annual ryegrass, **8583**

Southern chinch bug, **4782, 7267, 8899, 9478**

Southern chinch bug
chemical control, **4782, 7267, 7268, 8902, 10982, 14379, 14397, 14398**

Southern chinch bug
St. Augustinegrass susceptibility: cultivar evaluation, **14398**

Southern June beetle (see June beetle, southern)

South German mixed bentgrass, **478, 3775, 7777, 9518, 10862, 11661, 11666, 11767, 11962, 12406, 16064, 16065**

Sowbug, **1847, 3042**

Soybean meal, **15697**

Sparryman peat
topdressing, **5611**

Spartina pecinata (see Sloughgrass)

S-(p-chlorophenylthiomethyl) *O*-diethyl phosphorodithioate (see Carbophenothion)

Specifications, **4003, 9461**

Specifications
airport construction, **1912**

Specifications
golf course construction, **11212, 12372**

Specifications
planting, **9444**

Specifications
sod transplanting, **2141, 9444**

Specifications
soil modification, **10969**

Specifications
sports field construction, **1637, 11200**

Specifications
turfgrass culture, **14982**

Spectrophotometric methods
turfgrass color evaluation, **15773**

Speedwell
chemical control, **443, 6628, 10996, 14082**: evaluation, **8189, 8191**

Speedwell, creeping, **1221, 1397**
chemical control, **32, 37, 1221, 1493, 6660, 14083**: DCPA, **1872, 1916, 2015**; endothall, **1235, 2633, 3999, 11047, 14876**; evaluation, **1782, 11046**

Speedwell, thymeleaf, **4743, 15706**
chemical control, **8852, 15696**

S.23 perennial ryegrass, **1396, 1789, 3903, 5948, 7309, 8343**
evaluation, **7191, 7284, 7287, 8338, 8350**

Sphagnum peat, **6689, 10029, 15550, 15552**

Sphecius speciosus (see Cicada killer)

Sphenophorus parvulus (see Bluegrass billbug)

Sphenophorus phoeniciensis (see Phoenix billbug)

Spider
chemical control, **12316**

Spider mite, **4779**
chemical control, **1639**

Spikelets, **14240**

Spiking, **587, 648, 673, 826, 1639, 5978, 7474, 9297, 11912**

Spiking
effects on: earthworms, **8469**; thatch control, **5523**

Spiking
greens, **555, 15725, 16224**

Spiking
localized dry spots, **731**

Spiral nematode, **137, 2241, 3250, 3779, 5011, 6606, 6337**

Spiral nematode
chemical control, **12060**

Spiral nematode
description, **5009, 12057, 12060**

Spiral nematode
injury symptoms, **927, 12042**

Spiral nematode
species susceptibility, **6607, 11345, 11668, 16106**: Kentucky bluegrass, **14052, 14458**

Spittlebug, **3696**

Spodoptera frugiperda (see Armyworm)

Sponge rubber
soil modification, **4506**

Spore, **3626a, 4712, 12673**

Sporobolus heterolepis (see Prairie dropseed)

Sporobolus neglectus (see Annual dropseed)

Sports field, **2325, 3454, 3456, 6392, 7244, 13690**

Sports field
construction, **1084, 1096, 1179, 1339, 1369, 1692, 1707, 1718, 1964, 4080, 4757, 5625, 5630, 6016, 6017, 6018, 6149, 6632, 6711, 8455, 10293, 14442, 14560, 16254**: book, **14032**; specifications, **1637, 7426, 11200**; timing, **1640, 1642, 1798**

Sports field
culture, **276, 825, 1504, 1651, 1670, 2834, 2861, 3460, 4080, 4125, 4130, 4309, 4464, 4516, 4609, 4748, 4750, 4751, 4752, 4757, 4785, 5263, 5425, 5729, 5730, 6260, 6540, 6555, 6572, 6588, 6591, 6632, 6711, 7234, 7244, 7416, 7426, 9169, 10043, 10046, 10048, 10235, 10257, 10293, 10612, 10892, 10893, 11728, 12033, 12293, 12732, 12762, 12777, 12867, 13165, 14560, 14745, 14746, 15207, 15486, 15521, 15564, 15579, 15941, 16000, 16403**: book, **2529, 5754, 9847, 9865, 9866, 9867, 14032, 14184, 14466**; bulletin, **2335, 3475, 5521, 7417, 7420, 7423, 9252, 11200, 12191**; cost analysis, **12111, 13045, 13046, 13939**; cultivation, **2134, 10257, 14464, 15521, 15564, 15981**; cutting height, **1682, 3459**; England, **5625, 8866, 10345, 11001, 11244**; Europe, **1935, 2472, 8546, 13063, 14225, 14991, 15753**; fertilization, **1434, 1964, 4125, 4241, 6662, 9211, 10215, 12732, 15208, 15244, 15449, 15521**; irrigation practices, **580, 7591, 14287, 15521**; mowing, **3459, 15521**; New Zealand, **15179, 15206, 15210, 15239, 15303, 15305, 15314, 15315, 15317, 15322**; rolling, **15286**; tall fescue, **12210**; topdressing, **1502**; weed control, **1082, 2987, 5605**; winter, **1866, 4749, 15167, 15171, 15172, 15175, 15240, 15243**

Sports field
design, **7416**

Sports field
domed: turfgrass culture, **1723, 1776**

Sports field
drainage, **378, 1561, 1601, 2126, 2426, 2857, 3852, 6572, 10612, 10998, 11292, 12855, 13690, 14745**

Sports field
establishment, **1038, 1500, 1651, 1944, 3460, 4757, 5424, 5630, 6018, 6144, 6149, 6588, 6632, 7416, 7426, 7743, 9554, 10257, 10293, 12517, 13165, 14560, 16128**: England,

10998, 10999, 13582; Europe, **1935, 8455, 9220;** methods, **15753;** seeding, **9025, 9154;** sodding, **9025;** soil preparation, **578, 2188, 13690;** state bulletin, **7420, 7423, 12191**

Sports field
grasses used, **1238, 1963, 1964, 2325, 2335, 3317, 4609, 5424, 5729, 6540, 6898, 9025, 9221, 11146:** cool season, **992, 1553, 2027, 3387, 4842, 5625, 6572, 10257, 10612, 10999, 13165, 13831, 15085, 16512;** England, **5625, 10924, 10999;** Europe, **2472, 6625, 8546, 8746, 14225, 15085;** Germany, **5345, 6392, 7284, 13819, 13822;** Netherlands, **8746;** seed mixtures, **996, 1964, 3459, 12485;** warm season, **8152, 10257, 10612, 13165, 15823, 16128**

Sports field
hard surface: maintenance, **1598**

Sports field
ice removal: rotary tiller, **1553**

Sports field
irrigation system, **7591**

Sports field
polystand, **1963, 12123:** secession, **8746**

Sports field
renovation, **276, 1325, 1392, 1592, 1848, 1900, 1902, 2014, 2861, 3368, 4125, 4453, 6898, 7368, 8120, 8290, 10044, 10280, 10283, 10293, 11146, 12063, 12851, 12854, 13825, 15486, 16027:** cost analysis, **13045;** New Zealand, **15182, 15183, 15227, 15322;** procedures, **8292, 8816, 12732**

Sports field
safety considerations, **6806, 15878, 15879**

Sports field
soil amendment, **2886, 3913, 4842**

Sports field
soil mix, **1964, 8450, 10157, 14442**

Sports field
soil modification, **2100, 2885, 4473, 4548, 9220, 10612, 11146**

Sports field
soil reaction, **1484, 3461**

Sports field
soils, **27, 2325, 3828, 6664**

Sports field
soil warming, **1692, 1724, 2440, 4547, 8449, 13850**

Sports field
summer overseeding: common bermudagrass, **11592**

Sports field
tarp cover: automatic roller, **8453**

Sports field
winter protection, **1552**

Sports Turf Research Institute, **1041, 4732, 15403**

Spot sodding, **1728, 10486**

Spotted spurge (see Spurge, spotted)

Spray applicators
certification: Michigan, **9720**

Sprayer, **217, 8654, 11291**

Sprayer
application technique, **6128, 6467, 10732, 14314, 15051, 15423, 16062**

Sprayer
calibration, **2879, 3575a, 5548, 5765, 6246, 7678, 7708, 7758, 7759, 9050, 10496, 10516, 11686, 11844, 11845, 12192**

Sprayer
experimental plot use, **4046, 14879**

Sprayer
helicopter, **5252**

Sprayer
maintenance, **1264, 1615, 2879, 11291:** clean-up, **6246, 6247, 6357**

Sprayer
nozzle type, **7708, 14615**

Sprayer
selection, **5640, 8654, 12192**

Sprayer
types, **1156, 1942, 2879, 7708, 8654, 11465, 11686, 12129, 12571, 14615, 14616, 15235, 15953, 16061, 16232**

Spreader, fertilizer, **5640**
calibration, **5548, 15767, 15797**

Sprig
certification, **8303**

Sprig
production, **7042**

Sprig
sprouting, **2731**

Sprig
storage, **3815**

Sprigging (see also Establishment, vegetative), **2609, 6248, 9601, 10131, 11741, 11867, 13567**

Sprigging
effects of: sprig storage, **3816**

Sprigging
equipment, **8520**

Sprigging
method, **7719, 9444, 13413:** planting depth, **3815, 3816;** rate, **5821**

Sprigging
post-planting care, **1623**

Sprigging
warm season species, **1191, 1700, 7719, 11798**

Spring-Bak® (see Nabam)

Spring dead spot, **1809, 1813, 4332, 6114, 6118, 6125, 6130, 9932, 9934, 13887, 15125, 15134, 15354, 16301**

Spring dead spot
causal organism, **10094, 13937, 15133, 15136**

Spring dead spot
chemical control, **8185, 13889:** evaluation, **6122, 13888, 15127**

Spring dead spot
control, **6118, 6120, 6137**

Spring dead spot
description, **6137, 15131**

Spring dead spot
effects of: thatch, **1700, 9969**

Spring dead spot
factors affecting, **10094, 10769, 13936**

Spring dead spot
injury symptoms, **6120, 8185, 15133, 15134**

Springfield creeping bentgrass, **1102, 10616**

Spring green-up
bermudagrass: cultivar evaluation, **14404**

Spring green-up
creeping bentgrass: cultivar evaluation, **854, 2564**

Spring green-up
effects of: cutting height, **1700, 14900;** gibberellin, **1240, 9419, 16134;** nitrogen fertilization, **9438, 12497;** potassium, **14440;** protective covers, **9437;** thatch removal, **1871, 1967, 2614**

Spring green-up
Kentucky bluegrass: cultivar evaluation, **2564**

Spring green-up
red fescue: cultivar evaluation, **2564**

Sprinkler head, **2809**

Sprinkler head
operation, **10931**

Sprinkler head
spacing, **1844, 12835**

Sprinkler head
types, **5059, 9725, 12835, 13678:** rotary pop-up, **1788, 5059**

Sprinkler head
water distribution, **2532**

Sprinkler irrigation
book, **6995**

Spurge
chemical control, **1700, 6331, 7261, 8408**

Spurge, prostrate
chemical control, **7260, 7537**

Spurge, spotted, **465**
chemical control, **1700, 3510, 10782, 12794, 12799**: DMPA, **9578, 9579;** evaluation, **9966, 10403, 12797, 12808, 14839**

Spurry, **4737, 8405**

S.59 red fescue, **1789, 8343**
evaluation, **7284, 8336, 8338, 8341, 8350**

Stabilized roadway (see Roadway, turfed, stabilized soil)

Stabilized soils (see also Roadway, turfed)
airfield, **16288**

Stabilized soils
bitumen, **4756**

Stabilized soils
turfgrass culture, **14467, 16242**

Stabilized soils
turfgrass establishment, **3585a, 3586a**

Stadium, domed (see Domed stadium)

Stagonospora maculata
on orchardgrass, **6804**

Stand (see Shoot density)

Starch
species variability, **4837, 14542**

Star-nosed mole, **4306**

Starweed, **4730**
bowling green, **10343, 15211**

Steam
soil sterilization, **2384, 4719, 8510, 12988, 15409**

Steel-cement pipe, **15080**

Steel pipe, **12913**

Steinach colonial bentgrass, **8336, 8338**

Steinach red fescue, **8336, 8341, 8350**

Steinach velvet bentgrass, **8336**

Steinacher Kentucky bluegrass, **9218**

Stellaria media (see Common chickweed)

Stem, **11366, 16465**

Stem
anatomy, **7577, 7585, 12101, 14240**

Stem
elongation, **9878**

Stem apex, **5952, 14085, 14087**

Stem borer, **15001**

Stem eyespot, **14006**

Stem rust, **3244, 12931**

Stem rust
chemical control, **1545, 1776, 3244**

Stem rust
Kentucky bluegrass: cultivar susceptibility, **3259, 3261**

Stem rust
species susceptibility, **3246, 3261**

Stenotaphrum secundatum (see St. Augustinegrass)

Stensballe Kentucky bluegrass, **9218**

Sterilant (see Soil sterilization)

Sterilization, soil (see Soil sterilization and Fumigation)

Sticking agents, **1196, 1639**

S.50 timothy, **1439, 1789, 5948, 8343**
evaluation, **7191, 8336, 8338, 8341**

S.52 timothy, **724**

Sting nematode, **5011, 5014, 6606, 8830, 10551, 11696, 11742, 11743, 11744, 11745, 12229**

Sting nematode
chemical control, **12040, 12058, 13913, 16103, 16105**

Sting nematode
description, **5009, 12057, 12059**

Sting nematode
factors affecting, **3116, 8331**

Sting nematode
injury symptoms, **12057, 12661, 16105**

Sting nematode
parasitic effects, **12050, 12562, 12563, 12662, 16101**

Sting nematode
species susceptibility, **6607, 9332, 11750, 12662, 16106**

Stipa spartea (see Porcupinegrass)

Stitchwort
chemical control, **4809, 5594, 8433**

Stolon, **12101, 12454, 12771**

Stolon
nematode control: hot water, **1899**

Stolon
production (see Stolon nursery)

Stolon growth
effects of: calcium, **12771, 13897;** day length, **16359, 16399;** gibberellic acid, **8666, 8668, 13022**

Stolon growth
storage effects, **14307**

Stolonizing (see also Establishment, vegetative), **2193, 2609, 2798, 3055, 3056, 3712, 4732, 8126, 8555, 9600, 10450, 11676, 11741**

Stolonizing
bentgrass, **3051, 3053, 11764, 12289**

Stolonizing
equipment, **8520**

Stolonizing
fairway, **7539**

Stolonizing
green, **2800, 3052, 3054, 4306, 4914, 4915, 5308, 5964, 7274, 7330, 11593, 12135**

Stolonizing
pelleted, **1492**

Stolonizing
procedures, **3710, 5241, 6346, 7043, 7108, 9832, 11010, 11593, 12329**

Stolonizing
warm season species, **1700**

Stolonizing
zoysiagrass, **6435, 9319**

Stolon nursery, **428, 754, 6570, 7043, 8555, 11010**
bentgrass, **293, 1289**

Stomata
chemical closure, **10481, 10483, 13669**

Stomata
distribution: leaf blade, **13623, 13624, 13625**

Stomata
opening: factors affecting, **8658;** species variation, **7740**

Stomatal density, **12548**

Stomatal density
Agrostis species, **13625**

Stomatal density
effects of: irrigation frequency, **10481, 13623, 13624;** light intensity, **13623, 13624;** temperature, **13623, 13624**

Stomatal density
effects on: smog injury, **8658;** wet wilt, **10483**

Stomatal density
factors effecting, **2069, 13623**

Stomatal density
water use relationships, **2677**

Straw mulch, **18, 1552, 2419, 2420, 2432, 2579, 2593, 2667, 2975, 3046, 3794, 5108, 6010, 6946, 8834, 13404, 14695**

Straw mulch
application rate, **3794, 7002**

Straw mulch
effects on: infiltration, **10165;** soil moisture, **2874, 3050, 7446;** soil temperature, **2874**

Straw mulch
erosion control, **2734, 3794, 6716, 10165, 13403**

Straw mulch
evaluation, **122, 1479, 2566, 5276, 6034, 6515, 6716, 12596, 13212, 13401, 13797, 14432**

Straw mulch
winter protection, **1135, 1243, 1639, 5590**

Stripe rust, **9894**

Stripe smut, **2862, 3254, 4187, 4653, 4710, 5940, 7082, 9072, 12931**

Stripe smut
chemical control, **1817, 7199, 7350, 7352, 7359, 11103, 11940, 11943, 15011, 15013, 15014:** benomyl, **4051, 11110, 12837;** evaluation, **1985, 2100, 6453, 7195, 7196, 7198, 7200, 7202, 7351, 7354, 7355, 7356, 7358, 7360, 7361, 8369, 9752, 9762, 15015**

Stripe smut
on cool season turfgrasses: bluegrass, **15670**

Stripe smut
on creeping bentgrass, **7627:** cultivar evaluation, **6445, 7805, 7808**

Stripe smut
cultural control, **7193:** urea, **9751**

Stripe smut
cultural factors affecting: mowing, **7201, 11019**

Stripe smut
description, **4710, 5940, 9094, 14624**

Stripe smut
development, **7807, 7811, 7817, 7819**

Stripe smut
effects of: fertilization, **6329, 7201, 7202, 7203;** temperature, **7808, 9086, 11939**

Stripe smut
effects on: flowering, **7810, 7812, 7815;** morphology, **7806, 7809**

Stripe smut
hosts, **4714, 7202, 14624**

Stripe smut
incidence, **7202, 11324**

Stripe smut
injury symptoms, **7193, 7804, 7807, 9892, 10853, 11937, 14624**

Stripe smut
innoculation techniques, **4714**

Stripe smut
on Kentucky bluegrass, **1732, 1776, 7818:** cultivar evaluation, **5509, 6290, 6317, 6328, 7193, 7195, 7196, 7201, 7203, 9087**

Stripe smut
races, **6450**

Stripe smut
sanitary control, **1908**

Stripe smut
seasonal variation, **7202**

Strip mine reclamation
crownvetch, **3214**

Strip sodding, **1728, 10442**

Structure, soil (see Soil structure)

Stubble mulch, **228**

Stubby root nematode, **1315, 5009, 5011, 6606, 6607, 8830, 9670, 11696, 11743, 11745, 16106**

Stubby root nematode
control, **12040**

Stubby root nematode
effects on: shoot growth, **12562, 12563, 12654**

Stubby root nematode
injury symptoms, **12057, 12562, 12654**

Stunt nematode, **1548, 2241, 3250, 14817**

Stunt nematode
chemical control, **9329**

Stunt nematode
distribution, **6607, 11668, 12228, 14565, 14822**

Stunt nematode
effects on: root growth, **14816, 14817;** shoot growth, **9326, 14817**

Stunt nematode
on Kentucky bluegrass, **7801, 14052, 14458**

Stylet nematode, **3779, 6337, 9330, 12050, 15023**

Styrofoam
mulch, **15751, 15752**

Styrofoam
soil amendment, **15752**

Submersion
effects, **10003, 12198**

Submersion
injury: factors affecting, **4600, 12186;** water temperature effects, **2655, 2700, 2701**

Submersion
low temperature: species tolerance, **2559, 2570**

Submersion
species tolerance, **4600, 4916, 10003:** evaluation, **2566, 2655, 2700, 2701, 3047, 10002**

Subsidence, soil
sod production, **1958, 4718**

Subsoiling, **2191**

Subsurface irrigation, **1605, 2722, 2881**
evaluation, **1639, 11276, 11948**

Subsurface moisture barriers, **11948**

Succession, **16360**
polystand: lawn community, **9225;** roadside community, **9129, 16316**

Succulence
diurnal variation, **14319**

Succulence
factors affecting, **2614, 10076, 11973**

Succulence
seasonal variation, **14319**

Sucrose
thatch decomposition effects, **10230**

Sugarcane mosaic virus, **12984**

Sugarcane mosaic virus
host range, **6184, 12986**

Sugarcane mosaic virus
on St. Augustinegrass, **3, 4329, 12986, 14740**

Sulfur, **5850, 6972, 6975, 9698, 10385, 11433, 11786, 11787, 11850, 16203**

Sulfur
carriers, **1803, 1890, 2683, 8049, 10351, 10352, 10864**

Sulfur
deficiency symptoms, **4227, 6975, 9712, 9717, 11790, 12362**

Sulfur
effects on: annual bluegrass invasion, **6686;** chemical composition, **9257;** disease development, **6750, 6975;** root growth, **12532;** shoot growth, **8636, 8758, 9257, 10352, 12532;** soil physical condition, **4754, 9971;** soil reaction, **2617, 11397, 12624**

Sulfur
evaluations,**2172, 2668, 2683, 6790**

Sulfur
fertilization, **2723, 10351**

Sulfur
soil relationships, **2683, 10159**

Sulfur
uptake: factors affecting, **8636, 15071**

Sulfur-coated urea, **157, 158, 1529, 1980, 14402, 14403**

Sulfur dioxide, **2679**
species tolerance, **3217**

Sulfuric acid, **2942, 8633**

Summer blight (see *Helminthosporium* leaf blotch)

Summer dormancy, **5487, 12688, 13375**

Summer dormancy
cultural factors affecting, **866, 1434**

Summer dormancy
effects on: carbohydrate reserves, **2566**

Summer dormancy
environmental factors affecting, **9320**

Summer dormancy
species evaluation, **5646, 9320**

Summer injury, **187, 5487, 6661**

Summer overseeding
with common bermudagrass: sports field, **11592**

Summer problems
causes, **6661**

Sun flects, **4579, 5654, 5658**

Sunturf bermudagrass, **1153, 1472, 1547, 7309, 8144, 8185, 9568, 11235, 12820**

Sunturf bermudagrass
adaptation, **8144, 16378**

Sunturf bermudagrass
description, **8144, 8212, 16331**

Sunturf bermudagrass
evaluation, **8154, 11232, 11882**

Superphosphate, **1558, 3339, 3462, 5634, 5678, 5684, 12520**

Superphosphate
effects on: soil reaction, **11024**

Superphosphate
evaluation, **2172, 5636, 7220**

Surfactant (see also Wetting agent), **3838, 4244, 10464**

Surfactant
effects on: herbicide effectiveness, **2027, 2412, 4244, 9402, 10051, 10052, 10464, 12283, 13528**

Surfactant
phytotoxicity, **2252, 8179**

Surfactant
types, **9660, 10464**

Surfactant
use, **9656, 10049**

Survey
golf course, **1658, 1721, 1743, 5286**: California, **4698, 4701;** Japan, **16290;** maintainence costs, **5739;** Oregon, **6592;** United States, **1864, 2089;** world, **12246**

Survey
sod industry, **1662, 1704**: California, **11216;** Florida, **3225, 13940;** Maryland, **2202;** Michigan, **7783**

Survey, turfgrass, **1604, 1939, 6884, 7974**

Survey, turfgrass
Arizona, **9010**

Survey, turfgrass
California, **4700, 7241, 8928, 8930, 15940**

Survey, turfgrass
Colorado, **12958, 14288**

Survey, turfgrass
economic value: Los Angeles, **2860**

Survey, turfgrass
Florida, **7974, 14401**

Survey, turfgrass
general trends, **14183**

Survey, turfgrass
Los Angeles County, **8929, 10946**

Survey, turfgrass
maintenance costs, **1719, 7935**

Survey, turfgrass
Maryland, **10557**

Survey, turfgrass
Nebraska, **1999, 5118**

Survey, turfgrass
New Jersey, **1111, 1120, 1375**

Survey, turfgrass
Ohio, **10628**

Survey, turfgrass
Oregon: parks, **9575**

Survey, turfgrass
Pennsylvania, **1702, 2608, 3077, 5168**

Survey, turfgrass
West Virginia, **7667**

Survey, turfgrass
Southern California, **7242**

Survey, turfgrass
Southern Florida, **13898**

Survey, turfgrass
Southern U.S.A., **10683**

Survey, turfgrass
Texas, **5844, 11723**

Survey, turfgrass
United States, **8676, 11723, 13215**

Survey, turfgrass
Virginia, **1658**

Survey, turfgrass
Washington, **6675, 6680, 6718**

Suwannee bermudagrass, **3571, 3574, 3581**

Sweden
cool season species: breeding, **9224**

Sweden
grasses used, **9223**

Sweden
sports field: soil warming, **9225**

Sweden
turf advisory service, **9227**

Switchgrass, **76, 9129**

Sydsport Kentucky bluegrass, **7287, 9218, 9226, 14813**

Synthetic-natural turf combinations, **2000**

Synthetic turf, **2796, 3606, 4005, 6253, 7216, 10415, 11734, 11736, 14957, 16410**

Synthetic turf
cost, **16410**

Synthetic turf
effects on: temperature, **2441, 10413**

Synthetic turf
on golf courses, **1875, 3219**

Synthetic turf
installation, **3606a**

Synthetic winter protection covers (see Winter protection covers)

Syringing, **1286, 4237, 6877, 10931**

Syringing
effects on: temperature, **4318, 5149, 5151, 10413**

Syringing
use: cooling, **2621, 2673, 2706, 12459**

Systematics, grass, **3376, 3380, 9142, 9143**
book, **6771**

Systemic fungicide, **7352, 8370, 10488, 13723, 15008, 15011, 15013**

Systemic fungicide
dollar spot control, **2631, 3103, 15022**

Systemic fungicide
stripe smut control, **15015**

Systemic pesticide, **2502, 16318**

2,4,5–T, **2118, 13779**

2,4,5–T
clover control, **3452, 4151, 4369, 4377, 4386, 4395, 5190, 16124:** evaluation, **4364, 4383**

2,4,5–T
spurge control, **7261**

2,4,5–T
weed control, **2726, 2914, 6367, 7022, 7538, 15422, 15424**

Take-all disease, **8955**

Tall fescue, **2523, 3832, 4226, 6264, 8171**

Tall fescue
adaptation, **3553, 4601, 4786, 6498, 12844:** low temperature hardiness, **1639, 2566, 2706, 10604, 12844, 15084**

Tall fescue
breeding, **3417, 3419, 3423, 3424, 3428, 3437, 3553, 3564, 8502**

Tall fescue
chemical composition, **3484, 6463, 6464**

Tall fescue
cultivars, **6498, 13823:** evaluation, **1186, 2560, 2566, 2574, 2583, 2584, 2603, 2617, 2631, 2632, 2658, 2698, 2704, 2706, 2707, 5313, 6207, 6310, 6879, 8550, 8647, 13437**

Tall fescue
culture, **1639, 2027, 6498:** cutting height, **3484, 5146, 10604, 16360;** fertilization, **7126, 14607;** irrigation, **5146**; nitrogen fertilization, **4644, 5146, 10604, 14383**

Tall fescue
description, **1513, 3553, 3832, 4008, 4277, 6498, 7947, 11354, 12193:** cytology, **3415, 3836, 4275, 8501, 8508, 11225;** rooting, **6498, 8399**

Tall fescue
diseases, **2851, 4334, 6207, 6462, 9095, 15672:** brown patch, **174, 2286, 9815**

Tall fescue
establishment, **7514, 10706, 13459**

Tall fescue
herbicide selectivity, **8695**

Tall fescue
pin nematode, **4217**

Tall fescue
seed germination: factors affecting, **8781**

Tall fescue
seedling drought tolerance, **16181**

Tall fescue
uses, **3553:** roadside, **248, 10233, 12596;** sand dune stabilization, **1700, 16456;** sports field, **2027**

Tall fescue-Italian ryegrass hybrid (see Italian ryegrass-tall fescue hybrid)

Tall fescue, weed
control, **2893, 4082, 11819, 16360**

Tall oatgrass
use: roadside, **936**

Tall wheatgrass
use: roadside, **2092**

Tamper, **620**

Tankage, **15697**
processed, **12265**

Tannery sludge, **11213**

Taraxacum officinale (see Dandelion)

Tarp cover
soil warming, **2439, 8455**

Tarp cover
sports field: automatic roller, **8453;** evaluation, **8455**

Taxonomy, grass, **3871, 4338, 8499, 11081, 12130**

Taxonomy, grass
book, **6771, 8127, 8128**

Taxonomy, grass
embryo characteristics, **12491**

Taxonomy, grass
root hair development, **12906**

2,3,6-TBA (see Trichlorobenzoic acid)

TBZ® (see Thiabendazole)

TCA, **2172, 2447**

TCA
bermudagrass control, **5351**

TCA
centipedegrass control, **11878**

TCA
perennial grass control, **5351**

TCNP
stripe smut control, **7356**

Tee, **830**

Tee
construction, **1013, 1625, 4939, 5216, 12395, 12398, 15971**

Tee
culture, **1972, 6281, 6527, 6829, 7369, 8328, 11461, 11517, 12371, 12398, 14248, 16187:** cost analysis, **3086**

Tee
design, **1625, 3961, 4455, 5868, 7489, 12398**

Tee
establishment, **1625, 11461**

Tee
grasses used, **2870, 4939, 5473, 6887, 6891, 6982, 7456, 10011, 11502, 11517, 12398:** bermudagrass, **3607, 3608, 11551, 11565, 11592, 11621, 16187;** cool season, **3672, 3673, 5624, 11461, 11622;** warm season, **11461, 11622;** zoysiagrass, **8970, 9568, 11447, 11551**

Tee
renovation, **1972, 12398, 12876**

Tee
traffic control, **1455, 3145, 8328**

Tee
types, **1318, 9940, 12445**

Telvar® (see Monuron)

Temik® (see Aldicarb)

Temperature, **503, 2643, 14319**

Temperature
adaptation: species variability, **2027,** 3035, 6068, 7522, **11903, 16361**

Temperature
diurnal variation, **10415, 10849, 11648, 11836, 14196, 14197, 15418**

Temperature
effects, **2027, 3035, 3751, 7598, 12965, 13951, 14611, 16353, 16373:** physiological, **2614, 8658, 8749, 13412, 14324, 15437;** vernalization, **3900, 3901**

Temperature
effects of: air pollution, **3744, 8658;** asphalt, **10413;** day length, **12089;** irrigation, **4944, 10415;** mulch, **2667, 9610;** shade, **8678, 9973;** slope exposure, **75, 9994;** syringing, **4318, 5149, 5151, 10413;** wind, **5149, 5151**

Temperature
effects on: annual bluegrass, **2707, 3035, 11276;** asparagine, **2694, 2697, 14323;** carbohydrates, **2248, 2295, 2360, 2614, 3365, 8651, 10000, 10228, 13400, 14450;** carbohydrate reserves, **88, 89, 90, 2362, 2363, 2707, 2977, 3364, 5150, 5333, 5336, 8649, 8651, 8652, 8778, 9999, 10000, 11673, 13409, 13410, 13427, 13428, 13948, 13951, 14323, 14450, 15437, 15438, 16430, 16433, 16465;** chemical composition, **169, 3329, 5330, 6052, 14323;** chlorophyll content, **11903;** cutting height, **2077, 11648, 15417;** disease development, **2545, 2546, 2817, 4980, 5402, 7814, 8858, 9086;** floral initiation, **9668, 16349, 16350;** flower development, **2275, 3669a, 3896, 3897, 3898, 3899, 3902, 3904, 5664, 6400, 7320, 7735, 7737, 9019, 9592, 9593, 10368, 12089, 12766, 12767, 12966, 14604, 16257, 16258, 16444;** glutamine, **2694, 2697, 8778, 14323;** growth, **2977, 3329, 3897, 6055, 6056, 7557, 7558, 8058, 12965, 13412, 16350, 16372, 16392;** growth habit, **11365;** herbicide effectiveness, **3623a, 12234, 12760, 14860;** leaf appearance rate, **12965, 14606;** leaf length, **2614, 3072, 5646, 8658, 12965, 14606;** leaf width, **2552, 2614, 8658, 12965, 14606;** low temperature discoloration, **16327, 16350, 16354;** nitrate content, **5215, 11673, 13774;** nitrate reductase activity, **2649, 8773, 8776, 8785;** nitrogen content, **8778, 14324;** nitrogen metabolism, **2694, 2697, 5215, 14323;** nitrogen uptake, **10067, 15437;** photosynthesis, **2614, 6052, 8314, 10228, 10640, 11936, 13410, 13427, 13428, 15435;** plant-water deficits, **10482, 11973;** protein, **8778, 14323;** *Pythium* blight, **10533, 10877, 10890;** respiration, **8778, 10228, 12220, 13409, 13410, 13427, 13428, 15434, 15435;** root growth, **2550, 2552, 2554, 2556, 2695, 2963, 3035, 3488, 4028, 4578, 7495, 7670, 9303, 9724, 10698, 12421, 12422, 12889, 13409, 13427, 13562, 14051, 14137, 14156, 14161, 14323, 14450, 14836, 15437, 16350, 16354;** root-shoot ratio, **14834, 14836;** seed germination, **205, 1855, 2674, 3035, 3327, 3821, 3822, 6112, 7507, 7672, 8086, 9036, 9972, 10134, 11276, 12159, 12889, 13570, 13573, 14051, 15654, 15843;** seedhead formation, **3035, 9019, 10367;** seedling emergence, **7507, 9322, 14191;** seedling growth, **3075, 4028, 6111, 7672, 7703, 9321, 14191;** seed viability, **3664a, 6393, 6409, 9030, 10367;** shoot density, **12089, 16430, 16433;** shoot growth, **88, 89, 90, 2234, 2275, 2360, 2361, 2362, 2363, 2614, 2617, 2707, 2944, 3035, 3365, 4247, 4578, 5150, 5333, 7495, 7496, 7737, 8550, 8649, 8651, 8652, 8658, 8778, 9178, 9303, 9724, 10000, 10228, 10697, 10698, 10700, 10704, 11673, 12005, 12006, 12889, 13409, 13427, 13562, 13951, 14323, 14450, 14604, 14836, 15437, 15438, 15650, 16327, 16338, 16350, 16354, 16414, 16430;** stomatal density, **8658, 13623, 13624;** submersion tolerance, **2617, 2700, 2707;** tillering, **2295, 3895, 3897, 7669, 7670, 8055, 10699, 10700, 10704, 12965, 14606, 16399, 16414;** vegetative development, **10695, 10699, 10705, 14579;** water use rate, **2677, 4107, 13623, 13624**

Temperature
insulation, turf, **6785**

Temperature
inversion, **15417**

Temperature
optimum, **2623, 4242, 11903**

Temperature
seasonal variation, **2481, 11836, 13925**

Temperature
soil (see Soil temperature)

Temperature
synthetic turf, **9022, 10413**

Temperature
vertical variation, **2480, 2481, 2509, 2552, 5031, 6069, 9022, 10415, 14193, 14196, 14197, 15417:** evaluation, **10703, 11836, 12614, 15418**

Temporary green (see Green, alternate)

Tennis court
culture, **823, 963, 1034, 1249, 1398, 1978, 2190, 4309, 10042, 10044, 10045, 10330**: Australia, **15288;** England, **7589, 12241, 12446, 13005, 14468;** fall, **1033, 1097, 1100;** New Zealand, **15167, 15169, 15206, 15214, 15216, 15233, 15238, 15252, 15272, 15296, 15305, 15308, 15309, 15311, 15313, 15314, 15315, 15317;** spring, **1072, 1088, 1177, 1775;** topdressing, **1482, 2263**

Tennis court
grasses used, **12485**

Tennis court
renovation, **1799, 1978, 12241**

Tennis court
rotation of play, **1034**

Tensiometer, **1491, 1549, 1639, 1780, 1967, 7643, 10209**

Tensiometer
construction, **12581**

Tensiometer
effects on: irrigation frequency, **10977**

Tensiometer
evaluation, **2678, 10950, 10972, 10976**

Tensiometer
irrigation control: shoot growth response, **14974**

Tensiometer
response time, **9003**

Tensiometer
salinity effects, **1700**

Tensiometer
soil moisture determination, **10202, 12634**

Tensiometer
use, **10958, 12581, 12630:** in irrigation **10184, 10208, 10211, 10212, 10943, 10950, 10954, 10976, 12188, 12584, 12586, 12587, 13529, 15569**

Terbacil
annual bluegrass control, **9533, 9537, 11256**

Terbutol, **8768**

Terbutol
annual bluegrass control, **5632, 9533, 9537**

Terbutol
crabgrass control, **2904, 5383, 5543, 5545, 8168, 8414, 8415, 9530, 9531, 9533, 9537, 9544, 10375, 10377, 10378, 10619, 13859, 14823, 14827**

Terbutol
selectivity, **8706, 8707, 12735, 13970**

Terminology
landscape, **2060, 10213**

Terminology
ornamental horticulture, **2060**

Terminology
turfgrass, **1107, 1463, 1666**

Terraces
construction, **487**

Terraclor® (see PCNB)

Tersan SP® (see Chloroneb)

2,4,5,6-tetrachloroisophtalonitrile (see Chlorothalonil)

0,0,0,0-tetraethyl S,S-methylene bisphosphorodithioate (see Ethion)

Tetrahydro-3,5-dimethyl-2h-1, 3,5-thiadiazine-2thione (see Dazomet)

Tetramethylthiuram disulfide (see Thiram)

Tetraploidy, **6046**

Thiabendazole
dollar spot control, **4203**

Tersan® (see Thiram)

Texture, leaf
cutting height effects, **9877**

Texture, leaf
nitrogen effects, **4840**

Texture, leaf
species evaluation, **16361, 16368**

Texture, soil (see Soil texture)

Texturf 1F bermudagrass, **1547, 7309, 7920, 9662, 10768, 10922, 16261, 16378**
evaluation, **8154, 11232, 11882**

Texturf 10 bermudagrass, **7309, 7920, 10922, 15442**
evaluation, **8154, 11882, 14906**

Thatch, **2869, 3651, 4300, 5452, 5505, 5878, 6698, 6908, 7161, 10273, 10290, 10301, 10603, 11163, 11576, 13099, 13233, 15336**

Thatch
biological control, **5852, 6693, 8043, 9067, 9436, 10227, 10303, 14045, 14297, 15891, 16004:** environmental factors affecting, **14230, 14231;** materials used, **2633, 10227, 10231**

Thatch
causes, **187, 2583, 2646, 3651, 3705, 3705a, 6693, 7161, 10607, 10620, 11190, 11265, 13044, 13319, 15665, 15830, 15859, 15890, 15892:** cultural practices affecting, **2165, 4905, 12928, 14698, 14730;** cutting height, **1154, 2574, 2603, 2707, 6713, 14900;** irrigation, **5497, 6687;** mowing, **2574, 5852, 6687, 14726, 14730;** nitrogen fertilization, **3001, 5497, 5498, 5523, 6687, 6713, 9273, 12629;** wetting agent, **2615, 5523**

Thatch
chemical composition, **2069, 2165, 2633, 5505, 7210, 7784, 9100, 9436, 10227, 10230, 10231, 10286, 10301, 10625, 11901, 12627, 13341:** lignin content, **9100, 10230**

Thatch
chemical control, **2610, 10230**

Thatch
control, **730, 773, 860, 3651, 3705a, 4035, 4145, 4300, 4433, 4484, 5448, 5452, 6698, 7161, 9066, 10271, 10273, 10282, 10607, 10620, 15665, 15890, 15892, 15897, 16170:** effects, **8161, 8179**; evaluation, **2615, 5479, 5523, 15070**

Thatch
cultural control, **1700, 2614, 4143, 5523, 9273, 14688:** burning, **10469**; coring, **2614, 2615, 5523, 10290, 10462, 15355;** cultivation, **2615, 5523, 14701, 15601**; fertilization, **5523, 9273, 10448;** liming, **1175, 2615, 5523;** mechanical removal, **1104, 5497, 5852, 6101, 6687, 6693, 6944, 8043, 10285, 10303, 10469, 11571, 12629, 13329, 14045, 14671, 14698, 14701, 14726, 14730, 14812, 15069, 15070, 15071, 15601, 15859, 15891, 15895, 15896, 16004**; topdressing, **1175, 2614, 2615, 5523, 9065, 11931**; vertical mowing, **2130, 2614, 11931, 14701, 15355**

Thatch
decomposition, **187, 2069, 2170:** chemical enhancement, **10227, 10230;** factors affecting, **9065, 9425;** microorganism activity, **10227, 14231, 14726, 14730**

Thatch
description, **2165, 2610, 9425**

Thatch
effects, **2583, 5852, 10303, 10620, 11265, 14726, 14730, 14812**

Thatch
effects of: clipping removal, **2603, 2707**; compaction, **12629, 13418;** earthworms, **2055, 12432, 12434;** herbicides, **12434, 14881**; insecticides, **12432, 12434;** soil moisture, **5497, 12629, 16080;** soil reaction, **2172, 3001, 4905**

Thatch
effects on: disease development, **61, 188, 1700, 2539, 2699, 5497, 9969, 12629;** rooting, **5497, 12629;** wear tolerance, **9782, 16386**

Thatch
measurement, **15072**

Thatch
prevention, **4786, 14699**

Thatch
removal: timing, **1871, 1967, 2614, 13329**

Thatch
species proneness, **5100, 12224, 13044, 13260:** bentgrass cultivars, **2564;** bermudagrass cultivars, **7922**

Thermal conductivity
soil, **6785**

Thermoperiodism
seed germination, **11262, 14761**

Thiabendazole
dollar spot control, **2633, 16212**

Thiabendazole
Fusarium blight control, **11111**

Thiamin
effects, **46, 47**

Thimet® (see Phorate)

Thiophonate
Fusarium blight control, **11107**

Thiourea, **2725**

Thiram, **708, 718, 729, 13637**

Thiram
algae control, **6197**

Thiram
brown patch control, **4681, 10410, 10846, 10891, 13071, 15123, 16292**

Thiram
copper spot control, **7390**

Thiram
disease control, **6864, 7337, 16291:** evaluation, **7959, 8059, 16298**

Thiram
dollar spot control, **8185, 9246, 10568, 10846, 13605, 14714, 15123, 15130**

Thiram
Fusarium blight control, **2547**

Thiram
red thread control, **16212**

Thiram
spring dead spot control, **13936**

Thiram
Typhula blight control, **2717, 4782, 7337**

Thistle, musk, **7544**

Thymeleaf speedwell (see Speedwell, thymeleaf)

Thymelicus lineola (see Skipper, Essex)

Ticks
chemical control, **3291, 4122**

Tifdwarf bermudagrass, **1639, 1700, 2612, 3519, 8757, 10764, 10766, 10768, 10783**

Tifdwarf bermudagrass
adaptation, **3483, 10773, 16413**

Tifdwarf bermudagrass
culture, **3601, 10764, 10766, 13968**

Tifdwarf bermudagrass
description, **3603, 10764**

Tifdwarf bermudagrass
evaluation, **3864, 8761, 11233**

Tifdwarf bermudagrass
herbicide phytotoxicity, **8022, 13970**

Tifdwarf bermudagrass
pests: billbug, **10983;** nematode, **7618**

Tifdwarf bermudagrass
uses: green, **3532, 3601, 10764;** lawn, **10764, 13344**

Tiffine bermudagrass, **1508, 3573, 7309, 7407, 10768, 11562, 12804, 12818, 12820, 15441**

Tiffine bermudagrass
adaptation, **3574, 7977**

Tiffine bermudagrass
culture, **7977**

Tiffine bermudagrass
description, **7638, 12817**

Tiffine bermudagrass
evaluation, **8154, 11232, 14899**

Tifgreen bermudagrass, **1153, 1472, 1489, 1508, 1547, 1639, 2490, 6840, 7309, 7692, 9568, 10768, 10783, 11235, 12820, 12822, 13560, 15441**

Tifgreen bermudagrass
adaptation, **2008, 2063, 3483, 6510, 7640, 7977, 16378, 16413**

Tifgreen bermudagrass
culture, **3576a, 3598, 6958, 7977:** fertilization, **7990, 7991, 8007, 8010, 8331, 8332, 10452, 15349**

Tifgreen bermudagrass
description, **2063, 8212, 11232, 12806, 12824, 15442**

Tifgreen bermudagrass
evaluation, **8154, 8791, 12823, 12824, 14899, 14906**: Japan, **8761, 11882**

Tifgreen bermudagrass
herbicide phytotoxicity, **3281, 3344, 3615a, 6266, 13970**

Tifgreen bermudagrass
pests: ground pearls, **15739;** nematodes, **7615, 7618, 8563, 12661**

Tifgreen bermudagrass
uses: green, **3598, 6958, 12806**

Tifhi bahiagrass, **7639**

Tiflawn bermudagrass, **1472, 3557, 3559, 3560, 3573, 7309, 7407, 7638, 11562**

Tiflawn bermudagrass
adaptation, **3574, 7977**

Tiflawn bermudagrass
culture, **7977, 8016, 8039**

Tiflawn bermudagrass
evaluation, **8154, 8522, 11232, 11882**

Tifway bermudagrass, **1472, 1489, 1547, 1639, 4074, 13560, 13970**

Tifway bermudagrass
adaptation, **7977, 16378, 16413**

Tifway bermudagrass
culture, **7977:** fertilization, **4033, 8039, 8042, 8048**

Tifway bermudagrass
description, **3583, 3602**

Tifway bermudagrass
dollar spot disease, **8050**

Tifway bermudagrass
evaluation, **8154, 11232, 11882, 14899, 14906**

Tile drains (see Drain tile)

Tillam® (see Pebulate)

Tillering, **6402, 10695, 11007**

Tillering
cultural factors affecting **15086:** cutting height, **3037, 7493, 7513, 8055, 8675, 9034, 9622, 10036, 12765, 16435;** growth regulators, **9484;** mowing, **2295, 7667, 9992, 10697, 11833, 15362;** mowing frequency, **1513, 9034, 12765, 12770;** nitrogen fertilization, **90, 2295, 5646, 6402, 8055, 9992, 10784, 11980;** phosphorus fertilization, **10784**

Tillering
development, **9179, 9182, 9624, 9627, 11359, 12457, 14576, 14831, 14834, 15339**

Tillering
effects of: herbicides, **6440;** shoot growth, **8447, 10336;** vernalization, **10022, 11023**

Tillering
effects on: carbohydrate reserves, **14576, 15362**

Tillering
environmental effects, **6402, 10696, 11018:** day length, **2295, 3897, 6402, 10022, 10696, 11015, 11020, 11023, 12967, 14606, 16399;** light intensity, **2295, 2533, 8055, 10697, 12961;** shading, **10696, 10697, 10699, 10702, 11980;** temperature, **2295, 3895, 3897, 7669, 7670, 8055, 10697, 10699, 10700, 10704, 12965, 14606, 16399, 16414**

Tillering
factors affecting, **6111, 6402, 9182, 11980, 14661, 14962**

Tillering
Kentucky bluegrass, **5646:** cultivar evaluation, **6328, 9634, 11020**

Tillering
longevity, **9179**

Tillering
rate, **10698, 14831**

Tillering
seasonal variation, **4594, 9180, 9181, 9699, 11951, 13527, 14576**

Tillering
species variation, **9430, 11920**

Tilletia contraversa (see Dwarf bunt)

Timothy, **4009**

Timothy
cultivars, **2129, 13823:** evaluation, **513, 2658, 5316, 5320, 7191, 7284, 7287, 8336, 8338, 8341, 13661, 13662**

Timothy
description, **1439, 1685, 5666, 11359, 11773:** haplocorm development, **13618;** tillering, **8055, 9179**

Timothy
seed germination, **3821**

Timothy mite, **10143**

Tipulidae family (see Crane fly)

Tires, **16477**

Tissue analysis (see also Tissue test), **6041, 7828**

Tissue test, **4658, 7214, 7217, 7840, 11527, 11613, 13043**

Tissue test
calcium, **11307**

Tissue test
determining nutrient needs, **7841, 12602, 12628**

Tissue test
factors affecting, **4282, 15117, 15327**

Tissue test
manganese, **10061**

Tissue test
nitrogen, **12957, 13862:** factors affecting, **4639, 6657, 9103, 11012, 11082, 15437;** nitrogen fertilization effects, **11672, 12726, 15985**

Tissue test
nutrient content, **1841, 4418, 6666, 6999, 9026, 11472, 11635, 14691, 15488:** evaluation, **4282, 4420, 10195, 10784, 11801, 12498, 14453, 15117, 15327, 15351, 16404;** factors affecting, **14486, 15116, 15328**

Tissue test
phosphorus, **11307, 11615**

Tissue test
potassium, **11614**

Tissue test
Purdue method, **11800**

Tobacco dust
nitrogen carrier, **7220**

Tobacco stems, **566**

Toban
dollar spot control, **3103**

Topdressing, **225, 628, 736, 833, 1029, 1839, 1887, 2151, 2171, 2458, 2799, 2934, 4034, 4321, 4768, 5303, 5626, 6933, 7571, 7576, 9687, 9958, 14924, 15970**

Topdressing
compost preparation, **3640a, 11666**

Topdressing
effects, **1175, 5523, 5902, 7555, 12883**

Topdressing
frequency, **7571, 14251**

Topdressing
fumigation, **2951, 4849, 4850, 9687, 10816, 11471, 13966**

Topdressing
golf course, **218, 6100, 6283**

Topdressing
green, **218, 341, 455, 483, 2805, 4300, 5965, 6280, 6282, 6940, 7165, 7866, 9687, 9829, 9834, 9925, 11515, 11583, 12468, 12470, 12550, 13982, 14250, 15170**

Topdressing
materials used, **583, 1225, 4289, 7241, 8747, 8748, 10363, 10974, 11470, 12472, 13984, 14251, 15541:** sand, **7245, 9383**

Topdressing
practices, **285, 11666, 11765, 13689, 15541:** application, **7571, 9687, 11471, 14112, 14251;** preparation, **1498, 4871, 9382, 9687, 9701, 11190, 11205, 13966, 14246, 14251, 14781;** rates, **833, 9378, 11121**

Topdressing
soil mix, **1194, 3567, 6893, 10539, 11190, 11583:** composition, **2003,** 3792, 4849, 4850, 6021, 6911, 9280, 9377, 9687, 11471, 12144, 14112, 14152, **14781**

Topdressing
sports field, **1502**

Topdressing
uses, **14112:** smoothing, **11691, 12472, 14251, 15541;** thatch control, **1700, 2614, 2615, 5505, 5523, 9065, 9067, 11931, 12472, 14251, 14698, 15541;** winter desiccation prevention, **7866;** winter overseeding, **11691, 13433, 13561**

Topdressing
weed control, **7469, 9371**

Topography (see Slope)

Topsoil, **9856, 15871**

Tordon® (see Picloram)

Tormentil, **4741**

Toronto creeping bentgrass, **742, 757, 989, 992, 993, 1289, 3057, 3058, 6840, 6950, 7008, 7309, 10637, 11165, 12698**

Toronto creeping bentgrass
adaptation: ice cover tolerance, **2559, 2582;** low temperature hardiness, **2570, 9408;** submersion tolerance, **2700, 2701**

Toronto creeping bentgrass
diseases, **854, 8096, 9564**

Toronto creeping bentgrass
evaluation, **5781, 9233, 9564, 10616, 10622, 10760, 11021, 11031, 11232**

Toronto creeping bentgrass
pests: root knot nematode, **7801, 7822**

Toronto creeping bentgrass
uses: fairway, **789, 815;** green, **854**

Tournament, golf
golf course preparation, **6382, 6394, 8266**

2,4,5–TP (see Silvex)

Toxaphene, **13776**

Toxaphene
armyworm control, **12437**

Toxaphene
insect control, **9467, 12178, 12437, 13483**

Toxaphene
Japanese beetle control, **7158, 12168, 12173, 12178, 13472**

Trace elements (see Micronutrients)

Tracenta colonial bentgrass, **1789**

Track
irrigation system design, **15342**

Track
layout specifications, **6605**

Tractor
comparisons, **16474, 16479, 16480, 16481**

Tractor
maintenance manual, **1889**

Traffic
airfield, **802, 803**

Traffic
control, **1455, 1997, 2001, 5868, 7414, 9936:** golf course, **2782, 2788, 3161, 5837, 13666;** methods, **5843, 8969, 9936, 12779, 12780, 15863**

Traffic
cultural adjustments, **12351, 12476, 13839**

Traffic
effects, **866, 1346, 3161, 4643, 6613, 10752, 12369, 12393, 12460, 13822, 14675:** soil, **10305, 15514, 15526;** soil compaction, **3390, 3604, 5976, 6843, 16183;** soil structure, **3788, 13445;** turfgrass, **3390, 3594, 4393, 5016, 5485, 11002, 16370**

Traffic
effects on: winter injury, **6699, 10774, 12476**

Traffic
simulation apparatus, **8746, 12039, 16183**

Traffic
species tolerance, **3024, 16377**

Traffic
types: shoe soles, **866, 1391, 1454, 5818, 16185;** vehicular, **1997, 14988**

Traffic
winter, **563, 1190, 2125, 2582, 2690:** green, **609, 1006, 1129, 1190, 3148**

Trail
design: roadside, **14445**

Training, turfgrass
cemetery foreman, **14095**

Training, turfgrass
golf course, **12846:** assistant superintendent, **3629a;** employees, **10477, 15772;** in service, **1268, 1596, 1814, 10183**

Training, turfgrass
technical, **3197, 4996, 8942**

Transition zone, **8785**

Transition zone
bermudagrass, **11565, 12356, 13658**

Transition zone
grasses used, **2744, 4801, 5228, 8786, 8795:** bentgrass, **5999, 9982, 10559;** tall fescue, **8715, 8717;** zoysiagrass, **9571, 12475**

Transition zone
turfgrass culture, **13239, 14257**

Transpiration, **3414, 7583, 12307, 15503**

Transpiration
control (see Antitranspirant)

Transpiration
diurnal variation, **3232**

Transpiration
environmental factors affecting, **3233, 7179, 15474, 15476, 15496, 15503:** temperature, **4107, 4225**

Transpiration
factors affecting, **2604, 2652, 5867, 11512, 11703, 13037, 15480, 15500**

Transpiration
herbicide effects, **13669, 14860**

Transplant rooting, sod, **2649, 2668, 2669, 10092**

Transplant rooting, sod
effects of: cutting height, **2672, 5234;** fertilizer placement, **6028, 8948;** nitrogen, **5233, 5581;** pre-emergent herbicide, **14838;** sod harvesting thickness, **2707, 4438, 4444, 4883, 5234, 6967, 8948, 10092, 11189, 15402;** sod soil type, **1958, 2603, 2631, 2633, 2707, 5508, 8944, 8945, 8948;** soil moisture, **8944, 8948;** soil warming, **8947, 9443;** underlying soil type, **2603, 2707, 5231, 5232, 8944, 8948**

Transplant rooting, sod
factors affecting, **2710, 3487, 5231, 5506, 9443**

Transplant rooting, sod
Kentucky bluegrass: blend evaluation, **2672, 2673;** cultivar evaluation, **2673, 2687**

Transplant rooting, sod
measurement technique, **8945**

Transplant rooting, sod
root initiation, **8649, 10092**

Transplant rooting, sod
seasonal variation, **2687**

Transplant rooting, sod
shear strength, **6806**

Trap (see Sand trap)

Tree, **3773, 8065, 8091**

Tree
care, **7491, 8204, 10414, 13454:** disease control, **11650, 13454, 13456;** fertilization, **1053, 1676, 8380, 9705;** golf course, **383, 1412**

Tree
golf course landscaping, **5096, 5862, 7055, 7064, 10188, 11281, 12097, 14732**

Tree
root competition, **7051, 8380, 8665, 15793, 15794, 15795, 15796**

Tree
root pruning, **1206, 7051**

Tree
selection, **10414, 12313**

Tree
windbreaks, **9875**

Treflan® (see Trifluralin)

Trex-san®
broadleaf weed control, **8427**

Tribulus terrestris (see Puncturevine)

Tribanil® (see Methabenzthiazuron)

Trichloma species, **2699**

Trichlorofon, **12437**

Trichlorofon
armyworm control, **12437**

Trichlorofon
chinch bug control, **8876**

Trichlorofon
sod webworm control, **11944, 12428**

Trichlorobenzoic acid, **3665a, 3666a, 10996**

Trichloronitromethane (see Chloropicrin)

2-(2,4,5-trichlorophenoxy) propionic acid (see Silvex)

2,3,6-trichlorophenylacetic acid
crabgrass control, **2729**

Trichodorus (see Stubby root nematode)

Tricholoma species (see Fairy ring)

Trifluralin, **5205, 5481, 6658**

Trifluralin
colonial bentgrass control, **6486**

Trifluralin
crabgrass control, **1782, 6380, 9529, 9530, 9531, 9548, 10375, 10378, 12760, 13803, 13859, 13877, 14491, 14823**

Trifluralin
nimbleweed control, **15160**

Trifluralin
selectivity, **4156, 12576, 13858**: Kentucky bluegrass, **13803, 15160**

Trifluralin
weed control, **4156, 8182**

Trifolium (see Clover)

Trifolium hybridum (see Alsike clover)

Trifolium repens (see White clover)

Trigone®
soil fumigation, **2880**

Trimec®
weed control, **2074**

Trimming
chemical, **2504**

Trinity red fescue, **972, 9152, 11165**

Triplex greenmower, **2810, 2948, 6970**

Trithion® (see Carbophenothion)

Troy Kentucky bluegrass, **7309**
evaluation, **6330, 8317**

Tufcote bermudagrass, **4788, 6287, 8154, 11232**

Tupersan® (see Siduron)

Turf conference (see Conference, turfgrass)

Turfgrass, **11432, 12956, 13159**

Turfgrass
adaptation (see Adaptation)

Turfgrass
breeding (see Breeding)

Turfgrass
definition, **6884**

Turfgrass
effects on: environmental quality, **2036, 2037, 11425, 11737, 12692, 12730, 12782, 13545, 14619, 15851, 16423**

Turfgrass
history (see History, turfgrass)

Turfgrass
identification (see Identification, grass)

Turfgrass
management (see Management, turf)

Turfgrass
morphology (see Morphology)

Turfgrass
problem diagnosis (see Problem diagnosis)

Turfgrass
renovation (see Renovation)

Turfgrass
research (see Research, turfgrass)

Turfgrass
selection, **2377, 4093, 4493, 6356, 9461, 10770, 11434, 11900, 13136, 13160, 13934, 14371, 16253, 16445**

Turfgrass
substitutes, **3680**

Turfgrass
uses, **3597, 10146, 13069, 14182**

Turfgrass color, **5769**

Turfgrass color
environmental effects, **10060, 16339:** temperature, **2006, 7559, 15909**

Turfgrass color
Kentucky bluegrass: cultivar evaluation, **6309, 14880**

Turfgrass color
measurement, **7559:** spectrophotometric methods, **2923, 15773**

Turfgrass color
nutritional effects, **12161, 14440, 15913:** magnesium, **8762, 12161;** nitrogen, **4840, 7559, 12220, 12757, 13813, 14103, 15118, 15909**

Turfgrass community, **2523, 12123, 12689, 16316, 16360**
factors affecting composition, **12678:** cultural, **7389, 8230, 16286;** fertilization, **2941, 3158, 3316, 5636, 16360;** mowing, **7220, 16360;** soil, **3159, 3179, 7389;** soil reaction, **5636, 11372;** soil salinity, **14959, 14960**

Turfgrass culture, **824, 1362, 1818, 2080, 2386, 3036, 3324, 3660a, 3755, 4142, 4215, 4441, 4457, 4475, 4476, 5242, 5626, 5727, 5822, 6838, 6844, 6913, 6949, 6971, 7077, 7497, 7635, 7760, 8681, 9021, 9048, 9371, 10080, 10284, 10307, 10840,**

11165, 11206, 11434, 11549, 11564, 11712, 13066, 13322, 13449, 13606, 14348, 14360, 14366, 14982, 15499, 15897, 15935, 15996, 16022, 16356

Turfgrass culture
Australia, **7586**

Turfgrass culture
book, **1430, 2688, 4007, 4295, 4554, 5326, 5743, 7031, 7319, 9229, 10097, 10098, 10460, 11137, 11199, 14184, 15316, 16112**

Turfgrass culture
California, **14350**

Turfgrass culture
Canada, **12035, 13966**

Turfgrass culture
China, **7000**

Turfgrass culture
contract maintenance, **5390, 15445**

Turfgrass culture
cool region, **4790, 8684**

Turfgrass culture
cool season turfgrasses used, **6585, 13529, 14350**

Turfgrass culture
cost analysis, **11196, 14657, 14806, 15557**

Turfgrass culture
cultivation (see Cultivation)

Turfgrass culture
cultural factors affecting, **11037, 13048, 14731**

Turfgrass culture
with deficient rainfall, **10294, 10299**

Turfgrass culture
effects, **3670, 5456, 5623, 10101, 14353, 15482:** of trees, **12313, 15794**

Turfgrass culture
Egypt, **13004**

Turfgrass culture
England, **3026, 5612, 5613, 5621, 5627, 5743, 6681, 9841, 9842, 11000, 14465**

Turfgrass culture
environmental factors affecting, **4242, 5486, 11541, 14731, 15361, 15546**

Turfgrass culture
Europe, **4526**

Turfgrass culture
with excessive rainfall, **15528, 15534**

Turfgrass culture
fall, **1888, 9433**

Turfgrass culture
fertilization (see Fertilization)

Turfgrass culture
Germany, **1696, 3018, 3019, 5343, 5344, 6391, 7304, 7725, 14253**

Turfgrass culture
Hawaii, **10961**

Turfgrass culture
historical development, **7760, 7770, 10563**

Turfgrass culture
irrigation (see Irrigation practices)

Turfgrass culture
Japan, **5326, 9112**

Turfgrass culture
lawn: state bulletin, **3846, 4982, 4994, 4995, 5389, 5586**

Turfgrass culture
Michigan, **2563, 2629**

Turfgrass culture
mowing (see Mowing)

Turfgrass culture
New Zealand, **6484, 15301**

Turfgrass culture
principles, **1247, 1450, 9021, 10312, 11165, 11169, 11173, 13597**

Turfgrass culture
problems, **2563, 6661, 8679, 9629, 10458, 10460, 11423, 11498, 15193, 15862, 15925:** diagnosis, **419, 1563, 10959**

Turfgrass culture
shade, **3590, 3592**

Turfgrass culture
soil factors affecting, **1906, 11037, 11399, 14731**

Turfgrass culture
South Africa, **10458, 10460**

Turfgrass culture
spring, **1790, 1794, 1885, 2455**

Turfgrass culture
summer, **6661, 9841, 9842**

Turfgrass culture
Sweden, **5324, 9224, 9229, 15642**

Turfgrass culture
USSR, **6340, 9256, 12969**

Turfgrass culture
United States, **2185, 4497, 14184**

Turfgrass culture
United States, Central Plains, **9223**

Turfgrass culture
United States, Northeast, **4144**

Turfgrass culture
United States, Northwest, **13463, 13464, 13529, 16023**

Turfgrass culture
United States, Western, **2801, 5819**

Turfgrass culture
warm regions, **2488, 9047, 13043, 13399, 15461**

Turfgrass culture
warm season turfgrasses used, **14350, 15455**

Turfgrass culture
wartime, **7766, 10847**

Turfgrass culture
winter, **1973, 16397**

Turfgrass establishment (see Establishment)

Turfgrass evaluation (see Evaluation, turfgrass)

Turfgrass Field Day (see Field Day, turf)

Turfgrass industry (see also Survey, turfgrass), **1120, 13763, 14288**

Turfgrass quality, **4408, 6455, 6897, 13232**

Turfgrass quality
components, **3672, 6890, 6901, 11151, 14213, 16196, 16250**

Turfgrass quality
cultural effects: cutting height, **12632, 15265;** fertilization, **2617, 2706, 2982, 9134, 11024, 12632, 13436, 14075;** irrigation practices, **10173, 14890**

Turfgrass quality
effects of: soil mix, **13896, 13902, 13907**

Turfgrass quality
environmental effects, **1744, 9047, 12207, 13906**

Turfgrass quality
evaluation, **4549, 14898, 15839, 16250**

Turfgrass science
book, **7319**

Turfgrass weevil, **2027, 3633a, 3635a, 3636a, 4147, 13499**

Turfgrass weevil
chemical control, **3634a, 3635a, 13499:** evaluation, **3628a, 3631a, 3632a, 3637a**

Turfgrass weevil
description, **3631a, 3632a, 3634a, 3638a, 4146**

Twin orchard creeping bentgrass, **11021**

Two-lined spittlebug, **14520**

Tylenchorhynchus (see Stunt nematode)

Tylenchorhynchus claytoni, **5757, 14393**

Tylenchorhynchus dubius (see Stylet nematode)

Tylenchorhynchus species, **11669**

Tylenchus species, **2859**

Typhula blight, **675, 720, 1208, 6650, 6699, 8342, 8345, 8373, 12545, 13736, 14968**

Typhula blight
bentgrass: cultivar susceptibility, **1776, 2566, 2592, 2676, 2704, 6318, 14617**

Typhula blight
chemical control, **21, 1283, 1487, 2649, 2704, 4683, 5918, 6114, 6748, 11943, 12936, 12937, 14302, 15011, 15014, 15018, 15477, 15483, 15485, 15589:** evaluation, **1518, 1545, 1776, 1967, 2100, 2577, 2578, 2591, 2595, 2605, 2617, 2620, 2633, 2650, 4209, 6336, 6667, 7337, 8100, 8373, 8741, 15017, 15019, 15020, 15590;** time of application, **2595, 2620, 2650, 2689, 15017, 15020, 15028**

Typhula blight
control, **4685, 6745, 7183, 8362**

Typhula blight
cultural practices affecting, **2699, 7193, 15589:** clipping removal, **2699;** cutting height, **2699, 14302**

Typhula blight
environmental factors affecting, **3942, 6739, 8362, 10423, 14302:** temperature, **3942, 6739, 14004**

Typhula blight
injury symptoms, **2646, 6132, 7193, 8362, 14302**

Typhula blight
Kentucky bluegrass: cultivar susceptibility, **8741, 14968, 15029, 15030**

Typhula blight
red fescue: cultivar susceptibility, **14968**

Typhula blight
species susceptibility, **3942**

Typhula graminum, **8397**

Typhula idahoenis (see *Typhula* blight)

Typhula ishikariensis (see *Typhula* blight)

Typhula itoana (see *Typhula* blight)

U-3 bermudagrass, **274, 866, 873, 884, 888, 890, 931, 940, 1027, 1073, 1472, 2372, 2834, 4093, 5236, 5433, 5440, 5890, 6862, 6875, 6893, 7309, 7403, 7407, 7692, 9152, 9153, 9304, 9598, 9617, 10922, 11165, 13462, 13560, 15441, 16261**

U-3 bermudagrass
adaptation, **4389, 5435, 5793, 6847, 6888, 7055:** low temperature hardiness, **960, 1404, 7057, 13658**

U-3 bermudagrass
bermudagrass mite susceptibility, **1489**

U-3 bermudagrass
culture, **5435, 6919, 7055, 7539, 16338:** on fairway, **13447, 13451**

U-3 bermudagrass
description, **8212, 16331, 16378**

U-3 bermudagrass
establishment, **1410, 5435:** plugging, **10132, 11539, 14367;** sodding, **11565;** stolonizing, **7539, 11798**

U-3 bermudagrass
evaluation, **8154, 8791, 11882, 14349, 14365, 16320**

U-3 bermudagrass
low temperature discoloration, **16327**

U-3 bermudagrass
spring dead spot, **15140**

U-3 bermudagrass
uses, **875, 5970, 13444:** fairways, **9278, 11551, 11554, 13445;** tees, **5970, 11551, 11565, 11592**

UF (see Ureaformaldehyde)

Uganda bermudagrass, **1472, 7309, 9568, 10126, 13445, 16261, 16331**

Uganda bermudagrass
description, **10126, 15442**

Uganda bermudagrass
evaluation, **8791, 11882, 16320**

United States Golf Association, **1361, 1416, 1417, 14211**

United States Golf Association
Green Section, **956, 1215, 1402, 2790, 14594:** activities, **1563, 6789, 6830, 6833, 6858, 6869, 6886, 11391;** Green Section Award, **1447;** history, **548, 549, 722, 764, 915, 7366, 15162;** research review, **5791, 6855, 7365, 10812, 11627, 12382;** visiting advisory service, **1402, 1415, 1448, 2803, 12948, 15998**

USGA Green Section Method
soil modification, **1401, 2802, 6881, 7902, 12373, 12376, 16048:** construction, **5861, 6394, 7060, 7902;** development history, **5884;** evaluation, **2795, 3338;** specifications, **1354, 1407, 1627, 5861, 7060, 7893, 7902, 12352**

Uramite® (see Ureaformaldehyde)

Urea, **1470, 1546, 1777, 2725, 2811, 2942, 3001, 3132, 3206, 5230, 5634, 7202, 9739, 10067, 12571, 16021**

Urea
effects, **4943, 5499, 6674**

Urea
effects on: soil reaction, **2614, 6674, 15064**

Urea
evaluation, **3528, 5636, 6574, 6579, 6595, 6790, 8699, 10861, 11185, 11213, 11905, 11907, 12567, 14402, 14403, 15118, 15697, 15787**

Urea
hydrolysis, **3270, 3818, 4919, 11871**

Urea
nitrogen efficiency, **13039, 15064, 15068**

Urea
phytotoxicity, **4120, 4218, 4219, 4220**

Urea
soil retention: nitrogen, **3267, 3270, 4101, 10133, 14118, 15064**

Urea
stripe smut control, **9751**

Urea
volitilization, **3818, 15062, 15064:** factors affecting, **1804, 4919, 8241, 13795**

Ureabor
soil sterilant, **8182**

Urea diamonium phosphate, **13039**

Ureaform, **5439**

Ureaformaldehyde, **136, 866, 873, 888, 979, 1075, 1163, 1237, 1241, 1307, 1382, 1434, 1470, 1488, 2027, 2100, 3206, 3699, 3700, 4646, 4647, 5030, 5196, 5439, 5503, 5634, 5806, 6922, 6934, 6954, 6957, 7341, 8198, 8199, 8729, 9045, 9058, 9059, 9085, 9790, 9958, 10583, 10589, 13386, 13776, 15065, 16021, 16285**

Ureaformaldehyde
application rate, **3699, 3700**

Ureaformaldehyde
effects, **3590a, 3591a, 5499, 7596, 11745, 16285**

Ureaformaldehyde
effects on: dollar spot, **12757;** growth, **3590a, 4113, 4550, 5180, 5181, 8730, 8915**

Ureaformaldehyde
evaluation, **838, 909, 2255, 2256, 2257, 3528, 4650, 4879, 4880, 4881, 5179, 5198, 5230, 5467, 5479, 5616, 5633, 5637, 5638, 5781, 5917, 6574, 6579, 6595, 6627, 7932, 7933, 8002, 8201, 8699, 10066, 11057, 11134, 11145, 11172, 11176, 11185, 11213, 11803, 11905, 11907, 12219, 12220, 12596, 13671, 14402, 14403, 15108, 15110, 15118**

Ureaformaldehyde
impurities: biuret, **3699, 3700**

Ureaformaldehyde
leaching, **7598, 7600**

Ureaformaldehyde
nitrification, **3855, 7600, 9085**

Ureaformaldehyde
nitrogen efficiency, **5637, 8915**

Ureaformaldehyde
nitrogen release, **6976, 8730, 9794, 14214:** factors affecting, **6263, 7598, 7601, 8006**

Ureaformaldehyde
properties, **6976, 7598, 7600, 10583, 12081**

Ureaformaldehyde
residual effects, **7599, 12081, 15064, 16123**

Ureaformaldehyde
roadside use, **2094, 11065, 11905**

Ureaformaldehyde
seedbed fertilization, **1546, 1687, 9055**

Ureaformaldehyde
soil reaction: nitrogen availability, **3205, 3855, 7598, 16285**

Ureaformaldehyde
urea-formaldehyde ratio, **2198, 14214, 14215, 16285**

Urethane seed mat (see Seed mat)

Ustilago cynodontis (see Inflorescence smut)

Ustilago cynodontis
on bermudagrass, **3808**

Ustilago striiformis (see also Stripe smut), **9398**

Vacuum cooling (see Sod shipping)

Vacuum sweeper, **1614, 1925**

Value
golf courses: California, **4698, 4701;** Georgia, **9254;** Oregon, **6592**

Value
sod industry: Florida, **3225;** USA, **1990**

Value, turf, **162, 6884, 11717, 13763**

Value, turf
California, **4700, 8928, 8930, 15940**

Value, turf
Colorado, **11723, 12958**

Value, turf
Florida, **14401**

Value, turf
Los Angeles County, **2860, 10946**

Value, turf
Maryland, **10557**

Value, turf
Michigan, **2629**

Value, turf
Nebraska, **1999, 3779**

Value, turf
Ohio, **10628**

Value, turf
Pennsylvania, **1702, 2608, 3077**

Value, turf
Southern California, **7242**

Value, turf
Texas, **5844**

Value, turf
Washington, **6680, 6718**

Value, turf
West Virginia, **7667**

Value, turf
United States, **5786, 8676, 11723, 13215, 13608**

Vapam® (see SMDC)

Vapor pressure deficit, **14193**

Variety (see Cultivar)

Vascular tissue, **3002**

Vascular tissue
in Festucoid grasses, **7790**

V-(1,1-dimethylpropynyl)-3,5 dichlorobenzamide (see Kerb ®)

Vegetative development, **9699, 14085**

Vegetative development
environmental effects, **14085:** light intensity, **10695, 10699, 10705, 14579;** temperature, **10695, 10699, 10705, 14579**

Vegetative propagation (see also Establishment, vegetative)

Vegetative propagation
American beachgrass, **2300**

Vegetative propagation
clones: mechanical methods, **16456**

Vegetative propagation
effects of: nitrogen, **10001**

Vegetative propagation
factors affecting, **10001**

Vegetative propagation
sanitary certification: warm season species, **12643**

Velvet bentgrass, **477, 479, 512, 2284, 3040, 3713, 7273, 11235, 11469, 11661, 11967, 12101, 12406, 14302**

Velvet bentgrass
adaptation, **83, 4885, 5483, 12510**

Velvet bentgrass
breeding, **4913, 11124**

Velvet bentgrass
cultivars, **4885, 8163, 10760, 11124, 12007, 13823:** evaluation, **1967, 4845, 8336, 8338, 8341, 8350, 10813, 10818, 10822, 10856, 11454, 11661, 11665, 13662, 16069**

Velvet bentgrass
culture, **500, 4905, 10710, 11479, 11542, 13580, 14173**

Velvet bentgrass
description, **4008, 4885, 7947, 8627, 9515, 9518, 10153, 11232, 12510, 15411**

Velvet bentgrass
diseases, **8336, 11661:** yellow tuft, **14531**

Velvet bentgrass
disease control, **20, 24**

Velvet bentgrass
effects of: 2,4-D, **15446**

Velvet bentgrass
establishment, **12289, 14276**

Velvet bentgrass
pests: sod webworm, **11663, 11665**

Velvet bentgrass
putting quality, **15722**

Velvet bentgrass
seed, **11963, 12101**

Velvet bentgrass
seed production, **724, 4846, 4897**

Velvet bentgrass
uses: green, **8612, 14173, 14276**

Velvetgrass, **7512**

Velvetgrass
chemical control, **39, 6580, 8939, 14082**

Verdure, **10076**

Vermiculite, **1379**

Vermiculite
soil amendment, **1225, 1157, 8018, 10090, 12010:** effects, **1879, 6346, 7170, 7987, 8037;** evaluation, **6412, 11644, 13896, 13905, 13906, 13907**

Vermiculite
topdressing, **1225, 5611**

Vermont creeping bentgrass, **302, 2450, 9258**

Vernalization, **3048, 5664, 5753**

Vernalization
effects on: rhizome development, **10022, 11015, 11016, 11023;** tillering, **10022, 11015, 11023**

Vernalization
species requirements, **536, 3901**

Vernalization
temperature effects, **3900, 3901**

Veronica filiformis (see Speedwell, creeping)

Veronica serpyllifolia (see Speedwell, thymeleaf)

Vertas meadow fescue, **7191, 8350**

Vertical column
soil modification, **2027**

Vertical mowing, **1178, 5626, 5978, 6526, 6892, 6923, 9482, 10182, 16262**

Vertical mowing
blade spacing, **10492**

Vertical mowing
crabgrass control, **6352**

Vertical mowing
effects on: annual bluegrass control, **16432;** annual bluegrass invasion, **16345, 16349, 16395;** localized dry spots, **5051;** polystand composition, **5510;** thatch control, **2130, 2614, 10603, 10947, 11193, 14688, 14698, 15355, 16262, 16400;** weed invasion, **5510**

Vertical mowing
equipment, **16264, 16483, 16487**

Vertical mowing
fairway, **3861, 4035**

Vertical mowing
frequency, **10492, 10495**

Vertical mowing
greens, **752, 773, 4236, 4300, 11560**

Vertical mowing
species tolerance, **5510, 10511**

Vertical mowing
timing, **5510, 16345, 16395, 16400**

Vertical mowing
uses, **16264**

Vertical mowing
warm season species, **10499, 15355**

Vertical mowing
weed control: establishment, **8836**

Vertical shoot growth
measurement: densitometer, **14897**

Vertical shoot growth rate (see also Shoot growth), **171**

Vertical trenching
soil modification: sports field, **2189, 4468, 4473, 4503, 4531**

Verticutting (see Vertical mowing)

Virginia creeping bentgrass, **301, 302, 352, 2453, 10860, 11419, 14185**

Virginia creeping bentgrass
evaluation, **388, 10862, 11661**

Viris perennial ryegrass, **9212, 9213**

Viruses, **1611, 3706, 12985, 13886, 15480**

Viscose-rayon cover
winter protection, **1967, 2100, 2148, 2623, 2675, 15559:** evaluation, **15559**

Visual pollution control
turfgrass function, **11737**

Vitamin B_1, **2551, 3847, 9196**

Vitamins, **626, 669**

Vitavax® (see Carboxin)

Vivipary, **8492**

Volatilization
nitrogen, **7302, 11972, 15062:** application rate effects, **8241, 9102;** factors affecting, **7302, 7344;** nitrogen carrier effects, **9102, 11243, 15064;** soil reaction effects, **15064**

Vorlex® **13724**

Vorlex®
soil fumigation, **2880, 3509, 7149**

Wall speedwell, **4743**

Warm season turfgrasses, **279, 913, 3042, 3578, 3811, 4243, 5135, 6154, 6205, 6838, 6888, 7407, 8014, 11574, 11611, 11705, 12007**

Warm season turfgrasses
adaptation, **7523, 7980, 8015, 11003, 15483**: California, **16366, 16393, 16448;** drought resistance, **3577, 3581;** shade, **8166, 9883**

Warm season turfgrasses
breeding, **3551, 8030, 8166**

Warm season turfgrasses
comparisons, **2936, 3676, 8009, 11700**

Warm season turfgrasses
culture, **8619, 8984, 10499, 14373:** fertilization, **8023, 8026, 9187, 11572, 11694, 12810**

Warm season turfgrasses
description, **13238, 13334, 15358, 15838, 16114:** root growth, **3535, 3563, 3571, 3577**

Warm season turfgrasses
establishment, **1700, 8166, 14537, 14538**

Warm season turfgrasses
evaluation methods, **1700, 6701**

Warm season turfgrasses
herbicide tolerance, **3498, 5504, 3508, 3510, 3511, 3515, 7969**

Warm season turfgrasses
nematode susceptibility: evaluation, **9890, 11742, 11750**

Warm season turfgrasses
species evaluation, **2466, 3305, 7982, 8015, 8025**

Warm season turfgrasses
uses, **3039, 7041, 7163, 8445, 8927, 10961, 14429, 14687:** golf course, **2372, 5970, 11966;** lawn, **3566, 10500, 11688**

Washington creeping bentgrass, **301, 302, 326, 352, 491, 742, 757, 989, 3713, 4840, 7309, 9258, 9844, 10837, 11235, 11419, 12158, 12698**

Washington creeping bentgrass
adaptation, **4581, 9408**

Washington creeping bentgrass
disease susceptibility, **388, 9564, 14923**

Washington creeping bentgrass
evaluation, **5781, 9233, 10616,**

10622, 10760, 10862, 11021, 11031, 11232, 11233, 11661, 11666, 16489

Wasps
chemical control, **12316**

Waste ash (see Fly ash)

Water, **1055, 5815, 6935, 10084, 10911**

Water
absorption, **5317, 12668:** factors affecting, **2642, 6493, 10105, 10644, 11059**

Water
conservation, **3348, 6837, 6841, 6860**

Water
cost, **5035**

Water
effects on: disease development, **6123, 7056, 16221;** seed germination, **3327, 15995**

Water
functions, **5798, 11562, 15561:** plant, **5826, 5832, 9260, 11512, 12856, 14123, 15768, 15769**

Water
location: magnetometer, **8446**

Water
management, **2339, 3471, 6909, 7171, 10296, 10535, 10911, 11869**

Water
penetration: wetting agent effects, **1045, 2673, 10902, 15791**

Water
plant effects, **11289, 12421, 13571**

Water
soil (see Soil water)

Water
soil effects, **1564, 6493, 6988**

Water
sources, **2929, 2930, 4775, 5027, 5061, 10911, 13746, 13923, 14287:** lake (see Lake); sewage effluent (see Sewage effluent, uses); well, **10535**

Water balance, **2604, 2652**

Water chickweed, **4737**

Water cycle, **10911**

Water deficit (see also Water stress), **2604**

Watering (see Irrigation)

Waterlogged soil, **6927, 12520, 15534**

Waterlogged soil
tolerance: bentgrass cultivars, **4881**

Waterlogged soil
turfgrass effects, **4581, 9084, 15534:** rooting, **6661, 15534**

Water quality, **1486, 41700, 3186, 4213, 5061, 11317, 11887, 13809, 15881, 16502**

Water quality
for irrigation, **15881, 16500:** salinity, **1780, 6261, 12583**

Water requirements (see Water use rate)

Water sedge
chemical control, **2951**

Water stress (see also Drought), **14123**

Water stress
effects, **188, 2434, 10294**

Water stress
effects of: nitrogen, **11973;** temperature, **233, 11973**

Water stress
effects on: disease development, **3799, 3804, 10890, 12736;** protein synthesis, **12092;** shoot density, **12758;** shoot growth, **9485, 11973, 12736**

Water table, soil
depth: shoot growth effects, **15003, 15924, 15972, 15973**

Water use rate, **9, 276, 720, 3229, 3230, 3231, 3334, 4775, 7174, 9854, 10532, 10672, 10673, 11533, 12068, 14131, 14132, 14194, 15467, 15768, 16001**

Water use rate
annual, **10522, 15769**

Water use rate
cultural practices affecting, **394, 6688, 6973, 15547:** cutting height, **2677, 7181, 10703, 13623, 13624, 15711;** irrigation frequency, **468, 2677, 10172, 13623, 13624**

Water use rate
daily, **9906, 9908, 10078, 14194**

Water use rate
effects of: antitranspirants, **11788;** nitrogen, **10172, 13623, 14194, 15710**

Water use rate
environmental effects, **277, 6492:** light intensity, **2677, 13623, 13624;** temperature, **2677, 13623, 13624**

Water use rate
factors affecting, **2069, 2170, 2604, 2652, 5055, 6493, 6860, 10069, 12630, 13623, 14194, 16407**

Water use rate
measurement, **2963, 4256, 6492, 7169, 7172, 9909, 10078, 10522, 12274, 12296, 12586, 14260, 14961, 16085**

Water use rate
soil effects: soil moisture, **5056, 5349, 13623;** soil oxygen, **7181, 9497**

Water use rate
species variation, **277, 5055, 9485, 11936, 14961, 15626, 15710**

Water vapor (see Atmospheric water vapor)

Waterway
establishment, **2287, 12490**

Waterway
grasses used, **2287, 7769**

Wear, **9782, 10287, 14650, 14654, 15059, 15863**

Wear
cultural practices affecting,

3912, 6806, 9782: cutting height, 6806, 9782, 16365, 16386

Wear
effects of, 3924, 5016: shoe sole type, 5816, 5824, 5827; thatch, 9782, 16386

Wear
evaluation: infrared photography, 16173; simulation apparatus, 12039, 16337, 16357

Wear
factors affecting, 4393, 7414, 16337, 13646, 16386

Wear
prevention, 4393, 16091

Wear
recovery: species evaluation, 6806, 16361, 16368, 16402, 16404

Wear
tolerance: bermudagrass cultivar evaluation, 3604, 8147, 16357; Kentucky bluegrass cultivar evaluation, 1815, 3117, 13663; polystand evaluation, 11129, 16365; species evaluation, 3788, 8981, 9028, 11002, 13664, 16346, 16347, 16357, 16361, 16368, 16386, 16402, 16404; species variation, 1454, 1489, 6806, 6894, 16369, 16372

Weather, 543, 2853, 3061

Weather
effects, 819, 5486, 13496

Weather
forecasting, 4928, 12435

Weed, 530, 1145, 1239, 2040, 3609, 3641, 3831, 4090, 4729, 5957, 6008, 6371, 9870, 13073, 13804, 14270

Weed
book: descriptions, 1014

Weed
description, 4729, 5971, 6825, 7022, 7587, 8232, 10393, 10553, 11779, 14159, 14166

Weed
dissemination, 530, 850, 4729, 6305, 7369, 7450, 7468, 7469, 10050, 10816, 14159, 14166

Weed
factors affecting, 15475, 16416

Weed
handbook, 12672, 14707, 15453

Weed
identification, 231, 3574a, 4249, 4730, 6373, 8977, 10216, 10552, 10553, 13631, 13632, 13633, 14545, 14870, 15453, 15763

Weed
kinds, 14413, 14414, 14416, 14984

Weed
seed germination, 416, 13573

Weed
seed identification, 11116

Weed
seed production, 14269

Weed control, 31, 176, 251, 379, 387, 426, 447, 581, 720, 1093, 1098, 1103, 1254, 1380, 1754, 1797, 1976, 2132, 2168, 2908, 3453, 3503, 3506, 3507, 3514, 3657, 3664, 3668, 3759, 3892, 4090, 4216, 4263, 4344, 4345, 4725, 4844, 4857, 4908, 5355, 5690, 5846, 6156, 6270, 6355, 6356, 6357, 6360, 6371, 6380, 6506, 6580, 6612, 6721, 7027, 7096, 7190, 7570, 7662, 7865, 7952, 8174, 8848, 8931, 9370, 9371, 9383, 9555, 9653, 10219, 10300, 10393, 10609, 10638, 11217, 11301, 11302, 11666, 11756, 11848, 11998, 12690, 12819, 13023, 13405, 13864, 13867, 14159, 14858, 15614, 16450

Weed control
aquatic, 1715, 10025, 13578

Weed control
book, 3683a, 6138

Weed control
broadleaf, 295, 1039, 1376, 2132, 2908, 3118, 3690a, 4059, 4133, 4135, 4607, 4805, 5689, 6359, 14415, 15081: evaluation, 2178, 3089, 5184, 5197, 5687

Weed control
bulletin, 268, 273, 4204, 4208, 6104

Weed control
burning, 699, 13816

Weed control
cemetery, 12968

Weed control
chemical, 401, 2136, 2394, 2442, 2726, 2751, 2911, 3892, 4154, 4264, 4267, 4607, 4608, 4661, 4771, 5090, 5434, 5676, 5706, 5707, 6155, 6354, 6359, 6360, 6361, 6363, 6367, 6480, 6481, 6590, 6631, 6684, 6816, 6825, 6826, 6827, 6835, 7022, 7240, 7250, 7294, 7296, 7298, 7369, 7588, 7592, 7700, 7752, 8138, 8164, 8633, 8635, 8926, 8927, 9240, 9259, 9364, 9370, 9449, 9483, 9513, 9540, 9664, 9852, 9941, 9979, 10096, 10170, 10218, 10355, 10374, 10393, 10606, 10782, 10827, 10830, 10851, 10868, 11096, 11130, 11133, 11140, 11509, 11523, 11596, 11779, 11828, 11935, 11949, 11950, 12032, 12115, 12250, 12280, 12281, 12385, 12442, 12671, 12799, 12959, 13024, 13156, 13578, 13760, 13781, 13833, 13836, 13883, 14083, 14084, 14159, 14427, 14428, 14627, 14669, 14863, 14875, 14971, 14928, 15032, 15053, 15639, 15703, 15854, 15974, 16076, 16153, 16259, 16375, 16396, 16492, 16496: application methods, 11, 1183, 3660, 6611, 7708, 11147, 11950, 13782, 15181; broadleaf, 2914, 4608, 5434, 5689, 6366; broadleaf evaluation, 2915, 3355, 3357, 3361; evaluation, 2672, 2684, 2914, 4436, 4470, 4893, 4911, 5596, 7293, 8171, 8187, 9876, 12769, 14079; fertilizer combinations, 795, 813, 7338,

13342; golf course, **1995, 2387, 3876**; green, **6480, 9513, 15275, 15300**; nonselective, **1995, 3655, 4867**; post-emergence, **3517, 3523**; principles, **2074, 7536, 12875**; recommendations, **2891, 3477, 3479, 3499, 6103, 6362, 6364, 6475, 6723, 6724, 7039, 7721, 7722, 7723, 8169, 8172, 8175, 8232, 8233, 8234, 8235, 9534, 9535, 9539, 9541, 9543, 9880, 9889, 10554, 10555, 10617, 11904, 12811, 13012, 13876, 14413, 14414, 14416, 14436, 14711, 15039, 15040, 15415**; roadside, **7799, 8182, 12273, 12919**; selectivity, **2069, 3440, 3892, 4157, 6155, 6818, 11599, 13017**; sports field, **1082, 5605**; spot treatment, **4828, 14795**; in warm season turfgrasses, **3517, 3522, 3523, 7965**; weedy grasses, **9941, 12699, 13114, 13512, 13749, 14913, 15293**; weedy grasses, annual, **3440, 3834, 6367, 13883**; weedy grasses, perennial, **2917, 3655, 3658, 4059, 4157, 5677, 6363, 6367, 9948, 14795, 14798**

Weed control
composting, **4854, 4861, 4870**

Weed control
crownvetch establishment, **5359, 12069**

Weed control
cultural, **362, 2164, 2324, 3596, 3664, 4485, 4857, 5622, 5623, 5740, 6367, 6483, 6825, 6835, 6947, 7155, 7240, 7369, 7534, 7882, 9049, 9158, 9300, 9364, 9664, 10292, 10613, 11140, 11147, 12794, 13140, 13338, 13836, 14166, 14863, 15482, 15487, 15893, 16076, 16166, 16321, 16375**: fertilization, **2136, 3785, 4911, 9049, 10843, 13074, 13333, 15482, 15525, 15726, 15727**; soil reaction, **483, 11666, 15698**

Weed control
England, **9559, 10997, 14082**

Weed control
environmental effects, **11175, 15127**

Weed control
establishment, **34, 425, 3540**

Weed control
evaluation, **3362, 5177, 5203, 6105, 6106,6108**

Weed control
fairway, **1384, 2865, 3453, 4813, 10169, 11491, 11493, 15959**

Weed control
fumigation, **5990, 6638**

Weed control
golf course, **2164, 2388, 7095, 9110, 9654, 10827, 11516, 11978, 12340, 14496**

Weed control
greens, **295, 8848, 10816**

Weed control
industrial grounds, **8513, 13879**

Weed control
Japan, **9110, 9764, 10122, 12801**

Weed control
lawn, **26, 3036, 3608a, 3619, 3690a, 4986, 6642, 6643, 7651, 9158, 9239, 9508, 9513, 9650, 10408, 10502, 13074, 13255, 13334, 14035, 14505, 16166:** bulletin, **250, 1229, 1562, 1959, 10870, 14224**; state bulletin, **1727, 1771, 5255, 7713, 7747, 8425, 9446, 10536, 11308, 11356, 11995, 12071, 14792, 14870**

Weed control
New Zealand, **11978, 15200, 15293**

Weed control
oil effects, **8171**

Weed control
park, **14858**

Weed control
principles, **11722, 11726**

Weed control
problems, **3668, 6363**

Weed control
recommendations, **3596a, 3601a, 3613, 3617, 3621a, 5202**

Weed control
roadside, **1575, 1700, 1717, 1826, 1832, 1833, 1933, 1934, 3654, 3660, 4302, 6051, 7155, 10992, 12489, 12919, 14601, 15405**

Weed control
sand trap, **1976, 1995, 4867**

Weed control
seedbed, **4854, 4861, 4870, 4903**

Weed control
sod production, **7147, 7964, 7965, 8275, 10406, 11303, 11842**

Weed control
state bulletin, **2039, 5354, 8977, 15706**

Weed control
Sweden, **15081**

Weed control
topdressing, **4849, 4850**

Weed control
warm regions, **1620, 7927, 8190, 9651, 9654, 10502, 11841, 11843, 12786, 12793, 12798, 12802, 12819, 14309, 14684**

Weed control
on warm season turfgrasses, **3524, 8159, 8984, 12803, 12809**

Weed control
weedy grasses, annual, **3691a, 4135, 5687, 6366, 7010**

Weed invasion, **7709, 9655, 16362**

Weed invasion
cultural practices affecting, **2633, 3652, 4882, 5510, 6947, 9300, 12807, 15458**: cultivation, **9295, 15524**; cutting height, **1422, 4632, 4634, 4636, 4646, 6308, 6309, 6317, 6637, 6713, 8724, 10064, 10617, 10622, 11330, 12840, 15524,**

16165; fertilization, 1304, 2617, 2632, 6308, 9295, 10816, 11130, 11192, 11768, 12676, 12701, 12705, 12717, 12719, 12840, 14128, 14984, 15524, 15728; irrigation, 9295, 10064, 12721, 12751, 12840, 14984, 15465, 15467, 15524; nitrogen carriers, 2650, 5634, 15729, 15787; nitrogen fertilization, 2631, 2941, 2942, 4634, 4657, 4840, 5636, 6309, 6317, 6637, 6713, 10617, 11330, 12726, 12747, 12751, 13813, 15729; soil reaction, 2172, 5634, 5636, 11666, 15787

Weed invasion
environmental factors affecting, 3648, 4882, 15459

Weed invasion
factors affecting, 3500, 6309, 9292, 13355, 15459

Weed invasion
species tolerance, 6304, 16165

Weeping lovegrass, 828, 5713

Weeping lovegrass
culture, 8181

Weeping lovegrass
sand dune stabilization, 16456

Weigrass Method
soil modification, 9206, 9211, 9220

Well (see Water, sources)

Western wheatgrass, 2772, 8810

Western wheatgrass
adaptation, 2770, 2771, 15054

Western wheatgrass
description, 4021, 7947

Western wheatgrass
roadside use, 2092

West Indian mole cricket, 15346

Wetting agent, 1423, 1542, 1549, 1687, 2775, 4565, 4958, 6004, 9842, 10897, 10898, 10900, 10903, 10904, 11163, 12530, 12759, 15791

Wetting agent
effects on, 5555, 9496, 10899, 10901, 10902, 10903, 10905, 12529, 12721, 14508, 15734: on fairy ring, 6727; infiltration rate, 2673, 9505, 10081, 10899, 10977, 11214, 15845; localized dry spots, 5051, 5523, 9496; root growth, 5419, 10738, 11678, 12744; seed germination, 5423, 10738; shoot growth, 5423, 10738, 12744, 15791, 15792; soil water movement, 10081, 10405, 10902, 11215, 14857, 14975, 15791; soil water retention, 4772, 10081; surface tension, 10899, 11214; thatching, 2615, 5523; turfgrass quality, 5523; wilting, 10482, 10896

Wetting agent
evaluation, 1491, 1700, 1780, 6637, 8242, 10979, 11853, 12720, 13919, 15791, 15792

Wetting agent
phytotoxicity, 5419, 5423

Wetting agent
uses, 1236, 2068, 6397, 9493 9496, 10899, 14857: dew removal, 6395; golf course, 2144, 12527, 13919, 14507

Wet wilt (see also Wilt), 1113, 8597, 10483, 11567, 15637

White clover, 1, 51, 534, 546, 2100, 3716, 4731

White clover
chemical control, 35, 923, 4149, 4755, 4760, 4893, 5602, 6357, 6650, 6940, 10782: 2,4-D, 766, 5603; endothall, 933, 7655, 11748, 11753; evaluation, 2566, 2901, 4809, 5500, 5530, 5603, 5777, 8188, 8422, 8435, 8436, 8852, 9530, 9533, 9537, 11131, 13770, 13860; 2,4,5-T, 438, 4364, 4374, 4377, 4382, 4383, 16124

White clover
cultural effects: nitrogen nutrition, 2943, 4634, 4657, 15697; phosphorus nutrition, 874, 4840

White clover invasion
cultural factors affecting, 4634, 4760, 15701

White grub (see Grub)

Wild celery
chemical control, 7264

Wild garlic, 597, 12070

Wild garlic
chemical control, 2890, 12070

Wild mustard, 9553

Wild onion, 4149

Wilmington bahiagrass, 3507, 3515, 10524, 10525

Wilt, 8831, 9569, 12721, 12933, 15637

Wilt
causes, 10482, 12423

Wilt
cultural practices affecting, 10072, 10482, 13918

Wilt
environmental factors affecting, 8018, 10481, 10482, 10483, 13918: light intensity, 10481, 10482, 10483

Wilt
prevention, 4492, 10481, 10483, 13918

Wilt
species proneness, 7168, 7169, 16082

Winchester bentgrass, 5712

Wind, 541

Wind
effects on, 683, 3759, 9994, 10828, 14929: spore dissemination, 683, 12673; sprinkler irrigation, 3829, 9725

Wind
environmental effects: cooling, 2621, 2706, 3335, 5149, 5759

Wind
modification: by plants, 1943, 9875

Wind
velocity, 6023, 15418: diurnal variation, 10849; factors

affecting, **75, 9875, 15418;** vertical variation, **6023, 10849, 15418**

Windburn (see Winter desiccation)

Wind erosion, **3008**

Wind erosion
control, **2761, 3793**

Windmillgrass, **1685**

Windsor Kentucky bluegrass, **1547, 3656, 5997, 7286, 11363, 12007**

Windsor Kentucky bluegrass
adaptation, **1815, 10614, 10633, 16097**

Windsor Kentucky bluegrass
description, **2021, 10022, 11023, 16096, 16435**

Windsor Kentucky bluegrass
establishment, **10022, 11023, 15774**

Windsor Kentucky bluegrass
evaluation, **6330, 7284, 9218, 9226, 10622, 10626, 10635, 11186, 11323, 11325, 11329, 14103, 14813**

Windsor Kentucky bluegrass
nutrient requirements, **9671, 13563**

Winter crown rot, **3271, 3272, 3273, 3942**

Winter crown rot
injury mechanism, **9404, 15366**

Winter crown rot
soil warming effects, **9404, 9408**

Winter crown rot
species susceptibility, **3942, 4331**

Winter desiccation, **355, 563, 877, 2620, 2689, 2690, 5893, 6940, 11484, 11488, 11605, 13846**

Winter desiccation
atmospheric, **10401, 11449, 11620, 15569**

Winter desiccation
creeping bentgrass: cultivar susceptibility, **9233**

Winter desiccation
factors affecting, **2078, 10401:** nitrogen, **9439, 14075**

Winter desiccation
protection, **6699, 7905, 11449, 11505, 11605, 11606, 12380, 12476, 15520, 16149:** methods, **2651, 12378, 15595;** plastic screen (see Plastic screen); protective cover, **2078, 2143, 2631, 2633, 2650, 2651, 2673, 5780, 9439, 10401, 11623, 12374, 12655, 15506, 15511, 15542, 15569, 15571, 15582;** protective cover, evaluation, **2623, 9437, 15519, 15593 15594;** topdressing, **2673, 11765**

Winter desiccation
soil drought, **15582**

Winter discoloration (see Low temperature discoloration)

Winter dormancy, **1216, 16359**

Wintergreen chewings fescue, **1958, 2612, 2649, 2707, 3918, 6294**

Winter green, **1729**

Winter hardiness (see Low temperature stress, hardiness)

Winterkill, **187, 188, 209, 1465, 1528, 1695, 1731, 1781, 2382, 2577, 2578, 2591, 2605, 2690, 4989, 5779, 6813, 7414, 7540, 7885, 7905, 8980, 10339, 10836, 11204, 11587, 12712, 13354, 13946, 14460, 14855, 15515, 15518, 15519, 15536, 16053**

Winterkill
of bermudagrass, **1275, 5858, 7540, 8145, 11633, 15354**

Winterkill
causes, **1358, 1511, 1514, 1519, 1582, 2169, 2568, 2690, 4989, 5778, 5780, 5849, 5864, 5893, 6067, 6510, 6699, 7073, 7074, 7890, 8943, 10390, 11449, 11620, 11623, 11816, 12353, 12378, 12400, 12476, 13491, 13581, 14003, 15516, 15543, 15569, 15571, 15582, 16149:** desiccation (see Winter desiccation); ice cover, **1597, 2562, 6229, 16139, 16140;** low temperature diseases, **2620, 2689, 2690, 5893, 11449;** traffic damage, **1190, 12353, 12400, 15161, 15571**

Winterkill
effects of: drainage, **3709, 10802;** fertilization, **9354, 10605**

Winterkill
factors affecting, **5779, 7073, 8978, 8979, 10605**

Winterkill
golf course, **1752, 2176, 12355**

Winterkill
green, **1129, 1190, 1870, 5858**

Winterkill
prevention, **1543, 1582, 1665, 2577, 2578, 2586, 2591, 2605, 2689, 2957, 5039, 5864, 7074, 9411, 11450, 11488, 12712, 14407, 15490, 15532, 15536, 16139:** covers, **2739, 9407, 10759, 13851;** greens, **7866, 10400;** ice removal, **10549;** soil warming, **2607, 9407;** species selection, **8980, 9407, 15354**

Winterkill
recovery program, **12353, 12400**

Winterkill
repair, **1582, 6682**

Winterkill
sod production fields, **1958, 1991**

Winter overseeding, **457, 541, 566, 958, 1012, 8537, 9014, 9288, 9289, 9480, 11347, 11444, 11585, 11612, 13652, 14327, 14430, 16187, 16240**

Winter overseeding
annual bluegrass control, **2100, 2311, 2312, 2918, 2919, 8031, 8032, 8442, 9429, 13561, 15326, 15356**

Winter overseeding
of bermudagrass, **8519, 9013, 9014**

Winter overseeding
cool season turfgrasses used, **429, 2100, 5834, 7076, 7785, 7994, 8736, 9014, 9290, 9481, 9675, 10756, 11508, 11603, 11621, 11625, 13118, 13119, 13121, 13307, 13407, 13899, 14532, 15349, 16241, 16356:** bentgrass, **5137, 9582, 11625;** bluegrass, **8733, 11625;** evaluation, **3212, 6019, 9012, 9675, 10454, 10520, 10817, 13407, 13420, 16028, 16032;** ryegrass, **8733, 12108, 14101;** ryegrass cultivar evaluation, **2100, 2211, 6496, 14979**

Winter overseeding
cost analysis, **14983, 14985**

Winter overseeding
diseases, **1487, 11724**

Winter overseeding
disease control, **676, 729, 9301, 15676**

Winter overseeding
golf course, **3213, 11621, 13237**

Winter overseeding
grasses used, **1489, 1547, 1639, 2377, 2492, 2494, 2495, 2498, 3343, 4243, 4567, 6524, 6970, 7053, 8033, 8164, 9289, 11601, 11608, 11633, 11724, 13269, 16114, 16119, 16120:** evaluation, **138, 1367, 1778, 2100, 2311, 2493, 2496, 2670, 3213, 5583, 6012, 7975, 8166, 8719, 9013, 9014, 9301, 9480, 9879, 10455, 10507, 10510, 10513, 11598, 11640, 11641, 11906, 11931, 13406, 13423, 13424, 13432, 13433**

Winter overseeding
green, **136, 2491, 2493, 2495, 9675, 10177, 10179, 11445, 16026**

Winter overseeding
herbicide phytotoxicity, **8032, 13561, 15326**

Winter overseeding
lawn, **10409, 13237, 13276, 13277, 14702:** grasses used, **6523, 13276, 13278, 13279, 13281, 13282**

Winter overseeding
procedures, **136, 144, 1492, 1639, 2494, 2498, 2841, 5139, 5834, 6014, 6523, 6524, 7053, 7076, 7785, 7994, 8736, 9296, 9675, 10175, 10176, 10520, 10756, 10774, 10883, 11406, 11478, 11504, 11508, 11598, 11601, 11608, 11724, 11731, 12108, 13119, 13305, 13420, 13425, 13432, 13433, 13435, 13561, 14677, 15462, 16032, 16046:** fertilization, **8035, 11404, 11478, 13435;** plantbed preparation, **1639;** seeding rate, **1639, 5834, 6524, 9675, 13406, 13407, 13423, 13432, 13899;** timing, **13406, 13425, 13432, 13899, 14681**

Winter overseeding
spring transition, **7076, 9731, 10521:** cultural effects, **10175, 10517, 10521, 11477**

Winter play
green damage, **4978, 6921, 8363**

Winter protection cover, **2689, 15515, 15532**

Winter protection cover
evaluation, **338, 1639, 1700, 1967, 2100, 2623, 2675, 2689, 5781, 15516, 15519, 15527, 15559, 15569, 15595**

Winter protection cover
green, **2051, 15595**

Winter protection cover
plastic screen (see Plastic screen)

Winter protection cover
polyethylene, **1492, 1965, 5774, 9408**

Winter protection cover
sports field, **2183**

Winter protection cover
uses, **2027, 15527**

Wireworm, **4611, 7029, 12542**

Wireworm
chemical control, **1570, 6071, 10893, 15334**

Witchgrass
chemical control, **4396**

Wood bluegrass, **1393, 3776, 4008, 9521, 16326**

Wood cellulose fiber
mulch (see Wood fiber mulch)

Wood chips, **172**

Wood chips
alternate surface, **7915**

Wood chips
mulch, **2667, 5042, 8987, 16462**

Wood chips
soil amendment, **9769**

Wood excelsior cover
winter protection, **1700, 1967, 2100**

Wood fiber mulch, **1768, 1787, 2268, 2420, 2975, 5108, 6010, 6946, 7184, 8215, 11316, 11371, 13212, 14695**

Wood fiber mulch
environmental effects, **2874, 3076**

Wood fiber mulch
evaluation, **3693, 3734, 6034, 6515, 8834, 11830, 12596, 13797, 13901**

Wood fiber mulch
winter protection, **1781, 15569**

Wood meadowgrass (see Wood bluegrass)

Wood shavings
mulch, **2667**

Woodsorrel, yellow, **15304**

Woodsorrel, yellow
chemical control, **4207, 7264, 7537, 8171**

Worm casts, **4722, 5647**

Woven paper net mulch, **1371, 1605, 2579, 2593**

Woven paper net mulch
evaluation, **1479, 12490, 12596, 13212**

Xanthophyll, **592**

Xiphinema (see Dagger nematode)

Xiphinema americanum, **5757**

Yarrow, **395, 4733, 7689**

Yarrow
chemical control, **5602, 5617, 7700, 10379, 11217, 11592, 14082:** evaluation, **4760, 11592, 12880, 15700**

Yellow bluestem, **10543**

Yellow nutsedge, **502, 2762, 7546, 7756**

Yellow nutsedge
chemical control, **2769, 3503:** in bermudagrass-bluegrass, **5225, 5237;** evaluation, **2762, 5226, 5229;** in Kentucky bluegrass-tall fescue, **5238**

Yellow suckling clover, **4731**

Yellow trefoil, **466**

Yellow tuft, **8096, 11766, 14530**

Yellow tuft
causes, **1690, 6909, 14531**

Yellow tuft
creeping bentgrass: cultivar susceptibility, **2564, 2566**

Yellow tuft
injury symptoms, **10853**

Yellow tuft
nematode association, **14530**

Yellow woodsorrel (see Woodsorrel, yellow)

Yield (see Shoot growth)

Yorkshire fog, **6487**

Yorkshire velvet bentgrass, **11665**

Zinc, **11786**

Zinc
carriers, **7135, 13522**

Zinc
deficiency symptoms, **1948, 9267, 9698, 9803, 10963**

Zinc
functions, **4807, 7671, 10963, 11785**

Zinc
organic soils, **14630**

Zinc
toxicity, **3150**

Zinc chelate, **13522**

Zinc ethylenebisdithio carbamate (see Zineb)

Zinc oxide
fungicide, **712, 15756**

Zinc sulfate, **7135, 13522**

Zineb, **2536, 7202, 16298**

Zonate eyespot, **4314, 5084**

Zonate eyespot
injury sumptoms, **9463, 10853**

Zonate eyespot
susceptible species, **5084, 5085**

Zoysiagrass, **413, 749, 765, 1165, 1316, 3127, 3579, 4243, 4412, 5573, 6047, 6142, 6513, 6951, 7000, 8535, 9151, 9662, 12877, 13272, 14544, 15358**

Zoysiagrass
adaptation, **1633, 2377, 3539, 3553, 3592, 3676, 3987, 4389, 4413, 4518, 4601, 5483, 5572, 5874, 6553, 6562, 6861, 6888, 6895, 8009, 16007, 16350, 16366:** low temperature hardiness, **1078, 1685, 2566, 6050**

Zoysiagrass
breeding, **3553**

Zoysiagrass
cultivars, **4413, 5273, 7396:** evaluation, **2203, 4401, 8009, 8761, 8765, 10922, 14687, 16347;** low temperature hardiness, **1700, 2566;** paper chromatography identification, **11229**

Zoysiagrass
culture, **1102, 3127, 4518, 6045, 6895, 7400, 8141, 11681, 14681, 16425:** cutting height, **16320;** fertilization, **6861, 8757, 8762, 12265, 12267;** Japan, **5274, 11236;** vertical mowing, **15355**

Zoysiagrass
description, **1489, 3553, 5874, 7175, 7947, 9424, 14361, 16117:** discoloration, **1127, 16352;** discoloration—carboxin treatment, **12976;** floral development, **11852, 11883**

Zoysiagrass
diseases, **4330, 15672:** rust, **1639, 2347, 6184, 8709, 9073**

Zoysiagrass
establishment, **1102, 2372, 4518, 5573, 7400, 9571:** cutting height effects, **2609;** gibberellic acid, **1271;** methods, **9602, 9632;** plugging, **3162, 6045, 6563;** seed, **1547, 2365, 14363;** in shade, **11906;** vegetative, **6141, 9319, 9652, 12475, 12481**

Zoysiagrass
evaluation methods, **6596**

Zoysiagrass
herbicide tolerance, **7995, 14952**

Zoysiagrass
iron chlorosis, **14440**

Zoysiagrass
pests, **8141:** hunting billbug, **8827, 14668;** nematode, **2756, 4969, 5757, 6607, 8686**

Zoysiagrass
in polystands, **7519**

Zoysiagrass
seed germination: factors affecting, **6048, 16513**

Zoysiagrass
uses, **413, 3553, 4409, 5874, 6861, 6893:** fairway, **6563, 6889, 7791, 12475, 12997, 12998, 13445;** golf course, **3115, 6143, 6937, 9935;** lawn, **4413, 5071, 11681, 12739, 16425;** tee, **3166, 9568, 11447, 11551**

Zoysiagrass rust, **6199, 7122, 7124, 14846**

Zoysiagrass rust
chemical control, **6726**

Zoysiagrass rust
zoysiagrass species susceptibility, **6185**

Zoysiagrass, weed
chemical control, **6207**

Zoysia japonica (see Japanese lawngrass)

Zoysia materella (see Manilagrass)

Zoysia species (see also Zoysiagrass)

Zoysia species
evaluation, **6050, 7404**

Zoysia species
identification: paper chromatography, **11230**

Zoysia tenuifolia (see Mascarenegrass)

Zwartberg Kentucky bluegrass, **9218, 14813**

Z-52 zoysiagrass (see Meyer zoysiagrass)